CARTER'S ADVANCED ACCOUNTS

CARTER'S

ADVANCED ACCOUNTS

A MANUAL OF BOOK-KEEPING AND ACCOUNTANCY FOR STUDENTS

SEVENTH EDITION

BY

DOUGLAS GARBUTT

M.Ed. (Leics.), A.C.I.S., A.C.M.A., A.M.B.I.M.

Professor and Head of the Department of Accountancy and Economics, Dundee College of Technology

[redacted]

[redacted]

Pitman

PITMAN PUBLISHING
128 Long Acre, London WC2E 9AN

A Division of Longman Group UK Limited

Seventh edition 1972, revised and reprinted 1974
First paperback edition 1976
Reprinted 1978, 1979, 1980, 1981, 1982 (twice),
1983, 1984, 1986, 1989 (twice)

[redacted]

Produced by Longman Group (FE) Ltd
Printed in Hong Kong

[redacted]

PUBLISHERS' PREFACE

THIS textbook was originally edited by the late Mr. Roger N. Carter, M.Comm., F.C.A., Lecturer in Accounting at the University of Manchester, and is still familiarly known as "Carter" by hundreds of thousands of practitioners, lecturers, and students.

A study of the book will fit the student of book-keeping for most of the ordinary public examinations in this subject. It contains considerably more than is necessary for examination purposes, and the student who is fully conversant with all the matters dealt with has no need to fear the result of such a test. Great pains have been taken to include all matters referred to in the syllabuses of the various examining bodies.*

Although the principles of double-entry book-keeping are universally accepted, there are, of course, differences of opinion as to the best methods of applying these principles. Where several ways of achieving the same result are in vogue, these have, in many instances, been given. It has been thought, also, that the inclusion of the more theoretical methods, as well as the practical methods, will have the effect of making the explanations clearer to the student of the subject.

Suitable exercises are given at the end of each chapter, and fully worked answers appear in the Key which is published separately.

One minor change which we hope will appeal to lecturers as exemplifying the principle of decimal classification is in the pagination system. Chapters are numbered 01 to 29 and each chapter is paged independently from 01. The first page is therefore 0101, the second 0102 and so on. This gives the author and publisher greater flexibility in keeping the book up-to-date. Any chapter may be revised without disturbing the entire pagination, since the system allows for expansion up to 99 chapters, each with 99 pages. Students may wish to be reassured that there is no intention of making full use of this capacity!

The sixth edition was partly decimalized because it was felt that this would assist lecturers and students during the dual currency period; the present edition has been fully decimalized.

HINTS REGARDING EXAMINATIONS

Many people who use this book will be preparing for examinations, and they would do well to remember that the real secret of success lies in adequate preparation. This involves hard work and practice in the months before the examination.

* Details of the ONC/D and HNC/D 1969 guideline Syllabuses covered by "Carter" are given on p. x of the Author's Preface.

During preparation the following plan is recommended—

First, a rapid reading of the subject matter, when the student obtains a broad general idea of the subject. This may be followed by a second reading and an attempt to master the details of procedure, law, and accounting treatment.

The study of accountancy has three main elements: commercial knowledge, law, and practical accountancy work. The ability to produce practical work is the ultimate test. The next stage, then, is for the student to work as many practical examples as he can. Reference to the answers or to the Key should only be made after a solution has been worked, otherwise you may become dangerously complacent.

Hasty, last-minute preparation for an examination is not recommended. Remember that the qualified man is expected to know his subject. Your knowledge will stay with you longer if you prepare over a reasonable period of time.

All students go through recognizable stages in learning. At first, the subject is difficult and complex. Learning may be slow. Then, suddenly, it seems, the bricks fit into place and the student feels himself progressing well. Alas, he may later come to another difficult patch, and is tempted to give up, but if he perseveres he will find after a time that he begins to progress again. So if you reach a "plateau of learning" don't give up!

At the same time, there is a limit to the amount of work which may be done at one time on one topic. After half an hour or an hour, the student may feel tired. If so, he should take a break or change his subject of study and come back to his knotty problem later. Even the knottiest problem may be far less fearsome after a rest!

Many candidates establish bad habits of working during their months of preparation, thinking that they will work neatly "on the day." This is bad policy. The candidate who establishes orderly and neat habits in working his questions goes into the examination confident, at least, of his ability to display his work well. He produces attractive work more quickly and with far less effort and he leaves his mind free to concentrate on the more important part of the examination—the accounting problems set by the examiners.

Many students are studying more than one subject at a time and they will naturally divide their time between the subjects so that each is given proper attention. It is best for the student to plan his study and to work steadily throughout the year, and he should be prepared to forgo some of the pleasures and entertainments he might otherwise enjoy. If his study is effective, he may well find it gives more rewards, in the end, whatever the examination results. But he should not cut himself off from society altogether—remember, all work and no play makes Jack a dull boy and it is the bright boys who are most likely to succeed.

When the examination approaches, however, a period of some weeks revision should be undertaken, and greater concentration on work may be quite acceptable in this period. Revise systematically, checking your past work and revising points which have caused difficulty. All examining bodies will supply copies of past papers, and these should be worked through. At least one paper in each subject should be worked in the time allowed, as far as possible under examination conditions.

If you have done your work of preparation well, you have nothing to fear in the examination room, but, again, make sure that you are free to concentrate on the problems set. Take a good supply of sharp pencils, a ruler, rubber, pens, and ink. Arrive in plenty of time and make sure you go to the right place. In other words, read the instructions sent by the examining body.

Examiners are looking for candidates they can pass. They do not set catch questions, but they do, in many cases, set questions which it is hard to answer fully in the time available. In most cases, the marks to be earned on a question are given and the candidates should divide the time available (less ten minutes or so for reading the questions and checking the answers at the end) between the questions in proportion to the marks to be earned. A candidate who attempts all the questions and gains average marks on all is more likely to pass than the candidate who answers one question fully but does not leave time to attempt the others!

Candidates, naturally, feel nervous when they first go into the examination room. They should read generally through the paper and get an idea of what the questions are about. Of the topics covered some, at least, should be familiar and one, perhaps, will stand out as one which the candidate feels able to solve. His best plan, then, is to answer that question before turning to a more careful reading of the others. The fact that one question has been answered reasonably well gives great confidence. On the whole, too, it is better to answer a short question first, rather than plunge straight into a long one merely because it is compulsory. Most accounting questions are practical, but where the essay form is used it is advisable to be as concise as possible. When comparisons or differences are asked for, a neat tabulated statement, graph, or chart will often give the best answer.

Examinees are strongly recommended to read carefully the examiners' reports which are published by most of the examining bodies. Many valuable hints are given in these, more especially regarding the more common errors to avoid.

Finally, take the examination test with a smile. Remember, it is provided to prove your mastery of the subject, and not to expose your lack of ability. Therefore, study to be master of the situation.

AUTHOR'S PREFACE TO THE SEVENTH EDITION

In this edition, the opportunity has been taken to up-date the book throughout in the light of changing legislation affecting business accounting. The edition is fully decimalized.

The major changes affect a number of chapters. The second chapter has been reorganized and expanded to give a clearer exposition of the preparation of final accounts and balance sheets from the trial balance and the cycle of accounting. For the first time, an explanation and example of the use of the work-sheet is included. The twelfth chapter has also been re-organized to expand and clarify the accounting treatment of hire-purchase, credit sale and leases (or rentals) as methods of financing the acquisition of assets. Some controversy has been aroused both in the UK and the USA over the way in which the extent to which firms are financing themselves by these methods may be concealed by the accounting methods which are widely used.

For a general manual such as *Carter's Advanced Accounts*, the treatment of taxation is a problem. It is no longer possible for a book such as this to serve as a guide to current tax rates. Should we therefore cut out the chapter on tax? Our attitude has been that we should not, but that we should change the character of the chapter a little so that it is a reasonably adequate and up-to-date exposition of the general tax system with tax rates as current as we can make them, but that we should deal with the problems of accounting for tax, rather than with the problems of computing liabilities for tax. These accounting problems are now dealt with under the general headings of direct and indirect taxation.

Under indirect taxation, we have included such taxes as SET and Purchase Tax, which were introduced in the last edition, but we have also introduced a reference to the Value Added Tax which is likely to replace them in 1974.

Direct taxation has been a problem since the Second World War, but at no time more than since 1965. Now we are promised some stability and simplification and we hope that in the future we shall be able to parallel that process in *Carter's Advanced Accounts*. But in the meantime, we have to deal with the system as it is, warts and all. In our last edition we introduced an exposition of the accounting treatment of the cash grants payable by the Board of Trade, which had just then been introduced. Now the grants are abolished! Should we therefore eliminate what was so lately introduced? We have decided not, for two reasons. The first may be pure accounting conservatism (from which the author normally shrinks)—if you like, a suspicion that it is too early yet to judge whether we have seen the last of cash grants.

The second reason is one of teaching principle: even if cash grants are abolished for our time, they still remain a possible way of providing incentives to industry (indeed they also still exist on a small scale) and they raise quite interesting problems of accounting, as could be seen by the contrasting recommendations of the Scottish, and the English and Welsh Institutes of Chartered Accountants. So they remain in, and we have added an exposition of the new first-year allowances and the pooling arrangements (again, we have not eliminated the explanation of balancing charges and allowances). Other detailed changes include the re-introduction of Schedule A and the elimination of Cases VII and VIII of Schedule D. Obviously, references are now to the 1968 and 1970 consolidating Capital Allowances, Income and Corporation Taxes and the Taxes Management Acts.

The final chapter on interpretation of accounts was generally welcomed by reviewers and teachers when it was introduced in the fifth edition. The opportunity has been taken to expand the diagram of funds flows in the firm and the ratios have been regrouped and reclassified.

ORDINARY AND HIGHER NATIONAL CERTIFICATE/DIPLOMA IN BUSINESS STUDIES

The new edition of Carter is closely related to the aims of the National Certificate/Diploma courses, which are to develop an understanding of accounting information in modern business. As far as possible, topics are treated in such a way that it is possible for the course tutor to vary the sequence and emphasis to accord with his own schemes of work.

The work in the Higher National Certificate/Diploma is intended to be much broader in its treatment than the Ordinary National Certificate/ Diploma and, in particular, to bring out the relationship of accounting to other subjects. For instance, it is suggested that the lecturer should bring out the relationship between accounting and economics. Whilst *Carter's Advanced Accounts* is most suitable for the Ordinary National level, lecturers will find that there are many points at which the treatment provides a firm foundation for a later broader treatment in the Higher National Certificate/Diploma. For example, on page 0101 the scope of accounting is defined in much wider terms than was customary in the past. The treatment of taxation in Chapter 28 also relates to the purposes of taxation in its direct and indirect forms.

As a guide to course planning, the topics in the syllabus and the related chapters are listed below.

Topics	Suggested Weight	Chapter in Carter
1. Principles of Accounting	15	01
Business entity		
Money measurement		
Cost concept		
Going concern concept		
Accrual and realization		
Conservatism, consistency and materiality conventions		
2. Basic Accounting Method	30	
Accounts and classification		01 *et seq.*
Balance sheet. Revenue accounts		02 *et seq.*
Capital and revenue expenditure		10
Depreciation		06
Accruals and pre-payments		02 *et seq.*
Reserves and provisions		02, 20, 22, 23, 24
Appropriations		17, 18, 21
3. Applications of Accounting Method	55	
Final accounts of different organizations including partnerships and companies		02, 10, 17, 18, 19, 20, 21, 22, 23, 24
Manufacturing accounts		16
Accounting for special purposes		04, 07, 08, 09, 11, 12, 13, 14, 26, 27, 28
Control accounts		05
4. Cost Accounting Method	30	15
Fundamental concepts		
Relation to financial accounting		
Absorption and marginal costing		
Job and process costing		
Standard costing		
Pricing policy		
5. Accounting for Future Profitability	30	
Budgeting		15
Variance analysis		
Breakeven analysis		
Capital budgeting including DCF		29

Topics	Suggested Weight	Chapter in Carter
6. Performance Evaluation and Control	25	
Concepts of capital employed Working capital Use of ratios Balance sheet and profit and loss analysis Funds flow statements		02, 29
Limited companies' capital structure		19, 20, 22
Dividend and retention policies		20, 21, 23, 24, 29
7. Data Processing and the Applications of the Computer	15	01
The place of the computer in accounting systems and introduction to mechanized accounting		
	200	

The weighting is 200 because the course should extend over two years.

ACKNOWLEDGEMENTS

THE author and publisher gratefully acknowledge the generosity of the following professional bodies in allowing quotations from their recommendations, publications, annual reports and examination questions.

Abbreviated titles are used in the text, as indicated, where extensive use is made:

	Abbreviated titles
The Institute of Cost and Management Accountants	Cost and Management or I.C.M.A.
The Institute of Chartered Accountants in England and Wales	I.C.A. or E & W or Chartered Accountants of England & Wales
The Institute of Chartered Accountants of Scotland	I.C.A. of S or Chartered Accountants of Scotland
The Institute of Chartered Accountants of Ireland	I.C.A. of I or Chartered Accountants of Ireland
The Association of Certified and Corporate Accountants	Certified Accountants or A.C.C.A.
The Institute of Bankers	Bankers or I.O.B.
The London Chamber of Commerce	L.C.C.
Chartered Institute of Secretaries	C.I.S. or Chartered Institute of Secretaries
Corporation of Certified Secretaries	C.C.S. or Corporation of Certified Secretaries
The Institute of Book-keepers and Related Data Processing	Institute of Book-keepers
Union of Lancashire and Cheshire Institutes	U.L.C.I.
Union of Educational Institutions	
Faculty of Teachers in Commerce	
West Riding of Yorkshire Examining Board	
Royal Sociey of Arts	R.S.A.

In addition to the acknowledgements to professional bodies above, we acknowledge the kind co-operation of Companies who have allowed us to use their annual reports, the Council of the Stock Exchange and the Registrar of Companies and his Deputy.

CONTENTS

	PAGE
PUBLISHERS' PREFACE	v
AUTHOR'S PREFACE TO THE SEVENTH EDITION	ix

CHAPTER 01

BASIC PRINCIPLES AND SYSTEMS OF ACCOUNTING

Principles and Standards	0101
Accounting Conventions	05
Accounts	06
Nature of Ledger Balances	06
Double Entry Book-keeping	08
Principal Books	08
Ledger	08
Cash Book	10
Trial Balance	14
Subsidiary Books	16
Petty Cash Book	16
Journal	16
Documents used in Commercial Transactions	17
Purchases Book	18
Sales Book	18
Purchases Returns Book	19
Sales Returns Book	20
Bill Books	20
Single Entry	21
Uses of Computers	25
Loose-leaf and Card Ledgers	29
Slip System of Book-keeping	30
Tabular System of Book-keeping	33

CHAPTER 02

REPORTING INCOME AND BALANCE SHEET POSITION

The Final Accounts (or income statement)	0201
Sections of the Income Statement	02
The Period of Account	02
Balance Sheet	02
Trading Account	04
Stock	04

Profit and Loss Account 0208
Provisions 11
The Balance Sheet 12
Assets 12
Liabilities 13
Capital 13
Preparation of the Final Accounts and Balance Sheet. The Accounting Cycle 16
Making Adjustments 17
Provisions for Bad or Doubtful Debts 20
Provisions for Discount 27
The Work-sheet 33
Closing Entries 35
Worked Examples 36
Special Points to Watch in Exercises 48
Adjustments and the Balance Sheet 50
Interpretation: Management Requirements 50

CHAPTER 03

THE CORRECTION OF BOOK-KEEPING ERRORS

Types of Errors 0301
Correction of Errors 02
Journal Entries 03
Corrections during the Accounting Year 03
Corrections after Final Accounts and Balance Sheets have been Prepared 05
Corrections after opening a Suspense Account 05

CHAPTER 04

BILLS OF EXCHANGE, PROMISSORY NOTES AND BANK SERVICES

Bills of Exchange 0401
Promissory Notes 28
Bank Notes 30
Bank Drafts 31
Paying Money through Bank Giro 31
Receiving Money through Bank Giro 33
Direct Debiting 36
IOU 37
Cheques 39

CHAPTER 05

ACCOUNTING SYSTEMS AND CONTROL ACCOUNTS

Sectional and Self-balancing Ledgers 0502
Control, Total or Adjustment Account 03
Principle of Proof 05
Procedures 30
Detection of Errors 31
Private Ledger 33

CHAPTER 06

√ DEPRECIATION OF FIXED ASSETS

1. Fixed instalment or straight line method . . 0604
2. Diminishing balance method . . 05
3. Sum of the years' digits method 06
4. Annuity system 11
5. Depreciation fund principle 14
6. Insurance policy system 18
7. Revaluation 20
8. Repairs, maintenance and depreciation fund or provision . 21
9. Depletion unit or production unit method . . 22
10. Combined methods . . . 23
Summary of Recommendations of the Institute of Chartered Accountants on Depreciation 23

CHAPTER 07

√ STOCK VALUATION AND CONTROL

Principles of Stock Valuation 0701
Cost 03
Market Value 05
Estimating Value of Stock 06
Fire Claims for Stock 07
Stock Control 09

CHAPTER 08

STOCK EXCHANGE TRANSACTIONS AND INVESTMENT ACCOUNTS

Stock Exchange Transactions 0801
Investment Accounts 15
Modification of Records for Capital Gains Tax 21

CHAPTER 09

CONSIGNMENT ACCOUNTS

Consignments Outwards 0901
Consignments Inwards 08

CHAPTER 10

REPORTING THE INCOME AND FINANCIAL POSITION OF CLUBS, SOCIETIES AND VOLUNTARY ASSOCIATIONS

Importance of Distinction between Capital and Revenue . . 1001
Apportionment between Capital and Revenue 02

CHAPTER 11

INCOMPLETE RECORDS

Single Entry 1102
Preparation of Final Accounts from Incomplete Records . . 05
Conversion to Double Entry 11

CHAPTER 12

FINANCING ASSET ACQUISITION; ROYALTIES; CONTAINERS

Financing Asset Acquisition 1201
Methods of Financing Acquisitions 01
Legislation Affecting Hire Purchase and Credit Sale . . 02
Parties to Financing Agreements 03
Accounting Treatment of Financing Agreements 04
Accounting by the Buyer or User 04
Misleading Use of Lease Finance 10
Problems of Calculating Interest 14
Accounting by the Dealer 19
Accounting by the Finance Company 28
Provision for Bad Debts 34
Royalty Accounts 34
Accounting for Containers and Cases 38

CHAPTER 13

DEPARTMENTAL ACCOUNTS

Allocation of Expenses by Means of Direct Analysis . . . 1304
Apportionment of Expenses According to Floor Space Occupied . 07
Apportionment of Expenses According to Turnover 09
Apportionment of Expenses According to the Number of Articles Sold 11
Separate Trading Accounts for Each Department 13

CHAPTER 14

BRANCH ACCOUNTS

Books kept by Head Office 1401
Retail Branches 04
Wholesale Branches 14
Books kept by the Branches 17
Foreign Branches 36
Conversion from and into Sterling 37
Forms of Foreign Remittances 38
Transactions in Currency 38
Problems of Conversion of Data 39
Inflation and Currency Fluctuation 43

CHAPTER 15

COST ACCOUNTING

Objects of Cost Accounts 1501
Analysis of Cost 02
Comparison between Cost and Financial Accounting 04
Systems of Cost Accounting 05
Classes of Cost Accounts 05
Cost Accounting Procedure 07
Overhead Apportionment 09
Overhead Absorption 11
Double-entry Cost Accounts 14
(*a*) Independent 14
(*b*) Standard 23
(*c*) Integrated 25
Direct or Marginal Costing 29
Total Cost Variation 30
Analysis of Semi-variable Costs 31
Comparison of Full and Marginal Costing 32
Break-even Analysis 34

Optimum Product Mix 1540
Contribution Charts 41
Joint and Common Costs 42
Problems in Break-even Analysis 43
Cost Estimating and Pricing 44
Subsidiary Books and Records in a Costing System . . 46
Cost Sheets 49
Materials, Labour and Methods of Wage Payment . . . 57

CHAPTER 16

DETERMINATION OF MANUFACTURING AND CONTRACT PROFITS

Manufacturing Accounts 1601
Contract Accounts 10

CHAPTER 17

PARTNERSHIP ACCOUNTS

Law of Partnership 1701
The Accounts 06
Limited Partnerships 26
Joint Ventures 29

CHAPTER 18

DISSOLUTION OF PARTNERSHIP

Profit on Realization 1805
Loss on Realization 07
Goodwill 20
Revaluation of Assets 21

CHAPTER 19

COMPANIES: FORMATION AND CAPITAL

Formation of Company 1904
Capital 18
Shares 19
Statutory and Statistical Books 20

CHAPTER 20

COMPANIES: RAISING OF CAPITAL

Issue of Shares and Debentures 2001
Accounting for Issues 02
Shares and Debentures Payable in Full 02
Shares and Debentures Payable by Instalments . . . 10
Convertible Loan Stock 15
Shares Over-subscribed 20
Calls in Arrear and in Advance 21
Forfeiture of Shares 22
Preliminary Expenses 27
Debentures as Collateral Security for Loan 27

CHAPTER 21

COMPANY EARNINGS

Interest 2103
Debenture Interest 03
Interest on Calls 05
Interest on Capital, Paid out of Capital 07
Corporation Tax 09
Dividends 09
Arrears of Dividend on Cumulative Preference Shares . . 15
Profits Prior to Incorporation 16
Loss Prior to Incorporation 18
Bonus Shares 18

CHAPTER 22

THE PUBLISHED ACCOUNTS OF COMPANIES

Recommendations on Accounting Principles 2202
Reserves, Provisions and Current Liabilities 02
Distinction Between a Provision and a Reserve 03
Reserve Funds 04
Secret Reserves 04
Balance Sheet Requirements: Sources of Funds 06
Uses of Funds 08
Profit and Loss Account Requirements 10
Loans to Officers 13
Directors Report 13

CHAPTER 23

COMPANIES: DEBENTURE REDEMPTION

Types of Debenture 2301
Redemption of Debentures 03
Conversion into New Debentures 12
Conversion of Debentures into Shares 12
Debentures Issued to a Bank 14

CHAPTER 24

COMPANIES: REDEEMABLE PREFERENCE SHARES

Issue and Redemption of Redeemable Preference Shares . . 2403

CHAPTER 25

BUSINESS SALES, PURCHASES, TAKE-OVERS, MERGERS, RECONSTRUCTIONS

Purchase of a Business 2501
Conversion of a Partnership into a Limited Company . 05
Amalgamation of Limited Companies 09
Amalgamation by Formation of a New Company, the Old Companies being Wound Up 10
Amalgamation by Formation of a "Holding Company" . 18
Amalgamation by Absorption 19
Amalgamation by the Acquisition of a Controlling Interest . 23
Reconstruction 23
Reorganization 24
Reduction of Capital 26
Group Accounts 31
Holding Companies 31
Preparation of the Consolidated Balance Sheet . . . 36
Consolidated Profit and Loss Account 45

CHAPTER 26

BANKRUPTCY, STATEMENT OF AFFAIRS, DEFICIENCY ACCOUNT, TRUSTEE'S ACCOUNTS

Bankruptcy 2601
Statement of Affairs 06
Deficiency Account 20
Trustee's Accounts 26

CHAPTER 27

LIQUIDATION

Voluntary Liquidation 2701
Liquidation by the Court 02
The Preparation of a Statement of Affairs in Compulsory Liquidation 03
Settling the List of Contributories 04
Liquidator's Cash Account 07

CHAPTER 28

ACCOUNTING FOR TAXES, LEVIES, ALLOWANCES AND GRANTS

Direct and Indirect Taxes 2802
Grants and Allowances 02
Accounting for Indirect Taxes 03
Redundancy Payments Scheme 06
Selective Employment Tax 16
Industrial Training Levies and Grants 20
Value-Added Tax 25
Direct Taxes 29
Definition of Income 32
Schedules 33
Surtax 37
Double Taxation Relief 37
Corporation Tax 38
Capital Gains Tax 38
Estate Duty 41
Direct Taxes on Businesses 42
Direct Tax on Employees, P.A.Y.E., National Insurance . . . 43
Accounting Treatment of P.A.Y.E. 52
Treatment of Corporation Tax 54
Imputation System 58
Dividends and Interest Received 59
Accounting for Capital Allowances and Investment Grants . . 62
Investment Grants 67
Capital Allowances and Depreciation 69
Providing for Deferred Taxation 75
The Treatment of Tax in Company Accounts 78
The Classification of Income Tax in the Balance Sheet . . 79
Adjustment of Accounts for Assessment of Income Tax . . 79
Partnership 81

CHAPTER 29

INTERPRETATION OF FINAL ACCOUNTS AND BALANCE SHEETS

Presentation of the Revenue Accounts and Balance Sheet . 2902
Ratios Calculated from the Revenue Accounts and Balance Sheet . 08
Profitability 10
Liquidity or Asset Use 16

Statements of Sources and Disposition of Funds 22
The Cash Budget, Forecast of Trading Account, Profit and Loss and Balance Sheet 40
Capital Expenditure Decisions 43
The Irrelevance of Book Values and Depreciation . . . 52

Appendix I
Table A Annual Present Value
Table B Cumulative Present Value
Table C Capital Recovery
Table D Sinking Funds

Appendix II
Decimal Conversion Table

Appendix III
Selected Reading List

Answers

Index

CHAPTER 01

BASIC PRINCIPLES AND SYSTEMS OF ACCOUNTING

Ah, how very sorely they're mistaken,
Who think that money doesn't count,
Fruitfulness turns into famine
When the kindly stream runs out.

BERTHOLDT BRECHT

Accounting is a discipline concerned with the recording, analysis, and forecasting of income and wealth of business and other entities. Generally it records in money terms the flow of economic values between or within economic entities, and it is applied in two main fields.

1. **Micro Accounting** is the field with which this book is mainly concerned and it covers business accounting (financial, managerial and cost accounting), governmental accounting, and household accounting.
2. **Macro Accounting** covers the fields of national income, input-output, balance of payments and money flow accounting. Although this book is concerned mainly with business accounting the principles applied are similar to those that are applied in the other fields, both micro and macro.

Accounting Principles are usually rules and conventions which have been adopted as a general guide to action by the accountancy profession. These principles are formulated in such a way that the practical details of accounting may differ greatly from one company to another. To secure acceptance, an accounting principle must be *useful* in coping with a practical recording problem, it must be reasonably *objective*, that is, provide a similar answer in the hands of qualified practitioners, and finally it must be *feasible*. That is, it should not be expensive to apply.

Accounting Standards. The Accounting Standards Steering Committee (A.S.S.C.) statements of Standard Accounting Practice describe methods of accounting approved by the Institutes of Chartered Accountants, the Institute of Cost and Management Accountants, and the Association of Certified and Corporate Accountants. So far as possible, the recommendations and definitions of these bodies have also been incorporated in this book.

Significant Departures. Where financial accounts significantly depart from Standards, the financial effects should be disclosed and explained unless this is impracticable or misleading.

Book-keeping is the science and art of correctly recording in the books all those business transactions that result in a transfer of money or moneys worth within or between entities.

There are seven basic concepts in accounting, all of which are exemplified in the many practical problems considered in this book. They are modified by three conventions. The concepts are—

1. The Business Entity

All accounts are kept in respect of business entities which are distinct from the persons who own or manage these entities. Sometimes the law makes the same distinction, as in the case of a limited company which is a separate legal entity from the shareholders or its Directors. In other cases the law does not make such a distinction, as in the case of partnership and sole traders, but even so, the books of account are kept so as to maintain the distinction. In the case of companies, partnerships and accounts for taxation there are statutory requirements on the form and content of the accounts to be prepared and the accountant must, therefore, have sufficient knowledge of the relevant legislation if he is to account effectively. Several chapters of this book are concerned with such statutory accounting.

2. Money as a Common Denominator

Accounting uses money to express certain facts about a business, and in such a way that they can be added or subtracted. For instance, the ownership of plant or equipment worth £10,000 can be added to the ownership of raw materials worth £20,000 and a useful expression of the wealth of the business is obtained.

3. The Cost Concept

The resources acquired by a business are called assets and normally the price paid to acquire an asset is recorded in the books and forms a basis for subsequent treatment. The result is that at any moment of time the values recorded in books do not necessarily reflect the current value of the assets.

The income of the business is measured by the difference between the value obtained for selling its products compared to the cost of the resources used in making them. The costs not yet expended are shown in the balance sheet.

4. The Going Concern Concept

In most cases the accounting system will treat the values on the assumption that the business will continue trading. If the business decides to liquidate or become bankrupt then a different approach to valuation is required.

5. The Dual Aspect Concept

This principle is the central core of modern accountancy. All business events are regarded as having a dual aspect. In the Balance Sheet, the dual aspect is *static* since it shows the state of the business at one moment of time. The accounts are *dynamic*, since they record changes in the state of the business. The *Balance Sheet* is the statement of the position of a person, firm or enterprise which shows on one side the assets being used by the business and on the other, the sources of those assets. The sources are of two kinds: (1) proprietors or owners capital and (2) liabilities or the claims of outsiders on the assets.

The Balance Sheet therefore takes the following form—

Liabilities
+
Proprietors' Capital } = Assets in use

The Business Transaction is a transfer of values. This value may be in the form of money, goods, or services and usually goods or services will be exchanged for money. In all business transactions *equal* values are exchanged. If Smith buys furniture for £400, he gives £400 in cash and receives furniture to that value. If Smith is to keep a double entry record of this transaction he must record each transaction in two accounts. In one will be shown value received, in the other, value given.

Accounts. An account is a form of record, originally kept in the Ledger. A page was taken for each account and the account was divided into two.

DEBIT (*Dr*)	CREDIT (*Cr*)
Value received	Value given

The debit side records value received; the credit, value given. In the case of Smith, above, the transaction would be recorded by debiting £400 to his Furniture account and crediting £400 to his Cash account.

Each transaction involves two entries in the same set of accounts, a *debit* entry and a *credit* entry. Every debit must have a corresponding credit, and vice versa.

Balancing. Accounts may be balanced at the end of a period or at any time when it is convenient.

The entries on the debit and credit sides of an account are unlikely to be equal. The balance is the difference between them. It is entered *twice*. Once *above the line*, i.e. above the totals. In this position it brings the smaller side to the same total as the larger. Once *below the line*, on the opposite side of the account. In this position it starts the new period of account.

CASH ACCOUNT

19..			£	19..			£
Jan	1	Capital	1,000	Jan	2	Purchases	20
					3	Expenses paid	10
					5	Balance c/d	970
			1,000				1,000
Jan	6	Balance b/d	970				

Advantages of Double Entry. These may be summarized as follows—

(*a*) **A Complete Record of Each Transaction.** When plant is purchased, wages paid, or discount received, etc., the business is affected in two respects by each transaction. As the number of transactions may be hundreds or thousands each day it would be impossible to keep track of all these aspects through single records. Double entry not only keeps records of personal accounts for debtors (who owe value to the firm) and creditors (to whom value is owed) but it also shows gains, losses, and assets held.

(*b*) **Control of the Business.** As the information in the accounts covers all aspects of its affairs, day-to-day control is made easier, and it is easier to see the trend of the changes which are taking place all the time.

(*c*) **A Check upon the Arithmetical Accuracy of the Clerical Work.** Since every debit has a corresponding credit, the total debits must at any time equal the total credits. Whether this be so or not is easily ascertained by means of a Trial Balance.

(*d*) **Preparation of Final Accounts and Balance Sheet.** As the accounts contain full information, it is easy to prepare the accounts needed at the end of the year or at convenient interim times. These assess the present position and show how that position has changed during the year.

6. The Accrual Concept

In accounting, the income accruing to the owner of a business is not necessarily the amount of cash actually received in a period of account. Any event which increases the proprietor's capital involves the accrual of income. Many difficult problems arise in deciding how much income has actually accrued in any period: these problems are dealt with in a number of chapters in this book, for instance, on joint ventures, company profits, royalties, hire purchase and treatment of containers. Accrual of income is always measured over a period of time which is normally the accounting year. This year may be broken down into interim periods in which reports are made to management or the share-holders. Companies quoted on the London Stock Exchange must publish interim statements of profits every six months.

Expenditure. Expenditure takes place whenever an asset or service is acquired. The acquisition may involve the immediate payment of cash, the payment of cash later or pre-payment.

Expense. Expenses are costs incurred in earning revenues. Those expenditures which may be charged against the revenues for a period will be considered as operating expenses. Expense implies a decrease in the proprietor's capital in the firm.

Cost. A cost is any monetary sacrifice whether or not this sacrifice has affected the proprietor's equity during a given accounting period. A cost is incurred when goods are produced, whether they are sold or not.

Expense, on the other hand, is cost which has expired and been charged against revenues. The accrual concept is applied both in ascertaining the revenues for a period and in ascertaining the expenses to be charged against the revenues.

7. The Realization Concept

Revenue is considered as earned on the day which is realized and this is when goods are transferred to the customer in exchange for a valuable consideration. The Accountant usually uses the date the product is shipped to the customer or the date on the invoice, whichever is the later. Difficult problems arise in deciding, for instance, how far income from hire purchase transactions has been realized.

ACCOUNTING CONVENTIONS

Since the accounting concepts stated above permit many differences in application to actual circumstances, three conventions are generally observed in interpreting them.

1. **Conservatism.** The first convention is that whilst the accountant will be prepared to anticipate possible future losses, he is not prepared to bring into account possible future profits however likely these may be. Obviously this cannot be carried to unreasonable ends but wherever a decision is to be made on the valuation of assets he will generally decide in favour of that valuation which underestimates the profits or the balance sheet values of the firm.

2. **Consistency.** This means that whilst certain alternatives are considered equally acceptable, the accountant having adopted one, must follow that method over a reasonable period of time. In the short run, for instance, one method of stock valuation may result in a higher profit for a firm but in the long run the profits shown will tend to be the same whatever the circumstances. Whilst changes of methods may be made it is accepted that these should not be made frequently nor for the purpose of mis-representing the profits of the firm.

3. **Materiality.** This means that the size of an amount will influence the treatment of it. Cumbrous controls and procedures should not be applied to items of small importance. Similarly, in presenting final accounts and balance sheets of a large company the figures will be rounded off to the nearest thousand or even million pounds. Items such as loose tools and small machines may be lumped together for balance sheet purposes if the value is relatively small in relation to the other assets. Some firms use "whole pound" accounting systems in which all items are rounded off to the nearest pound. In management accounting it is usually better to have early results rather than to wait for more accurate results which come too late to influence management decisions.

ACCOUNTS

An account is a ledger record, in a summarized form, of all the transactions that have taken place with the particular person or value specified; as J. T. Brown's account, Plant account, Wages account. There are two main divisions of accounts—

1. **Personal Accounts** comprise both debtors and creditors. Debtors are people who owe money, e.g. persons to whom the firm has sold goods or services. Creditors are people to whom money is owing, e.g. persons from whom the firm has bought goods or services.

2. **Impersonal Accounts** include both real and nominal accounts.

(*a*) **Real** or **Property Accounts** are those that refer to *assets*; such as plant and machinery, stock-in-trade, cash, etc.

(*b*) **Nominal Accounts** are those that relate to *gains and losses*; such as discounts, wages, rent, rates, sales, purchases, etc.

Some accounts though *impersonal* in name are really *personal* in significance. For instance, the Capital account and Drawings account are personal accounts either of the proprietor of the business or of the partners who are creditors of the concern for the amount of their capitals, and debtors to the extent of their drawings. An account for outstanding items, though *impersonal* in name, is really a *personal* account, being merely the account of unnamed creditors or debtors.

Some accounts are both *real* and *nominal*; as, for example, the Sales account, which is a real account so far as the goods themselves are concerned, but nominal in relation to the gain or loss arising from the sales.

NATURE OF LEDGER BALANCES

Debit Balances. The *debit* balances in a ledger may be classified as assets, expenses, or losses. If they denote debts, or tangible expenditures, such as plant, fixtures, etc., they are assets. If their value expires in the accounting period they are expenses or losses.

Credit Balances. The *credit* balances that are in a ledger must be either liabilities or gains. If they denote indebtedness, e.g. accounts payable, they are liabilities; if they represent income, such as a discounts received, they are gains.

The above distinction is of the utmost importance in the preparation of a Profit and Loss Account and Balance Sheet, as gains, expenses, and losses are entered in the former, and assets and liabilities in the latter.

The distinction between Revenue and Capital is important and a fuller treatment may be found on p. 1001.

Revenue items are those the full benefit of which is received in the normal accounting period, e.g. rent, wages, etc.

Capital items are those the benefit of which is received over a number of accounting periods, e.g. plant, equipment, etc.

Capital and revenue items must always be recorded in separate accounts.

QUESTIONS

1. Define "book-keeping." What are its objects?
2. What is capital? What is a deficiency? Explain the terms "trading," "fixed," "floating," "circulating," and "working" capital.
3. What are "assets"? Explain the following terms: "fixed," "current," "liquid," "wasting," "fictitious" assets. Give examples showing that "fixed" assets may sometimes be "current," and vice versa.
4. What is meant by an "account"? What two main divisions of accounts are there, and how are they subdivided? Explain what is meant by "real" and "nominal" accounts and give examples of them. Show by means of examples how some impersonal accounts may be personal in meaning, and also how some accounts may be both real and nominal.
5. Explain briefly the dual aspect theory of accounting the "debit" and "credit."
6. What are the principal advantages of "double entry"?
7. Explain the signification of the debit and credit balances in a ledger. Why is their proper classification of great importance?

Accounting Methods. The most widely used accounting procedure is the double entry method which is used mainly throughout this book. However, the dual aspect principle is a powerful analytical tool which can be applied to data irrespective of how it was collected: for instance, Chapter 04 of this book shows how a set of final accounts can be produced from incomplete data. In many small businesses a simple procedure of single entry with analysis columns is quite sufficient for normal purposes.

Manual Methods. Firms which use a complete set of accounts may, these days, complete their records by multiple posting methods which enable simultaneous entries to be made into accounts and various subsidiary records at one time.

Mechanization. Most firms use accounting equipment, punch cards and computers, all of which obviate the need for the laborious and time-consuming procedures of entering each item in two accounts. Despite these developments there is no substitute for a full understanding of the dual aspect principle to enable the accountant or analyst to thread his way through the maze of data which a modern business requires.

Systems Design. With the increasing size and complexity of businesses an increasing use is being made of computers. If these are to be used effectively, it is necessary to ensure that the firm has well-designed systems, procedures and methods.

A system is a complex set of relationships between a number of components. These components may be managers, or resources such as materials or facilities such as plant and machinery. Every business may be regarded as a set of systems and sub-systems, interrelated to a greater or lesser degree.

A procedure is the set of clerical activities through which a company's activities are controlled and which provides information to management.

Methods are the means by which the system is implemented.

An effective system design should be based on an overall view of the firm and should provide information for all users of the system whilst eliminating any overlapping and maintenance of duplicate records.

Fig. 01.1 illustrates one part of the accounting system of a business. Similar charts may be produced for other parts of the system and in this way overall co-ordination may be obtained.

DOUBLE ENTRY BOOK-KEEPING

The books utilized for book-keeping fall naturally into two divisions—

1. (*a*) **Principal Books,** namely Ledger and Cash Book. These are the main books and those in which the double-entry system of accounts is kept. The cash book contains the cash and bank accounts. All other accounts are in the ledger.

(*b*) **Subsidiary Books,** or books of first or original entry, such as Journal, Purchases Book, Sales Book, etc. Many details are recorded in these books, before the amounts concerned are entered in ledger accounts.

The journal was the only subsidiary book, at first, and the others were split off from it later.

2. **Statistical or Memorandum Books.** These are books in which are entered the numerous details connected with the business operations which cannot conveniently be recorded in the other books. Examples of these are the Policy Registers of an insurance company, the Cost Books and Stock Books, etc., of a manufacturing firm.

They are similar in purpose to subsidiary books, except that items are not posted from them to the ledger.

PRINCIPAL BOOKS

Ledger

Nature and Use. With the cash book, the ledger is the principal book of account. These two contain all the accounts of a business and are kept on the double-entry system: all transactions affect two accounts—one is debited (receives value) the other is credited (gives value).

Rulings of Ledgers. Many different rulings are met with in business. The most usual have columns for datc, particulars of transactions, folio, and amount. Multiple columns may be used for departments, foreign currencies, quantities, types of expenditure and so on.

Index. In order to facilitate reference to the accounts contained in it, each ledger is furnished with an alphabetical index, which is either at the commencement of the ledger or bound as a separate book, or in the form of a card index.

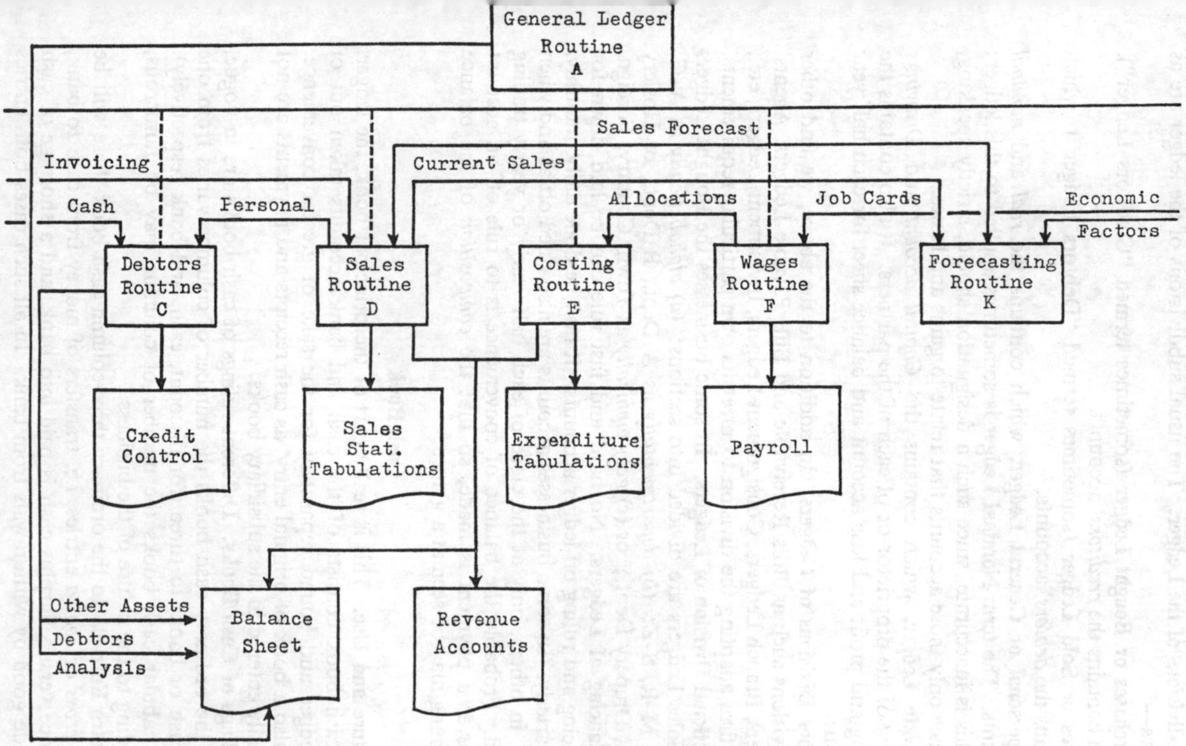

FIG. 01.1. Construction of Overall Plan

(Reproduced from "An approach to systems design" by R. Mitchell, *The Accountant*, 21st Jan. 1967).

Subdivisions of the Ledger. The usual subdivisions of the ledger are as follows—

Purchases or Bought Ledger (sometimes termed "Creditors Ledger"), which contains the *creditors'* accounts.

Sales or Sold Ledger (sometimes termed "Debtors Ledger"), which contains the *debtors'* accounts.

Impersonal or General Ledger, which contains the *real* and *nominal* accounts. The term **Nominal Ledger** is sometimes applied to this ledger; but this is inaccurate, since such a designation should, strictly speaking, embrace only those accounts that relate to gains and losses.

Private Ledger, which contains the *Capital account* and *Drawings account* of the proprietor or of each of the partners. It also contains the trading and profit and loss account and balance sheet for each half year or year.

Other Divisions of Ledgers. In addition to the above, we find other subdivisions such as Bills Receivable and Bills Payable Ledgers, Agents' Ledgers, Branch Ledgers, Consignment Ledgers, Investment Ledgers, etc., each firm adapting the division to meet its own particular requirements.

Sectional Division of Ledgers. In some businesses the Bought Ledgers and Sales Ledgers are divided into sections: (*a*) *alphabetically* as A–G, H–L, M–R, S–Z; (*b*) *departmentally* as A Dept., B Dept., or Hosiery Dept., Drapery Dept.; or (*c*) *geographically* as Town, Country, Foreign.

Balancing of Ledgers. No hard and fast rule can be laid down for balancing and ruling off ledger accounts. It may be done daily, monthly, or quarterly. In some businesses accounts are also ruled off as and when paid; in others, only at the close of each half-yearly or yearly trading period. Probably the balance of convenience is to rule off an account whenever a payment is made, so that the *composition* of the balance remaining may be seen at a glance.

Cash Book

Nature and Use. This is really part of the principal book, the ledger. The cash book consists of the cash and bank accounts taken out of the ledger and bound separately for the sake of greater convenience. It is also a book of original entry, as cash receipts and payments are not normally entered in the subsidiary books.

Rulings of Cash Books. Different rulings of cash books are in vogue. With the ordinary cash books the number of columns varies from one (for cash or bank) to three (for discount, cash, and bank respectively). With tabular cash books the number of columns may be numerous, according to the nature of the business.

Contra Entries. In the ordinary three-column cash book there will be some *cross* or *contra* entries, i.e. transfers of money from cash to bank, and vice versa. Surplus cash is paid into bank, and a shortage of cash is made good by withdrawals from bank. In all such cases both entries occur in the cash book and no ledger entry is required. This is indicated by a contra sign (ø) in the folio columns.

Cash Discounts. These are deductions made from accounts receivable and payable at the time of settlement. Cash Discount may be allowed by a seller if goods are paid for within a short period.

The amounts are recorded in special discount columns which are memorandum columns only. The individual amounts are posted to the ledger at the same time as the cash items. The totals are posted to a "Discount Allowed" or "Discount Received" account in the ledger, as appropriate, so that the amounts lost or gained on discount may be seen.

Treatment of Cheques. In some businesses all cheques received are entered in the cash column; in others they are entered direct into the bank column. Again, in some businesses, cheques received from customers are endorsed on to creditors. Such cheques must, both when received and also when paid away, be entered in the cash columns.

Posting to Ledger. All items in the cash book (excepting balances and contra entries) are posted into the Ledger. The receipts on the debit side of the Cash Book are posted to the *credit* of the ledger accounts affected; and the payments on the credit side of the cash book are posted to the *debit* of the ledger accounts concerned. The cash and discount are frequently added together and posted as "Cash, etc."

Balancing the Cash Book. To avoid the trouble of continually carrying forward large amounts on each side, as well as the possibility of error, the cash book is balanced at least once a month, and the balances are carried down to the new period.

Bank Cash Book. An alternative to the three-column cash book (Discount, Details, Bank) is known as the "Bank Cash Book." All money received is paid into the bank intact, and all payments except petty cash payments are made by cheque. The debit side of the cash book is written up from printed and numbered carbon copy receipts, and the credit side from the counterfoils of the cheques paid away. No cross entries are necessary; when money is paid into the bank the amount is simply extended into the bank column; and when money is drawn for petty cash, the amount is credited out of this cash book and posted to the debit side of a separate Petty Cash Book.

Cash Systems. Many kinds of cash book are in use. As the journal has been superseded by a number of subsidiary books which contain transactions peculiar to them, so also has the cash book proper been adapted.

Sometimes the cash book is composed of two books, "Cash Received" and "Cash Paid," with a third or Private Cash Book in which to show the balance. These books are again subject to division as determined by the circumstances of the business. The cashier may have "Received" and "Paid" Cash Books corresponding to debtors and creditors for different localities, etc. Again, a "Cash Paid" Book may be used for control over "real" expenditure, and a further one for expenditure on "fixed" charges. Whenever transactions in cash in any particular direction assume sufficient importance then special provision for their control in the cash system will be needed. A cash system develops side by side with a business, and only a thorough knowledge of practical conditions can indicate the best system of control.

The cash system of a life assurance office provides the following cash books and registers for control over money received and paid through its offices and agencies.

A General Cash Book, for daily totals, with two subsidiary cash books, namely, "Cash Received " and "Cash Paid."

1. The *Cash Received Book* is provided with the following columns—

(*a*) Premiums. (*b*) Interest. (*c*) Dividends on loans and investments. (*d*) Loans repaid. (*e*) Branch and agency remittances. (*f*) Consideration for annuities.	The amounts entered in the respective columns are, in turn, supplied from "subsidiary" cash books. Examples of these are— 1. H.O. Premium Cash Book. 2. Agency Remittances Cash Book. 3. Loans Cash Book, etc.

2. The *Cash Paid Book* is provided with the following columns—

(*a*) Claims. (*b*) Annuities. (*c*) Bonuses. (*d*) Surrenders. (*e*) Loans. (*f*) Investments. (*g*) Reassurances. (*h*) Management expenses, etc. (*i*) Sundry Expenses.	The amounts entered in the respective columns are, in turn, supplied from "subsidiary" cash books. Examples of these are— 1. "Claims" Cash Books (Ordinary and Industrial). 2. Loans on Policies Cash Book. 3. Annuities Cash Book. 4. Surrenders. 5. Petty Cash Book, etc.

Reconciliation Statement. This is a statement drawn up so as to agree the bank balance *as shown by the Bank Statement*, with the bank balance *as shown by the bank column of the cash book*. The reconciliation statement is usually copied into the cash book at the end of the month as a record. The two balances seldom agree. Cheques paid to creditors are entered in the cash book as at the date they are drawn, but will not be shown in the bank statement until the creditors have cleared them. Again, cheques paid into the bank do not always appear in the bank statement on the same date; these statements are usually made up on the following day. These items furnish the material for the adjusting entries as shown in the example below.

RECONCILIATION STATEMENT

	£	£
Bank balance as per bank statement		550
Add Cheques, etc., paid in, not credited		67
		617
Deduct Cheques paid away, not yet presented—		
Smith & Son	16	
Jones & Co.	23	
Brown & Roberts	10	49
Bank balance as per cash book		568

Where the balances are overdrafts the position is of course reversed, cheques paid in but not credited being *deducted* and those not presented for payment being *added*. Items such as bank charges frequently appear in the bank statement and in practice are immediately entered in the cash book and a new balance struck before the reconciliation is attempted. For examination purposes this cannot be done, and the effect of such items must be allowed for in the agreement by cancelling their effect on the bank statement balance.

An example covering this point and showing a reconciliation between an *overdraft* in the bank statement and a *debit balance* in the cash book is set out below.

RECONCILIATION STATEMENT

	£	£
Balance being overdraft as per bank statement		249
Less Cheques paid in not credited		194
		55
Add Cheques not presented—		
E. J. Read	16	
R. Edwards	50	66
		121
Less Bill payable met not entered in cash book	188	
Payment under banker's order not entered in cash book	25	213
Balance as per cash book		92

Trial Balance

A Trial Balance is a schedule or list of balances, both debit and credit, extracted from the accounts in the ledger, and including the cash and bank balances from the cash book.

Object of the Trial Balance. Under double entry, the total debits in the ledger must be equal to the total credits, and the trial balance is the recognized method of ascertaining whether this is so or not. The trial balance, being a summary of the ledger, is also used as material for preparing the trading and profit and loss account and balance sheet.

Ways of Constructing a Trial Balance. A trial balance can be constructed in two ways: (1) by means of totals, (2) by means of balances. The first method is rarely used. The usual method is to take out the balances of accounts, ignoring those accounts in which the amounts on the one side correspond with the amounts on the other side. Some business houses, however, take out the trial balance in compound form, i.e. the totals and balances side by side. It has the advantage of revealing compensating errors, for the total of the debit column of the trial balance must then agree with the total of those subsidiary books that are posted to the debit of accounts in the ledger together with the closing cash balance but omitting the cash balance in the opening entries; and the total of the credit column of the trial balance must likewise agree with the total of those subsidiary books that are posted to the credit of accounts in the ledger. Where, after repeated attempts, the totals of the trial balance cannot be made to agree, the difference is, in practice, put temporarily to a special account entitled "Suspense Account," or "Error in Books," to await developments. The adjustment of such errors when found in a subsequent period is dealt with in Chapter 03.

Trial Balance not an Absolute Proof. The trial balance is a proof only of the *arithmetical* accuracy of the postings; and even so, it is only prima facie evidence of such accuracy. Certain classes of mistakes, as under, are not shown by the trial balance prepared of balances only—

1. OMISSION OF ENTRIES. If both the debit and credit entries of a transaction have been omitted, the trial balance will not be affected, and will not, therefore, reveal the error.

2. COMPENSATING ERRORS. If one account has been under- or over-debited or credited with a certain amount, say £20, and another account has been under- or over-debited or credited with the same amount, it will not prevent the agreement of the trial balance. Hence, the error will not be revealed.

3. MISPOSTING OF ACCOUNTS, OR ERRORS OF COMMISSION. If £100 has been posted to the credit of R. Smith instead of to the credit of F. Smith, or if £50 has been debited to F. Brown instead of F. Rogers, such a mistake does not throw out the trial balance.

4. ERRORS OF PRINCIPLE. If an item of revenue expense is debited to an asset account (or vice versa), the error does not affect the agreement of the trial balance, and thus is not revealed.

Common Errors in Trial Balances. The reason why the totals of many trial balances cannot be agreed at the first attempt is very often due to one or more of the following errors—

1. Debit balances in the ledger having been entered in the credit column of the trial balance, and vice versa.
2. Balances missed in extracting lists of debtors or creditors.
3. Bad figures.
4. Errors in calculations when "striking" the balances.
5. Transposition of figures—£18 for £81, £7·81 for £1·87.
6. The purchases book and sales book totals not posted to the purchases and sales accounts respectively.
7. The discount totals in the cash book either not posted to the Discount Account, or *misposted*, the sides being frequently reversed in error.
8. Cash and bank balances, as per the cash book, omitted from the trial balance, or entered in the credit column instead of the debit, an error caused by the balances on the credit side of the cash book not having been brought down to the debit side thereof.

In the examination room particularly, the sight of a trial balance which disagrees may be very unnerving. A rather wild search often ensues (probably in the hope of "stumbling" across the error). It is not a difficult task to prepare a plan of action in such an emergency and the following is recommended:

1. Add up both sides again; there may be an error in the addition of the trial balance itself.
2. Find the actual difference and divide by two. If this new figure is to be found in the trial balance it is almost certainly on the wrong side. The placing of a figure on the wrong side throws the trial balance out by double the amount.
3. Check for "transposed" figures, e.g. 39 instead of 93.
4. Glance quickly through for obvious errors such as capital, goodwill, stock, and cash balance on the wrong side, and see that discounts have not been overlooked.
5. Check the figures again from the ledger and cash book but this time total the items, divide by two and try to find sufficient credit items to equal the figure obtained. The other balances will be debits.

Construction of Trial Balance from List of Balances. Examination questions are sometimes set asking for the preparation of a trial balance from a given list of balances. This means that the items have to be sorted into debits and credits, the totals of which must agree. The procedure is not so simple as it looks at first sight, as students find when they actually essay the task. The following rules will be found useful—

1. Assets, losses, and expenses are debit balances.

2. Liabilities, gains, and profits are credit balances.

Thus purchases, wages, rent, etc., will be entered in the *Dr.* column of the trial balance; and sales, discounts received, interest received, etc., will be entered in the *Cr.* column. Again, stock, plant and machinery, bills receivable, etc., being assets, will be placed in the *Dr.* column; while capital, loans, bills payable, etc., being liabilities, will be placed in the *Cr.* column.

In items such as interest and discount it should be stated whether they have been received or paid; while the balances of personal accounts must be indicated as either *Dr.* or *Cr.* Sometimes the two sides of the trial balance do not agree by a large amount, and if there is no capital mentioned, the difference should be entered as such. In some cases, the question paper states that a business is purchased for a certain sum, but the net assets taken over (i.e. total assets less liabilities) amount to a smaller sum than the purchase price. The difference, of course, is goodwill.

SUBSIDIARY BOOKS

Petty Cash Book

In many firms, it is convenient for various responsible persons to hold a small amount of cash from which they may pay out small sums of money. This is known as "petty cash."

Imprest System. A common method of keeping the petty cash is what is known as the "Imprest System," by means of which a certain sum of money is definitely "retained" or "held" for petty cash expenditure. At the end of the month a cheque is drawn for the exact sum spent, so that the imprest amount is always in hand at the commencement of each month. The expenditure is recorded in a tabular petty cash book, and at any time the person responsible must be able to produce cash or vouchers explaining how the difference has been spent. A column is kept for each type of expense and the totals posted direct from the petty cash book to the expense account in the general ledger. Other methods of recording petty cash are also used.

Journal

The Journal or Day Book was originally a daily record into which all transactions were entered, classified into debits and credits and then posted or entered in the ledger accounts.

Nature and Use. Today the journal, if used at all, is used for the following transactions—

1. The purchase and sale of assets on credit.
2. Opening and closing entries.
3. The correction of errors.
4. Transfer between accounts.
5. Any other items not recorded in another book of original entry.

The following example will illustrate the form—

Feb. 12 A. Jones purchases plant £1,000 on credit from Machine Tools Ltd.

	JOURNAL	*Dr*	*Cr*
19..		£	£
Feb 12	Plant account	1,000	
	To Machine Tools Ltd. account		1,000
	Being the purchase of plant on credit for use in Department XYZ, in accordance with Directors' Minute No. .. of 10th January, 19..		

The Narration is a short explanation of the nature of the transaction which should always be given before the journal entry is closed. This is particularly so in the case of correction of errors as the nature of the entries would not otherwise be clear. For examination purposes a narration is essential.

Posting the Journal. When the journal entries have been completed, they are posted to the ledger. In the above example, plant account would be debited £1,000 and Machine Tools Ltd. account credited.

Documents used in Commercial Transactions

Every firm has its own peculiarities and will use forms designed to meet its own needs. However, the following documents are in general use in connexion with the purchase and sale of goods.

Invoice. The invoice states the quantity, price, and value of goods supplied in a transaction. It is sent by the seller to the buyer, and usually states the discounts allowable (trade and cash) and the terms of trade (the conditions under which payment is expected).

Debit Note. A seller uses a debit note if, for any reason, the amount stated on one of his invoices was too little. He will not send a new invoice, but merely send a debit note for the difference. Similarly, a purchaser who is returning goods to the seller may send a debit note with them to show that he expects the seller to bear the charge.

Credit Note. The credit note is sent by a seller when the amount stated on one of his invoices is too large.

Statement. Most firms send out a monthly statement to debtors. It shows the value of goods invoiced, *plus* debit notes, *minus* credit notes and amounts of cash paid, with the balance owing.

E. & O.E. Most documents are sent out on this basis—errors and omissions excepted.

Copies of the above documents may also be used for Warehouse Notes, Advice Notes, and Delivery Notes.

The invoice, debit note, and credit note provide the information from which the subsidiary books are entered up. In some modern systems, copies of these documents are filed, and in this form make up a subsidiary book.

Purchases Book

Nature and Use. All goods purchased for resale *on credit*, i.e. not paid for at the time of sale, are entered in the purchases book.

The usual purchases book, like the journal, uses two columns, but the first column records *details*, the second column, *totals*. For example, A. Jones records the purchase of goods on credit from A. Marshall, sports outfitter.

PURCHASES BOOK

		Details £	Totals £
19..			
Jan 10	*A. Marshall*		
	10 Footballs, leather P.Q.9, @ £4	40	
	6 Tennis racquets, Slaz Ltd., @ £5	30	
		70	
	Less Trade Discount	7	63

Trade discount is a reduction of the price of the goods and is usually deducted in the purchases book.

Posting the Purchases Book. The net amount of the invoices will be posted to the ledger as follows—

Credit the personal accounts of the sellers with the individual amounts which Jones owes them (£63 credited to Marshall, above).

Debit the purchases account with the *total* for the day.

More complicated rulings may be used where an analysis of purchases, into various classes, is required.

The purchases book may take the form of a Bought Book, Bought Day Book, or Invoice Book, and assets and expenses may be entered in it, in which case, it is essential to distinguish between the different types of transactions involved.

Sales Book

Nature and Use. In this book are recorded all goods sold *on credit*. The rulings and use are similar to that shown under "Purchases Book." If a regular credit customer happens to pay cash down for some particular goods in order to reap the benefit of a cash discount, it is best for such sale to be passed through the Sales Book in the usual way, so that the customer's account may be a full record instead of a partial one.

Odd and Even Day Books. In some businesses where bound books are used, the custom exists of keeping *odd* and *even* day books; that is to say, all transactions on even dates, such as 2nd, 4th, 6th, etc., will be entered in one book; and all transactions on odd dates, such as 1st, 3rd, 5th, etc., will be entered in another book. This ensures the clerical work being up to date, for the ledger clerk can be using one day book to post up the previous day's transactions, while the invoice clerk is using the other day book to write the current day's transactions.

Posting the Sales Book. The net amounts of the invoices are posted to the ledger as follows—

Debit the personal accounts of the customers with the value of sales to them.

Credit Sales Account with the total for the day.

More complicated rulings may be used.

Trade Discount. The list price of goods is the *gross selling price*. From this is deducted the trade discount, to give the *net selling price*. Unlike cash discount, trade discount is never entered in the accounts.

Sales Journal. This is a form of sales book adopted in those businesses where carbon-copy invoice books are in use. No details are entered in it, but merely the date, name, and total of each transaction, columns being provided for the purpose of analysis. Reference is made to the detail by quoting the number of the invoice or the folio or page of the copy book. The following is an example—

SALES JOURNAL

Date	No. of Invoice	Name	Led. Fol.	Total	Mantles	Dress Materials	Felts

Purchases Returns Book

Nature and Use. This book, called also "Returns Outwards Book," records all returns of goods *bought*. The reason for return may be that the goods are of the wrong kind, or not up to sample, or because they are damaged. The ruling of the book will naturally be identical with the ruling of the purchases book. Allowances claimed for breakages, short weight, overcharge, etc., are usually dealt with in the same book. Quite frequently this will be found at the back of the purchases day book.

Debit Note Book. A specially printed Memorandum Book is generally utilized. Debit notes with full particulars are sent to the parties concerned, the counterfoils providing the material for writing up the returns book.

Posting Purchases Returns. The entries are—

Debit the person in the bought ledger to whom goods have been returned or from whom an allowance has been claimed, with the individual amount.

Credit the total at the end of the month to purchases returns account in the general ledger.

Allowances which are not actual returns, i.e. abatement in price, claims for broken or damaged articles, etc., may be posted to a separate Allowances account. Returns and allowances are deducted from purchases in the final accounts.

Sales Returns Book

Nature and Use. This book, termed also "Returns Inwards Book," is used for the purpose of recording all returns of goods *sold.* The circumstances necessitating the return of the goods may be that they are of the wrong description, or of inferior quality, or damaged. The ruling of the book will, of course, correspond with that of the sales book. Allowances claimed in respect of short delivery, breakage, overcharge, etc., are usually included in the same book. The back of its corresponding day book is sometimes used for such returns, etc.

Credit Note Book. A specially printed counterfoil memorandum book is in common use. Credit notes, printed in red ink, with full details, are sent to the customers concerned, the counterfoils supplying the necessary particulars for writing up the returns book. Since, however, these items arise from claims by customers, another method is to *file the claims* and enter up the returns book from the file. This ensures that all credits are bona fide claims and obviates the possibility of an amount being collected and embezzled and then entered as "Returns."

Posting to Ledger. For items of allowances other than actual returns, a separate "Allowances Account" is sometimes kept in addition to a Returns Account, and closed at balancing time to the Trading Account through the Sales Account.

Posting Sales Returns. The entries are—

Credit in the sales ledger the account of the person who returned goods.

Debit the total at the end of the month to sales returns account.

Bill Books

Nature and Use. These are two subsidiary books, called Bills Receivable Book and Bills Payable Book respectively, used for the purpose of recording details of bills of exchange. (See Chapter 04.)

QUESTIONS

1. Define the term "journal." Explain why the journal has been gradually superseded by other "books of original entry."
2. Explain the present-day use of the journal. Why is it important that transfers should always be made by means of journal entries? What is meant by "narration"?
3. Explain the nature and use of the purchases book. What other names has it? How should *cash* purchases be treated?
4. What are "trade" discounts, and how should they be treated in books? Give examples of some common errors in the purchases book.
5. Explain the nature and use of the sales book. How should *cash* sales be dealt with?
6. Explain the practice of keeping "odd" and "even" day books, and its advantages.
7. Explain, with facsimile ruling, the nature and use of a "sales journal."
8. Explain the nature and use of a purchases returns book. What other name has it? What is a debit note?
9. Explain the nature and use of a sales returns book. What other name has it? What is a credit note book?

SINGLE ENTRY

The traditional system of accounting involves two entries, a debit and credit, in two different accounts and implies, therefore, some duplication of effort. Whilst this may be justified in some circumstances to guard against fraud, it is generally to be avoided and a variety of means may be employed.

Analysed Cash Books. A common system in small businesses is to maintain only a cash book, with analysis columns for each type of receipt or payment. Whilst this still requires two entries, they are made on the same document. Many firms produce standard rulings suitable for various types of businesses. An example produced by Kalamazoo Ltd., is shown in Figure 01.2. This provides for the common type of public-house receipts and payments and there are spare columns to allow some adaptation to individual needs. Where a business is small and mainly on a cash basis such a record is adequate but it must be supplemented by information concerning creditors and assets when the periodic statement of income and the Balance Sheet position is prepared.

Multiple Posting. Where a business is somewhat larger and credit sales and purchases are the norm, but the clerical work is still insufficient to justify mechanization, then a standardized system may be used in conjunction with a "peg-board." This board allows the accurate location of documents one over the other and carbon or "no-carbon required" stationery is used to give posting of several records at one writing. For instance, the receipt of a cheque may be recorded simultaneously in the cash book and in the personal account and monthly statement of the customer. Once the routine has been learned such systems are highly economical. A full set of double-entry accounts and subsidiary records is maintained and a trial balance can be extracted when the periodic accounts and Balance Sheet are required.

Punched Cards and Tape. In the larger businesses, punched card and tape records may be used alone or in conjunction with a computer. In this case, only a single entry is made in respect of each transaction but it is coded in such a way that each type of information required e.g. sales, cash received, acquisition of assets, revenue expenses can be extracted by analysis of the cards.

Figure 01.3 shows the general layout of an ICT 40 column card. The more common system gives 80 columns.

Cards are divided horizontally into rows, each with digits 0 to 9. The card can, also, be punched in two other positions in the blank space above 0, thus allowing numbers 11 and 12 to be punched, if required (this is necessary where non-decimal currency is used, for instance).

The system is set up by dividing the card into "fields," with one for each characteristic or type of information. The field must allow the maximum piece of information to be punched. For instance, if the date is

Manager..House...........................Cash in Hand..Year Ending...............Sept. 19...............

Week Ending	Total Takings	Bar Takings	State Insurance	Sundry Expenses	Amount Banked	Remarks	Staff Hours	Insurance Stamps

FIG. 01.2. MANAGEMENT HOUSE TAKINGS AND EXPENSES

(*Note:* The above Account has been condensed and would normally contain many other items such as Wages, Sundries, Fuel and Heating, Cleaning and Materials, etc.).

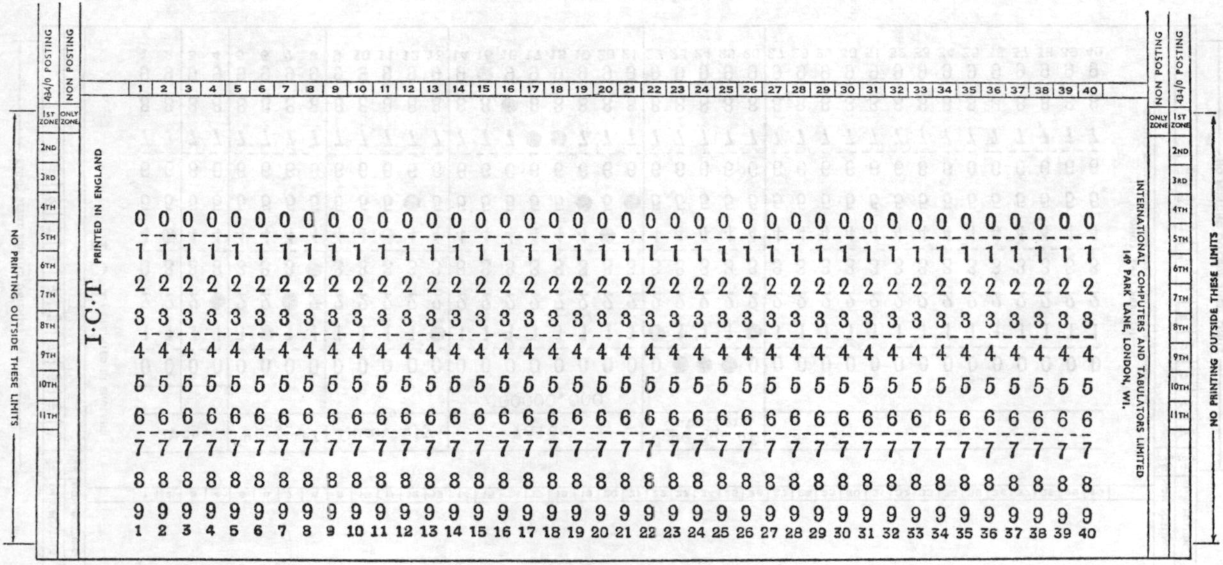

NO PRINTING OUTSIDE THESE LIMITS
434/0 POSTING
NON POSTING
1ST ZONE
ONLY ZONE
2ND
3RD
4TH
5TH
6TH
7TH
8TH
9TH
10TH
11TH
I·C·T
PRINTED IN ENGLAND
INTERNATIONAL COMPUTERS AND TABULATORS LIMITED
149 PARK LANE, LONDON, W1.

FIG. 01.3

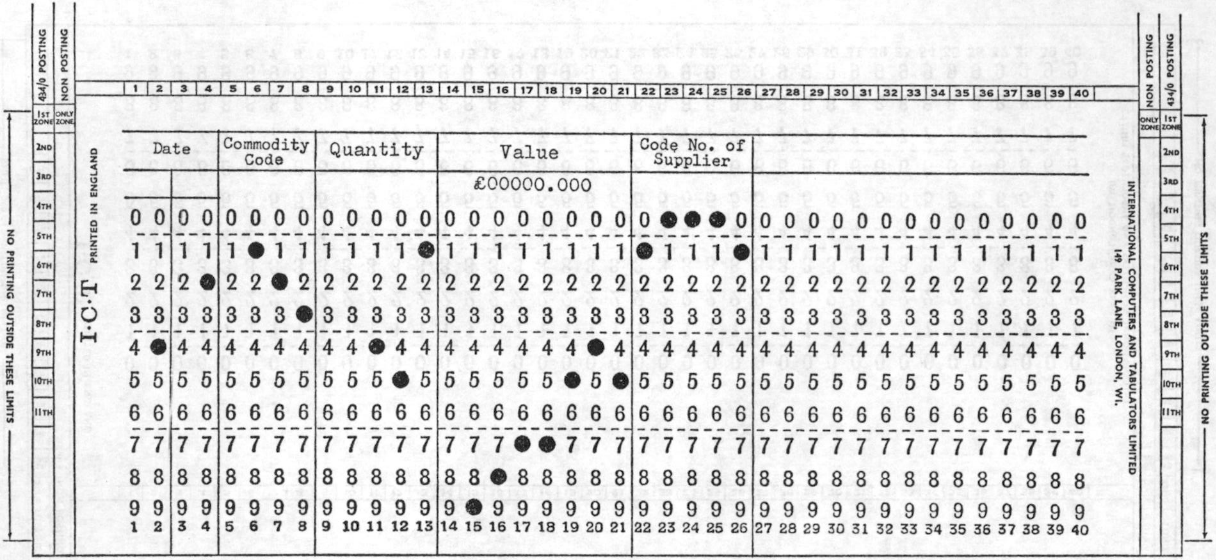
434/0 POSTING
NON POSTING
NO PRINTING OUTSIDE THESE LIMITS
I·C·T
PRINTED IN ENGLAND
Date
Commodity Code
Quantity
Value
£00000.000
Code No. of Supplier
INTERNATIONAL COMPUTERS AND TABULATORS LIMITED
149 PARK LANE, LONDON, W1.

FIG. 01.4

4th February, 1968, the requirements will vary according to the life of the cards, as follows—

Days only recorded—two columns needed (max. days 31).

Days and months—four columns needed (max. days 31, max. months 12) and so on.

The coding of the 4th February would then be—

04	(days only)
0402	(days and months)
040268	(days, months and years)

Notice that it is probably unnecessary to record the centuries!

A simple example of fields might be as shown in Figure 01.4. This has two fields for the date, a commodity code, the quantity, the value and the code number of the supplier.

The commodity code allows coding up to reference number 9,999 and the quantity may be up to 99,999 units.

The numbers omitted indicate where holes would be punched on a card if a delivery was made with the following details—

Code	0402	4th February
	0123	Commodity N° 123
	00451	Four hundred and fifty one units
	09877545	Valued at £9,877·545
	10001	Supplied by D. Smith (Code 10001)

Sorting. The cards may be sorted in a variety of ways. For instance, they could be arranged in date order; they could be arranged in commodity order and this would give the total purchases of that commodity on certain dates or over certain periods; they could be sorted by supplier or by any combination of these.

Tabulation. After sorting, a tabulator may be used to print out the information, and this could print the amount of each purchase by commodity or supplier and this may also be totalled.

If a card is punched whenever a purchase is made, it is also possible to provide for these to be punched in a "paid" column or a new card can be punched for receipts or payments. The tabulator can then provide the net amount owed or owing at the end of a period and this can be automatically punched into a summary card.

USES OF COMPUTERS

The use of computers is now so widespread that there are very few people who are not affected by their use. Bank Statements, bills for electricity and gas, payments for rates and other services are handled by computer systems. It is commonplace that computer capacity is increasing, but also the costs of computers are falling dramatically and the physical size for a given capacity is now almost infinitesimal compared to the early computers. This implies a growing use of computers in all kinds of business whether large or small, in schools, and in firms and personal uses.

The idea of a computer as an electronic "brain" underestimates the value of the human brain which is unrivalled in its ability to handle complexity and in its adaptability, and overestimates the capacity of the electronic computer whose main virtues are predictability and reliability in use.

Types of Computer. There are two types of computer: *digital* and *analogue*. The digital computer operates on circuits which either pass current or do not, and these conditions may be represented by binary notation which has only two symbols a one and a zero. Because of this, binary notation, if written, requires many more places as can be seen below—

Notation	
Decimal	*Binary*
0	0
1	1
2	10
3	11
4	100
5	101
6	111
7	1000
8	1001
9	1011
10	1111

The analogue computer represents information on scales with a continuous range of values. Input values can be set for a number of variables in accordance with mathematical relationships, and the resultant value can be read on output scales. Most general purpose computers are digital, but some are constructed for special scientific purposes. Analogue computers are special-purpose machines, although a slide rule is a manually operated analogue computer. Figure 01.5 shows the general scheme for a general purpose digital computer. The functions are as follows—

1. *Stores data.* A computer can store a vast quantity of information internally and externally.

2. *Arithmetic operation.* The machine adds and substracts at the speed of light 186,000 miles per second and, by repetition, will give multiplication and division. All mathematical operations are broken down into these fundamental operations.

3. *Control of operations.* This is the significant difference between a computer and other machines. It can compare for sign (plus or minus), for equality, and also in terms of relative size. Control operations are performed in accordance with programs situated in the control unit. A program states, in great detail, the steps required to accomplish each function, and these steps are then converted into instructions in the

standard language which the machine uses or "recognizes." Coded instructions may be held in the computer during a particular run and returned to an external store when the run is completed. The control unit executes

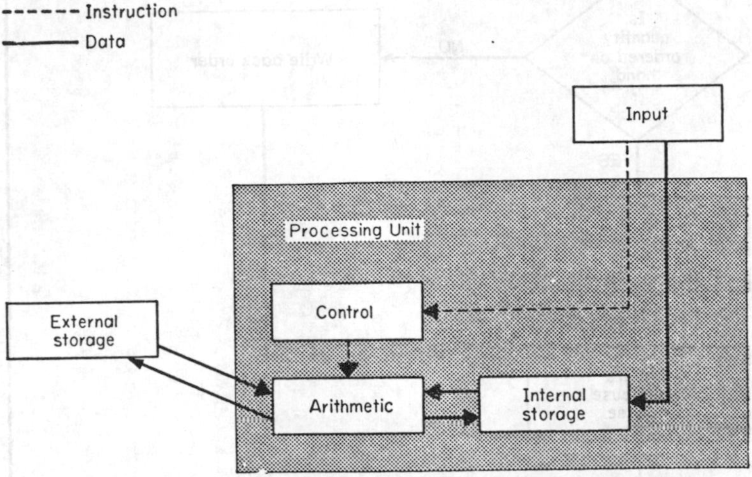

Fig. 01.5. Computer Schematic

each instruction in turn and determines which command to execute next. Figure 01.6 shows an example of command sequences used in a stock control routine.

Input. Each letter, symbol, e.g. £, %, 1, 2, etc., is called a character in the code, and the power of the computer is measured by the number of characters per second that it can process. Input and output of data is the slowest part of a computer operation according to the method used. Punch cards can handle 1,300 characters per second, and magnetic tape 300,000 characters per second. One tape of 2,400 feet holds 40 million characters.

MICR is Magnetic Ink Character Recognition, and this is faster because the characters can be read by machine, e.g. the cheque and account number on clearing-bank cheques. Some systems also allow direct entry through a typewriter. This is often associated with a visible output, e.g. the airline reservation system which provides input and output for any clerk or agent, allows him to see the state of booking for any flight, to make reservations, and to change reservations.

Output. Output may be provided in the forms used for input, but also may be printed, in the form of charts, visual display, or even a tape file with spoken sounds.

Storage. Since a machine can use 100,000 or more pieces of information per second, the time it takes to get new information, i.e. the access

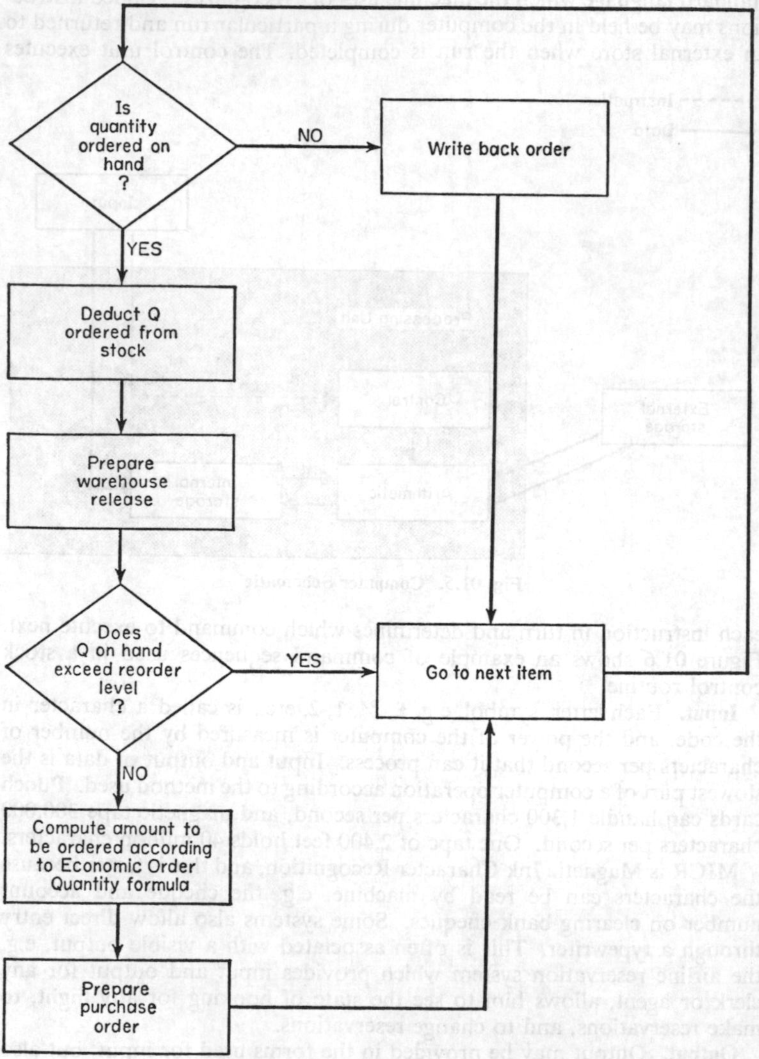

FIG. 01.6. **Order Processing Procedure**

time, is critical. Internal storage of data gives faster access, but is relatively costly. External storage on tape drives may need access time of minutes. An access time of less than one-half of a second to 3 to 100 million characters can be obtained by using discs. Even a medium-sized computer might also use magnetic tape and 200 cells or strips give a storage of 400 million characters.

Computer Languages. There are a number of computer languages of which the best known are, perhaps, COBOL and FORTRAN. These languages allow a programmer to instruct the computer on the operations it is to perform and the kind of data which it is to accept. A simple language is BASIC, and instructions in BASIC are put through a compiler which translates a language to the language which the computer uses. All languages have standardized operations or elements, e.g. sort in alphabetical order, raise to the *n*th power. There are also many standardized programs available, e.g. preparation of pay-roll including calculation of income tax and other deductions.

Modes of Processing. The following methods of presenting information to the computer processing may be used—

(*a*) *On-line or Real-time*. In this mode each user is able to feed information directly to the computer and to elicit immediate responses. The airline reservation system is an example already quoted.

(*b*) *Off-line or Batch Processing*. This is a less expensive method. Programs and data are put on the machine for a particular operation and processed in batches. This is well suited to routine, repetitive computing tasks.

(*c*) *Time-sharing*. This is a form of on-line service in which a large number of users have direct access to a large computer which is able to work on several programs "simultaneously." In fact, the users form a queue, but the waiting time is usually so short that none of them is made aware of this. Standard programs are available, and it is also possible to write programs and to have the computer store them without other users being able to gain an access.

LOOSE-LEAF AND CARD LEDGERS

Loose-leaf Ledgers consist of sheets ruled like the pages of an old-style bound ledger, such sheets being inserted or abstracted from an expanding binder as and when required. A certain number of sheets are printed and numbered; and a register is kept which shows when and to whom they were issued. The sheets are arranged alphabetically, A1, A2, A3, etc., B1, B2, B3, etc., C1, C2, C3, etc., and the number given to a customer when an account is opened for him always appears on all sheets relating to this particular customer. Thus, suppose James Smith is the twenty-third customer whose name begins with S; then S23 will always appear on the ledger sheets of James Smith's account, and as further sheets are added they will be numbered S23/1, S23/2, S23/3, etc. The ledger sheets are kept in two distinct binders or holders, one for *live* or *current* accounts and the other for *dead* or *closed* accounts. If the transaction is a chance one, the customer's account, when paid, is transferred to the closed section; if it is followed later on by further transactions, the account is retransferred to the current section. **Card Ledgers** are on exactly the same principle, the cards, however, being kept in special trays or drawers. The loose-leaf binders and the card trays or drawers are generally fitted with patent locking devices, the keys of which can be retained by someone in authority. Though very suitable for the personal accounts of debtors and creditors, they can also be used to advantage for statistical records, such as cost accounts, register of members of a joint stock company, etc.

Advantages. The advantages claimed for loose leaf and card ledgers are as follows—

1. The current ledger is not cumbered with dead or closed accounts, as the latter are taken out and filed separately; neither does it contain a number of blank pages.
2. There is no need for an index, the cards and leaves being arranged alphabetically.
3. The ledgers are continuous or "perpetual." Extra leaves or cards are added for each new account.
4. The work of posting, rendering statements, or taking out balances can be performed much more quickly, as sheets can be allotted to a number of clerks simultaneously.
5. An account is continuous, not scattered over many pages of a bound ledger.
6. When accounts are the subject of litigation, to produce a few loose leaves or cards instead of bound books is easier for the court and the litigant, and it would not bring the clerical work to a standstill owing to the books being away.

Disadvantages. The principal disadvantages of loose leaf and card ledgers are—

1. The cards or leaves may be accidentally or wilfully lost or destroyed.
2. Fresh cards or leaves may be fraudulently substituted for others, in order to commit or conceal fraud.

SLIP SYSTEM OF BOOK-KEEPING

Nature and Use. The "slip" system of book-keeping is really a reintroduction of the earliest methods of "book-keeping without books," that is, a recording on loose sheets of paper of transactions usually entered in subsidiary books. In its widest sense the term includes also loose-leaf and card ledgers.

Under the old-style system of book-keeping, transactions are recorded in books of original entry, and these transactions have to be copied into the ledger. The copying process has to be continued in other books according to the complexity of the transactions and the requirements of the business itself. The object of the slip system is to do away with this constant re-copying, by making the original record serve all the purposes of book-keeping. Thus, a carbon copy of an invoice may serve the purpose of both day book and ledger account. The counterfoils of receipts and cheques may be posted direct to the ledger accounts affected, thus avoiding the copying into the cash book, and the subsequent copying from there into the ledger. Naturally, there are many variations of detail in practice, a constant compromise, so to speak, between principle and convenience. The slip system has been adopted by banks for many years, the numerous customers' accounts being regularly posted up from original "dockets," such as paying-in slips, cheques, etc.

Advantages. The following advantages are claimed for the slip system of book-keeping—

1. Saving of time and labour, as it reduces the number of subsidiary books.

2. Ledgers can be posted more promptly, as the slips can if necessary be distributed among several ledger clerks simultaneously.

3. The minimizing of the risk of error, as much copying into intermediate books is dispensed with.

4. Ready reference from the ledger direct to the original slips.

Slip Day Book Sales. A large book is generally used with at least three or four printed and numbered invoice forms on a page. Carbon copies are obtained each time an invoice is made out. Postings are made from the carbon facsimiles (which are also detachable), *direct* to the personal accounts in the ledger. References are made in the ledger to the number of the posting slips, which are then carefully filed alphabetically, and in order of date. If subsequent reference is likely to be frequent, the detail itself is often copied into the ledger so as to avoid the constant turning up of slips. The amount of each invoice is extended into money columns provided on the counterfoils, or entered on a summary sheet against its corresponding number, or into a specially ruled dissection book if dissection is necessary; and the totals of the counterfoils, summary sheet, or dissection book are posted periodically to the sales account. In some cases, however, the amount of each slip is posted direct to the sales account.

A simple form of such day book is in use in most retail shops. Carbon copy "bills" or invoices are made out for each sale, one copy being given to the customer and the other handed in at the cash desk. Each form is numbered, and the amount of each sale is registered on a summary sheet at the back of the book, so that the total sales may be ascertained daily or periodically. Where dissection is imperative, the carbon duplicates are usually on different coloured papers, according to the departments making the sales and dissection is easily carried out, by simply sorting the slips into their different colours and then totalling them. Under this system, one of the commonest errors is guarded against, namely, the sending out of an invoice without any record of the sale being made in the day book. The principal objections to the ordinary bound day book are the length of time taken to compile it, lack of facilities for dissection, and the uncertainty as to whether the entries made therein correspond exactly with the invoices sent out to the customers.

Purchases. Invoices for assets and expenses are filed and, as when paid for at time of purchase, the personal side is ignored by posting the payment in the cash book direct to the asset or expense account involved. Thus, suppose on the 15th of the month we bought some stationery from Brown & Co. When the invoice was received it would simply be filed, and at the end of the month when the account was paid, the entry in the cash book would be *By Stationery* (*Brown* & *Co.*), which would be posted direct to the stationery account. This saves a considerable amount of entering up in the purchases book and is, perhaps, quite satisfactory in those businesses where the items are few and it is the custom to pay all such accounts at the end of the month.

Slip Cash Book. Where numerous subsidiary cash books are in use, a great saving of labour may be effected by the adoption of the slip system. An ordinary sized Cash Received Book is employed, having three or four printed and numbered carbon copy receipt forms on a page, which are provided with numbered counter-foils ruled with money columns. The carbon duplicates are detached and handed to the ledger clerks concerned for posting to the various personal accounts, after which they are filed alphabetically and in order of date. The totals of the counterfoils serve as a check on the debit side of the general cash book, and also for the purpose of compiling adjustment accounts for "self-balancing ledgers." The practice of using carbon receipts obviates the risk of money being received and acknowledged without any record being made of it. It is not, however, an infallible safeguard against embezzlement, as the receipts may be fraudulently altered; but it is a sufficient safeguard, inasmuch as alteration or erasure can be more or less easily detected.

As regards a Cash Paid Book, the same system could be employed, i.e. each page would contain three or four cheque forms provided with detachable duplicates, and with counterfoils ruled with money columns. The duplicates would be used for the purpose of posting to the bought ledger and impersonal ledger accounts, while the counterfoils when totalled would act as a check on the credit side of the general cash book.

Slip Ledger. Where it is desired to make the original slip serve all the purposes of book-keeping, the sale slips are not filed away in order of date, but are sorted into alphabetical order and placed in separate files or drawers. The personal account of each customer, therefore, consists of loose slips. When transactions are settled, the slips are removed to another set of files or drawers. This system is only suitable for businesses where the number of customers is very numerous, but the transactions with each only few in number, e.g. where the customers are chance and not regular ones. It may also be used for businesses where the accounts are nominally on a cash basis, but where it is sometimes necessary to give regular customers seven to ten days' credit. The advantages of this method are that it is absolutely direct, there being no intermediate entry between the original slip and the ledger; also it obviates the risk of error arising from copying. A typical slip system flow chart is shown in Figure 01.7.

TABULAR SYSTEM OF BOOK-KEEPING

The tabular or columnar system, by permitting columns for each kind of item, allows continuous analysis or classification, thereby saving the trouble of periodical dissection and summarizing. The arithmetical accuracy of the analysis can be verified by means of cross-casting. It is particularly suitable where transactions are of a regular type and frequent in occurrence.

Advantages. The system is simple in application, and can be adapted to almost any book of account or a statistical book. It economizes time and saves labour. Tabulated details are often of great importance, and serve many useful purposes in modern business, for comparison and estimating.

Disadvantages. The disadvantages are that the books required are often unwieldy; and items may easily be analysed into wrong columns and thus vitiate the whole of the results.

Tabular Books of Account. Examples of tabular subsidiary books will be found in departmental purchases and sales books, in the journal, cash book, petty cash book, and purchases book shown in the working of the exercise on self-balancing ledgers; in the trustee-in-bankruptcy's cash book. Examples of tabular ledger accounts are given in the sections dealing with departmental accounts, branch accounts, and investment accounts. Examples of tabular ledgers will be found in the sections on cost ledger, stores ledger, share ledger, bills receivable and payable ledgers.

Tabular Statistical Books. Examples of these are seen in the application, allotment, and call books, in the register of transfers, etc., of a company; in the policy registers of an insurance company; in cost accounts in the wages analysis book, the allocation of stores issued book, stores received and stores issued books, etc.; in the register of investments of an investment company, etc.

QUESTIONS

1. What are "cash" discounts, and how should they be treated in the books? What variations are there in practice with regard to the treatment of cheques?
2. How should cash sales be treated in the cash book?

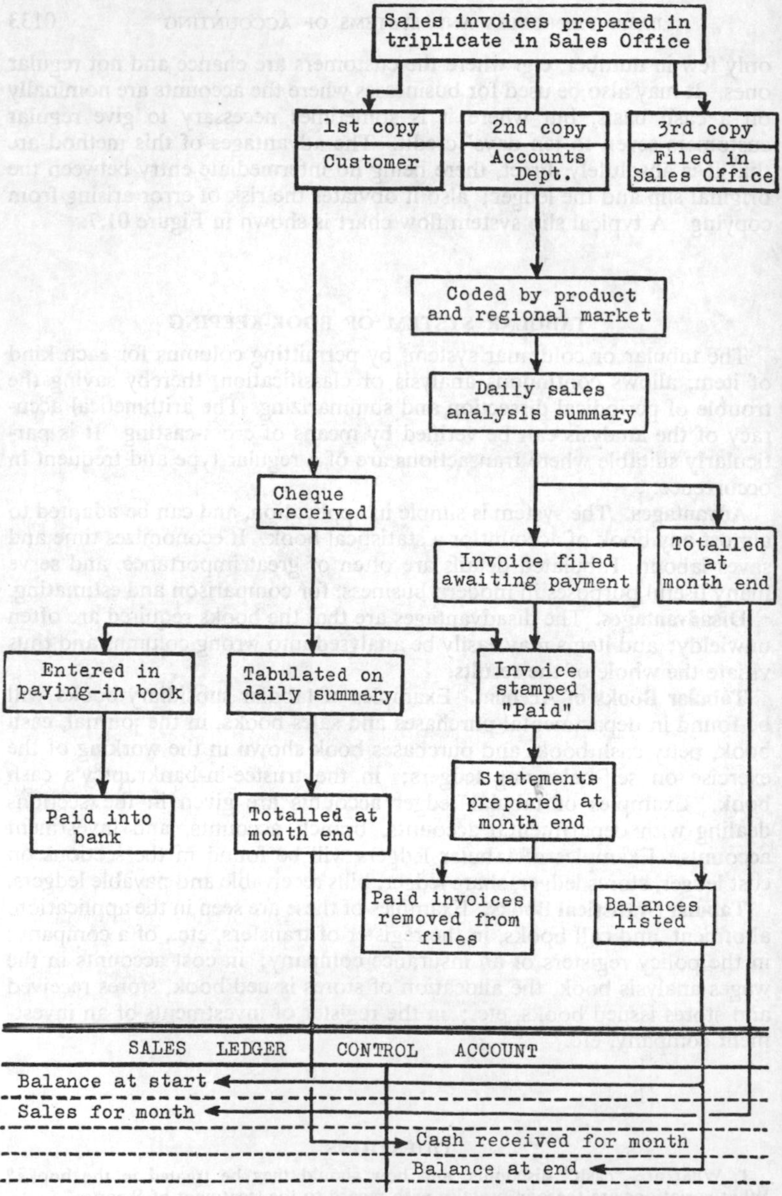

FIG. 01.7. Slip System Flow Chart

3. How is the cash book posted to the ledger as regards: (*a*) receipts, (*b*) payments, (*c*) discounts? When is the cash book balanced, and why?

4. Explain briefly the nature and use of a "bank cash book." Submit an example and make six specimen entries therein.

5. What is a reconciliation statement or account?

6. Explain briefly the nature and use of a petty cash book.

7. What is mean by the Imprest System of keeping the petty cash? Give a short account of its operation and advantages.

8. What is a ledger? Explain its form and use.

9. What is a cash book? Explain its use. Is the cash book a "principal" or a "subsidiary" book? Give reasons for your answer.

10. Explain the terms "cash," "contra," "Dr." and "Cr." in a cash book.

11. Name the usual subdivisions of the ledger, and give a short description of each. What mistake is sometimes made with reference to the use of the term "nominal ledger"?

12. What other divisions of ledgers are sometimes met with? Explain the "sectional" divisions of ledgers. When should ledgers be balanced?

13. Describe briefly the nature and use of "loose leaf" and "card" ledgers.

14. Enumerate the advantages and disadvantages of loose leaf and card ledgers as compared with the ordinary ledgers.

15. Write a short description of the "slip system" of book-keeping or accounting. What advantages are claimed for it?

16. What is a trial balance? What is the object of it?

17. In how many ways can a trial balance be constructed? Explain each method and the advantages attaching thereto.

18. What errors are not disclosed by the trial balance in its modern form?

19. Describe some of the common errors which prevent the agreement of trial balances.

EXERCISE 01

1. Journalize the following—

(*a*) 15th January. Exchanged 3 carpets, valued at £40 each, for 2 office desks worth £120.

(*b*) Exchanged, on 17th January, office safe, valued at £200, for typewriter worth £180.

2. Enter the following transactions into a suitable purchases book, showing discounts in full detail—

		£
Jan 1	Bought of A. Brown, 20 bags of coffee, less 10 per cent trade discount, net	72·90
5	Purchased from R. Smith & Co., 12 cases of sugar, less 12½ per cent trade discount, net	42·70
Jan 9	Bought of T. Titus, 6 chests of tea, less 20 per cent trade discount, net	36·60
15	Bought of O. Omicron & Son, 20 bags of coffee, less 7½ per cent trade discount, net	74·74
23	Purchased of P. Peters Ltd., 20 cases of sugar, less 5 per cent trade discount, net	57·95
27	Bought of L. Lucas, 12 bags of cocoa, less 25 per cent trade discount, net	28·73

3. Set out below are extracts from the cash book (bank columns only), and bank statement of J. Bull. Prepare a "reconciliation statement" as on 31st December.

CASH BOOK

19..			£	19..			£
Dec	1	Balance	458·20	Dec	2	Wages	48·00
	4	J. Smith & Co.	51·50		4	Petty Cash	10·00
	7	Brown Bros.	104·45		9	Self (Private)	100·00
	9	George White & Son	44·90		14	J. Tucker	284·15
	11	Buller & Co.	124·15		16	Wages	51·00
	29	Plumer & Co.	98·00		20	Cheque Book	0·25
	30	P. Methuen	208·80		30	Chermside & Co.	41·00
	31	Cronje & Co.	84·70		31	Salaries	35·00
						Wages	49·00
						Hunter & Co.	101·25
						Balance c/d	455·05
			1,174·70				1,174·70
19..							
Jan	1	Balance b/d	455·05				

BANK STATEMENT

(J. Bull in A/c with the Blankshire Bank)

19..			£	19..			£
Jan	1	Self	50·00	Dec	31	Balance forward	205·80
		Comm. on Scotch Draft (Plummer & Co.)	0·05	19..			
	2	Hunter & Co.	101·25	Jan	1	Plumer & Co.	98·00
		P. Carew	48·05			Cronje & Co.	84·70
	3	Comm. on Scotch Draft (J. Dundonald)	0·05			J. Dundonald	49·75
		Unpaid Draft (Cronje & Co.)	84·70			P. Methuen	208·80
		Chermside & Co.	41·00		6	J. Smith & Co.	48·67
		Wages	52·00				

(*London Chamber of Commerce.*)

4. From the following figures prepare a draft bank reconciliation statement—

	£
Balance shown in bank sheet	1,123·25
Balance shown in cash book	968·15
Cheques paid in but not yet credited	72·00
Cheques outstanding (unpresented)	240·30
Bank charges omitted from cash book	20·05
Bank interest credited, not in cash book	2·35
Cheque book omitted from cash book	0·60

How would you proceed to locate the error disclosed by the statement?

(*Chartered Institute of Secretaries.*)

5. Approaching the last week of his financial year to 31st October, 19 . ., P. Wrigley's ledger accounts show the following balances—

		Dr £	*Cr* £
Capital			1,065
Furniture and fittings		276	
Stock		1,099	
Motor vehicles		992	
Establishment expenses		1,072	
Selling and distribution expenses		1,419	
Purchases	totals to end of September	10,118	
Sales	totals to end of September		15,928
Discounts allowed	totals to end of September	377	
Discounts received	totals to end of September		245
J. Harcourt		229	
H. Gould		141	
S. Scott Ltd.			303

The sales and purchases day books for the month of October to date showed totals of, respectively, £1,078 and £726 and the figures for October brought forward in the cash book were—

	Discount £	Cash £	Bank £
Debit side	29	209	2,931
Credit side	25	187	787

Transactions during the ensuing week were—

Received payment from Harcourt, less £9 discount.
Sold goods on credit to H. Gould £89.
Paid cash for sundry office expenses £11.
Bought goods for cash £32.
Received £100 on account from H. Gould.
Sold goods for cash £185.
Paid Scott's account by cheque, being allowed £12 discount.
Purchased further goods from S. Scott Ltd. £77.
Withdrew cash for private purposes £15.
Bought new furniture for office, paying by cheque £20.
Drew cheque for wages £144 (£66 for office staff, £78 for "outside" staff).
Paid into bank cash and cheques to total of £436.
Sold goods on credit to T. Richie £54.

You are required to enter the opening balances and other figures direct into their relevant books and thereafter to make the necessary original entries in respect of the week's transactions and to close and fully post to the ledger the various books of original entry.

It should be noted that *no* trial balance is called for.

(*London Chamber of Commerce.*)

6. Make the journal entries necessary to record the following in the books of John Farmer, a wood merchant—

(*a*) Commission at the rate of 2½ per cent on a turnover of £9,342·35 due to Mr. Low, one of his travellers.

(*b*) Solicitor's charges of £9·20 for the collection of a debt of £87·55 due from H. Smith (a customer), the charges having been deducted from the amount of the debt, and the balance paid to Farmer on 30th August, 19 . .

(*c*) The taking over from a customer (D. Harris) of a second-hand car, valued at £40, in reduction of the amount owing by him.

7. The following transactions take place in the course of trading of a merchant, P. Holland. In respect of each you are required to state which ledger account would be debited and which credited and, with regard to the accounts named, whether the account is a personal account (P), a real account (R), or a nominal account (N).

Your answer should be tabulated in the form—

Date|P, R, or N|Account Debited|Account Credited|P, R, or N

19..
Aug 1 T. Ware paid his account by cheque.
2 Payments made for wages and petty expenses.
5 Purchased goods on credit from Valentine & Co.
7 Received an invoice from Office Equipment Ltd. in respect of a desk purchased from them.
P. Jackson paid his account by cash, being allowed discount for prompt payment.
8 Valentine & Co. agreed to make an allowance in respect of faulty goods supplied.
9 The proprietor drew a cheque for his private expenses and also took some goods from stock for his personal use.
11 Goods supplied on credit to K. Barford.
12 Cash and cheques paid into bank.
14 Sent cheque to Electricity Board in payment of account for electricity.

(*London Chamber of Commerce.*)

8. The system in force for the recording of the transactions of Jarrow & Jersey Ltd. is that all invoices, whether for goods or for services, are entered in the purchases journal, the entries in that journal being analysed to furnish the totals for posting to the impersonal ledger.

Rule a purchases journal which would give the details required, enter the following invoices, and show the totals under each heading—

19..		£
Jan 1	Leek & Co.—raw materials	176·25
	Postmaster-General—telephone	22·25
	Leigh & Co. Ltd.—raw materials	283·34
	Electricity Board—light and power	157·21
	Luton Bros.—raw materials	530·39
	Ashby S.S. Co.—freight	126·50
	Melton & Son—carriage	53·52
	J. Mowbray—raw materials	510·00
	Morpeth Ltd.—rent	300·00
	Road Services—carriage	58·49
	A. Malvern—printing	27·39
	Leek & Co.—raw materials	520·00

(*R.S.A.*)

9. In the books of Dundee & Co. is an account for J. Blythe in both the bought and sales ledgers.

On 28th February, 19.., the bought ledger account showed a credit balance of £260 and the sales ledger account was closed.

During the month of March, 19.., the following transactions took place—

19..
Mar 4 Sold goods on credit to Blythe for £285.
10 Purchased goods on credit from Blythe for £75.
12 Paid Blythe the balance due on the 1st day of the month *less* 2½ per cent cash discount, by cheque.
17 Blythe returned goods and Dundee & Co. issued a credit note for £15.

Mar 20 Sold goods on credit to Blythe for £290.
24 Purchased goods on credit from Blythe for £120, *less* a trade discount of 10 per cent.
26 One-half of the goods purchased on the 24th were returned to Blythe and an allowance of the cost of such goods made by Blythe.

Complete the accounts of J. Blythe in the books of Dundee & Co., showing the balance outstanding on each account at the end of the month.

(*R.S.A.*)

10. A. Atherstone carries on business as a manufacturer of hats and he requires the following details of his sales at the end of each week—

(*a*) Total sales;
(*b*) „ „ in the United Kingdom;
(*c*) „ „ abroad;
(*d*) „ „ of felt hats;
(*e*) „ „ of helmets.

During the week ending 7th January, 19.., the invoices issued were—

19..				£
Jan 2	A. Dalston	United Kingdom	helmets	355
	M. Salisbury	Rhodesia	felts	297
3	L. Kaus	Nigeria	„	201
	London & Co.	United Kingdom	„	674
4	J. Brighton	„ „	„	320
5	C. Kingston	Jamaica	„	254
	K. Rugby	United Kingdom	„	172
6	B. Karachi	India	helmets	301
	S. Sydney	Australia	felts	283
7	C. Cardiff	United Kingdom	„	348

Rule a sales journal that would give the information required, enter the above-mentioned invoices, and show the totals for the week ending 7th January, 19...

(*R.S.A.*)

11. A firm maintains a petty cash book with headings to the analysis columns of Postages, Motor Expenses and Travelling, Stationery and Advertising, Office Expenses and Sundries, and "Ledger."

During a typical week's activities the following outgoings fall to be recorded in the petty cash book—

19..			£
Mar	9	Postage stamps purchased	0.50
		Boy's fares in delivering parcel	0·08
	10	Cost of registered letter	0·05
	11	Petrol for van	0·72
		Advertisement in local paper	0·56
		Paid for tea and milk for office staff	0·17
	12	Paid creditor (B. Settle) his balance due	0·95
		Traveller's order book bought	0·20
	13	Paid for postage stamps	1·00
		Postage on parcel	0·17
		Petrol and oil for van	1·13
	14	Paid office cleaner	0·75

The book is operated on the imprest system with a float of £10, reimbursement being made to the petty cashier at the end of each week.

You are required—

(*a*) to write up the petty cash book from the information given and bring down the balance as on 16th March,

(*b*) to state how the "double entry" is effected in the firm's books relative to the petty cash items.

(*London Chamber of Commerce.*)

12. John Foster's position at 31st January, 19.., is reflected in the following balances: Cash in hand £23·25, Stock of goods £201, Motor-car £303, Office fixtures and fittings £47·50, Bank overdraft £158·25, Sundry debtors: H. Earle £89·15, P. Lord £45·60, Trade creditor: £95·50. (Supermarkets Ltd.).

During the following week the undermentioned transactions ensued in connexion with Foster's business—

	£		£
Invoices were issued to—		*Invoices were received from—*	
P. Lord	35·90	Debrett & Co.	35·33
A. Duke	24·00	Supermarkets Ltd.	40·50
L. Marquis	49·80		
		A Credit Note was received from—	
Payments were received from—		Supermarkets Ltd.	8·75
P. Lord (discount allowed £2·16)	43·44		
A. Duke (in settlement)	22·80	*Cheques were drawn for—*	
R. Baron (for old desk)	7·50	Supermarkets Ltd. (in settlement of opening balance)	90·00
Cash sales	133·85	Courtier Bros. (for new desk)	20·50
Cash was paid for—		Rent	15·50
Goods purchased	27·90	Foster's private purposes	10·00
Office expenses	11·04		
Wages	19·50		

and cash and cheques totalling £148·65 were paid into the bank.

You are to open Foster's books through the medium of an entry in the journal, to write up his cash book for the week, and to make *all* relevant entries in the ledger. No day books are required to be written up since it is intended that the details of credit transactions given above shall themselves constitute the original entry of these transactions.

Cash book and accounts should be balanced off as necessary but no trial balance is required.

(*London Chamber of Commerce.*)

13. Messrs. Judex, a retail shop, buy goods from Girlswear Ltd., a wholesale company. Messrs. Judex, who prepare accounts annually to 31st December, enter all invoices in detail in their purchase day book, posting only the monthly totals to the credit of the suppliers' accounts in the bought ledger. Girlswear Ltd., who use a system of mechanized accounting, send out statements made up to the 20th of each month.

The following are the statements received by Messrs. Judex from Girlswear Ltd. for the months ended 20th December, 19.., and 20th January, 19.1—

Date		Particulars	Debits £	Credits £	Balance £
Nov	20	Previous balance			19·30
	21	Goods	3·25		22·55
	29	,, ...	2·75		25·30
Dec	7	,, ...	3·96		29·26
	11	,, ...	1·17		30·43
	12	Cash		18·80	
	12	Discount		0·47	11·16
	17	Goods	1·25		12·41
Dec	20	Previous balance			12·41
	21	Goods	1·95		14·36
	31	,, ...	5·96		20·32
Jan	2	Returns		1·65	18·67
	9	Goods	6·15		24·82
	16	Cash		12·10	
		Discount		0·31	12·41

You find that the returns shown on the above statement as credited on 2nd January, 19.1, were entered in Messrs. Judex's day book as on 30th December 19..; otherwise the statements agree with the books in all material respects as to dates and amounts throughout the year.

(*a*) Show the account of Girlswear Ltd. as it will have appeared in the ledger of Messrs. Judex for the month of December, 19.., including the opening and closing balances.

(*b*) Explain how Messrs. Judex would have to modify their book-keeping procedure in order that the account should periodically show no balance, thus proving its correctness without the necessity of comparing it in detail with the statements from suppliers.

(*R.S.A.*)

14. The following is a copy of the rent and rates account of Ilex Ltd. for the year ended 31st October, 19.1, as it appears in the company's ledger—

			£				£
19..				19..			
Nov	8	Bank, Rates to 31/3/.1	977·28	Oct	31	Balance b/fwd. (see note below)	1,162·48
		,, Rent to 29/9/.. .	750·00				
19.1				19.1			
Jan	20	,, Rent to 25/12/.. .	750·00	Oct	31	P. & L. A/c	5,549·33
Apr	18	,, Rates to 30/9/.1	977·28			Balance c/fwd.	869·60
		,, Rent to 25/3/.1 .	750·00				
Jul	28	,, Rent to 24/6/.1 .	1,000·00				
Oct	29	,, Rates to 31/3/.2 .	1,043·52				
		,, Rent to 29/9/.1 .	1,000·00				
	31	Balance c/fwd. . .	333·33				
			7,581·41				7,581·41

NOTES—

1. Rents accrued at the opening and closing dates are calculated by apportionments in round months, i.e. ignoring the odd days between the quarter days and following ends of the calendar months.

2. The balance brought forward at 31st October, 19.., consisted of four months' rent at the rate of £3,000 per annum and one month's rates.

You are required—

(*a*) to calculate the "split" of the total charge for the year as between rent on the one hand and rates on the other, and

(*b*) to explain a method of book-keeping, the use of which would give the analysis in question without the necessity of opening any separate account.

(*R.S.A.*)

15. James Edwards is manager of a farm. He lives with his family in the farmhouse, and the terms of his employment provide, as regards heating and lighting, that he is to be chargeable personally with one-half of the total expenditure on coal and coke and one-quarter of the electricity.

The farm's accounting year ends on 31st March, and the following were the payments made during the year ended 31st March, 19.1—

(*a*) through the farm bank account—

19..			£
May	19	Electricity to 19th April	29·39
Jun	17	Coal and coke	13·75
Nov	14	Electricity to 13th October	17·33
Dec	10	Coal and coke	22·65
19.1			
Feb	14	Electricity to 15th January	23·63
Mar	5	Coal and coke	17·60

(*b*) through Edwards's personal bank account (through an oversight)—

19..			
Aug	25	Electricity to 20th July	13·15

£24 was estimated to be due for electricity used up to 31st March, 19.., and £26 up to 31st March, 19.1. Stocks of coal and coke on hand at 31st March, 19.., were valued at £12 and at 31st March, 19.1, at £15.

Write up the heating and lighting account in the farm's books for the year ended 31st March, 19.1, and show the relevant entries in Edwards's personal account.

To what extent do any of the above items illustrate accounting principles?

(*R.S.A. Modified.*)

16. Briefly explain the principles of the columnar or tabular system of book-keeping.

Illustrate the advantages of this system by means of *pro forma* rulings of a cash book, or other book of first entry, suitable for use in a small hotel.

(*London Chamber of Commerce.*)

17. Prepare a form of a columnar ledger suitable for use in a small hotel, and enter the following details—

Tuesday, 17th January: Visitors' accounts—J. Hughes (Room 1): balance from previous day £1·63; apartments £2·50; breakfast 18p; lunch 29p; dinner 39p; wine 45p; spirits 15p; cigars 8p; postages 5p; laundry 40p. F. J. Griffiths (Room 5); apartments £2·50; breakfast 40p; tea 80p; supper 50p; liqueurs 25p; minerals 10p; bath 10p; fire 20p. J. E. Eliott (Room 3): balance from previous day £2·85; breakfast 18p; 'bus to station 5p; cash received in settlement of bill, £3·08.

(*London Chamber of Commerce.*)

18. Give the ruling of a rates ledger suitable for a water company or municipal body, and illustrate its use by inserting a few items. (*Chartered Accountants.*)

19. Draw up the form of a tabular day book suitable for a hotel; also make three entries therein.

20. On 1st July, 1964, Jack Newton took his savings and some material he found in his father's garage and started business for himself. It wasn't a large business but it did give him the pleasure of being his own boss and combined the inside work of manufacturing with the outside work of selling. His product was a wooden crane which was priced to retail at £1. It was a realistic toy intended for boys aged 4 to 8 years. Mr. Newton was an energetic person and he soon had production moving, despite difficulties with the lifting mechanism. However, these were soon resolved. Mr. Newton did all the work himself and employed no labour.

At the end of the first six months trading, Mr. Newton took pride in his first profit and loss statement. He hoped that it would be the forerunner of a long series of reports showing profitable operations.

PROFIT AND LOSS STATEMENT FOR THE SIX MONTHS ENDING 31ST DECEMBER, 1964

	£	£
Net Sales		1,840
S Opening stock 1. 7. 64	100	
Materials purchases	1,000	
Wages	2,500	
Rent	300	
	3,900	
Less Stock unsold on 31. 12. 64	2,925	
Cost of goods sold		975
GROSS PROFIT		865
Expenses		
Advertising and selling	295	
Interest	25	
		320
NET PROFIT		£545

S Materials brought from Newton's father's garage.

Mr. Newton's Balance Sheet as at 31st December, 1964, appeared as follows—

	£	£
Assets		
Cash	70	
Y Debtor	100	
Stock at cost	2,925	
		3,095
Less Liabilities		
Loan: S. O. Newton	1,000	
Creditors	895	
		1,895
NET WORTH		£1,200

Y Debtor was for a sale made on 15th October, 1964, not yet paid.

What were Jack Newton's achievements and prospects? What plan of action would you advise to deal with his immediate problems?

(Case material of the Management Case Research Programme of the Department of Production and Industrial Administration, Cranfield. *Department of Education and Science*, September, 1965.)

CHAPTER 02

REPORTING INCOME AND BALANCE SHEET POSITION

Hovering between the profit and the loss
In this brief transit where the dreams cross.

T. S. ELIOT

Final Accounts. The form of final accounts for an organization varies according to the nature of the activity covered, the needs of management in the way of information, and the entity accounted for e.g. sole trader, partnership or company.

A trading firm prepares a trading and profit and loss account, a manufacturing business prepares a manufacturing account in addition to these; a social club prepares an income and expenditure account; professional men usually prepare only a profit and loss account.

Revenue Accounts. All the above forms of account are collectively known as Revenue Accounts or, in American practice, Income statements. In them, the revenue expenditure is deducted from revenue income to show the profit (surplus) or loss (deficit).

Source of Information. The amounts shown in the final revenue accounts are transferred from the revenue accounts in the ledger.

Capital Accounts. These accounts show items which are not of a revenue nature. The balances on such accounts are carried forward from one period to the next. They are *not* transferred to revenue at the end of the period. In order to give a complete picture of an organization's affairs, they are listed at the end of a period in the balance sheet. (See also pp. 1918 and 1919.)

THE FINAL ACCOUNTS (OR INCOME STATEMENT)

This chapter is concerned with the most general form of final accounts, the trading and profit and loss accounts which are generally presented in conjunction with a balance sheet for a trading (merchandizing) enterprise.

Like all accounting reports, the form of the accounts will vary according to the type of business and the requirements of management, but the following sequence is typical.

Sales and other operating revenues.

Less **Cost of Goods** sold.

Leaving **Gross Profit.** This is the excess of sales revenues over the buying cost of the goods sold and direct expenses of acquiring them (such as carriage inwards or importing costs).

Less **Operating Expenses,** often divided into administrative, selling and general expenses.

Leaving **Operating Profit.** This is the excess of gross profit over operating expenses.

Add **Other income** (non-operating). This is items of income arising from secondary activities such as interest and rent received by a company whose main business is not finance or property.

Less **Other Expenses.** These are items of expense arising from incidental activities or in the nature of financing costs, such as the payment of interest. Leaving **Net Profit Before Tax.**

Less **Corporation and Income Tax.** This is a provision for the relevant liability for tax which will eventually arise on the profits of the firm.

Leaving **Net Profit After Tax.** This is the residual income which remains after meeting related costs, expenses and provisions.

Gross Loss. If the cost of goods sold exceeds the sales income, there will be a gross loss.

Net Loss. This is either: (1) excess of selling and management expenses over gross profit or (2) the gross loss plus selling expenses and management expenses whenever there is no gross profit.

Sections of the Income Statement

The first section of the above statement, Sales less Cost of Goods sold, leaving Gross Profit is known as the Trading Account.

The following section, Gross Profit less Operating and other expenses, plus other income, less tax leaving Net Profit after tax is known as the Profit and Loss Account.

A further section, the Profit and Loss Appropriation Account may show the distribution of the profit is the owners or the form of its retention in the business.

Distinction between a Trading Account and a Manufacturing Account. A manufacturing account deals only with *raw materials*, work-in-progress and manufacturing expenses. A trading account deals only with *finished goods*, i.e. goods ready for sale, whether they are manufactured or purchased. The cost of goods manufactured and sold as shown in the manufacturing account is transferred to the debit of the trading account.

THE PERIOD OF ACCOUNT

The trading and profit and loss account must be drawn up for a period, which is usually a year. Interim accounts may be prepared monthly or quarterly and, in the case of companies whose shares are quoted on the London Stock Exchange, must be published half-yearly.

BALANCE SHEET

A balance sheet is a statement drawn up at the end of each trading or financial period, setting forth the various assets and liabilities of the concern as at the final date. Technically, it is better described as a classified summary of the debit and credit balances existing in the ledger after the profit and loss account has been constructed. In fact a balance sheet often contains items which are neither assets nor liabilities.

Difference between a Trial Balance and a Balance Sheet. A trial balance is a list of *all* the ledger balances, not only assets and liabilities, but also gains and losses. A balance sheet is a list of a *part* only of the ledger balances, i.e. those remaining after the revenue items have been dealt with.

Controversy *re* Form and Headings of Balance Sheet. In the ledger, the assets appear on the debit or left-hand side, and the liabilities on the credit or right-hand side. Since the balance sheet purports to represent the state of affairs *as shown by the books* of the business, it might be argued that the assets and liabilities should appear on the same sides of the balance sheet as the sides they are on in the ledger. But, in the English form of balance sheet, the sides are reversed. This is no doubt owing to the mistaken idea that the balance sheet is an *account*, whereas it is really only a *statement*. For this reason it is quite wrong to head the sides of a balance sheet as "*Dr.*" and "*Cr.*". The more technically correct form is in use by American, and by some English and Scottish, accountants, assets on the left, liabilities on the right.

Not only upon the form, but also upon the nomenclature of the balance sheet, there has raged a protracted and, at times, acute controversy. Because many items, such as reserves, sinking funds, preliminary expenses, income received in advance, deferred revenue expenditure, etc., can hardly be reconciled with the headings "Assets" and "Liabilities," such general headings are not recommended. It is better to group the items under two main headings Sources and Uses of funds, and to use sub-headings for each group, e.g. *Uses*; Fixed Assets, Current Assets: *Sources*; Capital and Reserves, Long-term Liabilities, Current Liabilities. An example of the modern form of balance sheet in vertical columns is shown on p. 0215–6. Many accountants consider this to be far more informative than the "two-sided" balance sheet. Notice how the significant totals are thrown into relief.

Matching Revenue Income and Expenses. The aim of an income statement must be to report all the revenue in the accounting period and to deduct from them all the expenses of earning those revenues. Not only must income be matched to expenses, but both must also be matched to the period of account.

Conservative Convention. The matching principle does not apply in all cases.

It is generally considered sound accounting policy to provide for any anticipated losses, but not to bring in any anticipated profits until they have actually been realized.

Adjustments. At the end of the accounts period, a trial balance will be extracted from the records and it will usually require some amendments to the items and amounts listed in order to match the revenue and expenses.

The changes required are called adjustments and after they have been made we have an adjusted Trial Balance from which the final accounts and Balance Sheet may be prepared. Accruals and *notional* or *non-cash* items such as Depreciation are adjustments.

If items are not included in the trial balance, a double entry is required for them. One will be in the trading and profit and loss account, the other in the ledger, and this will create a balance which is listed in the balance sheet.

The Accrual Concept. The expenses charged against revenues in any accounting period include the cost of goods sold, the wages and salaries earned and the value of services, supplies and assets used or consumed, irrespective of when the expense was authorized or paid. Expenses will normally include some items brought forward from earlier periods and will have excluded some carried forward to later periods.

The Realization Concept. Income is considered to have been earned when it is realized and this is normally the time at which the product is dispatched or invoiced to the customer, whichever is later. Two exceptions are gold-mining where the income is recognized as soon as the ore is smelted and hire-purchase where income from a transaction may be deferred in part to coincide with the receipt of instalments.

CONTENTS OF THE FINAL ACCOUNTS AND BALANCE SHEET

(a) Trading Account

This is an account constructed for the purpose of finding the *gross* profit. On the *debit* side are placed the stock at start, i.e. at the commencement of the period to which the account relates, the purchases, carriage inwards, and wages. On the *credit* side are placed the sales and the closing stock. The excess of the credit side over the debit side is the *gross profit*; if there is an excess of the debit side over the credit side, that is a *gross loss*. This balance is transferred to the Profit and Loss Account.

Stock

Stocks may represent three types of item—

1. Raw materials and supplies.
2. Work-in-progress.
3. Finished goods.

Stocks in the trading account represent finished goods unsold at the opening of the trading period (stock at start) and at the end of the trading period (stock at close).

Cost of Goods Sold. An alternative treatment to the one above is to show the cost of goods sold in the trading account as follows—

Example 1

TRADING ACCOUNT

	£		£
Stock at start	600	Sales	6,000
Add Purchases	5,000		
Goods availabe for sale	5,600		
Stock at close	800		
Cost of goods sold	4,800		
Gross profit	1,200		

Materials Consumed. Where raw materials, such as coal, stationery, etc., have been used, the same calculation as above is used to find their cost, thus—

Example 2

	£
Opening stock	3,000
Add Purchases	8,500
	11,500
Less Closing stock	2,450
Materials consumed	9,050

This example could appear in the trial balance in two ways—

	£	
1. Stock	3,000	*Dr.* balance
Purchases	8,500	*Dr.* balance
With closing stock	2,450	stated for adjustment purposes.

	£	
2. Materials consumed	9,050	*Dr.* balance
Closing stock	2,450	*Dr.* balance
No adjustment required.		

The second treatment provides one exception to the general rule that the stock at finish is always *outside* the trial balance. The student must, therefore, remember that the stock at finish does *not* in such cases appear in the trading account, but *only* in the balance sheet. The trading account, under such circumstances, assumes the following form—

TRADING ACCOUNT

	£		£
Materials Consumed	9,050	Sales	16,720
Wages	2,000		
Balance (Gross Profit)	5,670		
	16,720		16,720

—the Balance Sheet (assets side) showing the item—Stock (at close), £2,450.

A distinction is sometimes made between consumable and non-consumable stores for accounting purposes.

Packages, Packing Material. In many businesses special packages and special packing are required before goods can be considered ready for sale. In such cases this item of expense should be debited to trading account, as it would undoubtedly be charged for when fixing the selling price of the goods. In other cases, the packing material may be looked upon as a selling expense and debited to profit and loss. Any unused stock should be credited in the ledger account, and shown as an asset on the balance sheet. Where no stock is stated—and this is often the case in examination papers—the whole amount should be assumed to have been used, and be written off in the trading or profit and loss account as the case may be.

Loose Tools. These are small hand tools, drills, etc., which are too small individually to warrant a separate asset account. Generally, loose tools appear only in manufacturing concerns, and are shown in a manufacturing account.

If they appear otherwise, the treatment depends on whether they are made in the firm or purchased from outside.

(*a*) *Made in the Firm.* The figures given will be opening and closing stock and these are respectively debited and credited to trading account.

(*b*) *Purchased from Outside.* In this case, opening stock, purchases and closing stock are given. The value of loose tools is calculated in the same way as cost of goods sold, and debited to profit and loss account.

In (*a*) it is assumed that the cost of materials and wages used in making the tools has been charged to trading account and, therefore, any change in the stock of tools should be dealt with in this account.

Work-in-Progress, Orders on Hand. This item denotes partly executed work. In manufacturing concerns it represents goods in process of manufacture, while in non-manufacturing concerns it may simply denote partly executed orders. A separate account may be opened for it in the ledger. The Work-in-Progress at start must be *debited* to the trading or manufacturing account, and the work-in-progress at finish *credited* to the trading or manufacturing account. The latter must also appear on the assets side of the balance sheet.

Purchases. This item denotes, in an ordinary business, the total of the cash and credit purchases of goods for resale; while, in a manufacturing concern, it represents the purchases of raw material for the purposes of manufacture. It is debited to trading account after deducting any purchases returns and allowances, the deduction being shown in the trading account itself.

Sales. This item represents the total of the cash and credit sales during the trading period. It is credited to trading account after deducting any returns and allowances in connexion therewith, the deduction being shown in the trading account itself.

Carriage. This is the charge made for conveyance of goods *by land*, in contradistinction to freight. Goods are sold either: (1) *carriage paid*, or (2) *carriage forward*. This means that in case (1) the *seller* pays the carriage, and in case (2) the carriage has to be paid by the *buyer*. Carriage inwards increases the cost of the goods purchased, and hence is debited to trading account. Carriage outwards is a selling expense, and is debited to profit and loss. In exercises and examination work, when carriage appears in the trial balance and is not specified as being either inward or outward, it is generally assumed to be *inward* and is debited to trading account. This is based on the legal aspect of the case, that goods are sold where they stand and the buyer pays carriage. If the student places the carriage in the profit and loss account, he should guard himself with a note explaining that he has assumed the carriage to be *outward*.

The same treatment applies to dock charges, duty, and freight.

Inwards—debit to trading account.

Outwards—debit to profit and loss account.

Duty. This includes both Customs and Excise duties. Customs duties are levied on goods imported and exported; excise duties are imposed on goods produced and consumed in the country itself.

Freight. Freight is the charge made for conveyance of goods *by sea*, as opposed to Carriage.

Wages. See p. 0209 for the distinction between wages and salaries.

When a separate manufacturing account is not prepared, such wages and salaries as form part of the cost of making the goods are debited to trading account. For instance, a boot and shoe manufacturer buys raw material, such as leather, and sells a manufactured article, viz., boots and shoes. He could not properly credit the sale of the manufactured articles, i.e. the boots and shoes, against merely the cost of the raw material, i.e. the leather. The sale of the manufactured article must, of course, be set off against the cost of the manufactured article, which is obviously the cost of the leather plus the wages paid to manufacture it into boots and shoes.

Again, take the case of a large rag merchant. He buys goods in one condition, and employs persons to wash, clean, sort, and pack them in another condition ready for sale. Although nothing is, so to speak, manufactured, yet such wages are undoubtedly trading wages; the expense had to be incurred before such goods were ready for sale.

Some accountants designate manufacturing wages as "productive," "remunerative," or "direct." When, therefore, the student finds a distinction made in the trial balance between wages and salaries, he should debit the wages to trading account, and the salaries to profit and loss. When salaries and wages appear as one item, they should be debited to profit and loss, being assumed to be "non-productive." The above direction must not, however, be construed dogmatically, as it is intended to indicate only general principles and main lines of procedure. Special cases arise which must be determined by their own peculiar circumstances, it being quite impossible to lay down any hard-and-fast rule.

Such terms as "unproductive," "unremunerative" wages should be avoided, as they are misleading.

Manufacturing Charges or Expenses. These are expenses of a miscellaneous description that directly increase the cost of the goods; for instance, the dressing and ironing of shirts and collars when made, the sizing of paper or leather, the purchase of chemicals, etc. When a separate manufacturing account is not prepared, such expenses are debited to trading account.

Royalties. These are payments made to a patentee, author, or landlord, for the right to use his patent, copyright, or land. If they are productive expenses, they are debited to the manufacturing account when there is one, or, alternatively, to the trading account.

QUESTIONS

1. Explain the meaning of the terms "profit" and "loss," distinguishing between "gross" and "net" in each case.
2. What is a trading account, and of what items does it usually consist?
3. State what the following items in a trading account represent: (1) stock, (2) work-in-progress, (3) purchases, (4) sales.
4. What is meant by a "materials consumed account," and how is the amount arrived at? Show, by means of *pro forma* examples, the difference in a trading account with and without this item.
5. Explain what is meant by the following items: (1) dock charges, (2) duty, (3) freight, (4) carriage. When are these items charged to trading account, and when to profit and loss account?
6. Explain the following: manufacturing charges, royalties, fuel. Should these be charged to trading account or to profit and loss account? Give reasons for your answer.
7. What considerations enter into the question as to whether packages and packing material should be charged to trading account or to profit and loss account?

(b) Profit and Loss Account

A profit and loss account is an account into which all gains and losses are collected. If the gains exceed the losses, the excess is the net profit; if the losses are greater than the gains, the difference is the net loss. Some accountants call this a "Loss and Gain Account."

Dock Charges, Duty, Freight, Carriage. As mentioned when dealing with the trading account, all *outwards* charges in connexion with such items are debited to profit and loss, because they are *selling* expenses.

Rent. Two rent accounts may be opened. Rent received is credited to rent receivable account; rent paid, to the rent account. At the end of the year, the profit and loss account is debited with rent paid and credited with rent receivable.

Ground Rent is the rent payable to the ground landlord for the use of the land on which the buildings have been erected. Income tax must be deducted from each payment of ground rent, but the full amount is debited to profit and loss. For a fuller treatment of the problem of taxation in accounts see p. 2801 *et seq.*

Rates and Taxes. Various indirect taxes are debited to profit and loss account. In addition to the general and water rates, there may be social security selective employment tax and training levy. Training grant may be offset against levy (see Chapter 28).

Salaries. This item denotes the weekly or monthly remuneration of the employees of the firm in return for their services. *Productive* salaries should be charged to trading account. Where the business is divided into departments, there is generally a similar subdivision of the salaries, e.g. office, travellers, and management salaries.

Salaries and Wages. Unless there is something to indicate the contrary, this item of expenditure is debited to profit and loss. The distinction between a salary and a wage is far from uniform. Some accountants distinguish by the *kind of work* done; payment for work of a mechanical nature is termed a wage, and payment for work of an administrative nature is called a salary. Other accountants differentiate by the *period of time* covered by the payment; hourly, daily, or weekly rates of pay are called wages, and yearly sums payable half-yearly, quarterly, or monthly, are termed salaries. Again, there are some to whom the criterion is the *amount* of the payment. A small weekly sum denotes a wage, and a large weekly or monthly sum represents a salary.

Partners' and Owners' Salaries should be dealt with separately, as they require special treatment when preparing the firm's accounts for income tax assessment.

Discounts—Cash. This item represents the cash allowances made when accounts are settled. "Discounts allowed" are a loss, and must be debited to profit and loss. "Discounts received" are a gain, and must be credited to profit and loss. The terms "discounts on purchases" and "discounts on sales" usually denote the *cash* discounts mentioned above.

Discounts—Trade. Trade discounts are a reduction from retail list price offered to the trade. They are usually of the order of ten to fifteen per cent.

Treatment of Discount. A purchase or a sale may be subject to both a trade *and* a cash discount; and unless the discount on such purchase or sale is labelled "cash" or "trade" it is not possible to state definitely what it really is. In some exercises, the size of the discount (over 5 per cent, probably trade), obtained by a rough calculation, may be sufficient indication as to the designation. Since trade discount is usually deducted from sales and purchases before they are entered in the books, any discount must (except in very special cases) be assumed to be *cash* discount.

Some accountants adopt the terms "discounts on purchases" and "discounts on sales" to denote *cash* discounts; but debit the discount on sales to trading account, and credit the discounts on purchases to profit and loss, these latter discounts being dependent on the financial resources of the business, while the former are in effect a reduction of the sales to the absolute net figures.

The student should always treat the two amounts for discount separately. The object of having two totals is to show the actual gain and loss by discount. On the other hand it may be desirable to subtract one lot of discount from the other, and to deal only with the balance.

Interest on Investment and Loans. Where interest has been paid on loans, *less tax*, the tax should be added and the gross amount shown in profit and loss account. Interest on investments will have been received *less* tax, and the gross amount should be shown again. Interest is usually divided into two accounts, interest receivable and interest payable, and both amounts may be carried to profit and loss, the former being credited, and the latter debited.

Commission. While carrying on business for itself, a firm may also do work for other firms; for which, of course, it *charges* a commission. The firm may likewise employ agents to sell the firm's goods, and in such cases would have to *pay* commission. Two accounts are usually kept, for Commission Receivable and Commission Payable respectively. The former may be credited to profit and loss as a gain, and the latter debited as an expense.

Insurance. This item includes all premiums payable to insurance companies for indemnity: (*a*) for loss of goods or property by fire, burglary, flood, etc.; (*b*) for breakage of plate glass windows; (*c*) for damages awarded under the Employers' Liability Act, etc. National insurance payments should preferably be dealt with in a separate account, the employer's contribution being debited to it. Insurance, being an expense, is debited to profit and loss.

Bank Charges. This item includes charges for cheque books, for keeping current accounts, for discounting bills, etc. Such expenses are losses and are, therefore, debited to profit and loss.

Legal and Accountancy Charges. Legal expenses comprise solicitors' fees, law charges, and expenses in connexion with the recovery of debts, in lawsuits, etc. Accountancy charges consist of the fees and expenses in connexion with the investigation or audit of the accounts and books. These expenses are debited to profit and loss.

Printing and Stationery. Expenditure under this heading consists of payments for paper, envelopes, invoices, statements, account books, etc. It often includes the cost of catalogues, samples, etc. Losses of this nature are debited to profit and loss.

Advertising. Most businesses incur expenditure under this heading, and many owe their success almost entirely to it. Sometimes contracts are entered into and paid for a period of years in order to obtain cheaper rates. Such an amount is then debited to an "Advertising Suspense Account," and written off proportionately each year. Profit and loss account is, of course, debited with such an expense.

Repairs. Repairs and small renewals or replacements relating to the premises, to the plant and machinery, to the fixtures, fittings, utensils, etc., are generally included under this heading; and such expenditure, being an expense, is debited to profit and loss.

Postage, Telegrams, and Bill Stamps. Expenditure of this nature is, like other losses, a charge against profits. Bill stamps are those used on bills of exchange.

Travellers' Commission and Expenses. In those businesses which employ a number of travellers remunerated by means of commission and expenses, such expenditure generally forms a separate item in itself. It is, of course, a debit to profit and loss.

Travelling Expenses. In some businesses much travelling is necessary either by principals or by travellers, and sometimes by subordinate officials. Expenditure of such a character is generally dealt with as a separate item of expense, and, like other losses, debited to profit and loss.

Office Expenses. These are miscellaneous expenses pertaining to the office and are debited to profit and loss account.

Trade Expenses. Generally speaking, these are expenses of a varied nature for which it is not worth opening separate accounts. They are, therefore, amalgamated under the above heading, or under some other similar term, namely, "General Expenses," "Petty Expenses," "Sundry Expenses." Except in a few isolated instances, therefore, trade expenses are debited to profit and loss, the term signifying merely miscellaneous *business* expenses and not *trading* expenses. The term is undoubtedly very ambiguous.

Unused Supplies. It often happens at balancing time that there are some unused stocks of printing and stationery, and of catalogues, sample books, circulars, posters and other advertising material. The value of these must be deducted from the amount spent for printing and stationery, advertising, etc., so that only the amount actually used is debited to profit and loss. The unused stocks of printing and stationery, advertising material, coal, coke, fuel, etc., must be shown as assets on the balance sheet.

Provisions

In addition to the specific expenses already discussed, most businesses will have some expenses which can only be estimated at the end of the accounting period. A provision is the estimated amount of a specific business expense. The main provisions are for depreciation, bad or doubtful debts and accounting fees.

Depreciation. This is the loss of value sustained by fixed assets, e.g. plant and machinery, buildings, furniture and fixtures. If the business is to be put on a sound financial basis, such loss must be estimated and charged against the profits before arriving at the balance called "net profit." The subject is dealt with at length in Chapter 05.

Audit Fee. A Provision for Audit Fee is generally made, so that the auditor's charges may appear in the set of accounts that he has been checking. Otherwise the audit fee for one year would appear in the next year's accounts, as the auditor cannot send in his account before he has done the work.

Bad or Doubtful Debts Provision. This is a charge made against profits in order to provide for possible bad debts when persons fail to pay the amounts owed by them.

Reserves and Provisions. The distinction between a provision and a reserve is important, but rather difficult because of a lack of uniformity in practice. The question is dealt with more fully on p. 2202.

QUESTIONS

1. What is a profit and loss account, and how does it differ from a trading account?
2. Explain the meaning of the following items when they appear in a profit and loss account: dock charges, duty, freight, carriage.
3. Why do rent, rates, and ground rent appear in the profit and loss account? How should ground rent be treated when it has been paid *less tax*? How would you deal with rent received from sub-lettings?
4. What are salaries, and how do they differ from wages? To what account would you charge the item "salaries and wages," and why?
5. What is meant by "discount"? Explain the terms "discounts allowed," "discounts received," "discounts on sales," "discounts on purchases." What different methods of treatment are in vogue with respect to the last two items?
6. What do the following items denote: interest, commission, bank charges? Into what two accounts are each of the former usually divided, and why?
7. Explain the meaning of the following: insurance, advertising, repairs, travelling expenses, and why they are charged to profit and loss.

(c) The Balance Sheet

The Balance Sheet is a statement on one hand of the assets (funds employed) in an accounting entity at a particular moment in time, and on the other hand, of the liabilities and proprietors Capital (sources of funds).

ASSETS

Assets are the property and possessions of a business, i.e. its stock, land, buildings, book debts, etc. They are classified according to their nature and are of various kinds—

Fixed Assets are those acquired and held permanently for the purpose of creating production capacity, as, for example, plant and machinery, lease, etc.

Current Assets are those assets such as cash, debtors and stocks that can easily be realized and are therefore readily available to discharge liabilities. Further examples are gilt-edged securities, bills receivable, stock-in-trade, etc.

The same asset may be either fixed or current according to the nature of the business. Thus, investments would be a current asset to a stock-jobber, but a fixed asset to an ordinary trader. Machinery would be a fixed asset to an ordinary manufacturer, but a current asset to a machinery trading company. It depends on whether the asset is held merely for the purpose of sale, or is intended to be kept in the business.

Tangible Assets are definite assets which can be seen and touched.

Intangible Assets cannot be seen and touched, although they may have value, e.g. goodwill, patents, and trade marks.

Fictitious Assets are debit balances—losses which have been carried forward from one period to the next, e.g. profit and loss account balance, preliminary expenses of a limited company.

Wasting Assets are fixed assets that depreciate through wear and tear, as, for example, plant and machinery; those whose value expires with lapse of time, such as patents and leases; also those that become exhausted or consumed through being worked, such as mines, quarries, etc. The expression is more generally applied to the last-named.

Liquid Assets are cash or items, such as marketable securities, which can be turned into cash quickly.

LIABILITIES

Definition. A liability is any amount which a business is legally bound to pay. It is a claim by an outsider on the assets of a business.

Long-term Liabilities are those payable in the future, but not within the next accounting period.

Debentures are long-term liabilities (see p. 2301).

Current or Short-term Liabilities are those payable within a short period —within the next accounting period, usually one year—or already due.

Bank Loans and Overdrafts. Strictly, both are current liabilities as the bank reserves the right to request payment at short notice, but in practice a loan is often obtained for several years.

CAPITAL

The term Capital has so many uses that it is impossible to give it a single definition.

Personal Capital or Net-Worth means the original fund with which a person entered a business, plus any profits retained in the business. It can also be calculated as the excess of assets over liabilities. An excess of liabilities over assets is called a **Deficiency.** In the case of a joint stock company the **Equity Capital** is the amount contributed by the shareholders, plus any retained earnings and minus any losses.

Trading Capital consists of the fixed and current assets.

Fixed Capital comprises all the fixed assets.

Current or Circulating Capital consists of the current assets, as defined on the previous page.

Money borrowed by means of ordinary loans, mortgages, debentures, bonds, etc., is frequently spoken of as **Loan Capital.**

The total of the proprietor's capital and the long-term loan capital is called the **Long Term Capital** or invested funds.

Working Capital is the amount that remains for the working or running of a business after the purchase price of the fixed assets has been paid. Thus, if a trader started with a capital of £20,000 and expended £12,000 of it in the purchase of buildings and plant, then the balance of £8,000 would constitute the *working* capital. In a going concern this is calculated as the excess of current assets over current liabilities.

It must be borne in mind that there is no fixed layout for a balance sheet although, as will be seen later, legislation does require that certain items shall appear as distinct and separate items. The actual order of the items is very much a matter of viewpoint of the accountants preparing it and the particular purpose it is to serve.

Order of Stating Assets and Liabilities on a Balance Sheet. The question often arises in the student's mind as to the order in which the assets and liabilities should be entered on the balance sheet. Which should come first? Which should follow? Which should come last? And what is the reason for any particular order?

Different methods are in vogue in business. By one method, the assets are stated in the *order of realizability*, that is, the order in which they can be converted into cash; while the liabilities are stated in the order in which they would be discharged, that is, paid off with the cash realized by the sale of the assets. The arrangement is then as follows—

BALANCE SHEET ON .... 19..

	£		£
Current Liabilities		*Current Assets*	
Sundry Creditors		Cash	
Bills Payable		Bills Receivable	
Bank Loan		Sundry Debtors	
Outstanding Expenses		Payments in Advance	
Income Received in Advance		Stock	
Long-term Liabilities		*Investments*	
Loan on Mortgages		(Give details)	
Capital Accounts		*Fixed Assets*	
Partners Current A/cs		Furniture & Fittings	
Capital A/cs		Plant & Machinery	
		Land & Buildings	
		Goodwill	

By another method, the assets and liabilities are stated in the *order of permanence*, the fixed assets and liabilities taking precedence of the floating assets and liabilities, as shown at the top of the following page.

The balance sheets of some commercial concerns, e.g. banks, partake of both methods, the assets being stated in the cash order and the liabilities in the order of permanence. Another variation is sometimes met with in practice. The current assets and liabilities are marshalled first, but the liabilities begin with the creditors, and the assets with the debtors. Cash is sometimes placed next to the bills receivable, and sometimes last of all.

BALANCE SHEET ON .... 19..

	£		£
Capital Accounts			
Capital A/cs		Goodwill	
Current A/cs		*Fixed Assets*	
Long-term Liabilities		Patents & Trade Marks	
Loans on Mortgage		Land & Buildings	
Current Liabilities		Plant & Machinery	
Bank Loan		Furniture & Fixtures	
Sundry Creditors		*Investments*	
Accrued items		(Give details)	
Bills Payable		*Current Assets*	
		Stock	
		Sundry Debtors	
		Payments in Advance	
		Bills Receivable	
		Cash	

In the case of a bank the cash is put first as showing its stability on the principle that the first item strikes the eye most.

An alternative form is the vertical Balance Sheet and the examples on pp. 0215–6 designates the two aspects as *User* and *Sources* of funds respectively. The funds in use are the total fixed and current assets minus the current liabilities. The sources of funds are the equity capital and reserves and would include the long term liabilities, if any.

What a Balance Sheet tells us. A properly drawn up balance sheet should give us information on four important points—

1. The nature and extent of the assets.
2. The nature and extent of the liabilities.
3. Whether the firm is solvent.
4. Whether the firm is overtrading.

Essentially, the Balance Sheet is a historical document which does not purport to show the realizable value of the fixed assets nor, normally, of the stock in trade. It is not, therefore a statement of the net worth of the undertaking. Nevertheless, it will be certified to give a true and fair view if it has been drawn up in accordance with generally accepted principles.

Solvency may be defined as an excess of assets over liabilities and in this sense, the balance sheet indicates, on historical data, whether such an excess exists. This does not mean, however, that the business is able to meet the current liabilities as they fall due.

Working Capital. Current Assets *less* Current Liabilities = Working Capital. The amount required varies enormously but any business which has no working capital is in a vulnerable position should the creditors demand payment. In general, working capital should at least equal current liabilities.

BLANK COMPANY LTD.

BALANCE SHEET AS AT 31ST DECEMBER, 19..

		£	£	£
USES OF FUNDS				
Intangible Assets				
Goodwill at cost		1,000		
Patents and Trade Marks at valuation at .... 19..		200	1,200	1,200
Fixed Assets				
	Cost	Depreciation	Net	
Land and Buildings	£8,000	2,000	6,000	
Plant and Machinery	4,000	1,000	3,000	
Fixtures and Fittings	1,300	1,050	250	
				9,250
Current Assets				
Stocks		1,360		
Sundry Debtors		480		
Bills Receivable		250		
Cash at Bank		650		
Cash in Hand		10		
			2,750	
Less **Current Liabilities**				
Sundry Creditors		1,000		
Expenses Outstanding		50		
Bills Payable		150	1,200	
Surplus of Current Assets over Current Liabilities [WORKING CAPITAL]				1,550
				12,000
SOURCES OF FUNDS				
REPRESENTING CAPITAL AND UNDISTRIBUTED PROFITS				
SHARE CAPITAL Authorized and Issued—10,000 Ordinary Shares £1 each fully paid			10,000	
RESERVES				
General Reserve		500		
Profit and Loss A/c		1,500	2,000	12,000
				12,000

Overtrading. A firm which has no working capital is said to be overtrading. In this position it is very vulnerable, and could be forced into bankruptcy if its creditors lose faith in its ability to pay.

PREPARATION OF THE FINAL ACCOUNTS AND BALANCE SHEET. THE ACCOUNTING CYCLE

In order to prepare the final accounts and Balance Sheet it will be necessary to complete the accounting cycle. The first three stages of the cycle have already been discussed, and we will now discuss the remaining three stages. The complete cycle has six stages:

(1) Journalising. Transactions are analysed and recorded and may be summarized ready for posting.

(2) Posting. The journal entries are recorded in the ledger accounts.

(3) Extracting a Trial Balance. The ledger accounts are listed and the accuracy of the records tested.

(4) Making the Adjustments. The adjustments to the trial balance are analysed in relation to the relevant items in the trial balance, using a work sheet when necessary and the data are rearranged into the form of final accounts and Balance Sheet required for the entity which is being accounted for.

(5) Closing Entries. Journal entries are prepared and posted to the ledger to bring the ledger balance up to date.

The profit is also posted to the Capital and any appropriations put into effect.

(6) Preparing a Post-closing Trial Balance. In practice, a post-closing trial balance will also be prepared to prove the accuracy of the closing entries.

Making Adjustments

A wide variety of adjustments and provisions may be necessary in preparing final accounts and in the following few pages some typical examples are dealt with to illustrate the principle. Other examples, such as provision for depreciation, may be found in later chapters.

Payments in Arrear. The end of an accounting period rarely falls at the end of a week. This means that many expenses have not been paid right up to the balancing date. For instance, several days' wages may be owing, rent may be due, etc., and the firm has a liability to pay the amount.

It is essential that the accounts for a year contain a year's expenses. This may be dealt with in two ways—

1. *Dr.* profit and loss account with the full amount payable.
   Cr. expense account with the amount actually paid.
   Cr. outstanding expenses account with amount owing.
2. *Dr.* profit and loss account with full amount payable.
   Cr. expense account with full amount payable.

The result of this is to create a balance in the expense account equal to the amount outstanding, which is carried forward as a credit balance on the individual expense account and shows as a current liability in the balance sheet.

Payments in Advance. Some payments, such as rates and insurance, must be paid in advance. On the balancing date, such an account will show more expense paid in a period than is due. Only the expense for the period should be charged to the profit and loss account. The balance is carried forward as an asset.

This may, again, be dealt with in two ways—

1. *Dr*. profit and loss account with the amount payable.
   Dr. payments in advance with the amount paid in advance.
   Cr. expense account with the amount actually paid.
2. *Dr*. profit and loss account with the amount payable.
   Cr. payments in advance with the amount payable.

The resulting balance is carried down to the debit of the expense account and will show as a current asset in the balance sheet.

The advantage of the first method in both cases above is that the full story may be shown in the journal entries.

Accruing Income. It sometimes happens that certain income has accrued due, though it is not yet payable, to the firm. Where part of the premises has been sublet, rent receivable up to the time of balancing must be calculated and taken as a profit to profit and loss. "Sundry debtors for rent" should be debited and "rent receivable" credited; or the accrued rent may be adjusted in the rents receivable account itself, by crediting the amount on one side, and bringing it down as a debit balance on the other side. There may also be some interest or dividends due on Consols or other investments. These should be debited, *less tax*, to an Outstanding Dividends Account, and credited to a Dividends on Investments Account, this latter account being duly transferred to the credit of profit and loss.

Apportionments. Expenses are sometimes paid which extend over two or three years, such as those for advertising. A proportionate amount must be calculated each year, and taken as a loss to profit and loss. It is also necessary to apportion any income received in advance, such as Apprentice Premiums, Royalties Received in Advance, etc. The income received should be divided by the number of years over which it extends, and this will give the amount to be taken to profit and loss as the *current* year's share of such income. The adjustment may be made either in the account itself, or by means of a journal entry, e.g. in the case of apprentice premium, debiting apprentice premium account and crediting an Unexpired apprentice premium account. The former method is usually adopted in practice.

Interest on Capital. This is a very usual adjustment where there are partners in a business. If the same amount of capital had been invested elsewhere, it would have earned interest, and the business is, therefore, charged with some rate, usually 5 per cent. Interest account is debited, and the partners' capital, drawings, or current accounts are credited with the amount. Such interest, however, is not necessarily paid to the partners; nevertheless, it operates as a loss to the business, being a charge against the profits, and as a gain to the partners, because it increases their capital. If placed to their current accounts it is then drawn out. (See also Partnership Accounts, Chapter 12.)

An example showing the journalizing of a number of adjustments, etc., will now be worked.

Example 3

G. Kenn's trial balance as at 31st December contained the following items—

	£
Plant and machinery	550
Office furniture	120
Bad debts provision	102
Apprenticeship premium . .	100
Sundry debtors	2,200

The following matters have to be taken into account before the preparation of the final accounts—

1. Depreciation of plant and machinery 10 per cent.
2. Depreciation of office furniture 5 per cent.
3. The bad debts provision is to be increased to 5 per cent on sundry debtors.
4. Rent accrued to date £33.
5. Rates £78 have been paid in advance.
6. £100 apprenticeship premium received previous 1st January is to be written off over five years in equal amounts.

Show the journal entries.

Solution 3

JOURNAL

		Dr	*Cr*
19..		£	£
Dec 31	Depreciation	55	
	Plant & Machinery		55
	Being 10% written off.		
	Depreciation	6	
	Office Furniture		6
	Being 5% written off.		
	Profit & Loss A/c	8	
	Bad Debts Provision		8
	Being amount required to bring provision up to 5%.		
	Rent	33	
	Rent Accrued		33
	Being balance carried forward.		
	Rates Prepaid	78	
	Rates		78
	Being balance carried forward.		
	Apprenticeship Premium . . .	20	
	Profit & Loss A/c		20
	Being yearly sum written off.		

Provisions for Bad or Doubtful Debts

How the Amount of the Provision is Ascertained. The amount of the provision is either the total of a specially compiled list of doubtful amounts, or a fixed percentage of the total debtors, or, in some cases a small percentage ($\frac{1}{2}$ per cent and upwards) of the turnover or total sales, based on past experience. The bad debts, however, usually stand in direct relation to the debtors and not to the total sales, and the last-named method is only applicable where the debts are very numerous, and where the bad debts may be considered to be uniformly in proportion to the trade done.

Object of Making a Provision. The object of making the provision is to show the debtors on the balance sheet at a realistic value if possible. It is misleading to show, say, £5,000 debtors as an asset on the balance sheet if at least 5 per cent of them, namely £250, are possible bad debts. On the balance sheet, therefore, the provision, although a credit balance, is not placed on the liabilities side, but is shown on the *assets* side as a deduction from the debtors.

Methods of Creating a Provision. Two methods are in use with regard to the construction of the Provision—

1. The amount of the provision is debited direct to profit and loss account, and credited to a bad debts provision account.

2. The provision is entered *twice* in the bad debts account. In effect, it is treated like a balance, debited above the line (the totals) and brought down to the credit side.

The advantage of the second way is that no separate provision account is needed and this method is widely used today. A serious objection, however, is that no distinction is made in the profit and loss account between bad debts and the provision.

Methods of Dealing with the Provision and the Bad Debts Account. There are two methods, as follows—

1. The bad debts are transferred direct to the profit and loss account, thus ignoring the provision created specially to meet them. Any extra amount required is debited to profit and loss account, and credited (or added) to the old provision. If the old provision is too large, the amount beyond what is required is debited to (or subtracted from) the provision, and credited back to profit and loss account.

2. The bad debts are debited to the provision made specially for them. Any bad debts beyond the amount of the provision must be debited to profit and loss account. Should the provision be greater than the amount of the bad debts, then the surplus will be carried forward to the new provision, and thus reduce the amount debited to profit and loss account in order to make the fresh provision.

Example 4

The bad debts provision at 1st January was £120. The bad debts during the year amounted to £105. The debtors at 31st December are £2,700. Make a new provision of 5 per cent.

Show the journal, ledger, profit and loss, and balance sheet entries.

Solution 4

First Method

JOURNAL

		Dr	Cr
19..		£	£
Dec 31	Profit & Loss A/c	105	
	Bad Debts		105
	Transfer of balance.		
31	Profit & Loss A/c	15	
	Provision for Bad Debts . . .		15
	Additional amount required to raise Provision from £120 to £135 (5% on £2,700).		

LEDGER

BAD DEBTS

19..		£	19..		£
Jan to Dec	Sundry Debtors . .	105	Dec 31	P. & L. A/c . . .	105

PROVISION FOR BAD DEBTS

19..		£	19..		£
Dec 31	Amount c/d . . .	135	Jan 1	Balance . . .	120
			Dec 31	P. & L. A/c . . .	15
		135			135
			19.1		
			Jan 1	Balance b/d . . .	135

PROFIT AND LOSS ACCOUNT (*Dr.* side).

	£	£
Bad Debts		105
Provision for Bad Debts (5% on £2,700) . . .	135	
Less Old Provision	120	
		15

BALANCE SHEET

Assets	£	£
Sundry Debtors	2,700	
Less Provision for Bad Debts	135	
		2,565

Alternative Method

JOURNAL

		Dr	Cr
		£	£
Dec 31	Profit & Loss A/c	120	
	Bad Debts		120
	Transfer of balance.		

LEDGER

BAD DEBTS

		£			£
19..			19..		
Jan to Dec	Sundry Debtors . .	105	Jan 1	Balance b/f . .	120
Dec 31	Provision (5% on £2,700) c/d	135	Dec 31	P. & L. A/c . .	120
		240			240
			19.1		
			Jan 1	Balance b/d . .	135

PROFIT AND LOSS ACCOUNT (*Dr.* side)

	£
Bad Debts	120

BALANCE SHEET

Assets	£	£
Sundry Debtors	2,700	
Less Provisions for Bad Debts	135	
		2,565

Example 5

On 1st January the provision for bad debts was £86. The bad debts during the year amounted to £115. The debtors at 31st December are £2,840, and a new provision of 5 per cent thereof is required. Make the necessary journal and ledger entries, and show the profit and loss account and balance sheet.

Solution 5

First Method

JOURNAL

		Dr	Cr
19..		£	£
Dec 31	Profit & Loss A/c	115	
	Bad Debts		115
	Transfer of balance.		
31	Profit & Loss A/c	56	
	Provision for Bad Debts . . .		56
	Additional amount required to raise provision from £86 to £142 (5% on £2,840).		

LEDGER

BAD DEBTS

		£			£
19..			19..		
Jan to Dec	Sundry Debtors . .	115	Dec 31	P. & L. A/c . . .	115

PROVISION FOR BAD DEBTS

		£			£
19..			19..		
Dec 31	Balance c/d . . .	142	Jan 1	Balance . . .	86
			Dec 31	P. & L. A/c . . .	56
		142			142
			19.1		
			Jan 1	Balance b/d . . .	142

PROFIT AND LOSS ACCOUNT (*Dr*. side)

	£	£
Bad Debts		115
Provision for Bad Debts (5% on £2,840) . .	142	
Less Old Provision	86	
		56

BALANCE SHEET

Assets	£	£
Sundry Debtors	2,840	
Less Provision for Bad Debts	142	
		2,698

Alternative Method

JOURNAL

		Dr	Cr
		£	£
Dec 31	Profit & Loss A/c	171	
	Bad Debts		171
	Transfer of balance.		

LEDGER

BAD DEBTS

		£			£
19..			19..		
Jan to Dec	Sundry Debtors . .	115	Jan 1	Balance b/f . . .	86
Dec 31	Provision (5% on £2,840 c/d)	142	Dec 31	P. & L. A/c . . .	171
		257			257
			19.1		
			Jan 1	Balance b/d . . .	142

PROFIT AND LOSS ACCOUNT (*Dr.* side)

	£
Bad Debts	171

BALANCE SHEET

Assets	£	£
Sundry Debtors	2,840	
Less Provision for Bad Debts	142	
		2,698

Example 6

On 1st January the provision for bad debts was £206. The bad debts during the year amounted to £55. The debtors at 31st December are £2,440, and a new provision of 5 per cent is required. Make the necessary journal and ledger entries, and show also the profit and loss account and balance sheet.

Solution 6

First Method

JOURNAL

		Dr	Cr
19..		£	£
Dec 31	Profit & Loss A/c	55	
	Bad Debts		55
	Transfer of balance.		
31	Provision for Bad Debts	84	
	Profit & Loss A/c		84
	Amount credited back to Profit and Loss A/c in order to reduce Provision from £206 to £122 (5% on £2,440).		

LEDGER

BAD DEBTS

		£			£
19.. Jan to Dec	Sundry Debtors . .	55	19.. Dec 31	P. & L. A/c . . .	55

PROVISION FOR BAD DEBTS

		£			£
19.. Dec 31	P. & L. A/c . . .	84	19.. Jan 1	Balance . . .	206
	Balance c/d . . .	122			
		206			206
			19.1 Jan 1	Balance b/d . . .	122

PROFIT AND LOSS ACCOUNT

	£			£
Bed Debts	55	Provision for Bad Debts—		
		Old Provision . . .	£106	
		Less New . . .	122	
				84

BALANCE SHEET

Assets	£	£
Sundry Debtors	2,440	
Less Provision for Bad Debts	122	
		2,318

Alternative Method

JOURNAL

		Dr	Cr
19..		£	£
Dec 31	Provision for Bad Debts	55	
	Bad Debts		55
	Transfer of balance.		
31	Provision for Bad Debts	29	
	Profit & Loss A/c		29
	Amount credited back to Profit and Loss A/c to reduce provision from £151 to £122 (5% on £2,440).		

LEDGER

Bad Debts

		£			£
19..			19..		
Jan to Dec	Sundry Debtors . .	55	Jan 1	Balance b/f . .	206
Dec 31	Provision (5% on £2,440 c/d)	122			
	P. & L. A/c . . .	29			
		206			206
			19.1 Jan 1	Balance b/d . . .	122

Profit and Loss Account

			£
		Provision for Bad Debts . .	29

Balance Sheet

		£	£
	Assets		
Sundry Debtors		2,440	
Less Provision for Bad Debts		122	
			2,318

The choice of method in many cases depends upon the views of the auditors who are to check the books. There is, however, one drawback to all the methods already illustrated; it is that no figure appears which represents the amount of debts provided against which have proved to be good by recovery, and from the point of view of the Inspector of Taxes this is rather important. This can be shown as follows—

Example 7

On 1st January the provision for bad debts was £155. During the year £41 of these proved to be bad while £85 was found to be good and £19 of debts were bad that were not provided for. A new provision of £211 is required.

Solution 7

BAD DEBTS

19..		£	19..		£
Dec 31	Bad Debt w/o . .	19	Dec 31	P. & L. A/c . . .	19

PROVISION FOR BAD DEBTS

19..		£	19..		£
Dec. 31	Sundry Debtors—Bad Debts w/o .	41	Jan 1	Balance b/d . . .	155
	P. & L. A/c—Debts recovered . . .	85		P. & L. A/c—amount required to increase Provision to £211 .	182
	Balance c/d . . .	211			
		337			337
			19.1		
			Jan 1	Balance b/d . .	211

PROFIT AND LOSS ACCOUNT

19..		£	19..		£
Dec 31	Bad Debts . .	19	Dec 31	Doubtful Debts recovered . . .	85
	Provision for Bad Debts	182			

(w/o = written off.)

Provisions for Discount

Provision for Discount on Debtors. This is a charge made against profits, in order to provide for an expected loss in the shape of discounts that will have to be allowed to the firm's debtors on payment of their accounts.

Provision for Discount on Creditors. This is an addition to the profits, to provide for those discounts expected to be received on payment of the firm's creditors.

Object of Making Discount Provisions. The object of making provisions for discount is that the debtors and creditors shall appear on the balance sheet at their true value; otherwise, we should be *overstating* both our assets and liabilities. For this reason, therefore, such provisions are usually shown on the balance sheet as deductions from the debtors and creditors respectively.

Arguments for and against Discount Provisions. Some accountants urge that discounts expected to be allowed, and received, should not be taken into account at all; that these discounts should, properly speaking, appear only in the same period as the cash receipts or payments to which they belong. One argument *for* them has already been mentioned, namely, the otherwise overstating of the debtors and creditors.

Another argument urged in their favour is that the debtors are the result of sales, and that on each sale a certain amount of profit has been taken credit for, even though the debt has not actually been paid, and the discount to be allowed to the debtor on payment of the account is really a reduction of that profit to a smaller amount, and should, therefore, fall in the same period as the one in which the profit has been shown; so that only the exact amount of profit on each sale shall be taken credit for. And if it be right thus to anticipate the profit on the sale (for the profit is not really made unless and until the debt is actually paid), it surely cannot be wrong to anticipate any loss that will be made in the realizing of such profit.

Methods of Making the Provisions. The provisions are made by means of a journal entry direct to profit and loss account. Another method is to debit or credit them to the discount account. The objection to the latter method is that these amounts are not *actual* discounts but only provisions.

How the Amounts of the Provisions are Arrived At. The discount provisions may be the amounts of specially compiled lists of discounts allowable and receivable, but, generally speaking, they are calculated by means of a fixed percentage on the amount of the outstanding debtors and creditors. Any new provisions that are made must, of course, be adjusted each year with the old ones, as we do not require double provisions. The method of treatment is similar to that adopted with provisions for bad debts dealt with earlier in this chapter.

Note on Provision for Discount on Debtors. The provision for discount on debtors should, properly speaking, be calculated on the *good* debtors, that is, on the amount of the debtors *less* the new bad debts provision (if any). A debt cannot be both good and bad. If we provide for its being bad, we shall not require discount on it. On the other hand, should the debt turn out good, then the amount we have provided for it as a bad debt will be much greater than the discount allowed on it.

To make *ample* provision for losses is all that is required: there is no object in making *excessive* provision.

Example 8

The sundry debtors at 31st December are £10,000. A bad debts provision of 5 per cent is made, and also a discount provision of 5 per cent. The discounts allowed during the year amounted to £350. The discount provision on 1st January was £400.

Show the journal, ledger, profit and loss, and balance sheet entries relating to discount.

Solution 8

First Method

JOURNAL

		Dr	Cr
19..		£	£
Dec 31	Profit & Loss A/c	350	
	Discounts Allowed		350
	Transfer of balance.		
31	Profit & Loss A/c	75	
	Provision for Discount on Debtors . .		75
	Amount required to raise old provision from £400 to £475 (5% on £9,500, viz. £10,000 *less* provision for bad debts £500).		

LEDGER

DISCOUNTS ALLOWED

19..		£	19..		£
Dec 13	Sundry Debtors . .	350	Dec 31	P. & L. A/c . . .	350

PROVISION FOR DISCOUNT ON DEBTORS

19..		£	19..		£
Dec 31	Balance c/d . . .	475	Jan 1	Balance . . .	400
			Dec 31	P. & L. A/c . . .	75
		475			475
			19.1		
			Jan 1	Balance b/d . . .	475

PROFIT AND LOSS ACCOUNT (*Dr.* side)

	£	£
Discounts Allowed		350
Provision for Discount on Debtors	475	
Less Old Provision	400	
		75

BALANCE SHEET

Assets	£	£
Sundry Debtors	10,000	
Less Bad Debts Provision	500	
	9,500	
Less Discount Provision	475	
		9,025

Alternative Method

JOURNAL

		Dr	Cr
19..		£	£
Dec 31	Profit & Loss A/c.	425	
	To Discount Allowed.		425
	Transfer of balance.		

LEDGER

DISCOUNTS ALLOWED

		£			£
19..			19..		
Jan to Dec	Sundry Debtors . .	350	Jan 1	Balance b/f . . .	400
Dec 31	Provision on Debtors (5% on £9,500 c/d) .	475	Dec 31	P. & L. A/c . . .	425
		825			825
			19.1		
			Jan 1	Balance b/d . . .	475

PROFIT AND LOSS ACCOUNT (*Dr*. side)

	£
Discounts Allowed	425

BALANCE SHEET

Assets	£	£
Sundry Debtors	10,000	
Less Bad Debts Provision	500	
	9,500	
Less Discount Provision	475	
		9,025

Example 9

On 1st January the provision for discount on creditors was £120. The discounts received during the year amounted to £104. The creditors at 31st December are £4,960, and a new provision of $2\frac{1}{2}$ per cent is required. Show the journal, ledger, profit and loss, and balance sheet entries relating to discount.

Solution 9

First Method

JOURNAL

		Dr	Cr
19..		£	£
Dec 31	Discounts Received	104	
	To Profit & Loss A/c		104
	Transfer of balance.		
31	Provision for Discount on Creditors . .	4	
	To Profit & Loss A/c		4
	Additional amount required to raise provision from £120 to £124 ($2\frac{1}{2}$% on £4,960).		

LEDGER

DISCOUNTS RECEIVED

19..		£	19..		£
Dec 31	P. & L. A/c . . .	104	Jan to Dec	Sundry Creditors . .	104

PROVISION FOR DISCOUNT ON CREDITORS

19..		£	19..		£
Jan 1	Balance . . .	120	Dec 31	Balance c/d . .	124
Dec 31	P. & L. A/c . . .	4			
		124			124
19.1					
Jan 1	Balance b/d . . .	124			

PROFIT AND LOSS ACCOUNT (*Cr.* side)

	£	£
Discounts Received		104
Provision for Discount on Creditors	124	
Less Old Provision	120	
		4

BALANCE SHEET

Liabilities	£	£
Sundry Creditors	4,960	
Less Provision for Discount	124	
		4,836

Alternative Method

JOURNAL

		Dr	Cr
19..		£	£
Dec 31	Discounts Received	108	
	Profit & Loss A/c		108
	Transfer of balance.		

LEDGER

DISCOUNTS RECEIVED

		£			£
19..			19..		
Jan 1	Balance . . .	120	Jan to Dec	Sundries . . .	104
Dec 31	P. & L. A/c . .	108	Dec 31	Provision on Creditors (2½% on £4,960 c/d) .	124
		228			228
19.1					
Jan 1	Balance b/d . . .	124			

PROFIT AND LOSS ACCOUNT (*Cr.* side)

	£
Discounts Received	108

BALANCE SHEET

Liabilities	£	£
Sundry Creditors	4,960	
Less Provision for Discount	124	
		4,836

Supposing we had placed the provisions in both examples in the discount account instead of in separate provision accounts, as is sometimes done, the discount would appear as under—

DISCOUNT

		£			£
19..			19..		
Jan 1	Balance . . .	120	Jan 1	Balance . . .	200
Dec 31	Sundries . . .	167	Dec 31	Sundries . . .	104
	Provision on Debtors c/d	224		Provision on Creditors c/d	124
				P. & L. A/c . . .	83
		511			511
19.1			19.1		
Jan 1	Balance b/d . . .	124	Jan 1	Balance b/d . . .	224

This method, although shown for the purpose of information, is not recommended to the student, as it is rather complicated; and it is also very confusing to have *two* balances in *one* account. From the commercial viewpoint, also, it is better to be able to see at a glance the amount of the discount allowed and of that received.

QUESTIONS

1. Define "bad debts provision."
2. How is the amount of the bad debts provision arrived at? What objection is there to taking a percentage of the sales?
3. What is the object of making a bad debts provision?
4. Explain briefly the different methods of treating the bad debts provision and bad debts respectively.
5. Define the following: "provision for discount on debtors," "provision for discount on creditors."
6. What is the object of making discount provisions?
7. State briefly some of the arguments *for* and *against* making provisions for discount.
8. What different methods are there of making the discount provisions?
9. How is the amount of the discount provision ascertained?
10. Should a discount provision be calculated on the full amount of the debtors or not? Give reasons for your answer.
11. Explain the meaning of the phrase "adjustments at balancing time." Give examples.
12. What outstanding liabilities have usually to be provided for at balancing time? What accruing income must also be brought to account?
13. What apportionments are usually necessary at the time of closing the books, and why? How is the balance sheet affected by such apportionments?
14. Explain what adjustments come under the following headings—

    (*a*) Provisions for expected losses.
    (*b*) Provisions for expected gains.

15. Why must depreciation of assets be charged against profits?
16. What adjustments are rendered necessary at balancing time, (*a*) through unused stocks of stationery, advertising material, etc., on hand, (*b*) through national insurance?

THE WORK-SHEET

In examples 3 to 9, which we have just looked at, adjusting entries were journalized and then posted to the ledger. Such practice is satisfactory where we are working with a short trial balance with few adjustments. In preparing the final accounts and Balance Sheet of larger enterprises, however, the possibilities of errors will be reduced by the use of a work-sheet.

The work-sheet is an accountant's working document. It is not part of the accounting records and it is usually prepared in pencil, so that changes and corrections may be easily made. The work-sheet consists of one or more sheets of multi-column analysis paper. The columns are used in pairs, one for debit and one for credit. A typical set of pairs might be as follows:

1. The unadjusted Trial Balance.

2. The adjustments.
3. The final accounts.
4. The Balance Sheet.

More pairs of columns may be used if a pair is taken for each final account. An example of the work-sheet is shown on page 0239.

The work-sheet is used in the following way.

(*a*) The unadjusted Trial Balance items are listed under the account titles and the amounts entered into the debit and credit cash columns.

(*b*) The adjustments are entered in the adjustment columns against the appropriate account. If an account is required which is not already listed in the trial balance, then it is listed below. For instance, in our example, depreciation is credited to each fixed asset and the total is debited to a depreciation expense account.

Note also that each adjustment is lettered *a*, *b*, and so on and each amount is given the appropriate letter.

Treatment of Stock. The stock in the trial balance is usually the amount at the start of the accounting period, and the closing stock is normally given outside the trial balance. It can be treated either as an adjustment or as a closing entry.

If closing stock is treated as an adjustment, then an additional item, Trading Account, is entered on the work-sheet and the following enteries are made:

Opening stock. *Dr*. Trading Account.
Cr. Adjustment column.
Closing stock. *Dr*. Adjustment column.
Cr. Trading account.

If closing stock is treated as a closing entry, no additional items is entered on the work-sheet, and closing stock is dealt with at the final stage (c) in the preparation of the work-sheet. This procedure is followed in our example.

When all adjustments have been made, a check on accuracy can be made by totalling the debit and credit columns, which must agree.

(*c*) The final stage in the preparation of the work-sheet is to transfer the adjusted amount for each item to the debit or credit columns of the Trading, Profit and Loss Account or the Balance Sheet. If closing stock is being treated as a closing entry, then the following entries are made:

Opening Stock. *Dr*. in Trading, Profit and Loss Account column.
Closing Stock. *Cr*. in Trading, Profit and Loss Account column.
Dr. in Balance Sheet column.

Where an item has been adjusted, the net figure is transferred. In our example, the total for James Robinson's Capital account is £10,000 + £500 = £10,500, and this is transferred to the Balance Sheet credit column. The total for Rates and taxes is £300 − £23 = £277 and this is transferred to the Trading, Profit and Loss Account debit column.

A row is left on the work-sheet to accommodate the item Net Income or Net Loss. The net income will be debited to the Trading, Profit and Loss column and credited to the Balance Sheet column. A loss would be credited to Trading, Profit and Loss and debited to the Balance Sheet.

CLOSING ENTRIES

Closing entries are recorded through journal entries, and record all the transfers of revenue accounts at the end of a period.

Whenever the net profit of a firm is to be shared in one way or another, the profit and loss account should be subdivided into two sections. The first section is that in which the net profit available is determined. This is the profit and loss account proper. The second section is the *Profit and Loss Appropriation Account*, which shows the way in which the profit is to be disposed of.

Partners generally have an agreement on how the profit is to be divided. In the case of companies, the directors determine how much of the profit available shall be distributed as profit, put to reserve, etc.

Income and Corporation Tax. For a full treatment of tax in accounts see separate chapter. Such taxes are appropriation of profit and cannot be taken into account when determining profit, i.e. they cannot be treated as expenses. The amounts put aside appear in the appropriation account.

Interest on Capital should generally be regarded as appropriation of profit, unlike interest paid on loans, which is an expense.

Salaries paid to Owners or Partners should also be regarded as an appropriation of profit.

Drawings. The owners of a business may take out cash for personal expenses or goods at cost price for their own use, and such items are debited to the appropriate drawings account. The corresponding credit is to cash account, or, in the case of goods, to trading account.

Drawings are not an appropriation of profit, nor are they an expense. They do not appear in the profit and loss account at all.

How Accounts are Closed. Nominal accounts, i.e. those denoting gains and losses, are closed by transfer to trading account or profit and loss. The entries are—

LOSSES: *Cr.* Nominal (expense) account; *Dr.* Profit and loss account.
GAINS: *Dr.* Nominal (gain) account; *Cr.* Profit and loss account.

Formula for Closing Entries. In actual practice, the closing entries are frequently made direct from the ledger accounts themselves to the trading and profit and loss account, which is written up at the back of the ledger; but, in examination work, it is often necessary to know how to make the requisite journal entries. All the items (except stock at finish, adjustments, etc.) are obtained from the trial balance. In business, the stock at finish can be ascertained only by actual stock-taking, but in an exercise it is definitely stated. Sometimes, there is no stock at start in the trial balance, and this fact greatly perturbs students. But it is quite in order. In the first year of business the capital may be all in money; everything has then to be bought; and so the first year's trading account will start with purchases instead of stock. There will, however, be a stock at finish. The method of procedure is, therefore, as follows—

1. *Debit* trading account with the total of the following: stock at start, purchases *less* returns, wages, carriage inwards, and *credit* each of these accounts.

2. *Credit* trading account with the total of sales *less* returns, stock at finish, and *debit* the accounts named.

3. Subtract the *debit* total of trading account from the *credit* total of trading account, and the balance will be the *gross* profit.

4. Carry down the amount of the gross profit to the credit of the profit and loss account, *debit* discounts received account, and other profit accounts (if any) with their respective amounts, and *credit* profit and loss account with the total of all these gains.

5. *Debit* profit and loss account with the total of all the losses shown in the various accounts, and *credit* each of the latter.

6. Subtract the *debit* total of profit and loss account from the *credit* total of profit and loss account, and the balance will be the *net* profit.

7. *Debit* profit and loss account, and *credit* capital account, with the amount of the *net* profit.

8. *Debit* capital account, and *credit* drawings account, with the amount of the drawings (if any).

In the event of a *gross loss*, this will be debited to profit and loss along with the other losses, as stated in No. 5.

In the event of a *net loss* capital account must be *debited* and profit and loss account *credited*, with the amount thereof—in fact, just the reverse procedure to No. 7.

Where there is an appropriation account, No. 7 would read: *Debit* profit and loss account and credit profit and loss appropriation account with the net profit. No. 8 would then read: *Debit* appropriation account, credit various capital accounts, reserves or income tax accounts with the amounts appropriated to these.

WORKED EXAMPLES

We now propose to give two exercises, one fairly easy and one more difficult, on the preparation of a trading and profit and loss account and balance sheet, and to show the full working. The student should not be content to follow the key mentally, but should actually work the exercise in his own books.

Method of Working Final Accounts—

1. If the figures given are not in trial balance form, they should be

sorted into debits and credits. Time may not allow a complete rewriting of the trial balance. In this case, list *all* the balances and divide the total by 2. Sort out the credit balances (they are usually fewer) and check that they equal half the grand total.

2. Mark with an asterisk those items which require adjustment, e.g. plant depreciation, payment in advance, etc. Prepare a work sheet for the more difficult problems.

3. Go through the balances marking as follows where they are to appear—

T—Trading; P—Profit and Loss; B—Balance Sheet.

Remember that adjustments appear twice, once in trading account or profit and loss account and once in the balance sheet.

4. Tick off the items as they are entered in the final accounts.

Example 10

From the following trial balance, extracted from the books of J. & J. Robinson, prepare a trading account and a profit and loss account for the year ended 31st December, 19.., and a balance sheet as on that date.

Charge depreciation on land and buildings account at 2½ per cent, on plant and machinery account at 10 per cent, and on furniture and fixtures at 10 per cent. Make a provision of 5 per cent on the sundry debtors for bad debts.

Carry forward the following unexpired amounts—

	£
1. Fire insurance	12
2. Rates and taxes . . .	23

Charge 5 per cent interest on capital, but not on drawings. Profits and losses are to be shared in the following proportions: James Robinson, five-ninths, Joshua Robinson, four-ninths.

The value of the stock as on 31st December, 19.., was agreed at £4,900. (*R.S.A.*)

TRIAL BALANCE

	£	£
James Robinson, Capital A/c		10,000
Joshua " "		8,000
Land and Buildings	12,000	
Plant and Machinery	5,000	
Furniture and Fixtures	1,000	
Carriage Inwards	400	
Wages	3,000	
Salaries	4,000	
Bad Debts Provision (as on 1st Jan., 19..). . .		100
Sales		40,000
" Returns	200	
Bank Charges and Interest	50	

TRIAL BALANCE (*contd.*)

	£	£
Fuel	250	
Rates and Taxes	300	
Discount A/c		450
Purchases	20,500	
„ Returns		500
Bills Receivable	800	
Trade Expenses	150	
Sundry Debtors	3,200	
„ Creditors		1,200
Stock (1st Jan., 19..)	5,200	
General Expenses	650	
Fire Insurance	100	
Cash at Bank and in hand	3,450	
	60,250	60,250

Solution 10

(1) Journal Entries for Adjustments

		JOURNAL	*Dr*	*Cr*
	19..		£	£
(*a*)	Dec 31	Depreciation	900	
		Land and Buildings		300
		2½% of £12,000		
		Plant and Machinery		500
		10% of £5,000		
		Furniture and Fixtures		100
		10% of £1,000		
(*b*)	31	Unexpired Fire Insurance	12	
		Fire Insurance		12
		Transfer of amount prepaid		
(*c*)	31	Unexpired Rates and Taxes	23	
		Rates and Taxes		23
		Transfer of amount prepaid		
(*d*)	31	Bad debt expense	60	
		Bad debts Provision		60
(*e*)	31	Interest on Capital	900	
		James Robinson, Capital		500
		5% on £10,000		
		Joshua Robinson, Capital		400
		5% on £8,000		

J. & J. Robinson. Work sheet for year ended 31st December 19...

Account titles	Trial Balance		Adjustments		Trading, Profit and Loss Account		Balance Sheet	
	Dr.	Cr.	Dr.	Cr.	Dr.	Cr.	Dr.	Cr.
	£	£	£	£	£	£	£	£
James Robinson Capital A/c		10,000		(*d*) 500				10,500
Joshua Robinson Capital A/c		8,000		(*d*) 400				8,400
Land and buildings	12,000			(*a*) 300			11,700	
Plant and machinery	5,000			(*a*) 500			4,500	
Furniture and Fixtures	1,000			(*a*) 100			900	
Carriage inwards	400				400			
Wages	3,000				3,000			
Salaries	4,000				4,000			
Bad debt Provision		100		(*d*) 60				160
Sales		40,000				40,000		
Sales Returns	200				200			
Bank charges and interest	50				50			
Fuel	250				250			
Rates and taxes	300			(*c*) 23	277			
Discount A/c		450				450		
Purchases	20,500				20,500			
Purchases Returns		500				500		
Bills Receivable	800						800	
Trade expenses	150				150			
Sundry debtors	3,200						3,200	
Sundry creditors		1,200						1,200
Stock (1st Jan. 19..)	5,200				5,200	4,900	4,900	
General expenses	650				650			
Fire insurance	100			(*b*) 12	88			
Cash at bank and in hand	3,450						3,450	
	60,250	60,250						
Depreciation			(*a*) 900		900			
Unexpired fire insurance			(*b*) 12				12	
Unexpired rates and taxes			(*c*) 23				23	
Bad debts expense			(*d*) 60		60			
Interest on capital			(*e*) 900		900			
			1,895	1,895				
Net Income					9,225			9,225
					45,850	45,850	29,485	29,485

(2) Closing Entries

JOURNAL

Date	Particulars		Dr	Cr
19..			£	£
Dec 31	Trading A/c		28,850	
	Stock (at commencement)			5,200
	Purchases	£20,500		
	Less Returns	500		
				20,000
	Carriage Inwards			400
	Wages			3,000
	Fuel.			250
	Balances transferred.			
31	Sales	£40,000		
	Less Returns	200		
			39,800	
	Stock (at close)		4,900	
	Trading A/c			44,700
	Balances transferred.			
31	Trading A/c (gross profit)		15,850	
	Discount		450	
	Bad Debts, New Provision . . .	£160		
	Less Old Provision	100		
				60
	Profit & Loss A/c			16,240
	Balances transferred.			
Dec 31	Profit & Loss A/c		6,115	
	Salaries			4,000
	Bank Charges			50
	Trade Expenses			150
	General Expenses			650
	Fire Insurance	£100		
	Less Amount c/f	12		
				88
	Rates & Taxes	£300		
	Less Amount c/f	23		
				277
	Depreciation—			
	Land & Buildings			300
	Plant & Machinery.			500
	Fixtures & Fittings.			100
	Balances transferred.			
	Profit & Loss Appropriation A/c . . .		900	
	Interest on Capital—			
	James Robinson			500
	Joshua Robinson			400
	Interest transferred.			
	Profit & Loss Appropriation A/c . . .		9,225	
	Capital James Robinson $\frac{5}{9}$			5,125
	„ Joshua Robinson $\frac{4}{9}$			4,100
	Respective shares of profit transferred.			

NOTE 1. As a distinction is made in the trial balance between trade expenses and general expenses, the former may be debited to trading account. The student should provide a note explaining that such expenses have been assumed to be productive or manufacturing expenses.

NOTE 2. Instead of showing the returns as deduction from the purchases and sales as above, some accountants prefer to transfer the returns to the purchases account and sales account respectively. The transfers would be made by journal entries, thus—

		Dr £	*Cr* £
Dec 31	Sales	200	
31	Sales Returns		200
31	Purchases Returns	500	
31	Purchases		500

TRADING ACCOUNT

For the Year Ended 31st December, 19..

	£	£		£	£
Stock (at start)		5,200	Sales	40,000	
Purchases	20,500		*Less* Returns	200	
Less Returns	500				39,800
		20,000	Stock (at finish)		4,900
Carriage		400			
Wages		3,000			
Fuel		250			
Balance (Gross Profit)		15,850			
		44,700			44,700

Profit and Loss Account

For the Year Ended 31st December, 19..

		£		£
Salaries		4,000	Trading A/c (Gross Profit)	15,850
Bank Charges		50	Discount	450
Trade Expenses		150		
General Expenses		650		
Fire Insurance	100			
Less Amount unexpired	12			
		88		
Rates & Taxes	300			
Less Amount unexpired	23			
		277		
Depreciation				
Land & Buildings 2½% of £12,000	300			
Plant & Machinery 10% of £5,000	500			
Furniture & Fittings 10% of £1,000	100			
		900		
Bad Debts Provision				
New Provision	160			
Less Old Provision	100			
		60		
Balance (Net Profit) c/d		10,125		
		16,300		16,300

Profit and Loss Appropriation Account

		£		£
Interest on Capital			Net Profit b/d	10,125
Jas. Robinson, 5% of £10,000	500			
Jos. Robinson, 5% of £8,000	400			
		900		
Balance (Share of Profit)				
Jas. Robinson, 5/9	£5,125			
Jos. Robinson, 4/9	4,100			
		9,225		
		10,125		10,125

BALANCE SHEET AS AT 31ST DECEMBER, 19..

		£			£
Capital—			Fixed Assets—		
James Robinson,			Land & Buildings .	£12,000	
1st Jan . .	£10,000		*Less* Depreciation	300	
Add Interest .	500				11,700
„ Share of Profit	5,125		Plant & Machinery	£5,000	
		15,625	*Less* Depreciation	500	
					4,500
Joshua Robinson,			Furniture & Fittings	£1,000	
1st Jan . .	£8,000		*Less* Depreciation	100	
Add Interest .	400				900
„ Share of Profit	4,100				
		12,500	Current Assets—		
			Stock		4,900
Current Liabilities			Trade Debtors .	£3,200	
Trade Creditors . . .		1,200	*Less* Bad Debts		
			Provision .	160	
					3,040
			Unexpired Fire Insurance .		12
			Unexpired Rates . .		23
			Bills Receivable .		800
			Cash at Bank and in hand .		3,450
		29,325			29,325

Example 11

A and B were in partnership as manufacturing ironmongers. Their capital accounts, as on 31st December, 19.., were equal. The partnership agreement provided that A should take £300 of the profits before B received any share. The balance was to be divided equally between them. During the year ended 31st December, 19.., drawings were made by A at the rate of £50 a month, and by B at the rate of £6 a week.

On 31st December, 19.., the ledger balances, in addition to those of the partners' capital and drawings accounts, were as shown below.

On 31st December, 19.., the stock in hand was valued and agreed at £6,928·20, the work-in-progress was certified at £301·31, and the loose tools at £406·66.

You are required to prepare a trading account and a profit and loss account for the year ended 31st December, 19.., and a balance sheet as on that date. Before preparing these accounts, it is necessary to take the following matters into consideration—

1. The auditors called the partners' attention to the fact that the leasehold premises had not been depreciated in the past. The lease has 15 years to run, and it is decided to write off the book value by equal annual instalments.

2. Ten per cent depreciation is to be written off plant and machinery as on 1st January, and 5 per cent off the additions made during the year.

3. £50 depreciation is to be written off furniture and fittings.

4. Wages account is found to include £47, paid to men who were occupied repairing machinery; and it is decided to transfer this amount to its proper account, and also to put through a transfer of £121·13 as representing the cost of material used out of stock for such repairs.

5. The unexpired portions of rates and insurance were, on 31st December, 19.., £27·12 and £14·02 respectively.

6. It is decided to create a provision for bad debts amounting to 5 per cent on the sundry debtors.

NOTE. No interest on capital or drawings to be provided.

BALANCES OF LEDGER ACCOUNTS, 31ST DECEMBER, 19..

	£
Cash at bank	280·14
,, in hand	37·71
Plant and machinery (including additions during the year of £345·10)	4,018·12
Furniture and fittings	273·72
Discount (debit balance)	47·16
Manufacturing wages	7,649·65
Salaries	962·67
Purchases	20,747·85
Carriage	467·25
Office expenses	212·31
Postage and stationery	42·76
Leasehold buildings	1,500·00
Sales	34,242·64
,, returns	347·67
Purchases returns	742·60
Stock (1st Jan., 19..)	6,738·00
Sundry debtors	9,261·63
Work-in-progress (1st Jan., 19..)	276·75
Advertising	117·85
Bad debts	135·15
Interest on temporary loan (repaid November)	6·35
Loose tools (1st Jan., 19..)	431·74
Rent, rates, and taxes	346·76
Insurance	92·21
Commission	114·50
Lighting and heating	102·23
Sundry creditors	2,136·94

(R.S.A.)

(In a question such as the above, the student should, if time permits, prepare a trial balance and, also, a work-sheet).

Solution 11

(1) Journal Entries for Adjustments

JOURNAL

Date	Particulars	Dr	Cr
19..		£	£
Dec 31	Depreciation	534·55	
	Lease		100·00
	$\frac{1}{15}$ of £1,500		
	Plant & Machinery		384·55
	10% £3,673·02 = £367·30, and 5% £345·10 = £17·25.		
	Furniture & Fixtures		50·00
	Amounts written off respectively.		
31	Repairs	168·13	
	Materials Used for Repairs		121·13
	Wages		47·00
	For repairs to machinery carried out by own workmen.		
31	Unexpired Insurance	14·02	
	Insurance		14·02
	Balance carried forward.		
31	Unexpired Rates	27·12	
	Rent, Rates, & Taxes		27·12
	Balance carried forward.		

(2) Closing Entries

JOURNAL

Date	Particulars		Dr	Cr
19..			£	£
Dec 31	Trading A/c		35,521·64	
	Stock			6,738·00
	Work-in-progress			276·75
	Loose Tools			431·74
	Purchases	£20,747·85		
	Less Returns	742·60		
				20,005·25
	Manufacturing Wages			7,602·65
	Carriage			467·25
	Balances transferred.			
31	Sales	£34,242·64		
	Less Returns	347·67		
			33,894·97	
	Materials Used for Repairs		121·13	
	Stock		6,928·20	
	Work-in-progress		301·31	
	Loose Tools		406·66	
	Trading A/c			41,652·27
	Balance transferred.			

(*contd. over*)

JOURNAL (*contd.*)

		Dr	Cr
19..		£	£
Dec 31	Trading A/c	6,130·63	
	Profit & Loss A/c		6,130·63
	Gross profit transferred.		
31	Profit & Loss A/c	463·08	
	Provision for Bad Debts		463·08
	5% of sundry debtors £9,261·63.		
31	Profit & Loss A/c	2,841·49	
	Discount		47·16
	Salaries		962·67
	Office Expenses		212·31
	Postage & Stationery		42·76
	Advertising		117·85
	Bad Debts		135·15
	Interest on Loan		6·35
	Rent, Rates, & Taxes		319·64
	Insurance		78·19
	Commission		114·50
	Lighting & Heating		102·23
	Depreciation		534·55
	Repairs		168·13
	Balances transferred.		
31	Profit & Loss A/c	300·00	
	A—Capital		300·00
	Preferential claim on profits.		
31	Profit & Loss A/c	2,526·06	
	A—Capital		1,263·03
	B— ,,		1,263·03
	Respective shares of profit transferred.		
31	A—Capital	600·00	
	A's Drawings		600·00
	Balance transferred.		
31	B—Capital	312·00	
	B's Drawings		312·00
	Balance transferred.		

Trading Account
For the Year Ended 31st December, 19..

	£	£		£	£
Stock, 1st Jan.		6,738·00	Sales	34,242·64	
Work-in-progress, 1st Jan.		276·75	*Less* Returns	347·67	
Loose Tools, 1st Jan.		431·74			33,894·97
Purchases	20,747·85		Materials used for Repairs		121·13
Less Returns	742·60		Stock, 31st Dec.		6,928·20
		20,005·25	Work-in-progress, 31st		
Manufacturing Wages	7,649·65		Dec.		301·31
Less Transfer to Repairs	47·00		Loose Tools 31st Dec.		406·66
		7,602·65			
Carriage		467·25			
Balance (Gross Profit) c/d		6,130·63			
		41,652·27			41,652·27

Profit and Loss Account
For the Year Ended 31st December, 19..

	£	£		£
Discount		47·16	Balance (Gross Profit) b/d.	6,130·63
Salaries		962·67		
Office Expenses		212·31		
Postage & Stationery		42·76		
Advertising		117·85		
Bad Debts		135·15		
Interest on Loan		6·35		
Rent, Rates, & Taxes	346·76			
Less Amount c/f	27·12			
		319·64		
Insurance	92·21			
Less Amount c/f	14·02			
		78·19		
Commission		114·50		
Lighting & Heating		102·23		
Depreciation—				
Lease, $\frac{1}{15}$ of £1,500	100·00			
Plant & Machinery, 10% £3,673·02	367·30			
Plant & Machinery, 5% £345·10	17·25			
		384·55		
Furniture & Fittings		50·00		
Repairs—				
Materials used	121·13			
Wages paid	47·00			
		168·13		
Provision for Bad Debts 5% £9,261·63		463·08		
Balance (Net Profit) c/d		2,826·06		
		6,130·63		6,130·63
A—Capital, as per agreement		300·00	Balance (Net Profit) b/d	2,826·06
Balance—				
A—Capital, ½	1,263·03			
B—Capital, ½	1,263·03			
		2,526·06		
		2,826·06		2,826·06

Another method of adjustment is to transfer the £121·13 (materials used for repairs) to the purchases account and state the amount net—also to set the £406·66 against the £431·74 (loose tools), showing a net figure of £25·08 as "consumption of tools," or "tools used." Similarly, "work-in-progress" is frequently adjusted with sales, and the item described as "production."

BALANCE SHEET AS AT 31ST DECEMBER, 19..

Liabilities	£	£	*Assets*	£	£
Sundry Creditors		2,136·94	Cash in hand	37·71	
Capital—			Cash at Bank	280·14	
A—1st Jan., 19..	9,000·00				317·85
Add Share of Profit	1,563·03		Sundry Debtors	9,261·63	
			Less Bad Debts Provision	463·08	
	10,563·03				8,798·55
Less Drawings	600·00		Stock		6,928·20
		9,963·03	Work-in-progress		301·31
B—1st Jan., 19..	9,000·00		Loose Tools		406·66
Add Share of Profit	1,263·03		Furniture & Fixtures	273·72	
			Less Depreciation	50·00	
	10,263·03				223·72
Less Drawings	312·00		Leasehold Buildings	1,500·00	
		9,951·03	*Less* Depreciation	100·00	
					1,400·00
			Plant & Machinery	4,018·12	
			Less Depreciation	384·55	
					3,633·57
			Rates unexpired		27·12
			Insurance unexpired		14·02
		22,051·00			22,051·00

SPECIAL POINTS TO WATCH IN EXERCISES

Period Covered by the Trading and Profit and Loss Account. This is a point that should be carefully noted by the student. If it is not definitely stated, it can usually be ascertained by comparing the dates of the stock at start and the stock at finish. Sometimes the rates for depreciation and the rate of interest on capital are stated to be *per annum*, and if the period covered by the trading and profit and loss account is only six months, i.e. for the half-year, such rates must be dealt with accordingly. The percentage for the bad debts provision or discount provision, however, will not be affected. If these are given as 5 per cent, they will be 5 per cent (actual) of the sundry debtors, whether the account is for six or for twelve months, the period of time making no difference to these particular items.

Stock at Finish in the Trial Balance. This occurs only when there is a materials consumed account in the trial balance or list of balances. Its special treatment under such circumstances has been pointed out in our remarks on the contents of the trading account, to which the student should refer (p. 0205).

Bad Debts Not Written Off. In some exercises the bad debts have not been written off, and the student is told to do this. The student thinks it quite simple, and promptly puts them in the profit and loss account.

More often than not, however, he fails to complete the double entry by making a corresponding deduction from the sundry debtors, with, of course, disastrous effects on the accuracy of his work. For example, take the following trial balance (condensed)—

TRIAL BALANCE

	£	£
Sundry debit balances	5,082	
,, debtors	2,560	
,, credit balances		7,642
	7,642	7,642

Suppose the bad debts not written off are £60, and that a bad debts provision of 5 per cent is required to be made. The bad debts provision would be 5 per cent of £2,500, and not 5 per cent of £2,560. In the balance sheet, therefore, we should have—

	£	£
Sundry Debtors	2,500	
Less Bad Debts Provision	125	
		2,375

Depreciation. Sometimes depreciation appears in the trial balance as an amount already written off some asset or assets. Students who have been accustomed to show the assets in the balance sheet, *less* depreciation do so in this particular instance, and, of course, find subsequently that the balance sheet totals do not correspond. To show the asset *less* depreciation, the depreciation must be *added back* again to the asset and then deducted. For example, take the following trial balance (condensed)—

TRIAL BALANCE

	£	£
Sundry debit balances	7,206	
Plant and machinery	1,350	
Depreciation of plant and machinery	150	
Sundry credit balances		8,706
	8,706	8,706

The depreciation of plant would be transferred to the profit and loss account, and the plant and machinery would be shown in the balance sheet thus—

	£	£
Plant and Machinery	1,500	
Less Depreciation	150	
		1,350

As the depreciation appears in the trial balance it must have been written off the plant and machinery, for there could not be one-sided entries in the ledger. The asset is, therefore, as its net figure and must not be further reduced.

ADJUSTMENTS AND THE BALANCE SHEET

Common Errors. As in the intermediate stage the students' great difficulty is to make the trial balance agree, so also in the advanced stage their great difficulty is to make the balance sheet agree. The outstanding liabilities are frequently omitted, and the apportionments are either omitted or else placed on their wrong sides. The wrong stock is often entered in the balance sheet. It should not be the stock in the trial balance, but the stock at finish. Sometimes the disagreement of the balance sheet totals is caused by the omission of the stock-in-trade altogether. In other cases, the balance sheet will not agree because the wrong bad debts provision has been deducted, namely, the old provision instead of the new one, i.e. the one to be made; or else merely the amount debited or credited to profit and loss in order to adjust the two provisions has been shown as the actual provision. For example—

PROFIT AND LOSS ACCOUNT (Debit side)

	£	£
Bad Debts Provision (5% on £5,000)	250	
Less Old Provision	120	
		130

and then in Balance Sheet—

	£	£
Sundry Debtors	5,000	
Less Bad Debts Provision	130	
		4,870

instead of—

	£	£
Sundry Debtors	5,000	
Less Bad Debts Provision	250	
		4,750

which is the correct amount.

QUESTIONS

1. What are closing entries?
2. Explain the term "balance sheet." What information should it afford? How does it differ from a trial balance?
3. What controversy is there respecting the form of the English balance sheet?
4. What two methods are there of marshalling the assets and liabilities on a balance sheet? Illustrate your answer by means of *pro forma* examples. What variations are sometimes met with?
5. Why are outstanding liabilities included in the balance sheet in addition to being debited in the profit and loss account or trading account?

INTERPRETATION: MANAGEMENT REQUIREMENTS

The modern tendency in accountancy is to design the form of accounts so that the maximum use may be made of the information contained in them. In particular, comparisons and ratios should be used as they give a better guide than absolute figures.

No ideal design may be prescribed: every business should have the form best suited to its needs. The most common ratios are discussed in Chapter 29.

Comparative Figures. The value of all ratios and figures is enhanced by comparison with the same items for previous years. Published accounts of companies must show comparative figures for the previous year. Some companies give figures for several previous years. In this way, trends may be more easily discerned. The figures must, however, be compiled on the same basis throughout, otherwise quite misleading results may be shown. This question is dealt with more fully in Chapter 29.

EXERCISE 02

1. A and B commenced trading in partnership on 1st January, 19.., bringing in capital amounting altogether to £20,000, and the partners' combined drawings during 19.. amounted to £2,000.

At the end of the year the firm's book-keeper produced accounts showing that a net profit of £3,000 had been made. On the partners considering these, A said, "These accounts must be wrong. We are heavily overdrawn at the bank, so our profit must have been less than our drawings."

Is A right or wrong? If wrong, explain where the fallacy lies and state how you think the position has (probably) come about.

(*R.S.A.*)

2. J. Bucks carries on business as a haulage contractor and the balances on his books at 31st March, 19.., were—

	£	£
Capital		**22,541**
Haulage receipts		**22,172**
Motor lorries (cost £20,000)	**18,000**	
Wages	**4,308**	
Office salaries	**3,164**	
Stocks at 1st April, 19..—		
Petrol and oil	**101**	
Spare parts	**357**	
Petrol and oil purchases	**5,613**	
Spare parts purchases	**1,776**	
Rents received		**220**
Insurances, licences, etc., of lorries	**1,086**	
Repairs to vehicles	**502**	
" " premises	**108**	
Office expenses	**288**	
Bad debts	**106**	
Provision for bad debts		**100**
Debtors	**5,927**	
Creditors		**1,067**
Plant and equipment (cost £1,000)	**800**	
Land and buildings, at cost	**3,000**	
Balance at bank	**964**	
	46,100	**46,100**

Prepare suitable final accounts for the year ended 31st March, 19.1, and balance sheet at that date, taking into consideration the following—

(*a*) Stocks on hand at 31st March, 19.1, were: petrol and oil £129; spare parts £486.

(*b*) Motor lorries are to be depreciated at 20 per cent on cost.

(*c*) Plant and equipment are to be depreciated at 10 per cent on cost.

(*d*) Insurance paid in advance at 31st March, 19.1, amounted to £123.

(*e*) Part of the building is let at £240 p.a. and the rent for March, 19.1, was received in the following month.

(*f*) During the year a new office was erected. The cost of the materials, £50, was included in repairs to premises accounts and the cost of the labour, £150, included in wages.

(*g*) Included in salaries account is £1,200, drawn by the proprietor of the business.

(*h*) The provision for bad debts is to be made up to £127.

(*R.S.A.*)

3. Rice and Baxter entered into partnership on 1st January with a capital of £30,000, £20,000 of which was contributed by P. Rice and £10,000 by F. Baxter. It was agreed that profits should be shared in proportion to capital introduced, and the drawings of the partners should be: Rice, £400, and Baxter, £200 per quarter on account of accruing profit. Should either partner draw more than the agreed amount, he was to be debited with not less than one quarter's interest on the sum drawn in excess. Each partner was to be entitled to interest on his capital at 5 per cent per annum. A bad debts provision of 2½ per cent of the sundry debtors was to be created.

The stock at 31st December was valued at £12,857.

From the above particulars and the following balances, prepare trading and profit and loss accounts for the year ended 31st December, and a balance sheet as at that date—

	£		£
P. Rice, Capital	20,000	Trade charges	460
F. Baxter, Capital	10,000	Sundry debtors	17,078
Cash at bank	2,418	Returns outwards	1,756
„ on deposit	1,000	P. Rice, Drawings	1,600
Purchases	35,640	F. Baxter, Drawings	1,000
Sundry creditors	3,920	Rent owing *Cr.*	160
Rent, rates, and taxes	700	Interest and discount *Dr.*	270
Bills payable	2,690	Salaries	1,200
Furniture and fixtures	500	Returns inwards	2,460
Sales	29,360	Bills receivable	3,560

4. On 30th June, Messrs. Lewis & Co. extracted the following balances from their books—

	£		£
P. Lewis, Capital	7,012	Cash in hand	20
T. Smithers, Capital	5,010	Petty expenses	312
Wages of workmen	5,340	Bad debts	119
Gas and electric light	80	„ „ added to provision	100
Commission and discount (*Dr.*)	420	Salaries	1,000
Debtors for rent	50	Purchases	28,381
Bills receivable	781	Sundry creditors	6,245
Bills payable	1,970	P. Lewis, Drawings	1,000
Stock, 1st July	9,645	T. Smithers, Drawings	400
Freight and carriage	158	Sundry debtors	9,036
Sales	37,500	Rent, rates, and taxes	1,500
Bad debts provision	230	Travelling expenses	364
Bank overdraft	739		

Stock on hand 30th June was valued at £11,774. Provide for salary £300 to be credited to T. Smithers. Profits are to be divided—seven-twelfths to Lewis and five-twelfths to Smithers. Prepare trading and profit and loss account and balance sheet as at 30th June (to nearest £), after allowing interest on capital at 5 per cent per annum.

5. J. Dover and K. Deal carry on business in partnership and the books of the firm at 31st December, 19.1, show the following balances—

	£	£
J. Dover, Capital		12,000
K. Deal, "		500
J. Dover, Drawings	3,413	
K. Deal, "	883	
Stock at 31st December, 19..	2,109	
Rents received		360
Cash in hand	50	
Balance at bank	1,789	
General expenses	467	
Sundry debtors and creditors	2,253	1,406
Fixtures and fittings	320	
Discounts allowed and received	376	127
Salaries	2,205	
Returns inwards and outwards	596	284
Freehold property	7,250	
Purchases and sales	14,813	21,972
Insurance	125	
	36,649	36,649

In the deed of partnership it was agreed that—

(*a*) K. Deal should be credited with a salary of £800 per annum.

(*b*) Capital should carry interest at 6 per cent per annum, but no interest should be charged on drawings.

(*c*) Profits and losses should be divided in the proportions of $\frac{5}{7}$ to Dover and $\frac{2}{7}$ to Deal.

It is ascertained that—

1. The stock at 31st December, 19.1, was valued at £2,624.

2. Rent accrued at 31st December, 19.1, amounted to £120 and was received at a later date.

3. A provision for bad debts of £85 is required.

4. Fixtures and fittings are to be depreciated at the rate of 10 per cent per annum on cost £400.

5. Included in insurance account is the sum of £50, paid in advance.

Prepare the firm's trading and profit and loss account for the year ended 31st December, 19.1, and balance sheet at that date.

(*R.S.A.*)

6. From the following balances and the undermentioned particulars, prepare Rocklyn & Co.'s trading and profit and loss account for the year ended 30th September and a balance sheet as on that date—

	£		£
Purchases	18,682	R. Rocklyn, Capital	10,840
Bad debts	196	" Drawings	800
Sales	49,240	P. Farmley, Capital	10,306
Repairs and renewals	1,140	" Drawings	700
General Expenses	920	Extension of works	3,000
Coal and coke	1,040	Rents received	300
Sundry debtors	9,300	Cash in hand	80
Travellers' salaries and Commission		Rates and Taxes	760
	1,300	Cash at bank	3,120
Discounts allowed	860	Clerks' salaries	960
Trade creditors	3,080	Wages of workmen	6,338
Stock, 1st October	7,960	Discounts received	390
Plant and machinery	7,000	Premises	10,000

Make a bad debts provision of £460, a discount provision on debtors of 2½ per cent; credit interest on capital at 5 per cent per annum; depreciate plant and machinery 5 per cent. Stock on hand, 30th September, valued at £3,372. Profits and losses to be shared equally.

7. The following trial balance was extracted from the books of Traders Ltd. at 31st December, 19..—

	£	£
Authorized and issued share capital 50,000 shares of £1 each		50,000
5 per cent debentures		20,000
Share premiums		12,500
Provision for bad debts, 1st January, 19..		400
Stock-in-trade, 1st January, 19..	23,500	
Purchases	120,000	
Sales		155,000
Trade debtors	14,200	
Trade creditors		6,100
Balance at bank	18,190	
General expenses	6,650	
Freehold property (at cost)	50,000	
Bad debts	820	
Wages and salaries	9,240	
Furniture and fittings (at cost)	3,000	
Provision for depreciation of furniture and fittings		600
Directors' fees	1,000	
Rates	250	
Debenture interest paid to 1st July, 19..	500	
Profit and loss account balance, 1st January, 19..		2,750
	247,350	247,350

The following matters are to be taken into account—

(*a*) Stock-in-trade 31st December, 19.., £24,700.
(*b*) Wages and salaries outstanding, 31st December, 19.., £240.
(*c*) Rates paid in advance, 31st December, 19.., £50.
(*d*) The provision for bad debts required at 31st December, 19.., is to be £350.
(*e*) Provide for depreciation of furniture and fittings at the rate of 5 per cent of cost.
(*f*) The directors propose to transfer £10,000 to reserve and to pay a dividend of 10 per cent on the issued capital. Ignore income tax.

You are required to prepare a trading and profit and loss account for the year 19.. and a balance sheet as at 31st December, 19...

(*R.S.A.*)

8. R. Poole and F. Winchley entered in partnership on 1st October, under the style of Poole & Co. The following balances (except one) were obtained from their books at 30th September, after the first year's trading—

Sundry debtors £7,360; R. Poole, drawings £800; F. Winchley, drawings £800; stock, 30th September, £4,900; salaries £940; carriage £450; discounts received £720; purchases £26,720; commission £660; plant and machinery £9,252 (after charging depreciation £1,026); freehold premises £3,000; trade creditors (including bills payable £1,500), £7,704; cash at bank £1,180; discounts allowed £1,064; rent, rates, and taxes £1,660; wages of workmen £5,480; general expenses £872; travelling expenses £520; goods sold £35,360.

Draw up a trial balance (bringing into account the capital, which the partners contributed equally), and prepare trading and profit and loss account, and balance sheet as at 30th September, after allowing interest on capital at 5 per cent per annum.

9. The bad debts provision on 1st January was £725·78. The bad debts during the year amounted to £630·52. The sundry debtors on 31st December are £16,368·67, and a new provision of 5 per cent is required. Show (both ways) the journal, ledger, profit and loss account, and balance sheet entries.

10. On 1st January the provision for discount on creditors was £120. The discounts received during the year amounted to £110. The creditors on 31st December are £4,950, and a new provision of 2½ per cent is required. Show (both ways) the journal, ledger, profit and loss account, and balance sheet entries relating to discount.

11. On 1st January the provision for discount on creditors was £160·67. The discounts received during the year amounted to £187·82. The creditors at 31st December £6,626·55, and a new provision of 2½ per cent is required. Show (both ways) the journal, ledger, profit and loss account, and balance sheet entries relating to discount.

12. John and Martin Seagrove trade as retail chemists. Martin Seagrove prepared the accounts and their profit and loss account and balance sheet for the year ended 30th September, 1966, was as follows—

PROFIT AND LOSS ACCOUNT

	£		£
Wages—			
John Seagrove	1,200	Sales to customers	7,074
Martin Seagrove	1,200	Receipts from the National	
Assistants	2,667	Health Executive	22,311
Purchases	21,402	Depreciation of shop fittings to	
Stock at 30th September, 1966	2,033	30th September, 1965	806
Rent of shop	850	Goodwill at cost	3,000
Purchase of new scales	65	Accruals at 30th September,	
Cash at bank	1,103	1965—	
Printing and stationery	169	Wages	15
Discounts allowed	17	Rent	30
Repairs and renewals	222	Electricity	10
Riding lessons for Martin Seagrove's daughter	30	Loan by John Seagrove to the business at 5% per annum	
Electricity	61	from 31st March, 1966	600
Profit carried down	2,827		
	33,846		33,846

BALANCE SHEET

	£		£
Capital Accounts at 30th September, 1965—		Profit brought down	2,827
John Seagrove	3,800	Overdrawn current accounts at 30th September, 1965—	
Martin Seagrove	1,900	John Seagrove	63
Stock at 30th September, 1965	1,872	Martin Seagrove	102
Debtors at 30th September, 1966	127	Discounts received	108
Creditors at 30th September, 1966	1,199	Shop fittings at cost, at 30th September, 1965	1,963
Rates and insurances	432	Bank charges	72
Prepaid at 30th September, 1965—		Income tax paid—	
Insurances	33	Schedule D for John Seagrove	400
		Schedule D for Martin Seagrove	370
		PAYE taxation for assistants	433
	9,363		6,338

You are given this additional information—

(*a*) Goods invoiced during the year of £47 were included in purchases but were not received until 4th October, 1966. The goods were not included in the stock at 30th September, 1966, nor were they paid for at that date.

(*b*) The item repairs and renewals includes the sum of £80 paid in cash for a new cash register. The previous cash register was traded-in for £20 in part-exchange, but is still carried in the books of the partnership at its original cost of £50, with accumulated depreciation of £42.

(*c*) Depreciation should be provided at 10 per cent per annum on the net book value of the shop fittings as adjusted by transactions during the year.

(*d*) Accruals and prepayments at 30th September, 1966, have not been included in the accounts set out above, and were:

	Accruals	*Prepayments*
	£	£
Wages	17	
Insurance		26
Rent	30	
Electricity	42	
Repairs	103	

(*e*) The brothers, John and Martin Seagrove, trading in partnership, share profits equally.

(*f*) A provision of £103 against doubtful debts is to be made, and an additional sum of £1,405 was due from the National Health Executive at 30th September, 1966.

You are required to prepare the profit and loss account and balance sheet in a more correct form, incorporating the additional adjustments. (*I.C.M.A.*)

13. The books of Black & White, who are equal partners, are balanced yearly as on 31st December. Before profits are ascertained and divided, 5 per cent interest is allowed upon partners' capital. Depreciation at the rate of 5 per cent is written off plant, and a provision of 5 per cent is made for bad and doubtful debts. One year's interest, at the rate of 4½ per cent, is due upon the loan on mortgage, and has not yet

been passed through the books. The stock on hand, as on 31st December, was valued at £3,225.

The following are the final balances as on 31st December—

	£		£
Purchases	16,450	Trade charges	400
Manufacturing wages	2,150	Premium on lease (6 years unexpired as on 1st January)	2,400
Sales	24,800	Sundry creditors	15,345
Black's Capital	5,000	Loan on mortgage	5,000
„ Drawings (including interest)	550	Freehold land and buildings	8,000
White's Capital	2,000	Plant	4,000
„ drawings (including interest)	350	Provision for bad and doubtful debts (as on 1st January)	600
Stock (as on 1st January)	3,000	Sundry debtors	13,100
Salaries	820	Cash at bank	1,200
Rates and taxes	325		

Prepare a trading and profit and loss account for the year ended 31st December, and a balance sheet as on that date. (*London Chamber of Commerce.*)

14. The books of William Jones & Co. were balanced as on 31st December, and a profit and loss account and balance sheet prepared. The profit for the year, as shown by these accounts, amounted to £2,481·33. The following mistakes had been made by the book-keeper during the year—

(*a*) A gas engine costing £450 had been debited to purchases instead of to machinery and plant.

(*b*) An amount of £15·64, received as a final dividend in the estate of G. Smith, the balance of whose account had, in a previous year, been written off as a bad debt, was standing to the credit of a newly-opened account under the same name, and was included amongst the sundry creditors in the balance sheet.

(*c*) A cheque amounting to £10·24, which had been returned dishonoured, was posted to the debit of allowances instead of to the account of B. Brown, from whom it was received.

(*d*) Goods amounting to £52·07 had been returned by R. Robinson, on 30th December, and were taken into stock, but the entries recording the return were not passed through the firm's books until 4th January of next year.

What adjustments would be necessary to rectify these errors, and how would they affect the above-mentioned profit? (*London Chamber of Commerce.*)

15. The rent and rates account in the ledger of Riley Brothers showed that on 31st December, 19. ., the rent for the quarter to Christmas was outstanding, and that the rates for the half-year ended 31st March, 19. ., amounting to £76·38 had been paid. During the ensuing year the following payments relating to rent and rates were made—

		£
Jan 4	Rent for Christmas quarter	90·00
Mar 29	„ „ Lady Day „	90·00
Jun 26	Rates for half-year ending 30th September, 19.1	74·70
Jul 7	Rent for Midsummer quarter	90·00
Sep 30	„ „ Michaelmas „	90·00
Dec 28	„ „ Christmas „	90·00

The rates for the half-year ended 31st March, 19.2, which amounted to £80·88, were paid on 6th January, 19.2.

You are required to show the rent and rates account as it would appear after the books for the year ended 31st December, 19.1, had been closed. Make any calculation in months. (*R.S.A.*)

16. A limited company makes up its accounts annually to 30th June and shows rent and rates as one item in the profit and loss account.

The rent is £2,000 per annum, payable quarterly, and the payments during 19../.1 were as follows—

Rent for quarter to—

30th June, 19..	Paid 10th July, 19..
30th September, 19..	„ 27th September, 19..
31st December, 19..	„ 6th January, 19.1
31st March, 19.1	„ 24th March, 19.1
30th June, 19.1	„ 28th June 19.1

The rates for the half-year to 30th September, 19.., amounted to £590, and were paid on 15th May, 19..; for the half-year to 31st March, 19.1, the amount was the same and was paid on 10th November, 19..; for the half-year to 30th September, 19.1, the amount was £610, paid on 20th May, 19.1.

Show the rent and rates account as it would appear in the company's ledger for the year to 30th June, 19.1.

17. James Thompson took over the business of an iron ore proprietor, the lease of the mines having fifteen years to run, on 1st January, and carried on the business for six months.

Make up his profit and loss account and balance sheet from the following figures without taking account of interest upon capital, but providing for the wasting of the lease, and writing off depreciation, at the rate of 5 per cent per annum from machinery and plant, providing £445 for bad debts, and allowing a discount of 2½ per cent from the debtors and creditors.

	£		£
James Thompson, Capital	20,000	Rent, rates, and taxes	2,330
„ „ withdrawals	800	Bank charges	200
Machinery and plant	3,522	Discounts allowed	850
Ore sales	36,700	Royalty	5,000
Cash at bankers	5,709	Lease	16,500
„ on hand	9	Coals	1,260
Allowances and returns	500	Sundry debtors	6,300
Salaries	939	Candles and oil	390
Wages	12,684	Repairs	360
Discounts received	75	Powder	372
Damages for breach of contract	100	Office furniture	100
Unpaid wages	286	Carriage and freight	913
Sundry creditors	8,000	Stock, 1st January	4,850
Unexpired insurances	40	Ropes used	53
		Timber used	1,280

The stock at 30th June amounted to £5,000. (*Chartered Accountants.*)

18. The following trial balance was extracted from the books of B. Ltd. as on 30th September, 19.1—

	£	£
Share capital, authorized and issued: 25,000 ordinary shares of £1 each		25,000
Directors' current accounts—		
Evans		680
Gilbert		390
Motor vehicles (cost £4,800)	2,880	
Freehold properties, at cost	20,000	
Profit and loss account—		
Balance at 30th September, 19..		7,360
Purchases	91,375	
Sales		118,400
Stock-in-trade, 30th September, 19...	10,750	
Loan from X Ltd., at 5 per cent per annum		5,000
Loan interest accrued at 30th September, 19..		250
Goodwill	3,000	
Bad debts	470	
Provision for bad debts, 30th September, 19..		140
Rent receivable		250
Trade debtors and creditors	13,560	9,310
Motor and delivery expenses	772	
General expenses	4,330	
Balance at bank	2,008	
Directors' salaries	4,750	
Wages and salaries	12,425	
Rates and insurances	460	
	166,780	166,780

You are given the following information—

(*a*) Stock-in-trade, 30th September, 19.1, £11,550.

(*b*) The provision for bad debts is to be increased to £300.

(*c*) Wages and salaries outstanding at 30th September, 19.1, £200.

(*d*) Rates and insurances paid in advance at 30th September, 19.1, £62.

(*e*) The item "rent receivable £250" includes £50 in respect of the period from 1st October, 19.1, to 31st December, 19.1.

(*f*) Provision is to be made for depreciation of motor vehicles at the rate of 20 per cent per annum (on cost).

(*g*) During the year to 30th September, 19.1, E, one of the directors, took goods (cost £175) out of business stock, for his own use. No entry for this matter has been made in the books.

You are required to prepare a trading and profit and loss account for the year to 30th September, 19.1, and a balance sheet as on that date. Ignore taxation.

(*Chartered Institute of Secretaries.*)

19. The book-keeper of H. N. Ltd. has prepared the following profit and loss account and balance sheet—

PROFIT AND LOSS ACCOUNT FOR THE YEAR TO 30TH JUNE, 19.3

	£		£
Wages & Salaries	7,233	Gross Profit	27,872
Rent & Rates	1,491	Discounts Received	1,248
Petty Cash	318		
General Expenses	2,000		
Salesmen's Commission	7,840		
Depreciation of Motor Vehicles	800		
Net Profit for year	9,438		
	29,120		29,120

BALANCE SHEET—30TH JUNE, 19.3

		£			£
Authorized and Issued Share Capital—			*Fixed Assets*		
16,000 shares of £1 each		16,000	Motor Vehicles		1,215
Less Calls in Arrear		100	*Current Assets*		
		15,900	Stock-in-trade	15,484	
Profit & Loss A/c—			Debtors	12,622	
Balance, 1st July, 19.2	340		Balance at Bank	4,480	
Net Profit for year	9,438				32,586
		9,778			
Current Liabilities		8,123			
		33,801			33,801

You are given the following information—

(*a*) The motor vehicles account is as follows—

19..		£	19.1		£
Jul 1	Cost of four vehicles at £1,000 each	4,000	Jun 30	Depreciation	800
			19.2		
			Jun 30	Depreciation	800
			Jul 1	Sale of one vehicle	385
			19.3		
			Jun 30	Depreciation	800

(*b*) Calls in arrear, £100, represents the final call of 25p per share on 400 shares. These shares were forfeited on 30th June, 19.3.

(*c*) During June, 19.3, one of the company's salesmen collected £516 from trade debtors and paid £412 to trade creditors. He retained the balance of £104 in settlement of commission due to him.

Discounts allowed by the trade creditors amounted to £14. No entries for the commission of £104 or for any of the above transactions have been made in the books.

(*d*) Stock was taken at the close of business on 4th July, 19.3, when the cost of the goods on the company's premises was £15,484. Goods purchased and received during the first four days of July amounted to £536, and goods sold and dispatched in the same period were invoiced at £750. A credit note for returns inwards, £40, dated

1st July, 19.3, and entered in the books on that date, was found to represent goods returned on 30th June. The gross profit on all goods is 20 per cent of selling price.

(*e*) The imprest system for petty cash is used by the company, and the amount of the imprest is £30. The cashier is reimbursed on the first day of each month. Payments out of petty cash in June, 19.3, were £26. All payments from petty cash are to be treated as general expenses.

You are required to redraft the profit and loss account and balance sheet (not necessarily in a form for publication). Ignore taxation.

(*Chartered Institute of Secretaries.*)

20. Fogbound Ltd. is a private company. The directors, Brown and Gray, each hold one-half of the share capital. The following trial balance was extracted as on 31st December, 19.2—

	£	£
Share capital, authorized and issued: 40,000 ordinary shares of £1 each		40,000
Motor-cars, at cost less depreciation to 31st December, 19.1	1,500	
Purchases	185,630	
Sales		217,140
Stock-in-trade, 31st December, 19.1	13,400	
Freehold properties, at cost	22,250	
Trade debtors and creditors	11,370	14,280
Bad debts	310	
Provision for bad debts, 31st December, 19.1		150
Rates and insurances	815	
Balance at bank	9,856	
Directors' current accounts—		
Brown	3,180	
Gray	2,965	
Car expenses	640	
Wages and salaries	14,935	
Printing and stationery	318	
Repairs to buildings	1,022	
Suspense account		33
General expenses	6,129	
Profit and loss account: balance at 31st December, 19.1		2,717
	274,320	274,320

You are given the following information—

(*a*) Stock-in-trade, 31st December, 19.2, £14,890.

(*b*) Wages and salaries outstanding, 31st December, 19.2, £366.

(*c*) Rates and insurances paid in advance, 31st December, 19.2, £176.

(*d*) The provision for bad debts is to be increased to £225.

(*e*) Stock of stationery, 31st December, 19.2, £118.

(*f*) The motor-cars were purchased on 1st January, 19... Depreciation has been written off at 20 per cent (on cost) per annum, and is to be calculated at the same rate for 19.2.

(*g*) The item repairs to buildings includes £450 for alterations and improvements.

(*h*) The directors' current account balances represent cash drawn by the directors during 19.2, less credit balances brought forward at 31st December, 19.1. It has been agreed that one-fifth of the car expenses and one-fifth of the depreciation of the cars should be charged to the directors, in equal proportions, in respect of private motoring. Brown and Gray are each entitled to a salary of £4,000 for the year 19.2.

(*i*) The difference on the books, £33, was found to be due to a failure to post an item in the returns inwards journal to the personal account of the customer.

You are required to prepare a trading and profit and loss account for the year 19.2, and a balance sheet as on 31st December, 19.2.

No dividend is proposed. Ignore taxation. (*Chartered Institute of Secretaries.*)

21. (i) A trader debits car expenses account with all expenses relating to his car, but the annual accounts of his business, made up to 30th June, are prepared on the basis that four-fifths of the use of the car is for business purposes and one-fifth is for private purposes.

Total payments (including tax, insurance, repairs and all running expenses) during the year to 30th June, 19.1, amounted to £327.

Prepayments and outstanding expenses were as follows—

	At 30th June 19..	At 30th June 19.1
	£	£
Tax and insurance paid in advance . . .	16	17
Unpaid bills for petrol and repairs . . .	37	61

Show the car expenses account for the year to 30th June, 19.1.

(ii) The final accounts of A Ltd. are made up to 30th June in each year.

B Ltd. and C Ltd. occupied buildings which were the property of A Ltd. On 30th June, 19.., B Ltd. paid to A Ltd. £150, representing rent for the month of July, 19... At the same date, C Ltd. owed to A Ltd. £180 for rent for the month of June, 19...

During the year to 30th June, 19.1, A Ltd. received from B Ltd. £1,500, representing rent for the ten months to 31st May, 19.1, and from C Ltd. £2,520, representing rent for the fourteen months to 31st July, 19.1. The rent due from B Ltd. for June, 19.1, was not paid until July, 19.1.

Show the rent receivable account in the ledger of A Ltd. for the year to 30th June, 19.1. There are no personal accounts for B Ltd. or C Ltd. in the books of A Ltd.

(*Chartered Institute of Secretaries.*)

22. Early in 1961 John Brown, the accountant, of Watson, Jackson Ltd., was preparing for a Board Meeting at which the Board intended to discuss the performance of the company in the previous year. In preparation for this meeting John Brown had asked his assistant to prepare some comparative data for 1960 and 1961 and the analysis produced is shown in Exhibit 1. Whilst John Brown was convinced that the figures produced were accurate in themselves he was not satisfied with the presentation. He therefore decided that some re-arrangement of the data would be necessary to bring out the salient points for the Board. One consideration in his mind was a feeling that, to some extent, the company had been chasing increased sales at the expense of excessive spending on salesmens' salaries, expenses and advertising and he would like to obtain some measure as to whether, in fact, his suspicions were correct. Another problem which concerned him was the rising cost of administration which he thought might have been disproportionate in relation to sales activity. He found it rather difficult to separate out these rises from normal operations from the changes which had occurred in certain other unusual items such as the sale of capital assets. At the same time he would like the statement to reflect the amount of profit which would be available for appropriation by the company in one way or another. In his experience it was possible to re-arrange trading and profit and loss account so as to bring out these significant relationships and he also found that an analysis in terms of percentages was welcomed by many of the Directors.

Prepare an analysis of the data and draft comments on it which might serve as a basis for John Brown's presentation to the Board Meeting. Your presentation should recognize any difficulties and if there are alternative presentations which you consider satisfactory these might also be prepared, at least in draft.

EXHIBIT 1

	1960 £	1961 £		1960 £	1961 £
Cost of Sales	30,000	35,000	Sales	50,000	60,000
Salesmen's Salaries	5,000	4,500	Interest Receivable	400	500
Salesmen's Expenses	1,200	1,500	Dividends Received	500	450
Advertising	1,100	3,000	Profit on Sale of Fixed Assets	100	550
Other Selling Expenses	700	1,000			
Office Salaries	5,000	8,500			
Rent, Light and Heat	1,200	2,400			
Other Office Expenses	800	1,100			
Interest Payable	100	200			
Discounts Allowed	400	600			
Net Profit	5,500	3,700			
	51,000	61,500		51,000	61,500

(*L.C.C. Modified.*)

CHAPTER 03

THE CORRECTION OF BOOK-KEEPING ERRORS

The good bookkeeper should know how to correct, or deviate as it is called in Florence, an entry which he may have posted by mistake in the wrong place.
At times you cannot be so diligent as to avoid mistakes.
As the proverb says "He who does nothing, makes no mistakes. But he who makes no mistakes does not learn."

LUCA PACIOLI—*Treatise on Bookkeeping*, 1494

THE dual-aspect principle in accounting makes it possible to check from time to time that correct entries of data have been made. In machine systems, a pre-list is made before items are posted to ledger accounts and the accuracy of each run of postings can be made.

In double-entry book-keeping a Trial Balance is drawn up periodically to provide a check on the accuracy of the books but also as a convenient working document in the preparation of the final accounts and Balance Sheet.

TYPES OF ERRORS

Certain errors will not affect the agreement of a Trial Balance, however. These are—

1. **Omission.** If a transaction is completely overlooked, both debit and credit entries will have been omitted and the Trial Balance will still agree.

2. **Commission.** If a debit or credit entry is made to the wrong account within the correct category, e.g. if T. Smith's account is debited instead of S. Smith, then the error does not affect the total of the debtors.

3. **Principle.** These errors imply an entry to a wrong account in the wrong category also, e.g. debiting Plant and Machinery (an asset account) with consumable stores (a revenue expense).

4. **Compensating.** If two or more errors cancel each other out, then the Trial Balance will still agree, e.g. (*a*) Brown credited £100, Purchases debited £10 (incorrect); (*b*) Plant debited £990 (incorrect), Machinery Ltd., credited £900.

Book-keeping errors which will affect the Trial Balance are those in which—

5. Only a single entry (or any odd number of entries) is made.

6. Two entries are made on the same side of the account i.e. two debits or two credits. For example Sales of £200 credited to Robinson and Sales.

7. The amounts posted do not agree, e.g. Purchases of £47 from Wilkinson, £47 debited to Purchases, £74 credited to Wilkinson. This type of error may also arise from mis-casting of subsidiary books.

Errors also arise in extracting the Trial Balance from the books—

8. One or more accounts showing a balance in the books are not extracted.

9. One or more accounts are listed more than once.

10. Balances are listed on the wrong side i.e. debits instead of credits.

11. The amount of one or more balances is mis-stated, e.g. £1·98 instead of £1·89.

12. The Trial Balance is incorrectly totalled.

CORRECTION OF ERRORS

Although the first four types of error do not affect the Trial Balance this does not imply that they will not be detected eventually. For instance, Mr. T. Smith will almost certainly refuse to pay an amount with which he has been incorrectly debited! The method of correcting each type of error must therefore be considered—

1. **Omission.** The correct debit and credit entries must be made.

2. **Commission.** A double entry to correct the error must be made, e.g. debit S. Smith, credit T. Smith.

3. **Principle.** A double entry to correct the error must be made, e.g. debit Consumable Stores, credit Plant and Machinery.

4. **Compensating.** This error is really two examples of type (7) below and should be treated accordingly.

5. **Single Entry (or odd number of entries).** This error is corrected by making the entry which was omitted.

6. **Two debits and Credits.** Normally, it is assumed that one of the entries made will be correct and that the other is made on the wrong side. The correction then requires the debit or credit of *twice the amount posted*, e.g. the Sales of £200 incorrectly credited to Robinson requires a debit of £400 to Robinson.

When an error of commission or principle has also been made, then correction requires debit or credit of the *amount concerned twice*, e.g. £200 to A. Robinson and £200 to B. Robinson.

7. **Amounts Posted Disagree.** A single entry to correct the error must be made, e.g. Wilkinson credited with £74 instead of £47 is corrected by a debit of £27 to Wilkinson.

8, 9, 10, 11 and 12. **Errors of Extraction.** Since the Trial Balance is a working document and not part of the accounts, correction of these errors is effected by making the appropriate changes in the Trial Balance until—

8. All the accounts are listed.
9. No accounts are listed more than once.

10. All balances are correctly identified as debits or credits.
11. All balances are correctly listed.
12. The Trial Balance is correctly totalled.

The possibility of errors of extraction should be fully eliminated before a search is made for other errors.

JOURNAL ENTRIES

The correction of errors will normally be recorded in the Journal so as to provide a record explaining the entries made in the ledger.

CORRECTIONS DURING THE ACCOUNTING YEAR

Since some errors can only be corrected by single entries, it follows that the Journal entry will show this and will therefore differ from the norm.

The Suspense Account. If the Trial Balance is correctly extracted from the ledger and still does not agree and if the errors are not discovered before the final accounts and Balance Sheet are prepared it will be necessary to open a Suspense or "Difference in Books" Account. This will be shown on the Assets side of the Balance Sheet if the difference is a debit and on the Liabilities side if it is a credit.

If a Suspense account has been opened, the errors which normally require only a single entry will then be effected by a double entry. One account is debited or credited to correct the error of the previous year and the corresponding credit or debit is made to Suspense account. The effect of this can be seen more clearly if we consider an example.

Example 1

(i) During 19.. the sales day book for the month of May has been short-cast by £100. (ii) The total of £25, in the discount column on the debit side of the cash book for August has not been posted. As a result of this the trial balance will be £100 short on the credit side and £25 short on the debit side. To make the books balance an entry is therefore made as follows—

Suspense Account

	19..		£
	Dec 31	Difference in books .	75

During 19.1 the first of these two errors is found and corrected as follows—

	Dr	*Cr*
	£	£
Suspense A/c	100	
Sales		100

This corrects the sales account and now leaves a debit balance on the suspense account of £25 waiting for the next error to be revealed. When this second mistake is found, the entries are—

	Dr	Cr
	£	£
Discounts Allowed . .	25	
Suspense A/c . . .		25

The suspense account is now closed.

From the example given it will be seen that so long as there is a balance on the suspense account there are still some errors not found.

Example 2

The trial balance of the books of a company, taken out as on 31st July, 19.., did not balance.

A detailed checking of the books disclosed the following errors—

(*a*) Purchases returns for April, £100, posted to the debit of purchases account.

(*b*) Sales day book for May under-cast by £10.

(*c*) Discounts received in June, £120, posted to the wrong side of discount account.

(*d*) A sale of £10·25 to J B was correctly entered in the sales book, but was posted to the credit of J B in the sales ledger as £5·50.

(*e*) £5 paid for repairs to machinery was entered in the total column of the petty cash book, but not extended in the appropriate analysis column, the totals of which were posted.

The correction of these errors enabled the books to be balanced, and you are required to give the journal entries necessary to correct them.

(*Chartered Institute of Secretaries, Intermediate.*)

Two solutions are shown. The first assumes that the corrections were made during the year. The other assumes they were made at the end of the year after raising a suspense account.

Solution 2a

Corrections During the Accounting Year

JOURNAL

		Dr	Cr
19..		£	£
(a)	*Purchases A/c*		100·00
	Correction of error in debiting the total of purchases returns to Purchases account		
	Purchases Returns A/c		100·00
	Correct posting of Purchases Returns incorrectly posted and cancelled in entry above		
(b)	*Sales*		10·00
	Correction of incorrect posting arising from under-cast of sales day book		
(c)	*Discounts A/c*		240·00
	Correction of error in debiting discounts on sales (discounts received) of £120, instead of crediting them		
(d)	*J.B.*	15·75	
	Correction of error in crediting £5·50 to J.B.'s account instead of debiting £10·25		
(e)	*Repairs to Machinery*	5·00	
	Correction of error due to item omitted from analysis column on Folio—of petty cash book		

CORRECTIONS AFTER FINAL ACCOUNTS AND BALANCE SHEET HAVE BEEN PREPARED

Solution 2b

Corrections after Opening a Suspense Account

JOURNAL

		Dr	Cr
19..		£	£
(a) Jul 31	Suspense A/c	100·00	
	Purchases		100·00
	Cancellation of amount debited to purchases a/c of total of purchases returns book in error.		
	Suspense A/c	100·00	
	Purchases Returns		100·00
	To give effect to correct posting of total of purchases returns cancelled in last entry.		
(b)	Suspense A/c	10·00	
	Sales		10·00
	To correct error of under-cast of sales day book for May on fo.		
(c)	Suspense A/c	120·00	
	Discounts Account		120·00
	Cancellation of amount debited to discount on sales a/c of total of discounts on purchases for June.		
	Suspense A/c	120·00	
	Discounts Account		120·00
	To give effect to correct posting of total of discounts on purchases cancelled in last entry.		

JOURNAL (*contd.*)

		Dr	Cr
		£	£
(*d*)	J B	5·50	
	Suspense A/c		5·50
	Cancellation of incorrect posting from sales day book on fo.		
	J B	10·25	
	Suspense A/c		10·25
	To give effect to correct posting of item in sales day book cancelled in last entry at the correct amount.		
(*e*)	Repairs to Machinery	5·00	
	Suspense A/c		5·00
	To give effect to posting of item omitted on fo. .... of petty cash book.		
		470·75	470·75

On the basis of the above corrections it is possible to calculate what the amount in the Suspense Account would have been when it was opened—

SUMMARY SHOWING AMOUNT OF THE ORIGINAL ENTRY IN THE SUSPENSE ACCOUNT

	£	£
Item (*a*) as per journal entry	100·00	
,, (*a*) ,, ,, ,, ...	100·00	
,, (*b*) ,, ,, ,, ...	10·00	
,, (*c*) ,, ,, ,, ...	120·00	
,, (*c*) ,, ,, ,, ...	120·00	
,, (*d*) ,, ,, ,, ...		5·50
,, (*d*) ,, ,, ,, ...		10·25
,, (*e*) ,, ,, ,, ...		5·00
	450·00	20·75
Amount of original entry in suspense a/c . . .		429·25
	450·00	450·00

Corrections of errors in these circumstances require both the Journal entries to correct the errors and amendment of the trading, profit and loss accounts and Balance Sheet.

Example 3

The following draft Balance Sheet as on 31st March, 1963, has been drawn up by F. Lupin who carries on a manufacturing business—

	£	£		£
Creditors—			Cash in hand	86
Trade	5,500		Balances at bank—	
Accrued Expenses	364		Current Account	400
		5,864	Deposit Account	1,600
Capital Account—			Debtors	4,700
Balance on 31st March, 1962	15,960		Stock	6,500
Add Net Profit for the year	3,700		Plant and Machinery	5,200
			Freehold Premises	4,800
	19,660			
Less Drawings	2,300			
		17,360		
Suspense Account		62		
		23,286		23,286

Upon going through the books you find the following facts—

1. Included in the cash in hand is an IOU given by the book-keeper for a loan to him of £50.
2. The balance on the bank current account is the figure shown on the bank statement as being the balance to F. Lupin's credit on 31st March, 1963. There were cheques, in total £62, which had not been presented at that date and hence the suspense account shown in the balance sheet.
3. Interest allowed on the deposit account at June and December, 1962, in total £50, had not been entered in the books.
4. A debit balance of £30 appearing in the sales ledger had been regarded as having been settled in contra prior to 31st March, 1963, but no adjustment had been made in the accounts concerned.
5. A credit balance on P. Stock's account £82 represented a payment made by P. Stock for goods sent to him before 31st March, 1963, but which had not been entered in the sales day book.
6. Debts amounting to £72 shown in the schedule of balances on the sales ledger were stated to be of no value while others totalling £180 were considered to be doubtful.
7. While the stock shown in the balance sheet purported to be the value of the stock in the factory at cost, the total of one page, £483, had inadvertently been omitted from the summary of the stock sheets.
8. No depreciation has been written off plant and machinery and it was agreed that provision should be made for £520 to remedy this omission.
9. An annual premium of £48 had been paid during the year in respect of fire insurance giving cover up to 30th June, 1963.
10. F. Lupin had taken goods from stock for his own use the cost of which was £90 and no record of this was shown in the books.

Show the journal entries to give effect to any amendments that may be necessary and give a summary of the adjustments to be made to the Profit and Loss Account for the year. Also prepare a revised Balance Sheet as on 31st March, 1963

(Certified and Corporate Accountants.)

Solution 3

JOURNAL	Dr	Cr
	£	£
(1) Loan A/c	50	
Cash		50
Correction of cash balance in respect of loan to book-keeper		
(2) Suspense A/c	62	
Bank		62
Correction of bank balance in respect of cheques not yet presented		
(3) Deposit A/c	50	
Profit and Loss A/c		50
Correction in respect of interest allowed but not recorded in the Deposit A/c		
(4) Creditors Ledger	30	
Debtors Ledger		30
Correction due to settlement by *contra* (name...............) not posted		
(5) Debtors Ledger (P Stock)	82	
Sales Account		82
Correction due to sale on.................. omitted from books		
(6) Profit and Loss A/c	252	
Debtors Ledger		72
Provision for doubtful debts		180
Provision for doubtful debts and bad debts written off		
(7) Stock A/c	483	
To Trading A/c		483
Correction of error in Stock due Omission of Folio............of stock sheets		
(8) Profit and Loss A/c	520	
Depreciation Provision		520
Provision for depreciation in Plant and Machinery omitted from final accounts		
(9) Prepaid fire insurance	12	
Profit and Loss A/c		12
Correction of error in writing off unexpired insurance at close of year		
(10) Drawings A/c	90	
Purchases A/c		90
Correction of error due to omission of goods drawn for proprietor's own personal consumption		

From this, the adjusted profit can be calculated—

		£	£
	Profit shown in Balance Sheet		3,700
Add	Interest on deposit (3)	50	
	Sales omitted (5)	82	
	Stock omitted (7)	483	
	Prepaid insurance	12	
	Drawings (10)	90	
			717
			4,417
Deduct	Bad and doubtful debts	252	
	Depreciation	520	
			772
	Adjusted profit		3,645

The resulting Balance Sheet will be—

BALANCE SHEET as on March 31st, 1962

	£	£		£	£
CAPITAL ACCOUNT—			FIXED ASSETS—		
Balance, 31st March, 1962	15,960		Freehold Premises		4,800
Add: Net Profit for the year	3,645		Plant and Machinery at cost	5,200	
			Less: Depreciation	520	
	19,605				4,680
Less: Drawings	2,390				9,480
		17,215			
CURRENT LIABILITIES—			CURRENT ASSETS—		
Creditors	5,470		Stock at cost	6,983	
Expense	364		Debtors £4,680		
		5,834	*Less:* Provision for bad debts 180		
				4,500	
			Prepayments	12	
			Loan Account	50	
			Balances at bank—		
			Current Account	338	
			Deposit Account	1,650	
			Cash in hand	36	
					13,569
		23,049			23,049

QUESTIONS

1. Describe briefly the various types of errors.
2. What are: (*a*) errors of omission, (*b*) errors of commission? How do they occur?
3. What are the particular functions of suspense accounts? In what circumstances are they employed?
4. When errors occur in one trading period and are not revealed until the next trading period, what method of correction is usually adopted? Give an example of the correction of such an error to illustrate your answer.

EXERCISE 03

1. A book-keeper balances his books monthly, and if at any time his books fail to balance he enters the difference temporarily in a "suspense account." On 31st December, 19.., the books were properly balanced, but on the following 31st January there was an excess debit of £11·47, the suspense account therefore being credited with this amount. During February the difference was found and accounted for as follows—

(*a*) Discount amounting to £1·28 had been allowed to a customer A and credited to his account, but no other entry made.

(*b*) Wages paid, amounting to £78·25 had been posted to the wages account as £87·25.

(*c*) A creditor's balance of £4·75 had been entirely overlooked when taking out the list of balances on 31st January.

(*d*) The remainder of the difference was due to a mis-cast in the sales day book.

Set out in journal entry form the corrections necessary to adjust the several accounts affected. (*R.S.A.*)

2. A difference on a set of books has been carried to a suspense account, and you are asked by the proprietor of the business to trace this difference. On investigation you find that it is caused by the following errors—

(*a*) A total in the sales day book of £765·87 was carried forward as £756·87.

(*b*) A payment of £1·92 for goods purchased from A. Brown & Son had been posted twice, once to the personal account and once to cash purchases.

(*c*) The June discounts received and allowed, amounting to £10·48 and £12·14 respectively, had been posted to the wrong sides of the discount account.

(*d*) A cheque for £40 paid to a customer for a car purchased from him had been posted to his credit in the sales ledger.

(*e*) The debit side of the general expenses account had been under-cast by £5.

Show the suspense account as it would appear after you have corrected the errors. (*R.S.A.*)

3. Mr. Charles Cantuar, a grocer, gives you the following balance sheet which he has drawn up, and asks you to correct it.

BALANCE SHEET OF MR. CHARLES CANTUAR
For the Year Ended 31st December, 19.1

Liabilities	£	£	*Assets*	£	£
Mr. Charles Cantuar's Capital account—			Furniture, Fixtures & Fittings etc., as at 31st Dec. 19..	780	
Balance b/f at 31st Dec., 19..	1,000		Freehold Premises as at 31st Dec., 19..	3,000	
Drawings added	512				3,780
Loan received from Mr. Eric Ebor	2,000				
		3,512	Sundry Debtors at 31st Dec., 19.1		3,437
Sundry Creditors at 31st Dec., 19.1	4,600		Cash in Hand		147
Bank Overdraft	146		Stock-in-trade at 31st Dec., 19.. as valued by Mr. Cantuar		1,641
		4.746			
Depreciation at 10% p.a.	78				
Current Account (being Charles Cantuar's credit balance not drawn out of business at 31st Dec., 19..)	513				
		591			
P. & L. A/c— Net profit for the year ended 31st Dec., 19.1		156			
		9,005			9,005

On checking his figures you find that they are correct, his net profit for the year ended 31st December, 19.., being correctly stated as £156. His stock figures were, according to his own valuations, £617 at 31st December, 19.1, and £1,641 at 31st December, 19. .

You are required to correct the errors he has made, and to show the balance sheet drawn up in the proper order and form. (*R.S.A.*)

4. The following errors were found in the books of C. Drew & Co., affecting the year ended 31st December, 19. .—

(1) £25, sales to H. Carver, had been posted to his account as £2·50.

(2) A purchase of £350, plant and machinery, had been posted to purchases account.

(3) In addition of the returns inwards book, a total of £787 had been carried forward as £878.

(4) The sales journal had been over-added by £68·25.

You are required to show—

(*a*) The adjusting journal entries necessary to correct these errors.

(*b*) The adjusted profit for the year (the profit before adjusting the errors being £3,553·86). (*R.S.A.*)

5. On preparing a trial balance as on 31st December, 19. ., a trader found that the debit balances exceeded the credits by £38·50. The following errors were subsequently discovered—

(*a*) A credit balance of £5·48 had been omitted from the list of balances in the bought ledger.

(*b*) A cheque for £3·75 received from a debtor had been correctly entered in the cash book, but posted to the personal account as £7·35.

(*c*) An allowance of 92p had been claimed from a creditor and entered in the personal account without the double entry being completed.

(*d*) Discounts received for November, totalling £17·20 had been posted to the debit of the discount account instead of the credit.

Draw up a statement showing the effect of these errors and ascertain what the "difference" in the books will be after correcting them.

(*R.S.A. and L.C. Com. Joint—B. of Ed. Endorsed Cert.*)

6. TRADING AND PROFIT AND LOSS ACCOUNT

For Year to 31st December, 19. .

	£		£
Stock	1,500	Sales	5,100
Purchases	3,100	Stock	1,200
Balance c/d	1,700		
	6,300		6,300
Expenses	680	Balance b/d	1,700
Balance to Capital	1,020		
	1,700		1,700

On the figures set out above, indicate—

(*a*) The percentage of gross profit on sales.

(*b*) The percentage of gross profit on cost of goods sold.

(*c*) The percentage of net profit on sales.

(*d*) The percentage of expenses on cost of goods sold.

7. What special instructions would you suggest should be given at the time of stock-taking to the clerks who are responsible for checking inwards invoices and have charge of the purchase book and purchase ledger, so as to ensure the accuracy of the figures representing purchases, expenses, and stock as appearing in the trading account for the period under review? *(R.S.A.)*

8. At a recent examination, the understated "balance sheet" was sent in by a candidate. Have you any criticism to offer upon it?

BALANCE SHEET

MESSRS. A. & B. 31ST DEC., 19..

Assets		£	*Liabilities*		£
Plant A/c		4,000	A's Capital	£3,000	
Debtors	£8,200		*Add* Interest	150	
Less Provision (31st Dec.)	410				3,150
		7,790	B's Capital	£2,000	
A's Drawings		300	*Add* Interest	100	
B's "		200			2,100
Repairs		120	Creditors		9,800
Stock (1st Jan.)	£3,200		A's Profits		1,800
" (31 Dec.)	4,000		B's "		1,800
		7,200	Depreciation of Plant		200
Cash		420	Reserve for Debtors (Jan.)		350
			Balance		830
		20,030			20,030

(London Chamber of Commerce.)

9. The undermentioned errors were made by the accounts department staff in the books of Black & Brown during the year ended 31st December—

(*a*) On 30th June, a builder's charge for the erection of a small shed, amounting to £198, was analysed in the purchases journal under the head of "repairs," and posted to that account.

(*b*) On 1st July a cheque for £18·12 received from James Smith was dishonoured, and was posted to "allowance account."

(*c*) On 12th August the total of the previous month's wages was debited to "manufacturing wages account." During the month some new machinery had been put down and the firm's own men had spent time thereon amounting to £141.

(*d*) On 28th December, goods to the value of £64 were returned by Francis White, and were taken into stock; but the returns were not entered in the books until 2nd January.

How would you adjust these errors, and how would they affect the annual accounts for the year ended 31st December? *(R.S.A.)*

10. The account of A. Buyer in the books of Wholesalers Ltd. showed a debit balance of £15·48 on 1st January, 19... The following transactions subsequently took place—

(*a*) On 10th January Buyer purchased goods (on credit) to the value of £40.

(*b*) On 13th January he returned £5 of them as not up to sample and was given credit for the same.

(*c*) On 5th February he forwarded a cheque in settlement of his account, deducting 5 per cent discount in respect of the January purchase for settlement within one month.

(*d*) On 18th May he paid a deposit of £100 on account of future purchases, in consideration of which he was to receive a discount of 10 per cent on gross purchases covered by this amount.

(*e*) On 23rd June he ordered goods to the (gross) value of £40, on 17th August goods to the value of £50, and on 29th August goods to the value of £60.

(*f*) In November Buyer was adjudicated bankrupt, and the statement of affairs showed that the creditors would probably receive 25p in the £. When closing their books at the end of December, Wholesalers Ltd. wrote the expected loss off the account.

(*g*) On 1st February, 19.1, a cheque for £10·28 was received from the trustee in bankruptcy in final settlement.

You are requested to write up Buyer's Account in the books of Wholesalers Ltd.

(*R.S.A.*)

11. The Sussex Manufacturing Co. Ltd. rent their factory from J. T. Berkshire for £720 per annum, payable quarterly in 1st January, 1st April, 1st July, and 1st October.

From the following information you are required to write up the rent and rates account as it would appear in the company's nominal ledger for the financial year ended 31st January, 19.2.

19.1		
Apr	1	Paid rent for quarter to date, J. T. Berkshire.
Jul	1	„ „ „ „ „ „
	1	„ rates to 30th September, 19.1, £86.
Oct	1	„ rent for quarter to date, J. T. Berkshire.
Dec	15	„ rates to 31st March, 19.2, £87.
	31	„ income tax due under Schedule A, £150
19.2		
Jan	1	„ rent due for quarter to date, *less* Schedule A income tax.

NOTE. Rates paid in December, 19.., £90 for six months to 31st March, 19.1. Apportionments to be made in months.

12. The following items of expenditure are incurred by a firm. State which are capital expenditure, and which are revenue expenditure—

(*a*) £43 paid in wages for the installation of an additional steam boiler to generate steam for driving machinery.

(*b*) £186 paid for replacing plant that is worn out and has no scrap value. The displaced plant stands in the books at £186.

(*c*) £200 paid for re-upholstering chairs in a cinema.

(*d*) The purchase of an additional new show case at a cost of £50.

(*West Riding of Yorkshire.*)

13. A trial balance, extracted from the books of Loose Ends Ltd. as on 30th June, 19.1, did not agree, and the amount of the difference was entered in a suspense account. A trading and profit and loss account was prepared on the basis of this trial balance and showed a net profit of £7,500.

The following errors were afterwards discovered and the difference was eliminated.

(*a*) A sales invoice for £235 had been completely omitted from the books.

(*b*) A bank overdraft of £94, which appeared as a credit balance in the cash book at 30th June, 19.1, had been omitted from the trial balance.

(*c*) A payment of £54 to Baker, a trade creditor, correctly entered in the cash book, had been debited to the personal account as £45.

(*d*) The debit side of wages account had been under-cast by £30.

(*e*) A provision of £16 for sundry expenses outstanding at 30th June, 19.., debited to sundry expenses account at that date, had not been brought forward to the credit of the account in the following period and no credit entry had been made in any other account.

(*f*) Discounts received from suppliers, £176, had been entered on the wrong side of the purchases ledger control account and the closing balance on this account was included in the trial balance.

(*g*) On 30th June, 19.1, goods valued at £12 (selling price) were returned by a customer. No entry had been made in the books and these goods had not been included in the closing stock. The cost of these goods was £9.

You are required to show—

(i) the entries in the suspense account, and

(ii) your calculation of the correct net profit.

(*Chartered Institute of Secretaries.*)

14. On 31st October, 19.., X Ltd. purchased a freehold property. Until that date the company had occupied part of the building at a rent of £840 a year. The other part was occupied by Y Ltd. at a rent, payable to the owner, of £252 a year. All rates and repairs were payable by the owner. The tenancy of Y Ltd. was continued on the same terms as before, after 31st October, 19...

The total amount paid by X Ltd. in connexion with the purchase of the property was £10,194. This represented the purchase price of the property with the following additions or deductions—

(i) Rates for the five months to 31st March, 19.1, paid by the vendor, £60.

(ii) Water rate for the month of October, 19.., outstanding at 31st October, £1.

(iii) Legal expenses £317.

(iv) Rent paid in advance, to the vendor, for the months of November and December, 19..—

By X Ltd. £140
By Y Ltd. £42

You are required—

1. to show the entries for the above matters (including cash) in the journal of X Ltd., and

2. to show the amount at which the property should appear in the balance sheet of X Ltd.

(*Chartered Institute of Secretaries.*)

15. A trading and profit and loss account for the year to 31st May, 19.., prepared by R. Heath, a trader, showed a net profit of £2,468. The balance at bank at 31st May, 19.., according to Heath's cash book, was £322.

You are informed that—

(*a*) Cheques from customers, amounting to £249, which were entered in the cash book on 31st May, were not credited by the bank until 3rd June.

(*b*) Cheques drawn by Heath on 28th May in favour of trade creditors, amounting to a total of £371, were not paid by the bank until after 31st May.

(*c*) On 15th May, Brown, a customer, had paid £117 into Heath's bank account, in full settlement of a debit balance of £120 in Heath's sales ledger, but no entry had been made in Heath's books.

(*d*) On 1st April, 19.., the bank paid, in accordance with a standing order from Heath, £180 for the rent of Heath's business premises for the three months to 30th June, 19... No entry for this payment had been made in Heath's books and no provision for outstanding rent had been made in the profit and loss account.

(*e*) A cheque for £42 from an insurance company, in settlement of a claim for fire damage to stock, had been paid into the bank and credited by the bank on 20th May, but no entry had been made in the cash book. Credit had been taken in Heath's profit and loss account for an estimated amount of £40.

(*f*) On 30th May a cheque for £24 was received from a customer in settlement of a sales invoice for £24. The cheque was paid into Heath's bank, and both the sale of the goods and the cheque were entered in the books in the normal way. On 31st May the customer returned the goods to Heath and instructed his bank not to pay the cheque, but no entries in respect of these matters have been made in Heath's books. These goods, the cost of which was £16, were not included in Heath's closing stock.

You are required to prepare statements showing—

(i) the balance which should appear in the cash book on 31st May, after making all necessary corrections,

(ii) a reconciliation of the corrected cash book balance with the balance shown by the bank statement, and

(iii) your calculation of Heath's net profits for the year to 31st May, 19..

(*Chartered Institute of Secretaries.*)

16. The following is a summary of the repairs and renewals account in the nominal ledger of a small manufacturing company—

	£	£
Payments of 3 monthly hire-purchase instalments on a new sanding machine		87
Costs of repositioning existing plant		28
Own labour used in the erection and equipment of a new boiler-house		74
Cost of demolition of the old boiler-house		100
Basic cost of the new boiler		865
Sundry fittings, joints and piping used in installing the new boiler		149
Hire of crane for the installation		25
Premium payable under boiler inspection contract		12
Consulting engineer's fees and expenses		63
Building contractor's account		
Erection of new boiler-house	800	
Re-asphalting of the factory yard	140	
Re-pointing the brickwork	48	
Painting the factory	210	
		1,198
Sundry general repairs to plant		302
Sundry general repairs to the buildings		142
		£3,045
Less Sale of old boiler and fittings for scrap		50
Balance per trial balance		£2,995

You are required—

(*a*) to show by means of journal entries what changes you would make to the account;

(*b*) if the treatment of any of the items seem debatable to you, to set out *brief* arguments in support of the treatment you adopt in part (*a*) of your answer;

(*c*) to prepare a schedule analysing the balance remaining on the repairs and renewals account, after putting through the journal entries. (*I.C.M.A.*)

17. The book-keeper of a firm, having been unable to agree the Trial Balance at 31st January, raised a Suspense Account, on which he entered the amount he was out of balance.

He then prepared a draft Balance Sheet into which he carried the amount of the Suspense Account.

The following errors were subsequently discovered in the books and duly rectified, thus balancing the books, the Suspense Account being adjusted accordingly—

(*a*) The addition of the analysis column in the tabular Purchase Journal posted to Goods Purchased for Re-sale Account was found to be £15 short, though the addition of the total column was correct.

(*b*) Goods bought from a supplier amounting to £5·50 had been posted to the credit of his account as £55.

(*c*) A dishonoured Bill of Exchange receivable for £200, returned by the firm's bank, had been credited to the Bank Account and debited to Bills Receivable Account.

(*d*) An item of £10·50 entered in the Sales Returns Book had been posted to the debit of the customer who returned the goods.

(*e*) Sundry items of Plant sold amounting to £300 had been entered in the Sales Day Book, the total of which book had been posted to the credit of Sales Account.

(*f*) An amount of £60 owing by a customer had been omitted from the Schedule of Sundry Debtors.

(*g*) Discounts amounting to £2·25 allowed to a customer had been duly entered in his account but not posted to Discount Account.

(*h*) An amount of £45, being rates treated as paid in advance in the previous year, had not been brought forward as a balance on the Rates Account.

(1) Show the Suspense Account as raised by the book-keeper with the adjusting entries you would find it necessary to make therein; and

(2) Explain what effect any of the above-mentioned errors would have on the profit shown in the Accounts if not rectified.

Assume the Purchase and Sales Ledgers to be self-balancing. (*L.C.C.*)

18. A. Ltd. is a small wholesaling company, whose trial balance at 31st March, 1966 was as follows—

	£	£
Share capital		4,000
Profit and loss account—1st April, 1965		300
Creditors control account		1,847
Debtors control account	2,631	
Land and buildings	1,500	
Equipment and vehicles at cost	2,444	
Accumulated provision for depreciation of equipment and vehicles to date		862
Stock of goods at 31st March, 1966	908	
Sales		9,791
Cash at bank	56	
Cost of goods sold	6,008	
Discount allowed and received	122	79
Rates and insurances	260	
Warehouse wages and expenses	845	
Office wages and expenses	751	
Director's salary	975	
Depreciation of equipment and vehicles for the current year	243	
	16,743	16,879

The records are found to require the following adjustments—

(i) A total in the "discount allowed" column of the cash book of £52 was entered correctly in the debtors control account, but debited as £25 in the discount allowed account.

(ii) An item of £80 for a new banding machine was incorrectly posted to warehouse wages and expenses. The depreciation on this capital item would be 10 per cent on the original cost.

(iii) A cheque for £43 for rates was entered in the cash book as £63, and posted as this amount to the nominal ledger.

(iv) A physical stock-taking revealed that the correct value to be placed on the stock of goods was £875.

(v) A cheque for £121 received from a debtor has been dishonoured, but no record has been made of this in the books.

(vi) PAYE taxation of £14 on warehouse wages, £12 on office wages and £25 on the director's salary was owing to the Inland Revenue on 31st March, 1966, but no provision had been made for this in the accounts.

(vii) A sales invoice of £83 was correctly entered and posted to the sales account, but omitted from the debtors control account.

(viii) A sales invoice of £13 was correctly credited to the sales account, but also credited to a creditors account for the same firm in the creditors ledger and the creditors control account.

You are required to—

(*a*) prepare journal entries correcting or adjusting these matters, with full narrations;

(*b*) show the nominal ledger suspense account, including the appropriate journal entries from part (*a*) of your answer.

(*c*) prepare a revised trial balance, showing the balances after these adjustments and corrections have been made; final accounts for the company are *not* required.

(*I.C.M.A.*)

19. A private company which has been trading for many years was converted into a public company on 1st January, 1960. Its financial year had always ended on 31st December.

It is proposed to make an issue of shares to the public. In the course of preparing the prospectus a firm of accountants examine the accounts for the ten years 1950 to 1959, and find a number of errors, viz—

(1) At the end of 1957 an arithmetical error has resulted in stock being overstated by £2,500.

(2) At 31st December, 1959, there still appears in the books a balance of £162 as due from a customer who went bankrupt in June, 1957. His creditors are unlikely to obtain anything from his estate. No provision had been made for doubtful debts.

(3) A new machine, bought at the beginning of 1957 for £750, has been erroneously depreciated by the diminishing balance method instead of by the straight line method, although the correct rate of 10 per cent per annum had been used.

(4) A second machine, identical in all respects with that mentioned above, was bought on 1st July, 1958, and was written off to Plant Repairs Account.

(5) In 1957 a provision was created for £625 damages payable by the company for breach of contract arising during that year from delivery of faulty goods. The action was settled in 1958 for £400. The balance of the provision is still being carried forward.

(6) Goods bought at the end of 1958 for £1,300 and paid for in 1959 were entirely omitted from the 1958 records. Both the goods and the liability to pay for them were left out of the Balance Sheet for 1958. Payment for and sale of the goods in 1959 were correctly recorded in that year.

The net profits for the years 1957 to 1959 shown in the uncorrected accounts for those years were—

1957, £7,475; 1958, £4,807; 1959, £6,177

After payment of dividends and taxation the balance on Profit and Loss Account carried forward at 31st December, 1959, is £9,233.

Draw up a schedule showing how you would arrive at the corrected profits for each of the three years, and the corrected balance on Profit and Loss Account at 31st December, 1959. Calculations can be approximated to the nearest £.

(*L.C.C.*)

CHAPTER 04

BILLS OF EXCHANGE, PROMISSORY NOTES AND BANK SERVICES

Never ask of money spent
Where the spender thinks it went
Nobody was ever meant
To remember or invent
What he did with every cent

ROBERT FROST

Methods of Payment (Giro systems). Giro is a word from the Greek "guris," meaning a circuit or turn, and it is used here to describe any system for circulating money.

The most important instrument for circulating money at the end of the 19th century was the Bill of Exchange and the main act dealing with various forms of money is the Bills of Exchange Act, 1882. A cheque is merely a special form of Bill.

Today, Bills are confined mainly to foreign trade and have been replaced by cheques and the Bank and the Post Office giro systems within the United Kingdom. Promissory notes are more widely used in the United States.

This chapter deals with—

- Bills of Exchange.
- Promissory notes.
- Bank notes.
- Bank drafts.
- Paying money through Bank giro.
- Receiving money through Bank giro.
- Direct debiting.
- IOU's.
- Cheques.

BILLS OF EXCHANGE

According to the Bills of Exchange Act, 1882, a bill of exchange is defined as—

> **An unconditional order in writing, addressed by one person to another, signed by the person giving it, requiring the person to whom it is addressed to pay on demand or at a fixed or determinable future time a sum certain in money to or to the order of a specified person or to bearer.**

An instrument which does not comply with these conditions, or which orders any act to be done in addition to the payment of money, is *not* a bill of exchange.

An order to pay out of a particular fund is not unconditional within the meaning of this section; but an unqualified order to pay, coupled with (*a*) an indication of a particular fund out of which the drawee is to reimburse himself or a particular account to be debited with the amount, or (*b*) a statement of the transaction which gives rise to the bill, is unconditional.

Advantages of a Bill. There are four principal advantages to a bill—

1. It enables an exporter to obtain cash soon after the goods are despatched.
2. It enables the buyer to defer payment until the goods are received or even later.
3. Because it is a negotiable instrument it can be used freely to settle debts with no greater risk than other forms of money.
4. It fixes the date for payment and if payment is not made a creditor can sue on the evidence of the Bill itself.

Kinds of Bills. There are two kinds of bills, inland and foreign. An *Inland Bill* is a bill which is or on the face of it purports to be (*a*) both drawn and payable within the British Islands, or (*b*) drawn within the British Islands upon some person resident therein. For the purposes of the Act, the term British Islands includes the Isle of Man and the Channel Islands. Any other bill is a *Foreign Bill.*

A Trade Bill is a bill of exchange drawn in the ordinary course of business and for value received, in contradistinction to an Accommodation Bill, i.e. one for which no value has been given.

Form of Bill. No particular form of words is required by the Act, and the following may be taken as a fair specimen of the usual business document—

£250 due 20th April, 19. .	Accepted payable at the County Bank Limited, Kingsway Branch M. Goodman.	LONDON, 17th January, 19. .
Three months		after date pay to
Mr. M. Bressloff		or order the sum of
two hundred and		fifty pounds, value
received		
To Mr. M. Goodman.		J. ROWELL.

They can be purchased in blank form from any legal stationers or post office.

Parties to a Bill. There are three parties to a bill—

1. *Drawer*, the person who is assumed to have written out the bill, i.e. the creditor to whom the money is owing. Compare this with a cheque, which is always drawn by the debtor.

2. *Drawee*, the person on whom a bill is drawn, and who, after acceptance, is called the *acceptor*. In the case of a cheque, the bank is the drawee.

3. *Payee*, the person to whom the money is payable. Sometimes the drawer and payee are one and the same person, as when the drawer asks for the money to be paid to himself. In the example given, J. Rowell is the drawer, M. Goodman the drawee, M. Bressloff the payee.

Immediate parties are those in direct relationship with each other, e.g. drawer and drawee (or acceptor), drawer and payee, endorser and his next endorsee.

Remote parties are all those not in direct connexion with each other, e.g. last endorser and first endorser, an intermediate endorsee and the acceptor, an intermediate endorser and the drawer or payee.

Draft and Acceptance. Before acceptance the bill is called a draft, which may, therefore, be defined as the unaccepted form of a bill of exchange. But after the drawee has written his signature across the face of it, it is termed an acceptance. It is called a bill at either stage.

Stamp Duty. Before 1961, bills of exchange were liable to an *ad valorem* stamp duty, but the Finance Act, 1961, abolished the old scales in favour of a flat duty of twopence. Stamp duty was abolished in 1971.

Legal Liability of Parties to a Bill. The liability of the parties to a bill arises in the following order—

1. The acceptor.
2. The drawer.
3. The endorser (or endorsers).

The acceptor is primarily liable on a bill to the drawer so long as the drawer retains it. On endorsement to a payee, the drawer then becomes liable on the bill as well as the acceptor. The subsequent endorsement over by a holder in due course who becomes an endorser, thereby creates his liability on the bill. The drawer and endorser are liable to compensate the holder or any subsequent endorser provided the requisite proceedings on dishonour have been duly taken.

Letters of Credit. It is possible for a customer to arrange for a Bank to pay or accept Bills on his behalf. This is called a "credit" and may be acknowledged formally by the Bank to the customer in a letter of credit.

Discount and Acceptance Houses. Certain firms in the City of London specialize in discounting and accepting Bills of Exchange. Their services are available both to Banks and to the general public.

Option of Treating Bill of Exchange as a Promissory Note. Where in a bill drawer and drawee are the same person, or where the drawee is a fictitious person or a person not having capacity to contract, the holder may treat the instrument, at his option, either as a bill of exchange or as a promissory note.

Sum Payable. The sum payable by a bill is a sum certain within the meaning of the Act, although it is required to be paid—

(*a*) With interest.
(*b*) By stated instalments.
(*c*) By stated instalments, with a provision that upon default in payment of any instalment the whole shall become due.

Where the sum payable is expressed in words and also in figures, and there is a discrepancy between the two, the sum denoted by the words is the amount payable as with a cheque.

Where a bill is expressed to be payable with interest, unless the bill provides otherwise, such interest runs from the date of the bill, or, if the bill is undated, from the issue of it.

Bill Payable on Demand. A bill is payable on demand—

(*a*) Which is expressed to be payable on demand, or at sight, or on presentation; or
(*b*) In which no time for payment is expressed.

Where a bill is accepted or endorsed when it is overdue, it is deemed a bill payable on demand as regards any such acceptor or endorser.

Bill Payable at a Future Time. A bill is payable at a determinable future time within the meaning of the Act which is expressed to be payable—

(*a*) At a fixed period after date or sight.
(*b*) On or at a fixed period after the occurrence of a specified event which is certain to happen, though the time of happening may be uncertain.

An instrument expressed to be payable on a "contingency" is not valid as a bill. A bill would be valid if made payable "two days after the death of Mr. X" because, however long he may live, Mr. X is sure to die. It would not be valid if made payable "two days after the marriage of Miss Y," because this event, however likely it may be, is not sure to happen.

Fine Bank Bills are Bills drawn and accepted by London banks and acceptance houses.

Agency Bills are drawn and accepted by London branches of overseas banks.

Foreign Domicile Bills are not dealt with in London: they are Bills drawn on and accepted by firms and individuals abroad.

Documentary Bills. If a Bill is accompanied by the other relevant documents to a movement of goods, e.g. insurance policy, bill of lading, etc. (See p. 0424) then it is a documentary bill.

Date of Bill. A bill is not invalid by reason of its not being dated, being ante-dated, post-dated, or dated on a non-business day (including Saturday and Sunday).

Where a bill expressed to be payable at a fixed period after date is issued undated; or where the acceptance of a bill payable at a fixed period after sight is undated, any holder may insert therein the true date of issue or acceptance, and the bill is then payable accordingly. And should the holder in good faith and by mistake insert a wrong date, the bill is not avoided thereby, but is still payable as if the date so inserted had been the true date. The holder who fills in a date after acceptance should notify the acceptor, so that the latter may know the exact date of maturity.

d/d. means days after date.
d/s. means days after sight.
m/d. means months after date.

Calculation of Time of Payment and Days of Grace. Under the 1882 Act, all bills except those payable on demand were subject to days of grace; that is, three extra days were allowed for payment beyond the date mentioned in the bill. These three days were abolished by the Banking and Financial Dealings Act 1971, and the bill is due and payable on the stated date or, if that is a non-business day, the next following business date.

Where a bill is payable at a fixed period after date, after sight, or after the happening of a specified event, the time of payment is determined by excluding the day from which the time is to begin to run and by including the day of payment. In the case of leap year, one more day must be allowed to the month of February.

Where a bill is payable at a fixed period after sight, the time begins to run from the date of the acceptance if the bill is accepted, and from the date of noting or protest if the bill be noted or protested for non-acceptance or for non-delivery.

The term "month" in a bill means calendar month. Thus, bills drawn on 28th, 29th, 30th, or 31st December at two months would all mature on the same date, nominally on 28th February, but legally on 3rd March (allowing for days of grace).

Overdue Bills. A bill of exchange is overdue if the period for which it was issued has expired. If it is payable on demand, then it would become overdue if it were not presented within a reasonable time. An overdue bill ceases to be a negotiable instrument. It may still be transferred from one person to another, but no one can give a better title than he has himself.

QUESTIONS

1. What is the legal definition of a bill of exchange?
2. How many kinds of bills are there? Distinguish them.
3. How many parties are there to a bill? Explain them, and distinguish between immediate and remote parties.
4. A B, of London, draws, on 1st April, a bill on C D of Liverpool for £336, payable 3 m/d. C D accepts, and makes the bill payable at the Royal Bank, Liverpool. Write out the bill, showing C D's acceptance.
5. State briefly some of the advantages of bills of exchange.
6. Distinguish between: (*a*) trade bill and accommodation bill; (*b*) draft and acceptance; (*c*) drawee and acceptor; (*d*) long bills and short bills.
7. On what date is a bill payable if the date on which it is due is a non-business day?
8. A trader has bills falling due on the following days (including days of grace)—(*a*) New Year's Day; (*b*) Good Friday; (*c*) Easter Sunday; (*d*) Easter Monday; (*e*) Whit-Monday; (*f*) August Bank Holiday; (*g*) Sunday after a special Saturday Bank Holiday; (*h*) Christmas Day; (*i*) Boxing Day.
   When are the bills actually payable in each case?
10. When is a bill payable: (*a*) on demand; (*b*) at a fixed or determinable future time?

Case of Need. The drawer of a bill, and any endorser, may insert in the bill the name of a person to whom the holder may resort in case of need, that is, in case the bill is dishonoured by non-acceptance or non-payment. Such person is called the *referee in case of need.* It is in the option of the holder to resort to the referee in case of need or not as he may think fit.

Acceptance. The acceptance of a bill is the signification by the drawee of his assent to the order of the drawer. This acceptance is effected by the drawee writing his signature across the face of the bill, though it is apparently quite legal if written on the back of it. The word "accepted" is generally prefixed, but it is not legally necessary.

Domicile. When the drawee on accepting a bill marks on it the *place* of payment, this is called the domicile of the bill. If no place is mentioned, the bill is payable at the acceptor's usual place of business.

Kinds of Acceptance. An acceptance may be either (*a*) general or (*b*) qualified.

A *general acceptance* assents without qualification to the order of the drawer. A *qualified acceptance* in express terms varies the effect of the bill as drawn. In particular, an acceptance is qualified which is—

(*a*) *conditional*, that is to say, which makes payment by the acceptor dependent on the fulfilment of a condition stated therein;

(*b*) *partial*, that is, an acceptance to pay part only of the amount for which the bill is drawn;

(*c*) *local*, that is, an acceptance to pay only at a particular specified place. An acceptance to pay at a particular place is a general acceptance, unless it expressly states that the bill is to be paid there only and not elsewhere;

(*d*) *qualified as to time*, as when a bill for two months is accepted for four;

(*e*) *the acceptance of one or more of the drawees*, but not all.

The holder of a bill may refuse to take a qualified acceptance, and if he does not obtain an unqualified acceptance he may treat the bill as dishonoured by non-acceptance.

NOTE. An acceptance on behalf of a firm or a limited company or in any fiduciary capacity should contain the name of the firm or company and be accepted for them, otherwise it may legally be held to be merely the personal acceptance of the party or parties signing; and this would render the latter personally liable on the bill. Thus acceptance should be—

For and on behalf of A B Co. Ltd.

....

Director.

And not—

....

Director of A B Co. Ltd.

Presentment for Acceptance. The presentment must be made by or on behalf of the holder, to the drawee or to some person authorized to accept on his behalf, at a reasonable hour on a business day and before the bill is overdue.

Where a bill is addressed to two or more drawees who are not partners, presentment must be made to them all, unless one has authority to accept for all, when presentment may be made to him only. Where the drawee is dead, presentment may be made to his personal representative. Where the drawee is bankrupt, presentment may be made to him or to his trustee. Where authorized by agreement or usage, a presentment through the Post Office is sufficient.

Presentment for acceptance is excused, and the bill may be treated as dishonoured by non-acceptance—

(*a*) Where the drawee is dead or bankrupt, or is a fictitious person, or a person not having capacity to contract by bill;

(*b*) Where after the exercise of reasonable diligence presentment cannot be effected.

The fact that the holder has reason to believe that the bill, on presentment, will be dishonoured does not excuse presentment.

Dishonour by Non-acceptance. When a bill is duly presented for acceptance and is not accepted within the customary time (usually twenty-four hours), it must be treated as dishonoured by non-acceptance, or else the holder will lose his right of recourse against the drawer and endorsers.

A bill is dishonoured by non-acceptance—

(*a*) When it is duly presented for acceptance and such acceptance is refused or cannot be obtained; or

(*b*) When presentment for acceptance is excused and the bill is not accepted.

When a bill is dishonoured by non-acceptance, an immediate right of recourse against the drawer and endorsers accrues to the holder, and no presentment for payment is necessary.

Recourse. This term denotes the right of a bona fide holder of a bill of exchange to require payment of it from some person other than the acceptor, that is, from any of the endorsers, or from the drawer.

Delivery of Bill. A bill of exchange, although complete in form, is, like a deed, of no effect against the parties to it until it has been properly delivered. If, therefore, a bill of exchange gets into circulation through being stolen from the drawer, acceptor, or endorsers, they will not be liable upon it except to a holder in due course.

Negotiable Instruments. Partly by custom (modern as well as ancient) and partly by statute law, certain documents, including bills of exchange, have acquired negotiability. The characteristics of negotiable instruments are—

(*a*) The property in them, and not merely the possession, passes by delivery.

(*b*) The holder in due course is not prejudiced by any defects of title on the part of the transferor or any previous holder, even though such prior party may have stolen the bill.

(*c*) The holder can sue upon them in his own name.

Generally speaking, if the holder's title can be made good through theft then the document is a negotiable one; if not, then it is not negotiable. The following are examples of negotiable instruments: coins of the realm, bills of exchange, bank notes, cheques, promissory notes, dividend warrants, share warrants, bearer debentures and scrip, and bonds of foreign and Colonial Governments.

Negotiation of Bill. A bill being a negotiable instrument may be transferred from one person to another, who then acquires all the rights in it. A bill, negotiable in its origin, continues to be negotiable, i.e. may be reissued, until it has been (*a*) restrictively endorsed or (*b*) discharged by payment or otherwise. Any holder may endorse over or transfer a bill unless the bill contains in the body thereof words prohibiting its transfer, or bears a restrictive endorsement. If a bill is payable to bearer, it is transferable simply by delivery; if payable to order, it is transferable by endorsement and delivery, that is, it requires the holder's signature on the back of it before being passed on. In any case, it is always advisable to obtain the endorsement of a transferor in order to make him liable as a party to the bill, which he would not be otherwise.

Endorsement. The requisites of a valid endorsement are that it must be written on the bill itself and be signed by the endorser. The simple signature of the endorser *without additional words* is sufficient. The endorsement is usually on the back of the bill, though quite legal if on the front of it. The number of endorsements may be so numerous that the space on the back of the bill is insufficient to contain all the signatures. In this case a slip of paper, called an *allonge*, may be pasted on to the bill to receive any further endorsements. The first person to sign afterwards should write his signature partly on the bill and partly on the allonge, in order to prevent the two being separated; otherwise, the first signature on the allonge might be fraudulently attached to a bill of a larger amount. An endorsement written on an allonge, or on a "copy" of a bill, is deemed to be written on the bill itself.

Where, in a bill payable to order, the payee or endorsee is wrongly designated, or his name is misspelt, he should endorse the bill as therein described, adding, *if he thinks fit*, his proper signature.

Kinds of Endorsements. An endorsement may be in blank or special. It may also contain terms making it restrictive. An *endorsement in blank* specifies no endorsee, and a bill so endorsed becomes payable to bearer. A *special endorsement* specifies the person to whom, or to whose order, the bill is to be payable, as "pay C D or order." A *restrictive endorsement* prohibits the further negotiation of the bill, as "pay C D only," or "pay C D for the account of E," or "pay C D or order for collection." Where any person is under obligation to endorse a bill in a representative capacity, he may endorse the bill in such terms as to negative personal liability. The endorsement "*sans recours*" (without recourse) is thus often used by persons who have been acting as agents and not principals. A *facultative endorsement* is one in which an endorser has, as regards himself, waived some or all of the holder's duties, such as presentment for payment, notice of dishonour, etc. Example—

Pay C D or order,
Notice of Dishonour waived.

A B.

An endorsement must not be partial or conditional; it must be for the whole bill; and if the endorsement *is* conditional the condition may be ignored by the payer.

Circuity of Action or Negotiation Back. Where a bill is negotiated back to the drawer, or to a prior endorser, or to the acceptor, such party may reissue and further negotiate the bill, but cannot enforce payment of the bill against any intervening party to whom he was previously liable. Thus, if Brown draws a bill and endorses it to Jones, Jones endorses to Roberts,

Roberts to Green, and finally Green endorses back to Brown before it is due, Brown can reissue and negotiate the bill but cannot enforce payment against Jones, Roberts, or Green. In like manner, if any other person becomes, for the *second* time, an endorser of the same bill, all endorsers between his first and second endorsements are discharged from liability.

Where a person signs a bill otherwise than as drawer or acceptor, he thereby incurs the liabilities of an endorser to a holder in due course. This is known as "backing" a bill.

Consideration. The words "for value received" are usually written in a bill, but are not legally necessary, as a bill is not invalid by reason that it does not specify the value given, or that any value has been given therefor. Moreover, every party whose signature appears on a bill is prima facie deemed to have become a party thereto for value. This assumption, however, may be rebutted by evidence to the contrary. Valuable consideration for a bill may be constituted by—

(*a*) Any consideration sufficient to support a simple contract;

(*b*) An antecedent debt or liability, whether the bill is payable on demand or at a future time.

If a bill which has been previously accepted for value received is ultimately handed to a person as a gift, the holder cannot recover the amount from his immediate transferor as no consideration has passed; he can, however, recover it from any of the other parties to the bill. If a bill be given for a wagering or gaming debt, the holder cannot sue the loser upon it as the consideration is illegal. But if the bill is transferred for value to a third person who is unaware of the gaming transaction, such third person can enforce payment.

Presentment for Payment. Except in a few special instances, a bill must be duly presented for payment, otherwise the drawer and endorsers will be discharged from their liability. A bill payable on demand must be presented within a "reasonable" time. A bill not payable on demand must be presented on the due date at the place of payment or address of drawee or acceptor mentioned in the bill; or if this is not specified, at the drawee's or acceptor's place of business if known; and if not, at his ordinary residence if known; and if not, at his last known place of business or residence, or wherever he can be found. Where authorized by agreement or usage, a presentment through the Post Office is sufficient. Presentment for payment is not necessary in order to make an *acceptor* liable.

Delay in presentment for payment is excused when the delay is caused by circumstances beyond the control of the holder of the bill. Presentment is excused where the drawee is a fictitious person, by express or implied waiver, and where, after the exercise of reasonable diligence, presentment cannot be effected. The fact that the holder has reason to believe that the bill will, on presentment, be dishonoured, does not dispense with the necessity for presentment.

Dishonour by Non-payment. A bill is dishonoured by non-payment (*a*) when it is duly presented for payment and payment is refused or cannot be obtained, or (*b*) when presentment is excused by the Act and the bill is overdue and unpaid. When a bill is dishonoured by non-payment, an immediate right of recourse against the drawer and endorsers accrues to the holder. When a bill is dishonoured by non-acceptance or non-payment, notice of dishonour must be given to the drawer and each endorser, or they will be discharged from their obligations. The notice may be given in writing or by personal communication. The return of a dishonoured bill to the drawer or an endorser is, in point of form, deemed a sufficient notice of dishonour. Notice must be given immediately after dishonour or within a reasonable time. Each party who receives notice of dishonour is allowed reasonable time to give notice to antecedent parties to the bill. Where a notice of dishonour is duly addressed and posted, the sender is deemed to have given due notice of dishonour, notwithstanding any miscarriage by the Post Office.

Noting and Protest of Bill. Where an inland bill has been dishonoured, it may, if the holder thinks fit, be noted for non-acceptance or non-payment as the case may be; but noting is not legally necessary to preserve the holder's rights against the drawer and endorsers. It is often done, however, in order to prevent any subsequent dispute as to the dishonour. A bill which has been protested for non-acceptance may be subsequently protested for non-payment. Provided a bill is duly noted on the day of its dishonour, or on the next succeeding business day, the protest may be extended subsequently as of the same date as the noting. A bill must be protested at the place where it is dishonoured, unless it has been presented through the Post Office, when it may be protested at the place to which it is returned by post. Where the acceptor of a bill becomes bankrupt or insolvent or suspends payment before it matures, the holder may cause the bill to be protested for better security against the drawer and endorsers.

Notary Public. This is a public officer whose duty is to certify deeds and other documents. The word "notary" is derived from the Latin *notarius* = a writer. The duties of a notary also include the presentation of dishonoured bills of exchange, and noting their non-acceptance or non-payment and afterwards protesting them if necessary.

Noting Charges. These are the notary's fees for re-presenting the bill, recording and certifying its dishonour, and, if required, drawing up the protest. When dishonoured bills are noted, the noting charges must be paid by the holder of the bill, who is entitled to recover them from the acceptor or from the person from whom he received the bill. The notary makes a copy of the bill in his register, and then writes on the bill itself the date, his charges, the letter or folio of his register, and lastly his initials. He, or his clerk, then re-presents the bill for acceptance, or payment, as the case may be. If it is dishonoured again, he gums on to the bill a small ticket or label containing his charges and the reason given for dishonour.

The following is an example—

NOTING TICKET

PETER BROWN & Co., NOTARIES, 6 ABBEY LANE, LONDON, E.C.3 NOTING CHARGES, £0·50. Refer to Acceptor

Other reasons given might be "No Orders," "No Advice," "No Effects," "No Instructions," or "No Funds."

When Noting or Protest is Necessary. Noting or protest is absolutely necessary in the following four cases—

1. Before a bill can be presented for payment to a referee in case of need.
2. Prior to an acceptance or payment for honour.
3. On dishonour of a bill by an acceptor for honour.
4. In the case of non-acceptance or non-payment of foreign bills.

Protest. This is the formal declaration in writing made by the notary public against the non-acceptor or non-payer of a bill of exchange. A protest must contain a copy of the bill, and must be signed by the notary making it, and must specify—

(*a*) The person at whose request the bill is protested;

(*b*) The place and date of protest, the cause or reason for protesting the bill, the demand made, and the answer given, if any, or the fact that the drawee or acceptor could not be found.

It is not necessary to protest a bill in order to make the *acceptor* liable.

Where a dishonoured bill or note is authorized or required to be protested, and the services of a notary cannot be obtained at the place where the bill is dishonoured, any householder or substantial resident may, in the presence of two witnesses, give a certificate signed by them, attesting the dishonour of the bill, and the certificate operates as if it were a formal protest of the bill.

QUESTIONS

1. Is it necessary: (*a*) for the drawer of a bill to insert the phrase "for value received," (*b*) for the acceptor of a bill to write the word "accepted," (*c*) for an endorser to write the word "endorsed," or (*d*) for an acceptor for honour to write the phrase "accepted for honour"? Give reasons for your answer in each case.

2. What are negotiable instruments? Name some. What are their three distinguishing characteristics?

3. How are bills of exchange negotiated? How can negotiation be restricted: (*a*) in drawing the bill, (*b*) in endorsing the bill?

4. What is meant by the acceptance of a bill? Explain: (*a*) general acceptance, (*b*) conditional acceptance, (*c*) partial acceptance, (*d*) local acceptance. In what other ways can the acceptance be qualified? Is a holder bound to take a qualified acceptance?

5. Explain the following: domicile, endorser, allonge, acceptor for honour, referee in case of need.

6. What is meant by endorsing a bill of exchange? When is it necessary, and when not? The following endorsements appear on some trade bills—

(*a*) Pay A B.
(*b*) Pay C D or order, A B
(*c*) Sans recours, G H.
(*d*) Pay E F only, C D.
(*e*) Pay C D, notice of dishonour waived, A B.

What kind of endorsements would you respectively call these?

7. What two things are necessary in order to constitute an acceptance a valid one?

8. When is presentment for acceptance necessary, and when is it excused?

9. What is meant by noting and protest of a bill of exchange? Is it always necessary?

10. Explain the terms: notary public, noting charges, noting ticket. What stamp is required on a protest? Can a householder draw up a protest?

Damages on Dishonour. Where a bill is dishonoured, the measure of damages, deemed to be liquidated damages, is as follows—

The holder may recover from any party liable on the bill, and the drawer who has been compelled to pay the bill may recover from the acceptor, and an endorser who has been compelled to pay the bill may recover from the acceptor or from the drawer, or from a prior endorser—

(*a*) The amount of the bill;

(*b*) Interest thereon from the time of presentment for payment if the bill is payable on demand, and from the maturity of the bill in any other case;

(*c*) The expenses of noting, or, when protest is necessary, and the protest has been extended, the expenses of protest.

Holder in Due Course. A holder in due course is a holder who has taken a bill, complete and regular on the face of it, under the following conditions, namely—

(*a*) That he became the holder of it before it was overdue, and without notice that it had been previously dishonoured, if such was the fact.

(*b*) That he took the bill in good faith and for value, and that at the time the bill was negotiated to him he had no notice of any defect in the title of the person who negotiated it.

Every holder of a bill is prima facie deemed to be a holder in due course.

Duty of Holder. Where the holder of a bill presents it for payment, he must exhibit the bill to the person from whom he demands payment, and when a bill is paid in legal tender the holder must forthwith deliver it up to the party paying it.

Acceptance for Honour Supra Protest. Where a bill of exchange has been protested for dishonour by non-acceptance, or protested for better security, and is not overdue, any person, not being a party already liable thereon, may, with the consent of the holder, intervene and accept the bill *supra* protest, for the honour of any party liable thereon or for the honour of the person for whose account the bill is drawn. A bill may be accepted for honour for part only of the sum for which it is drawn. An acceptance for honour *supra* protest, in order to be valid, must (*a*) be written on the bill, and indicate that it is an acceptance for honour, (*b*) be signed by the acceptor for honour. Such an acceptance is as follows—

Accepted supra *protest*, or *Accepted for the honour and account of* ....(drawer or endorser) *with £*.................. *noting charges and expenses.*

M. Collado

Where an acceptance for honour does not expressly state for whose honour it is made, it is deemed to be an acceptance for the honour of the drawer. Where a bill payable after sight is accepted for honour, its maturity is calculated from the date of the noting for non-acceptance, and not from the date of the acceptance for honour.

Where a dishonoured bill has been accepted for honour *supra* protest, or contains a referee in case of need, it must be protested for non-payment by the drawee (if he refuses payment on presentment of the bill to him) before it is presented for payment to the acceptor for honour, or referee in case of need. When a bill of exchange is dishonoured by the acceptor for honour, it must be protested for non-payment by him.

Payment for Honour Supra Protest. Where a bill has been protested for non-payment, any person may intervene and pay it *supra* protest for the honour of any party liable thereon, or for the honour of the person for whose account the bill is drawn. Payment for honour *supra* protest, in order to operate as such and not as a mere voluntary payment, must be attested by a notarial act of honour which may be appended to the protest or form an extension of it.

Alteration of Bill. Where a bill or acceptance is materially altered without the assent of all parties liable on the bill, the bill is avoided except as against a party who has himself made, authorized, or assented to the alteration, and *subsequent* endorsers. In particular the following alterations are material: any alteration of the date, the sum payable, the time of payment, the place of payment, and where a bill has been accepted generally, the addition of a place of payment without the acceptor's assent. Alterations on a bill should, therefore, be initialed by all parties to the bill.

Lost Bill. Where a bill has been lost before it is overdue the person who was the holder of it may apply to the drawer for another bill of the same tenor, giving security to the drawer, if required, to indemnify him against all persons whatever in case the bill alleged to have been lost is found again. If the drawer, on request, refuses to give such duplicate bill, he may be compelled to do so.

Forgery. No title to a bill can be made through forgery. A transferee acquires no rights through a bill which bears a forged signature of either drawer, acceptor or endorser even though he had no knowledge of the forgery. He can, however, demand repayment of the amount he has paid for the bill from his transferor.

Discharge of Bill. A bill is discharged, i.e. all rights of action on it extinguished, by payment in due course by or on behalf of the drawee or acceptor. "Payment in due course" means payment made in legal tender *at* or *after* the maturity of the bill to the holder thereof in good faith and without notice that his title to the bill is defective. If a cheque is tendered in payment of a bill, the bill will be retained until the cheque is met, as cheques are not legal tender. Payment by the acceptor *before* maturity does not discharge the bill, and the acceptor may reissue it. Payment by the drawer or an endorser does not discharge a bill. Where a bill payable to, or to the order of, *a third party* is paid by the drawer, the drawer may enforce payment thereof against the acceptor, but may not reissue the bill. Where a bill is paid by an endorser, or where a bill payable to *drawer's order* is paid by the drawer, the party paying it is remitted to his former rights as regards the acceptor or antecedent parties, and he may, if he thinks fit, strike out his own and subsequent endorsements, and reissue the bill.

When the acceptor of a bill is or becomes the holder of it at or after its maturity, in his own right, the bill is discharged. When the holder of a bill at or after its maturity, by express waiver in writing, or by delivering up the bill to the acceptor, absolutely and unconditionally renounces his rights against the acceptor, the bill is discharged. Where a bill is intentionally cancelled by the holder or his agent, and the cancellation is apparent thereon, the bill is discharged.

Moratorium. This term, which is a Latin word derived from *morari* = to delay, denotes a legal authorization to delay for a stated time the payment of certain specified debts or obligations.

The promulgation of a moratorium is to allow debtors on bills of exchange, particularly firms who are unable to obtain payment from foreign debtors, time to collect the necessary funds to meet their own obligations, and thus save themselves from bankruptcy.

Accommodation Bills. An accommodation bill is a bill put into circulation in order to raise money on it by the process of discounting. It differs from an ordinary trade bill in that no value has been received for it. Accommodation bills are also known as "fictitious bills," "kites," "windmills," and "finance bills."

Method of Procedure. Bills may be drawn for the accommodation of either drawer or acceptor, or for the mutual accommodation of both. The discount charges are borne by the party or parties receiving the proceeds of the bill. The party accommodated engages—

(*a*) to provide funds for the payment of the bill at maturity;
(*b*) to indemnify the accommodating party should the latter be compelled to pay the bill.

Discharge of Bill. Where an accommodation bill is paid in due course by the party accommodated the bill is discharged. Unlike a trade bill, the principal debtor is not necessarily the acceptor, but the party accommodated.

Bills of Exchange Transactions. Transactions in bills of exchange beyond the elementary stage seem a source of difficulty. The student may be unable to decide which set of entries belong to which party.

Practical problems of this kind are best dealt with a step at a time. Perhaps two examples of transactions in accommodation bills will more clearly explain the method of handling such transactions.

Example 1

On 1st January A draws on B for his personal accommodation a bill at three months for £200 which he immediately discounts with his banker. The banker charges 5 per cent. On maturity, A honours his obligation to B by cheque, with which B meets the bill. Show the entries in the books of both parties.

Method of Procedure and Solution 1

It must first be determined "whose books shall be prepared *first*—A's or B's." Take A's standpoint, and the transactions he is concerned with, are as follows.

1. A draws on B.
2. A discounts B's acceptance, being charged discount at 5 per cent.
3. A remits cheque to B.

The accounts will be as under—

A's LEDGER

BILLS RECEIVABLE

19..			£	19..			£
Jan	1	B	200·00	Jan	1	Bank . . .	200·00

B

19..			£	19..			£
Apr	4	Bank . . .	200·00	Jan	1	Bills Receivable .	200·00

BANKERS' DISCOUNT

19..			£				
Jan	1	Bank . . .	2·50				

BANK

19..			£	19..			£
Jan	1	Bills Receivable .	200·00	Jan	1	Discount Charges .	2·50
				Apr	4	B . . .	200·00

The entries in the bank account agree with the method of entry as shown in the bank pass book. An alternative method is to utilize the discount column on the debit side, and extend the net amount of the bill in the bank column, so—

CASH BOOK (*Dr.* side)

Date	Particulars	Fo.	Discount	Bank
19..			£	£
Jan 1	Bills Receivable		2·50	197·50

NOTE. The discount is calculated on the period the bill has to run.

Now that A's books have been prepared it is a simple matter to deal with the transactions as they affect B. B is concerned with the following transactions—

1. Accepts A's draft.
2. Receives £200 from A.
3. Honours his acceptance.

The following are the accounts he will prepare—

B's LEDGER

A

19..		£	19..		£
Jan 1	Bills Payable . . .	200	Apr 4	Bank	200

BILLS PAYABLE

19..		£	19..		£
Apr 4	Bank	200	Jan 1	A	200

BANK

19..		£	19..		£
Apr 4	A.	200	Apr 4	Bills Payable . . .	200

Example 2

On 1st January A and B draw on each other at three months for £200. They discount each other's bills, the banker's discount charges being 5 per cent per annum. On the due date of the bills meets his own acceptance. Show the accounts in the books of both parties.

Method of Procedure and Solution 2

Take A's viewpoint, and the transactions develop in the following order—

1. A draws on B.
2. A accepts B's draft.
3. Discounts B's acceptance.
4. Honours own acceptance.

A's ledger will show the following accounts—

A's LEDGER

B

			£				£
19..				19..			
Jan	1	Bills Payable	200·00	Jan	1	Bills Receivable	200·00

BILLS RECEIVABLE

			£				£
19..				19..			
Jan	1	B	200·00	Jan	1	Bank	200·00

BILLS PAYABLE

			£				£
19..				19..			
Apr	1	Bank	200·00	Jan	1	A	200·00

BANKERS' DISCOUNT

			£				
19..							
Jan	1	Bank	2·50				

BANK

			£				£
19..				19..			
Jan	1	Bills Receivable	200·00	Jan	1	Discount Charges	2·50
				Apr	1	Bills Payable	200·00

Having established the position of A in regard to the question, we have now to indicate the transactions as they affect B; they are as follows—

(*a*) B draws on A.
(*b*) B accepts A's draft.
(*c*) Discounts A's acceptance.
(*d*) Honours own acceptance.

As will be seen, the accounts B will raise are parallel to those of A.

Example 3

Dishonour. J failed to honour his acceptance to A of Bill No. 14 for £200 on the due date. The noting charges were £0·25. Show the necessary book-keeping records in connexion therewith. There are several circumstances under which dishonour may arise; state these, and show accounts applicable to the different circumstances of dishoonur.

Method of Procedure and Solution 3

The accounts to be drawn up are those of the "drawer." Avoid speculating at this point as to the relation of any of the other parties to the bill on the subject of dishonour. All the entries should be viewed from the drawer's position. The next step is to put down in order the circumstances under which J's acceptance may be dishonoured, which are as follows—

(*a*) The bill is still in the hands of the drawer.
(*b*) The bill has been since discounted with the banker.
(*c*) The bill has been handed to the banker for collection.
(*d*) The bill has been previously endorsed over to a creditor.

The following solution is given in the form of journal entries.

1. On dishonour when the bill is still in the hands of the drawer.

A's BOOKS
JOURNAL

		Dr	*Cr*
		£	£
	J	200·00	
	Bills Receivable		200·00
	Cancellation of Bill No. 14.		

The noting charges will be the subject of a cash book entry as under—

CASH BOOK (*Cr*. side)

		Office
		£
	J (noting charges on dishonour)	0·25

2. On dishonour when the bill has since been discounted with banker; and

3. On dishonour when the bill has been sent to the banker for collection.

CASH BOOK (Bank Account) *Cr*

		£
	J (Dishonoured Bill and noting charges)	200·25

Should the "drawer" and not the banker get the bill noted, then the "Office" column would show £0·25 for noting charges, and the "Bank" column would show £200—the amount of the bill.

4. On dishonour when the bill has been endorsed over to a creditor.

JOURNAL

		Dr	Cr
		£	£
	J	200·25	
	A. Creditor		200·25
	For amount of bill and noting charges.		

Renewal. After dishonour it is frequently the case that bills are renewed, i.e. the existing bill is cancelled, as mentioned above, and a new one is made out for the whole or part of the amount owing and including interest. The book-keeping entries necessary are—

(1) For Bills Receivable	(2) For Bills Payable
JOURNAL	JOURNAL
T *Dr* Bills Receivable Cancellation of bill.	Bills Payable *Dr* M Cancellation of bill.
T *Dr* Interest Interest charged for extended period of credit.	Interest *Dr* M Interest charged for extended period of credit.
Bills Receivable *Dr* T For new bill, including interest.	M *Dr* Bills Payable For new bill, including interest.
Interest on bills receivable is a *gain.*	Interest on bills payable is a *loss.*

Example 4

In exercises it is not unusual to meet with this transaction: "Endorsed B's acceptance over to Q in consideration of which Q credited my account with £195; the bill was drawn for £200." This transaction includes a charge for interest on the bill. It is obvious that Q must charge for the period he has to wait before he can encash B's acceptance (assuming he waits till date of maturity). The entries will be as follows—

JOURNAL

		Dr	Cr
		£	£
	Q	200	
	Bills Receivable		200
	Endorsement of B's acceptance.		
	Interest	5	
	Q		5
	Interest charged on unexpired term of bill (loss).		

Bill Books. Where a firm frequently deals with bills of exchange, special subsidiary books are used to record details of bills payable and receivable.

The precise form will depend upon the type of business.

The books may be memorandum books, in which case journal entries are required for all transactions.

They may be part of the double entry, in which case the debit entry in bills receivable book will be posted to the credit of the person sending it. The entry in the bills payable book is a credit, with a corresponding debit to the personal account of the drawer.

Columns may be added for discounts if all bills receivable are discounted.

QUESTIONS

1. What is meant by presentment for payment? When is it necessary, and when not? When is delay in presentment excused?

2. When is a bill dishonoured: (*a*) by non-acceptance, (*b*) by non-payment?

3. What is meant by notice of dishonour? When is it necessary, and when is it excused?

4. Explain the terms: holder in due course, recourse, damages on dishonour, payment for honour *supra* protest.

5. Bills are drawn as under—

(*a*) Payable in three months provided the goods turn out satisfactory.

(*b*) Payable one month after the drawer's marriage (the marriage actually takes place).

(*c*) Payable as soon as the ship reaches the port of Liverpool (the ship duly arrives in port).

(*d*) Payable ten days after a certain person's death.

(*e*) Payable out of a particular fund.

State, with reasons in each case, whether the above bills are valid or not.

6. How do the following affect the parties to a bill of exchange?—

(*a*) Material alterations, (*b*) forgery, (*c*) non-delivery of bill, (*d*) loss of bill?

7. In what ways can a bill be discharged?

8. What are the legal liabilities respectively of—

(*a*) Drawer, (*b*) acceptor, (*c*) endorser, (*d*) acceptor for honour?

9. Explain the method of procedure with regard to accommodation bills. What is the legal liability of an accommodation party?

10. Explain the meaning of fictitious payee. How does the absence of a date affect a bill? Does any mention of interest affect a bill?

Foreign Bills. According to Sect. 4 of the Bills of Exchange Act a "foreign" bill is any other bill which does not come within the definition of an inland bill. It is generally defined as "a bill drawn in one country but payable in another." Foreign bills are usually drawn in sets of three, called "vias," and generally contain the phase "value received" or "value in account." Each via is numbered, and stipulates that it is to be paid only if the other two vias are unpaid. To minimize the risk of loss, and to avert the delay arising therefrom, the three forms are dispatched at different times.

Form of Bill. There is no particular form of bill required by the Act. Below is a specimen in common use.

> LONDON,
> Exchange for £800. 21st *January*, 19..
>
> Thirty days after sight pay this First of Exchange (Second and Third of same date and tenor unpaid) to Messrs. Carpentier et Cie, or order, eight hundred pounds, value in account.
>
> J. ROWELL.
>
> To Messrs. Hachette Frères,
> Lyons.

Sum Payable. In addition to the cases mentioned under Inland Bills, the sum payable by a bill is a sum certain within the meaning of the Act, although it is required to be paid—

According to an indicated rate of exchange, or according to a rate of exchange to be ascertained as directed by the bill.

The sum for which a foreign bill is drawn is often stated in the currency of the country where it is payable. Where a bill is drawn out of, but payable in, the United Kingdom, and the sum payable is not expressed in the currency of the United Kingdom, the amount, in the absence of some express stipulation, is calculated according to the rate of exchange for sight drafts at the place of payment on the day the bill is payable.

Bill in a Set. Where a bill is drawn in a set, each part of the set being numbered, and containing a reference to the other parts, the whole of the parts constitute one bill. The acceptance may be written on any part, and it must be written on one part only. Any person who accepts, or any person who endorses, more than one part will be liable on those parts as if they were separate bills. With these exceptions, where any one part of a bill drawn in a set is discharged by payment or otherwise, the whole bill is discharged.

Sola. This term, or "sola draft," "sola of exchange," appearing on a bill of exchange means that it is the sole or only bill, i.e. that the bill has not been drawn in a set. With near countries, nowadays, one copy, or a first and second of exchange, are often deemed sufficient, as the mail service is more regular and reliable than in former times.

Foreign Bills Drawn in Sterling. The custom has long prevailed amongst English merchants of drawing on their foreign customers in the home currency instead of in the currency of the country where the bill is payable, and of stipulating that the bill shall be paid at the rate of exchange ruling on the day of the first London endorsement. An example is shown below.

£227·16

LIVERPOOL,
15th September, 19..

Three months after date pay this First of Exchange (Second and Third of same date and tenor unpaid) to Signor F. Spraghetti, or order, the sum of two hundred and twenty-seven pounds and sixteen pence, at the rate of exchange as per first London endorsement, value received, and charge to account as per advice.

ROGERS & SON.

To Signori Bellami & Cia.
Genoa.

When the bill is sold the endorsement would be similar to the following—

Pay T. Ruelli & Co., or Order, at the exchange of 1,750 *lire for* £1 *sterling*.

The buyer, i.e. the London banker or broker, will write the rate of exchange and the currency amount on the bill underneath the sterling figures; and this information will be sent by the drawer to the drawee, so that the latter may verify the exchange and know what amount he will eventually have to pay. The great advantage of this method to the drawer is that he obtains the cash for the full amount of his invoice, and thereby obviates the risk of loss in exchange. The custom seems to have originated from the violent fluctuations of exchange in time of war or panic, and the consequent desire of the drawer to protect himself against the resultant loss. The foreign merchant thus bears the loss arising from exchange; for no matter how low exchange falls, he must provide a sufficient amount of the foreign currency to purchase a bill for the required sterling sum. At the same time, however, he stands a chance, should the rates be favourable, of making a profit on exchange.

Stamp Duty. On bills drawn in the United Kingdom and payable abroad, and on bills drawn abroad and payable in the United Kingdom, no stamp duty is now payable.

Stamps may be required by the laws of foreign countries, and are usually affixed by the foreign customer and debited to the account of the English merchant.

Usance. It is customary for foreign bills to be made payable at one or more "usances," i.e. time of payment as fixed by custom. For instance, the usance between London and New York is sixty days after sight.

After Sight. Foreign bills are generally drawn payable at so many *days* "after sight." This ensures the drawee having the benefit of the full period of time after acceptance, an important point when the acceptor is abroad

The acceptor of such bills must, therefore, sight or date his acceptance, as the time for maturity begins to run from the date of such acceptance and not from the date on which the bill was drawn. The following is an example of a foreign bill duly sighted.

Exchange for $4,000.

LONDON,
21st January, 19. .

At sixty days' sight pay this First of Exchange (Second and Third of same date
and tenor unpaid) to the order of Mr.
James Retrop the sum of four thousand
dollars, value received, and place
to account as advised.

Sighted 28 January, 19. .
Accepted payable at
National Bank, New
York,
A B & Co.

To Messrs. A B & Co.
New York.

R. BRABY.

Noting and Protest. Where a foreign bill has been dishonoured by non-payment or non-acceptance, it must be protested, otherwise the drawer and endorsers are discharged. The noting and protest is the only recognized evidence of dishonour in many foreign courts.

Conflict of Laws. Where a bill drawn in one country is negotiated, accepted, or payable in another—

(*a*) The validity of the bill as regards requisites in form is determined by the law of the place of issue, and as regards the supervening contracts, such as drawing and endorsement, by the law of the place where such contract was made.

(*b*) The duties of the holder with respect to presentment for acceptance or payment, etc., are determined by the law of the place where the act is done or the bill dishonoured.

(*c*) The due date of the bill is determined according to the law of the place where it is payable.

Documentary Bills. A Documentary Bill is a foreign bill having certain "documents of title" attached. The documents are usually the invoice of the goods, the bill of lading, insurance policy, and, sometimes, a letter of hypothecation.

Nature and Use of Documents Attached. Foreign bills, especially those relating to shipping orders and consignments, are discounted or sold before they are accepted. The banker is thus taking a considerable risk, and seeks to protect himself by obtaining possession of the relative shipping documents.

The invoice is required in order to identify the goods, and must be produced to the customs officials at the port of delivery. The bill of lading, duly endorsed, gives the banker a title to the goods; and the shipping company will deliver only in exchange for the bill of lading. The insurance policy, duly endorsed, is the banker's security for indemnity in case the goods are lost owing to the perils of the sea. The letter of hypothecation pledges the goods as security for the payment of the bill, by giving the banker the right, in the event of the bill being dishonoured by non-acceptance or non-payment, to dispose of the goods and to charge any deficiency to the drawer. Documentary bills are also bought and sold by bill brokers. They form a convenient means of settling debts in the countries where the bills are payable, the documents attached affording security to the purchaser.

Letter of Hypothecation. Letters of hypothecation are seldom used nowadays, the banker referring, on dishonour, to the drawer for instructions, repayment of bill, and disposal of goods. This is more particularly the case where the drawer keeps a substantial current account with the bank concerned.

LETTER OF HYPOTHECATION

LONDON,
20*th June*, 19..

THE SAFE BANK LTD.
Hillcorn, E.C.2.

Dear Sirs,

We send you enclosed bill for £600 at 90 days' sight drawn by us on Messrs, Roberts & Son, Wellington, New Zealand. In consideration of your advancing to us thereon 80 per cent, namely £480, we hand you the following set of shipping documents—

Invoice for 20 Cases of Goods, value £600, in triplicate;

Bill of Lading for above 20 cases marked [R. & Son] 626/45, in triplicate;

Policy of Marine Insurance for £650, in duplicate.

Freight on the goods has been paid by us.

In the event of the said bill being dishonoured, we authorize you to sell such goods for our account and at our risk, and to charge us with the usual expenses and commission.

Yours faithfully,
F. FRANCIS & CO.

Method of Procedure. The banker, having discounted the bill, or made the required advance, generally 80 to 90 per cent *less* charges, forwards the

No. 356. LONDON,
Exchange for £600 *20th June*, 19..

Ninety days after sight of this First of Exchange (Second and Third of same date and tenor unpaid) pay to us or our order the sum of six hundred pounds, value received against [R. & Son] 626/45 = 20 Cases of Goods per S.S. *Crown Prince*, and place to account as advised. Shipping documents attached to be surrendered on payment.

To Messrs. Roberts & Son,
Wellington,
New Zealand.

F. FRANCIS & Co.

The above bill would be endorsed—

Pay to the Safe Bank Ltd., or Order,
F. Francis & Co.

No. 764. LONDON,
Exchange for £450. *4th January*, 19..

Sixty days after sight of this First of Exchange (Second and Third of same date and tenor unpaid) pay to our order the sum of four hundred and fifty pounds sterling, payable at the National Bank of India's drawing rate for demand drafts on London, with interest at six per cent per annum added thereto from date hereof to approximate due date of arrival of the remittance in London, value received against [S.S. & S.] 623/37 = 15 bales of Cotton Goods per S.S. *Queen Maud*. Shipping documents attached to be surrendered on acceptance.

S. SELLER & SON.

To Messrs. Byjamji & Co.,
Bombay.

The above bill would be endorsed by the drawers, thus—

Pay The National Bank of India, or Order,
S. Seller & Son.

bill (the first copy being duly stamped), together with the original documents attached, to his branch or agent at the place of destination of the goods. A second set is sent by the next mail, the third set being retained by the banker. When the goods arrive they are unshipped and stored in the dock warehouses by the banker's agent, who calls upon the drawee for acceptance or payment of the bill, in return for which he surrenders the documents. Where the drawee is a trader of good financial standing, the banker's agent will release the goods as soon as the bill has been accepted; in such cases the bill generally contains the clause "*documents attached to be surrendered on acceptance*." In other cases the agent will be instructed to obtain not only acceptance, but payment of the bill at maturity, before releasing the goods. The abbreviations D/P and D/A are used to indicate whether the documents are to be released to the drawee against payment or acceptance respectively.

With some indents (shipping orders from abroad) the bill is drawn at such a period that maturity of the bill will coincide with the arrival of the goods. If the customer so desires, he may pay the bill by instalments, obtaining in return a corresponding portion of the goods. Where the customer wishes to secure possession of the whole of the goods before maturity of the bill, in order to take advantage of a favourable market, he may retire the bill under rebate, that is, a cash discount for the unexpired term of the bill. The banker's charges include, not only commission and cost of stamp that may be necessary in the foreign country, but also interest from the date of the bill up to maturity. And hence, if the bill is paid before the due date, the banker will be quite willing to forgo the unearned portion of the interest.

Bills drawn in sterling, and not in the currency of the country whence they are forwarded, are payable at some specified rate of exchange; and in such cases the banker's charges may be covered by the rate of exchange at which he buys the bill. Sometimes, the amount to be paid is the amount of the bill, plus interest on it up to the time when the remittance in payment reaches London, or other place of making the original advance. On receipt of advices that the bill has been duly honoured, the banker will pay the remaining 10 or 20 per cent due on the bill. Documentary bills are used principally in the import and export trade, both of which are virtually financed by means of these bills under the above-mentioned procedure. Inward and outward shipments are also made against bills drawn payable at sight, but more usually against bills drawn at ordinary usance.

Specimens of Documentary Bills. Opposite are fair specimens of the documentary bills in ordinary use—

The number in the top left corner is entered by the person drawing the bill (usually the drawer) and is merely the next available number in his bill book. Once a bill goes into circulation it is always referred to by its number.

Whenever a bill is taken from circulation, by payment, dishonour, or renewal, its fate must be recorded in the bills receivable or bills payable book in order that a check can be kept on the accuracy of the corresponding impersonal ledger account.

QUESTIONS

1. Define a foreign bill.
2. On 15th March, B. Brown, of Melbourne, drew on A. Archer, of London, at 60 d/s for £275, on account of 36 bales of wool marked as shown, shipped per S.S. *Retrop*, and attached the usual documents which were to be surrendered on acceptance of bill. Write out the bill in each of its three vias.

3. Explain the following terms: usance, letter of hypothecation, protest.
4. A bill is drawn in Germany, accepted in France, and paid in England. To what parts of the bill would the different laws apply?
5. Why are foreign bills often drawn in the home currency? When the amount of a foreign bill is not expressed in sterling, how is its value determined for the purpose of payment?
6. Why are foreign bills drawn "after sight"? How does this affect the acceptance of a long bill? Give an example of a foreign bill drawn "after sight" and duly accepted.
7. "Foreign bills, unless drawn on a near country, are not sent for acceptance and return." Explain this, and the procedure with regard to such bills.
8. Are bills liable to stamp duty? What is the position if bills are liable to duty in a foreign country?
9. Give an example of a documentary bill. Explain the object of such bills, and the usual method of procedure with regard to them.

PROMISSORY NOTES

According to the Bills of Exchange Act, 1882, a promissory note is defined as—

> **An unconditional promise in writing made by one person to another signed by the maker, engaging to pay, on demand or at a fixed or determinable future time, a sum certain in money, to, or to the order of, a specified person or to bearer.**

Promissory notes are used chiefly for loan transactions. Like bills of exchange, they are negotiable instruments, and can be transferred for value. They are sometimes discounted, and are subject to days of grace, unless payable on demand. Promissory notes which are payable *to bearer* on demand for a sum that is greater than £1 and less than £5 are void in England.

Form of Note. There is no special statutory form of promissory note, but a typical specimen is shown on the following page. A market in company promissory notes denominated in dollars was started in London in 1970. The notes are known as Euro-commercial paper and are sold at ¼% above bank certificates of deposit.

Stamp Duty. The stamp duty on promissory notes was abolished in 1971.

£120	LONDON, *1st July*, 19..

> Two months after date I promise to pay to Mr. T. Green, or order, the sum of one hundred and twenty pounds, for value received.
>
> Y. YELLOW

Parties to a Note. There are only two parties to a promissory note, and these are—

(*a*) *Maker*, the party who writes out the note, i.e. the debtor. In the example given Y. Yellow is the maker.

(*b*) *Payee*, the person to whom the money is payable, i.e. the creditor. In the example given T. Green is the payee.

Kinds of Notes. Promissory notes are of two kinds, *inland* and *foreign*. An *inland note* is one which is, or on the face of it purports to be, both made and payable within the British Islands. Any other note is a *foreign note*.

Difference between Promissory Note and Bill of Exchange. The following points of difference should be carefully noted—

1. A note is a *promise* to pay, a bill is an *order* to pay.
2. Bills are often drawn *in sets*, notes are made *singly*.
3. There are *three* parties to a bill, but only *two* to a note.
4. A bill is drawn by the *creditor*, a note is made out by the *debtor*.
5. A bill requires *acceptance*, a note does *not*.
6. Foreign bills when dishonoured must be *protested*, foreign notes need *not*.

Joint Notes, Joint and Several Notes. By Sect. 85 of the Bills of Exchange Act—

> 1. A promissory note may be made by two or more makers, and they may be liable thereon jointly, or jointly and severally according to its tenor.
>
> 2. Where a note runs, "I promise to pay," and is signed by two or more persons, it is deemed to be their joint and several note.

On page 0430 is a specimen of a joint note.

To convert this into a joint and several note it would have to be amended to read, "I promise to pay," or "We and each of us promise to pay," or "We jointly and severally promise to pay." A joint and several note has a great advantage over a mere joint note, because it enables the holder to sue the makers not only jointly but also individually.

£100	LONDON, 25*th February*, 19..

Four months after date we promise to pay to Mr. R. J. Porters the sum of one hundred pounds, value received.

W. MARSHMAN.
T. BAYES.

Note Payable on Demand. Like a bill of exchange a note is payable on demand—

(*a*) Which is expressed to be payable on demand, or at sight, or on presentation; or

(*b*) In which no time for payment is expressed.

Presentment for Payment. Where a promissory note is in the body of it made payable at a particular place, it must be presented for payment at that particular place in order to render the maker liable. In any other case, presentment for payment is not necessary in order to render the *maker* liable. Presentment for payment is necessary in order to render an *endorser* liable.

Liability of Maker. The maker of a promissory note by making it—

(*a*) Engages that he will pay it according to its tenor.

(*b*) Is precluded from denying to a holder in due course the existence of the payee and his then capacity to endorse.

Promissory Note and Collateral Security. By Sect. 83 (3) of the Act, "A note is not invalid by reason only that it contains also a pledge of collateral security with authority to sell or dispose thereof."

Bills of Exchange Act and Promissory Notes. The provisions of the bills of Exchange Act apply also to promissory notes, with the following exceptions—

(*a*) Presentment for acceptance; (*b*) Acceptance; (*c*) Acceptance *supra* protest; (*d*) Bills in a set; (*e*) Protest on dishonour.

In applying the provisions of the Act, the maker of a note is deemed to correspond with the acceptor of a bill, and the first endorser of a note is deemed to correspond with the drawer of an accepted bill payable to drawer's order.

Foreign Promissory Notes. A foreign note is any note that does not come within the definition of an inland note. On page 0431 is a specimen.

BANK NOTES

These are promissory notes, payable to bearer on demand, issued by English, Scottish, and Irish banks. They may be reissued after payment and usually are, except by the Bank of England.

BILLET À ORDRE

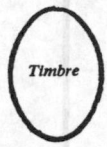

PARIS, *le* 15 *Janvier*, 19..	Bon pour Francs 2,500.
Timbre	A deux mois de date je payerai à Monsieur Paul Coppée, ou à son ordre, la somme de francs deux mille cinq cents, valeur reçu en espèces.
	LOUISE PEINE.

The Bank of England now has the monopoly of note issue for England and Wales.

Amounts for which Notes may be issued. In England and Wales notes are issued for sums of £1, £5, £10 and £20. Scottish and Irish notes are issued for sums of £1 upwards.

Legal tender. Bronze (copper) coins with values up to and including 2p are legal tender up to 20p.

Cupro-nickel (silver) coins with values up to and including 10p are legal tender up to £5. The 50p coin is legal tender up to £10.

Good tender must be the exact or a higher amount, provided change is not demanded.

Bank Notes Negotiable Instruments. Bank of England notes are legal tender for all amounts. As they are negotiable instruments the holder of a bank note, provided he has taken it bona fide and for value, can retain it against everybody, even the lawful owner. The bank may have "stopped payment" of certain stolen notes, but is nevertheless liable to a bona fide holder for value. For greater safety, when being sent by post, bank notes can be cut in halves, one half being forwarded by one post, and the other by a later one. The halves must be pasted together before being presented for payment, but the mutilation does not affect their negotiability.

BANK DRAFTS

Bank drafts are bills of exchange drawn by one banker on another. As any person can buy from a banker a draft payable in any part of the United Kingdom, or in any country abroad, they form a convenient means of remitting money. They possess a certain security against fraud, inasmuch as the other bank is notified of the amount of the draft. On inland drafts a small commission is charged, but with foreign drafts this will be covered by the rate of exchange at which they are purchased.

PAYING MONEY THROUGH BANK GIRO

The bank giro system has great advantages when making numerous payments at any one time. Instead of posting individual cheques to payees,

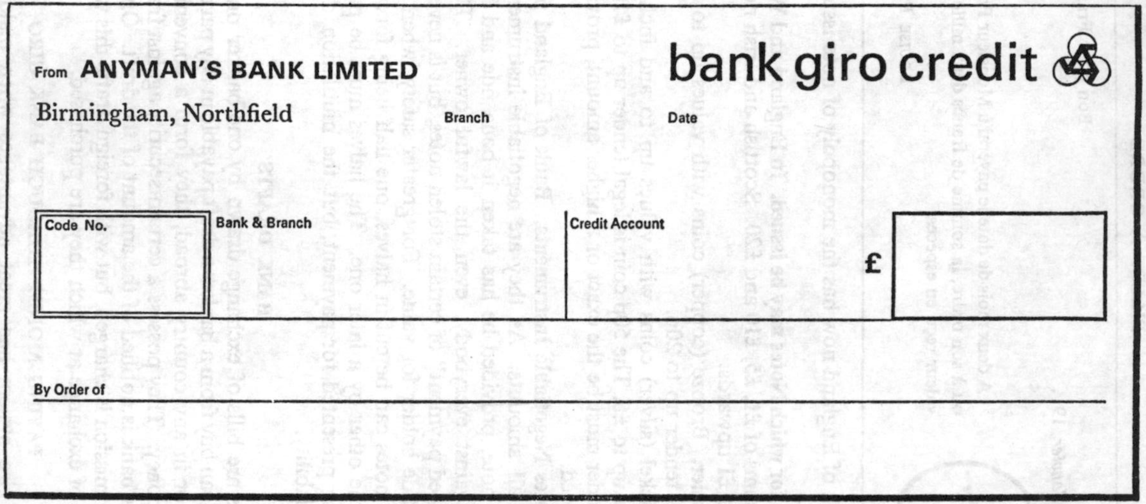
From ANYMAN'S BANK LIMITED

Birmingham, Northfield

Branch

Date

bank giro credit

Code No.

Bank & Branch

Credit Account

£

By Order of

FIG. 04.1

one cheque is sent to the Bank to cover all the payments. This saves time, stationery costs, bank handling charges, and accounting and administrative costs.

1. **How to Make Payments.** A bank giro credit form is completed for each payment, giving the payer's name, the sum due, and the payee's name and bank or the payee's bank branch sorting code number. (Standard forms are supplied free by banks, or special versions subject to certain requirements on layout, size, etc.)

2. Where more than six payments are made together, commercial users are asked to list them on a schedule (also provided free by the banks).

3. A cheque for the total amount is drawn by the payer. Alternatively, a suitable authority to cover payment may be incorporated in the schedule.

4. Forms, schedule and cheque are taken or posted to the payer's bank branch.

5. The bank distributes the credits through the system. Normally these are credited to payees' accounts on the second working day after being paid in, or on the third working day if paid in on a Friday or Saturday. Direct credits to the payees' bank branches may be made for a fee.

No handling charge is made for transfers through the system between any two bank accounts and no charge is made for stationery.

A bank giro credit form, designed for computer use, can be seen in Fig. 04.1.

RECEIVING MONEY THROUGH BANK GIRO

Simple Handling. Bank giro offers the advantages to the payee that instead of handling a variety of cheques, postal orders, money orders and cash, payments come direct to the bank and the payee receives the relevant credit form for each item received.

Payment Advice. Advice of credits received can be sent as they enter the account each day, or weekly, or at any specified interval. A special reference number on the credits may be used to identify the payments.

Encouraging Payment. Experience has shown that the easier it is for customers to pay by bank giro, the more readily will they do so. A detachable bank giro credit may be sent as part of a regular invoice. By pre-printing as many details as possible the customer is encouraged to make an early settlement of his account. This method has the advantages that—

(*a*) Customers do not pay any handling charges to their banks.

(*b*) People without a bank account may make payment in cash through any branch of any bank. The service is free unless the account into which payment is made is held in a different bank, when officially a charge of 2p per entry may be made.

Collection from Agents. If agents are employed to collect cash it is convenient to provide them with bank giro credits. They then pay the

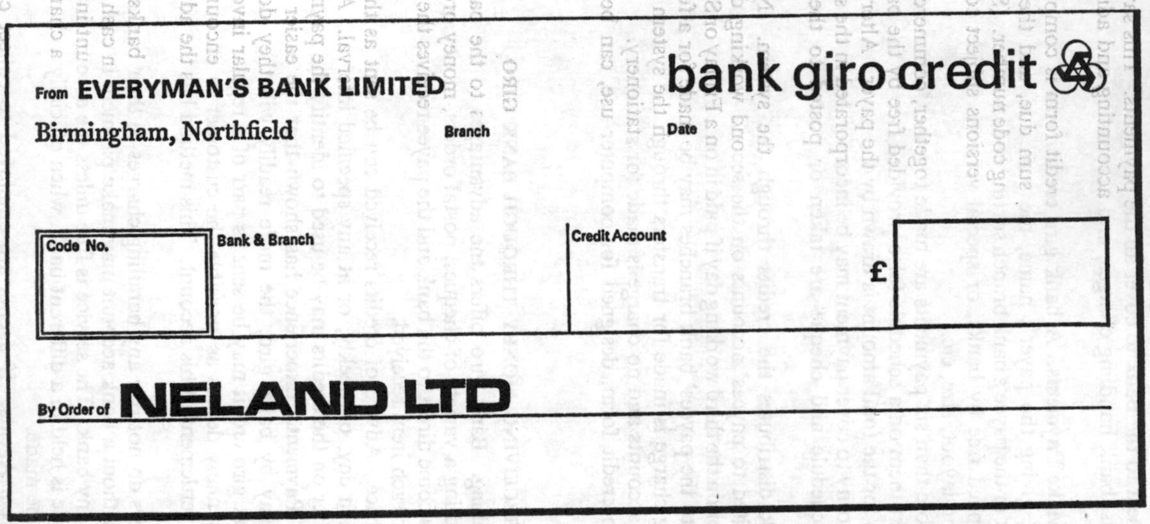
bank giro credit

From EVERYMAN'S BANK LIMITED

Birmingham, Northfield

Branch

Date

Code No.

Bank & Branch

Credit Account

£

By Order of NELAND LTD

FIG. 04.2. A Bank Giro Credit for Neland Ltd., designed to be used on computer or typewriter

cash direct into the company's account. No charge is made for this service.

Individual Design. So long as certain basic requirements of size and layout are followed, the design of the form can be varied at will, as seen in Figs. 04.2 and 04.3—

(a) The front may be used to show discounts, etc.

(b) The back may be used for special messages, account references or orders from, say, a home shopper to a mail order house.

The Standing Order. The banker's order or standing order is used to ensure that subscriptions, mortgage or rent payments, insurance premiums and hire-purchase instalments are paid punctually as they fall due. A stamped authorization is given to the bank to make payments of a fixed amount at a stipulated time. Payments under standing orders of this kind are initiated by the payer, and are generally best suited to regular payments of uniform amounts.

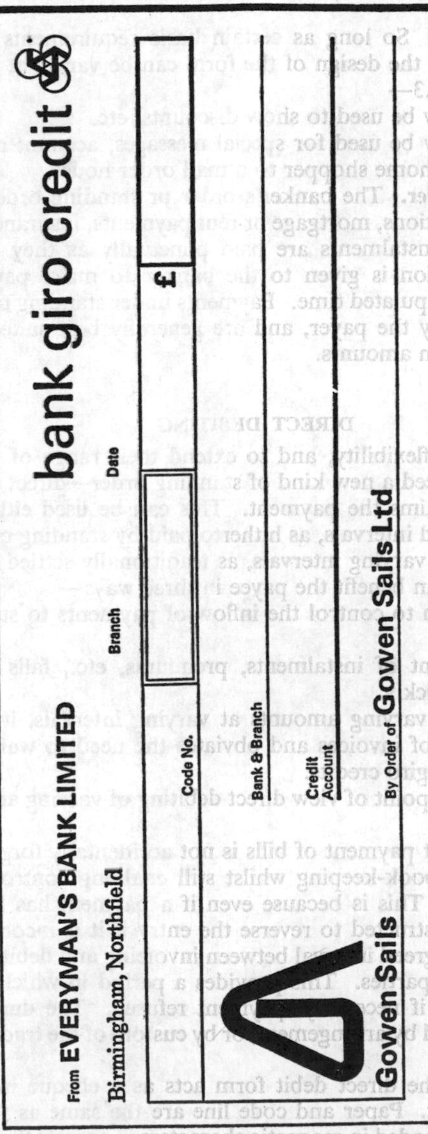

FIG. 04.3. A Bank Giro Credit for Gowen Sails Ltd., designed for address-plate use

DIRECT DEBITING

To achieve greater flexibility, and to extend their range of services, the banks have introduced a new kind of standing order—direct debiting—in which the payee claims the payment. This can be used either for fixed amounts due at fixed intervals, as hitherto paid by standing order, or for varying amounts at varying intervals, as traditionally settled by cheque.

Direct debiting can benefit the payee in three ways—

(a) It enables him to control the inflow of payments to suit his book-keeping procedures.

(b) If the payment of instalments, premiums, etc., falls into arrear, this is shown up quickly.

(c) If applied to varying amounts at varying intervals, it ensures the prompter payment of invoices and obviates the need to wait for receipt of cheques or bank giro credits.

From the payer's point of view direct debiting of varying amounts gives two benefits—

(a) It ensures that payment of bills is not accidentally forgotten.

(b) It simplifies book-keeping whilst still enabling control to be kept over the accounts. This is because even if a payment has been debited the Bank can be instructed to reverse the entry if it is incorrect. Again, there might be an agreed interval between invoicing and debiting mutually acceptable to both parties. This provides a period in which queries can be dealt with and, if necessary, payment refused. The duration of the interval may be fixed by arrangement or by custom of the trade, or notified on the invoice.

Specifications. The direct debit form acts as a cheque in that it is a debit to an account. Paper and code line are the same as for a cheque. Direct debits are encoded in magnetic characters in exactly the same way as

cash direct into the company's account. No charge is made for this service.

Individual Design. So long as certain basic requirements of size and layout are followed, the design of the form can be varied at will, as seen in Figs. 04.2 and 04.3—

(*a*) The front may be used to show discounts, etc.

(*b*) The back may be used for special messages, account references or orders from, say, a home shopper to a mail order house.

The Standing Order. The banker's order or standing order is used to ensure that subscriptions, mortgage or rent payments, insurance premiums and hire-purchase instalments are paid punctually as they fall due. A stamped authorization is given to the banker to make payments of a fixed amount at a stipulated time. Payments under standing orders of this kind are initiated by the payer, and are generally best suited to regular payments of uniform amounts.

DIRECT DEBITING

To achieve greater flexibility, and to extend their range of services, the banks have introduced a new kind of standing order—direct debiting—in which the payee claims the payment. This can be used either for fixed amounts due at fixed intervals, as hitherto paid by standing order; or for varying amounts at varying intervals, as traditionally settled by cheque.

Direct debiting can benefit the payee in three ways—

(*a*) It enables him to control the inflow of payments to suit his book-keeping procedures.

(*b*) If the payment of instalments, premiums, etc., falls into arrear, this is shown up quickly.

(*c*) If applied to varying amounts at varying intervals, it ensures the prompter payment of invoices and obviates the need to wait for receipt of cheques or bank giro credits.

From the payer's point of view direct debiting of varying amounts gives two benefits—

(*a*) It ensures that payment of bills is not accidentally forgotten.

(*b*) It simplifies book-keeping whilst still enabling control to be kept over the accounts. This is because even if a payment has been debited the Bank can be instructed to reverse the entry if it is incorrect. Again, there might be an agreed interval between invoicing and debiting mutually acceptable to both parties. This provides a period in which queries can be dealt with and, if necessary, payment refused. The duration of the interval may be fixed by arrangement, or by custom of the trade, or notified on the invoice.

Specifications. The direct debit form acts as a cheque in that it is a debit to an account. Paper and code line are the same as for a cheque. Direct debits are encoded in magnetic characters in exactly the same way as cheques. The basic codings are pre-printed in bulk by—or on behalf of—the payee. A further code, for the amount payable, is added when the direct debit is paid into the bank by the payee, or by the payee's own encoding equipment.

Forwarding and Crediting. When presenting direct debits, first sort them into bank order and then send them to the Head Office or main London office of each of the banks to be debited. The debits are normally forwarded to bank branches on the first working day after being lodged, and charged to individual accounts on the following day (excluding weekends). The payee is also credited on this day. Alternatively, if numbers are small, they can be paid into your own bank branch, and cleared exactly as ordinary cheques.

A Direct Debit form can be seen in Fig. 04.4.

IOU

An IOU is a written memorandum or acknowledgement of indebtedness. The letters IOU are a contraction for the phase "I owe you," the sounds of both being identical. The following is an example—

		LONDON, 10*th January*, 19..
To Mr. Alfred Brown,	IOU £30	
		WILLIAM THORNYCROFT.

Points to be Noted. An IOU is neither a receipt nor an agreement. It should not contain any promise or date of repayment, otherwise it becomes a promissory note. It is not a negotiable instrument. In a court of law it is accepted as evidence only of an account stated between the parties mentioned, but not of the amount named. The amount is sometimes written in words as well as in figures.

QUESTIONS

1. What is the statutory definition of a promissory note? For what purpose are such notes used, and in what respects do they: (*a*) resemble, (*b*) differ from, bills of exchange?
2. Is stamp duty required on promissory notes? How many parties are there to a note, and who are they?
3. How many kinds of notes are there? Give an example of each.
4. What is: (*a*) a joint promissory note, and (*b*) a joint and several promissory note? Give an example of each. Why are the latter preferable?
5. When is a note payable on demand? Must a note be presented for payment? Can a valid note contain any reference to a collateral security?
6. What is the legal liability of the maker of a note? How far does the Bills of Exchange Act apply to promissory notes? To whom do the drawer and acceptor of a note correspond in a bill of exchange?

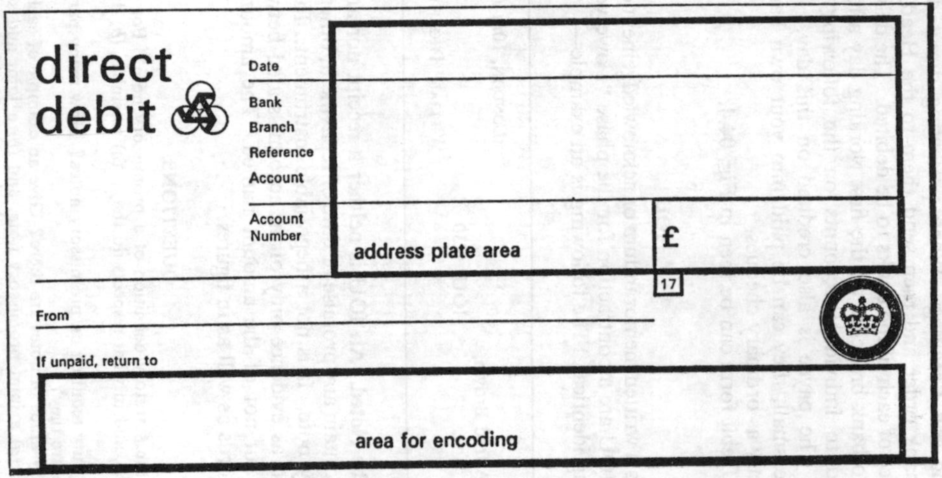
direct debit

Date

Bank

Branch

Reference

Account

Account Number

address plate area

£

17

From

If unpaid, return to

area for encoding

FIG. 04.4

7. What are bank notes? For what amounts may they be issued, and by whom? Suppose a bank note be stolen, and is afterwards traced to a bona fide holder for value, what is his position?

8. What are bank drafts, and for what purpose are they used?

9. What is an IOU? Give an example. Is it legal evidence of debt?

CHEQUES

By the Bills of Exchange Act, 1882, a cheque is "a bill of exchange drawn on a banker payable on demand," and, with a few exceptions, the provisions of the Act applicable to bills of exchange payable on demand apply also to cheques.

The following is a specimen of a cheque—

No. 365,907 **6 *Jan.*, 19..**	**No. 365,907. LONDON, 50–30–17** ***6th January*, 19..**
Retrop & Co.	**THE ENGLISH BANK LIMITED** **LONDON, E.C.**
a/c	**Pay to *Messrs. Retrop & Co.* or Order** **the sum of *seventy-six pounds.***
rendered.	**£76**
£76	**503017 1897243 ARTHUR J. BROWNLEY.**

Great care should be exercised in the drawing of cheques. The banker is liable to the drawer for any loss resulting from his paying a cheque with a forged signature or one fraudulently altered, but the *drawer* is liable for contributory negligence. This means that if he makes the fraudulent alteration easier by his own carelessness the drawer, and not the banker, will have to suffer the loss of the additional amount which has been paid out on the cheque.

The form is perforated ready for division into two parts. The smaller portion, called the *counterfoil*, is retained in the cheque book for reference. The larger portion, called the *cheque*, is forwarded to the payee mentioned thereon. In the case of large firms and of limited companies, the names of such firms or companies are often printed at the top of their cheques, and in fact the whole of the cheque is specially printed as required by the firm.

Bearer Cheques. A bearer cheque is one payable to bearer, i.e. that can be cashed or negotiated without previous endorsement.

Order Cheques. An order cheque is one payable to a certain person's order. It must be endorsed before it can be cashed or transferred. The endorsement by the payee turns an order cheque into a bearer cheque unless the payee endorses it payable to the order of someone else.

Open Cheques. An open cheque is one that has not been crossed, i.e. one that can be cashed over the counter.

Stale Cheques. A stale cheque is one that has been drawn for some time previous to presentation for payment, i.e. one that is some months old.

Alterations on a Cheque. All material alterations must be initialled by the drawer. Owing to forgeries in this respect, some bankers require full signatures instead of mere initials. Only the drawer may alter a cheque from order to bearer, but either the holder or drawer may alter a bearer cheque to an order cheque. The latter alteration does not require initialing. Where the amount expressed in words does not agree with the amount expressed in figures, the banker is bound *by the words*. Many bankers, however, return such cheques for correction.

Post-dated Cheques. These are cheques that bear a date later than the current date on which they are drawn. They cannot, however, be cashed before the proper date. If they are paid in to a bank for collection the banker will return them, unless instructed to keep them and treat them as short bills. If a banker inadvertently pays a post-dated cheque, he must not debit his customer's account with the amount immediately, but must wait until the date entered on the cheque. By the Act a cheque "is not invalid by reason only that it is post-dated." In book-keeping, post-dated cheques are entered "short" (i.e. the amounts not extended into the money columns) in the cash book, in order to prevent their being lost sight of; on the proper date they can then be entered in the accounts in the usual way.

Fictitious or Non-existing Payee. Where a cheque is payable to a fictitious or non-existing payee, such as a cheque drawn payable to *Wages*, *Petty Cash*, or *Order*, it may, by Sect. 7 of the Bills of Exchange Act, 1882, be treated as a cheque payable to bearer.

Crossed Cheques. The provisions of the Bills of Exchange Act with reference to the crossing of cheques are found in Sects. 76 to 78, and are as follows—

By Sect. 76—

1. Where a cheque bears across its face an addition of—

(*a*) The words "and company" or any abbreviation thereof between two parallel transverse lines, either with or without the words "not negotiable"; or

(*b*) Two parallel transverse lines simply, either with or without the words "not negotiable"; that addition constitutes a crossing, and the cheque is crossed generally.

2. Where a cheque bears across its face an addition of the name of a banker, either with or without the words "not negotiable," that addition constitutes a crossing, and the cheque is crossed specially and to that banker.

By Sect. 77—

1. A cheque may be crossed generally or specially by the drawer.
2. Where a cheque is uncrossed, the holder may cross it generally or specially.
3. Where a cheque is crossed generally, the holder may cross it specially.

4. Where a cheque is crossed generally or specially, the holder may add the words "not negotiable."

5. Where a cheque is crossed specially, the banker to whom it is crossed may again cross it specially to another banker for collection.

6. Where an uncrossed cheque, or a cheque crossed generally, is sent to a banker for collection, he may cross it specially to himself.

Sect. 78 enacts—

A crossing authorized by this Act is a material part of the cheque; it shall not be lawful for any person to obliterate or, except as authorized by this Act, to add to or alter the crossing.

The above provisions apply also to dividend warrants (Sect. 95).

By the Finance Act, 1883, Sect. 17, the provisions of the Bills of Exchange Act as to crossed cheques are also extended to

. . . any document issued by a customer of any banker, and intended to enable any person to obtain payment from such banker of the sum mentioned in such document.

Thus money orders, postal orders, demand drafts, etc., are generally crossed when sent by post or paid into a bank for collection. Such documents, however, are not rendered "negotiable."

It should be noted that the words "and Co.," or "not negotiable," do not alone form a crossing, but are merely additions to a crossing; whereas two parallel transverse lines on a cheque do, in themselves, constitute a crossing.

Specimens of Crossings. On p. 0442 are examples of some of the commonest crossings.

Cancellation of Crossing. Although contrary to the provisions of the Act, the crossing of a cheque can be, and often is, cancelled by the drawer writing in the crossing the words "*pay cash.*" Payees who have no banking accounts frequently ask for this to be done. Cheques to impersonal payees, such as Salaries and Wages, Petty Cash, etc., are sometimes crossed by mistake, and have consequently to be reopened. Such opening of a crossing needs to be authenticated by the full signature of the drawer.

Object of Crossing a Cheque. The object of crossing a cheque is to prevent its being cashed over the counter by anyone who might accidentally or fraudulently obtain possession of it. A crossed cheque will not be paid to anyone except a banker; and if the banker's name is added in the crossing, then payment will be made only to that particular banker. The practice of crossing originated as a Clearing House custom, and was eventually recognized by law.

Not Negotiable. A cheque being a negotiable instrument, any bona fide holder can retain it, even though the cheque has been lost or stolen. To protect the owner against damage by loss or theft, the words "not negotiable" may be written on the cheque by the drawer or by any holder. The addition of these words does not, therefore, *prevent* the further transfer

GENERAL CROSSINGS

1. (two parallel lines)
2. & Co.
3. Not Negotiable
4. Not Negotiable & Co.
5. Under Ten Pounds & Co.
6. & Co. A/c Payee Only
7. Not Negotiable & Co. Under Twenty Pounds
8. Not Negotiable & Co. A/c Payee Only

SPECIAL CROSSINGS

9. Lloyds Bank Ltd. Not Negotiable
10. Lloyds Bank Ltd. A/c Westminster Hospital
11. Not Negotiable Lloyds Bank Ltd. Under Twenty Pounds
12. Not Negotiable Lloyds Bank Ltd. A/c Payee Only

of the cheque, but is a warning to any person taking it that he may not get a good title.

If the cheque has been found or stolen and passed on to another person, the holder's title is defective, even if he has given value for it; he can legally be made to restore the cheque to its rightful owner.

It should be noted that the phrase "not negotiable" applies, legally, only to crossed cheques. Other documents could, of course, be marked "not negotiable," but it would have no legal effect.

Account Payee Only. Bankers have been in the habit of ignoring this crossing, because it was not found, or provided for, in the Bills of Exchange Act. But custom seems likely to prevail, and, as with other cases of the *lex mercatoria*, eventually to graft itself upon the law. The object of it is still further to protect the drawer against damage should the cheque be lost or stolen. It constitutes a distinct notice to a receiving banker that the drawer desires the cheque to be placed to the credit of a certain account. And if a banker disregards this direction, he renders himself liable to an action for "negligence."

Endorsement of Cheques. Endorsing is the signing of the payee's name on the back (Latin *dorsum* = back) of the cheque, though apparently it is quite legal if the payee signs his name on the front of the cheque. Bearer cheques do not require endorsing, though endorsements are sometimes obtained, in order to make the transferor a party to the cheque. The Cheques Act, 1957, did away with the need to endorse order cheques paid into a bank account by the payee. If a payee negotiates a cheque, however, endorsement will be required.

Revocation of Banker's Authority to Pay. The duty and authority of a banker to pay cheques drawn on him by his customer are determined by—

(*a*) Countermand of payment.
(*b*) Notice of the customer's death.
(*c*) Notice of his insanity, legally declared.
(*d*) Notice of an act of bankruptcy on the part of the customer.
(*e*) Receipt of a garnishee order.

Want of funds, or any irregularity in the drawing or endorsing of the cheque, will also cause a banker to stop payment (see later under "Dishonoured cheques").

Cheque not Legal Tender. A cheque, it should be noted, is not legal tender. The only paper money that is legal tender in England and Wales is the Bank of England Note.

Property in Cheques. A paid cheque is, legally, the property of the drawer. Some banks return the paid cheques at periodical intervals; others do not.

Forgery. A forged cheque is one on which the name of the payee or the amount of the cheque has been falsified, or on which the signature of the drawer is not genuine. A banker is liable for any loss caused by his paying a cheque on which the signature of the drawer has been forged; but he is not liable for any loss caused by his paying a cheque bearing a forged endorsement.

Evidence of Receipt. Sect. 3 of the Cheques Act, 1957, provides that a cheque which appears to have been paid by the banker on whom it is drawn is evidence of receipt by the payee. Endorsement is unnecessary.

Cheques sent through the Post. If the drawer makes the post office his agent he must bear any loss arising from the miscarriage of the cheque. If, however, the payee has requested a cheque to be sent by post, the Post Office becomes the agent of the payee, who is, therefore, liable for any loss.

Cheque Stamp and Cheque Books. A piece of ordinary writing paper ordering a banker to pay money, is legally a "cheque."

The usual practice of bankers is to supply their customers with books of specially printed and numbered cheque forms. The object of this is the prevention of forgery. Bankers make no charge for the book of forms. Fresh cheque books are obtained by the customer filling up and presenting the bank's printed application forms.

Dishonoured Cheques. A dishonoured cheque is one which a banker, for some reason or other, has refused to pay on presentation. Such cheques generally have some explanatory phrase written on them, as follows—

No assets, N/A.
No effects, N/E.
Refer to drawer, R/D.
Not sufficient (funds), N/S.
Insufficient funds, I/F.
Endorsement irregular.
Words and figures differ.
Drawer's signature differs (i.e. from that in Bank's signature book).
Alterations require drawer's signature.
Drawer deceased.
Receipt (i.e. on cheque) requires stamp.
Account closed.
Cheque mutilated.
Effects not cleared. Present again.
Post-dated.
Payment stopped, or Orders not to pay.

Dishonoured cheques may, of course, be noted, and those bearing foreign endorsements may be protested.

Lost Cheque. Where a cheque has been lost, the holder can compel the drawer to give him a new cheque, but must give security to the drawer, if required, to indemnify him in case the lost cheque should be found and negotiated. The cheque should be marked "Duplicate," and the paying banker instructed to pay it.

In 1967, approximately 3,500,000 cheques were paid into United Kingdom banks every day. Despite the giro arrangements which eliminate many cheques in commercial transactions, their use in personal transactions continues to increase.

Points of Difference between Cheques and Bills. Although a cheque is *legally* a bill of exchange, the following differences exist—

1. A bill requires acceptance. A cheque is never accepted by a banker. The acceptor of a bill is liable to the holder for refusing payment of it.

2. The drawer of a bill is discharged from liability by delay in presenting it for payment; the drawer of a cheque is not.

3. Notice of dishonour is necessary in the case of a bill not being met, but not in the case of a cheque.

There is a contingent liability when a bill has been discounted before the close of the books for the year but the maturity date falls in the next financial period.

Example 5

A receives a three months' bill from B for £100 dated 1st October at three months after date and therefore due for payment on 4th January. On 1st November he discounts this bill with his banker, the discount charge being £1.

LEDGER

B

19..			£	19..			£
		Goods	100	Oct	1	Bill Receivable No... . . .	100

BILLS RECEIVABLE

19..			£	19..			£
Oct	1	Bill Book . . .	100	Nov	1	Bank, Bill Receivable No.. discounted . .	100

BANKERS' DISCOUNT

19..			£				
Nov	1	Bank	1				

CASH BOOK

19..		£	19..		£
Nov 1	Proceeds of Bill Receivable No. .. discounted . .	100	Nov 1	Discount charge on Bill Receivable . .	1

It will be seen from this example that on the receipt of the bill by A the debt was converted in the books from a personal debt owing by B (and appearing as one of the sundry debtors) to an impersonal debt in the form of a bill of exchange, and in so far as A still held it he had no liability on it. On the discounting of it on 1st November two things happened. The bill disappeared from the books as such and its identity was lost in the balance at the bank. At the same time, by negotiating it to his banker A made himself liable to repay the £100 to the bank in January in the event of B's failing to pay at maturity. This liability on the part of A therefore exists at 31st December, but does not show in the books and cannot appear among the assets and liabilities on the balance sheet. The only way in this case is to show the item as a footnote as follows—

BALANCE SHEET

Liabilities	£	*Assets*	£

Contingent Liability for bill under discount £100

In order to arrive at this figure it is necessary to obtain a list of all bills discounted before the date of the account but maturing afterwards.

The significant differences between these methods of payment is in the direction in which money instruments flow and the way in which payment is authorized.

In practice, this can make a considerable difference to the paper work required and, therefore to the cost of payment. Each system will also involve a differential delay in effecting settlement which will give rise to considerable differences in costs.

To clarify the relationships, the charts shown in Fig. 04.5 have been constructed.

Computer Based Direct Debit Service. Organizations such as insurance companies, building societies and hire purchase companies whose income

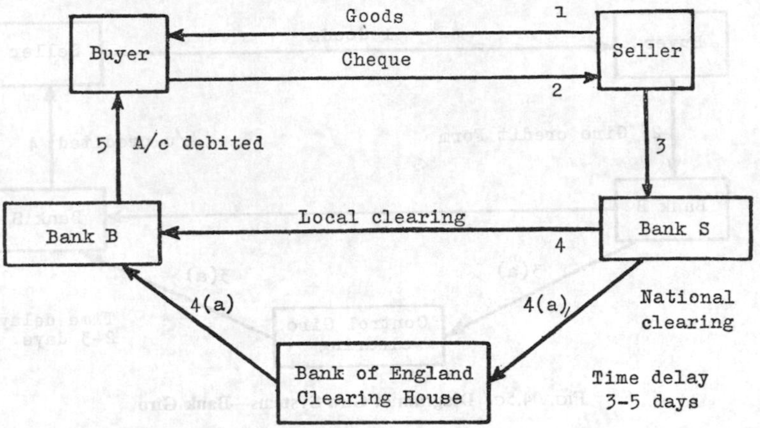

FIG. 04.5A. Diagram of Giro Systems—Cheque System

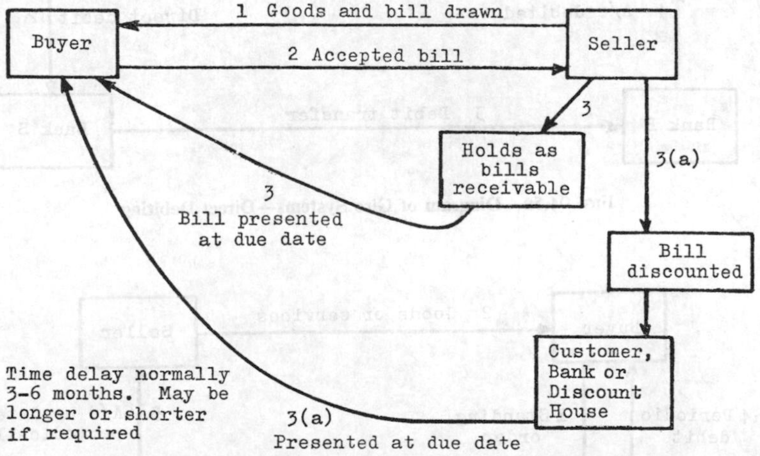

FIG. 04.5B. Diagram of Giro Systems—Bills of Exchange

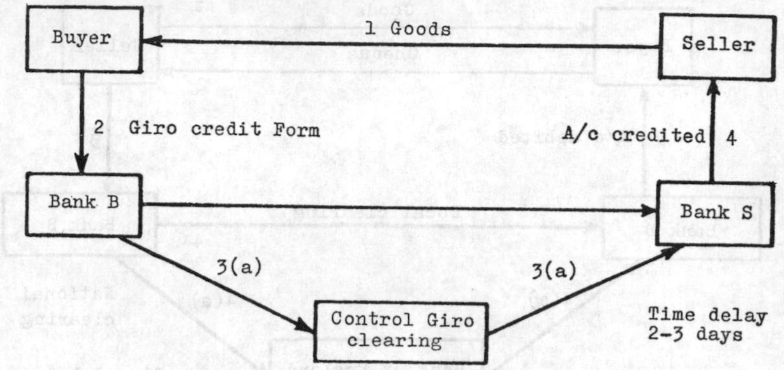

FIG. 04.5C. **Diagram of Giro Systems—Bank Giro**

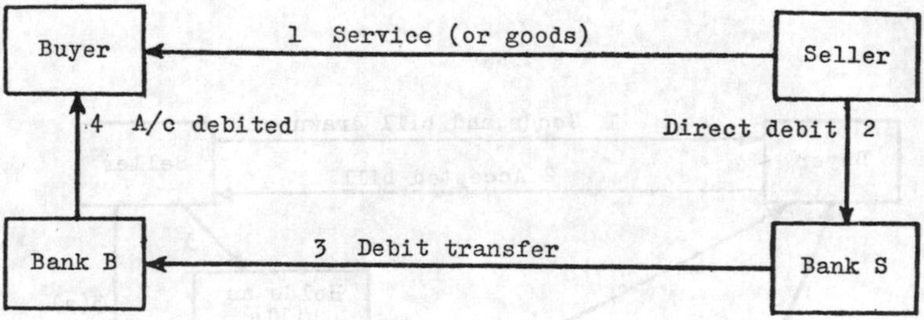

FIG. 04.5D. **Diagram of Giro Systems—Direct Debiting**

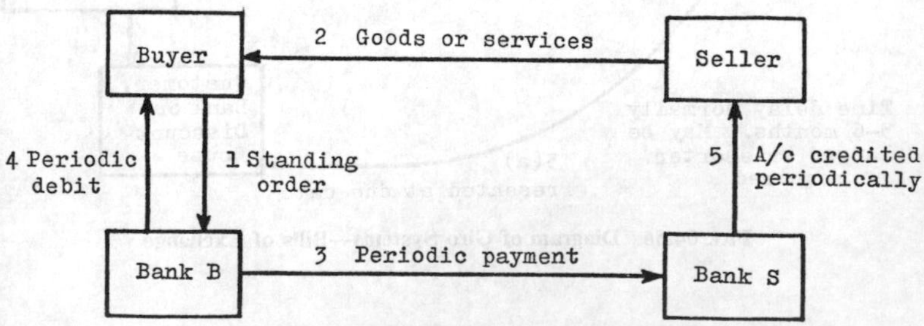

FIG. 04.5E. **Diagram of Giro Systems—Standing Order**

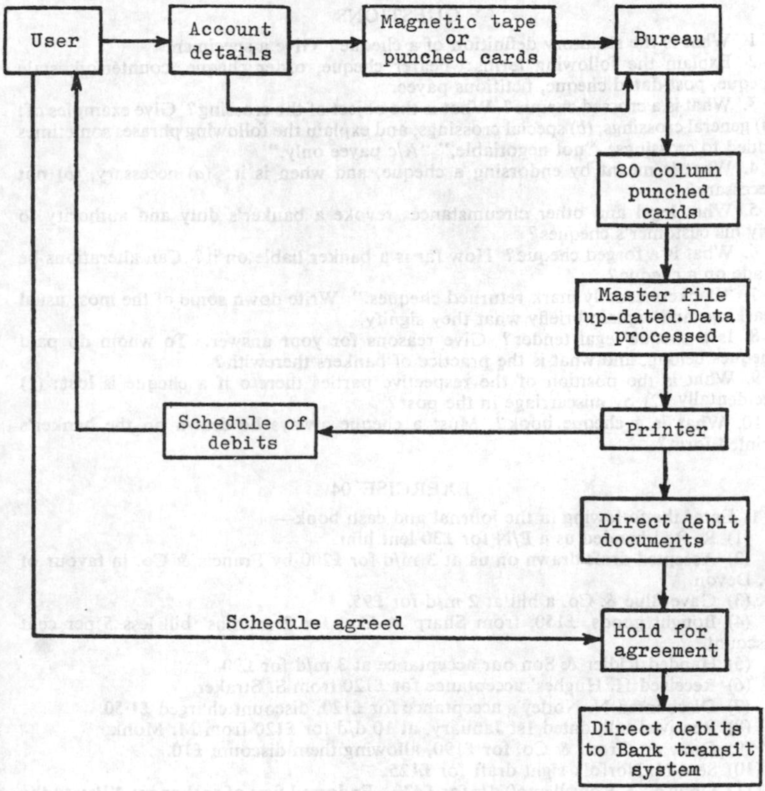

FIG. 04.6. **Diagram of Direct Debit Service**

consists largely of regular monthly, quarterly and annual payments will make considerable use of the direct debit system.

In 1967, one of the large computer firms offered a bureau service for direct debits based on their own 80 column punched card equipment.

The user may supply details of accounts direct to the bureau or may send the data on magnetic tape or punched cards. The Bureau will, if necessary, convert the data to 80 column cards and then produce direct debits for each customer. A schedule of these is sent to the user for agreement before the direct debit documents are forwarded to the Banks.

Use of the bureau service will usually be cheaper than a manual system and may also be cheaper for firms with automatic data processing equipment which is incompatible with the bank system.

This system is shown in Fig. 04.6.

QUESTIONS

1. What is the statutory definition of a cheque? Give a specimen.

2. Explain the following terms: bearer cheque, order cheque, counterfoil, stale cheque, post-dated cheque, fictitious payee.

3. What is a crossed cheque? What is the object of the crossing? Give examples of: (*a*) general crossings, (*b*) special crossings, and explain the following phrases sometimes added to crossings: "not negotiable," "A/c payee only."

4. What is meant by endorsing a cheque, and when is it: (*a*) necessary, (*b*) not necessary?

5. What legal and other circumstances revoke a banker's duty and authority to pay his customer's cheques?

6. What is a forged cheque? How far is a banker liable on it? Can alterations be made on a cheque?

7. "Bankers usually mark returned cheques." Write down some of the most usual markings and explain briefly what they signify.

8. Is a cheque legal tender? Give reasons for your answer. To whom do paid cheques belong, and what is the practice of bankers therewith?

9. What is the position of the respective parties thereto if a cheque is lost: (1) accidentally (2) by miscarriage in the post?

10. What is a cheque book? Must a cheque always be drawn on the banker's printed form?

EXERCISE 04

1, Enter the following in the journal and cash book—

(1) R. Red handed us a P/N for £30 lent him.

(2) Accepted draft drawn on us at 3 m/d for £200 by Francis & Co. in favour of D. Devon.

(3) Gave Blue & Co. a bill at 2 m/d for £95.

(4) Bought goods, £150, from Sharp & Co., for 2 months' bill less 5 per cent discount.

(5) Handed Ridler & Son our acceptance at 3 m/d for £90.

(6) Received H. Hughes' acceptance for £120 from S. Straker.

(7) Discounted N. Notley's acceptance for £120, discount charged £1·50.

(8) Received bill, dated 1st January, at 10 d/d for £120 from M. Monk.

(9) Drew on Green & Co. for £190, allowing them discount £10.

(10) Sent N. Norfolk sight draft for £125.

(11) Drew on J. Rowell at 60 d/s for £420. Endorsed first of exchange: "Pay to the order of M. Goodman," and forwarded it to the latter.

(12) Henry & Co.'s P/N for £40 duly taken up.

(13) Sold goods, £120, to B. Blunt, for 2 months' bill, less $2\frac{1}{2}$ per cent discount.

(14) Sold goods for £150 to York & Son, and received in payment our own acceptance to Bull & Son for £150 due today.

(15) Our P/N to M. Martin for £120 redeemed today.

(16) Discounted G. Graham's acceptance for £150, due 3 months hence, with Sheffield, Sons & Co., bill brokers, discount rate $3\frac{3}{4}$ per cent.

(17) Sent Perrier Frères, Paris, 7 days' draft for £100.

(18) Accepted Dark & Co.'s draft for £285, being allowed discount £15.

(19) Provide solutions to the following—

(*a*) Sketch the form of a bill of exchange, inserting all details therein that will show it to be a negotiable instrument. Further, prepare the necessary accounts in support of the transactions from the viewpoints of the several parties thereto.

(*b*) A bill drawn on B for £100 was endorsed over to K, who subsequently presented it to B for payment, but was unsuccessful. K thereupon noted the bill. Prepare the accounts required by the above transactions, as they affect: (i) the drawer, and (ii) K.

(*c*) B draws on F for £100. On maturity the bill is dishonoured. Show the book-keeping records on dishonour in B's books which would apply under three different circumstances.

2. Record the following in journal and cash book—

(1) Blue & Black's acceptance for £200 renewed for 3 months, plus interest at 5 per cent.

(2) G. Gulliver's acceptance for £450, due this day, returned dishonoured. Noting charges 25p.

(3) Wilson & Jones retire their acceptance for £420 by cheque £120, and a new bill at 1 m/d for the balance plus interest at 5 per cent.

(4) L. Lambe's acceptance for £460, due this day, notified by our creditors (Charles & Son) as being dishonoured, noting charges paid by them 28p. Withdrew same in exchange for our cheque.

(5) Retired our acceptance to Brockwell & Haigh for £630 by cheque £230, and a new bill at 2 m/d with interest at 4 per cent for the balance.

(6) Our acceptance to Locke & Co. for £300 renewed for 4 months, plus interest at 3½ per cent.

(7) Our own acceptance to Dawson Bros. for £345 dishonoured (through omitting to instruct bankers to pay). Dawson Bros. send us debit not for £345·54, including noting expenses. We settle this by cheque.

(8) Needham & Co.'s acceptance for £425, due this day, returned by bank dishonoured, with noting charges 20p, and expenses 18p.

(9) Frame & Son's acceptance for £1,055 due this day, returned by bank dishonoured, with noting expenses £1·20. Renewed same for 5 months with interest at 6 per cent, noting expenses, and interest.

3. Write up in the books of both parties the ledger accounts (including cash) for the following transactions in bills—

(*a*) On 1st January, S. Silverman accepts a 3 months' bill for £125, drawn on him by G. Goldstein for the latter's benefit. Goldstein discounts the bill at the rate of 3½ per cent, and at maturity forwards Silverman a cheque with which to meet the bill.

(*b*) On 1st March, P. Paterson and I. Ingram draw on one another at 3 months for £135 for their mutual convenience. They discount each others' bills at the rate of 4 per cent, and, at maturity, each meets his own acceptance.

(*c*) On 1st February, H. Hooker accepts a three months' bill for £115 drawn on him by E. Evans for their mutual accommodation. The bill is then discounted by Evans at the rate of 3¾ per cent, and half the proceeds handed to Hooker. At maturity Evans sends a cheque to Hooker, who then pays the bill.

4. Darlow & Walsh are the acceptors of a bill of four months date for £659·75, due on the 24th January. A few days before it matured, Darlow & Walsh found they could not meet it and wrote to the drawers, Earle & Creasey, requesting them to renew the bill for three months, adding interest at 5 per cent per annum. The drawers (Earle & Creasey) expressed their willingness to do so conditionally upon Darlow & Walsh lodging security with them for the amount of the renewed bill. Darlow & Walsh offered as security five customer's bills, viz.—

(1) H. G. Bourner & Co.'s bill £209·58, due 14th February.
(2) Neville & Co.'s bill £173·24, due 26th February.
(3) James Hordarn & Co.'s bill £89·75, due 25th March.
(4) George Blakey & Co.'s bill £82·80, due 19th April.
(5) Smith, Wilks & Co.'s bill £112·65, due 26th April.

Each of the above five bills was discounted by Earle & Creasey's bankers, and Darlow & Walsh's renewed bill was paid into the bank one month after its acceptance. Bills 1, 2, and 4 were duly honoured. Bill 3 was dishonoured and returned to Earle & Creasey, who drew a cheque for its amount, plus 50p noting expenses. Darlow & Walsh, on being called upon, made good this amount ten days later.

Bill 5 reached maturity the same day as Darlow & Walsh's renewed bill, and both were dishonoured.

(*a*) Draw the renewed bill, adding £1·50 for expenses, also 5 per cent interest for the term of the bill's currency.

(*b*) Show Earle & Creasey's journal entries.

(*c*) Show Darlow & Walsh's account as it appears in Earle & Creasey's ledger.

(*West Riding of Yorkshire.*)

5. (*a*) A bill for £105 is drawn at 6 months from the 1st October, by Smith on Rhodes, and accepted by the latter payable at X Bank. When does this bill become due for payment?

(*b*) On the 11th December, Smith discounts the bill with Hurst, and receives £100 cash.

(*c*) The bill is dishonoured on maturity, but is taken up by Smith on the 4th April.

Show by means of the Journal the necessary entries to record the above transactions (*a*), (*b*), and (*c*)—in Smith's books.

6. Jones, for the mutual and temporary accommodation of himself and Brown, draws upon the latter a bill of exchange at 3 months for £600, dated 1st January. Jones discounts this bill immediately at his bankers, the rate of discount being 5 per cent, and hands half the proceeds to Brown.

Brown, for a similar purpose, and at the same time, draws a bill at 3 months on Jones for £300. This he discounts at his bankers at 5 per cent, and hands half the proceeds to Jones. Brown becomes a bankrupt on 31st March, and a first and final dividend of £0·25 in the £ is paid on his estate on 30th June.

Write up Brown's account in Jones' book. Assume, in each case, that one half of the charge for discounting the bill is chargeable to Brown and one half to Jones.

(*London Chamber of Commerce.*)

7. You are preparing the balance sheet of a limited company of which you are the chief accountant, and find that there are bills under discount amounting to £10,750. On going through the books you discover facts which point to the probability that £1,000 worth of these bills will be dishonoured on maturity, but that there is a reasonable chance of eventually receiving 50p in the £ on the £1,000. How would you deal with these bills under discount, and how should they appear in the company's published accounts? (*London Chamber of Commerce.*)

8. On 1st January, A owes B £6,000, for which B receives two acceptances from A, one for £2,000 payable in 2 months, the other for £4,000 payable in 4 months, in each case from 1st January. B duly discounts both these acceptances with his bankers on 3rd January at 4 per cent.

Before the first bill becomes due, A requests B to assist him in taking it up by providing him with £1,000 in cash, and drawing a third bill on A for that amount at 3 months from the due date of the first bill, plus interest at 5 per cent per annum; B agrees to this proposal and advances the money, discounting the bill with his bankers at 4 per cent.

A week before the second bill for £4,000 falls due A again asks B to assist him to the extent of £2,500. B, however, is not in a position to do this, and, as his bankers will not discount any more of A's acceptances, he arranges with A to draw on him (B) two bills for £1,131·83 and £1,408·17 at 2 months and 3 months respectively from the due date of the £4,000 bill. B duly accepts these two bills and remits them to A, who discounts them with his bankers at 4 per cent, and assisted by the proceeds, duly meets the £4,000 bill. B also meets his two bills on maturity. On 4th June A becomes bankrupt, leaving his third bill unpaid. Make the necessary entries in B's books to give effect to the above transactions.

(*London Chamber of Commerce.*)

9. From the following particulars compile detailed bills receivable and payable books, and post them to proper ledger accounts—

(N.B. All our acceptances were made payable at our bankers, Royal Bank.)

Mar 2 Drew on Green & Golding at 1 m/d for £152, allowing them discount £8. Bill No. 129.

3 Received Green & Golding's acceptance, payable at the Safe Bank, City. Accepted Philips & Son's draft of the 2nd inst., at 2 m/d in favour of Ogden & Co., £237·67 Bill No. 95.

9 Received of Ellis & Co., J. Thomson's acceptance to them for £85·85, dated 9th January, at 2 m/d, payable at Union Bank, Holborn.

12 Gave Lonsdale & Sons our acceptance, dated 11th inst., at 10 d/d for £125. Received Pavey & Lord's acceptance of our draft of yesterday at 3 m/d for £120·65, payable at Bank of England, Liverpool.

16 Allott, Jones & Co. forward me B. Bunker's acceptance to them for £185, payable at Midland Bank. Bill drawn 15th February, at 60 d/s, acceptance being dated 28th February.

21 Received Sowerby & Wade's draft on us of the 19th inst., at 1 m/d, in favour of Lewry & Son for £166·06, discount allowed, £8·75. Returned same duly accepted.

22 Drew on Bayes & Kerry at 4 m/d, for £214·48, allowing discount, £11·30.

23 Received Bayes & Kerry's acceptance, payable at Parry's Bank, City.

27 Received Green & Noel's draft on us of yesterday's date for £299·75, at 3 m/d, with interest at 5 per cent. Returned it duly accepted.

30 Returned, duly accepted, T. Nicholson's draft on us, dated 29th inst. at 4 m/d, for £66·60 in favour of Gardner & Isbister.

31 B. Bearon forwards u L. Levar's acceptance to H. Moore for £116·12. Bill dated 29th January, at 2 m/d, and payable at Joint Stock Bank, Leeds. Accepted G. Graham's draft on us, dated 21st March, at 90 d/s, for £134·65, discount allowed £7·08.

Bill No. 130 was duly met. No. 132 was discounted. No. 134 was dishonoured. No. 131 was endorsed over to Mandrakes Ltd. on 8th June. Acceptance No. 96 was duly honoured, and No. 95 was renewed on 2nd May.

10. What is meant by "renewing" a bill? Give, in both parties' books in each case, the journal entries for the following—

(*a*) Welt and Dray renew a bill for £126·78 for their customer, F. Frost, for $2\frac{1}{2}$ months with interest at $3\frac{3}{4}$ per cent.

(*b*) S. Storm, a creditor of Jenkins & Co., renews a bill for £226·74 for $3\frac{1}{2}$ months, with interest at $4\frac{3}{4}$ per cent.

11. T. Talbot receives his customer's acceptance for £120. State the different ways in which he can deal with this bill, and give the journal and cash book entries for each way. Assuming the bill to be dishonoured in each case, give the necessary journal and cash book entries.

12. Give a written explanation of a method of procedure in dealing with bills of exchange transactions which, in your judgement, would ensure a clear grasp of the facts. Support your answer by solutions—with notes—to the following problems.

(1) S, who discounted a bill he had drawn on J, has been notified by his banker that J failed to meet it on presentment for payment.

(2) M and B draw on each other for £100 on 1st March. Each discounts the other's bill and, at maturity, each party honours his acceptance. The bankers charged 5 per cent for discounting.

(3) L drew on M; endorsed over to N; but on the advice of N that M was unable

to pay, L met the bill. Show the records in: (*a*) L's books, (*b*) M's, and (*c*) N's books respectively.

13. Write up in the several books to which they properly belong, the following transactions—

19..

Jan 2 Sold James & Co. 20 tons steel bars at £5·20 f.o.b.
Paid carriage thereon at 25p per ton, by cheque on Provincial Bank.
Received cheques—J. Tasker £47·50; W. Methley £39·75; and from J. Moulton £43·80 in payment of his account after deducting 2½ per cent discount.
6 Received from W. Lyons 150 tons pig iron at £2·20, less 3 per cent—remitted him acceptance at 3 months, dated 1st January.
7 Received from J. Kitson his acceptance at 4 months, dated 4th inst., for £178·50, in payment of his account.
9 Gave cheques for—rent, £100, quarter year due 1st January; salaries, £25; and for wages, £75.
11 Received from Provincial Bank J. Butler's dishonoured acceptance for £35·35, with 50p expenses. (*London Chamber of Commerce.*)

14. William Ashton is a shipbuilder. On 1st January he had a capital of £23,760 bills payable current No. 135, £640, No. 136, £732, No. 137, £320, and having received on account of ships in progress, *Owl*, £6,849, and *Hawk* £3,500. A mortgage to P. Piper for £8,000 existed on his works and plant, which were valued as follows: freehold works and buildings £9,127, fixed plant and machinery £7,826, dry dock £6,284, loose plant and rolling stock £2,788.

He owed to Brown & Co. £848, Jones & Co. £1,653, Robinson & Co. £984. He had cash at bankers £2,796, and in office £123. His bills receivable in hand were No. 186, £330, No. 187, £546, No. 188, £490.

He had three ships under construction, on which he had expended in work and materials, *Owl* £7,126, *Hawk* £4,291, *Sparrow* £835. The stock of stores and materials on hand, valued at cost price, was £4,724.

You are required to make the necessary opening entries.

(*R.S.A. modified.*)

15. On 1st September, 19.., V. Whiting drew on R. Salmon a bill of exchange for £1,500 in settlement for goods supplied. The bill, which was expressed payable four months after date, was accepted next day, and was discounted on 3rd September with R. Sturgeon for £1,460. Shortly before the due date Salmon advised Whiting he would be unable to meet the bill, but could provide £500 towards it; accordingly Whiting advanced Salmon the balance of £1,000. In return he received from him, on 1st January, 19.1, a new bill payable after six months, to cover the principal sum, together with interest at the rate of 5 per cent per annum.

Set out these transactions as they would affect Whiting's cash book and ledger. Entries in the journal or subsidiary books are not required.

(*London Chamber of Commerce.*)

16. H. Timber Ltd., imports large quantities of timber and re-exports a certain amount of it. Payment is normally by bills of exchange, drawn in £ sterling, with discount charges being borne by the drawer.

These are some of the company's transactions—

19..

Feb 1 Bought timber costing £84,000 from the S Timber Corporation; accepted a bill of exchange for that amount at 60 days after sight.
14 Bought timber costing £120,000 from the L Timber Agency; accepted a bill of exchange drawn on 31st January for 90 days after date.
28 Sold timber for £80,000 to the F Timber Co., drawing a bill on them for £70,000 for 30 days after date.

March 16 Accepted bill returned by F Timber Co., which was discounted with the bank of H Timber Ltd. at 2 per cent discount.

18 Reached agreement with the L Timber Agency for an allowance of £7,000 in respect of a previous defective consignment of timber.

22 Sold timber to P for £24,000, drawing on him a bill of exchange for £4,000 at 14 days and another for £20,000 at 90 days.

29 Accepted bills returned by P; the £20,000 bill was discounted with the bank at 2 per cent discount.

April 1 Cheque (in £ sterling) received from the F Timber Co. for the balance of their account.

5 Received notice from the bank that the cheque from the F Timber Co. has not been met and that the bill discounted on 16th March has been dishonoured.

12 Drew an accommodation bill on M Bros. for £100,000 at 90 days; the bill was discounted with the bank at 2 per cent. In return accepted a bill drawn by M Bros. for £102,000 at 60 days.

14 Bought timber for £67,000 from the L Timber Agency; accepted a bill dated 1st April at 60 days for £60,000.

Assuming that all the bills are met on their due dates (excepting where the contrary is stated), and ignoring any additional bank charges on the various transactions, you are required to write up the appropriate personal ledger accounts and nominal legder accounts of H Timber Ltd. The company's financial year ended on 30th April, 1966, and you should carry down the balances at that date. Ignore days of grace. *(I.C.M.A.)*

17. John Nightingale, East Street, Sheffield, sells to the Low Moor Iron Co., on 4th March, 20 tons of Scotch iron at £4·50 per ton; 10th March, 50 tons of Swedish iron at £4·40 per ton; 19th March, 40 tons of hematite iron at £4·20 per ton; and receives, 30th March, £200 on account, and on 2nd April, a bill of exchange at three months for £250.

(*a*) Make out an invoice of the first transaction.

(*b*) A statement of account on 12th July; and

(*c*) Draw the B/E mentioned above, make it payable in Leeds, and write upon it an acceptance for payment at the Leeds Joint Stock Bank Ltd.

(*d*) Also rule a form of John Nightingale's bill book, and enter in it the particulars of this bill.

What entries would appear in the Low Moor Iron Co.'s books in respect of the B/E mentioned in the foregoing question? *(West Riding of Yorkshire.)*

18. X owed Y £1,555 for goods supplied. The account was settled on 1st October, 19.., by X giving Y a cheque for £305, a three months' bill of exchange for £600, and a five months' bill for the balance.

The first bill was met when due and at the same time the second was withdrawn in consideration of two further bills, equal in amount, due on 1st June, 19.1, and 1st September, 19.1, respectively. Interest on the renewal was payable forthwith in cash, calculated at the rate of 4 per cent per annum.

Show the above transactions as they would appear in Y's ledger and cash book up to March, 19.1. Ignore days of grace and calculate the interest on the basis of months. *(R.S.A.)*

19. Record the following matters in the cash book of Jonas Wilkinson—

Jun 4 Discounted at bank bill receivable for £400, the discount charge being £4·20.

6 An amount of £360 due to Frank Kilner paid by cheque, 2½ per cent discount being deducted.

10 Bank charges, the cost of which (£2) was charged against the banking account.

13 Received from William Dawson in cheques, postal orders and cash £77·12, and allowed him discount £2·35.
15 Paid into Bank £70.
17 Drew and cashed cheque to make the following payments—

	£
Stationery . . .	3·40
Petrol and oil . . .	6·50
Wages . . .	15·00
Amount of cheque . .	24·90

Jun 18 A. Brewer's cheque for £20 received from William Dawson on the 13th inst. is returned by the bank marked "R/D."
30 The bank pass book shows £3·40 to have been credited on this date for interest.

Balance the book, and carry down the balances.

(*Faculty of Teachers in Commerce.*)

20. A draws a bill of exchange on B, for goods supplied, for £10,000, dated 1st January, at six months, and, on B's acceptance of the same, discounts it with C on 4th January, at 5 per cent per annum. The bill is dishonoured at B's bankers on presentation, the charges for noting and expenses being 25p. B pays A cash £4,000 on account on 5th July, and accepts three bills for the balance then due, together with interest at 5 per cent per annum, of equal amounts, payable at two, four, and six months respectively. Show these transactions in A's Ledger. (*Chartered Accountants.*)

21. H. Brown commenced to trade on 1st July, 19.., with a balance at bank of £200. His diary recorded the following transactions—

19..
Jul 1 Bought goods from F. Green for £284.
7 Sold goods to G. White for £90.
8 Sent Green cheque for £84 and accepted bill drawn by him at two months for £100.
10 Drew bill on White at one month for £90 and discounted it at the bank for £88.
24 Sold goods to A. Gray for £120.
26 Received cheque from Gray for £40 and a bill accepted by him at one month for £80. Endorsed this bill on to Green in part settlement of his account.
Aug 11 Gray returned goods invoiced to him for £30 against a credit to him of £18. These goods had been damaged and were taken into stock at £10.
14 White's bill returned dishonoured.
18 Agreed with White that he return and be credited with goods invoiced to him for £60 and that he pay the balance on his account less 10 per cent. This he did. The returned goods were in good condition and were taken back into stock at their original cost.
20 Returned goods to Green invoiced by him for £30.

Except for White's bill, all bills were duly honoured on maturity.
You are required to prepare in respect of these transactions—

(*a*) the personal ledger accounts, bills receivable account, bills payable account, and cash book in Brown's books, bringing down any balances as on 30th August, 19.., and

(*b*) a statement showing the profit or loss arising therefrom assuming that stock is taken at cost and that all goods were sold at cost plus 50 per cent.

(*Chartered Accountants.*)

22. On 3rd January Q purchased from P goods to the value of £600 and settled the account by means of three bills of exchange for £200 each due respectively in two, three, and four months. A week later P discounted the first of the three with his bank, receiving £199·28; the others he held.

The first two bills were paid at maturity. The third Q was unable to meet, and it was retired by arrangement, Q paying £50 in cash and giving P a fresh bill for three months to cover the balance with interest at the rate of 5 per cent per annum. P discounted this on 10th May for £150·30.

Set out the entries recording the above in P's ledger. (The cash book is not required.)
(R.S.A.)

CHAPTER 05

ACCOUNTING SYSTEMS AND CONTROL ACCOUNTS

Roll on, thou deep and dark blue Ocean—roll!
Ten thousand fleets sweep over thee in vain;
Man marks the earth with ruin—his control
Stops with the shore.

LORD BYRON—*Childe Harold*

THE method of accounting described in Chapter 01 is the traditional one which has been in use for many centuries. Whilst it can still be found in many small businesses, it is by no means the only method in use.

The objectives of an accounting procedure may be stated as to maintain accurate records at minimum cost; to facilitate the rapid extraction and reporting of accounting information; and to safeguard the business against theft, fraud and misappropriation.

Whilst the general skill of systems design is outside the scope of this book, the main types of accounting procedures must be considered so as to familiarize the student with the accounting aspect.

The dual-aspect principle of accounting permits the expansion of the number of accounts maintained into hundreds and thousands without losing the principle of reconciliation through the Trial Balance or a similar device such as a pre-list. Moreover, it is possible to employ a large number of clerks or machine operators whilst maintaining close control of accuracy. Division of the work in this way also permits cross-checks which help to prevent fraud and theft.

The need to safeguard against theft and fraud conflicts with the aims of minimum cost and rapid retrieval of information. Practicable procedures make fraud difficult but are never fool-proof and do not therefore obviate the need for management and auditing vigilance.

When working text-book exercises, thirty or forty is, in all probability, the maximum number of accounts in use but, irrespective of the *number*, there are only three types—

1. **Real Accounts.** Assets and liabilities, other than the personal accounts of debtors and creditors.
2. **Nominal Accounts.** All those accounts which form the trading and

profit and loss accounts (excepting the stock account, which is included among the assets).

3. **Personal Accounts.** E.g. debtors and creditors.

These forty or so accounts may be representative of many thousands in an actual set of books. A comparative table will illustrate this best.

	In Exercises	In Practice
Real A/cs	6	20
Nominal A/cs	20	60
Personal A/cs—Debtors	8	10,000
Creditors	4	200
TOTAL	38	10,280

Two facts stand out from these figures. Firstly, there is a great difference between the two numbers of personal accounts. Secondly, at the end of a period of accounts, if a single trial balance for all the accounts is prepared and found not to agree, then the search for the reason for disagreement may be long and tedious, and all accounting staff concerned with posting would have to be involved in the process of checking their own work and that of others.

As a single ledger expands with the growth of the business, all the additional work falls on the personal accounts especially on the debtors' accounts. Imagine the posting of 100 sales. This necessitates 100 debits to the personal accounts of customers and *only one* credit monthly to the sales account. Multiply this by ten, and the result will be 1,000 debits to customers but still only one credit. As a result, Sections 1 and 2 scarcely expand at all as to the *number* of postings, whilst Section 3 grows to such an extent that other ledgers are necessary.

If a sales clerk can handle 300 accounts, with 1,500 customers it would be necessary to have five sales ledgers divided more or less into the following sections of the alphabet A–D, E–H, I–L, M–R, and S–Z. With two bought ledgers and a general ledger, our system of books now includes eight ledgers in place of the single ledger with which we started.

Sectional Balancing. The problem of the large number of accounts is solved by dividing the accounts into sections. Each section is made self-balancing, so that proof of accuracy is incorporated into each section. Proof of accuracy means a trial balance and this in its turn demands double entry. Therefore, *every* ledger or section must have *complete double entry*.

A self-balancing ledger is one whose balances, when extracted, form a complete trial balance. The expression "self-balancing" ledger is scarcely strictly accurate. A more satisfactory definition is separately balanced by means of an aggregate account.

How Ledgers are made Self-Balancing. Where several ledgers are in use, it is obvious that they will not balance of themselves, because the balances they contain will be one-sided. Thus, the bought ledger will comprise all *credit* balances, the sales ledger all *debit* balances, and so on. Ledgers have, therefore, to be made self-balancing by means of an ingenious device called, an Adjustment, Control or Total Account.

CONTROL, TOTAL OR ADJUSTMENT ACCOUNT

This is an extra account inserted in the ledger or section of accounts to make it self-balancing.

Items are posted to the individual ledger accounts in the usual way, but when the postings are complete, the *total* is posted to the *opposite* side of the control account.

At the end of a period, the balance on the control account will be equal and opposite to the sum of balances on the ledger accounts, thus proving the ledger and allowing a trial balance to be extracted from *each* ledger or section.

All these accounts are total accounts. The term control accounts, is sometimes applied to them all and sometimes only to the total accounts in the general ledger, in which case, the total accounts in the other ledgers may be called adjustment accounts.

The Private Ledger. The same principle can be used to preserve the confidentiality of some accounts, for instance in a private firm where the owners wish to keep knowledge of their profits, capital accounts, drawings and salaries from the accounting staff. A separate cash account must be opened and all the vouchers associated with the secret transactions retained and posted by the owner or one of the partners. The private ledger thus incorporates a cash account, all other secret accounts, and a total account to make it self-balancing. The general ledger has a single Private Ledger Account to which totals are debited or credited.

The following diagram illustrates the way in which the single general ledger is broken down into sections under sectional balancing—

Non-sectional:	*Sectional:*
A. General Ledger	*A. General Ledger*
1. Real A/cs	1. Real A/cs
2. Nominal A/cs	2. Nominal A/cs
3. Personal A/cs	Sales A/c
(*a*) Debtors	Purchases A/c
(*b*) Creditors	3. Total Debtors
	Total Creditors
	B. Sales Ledger
	Containing—
	(*a*) Personal A/cs for each customer
	(*b*) Control A/cs for totals posted
	C. Bought (*or Purchases*) *Ledger*
	Containing—
	(*a*) Personal A/cs for all suppliers
	(*b*) Control A/cs for totals posted

To illustrate the principle, we will take a simple example of the posting of a sales, a purchase and the receipt and payment of cash showing the non-sectional and sectional postings.

Example 1

On 5th January, the Blitz Record Company purchases one ton of plastic powder for £10, from Raver Plastics Ltd., and on the same day it sells records to the value of £50 to the Hampstead Record Shop. £40 was received on account of sales on 15th February and £5 paid on account of the plastic powder on 1st February. These transactions may be recorded as follows—

In a non-sectional ledger

PURCHASES ACCOUNT

19..		£			
Jan 5	Goods (Raver Plastic Ltd.)	10			

SALES ACCOUNT

			19..		£
			Jan 5	Goods (Hampstead Record Shop)	50

RAVER PLASTICS LTD.

19..		£	19..		£
Feb. 1	Cash	5	Jan 5	Purchases	10

HAMPSTEAD RECORD SHOP

19..		£	19..		£
Jan 5	Sales	50	Feb 15	Cash	40

CASH ACCOUNT

19..		£	19..		£
Feb 15	Hampstead Record Shop	40	Feb 1	Cash (Raver Plastics Ltd.)	5

In a sectional ledger

(*A*) *General Ledger*

PURCHASES ACCOUNT

19..		£			
Jan 5	Total Creditors Account	10			

SALES ACCOUNT

			19..		£
			Jan 5	Total Debtors Account	50

CASH ACCOUNT

19..		£	19..		£
Feb 15	Total Debtors Account	40	Feb. 1	Total Creditors Account	5

SALES LEDGER CONTROL (TOTAL DEBTORS) ACCOUNT

19..		£	19..		£
Jan 5	Sales	50	Feb 15	Cash	40

BOUGHT LEDGER CONTROL (TOTAL CREDITORS) ACCOUNT

19..		£	19..		£
Feb 1	Cash	5	Jan 5	Purchases	10

(*B*) *Sales Ledger*

HAMPSTEAD RECORD SHOP

19..		£	19..		£
Jan 5	Sales Ledger Control Account	50	Feb 15	Sales Ledger Control Account	40

GENERAL CONTROL LEDGER ACCOUNT

19..		£	19..		£
Feb 15	Sundry Debtors (Hampstead Record Shop)		Jan 5	Sundry Debtors (Hampstead Record Shop)	50

(*c*) *Bought* (*or Purchases*) *Ledger*

RAVER PLASTICS LTD.						GENERAL LEDGER CONTROL ACCOUNT					
19..		£	19..		£	19..		£	19..		£
Feb 1	Bought Ledger Control Account	5	Jan 5	Bought Ledger Control Account	10	Jan 5	Sundry Creditors (Raver Plastics Ltd.)	10	Feb 1	Sundry Creditors (Raver Plastics Ltd.)	5

The trial balance under each system would appear as follows—

TRIAL BALANCE(S)

Non-sectional

	Dr.	Cr.
(*A*) *General Ledger*	£	£
Purchases	10	
Sales		50
Cash	35	
Hampstead Record Shop .	10	
Raver Plastics Ltd. . .		5
Totals . . .	55	55

Sectional

	Dr.	Cr.
(*A*) *General Ledger*	£	£
Purchases	10	
Sales		50
Cash	35	
Sales Ledger Control (Total Debtors) . . .	10	
Bought Ledger Control (Total Creditors) . .		5
Totals . .	55	55
(*B*) *Sales Ledger*		
Hampstead Record Shop .	10	
General Ledger Adjustment Account . .		10
Totals . .	10	10
(*C*) *Bought Ledger*		
Raver Plastics Ltd. . .		5
General Ledger Adjustment Account . . .	5	
Totals . . .	5	5

Principle of Proof of Control Account. The principle of check underlying the adjustment account is that *the whole must be equal to the sum of all its parts.*

Sectional Balancing. This term is sometimes applied to systems where control accounts are kept as memorandum accounts only and do not form part of the double entry.

Self-balancing Ledgers, strictly speaking, are those in which the control accounts form part of the double entry. In this system, control accounts must be used in pairs and each item will involve four entries instead of two. The principle may be seen more clearly if the entries for a sale are compared—

Normal ledger entries	*Self-balancing ledger entries*	
1. *Cr.* Sales account	*Cr.* Sales account *Dr.* Sales ledger total account	in general ledger.
2. *Dr.* Personal account of debtor	*Dr.* Personal account of debtors *Cr.* (in total) General ledger adjustment account	in sales ledger.

Obviously, control or total accounts are posted periodically with totals. The following examples are illustrative.

Bought Ledger. This account would appear in the general ledger. Control accounts are constructed for each subdivision if there are several bought ledgers. All the items have been posted in detail in the bought ledger. In the bought ledger there would be a corresponding account having the items on the opposite sides, thus—

(1) General Ledger

Example 2

BOUGHT LEDGER CONTROL ACCOUNT

19..		£	19..		£
Jan 31	Cash	543	Jan 1	Balance (total of creditors as at this date)	2,607
	Discount	18	31	Purchases	741
	Bills Payable	396			
	Returns & Allowances	41			
	Balance c/d	2,350			
		3,348			3,348
			Feb 1	Balance b/d	2,350

(2) Bought Ledger

GENERAL LEDGER CONTROL ACCOUNT

19..		£	19..		£
Jan 1	Balance (total of creditors as at this date)	2,607	Jan 31	Cash	543
31	Purchases	741		Discount	18
				Bills Payable	396
				Returns & Allowances	41
				Balance c/d	2,350
		3,348			3,348
Feb 1	Balance b/d	2,350			

The above balance would, of course, be equal to the sum of the separate bought ledger balances, and thus prove the bought ledger. Special items, such as transfers of contra accounts, cancelled bills, interest on renewed bills or on overdue accounts, etc., which have been posted direct from the journal, and debited or credited to any of the personal accounts in the bought ledger, must also be debited or credited to these adjustment accounts.

Sales Ledger. Control accounts are constructed for the sales ledger, and also for each of its subdivisions if there are several sales ledgers. The following is an example—

(1) General Ledger

Example 3

SALES LEDGER CONTROL ACCOUNT

			£				£
19..				19..			
Jan	1	Balance (total of debtors as at this date)	7,416	Jan	31	Cash	3,716
	31	Sales	3,028			Discount	169
		Cash (dishonoured bills and charges)	54			Bills Receivable	316
						Returns & Allowances	74
						Bad Debts	124
						Balance c/d	6,099
			10,498				10,498
Feb	1	Balance b/d	6,099				

The above account would appear in the general ledger. In the sales ledger there would be a corresponding account, but having the items on the opposite sides in order to make a double entry by these two accounts, thus—

(3) Sales Ledger

GENERAL LEDGER CONTROL ACCOUNT

			£				£
19..				19..			
Jan	31	Cash	3,716	Jan	1	Balance (total of debtors as at this date)	7,416
		Discount	169		31	Sales	3,028
		Bills Receivable	316			Cash (dishonoured bills and charges)	54
		Returns & Allowances	74				
		Bad Debts	124				
		Balance c/d	6,099				
			10,498				10,498
				Feb	1	Balance b/d	6,099

The above balance would, of course, be equal to the sum of the separate sales ledger balances, thus checking or proving the sales ledger. Special items, such as transfers of contra accounts, interest on renewed bills or on overdue accounts, cancelled bills, etc., which have been posted direct from the journal, or items such as carriage paid out on empties or returns, etc., which have been posted from the petty cash book, and have been debited or credited to any of the personal accounts in the sales ledger, must also be debited or credited to these adjustment accounts.

QUESTIONS

1. Define the term "self-balancing ledger."
2. State briefly the object of self-balancing ledgers.
3. What is the chief advantage of self-balancing?
4. How are ledgers made self-balancing?
5. Explain the nature and construction of a "control account."
6. State briefly the principle of proof underlying the control account.
7. Submit *pro forma* control accounts for proving the bought ledger.
8. Submit *pro forma* control accounts for proving the sales ledger.
9. Explain the connexion between adjustment accounts and total checking accounts.

Rulings of Subsidiary Books. Where there are several bought ledgers and sales ledgers in use, extra columns will be required in the purchases and sales books, returns books, bills books, cash book, etc., for the purpose of analysing the items under the ledgers to which they have been posted. These columns will be in addition to the departmental columns (if any). Where the number of ledgers is very large, separate subsidiary books will be required for each ledger. See examples on the following pages.

Perhaps the most important point to bear in mind in connexion with the analysis of the subsidiary books is that *every* item is analysed, although only those figures affecting the bought and sales ledgers are actually required for self-balancing purposes. If partial analysis only is done, there is no check on the totals of the analysis columns by the simple method of cross-casting.

BANK CASH BOOK

Dr RECEIPTS

Date	Particulars	Fol.	Discount	Details	Bank	Sales Ledgers		
						A–K	L–R	S–Z

PAYMENTS *Cr*

Date	Particulars	Fol.	Discount	Details	Bank	Bought Ledgers		
						A Dept.	B Dept.	C Dept.
						Town	Country	Foreign

NOTE 1. It is not essential to analyse the general ledger items as in the worked example, although if this is not done there is no figure against which to check the cross-cast of the analysis columns. Where there are several bought ledgers and sales ledgers, the columns can be used to greater advantage as shown above.

NOTE 2. The bought ledger column on the receipts side and the sales ledger column on the payments side, shown in the worked example, can also be dispensed with, as the items are not very numerous, and can be easily picked out when the monthly adjustment accounts are constructed. But there is again the drawback mentioned above. The *full* analysis is strongly recommended even although it may necessitate the use of separate cash books for receipts and payments and in consequence a private cash book to summarize them.

SALES BOOK

Date	Particulars	Led. Fol.	Total	Ledgers			Mantles	Dress Materials	Felts
				A–K	L–R	S–Z			
			(1)	(2)	(3)	(4)	(5)	(6)	(7)

The total of column No. 1 will be used twice—first to the credit side of the sales account, and then to the debit side of the sales ledger adjustment account in the general ledger.

If departmental accounts are being kept, the totals of columns 5, 6, and 7 will be taken to their respective sales accounts in the general ledger, but the total of No. 1 will still be debited to the sales ledger adjustment account.

The totals of Nos. 2, 3, and 4 will be posted to the *credit* side of the general ledger adjustment accounts in the sales ledgers concerned.

PURCHASES BOOK

Date	Particulars	Led. Fol.	Total	Ledgers			Departments		
				Town	Country	Foreign	No. 1	No. 2	No. 3
			(1)	(2)	(3)	(4)	(5)	(6)	(7)

For the purpose of self-balancing, the total of No. 1 column will be posted to the credit of the bought ledger adjustment account in the general ledger, and the totals of columns 2, 3, and 4 to the debit of the general ledger adjustment accounts in the respective purchases ledgers.

Example 4

From the following particulars write up the journal, tabular purchases books, sales book, returns books, bank cash book, petty cash book, and bill books. Post to proper ledgers, make them self-balancing, and extract trial balances—

R. Retrop commenced the month with the following assets and liabilities—

19..				£
Jul	1	Petty cash in hand		20
		Cash at National Bank Ltd.		1,757
		Stock-in-trade		1,756
		Bills receivable (Nos. 120–125)		856
		A. Archer Ltd.	*Dr*	317
		B. Brown	*Dr*	426
		D. Dunlop & Co.	*Dr*	396
		Evans Bros.	*Dr*	675
		F. Finch & Son	*Dr*	87
		Garnet, Son & Co.	*Dr*	219
		H. Henry	*Cr*	430
		I. Isaacs Ltd.	*Cr*	361
		J. Jones & Co.	*Cr*	212
		Korper Bros.	*Cr*	86
		L. Lewin & Sons	*Cr*	216
		Martin, Son & Potter	*Cr*	76
		Outstanding rent	*Cr*	28
		Plant and machinery		4,216
		Furniture and fixtures		607
		Bills payable (Nos. 48–50)		428

His transactions for the month were—

19..			£
Jul	2	Bought goods of H. Henry	217
	3	Bill receivable No. 121 (accepted by F. Finch & Son) returned dishonoured	65
	4	Received bill (No. 126) from A. Archer Ltd., P. Green's Acceptance dated 2nd July at 1 month, payable at Coutts', City	302
		Discount allowed	15
		Paid fire and employers' liability insurance	15
	5	Sold goods to A. Archer Ltd.	132
		Received cash from F. Finch & Son	65
		Paid wages	31
		Bought National Insurance Stamps	10
		Cash sales	16
	7	Received cash for bill receivable No. 123	157
	9	Purchased goods of I. Isaacs Ltd.	84
		Received cash from B. Brown for amount of account less 5 per cent. Write him that we could allow 2½ per cent, and would carry the balance forward.	
Jul	10	Bought furniture of Ridler & Co.	100
	11	Accepted I. Isaac's draft at 1 m/d (No. 51) dated 10th July	343
		Discount allowed	18
		Paid life assurance premium	10

19..			£
	12	Sold goods to B. Brown £424, less trade discount of 25 per cent	318
		Paid wages	34
		Sent bill No. 120 to bank for collection	125
		G. Goodman's acceptance (No. 124) £125, renewed for 3 months with interest at 5 per cent. New bill No. 127 payable at Bank of England, Gloucester	126
		Cash sales	15
	14	Purchased goods of L. Lewin & Sons	72
		Bill receivable No. 120 (accepted by D. Dunlop & Co.) returned by bank dishonoured	125
		Noting charges paid by bank	1
	15	D. Dunlop & Co. return damaged goods	10
	16	Received cash from D. Dunlop & Co. on account	200
		Bought coal of Midland Colliery Co.	25
		Paid carriage on same	5
	17	Sold goods to D. Dunlop & Co.	97
		Paid Ridler & Co. amount of account less 5 per cent	
	18	Renewed my acceptance to M. Masters (No. 48), £150 for 3 months with interest at 5 per cent. New bill No. 52	
	19	Bought goods of J. Jones & Co.	224
		Paid wages	29
		Received cash from Evans Bros. for amount of account at 1st July, less 5 per cent	
		Cash sales	10
	21	Bought of Stationery Supplies Co., stationery	27
		Paid Korper Bros.	82
		Discount deducted 5 per cent	4
	22	Returned to J. Jones & Co. goods not up to sample	8
		F. Finch & Sons accepted our draft at 2 months, bill No. 128, dated 20th July, payable at Lloyds, Chatham	83
		Discount allowed	4
		Sold goods to Evans Bros.	206
		Drew for self	50
	23	Purchased goods of Korper Bros.	86
		Sent Garnet, Son & Co's acceptance (No. 122) to H. Henry on account	200
		Bill payable No. 49 paid by bank	216
		Paid J. Jones & Co.	204
		Korper Bros. write and say they can allow only 2½ per cent discount, and will carry balance forward	
	24	Cash purchases	21
	25	Discounted bill receivable No. 125	184
		Bankers' charge for discounting	1
		Sold goods to F. Finch & Son	287
		Accepted L. Lewin & Sons' draft at 2 m/d (bill No. 53) in favour of N. Nash, dated 24th	211
		Discount allowed	5
Jul	26	Paid Martin, Son & Potter their account as at 1st July, less 2½ per cent discount	
		Paid wages	32
		Sold old plant (value in books £85) for cash	70
		Till takings	10

19..		£
28	Paid rent to June last	28
	Received demand note for rates	17
	Bill receivable No. 122 (accepted by Garnet, Son & Co.) returned by H. Henry dishonoured	
	Noting charges paid by him	1
29	Bought goods of Martin, Son & Potter, less trade discount of 10 per cent . . . *net*	240
30	Received Cash from Garnet, Son & Co.	201
	Paid H. Henry	201
31	Sold goods to Garnet, Son & Co.	79
	Paid for stationery	13
	Paid salaries for month	41
	Till takings	4
	Petty cash expenses	13

Solution 4

PRIVATE JOURNAL

19..		£	*Dr* £	*Cr* £
Jul 1	Petty Cash		20	
	Bank		1,757	
	Stock		1,756	
	Bills Receivable		856	
	Sales Ledger Adjustment A/c		2,120	
	A. Archer Ltd.	317		
	B. Brown	426		
	D. Dunlop & Co.	396		
	Evans Bros.	675		
	F. Finch & Son	87		
	Garnet, Son & Co.	219		
	Plant and Machinery		4,216	
	Furniture and Fixtures		607	
	Brought Ledger Adjustment A/c			1,409
	H. Henry	430		
	I. Isaacs Ltd.	361		
	J. Jones & Co.	212		
	Korper Bros.	86		
	L. Lewin & Sons	216		
	Martin, Son & Potter	76		
	Outstanding A/cs	28		
	Bills Payable			428
	Capital			9,495
			11,332	11,332
	For sundry assets and liabilities as at this date			

JOURNAL

Date	Particulars	Dr	Cr	Bought Ledger Dr	Bought Ledger Cr	Sales Ledger Dr	Sales Ledger Cr
19..		£	£	£	£	£	£
Jul 3	F. Finch & Son	65				65	
	Bill Receivable		65				
	Dishonoured bill No. 121 cancelled.						
12	G. Goodman	125				125	
	Bill Receivable		125				
	Bill No. 124 cancelled.						
12	G. Goodman	1				1	
	Interest		1				
	Interest on £125 for 3 mos. at 5%.						
17	Ridler & Co.	5		5			
	Furniture		5				
	Discount allowed 5%.						
18	Bill Payable	150					
	M. Masters		150		150		
	Bill No. 48 cancelled.						
18	Interest	2					
	M. Masters		2		2		
	Interest on £150 for 3 mos. at 5%.						
23	H. Henry	200		200			
	Bill Receivable		200				
	Bill No. 122 endorsed over to him.						
23	Discounts Received	2					
	Korper Bros.		2		2		
	Discount deducted in error.						

JOURNAL (*continued*)

Date	Particulars	Dr	Cr	Bought Ledger		Sales Ledger	
				Dr	Cr	Dr	Cr
19..		£	£	£	£	£	£
	Brought forward	550	550	205	154	191	
Jul 26	Loss on Sale of Plant	15					
	Plant & Machinery		15				
	Loss on sale transferred.						
28	Garnet, Son & Co.	201				201	
	H. Henry		201		201		
	H. Henry's acceptance bill No. 122 dishonoured, noting charges £1.						
		766	766	205	355	392	

NOTE. As, in practice, journal entries are often very few, the analysis is left until the end of the month, being entered below the total as follows—

	Dr	Cr
	£	£
SALES LEDGER	392	
BOUGHT LEDGER	205	355
GENERAL LEDGER	169	411
	766	766

This has the advantage that it can be checked against the totals.

PURCHASES BOOK

Date	Particulars	Details	Totals	Purchases	Rent, Rates, etc.	Coal	Furniture and Fixtures	Stationery
		£	£	£	£	£	£	£
19.. Jul 2	H. Henry Goods		217	217				
9	I. Isaacs Ltd. Goods		84	84				
10	Ridler & Co. Furniture		100				100	
14	L. Lewin & Sons Goods		72	72				
16	Midland Colliery Co. Coal		25			25		
19	J. Jones & Co. Goods		224	224				
21	Stationery Supplies Co. Stationery . . .		27					27
23	Korper Bros. Goods		86	86				
28	Outstanding A/cs Rates		17		17			
29	Martin, Son & Potter Goods . . . . *Less* Trade Discount 10% .	267 27	240	240				

PURCHASES RETURNS BOOK

		£	£
19..			
Jul 22	J. Jones & Co.		
	Goods not up to sample		8
			8

SALES BOOK

		£	£
19..			
Jul 5	A. Archer Ltd.		
	Goods		132
12	B. Brown		
	Goods	424	
	Less Trade Discount, 25%	106	
			318
17	D. Dunlop & Co.		
	Goods		97
22	Evans Bros.		
	Goods		206
25	F. Finch & Son		
	Goods		287
31	Garnet, Son & Co.		
	Goods		79
			1,119

SALES RETURNS BOOK

		£	£
19..			
Jul 15	D. Dunlop & Co.		
	Goods damaged		10
			10

BANK CASH BOOK

Receipts

Date	Particulars	Discount	Details	Bank	Bought Ledger	Sales Ledger	General Ledger
19..		£	£	£	£	£	£
Jul 1	Balance			1,757			1,757
5	F. Finch & Son		65			65	
	Cash Sales		16	81			16
7	Bill Receivable No. 123			157			157
9	B. Brown	11		404		415	
12	Bill Receivable No. 120		125				125
	Cash Sales		15	140			15
16	D. Dunlop & Co.			200		200	
19	Evans Bros.	34	641			675	
	Cash Sales		10	651			10
25	Bill Receivable No. 125			184			184
26	Plant		70				70
	Cash Sales		10	80			10
30	Garnet, Son & Co.			201		201	
31	Cash Sales			4			4
		45		3,859		1,556	2,348
Aug 1	Balance b/d			2,528			2,528

BANK CASH BOOK

PAYMENTS

Date	Particulars	Discount	Details	Bank	Bought Ledger	Sales Ledger	General Ledger
19..		£	£	£	£	£	£
Jul 4	Insurance			15			15
5	Wages			31			31
	Insurance stamps			10			10
11	Drawings			10			10
12	Wages			34			34
14	D. Dunlop (bill)			126		126	
16	Coal (carriage)			5			5
17	Ridler & Co.			95	95		
19	Wages			29			29
21	Korper Bros.	4		82	86		
22	Drawings			50			50
23	Bill payable No. 49			216			216
	J. Jones & Co.			204	204		
24	Cash purchases			21			21
25	Banker's discount			1			1
26	Martin, Son & Potter	2		74	76		
	Wages			32			32
28	Outstanding rent			28	28		
30	H. Henry			200	200		
31	Stationery			13			13
	Salaries			41			41
	Petty cash			13			13
	Balance c/d			2,528			2,528
		6		3,859	690	126	3,049

BILLS RECEIVABLE BOOK

Date	No. of Bill	From Whom Received	Led. Fol.	Discount	Amount of Bill	Date of Bill	Term	Due Date
19..				£	£			
Jul 4	126	A. Archer Ltd.		15	302	Jul 2	1 m/d	Aug 5
12	127	G. Goodman			126	11	3 m/d	Oct 14
22	128	F. Finch & Son		4	83	20	2 m/d	Sep 23
				19	511			

BILLS PAYABLE BOOK

Date	No. of Bill	To Whom Given	Led. Fol.	Discount	Amount of Bill	Date of Bill	Term	Due Date
19..				£	£			
Jul 11	51	I. Isaacs Ltd.		18	343	Jul 10	1 m/d	Aug 13
18	52	M. Masters			152	17	3 m/d	Oct 20
25	53	L. Lewin & Sons		5	21	24	2 m/d	Sep 27
				23	706			

NOTE. Where bills are more numerous or where there are several bought and sales ledgers, the analysis can be done at the end of the month as in the case of the journal (see previous page).

BOUGHT OR CREDITORS' LEDGER

H. HENRY

19..			£	19..			£
Jul	23	Bills Receivable	200	Jul	1	Balance	430
	30	Cash	200		2	Goods	217
					28	Garnet, Son & Co.	200

KORPER BROS.

19..			£	19..			£
Jul	21	Cash	82	Jul	1	Balance	86
		Discount	4				
			86				86
				Jul	23	Discount	2
						Goods	86

I. ISAACS LTD.

19..			£	19..			£
Jul	11	Bills Payable	343	Jul	1	Balance	361
		Discount	18		9	Goods	84

J. JONES & CO.

19..			£	19..			£
Jul	22	Returns	8	Jul	1	Balance	212
	23	Cash	204		19	Goods	224

L. LEWIN & SONS

19..			£	19..			£
Jul	25	Bills Payable	211	Jul	1	Balance	216
		Discount	5		14	Goods	72

MARTIN, SON & POTTER

19..			£	19..			£
Jul	26	Cash	74	Jul	1	Balance	76
		Discount	2				
			76				76
				Jul	29	Goods	240

M. Masters

Date	Particulars	£	Date	Particulars	£
19..			19..		
Jul 18	Bills Payable	152	Jul 18	Bills Payable	150
				Interest	2
		152			152

Midland Colliery Co.

Date	Particulars	£	Date	Particulars	£
			19..		
			Jul 16	Coal	25

Stationery Supplies Co.

Date	Particulars	£	Date	Particulars	£
			19..		
			Jul 21	Stationery	27

Ridler & Co.

Date	Particulars	£	Date	Particulars	£
19..			19..		
Jul 17	Cash	95	Jul 10	Furniture	100
	Furniture	5			
		100			100

Outstanding Accounts

Date	Particulars	£	Date	Particulars	£
19..			19..		
Jul 28	Cash	28	Jul 1	Balance	28
			Jul 28	Rates, etc.	17

General Ledger Control Account

Date	Particulars	£	Date	Particulars	£
19..			19..		
Jul 1	Balance	1,409	Jul 31	Returns	8
31	Goods	1,092		Cash & Discount	690
	Transfers as per Journal	355		Bills Payable	706
				Discount	23
				Transfers as per Journal	205
				Balance c/d	1,224
		2,856			2,856
Aug 1	Balance b/d	1,224			

SALES OR DEBTORS' LEDGER

A. ARCHER LTD.

			£				£
19..				19..			
Jul	1	Balance . . .	317	Jul	4	Bills Receivable . .	302
						Discount . . .	15
			317				317
Jul	5	Goods . . .	132				

B. BROWN

			£				£
19..				19..			
Jul	1	Balance . . .	426	Jul	9	Cash	404
						Discount . . .	10
						Balance c/d . .	10
			426				426
Jul	9	Balance b/d . .	11				
	12	Goods . .	318				

D. DUNLOP & CO.

			£				£
19..				19..			
Jul	1	Balance . . .	396	Jul	15	Returns . . .	10
	14	Cash (dishonoured bill)	126		16	Cash	200
	17	Goods .	97				

EVANS BROS.

			£				£
19..				19..			
Jul	1	Balance . . .	675	Jul	19	Cash	641
						Discount . . .	34
			675				675
Jul	22	Goods . . .	206				

F. FINCH & SON

			£				£
19..				19..			
Jul	1	Balance . . .	87	Jul	5	Cash	65
	3	Bill Receivable dis-honoured) . .	65		22	Bill Receivable . .	83
						Discount . . .	4
			152				152
Jul	23	Goods . . .	287				

Garnet, Son & Co.

19..			£	19..			£
Jul	1	Balance	219	Jul	30	Cash	201
	28	H. Henry	201				
	31	Goods	79				

G. Goodman

19..			£	19..			£
Jul	12	Bill Receivable	125	Jul	12	Bill Receivable	126
		Interest	1				
			126				126

General Ledger Control Account

19..			£	19..			£
Jul	31	Cash and Discount	1,556	Jul	1	Balance	2,120
		Returns	10			Cash (dishonoured bill)	126
		Bills Receivable	511			Transfer as per Journal	392
		Discount	19			Goods	1,119
		Balance c/d	1,661				
			3,757				3,757
				Aug	1	Balance b/d	1,661

IMPERSONAL or GENERAL LEDGER

Stock

19..			£				
Jul	1	Balance	1,756				

Plant and Machinery

19..			£	19..			£
Jul	1	Balance	4,216	Jul	26	Cash	70
						Loss on Sale	15

Furniture and Fixtures

19..			£	19..			£
Jul	1	Balance	607	Jul	17	Ridler & Co.	5
	31	Sundry Crs.	100				

Bills Payable

		£			£
19..			19..		
Jul 18	M. Masters	150	Jul 1	Balance	428
23	Cash	216	31	Sundry Crs.	706

Bills Receivable

		£			£
19..			19..		
Jul 1	Balance	856	Jul 3	Finch & Son	65
			7	Cash	157
			12	Cash	125
				G. Goodman	125
			23	H. Henry	200
			25	Cash	184
		856			856
Jul 31	Sundry Drs.	510			

Purchases

		£			£
19..					
Jul 24	Cash	21			
31	Sundry Crs.	923			

Purchases Returns and Allowances

		£			£
			19..		
			Jul 31	Sundry Crs.	8

Salaries

		£			£
19..					
Jul 31	Cash	41			

Sales

		£			£
			19..		
			Jul 5	Cash	16
			12	Cash	15
			19	Cash	10
			26	Cash	10
			31	Cash	4
				Sundry Drs.	1,119

Sales Returns and Allowances

		£			£
19..					
Jul 31	Sundry Drs.	10			

Wages

			£
19..			
Jul	5	Cash	31
	12	Cash	34
	19	Cash	29
	26	Cash	32

Health Insurance Stamps

			£
19..			
Jul	5	Cash	10

Insurance

Jul	4	Cash	15

Rent, Rates, and Taxes

			£
19..			
Jul	31	Sundry Crs. . .	17

Printing and Stationery

			£
19..			
Jul	31	Cash	13
		Sundry Crs. . .	27

Coal

			£
19..			
Jul	16	Cash (Carriage) . .	5
	31	Sundry Crs. . .	25

Loss on Sale of Plant

			£
19..			
Jul	26	Plant and Machinery .	15

Discounts Allowed

			£
19..			
Jul	31	Sundry Drs. . .	45
		Sundry Drs. . .	19

Discounts Received

19..			£	19..			£
Jul	23	Korper Bros. . .	2	Jul	31	Sundry Crs. . .	6
						Sundry Crs. . .	23

Banker's Discount

19..			£				
Jul	25	Cash	1				

Interest Receivable

				19..			£
				Jul	12	G. Goodman . .	1

Interest Payable

19..			£				
Jul	18	M. Masters . .	2				

Sundry Expenses

19..			£				
Jul	31	Petty Cash . . .	13				

BOUGHT LEDGER CONTROL ACCOUNT (OR ADJUSTMENT ACCOUNT)

19..			£	19..			£
Jul	31	Returns	8	Jul	1	Balance	1,409
		Cash and Discount	690		31	Goods	1,092
		Bills Payable	706			Transfers as per Journal	355
		Discount	23				
		Transfers as per Journal	205				
		Balance c/d	1,224				
			2,856				2,856
				Aug	1	Balance b/d	1,224

SALES LEDGER CONTROL ACCOUNT (OR ADJUSTMENT ACCOUNT)

19..			£	19..			£
Jul	1	Balance	2,120	Jul	31	Cash and Discount	1,556
	31	Cash (dishonoured bill)	126			Returns	10
		Transfers as per Journal	392			Bills Receivable	511
		Goods	1,119			Discount	19
						Balance c/d	1,661
			3,757				3,757
Aug	1	Balance b/d	1,661				

PRIVATE LEDGER

CAPITAL

				19..			£
				Jul	1	Balance	9,495

DRAWINGS

19..			£				
Jul	11	Cash	10				
	22	Cash	50				

TRIAL BALANCE (BOUGHT LEDGER), 31ST JULY, 19..

	£	£
I. Isaacs Ltd.		84
H. Henry		447
J. Jones & Co.		224
Korper Bros.		88
L. Lewin & Sons		72
Martin, Son & Potter		240
Midland Colliery Co.		25
Stationery Supplies Co.		27
Outstanding a/cs		17
General ledger adjustment a/c	1,224	
	1,224	1,224

TRIAL BALANCE (SALES LEDGER), 31ST JULY, 19..

	£	£
A. Archer Ltd.	132	
B. Brown	329	
D. Dunlop & Co.	409	
Evans Bros.	206	
F. Finch & Son	287	
Garnet, Son & Co.	298	
General ledger adjustment a/c		1,661
	1,661	1,661

TRIAL BALANCE (GENERAL LEDGER), 31ST JULY, 19..

		£	£
	Stock	1,756	
	Plant and machinery	4,131	
	Furniture and fixtures	702	
	Bills payable		768
	Bills receivable	511	
	Purchases	944	
	Purchases returns and allowances		8
	Salaries	41	
	Sales		1,174
	Sales returns and allowances	10	
	Wages	126	
	National insurance stamps	10	
	Insurance	15	
	Rent, rates, and taxes	17	
	Printing and stationery	40	
	Coal	30	
	Loss on sale of plant	15	
	Discounts allowed	64	
	Discounts received		27
	Banker's discount	1	
	Interest receivable		1
	Interest payable	2	
	Sundry expenses	13	
	Bought ledger adjustment a/c[1]		1,224
	Sales ledger adjustment a/c[2]	1,661	
P.L.	Capital		9,495
	Drawings	60	
C.B.	Cash at bank	2,528	
P.C.B.	Petty cash in hand	20	
		12,697	12,697

[1] On the balance sheet this item will appear as sundry creditors.
[2] On the balance sheet this item will appear as sundry debtors.

Procedure where there are Several Purchases and Sales Ledgers. In large concerns where there are several purchases and sales ledgers in use, the subsidiary books are ruled with departmental columns. Separate analysis sheets or books are provided, in which the amounts in the subsidiary and cash books are dissected. Thus, items in Ledger No. 1 would, when posted, have the figure 1 prefixed to the folio and so on. The analytical columns are totalled horizontally and vertically to check the analysis. Separate adjustment accounts can be prepared for each ledger, or the whole lot may be constructed in tabular form. The combined total of the balances of the adjustment accounts provides the total amount of debtors and creditors for the balance sheet. This principle is fully illustrated in the chapter on Departmental Accounts.

Contra Account. This means that we have both bought from, and sold to, the same person; and that while he is our *debtor* for the goods we have sold to him, and his account appears in the sales ledger, yet he is also our *creditor* for the goods we have bought from him, and his "contra" account, appears in the bought ledger. Settlement may be effected by deducting one account from the other, and paying, or being paid the balance. Hence the smaller account must be transferred to the greater, either the bought ledger account to the sales ledger account as the case may be. These transfers must be passed through the journal and analysed into their proper columns.

Contra Balances in Ledgers. Strictly speaking, the bought ledger should contain all *credit* balances, and the sales ledger all *debit* balances, yet in practice it sometimes happens that in some of the bought ledger accounts there are sundry small *debit* balances, and also that in the sales ledger accounts there are sundry small *credit* balances. Take the case of the sales ledger. Accounts often include charges for packages. An account is settled in cash, and subsequently when the packages are empty they are returned and have to be credited. At balancing time there may be no debit in the account to offset this credit. Mistakes are occasionally found after accounts have been settled, and their rectification sometimes involves the crediting of such accounts with a certain amount. These small credit balances are sometimes deducted from the total debtors, and only the net amount of the debtors shown in the balance sheet. And likewise with the bought ledger, the total of the small debit balances appearing in it is sometimes deducted from the creditors, and only the net amount of the creditors shown in the balance sheet. Some accountants, however, bring down both debit and credit balances, and also show them on the balance sheet. For example, suppose the bought ledger balances to amount to £3,466·00 after deducting £9·75, the total of sundry *debit* balances therein, and the sales ledger balances to amount to £8,457·45 after deducting £5·40, the total of sundry *credit* balances therein, the adjustment accounts in the general ledger would appear as follows—

BOUGHT LEDGER CONTROL ACCOUNT (OR ADJUSTMENT ACCOUNT)

		£			£
19..			19..		
Jan 1	Balance	9·75	Jan 1	Balance	3,475·75

SALES LEDGER CONTROL ACCOUNT (OR ADJUSTMENT ACCOUNT)

		£			£
19..			19..		
Jan 1	Balance	8,462·85	Jan 1	Balance	5·40

The balance sheet would be as under—

BALANCE SHEET

Liabilities	£	£	*Assets*	£	£
Sundry Creditors as per Bought Ledger	3,475·75		Sundry Debtors as per Sales Ledger	8,462·85	
Add Sundry *Cr.* bal. in Sales Ledger	5·40		*Add* Sundry *Dr.* bal. in Bought Ledger	9·75	
		3,481·15			8,472·60

Under the other method it would appear—

BALANCE SHEET

Liabilities	£	*Assets*	£
Sundry Creditors	3,466·00	Sundry Debtors	8,457·45

As can be seen, the final result in each case is a *net* debit of £4,991·45, so that the double entry is not affected in any way. But by the two balances method we show the true financial position, i.e. the *exact* amount of debtors and creditors.

DETECTION OF ERRORS

Since this is a primary aim in maintaining control accounts, examiners frequently set examples in which an error has been made.

Example 5

A.B.C. Ltd., maintains self-balancing ledgers. From the details given below you are required to construct the Control Accounts in respect of the Purchases and Sales Ledgers for the year ended 31st December, 1959.

The differences on the Control Accounts should be inserted and the possible causes of the errors should be indicated—

	£
Purchases	15,327·75
Bad Debts written off	220·50
Bills Payable accepted	2,170·50
Bills Receivable drawn	5,020·55
Interest Charged to Customers	7·25

Purchases Returns	89·30
Payments to Creditors	12,538·50
Receipts from Debtors	14,308·00
Bills Receivable dishonoured	575·00
Discounts Allowed	526·00
Discounts Received	327·40
Sales Returns	301·20
Cash repaid to Debtors	75·20
Cheques from Debtors returned unpaid . . .	25·00
Sales and Purchases Ledgers contras	1,017·60
Bills Receivable discounted	4,785·00
Bills Payable retired for non-payment	150·00
Sales	20,051·40
Bad Debts recovered (included in cash from Debtors) .	8·25

Creditors Balances at—

1st January, 1959	5,762·20 (Credit)
1st January, 1959	10·40 (Debit)
31st December, 1959	5,095·55 (Credit)
31st December, 1959	9·50 (Debit)

Debtors' Balances at—

1st January, 1959	7,521·30 (Debit)
1st January, 1959	50·25 (Credit)
31st December, 1959	6,892·25 (Debit)
31st December, 1959	73·15 (Credit)

(*London Chamber of Commerce.*)

Solution 5

The two control accounts may be constructed as follows—

PURCHASES LEDGER CONTROL A/C

		£			£
1959			1959		
Jan–Dec	Bills payable . . .	2,170·50	Jan 1	Balance . . .	5,751·80
	Purchases returns . .	89·30		Purchases . . .	15,327·75
	Cash (payments to creditors) . . .	12,538·50		Bill payable retired	150·00
	Discounts received . .	327·40			
	Sales Ledger control (contras) . . .	1,017·60			
	Difference in books	0·20			
Dec 31	Balance c/d	5,086·08			
		21,229·55			21,229·55
			1960		
			Jan 1	Balance b/d	5,086·05

SALES LEDGER CONTROL A/C

		£			£
1959			1959		
Jan 1	Balance	7,471·05	Dec 31	Bad debts w/o . .	220·50
Jan–Dec	Interest	7·25	Jan–Dec	Bills receivable . .	5,020·55
	Bill receivable dishonoured	575·00		Cash (receipts from debtors) . . .	14,308·00
	Cash repaid to debtors .	75·20		Discounts allowed . .	526·00
	Cash (dishonoured cheques)	25·00		Sales Returns . .	301·20
	Sales	20,051·40		Purchases Ledger control (contras) . .	1,017·60
	Bad debts recovered .	8·25		Difference in books	0·20
			Dec 31	Balance c/d . . .	6,819·10
		28,213·15			28,213·15
Jan 1	Balance b/d	6,819·10			

Since the difference is equal and opposite, it seems most likely that the amount of the *contras* has been understated by twenty pence, and that it should have been £1,017·80.

QUESTIONS

1. Submit rulings of the purchases and sales books where the nature of the business necessitates departmental analysis as well as self-balancing ledgers.
2. Submit rulings of a cash book suitable for a business that divides its ledgers into sections: (*a*) alphabetically, (*b*) departmentally.
3. Submit *pro forma* journal entries for constructing the adjustment accounts relative to the bought ledger.
4. Submit *pro forma* journal entries for constructing the adjustment accounts relative to the sales ledger.
5. Supposing there are several small *debit* balances in the bought ledger, how should they be treated in preparing the adjustment account?
6. Supposing there are sundry small *credit* balances in the sales ledger, how will they affect the preparation of the adjustment account?
7. How will personal items in the petty cash book affect the adjustment accounts?
8. How are *contra* accounts in the bought ledger dealt with when preparing the sales ledger adjustment accounts?
9. When the number of ledgers in use is too large for analytical columns to be provided in the cash and subsidiary books, how is the material for control accounts obtained?

PRIVATE LEDGER

It will be noticed in the worked example that the private ledger contains only the capital and drawings accounts. This ledger is often kept confidentially, and may include other accounts of a private nature, such as loans, and in some cases the bank balance, and the stock. Without knowing the value of the stock at the commencement and at the end of a period, it would be impossible for any clerk to arrive at the gross or net profit, even though he had access to all the other information. An earlier method of division of accounts, which is still to be found in many businesses, is to keep all the nominal and real accounts in the private ledger. Another method is to keep all the expense accounts in a nominal ledger, and to put all the real or property accounts, e.g. plant and machinery, bills, stock, etc., into the private ledger.

Private Ledger Account. To preserve confidentiality a private ledger control account, is opened at the end of the general ledger, and credited with the net balance of all the accounts in the private ledger. All items that should be posted to the private ledger are then debited or credited to the private ledger account instead. The balance of the private ledger account thus enables the trial balance to be completed without reference to the private ledger itself. At balancing time the professional accountant, who makes up the profit and loss account and balance sheet, analyses the private ledger account and posts the details to the proper accounts in the private ledger. He closes the private ledger account for the past period by writing

"*Transfer to Private Ledger*," and reopens it by writing "*Balance*" the net amount for the new period.

The following example will serve as an illustration of the above procedure—

Example 6

IN GENERAL LEDGER

Private Ledger Account

19..		£	19..		£
Feb 15	Cash	100·00	Jan 1	Balance	2,175·15
Apr 20	"	100·00	Jun 30	Cash	1,000·00
Jun 25	"	100·00	Dec 31	Cash Book totals	6,792·70
Sep 17	"	100·00		Interest	275·00
Nov 20	"	100·00			
Sep 25	" (R. Brown)	500·00			
Dec 31	Cash Book totals	7,597·80			
	Transfer to Private Ledger	1,645·05			
		10,242·85			10,242·85
			Jan	Balance	2,834·00

IN PRIVATE LEDGER

Bank

19..		£	19..		£
Jan 1	Balance	1,200·00	Jan to Dec	Cash Book totals	6,792·70
Jan to Dec	Cash Book totals	7,597·80	Dec 31	Balance c/d	2,005·10
		8,797·80			8,797·80
19.. Jan 1	Balance b/d	2,005·10			

Loan from R. Brown

19..		£	19..		£
Sep 25	Cash	500·00	Jan 1	Balance	1,000·00
Dec 31	Balance c/d	500·00			
		1,000·00			1,000·00
			Jan 1	Balance b/d	500·00

Drawings

19..		£	19..		£
Jan to Dec	Cash	500·00	Dec 31	Capital	500·00

Stock

19..		£	19..		£
Jan 1	Balance	2,624·85	Dec 31	Trading A/c	2,624·85
Dec 31	Trading A/c	2,289·75			

CAPITAL

19..		£	19..		£
Dec 31	Drawings . . .	500·00	Jan 1	Balance . . .	5,000·00
	Balance c/d . . .	6,629·85	Jun 30	Cash . . .	1,000·00
			Dec 31	Interest . .	275·00
				Profit & Loss A/c .	854·85
		7,129·85			7,129·85
			Jan 1	Balance b/d . . .	6,629·85

QUESTIONS

1. What is meant by the term "*contra* account"?
2. How are *contra* accounts usually settled? What exceptions are there?
3. How does the transfer of *contra* accounts affect the control accounts for the bought and sold ledgers respectively? Should such transfers be made direct from one ledger account to the other? Give reasons for your answer.
4. How are the sundry *debit* balances in a bought ledger, and the sundry *credit* balances in a sales ledger, sometimes shown in the balance sheet, and why? Give examples. How do such balances arise?
5. What differences of opinion exist in practice with regard to the question as to what accounts should be kept in the private ledger?
6. What is the modern tendency with regard to the ledgering of nominal and real accounts?
7. How can the bank balance be kept from the knowledge of the staff? Why is the stock account sometimes kept in the private ledger?
8. Explain how a set of books may be kept and balanced by means of a monthly trial balance without giving the book-keeper access to the private ledger.
9. Give an example of the working of a private ledger account in the general ledger and show the corresponding accounts in the private ledger.

EXERCISE 05

1. What do you understand by the "sectional" system of balancing ledgers?

In the business of X, Y, Z & Co., the following books are in use: 1 "bought" ledger, 2 "sold" ledgers ("town" and "country"), 1 "private and nominal" ledger, 1 "bank" cash book, 1 petty cash book, 2 sales books ("town" and "country"), 1 purchases book, and 1 journal. Explain briefly what alterations (if any), it would be necessary to effect in these books in order to introduce the "sectional" system of balancing. *(London Chamber of Commerce.)*

2. The following books are in use in a printing business, and are properly kept upon the ordinary double-entry system: cash book (bank items only), petty cash book (for all *cash* payments), purchases journal, sales journal, two personal ledgers ("A", town debtors, and "B," country debtors), bought ledger, and nominal ledger.

You are asked to rearrange the system of book-keeping so that every ledger may be self-balancing. How would you effect this? *(London Chamber of Commerce.)*

3. Briefly describe the uses of the journal; and give particulars of the entries you would expect to find in the journal of a business in which the "sales" and "bought" ledgers were balanced independently, by means of adjustment accounts. *(London Chamber of Commerce.)*

4. John Garside keeps his sales ledger upon the "self-balancing" principle. Prepare the necessary "adjustment account" as on 31st January, from the undermentioned particulars—

			£
Jan	1	Total debtors' debit balances at this date were	12,542
	31	" goods sold to customers for the month	21,658
		" " returned by customers for the month	942
		" cash received from customers for the month	15,621
		" discount allowed to customers for the month	968
		" acceptances received from customers, during the month	3,471
		Total acceptances dishonoured by customers during the month	542

(*R.S.A.*)

5. Give suitable rulings for the sales journal of a wholesale business comprising three departments, viz.: "mantles," "dress materials," and "felts." There are two sales ledgers in use, viz.: "town" and "country," and each ledger is kept upon the self-balancing principle. (*London Chamber of Commerce.*)

6. Rule a form of cash book which would be necessary in a business in which a general ledger, two bought ledgers and two sold ledgers are in use, all these ledgers being "self-balancing." Explain briefly how you would put into practice the principles of "self-balancing" ledgers in connexion with this cash book.

(*London Chamber of Commerce.*)

7. Illustrate the sectional system of self-balancing ledgers by posting direct from the exercise given below, all the items necessary to form a complete sales ledger, render it self-balancing, and take out a trial balance. Ignore any items not affecting the sales ledger.

On 1st March, Samuel Sparrow, merchant, had cash in hand £360; goods on hand £450. Debtors: James Crow £220; Thomas Finch £150; John Jay £270. Creditors: Louis Lark £180; Robert Rook £200.

			£
Mar	1	Samuel Sparrow drew cash for self	20
	2	Received Cash from J. Crow	210
		Discount allowed in addition	10
	3	Paid for postages	1
	4	Cash purchases	210
	6	Sold goods to J. Crow	175
		Charged him for carriage paid on above goods	1
	7	Received cash of T. Finch	147
		Discount allowed in addition	3
	8	Paid rates	40
	9	Cash sales	130
	10	T. Finch bought goods	180
	11	Sales to L. Lark	50
	13	Paid L. Lark, cash	127
		Received discount from him	3
	14	Sales to R. Robin	135
	15	Purchases from L. Lark	215
	16	Paid R. Rook cash	195
		Received discount from him	5
	17	Received cash from R. Robin	35
	18	J. Crow bought goods	28
	20	R. Rook sold me goods	165
	21	Received cash of John Jay in full settlement	255
		Wrote off his balance as bad debt	15
	22	Bought goods of Charles Wren	54
	23	Received cash for a bad debt written off two years ago	27

		£
24	Purchases from R. Rook	45
25	Paid R. Rook cash	100
27	Received cash from J. Crow	77
28	Paid wages	16
29	Paid rent	25
31	Interest on capital	4
	Stock on hand	529

8. The following totals are taken from the books of Dover & Dudley—

19..		£
Jan 1	Credit balances in purchases ledger	5,926
	„ „ „ sales ledger	134
	Debit balances in purchases ledger	56
	„ „ „ sales ledger	10,268
Dec 31	Sales	71,504
	Purchases	47,713
	Cash received from customers	69,872
	Cash paid to creditors	47,028
	Sales ledger balances written off as bad	96
	Sales returns and allowances	358
	Purchases returns and allowances	202
	Discounts allowed	1,435
	„ received	867
	Purchase ledger credits transferred to sales ledger	75
	Legal expenses charged to customers	28
	Credit balances in sales ledger	101
	Debit balances in purchases ledger	67

Prepare separate purchases ledger control and sales ledger control accounts, as they would appear in the general ledger of the firm, showing the balances carried forward to the following year. (*R.S.A.*)

9. From the following particulars write up A. Allott's bought ledger for the month of January, and make it self-balancing. Take out a trial balance in order to prove the accuracy of your work.

Ledger balances as at 1st January: S. Smith £210; B. Brown £160; J. Jones £80; T. Thompson £60; H. Hewitt £180; L. Lovejoy £200.

His transactions for the month were as follows—

		£
Jan 3	Bought of S. Smith goods	80
5	Paid L. Lovejoy (discount £10)	190
10	Bought of B. Brown goods	150
11	Returned goods to J. Jones	15
12	Paid H. Hewitt on account	50
14	Accepted B. Brown's draft (discount £5)	75
17	Bought of J. Jones goods	60
19	Paid T. Thompson (discount £2)	58
21	Bought of T. Thompson goods	70
23	Paid J. Jones on account	40
24	Bought of H. Hewitt goods	180
25	Paid B. Brown (discount £4)	76
26	Accepted H. Hewitt's draft (discount £3)	70
28	Returned goods to L. Lovejoy	20
30	Bought of L. Lovejoy goods	160
31	Paid S. Smith (discount £10)	200

10. From the following particulars write up P. Zucker's bought ledger for the month of March. and make it self-balancing. Prove the accuracy of your work by drawing out a trail balance as at the end of the month.

The creditors' balances as at 1st January were: L. Luke £270; M. Matthew £440; J. John £190; M. Mark £210; P. Paul £150; S. Silas £360.

Zucker's transactions for the month were as follows—

			£
Mar	4	Bought of L. Luke goods	250
	6	Paid to S. Silas on account	80
	11	Bought of M. Matthew	65
	12	Accepted L. Luke's draft (discount £8)	152
	13	Returned goods to P. Paul	28
		Paid P. Paul (discount £6)	116
	18	Bought of J. John goods	75
	20	Paid M. Mark (discount £10)	200
	22	Bought of M. Mark goods	130
	24	Paid J. John (discount £9)	181
	25	Bought of P. Paul goods	50
		Accepted S. Silas' draft (discount £10)	190
	26	Paid M. Matthew on account	100
	27	Returned goods to M. Matthew	38
	30	Bought of S. Silas goods	160
	31	Paid L. Luke on account	50

11. You are required to write up, from the following particulars, E. Brockwell's sales ledger for the month of July. Make it self-balancing, and prove the accuracy of your work by means of a trial balance at the end of the month.

The opening ledger balances on 1st July were: B. Beard £126; C. Cowan £137; D. Doggett £85; E. Eley £97; F. Foxwell £175; G. Graves £186.

The following were his transactions for the month—

			£
Jul	3	Sold goods to B. Beard	62
	4	G. Graves returned goods	23
	5	Received from G. Graves (discount £9)	154
	6	F. Foxwell accepted our draft (discount £4)	90
	10	Sold goods to C. Cowan	74
	12	Received cash from F. Foxwell on account	50
	17	Sold goods to D. Doggett	165
	19	Received from E. Eley (discount £5)	92
	21	Sold goods to E. Eley	120
	23	Received from D. Doggett (discount £5)	80
		C. Cowan returned goods	16
	24	Sold goods to F. Foxwell	88
	25	Received from C. Cowan (discount £2)	54
	26	B. Beard accepted our draft (discount £3)	63
	30	Sold goods to G. Graves	100
	31	Received from B. Beard on account	40

12. The accountant of Benux Ltd. divides the company's sales ledgers into four sections for the purposes of balancing, with a separate control account for each. All the sections are supposed to be balanced monthly, and in fact were balanced at 30th September, 19. ., but, owing to pressure of work, differences arising in the following

months were not located and corrected at the time. The following table sets out the totals of the schedules of balances and of the control balances for each section at the end of October, November, and December, 19. ., respectively—

	Section 1	*Section* 2	*Section* 3	*Section* 4
	£	£	£	£
Oct 31				
Total of Schedules—				
Debits . . .	763·25	931·75	591·15	807·35
Credits . . .	*nil*	26·25	5·90	*nil*
Control balance . .	775·00	905·50	573·50	811·25
Nov 30				
Totals of Schedules—				
Debits . . .	873·45	890·15	732·25	951·10
Credits . . .	3·45	26·45	5·90	7·25
Control balance . .	870·00	863·70	726·35	947·75
Dec 31				
Totals of Schedules—				
Debits . . .	860·65	841·15	690·45	986·30
Credits . . .	3·25	17·65	5·90	7·50
Control balance . .	857·40	817·65	684·55	972·70

State the various inferences that can be drawn from an analysis and comparison of the foregoing figures and in which section(s) for what month(s) the postings should be checked in order to get books in proper balance again. (*R.S.A.*)

13. On 1st January Graham and Winder, who were equal partners in a business, possessed the following assets and liabilities: stock £2,750; cash £1,725; plant and machinery £2,550; creditors £1,720; debtors £2,645. The debtors and creditors were as follows—

Debtors	£	*Creditors*	£
Moore . . .	574	Horsham . .	236
Roberts . . .	206	Piggott . . .	350
Harrison . . .	495	Manton . . .	272
Squires . . .	369	Coles . . .	314
Farrow . . .	573	Day . . .	285
Lonsdale . . .	428	Bullen . . .	263

The following were their transactions for the month of January—

	Sales	*Cash Received*	*Discount Allowed*
	£	£	£
Moore	276	546	28
Roberts	365	196	10
Harrison	198	466	29
Squires	457	351	18
Farrow	584	545	28
Lonsdale	343	407	21

	Purchases	*Cash Paid*	*Discount Received*
	£	£	£
Horsham	274	225	11
Piggott	298	333	17
Manton	237	259	13
Coles	196	299	15
Day	189	271	14
Bullen	285	250	13
Sundry Expenses		263	
Graham		35	
Winder		35	
Salaries		75	
Wages		125	

Record the above transactions in their proper ledgers, make them self-balancing, and extract trial balances. Close the books as at 31st January. Provide £100 for bad debts, £125 for outstanding sundry expenses, and provide for depreciation of plant and machinery at the rate of 12 per cent per annum. Charge also interest on capital at 5 per cent per annum. Stock in hand 31st January was £3,150.

14. H. Holland is in business, and on 1st January his assets and liabilities are: cash £50; bank £870; stock £1,000; bills receivable £375; furniture and fixtures £200; plant and machinery £1,700; A. Arthur, *Dr.*, £275; B. Brown, *Dr.*, £362; F. Flower, *Dr.*, £250; C. Cook, *Dr.*, £873; bills payable £420; D. Dunlop, *Cr.*, £175; G. Garnet, *Cr.*, £130; E. Ernest, *Cr.*, £85; F. Franklin, *Cr.*, £220.

His transactions for the month are as follows—

			£
Jan	4	Sold to A. Arthur goods	360
		Paid wages	127
	7	Bought from D. Dunlop goods	620
	10	Received from B. Brown (discount £18)	344
	11	Paid wages	131
	13	Sold to B. Brown goods	250
		Paid D. Dunlop (discount £10)	165
	14	Bought from E. Ernest goods	460
	15	Received from A. Arthur (discount £13)	262
		B. Brown returned goods	20
		F. Flower accepted our draft (discount £12) Bill No. 59, dated 13th January at 2 m/d	238
		Paid acceptance No. 86	270
	16	Bill receivable No. 56 duly met at bank	120
		Paid to E. Ernest (discount £3)	82
	18	Sold to F. Flower goods	210
		Paid wages	142
	19	Paid acceptance No. 85	150
	21	Bought from F. Franklin goods	275
	22	Accepted G. Garnet's draft (discount £6). Acceptance No. 87, dated 21st January, at 2 m/d	124
		Received from C. Cook (discount £43)	830
	23	Paid F. Franklin (discount £10)	210
		Received payment of bill No. 57	155

Jan		£
24	Bill No. 54, accepted by A. Arthur, returned by bank dishonoured, noting charges, £1	156
	Bought from G. Garnet goods	220
	Returned to F. Franklin goods	10
25	Paid wages	130
26	Bill receivable No. 58 duly met	100
27	Sold to C. Cook goods	320
	Drew for self	150
31	Ready money purchases	24
	Paid salaries	242
	Paid rent, rates, and taxes	270
	Paid trade expenses	170
	Ready money sales for month	127

You are required to record the above transactions in the proper subsidiary books, post to separate ledgers and make them self-balancing, and to verify the accuracy of your work by extracting trial balances as at the end of the month.

15. In order to locate the difference on the trial balance of King and Cross at 30th June, 19.1, it was decided to prepare purchases and sales ledger total (or control) accounts.

From the following details, prepare these accounts to show where an error may have been made—

19..			£
Jul	1	Purchases ledger balances	5,982
		Sales ledger balances	9,872
		Totals for year ending 30th June, 19.1—	
		Purchases journal	77,281
		Sales journal	99,831
		Returns outwards journal	1,324
		Returns inwards journal	2,278
		Cheques paid to suppliers	73,050
		Petty cash paid to suppliers	39
		Cheques and cash received from customers	92,980
		Discounts allowed	2,910
		Discounts received	1,067
		Bad debts written off	198
		Customers' cheques dishonoured	15
		Balances on the sales ledger set off against credit balances in the purchases ledger	518

The list of balances taken from the purchases ledger shows a total of £7,265 and that from the sales ledger a total of £10,829.

(*R.S.A.*)

16. Moda-Styles Ltd. (the company) sell Furniture for cash, allowing 5 per cent cash discount, and on credit, NETT. Customers Debts are formally assigned to Moneybag Ltd.—a Finance House—who immediately advance 80 per cent thereof to the company and the balance of 20 per cent when debts are collected in full by the company and paid over to Moneybag Ltd. who retain 1 per cent for Finance Charges.

From the following particulars of transactions in the year to 31st December last, show the Sales Ledger Control or Adjustment Account and the Moneybag Ltd.

Advances Account in the company's General Ledger—assuming all debts are retained on to books till finally collected (ignoring delays in transit of cash).

	£
Trade Debtors at beginning of year	20,000
Advances from Moneybag Ltd. on above debts, brought forward	16,000
Sales on credit during year	10,000
Cash Received—	
Cash sales (£5,000) less Discount (£250)	4,750
From customers—in full settlement	22,000
Advances from Moneybag Ltd.—	
(i) 80 per cent advances	8,000
(ii) 20 per cent advances (£4,400) less charges (£220)	4,180
Cash Paid—	
Cash collected per *contra* paid to Moneybag Ltd.	22,000

(*L.C.C.*)

17. From the following figures of a firm of retailers, prepare Sales Ledger and Bought Ledger Control Accounts for the three months ended 30th June, 1963.

	£
Sundry Debtors Balances as at 1st April, 1963	2,046·60
Sundry Creditors Balances as at 1st April, 1963	1,114·45
Cash received from Debtors	11,990·95
Cash paid to Creditors	7,512·15
Purchases	8,713·55
Discounts Received	199·50
Sales	12,940·85
Bad Debts written off	47·50
Returns Inwards	89·15
Returns Outwards	201·05
Interest charged to Debtors	3·55
Cheques from Debtors Dishonoured	59·62
Discounts Allowed	240·70
Bills Payable Accepted (including Renewals)	750·75
Bills Payable upon Renewal	190·00
Interest on Bills Payable Renewed	1·75

(*L.C.C.*)

18. The X Y Company Limited keep their ledgers on the "self-balancing" system. On 31st December the sales ledger account in the private ledger showed a debit balance, brought down 31st December of the previous year of £4,031. During the year the total sales were £35,422, and returns inwards were £625. The cash received during the year and posted to the sales ledger was £31,125. The discounts allowed on accounts in the sales ledger amounted to £1,314. Transfers from the bought ledger to the *Cr.* of sales ledger accounts £720. Transfers from the sales ledger to the *Dr.* of bought ledger accounts £1,052. Bills receivable posted to the sales ledger £2,035. Write up the sales ledger account and show the balance brought down at 31st December. What does this balance represent? (*Chartered Accountants.*)

19. Up and Down are trading in partnership. The sales ledger is separately balanced by means of a control account in the nominal ledger, but the bought ledger is not, the number of accounts and volume of transactions not being thought large enough to justify it.

You are required to set out journal entries at the close of the year to adjust or correct the following matters, using the standard journal ruling or a special one, whichever you prefer—

(*a*) Trading stock valued (at cost price to the firm) at £27·50 was taken by Down for his personal use. £15 of this was entered by the book-keeper in the sales day book and posted to an account which is still open in Down's name in the sales ledger. The remaining £12·50 has not been dealt with at all.

(*b*) A sum of £7·75 had been received from the liquidator of Pages Ltd. and posted to the credit of that company's account in the sales ledger after the previous debit balance had been wholly written off as bad.

(*c*) The book-keeper had wrongly entered in the returns inward book £4·06 as the value of returns from M. Queen and posted it. When Queen received his statement he had pointed out that the amount should have been £4·66, whereupon the book-keeper had corrected the ledger account but had done nothing else.

(*d*) A debit balance of £14·85 in the name of James & Sons in the sales ledger is to be set off against a credit balance in the name of the same firm in the bought ledger.

(*R.S.A.*)

CHAPTER 06
DEPRECIATION OF FIXED ASSETS

I withdraw penny minutes, shilling hours,
Continually from my bank of days
And priceless promissory notes of time
I squander. Credit dwindles and always
Time leaks. It is not possible to freeze
This current and no statements of account
Are issued. Total capital of days
Is from the first unknown. I know they grant
No interest. Time's bank invests in me
A finite sum to multiply.

ANNA ADAMS

Acquisition of Assets. Expenditure on acquiring assets which will be held over several periods with the object of earning revenue is treated as capital expenditure, or capitalized. Such expenditures include the price paid, freight and insurance, installation costs, legal costs and all costs of putting the assets into productive service. The cost of a machine tool includes bedding down, laying foundations and so on. Fixed assets unlike stock-in-trade, are not acquired for sale in the normal course of business which means that a fixed asset for one business may be stock-in-trade for another. For instance, buildings are normally fixed assets but may be stock-in-trade for a property dealer.

Fixed assets are normally recorded in the books at cost and periodical allowances made for that cost: this allowance is the depreciation, amortization or depletion. If a machine costs £5,000 and is sold for scrap after 5 years for £500 then the total depreciation is £4,500. This might be calculated as £900 per annum for the five years.

Depreciation is a cost of conducting the business and the costs must include an allowance for depreciation if the profits or losses are to be shown accurately whilst the assets are in use.

Types of Fixed Assets. The main types of fixed assets are—

1. Land and Buildings. Factories, offices, houses, wharves and warehouses, etc. Land does not deteriorate and is not usually depreciated. Buildings depreciate slowly, if at all.

2. Natural Resources. Mines, quarries, oil, coal, and gas deposits, etc. These are sometimes called wasting assets since they become worthless when the deposits or resources have been depleted.

3. PLANT, MACHINERY AND EQUIPMENT. Machines, tools, heating and ventilating plant, accounting machines, furniture, computers, etc. This is the main class of assets subject to depreciation.

4. LEASEHOLDS, PATENTS AND COPYRIGHTS. These rights have a limited life and their cost is written off over that life. Provisions in respect of leases must take account of the cost of the dilapidations payable by the tenant at the end of the lease.

Reasons for Charging Depreciation. Unless assets are depreciated their value may sometimes be overstated on the Balance Sheet. Assets such as plant and machinery are held for the purpose of earning income, and the loss arising on those assets through wear and tear is undoubtedly an expense against such income. If depreciation was not provided for by charges against profits, additional capital would have to be raised whenever the necessity for replacing the asset arose.

Assessment of Depreciation. This involves three factors—

1. *The original or historic cost*—this is known.
2. *The estimated life of the assets*—this can be estimated within limits.
3. *The estimated scrap, residual or break-up value*—this can also be estimated.

How long an asset may be useful to a firm or what value it will realize, if any, when it is eventually disposed of, can only be guessed. Depreciation is, therefore, an estimate and students should recognize this by rounding off all calculations.

Causes of Depreciation. The chief causes are—

1. *Wear and tear*—loss of value from use.
2. *Obsolescence*, i.e. machinery rendered out of date by later inventions.
3. *Passage of time*. Whatever the condition of an asset it loses value according to age.
4. *Superfluity*. Some plant may be superfluous to requirements if productions plans change. This leads to loss of value.
5. *Physical factors* may lead to depreciation in value of assets, e.g. dampness, floods, excessive heat, etc.
6. *Fluctuation in prices*. If there is a general change in prices or foreign exchange rates, the money value of assets, both new and second hand, will also change. This may give rise to appreciation of value or to a loss.

Appreciation is the opposite of depreciation, and means a permanent increase in the value of an asset. Land and property are more liable to appreciation than other assets. On the conservatism convention, appreciation may be ignored until assets are sold and the profit is realized in hard cash. In practice, this may make a balance sheet highly misleading.

Repairs, Renewals, and Replacements. To repair means to restore, to make efficient for all practical purposes. To renew, means to discard an asset, or some part of it, and to replace with a similar or improved asset or part. It has been argued that, if proper provision is made for repairs and renewals, there is no need to provide for depreciation.

Methods of Depreciation. There are various methods of calculating depreciation—

1. Fixed instalment method.
2. Diminishing or reducing balance method.
3. Sum of the years' digits.
4. Annuity system.
5. Depreciation fund method.
6. Insurance policy system.
7. Revaluation.
8. Repairs, maintenance and depreciation fund or provision.
9. Depletion unit or production unit method.
10. Combined methods.

Since the principle is the same as that of the depreciation fund, this chapter also deals with—

11. The Sinking fund.

Book-keeping Treatment. There are two fundamental methods of treating depreciation in book-keeping.

1. *Credit* asset account } with amount written off each
Debit depreciation expense account } year.

When all assets have been depreciated for the year, the depreciation account is closed—

Credit depreciation expense account } with total written off all assets.
Debit profit and loss account }

2. *Debit* profit and loss account } with amount provided for
Credit depreciation provision account } the year.
(for each asset) }

In the first method the book value of the asset in the asset account decreases each year. Example 1 on p. 0604 shows this method applied to a lease.

In the second method, the book value of the asset in the asset account remains constant, but the depreciation fund increases in value each year. Example 8 on p. 0615 shows this method applied to a lease also. In the balance sheet the depreciation fund could be shown on the liabilities side, but it is usually deducted from the value of the asset on the assets side.

Provided the same values are taken, both methods would show the same results, and both are found in practice. Concurrently with all or any of the book-keeping methods just mentioned (and whichever principle of arriving at the charge is used) a specific sum may be set aside either in cash or by way of investment so as to provide liquid funds at the end of the stated period of time. This is the sinking fund principle.

1. Fixed Instalment or Straight Line Method

Under this system, a fixed proportion of the original capital outlay is written off annually in order to reduce the asset to zero or residual value at the end of the period.

Example 1

A lease is purchased for a term of four years for the sum of £320. Show how the lease account would appear in the ledger during this period, depreciation being written off by equal instalments each year.

Solution 1

In four years £320 has to be written off, which gives us £80 each year to write off the original cost. As a percentage of original cost this is $\frac{80}{320} \times 100 = 25$ per cent. A journal entry would be made each year for four years, thus—

	Dr	*Cr*
Depreciation	£80	
Lease		£80

The amount of the lease account not written off would appear on the assets side of the balance sheet.

		£	£
Year 2	Lease at cost	320	
	Less Amount written off . . .	160	
	Book value		160

LEASE

Year		£	Year		£
1	Cash	320	1	Depreciation	80
				Balance c/d . . .	240
		320			320
2	Balance b/d . . .	240	2	Depreciation	80
				Balance c/d . . .	160
		240			240
3	Balance b/d . . .	160	3	Depreciation	80
				Balance c/d . . .	80
		160			160
4	Balance b/d . . .	80	4	Depreciation	80

Example 2

Plant purchased for £4,000 has an estimated life of three years and an eventual disposal value of £400.

Solution 2

PLANT

Year		£				
1	Cash	4,000				

DEPRECIATION ON PLANT PROVISION

Year		£	Year			£
2	Balance c/d . . .	2,400	1	P. & L. A/c . . .		1,200
			2	P. & L. A/c . . .		1,200
		2,400				2,400
			3	Balance b/d . . .		2,400
				P. & L. A/c . . .		1,200

No further provision would be made, and so long as the asset is retained in the firm it will appear on the balance sheet as—

	£	£
Plant at cost	4,000	
Less Depreciation Provision . . .	3,600	
		400

2. Diminishing balance method

By this method a fixed rate per cent is written off the reducing balance of the asset account each year. Often this system is adopted for plant and machinery, furniture, fixtures, fittings, etc., as such assets have a long life and one which it is difficult to estimate.

Advantages. The advantage of this method of depreciation is that it tends to give a fairly even charge against revenue each year. For while depreciation is heavy during the first few years, this is counterbalanced by the repairs being light; and in the later years, when repairs are heavy, this is counterbalanced by the decreasing charge for depreciation.

Mathematical Formula. The rate per cent to write off the diminishing value each year is found by means of the following formula—

$$P \times \left(\frac{100 - r}{100}\right)^n = RV$$

where P denotes the principal, r the required rate per cent, n the number of years, and RV the residual value.

As a rough rule of thumb, *twice* the straight line depreciation rate may be taken, e.g. asset with 10 year life—20 per cent. This method is therefore sometimes called the double-declining method.

Example 3

Machinery is bought for £2,000. Its life is estimated to be six years, and its break-up value at the end of the period £356. Show the machinery account for the six years, writing off depreciation at a fixed rate per cent on the diminishing or reducing value of the asset.

Solution 3

According to the formula: $2{,}000 \times \left(\frac{100 - r}{100}\right)^6 = 356$, which, when reduced, gives

$$r = 100 - 100\sqrt[6]{0{\cdot}178} = 100 - 100\,(0{\cdot}7500) \text{ approx.;}$$

hence $r = 100 - 75 = 25$ per cent approx.

The ledger account of the asset will be as follows—

MACHINERY

Year		£	Year		£
1	Cash . . .	2,000	1	Depreciation . . .	500
				Balance c/d . . .	1,500
		2,000			2,000
2	Balance b/d . . .	1,500	2	Depreciation . . .	375
				Balance c/d . . .	1,125
		1,500			1,500
3	Balance b/d . . .	1,125	3	Depreciation . . .	281
				Balance c/d . . .	844
		1,125			1,125
4	Balance b/d . . .	844	4	Depreciation . . .	211
				Balance c/d . . .	633
		844			844
5	Balance b/d . . .	633	5	Depreciation . . .	158
				Balance c/d . . .	475
		633			633
6	Balance b/d . . .	475	6	Depreciation . . .	119
				Balance c/d . . .	356
		475			475
7	Balance b/d . . .	356			

3. Sum of the years' digits method

This method of calculating depreciation is an alternative diminishing balance method. The years in the life of the asset are added: for instance, on a five-year life, the sum is $1 + 2 + 3 + 4 + 5 = 15$. The total amount to be depreciated is then divided by this sum of the years digits: for instance, if an asset costing £16,000 were expected to have a residual value of £1,000, then on a five-year life, each unit would be £1,000.

The depreciation is then allocated to each of the five years in proportion to the reverse order: that means, on a five-year life, that the first year will attract 5 fifteenths, the second year 4 fifteenths, and so on, as follows:

		Annual Depreciation
Year 1	5/15 of £15,000	£5,000
Year 2	4/15 of £15,000	£4,000
Year 3	3/15 of £15,000	£3,000
Year 4	2/15 of £15,000	£2,000
Year 5	1/15 of £15,000	£1,000
		£15,000

QUESTIONS

1. Define depreciation.
2. What are the causes of depreciation?
3. State briefly some of the reasons for charging depreciation.
4. Explain the meaning of the following terms: "life" of an asset, "residual," or "break-up" value, to scrap, obsolescence. How is the loss sustained by obsolescence treated?
5. State briefly what is meant by: repairs, renewals, and replacements.
6. What entries may be made in the books when an asset is depreciated?
7. What methods of depreciation are there?
8. Explain briefly the nature and use of the "fixed instalment" method of depreciation. Can this method be used for all assets?
9. Explain briefly the "diminishing balance" method of depreciation. What advantages does this method possess?

Depreciation of Additions to an Asset. The question of how to treat additions to an asset, when writing off depreciation on the first occasion after such addition, is rather a complex one. Owing to conflicting views, no less than three different methods obtain. The additions are—

1. Ignored, by writing depreciation off the balance of the asset account as at the *beginning* of the year.
2. Included, by writing depreciation off the balance of the asset account as at the *end* of the year.
3. Depreciated *proportionately*, a machine purchased about the middle of the year being written down at *half* the annual rate, and so on.

Example 4

Machinery is bought for a sum of £2,000. Additions are made in June in the second year to the extent of £200, and in March of the third year to the amount of £160. Show, by means of ledger accounts, the various methods of dealing with the additions when writing off annual depreciation at the rate of 10 per cent on the diminishing balance.

Solution 4

First Method

PLANT AND MACHINERY

		£			£
1st yr.	Cash	2,000	1st yr.	Depreciation, 10% £2,000	200
				Balance c/d	1,800
		2,000			2,000
2nd yr.	Balance b/d	1,800	2nd yr.	Depreciation, 10% £1,800	180
	Cash (June)	200		Balance c/d	1,820
		2,000			2,000
3rd yr.	Balance b/d	1,820	3rd yr.	Depreciation, 10% £1,820	182
	Cash (March)	160		Balance c/d	1,798
		1,980			1,980
4th yr.	Balance b/d	1,798			

Second Method

PLANT AND MACHINERY

		£			£
1st yr.	Cash	2,000	1st yr.	Depreciation, 10% £2,000	200
				Balance c/d	1,800
		2,000			2,000
2nd yr.	Balance b/d	1,800	2nd yr.	Depreciation, 10% £2,000	200
	Cash (June)	200		Balance c/d	1,800
		2,000			2,000
3rd yr.	Balance b/d	1,800	3rd yr.	Depreciation, 10% £1,960	196
	Cash (March)	160		Balance c/d	1,764
		1,960			1,960
4th yr.	Balance b/d	1,764			

Third Method

PLANT AND MACHINERY

		£				£
1st yr.	Cash	2,000	1st yr.	Depreciation, 10% £2,000 .		200
				Balance c/d . . .		1,800
		2,000				2,000
2nd yr.	Balance b/d . . .	1,800	2nd yr.	Depreciation, 10% £1,800 . .	£180	
	Cash (June) . . .	200		10% for 6 months on £200 . .	£10	
						190
				Balance c/d . . .		1,810
		2,000				2,000
3rd yr.	Balance b/d . . .	1,810	3rd yr.	Depreciation, 10% £1,810 . .	£181	
	Cash (March) . . .	160		10% for 9 months on £160 . .	£12	
						193
				Balance c/d . . .		1,777
		1,970				1,970
4th yr.	Balance b/d . . .	1,777				

Sale of Assets. When an asset is sold, there will usually be a profit or loss, depending on whether the proceeds exceed the book value of the asset. The book value of the asset is the original cost of asset *less* depreciation provided for the particular asset since purchase.

This profit or loss must be taken out of the asset account (usually to profit and loss account) and this can be done in two ways—

(*a*) *If depreciation has been credited to the asset account*—

(i) *Dr.* cash account / *Cr.* asset account } with amount realized on sale of asset.

(ii) If there is a profit—

Dr. asset account / *Cr.* profit and loss account } with profit realized on sale.

Naturally, entry (ii) is reversed for a loss.

Example 5

Plant is bought for £15,000, depreciated at 20 per cent on cost for two years and then sold for £10,000.

Solution 5

PLANT

Year		£	Year		£
1	Cash . .	15,000	1	P. & L. A/c (Depreciation)	3,000
2	P. & L. A/c (profit on sale)	1,000	2	P. & L. A/c (Depreciation)	3,000
			2	Cash (Proceeds of sale) .	10,000
		16,000			16,000

(*b*) ***If depreciation has been carried to a depreciation provision.*** **This is best dealt with by opening a sale of plant account, to which are transferred the original cost of the asset and the accumulated depreciation on the asset.**

Example 6

Taking Example 5, assume that the plant is part of a grand total of £55,000 plant, on which £35,000 depreciation has been provided.

Solution 6

PLANT

Year		£	Year		£
2	Balance . . .	55,000	2	Sale of Plant A/c .	15,000

DEPRECIATION ON PLANT FUND

Year		£	Year		£
2	Sale of Plant A/c .	6,000	2	Balance . . .	35,000

SALE OF PLANT ACCOUNT

Year		£	Year		£
2	Plant A/c . . .	15,000	2	Depreciation Fund .	6,000
2	P. & L. A/c . . .	1,000	2	Cash . . .	10,000
		16,000			16,000

Calculation of Depreciation. The amount of depreciation to be charged depends upon the policy adopted in charging additions. Whatever policy is adopted on additions should be applied to sales also. As an example refer to the accounts in Example 4. Assume that half of the machinery bought for £2,000 in Year 1 is sold the next year, on 1st October, for £500.

(i) If depreciation is written off the balance on the asset account at the *beginning* of the year.

		£	
Cost of Asset		1,000	
Less Depreciation 10 per cent—			
Year 1	£100		
„ 2	90		
		190	
Book value		810	∴ Loss £310

However, it must be noted that the £90 will not be charged to profit and loss account until the end of the year, when it is included in the £180 charged.

(ii) If depreciation is written off the balance of the asset account at the *end* of the year.

	£	
Cost of Asset	1,000	
Less Depreciation 10 per cent—		
Year 1	100	
Book value	900	∴ Loss £400

(iii) If depreciation is written off proportionately.

		£	
Cost of Asset		1,000	
Less Depreciation 10 per cent—			
Year 1	£100		
Year 2 for 9 months	67		
		167	
Book value		833	∴ Loss £333

Again, the £67 is not charged to profit and loss account until the end of the year, when the amount charged would be—

		£
10 per cent on £900	=	90
„ „ „ „ £900 for 9 months	=	67
„ „ „ „ £200 „ 6 „	=	10
		167

4. Annuity System

Under the annuity system the purchase of the asset is regarded as an investment of capital which, if employed for other purposes, would be earning a certain rate of interest. Interest at this fixed rate is, therefore, added to the cost of the asset account each year. The asset and interest are then written down by equal annual instalments until extinguished. This method is used principally for leases involving considerable outlay spread over a number of years, when it is not desired to replace them at the end of the period. Conceptually, it is the best method for calculating depreciation on all assets, although it is not widely used.

Calculation of the Depreciation Charge. The amount to be written off yearly by the Annuity method (i.e. Principal + Interest − Instalment) can be easily calculated from the following formula for £1—

$$\frac{1}{\dfrac{(1 + \text{Interest})^n - 1}{\text{Interest}}} + \text{Interest, or } \frac{\text{Interest}}{\text{Compound Interest}^n} + \text{Interest}$$

where n = number of years. This gives us for five years, at 5 per cent, $\frac{0{\cdot}05}{0{\cdot}276281} + 0{\cdot}05$ or $0{\cdot}180975 + 0{\cdot}05$, that is $0{\cdot}230975$; and so on for other rates and years.

To obviate the need for extensive calculations, a table of capital recovery factors may be used. Table C in Appendix I gives the factors for a range of interest rates for up to fifty years life. The factor multiplied by the original cost gives the required annual depreciation charge.

Book-keeping treatment. Since the interest charged to the asset is purely notional, it cannot be credited directly to the profit and loss account. Instead, it is credited to the Depreciation expense account, which is usually re-named the depreciation and interest account. This system results in an increasing charge against revenue each year; for, while the depreciation that is debited remains constant, the interest being credited will diminish each year.

The following entries will be made:

On acquisition of the asset:

Debit asset account.
Credit cash or suppliers account.

At each year end:

Interest is calculated on the balance standing in the asset account at the beginning of the year and the entries made.
Debit asset account with the notional interest.
Credit interest and depreciation account.
Depreciation will be a constant sum, calculated as indicated above and the entries to be made are:
Debit interest and depreciation account.
Credit asset account (or depreciation provision).
The interest and depreciation expense will then be charged to profit and loss account and the entries are:
Debit profit and loss account.
Credit interest and depreciation expense account.

If, at the expiration of a lease, dilapidations have to be provided for, this can best be done by means of the sinking fund method explained later on in this chapter.

Example 7

A lease is purchased for a term of seven years by payment of £3,000. It is proposed to depreciate the lease by the annuity method, charging 4 per cent interest. Show the ledger account of the asset during this period.

Solution 7

Reference to Table C shows that the amount for £1 for seven years at 4 per cent is 0·1666. Multiplying this by £3,000, we get £499·8 or £500, approximately.

LEASE

Year		£	Year		£
1	Cash	3,000	1	Depreciation	500
	Interest (4% on £3,000)	120		Balance c/d	2,620
		3,120			3,120
2	Balance b/d	2,620	2	Depreciation	500
	Interest (4% on £2,620)	105		Balance c/d	2,225
		2,725			2,725
3	Balance b/d	2,225	3	Depreciation	500
	Interest (4% on £2,225)	89		Balance c/d	1,814
		2,314			2,314
4	Balance b/d	1,814	4	Depreciation	500
	Interest (4% on £1,814)	73		Balance c/d	1,387
		1,887			1,887
5	Balance b/d	1,387	5	Depreciation	500
	Interest (4% on £1,387)	55		Balance c/d	942
		1,442			1,442
6	Balance b/d	942	6	Depreciation	500
	Interest (4% on £942)	38		Balance c/d	480
		980			980
7	Balance b/d	480	7	Depreciation	500
	Interest (4% on £480)	20			
		500			500

NOTE. There is often a small adjustment to make in the last year.

5. Depreciation Fund Principle

Under this method the asset is allowed to stand in the books at its original cost. A fixed amount, called the sinking fund instalment, is debited to profit and loss each year; and a corresponding amount of cash is invested every year in securities, the amount being enough to accumulate, at compound interest, to the sum required to replace the asset. This system is rarely used in industry today since the funds can usually be employed at a higher rate of profit by the firm itself. Investment in outside securities is unlikely to be more profitable.

The principle, however, is still used for redemption of capital purposes, as outlined in Chapter 23 (p. 2306–10).

Other Terms. The depreciation fund account is also called an amortization fund account, sinking fund account or redemption fund account. The first term is more appropriate to the writing off of intangible expenditure, that is not represented by assets, e.g. debenture discount; the last two terms are more suitable for the repayment of loans and debentures. Depreciation fund account is the best term to use in connexion with the replacement of a wasting asset.

Object of Investing Cash. The object of investing cash each year and allowing it to accumulate is that the fund becomes available (on realizing the investments) when it is required. Otherwise the cash required at the end of the period would have to be taken from the ordinary bank balance this might cause serious inconvenience to the business, and if the amount were very large, might cripple it. The effect of the sinking fund investment, therefore, is that it provides the money outside the business, and prevents any disturbance of the financial position.

Entries for a Depreciation or Sinking Fund. The twofold nature of the operation can best be seen in the basic entries involved.

(i) *Dr.* profit and loss account } with annual amount provided for
Cr. depreciation fund account } depreciation.

(ii) *Dr.* investment account } with equivalent amount of cash invested.
Cr. cash account }

If the interest earned by the investment were ignored, the above entries would suffice, but in fact the amount set aside each year takes into account the rate of interest expected on the investment. In the second and succeeding years, then, the following entries are made—

(iii) *Dr.* cash account } with interest received.
Cr. depreciation fund account }

(iv) *Dr.* investment account } with interest invested (this is combined
Cr. cash account } with (ii) above).

At the end of the funding period, the entries are—

(v) *Dr*. depreciation fund account } with accumulated provision, thus
Cr. asset account } closing asset account.

(vi) *Dr*. cash account } with amount of cash realized on sale of
Cr. investment account } investments.

Note that the last instalment of depreciation may need to be adjusted slightly to provide the exact total required in the fund. The last instalment of cash is not invested, but the entries may be made.

Sinking Fund Depreciation Tables. The sinking fund amount is calculated from tables based on the following formula—

$$\frac{1}{\dfrac{(1 + \text{Interest})^n - 1}{\text{Interest}}} \quad \text{or} \quad \frac{\text{Interest}}{\text{Total amount of Compound Interest in } n \text{ years}}$$

This gives the amount to be set aside yearly, at a given rate of interest, to provide £1 at the end of *n* or the given number of years.

For five years at 5 per cent the amount shows $\frac{0{\cdot}05}{0{\cdot}276281}$ or 0·180975 and so on for other years at other rates.

Table D in Appendix I gives the sinking fund factors for a range of interest rates for up to 50 years of asset life.

Example 8

£3,000 is paid for a lease for a term of seven years. It is desired to write off this amount by means of the depreciation fund system, it being necessary to raise a similar amount, at 4 per cent compound interest, in order to replace the lease at the end of the period. Show the ledger accounts dealing with this matter.

Solution 8

Referring to Table D, we find the amount required to be invested yearly at 4 per cent in order to produce £1 at the end of seven years is 0·1266. The amount required to produce £3,000 will, therefore, be £3,000 × 0·126609, which gives us £379·827, or £380 to the nearest £1.

The reason why the depreciation fund investment account does not, on the balance sheet, always correspond in amount with the depreciation fund account is that the instalment is charged against profits at the end of the year (say 31st December), but the corresponding investment of cash may not take place until the first month (say January) of the succeeding year. For the sake of clearness, however, the dates in the worked example have been made to agree.

The ledger accounts would appear as under—

LEASE

			£				£
1st yr.				7th yr.			
Jan	1	Cash	3,000	Dec	31	Depreciation Fund A/c	3,000

DEPRECIATION FUND

		£			£
1st yr.			1st yr.		
Dec 31	Balance c/d . . .	380	Dec 31	P. & L. A/c . . .	380
2nd yr.			2nd yr.		
Dec 31	Balance c/d . . .	775	Jan 1	Balance b/d . . .	380
			Dec 31	Cash (Interest) . .	15
				P. & L. A/c . .	380
		775			775
3rd yr.			3rd yr.		
Dec 31	Balance c/d . . .	1,186	Jan 1	Balance b/d . . .	775
			Dec 31	Cash (Interest) . .	31
				P. & L. A/c . .	380
		1,186			1,186
4th yr.			4th yr.		
Dec 31	Balance c/d . . .	1,613	Jan 1	Balance b/d . . .	1,186
			Dec 31	Cash (Interest) . .	47
				P. & L. A/c . .	380
		1,613			1,613
5th yr.			5th yr.		
Dec 31	Balance c/d . . .	2,057	Jan 1	Balance b/d . . .	1,613
			Dec 31	Cash (Interest) . .	64
				P. & L. A/c . .	380
		2,057			2,057
6th yr.			6th yr.		
Dec 31	Balance c/d . . .	2,519	Jan 1	Balance b/d . . .	2,057
			Dec 31	Cash (Interest) . .	82
				P. & L. A/c . .	380
		2,519			2,519
7th yr.			7th yr.		
Dec 31	Amount transferred to Lease A/c. . .	3,000	Jan 1	Balance b/d . . .	2,519
			Dec 31	Cash (Interest) . .	101
				P. & L. A/c . .	380
		3,000			3,000

Depreciation Fund Investment[1]

		£			£
1st yr.			1st yr.		
Dec 31	Cash	380	Dec 31	Balance c/d	380
2nd yr.			2nd yr.		
Jan 1	Balance b/d	380	Dec 31	Balance c/d	775
Dec 31	Cash (Instalment and Interest)	395			
		775			775
3rd yr.			3rd yr.		
Jan 1	Balance b/d	775	Dec 31	Balance c/d	1,186
Dec 31	Cash	411			
		1,186			1,186
4th yr.			4th yr.		
Jan 1	Balance b/d	1,186	Dec 31	Balance c/d	1,613
Dec 31	Cash	427			
		1,613			1,613
5th yr.			5th yr.		
Jan 1	Balance b/d	1,613	Dec 31	Balance c/d	2,057
Dec 31	Cash	444			
		2,057			2,057
6th yr.			6th yr.		
Jan 1	Balance b/d	2,057	Dec 31	Balance c/d	2,519
Dec 31	Cash	462			
		2,519			2,519
7th yr.			7th yr.		
Jan 1	Balance b/d	2,519	Dec 31	Cash (*proceeds of realization of investments*)	3,000
Dec 31	Cash	481			
		3,000			3,000

NOTE 1. The cash instalment at the end of the last year will not be invested, but will be transferred to the investment account money so that the full amount will be in hand with which to purchase the new lease.

NOTE 2. The lease account and the depreciation fund investment account will appear on the assets side of the balance sheet until the end of the period. The depreciation fund account will show on the liabilities side of the balance sheet until the end of the period; or, better still, on the assets side as a deduction from the lease.

[1] As the funds would probably be invested in *various* securities, there would be several accounts amounting to this in the aggregate.

The balance sheet will be as follows—

BALANCE SHEET

Liabilities	£	Assets	£
(Year 1) Depreciation Fund Account	380	(Year 1) Depreciation Fund Investment Account	380
(Year 2) Depreciation Fund Account	775	(Year 2) Depreciation Fund Investment Account	775

Income Tax on Interest from Investments. In the worked example, the investments have been taken at par, and income tax has been ignored for the sake of simplicity, but, in practice, interest on investment would be received *less tax*. Certain types of investment, such as unit trusts, may permit a standing instruction for automatic re-investment of the interest. In such cases a cash book entry as previously shown would not be required, but a journal entry would be necessary to debit the investment account and credit the depreciation fund account with the amount of such interest. If interest is remitted, then the company must re-invest the interest received.

To provide for the amount lost because of tax, an additional provision will be required each year. This is debited to profit and loss and credited to the Depreciation Fund account. A corresponding cash investment must be made.

6. Insurance Policy System

Under this method an insurance policy is taken out for the amount required to replace the asset at the end of its life. The procedure is like the depreciation fund system, except that the cash, instead of being invested in gilt-edged securities, is paid away in premiums to the insurance company. Although the interest thus obtained is lower, there is not the risk of loss on realization, as in the case of outside investments subject to market fluctuations.

Entries in the Books. Two methods of recording are used. In some cases the amount paid as a yearly premium is debited to lease policy account, and is regarded as an investment which increases by the addition of interest each year. At the date of the maturity of the policy the amount standing to the debit of the lease policy account would agree (approximately) with the amount received from the insurance company. If, however, a balance were shown, this could readily be adjusted. In the event of the policy being surrendered before maturity, the amount actually received would be credited to the lease policy account, and any loss shown on this account would be written off.

(*a*) *When the policy is valued at premiums paid plus interest* the entries in the books will be—

(i) *Dr.* lease policy account / *Cr.* cash account — with annual premiums paid to insurance company.

(ii) *Dr.* profit and loss account / *Cr.* lease redemption fund account — with annual amount provided for depreciation at the end of the year.

The provision may be increased so as to provide for dilapidations, if the firm is liable for these at the end of the lease.

As insurance premiums are payable in advance, the first entry will be made at the beginning of the year. The second entry is made at the end of the year—

(iii) *Dr.* lease policy account / *Cr.* lease redemption fund account — with interest at the rate expected.

When the policy matures—

(iv) *Dr.* cash account / *Cr.* lease policy account — with the cash received.

Any balance remaining on the lease policy account may be written off to profit and loss account.

The accounts are finally closed by—

(v) *Dr.* lease redemption account / *Cr.* lease account — with transfer of accumulated provisions.

During the period, the lease account and the lease policy account will figure on the assets side of the balance sheet, while the lease redemption (or depreciation) fund account will be shown on the liabilities side of the balance sheet.

(*b*) *When the policy is valued at surrender value*. If a policy is given up before maturity, only the surrender value is payable. In the early years, the surrender value may be less than the premiums paid. In later years it should be more.

If the policy account is kept at surrender value, the entries are as follows—

(i) and (ii) as above.

(*a*) Where surrender value is *less* than the amount paid—

(iii) (*a*) *Cr.* policy account / *Dr.* lease redemption account — with amount necessary to bring policy account to surrender value.

(*b*) Where surrender value exceeds premiums paid—

(iii) (*b*) *Dr*. policy account.
Cr. lease redemption account.

At the end of the period, a profit will be shown on the policy account and this also is transferred to lease redemption account.

The final entries are the same as (iv) and (v) above.

7. Revaluation

Revaluation is used in two main circumstances—

(*a*) It is adopted for assets which cannot always be conveniently dealt with under normal methods of depreciation, e.g. livestock, casks, bottles, packages, loose tools, patterns, models, moulds, trade marks, copyrights, investments, etc. In this case the calculation will be as follows—

	£
Opening stock £10,000	10,000
Add Purchases during the year	150,000
	160,000
Less Closing stock	15,000
Consumed in year	£145,000

The difference arising from the valuation of the opening and closing stock is debited to Profit and Loss account. Should there be a favourable difference then this could be credited to the Profit and Loss account. It is normally expected that with this type of asset there will be a debit to Profit and Loss representing the value of the assets used during the year.

(*b*) The second context in which revaluation is used is in the case of such items as land and buildings where appreciation of the asset may have taken place.

For example, if land is bought for £18,000 cash on the 1st January, 1952 then it will be recorded at that cost in the accounts. If a revaluation is undertaken on the 1st January, 1968 and this shows that the current value is now £30,000 then the revaluation will be affected by debiting the land account with the appreciation of £12,000 and crediting the same amount to capital reserve (or profit on revaluation of land). The accounts will be as follows—

(*a*) LAND ACCOUNT

		£	
1952			
Jan 1	Cash	18,000	
1968			
Jan 1	Capital Reserve	12,000	

Capital Reserve (Profit on revaluation of land)

					£
			1968		£
			Jan 1	Land	12,000

Disadvantage of this Method. One disadvantage of writing off depreciation by this revaluation process is that while the asset is rendering virtually the same services to the business year by year, the business is charged with very unequal sums each year in respect of these services. (See p. 0206 for treatment of loose tools.)

8. Repairs, Maintenance and Depreciation Fund or Provision

As the name implies, in this method a single amount is debited to profit and loss account annually for repairs, maintenance, and depreciation and a Repairs and Depreciation Fund or Provision account credited.

Additions to assets are debited to plant account, and payments for repairs and maintenance are debited to depreciation fund or provision.

The credit balance of the depreciation account shows the net amount set aside for depreciation and repairs. A debit balance shows that the provision has not been adequate. When this method is used, the assets should be revalued periodically, and it may also be necessary to vary the annual amount set aside.

Example 9

A firm acquired plant for £10,000 on 31st December, 19.. and added £1,000 worth on 31st December, 19.1. A further addition worth £2,000 was made on 31st December, 19.2. Allow straight line depreciation at 5 per cent on original cost. The firm keeps a Depreciation, Repairs and Maintenance Fund. Spending on Repairs and Maintenance were: 19.1 £50, 19.2 £100, 19.3 £300. Show the accounts.

Solution 9

PLANT

19..		£			
Dec 31	Cash	10,000			
19.1					
Dec 31	Additions	1,000			
		11,000			
19.2					
Dec 31	Additions	2,000			
		13,000			

DEPRECIATION, REPAIRS, AND MAINTENANCE FUND

		£			£
19.1			19.1		
Dec 31	Repairs and Renewals .	50	Dec 31	P. and L. A/c 5% on £10,000 . . .	500
	Balance . . .	450			
		500			500
19.2			19.1		
Dec 31	Repairs and Renewals .	100	Dec 31	Balance . . .	450
	Balance . . .	900	19.2		
			Dec 31	P. & L. A/c 5% on £11,000 . . .	550
		1,000			1,000
19.3			19.2		
Dec 31	Repairs and Renewals .	300	Dec 31	Balance . . .	900
	Balance . . .	1,250	19.3	P. & L. A/c 5% on £13,000 . . .	650
		1,550			1,550
			19.3		
			Dec 31	Balance . . .	1,250

9. Depletion Unit or Production Unit Method

Where an asset, such as a quarry or mine, will eventually be worked out, it is called a wasting asset. Such assets may be depreciated by charging depreciation by the unit extracted.

Example 10

The rights to work a gravel pit cost £70,000 and the firm agreed to reinstate the land after working at an estimated cost of £10,000. The estimated yield of the pit is 700,000 tons. Output is—

Year 1 7,000 tons
Year 2 21,000 ,,

GRAVEL PIT ACCOUNT

Year		£	Year		£
1	Cash	70,000	1	P. & L. A/c . . .	700
				Balance . . .	69,300
		70,000			70,000
2	Balance	69,300	2	P. & L. A/c . . .	2,100
				Balance . . .	67,200
		69,300			69,300
3	Balance	67,200			

The cost of reinstatement should be separately provided.

PROVISION FOR PIT REINSTATEMENT

		Year		£
		1	P. & L. A/c . . .	100
		2	P. & L. A/c . . .	300

The same principle is applied to certain classes of machine where depreciation is calculated as a rate per unit produced.

Example 11

A press has an estimated output of 1,000,000 parts over its life. Original cost £500,000. The output is—

Month 1 10,000 parts
Month 2 15,000 „

MACHINE ACCOUNT

		£			£
			1st yr.		
1st yr.	Cash . . .	500,000	Month 1	P. & L. A/c . .	5,000
			„ 2	. „ „ „ .	7,500

When the number of units produced is high and the rate of production fairly constant, the rate may be calculated according to hours worked.

10. Combined Methods

Various methods may be combined in order to give more accurate depreciation rates. For instance, the depreciation on a machine might be split, part being on a straight-line annual basis and the other part on production hours worked.

SUMMARY OF RECOMMENDATIONS OF THE INSTITUTE OF CHARTERED ACCOUNTANTS ON DEPRECIATION

1. A *consistent* basis should be used.

2. Assets should be shown in the balance sheet at cost less aggregate depreciation.

3. Appropriate bases for particular assets are recommended—

(*a*) Goodwill and freehold land—

No depreciation except as in (*d*) below.

(*b*) Freehold buildings, plant and machinery, tools and equipment, ships, transport vehicles, and similar assets which are subject to depreciation by reason of their employment in the business generally on a straight-line basis but see (*c*), below.

(*c*) Leaseholds, patents, and other assets which become exhausted by the effluxion of time—

A straight-line basis. Loose tools, jigs, patterns, etc., by revaluation. Lease provision must provide for dilapidations also. Annual premiums provide a satisfactory debit to profit and loss account if the insurance policy method is used.

(*d*) Mines, oil wells, quarries, and similar assets of a wasting character which are consumed in the form of basic raw material or where the output is sold as such—

No specific method, but if no provision is made, shareholders should be informed.

Amounts set aside for obsolescence or for increased replacement costs are reserves, not provisions.

Rates of Depreciation Generally Adopted. The following are the rates of depreciation generally adopted, though it is quite possible that special circumstances may make them higher or lower—

Freehold Land and Buildings, 1%–3% p.a.

Leasehold Land and Buildings, written off over the period of the lease.

Plant and Machinery, 5%–25% p.a.

Vans and Motor Lorries, etc., 10%–25% p.a.

Patents (life 16 years), $\frac{1}{16}$ of original cost each year. There is, sometimes, as with trade marks, a residual value in the form of goodwill caused by the trade these things have created.

Furniture, Fixtures, and Fittings, 2½%–7½% p.a.

Blast Furnaces, Gas Retorts, and Chemical Plant (subject to rapid depreciation and constant repair with little or no break-up value), the original cost divided by the number of years' life.

Engines (*movable*), 10%; (*fixed*), 7½% p.a.

Boilers (*high pressure*), 15%; (*low pressure*), 10% p.a.

Driving Gear, 5%–7½% p.a.

Rolling Stock—

Locomotives, 10% p.a.

Wagons (life about 15 years), 7½% p.a.

Ships (life about 20 years), 5% p.a.

Casks (in breweries, distilleries, oil refineries), 10%–20% p.a., or revalued yearly.

The above rates, except where otherwise stated, are for depreciation on diminishing balances, normal conditions and hours of working being assumed.

QUESTIONS

1. What methods are there in vogue with reference to the depreciation of "additions" to an asset?

2. Explain briefly the nature and use of the "annuity system" of depreciation. What disadvantage attaches to it?

3. Explain briefly the nature and use of the "depreciation fund principle" of depreciation. What other terms are used for depreciation fund?

4. What object is sought by investing cash on account of a depreciation fund? Is profit ever invested?

5. In what different ways can provision be made for depreciation of a lease? Give examples.

6. How is the loss of interest on investments, by reason of income tax, adjusted in depreciation funds and sinking funds?

7. Explain briefly the nature and use of the "insurance policy system" of depreciation.

8. What is surrender value?

9. List the methods of depreciation.

11. Sinking Funds

A sinking fund is either (i) a charge against profits in order to provide for the replacement of a wasting asset such as a lease, plant and machinery, etc., or (ii) an appropriation of profits to repay a liability such as a loan or debentures. In each case, however, there is a corresponding amount of *cash* invested, so that the sinking fund may be immediately available, when required, by realizing the investments An example of a sinking fund to replace an asset has already been given, and an example of a sinking fund to repay a liability is shown hereunder—

Example 12

A sum of £6,000 is borrowed for a term of six years. It is resolved to provide for its repayment by means of a sinking fund, reckoning interest at 3 per cent per annum. Show the ledger accounts thereof over the whole period.

Solution 12

LOAN REDEMPTION FUND INVESTMENT

Year		£	Year		£
1	Cash	927	1	Balance c/d	927
2	Balance b/d	927	2	Balance c/d	1,882
	Cash (Instalment plus Interest)	955			
		1,882			1,882
3	Balance b/d	1,882	3	Balance c/d	2,865
	Cash	983			
		2,865			2,865
4	Balance b/d	2,865	4	Balance c/d	3,878
	Cash	1,013			
		3,878			3,878
5	Balance b/d	3,878	5	Balance c/d	4,921
	Cash	1,043			
		4,921			4,921
6	Balance b/d	4,921	6	Cash	6,000
	Cash	1,079			
		6,000			6,000

LOAN

Year		£	Year		£
6	Cash (repaid) . . .	6,000	1	Cash (borrowed) . .	6,000

LOAN REDEMPTION FUND

Year		£	Year		£
1	Balance c/d . . .	927	1	Appropriation A/c . .	927
2	Balance c/d . . .	1,882	2	Balance b/d . . .	927
				Cash (Interest) . . .	28
				Appropriation A/c .	927
		1,882			1,882
3	Balance c/d . . .	2,865	3	Balance b/d . . .	1,882
				Cash (Interest) . . .	56
				Appropriation A/c . .	927
		2,865			2,865
4	Balance c/d . . .	3,878	4	Balance b/d . . .	2,865
				Cash (Interest) . .	86
				Appropriation A/c . .	927
		3,878			3,878
5	Balance c/d . . .	4,921	5	Balance b/d . . .	3,878
				Cash (Interest) . . .	116
				Appropriation A/c . .	927
		4,921			4,921
6	Transfer to General Reserve A/c . . .	6,000	6	Balance b/d . . .	4,921
				Cash (Interest) . . .	147
				Appropriation A/c . . (Adjustment made)	932
		6,000			6,000

Income Tax. As previously mentioned, the interest on the investments is received *less tax* at the current rate for unearned income. To provide for this loss, a similar amount is debited to the appropriation account and credited to the loan redemption fund account. The ledger account of the previous example would then appear as shown below—

LOAN REDEMPTION FUND

Year		£	Year		£
1	Balance c/d	927	1	Appropriation A/c	927
2	Balance c/d	1,882	2	Balance b/d	927
				Cash (Interest *less* tax)	21
				Appropriation A/c (tax)	7
				Appropriation A/c	927
		1,882			1,882
3	Balance c/d	2,865	3	Balance b/d	1,882
				Cash (Interest *less* tax)	42
				Appropriation A/c (tax)	14
				Appropriation A/c	927
		2,865			2,865
4	Balance c/d	3,878	4	Balance b/d	2,865
				Cash (Interest *less* tax)	65
				Appropriation A/c (tax)	21
				Appropriation A/c	927
		3,878			3,878
5	Balance c/d	4,921	5	Balance b/d	3,878
				Cash (Interest *less* tax)	87
				Appropriation A/c (tax)	29
				Appropriation A/c	927
		4,921			4,921
6	Transfer to General Reserve	6,000	6	Balance b/d	4,921
				Cash (Interest *less* tax)	110
				Appropriation A/c (tax)	37
				Appropriation A/c (Adjustment of 1d.)	932
		6,000			6,000

NOTE. The rate of tax has been taken as £0·25 in the £ for convenience.

Difference between a Sinking Fund to replace a Wasting Asset, and a Sinking Fund to repay a Liability. The difference should be very carefully noted by the student. A sinking fund to replace a wasting asset is a *charge against* profits, because the accumulations out of revenue are required, at the end of the period, to extinguish the asset account. In this way the asset is depreciated in its entirety at the end of the period. The sinking fund instalment, being equivalent to the annual depreciation, is debited to the *profit and loss account*, and not to the appropriation account. In the case, however, of a sinking fund to repay a liability, the accumulated profits remain unused at the end of the period. They are freely available for paying dividends if enough cash is available in the firm, but as it is not usually, the amounts are transferred to general reserve until cash is available. This shows that they are appropriations of profit. Hence the sinking fund instalment, in such cases, is debited to the *appropriation account*, and not to the profit and loss account.

Depreciation and Taxation. Depreciation, as such, is not allowed as an expense for tax purposes. Instead, capital allowances are given for certain types of assets. In some cases, cash grants may be paid for approved capital expenditure by the Board of Trade.

Most business will claim the maximum capital allowances for which they are eligible, and this does not affect their treatment of depreciation, which will remain at the rate selected for ordinary commercial purposes based on the expected life and residual value at the time of disposal.

Change of Depreciation Policy. It sometimes happens that management policy on depreciation is changed. For instance, directors might decide to switch from the straight-line to the diminishing balance method, or to adopt a different policy on acquisitions, disposals and trade-ins. The result may be implemented retrospectively so that an adjustment of the asset and depreciation accounts is required. The treatment of depreciation will also affect the profits as previously stated and an adjustment must be made to the retained profits or reserves.

Example 13

The following example is a typical examination question—

On 1st January, 1963, Suburban Transport Co. Ltd., began to operate lorries in connection with their business. Depreciation was provided at the rate of 20 per cent per annum on their net book value at the commencement of each year. When a lorry was replaced, the "trade-in" price of the old lorry was deducted from the cost of the new lorry and the net amount capitalized.

The Lorries Account appears in the books thus—

			£				£
1963				1963			
Jan	1	Lorry No. 1 . .	1,000	Dec 31	Depreciation . .		200
Jul	1	Lorry No. 2 . .	1,400		Balance . . .		2,200
			2,400				2,400
1964				1964			
Jan	1	Balance . . .	2,200	Dec 31	Depreciation . .		440
					Balance . . .		1,760
			2,200				2,200
1965				1965			
Jan	1	Balance . . .	1,760	Dec 31	Depreciation . .		352
Apl	1	Lorry No. 3 . .	800		Balance . . .		2,808
Oct	1	Lorry No. 4 . .	600				
			3,160				3,160
1966							
Jan	1	Balance . . .	2,808				

The Directors agreed that this method was misleading and they decided that the account should be reconstructed so as to provide depreciation at the rate of 20 per cent per annum on cost as from the date of purchase, also that a separate account should be opened for the provision for depreciation.

You ascertain that the "trade-in" price of Lorry No. 1, which was replaced by Lorry No. 3, was £800 and that of Lorry No. 2, which was replaced by Lorry No. 4, was £500.

(London Chamber of Commerce)

Solution 13

The accounts must be revised to separate the cost of lorries from the depreciation provided and it will be useful to draw up a Sale of Lorries account since this will bring out the double entry in respect of the sale of lorries and the trade-in values.

Depreciation on the new basis is computed as follows—

	£
1963	
Lorry No. 1 £1,000 × 20% for 1 year	200
Lorry No. 2 £1,400 × 20% for 6 months	140
	£340
1964	
Lorry No. 1 £1,000 × 20% for 1 year	200
Lorry No. 2 £1,400 × 20% for 1 year	280
	£480

1965		
Lorry No. 1 £1,000 × 20% for 3 months	. . . . . .	50
Lorry No. 2 £1,400 × 20% for 9 months	. . . . . .	210
Lorry No. 3 £1,600 × 20% for 9 months	. . . . . .	240
Lorry No. 4 £1,100 × 20% for 3 months	. . . . . .	55
		£555

The lorries account will show all acquisitions and disposals at cost as follows—

Lorries Account

Date			£	£	Date		£
1963				£	1963		£
Jan 1	Lorry No. 1—Cash			1,000	Dec 31	Balance c/d	2,400
Jul 1	Lorry No. 2—Cash			1,400			
				2,400			2,400
1964					1965		
Jan 1	Balance b/d			2,400	Apl 1	Sale of Lorries A/c	1,000
1965					Oct 1	Sale of Lorries A/c	1,400
Apr 1	Lorry No. 3—Cash		800				
	Sale of Lorries A/c		800				
				1,600			
Oct 1	Lorry No. 4—Cash		600				
	Sale of Lorries A/c		500		Dec 31	Balance c/d	2,700
				1,100			
				5,100			5,100
1966							
Jan 1	Balance b/d			2,700			

The Depreciation account will show the credit of the annual provision, as calculated above. Whenever a lorry is disposed of, the accumulated depreciation will be transferred to the sale of lorry account by a debit to Depreciation account and a credit to sale of lorry. The sale account is also credited with trade-in value or cash received. Any difference will be a profit or loss on sale.

The result in the example is—

Provision for Depreciation of Lorries Account

Date		£	Date		£
1963		£	1963		£
Dec 31	Balance b/d	340	Dec 31	Profit and Loss A/c	340
1964			1964		
Dec 31	Balance b/d	820	Jan 1	Balance b/d	340
			Dec 31	Profit and Loss A/c	480
		820			820
1965			1965		
Apl 1	Sale of Lorries A/c	450	Jan 1	Balance b/d	820
Oct 1	Sale of Lorries A/c	630	Dec 31	Profit and Loss A/c	555
Dec 31	Balance c/d	295			
		1,375			1,375
			1966		
			Jan 1	Balance b/d	295

SALE OF LORRIES ACCOUNT

		£			£
1965			1965		
Apl 1	Lorries Account . . .	1,000	Apl 1	Depreciation Account . .	450
	Profit and Loss A/c—			Lorries A/c	800
	Profit on Sale . . .	250			
		1,250			1,250
Oct 1	Lorries Account . . .	1,400	Oct 1	Depreciation Account . .	630
				Lorries Account . . .	500
				Profit and Loss Account—	
				Loss on Sale . . .	270
		1,400			1,400

The changes which have occurred may be analysed to show the adjustment to profits.

DEPRECIATION CHARGE

	Old	New	Reduction of profit
	£	£	£
1963	200	340	140
1964	440	480	40
1965	352	555	203
Total reduction in reported profits			383

In addition to the reduction in reported profits on profit and loss account of £383, there will be a profit on sale of lorries of £250 and a loss of £270 in 1965, giving a net decrease of £403 (£383 + £20). This corresponds to the change in the book value of the lorries—

	£	£
Net book value under old method . . .		2,808
Net book value under new method . .		
Cost of lorries	2,700	
Less Depreciation	295	
		2,405
Decrease in book value		403

QUESTIONS

1. Explain briefly the nature and use of the "revaluation process" of depreciation. What disadvantages attach to it?

2. State briefly the rates generally adopted in the case of some of the more general assets.

3. What is a sinking fund? Must there be an investment of cash in connexion therewith?

4. State briefly the difference between a sinking fund to replace a wasting asset, and a sinking fund to repay a liability.

5. What is a provision? Name some of the more usual ones.

6. What is a reserve fund? How does it differ from a reserve account?

7. Differentiate between a reserve, a reserve account, a reserve fund, and a sinking fund.

EXERCISE 06

1. A lease is purchased for a term of four years by payment of a sum of £440. Show how the lease account would appear in the books during this period, depreciation being written off by equal annual instalments.

2. Machinery is bought for £3,000. Its life is estimated to be six years, and its break-up value at the end of this period £534. Show the machinery and depreciation accounts for the six years, writing off depreciation at a fixed rate per cent on the diminishing or reducing value of the asset.

3. Machinery is purchased for a sum of £3,000. Additions are made in June of the second year to the amount of £250, and in March of the third year to the extent of £320. Show by means of ledger accounts the various methods of dealing with these additions when writing off the annual depreciation, the rate of which is 10 per cent on the balance of the plant and machinery account.

4. A lease is purchased for a term of seven years by payment of £2,000. It is proposed to depreciate the lease by the annuity method, charging 5 per cent interest. Show the ledger account of the asset during this period.

5. £2,000 is paid for a lease for a term of seven years. It is desired to write this amount off by means of the depreciation fund method, it being necessary to invest a similar amount, at 5 per cent compound interest, in order to replace the lease at the end of the period. Show the ledger accounts dealing with this matter.

6. A firm possesses investments valued at the commencement of the year at £10,586. At the end of the year the investments are revalued at market price and they are then found to be worth £8,972. How (if at all) would you deal with the matter in the firm's books and balance sheet? Supposing they had been valued at £11,000, how would you deal with the matter?

7. An engineering firm has loose tools valued at the commencement of the year at £1,026. At the end of the year, stock is taken and the loose tools are found to amount to £1,207. How would you deal with this matter in the firm's books? Supposing they had been valued at £987, how would you deal with the matter?

8. A repairs and renewals provision is created by charging revenue each year with a fixed sum of £200. The repairs and renewals for the ensuing four years are: (1) £159; (2) £125; (3) £269; (4) £225. Show the journal, ledger, and balance sheet entries relating to the above.

9. When calculating the annual sinking fund to replace the cost of a lease or other terminable benefit, why should compound interest be taken into account, thereby making the amounts carried to the fund in the earlier years comparatively small, and in the later years comparatively large, instead of setting aside equal annual sums?

(*Chartered Accountants.*)

10. On 1st January the M N Co. Ltd. purchased the lease of certain premises for £1,000. The directors decided to form a sinking fund to accumulate this amount at the end of the lease, which had five years to run, the rate of interest being taken at 3 per cent. The requisite sum is to be transferred annually from profit and loss account, and a corresponding amount invested in securities producing the required rate of

interest. According to the tables, £0·1884 per annum amounts to £1 in five years at 3 per cent. Write up the sinking fund account, the sinking fund investment account, and the interest account for the first three years. You may show your calculations in decimals. (*Chartered Accountants.*)

11. What is a "depreciation fund"? Give two examples showing how a company could create a "depreciation fund?"

12. The directors of the Old Time Spinning Company decide to replace entirely their plant, which is now out of date. Having advertised for tenders for the new machinery they require, they accept that sent in by A B & Co., amounting to £8,850.

The old machinery and plant account stood in the books of the company at £5,400. There was also a depreciation fund in the books, the accumulated credit balance of which amounted to £1,050. Some of the materials composing the old machinery were found to be in good condition, and A B & Co. agreed to take over shafting, etc., valued at £550, for use again; whilst the remainder was put up to auction and realized £1,200 (net).

Make the entries necessary to record these transactions in the books of the Old Time Spinning Company, and state how you would deal with the balance of the old "machinery and plant account." (*London Chamber of Commerce.*)

13. A company having a lease standing in their books at £5,000 decide to provide for depreciation by taking out a policy for leasehold redemption. How would you deal with the annual premiums in the books; and how would you adjust the accounts when the lease expires and the policy matures? (*R.S.A.*)

14. On 1st January, 19.., a manufacturer buys plant £2,000; on 1st July, 19.1, he buys new plant £400, and on 31st December he sells for £160 plant costing 1st January, 19.., £300. On 1st April, 19.2, he buys new plant £280, and on 1st October, 19.3, sells for £70 plant costing 1st July, 19.1, £120. His plant is depreciated in the books annually at 31st December at the rate of 5 per cent per annum on the original cost. At 31st December, 19.3, he wishes to alter this method, for the whole period, to 7½ per cent per annum on the diminishing value. Prepare machinery and depreciation accounts showing the result of both methods.

15. A firm carries on business as funeral directors and motor hirers and make up their accounts to 31st March, each year.

In such accounts provision for depreciation of motor vehicles has been made at 25 per cent of the reducing balance and when a vehicle has been bought a full year's charge has been made for the year in which the purchase took place.

In the balance sheet as on 31st March, 1963, motor vehicles appeared as follows—

	£
At cost	12,840
Less Depreciation	6,580
	£6,260

The details of the purchases of motor vehicles are as follows—

	£
In the year to 31st March, 1959	3,850
,, ,, ,, ,, ,, 1960	2,210
,, ,, ,, ,, ,, 1962	2,580
,, ,, ,, ,, ,, 1963	4,200
	£12,840

During the year ended 31st March, 1964, motor vehicles were sold as follows—

					£		£
Vehicle A	bought	2nd July,	1958,	cost	1,000	sold for	300
" B	"	30th June,	1959,	"	1,280	" "	420
" C	"	4th Sept.,	1961,	"	920	" "	500
					£3,200		

purchases were made—

Vehicle L	880
" M	940
" N	960
	£2,780

Separate accounts are kept in the nominal ledger for (*a*) motor vehicles at cost, (*b*) provision for depreciation and (*c*) disposal of vehicles.

The partners have agreed that the basis of the calculation of the annual charge for depreciation shall be altered to 20 per cent of the original cost of each vehicle and for the accumulated provision for depreciation as at 31st March, 1963, to be amended in accordance with the new basis.

You are required—

1. To prepare statements showing—

(i) what additional provision for depreciation will be required on 31st March, 1963, for the past years as a result of the alteration of the basis,

(ii) the charge for depreciation for the year ended 31st March, 1964, and

(iii) the profit or loss on the disposal of motor vehicles during the year ended 31st March, 1964.

2. To make the necessary entries in the nominal ledger as regards these matters. (*A.C.C.A.*)

16. A trading company takes out a capital redemption policy with an insurance company to provide for a wasting asset, paying £80 per annum premium. The premium is to be provided out of revenue. Give examples showing the entries to be made in the books of the trading company (1) annually, and (2) upon payment of the capital sum by the Insurance Company. (*Chartered Accountants.*)

17. On 31st December the City Trading Co. Ltd. had a debenture reserve fund of £50,000, represented by investments amounting to £59,000 2½ per cent Consols. The company also had a balance in the bank on current account at 30th June following of £6,000. The debentures, amounting to £50,000, were paid off on 30th June. To provide for this the Consols were realized at 83 net, and the proceeds paid into the bank on 30th June. Record the above transactions in the books of the company, and show the ledger accounts affected. (*Chartered Accountants.*)

18. A company insured for its own benefit the life of the managing director for £10,000, at an annual premium of £250. How would you expect the outlay to be dealt with in the accounts submitted to you for audit? (*Chartered Accountants.*)

19. The following is an analysis of the plant and machinery owned by P. Ltd. on 31st December, 1959, showing the annual depreciation rates—

Depreciation rate (calculated on cost)	Year of Purchase	Cost £	Depreciation to Date £	Net £
5%	bought 1940 or earlier .	8,500	8,500	—
„	„ 1941 or later .	46,500	20,200	26,300
10%	„ 1950 or earlier .	18,200	18,200	—
„	„ 1951 or later .	53,300	28,250	25,050
		126,500	75,150	51,350

The company's practice is to charge a full year's depreciation on any machine in the year of purchase regardless of the actual date of purchase and, conversely, to charge no depreciation in the year of sale or scrapping.

Apart from depreciation proper, a machinery renewals reserve is being built up by annual appropriations of amounts equal to $2\frac{1}{2}$ per cent of the cost of all machinery in use at the end of each accounting year and any profits or losses realized on the sale or scrapping of any machines are credited or debited (as the case may be) to this account. The balance of this reserve on 31st December, 1959, was £7,970.

During the year ended 31st December, 1960, the following transactions took place—

(*a*) A new machine (depreciation rate 10 per cent) was bought for £5,600.

(*b*) Old machinery (depreciation rate 5 per cent), bought in 1936 for £800, was taken out of service.

(*c*) A machine (depreciation rate 10 per cent), bought in 1953 for £4,300, was sold for £1,725.

Write up the plant and machinery account (maintained at cost), the corresponding depreciation account, and the machinery renewals reserve. Also, show how the position should appear in the published balance sheet at 31st December, 1960.

(*R.S.A.*)

20. X. Ltd. purchased plant and machinery, as follows—

Date	*Cost* £
1st January, 19..	8,000
1st July, 19.1	10,000
1st October, 19.2	4,200

On 1st January, 19.2, part of the machinery purchased on 1st January, 19.., was sold for £2,000. The cost of this machinery was £3,000.

Depreciation is provided, at the rate of 10 per cent per annum, by the straight-line method. The company's accounting year ends on 31st December.

You are required—

(i) To show the plant and machinery account for each of the three years 19.., 19.1, and 19.2, assuming that no separate "provision for depreciation" account is kept.

(ii) To show the plant and machinery account and other relevant accounts for each of the three years 19.., 19.1, and 19.2, assuming that plant and machinery is retained in the books at cost and that depreciation is credited to a separate "provision for depreciation" account.

(iii) To show how the plant and machinery would appear in the balance sheet at 31st December, 19.2.

NOTE. Your answers to (i) and (ii) should be headed "First Assumption" and "Second Assumption" respectively. (*Chartered Institute of Secretaries.*)

21. Nerine Ltd. owns a quantity of plant, not enough to justify the use of a plant ledger but of sufficient value to make careful and accurate records necessary. This is done by listing in a book, kept for the purpose, the description and cost of each item purchased, keeping a separate page for each year and using analysis columns to divide the totals according to the varying depreciation rates applied. The "fixed instalment" method of depreciation is used.

An annual summary is drawn up and agreed with the balance of the plant and machinery account (maintained at cost) each year and the aggregate depreciation is calculated from another annual summary, derived from the first in the manner illustrated by the undermentioned statements, which show the position at 31st December, 19.8—

SUMMARY OF PLANT (AT COST), 31ST DECEMBER, 19.8

Year of Purchase	Total	Depreciation Rate 5%	10%	20%
	£	£	£	£
19..	7,400	5,800	—	1,600
19.4	950	—	950	—
19.7	400	400	—	—
19.8	1,920	1,680	—	240
	10,670	7,880	950	1,840

SUMMARY OF DEPRECIATION, 31ST DECEMBER, 19.8

Year of Purchase	Number of Years Depreciation	Total	Depreciation Rate 5%	10%	20%
		£	£	£	£
19..	9	4,210	2,610	—	1,600
19.4	5	475	—	475	—
19.7	2	40	40	—	—
19.8	1	132	84	—	48
		4,857	2,734	475	1,648

During 19.9 the company bought three machines, costing £800, £1,960, and £380 respectively, and to which respective depreciations rates of 5 per cent, 10 per cent, and 20 per cent are to be applied, and sold for £450 one machine which had been bought in 19.. for £660 and depreciated at the rate of 5 per cent per annum.

You are required to—

(*a*) draw up summaries, in the form shown above, showing the position at 31st December, 19.9, and

(*b*) calculate the depreciation charge for the year. (*R.S.A.*)

22. The A.B.C. Co. Ltd. showed the following cost values in its books at the year ended 31st December, 19.3—

	£
(*a*) Freehold land	20,000
(*b*) Freehold buildings	100,000
(*c*) Plant and machinery	75,000
(*d*) Motor-cars	15,000
(*e*) Office appliances	5,000

The rates of depreciation as used by the company, are—

(*b*) 2 per cent fixed instalment
(*c*) 15 „ „ reducing balance
(*d*) 25 „ „ „ „ .
(*e*) 25 „ „ „ „

(i) Show the ledger accounts for each asset as at 31st December, 19.3, assuming that the whole of the assets were purchased on 1st January, 19.., and that depreciation has been taken for each year.

(ii) Show the journal entries required to record the following transactions, all of which took place after three years' depreciation had been charged—

(*a*) an item of plant which cost £500 was scrapped with no residual value;
(*b*) a motor-car which cost £800 was sold for £350;
(*c*) an office machine which cost £200 was sold for £75.

(iii) Show the necessary journal entries to correct the following—
In the original figure of £5,000 for office appliances, an item of plant costing £160 had been wrongly included. The error was noticed after 31st December, 19.3.
(*Cost and Management Accountants.*)

23. The following trial balance was extracted from the books of James Eyre, a trader, at 31st December, 19..—

TRIAL BALANCE, 31ST DECEMBER, 19..

	£	£
Capital account		10,270
Stock-in-trade, 1st January, 19..	4,930	
Furniture and fittings	350	
Motor-vans	1,058	
Purchases	58,200	
Sales		71,350
Trade debtors	7,818	
Trade creditors		5,212
Bad debts	382	
General expenses	848	
Provision for bad debts, 1st January, 19..		180
Wages and salaries	8,160	
Discounts allowed	1,413	
Discounts received		891
Balance at bank	1,424	
Drawings	2,205	
Motor expenses	475	
Rent and rates	640	
	87,903	87,903

The following matters are to be taken into account—

1. Stock-in-trade, 31st December, 19.., £5,780.
2. Wages and salaries accrued, 31st December, 19.., £217.
3. Rates paid in advance at 31st December, 19.., £15.

4. The motor vans account appeared in the ledger as follows—

MOTOR VANS

19..		£	19..		£
Jan 1	Balance (old van) . .	240	Jan 1	Cash—sale of old van .	182
	Cash—cost of new van .	1,000	Dec 31	Balance . . .	1,058
		1,240			1,240
Dec 31	Balance . . .	1,058			

Provide depreciation on the new van at the rate of 20 per cent per annum.

5. The provision for bad debts is to be increased to £200.

6. After the above trial balance had been prepared, it was found from the bank statement that no entries had been made in Eyre's books for: (*a*) bank charges £4, and (*b*) a payment of £24 made under standing order by Eyre in respect of household equipment for his private residence.

You are required to prepare a trading and profit and loss account for the year 19.. and a balance sheet at 31st December, 19... Ignore depreciation of furniture and fittings. (*Cost and Management Accountants.*)

24. An old-established company engaged in manufacture owns a quantity of machinery. All the machines have a useful life of ten years and depreciation is provided at the rate of 10 per cent per annum calculated on cost, a full year's depreciation being provided in the year of purchase.

The following statement shows the analysis of the machinery in use on 31st December, 1960—

Year of Purchase	Cost £	Year of Purchase	Cost £
1951	20,000	1956	26,000
1952	24,000	1957	30,000
1953	22,000	1958	34,000
1954	26,000	1959	36,000
1955	28,000	1960	32,000

Supposing that in each of the four following years every machine is scrapped on reaching the end of its tenth year of life, and replaced, and that every replacement cost 50 per cent more than the original cost of the machine it replaces—

(*a*) Calculate the yearly depreciation charge for each of the years 1961 to 1964 inclusive.

(*b*) Show the entry relating to machinery in the company's balance sheet (giving the minimum statutory information) as on 31st December, 1964.

(*c*) Supposing that in 1961 and onwards the company's directors, in view of the continuing increase of replacement cost and anticipating that it would continue, decided to charge against profits an amount equal to 15 per cent of the cost of machinery employed, instead of 10 per cent as hitherto, show how the position would be reflected in the balance sheet as on 31st December, 1964. What would be the directors' object in taking this step?

(*R.S.A.*)

25. How would you treat, in a manufacturer's books, works held under a lease of which twenty years remained unexpired, the consideration for which stood in the ledger at £3,500; and how would you treat patent rights expiring in ten years, the consideration for which stood in the same trader's ledger at £850?

(*London Chamber of Commerce.*)

26. In preparing the profit and loss account of a manufacturing firm, what different methods are there of providing for the waste of an asset owing: (*a*) to wear and tear, as in the case of machinery; or (*b*) effluxion of time, as in the case of a building erected upon leasehold land?

What method do you favour for providing for such waste, and why? State briefly what entries would be required to carry your suggestions into effect.

(*London Chamber of Commerce.*)

27. The following balances composed the balance sheet of John Brown Limited: cash £6,000, bills receivable £1,200, sundry debtors £2,500, stock £5,000, capital £10,000, bills payable £800, sundry creditors £1,400, divisible profit £2,500.

It was resolved to start a reserve fund with such an amount of the balance of profit as would, when invested, purchase £1,500 Consols at 85 (charges neglected).

You are requested to give the necessary journal entries to effect this; then set out ledger accounts for investments, reserve fund, and profit and loss; also draw up a new balance sheet showing these changes.

28. Describe a municipal corporation's sinking fund—

(*a*) As to method of contributions to same.

(*b*) As to interest received on instalments invested. (*U.L.C.I.*)

CHAPTER 07

STOCK VALUATION AND CONTROL

From his brimstone bed at break of day
A walking the Devil is gone,
To visit his snug little farm the earth,
And see how his stock goes on.

SAMUEL TAYLOR COLERIDGE—*The Devil's Thoughts*

Stock or Inventory. The American Institute of Accountants defines the term inventory as "the aggregate of those items of tangible property which (1) are held for sale in the ordinary course of business, (2) are in process of production for such sale or (3) are to be currently consumed in the production of goods or services to be available for sale." In the United Kingdom, inventory is usually referred to as stock-in-trade or work-in-progress.

Types of Stock. Stock may consist of—

(i) Raw materials and supplies to be consumed in production;
(ii) Work-in-progress, or partly manufactured goods;
(iii) Finished stock or goods ready for sale.

A study of 1,800 industrial concerns in the United Kingdom in 1966 showed that 29 per cent of the Balance Sheet Assets (net of accumulated depreciation) were held in the form of stocks.

PRINCIPLES OF STOCK VALUATION

Stocks are valued in a fundamentally different way from Fixed Assets: the latter are usually valued at cost less accumulated depreciation; less frequently they are revalued by independent valuation.

No method of stock valuation is suitable for all types of business in all circumstances. The I.C.A. of E. & W. recommend that stock be valued at cost less any part of cost which needs to be written off when net realizable value or the replacement price is lower than cost, i.e. at *the lower cost or market value*. A survey of the I.C.A. of S. in 1968 showed, however, that 20 per cent of their sample companies valued their finished goods at selling price less appropriate adjustments.

The effect of the application of this formula is to exclude possible profits which have not actually been realized but to take into account any possible losses—

Example 1

	Cost	Market Value	Valuation Taken	
	£	£	£	
A	5,000	4,800	4,800	Loss of £200 anticipated.
B	30,000	35,000	30,000	Possible profit of £5,000 ignored.

The valuation put on stock affects the gross profit on trading—

	Stock at Cost		*Stock at Market Valuation*	
	£	£	£	£
Sales . . .		200,000		200,000
Opening Stock . .	25,000		25,000	
Purchases . . .	110,000		110,000	
	135,000		135,000	
Less Closing Stock .	30,000		35,000	
		105,000		100,000
Gross Profit . . .		95,000		100,000

A relatively small difference in the valuation of stock may have a considerable effect on the net profit, and may turn a net loss into a net profit.

As the closing stock of one year is the opening stock of the next it is perfectly true that ultimately the "truth will out." If profit is increased one year, the following year's profit is correspondingly reduced. But even in this case, it is possible that the *trend* of profit will be misrepresented.

Example 2

The net annual sales of a company are £20,000. The cost of goods sold over a year is—

	Year 1	Year 2	Year 3	*Total Profit*
	£	£	£	
(*a*) Opening Stock . .	2,000	3,000	3,000	
Purchases . . .	10,000	10,000	10,000	
	12,000	13,000	13,000	
(*b*) Closing Stock . .	3,000	3,000	2,500	
Cost of Goods sold . .	9,000	10,000	10,500	
Gross Profit . . .	11,000	10,000	9,500	£30,500

If we assume that at the end of Year 1 and Year 2 the market value of the stocks was £2,000 but that the other valuations remain the same, the result is—

	Year 1	Year 2	Year 3	*Total Profit*
	£	£	£	
Opening Stock	2,000	2,000	2,000	
Purchases	10,000	10,000	10,000	
	12,000	12,000	12,000	
Closing Stock	2,000	2,000	2,500	
Cost of Goods sold	10,000	10,000	9,500	
Gross Profit	10,000	10,000	10,500	£30,500

Although the overall profit is £30,500 in each case, the trend is in the opposite direction.

This also emphasizes the rule that *in stock valuation, the method used should be consistent.* If frequent changes in the method of valuing stock are made, it is possible to produce a completely false picture of earnings.

In applying the valuation at cost or market value, whichever is the lower, differences in interpretation may arise.

The first difference may arise if a number of items of stock are held. Cost or market value may be compared item by item *or* on a group basis. Either basis is acceptable, provided it is applied consistently.

Example 3

A firm holds the four items of stock the relative costs and market values of which are given below. Give the stock valuation.

Solution 3

	Cost	Market Value	Lower of Cost or Market Value
	£	£	£
A	20,000	25,000	20,000
B	30,000	28,000	28,000
C	5,000	8,000	5,000
D	10,000	6,000	6,000
	65,000	67,000	59,000

(*a*) Taken on a group basis, cost £65,000 is the lowest valuation.
(*b*) On an individual basis, the valuation is £59,000.

Cost

The cost of stock is—

(i) direct expenditure on goods bought for re-sale, and materials and components used in manufacturing finished goods; to this may be added—

(ii) direct expenditure incurred in bringing stock to its existing location or condition, e.g. direct labour, transport, etc.

(iii) indirect or overhead expenditure incidental to the class of stock concerned (if any).

The I.C.A. of S. survey showed that for manufacturing companies the following proportions used each cost basis: (a) Direct expenditure only 28 per cent. (*b*) Direct cost plus factory overhead 38 per cent. (*c*) Direct cost plus factory and administrative overhead 34 per cent.

Valuing stock has two aspects: (*a*) determining the quantity held; (*b*) deciding the price of the quantity held.

(*a*) **Quantity Held.** This may be found by physical stock-taking, in which the quantity of each item is checked.

In many businesses, there are so many items of stock that a once-a-year stock-taking is too large an undertaking. In such cases, a system of continuous stock-taking is used, and a proportion of the stock is checked each day. If the value of the stock held is calculated continuously, this means that a perpetual inventory is available, and the value of stock can always be ascertained.

Some industries still take stock by technical estimate, a method which should be avoided where possible.

(*b*) **Prices.** The following is a list of the more usual methods of pricing—

(i) FIRST IN, FIRST OUT. (F.I.F.O.) This method assumes that items of stock are used in the same order as they come into the business. Any stock remaining, therefore, will be valued at the actual prices paid for the latest equivalent quantities received. The method is sound and widely used.

(ii) LAST IN, FIRST OUT. (L.I.F.O.) Is the reverse of F.I.F.O. as it assumes that issues are made from the latest items received into the business. Stock will therefore be valued at a price paid for the earliest items received from which the stock could have been drawn. Whilst this method is common in the United States it is rarely used in the U.K.

Example 4

			VALUATION	
Date	*Receipts*	*Issue*	*F.I.F.O.*	*L.I.F.O.*
1 Jan	200 @ £0·50			
2 Jan	300 @ £0·60	350	200 @ £0·50 150 @ £0·60 } £190	300 @ £0·60 50 @ £0·50 } £205

The F.I.F.O. valuation of stock will be 150 @ £0·60 = £90
The L.I.F.O. „ „ „ „ „ 150 @ £0·50 = £75.

(iii) SPECIFIC PRICE. Certain types of stock can be readily identified and the cost of each item ascertained, e.g. motor-cars held by a car dealer. In such cases the specific price is taken.

(iv) AVERAGE PRICES. In industries where large numbers of small items of stock are purchased at fluctuating prices, an average price may be used for pricing issues. In such cases, the same average price may be used to calculate the cost of stock.

(v) STANDARD PRICE. In manufacturing or processing industries where several operations are involved or goods are produced on mass production lines, stock is valued on a predetermined or budgeted basis. Stock may be valued at the same prices, provided standards are kept up to date.

(vi) ADJUSTED SELLING PRICE. In this case stock is valued at current selling prices less the estimated profit margin and less the estimated cost of disposal.

(vii) WORK-IN-PROGRESS COST. The cost of work-in-progress is difficult to determine, but may be defined as prime cost actually incurred plus a fair cost of overhead incurred. Where a costing system is in existence, the actual overhead incurred may be accurately determined. Otherwise an estimate must be made.

Market Value

The market value of stock can be taken as—

(i) The "replacement value" or the cost of replacing the stock at the accounting date.

(ii) The "net realizable value" for which the stock can be sold in the ordinary course of business less reasonably predictable costs of completion and disposal.

(iii) The net realizable value, as in (ii) but less an allowance for the normal profit margin. The valuation produced by (ii) is the "ceiling" and by (iii) the "floor" net realizable value.

Example 5

(i) If 200 items were purchased at £0·50 each and the current purchase price is £0·60 each, the replacement value is 200 @ £0·60 = £120 (stock would be valued at cost £100).

(ii) Work-in-progress consists of 1,000 parts intended for a main assembly, which can be sold in the open market at £1 each. To sell them will involve expenses of £20. "Ceiling" Net realizable value is £1,000 less £20 = £980.

(iii) Work-in-progress has cost, to date—

	£
Prime Cost	300
Proportion of Overhead . .	200
Cost to date	500

The value of the finished product is £800, and it is estimated that the following cost will be incurred before the item is disposed of—

	£
Prime Cost	120
Overhead	80
Additional Factory Cost	200
Administration Cost	50
Selling and Distribution	100
Anticipated additional cost	350
Normal profit margin 10% on £800	80
	430

"Floor" net realizable value of work-in-progress £800 − £430 = £370. "Ceiling" net realizable value would be £450. British Accountants would normally value the stock at £450.

Base Stock Valuation. This method, used in some industries, values stock at a fixed figure at or under original cost.

American Accountants value stock at replacement value when that falls between the "floor" and "ceiling" realizable values but will not take a value higher than "ceiling" or lower than "floor."

Estimating Value of Stock

Where a firm has standardized prices and a uniform rate of profit, there is no need for physical stock-taking, as the value of the closing stock can be estimated. This principle is dealt with in connexion with Branch Accounts on p. 1401.

If the opening stock and purchases (at cost) are added together the resulting figure is the cost of goods available for sale. If the cost price of sales (sales *less* the estimated profit) is deducted from the goods available for sale, the result must be the cost price of those goods still unsold.

Example 6

A firm obtains a gross profit of 30 per cent on sales, on its range of products sold at fixed prices. On 1st January the stock (at cost) was £4,000. Purchases for the month £1,200 (at cost). Sales were £1,500 for the month. Estimate the closing stock.

Solution 6

		£
Opening stock (at cost)		4,000
Add Purchases		1,200
		5,200
Sales (at selling price)	£1,500	
Deduct Estimated profit	450	
Cost price of sales (*deduct*)		1,050
Estimated closing stock at cost		4,150

The sales figure taken must be the normal selling price if the results are to be accurate. If some goods are known to have been sold at reduced prices and if allowances and discounts have been given, these must be added back to obtain a normal sales figure from which the normal rate of profit can be deducted.

Example 7

On 1st April stock at cost £3,000. Purchases £1,500. Sales were £1,000, and the normal rate of gross profit on cost price is 25 per cent. However, it is known that allowances of £200 have been made to customers. Calculate closing stock.

Solution 7

		£
Opening stock		3,000
Purchases		1,500
Available for sale		4,500
Sales	£1,000	
Add Allowances	200	
"Normal" sales	1,200	
Less Estimated profit (20% on S.P.)	240	
Cost price of sales (*deduct*)		960
Estimated closing stock at cost		3,540

FIRE CLAIMS FOR STOCK

This method of stock valuation is used when a trader suffers loss of stock through fire and the value of the stock destroyed is unknown. In such cases, records are often incomplete, yet an effort must be made to make a realistic estimate of the loss suffered.

The average rate of gross profit is obtained by examining the trading accounts for the previous years. The opening stock for the period since the last accounts can be obtained from the last balance sheet. Copies of these documents will usually be in the hands of auditors and/or the Inspector of Taxes.

If records of sales have been destroyed, customers may be circularized and the approximate level of credit sales estimated. If the ratio of cash to credit sales in past periods is calculated, the approximate cash sales for the period may also be calculated.

Suppliers should be circularized for an estimate of purchases in the period.

When the value of the stock has been calculated the value of any stock salvaged must be deducted from it to give the extent of the insurance claim. Usually, the value of the stock held will exceed the amount insured against. In such cases, the insurance company will meet the same proportionate share of the loss as the sum insured against bears to the stock carried.

If the closing stock is £4,000, whilst £3,000 is the limit of the insurance company's indemnity and £800 of stock was salvaged, the total loss is £3,200 of which the insurance company will pay £3,200 × $\frac{3,000}{4,000}$ = £2,400.

Example 8

On 1st April, 19.2, fire destroyed the stock of Sureglaze Ltd. The books gave the following details—

	£
Sales for the year to 31st December, 19.1 . . .	122,000
Stock on balance sheet at 31st December, 19.1	30,040
Purchases between 1st January, 19.2, and 1st April . . .	29,880
Sales between 1st January, 19.2, and 1st April	47,200
Stock at cost at 31st December, 19..	35,440
Purchases for year ended 31st December, 19.1	83,080

The value of the stock on 31st December, 19.1, included an item costing £1,440, which had been written down to £800. It was sold in February for £1,400. Apart from this, the gross profit ratio has stayed constant. Stock salvaged realized £4,084.

Calculate the amount of insurance claim for stock.

Solution 8

The first step is to draw up a Trading Account for the last full year, 19.1, in order to calculate the normal profit ratio.

TRADING ACCOUNT FOR YEAR ENDED 31ST DECEMBER, 19.1

	£			£
Opening Stock. . . .	35,440	Sales . . .		122,000
Purchases	83,080	Closing Stock .	£30,040	
Normal Gross Profit . .	34,160	*Add* Reduction .	640	
				30,680
	152,680			152,680

Normal gross profit ratio to sales $\frac{34,160}{122,000} \times 100 = 28$ per cent.

The next step is to calculate the cost of goods which were available for normal sale in the period and to compare this to the sales known to have been made, at cost. Any difference will be the stock loss.

To calculate the normal sales for 19.1, the stock written down to £800 must be taken in closing stock at its normal full cost, i.e. £1,440. As the same stock was sold for £1,400, which is below cost, the item has been excluded both from the goods available for sale and the sales. An alternative would be to leave the item in, but the sales figure would then have to be increased by the amount necessary to yield 28 per cent on the sales figure over a cost of £1,440, remembering that the sales figure already includes £1,400 realized on the item.

CALCULATION OF STOCK LOSS ON 1ST APRIL, 19.2

		£
Opening Stock		30,680
Purchases		29,880
		60,560
Exclude stock sold below cost		1,440
Goods available for normal sales in period		59,120
Sales	£47,200	
Exclude stock sold below cost	1,400	
	45,800	
Less Normal Gross Profit, 28%	12.824	
Cost of Goods sold		32,976
Closing stock (estimated)		26,144
Deduct amount realized on salvaged stock		4,084
Insurance loss		22,060

The loss of £22,060 is the amount on which the insurance claim will be based. Policies often limit the claim to a percentage of the loss. If that percentage were 60 per cent then the firm would claim £13,236. The difference of £8,824 would be written off as a loss in the profit and loss account. The entries are:

Debit Cash (or Insurance Company) £13,236.

Profit and loss £8,824.

Credit Stock £22,060.

The balance in the stock account would be debited to the Trading Account in the normal way.

STOCK CONTROL

The primary concern in the management of stock control must be to provide the right goods in the right condition at the right price in the right place at the right time.

This means that control procedures should—

1. Retain stock at appropriate levels.
2. Safeguard stock against loss or misuse.
3. Ensure that stock is properly used in business operations.
4. Ensure that stock is duly accounted for.

Management must control the procedures for purchasing and controlling stock in such a way that an optimum balance is obtained between efficient control and economy. Such a system must be designed in the light of the individual needs of the business.

From the accounting point of view the criteria to be borne in mind are the value of the stock, its susceptibility to misappropriation and the usable life.

An adequate system of control must aim to achieve the following objectives—

1. Elimination of the delivery of incorrect stock, as regards type, quantity or quality.
2. Reduction or elimination of pilfering.
3. Control of movement showing sales per product.
4. Avoidance of holding of slow-moving stock which, apart from tying up money, may be completely wasted by obsolescence.
5. Increased facilities for taking a physical stock at short periods.
6. Provision of a check on over-ordering when demand may fall off.
7. Prevention of the passing of invoices for payment without the receipt of the relative goods.
8. Prevention of goods being charged at incorrect prices.

It is not suggested that this is an exhaustive list of the advantages to be obtained, or that the following remarks are in any way a complete answer to this most important question. Every business has problems peculiar to itself.

1. **Elimination of the Delivery of Incorrect Stock, as regards Type, Quantity, or Quality.** All deliveries of goods should be checked against the copy order when they are received and discrepancies noted. The person ordering the goods is responsible for certifying that they are up to standard.

2. **The Reduction or Elimination of Pilfering.** The key factor here is the relationship between unit value and bulk. If goods are easily portable, of small bulk, and of high value then they will be more likely to misappropriation. Greater security may be exercised on the issue of goods which fall within this category. Where goods are of high bulk and of little value, free access to their use may be allowed but where the opposite is the case a tighter control over access to stores and authorization of issues is necessary.

A physical check of stock may be made at random and at irregular intervals, to provide a moral check on pilfering of stock in the same way as the audit may prevent pilfering of cash.

3. **Control of Movement Showing Sales per Product.** Regular analysis of sales and purchases will indicate changes in demand. If excess stocks are being ordered, this can be checked.

Excessive analysis should be avoided and a periodic check made to see whether information produced is being used.

4. **Avoidance of Holding of Slow-moving Stock.** This can be obtained by marking on each of the stock record cards a minimum and maximum quantity. The minimum is the lowest quantity to which the particular line should be allowed to drop if deliveries are to be maintained, and in arriving at this figure the factors to be considered are the speed at which it is used or sold, the length of time required for delivery on the part of the suppliers and the possibility of late delivery or abnormal usage.

The maximum is the figure above which it may be considered an excessive stock is being carried, and according to the particular business or article may represent several months' stock. Where stock moves more rapidly or more slowly, the store or stock keeper is responsible for reporting immediately for the necessary action on the part of the purchasing department. If stock is moving more rapidly, the quantity normally ordered or put into production can be increased to maintain the stock. Conversely the purchasing can be reduced and when necessary the stock disposed of as a clearance line.

The factors to be considered in fixing the maximum are the rate of consumption; time for delivery; the amount and cost of capital tied-up; the risks of deterioration and obsolescence; the cost of storage; price fluctuations; fire hazards and the economic order quantities.

5. **Increased Facilities for Taking a Physical Stock at Short Periods.** For the purpose of preparing interim trading and profit and loss accounts, stock is quite frequently estimated, but it is obvious that a correct stock-taking is the ideal at which to aim. If the system of recording stock is kept up to date with the monetary value shown against the balances, stock sheets or books can be quickly prepared.

6. **Provision of a Check on Over-ordering when Demand may Fall Off.** The minimum and maximum stocks must be revised periodically. This can be done by the regular inspection of groups of stock cards when alterations can be made as seems necessary.

7. **Prevention of the Passing of Invoices for Payment Without the Receipt of the Relative Goods.** This is particularly important when regular deliveries are received of the same goods and in the same quantities. One satisfactory method of attaining this object is to allot letters to the various sections of the stores or stock and a number to each delivery. No invoice should be passed through the books without the delivery note being attached which bears this number and letter, and to indicate that the order has been marked off, the order number appearing on the invoice should be marked through.

8. **Prevention of Goods being Charged at Incorrect Prices.** This can only be done by insisting that every invoice is checked against the corresponding order or quotation and that orders issued always have prices inserted.

Problems in Accounting for Stocks. Problems in determining the value of stock held may arise because of—

1. Discrepancies between physical stocks and stock records. The differences are usually but not invariably unfavourable.

2. Differences in the timing of receipts of stock and the documentation, e.g. invoices may not have been received.

3. Errors in accounting or stock-taking.

4. Failure to complete stock-taking at the end of the accounting period. In this case, the stock can only be calculated by adjusting for subsequent receipts and issues.

Example 9

This example illustrates some of these problems—

A business prepares accounts annually to 31st March, and stock-taking takes place during the following week-end.

In 1965, 31st March, fell on a Wednesday, stock-taking commenced on 3rd April, and the value of stock then actually on the premises was found to be £15,918. You ascertain the following additional facts—

1. Goods outwards are entered in the Sales Day Book as on the day of dispatch.

2. Goods inwards are entered in the Bought Day Book as on the date of the invoice.

3. Sales during the period 1st–3rd April, as shown by the Sales Day Book and the Cash Sales Book, amounted to £200.

4. Purchases during the same period as shown by the Bought Day Book amounted to £151, but, of these, goods to the value of £53 were not received until after 3rd April.

5. Goods invoiced during March and not received until April totalled £160. Of these, goods to the value of £130 were actually received during the period 1st–3rd April and £30 after 3rd April.

6. The average ratio of gross profit to turnover is 25 per cent.

You are instructed to ascertain the value of the stock as on 31st March, 1965, for inclusion in the year's accounts.

(*London Chamber of Commerce.*)

Solution 9

Working back from the stock actually found on 3rd April, it is necessary to add back issues (Sales at cost) made on Thursday and Friday 1st and 2nd April, and to deduct receipts (Purchases received) on those days. These may have been recorded in March or during 1st–3rd April.

The calculation is as follows—

			£
Value of stock on 3rd April			15,918
		£	
Add back	Sales during 1st–3rd April	200	
Less	28 % Gross profit	50	
Sales at cost			150
			16,068
Deduct	Purchases recorded during 1st–3rd April	151	
Less	Goods not yet received	53	
			98
			15,970
Deduct	Purchases recorded in March but received during 1st–3rd April		130
Stock on 31st March, 1965			15,840

This figure is the stock in hand, invoiced on 31st March, 1965. It does not include £30 invoiced but not received until after 3rd April.

The second example, the opening stock is known and it is necessary to calculate from the records of sales and purchases what the stock-level should be at the end of the period.

Example 10

Nokair Ltd. does not keep records of stock movements. A physical stocktaking is made at the end of each quarter and priced out at cost. This figure is used for compiling quarterly accounts. Draft accounts have been prepared for the year ended 30th June, 1965, and the figure for the closing stock included in such accounts was that disclosed by the stocktaking made on 31st March, 1965, details of the stock taken on 30th June, 1965, having been mislaid and cannot be found. The company operates on a gross profit margin of $33\frac{1}{3}$ per cent of cost.

You have ascertained the following facts—

(*a*) The total of the sales invoiced to customers during April, May and June, 1965 was £53,764. This figure includes £4,028 relating to goods despatched on or before 31st March, 1965. The total of the goods despatched to customers before 30th June, 1965 but invoiced in the following month was £5,512.

(*b*) The total of purchase invoices entered in the Bought Day Book during April, May and June, 1965 was £40,580 and this figure includes £2,940 in respect of goods received on or before 31st March, 1965. Invoices relating to goods received in June, 1965 but which were not entered in the Bought Day Book until July, 1965, totalled £3,880.

(*c*) The value of the stock at cost on 31st March, 1965 was £42,640.

(*d*) In the stock sheets at that date—

1. the total of one page was over-cast by £85.
2. 120 items, the cost of which was £2·00 each, had been priced out at 20p each.
3. the total of the stock in one section which was £5,260 had been included in the summary as £5,620.

Show how you would arrive at the figure for the stock, at cost, as on 30th June, 1965.

(*Certified and Corporate Accountants.*)

Solution 10

In this case, the sales must be adjusted so that the cost value of stocks despatched during the period can be calculated. Goods despatched but not invoiced must be added: goods invoiced but not despatched must be deducted. The Cost of Sales can be calculated by deducting the normal profit margin.

The opening stock must be adjusted by adding back the under-valuation and deducting the two errors which over-valued the stock. The adjustment of purchases is then as in the previous example.

The difference between the cost of stock plus purchases minus cost of sales will be stock at cost at the end of the period, as follows—

NOKAIR LTD.

STATEMENT SHOWING AMOUNT OF STOCK, AT COST, ON 30TH JUNE, 1965

		£
Sales—April, May and June, 1965		53,764
Add Goods dispatched before 30th June, invoiced in July		5,512
		59,276
Less Goods dispatched on or before 31st March, included in sales		4,028
Adjusted sales		55,248
Gross profit margin 25%		13,812
Cost of sales		£41,436
	£	£
Stock at cost at 31st March, 1965		42,640
Add Error in valuation (120 × 36s)		216
		42,856
Less Error in casting	85	
Error in posting to summary	360	
		445
Adjusted stock at 31st March		42,411
Add Purchases—April, May and June, 1965	40,580	
Goods purchased in June but entered in July	3,880	
	44,460	
Less Goods purchased on or before 31st March, included in purchases	2,940	
		41,520
		83,931
Less Cost of sales, as shown above		41,436
Stock at cost, as on 30th June, 1965		£42,495

QUESTIONS

1. What is a manufacturing account? With what items does it deal?
2. Explain the meaning of the terms "prime cost" and "cost of production."
3. What is meant by "overhead"? What are its two usual divisions?
4. What expenditure is included under: (*a*) works overhead, (*b*) administration overhead?
5. At what price should goods manufactured in one's own factory be charged to the selling department? What different views are there on this point?
6. What are the main advantages of a good stock control system?

7. List the different interpretations of "market value."
8. Why must the basis of stock valuation be consistent?
9. What is F.I.F.O.?
10. State how you would value work-in-progress.

EXERCISE 07

1. State concisely how you would deal with the following matters in preparing the accounts of a manufacturing company—

(1) The current replacement cost of a raw material is £0·75 per lb. A quantity in stock was bought for £1 per lb. At the latter price the material represented one-quarter of the cost of a finished product, selling at a profit of 20 per cent on the selling price.

(2) Stock of a finished product which cost £100,000 has a current market value of £60,000, but contracts have previously been made to sell half the stock at prices which, after deduction of selling expenses, will show a profit on cost of £15,000.

(3) Contracts have been made to sell 100,000 lbs. of a finished product at £0·50 per lb. At that time raw material sufficient for half that quantity was bought at £0·25 per lb. No contracts have been made to buy the balance and the current price of raw material is £0·37 per lb.

(4) A sum of £10,000 has been received as compensation for cancellation of a contract of sale with a wholesaler. The manufacturing company is still bound by a contract to buy 30,000 lbs. of raw material which would have been required for the cancelled sale contract. This has now fallen in price by £0·50 per lb. *(L.C.C.)*

2. The stock-in-trade of C D Ltd. is classified in four groups. The following is a summary of the stock list at 31st December, 19.1—

	Cost	Market Value
	£	£
Group 1	1,000	1,200
2	500	400
3	1,800	2,200
4	1,600	1,150

(i) You are required to compute the two amounts at either of which, by two alternative methods of applying the formula "cost or lower market value," the whole stock might properly be valued for purposes of the annual accounts.

(ii) If the directors, after using, for 19.. and earlier years, one of the methods referred to above, decided to adopt the other of the two methods for the annual accounts of 19.1, how should the matter be dealt with, in order to comply with the requirements of the Companies Act, 1948? *(Institute of Bankers.)*

3. The annual accounts of Smokescreens Ltd. are made up to 31st December in each year.

The stock-in-trade at 31st December in each year up to and including 19.2 was brought into the annual accounts at cost, less 10 per cent. During 19.3 it was decided that in future stock should be brought into the annual accounts at cost, without any deduction (unless market value should be lower), and accordingly the stock at 31st December, 19.3, was taken, for purposes of the annual accounts, at cost. The stock at 31st December, 19.2, was charged to the trading account of 19.3, in the usual way, at the amount at which it stood in the books.

The following figures are taken from the company's books—

	Stock-in-trade at 31st Dec.	Net Profit for Year	Credit Balance Carried Forward on P. & L. A/c at 31st Dec.
	£	£	£
19..	18,000	—	15,400
19.1	27,900	9,200	24,600
19.2	21,600	10,600	35,200
19.3	35,000	11,500	46,700

You are required—

(*a*) to redraft the above table, setting out all the items at the amounts at which they would have appeared in the company's books if stock-in-trade had, at all relevant dates, been taken at cost, and

(*b*) to point out, very briefly and without any discussion of the principles of stock valuation, the significance of the contrast between the original amounts and the revised amounts of net profit. (*Institute of Bankers.*)

4. A retail trading company sells goods at prices which are normally 25 per cent above cost. Goods which cannot be sold at the normal selling price are "marked down" to a lower selling price.

The following figures were extracted from the company's books at 31st December, 19..—

	£
Stock-in-trade, 1st January, 19.., at cost	2,400
Purchases for the year 19..	42,100
Sales for the year 19..	49,965

The stock at 1st January had been marked down to £2,930, and the goods were afterwards sold for that amount, which is included in the sales shown above (£49,965).

Certain goods purchased during 19.. at a cost of £8,600 (included in purchases £42,100) had been marked down to £10,120. Some of these goods (cost £100, marked down to £85) remained in stock at 31st December, 19.., but the rest had been sold at the reduced prices to which they had been marked down. These sales are included in the figure £49,965 above. You are required—

(*a*) to show your calculation of the stock at 31st December, 19.., at cost price, and

(*b*) to prepare a trading account for the year 19.., bringing in the closing stock at the lowest amount consistent with the principle of valuation at cost or lower market value. You are to assume that "market value" means the price for which goods can be sold and that all stock not marked down can be sold at its normal selling price. (*Institute of Bankers.*)

5. A retail firm was unable to take stock until several days after the close of the financial year. Between the dates of the end of the financial year and the actual stock-taking the following transactions occurred—

	£
Goods were sold amounting to	290
Returns outwards amounted to	14
Goods received and passed through Purchase Day Book	128
Goods received for which no invoices arrived until after the Stock had been taken	35
The total amount of the Stock as shown by the inventory was	13,190

Assuming the average gross profit to be 25 per cent, at what figure should the Stock be included in the Balance Sheet? (*L.C.C.*)

6. A company sells four product groups A, B, C, and D at a profit of 10, 8, 12, and 20 per cent on cost respectively. At 31st March, 19.. (the end of the company's financial year), the stocks at cost were as follows—

	£
A	8,500
B	23,200
C	16,500
D	9,200

During April, 19.. the purchases and sales were as follows—

	Purchases	Sales
	£	£
A	24,600	25,010
B	49,700	61,784
C	38,600	40,742
D	29,400	31,770

It was necessary during that month to make certain sales at less than normal prices. These (which are included in the above sales figures) were as follows—

	Sales at Normal Prices	Rate of Discount
	£	%
A	800	50
B	400	25
C	1,000	25
D	200	75

You are required, from the above information, to prepare the trading account of the company for the month ended 30th April, 19...

(Cost and Management Accountants.)

7. You are preparing the accounts of P. Snow for the year ended 31st March, 1963. In carrying out your investigation of the books for that purpose, you find that all invoices relating to sales and purchases and credit notes bearing dates in March 1963 had been entered in the books but that such documents bearing dates in April 1963 had been dealt with as though they related to the year commencing 1st April, 1963.

It had been impossible to actually take stock until 5th April, 1963, and the summary of the stock sheets showed the value of the total stock at cost at that date to be £16,420.

The rate of gross profit earned was 20 per cent on selling prices.

You find that—

(1) For the period 1st April, 1963, to 4th April, 1963, sales and sales returns were £730 and £85 respectively and all the invoices and credit notes relating thereto bore dates in April 1963.

(2) Suppliers had sent in goods during the four days to 4th April, 1963, invoices relating to such bearing dates in March 1963 amounted in total to £340 and those bearing dates in April 1963 to £180.

(3) An item of 200 articles priced at 80p each had been extended as £100.

(4) The total of one stock sheet amounting to £300 had not been carried to the summary and the total of another, namely £150, had been included in the summary as £180.

(5) Goods to the value of £325 at selling price had been sent, prior to 31st March, 1963, to a customer on approval. No entries as regards this transaction had been made in the books and neither were the goods included in the stock.

Show how you would arrive at the figure for stock to be inserted in the accounts for the year ended 31st March, 1963. *(A.C.C.A.)*

8. On 2nd August, 19.1, a fire destroyed the premises, but not the books and records of the Eversafe Company. The books disclosed the following details—

	£
Sales for year to 31st March, 19.1	61,000
Stock per balance sheet 31st March, 19.1	15,020
Purchases from 1st April, 19.1, to 2nd August 19.1	14,940
Sales from 1st April, 19.1, to 2nd August, 19.1	23,600
Stock at cost, 31st March, 19..	17,720
Purchases year to 31st March, 19.1	41,540

The value of stock at 31st March, 19.1, was arrived at after writing down to £400 an item which cost £720. This was sold in May, 19.1, for £700. Apart from this transaction, the gross profit ratio has remained constant. The salvage stock was valued at £2,042.

You are required to calculate the amount of the insurance claim for loss of stock.

(*Cost and Management Accountants.*)

9. A. Smith is a sole trader in a retail business and on 29th May, 1965, a fire occurred which destroyed all his stock, fixtures and fittings, financial books and papers, with the exception of a file of unpaid invoices and his cash box containing the float, which he had taken home with him.

The fire insurance covered loss of stock, at cost, not exceeding £3,000 and fixtures and fittings to the value of £500. He had not insured against loss of profit.

Smith's last Balance Sheet, made up to 3rd April, 1965, was as follows—

	£	£		£
Capital		3,000	Fixtures and Fittings	600
Creditors			Stock at cost	2,400
Goods	200		Balance at Bank	250
Expenses	60		Cash in till	10
		260		
		3,260		3,260

He had banked all his takings up to the close of business on 29th May, 1965, with the exception of—

(1) £20 per week paid for Wages.
(2) £10 per week for his own living expenses.
(3) A float of £10 kept in the cash box.

All payments for stock purchases and business expenses (other than wages) had been made by cheque.

The selling price of his goods was calculated by adding 30 per cent to the cost price.

An analysis of his Bank Statements for the eight weeks to 29th May, 1965, was as follows—

	£		£
Balance at 3rd April, 1965	205	Creditors for Goods	1,240
Suppliers for goods returned	40	Expenses	200
Weekly Bankings	1,840	Balance at 29th May, 1965	690
	£2,130		£2,130

The unpaid invoices on 29th May amounted to—

	£
Goods	160
Expenses . .	40

You are required to prepare—

(*a*) A statement of claim for loss of stock.

(*b*) Smith's Profit and Loss Account for the eight weeks ended 29th May, 1965, and a Balance Sheet as on that date, assuming that the claims for stock and fixtures are agreed.

10. As accountant you are concerned as to the amount of working capital invested in raw material stocks, and would like to see it reduced if possible.

The works manager, for his part, wishes to be sure that these stocks never fall too low.

You therefore agree to meet each other to discuss the possibility of fixing—

(*a*) Maximum.
(*b*) Minimum stock levels.

List the factors which in your opinion should be taken into consideration in fixing (*a*) and (*b*), and outline the procedure you would recommend for implementing the scheme of stock control. (*A.C.C.A.*)

11. Arnold, Ltd., insured for Consequential Loss for £18,000.

The net profit for the year ended 31st December was £6,000 and the Insurable Standing Charges £15,000, but only £14,000 was included in the definition of Insured Standing Charges.

The period of indemnity is six months and the fire occurred on 1st April and the interruption continued till 31st July.

Additional Cost of Working to mitigate the effect of the damage is £2,000 and the saving in Insured Standing Charges is £200.

	Turnover last financial year	Turnover for financial year in which the damage occurred	Reduction in period of interruption
	£	£	£
Jan–Mar	25,000	25,600	
Apr–Jul	20,000	6,000	14,000
Aug–Dec	35,000	37,400	
	£80,000	£69,000	

The damage caused was severe, and but for the expenditure of the above £2,000 the business would have shut down for the period after the fire till 31st July, but by that time full restoration of normal conditions would have been effected.

Show details of draft claim against the insurance company.

12. Discuss the familiar rule which asserts that the accounting basis for the valuation of stock-in-trade should normally be the lower of cost or current market value, indicating the accepted modern interpretations of the expressions "cost" and "market value."

13. The following information relates to three departments whose stocks are controlled at selling prices.

Dept.	Weeks	Purchases	Sales	Sales Value of Price Reductions Authorized	Stock at Beginning	Sales Value of Stock at Beginning
		£	£	£	£	£
A	1–4	2,900	3,800	400	3,500	4,200
	5–8	3,300	4,100	200	—	—
	9–12	3,100	3,700	—	—	—
B	1–4	2,200	2,700	100	2,800	3,500
	5–8	2,000	2,300	—	—	—
	9–12	2,300	2,900	300	—	—
C	1–4	1,400	1,800	—	1,900	2,470
	5–8	1,600	2,100	100	—	—
	9–12	1,800	1,900	200	—	—

What was the value at cost of the stock in each department at the end of each 4-weekly period? Show your workings in the form of a tabulation. Work to the nearest £. (*Cost and Management Accountants.*)

14. Lyre & Co. were in business with two departments: Music and Records; and Musical Instruments.

The accounts for the year ended 31st March, 19.1, showed the following departmental figures—

	Stock 1/4/..	Purchases	Sales	Stock 31/3/.1
	£	£	£	£
Music and Records	5,000	20,000	30,000	4,000
Musical Instruments	7,000	8,000	12,000	6,000

On 30th June, 19.1, the premises and stock therein were entirely destroyed by fire. The books were not destroyed and showed the following figures for the period 1st April to 30th June, 19.1—

	Stock 1/4/.1	Purchases	Sales	Cost of goods in Hands of Customers on Sale or Return
	£	£	£	£
Music and Records	4,000	5,000	9,000	None
Musical Instruments	6,000	2,500	4,000	200

You are required to compute the value of the stock destroyed by fire, assuming the same profit percentages as those disclosed for the year ended 31st March, 19.1. (*Chartered Accountants.*)

15. For the current year a trading account stands thus—

	£		£
Cost of Materials	5,000	Sales	10,000
Wages	3,000		
Discount	500		
Expenses	1,500		
	10,000		10,000

State the above costs as percentages on turnover.

As this leaves no profit, the trader considers how he can improve matters, and finding that he cannot advance his selling prices he will aim at increasing the turnover by £2,000, and reducing the percentage costs on turnover by materials 2, wages 1, discount 2: the expenses remain at the same amount.

Show his trading account for the next year on the basis of these alterations.

(*West Riding of Yorkshire.*)

16. After the close of business on 28th February, 19.., a fire occurred on the premises of C. Brett, a sole trader carrying on business in a retail shop. It was found that all the stock had been destroyed or damaged. A comprehensive fire policy included cover for loss of stock, at cost, not exceeding £400. Brett had not insured against loss of profit.

The only records Brett kept, apart from his "bank statement" were files of paid suppliers' statements and unpaid invoices for goods purchased, together with a note book in which he recorded a few sales to special customers who paid by cheque. Cash received for cash sales was paid into the till, out of which Brett paid certain amounts of which he kept a rough record, the balance at the end of each week being paid into the bank after retaining a float of £10. All suppliers of goods were paid by cheque.

Brett had prepared a balance sheet as on Saturday, 3rd January, 19.., as follows—

	£		£
Capital	572	Fixtures and Fittings (net)	350
Suppliers	74	Stock, at cost	180
Creditors for Expenses	38	Debtors	48
		Balance at bank	96
		Cash in hand	10
	684		684

An analysis of the bank statements for the eight weeks to 28th February, 19.. was as follows—

	£		£
Balance 5th January, 19..	96	Suppliers of Goods	585
Special Customers	67	Expenses	29
Suppliers for goods returned	24	Balance 28th February, 19..	40
Weekly bankings	467		
	654		654

Brett estimates that during the eight weeks the total amounts paid out of the till, before making the weekly bankings, were: drawings £75, wages and national insurance £48, sundry shop expenses £28 and a special price allowance on goods sold to a customer £5.

You ascertain that at the close of business on 28th February, 19.., the balance in the till was £10, suppliers' unpaid invoices amounted to £89, special customers owed £38 and creditors for expenses were £44.

The whole of the stock salvaged was afterwards sold to a dealer for £40.

The usual percentage of gross profit on sales for this class of business can be taken to be 30 per cent. You are required to—

(*a*) prepare a statement for submission to the insurance company to substantiate a claim for loss of stock by fire, and

(*b*) prepare Brett's balance sheet as on 28th February, 19.., and the profit and loss account for the eight weeks ended on that date, assuming the claim is admitted. (*Chartered Accountants.*)

17. An engineering company records prices as well as quantities in its stores ledger and the following is a summary of the receipts and issues of 20-foot angle irons during the half-year ended 30th June, 19..—

Stock on hand, 1st January . . .	**600 valued at 75p each**
Taken into store during January . .	**1,200 invoiced at 80p each**
" " " " April . . .	**600 " " 85p each**
Issues, during—	
January	**none**
February	**450**
March	**900**
April	**none**
May	**none**
June	**700**

Write up the stores ledger account for the half-year: (*a*) on the basis that all issues are charged out at cost on the "first-in-first-out" method, and (*b*) on the basis that all issues are charged out at the average cost of the balance of goods in stock at the date of issue. (*R.S.A.*)

18. A summary of the audited balance sheet of The Betta Traders Ltd. as on 30th June, 1961, was as follows—

	£		£
Share Capital—		**Office Furniture and Equipment**	
Authorized and Issued .	**25,000**	**at cost . . . . .**	**6,253**
General Reserves inclusive of the balance on Profit and Loss Account	**39,216**	***Less* Depreciation . .**	**2,948**
			3,305
Sundry Creditors . . .	**9,104**	**Stock on hand, at cost . .**	**30,478**
		Sundry Debtors . . .	**29,642**
		Cash at Bank . . .	**4,895**
	68,320		**68,320**

After the close of business on 30th September, 1961, a fire occurred on the premises and the cash-book and nominal ledger were destroyed together with a till which contained that day's takings.

You are able to ascertain that at the time of closing on 30th September, 1961—

(*a*) Balances were—Bank, after the adjustment of outstanding items, £6,020, Sundry Debtors £49,724 and Trade Creditors £12,563.

(*b*) The transactions during the period 1st July, 1961, to 30th September, 1961, were: Purchases, less returns £225,353, Cash and credit sales, less returns £383,791, Wages and salaries £36,532, General expenses, £96,975, Depreciation provided £80, Accounting machine purchased £820 and dividend, declared prior to 30th June, 1961, paid 4th July, 1961, £2,000.

(*c*) The whole of the takings had been paid into the bank with the exception of those lost in the fire.

(*d*) The value of the stock on hand on 30th September, 1961, at cost, was £22,672.

Being instructed by the insurance company to ascertain the loss of cash resulting from the fire, prepare—

(1) A statement setting forth your computation of such loss.

(2) Trading and Profit and Loss Account for the three months ended 30th September, 1961, and a balance sheet as on that date, assuming that the claim for lost cash as computed by you will be fully admitted by the insurance company. (*A.C.C.A.*)

19. The accounting year of Syntax Ltd. ends on 31st March and the company's custom is to take stock on the following Saturday. In 19.. 31st March fell on a Tuesday, and stock was taken on 4th April, when the value of the physical stock on hand at the end of the day, all at cost, was found to amount to £18,591.

You are informed that all sales are invoiced out and dispatched on the date of sale and that all purchases are entered in the bought day book according to the dates shown on the invoices, regardless of the date on which the consignment in question may have actually been received.

According to the financial books purchases during the period 1st–4th April amounted to £491 and sales to £932.

Comparison of the invoices with the goods inwards book discloses the following facts—

(1) Of goods actually received in March £121 were charged on invoices dated between 1st and 4th April and £8 on 8th April.

(2) Of goods actually received during the period 1st–4th April £106 were invoiced in March, £246 between 1st April and 4th April, and £34 on or after 5th April.

(3) Of goods not received until after 4th April, none were invoiced in March but £123 were invoiced during the period 1st–4th April.

You may assume that the average ratio of gross profit to sales is 25 per cent. There were no returns during the period, either inwards or outwards.

You are required to show what adjustment (if any) is required to the purchases account, and the value of the stock on hand at the close of business on 31st March for inclusion in the accounts. *(R.S.A.)*

20. A clothing manufacturer commenced business on 1st January, 19... Textile materials used include two types, A and B. During the six months to 30th June, 19.., purchases were as follows—

Jan	1	1,000	yards of type	A	at £0·50	a yard.
	6	1,600	,, ,,	B	,, £0·75	,,
Mar	18	2,300	,, ,,	A	,, £0·60	,,
Apr	16	3,000	,, ,,	B	,, £0·80	,,
May	26	800	,, ,,	A	,, £0·40	,,

Issues from the store-room to the factory were as follows—

Jan	7	700	yards of type	A.
	12	1,200	,, ,,	B.
Mar	28	1,420	,, ,,	A.
Apr	22	2,860	,, ,,	B.
Jun	1	1,580	,, ,,	A.

Materials were charged to the factory at cost, on the "first in, first out" principle, and stocks were valued on the same basis for purposes of the trading account for the six months to 30th June, 19.., and balance sheet as on 30th June, 19...

You are required to set out accounts, in debit and credit form, with columns for quantities and money values, for each of the two materials, for the six months to 30th June, 19... The closing balances on these accounts should represent the amounts to be included in the trading account and in the balance sheet.

(Chartered Institute of Secretaries.)

21. Weston Ltd., an engineering company, records prices as well as quantities in its stores ledger. The following are the details of the receipts into and issues from store in 6 in. steel bolts during the year ended 31st December, 19...

On 1st January, 19.. there were in store 1,800 bolts, priced at 20p each and receipts and issues during the year were as follows—

Receipts—	
March	3,000 invoiced at 30p each
September	2,000 ,, ,, 18p each
Issues—	
February	1,200
April	2,000
June	600
November	2,200

Write up the account in question in the stores ledger on the alternative assumptions that issues are priced—

(1) On the "first in, first out" principle.
(2) On the "last in, first out" principle.

(*Chartered Institute of Secretaries.*)

CHAPTER 08

STOCK EXCHANGE TRANSACTIONS AND INVESTMENT ACCOUNTS

I shall not want Capital in Heaven
For I shall meet Sir Alfred Mond.
We two shall lie together, lapt
In a five per cent Exchequer Bond

T. S. ELIOT

STOCK EXCHANGE TRANSACTIONS

THE Stock Exchange is a specialist institution and the book-keeping, whilst still following double-entry rules, is unlike that of any other business. Any student who intends to enter the office of a stockbroker or stockjobber will find it necessary to make a particular study of this branch of accounting.

The Stock Exchange Council requires all member firms to keep proper books of account and detailed records of transactions and finances. An annual balance sheet signed by all the partners must be submitted to the Council and an independent accountant must report on whether these requirements have been fulfilled. The purpose of this section is not to describe a complete accounting system for Stock Exchange firms, but merely to outline the main features.

A *stockbroker* is an agent who takes instructions from his clients. Each purchase or sale is executed by him with a stockjobber so that, with few exceptions, every transaction is recorded as a purchase from, or sale to, a jobber by the broker's clients. As evidence that the transaction has been carried out, a bought or sold contract note is sent by the broker to his client, all charges and commission being added to a purchase or deducted from a sale. The charges and commissions are as follows—

1. **The Contract Stamp.** In 1970 the stamp duty on contract notes for or relating to the sale or purchase of any stock or marketable security was nil on a value of £100 or less. It was 10p on amounts up to £500; 30p up to £1,500; and 60p on amounts exceeding £1,500.

2. **Transfer Stamp Duty.** In 1970 an additional scale of stamp duty was payable according to the following scale—

Consideration not exceeding £5	5p
Exceeding £5 and not exceeding £10 . . .	10p
Exceeding £10 and not exceeding £20 . . .	20p
Exceeding £20 and not exceeding £30 . . .	30p
Exceeding £30 and not exceeding £40 . . .	40p

Exceeding £40 and not exceeding £50 . . .	50p
Exceeding £50 and not exceeding £60 . . .	60p
Exceeding £60 and not exceeding £70 . . .	70p
Exceeding £70 and not exceeding £80 . . .	80p
Exceeding £80 and not exceeding £90 . . .	90p
Exceeding £90 and not exceeding £100 . . .	£1·00

Thence 20p for every additional £20 or part up to £300 consideration. Over £300 the duty is 50p for every £50 or part.

From the above it is seen that for a transaction of £5 the duty is 2 per cent, but for transactions over £5 it is 1% or less.

3. **Brokers' Commission.** The scale of minimum stock exchange commissions varies according to the type of security dealt in.

A (1) Securities quoted *vide* the following headings in the official list—

British Funds, etc. Securities issued by the International Bank for Reconstruction and Development Securities issued by the Inter-American Development Bank Corporation and County Stocks—Great Britain and Northern Ireland Public Boards, etc.—Great Britain and Northern Ireland Commonwealth Government and Provincial Securities Commonwealth Corporation Stocks	$\frac{3}{8}$ per cent on Stock up to £10,000 Stock. $\frac{1}{4}$ per cent on Stock on any balance in excess of £10,000 Stock.

See also A (2) below.

A (2) (i) Securities of or guaranteed by Commonwealth Governments, Provinces or Corporations—

Bonds to Bearer either expressed in a currency other than Sterling or carrying an option for payment at a fixed rate in a currency other than Sterling, where the price is over 100. (ii) Annuities (dealt in per unit of Annuity) issued by any of the Bodies mentioned in A (1) above (iii) Bank of Ireland Stock	$\frac{3}{8}$ per cent on consideration.

B Debentures and Bonds and any other securities representing loans (Debenture Stocks, Loan Stocks, Notes, Annuities, etc.) other than those included in Section A above.

Registered	$\frac{3}{4}$ per cent on consideration.
Loans quoted in London expressed or optionally payable in a foreign currency other than of a Scheduled Territory	$\frac{1}{4}$ per cent on consideration.
Other Bearer Securities	$\frac{1}{2}$ per cent on consideration.

C Stocks and Shares Registered or Bearer other than those included in Section A, B or (D) whether partly or fully paid up

Price	*Commission per Unit or Share*
Up to 7½p	At discretion
Over 7½p to 15p	$\frac{1}{16}$p
Over 15p to 30p	⅛p
Over 30p to 60p	¼p
Over 60p to 110p	½p
Over 110p to 200p	1p
Over 200p to 275p	1½p
Over 275p to 350p	2p
Over 350p to 450p	2½p
Over 450p to 550p	3p
Over 550p to 700p	4p
Over 700p to 900p	5p

With 1p increase for every 200p in price or portion thereof.

D Shares or Units of Stock, Registered or Bearer (other than Shares included in Section E). . . . . . . 1¼ per cent on Money.

E Shares of Companies incorporated in the United States of America or Canada (whether dealt in in London on a Dollar or Sterling basis), with the exception of Shares which are transferable by Deed of Transfer.

The Dollar prices set out in the scale below relate to transactions done for settlement in Sterling (including any premium paid or received).

For the purpose of applying the scale of transactions effected in overseas markets where payment is made and received in Dollars, the American or Canadian Dollar price is to be converted into the Sterling equivalent at the current rate of exchange.

Price 25 cents (5p) or under . At discretion. Thereafter on a rising scale.

F Securities of New Issues passing by delivery in scrip form or by letters of Renunciation—

(*a*) Sales and purchases of shares and units of stock included in section D and registered Stocks (quoted per cent) included in Section C
1¼ per cent on consideration.

(*b*) Sales and purchases of Debentures and Bonds, etc., included in Section B
¾ per cent on consideration.

(*c*) Sales and purchases of Securities included in Section A—
At discretion until Security is fully-paid and then at the rate laid down in Section A.

G "Givers" of option money for more than one Account — As on bargains.
"Takers" of option money for more than one account — Half the above scale.

Options for one Account or less
Powers of Attorney for Inscribed Stock
Probate and other Valuations
Securities Made-up or Made-down
Short-dated Securities (having Five Years or less to run)*
} At discretion.

* NOTE: Not applicable in the case of securities in default.

Transfers of Stocks and Shares

Small Bargains—

No lower Commission than £2 may be charged except in the case of—

(*a*) Transactions on which the Commission may be at discretion.

(*b*) Transactions amounting to less than £100 in value on which a Commission of not less than £1 must be charged.

(*c*) Transactions amounting to £10 or less in value on which the Commission may be at discretion.

£5,000 *Rule*

In the case of a transaction in which the consideration exceeds £5,000, full commission must be charged up to that amount but a broker may at his discretion charge half the Standard Rate on the excess. This rule is not permissible where commission is shared with an Agent.

£50,000 *Rule*

In the case of a transaction in not less than £50,000 Stock of a security included in Section A (1), i.e. British Government Securities and certain other stocks, with less than 10 years to run, a reduced charge on the entire amount of not less than $\frac{1}{8}$ per cent on stock may be conceded, if the commission is divisible with an agent. If the commission is not divided with an agent, the rate is $\frac{1}{16}$ per cent on stock.

The normal rate of commission on shares in a company is $1\frac{1}{4}$ per cent with a minimum of £2.

4. **Registration Fee.** Some companies still charge £0·125 for registering a transfer, but many have dropped the charge. The buyer's broker informs the company of the transfer, and they issue a new share certificate and dividend mandate.

It is from this point that each item enters the books of accounts which may be divided into two main sections—

Ledgers. Impersonal and Private Ledger or Ledgers; Clients Ledgers; Jobbers Ledgers; Brokers Ledger; Investment Ledger (to record the Broker's own investments); Dividends and Rights.

Books of Original Entry. Day Books (not divided into Sales and Purchases as with a commercial business); Cash Book; Journal; Stamps and Fees; Tickets Payable; Tickets Receivable; Contango Journal.

Whether the transaction is a speculation, as the result of which the client hopes to make a quick profit, or a genuine investment, does not effect the entries from the point of view of the broker, and the following example will serve as a general illustration.

Example. Bernard Hartley instructs his broker to purchase 300 Barclays Bank Ltd. Ordinary shares. The transaction is duly carried out at the price of 400p per share with C. Bowyer, a jobber. Show the bought contract note and the entries in the books of the broker.

Had this transaction been a sale by the client the entries would, of course, have been reversed and the item of £12·13 for transfer stamps and fees would not have appeared on the contract note, as these expenses

CONTRACT NOTE

NAME OF BROKER — ADDRESS

LONDON, E.C.2.

14th January, 19..

To *Bernard Hartley, Esq.*

We have this day BOUGHT as per your Order, for settlement in Cash—subject to the Rules, Regulations, and Customs of the London Stock Exchange.

		£	£
300 *Ordinary Shares Barclays Bank Ltd.*	PRICE @ 400p . . .	1,200·00	
	BROKERAGE 2½p *per share* .	7·50	
	CONTRACT STAMP . .	0·30	
	TRANSFER STAMP AND FEE .	12·13	
			1,219·93

In view of the introduction of Capital Gains Tax, it is essential that ALL Contract Notes and Statements should be retained by clients.

30p CONTRACT NOTE

(Signature of Broker)

Member of the Stock Exchange, London, E.C.2.

E. & O. E.

are paid by the buyer. The brokerage and contract stamp would be deducted instead of added and would therefore read—

	£	£
Price @ 400p	—	1,200·00
Brokerage 2½p per share	7·50	
Contract stamp	·30	7·80
		1,192·20

The transfer stamp is in fact paid for by the selling broker who prepares the transfer, but he is reimbursed when the transfer is delivered to and paid for by the buying broker. On the first page of this chapter it was stated that a stockbroker is an agent who merely carries out orders. It should perhaps be added that in accordance with the rules of the London Stock Exchange he is the principal in all dealings on the market, but this merely means that he is liable for all purchases made by him and if his clients

DAY BOOK

1 *Dr* | *Cr* 1

Date	Particulars	Fo.	Seller		Cont. Stp.	Stps. & Fees	Commn.	Buyer	Fo.	
				£	£	£	£			£
	300 Barclays Bank Ord.	21	C. Bowyer . . .	1,200·00	0·30	12·13	7·50	Bernard Hartley . .		1,219·93

Note 1. Posted *Dr*. to *Cr*. and *Cr*. to *Dr*.
Note 2. Entries are made in this book from counterfoils of the contract notes.

JOBBERS LEDGER

21 *Dr* *C. Bowyer* | *Cr* 21

Date	Barclays Bank Ord.				Price	Fo.	£	Date	Barclays Bank Ord.				Price	Fo.	£
	300				400p	T.P.61	1,200·00		300				400p	D.B.1	1,200·00

Note 1. Had the transaction been a sale the debit entry would be made from the day book, and the credit entry from the tickets receivable book.
Note 2. It does not follow that the ticket passed will be at the same price as that at which the transaction was done. If the price is different the amount by which the two sides disagree will be paid to or received from the Jobber as a "difference" on settlement. The amount will, of course, be recovered when the transfer is paid for.

CLIENTS LEDGER

51 *Dr* | *Cr* 51

Date		Price	Fo.	£	Date		Price	Fo.	£
	300 Barclays Bank Ord. shares . .	400p	D.B.1	1,219·93		Cash			1,219·93

TICKETS PAYABLE

61 *Dr* | *Cr* 61

Date	No.	Stock or Shares	To Whom Paid	Stamp £	£	Date	No.	Stock or Shares	To Whom Given	Stamp £	£
	28	300 Barclays Ord..	C. Bowyer . .	12·13	1,200·00		28	300 Barclays Ord..	C. Bowyer . .	12·13	1,200·00

This side is entered from the tickets received on the transfers at the time of delivery.

This side is entered from the counterfoils of the tickets or "names" issued.

CASH BOOK

Dr | *Cr*

Date	Name		£	Date	Name		£
	Bernard Hartley		1,219·93		C. Bowyer		1,212·13

In practice separate cash books are generally used for receipts and payments.

are unable to meet their commitments he must take the stock or shares himself and pay for them. Further points in connexion with the jobbers ledger and ticket books must be considered before passing on to the other books included in the set.

Jobbers Ledger. The somewhat unusual ruling is necessary to enable the clerk responsible to see at a glance when any particular account is closed. Each jobber operates in a group of securities known as a "market" and for every purchase or sale by a broker a ticket must be passed between them with the result that at balancing time—fortnightly under normal conditions—the total number of shares or amount of stock on the one side must be the same as on the other. If, when this is so, the money columns do not agree a cheque will pass for the difference. In the illustration given, one "ticket" or "name" was passed by the broker for the 300 shares and a transfer delivered for this one item. In actual fact the jobber may not be able to deliver in one "lot" and is therefore compelled to split the ticket into two or more smaller numbers. This will not affect the debit entry in the jobbers ledger, but it will cause additional entries on the debit side of tickets payable and that, in its turn, may be the cause of a journal entry.

Tickets Payable. When a ticket is split the price per share or other unit on the original must always be used on the counterparts so that, errors apart, the total of the right-hand column on both debit and credit sides of the ticket book will be the same when all deliveries have been made, but some variation in the total stamp duty payable may result. In this case the jobber from whom the original purchase was made is responsible to the buying broker to reimburse him the excess as well as any additional registration fees caused thereby.

Reference to the original contract note will show that the transfer stamp duty was £12·00 and the registration fee £0·13. Had delivery been made in three smaller lots, the stamp duty might have amounted to, say, £13·20 and, of course, the registration of three transfers would cost £0·38. This difference of £1·20 will be claimed by the broker from C. Bowyer and this is known as claiming "splits." This will necessitate a journal entry, to which reference is made under that heading.

The remaining books mentioned in the early part of the chapter will now be considered briefly, as they are of special interest only to the person entering this branch of business and it is not considered necessary to illustrate them.

Brokers Ledger. Generally speaking this takes the place of the jobbers ledger under certain conditions. There are Stock Exchanges in the major provincial cities and according to their geographical position certain types of shares may have an even more active market than in London. As an instance a broker in London on receiving an order to buy or sell shares in a bicycle manufacturing company may find London a difficult market, and that he can deal to better advantage on the Birmingham

Exchange. In this case he will place his order with a broker in Birmingham (provincial exchanges do not differentiate between brokers and jobbers) and in consequence the entry will be between the brokers ledger and clients ledger.

Investment Ledger. This will be dealt with under "Investment Accounts."

Dividends and Rights. The terms have already been dealt with in the chapter on Company Accounts and will therefore be understood. Many weeks must sometimes elapse between the date of a purchase or sale on the Stock Exchange and the eventual registration of the transfer by the buying broker, so that although the purchase was made cum dividend and/or rights, the seller remains on the register of members and will therefore receive the dividend warrant or rights from the company. In this case the broker acting for the buyer will claim them from the jobber or broker giving delivery. Entries will be made from the journal and cash book and the headings of the accounts are the names of the securities.

Journal. Three main types of entries are to be found in this book as the result of "splits," dividends and rights, and dealings with the Stock Exchange Clearing House. The first two have been explained above, and the entries can be visualized by the student without difficulty. The object of a Clearing House is to eliminate a great deal of routine work. A simple illustration will make this clear. Under normal conditions the market in mining shares is very active and in the course of one "account"—a fortnight—many hundreds of transactions may be executed by one broker in one particular share alone and with possibly several jobbers.

Assume the position to be as follows—

ARIZONA COPPER MINES

	No. of Shares	*Buyer*	*Seller*
1	250	Jobber A	Client
2	750	do.	do.
3	350	Client	Jobber B
4	500	Jobber B	Client
5	500	do.	do.
6	1,000	Jobber C	do.
7	250	Client	Jobber A
8	1,000	do.	do. C

The first and seventh items and the sixth and eighth will cancel out so that the passing of names is not necessary, but in respect of the others the broker will need to pass one ticket for 350 shares and receive tickets for 750, 500, and 500. Not only so but with an active market the 250 shares sold to Jobber A may have changed hands many times in the interim, so that if names are being passed this particular one may have to pass from, say, X to P to D to R to A and it is obviously quite unnecessary for it to go by such a circuitous route if arrangements can be made for putting X directly into touch with the selling broker.

This is done by all members sending details of their transactions to the

Clearing House, and here all such intermediate parties can be struck out. Where names are not received from or passed to jobbers as a result of the elimination, the jobbers' ledger account must be closed by a journal entry.

Contango Journal. A speculator who instructs his broker to buy securities he does not wish to pay for, or "take up" as it is termed, but in the hope that he will be able to sell at a profit, is a "bull."

Alternatively a speculator who sells stock or shares he does not possess in the belief that a fall in price is imminent which will enable him to buy back at a lower price before he has to deliver the securities, is known as a "bear."

If either operator finds he is unable to "close" his speculation before the end of the account when he should take up or deliver the shares or stock, he may ask his broker to defer the settlement until the next Pay Day, and if the broker can arrange it, he is said to "carry-over" the deal.

Contango is the interest charged to a bull operator for the privilege of being allowed to postpone the taking up of the stock from one account to another.

Backwardation is the charge made to a bear operator for the privilege of being allowed to postpone delivery until the following account.

As to whether the bull will have to pay contango, or the bear backwardation, depends upon the state of the market.

"Carrying-over" may be defined as a sale or purchase in the old account followed by a repurchase or resale in the new account at prices fixed by the Stock Exchange Committee, called "making up" prices. When this takes place it follows that the ticket does not have to be passed, and in order to close and reopen the accounts in the jobbers and clients ledgers, a journal entry is necessary and a special journal is kept for this purpose.

Coding of Securities. A Working Party was set up in September, 1966, on the initiative of the Council of the Stock Exchange, with representatives of other bodies concerned with the processing of data relating to Securities, to evolve a standard system of Coding and alphabetic abbreviation for securities dealt in and held within the United Kingdom.

The Working Party recommended—

(*a*) That a revised numeric code be introduced, based on the existing Stock Exchange Code, but covering a much wider range of securities including those quoted on major Overseas Stock Exchanges.

(*b*) That a uniform system of alphabetic abbreviation be devised both for the names of companies and other issues of securities, and for the description of individual stocks, with a maximum overall length of 45 characters.

(*c*) That all those concerned with using computers for the processing of securities be encouraged to make use of the standard code and abbreviations and that their use be generally accepted by all concerned in securities documentation.

The Working Party propose in due course to make suggestions for a further standard coding system categorising securities by industry, etc., when the details of the industrial classification at present being compiled by the Institute of Actuaries have been settled. This will be separate and distinct from the identifying numerical code.

The Council of the Stock Exchange accepted the responsibility of compiling, publishing and maintaining a code book incorporating the standard code and abbreviation for every security quoted in the United Kingdom and Ireland, and all British Unit Trusts. As this is completed, the system will be extended by stages to cover the categories of foreign securities recommended by the Working Party.

It is hoped that the standard code and abbreviation will be adopted by all computer users and others. If companies print the security code number in association with their full titles on dividend warrants and certificates registrars will be able to accept transfers made out in the abbreviated form coupled with the code number.

Numeric Identifying Securities Code. The basic form of the identifying code will be as follows—

Block identifier	*Item identifier*	*Check digit*
(1 digit)	(5 digit)	(1 digit)
0–9	00002–99999	0–9

The block identifiers are as follows—

(i) 0-*series* (*even numbers only*). All U.K. quoted securities and Unit Trusts (including Overseas Securities quoted in U.K.). The 5 digit item identified will in almost all cases be that assigned within the existing code.

(ii) 0-*series* (*odd numbers*). Temporary Lines for new issues and other temporary variants of the above.

(iii) 1-*series.* Reserved for independent allocation by users for unquoted British securities.

(iv) (*a*) 2-*series.* For official allocation by the centre to all securities quoted on the New York, Toronto, and American Stock Exchanges; (*b*) 3-*series.* Reserved for independent allocation by users to other North American securities.

(v) (*a*) 4-*series.* For official allocation to all securities except local Provincial and Municipal Bonds quoted on Amsterdam, Brussels, Frankfurt, Milan, Paris and Zurich Stock Exchanges; (*b*) 5-*series.* Reserved for independent allocation to other European securities.

(vi) (*a*) 6-*series.* For official allocation to all stocks quoted on Johannesburg, Australian, and Tokyo Stock Exchanges; (*b*) 7-*series.* Reserved for independent allocation to other miscellaneous overseas securities.

(vii) 8-*series.* Spare, reserved for Stock Exchange use.

(viii) 9-*series.* Spare, reserved for allocation by independent users for non-Stock Exchange items (e.g. currencies, Local Authority Mortgages, etc.).

The check digit is used for computer checking of inputs.

Calculations. A stockbroker must, of course, at all times be prepared to give professional advice to his clients, not only as to the advisability of purchasing securities but in suggesting a change of holdings in order to produce a higher income. This involves the calculation of "yields," and in the case of securities being redeemed on a specified date there will be two calculations—one representing the *flat yield* and the other the *yield on redemption.*

Example 1

A stock which pays a $4\frac{1}{2}$ per cent dividend every year can be bought at $109\frac{7}{8}$ for each £100 stock. Find, *to the nearest penny*, what rate of interest that would be on each £100 invested. (*R.S.A.*)

Solution 1

In this case £$109\frac{7}{8}$ is the cash price of £100 stock, and £100 stock yields an annual income of £4·50.

In other words, £$109\frac{7}{8}$ (cash) must be invested to obtain an income of £4·50. We have to find the income obtained by investing £100 (cash).

And this income is—

$$£4{\cdot}5 \times \frac{100}{109\frac{7}{8}} = \frac{£4{\cdot}5 \times 800}{879} = £4{\cdot}096 = £4{\cdot}10$$

Example 2

A 3 per cent stock can be bought for £$98\frac{5}{8}$ for each £100 stock, and a 4 per cent can be bought for £$107\frac{3}{4}$ for each £100 stock. If a man buys £4,000 of the 3 per cent stock and £2,000 of the 4 per cent stock, find, *to the nearest penny*, how much interest he gets, on an average, on each £100 invested. (*R.S.A.*)

Solution 2

Since the man buys £4,000 (stock *not* cash) of 3 per cent stock, and each £100 of this stock yields £3 income, his total income from this stock is £3 × 40 = £120.

Similarly, his total income from £2,000 (stock *not* cash) of 4 per cent stock is £4 × 20 = £80.

Hence from both investments his total income is £200.

We have next to find the total sum invested, i.e. the total cost (cash) of the stock.

Now, since each £100 (stock) of the 3 per cent stock cost £$98\frac{5}{8}$ (cash), £4,000 (stock) of this stock cost

$$£98\tfrac{5}{8} \times 40 = £3{,}945 \text{ (cash).}$$

Also, in the same way, £2,000 (stock) of the 4 per cent stock cost £$107\frac{3}{4}$ × 20 = £2,155 (cash).

Hence the total cost of the stock bought, i.e. the total cash invested, is

$$£3{,}945 + £2{,}155 = £6{,}100.$$

Now, we have found that an investment of £6,100 yields a total income of £200.

The average yield for each £100 (cash) invested is, therefore—

$$£200 \div 61 = £3{\cdot}279 = £3{\cdot}28$$

Example 3

On 14th April last, a man bought £250 of 4 per cent debenture stock at $104\frac{3}{4}$. In addition to the purchase price he had to pay the following charges—

Stamp and fee	£2·80
Brokerage, $\frac{3}{4}$ per cent of the purchase price.	
Contract stamp	£0·10

The interest on this stock is paid in equal half-yearly instalments on 1st January and 1st July. What interest had accrued up to the date of the purchase? Deduct the accrued interest from the sum of the purchase price and charges. Then calculate to the nearest shilling the annual yield per £100 invested. (*R.S.A.* (*modified*).)

Solution 3

The period 1st January to 14th April includes

$$(30 + 28 + 31 + 14) \text{ days, that is 103 days.}$$

Now the interest on £250 for 103 days at 4 per cent per annum is—

$$\frac{£250 \times 103 \times 4}{100 \times 365} = \frac{£206}{73} = £2{\cdot}822.$$

		£
The purchase price is $£104{\cdot}75 \times 2{\cdot}5\text{p} = £104{\cdot}75 \times \frac{10}{4}$	=	261·875
Brokerage, $\frac{3}{4}$ per cent of £261·875	=	1·964
Other charges	=	2·900
Total	=	266·739

Deducting from this total the accrued interest (since this comes to the purchaser on 1st July), we get as the net cost of the stock £266·739 − £2·822 = £263·917. Also the annual income from £250 of 4 per cent stock is £4 × 2·5p = £10.

Hence the investment of £263·917 (cash) yields an annual income of £10.

And therefore an investment of £100 (cash) yields annually—

$$\frac{£10 \times 100}{263{\cdot}917} = £3{\cdot}79 \text{ (approx.)}$$

Example 4

A person owns £2,500 of $4\frac{1}{2}$ per cent stock. He sells out at $108\frac{1}{2}$ and invests the proceeds in $5\frac{1}{2}$ per cent stock at 124. What change in annual income results?

Solution 4

Since the annual income from £100 of this $4\frac{1}{2}$ per cent stock is £4·50, that from £2,500 of this stock is £4·50 × 25 = £112·50.

On selling out at $108\frac{1}{2}$, the holder of this stock reveives £108·50 for each £100 stock sold.

Hence for £2,500 stock he receives in all £108·50 × 25 = £2,712·50 (cash).

Now for each £100 of $5\frac{1}{2}$ per cent stock bought he pays £124 (cash). That is, £124 (cash) so invested yields £5·50 income.

Therefore £2,712·50 (cash) invested produces $\frac{£5{\cdot}5 \times 2{,}712{\cdot}50}{124}$ income = $\frac{£11 \times 5{,}425}{4 \times 124}$ income = $\frac{£1{,}925}{16}$ income = £120·31 income.

The change in income is therefore an increase of £120·31 − £112·50 = £7·81.

Example 5

A man who has £3,500 of $3\frac{1}{2}$ per cent stock sells out at $101\frac{7}{8}$ and reinvests the cash realized in a 5 per cent stock, thus gaining £23·33 in annual income. At what price does he buy the 5 per cent stock?

Solution 5

The annual income from £3,500 $3\frac{1}{2}$ per cent stock is £3·50 × 35 = £122·50.

The income from the 5 per cent stock is therefore £122·50 + £23·33 = £145·83.

Now the cash realized by the sale of the $3\frac{1}{2}$ per cent stock is $£101\frac{7}{8} \times 35$ = $£3{,}535 + £30\frac{5}{8} = £3{,}565\frac{5}{8}$.

Hence, $£3{,}565\frac{5}{8}$ invested in 5 per cent stock yields annually £145·83.

We have to find the sum (cash) that, so invested, yields £5.

And this sum is $\frac{£3{,}565\frac{5}{8} \times 5}{145\frac{5}{6}} = \frac{£3{,}565\frac{5}{8}}{29\frac{1}{6}} = \frac{£28{,}525 \times 6}{8 \times 175} = \frac{£489}{4} = £122\frac{1}{4}$.

The 5 per cent was bought at $122\frac{1}{4}$.

Example 6

What percentage change in annual income is effected by selling a $3\frac{1}{2}$ per cent stock at $94\frac{1}{2}$ and reinvesting the cash realized in a $4\frac{1}{2}$ per cent stock at $112\frac{1}{2}$?

Solution 6

Each £100 of the original stock held yielded £3·50 annual income, and when sold realized $£94\frac{1}{2}$ (cash).

Now to obtain $£4\frac{1}{2}$ annual income from the second ($4\frac{1}{2}$ per cent) stock, it was necessary to buy £100 stock, and this cost £112·50 (cash). Hence, £94·50 (cash) invested in this stock yielded as annual income $\frac{£4{\cdot}50 \times 94{\cdot}50}{112{\cdot}50}$ = $\frac{£4{\cdot}50 \times 189}{225} = \frac{£186}{50}$ = £3·78.

Expressing the income from the second stock as a percentage of that from the first stock, we get $\frac{£3{\cdot}78 \times 100}{£3{\cdot}5}$ per cent = $\frac{378}{3{\cdot}5}$ per cent = 108 per cent.

The increase required is therefore 8 per cent.

Example 7

Calculate the yield of a redeemable security, such as 5 per cent debentures redeemable at par 10 years hence and purchased for £93.

Solution 7

The main problem here is how to treat the profit of £7 per cent on redemption.

A common method is to attribute the increase in the capital value equally over the whole period: that is, in this case to assume that £0·70 is added to the capital annually. The average annual return is, therefore, £5·70. But this has to be related to the average of the annual capital, which increases year by year from £93 to £100 at the end of the tenth year. Thus, assuming £0·70 is added in each year, in successive years the capital is £93, £93·70, £94·40 . . . £99·30, giving an average of £96·15. The effective yield for each unit of capital can then be ascertained by dividing the annual return (£5·70) by the average capital (£96·15); thus, yield $= (5{\cdot}70 \times 100) \div 96{\cdot}15 = 5{\cdot}9$ per cent approximately.

INVESTMENT ACCOUNTS

Investment accounts are usually ruled specially with three columns on each side, so that the nominal value of the investment, the principal or capital value, and the periodical interest or dividends, may be seen at a glance. Where the interest or dividend is payable at fixed dates, such dates are recorded at the head of the Investment Account.

Entries in the Accounts. When the investment is purchased, the nominal value will be entered in the Nominal Value column and the actual cost in the Capital column. As the dividend or interest is received, the cash will be debited in the cash book and posted to the credit of the Income column of the investment account. At balancing time, the total receipts from each investment will be transferred to a dividends and interest account and finally to profit and loss account. Where fixed dividends have accrued, but have not been actually received, the amount should at balancing time be entered in the Interest or Dividends column and brought down as a debit balance in the same column.

The adjustment in investment accounts is made in the same way as prepayments for insurances in commercial accounts, where the amount paid in advance is credited to the expense account and carried down as a debit to the new trading period.

But accruals of income should only be made in the case of interest due at fixed dates on British Government securities, the payment of which is certain. Debenture interest and dividends *must not* be accrued unless actually declared as payable. It does not follow that because debentures or shares carry a fixed preferential or even guaranteed payment it will be forthcoming.

Example 8

P. Ruthven holds £6,000 worth of 2½ per cent Consols, which cost him, including brokerage and expenses, £4,797·32. Show the ledger account

Solution 8

2½% CONSOLS

Dividends payable on 5th Jan., 5th April, 5th July, and 5th Oct.

Dr | *Cr*

Date	Particulars	Nominal	Dividends or Interest	Capital or Principal	Date	Particulars	Nominal	Dividends or Interest	Capital or Principal
19..		£	£	£	19..		£	£	£
Jan 1	Balance	6,000·00	28·60	4,768·72	Jan 5	Cash— Quarter's Dividend to date. £37·50 – ; [1]*Less* tax at 20% 7·50 –		30·00	
Dec 31	Transfer to Dividends & Interest A/c . . .		120·00		Apr 5	Cash (ditto) . . .		30·00	
					Jul 5	" " . . .		30·00	
					Oct 5	" " . . .		30·00	
					Dec 31	Balance c/d . . .	6,000 – –	28·60	4,768·72
		6,000·00	148·60	4,768·72			6,000 – –	148·60	4,768·72
19.1									
Jan 1	Balance b/d . . .	6,000 – –	28·60	4,768·72					

Note. The accruing dividend at the commencement of the year is obtained by taking $\frac{87}{365}$ of £120, the yearly dividend less tax at 20%. Some accountants prefer to take $\frac{87}{92}$ of the quarterly dividend less tax. It makes no difference to the yearly income from the investment, as the same amount has to be carried forward again at the end of the year.

[1] *This rate of tax is used for convenience only.*

of the investment for one year, dividends being payable on 5th January, 5th April, 5th July, and 5th October.

(*For* **Solution 8** *see opposite page*)

Purchase of Investments. When investments are purchased cum div. (that is, including dividends accrued)—and the price is always cum div. unless otherwise stated—it will be necessary to ascertain the amount of the accrued dividend, less tax, and to enter it in the Interest or Dividends column of the investment account; and also to *deduct* the amount from the opening price of the investment. The balance of the purchase price will represent the capital cost to be entered in the Capital or Principal column. When the dividend or interest on the investment is received, it will be credited in the Interest or Dividend column. The offset on the debit side of the same column will have the effect of reducing the dividend to the amount receivable for the time the investment has been held. When stocks, shares, etc., are purchased cum div., such an adjustment should always be made in private accounts. It would not be proper to show an investment as earning six months' income if we held the investment for only *two* months.

Sale of Investments. When investments are sold cum div.—it will likewise be necessary to ascertain the amount of the accrued dividend, up to date of sale, less tax, and to enter it in the Interest or Dividends column. Such an adjustment must be made, because the sale price will include the accruing dividend. The balance of the money received, after deducting the accrued dividend or interest, will represent the capital amount to be entered in the Capital or Principal column.

Profit or Loss on Sale of Investments. When the whole of an investment is sold, the difference of the Capital columns will represent profit or loss on such sale. When only part of an investment is sold, the balance of the holding should be brought down *at cost*. In practice this may be all but impossible if many purchases and sales take place. An average price must then be used. Any difference between the Capital columns will denote profit or loss on the sale. This profit or loss is transferred to a separate account entitled Profit (or Loss) on Sale of Investments. As this profit is of a capital nature, the account should be closed at balancing time by transfer to a reserve or in reduction of an intangible asset.

Balancing Investment Accounts. When the investment account is balanced at the end of each year, the balance should be brought down *at cost* (including brokerage and expenses). Where the market value of the investments on the date of balancing is above cost, no credit should be taken for the enhanced price; but where the market value is below cost, a reserve for depreciation should be made.

Where, at a balance sheet date, investments are valued at cost, the

4% BEARER BONDS

Date	Particulars	Nominal	Income	Capital	Date	Particulars	Nominal	Income	Capital
		£	£	£			£	£	£
19.. Feb 1	Cash— Bonds at 95 cum div., *plus* brokerage ½%.	10,000·00	16·67	9,533·93	19.. Mar 31	Cash— Dividend . . £100 *Less* Tax . . 50		50·00	
Dec 31	Increase Tax A/c (on accrued dividend) .		16·67		May 1	Cash— Sale of £3,000 Bonds at 97 cum div., *less* brokerage at ½% and stamp 60p .	3,000·00	5·00	2,889·40
Dec 31	Profit & Loss A/c . .		286·66		Jun 30	Cash— Dividend (on £7,000 Bonds) . . £70 *Less* Tax . . 35		35·00	
	Profit & Loss on Investments A/c (profit on sale)			29·22	Sep 30	Cash (ditto) . . .		35·00	
					Dec 31	,, ,, . . .		35·00	
						Income Tax A/c . .		160·00	
						Balance (at cost) c/d . .	7,000·00		6,673·75
		10,000·00	320·00	9,563·15			10,000·00	320·00	9,563·15
19.1 Jan 1	Balance (at cost) b/d	7,000·00		6,673·75					

balance sheet should preferably include a note indicating the position as regards market value—with or without giving the actual figure.

In the case of companies, the Companies Act, 1948, requires that investments be classified as (i) trade investments; (ii) other investments.

The "other investments" must be subdivided into quoted and unquoted, and a distinction must be drawn between those quoted investments which have been granted a quotation or permission to deal in a recognized Stock Exchange, and those which have not. The aggregate market value of quoted investments must be stated and, if lower, the Stock Exchange value.

Example 9

A company purchased on 1st February, 19. ., £10,000 of 4 per cent bearer bonds at 95, dividends being payable quarterly, the next being due on 31st March. Brokerage of ½ per cent was charged.

On 1st May £3,000 worth of stock was sold for cash at 97, less brokerage ½ per cent and contract stamp 60p.

Show the ledger account of the investment, recording the above transactions and the receipt of the dividends, and showing the balances on 31st December. Income tax may be taken at 50%.

Solution 9

(The worked account is shown on p. 0818.)

The original cost of the investment is—

	£
£10,000 bonds at 95	9,500·00
Brokerage, ½ per cent on nominal value . .	50·00
Contract stamp	0·60
	9,550·60

This cost includes the accrued dividend for one month at 4 per cent per annum, less tax, which is £16·67. The balance of the cost, £9,533·93 is the capital cost of the investment.

A similar calculation must be made when any part of the investment is sold.

At the end of the year, the investment remaining must be valued at cost, that is, seven-tenths of £9,533·93 = £6,673·75. The income is transferred to profit and loss account gross, that is, without deduction of tax, but as the dividends are received net, after deduction of tax, the income column must be credited with the tax suffered. The corresponding debit is to the income tax account. For a fuller explanation, see p. 2879 (Treatment of Income Tax in Accounts).

Bonus Shares and Rights Issues. Companies with substantial reserves may issue bonus shares to shareholders, and companies which wish to raise fresh capital may do so by means of "rights" issues which give existing shareholders the right to subscribe to the new shares in proportion to their existing holdings. These questions are dealt with in Chapter 25 from the point of view of the company raising the capital or issuing the shares, but here we are concerned with the problems of the investor.

BONUS SHARES will be recorded when the issue is authorized at nominal value. No entry is needed in the Capital column of the account because no additional cost is incurred. If shares of nominal value £10,000 were purchased for £16,000 and subsequent bonus shares £5,000 received, the investor would then hold shares of nominal value £15,000 at a cost of £16,000.

RIGHTS ISSUES are usually valuable to the investor, and if he is unable or unwilling to take up the rights himself, he will be able to sell the rights on the open market. The proceeds of any such sale of rights should be treated as a capital return which reduces the original cost of the investment. For instance, an investor holding shares of nominal value £15,000, which cost him £16,000, is offered the right to subscribe for a further £5,000 shares (this would be a "one-for-three rights issue") at £1·20 per £1 share. If the investor takes up the rights, he will pay £6,000 and acquire additional shares of £5,000 nominal value. His total investment will then be—

	Nominal	Capital (cost)
	£	£
Original investment	15,000	16,000
Rights, taken up	5,000	6,000
TOTAL	20,000	22,000

If, on the other hand, the investor sells the rights for 30p per share, the result will be—

	Nominal	Capital (cost)
	£	£
Original investment	15,000	16,000
Rights, sold		1,500
TOTAL	15,000	14,500

The following worked example illustrates these points—

Example 10

On the 30th June, 19. ., the entry "5,000 shares of £1 each in Ho Kay Ltd. £6,250" was shown in the books of The Awl-Right Investment Co. Ltd.

At a meeting held on 13th November, 19. ., Ho Kay Ltd. decided—

(*a*) to make a bonus issue of two fully paid shares for every four shares held on 31st October, 19. . .

(*b*) to give its members the right to make application for two shares for every five shares held on 31st October, 19.., at the price of £1·20 per share, the applicant to pay 60p per share when applying for the shares on or before 26th November, 19.., and a further 60p per share by 15th February, 19.1.

A condition attached to the resolution was that the new shares resulting from the above-mentioned clauses were not to participate in the dividend for the year ended 31st March, 19.1.

In due course The Awl-Right Investment Co. Ltd. received the bonus shares and took up under the rights issue 1,400 shares, making payment therefore on the due dates. The rights to the shares remaining and available to it under the latter issue were sold on 21st November, 19.., for 35p each.

At the annual general meeting held on 30th June, 19.1, Ho Kay Ltd. declared a dividend of 15 per cent, less income tax at 42·5 per cent, for the year ended 31st March, 19.1, and the same was expressed to be payable forthwith.

Write up the investment account as it should appear in the books of The Awl-Right Investment Co. Ltd., incorporating the transactions mentioned and bringing down the balance. (See p. 0822.)

(*Association of Certified and Corporate Accountants.*)

MODIFICATION OF RECORDS FOR CAPITAL GAINS TAX

The capital gains tax is dealt with in the chapter on Taxation but the modifications to the Investment Ledger if the information required is to be recorded are best considered at this point.

All gains on the acquisition and disposal of investments are taxed at a fixed rate according to whether they are short-term or long-term. Short-term gains are those realized within twelve months of acquisition and they are dealt with on an individual basis. That is, the cost of acquiring the specific shares is matched against the proceeds of sale. Long-term gains are dealt with on a "pool" or group basis. For this reason, the Investment Ledger Account must provide for recording the shares at acquisition and then for transfer to the pool after twelve months, if they have not been disposed of in the meantime.

To simplify the illustration, only the Capital items are shown in the Investment Account and the analytical method of recording is shown.

The entries and the transactions shown in the illustration are as follows—

6th April, 1969. The account shows a balance of 2,500 £1 Ordinary shares valued at cost at £2,480. These balances are entered in the Investment Account nominal and actual (debit) columns and in the Nominal and Pool Cost columns in the long-term section of the Capital Gains Tax Record.

THE AWL-RIGHT INVESTMENT CO. LTD. £1 SHARES IN HO KAY LTD.

Date	Particulars	Nominal	Income	Capital	Date	Particulars	Nominal	Income	Capital
		£	£	£			£	£	£
19..					19..				
Jul 1	Balance b/d . . .	5,000		6,250	Nov 21	Cash: Sale of rights to 600 shares at 35p each .			210
Nov 13	Bonus Issue . . .	2,500							
26	Cash: Application money on 1,400 shares, under rights issue, at 60p each.	1,400		840					
19.1					19.1				
Feb 15	Cash: Final call money, on shares taken under rights issue, at 60p each.			840	Jun 30	Cash: Dividend of 15 per cent *less* tax for the year ended 31st March, 19.1.		431	
Jun 30	P. & L. A/c . . .		750			Income Tax A/c: Tax deducted from dividend .		319	
						Balance c/d . . .	8,900		7,720
		8,900	750	7,930			8,900	750	7,930
19.1									
Jul 1	Balance b/d . . .	8,900		7,720					

20th August, 1969. 1,000 £1 Ordinary shares were purchased for £1,500 and these amounts were entered in the Nominal and Actual Cost columns of the Investment account and of the short-term Capital Gains Tax record.

6th April, 1970. The Investment account is balanced and shows that 3,500 shares at a cost of £3,980 are held at that date.

1st June. A further purchase of 1,000 shares for £1,250 is entered in the Investment account and the short-term Capital Gains record.

21st August. After a lapse of twelve months, the shares acquired on 20th August, 1969, can be transferred from the short-term to the long-term Capital Gains Tax record. A minus entry is made in the short-term columns and a plus entry in the long-term columns. This is totalled to show the pool as 3,500 £1 Ordinary shares at a pool cost of £4,160.

1st October. The sale of 1,700 £1 Ordinary shares at a price of £2 per share gives rise to a short-term and a long-term transaction. The sale of 1,000 shares is treated as a short-term disposal and the balance of 700 as a long-term disposal.

Since the short-term disposal is treated as a separate item, the gain on that disposal can be calculated as follows—

	£
1,000 shares disposed of for £2 each . . .	2,000
,, ,, at acquisition cost	1,270
Short-term capital gain	730

The gain on the pooled shares is calculated—700 shares disposed of came out of the long-term pooled cost.

The disposal price is £2 each, that is £1,400 and the shares take $\frac{700}{3,500}$ = 1/5th of £4,160 as the pool cost of acquisition, that is £832.

The calculation of the Capital gain is therefore—

	£
700 shares at £2 each	1,400
Pool cost of acquisition	832
Long-term capital gain	568

6th April, 1971. The Investment account is balanced and at that date the investment is 2,800 shares. A pool cost of £3,328 for these shares is shown in the Capital Gains Tax record.

In the Investment Account, however, the valuation of the shares sold and the balance held, at cost, may be on a first-in first-out basis; at specific cost or on an average basis.

The cost of the shares held on 1st June, 1970, was—

		£
2,500	at	2,480
1,000	,,	1,500
1,000	,,	1,250
4,500		5,230

The cost of the sale of 1,700 on 1st October can be calculated as follows—

F.I.F.O. Basis. Cost of shares disposed of—

$$\frac{1,700}{2,500} \times \frac{£2,480}{1} = £1,686 \text{ approx.}$$

The balance held will then be valued at £3,544.

Specific Cost. This would depend on which numbered shares were disposed of but if they were the 1,000 acquired for £1,500 plus 700 of the old holding, the calculation would be—

	£
700 of old holding at $\frac{700}{2,500} \times$ £2,480 . . .	694
1,000 at £1,500	1,500
Total . .	2,194

The balance held will then be valued at £3,036.

Average Cost. On the average cost basis, the cost of disposals would be—

$$\frac{1,700}{4,500} \times \frac{£5,230}{1} = £1,976 \text{ approx.}$$

On the basis the balance is valued at £3,254.

Naturally, the valuation of the disposal cost affects the profit shown as follows—

	Basis of valuation of disposal		
	F.I.F.O.	Specific	Average
	£	£	£
Sales value	3,400	3,400	3,400
Cost of disposal	1,686	2,194	1,976
Profit on sale . . .	1,714	1,206	1,424

FAIR AND WHETHER COMPANY LTD. £1 ORDINARY SHARES

Investment Account						Capital Gains Tax Record				
						Short-term		Long-term		
Date	Item	Ref.	Nominal Value	Debit Actual Cost	Credit Proceeds	Nominal	Actual Cost	Nominal	Pool Cost	Remarks
			£	£	£	£	£	£	£	
1969										
Apr 6	Balance	b/f	2,500	2,480				2,500	2,660	Market value 21s.
Aug 20	Purchase		1,000	1,500		1,000	1,500			
1970										
Apr 5	Balance	c/d			3,980					
				3,980	3,980					
Apr 6	Balance	b/d	3,500	3,980						
Jun 1	Purchase		1,000	1,250		1,000	1,250			
			4,500			2,000	2,750			
Aug 21	Transfer					−1,000	−1,500	1,000	1,500	Pool on 21st August, 1970
								3,500	4,160	
Oct 1	Sale		−1,700		3,400	−1,000	−1,250	−700	832	Pool on 1st October, 1970
	P. & L. A/c			1,714						
Apr 5	Balance	c/d			3,544			2,800	3,328	
				6,944	6,944					
1971										
Apr 6	Balance	b/d	2,800	3,544						

These figures compare with the gains for tax purposes which were—

	£
Short-term gain	730
Long-term gain	568
Total gain . . .	1,298

and it can be seen that in each case the calculation differs. It is the Investment Account which will show the profit for accounting purposes and, in the example, it has been assumed that the Investor has dealt with the shares on a F.I.F.O. basis.

Holdings on 6th April, 1965. Investments held when the Act was introduced are valued at cost of acquisition or at the market value on the 6th April, 1965, for capital gains tax and a separate record of these holdings should be kept. Extel's Capital Issue Volume gives prices up to 5 places of decimals which are accepted by the Inland Revenue.

Capital Gains and Losses. Since, in certain circumstances gains and losses can be offset on the short or the long-term basis, a separate record must be kept of such gains and losses and, in particular, of losses carried forward.

QUESTIONS

1. Describe briefly the books of a stockbroker.
2. What is the function of the tickets payable book?
3. Under what circumstances may the jobbers ledger not enter into the recording of a transaction?
4. Why is it necessary to have a dividends and rights ledger?
5. What are the main types of items passed through the journal in a stockbroker's office?
6. State what you understand to be the function of the Stock Exchange Clearing House.
7. What do you understand by a "bull" and a "bear" in connexion with stock and share dealing?
8. What is meant by contango and backwardation?
9. What are investment accounts? What special ruling is required? Explain the meaning of the terms cum div. and ex div., and their effect on the investment account.
10. How are investment accounts balanced?

EXERCISE 08

1. A man having £500 to invest buys 200 shares in a company at £1·75 per share, and with the remainder buys 2½ per cent Consols at 75 (brokerage, etc., included). The shares pay an annual dividend of 10p a share. Find the total income. (*R.S.A.*)

2. A man buys shares at £1·25 each ex dividend. At the end of the year a dividend of 5p per share is declared. He then sells them ex dividend at £1·30 per share. What rate of interest has he received on the money invested? Answer to the nearest penny. (*R.S.A.*)

3. A man bought £300 of $3\frac{1}{2}$ per cent stock at $105\frac{5}{8}$ and also £600 of $4\frac{1}{2}$ per cent stock at $117\frac{3}{8}$. Find, to the nearest penny, the average interest received on each £100 invested. (*R.S.A.*)

4. A man buys £750 of 4 per cent stock at $115\frac{1}{2}$ and in addition to the purchase price pays the following charges: brokerage, $\frac{3}{4}$ per cent on the consideration; stamp, £9; contract stamp, 10p; registration fee, 13p. At what rate per cent per annum does he receive interest on his investment?

5. A man bought £2,000 of $3\frac{1}{2}$ per cent stock at $101\frac{3}{8}$, and afterwards sold it at $103\frac{1}{2}$. He paid brokerage at $\frac{3}{4}$ per cent on the consideration in each transaction, and the contract stamp on each occasion cost 60p. At the time of purchase there were the following additional charges: stamp, £20·50; registration fee, 13p. By how much was the man's capital increased as a result of the transaction?

6. The holder of £3,500 Conversion Loan ($3\frac{1}{2}$ per cent) sells out at $106\frac{5}{16}$ and invests the cash realized in a 4 per cent stock at 115. What is the change in his annual income, brokerage at $\frac{3}{8}$ per cent on the stock being charged in each transaction?

7. As a speculation, a man bought 500 £1 shares of a company at 150p each (brokerage 1p per share). He received dividend at 10 per cent less income tax at 25 per cent, and was allowed to take up 50 new shares (ranking equally with those already issued) at 125p per share, free of brokerage. He sold all the shares at 130p each (brokerage 1p per share). What did he lose by these transactions? (*R.S.A.*)

8. The dividends on a certain 4 per cent debenture stock are paid in two equal half-yearly instalments at the end of June and December. At the end of April an investor purchased £250 of this stock at $104\frac{1}{4}$. In addition to the purchase price, he had to pay £2·93 stamp and fee, brokerage $\frac{3}{8}$ per cent of the purchase price, contract stamp 10p. What interest had accrued on the £250 stock during the four months preceding the date of purchase? Adding the charges and deducting the accrued interest, calculate the net cost. Hence, ignoring the matter of the future redemption of the stock, find the annual yield in £p per £100 invested. (*R.S.A.*)

9. The George C. Waud Finance Corporation Ltd. hold a large number of investments. Explain briefly what records you would advise the company to keep relative to their investments. Give a *pro forma* ruling of the ledger account you recommend, and enter therein not more than six items. (*London Chamber of Commerce.*)

10. Show by the ledger entries *only* what the total amount of an investment account would be at the end of six years' compound interest (yearly) $2\frac{1}{2}$ per cent—neglect fractions of a penny. The amount invested *yearly* is £250.

11. Prepare the necessary accounts, relative to the undermentioned investment, which would appear in W. A. Richardson's ledger—

On 1st June, Richardson purchased £5,000 New Zealand 3 per cent (1945) stock at $85\frac{1}{2}$ plus $\frac{3}{8}$ per cent brokerage and £43·73 stamps, etc. On 3rd April, 2 years later, Richardson sold £4,000 of the Stock at 89, and paid £36·60 expenses.

Interest upon the stock is payable half-yearly on 1st April and 1st October, less tax (to be taken at 25p in the £). (*R.S.A.*)

12. Ulrich Brunner purchased, on 3rd August, £1,150 Canadian Western Railway Co. 5 per cent debenture stock at $85\frac{1}{2}$, and paid £19·05 for stamps, commission, etc. On 29th April next, Mr. Brunner sold the Stock at 88 and paid £18·39 expenses. The debenture interest is payable half-yearly, on 1st April and 1st October, less tax (to be taken at 25%). Prepare the accounts, showing the history of this investment, as it should appear in Mr. Brunner's ledger. (*London Chamber of Commerce.*)

13. Describe the best method of keeping the accounts relating to the investments of an individual or a firm, and record the following transactions in the books you would recommend—

On 3rd May, Robert Rene bought £2,000 Arcadian Government 5 per cent bonds at 95 plus $\frac{3}{8}$ per cent, brokerage and £19·60 stamps.

On 30th September of the following year he sold £1,000 of these bonds at 98 less £13·55 expenses. Interest on the bonds is payable on 1st January and 1st July in each year

Ignore all questions of income tax. (*R.S.A.*)

14. The following transactions AB had with his London broker, John Statham—

On the 18th March he buys £15,000 New Zealand $3\frac{1}{2}$ per cent 1940 stock at $106\frac{3}{4}$, £7,000 Victoria 4 er cent 1881 Inscribed at $104\frac{5}{8}$, and £5,000 Natal 4 per cent Inscribed 1937 at $119\frac{1}{4}$. On these transactions the broker charges a commission of $\frac{3}{8}$ per cent.

On the 25th March he sells the New Zealand stock at $107\frac{1}{4}$ and the Natal stock at $120\frac{1}{2}$, the Victoria stock being carried forward, contango being charged of three-eighths.

You are asked to show how these transactions would appear in John Statham's ledger. (*London Chamber of Commerce.*)

15. F. Reynolds holds £10,400 of $2\frac{1}{2}$ per cent Consols, which cost him, including brokerage and expenses, £8,333·10. Show the ledger account of the investment for one year, dividends being payable on 5th January, 5th April, 5th July, and 5th October.

16. A company purchased on 1st March £24,000 of 4 per cent Blank preference stock at 90, dividends being payable on 31st March, 30th June, 30th September, and 31st December. Stamps and expenses amounted to £216·73, and brokerage of $\frac{3}{4}$ per cent was charged. On 1st June, £6,000 of stock was sold for cash at 92, less brokerage three-eighths and stamp 60p. On 1st September, another £6,000 of stock was sold for cash at 91 ex div. less brokerage $\frac{3}{8}$ per cent and stamp 60p. The market price on 31st December, the date of the annual balance sheet, was 89. Show the ledger account of the investment recording the above transactions and the receipt of the quarterly dividends, and balance it as on 31st December. Ignore tax.

17. Philip Snowflake had the undermentioned transactions with his broker on the London Stock Exchange—

On 16th July he bought £15,000 Mexican ordinary at $46\frac{3}{4}$; on 21st July, £14,000 South-Eastern at $32\frac{1}{8}$; on 23rd July, £16,000 North-Western at $69\frac{7}{16}$. On these transactions the broker charged a commission of $\frac{3}{8}$ per cent. On 24th July, Snowflake sold the South-Eastern at 34. On 30th July, Snowflake carried forward the Mexican ordinary and North-Westerns at 47 and $69\frac{11}{16}$ respectively, contango being charged at $\frac{3}{4}$ per cent, on each stock.

Show Snowflake's account in the broker's ledger.

18. You are required to write up the investment and investment income accounts from the undernoted information, differentiating carefully between capital and revenue and showing the net profit or loss on the series of transactions. Ignore income tax.

2,400 Ordinary shares in Harrod and Evans Ltd.
Purchased 10th April, 19. . at £4·30 a share.
Sold 10th January, 19.1 at £4·65 a share.
Interim dividend of 10 per cent paid 10th May each year.
Final dividend of 15 per cent paid 10th November, 19. . .

9,000 8 per cent preference shares in Warring and Wallis Ltd.
Purchased 30th September, 19. . at £1·65 a share.
Sold 30th April, 19.1 at 175p a share.
Dividends paid 31st July and 31st January.

(*Cost and Management Accountants.*)

19. On 1st October, 19.., A. B. Ltd. purchased £2,400 3 per cent Government stock, cum dividend at 75.

Interest on this stock is paid half-yearly on 1st March and 1st September.

On 1st May, 19.1, the company sold £800 of the stock, cum dividend, at 80. On 1st August, 19.1, a further £1,200 stock was sold, ex dividend, at 76½.

When investments are bought or sold, suitable apportionments to distinguish between capital and income are made in the company's books. All investments held by the company appear in the books at cost, and it is the company's practice to bring investments into the balance sheet at cost.

The accounting year of the company ends on 30th September.

You are required to set out the account for 3 per cent Government stock for the year to 30th September, 19.1, balancing the account at the latter date. Each side of the account is to be provided with separate columns for capital and income respectively.

Apportionments are to be made in months.

Interest accrued during the month of September, 19.1, is to be ignored. Ignore income tax and brokerage. (*Institute of Bankers.*)

20. On 31st March, 1962, the investments held by The Secure Investment Trust Ltd., included 8,000 fully paid Ordinary Shares of £1 each in Safety Devices Ltd., such shares appearing in the books at £8,800. It is not the practice of the trust to make apportionments either of dividends received or receivable.

The trust sold 1,500 shares on 31st May, 1962, for £2,130.

On 15th August, 1962, Safety Devices Ltd.—

(*a*) Issued by way of a bonus issue two fully paid shares for every four held on 31st July, 1962.

(*b*) In respect of shares held on 31st July, 1962, gave the right to such shareholders to apply for three shares for every five so held, at the price of £1·10 per share, 60p being payable on application made on or before 30th September, 1962, and the balance on or before 30th November, 1962.

The shares issued under (*a*) and (*b*) above were precluded from participating in the dividend for the year ended 31st July, 1962.

The bonus shares were duly received by The Secure Investment Trust Ltd. and it took up 2,350 shares under the rights issue. On 22nd August, 1962, it sold the remaining shares to which it was entitled for 20p per share and paid, on the due dates, for the shares it had taken up itself.

On 30th November, 1962, Safety Devices Ltd. declared and paid a final dividend of 25 per cent, less income tax, for the year ended 31st July, 1962, and on 1st March, 1963, an interim dividend of 5 per cent, less income tax, for the year ending 31st July, 1963.

Show the Investment Account for the year ended 31st March, 1963, as it would appear in the books of The Secure Investment Trust Ltd.

N.B. Income tax to be taken as being 40 per cent and expenses of sale are to be ignored. (*A.C.C.A.*)

CHAPTER 09

CONSIGNMENT ACCOUNTS

Unreal City
Under the brown fog of a winter morn
Mr Eugenides, the Smyrna merchant
Unshaven, with a pocket full of currants
C.i.f. London: documents at sight

T. S. ELIOT—*The Waste Land*

CONSIGNMENTS OUTWARDS

AN Outward Consignment is the dispatch of a quantity of goods from one place to another, usually to some country or place abroad, for the purpose of sale by an agent on commission.

Consignor. A consignor is a person who forwards the goods for sale.

Consignee. A consignee is the person to whom the goods are forwarded for sale.

Commission. This is the remuneration of the consignee for selling the goods, usually a percentage on sales value.

Differences between a Consignment and a Sale. There are two principal differences between a consignment and a sale. When goods are *sold* to a person, the property in them passes to that person; when goods are *consigned* to a person the legal ownership of the goods remains in the consignor. Hence the person to whom goods are sold is a *debtor*; but the person to whom goods are consigned is merely an *agent*. Again, a consignment is returnable if it cannot be marketed; but goods sold are not returnable except for some special reason, such as damage or of being of the wrong kind.

Difference between a Consignment and Goods on Sale or Return. In the case of a consignment the person to whom the goods are sent is an *agent* of the sender; but in the latter case, the person to whom the goods are sent is merely an *optional purchaser*.

Special Consignment Books and Marks. When consignments are very numerous, a special "Consignment Day Book" and a separate "Consignment Ledger" are generally kept. The total of the consignment day book is credited monthly to a "Goods on Consignment Account" in the general ledger. In examination work a journal entry is usually sufficient. Consignments are distinguished by the name of the consignee, or by the name of the place to which the goods have been consigned, or by a special letter or number, or by both; for example, "Consignment to A. Smith," or "Consignment to Calcutta," or "Consignment No. Ad 46."

Pro Forma Invoice. When goods are consigned, a *pro forma* invoice is forwarded with them giving particulars as to the nature of the goods, number, and/or quantity, weight, measurement, prices, marking, packing, etc. The goods are dealt with in the consignor's books usually at cost price, but the invoice to the consignee is usually made out at a higher figure. If the consignment has been entered up in the consignor's books at figures in excess of cost (which would be irregular) credit will have been taken for profit before it has been realized. If, at balancing time, the consignment is still unsold, such profit must, of course, be transferred to a "Consignment Suspense Account."

Expenses on Consignment. In consigning goods abroad certain expenses will be incurred, namely, carriage or cartage to the dock, dock dues, freight, marine insurance, etc. All these expenses must be charged direct to the consignment account.

When the goods reach their destination there will be further disbursements, namely, dock dues, unloading and cartage, fire insurance, warehouse or storage rent, auction room expenses, brokers' fees, etc. These expenses will be defrayed by the consignee, and debited in his books to the personal account of the consignor. When settling with the consignor, the consignee will deduct all these charges, and also his selling commission on the *gross* amount of the sales, and remit only the balance, less, of course, any advance or previous payment on account.

Advance on Consignment. In some cases, it is usual for the consignee to remit a certain sum of money as an advance against the consignment. This is not a part payment, but merely an advance by way of security for the large amount of goods forwarded to the consignee. An advance should *not* be put to the credit of the consignment account, as it is not part of the proceeds of it. It should be posted to the credit of the consignee's personal account. It thus figures in the books as a liability. This is the correct position, for if the consignee does not sell the goods, the money will have to be repaid to him. On the balance sheet, the advance is shown sometimes as a liability, and sometimes as a deduction from the consignment on the assets side since, in the event of the consignee selling the goods, the advance will count as part payment.

Bills Drawn against Consignments. In some cases the consignor will draw a bill on the consignee for a large portion of the value of the consignment, and discount or sell it, so that he is not prevented from having the use of the money until the goods are actually sold and paid for. The bill is known as a *documentary bill*, and the procedure has been fully explained under Foreign Bills in Chapter 04. The discount or exchange charged by the bankers for cashing the bill may be dealt with in two different ways. If regarded as an ordinary financial expense, it is charged to profit and loss account; if looked upon as a special expense in connexion with the consignment, it is debited to the particular consignment account.

Del Credere Commission. To prevent any losses by bad debts falling upon the consignor, the latter sometimes arranges to pay the agent an extra commission, called a del credere (dĕl krĕd′-ĕr-e) commission. In return for this, the agent guarantees the proceeds of the consignment after the goods are sold, that is to say, the agent will pay the consignor whether he himself receives payment or not.

Account Sales. This is a document showing the gross and net proceeds of the consignment sold by the consignee for the account of the consignor, and detailing the various expenses and charges in connexion therewith. The following is an example—

ACCOUNT SALES

of 30 cases of Fancy Goods ex S.S. *Stormy Petrel* sold by Trumper & Co., of Wellington, New Zealand, for the account and risk of Messrs. Williams & Sons, London.

		£	£
W. & S.L. / 1–15	15 cases of Fancy Goods	12	180
W. & S.L. / 16–30	15 cases "	15	225
			405
	Less Charges and Expenses–		
		£p	
	Transport	4·50	
	Storage	6·75	
	Insurance	8·50	
	Commission 5% on £405	20·25	
			40
			365
	Less Advance		200
			165
	E. & O. E. Sight draft for £165 herewith Trumper & Co., Wellington. 12th March, 19..		

In some cases, the consignee pays the outward freight and insurance, and these two items also then appear on the account sales.

Account Sales in Currency. Where the account sales is rendered in currency, it must be converted into sterling at the rate ruling on the day when the account sales is received. Should payment be made at a later date, and a different rate be current when the money is actually received, a journal entry must be made transferring any profit or loss on exchange either to a "Difference in Exchange Account," or, if preferred, back to the consignment account. Both methods are used.

Account Current between Consignor and Consignee. Sometimes interest is brought into account with respect to the transactions connected with the consignment, thus introducing an account current between the two parties. The consignee will charge interest on the various sums of money paid out, on advances and on remittances on account, and will likewise allow interest on the proceeds of the consignment, the interest running in each case up to the final date of settlement.

Formula for Consignment Outwards—

1. *Debit* consignment account, and *credit* a goods on consignment account, with the cost price of the goods by means of journal entry.

2. Debit consignment account with the freight, insurance, and other charges paid or payable by the consignor, and credit cash, if paid, or a personal account if unpaid.

3. Debit cash or bills receivable account with the amount of any advance received, and credit personal account of consignee.

4. When the account sales is received—

(*a*) Debit the consignee's personal account and credit consignment account with the gross proceeds.

(*b*) Debit consignment account and credit consignee's personal account with the latter's expenses and commission.

Alternatively, the *net* proceeds may be debited to the consignee and credited to the consignment account. The result is the same.

5. Balance the consignment account and transfer the balance to profit and loss account. Any stock unsold must be credited before balancing and brought down to the debit side.

6. Debit cash or bills receivable account with any cash or bill received in settlement, and credit consignee.

7. Close goods on consignment account by transfer to trading account.

When the goods are only partly sold, then the unsold stock, *plus* a proportionate amount of the freight, insurance, and other non-recurring charges, must be credited and carried down in the consignment account. The commission is a recurring charge and must not, therefore, be so apportioned. This unsold stock, plus charges, will be shown as an asset on the balance sheet. If the consignment expenses were not apportioned, the freight and insurance of the *whole* of the goods would be charged against the sale of *part* of them. If, at balancing time, no part of the consignment is sold, then the amount of the consignment account, i.e. cost of the goods *plus* expenses, will be shown on the balance sheet as an asset under the heading of "goods" or "stock on consignment."

It by no means follows that if half of a consignment of £500 (£250) has been sold for £400 that there is a profit of £150. It may be that the consignment was a pure speculation and that the remaining goods will have to be almost given away.

In the illustration just given the stock has been entered at the figure given in the example, and the amount of the expenses to be carried forward calculated on the basis of the proportion of the closing stock stated to the total value of the goods consigned. As an alternative to this the *quantity* of goods shipped and remaining unsold is given, or possibly, in examination questions, the amount or number of units unsold is not stated. When this is so, a memorandum column must be included in the consignment account, so that it can be seen at a glance how many units have not been sold, in order to calculate the stock and expenses to carry forward. Stock should be valued at cost or market value, which ever is lower.

Example 1

Consigned goods value £825 to R. Lake, of Melbourne. Paid freight, etc., £65 and insurance, £40. Drew on R. Lake at 3 m/d for £300 as an advance against consignment, and discounted the bill for £296. Received account sales from R. Lake showing that part of the goods had realized gross £835, and that his expenses and commission amounted to £87. The stock unsold was valued at cost price, at £275. Received draft at two months from R. Lake for amount due. Make the necessary entries in the consignor's journal, cash book, ledger, etc., to record the above transactions.

Solution 1

JOURNAL

		Dr	*Cr*
		£	£
	Consignment A/c	825	
	Goods on Consignment		825
	Value of goods forwarded to R. Lake, of Melbourne.		
	R. Lake	835	
	Consignment A/c		835
	Gross proceeds as per account sales.		
	Consignment A/c	87	
	R. Lake		87
	Expenses and commission as per account sales.		

CASH BOOK

	£		£
Bills Receivable	300	Consignment A/c—	
		Freight	65
		Insurance	40
		Discount on Bill . . .	4

BILLS RECEIVABLE BOOK

Date	No. of Bill	From Whom Received	Led. fol.	Discount	Amount of Bill	Date of Bill	Term	Due Date
					£			
		R. Lake .			300		3 mos.	
		R. Lake .			448		2 mos.	

LEDGER

Consignment to R. Lake, Melbourne

	£		£
Goods	825	R. Lake	£835
Cash (Freight)	65	Stock £275	
,, (Insurance)	40	Expenses $\frac{275}{825}$ of £105 = 35 } c/d	310
,, (Discount on Bill)	4		
R. Lake (Expenses & Commission)	87		
P. & L. A/c (profit)	124		
	1,145		1,145
Balance b/d	310		

Goods on Consignment

	£		£
Trading A/c	825	Consignment A/c	825

R. Lake

	£		£
Consignment A/c	835	Bills Receivable	300
		Consignment A/c	87
		Bills Receivable	448
	835		835

Trading Account

			£
		Sales	xxx
		Goods on Consignment	825

Profit and Loss Account

			£
		Trading A/c (gross profit)	x
		Consignment A/c (net profit)	124

Treatment of Stock Losses. A further problem arises when the question introduces the loss or damage of stock.

If the loss is not insured against, it should be dealt with by crediting consignment account and debiting loss of goods on consignment account.

This loss is written off to Profit and Loss account at the year end. If the loss is ignored, the normal profit on the consignment will be understated. The final effect on the profit and loss account must be the same.

Where the loss or damage is covered by insurance the amount will be credited to consignment account and debited to insurance account. In cases of this kind care must be exercised in getting the correct proportion of the expenses to be carried forward when there is still some stock on hand.

The value of the closing stock is made up of two parts as follows—

1. A proportion of the value of the whole consignment, as in the previous example, plus expenses incurred on all the goods.
2. A proportion of the expenses applicable after the loss.

Example 2

One thousand crates of goods are consigned, cost £8,000; 100 crates are lost in a fire. Expenses are—

	£
Prior to fire	250
After fire	180

The stock carried forward is 200 crates, cost £1,600 ($\frac{1}{5}$th of £8,000).

Closing Stock Valuation

	£	£
Cost of goods	1,600	
Prior expenses $\frac{200}{1,000} \times £250$	50	
Subsequent expenses $\frac{200}{900} \times £180$	40	
		1,690

Insurance claim for loss. Equally, the claim for insured loss or damage may also include a proportion of the expenses, depending on the terms of the policy. If expenses are admissible then, clearly, only the fair proportion of the *prior* losses would be added to original cost. In Example 2, the calculation would be:

	£
100 crates, cost	800
Plus prior expenses $\frac{100}{1,000} \times 250$	25
	825

Profit and Loss on consignment. When an agent receives del credere commission and is responsible for bad debts, it may be desirable to open a Profit and Loss on Consignment account. This is credited with the commissions due and debited with any bad debts. The balance is transferred to general profit and loss account.

QUESTIONS

1. What is meant by an outwards consignment?
2. Explain the following terms: consignor, consignee, commission.
3. What is the difference between a consignment and a sale of goods?
4. What is the difference between a consignment and goods on sale or return?
5. How are consignments distinguished when they are very numerous?
6. Explain the use of a *pro forma* invoice in connexion with consignments.
7. What are the usual expenses in connexion with a consignment outwards, and how are they treated: (*a*) when paid, (*b*) when not paid?
8. What is meant by an advance on consignment, and how should it be treated in the books?
9. Explain the terms, "bills drawn against consignments," "del credere commission."
10. What is an account sales, and what entries are necessary in the books when one is received? What further steps will be necessary if the account sales is rendered in currency?
11. How and when is a consignment account balanced, and when does it appear on the balance sheet?

CONSIGNMENTS INWARDS

An Inwards Consignment is simply the reverse of the outwards consignment, that is, as it appears in the books of the consignee.

Difference between an Inwards Consignment and a Purchase. When a firm buys goods, the property in the goods passes to them; but when they receive a consignment, the ownership of the goods does not pass. It remains vested in the consignor. In the first case, the seller is the *creditor*, and the buyer the *debtor*; in the second case, the supplier is the principal, and the recipient is his *agent*, becoming the debtor only if the goods are sold. An inwards consignment is returnable if it cannot be sold; a purchase of goods is not.

Difference between an Inwards Consignment and Sale of Goods on Commission. With an inwards consignment the firm receives actual possession of the goods, but in the other case they merely sell from samples. When a sale on consignment takes place, this is recorded in the normal way by debiting the buyer and crediting sales on consignment. In the latter case, the firm passes the order on to the principal, booking up only expenses and commission.

Advance on an Inwards Consignment. On receiving possession of the goods, the agent may forward the consignor a sum of money, or allow him to draw on them, as an advance against the consignment. The advance is debited to the personal account of the consignor, and appears in the books as an asset, being an amount repayable in the event of the firm not being able to dispose of the goods.

Two Methods of Dealing with an Inwards Consignment. The first method is to make no entry in the financial books when a consignment is received. No liability has been contracted and none is shown. The receipt of the goods is, therefore, recorded merely in a memorandum "consignment inwards" or "consignment stock" book. All expenses paid out in connexion with the goods, such as dock dues, customs duties, unloading, fire insurance, cartage, storage, warehouse rent, are debited to the personal account of the consignor. The sales of the goods, either for cash or on credit, are credited to the consignor's account, which is also debited with any advance and with the commission for selling the goods. The balance of the account shows the final amount due to the consignor, which is settled either by a sight draft or a bill. It is from this account that the account sales is sometimes prepared.

The second method is, on receipt of the goods, to open a consignment inwards account and debit it with the invoice value of the goods, at the same time crediting the consignor's account. Although the relationship of debtor and creditor does not as yet exist between the parties to the consignment, this procedure can be justified on the ground that it reflects the legal liability of the agent to account to his principal. A mere memorandum is insufficient and unsatisfactory. The consignment inwards account is debited with all expenses and with the selling commission, and credited with all sales of the goods. The balance of this account shows a profit made on the consignment, and is transferred to the personal account of the consignor. This latter account is debited with any advance, and is closed by being debited with the final draft of bill in full settlement.

Formula for an Inwards Consignment (Principal Method)—

1. On receipt of the goods, no entry.

2. On payment of the various expenses connected with the consignment, *credit* cash, *debit* consignor.

3. On sending an advance, *debit* consignor, *credit* cash or bill payable as the case may be.

4. On selling the goods pertaining to the consignment—

(*a*) For cash, *debit* cash, *credit* consignor.

(*b*) On credit, *debit* person to whom goods sold, *credit* consignor.

5. *Debit* consignor, *credit* commission account with the amount of the commission due, by means of journal entry.

6. Close consignor's account by *debiting* it with the final bill or draft in settlement.

Formula for an Inwards Consignment (Alternative Method)—

1. On receipt of the goods, *debit* consignment inwards account, *credit* consignor, by means of journal entry.

2. On payment of the various expenses connected with the consignment, *credit* cash, *debit* consignment inwards account.

3. On sending an advance, *debit* consignor, *credit* cash or bill payable as the case may be.

4. On selling the goods pertaining to the consignment—

(*a*) For cash, *debit* cash, *credit* consignment inwards account.

(*b*) On credit, *debit* person to whom goods sold, *credit* consignment inwards account by means of journal entry.

5. *Debit* consignment inwards account with the selling commission as arranged, *credit* commission account, by means of journal entry.

6. Balance the consignment inwards account, and transfer balance to consignor's personal account. Any unsold stock must be entered on the *credit* side, and brought down as a *debit* balance after ruling off the account.

7. Close consignor's account by *debiting* it with the final bill or draft in settlement. The value of any unsold stock must be entered on the *debit* side, and brought down as a *credit* balance after ruling off the account.

One great objection to this alternative method is that the full amount to the credit of the consignor might get paid to him though the goods were not realized.

Example 3

Received consignment of goods from J. Rowell valued at £760. Terms: agent's commission 5 per cent on all Sales; del credere commission 2½ per cent on credit transactions. Paid customs duties £23·75; landing charges and carriage £8·75; fire insurance £9·50. Sent J. Rowell an advance of £225. Sold part of Rowell's consignment to H. Thompson for £420, part for cash £475, and took part value £200 into stock for our own use. Paid brokerage 1½ per cent, £12. Sent J. Rowell an account sales, and sight draft for balance due. The stock remaining unsold was valued at £200. Make the necessary subsidiary book entries, and show the ledger accounts.

1. Principal Method

JOURNAL

	Dr	Cr
	£	£
J. Rowell	65·25	
Commission		65·25
5% agent's commission on £1,095 = £54·75		
2½% del credere commission on £420 = £10·50		
J. Rowell	42·00	
Cash		42·00
Customs duties, landing charges and fire insurance		
J. Rowell	225·00	
Cash		225·00
H. Thompson	420·00	
J. Rowell		420·00
Sale of part of the inwards consignment		
Cash	475·00	
J. Rowell		475·00
Purchases	200·00	
J. Rowell		200·00
J. Rowell	12·00	
Cash		12·00
J. Rowell	750·75	
Cash		750·75

CASH BOOK

	£		£
J. Rowell	475·00	J. Rowell expenses	42·00
		J. Rowell (advance)	225·00
		,, (brokerage)	12·00
		J. Rowell	750·75

LEDGER

J. Rowell

		£		£
Cash—			Cash	475·00
Customs Duties		23·75	Purchases	200·00
Landing Charges		8·75	H. Thompson	420·00
Fire Insurance		9·50		
Cash (advance)		225·00		
„ (Brokerage)		12·00		
Commission		65·25		
Cash		750·75		
		1,095·00		1,095·00

MEMORANDUM CONSIGNMENT STOCK ACCOUNT

J. Rowell

Date		Qty	£	Date		Qty	£
	Consignment		760		H. Thompson		247
					Cash		277
					Purchases		118
					Balance c/d		118
			760				760
	Balance b/d		118				

Since the cost of stock disposed of in each transaction is not given, it has been assumed that cost is proportional to the (selling) value given.

2. Alternative Method

Those entries which would be the same have not been repeated.

JOURNAL

	Dr	Cr
	£	£
Consignment Inwards	760·00	
J. Rowell		760·00
Receipt of goods on consignment		
J. Rowell	65·25	
Consignment Inwards		
H. Thompson	420·00	
Consignment Inwards		
Cash	475·00	
Consignment Inwards		475·00
Purchases	200·00	
Consignment Inwards		200·00
Cash	12·00	
Consignment Inwards		12·00

CASH BOOK

	£		£
Consignment Inwards	475·00	Consignment Inwards—	
		Customs Duties	23·75
		Landing & Carriage	8·75
		Fire Insurance	9·50
		J. Rowell	225·00
		Consignment Inwards—	
		Brokerage	12·00
		J. Rowell	750·75

LEDGER

Consignments Inwards

	£		£
J. Rowell	760·00	Cash	475·00
Cash (Customs Duties)	23·75	Purchases	200·00
,, (Landing & Carriage)	8·75	H. Thompson	420·00
,, (Fire Insurance)	9·50	Stock unsold c/d	200·00
Commission	65·25		
Cash (Brokerage)	12·00		
Balance transferred to J. Rowell's A/c	415·75		
	1,295·00		1,295·00
Balance b/d	200·00		

J. Rowell

	£		£
Cash	225·00	Consignment Inwards A/c	760·00
,,	750·75	Transfer from Consignment Inwards A/c	415·75
Balance (Stock) c/d	200·00		
	1,175·75		1,175·75
		Balance b/d	200·00

QUESTIONS

1. Define a consignment inwards. How does it differ from a consignment outwards?
2. Explain the difference between a consignment inwards and: (*a*) a purchase of goods, (*b*) an ordinary sale of goods on commission.
3. What two methods are there of treating an inwards consignment? Outline them briefly.
4. Supposing part of an inwards consignment is taken by the consignee for his own use, how should it be dealt with in his books?
5. How does the consignee recoup himself for his expenses connected with the consignment, and how does he obtain his commission?
6. When a consignee renders an account sales, what entries will be necessary in his books? How is an advance on consignment treated in his books?

EXERCISE 09

1. Richard Random and Sons shipped goods to Paul Gold, their agent at Capetown, on 1st September, and sent therewith a *pro forma* invoice for £578 (goods £500, freight £60, and insurance £18). On 28th October Paul Gold sent home an account sales, from which it appeared that a portion of the goods had realized £460; and, deducting expenses £10 and commission £25, he enclosed a draft at three months for the balance. The stock remaining unsold amounted, at invoice prices plus expenses, to £280. On 2nd November he sent home another account sales, which showed that the balance of the consignment had realized £320; which, less £8 expenses and £10 commission he remitted by a three months' draft.

Show how the above transactions should appear in the books of Richard Random and Sons. *(R.S.A.)*

2. What is an "account sales"? In what particulars (if any) does it differ from a "consignment account"?

On 15th October Delmaine Bros., London, shipped to Donnison & Sons, Port Elizabeth, 60 cases of mixed Sheffield goods. These goods were invoiced *pro forma* at £300 per case.

The London payments in connexion with this consignment were: insurance, £100; freight, £540; sundry charges, £30.

The payments made by Donnison & Sons, in South Africa, were: storage, £160; landing charges, £60; insurance, £20.

On 15th December Donnison & Sons sold 30 cases of goods at £450 per case; on 17th December, 25 cases at £500 per case; and on 19th December, the balance of the consignment at £510 per case. All the above sales were effected for prompt cash. A commission is payable to Donnison & Sons of 2 per cent on all sales plus $1\frac{1}{2}$ per cent del credere commission.

On 1st November Delmaine Bros. drew a bill on Donnison & Sons for £10,000. This draft was duly accepted.

Prepare an account sales showing the result of the above consignment, and show how the transactions would appear in the books of Delmaine Bros.

(London Chamber of Commerce.)

3. J. Moss & Co., London, consign goods to the cost amount of £1,500 to their agent, J. Solomon, Hong Kong, on which they pay freight, insurance, and charges £55, drawing on him at 90 days for £1,300. They discount the bill at Lloyds Bank, being charged £15 therefor. They receive account sales of the consignment for £1,729, less agent's commission, etc., £71, and a draft on the Bank of Hong Kong for the balance.

Record the above transactions in the books of J. Moss & Co.

(London Chamber of Commerce.)

4. FK Ltd. acts as agent for GL Inc. of New York, to sell micrometers made by the latter firm. The goods are sent to FK Ltd. on a pro-forma invoice, and stored by them pending sale, but the goods (and the resulting sales and debtors) do not become the property of FK Ltd. at any time.

FK Ltd. is entitled to deduce a commission of 10 per cent on the cash remitted to GL Inc., after deducting the expenses paid directly on their behalf and also the commission itself.

On 9th February, 1966, a consignment of 50 micrometers was received, which had a sterling sales price of £8 each. Customs duty and entry expenses amounted to £16, and £11 was paid on 17th March for insurance and carriage.

The following sales were made on behalf of GL Inc.—

Feb 16	6	micrometers to	AB Ltd.
24	7	„ „	CD Ltd.
Mar 22	2	„ „	AB Ltd.
31	12	„ „	JP Ltd.
Apr 13	7	„ „	KT Ltd.
29	4	„ „	JP Ltd.

At 30th April, two micrometers were found to be damaged, in circumstances which were admitted to be the fault of FK Ltd. At that date all the debtors had paid except JP Ltd., who had paid nothing.

(*a*) Prepare the memorandum consignment stock account and consignor's personal account in the books of FK Ltd. for the period to 30th April, 1966, and an account sales (in sterling) to be sent to GL Inc. with the money due to it.

(*b*) Describe briefly what changes you would have made in your answer had FK Ltd. been a *del credere* agent (i.e. one who guarantees that the debt will be paid). What additional information would you require to calculate the commission in these circumstances? (*C.M.A.*)

5. You are required to write up all of the transactions given below in the ledger accounts of Q, including an account that shows the amount of profit or loss made by Q on the transactions.

Q is an agent who acts for a number of overseas manufacturers. On 12th February, 1969 he receives, as agent, 800 transistor radios from R of Japan which have a cost price of £6 each, and which he is instructed to sell for £10 each subject to any discounts, which he has discretion to allow. On the same day he pays customs duty of £1,019 and carriage and insurance of £127 on the consignment.

Q's agreement with R provides that he shall be entitled to reimbursement of any expenses that he pays on behalf of R and that he shall be entitled to a commission of 5 per cent of the amount of the sales after deducting any discounts and a further 2 per cent commission for agreeing to bear any bad debts that might arise from the sale of the transistor radios.

Q effects the following sales of transistor radios:

Date	Quantity	Customer	
28th February	200	L	A special trade discount of 5% was given to L
9th March	100	M	
18th March	50	N	
23rd April	200	M	
11th May	150	N	

The financial year of both Q and R ends on 30th June, 1969 and on that date Q prepares an account sales which he sends with a remittance for the amount due to R. M and N have paid their debts, but L has been declared bankrupt and has paid a final dividend of fifteen shillings in the £1 to all his creditors. (*C.M.A.*)

6. From the following particulars calculate the value of stock of goods on consignment at 30th June, 1959—

	£
Goods Consigned (100 units) at cost	9,000
Goods Lost in Transit (2 units), Insurance recovered	250
Goods Sold (80 units) realized	10,800
Consignor's Expenses	602
Consignee's Expenses (including £200 for Selling Expenses and £540 Commission)	950

Show full details of your calculations which may be approximated to the nearest £.

(*London Chamber of Commerce.*)

7. A manufacturer, J. Sheffield, has an agent, D. Durban, in South Africa, whose account in Sheffield's books showed a debit balance of £1,000 on 1st October, 19...

On that date J. Sheffield forwarded to Durban a consignment of 100 cases of goods together with a *pro forma* invoice showing cost at £10 per case. At the same time Sheffield paid transport charges £68 and insurance £5.

On 30th January, 19.1, an account sales was received from the agent showing that 60 cases had been sold for £15 each and that the agent had paid landing charges £68 and import duty £100.

On 28th February, 19 1, a further account sales was received showing that the balance of the consignment had been sold at £15 per case.

The agent was entitled to a commission of 5 per cent of the gross sales.

Record these transactions in the ledger of J. Sheffield, showing the profit or loss on the consignment. *(R.S.A.)*

8. On 1st January, 19.., H. Brown & Co. consigned to Hertz & Co., of Hamburg, per S.S. *Fortuna*, goods valued *pro forma* at £357, incurring expenses as follows: shipping charges £6·50; insurance £1·12; freight, £7·63. On 17th February, H. Brown & Co. received from Hertz & Co. an account sales, showing that the consignment had realized £540 gross, and that their expenses and charges were £41·50 for which they enclosed a sight draft on the Anglo-Foreign Bank Ltd. Say in what book you would record the dispatch of this consignment and make the entry. Also, make the account as it would appear in the books of H. Brown & Co.

(London Chamber of Commerce.)

9. Goods costing £3,200 were sent on consignment by H. Azard, Limited on 1st May, 1969, to Frank Seller in Australia. On the same date expenses paid in cash by H. Azard, Limited in respect of the goods were freight £124 and insurance £100. On receipt of the goods on 1st June, 1969, a bill was drawn by H. Azard, Limited on Frank Seller for £1,500, payable in three months' time, which was discounted by the company for £1,480 on 10th June. An account sales received from Frank Seller on 31st July, 1969, disclosed that he had made sales amounting to £4,100 and that he had goods on hand to the value of £400, at original cost. It further showed that he had made deductions for commission on sales to date of £120 and for selling expenses £50.

The balance due for goods was settled by Frank Seller by means of a two-month bill accompanying the account sales which H. Azard, Limited discounted with its bank, being charged £24 for such service.

Show the ledger accounts, other than case accounts, in the books of H. Azard, Limited and Frank Seller in which these transactions would be recorded and make the relative entries therein. *(A.C.C.A.)*

10. Make entries showing how the transactions detailed below are recorded in the books of the consignor and consignee respectively.

J. M., of Hull, consigns goods to the amount of £1,200 to his agent, L. R., of London, on which J. M. pays all outward charges, amounting to £50. J. M. draws on L. R. at 60 days for £1,000. Subsequently, L. R. sends an A/S to his principal, indicating that the consignment yielded £1,700, less expenses and commission, which were £85.

11. On 10th March, 19.., Robert Prentice & Co. Ltd. dispatched to their agent in Johannesburg 12 cases of hardware to be sold for their risk and account. The *pro forma* invoice amounted to £945·50. On arrival at Durban the agent, Mr. John Rowland, made the necessary entry to clear them and paid dock dues, and wharf charges of £40 and duty at the rate of 20 per cent.

One case was damaged and on production of the surveyor's certificate, Rowland obtained a cheque for £10 as compensation.

Sales were subsequently made as follows—

			£
May 16	Sold for cash	.	50·00
31	,, to R. Edwards	.	250·50
Jun 9	,, ,, K. Lane	.	200·00
24	,, ,, D. Carden	.	90·50

An account was rendered by Rowland as at June 30th when the value of unsold stock was £630·00.

Commission of 10 per cent was agreed upon by Prentice.

Show the ledger of Rowland and the A/S rendered by him.

12. Post the following items to their respective accounts, and draw up a capital account, profit and loss account, and balance sheet as at 31st December.

A merchant's books showed his position on 1st January to be as follows—

		£
Cash at bankers		1,756
Bills receivable in hand		3,250
Wool and other produce in hand	£45,200	
Less Advances received thereon	39,000	
		6,200
Bill payable due in the following year		7,500
Consignments to Australia		10,000
Bank of Australia, amount due for advances against consignments		8,000
Sundry creditors, amount due to them		3,500

During the year following the merchant had the following transactions—

	£
Goods purchased for export	24,000
Freight paid thereon	2,760
Insurance paid	250
Proceeds of sale of goods exported as per account sales rendered by agents	22,500
Exported goods remaining in hands of agents at close of year	5,700
Bills receivable received from agents in respect of exported goods sold	21,000
,, payable accepted against goods purchased for export	20,000
Cash paid for goods purchased for export	1,500
Bills payable paid at maturity	24,000
,, receivable paid at maturity during the year, and placed by bankers to credit of banking a/c	7,500
,, receivable discounted during the year, £15,000 and proceeds, *less* £450 discount paid into banking a/c	14,550
Wool and other produce sold during the year, proceeds in cash paid into banking a/c	50,000
Advances on ditto repaid	39,000
Interest paid on such advances	950
Consignments to Australia realized, and net proceeds received by merchant in cash, and paid into banking a/c	9,350
Advances against consignments repaid to Bank of Australia with interest thereon	8,400
Office expenses, salaries, and rent paid	2,350
Private drawings of merchant	1,500

(*Institute of Bankers.*)

13. John James bought goods of Edward Rhodes, the invoice value of which amounted to £367·50. A discount of 7½ per cent was to be allowed off the account. One-half the net sum was to be paid in cash, and Rhodes was to draw at 3 months upon James for the balance, plus 1 per cent for commission and at 4 per cent for

discount. The transaction was carried out, and the cash was duly paid, but, shortly before the bill fell due, James, on the plea that the goods were not wholly disposed of, proposed to Rhodes to pay £50 in cash, to have the present bill withdrawn, and to give his acceptance for the balance, plus £1·50 per cent Commission and 6 per cent discount. This was agreed to. The £50 was paid in due course, and the second acceptance met at maturity.

Make the journal and cash book entries, giving effect to this transaction, and prepare James's account as it should appear in Rhodes's ledger, assuming his books to have been properly kept. *(London Chamber of Commerce.)*

14. The Midland Steel Company Limited consigned to its Australian agents, Murray & Co., of Sydney, 125 tons of steel bars per S.S. *Tantallon Castle*. Murray & Co. paid for landing charges £15, carting £10, warehousing £6, insurance £1, and advertising £5. On 1st July, they sold the steel by auction as follows—

25 tons at £10 per ton
30 tons at £9·50 per ton
30 tons at £9·25 per ton
40 tons at £9·00 per ton

They charged commission at 5 per cent. Make out in proper form the account sales rendered by Murray & Co. to the Midland Steel Company Limited, showing the balance due, for which Murray & Co. sent a bill at 30 days after sight, and record the transactions in the books of Murray & Co. *(Chartered Accountants.)*

15.

	£
Lewis & Co. sell and ship to Armstrong & Sons of Iquique, sundry goods invoiced as costing	1,004
Freight, insurance and dock charges were	90
Buying and shipping commission charged was	30
Total of invoice was	1,124

Lewis & Co. drew on Armstrongs for that amount and secured an advance of £650 from the bankers through whom they were forwarding the documents. The draft was duly accepted.

At due date of draft Armstrongs paid one-half and gave a bill for the balance, plus 6 per cent interest per annum for 6 months.

The bankers were repaid their advance by Lewis & Co., and the extended bill was met at maturity by Armstrongs.

Frame journal entries to record properly the whole of the above transactions in the books of—

1. Lewis & Co.
2. Armstrong & Sons.

Narrations are essential. *(Civil Service.)*

16. Make out for Stephens & Son, London, an account sales of 65 casks of fine Lard marked "A1," sold at £40 per cwt. for 20 cwt. The lard was shipped per S.S. *Rameses* from Williams & Co., of New York. The following charges were incurred—

	£
Freight as per bill of lading	15
Marine insurance and Customs dues	20
Unloading, weighing, etc.	5
Expenses of sale	12
Fire insurance	13
Brokerage 10 per cent	
Commission 5 per cent.	

17. On 1st March, W. Williams, a merchant carrying on business in London, consigned to his agent, S. Siegfried, of Hamburg, 1,000 tons of iron, invoiced *pro forma* at £5 per ton. On 1st May he received an account sales showing that the whole of the consignment had realized 69,420 marks. Siegfried's disbursements amounted to 1,425 marks, and his commission was 2½ per cent on the gross proceeds. Siegfried remitted a bill in currency at 2 m/d for the amount due. The carriage, cartage, freight, and insurance paid by Williams in connexion with the consignment amounted to £120. Assume the average value of the mark to be 10p, but that on the date the bill was paid the rate of exchange was 11 marks to the £ sterling. Record the above transactions in W. Williams' books.

18. Messrs. Lux and Lucifer, Birmingham, consign on 1st February, to M. Marconi, of Milano, 500 "Radiant" electric lamps, invoiced at £1 each, and pay freight £5, and insurance £3. One hundred and twenty-five lamps are damaged and rendered worthless by storm, and M. Marconi receives £72 in settlement from underwriters. He sells 250 lamps for £260, and on 4th April sends account sales and bankers' draft for balance due to the consignors, after charging his agency expenses £4, and commission £17. Give the accounts as they would appear in Lux and Lucifer's ledger.

(*West Riding of Yorkshire.*)

19. On 1st July, 19.., Jones Bros. of London consigned per S.S. *Thames* 1,000 tons of ash to Cham & Son, their agents in Calcutta, at the invoice price of £1·95 per ton.

Against this consignment they drew a bill at sixty days' date on the consignors for £750. They paid freight of £0·70 per ton and insurance of £40, together with railway charges of £53, and loading charges of £20.

The consignment was received in Calcutta on 7th August, and the bill was accepted. Dock dues of 520 rupees, and other expenses on the consignment, 346 rugees, were paid by Cham & Son.

During the ensuing week they sold 400 tons at 40 rupees per ton, 350 tons at 42 rupees per ton, and the balance at 44 rupees per ton.

They rendered an account sales for the proceeds, including their commission of 2 per cent on sales, on 14th August and, on the same date remitted a draft on London for the sterling equivalent of the balance of the net proceeds. This was received by Jones Bros. on 9th September.

Assuming that the rupee was worth 7½p throughout—

(*a*) Show these transactions in the ledger accounts of Jones Bros.

(*b*) Draw up the account sales for the consignment. (*R.S.A.*)

20. On 1st January A. Stevenson bought goods value £1,100 and consigned them to L. Lanng as a joint speculation, profits being divisible equally. On the same date he paid carriage and freight £70; insurance, etc., £25·20; and drew on Lanng at two months for £600 on account, discounting the bill on 4th January for £597·50. On receipt of the goods on 1st February Lanng paid dock dues and cartage £30; and government duty, insurance, etc., £40. On 31st May Stevenson received an account sales showing that on 30th April the goods had realized gross £1,640, and that Lanng's disbursements made on the same date were: storage £30; sundries, brokerage, and expenses of sale £100. Lanng also enclosed a sight draft for amount due at 31st May. Prepare a general statement showing the result of the venture, and write up the accounts in Stevenson's and Lanng's ledgers respectively. Interest is to be brought into account at the rate of 5 per cent per annum.

CHAPTER 10

REPORTING THE INCOME AND FINANCIAL POSITION OF CLUBS, SOCIETIES AND VOLUNTARY ASSOCIATIONS

Carlyle and Milnes were talking . . . of the Administration just formed by Sir Robert Peel, and Milnes was evincing some disappointment . . . that he had not been offered a post in it. 'No, no,' said Carlyle, 'Peel knows what he is about; there is only one post fit for you, and that is the office of perpetual president of the Heaven and Hell Amalgamation Society.'

T. E. WEMYSS REID—*The Life of Lord Houghton*

Importance of Distinction between Capital and Revenue. In principle, the accounts of a club or society should be kept along the same lines as for a business entity, but in practice many confused "accounts" are presented by amateur treasurers. These documents often reflect an imperfect understanding of the basic distinctions between capital and revenue and of the difference between the Income and Expenditure and the Receipts and Payments Accounts.

Capital Expenditure consists of expenditure the benefit of which is not fully consumed in one period, but spread over several periods. It includes assets acquired for the purpose of earning income, or increasing the earning capacity of the business; for example, land and buildings or additions thereto, patent or mining rights, plant and machinery or additions thereto. The actual installation cost, in addition to the invoice price, should also be capitalized. Capital items appear in the balance sheet.

Revenue Expenditure consists of expenditure incurred in one period of account, the full benefit of which is consumed in that period. It includes such items as: replacements, repairs, renewals, depreciation of the fixed assets, and also the current expenses of carrying on the business, such as rent, rates and taxes, wages and salaries, carriage, insurance, and other trade charges. Such items appear in the trading, profit and loss accounts or some other form of revenue account.

Deferred Revenue Expenditure is expenditure which would normally be treated as revenue expenditure which is not written off in one period. Exceptional expenditure on an advertising campaign might be treated in this way.

In the following examples a distinction has been drawn between capital and revenue items in order to illustrate the subject further—

Installation of electric light and telephone	Capital
Annual charges for maintenance	Revenue
Purchase of new plant	Capital
Repairs to motor vehicles	Revenue
Depreciation on plant	,,
Purchase of leasehold premises	Capital
Ground rent on premises	Revenue
Purchase of patent rights	Capital
Renewal fees for patents	Revenue
Purchase of new vehicles	Capital
New tyres to vehicles	Revenue
Sale of old plant (depreciated value in books, £135) for £70 and purchase of new plant £320 in place of it—	
Loss on sale of old plant £65	Revenue
Cost of new plant £320	Capital

The above are only general rules, as it is quite impossible to draw a hard and fast line. Circumstances sometimes arise which make the question a very complicated one. Repairs are usually a revenue charge; but if we purchase second-hand plant, and pay for some immediate repairs necessary to make it efficient for our purpose, then such repairs become capital expenditure, and must be added to the plant as part of its cost. Wages are a revenue item; but the wages paid to workmen to erect and fit some new machinery the firm has bought must be considered as an addition to the cost of the machinery. *Legal expenses* are a revenue charge; but the legal expenses for conveyancing when purchasing a works must be treated as part of the cost of the works. Transport charges are usually a revenue item; but payments made for transporting on any plant and machinery are added on as part of the cost. *Interest on Capital* during the construction of works or buildings or plant may also be capitalized. *Parliamentary Expenses* incurred in the promotion of bills for the establishment of public utility undertakings, etc., are also allowed to be capitalized.

Apportionment between Capital and Revenue. With some items of expenditure it may be necessary to make an apportionment, i.e. to charge so much to capital, and to write off the balance. This may be the case with alterations, improvements, and extensions of premises or plant. To capitalize the whole of the expenditure may not always be prudent, as the value of the premises or plant may not be enhanced by anything like the amount of money spent. Speaking generally, the safe policy to adopt seems to be *not* to capitalize *permanently* any expenditure which is not represented by assets, although legally it may be done. A manufacturer who finds it necessary to scrap his plant and machinery, and replace it with newer and better inventions will incur a loss on the sale of the obsolete plant. Is this part of the cost of the new equipment? Undoubtedly not, and it should not generally be capitalized.

Capital Receipts in a business comprise capital paid in by partners, or, in the case of a joint stock company, sums received from shareholders or debenture holders; loans; the proceeds of sale of any of the assets; etc.

Similar receipts by clubs or associations are life subscriptions; entry fees; government grants and subventions; legacies ane endowments.

Revenue Receipts, in a business are cash from sales, discounts received, commission, interest on investments, transfer fees, etc. Similar receipts by clubs or associations are annual subscriptions; sales of beer, wines and spirits; sale of golf clubs and balls; charges to other clubs for use of premises, etc.

Club Accounts. It is usual to present to members—

1. A summarized cash account called the Receipts and Payments Account. This shows actual cash receipts and payments during the accounting period and the balance is cash in hand or an overdraft.

2. A statement of the results of operations during the year called the Income and Expenditure Account. This is drawn up on the same lines as a Profit and Loss Account, and it shows the income arising and the expenditure incurred during the accounting period, irrespective of whether these have actually been received or paid during the period.

If operations have been profitable there will be a surplus, otherwise there will be a deficit.

Note re Hospital Accounts. The majority of hospitals in the National Health Service are required to keep records to conform to the instructions and regulations issued by the Treasury and the Minister of Health. These records may be complete departmental accounts or simple cash records. They necessitate the preparation of annual estimates of capital and maintenance expenditure and income, and also the keeping of impersonal accounts and the preparation of annual accounts. The day-to-day work is usually of the simplest nature, viz. a "receipts and payments" account (analysed if required), the expenditure being posted to the appropriate accounts. Grants from the Treasury are shown on the debit side of the receipts and payments account and posted to the ledger, and a trial balance prepared.

With a view to keeping expenditure within the approved estimates without hindering efficiency, budgetary control is being more widely developed, with advantage to the country as a whole and to the individual organization.

In the case of voluntary hospitals or where voluntary gifts and funds operate, full details of the sources must be given on a separate schedule of income and expenditure.

Difference between an Income and Expenditure Account and a Receipts and Payments Account. The following points of difference should be carefully noted by the student. An income and expenditure account deals with the *whole* of the income and expenditure for the year, whether actually received and paid, or not. All accruing income and all outstanding expenses that belong to the period covered by the account must be included before any balance is struck. A receipts and payments account, on the other hand, deals with only *part* of the income and expenditure for the year, namely, that part actually received and actually paid. Again, an income and expenditure account contains income and expenditure of the *current* year only. A receipts and payments account may contain the balance of cash in hand at the commencement and at the close of the year, and it will also contain all cash received and paid during the year. It may comprise, not only income and expenditure for the *current* year, but also for the *previous* year, and even for the *succeeding* year. Further, the balance (if any) of a receipts and payments account denotes merely the cash in hand; the balance of an income and expenditure account represents the surplus for the year, or the deficit as the case may be.

Errors in Published Accounts. It is not unusual to find some published "income and expenditure accounts" showing the income on the debit and the expenditure on the credit, and containing the balance from the previous year; in some cases they are even called "balance sheets." The nomenclature of such accounts is, of course, quite wrong and very misleading. A proper income and expenditure account shows the *expenditure* on the *debit* and the *income* on the *credit*, and does *not* include any balance from the *previous* year, which would simply make it impossible to arrive at the true income or expenditure for the *current* year.

QUESTIONS

1. Why is the distinction between capital and revenue of great importance in accounting?

2. Define "capital expenditure." Give examples.

3. What is meant by "revenue expenditure"? Give examples.

4. Discriminate, in the following cases, between "capital" and "revenue" expenditure respectively—

(*a*) Purchase of leasehold premises.
Annual depreciation of lease.
Annual repairs.
Annual ground rent.
(*b*) Installation of heating and ventilating apparatus.
Annual charge for maintenance.
(*c*) Purchase of additional furniture.
Annual depreciation.
Annual repairs.

(*d*) Purchase of patent rights.
Annual depreciation.
Annual renewal fees.

(*e*) Sale of old machinery (depreciated value in books £275) for £80, and purchase of new machinery £1,050 in place of it.

(*f*) Purchase of second-hand pumps (additional).
Wages paid to own workmen to fix.
Immediate repairs to make efficient.
Cost of immediate painting.

5. Give some examples of "revenue" expenditure becoming, under certain circumstances, "capital" expenditure.

6. Is it ever necessary to apportion one and the same lot of expenditure between both capital and revenue? Illustrate your answer by examples.

7. What is the safe rule to follow as regards "capital," in difficult questions of apportionment?

8. Is there any risk attaching to the non-discrimination between "capital" and "revenue" in the case of receipts?

9. Define "capital receipts." Give examples.

10. Explain what is meant by the term "revenue receipts." Give examples.

11. Define "revenue account."

12. What is a "receipts and payments account"?

13. Explain the term "receipts and expenditure account."

14. What do you understand by an "income and expenditure account"?

15. Is there any difference between an income and expenditure account and a revenue account? Give reasons for your answer.

The wide variety of clubs and societies makes it impossible to prescribe a uniform system of accounts although, in general, a record of receipts and payments, suitably analysed, will be sufficient.

This should be kept by the Treasurer who must then obtain, at the end of the accounting period, a statement of all items of income and expenditure which have been paid in advance or are in arrear. This information may be obtained from his own records and from the various officers of the club who have authority to make payments. All balances of petty cash held by officers must also be checked.

Example 1

The following information was collected by the Treasurer of the Welcome Club and from it he prepared an Income and Expenditure Account for the year ended 31st December, 19.., and a Balance Sheet at the end of the year—

	£
Capital account as per last balance sheet	1,873
Library books	225
Furniture, fixtures, and fittings	476
Glass, cutlery, china, house and table linen	286
Annual subscriptions	675
Printing, stationery, and stamps bought	354
Hire of hall (*Cr.* balance)	185
Cost of entertainments	72

	£
Billiard room receipts	216
Rent, rates, and taxes	124
Cash in hand	27
Cash at bank	224
Cash on deposit at 5 per cent	500
Profit on sale of wines and spirits, beer, minerals, cigars and tobacco, during the year	100
Secretary's honorarium	160
Sales of tickets for entertainments	145
Salaries of staff	246
Entrance fees	215
Sale of tickets for annual dinner	80
Gas and electric light	66
Sundry creditors	163
£600 2½ per cent Consols	450
Dividend on Consols, *less* tax	7
Audit fee	21
Interest on bank deposit	25
Repairs, cleaning, and washing	118
Cost of annual dinner	67
Newspapers and magazines	58
Stock of wines and spirits, beer, minerals, cigars and tobacco, 31st Dec., 19..	210
Stock of stationery, 31st Dec., 19..	46

Depreciate library books, furniture, glass, cutlery, etc., 10 per cent. Of the subscriptions £20 is paid in advance, and £12 is in arrear. £17 is owing for salaries of staff. (See pp. 1007–08.)

Special Items in Income and Expenditure Accounts. Instructions are, as a rule, given in the exercises as to the treatment of special items. Extraordinary expenditure is generally spread over a period of years. Donations and subscriptions are usually credited to income, and legacies to capital. The rules of the association or institution may, however, provide that a certain portion of the donations and entrance fees, or other sources of income, shall be capitalized. Life membership of a club may sometimes be obtained by payment of a lump sum, which should be credited to a separate fund and a fair proportion credited to income in subsequent years. Legacies and endowments may, in certain cases, be for a definitely specified purpose, and will then require special accounts; while the income will also require to be separately treated. By way of illustration, the following example is a part of Question 4 on p. 1016 at the end of this chapter.

Example 2

The balance sheet of the Society of Wiseacres at 31st December, 19.., included an item "Lecture Endowment £512," representing a legacy of £500, the income from which was to finance an annual lecture and £12 income which had not been spent. Investments which cost £4,350 also included £500 held on account of the lecture endowment. An investment income of £208 included £25 in respect of the lecture endowment investment and £28 out of total lecture fees and expenses of which £225 was for the relevant lecture.

THE WELCOME CLUB

INCOME AND EXPENDITURE ACCOUNT FOR THE YEAR ENDED 31ST DECEMBER, 19..

Expenditure	£	£	*Income*	£	£
Printing, Stationery & Stamps	354		Annual Subscriptions	675	
Less Stock c/f	46		*Add* Amount due	12	
		308		687	
Cost of Entertainments		72	*Less* paid in advance	20	
Rent, Rates & Taxes		124			667
Honorarium to Secretary		160	Hire of Hall		185
Gass & Electric Light		66	Billiard Room Receipts		216
Salaries of Staff	246		Profit from Sale of Wines & Spirits, Beer, Minerals, Cigars, etc.		100
Salaries of Staff due	17		Sale of Tickets for Annual Dinner		80
		263	Entrance Fees		215
Audit Fee		21	Sale of Tickets for Entertainments		145
Repairs, Cleaning & Washing		118	Dividends on Consols *less* tax		7
Cost of Annual Dinner		67	Interest on Bank Deposit *less* tax		25
Newspapers & Magazines		58			
Depreciation—					
Library Books, 10%, £225	23				
Furniture, etc., 10%, £476	48				
Glass, Cutlery, etc., 10%, £286	29				
		100			
Balance (Surplus of Income over Expenditure for the year)		283			
		1,640			1,640

THE WELCOME CLUB

BALANCE SHEET AS AT 31ST DECEMBER, 19..

Liabilities	£	£	*Assets*	£	£
Sundry Creditors		163	Cash in hand	27	
Subscriptions paid in advance		20	Cash at Bank	224	
Outstanding Expenses		17	Cash on Deposit	500	
Capital—					751
Balance, 1st Jan.	1,873		£600 $2\frac{1}{2}$% Consols		450
Add Surplus for Year as per Income &			Outstanding Subscriptions		12
Expenditure A/c	283		Library Books	225	
		2,156	*Less* Depreciation	23	
					202
			Furniture, Fixtures, etc.	476	
			Less Depreciation	48	
					428
			China, Glass, Cutlery, House & Table Linen	286	
			Less Depreciation	29	
					257
			Stock of Stationery		46
			Stock of Wine & Spirits, Beer, Minerals, Cigars and Tobacco		210
		2,356			2,356

The accounts for both capital and revenue of the endowment should be separated from the general accounts as follows—

THE SOCIETY OF WISEACRES

LECTURE ENDOWMENT (CAPITAL) FUND

		19.1	£
		Jan 1 Balance	500

LECTURE ENDOWMENT INVESTMENT

19.1	£		
Jan 1 Cash	500		

LECTURE ENDOWMENT INCOME AND EXPENDITURE ACCOUNT FOR THE YEAR ENDED, 31ST DECEMBER, 19.1

	£		£
Cash (lecture fees and expenses)	28	Balance b/f. . . .	12
Balance c/f	9	Cash (investment income) .	25
	37		37

EXTRACT FROM BALANCE SHEET OF THE SOCIETY OF WISEACRES ON 31ST DECEMBER, 19.1

		£		£
Lecture Endowment Fund	£500		Lecture Endowment Investment, at	
Balance on Income c/f . .	9		cost	500
		509		

NOTE. The balance shown on the general investment account will be £3,850. In the general income and expenditure account, income from investments credited will be £183 and the lecture fees and expenses debited will be £197.

Trading Activities. Many clubs run bars, restaurants and other commercial activities and a separate trading account should be prepared to show the results of each activity. The profit or loss is carried to the general income and expenditure account.

Apportionment. Some items of expenditure may be partly concerned with trading and partly with the general purposes of the club, and the total should be divided fairly between them; for example, club stewards' wages may be shared one-third to bar and two-thirds to general income and expenditure.

Payments in Kind. Employees may be entitled to free meals, and the value of such meals should be calculated. The amount is *income* to the restaurant account (which is credited) and *expenditure* to the general account (which is debited).

The following example illustrates these points—

Example 3

The following is an account of the receipts and payments of the Henton Social Club for the year to 31st December, 19.1.

RECEIPTS AND PAYMENTS ACCOUNT

	£		£
Balance at Bank, 1st Jan., 19.1	700	Payments for Restaurant and Bar Supplies	10,000
Annual subscriptions—		Wages	3,400
For the year 19..	240	Lighting and Heating	460
" " " 19.1	3,670	Secretary's Expenses	370
" " " 19.2	30	General Expenses	2,015
Restaurant and Bar Sales	12,000	Payments on account of New Furniture	300
Interest on 3½% War Loan	105	Balance at Bank, 31st Dec., 19.1	500
Life Membership Subscriptions	300		
	17,045		17,045

You are given the following information—

(i) Stock of restaurant and bar supplies—

At 31st December, 19..	£820
" " 19.1	£2,000

(ii) Creditors for restaurant and bar supplies—

At 31st December, 19..	£900
" " 19.1	£1,080

(iii) In addition to the bank balance and the stock mentioned in (i) above, the assets of the Club at 31st December, 19.., were—

Furniture, valued at	£2,000
£3,000 3½% War Loan, at cost	£3,100
(Ignore current market value of this investment)	
Lease of Club premises, valued at	£2,500

The lease has 10 years to run from 31st December, 19..

(iv) During 19.1, new furniture was purchased at a cost of £500.

(v) In December, 19.., £40 was received in respect of annual subscriptions for the year 19.1.

(vi) At 31st December, 19.1, the Club owed £10 to the secretary for his expenses. Nothing was owing to the secretary at 31st December, 19.., but he is entitled to free meals valued at £50 per year.

(vii) Bills outstanding for lighting and heating at 31st December, 19.., amounted to £60. These bills were paid during 19.1, and nothing was outstanding in this respect at 31st December, 19.1.

(viii) On 1st January, 19.1, the rules of the Club were amended to make provision for life membership at a subscription of £30 per life member. It was also provided that 10 per cent of each life member's subscription should be transferred annually to income and expenditure account, and that the first of these transfers should be made in the year during which the subscription should be received.

You are required to prepare a restaurant and bar trading account, a general income and expenditure account for the year to 31st December, 19.1, and a balance sheet at 31st December, 19.1.

No credit is to be taken for any subscriptions in arrear at 31st December, 19.1, and you may assume that this principle was followed in the preparation of the accounts for the year 19...

Ignore depreciation of furniture.

HENTON SOCIAL CLUB

Restaurant and Bar Trading Account for 19.1

		£		£
Supplies—				
Stock on 1st Jan. .	£820		Sales	12,000
Purchases .	10,180		Secretary's meals . . .	50
	11,000			
Less Stock 31st Dec. .	2,000			
		9,000		
Gross profit		3,050		
		12,050		12,050

General Income and Expenditure Account for the Year Ended 31st December, 19.1

		£			£
Wages		3,400	Gross profit on Restaurant and		
Lighting and Heating	£460		Bar		3,050
Less Arrears from 19..	60		Subscriptions received—		
		400	For 19.. . . .	£240	
General Expenses . . .		2,015	For 19.1 . . .	3,670	
Secretary's Expenses—			For 19.1 (in 19..)	40	
	£370				3,950
Add Accruals . .	10		Life Members (proportion)		30
Meals .	50		Interest on War Loan . .		105
		430			
Lease Amortization . . .		250			
Surplus for Year . . .		640			
		7,135			7,135

Balance Sheet on 31st December, 19.1

		£			£
Capital Fund	£8,120		*Fixed Assets*		
Add Surplus for Year	640		Leasehold Premises	£2,500	
		8,760	*Less* Amortization	250	
Life Subscriptions	£300				2,250
Less Transfer to Income	30		Furniture at Cost		2,500
		270	War Loan, 3½%, at cost		3,100
Current Liabilities			*Current Assets*—		
Creditors—			Stock		2,000
Trade	£1,080		Cash in Hand		500
On Furniture	200				
Secretary	10				
Subscriptions in Advance	30				
		1,320			
		10,350			10,350

Notes—

(*a*) The opening balance on the capital fund may be calculated from the total of assets at the beginning of the year, less the liabilities at that time, i.e. £9,120 − £1,000 = £8,120.

(*b*) The purchases may be calculated: Payments for bar supplies £10,000, *deduct* creditors at start of year £900, *add* creditors at end of year £1,080.

Accumulated Fund. The fund corresponds to the capital and reserves of a company and the capital in a partnership or sole trader and it may be necessary to calculate the opening Balance Sheet position before preparing the accounts for the period.

Example 4

The treasurer of the Country Farmers' Club has prepared from the bank statements the following Receipts and Payments Account for the year ended 31st January, 1963—

Receipts	£	£	*Payments*	£	£
Cash at 1st February, 1962—			Billiards equipment purchased		80
In hand	30		Purchases for bar		2,910
At bank as per bank statements—			Rates, telephone and insurance		112
Current Account	98		Wages		420
Deposit Account	226		Printing, stationery, etc.		92
		354	Cash at bank on 31st January, 1963 as per bank statements—		
Subscriptions		96			
Billiards takings		125		£	
Takings from bar		3,840	Current Account	623	
Interest on bank deposit account		10	Deposit Account	188	
					811
		4,425			4,425

The following additional information was obtained—

	On 31st January, 1962	On 31st January, 1963
	£	£
Rates and Insurance paid in advance .	28	32
Telephone charges owing . . .	16	19
Subscriptions due but not paid . .	18	14
Subscriptions paid in advance . .	6	4
Value of stock in bar . . .	178	184
Cheques issued for purchases for bar were unpresented	40	54

The original billiards equipment cost £350.

You also find that—

(1) the takings from the bar on 31st January, 1963, amounting to £64, were in the treasurer's hands and were paid into the bank on 2nd February, 1963;

(2) depreciation of 10 per cent is to be written off the cost of the original billiards equipment and the additions thereto;

(3) the barman is entitled to a commission of 5 per cent on the gross profit from the bar before any charge is made for wages;

(4) a donation of a barrel of beer costing £14 has been made to the local agricultural show.

You are requested to—

(*a*) compute the balance of the Accumulated Fund of the club as on 31st January, 1962; and

(*b*) prepare Income and Expenditure Account for the year ended 31st January, 1963, and the Balance Sheet as on that date. (*A.C.C.A.*)

Solution 4

(*a*) The accumulated fund at 31st January, 1962, can be calculated by extracting the information on the assets and liabilities at that date—

COMPUTATION OF ACCUMULATED FUND
ON 31ST JANUARY, 1962

	£	£
Cash in hand		30
Cash at Bank—Current Account	98	
Less Unpresented cheques	40	
	—	58
Deposit Account		226
Subscriptions due but not paid		18
Rates and insurance paid in advance		28
Bar stock at valuation		178
Billiards equipment at cost		350
		888
Less Subscriptions paid in advance	6	
Telephone charges owing	16	
	—	22
		866

(*b*) The accounts can then be prepared as follows—

INCOME AND EXPENDITURE ACCOUNT

For the year ended 31st January, 1963

	£		£	£	£
Wages	420	Bar Profit—			
Commission to Barman . . .	50	Sales . . .		3,904	
Rates, Telephone and Insurance .	111	Donation . . .		14	
Printing, Stationery, etc. . . .	92				
Donation to Local Agricultural Show .	14			3,918	
Depreciation	43	Opening stock	178		
Excess of Income over Expenditure .	499	Purchases . . .	2,924		
			3,102		
		Less: Closing stock	184		
				2,918	
					1,000
		Subscriptions . .			94
		Billiards Takings . .			125
		Bank Deposit Interest .			10
	1,229				1,229

BALANCE SHEET

at 31st January, 1963

	£	£		£	£
Accumulated Fund			Fixed Assets—		
At 1st February, 1962 .	866		Billiards Equipment—		
Excess of Income over Expenditure for the year . . .	499		At Cost . . .	430	
		1,365	*Less:* Depreciation .	43	
					387
Current Liabilities—			Current Assets—		
Subscriptions in advance .	4		Bar Stock	184	
Telephone	19		Subscriptions due . . .	14	
Barman's commission . .	50		Prepayments	32	
		73	Balance at bank—		
			Deposit Account . . .	188	
			Current Account . . .	569	
			Cash in hand	64	
					1,051
		1,438			1,438

If the accounts for subscriptions and rates, etc., were prepared, they would show the following data—

	Subscriptions £	*Rates, Telephone and Insurance* £		*Subscriptions* £	*Rates, Telephone and Insurance* £
Balances, brought down, 31st January, 1962 .	18	28	Balances, brought down, 31st January, 1962 .	6	16
Cash		112	Cash	96	
Balances, carried down, 31st January, 1963 .	4	19	Balances, carried down, 31st January, 1963 .	14	32
Income and Expenditure Account . . .	94		Income and Expenditure Account . . .		111
	116	159		116	159

EXERCISE 10

1. What is the chief difference between a "receipts and payments account" and an "income and expenditure account"? In what undertakings are these forms of accounts respectively made use of? (*R.S.A.*)

2. Is there any difference between a receipts and payments account and an income and expenditure account?

The following particulars relate to the Chilworth Literary Society for the year ended 31st December: subscriptions received £110; interest received on investment £38; net proceeds received from lectures and concerts £232; rent paid for use of hall £21; petty cash payments £10; advertising paid £21; printing expenses paid £12.

The Society holds ten 4 per cent debentures of £100 each in the Universal Library Ltd. As on 31st December, the Society owed £8 for rent of hall and £10 for printing.

Prepare the Society's annual statements of account for the year ended 31st December. (*London Chamber of Commerce.*)

3. During the long vacation of 1965, the University of Barsetshire Aqualung Club organized an expedition to investigate the marine life about the shores of the Pongo Islands. The following is a summary of the expedition's British bank pass-sheets—

Receipts	£	Payments	£
Donation from the "Barsetshire Echo"	30	Payment to travel agent for fares of 14 members of £40 each	560
Contribution from the Barsetshire University Athletics Union	130	Additional equipment	34
Receipts from members—		Printing, stationery and postages	6
14 deposits of £5 each	70	Cost of visas	21
10 balances of contribution of £60 each	600	Bank charges and cheque books	2
		Group insurance	30
		Hire of boats	25
		Medical supplies	18
		Food	73
		Maps and charts	4
		Cash drawn by the expedition's leader	50
		Balance at 30th September, 1965	7
	830		830

The expedition leader has prepared the following summary of his cash expenditure (which has been converted to £ sterling)—

Receipts	£	Payments	£
Cash from bank	50	Food	36
Balance of contribution from one member	60	Wages of local crew	40
Leader's own personal travellers cheques	30	Hire of tents, etc.	24
		Repairs to equipment	16
		Leader's own personal expenses	14
		Balance of cash, retained by leader after the return	10
	140		140

At 1st October, 1964, the Aqualung Club owned equipment valued at £80 and had a petty cash balance of £4. On 30th September, 1965, the equipment, including that brought back by the expedition, was valued at £70, and one-half of the resulting depreciation was attributable to the expedition. The petty cash stood at £7.

Also at 30th September, 1965, two members of the expedition owed the balance of their contributions. In addition, a member had been unable to join the expedition: his deposit was forfeited to the club, but £35 was recoverable from the travel agent in respect of part of his fare.

Apart from the expedition, the activities of the club have not been extensive. A subscription of 5p each has been collected from 40 members during the year, and this together with a donation of £10 from the honorary president and a grant of £3 from the University Athletics Union was put into the petty cash. From this stationery and postages accounted for £4, repairs to equipment £6, and the difference between the resulting balance and the actual cash in hand had been spent on the entertainment of visiting teams.

You are required to prepare—

(*a*) The income and expenditure account of the club for the year ended 30th September, 1965, showing as a separate item the surplus or deficit on the expedition.

(*b*) A balance sheet on that date. (*C.M.A.*)

4. The Society of Wiseacres organizes study groups and lectures for its members, and publishes a quarterly journal *Lucidity*. The following is a summary of the receipts and payments of the society for the year 19.1.

RECEIPTS AND PAYMENTS ACCOUNT

		£		£
Balance at Bank, 1st Jan., 19.1		475	Rent	300
Annual Subscriptions—			Salaries	975
For 19..	£36		Lecture Fees and Expenses	225
19.1	1,582		Cost of Printing *Lucidity*	1,024
19.2	124		Stationery and Postage	246
		1,742	General Expenses	369
Sales of and Subscriptions to *Lucidity*		847	New Office Equipment	65
Advertising Receipts		533	Balance at Bank, 31st Dec., 19.1	601
Income from Investments		208		
		3,805		3,805

You are given the following information—

(i) Subscriptions for the 19.1 issues of *Lucidity* received in 19.. were £217 and subscriptions for 19.2 issues received in 19.1 were £198.

(ii) At 31st December, 19.., £93 had been received in respect of annual subscriptions to the society for 19.1.

(iii) Amounts owing to the printers of *Lucidity* were—

	£
At 31st December, 19..	249
At 31st December, 19.1	287

(iv) Amounts owing to the society for advertisements in *Lucidity* were—

	£
At 31st December, 19..	76
At 31st December, 19.1	108

(v) £113 of the cost of stationery and postages was in connexion with *Lucidity*.
(vi) Salaries outstanding were—

	£
At 31st December, 19.. . .	80
At 31st December, 19.1 . .	85

(vii) The balance sheet of the society at 31st December, 19.., included an item "Lecture Endowment £512," representing a legacy of £500, the income from which was to finance an annual lecture, and £12 income which had not been spent.

(viii) In addition to the bank balance and debtors for advertisements, the assets of the society at 31st December, 19.., were—

	£
Office furniture and equipment, at cost . .	650
Investments, at cost (£500 of which represented investments held on account of the lecture endowment)	4,350

(ix) £25 of the investment income was in respect of the lecture endowment investment and £28 of the lecture fees and expenses was in respect of the relevant lecture.

You are required to prepare a profit and loss account for *Lucidity* for the year 19.1, a general income and expenditure account for the year 19.1 (including profit or loss on *Lucidity*) and a balance sheet at 31st December, 19.1.

Subscriptions in arrear at the end of any year are taken into account in the year in which they are received. Taxation and depreciation of fixed assets are to be ignored.

(*Chartered Institute of Secretaries.*)

5. The Games Sports Club was started on 1st March, 1963, and on 29th February, 1964, the Cash Account for the year was as follows—

Receipts	£	Payments	£
Subscriptions, 1963–64 . .	945	Rent and Rates	150
,, 1964–65 . .	52	Stationery, Printing, etc. . .	76
Entrance Fees	236	Equipment	240
Bar Takings	1,012	Furniture Purchased . .	466
Sundries	19	Salaries and Wages . . .	260
Locker and Equipment Hire .	97	Bar Purchases	795
Post Office Interest . . .	4	Post Office Deposit . . .	225
Gifts for Purchase of Furniture .	200	General and Sundry Expenses .	207
		Newspapers and Magazines .	18
		Cash at Bank	100
	£2,565		£2,537

You are required to prepare an Income and Expenditure Account for the year ended 29th February, 1964, and Balance Sheet at that date, taking into consideration the following—

£5 owing by Members for Hire of Equipment.
Bar Creditors at 29th February, 1964, £5.
General Expenses unpaid, £10.
Depreciate Equipment by £20 and Furniture by £46.
Bar Stock at 29th February, 1964, Nil. (*L.C.C.*)

6. The secretary of the Woodland Hockey Club gives you the following summary of his cash book for the year ended 31st May, 1969:

	£		£
Balances at commencement of year:		Rent	234
At bank	63	Printing and stationery	18
In hand	10	Affiliation fees	12
Subscriptions:		Captain's and secretary' expenses	37
Supporters	150	Refreshments for visiting teams	61
Supporters 1969–70 season	20	Annual social	102
Fees per game	170	Equipment purchased	26
Annual social	134	Balances at close of year:	
		At bank	49
		In hand	8
	547		547

The secretary also gives you the following information:

	31st May 1968 £	*31st May* 1969 £
Amounts due to the club:		
Supporters' subscriptions	14	12
Fees per game	78	53
Re annual social	6	—
Amounts owing by the club:		
Rent	72	54
Printing	—	3
Secretary's expenses	4	8
Refreshments	13	12

On 31st May, 1968 the club's equipment appeared in the books at £150. It is desired that $12\frac{1}{2}$% be written off the book value of the equipment as it appears on 31st May, 1969.

You are required to:

(1) show your computation of the club's Accumulated Fund as on 31st May, 1968.
(2) Prepare the Income and Expenditure Account showing the result for the year ended 31st May, 1969, and the Balance Sheet as on that date.

7. Cane and Chalk carry on a boarding school for boys in partnership, the former's share of the profits being two-thirds and the latter's one-third.

The following trial balance was extracted from the books as on 31st July, 1961, the end of the scholastic year—

	Dr £	*Cr* £
Cash at bank	3,860	
Capital Accounts—		
Cane		2,100
Chalk		1,700

	Dr	Cr
	£	£
Drawings—		
Cane	1,200	
Chalk	750	
Fixtures and Fittings, as at 31st July, 1960	640	
Fees and additionals		11,500
Laundry	910	
Lighting and heating	520	
Purchases—		
Food	3,510	
School requisites	210	
Repairs	350	
Salaries and Wages	2,870	
Stationery and Printing	300	
Stocks on hand on 31st July, 1960—		
Food	110	
School requisites	40	
Fuel	30	
	15,300	15,300

Additional information is as follows—

(*a*) Accounts for fees and additionals are sent out at the beginning of each term and the fees, other than the additionals, are payable in advance. The additionals included are those for the previous term. All amounts due at 31st July, 1961, had been received except £113 and of this amount £40 was regarded as unobtainable and was to be written off. The additionals for the last term of the scholastic year amounted to £375.

(*b*) The premises are owned by Cane and he is to be credited with a rent of £460 for the use the school makes of them.

(*c*) Included in repairs is an amount of £20 solely in respect of repairs to the residential portion of the premises occupied by Cane.

(*d*) The stocks of food, fuel and school requisities on 31st July, 1961, were £140, £50 and £30, respectively.

(*e*) On 31st July, 1961, there was owing for food £149, for laundry £72 and for printing £10.

(*f*) Fixtures and fittings are to be depreciated by 10 per cent.

(*g*) Provision is to be made for commission payable to the senior master which is 5 per cent of the net. profit remaining after charging such commission.

Partners' capital accounts do not carry interest.

Prepare an Income and Expediture Account for the year ended 31st July, 1961, and draw up a Balance Sheet as at that date. (*A.C.C.A.*)

8. The Greybeards Society provides a programme of lectures for its members and publishes a quarterly magazine. The following is a summary of the receipts and payments of the society for the year 19.1.

RECEIPTS AND PAYMENTS ACCOUNT

		£		£
Balance at Bank, 1st Jan., 19.1 .		360	Rent	150
Annual Subscriptions—			Salaries	825
For 19.. . .	£17		Stationery & Postages .	215
„ 19.1 . .	1,224		New Typewriter . . .	75
„ 19.2 . .	149		Lecture Fees	135
		1,390	General Office Expenses .	215
Sales of magazine . . .		560	Magazine Expenses—	
Magazine Advertisements . .		640	Payments to printers . .	950
Income from Investments . .		150	Balance at Bank, 31st Dec., 19.1.	535
		3,100		3,100

You are given the following information—

(i) Amount owing to printers for magazine expenses—

	£
At 31st December, 19..	216
„ „ „ 19.1	304

(ii) The amount owing to the printers at 31st December, 19.1, included £63 for a quantity of paper, which was to be used for the first issue of the magazine in 19.2.

(iii) Amount owing to the society for advertisements in the magazine—

	£
At 31st December, 19..	78
„ „ „ 19.1	57

(iv) In December, 19.., £122 was received in respect of annual subscriptions for 19.1.

(v) £94 of the cost of stationery and postages was in connexion with the magazine.

(vi) Salaries outstanding at 31st December, 19.1 amounted to £65.

(vii) In addition to the bank balance and debtors for advertisements, the assets of the society at 31st December, 19.., were—

	£
Office furniture and equipment, at cost . . .	525
Investments, at cost.	2,800

You are required to prepare—

(*a*) a profit and loss account for the magazine for the year 19.1 (showing items relating to the magazine only), and

(*b*) a general income and expenditure account for 19.1 (including profit or loss on the magazine), and

(*c*) a balance sheet at 31st December, 19.1

NOTES. It is the practice of the society to ignore, for purposes of the annual accounts, subscriptions due, but not received, the current market value of the investments, and depreciation of furniture and equipment. Ignore taxation.

9. Misses Prim and Proper are in partnership as proprietors of a girls' boarding school, sharing profits: Miss Prim three-fifths, Miss Proper two-fifths.

The trial balance extracted from their books as on 31st July, 19.1, which coincided with the end of the summer term, was as follows—

	£	£
Capital—		
Miss Prim		1,500
Miss Proper		1,200
Fixtures and fittings, at cost	560	
,, ,, ,, provision for depreciation		360
Stocks at 31st July, 19. .—		
Food	80	
Fuel	40	
Purchases—		
Food	2,680	
Fuel	360	
Salaries and wages	2,400	
Repairs	240	
Laundry	720	
Stationery	180	
Drawings—		
Miss Prim	950	
Miss Proper	600	
Fees and extras		8,840
Balance at bank	3,090	
	11,900	11,900

You are given the following additional information—

(1) On 31st July, 19.1, stocks of food and fuel were £120 and £30 respectively.

(2) On 31st July, 19.1, amounts owing for food and laundry were £90 and £60 respectively.

(3) Fees, other than extras, are payable in advance, and accounts are sent out at the beginning of each term. Each account includes extras for the previous term. At 31st July, 19.1, all amounts due had been received with the exception of £84, of which £34 was to be written off. Extras for summer term, 19.1, were £300.

(4) No interest is to be credited on capital accounts.

(5) Miss Prim, who owns the premises, is to be credited with £400 for the use of these.

(6) Repairs include £40 for the purchase of a typewriter, which is to be capitalized under fixtures and fittings.

(7) Depreciation of fixtures and fittings is to be provided at the rate of 5 per cent per annum on cost at the end of the year.

(8) Miss Truelove, the senior mistress, is entitled to 5 per cent of the net profits after charging such commission.

You are required to prepare—

(*a*) an income and expenditure account for the year ended 31st July, 19.1, and
(*b*) a balance sheet as on that date. (*Chartered Accountants.*)

10. The following is the published account of a provincial charitable school—

BALANCE SHEET

For the Year Ending 31st December, 19..

		£			£
Government Grants—			Alterations & Repairs		76
Ordinary	£2,060		Salaries & Wages		754
Special	120		Washing & Cleaning		287
		2,180	Fuel, Lighting, & Heating		126
Councils' Grants—			Furniture		296
Ordinary	£1,026		Clothing		317
Outfits	55		Printing & Stationery		88
		1,081	Outfits		76
Subscriptions		126	Rates, Taxes & Insurance		85
Interest		19	Boys' Reward		20
Receipts from Band		72	Medical Expenses		43
Sundry Profits		126	Band Expenses		175
Profits of Farm		98	Loss on Workshops		26
Profits of Gardens		29	Travelling Expenses		63
Balance (Loss for year)		255	Cost of Entertainments		36
Rents of Land		156	Provisions		1,027
			Postages		36
					3,531
			Special Expenditure—		
			New Drainage	£475	
			Improvements to Premises	136	
					612
		4,142			4,142

What criticism have you to offer on the above?

11. From the following particulars of the "Lumley" Aviation Club prepare revenue account for the year ended 31st December.

***Receipts for the Year*. Subscriptions £1,272. Interest on investments £44. Proceeds of sale of journal £175.**

***Expenditure for the Year*. Salaries £327. Deputation expenses £40. Annual dinner and entertainment £72. Journal expenses £146. Postages £15. General expenses £10. Printing and stationery £37. Year book expenses £136. Rent, rates, and taxes £346. Fuel, lighting, and cleaning £56. Lecture expenses £75. Legal expenses £7. Auditors' fees £10.**

12. From the following particulars make up a receipts and payments account for the year ending 31st December—

	£
Cash in hand and at bank 1st January	274
Subscriptions for the year	45
Purchases of furniture during the year	25
Stationery and printing during year	14
Postages and petty expenses during year	10
Receipts from sale of tickets for annual dinner	66
Expenses of annual dinner and entertainment	47
Grants made for benevolent purposes	15
Engraving coat of arms	3
Interest on bank deposits	3

13. The following is a summary of the Cash Book of the Near Country Club.

Receipts	£	Payments	£
Balance at Bank 1st April, 1963	237	Staff Wages	669
Members Subscriptions .	1,786	Bar supplies	2,520
Entrance Fees . . .	160	Rent for $1\frac{1}{2}$ years to 30th June, 1964	390
Bar Takings	2,840	Rates	110
Competition Receipts .	382	Secretary's Salary . . .	156
Loan from Treasurer . .	4	Lighting, Heating and Cleaning.	385
		Competition Prizes . . .	185
		Printing, Postages and Sundries.	300
		Deposited with Building Society	400
		Balance at Bank 31st March, 1964	294
	5,409		5,409

The assets of the club on 1st April, 1963, were furniture and equipment £2,400, bar stocks £130, and prizes in hand £40; £260 was owing for bar supplies.

On 31st March, 1964, the bar stocks were £150, prizes £25 and £280 was owing for bar supplies.

It appeared from the register of members that subscriptions unpaid at 31st March, 1964, totalled £50.

Subscriptions received during the year under review included £35 in respect of the previous year and £20 in respect of the year beginning 1st April, 1964.

The secretary is to be allowed £25 per annum for the use of his own motor car in connexion with the club's affairs.

Interest on the Building Society Deposit for the year to 31st March, 1964, was received on 1st April, 1964, amounting to £12.

It was agreed that the steward of the club should receive a bonus of 5 per cent of bar takings in excess of an average of £200 per month for the year to 31st March, 1964.

Write off depreciation on furniture and equipment at 10 per cent per annum.

Prepare an account showing the profit on the bar, an Income and Expenditure Account for the year and a Balance Sheet as at 31st March, 1964.

(A.C.C.A.)

14. Would you consider the following chargeable to capital expenditure or revenue? Give reasons for your answers.

(*a*) Premium given for a lease.
(*b*) Cost attending the obtaining of a mortgage.
(*c*) Commission on issue of debenture bonds.
(*d*) Commission on issue of debenture stock.
(*e*) Accrued dividends or interest included in the cost price of an investment.

15. The Balance Sheet of The Artisan Golf Club as on 31st December, 1963 was as follows—

	£	£		£	£
Current Liabilities—			**Fixed Assets—**		
Purchases—			Plant and Tools at valuations		75
Bar	147		Furniture and Fittings at cost less depreciation		840
Catering	45		**Current Assets—**		
Light and Heat	88		Stock on hand—		
Rent	280		Bar	410	
Excise Duty	53		Catering	25	
Subscriptions in advance	206		Debtors for catering	12	
		819	Subscriptions in arrear	43	
Accumulated Fund		1,272	Rates and Insurance in advance	181	
			Cash at bank	505	
					1,176
		2,091			2,091

A summary of the cash book for the year 1964 is as follows—

	£	£		£	£
Balance at bank		505	Purchases—		
Takings—			Bar	2,720	
Bar	3,680		Catering	974	
Catering	982				3,694
		4,662	Wages and Salaries—		
Subscriptions		2,276	House	826	
Locker rents		64	Course	1,435	
Green fees		373			2,261
			Rent, Rates and Insurance		852
			Light and Heat		206
			Printing and Stationery		59
			Telephone and Postages		81
			Course maintenance		238
			General house expenses		94
			Excise Duty		53
			Balance at bank		342
		7,880			7,880

On 31st December, 1964—

The club was owing—

Bar Purchases £165, Catering purchases £32, Rent £280, Light and Heat £74 and Excise Duty £60.

Subscriptions paid in advance amounted to £220.

Rates and insurance paid in advance amounted to £198.

Members were owing—

Catering accounts £16, Subscriptions £40.

Stocks on hand were—Bar £442, Catering £34.

10 per cent is to be written off the book value of the furniture and fittings.

Prepare—

1. Income and Expenditure Account for the year ended 31st December, 1964; and
2. Balance Sheet as on that date.

CHAPTER 11

INCOMPLETE RECORDS

Ah, take the Cash, and let the Credit go,
Nor heed the rumble of a distant Drum!

EDWARD FITZGERALD—*The Rubáiyát of Omar Khayyám*

THE object of this chapter is to consider the problems of preparing an income statement and Balance Sheet in circumstances when a business has not kept complete records leading to a Trial Balance, and what must be done to carry out the conversion to double entry.

One can develop a very good mental picture of the state of affairs existing when books are kept in a haphazard way, by visualizing the place where they are to be found, and the outlook of the proprietor. In all probability it will be a small local shopkeeper, wholesaler or manufacturer in a very small way, with premises in keeping, and a connexion which just gives him a living, year in and year out.

In support of the fact that such exist, one has only to take note of the advertisements for audit clerks with experience in the preparation of accounts from *incomplete records*.

The matters of outstanding importance to the proprietor of a business of this type are three in number—

1. What money has he in the bank?
2. How much money is owing to him and by whom?
3. What does he owe for goods purchased on credit, and the important items of expenditure such as rent, rates, and wages?

It follows that he will keep only such books as are necessary to show this, and in all probability they will consist of a cash book and ledger.

The cash book may or may not be written up correctly, as he can rely on his pass book for the figure he wants, but the ledger will generally have accounts opened for every person to whom goods are sold on credit, and each account will be debited, direct, without the intervention of a book of original entry. It is unlikely that creditors' accounts will be opened, as he will keep his "bills" on a clip, and remove them as paid. In the case of the debtors, he will not feel the need for posting cash received, as he will open the ledger and write the word *paid* each time.

The shortcomings of this type of account keeping are that no records will appear of—

1. Capital.
2. Creditors.
3. Assets (other than debtors).
4. Expenses.
5. Total sales and purchases.

SINGLE ENTRY

The system described is often called the single entry system but technically this is a misnomer, since its vital feature is its incomplete classification and recording. Some single entry systems based, for instance, on punched cards, give complete records by multiple classification. (See p. 0121.)

Preparation of a Statement of Affairs. What is involved in the task of finding results in the form of profit or loss from such incomplete figures?

The basic approach is related to the comparison of the opening and closing Balance Sheet position.

The difference between assets and liabilities on the Balance Sheet is the capital or net worth, and subject to any adjustments required for drawings, or the introduction of fresh money, a change of capital from one period to another will represent the profit or the loss. The first objective is, therefore, to build up a Statement of Affairs with the assistance of the proprietor. This statement must collect all the missing items, as listed above, which affect the opening and final position.

The valuation of premises should create little difficulty and any plant or machinery, fixtures or fittings can be calculated on the original cost which the owner will probably know, or he must be asked either to have them valued or to estimate the value to the best of his ability. Stock must be taken, the debtors will appear in the ledger, and the creditors can be ascertained from the file or clip of unpaid invoices and statements. To obtain the cash balance, the cash book will have to be written up with the aid of the pass book and cheque book.

Furnished with this information, and an estimate of the amount of the proprietor's capital at the commencement of the period under consideration, a statement can be built up, and the profit or loss ascertained.

From the following examples it will be seen that the steps involved in answering such a question are as follows—

1. Find the difference between the opening and closing capitals, which gives apparent profit.
2. Adjust this apparent profit by adding withdrawals or amount by which fixed assets have been appreciated, and deducting depreciation to

be written off, bad debts provisions or increases of capital by the introduction of further cash.

3. Draft the new statement of affairs.

As an example, the following is an adaptation of a single-entry question set in an Intermediate Paper of the Royal Society of Arts—

Example 1

A manufacturer, Philip Morgan, kept an incomplete set of records. The position of the business at the 31st December, 19.., revealed the following—

	£
Freehold premises	1,000
Plant and machinery	600
Stock-in-trade	1,300
Sundry debtors	1,750
Cash at bank	300
Sundry creditors	1,875

At 1st January, 19.., his capital was £5,500. Prepare a statement of affairs showing his position at 31st December, 19.., and ascertain his profit or loss for the year.

Solution 1

STATEMENT OF PROFIT AND LOSS

For the Year Ended 31st December, 19..

19..		£	19..		£
Dec 31	Sundry Liabilities	1,875	Dec 31	Sundry Assets	4,950
	Capital at this date c/d	3,075			
		4,950			4,950
19..			19..		
Jan 1	Capital at commencement	5,500	Dec 31	Capital b/d	3,075
				Loss for year	2,425
		5,500			5,500

STATEMENT OF AFFAIRS AS AT 31ST DECEMBER, 19..

Liabilities		£	*Assets*	£
Capital—			Freehold Premises	1,000
Balance at 1st January	£5,500		Plant & Machinery	600
Less Loss for year	2,425		Stock	1,300
		3,075	Sundry Debtors	1,750
Sundry Creditors		1,875	Cash at Bank	300
		4,950		4,950

No cognizance has been taken of the fact that the owner must have drawn out money for his private use, and in many cases used some of his stock in his household. Depreciation of fixed assets should also be allowed for.

The necessary adjustments must be made in the statement of profit and loss, and, of course, on the balance sheet.

A further example with adjustments of this nature should make the position clear.

Example 2

The following statement of affairs has been drawn up to give the financial position, as on 31st March, 19.1, of A. Brown, who keeps an incomplete set of records.

STATEMENT OF AFFAIRS AS AT 31ST MARCH, 19.1

Liabilities	£	*Assets*	£
Capital	6,192	Fixtures	250
Creditors	742	Stock	2,305
		Debtors	4,176
		Cash	203
	6,934		6,934

His capital at 31st March, 19.., was £5,659.

Brown transferred £50 a month from his business banking account to his private banking account, by way of drawings, and has taken £25 worth of stock for private use. His private car was sold for £180, and the proceeds paid into the business. He has agreed that his fixtures should be written down by £50.

Calculate Brown's profit for the year, and re-draft the Statement of Affairs as at 31st March, 19.1.

Solution 2

STATEMENT OF PROFIT AND LOSS

For the Year Ended 31st March, 19.1

	£		£
Creditors	742	Sundry Assets at 31st March, 19.1	6,934
Capital at 31st March, 19..	5,659		
Balance c/d	533		
	6,934		6,934
Sale of private car	180	Balance b/d	533
Depreciation of Fixtures	50	Drawings	600
Net Profit	928	Goods withdrawn	25
	1,158		1,158

STATEMENT OF AFFAIRS, AS AT 31ST MARCH, 19.1

Liabilities		£	*Assets*		£
Capital—			Fixtures at 31st March, 19..	£250	
Balance at 31st March, 19..	£5,659		*Less* Depreciation	50	200
Add New Capital	180				
Net Profits for year	928		Stock		2,305
	6,767		Sundry Debtors		4,176
Less Drawings	625		Cash		203
		6,142			
Sundry Creditors		742			
		6,884			6,884

PREPARATION OF FINAL ACCOUNTS FROM INCOMPLETE RECORDS

Many examination questions require the preparation of trading account, profit and loss account, and balance sheet from incomplete records, and this may involve the calculation of some figures, which usually include the sales and purchases. In these cases, the information given will be for cash received or paid, opening and closing value of debtors or creditors. The sales figure is calculated as follows—

	£
Cash received from debtors	15,000
Less opening value of debtors	2,000
Cash received for sales in current period	13,000
Add closing value of debtors	1,500
VALUE OF SALES IN THE PERIOD	14,500

The purchases may be calculated in the same way from the cash paid and the opening and closing values of creditors. In other cases, no record of takings may be kept, and the amount must be calculated from an assumed rate of gross profit. The first step is to calculate cost of goods sold (see p. 0706–7) and then add the assumed rate of profit.

Example 3

If the rate of gross profit is 25 per cent on cost, cash paid for goods in the year £10,000, opening creditors £2,000, closing creditors £2,500, opening stock £3,250, closing stock £2,750, the calculation is as follows—

	£
Cash paid to creditors	10,000
Less opening value of creditors	2,000
	8,000
Add closing value of creditors	2,500
Purchases	10,500
Add opening stock	3,250
	13,750
Less closing stock	2,750
Cost of goods sold	11,000
Add 25% on cost (= 20% on S.P.)	2,750
TAKINGS (SALES)	13,750

The next problem is taken from a London Chamber of Commerce examination paper.

Example 4

A retail tobacconist and confectioner pays into his Bank Account the amount of his cash takings, after retaining £10 per week for personal use and after payment of wages and expenses, which for the year to 31st March, 1962, were as follows—

	£
Wages of Staff	1,200
Goods	220
Cleaning	75
Carriage	35
Incidentals	20

The transactions in his Bank Account during the year were—

	£
Balance, 1st April, 1961	2,000
Lodgements—	
From Shop Takings (Cash)	30,100
Wholesale Accounts—Sales (Cheques)	4,800
Defence Bond Interest	30
	36,930

Payments—

	£
Goods	30,830
Rent	400
Rates of Shop	345
Rates of Private House	55
Lighting and Heating—Shop	200
House	20
Telephone, Stationery and Advertising	150
Shop Incidentals	70
Insurance, Fire, Plate Glass, etc.	60
Insurances, Life and Endowment	30
Repairs	150
New Fixtures	600
Accountancy Charges	40
Income Tax, Schedule D	900
Personal Accounts—School Fees, etc.	180
Balance, 31st March, 1962	2,900
	36,930

Debtors, Creditors and Stocks were—

	1st April, 1961 £	31st March, 1962 £
Creditors—Goods Purchased	2,900	3,195
Expenses—Rent	80	
Electric Light	25	30
Telephone, Stationery, etc.	45	65
Accountancy	40	40
Debtors—Wholesale Accounts	490	430
Stocks	2,050	1,875

Prepare a Trading and Profit and Loss Account for the year to the 31st March, 1962, and Balance Sheet as at that date.

Solution

The Sales figure can be calculated as—

		£
Lodgements		
Shop takings		30,100
Add back personal drawings		520
Add back expenses paid		1,550
Cash sales		32,170
Wholesale accounts	4,800	
Less opening debtors	490	
	4,310	
Add closing debtors	430	
Sales on credit		4,740
Total Sales		36,910

Working on similar lines, the Purchases are—

	£
Payments for goods	30,830
Less opening creditors	2,900
	27,930
Add closing creditors	3,195
	31,125
Add cash payments	220
Total Purchases	31,345

Although it may be assumed that the trader is responsible for internal repairs (and decorations) of the rented shop, it is assumed that this substantial expense refers to his own house. If this is not the case, then that proportion of expense which applies to the shop should be charged against the business profit.

The calculation of the other expenses payable is—

Rent

	£
Paid	400
Deduct amount due on 1st April, 1961	80
	320
Add Rates of shop	345
	665

Lighting and heating

		£
Paid		200
Less owing on 1st April, 1961	25	
Add owing on 31st March, 1962	30	5
		205

Telephone, etc.

		£
Paid		150
Less owing on 1st April, 1961	45	
Add owing on 31st March, 1962	65	
	—	20
		170

The personal expenses paid by the firm are chargeable to the proprietor as drawings. They are not a business expense. The items involved are—

	£
Personal drawings	520
Rates of private house	55
Lighting and heating house	20
Repairs	150
Life and Endowment insurances	30
Income tax—Schedule D	900
Personal accounts	180
	1,855
Less Defence Bond interest	30
	1,825

Using the information on assets and liabilities at the opening and closing dates, it is possible to draw up a statement of the capital and the change which has occurred in it.

		1st April, 1961		31st March, 1962
Capital in business				
Assets		£		£
Cash in bank		2,000		2,900
New fixtures				540
Debtors		490		430
Stocks		2,050		1,875
		4,540		5,745
Liabilities	£	£	£	
Trade Creditors		2,900	3,195	
Expense				
Rent	80		30	
Electricity	25		65	
Telephone, etc.	45			
Accountant	40	190 / 3,090	40	3,330
Capital fund (in business)		1,450		2,415

A Trading, Profit and Loss Account for the year and the Balance Sheet on 31st March, can then be prepared, and the profit shown should, of course, confirm the above calculation.

A RETAIL TOBACCONIST AND CONFECTIONER

Trading and Profit and Loss Account for the Year Ended 31st March, 1962

	£		£
Opening stocks	2,050	Sales	36,910
Purchases	31,345		
Add Carriage	35		
	33,430		
Less Closing stocks	1,875		
	31,555		
Wages of staff	1,200		
Gross profit	4,155		
	36,910		36,910
Cleaning	75	Gross profit	4,155
Incidentals	90		
Rent	665		
Lighting and Heating	205		
Telephone, etc.	170		
Insurances	60		
Accountancy charges	40		
Depreciation on fixtures 10%	60		
Net profit on trading	2,790		
	4,155		4,155

Balance Sheet on 31st March, 1962

	£	£		£	£
Capital on 1st April, 1961	1,450		*Fixed assets—*		
Add Profit for year	2,790		Fixtures at cost	600	
	4,240		*Less* Depreciation	60	
Less Drawings	1,825				540
			Current assets—		
			Stock		1,875
Capital on 31st March, 1962		2,415	Debtors		430
Current liabilities—			Cash at Bank		2,900
Trade creditors		3,195			
Expense creditors		135			
		5,745			5,745

Another problem which may arise is that the takings shown by the cash book cannot be reconciled with takings calculated as above. The proprietor may agree to regard this discrepancy as drawings.

Example 5

In Example 3 above, the cash book showed lodgements of £12,100, and the proprietor stated that business expenses amounting to £450 had been paid but not shown in the cash book; then drawings would be £1,200 (£12,100 + £450 = £12,550, deducted from £13,750).

CONVERSION TO DOUBLE ENTRY

The amount of work to be done to convert to double entry a set of books which are in an incomplete state will differ with almost every set of books.

Perhaps it is best to take an extreme case. If the books being dealt with are those of a trader who has made no attempt at all at even partial double entry, and that we are supplied with a cash book more or less correctly written up but not posted, a ledger containing accounts of all debtors, entered correctly on the debit side as regards sales, and on the credit side in respect of returns, but with no cash posting. Other than that, the invoices for purchases and expenses have been dealt with on a cash basis, so that there is no bought ledger. The objective is to complete the double entries and draw up a trial balance. If a schedule of the missing figures is prepared the task should be somewhat simplified.

The schedule would read somewhat as follows—

1. Cash book not balanced or agreed with the pass book.
2. Cash book not posted.
3. Total sales and returns not entered.
4. No bought ledger in use, but invoices and receipts available.
5. Total purchases and returns not entered.
6. No stock account in the ledger.
7. No assets in the ledger.
8. No capital or drawings accounts opened.
9. No expense accounts.

The work will proceed along these lines—

Cash Book. From the pass book, paying-in book counterfoils, and cheque counterfoils, enter up the cash book and prepare a reconciliation statement. Post all items from the cash book. This will provide entries for the sales account as far as cash sales are concerned, close all debtors accounts in so far as they are paid, and supply the debit entries in the ledger for expenses, drawings, and payments to creditors for purchases.

Sales Ledger. The cash having been posted, the debit and credit entries for sales and returns can be extracted on to analysis paper, or into a day book to supply the total figures for the impersonal accounts. At the same time the unpaid items can be noted down for the sundry debtors figure. Any sales not entered will have to be dealt with and added to the list of debtors.

Bought Ledger. Although it may be possible to avoid entering the invoices or the cash by marking off the invoices and receipts to the cash book and entering only those unpaid, the work will be more satisfactory if all items are entered and the totals for the impersonal accounts and sundry creditors obtained by extraction in the same manner as was done with the sales ledger.

Asset Accounts. Accounts for premises (if owned), plant and machinery, fixtures and fittings, vehicles owned, and stock, must be opened and the requisite figures obtained from the proprietor, or, if recently acquired, from the invoices. As an alternative, many of the figures might be obtained by application to the suppliers, and the question of depreciation must then be dealt with.

In the case of the opening stock, the proprietor's estimates will have to be accepted, whilst an actual stock-taking will provide the figure for the balance sheet.

Liabilities. The sundry creditors having been obtained, the owner of the business must supply any information as to loans, whilst the accrued items can be calculated from the impersonal accounts, which are now in the ledger as the result of posting the cash book.

Trial Balance. It should be possible to prepare a trial balance at this point, and although one cannot guarantee its accuracy, the difference will be entered as capital, and an account opened accordingly in the ledger.

In many cases much of this work will not be necessary, but the programme has been planned on the assumption that the very minimum amount of book-keeping is being done in the books under consideration.

Modifications in this routine must be made in the light of the missing information in the particular set of books to be converted.

QUESTIONS

1. State briefly the disadvantages of incomplete methods of bookkeeping.
2. Describe the steps you would take in order to prepare a trading account, profit and loss account, and balance sheet from an incomplete set of records. *(London Chamber of Commerce.)*
3. Describe briefly how you would convert an incomplete set of records to the double-entry system. *(R.S.A.)*
4. In what kind of business would you expect to find incomplete records?
5. Should all businesses maintain accounting records on double-entry lines or is there sometimes a case for incomplete records?

EXERCISE 11

1. From the following particulars, prepare a trading and profit and loss account for the year ended 31st March, 19.1, and a balance sheet as at that date.

BALANCE SHEET AS AT 31ST MARCH, 19..

	£			£
Capital	200,000	Buildings		100,000
Loan	50,000	Plant & Machinery		68,250
Creditors	16,262	Stock		67,750
Bank Overdraft	2,167	Debtors	£10,700	
		Less Provision for for Bad Debts	1,070	
				9,630
		Profit & Loss A/c		22,799
	268,429			268,429

CASH SUMMARY FOR YEAR ENDED 31ST MARCH, 19.1

	£		£
Cash Sales	10,626	Bank Overdraft b/f.	2,167
Debtors	121,004	Creditors	92,636
		Wages	10,607
		Trade Expenses	15,206
		Loan Interest	2,100
		Bank Balance c/f	8,914
	131,630		131,630

The books disclose the following totals—

Discounts allowed for the year, £3,202; discounts received, £2,006; purchases, £95,585; sales, £124,756.

Stock at 31st March, 19.1, stood at £70,100; debtors at £11,250; and creditors at £17,205.

Depreciation is to be written off plant and machinery at 10 per cent and a provision of 10 per cent of debtors outstanding is to be kept against bad debts. Insurance premiums of £62 have been paid in advance and included in trade expenses.

(*Chartered Institute of Secretaries* (*adapted*).)

2. A solicitor set up in practice on 1st January, 19... His cash receipts from clients during 19.. amounted to £619 and during 19.1 to £1,042, his expenses in the respective years being £196 and £248.

Fees owing to him from clients unpaid at the end of 19.. amounted to £173 and at the end of 19.1 to £281.

Ascertain his net earnings for each year.

3. Frost and Snow are in partnership, and share profits and losses in the proportions of 3 and 2. They keep incomplete records. On 31st December,19.., a statement of affairs was prepared and showed the following position—

Liabilities	£	*Assets*	£
Capital—		Plant & Machinery	5,400
Frost	10,000	Stock	4,987
Snow	4,000	Sundry Debtors	6,723
Loan—Frost	2,000	Cash at Bank	1,766
Sundry Creditors	2,876		
	18,876		18,876

On 31st December, 19.1, their assets and liabilities were—

	£
Sundry debtors	7,367
„ creditors	3,213
Plant and machinery	5,400
„ „ „ additions	2,000
Bills receivable	1,000
Stock	4,813
Cash at bank	1,399

You are required to ascertain the amount of the firm's profit or loss for the year ended 31st December, 19.1, and to prepare a statement of affairs as at that date after taking into consideration the following—

(*a*) Depreciation on plant and machinery, including additions, is to be provided at the rate of 9 per cent per annum.

(*b*) On 1st October, 19.1, Frost increased his loan by £2,000 in order to pay for additional machinery, the installation of which had been completed on the previous day.

(*c*) Interest on the loan is to be allowed at 5 per cent per annum.

(*d*) During the year Frost and Snow drew £1,243 and £1,030 respectively.

(*R.S.A.* (*adapted*).)

4. Edge and Jones, trading in partnership in a small retail business, and sharing profits in the ratio of three to two, keep their books by "single entry." The following statement of affairs shows their position at 31st March, 19..—

	£		£
Capital Accounts—		Furniture & Fittings	920
Edge	3,519	Motor Van	350
Jones	1,904	Stock	3,874
Creditors	271	Debtors	72
		Bank & Cash	478
	5,694		5,694

You ascertain that—

(*a*) On 31st March, 19.1, the cash and bank balances amounted to £249, debtors to £88, and creditors to £299, while the stock was valued at £3,985.

(*b*) During the year the motor van had been sold for £390 and replaced by a new one costing £740. The partners wish £150 to be written off the new van for depreciation and £40 off the furniture and fittings.

(*c*) Edge's cash drawings during the year amounted to £1,230 and he had taken for personal use goods valued at £40, while Jones had drawn £680 in cash and goods valued at £35.

Ascertain the net profit for the year ended 31st March, 19.1, and the balances of the partners' capital accounts.

(*R.S.A.*)

5. A keeps incomplete records. On 1st January his capital was £6,900. An analysis of his cash book for the year gives the following particulars—

Debit Side	£
Received from Sundry Debtors	6,000
Paid in on Capital A/c	500

CREDIT SIDE	£
Due to bank, 1st January	740
Payments to sundry creditors	2,500
General expenses of business	1,000
Wages	1,550
Drawings	300
Balance at bank, 31st December	400
„ in hand	10

Debtors at 1st January were	£5,300,	and at 31st December were	£8,800
Creditors „ „ „	£1,500	„ „ „	£1,950
Stocks „ „ „	£1,700	„ „ „	£1,900
Plant and machinery „	£2,000	„ „ „	£2,000
Furniture and fittings „	£140	„ „ „	£140

From the above material prepare a profit and loss account for the year ended 31st December, and a balance sheet at that date, after providing 5 per cent interest on capital (ignoring payments in and drawings), 10 per cent depreciation on plant, 5 per cent depreciation on furniture, and a provision of 5 per cent on sundry debtors.

(*Chartered Accountants.*)

6. David Fisher carries on a grocery business and does not keep his books on a double-entry basis. The following particulars have been extracted from his books—

	1st July, 19..	30th June, 19.1
	£	£
Plant and machinery	900	900
Stock	400	350
Sundry debtors	100	150
„ creditors	250	200
Cash in hand	8	6
„ at bank	225	250

The following transactions took place during the year ended the 30th June, 19.1—

	£
Wages	300
Sundry expenses	125
Printing, stationery, and advertising	56
Rent and rates	125
Heating and lighting	39
Cash received from customers	4,125
„ paid for purchases	3,217
„ withdrawn from business for own use	156
Carriage	84
Purchases returns	50

During the year Fisher had taken goods from his business for his own consumption which amounted to 75p per week, and had not paid any money into the business for them.

Prepare balance sheet as at the 1st July, 19.., and trading and profit and loss account for the year ended 30th June, 19.1, and balance sheet at 30th June, 19.1.

(*Corporation of Certified Secretaries.*)

7. A H has a building and house-repair business. On 30th September, 1963, his balance sheet was—

	£		£ Cost	£ Depreciation	£
Proprietor's capital	4,000	Plant	1,102	292	810
Loan account	1,000	Motor vehicles	700	120	580
Trade creditors	340				
			1,802	412	1,390
		Work in progress		3,600	
		Less deposits		460	
					3,140
		Stock			620
		Debtors			170
		Cash			20
	5,340				5,340

During the winter of 1963, his wife, who acted as his bookkeeper, died, and since then the books of account have not been properly kept.

At 30th September, 1966, A H is able to make the following estimate of his financial position—

	£
Plant (at cost less depreciation)	1,750
Motor vehicles (at cost less depreciation)	600
Work in progress	5,150
Deposits	710
Stock	1,455
Debtors	205
Cash	1,085
Trade creditors	508

During the period since the last balance sheet, these additional events have occurred—

(1) A H has withdrawn £15 in cash each week.

(2) A cement-mixer, with a book-value of £60 at 30th September, 1965, was traded in for £10 on 1st October, 1965, for another costing £250; the balance of the purchase price was covered by a hire-purchase transaction involving 24 monthly payments of £12 commencing 1st November, 1965. All instalments have been paid as they became due on the first day of each month.

(3) The loan account shown on 30th September, 1963 has been paid off.

(4) A fire destroyed some work in progress which was still at the risk of the builder; this was not adequately covered by insurance, and the resultant loss was estimated to have been £400.

(5) Early in 1964 A H sold his house and furniture for £6,000 and went to live with his married daughter. The money received has been merged into the business funds.

(6) During the period under consideration, A H has paid three income tax assessments from the firm's bank account, amounting in all to £1,070.

You are required to calculate as accurately as possible the trading profit of the business of A H for the period from 1st October, 1963 to 30th September, 1966, clearly distinguishing the normal trading profit from the exceptional or non-trading items.

(*C.M.A.*)

8. V. Coy began in business as a retail pharmacist on 1st January, 1962. He has not kept a full set of books but most of his sales have been for cash and a ledger kept for all sales on credit, but no sales day book.

In addition to withdrawing £8 each week for himself, he has also made the following small payments in cash before paying his takings into the bank.

	£
Salaries and National Insurance (as Employer)	214
Petty Expenses	40
Sundry Purchases for resale	20

From a summary of the banking account you obtain the following information—

Lodgements—

Transfer from Deposit Account	£
V. Coy as Capital	1,500
Cash sales after deducting cash payments	7,000
Receipts from Ledger Account customers	1,466

Payments by Cheque—	£
Fixtures and Fittings	323
Solicitor's Costs *re* Lease	52
Rent, Rates and Insurance	220
Assistants' Salaries	660
Purchases for resale	7,420
Electricity	42
Personal Expenses	75
Stationery and Advertising	120

You further find that at 31st December, 1962—

	£
1. Customers debts were	206
2. V. Coy's liabilities were—	
Goods for resale	440
Lighting and Heating	11
3. Rates and Insurance had been paid in advance	14

Stock had been valued at 31st December, 1962, in the sum of £800 and V. Coy informed you that goods costing £78 had been taken by him from stock for his own use.

You are required to construct cash and bank accounts and to prepare a Trading and Profit and Loss Account for the year together with the Balance Sheet as at 31st December, 1962. (*A.C.C.A.*)

9. **A retail business, left to M. Oliver by his uncle, was valued for estate duty purposes at £1,084 comprised as to £520 for the fixtures and goodwill, £160 for the stock and £404 cash at bank.**

He decided to carry on the business and for that purpose rented a shop with rooms over in which he lived. He commenced trading on 1st November, 1961, after having the cash at bank transferred into an account in his own name.

He kept a record of the amounts owing to him in a note book and this was the only record he kept. All cash payments and his personal drawings were taken from the till and the cash remaining was paid into the bank at irregular intervals. He settled all accounts for purchases of goods by cheque.

An analysis of his bank account for the year ended 31st October, 1962, is as follows—

Banking—	£	Cheques drawn—	£
Proceeds of National Savings Certificates cashed	130	Purchases of goods	2,710
Cheques received for sales on credit	320	Cash register	60
Other lodgements	2,642	House furniture	147
		Rent, 11 months to 30th September, 1962	220
		Lighting and Heating	54
		Fire insurance premium, cover for year to 31st December, 1962	36

Cash payments made from the till were estimated to be per week—wages £7, shop expenses £4 and personal drawings £8.

On 31st October, 1962, Stock on hand at cost was £245, debtors were £92, the amount owing to suppliers was £335 and the cash in hand was £14. There was also owing £12 for lighting and heating.

It can be assumed that as regards rent, lighting and heating and fire insurance the proportion applicable to the shop was two-thirds and to the house portion of the premises one-third.

From the above information prepare a Trading and Profit and Loss Account for the year ended 31st October, 1962, and a Balance Sheet as on that date.

(A.C.C.A.)

10. A. Naylor is a retail ironmonger and does not keep a complete set of accounting records. A summary of his Banking Account and Cash Book for the year to 31st March, 1962 was as follows—

Receipts	*Cash* £	*Bank* £
Balance in hand 1st April, 1961	15	
Balance at Bank 1st April, 1961		2,103
Cash Sales		3,290
Credit Sales		2,960
Rent of room sublet	52	
Proceeds of Sale of Old Fixtures (written down value £30)	10	
Additional capital introduced		150
Income Tax Schedule "D" refunded		25
Cash from Bank	1,218	
	1,295	8,528

Payments	£	£
Purchases for resale		4,220
General Expenses	60	200
Rents and Rates		295
Wages	560	
Personal Drawings	650	
Income Tax Schedule "D" 1961/62		300
Cost of new showcases		160
Cash from Bank		1,218
Balance at Bank 31st March, 1962		2,135
Balance in hand 31st March, 1962	25	
	1,295	8,528

Inspection of the Credit Sales Invoice Books showed that customers owed £1,250 on 1st April, 1961 and £1,560 on 31st March, 1962 of which £58 and £68 respectively were expected to be bad debts.

Examination of the paid invoices for purchases disclosed creditors of £950 at 1st April, 1961 and £1,060 at 31st March, 1962.

Naylor estimates that he had taken goods from stock for his own domestic use costing £26 during the year, and had not paid for them.

At the beginning of the year the Shop Fixtures and Fittings on which depreciation is charged at 5 per cent per annum, stood at £570.

Stock was valued at £950 on 1st April, 1961 and £900 on 31st March, 1962.

You are required to prepare a Trading and Profit and Loss Account for the year to 31st March, 1962 and a Balance Sheet as at that date, together with a Statement of Capital at 1st April, 1961. *(A.C.C.A.)*

11. On 1st January, 19.., the total of the debtors appearing in a trader's sales ledger was £1,537. During the year 19.. the total cash received in respect of cash and credit sales was £5,731, discount allowed amounted to £218 and accounts amounting to £37 were written off as bad. The total of the debtors on 31st December 19.., was £1,732.

Prepare a statement showing the amount of the net sales for the year. *(R.S.A.)*

12. On 1st January, 1965 Jack won £6,000 and decided to buy a freehold garage with car hire business. The consideration was £6,500 which included in addition to legal costs of £174, fittings and equipment £190, three private cars valued at £1,380, debtors £90, petrol and spares £298, licences and insurances pre-paid £62, less electricity due £28. The balance of £500 was loaned to Jack by his wife.

Only memorandum records are kept and the following facts are ascertained—

(1) Jack buys from a dealer for his personal use a car costing £520, and uses petrol costing £40.

(2) One of the cars originally valued at £350 was sold for £375 and a new car purchased for £580.

(3) Personal drawings amounted to £420.

(4) Jack has repaid £300 to his wife.

(5) Additional equipment was purchased costing £165.

(6) Of debtors taken over, only £60 proved to be collectable and further bad debts of £45 were incurred and written off during the year.

(7) During the year Jack started a travel agency and he had collected deposits in respect of future bookings amounting to £150 of which £130 had been forwarded to his principals.

At the end of the year cash in hand was £267, creditors for spares and petrol £66, prepayments £78, petrol and spares £193, debtors £57. Depreciation at the rate of 20 per cent is to be provided on all vehicles in use at the end of the year, and at the rate of 15 per cent on fittings and equipment.

You are to prepare—

(*a*) a calculation of trading results for the year;

(*b*) a balance sheet of the business as at 31st December, 1965. *(C.M.A.)*

13. D. Burton started a retail business on 1st April, 19... The only records he kept consisted of entries in a rough diary. Out of the takings he paid the wages of an assistant, sundry cash disbursements, and his own drawings. After retaining £4 as a float he paid the remainder of the takings into the bank each week. All sales were made for cash and D. Burton fixed his selling prices by adding 20 per cent to the cost. The gross takings amounted to £5,124.

During the year to 31st March, 19.1, the payments out of takings were £244 for assistant's wages and £50 for sundry trade disbursements. The remainder of the takings unbanked, apart from the float, represented D. Burton's own drawings.

After the usual reconciliation was made, a summary of his bank account for the year was as follows—

	£
Lodgements—	
Cash paid in by way of capital	250
Takings paid in	4,466
Loan from a brother free of interest	200

	£
Cheques drawn, etc.—	
Fixtures and fittings	230
Purchases	4,079
Rent and rates	70
Insurance	20
Lighting and heating	12
Bank charges	10

At 31st March, 19.1—

(*a*) There were creditors for goods £356 and for lighting and heating £6.

(*b*) Rent had been paid in advance to the extent of £5.

(*c*) The value of stock on hand was £165.

D. Burton requests you to depreciate fixtures and fittings by 10 per cent.

From the above particulars prepare a trading and profit and loss account for the year ended 31st March, 19.1, and draw up a balance sheet as on that date. (*R.S.A.*)

14. P. Roff opened a small retail shop on 1st April, 19... Sales were made only for cash and, after certain outgoings had been paid out of the till and a cash float of £5 retained, the remaining cash was paid into the bank weekly. Suppliers' accounts were settled by cheque.

An analysis of his bank statements for the year ended 31st March, 19.1, is as follows—

	£
Bankings—	
Paid in to commence business	1,000
Total of weekly lodgements	4,020
	5,020

	£
Cheques drawn, etc—	
Fixtures, fittings, etc	500
Purchases	3,736
Rent, rates, postage, and insurance	235
Electricity and gas	23
Paper bags, etc.	18
Bank charges	5
Balance at 31st March, 19.1	503
	5,020

The outgoings paid out of the till totalled £250 for the year, made up of wages £200, stationery £12, sundry trade expenses £38. Since he kept no record of takings, Roff agrees that the preparation of the accounts can be based on the assumption that the rate of gross profit is 25 per cent of the sale price of goods sold. Roff further agrees that the remainder of the estimated takings not otherwise accounted for can be taken as being personal drawings.

On 31st March, 19.1, the value of goods on hand on a cost basis was £300 and the stock of paper bags, etc., was valued at £5. The outstanding liabilities were: suppliers £239, electricity £10, incidentals £5, and paper bags £2. Rent and insurance paid in advance amounted to £10. Depreciation at the rate of 10 per cent per annum is to be written off fixtures, fittings, etc.

Prepare trading and profit and loss accounts for the year ended 31st March, 19.1, and balance sheet as at that date. (*R.S.A.*)

15. B. Gunn has prepared the following Statement of his Assets and Liabilities at 30th September, 1965.

	£	£		£	£
Capital as at 1st October, 1964	7,500		Freehold Land and Buildings at cost less Depreciation		3,500
Profit for the year	4,000	11,500	Plant and Machinery at cost less Depreciation		2,960
Loan at 6½% per annum		2,000	Investments at cost		1,400
Trade Creditors		3,760	Stock on Hand		3,640
			Sundry Debtors	4,840	
			Less Provision for doubtful debts	560	4,280
			Balance at Bank, per Cash Book		1,440
			Cash in Hand		40
		17,260			17,260

On making enquiries you find that—

(i) The Freehold Land and Buildings and Plant and Machinery are to be written down to £3,000 and £2,750 respectively.

(ii) The Sundry Debtors include £240 considered worthless and others estimated to be doubtful to the extent of £640.

(iii) The Stock Sheets had been undercast by £1,000 and a quantity of finished goods overvalued by £420.

(iv) B. Gunn has taken £4 per week as personal drawings from his cash sales but no record has been made of this in his books.

(v) No provision has been made for the half year's loan interest due on 30th September, 1965.

(vi) The Bank Statement showed entries for Bank Charges £56 and dividends credited £75, but these were omitted from the Cash Book. Monthly payments to B. Gunn of £100 by Standing Order had also not been recorded in his books.

(vii) Electricity Charges accrued were estimated at £55 and Insurance paid in advance at £26, but no adjustment had been made in the records.

You are required to prepare—

(i) A Statement showing the necessary adjustments to the Profit for the year.

(ii) A corrected Balance Sheet as at 30th September, 1965, showing details of the alterations in Gunn's original figures. (*A.C.C.A.*)

Income Tax is to be ignored.

16. A. Bamford began trading as a wholesale grocer on 1st July, 1961. A summary of his banking transactions for his first year was as follows—

	£
Paid to Bank	£
Capital Introduced	4,000
Receipts from credit customers	2,164
Cash Sales (*less* Cash payments)	2,816
Cheque Payments	£
Purchase of Shop Premises	1,960
Paid for Fixtures and Fittings	760
Purchases for resale	4,740
Rent and Rates	360
Lighting and Heating	120
Other business expenses	270

Bamford keeps a cash book in which he records cash payments made out of cash sales, and these were—

	£
Personal Drawings	760
Travelling expenses	42
Wages of employee	460
Petty business expenses	64

Apart from these payments the cash sales were all banked intact.

Cash discounts allowed to credit customers were £56, and by suppliers £42. Bad debts written off during the year were £24.

At 30th June, 1962, inspection of the sales ledger showed £564 owing by customers while liabilities to suppliers amounted to £670.

Stock on hand was valued at £587 and depreciation of fixtures and fittings was estimated at 10 per cent per annum.

Prepare total Cash and Bank accounts, Trading and Profit and Loss account for the year to 30th June, 1962, and Balance Sheet as at that date. Also state the average percentage of gross profit on the sales.

17. W. Painter commenced trading on 1st May, 1961. He prepared a set of accounts for his first year in business which were as follows—

TRADING AND PROFIT AND LOSS ACCOUNT FOR THE YEAR ENDED 30TH APRIL, 1962

	£		£
Cost of goods sold	12,240	Sales	20,500
Salaries	2,560		
Rates, lighting and heating	380		
Drawings	1,400		
Sundry expenses	1,840		
Depreciation	90		
Reserve for bad debts	460		
Net profit	1,530		
	20,500		20,500

BALANCE SHEET AS ON 30TH APRIL, 1962

	£	£		£	£
Sundry creditors		3,400	Cash in hand and at bank		1,420
Capital Account—			Sundry debtors	3,230	
Cash introduced	9,750		*Less* Reserve for bad debts	460	
Add Profit for year	1,530				2,770
		11,280	Stock on hand		4,080
			Freehold premises, at cost		5,600
			Fixtures, Fittings, etc., at cost	900	
			Less Depreciation	90	
					810
		14,680			14,680

He asks you to check his accounts and hands you his books for that purpose. In the process of checking you find that—

(1) The entries relating to goods sold in April 1962 amounting to £80 had been made in the month of May 1962.

(2) Goods to the amount of £360 delivered to the business on 28th April, 1962, had been included in the closing stock, but the entries relating thereto had been made in the purchases for May 1962.

(3) Goods bought and paid for during the year and entered in purchases included some which were left with the supplier until delivery was requested. At 30th April, 1962, these amounted to £420 but no entry had been made as regards them in the stocktaking at that date.

(4) Sundry expenses included a sum of £120 expended on a cash register.

(5) An amount of £22 was owing at 30th April, 1962, in respect of lighting and heating which had not been taken into account.

(6) Goods taken by W. Painter from stock for his own requirements during the year amounted to £150.

Upon acquainting W. Painter with your findings, he asks you to draw up amended accounts. Set forth the amended accounts and balance sheet which you would submit in compliance with this request. (*A.C.C.A.*)

18. A. York is a trader who does not keep a complete set of books.

On 1st May, 1963 his debtors were £4,900 and his creditors £1,500. On the same date his Capital was £6,500, plant and machinery was valued at £2,000, furniture and fittings at £140 and stock at £1,700.

A summary of his cash book for the year to 30th April, 1964 showed the following totals.

	Cash	*Bank*
	£	£
Credits		
Due to Bank at 1st May, 1963		740
Payments to Creditors for Purchases	250	2,250
General Expenses	100	900
Wages	775	
Drawings by A. York	104	600
Income Tax 1963/64		126
Rent of Shop (£25 in advance)		450
Debits		
Receipts from Debtors for Sales		4,250
Sale of Machinery	260	
(Book Value 1st May, 1963, £200)		
Rent of Warehouse sublet	78	
Cash Sales	1,000	750
Cash Capital introduced 1st November, 1963		500

The debtors and creditors respectively amounted to £8,800 and £1,950 at 30th April, 1964 and stock was valued at £1,900 on that date.

Cash Discounts allowed to debtors were £46, and received from creditors were £162.

A. York had included in the general expenses £26 for electricity supplied to his private house.

Doubtful debts were estimated at £40, and depreciation on unsold plant has to be provided for at 10 per cent per annum.

You are required to prepare—

A Total Sales Account,

A Total Purchases Account,

Trading and Profit and Loss Account for the year and Balance Sheet as at 30th April, 1964.

19. On 1st January, 1965, G. Green began trading as a Retailer and opened a banking account on that date, into which he later paid all his takings periodically after making various payments in cash, and retaining £5 for a cash float. These cash payments and all other transactions are entered in a diary, but no other records are kept. From the diary you obtain the following summary of the transactions—

Bank—

Encashed National Savings Certificates realizing £1,750.
Paid (January 1st) six months rent in advance £130.
Paid Insurance on stock for year to 31st December, 1965, £24.
Purchased (1st February) Motor Van cost £600.
Paid for Stocks £864 after deducting £22 discount.

Cash—

Sales £1,086.
Paid to Bank £870.
Purchases for Stock £45.
Personal Expenditure and Drawings £91.
Sundry Expenditure £20.

You also ascertain the following facts from Mr. Green—

Stock at 31st March, 1965, £407.
Debtors at 31st March, 1965, £20.
Goods supplied but not paid for £200.

At the start of business, Mr. Green brought fixtures, valued at £150, into the business. These are to be depreciated at 10 per cent per annum of their value. The Motor Van is to be depreciated at 25 per cent per annum of cost.

From the above summary, compile the Trading and Profit and Loss Account for the three months to 31st March, 1965, and Balance Sheet as at that date.

(*A.C.C.A.*)

20. Robinson owned a petrol-filled station and employed a manager, Rogers, who had complete charge of the site. Rogers commenced work on the 1st December, 1968 at a salary of £40 per week. On 22nd February, 1969 Robinson received an urgent message that Rogers had absconded and ordered an immediate investigation into any defalcation by Rogers.

The following facts are available:

(*a*) The station sells four grades of petrol:

A retailing at 33p per gallon.
B retailing at 32p per gallon.
C retailing at 31p per gallon.
D retailing at 30p per gallon.

(*b*) Stocks of petrol on the 30th November, 1968 and 22nd February, 1969 were:

A at 30th November, 1968 2,500 gallons: 22nd February, 1969 500 gallons.
B at 30th November, 1968 2,000 gallons: 22nd February, 1969 1,000 gallons
C at 30th November, 1968 3,500 gallons: 22nd February, 1969 1,500 gallons
D at 30th November, 1968 500 gallons: 22nd February, 1969 200 gallons.

(*c*) The petrol company which supplies the station made the following deliveries for the 12 weeks from 1st December, 1968 to 22nd February, 1969:

A 10,000 gallons
B 30,000 gallons
C 18,000 gallons
D 6,000 gallons

(*d*) There was a cash float of £50 at 30th November, 1968 but on 22nd February, 1969 the till was empty.

(*e*) The bank statement for 12 weeks to 22nd February, 1969 showed total takings banked of £19,005.

(*f*) The following items were paid direct from the till before the takings were banked.

(i) Rogers' salary.
(ii) Wages at £60 per week.
(iii) Petty cash expenses average £10 per week.
(iv) Rent of site £25 per week.

(*g*) The employees informed Robinson that they had not received their wages for the week ended 22nd February, 1969.

(*h*) No rent had been paid for the last four weeks up to the date of Rogers' departure.

You are required to compute the amount of money misappropriated by Rogers.

(*A.C.C.A. modified.*)

CHAPTER 12

FINANCING ASSET ACQUISITION; ROYALTIES; CONTAINERS

These gears which ran in oil for week
By week, needing no look, now will not work;
Those manors mortgaged twice to pay for love
Go to another.

W. H. AUDEN

FINANCING ASSET ACQUISITION

SO FAR in this book we have assumed that the entities for which we accounted have acquired their fixed assets by payment of cash or, at least, on normal, short-term credit terms, perhaps monthly or less.

In fact, however, many firms sell or buy fixed assets on longer payment terms. They may also offer or take advantage of leasing or rental arrangements which allow them to acquire the use of assets without actually having to buy them. Naturally, these special financial relationships give rise to accounting problems.

Government Control of Finance. Under the Control of Hiring Order, 1964 and the Control of Hiring (rebates) Order, 1960, the Government has the power to control the terms offered. Amendment Orders are promulgated from time to time stipulating minimum deposits and maximum repayment periods for hire purchase and credit sale agreements.

Orders usually list assets covered by the order and usually a different minimum deposit and repayment period will be stipulated for various groups of assets.

Three basic types of contract can be identified and the accounting methods adopted should reflect the particular legal relationship.

METHODS OF FINANCING ACQUISITIONS

1. **Credit Sale.** This involves a contract of sale with payment by instalments. Ownership of the goods passes on delivery by the supplier and a binding debt is created which cannot be avoided by returning the goods. The differences between this and normal credit terms are:

(*a*) the payments are made in a number of instalments, commonly nine monthly payments.

(*b*) a charge may be made for interest on the amount payable.
(*c*) the seller of the goods may use the services of a finance house to provide finance for this type of sale.

For consumer goods, this type of arrangement has been used to circumvent the restrictions placed on hire purchase contracts. For industrial goods it is a common service provided by sellers, often supported by Government loans, if the sums required are very large.

2. **Hire Purchase.** The hire-purchase system is a system under which money is paid for goods by means of periodical instalments, with the view of ultimate purchase. All money being paid in the meantime is regarded as payment for hire; and the goods become the property of the buyer only when all the instalments have been paid. On the fulfilment of certain conditions, normally the payment of an agreed number of instalments, the customer becomes entitled to exercise an option to purchase. Until this option is exercised the goods remain the property of the supplier. Usually, the option is to pay a small nominal sum with the final hire payment.

The original purpose of hire-purchase agreements was to avoid the necessity of complying with the statutory requirements relating to money-lenders and bills of sale.

3. **Rental or Lease.** The customer enters into a hire agreement for goods, normally for a fixed minimum period with arrangements for renewal. The agreement does not provide the hirer with an option to purchase; the goods remain the property of the supplier, who may undertake to keep them in working order and they are returned to him on termination of the agreement. After a stipulated period, the rental is normally decreased.

LEGISLATION AFFECTING HIRE PURCHASE AND CREDIT SALE

In addition to the government control of finance, the terms of contracts are governed by—

1. **The Advertisements (Hire-purchase) Act, 1957.** This is designed to prevent the display of misleading hire-purchase and credit sale advertisements.

The advertisement must state (1) the exact amount of the deposit or the proportion of the total price which is represented by it; (2) the amount of each instalment; (3) the total number of instalments payable; (4) the length of the period in respect of which each instalment is payable; (5) the number of instalments payable before delivery of the goods; and (6) the sum which represents the cash price of the goods. Non-compliance with the provisions of the Act will make the offending dealer liable to a fine not exceeding £50 for a first offence and one of £100 for any subsequent offence.

2. The Hire Purchase Act, 1964. This makes important amendments to three earlier Acts. It came into force on 1st January, 1965.

The hirer has a right of termination subject to notice in writing and payment of any instalments in arrears up to half the purchase price of the goods. But the court may order a lessor to make-up payment if it would cover the loss caused to the owner by the premature termination of the agreement.

Part III of the Act protects the person who purchases a motor vehicle in good faith and without notice that it is subject to a hire purchase or conditional sale agreement under which the ownership has not passed to the person who disposes of it. Normally the finance company has security for its money because the hirer is prevented from passing a good title to the goods to a third party until he has paid all instalments and has exercised the option to purchase.

3. Hire Purchase Acts, 1965. This Act repealed the Acts of 1938 and 1954 and all of the 1964 Act except for Part III. It applies to all transactions of up to £2,000. This is large increase on the £300 in the previous legislation. The hire purchase agreement legally binds the hirer and the owner of the goods. It is signed by the hirer and the owner of the goods over a sixpenny stamp and sets out the terms under which the goods are hired.

A statutory notice must be inserted in the agreement setting out (*a*) the rights of the hirer to terminate on terms set out in the Act, (*b*) the rights of the owner to repossess. This is restricted after one third of the hire purchase price has been paid. Warranties and conditions as to quality of goods are imposed upon the owner: the goods must be saleable and reasonably fit for their purpose unless such a warranty is excluded in the agreement and this was brought to the notice of the hirer before he signed it.

Parties to financing agreements

There are normally three parties to agreements of this nature.

1. The Buyer or User. Under credit sale, the property in goods passes immediately the contract is signed. Under hire purchase, the buyer is first the hirer and ownership only passes if and when he exercises his option to buy. Under lease and rental arrangements the user never becomes the owner.

2. The Dealer. The firm which sells the goods and then introduces the buyer to the finance company if hire purchase or credit sale finance is needed.

Under leasing or rental arrangements the dealer negotiates the terms or, if they are standard, obtains the customer's agreement to them. In addition to selling or providing goods for lease or rental, dealers may also provide after sales service. In many cases they will be responsible for collecting instalments or lease payments and for repossessing goods if the terms are breached.

3. **The Finance Company.** If hire purchase finance is required by the buyer then the goods are actually sold by the dealer to the finance company. Then the ownership passes from the finance company to the hirer when the option to purchase is exercised.

Each agreement involves two quite separate contracts—

1. A contract of sale between dealer and finance company and,
2. A contract of hire between finance company and hirer.

If credit sale terms are arranged with a finance company, then, of course, the buyer owns the goods from the start but in effect borrows the unpaid balance of the purchase price from the finance house, although the dealer acts as the agent for the latter.

In the case of lease or rental agreements, if a finance company is involved, then the dealer sells the goods to them. Again, he may act as their agent in collecting the rental payments from the user.

In many cases, a manufacturer may also act as a finance company.

Sources of Finance. Finance companies often use Bills of Exchange. Bills are drawn by finance companies on banks and acceptance houses under acceptance credit lines. The bank or accepting house receive commission carying in accordance with the finance company's standing and the company can then discount the bills in the money market.

Otherwise their sources of finance are shareholders and depositors.

Capital Allowances. If the assets are subject to Capital allowances and grants, these are normally claimed by the company owning the asset.

Duration of Contracts. Contracts are normally up to three years for cars and five years or more for industrial plant and equipment.

ACCOUNTING TREATMENT OF FINANCING AGREEMENTS

It is proposed to deal with each type of agreement, credit sale, hire purchase and lease or rental, first from the view-point of the buyer or user. The examples used will adopt a simplified treatment of interest.

We will then go into the problems of calculating interest before going on to the accounting treatment in the books of the dealer.

Finally, we will discuss methods of accounting for the finance company.

Accounting by the buyer or user

(*a*) Credit sale and hire purchase

Despite the legal form of the contract, hire purchase of an asset is normally accounted as a purchase of a depreciable fixed asset coupled with the raising of finance. For this reason, the credit sale and hire purchase agreements can be considered together here. The instalments paid are regarded as partly capital payment and partly payment of interest. The three different methods of recording the payments in the buyer's books, which are shown here, arise from different accounting treatment of the two elements in the payments.

Method 1. The full cash value of the asset is brought into the books at the start, the vendor being treated as a creditor for that amount. Interest is treated as being paid and credited to vendor at the time of each instalment. With this method the asset can be depreciated from the start.

Method 2. No entry is made until the first instalment is paid, when the appropriate share is debited to the asset and to interest. The full cost price of the asset accumulates over the period of payment. With this method, depreciation can only be charged after the payment of the first instalment.

Method 3 is a variant of the first method. Whilst the full cash value of the asset is debited to the asset account, the vendor is credited with the full amount of instalments payable. The difference is debited to an interest suspense account. When each periodic payment is made, the vendor is debited with the full amount of instalments, and at the same time the appropriate amount of interest is transferred from interest suspense to interest expense account.

Whilst all of these methods may be encountered in practice, the first and third methods are to be preferred for accounting purposes. So far as hire purchase goes, the methods rely on the common sense of the situation rather than the strict legal aspect of it because title is not acquired by the purchaser until the final instalment.

To illustrate the methods used, one simple example is used throughout, and for the sake of simplicity, it is assumed that the interest is paid in equal instalments.

Example 1

D. Broke purchases a machine from A. Vendor, cash price £600, agreeing to pay for it in three equal instalments, at a nominal rate of 10 per cent.

The calculations are—

	£
Cash price	600
Charges 10 per cent for 3 years	180
Hire-purchase price	780
Annual payment	260

Depreciation should be allowed at 10 per cent of cost.

Solution: Method 1

Entries required—

Dr. Asset } with cash price.
Cr. Vendor }

Dr. Vendor } with instalment paid.
Cr. Cash }

Dr. Interest } with interest accrued at time of each payment.
Cr. Vendor }

MACHINERY ACCOUNT

		£			£
Year 1			Year 1		
Jan 1	Vendor	600	Dec 31	P. & L. A/c (Depreciation)	60
			Year 2		
			Dec 31	„ „ „	60
			Year 3		
			Dec 31	„ „ „	60

VENDOR'S ACCOUNT

		£			£
Year 1			Year 1		
Dec 31	Cash	260	Jan 1	Machinery	600
Year 2			Dec 31	Interest	60
Dec 31	„	260	Year 2		
Year 3			Dec 31	„	60
Dec 31	„	260	Year 3		
			Dec 31	„	60

CASH ACCOUNT

					£
			Year 1		
			Dec 31	Vendor	260
			Year 2		
			Dec 31	„	260
			Year 3		
			Dec 31	„	260

INTEREST ACCOUNT

		£			£
Year 1			Year 1		
Dec 31	Vendor	60	Dec 31	P. & L. A/c	60
Year 2			Year 2		
Dec 31	„	60	Dec 31	„ „	60
Year 3			Year 3		
Dec 31	„	60	Dec 31	„ „	60

In the balance sheet, the asset will show at the end of the first year—

	£	
Cost of Machinery on Hire Purchase	600	
Less Balance owing to Vendor	400	
	200	
Less Depreciation	60	
		140

Solution Method 2

The entries required in this case are—

(i) No entry is made until payments are actually made.
(ii) In respect of each instalment—

The capital element in the price is debited to the asset account;
The interest element is debited to an interest account;
The vendor is credited with the full amount.

Machinery Account

		£			£
Year 1			Year 1		
Dec 31	Vendor	200	Dec 31	P. & L. A/c (Depreciation)	60
				Balance c/d	140
		200			200
Year 2			Year 2		
Jan 1	Balance b/d	140	Dec 31	P. & L. A/c (Depreciation)	60
Dec 31	Vendor	200		Balance c/d	280
		340			340
Year 3			Year 3		
Jan 1	Balance b/d	280	Dec 31	P. & L. A/c (Depreciation)	60
Dec 31	Vendor	200		Balance c/d	420
		480			480
Year 4					
Jan 1	Balance b/d	420			

Vendor's Account

		£			£
Year 1			Year 1		
Dec 31	Cash	260	Dec 31	Machinery & Interest	260
Year 2			Year 2		
Dec 31	"	260	Dec 31	" " "	260
Year 3			Year 3		
Dec 31	"	260	Dec 31	" " "	260

Interest Account

		£			£
Year 1			Year 1		
Dec 31	Vendor	60	Dec 31	P. & L. A/c	60
Year 2			Year 2		
Dec 31	"	60	Dec 31	" "	60
Year 3			Year 3		
Dec 31	"	60	Dec 31	" "	60

Cash Account

					£
			Year 1		
			Dec 31	Vendor	260
			Year 2		
			Dec 31	"	260
			Year 3		
			Dec 31	"	260

At the end of the first year, the asset will be shown in the balance sheet as follows—

	£	
Machinery at cost		
(Proportion of hire-purchase price paid) . .	200	
Less Depreciation	60	
		140

Solution Method 3

The entries required in this case are—

(i) On acquiring the asset—

Debit full cash value to the asset account;
Credit the vendor with the hire-purchase price;
Debit an interest suspense account with difference between cash and hire-purchase price.

(ii) When instalments are paid—

Credit cash;
Debit vendor with the full instalment.

The interest element in the instalment is then dealt with by debiting interest account and crediting interest suspense account.

MACHINERY ACCOUNT

			£				£
Year 1				Year 1			
Jan	1	Vendor	600	Dec	31	P. & L. A/c (Depreciation) .	60
				Year 2			
				Dec	31	,, ,, ,, .	60
				Year 3			
				Dec	31	,, ,, ,, .	60

VENDOR'S ACCOUNT

			£				£
Year 1				Year 1			
Dec	31	Cash	260	Jan	1	Machinery and Interest Suspense A/cs	780
Year 2							
Dec	31	,, ...	260				
Year 3							
Dec	31	,, ...	260				

INTEREST SUSPENSE ACCOUNT

			£				£
Year 1				Year 1			
Jan	1	Vendor	180	Dec	31	Interest	60
				Year 2			
				Dec	31	,, ...	60
				Year 3			
				Dec	31	,, ...	60

INTEREST ACCOUNT

			£				£
Year 1				Year 1			
Dec	31	Interest Suspense A/c . .	60	Dec	31	P. & L A/c	60
Year 2				Year 2			
Dec	31	,, ,, ,, . .	60	Dec	31	,, ,, ...	60
Year 3				Year 3			
Dec	31	,, ,, ,, . .	60	Dec	31	,, ,, ...	60

CASH ACCOUNT

	Year 1			£
	Dec 31	Vendor	. . . . .	260
	Year 2			
	Dec 31	"	. . . . .	260
	Year 3			
	Dec 31	"	. . . . .	260

The balance sheet at the end of the first year will show—

		£	
Machinery at cost		600	
Less Owing to Vendor	£520		
Deduct Interest in Suspense . . .	120		
		400	
		200	
Less Depreciation		60	
			140

(*b*) **Lease or rental of assets**

We stated above that a hire purchase agreement should normally be accounted for in the same way as a credit sale. However, the legal relationship would allow a user to account for a hire purchase initially in the same way as a lease.

Method 1

For the user, the normal method of accounting for leases is to treat each payment as an expense. The entries would be:

Debit lease, rental or hire purchase expense account.
Credit Cash.

At the end of the year, the expense would be charged to the appropriate part of the income statement. For example equipment leased and used in a factory would be charged to manufacturing account, a warehouse leased might be charged to trading account and a computer leased by head office charged to profit and loss. The entries would be:

Debit income statement.
Credit lease, rental or hire purchase account.

On this basis, if A. Vendor offers to lease the machine to D. Broke for £260 per annum for three years, with a subsequent nominal rental of £10 per annum, the accounts would show:

MACHINERY LEASE EXPENSE

Year 1			£	Year 1				£
Jan 1	Cash	. . . . .	260	Dec 31	P. & L. a/c	. . . . .		260
Year 2				Year 2				
Jan 1	Cash	. . . . .	260	Dec 31	P. & L. a/c	. . . . .		260
Year 3				Year 3				
Jan 1	Cash	. . . . .	260	Dec 31	P. & L. a/c	. . . . .		260
Year 4 et seq.				Year 4 et seq.				
Jan 1	Cash	. . . . .	10	Dec 31	P. & L. a/c	. . . . .		10

PROFIT AND LOSS ACCOUNT

Year 1			
Machinery lease expense	260		
Year 2			
Machinery lease expense	260		
Year 3			
Machinery lease expense	260		
Year 4 et seq.			
Machinery lease expense	10		

CASH ACCOUNT

		Year 1	
		Jan 1 Machinery lease expense . .	260
		Year 2	
		Jan 1 Machinery lease expense . .	260
		Year 3	
		Jan 1 Machinery lease expense . .	260
		Year 4 et seq.	
		Jan 1 Machinery lease expense . .	10

In the case of a hire purchase acquisition, in this method, the first three years of the agreement would be accounted for in exactly the same way as above but a final entry would be required at the end of the agreement when the final purchase option was exercised. The entries would be:

Debit asset account.
Credit cash account.

Let us suppose the machinery in our example may be purchased for £1 at the end of the three-year hiring period. When the final option to purchase was exercised, the entries would be:

CARS

	£		
Dec 1 Cash	1		

CASH

			£
		Dec 1 Cars	1

MISLEADING ACCOUNTING FOR FINANCE

The treatment of lease financings as an expense may mislead shareholders, creditors or other outside parties because it does not reveal in the accounts the degree to which a firm is using leases as a means of obtaining finance. Whilst the actual payments are shown as expenses, the actual commitment to future payments is not shown as a liability.

There are two ways in which the situation might be remedied. The first would be to account for leases in the same way as credit sales. The entries under each method would be slightly modified, as follows:

Method 2

Dr. Leased assets *Cr.* Lessor	with cash price.
Dr. Lessor *Cr.* Cash	with instalments paid.
Dr. Leased machinery expense *Cr.* Lessor	with the interest element in the lease payment.
Dr. Leased machinery expense *Cr.* Leased machinery	with the capital element in the lease payment.
Dr. Profit and Loss *Cr.* Leased machinery expense	with the expense for the year.

After the end of the primary leasing period, the nominal lease payment would be debited direct to Leased machinery expense.

Let us assume that D. Broke leases the machine from A. Lessor for £260 per annum, but accounts for the lease as if it were a credit sale. The accounts would show:

LEASED MACHINERY

		£			£
Year 1			Year 1		
Jan 1	A. Lessor	600	Dec 31	Leased machinery expense	200
			Year 2		
			Dec 31	Leased machinery expense	200
			Year 3		
			Dec 31	Leased machinery expense	200

A. LESSOR

Year 1			Year 1		
Jan 1	Cash	260	Jan 1	Leased machinery	600
Year 2			Dec 31	Leased Machinery expense	60
Jan 1	Cash	260	Year 2		
Year 3			Dec 31	Leased Machinery expense	60
Jan 1	Cash	260	Year 3		
			Jan 1	Leased Machinery expense	60

LEASED MACHINERY EXPENSE

Year 1			Year 1		
Dec 31	Lessor and leased machinery	260	Dec 31	P. & L. a/c	260
Year 2			Year 2		
Dec 31	Lessor and leased machinery	260	Dec 31	P. & L. a/c	260
Year 3			Year 3		
Dec 31	Lessor and leased machinery	260	Dec 31	P. & L. a/c	260
Year 4					
	Cash	10			

CASH ACCOUNT

					£
			Year 1		
			Jan 1	A. Lessor	260
			Year 2		
			Jan 1	A. Lessor	260
			Year 3		
			Jan 1	A. Lessor	260
			Year 4 et seq.		
			Jan 1	A. Lessor	10

At the end of Year 1, the Balance Sheet of D. Broke would show on the assets side:

	£	£
Leased machinery	400	
Owing to A. Lessor . . .	400	0

Method 3

The previous example brings out the problem of the second method. This method gives a little more information in the Balance Sheet, but it assumes that the asset has, in effect, a useful life equal to the primary term of the lease. The third method writes off the lease expense taking into account the expected useful life of the asset.

The entries requires are:

Dr. Leased assets *Cr*. Lessor	With cash price.
Dr. Lessor *Cr*. Cash	With instalments paid.
Dr. Leased machinery expense *Cr*. Lessor	With the "interest" element in the lease payment.
Dr. Leased machinery expense *Cr*. Leased machinery	With an amount equal to the depreciation chargeable, if the asset were owned.
Dr. Profit and Loss *Cr*. Leased machinery expense	With the expense for the year.

In our example let us assume that the asset has an expected ten-year life with no residual value and that D. Broke uses the straight line depreciation method.

The accounts for the first four years will now show:

LEASED MACHINERY

			£				£
Year 1				Year 1			
Jan	1	A. Lessor	600	Dec	31	Leased machinery expense	60
				Year 2			
				Dec	31	Leased machinery expense	60
				Year 3			
				Dec	31	Leased machinery expense	60
				Year 4 et seq.			
				Dec	31	Leased machinery expense	60

LEASED MACHINERY EXPENSE

Year 1				
Dec	31	Lessor and leased machinery	120	
Year 2				
Dec	31	Lessor and leased machinery	120	
Year 3				
Dec	31	Lessor and leased machinery	120	
Year 4 et seq.				
Dec	31	Lessor and leased machinery	70	

A Lessor's and the Cash Account will be the same as in Method 2.

At the end of Year 1 the Balance Sheet of D. Broke would show, on the assets side:

	£
Leased machinery	540
Owing to A. Lessor	400
Net leased assets	140

The strong objection to this method is that it shows in the Balance Sheets assets which are not owned by the entity.

Method 4

This method tries to combine the advantages of all the other methods. Basically, the accounting treatment is that of the first method. The lease payments are treated as an expense in the year in which they are paid.

At the same time, memorandum accounts are opened to show the total lease liabilities and the book value of the leased assets.

The entries are:

Dr. Leased machinery expense *Cr*. Cash *Dr*. P. & L. a/c *Cr*. Leased machinery expenses	With lease payments.

The memorandum entries would be:

Dr. Leased machinery *Dr*. Lease interest suspense *Cr*. Lessor	With full amount payable under the lease.
Dr. Lessor	—annually with full amount of lease payments.
Cr. Leased machinery	—with an amount equal to the interest chargeable if the asset were owned.
Cr. Lease interest suspense	—with the interest element in the lease payment.

The debit to the Lessor account will be larger than the two credits if the asset has a longer life than the primary lease period. If it is desired to maintain the double entry principle, the balance may be credited to a leased machinery equalization account. When the lease payments revert to the nominal level, the difference will be debited to the equalization account.

The memorandum data may then be appended as a footnote to the Balance Sheet in the following way:

	£
Cost value of leased assets	600
Less notional depreciation	60
Book value of Leased assets	540
Less amount owing to Lessor	400
Net leased assets	140

PROBLEMS OF CALCULATING INTEREST

The above examples considerably simplify the treatment of interest in order to simplify the presentation.

Apportionment of Interest and Income. The following approaches may be used—

1. **Equal Instalment or Straight Line Method.** This is the method already illustrated.

Interest from finance charges is treated as accruing evenly over the life of each agreement and no attempt is made to relate the interest to the time over which the capital is outstanding.

If this method is used by the Finance House, it underestimates the interest receivable in the early years of a contract and since an important cost is the cost of borrowing finance it does not relate revenue directly to the expense incurred in earning it. Its advantage is that by reasons of its conservative nature it makes some provision against the many unforeseeable factors including the risk of bad debts. The distortion will be most marked when a company is expanding or contracting.

2. **The Actuarial Method.** Study of this method may be deferred until the student has studied the use of present value factors (Appendix I).

This method is based on the allocation of interest in proportion to the reducing balance of capital outstanding at any given time.

The calculation can be made by using the present value factors (Tables A to D in Appendix I).

The following example illustrates the calculation for a buyer.

Example 3

An electronic computer is offered for sale, on the following terms: £4,000 on delivery, plus—

£4,000 at the end of each of the following 4 years
£5,000 at the end of the fifth year after delivery

Assuming that interest at 6 per cent compound is allowed for, calculate from the information given below the equivalent price which would be appropriate, if payment were to be made in full on delivery.

Solution 3

From Table B, the amount required to produce an annuity of £1 is—

4 years . . .	£3·4651
5 years . . .	£4·2124

From Table A, the present value of £1 payable a number of years hence is—

4 years . . .	£0·79209
5 years . . .	£0·74726

(A.C.C.A.)

The total payment over the period, which is presumed to include a charge for 6 per cent interest is—

	£
On delivery	4,000
Four instalments of £4,000 each at the end of the next four years .	16,000
Final payment at the end of the fifth year	5,000
	£25,000

The present value of the delivery charge is £4,000. The present value of the four instalments at 6 per cent can be found by using the factor from Table B—

$$£4{,}000 \times 3{\cdot}4651 = £13{,}860$$

The present value of the fifth payment must be calculated using the factor from Table A—

$$£5{,}000 \times £0{\cdot}74726 = £3{,}736$$

The equivalent payment today would be—

$$£4{,}000 + £13{,}860 + £3{,}736 = £21{,}596$$

Whether the computer is bought on hire purchase or not, this is the cost price which should be taken.

The annual interest can be calculated approximately by assuming that each instalment is used first to meet the interest on the outstanding capital and the balance applied to pay off the capital.

The initial capital borrowed is the present value of the deferred payments: £13,860 plus £3,736—

Year	Capital £	Interest 6% paid £	Capital repaid £	Instalment £
1	17,596	1,056	2,944	4,000
2	14,652	879	3,121	4,000
3	11,531	692	3,308	4,000
4	8,223	493	3,507	4,000
5	4,716	283	4,717	5,000

The error of £1 is due to rounding.

The accounting entries, if it is hire-purchased and accounting method 3 is used will be—

COMPUTER ACCOUNT

		£			£
Year 1 Jan 1	Vendor	21,600	Year 1	Dec 31 Profit and Loss (Depreciation) . .	4,320
			2	" " " " "	4,320
			3	" " " " "	4,320
			4	" " " " "	4,320
			5	" " " " "	4,320
		£21,600			£21,600

VENDOR'S ACCOUNT

Year		£	Year		£
1	Jan 1 Cash	4,000	1	Jan 1 Computer and Interest Suspense Accounts .	25,000
	Dec 31 "	4,000			
2	" " "	4,000			
3	" " "	4,000			
4	" " "	4,000			
5	" " "	5,000			
		25,000			25,000

INTEREST SUSPENSE ACCOUNT

	£		£
Year 1 Vendor's Account	3,400	Year 1 Interest paid A/c	1,056
		2 " " "	876
		3 " " "	692
		4 " " "	493
		5 " " "	283
	3,400		3,400

The original cost has been rounded to £21,600 to compensate for rounding errors.

HIRE PURCHASE INTEREST PAID ACCOUNT

		£			£
Year 1	. . . .	1,056	Year 1	Profit and Loss A/c . .	1,056
2	. . . .	876	2	" " " . .	876
3	. . . .	692	3	" " " . .	692
4	. . . .	493	4	" " " . .	493
5	. . . .	283	5	" " " . .	283
		3,400			3,400

CASH ACCOUNT

				£
	Year 1	Jan 1	Vendor . . .	4,000
		Dec 31	" . . .	4,000
	2	" "	" . . .	4,000
	3	" "	" . . .	4,000
	4	" "	" . . .	4,000
	5	" "	" . . .	5,000

At the end of the first year the computer would appear on the asset side of the Balance Sheet as follows—

	£
Computers in course of hire-purchase	21,600
Less Depreciation	4,320
	17,280

The Vendor would appear on the liabilities side as follows—

		£
Hire purchase liability on computer		17,000
Less interest in suspense	£3,400	
Less paid in year	1,056	
		2,344
		14,656

For the purpose of the balance sheet the balance of the vendor's account less the balance of the interest suspense account may be deducted from the asset, with the following result—

	£
Computer after depreciation	17,280
Less liability	14,656
	2,624

This is the net capital expenditure—

	£
Payments	8,000
Less interest and depreciation	5,376
	2,624

3. **Sum of the Digits Method.** (Sometimes called the "Rule 78"). This method produces an approximation to the results of the actuarial method. Income from finance charges is distributed over the lives of agreements arithmetically in proportion to the reducing balances outstanding. If the amount of H.P. charge attributable to the last instalment is £x, then the amount attributable to the penultimate instalment will be £$2x$; that attributable to the antepenultimate instalment £$3x$, etc. In an agreement involving twelve equal monthly instalments the total income from finance charges would be £x + £$2x$ + £$3x$ + £$4x$ + . . . £$12x$ = £$78x$. The first repayments under such an agreement would be computed to contain $\frac{12}{78}$ of the total income from finance charges, the second instalment $\frac{11}{78}$ and the last instalment $\frac{1}{78}$ (hence the "Rule of 78").

Applying this method to the first example on p. 1205, the total charge is £180 payable over three years. The sum of the digits is 1 + 2 + 3 = 6 and the income for each year will be—

Year		£
1	$\frac{3}{6}$ths of £180	90
2	$\frac{2}{6}$ths of £180	60
3	$\frac{1}{6}$th of £180	30
		180

The interest will be taken into account accordingly.

4. **Batching.** The system of accounting and the volume of current agreements may make it impracticable to apply the sum of digits method to each agreement individually. In such circumstances it is customary to batch agreements for treatment in total, each batch being grouped in appropriate categories according to the calendar months in which they were entered into, the rate of hire purchase charges and the unexpired periods over which they run. Totals are thus obtained for each month for each type of agreement and the necessary computations are then applied to the batch totals.

5. **The Direct or Arbitrary Percentage Method.** Some finance houses adopt a method of carrying forward as deferred income at the end of each accounting period a percentage of the outstanding balances on instalment credit accounts. At its crudest, the same percentage is applied from year to year in an arbitrary manner which takes no account of variations in the composition and nature of the accounts outstanding. The results are apt to be inaccurate and unreliable, and the method is not, therefore, recommended.

ACCOUNTING BY THE DEALER

(*a*) Instalment payment and credit sale

Difference between Hire-purchase and Credit Sale. Under the hire-purchase system the property in the goods does not pass to the buyer, but remains vested in the seller until the last instalment has been paid; and if default is made in payment the seller can take possession of the goods or secure their return. Under the instalment-payment system of purchase, however, the property in the goods passes at once to the buyer. He actually owns the goods, although payment for them is to be spread over a series of years. If default is made in payment, the seller cannot re-take possession of the goods; he can only sue for the balance of the debt.

Accounting Methods. Despite the legal distinction, it was explained on p. 1204–5 that the hire-purchase transactions are often treated as credit sales. It would be possible for a seller to take the same view and adopt the corresponding treatment.

Solution: Method 1

LEDGER

THE X. CO. LTD.

Year		£	Year		£
1	Sundries	2,600	1	Cash	600
	Interest	130		Balance c/d	2,130
		2,730			2,730
2	Balance b/d	2,130	2	Cash	600
	Interest	106		Balance c/d	1,636
		2,236			2,236
3	Balance b/d	1,636	3	Cash	600
	Interest	82		Balance c/d	1,118
		1,718			1,718
4	Balance b/d	1,118	4	Cash	600
	Interest	56		Balance c/d	574
		1,174			1,174
5	Balance b/d	574	5	Cash	603
	Interest	29			
		603			603

Entries in the Vendor's Books. The only difference between this transaction and a normal sale on credit is that interest is charged to the customer. Two methods may be adopted. Under method 1, entries will be made debiting the purchaser and crediting the sales account with the *cash sale value* of the goods. Periodically, as arranged, the purchaser will be debited with interest on the balance outstanding, the amount of the interest being credited to interest account. Cash will be debited with the instalment when received, and the amount will be credited to the purchaser, as in the example on page 1219.

Example 4

The X Co. Ltd. purchases on the instalment-payment plan a number of coal wagons, to be paid for by four annual instalments of £600 each and a final instalment to discharge the balance. The cash value of the wagons amounts to £2,600, and the wagon company charges interest at the rate of 5 per cent per annum on yearly rests.

Write up the purchaser's account as it would appear in the books of the vendor.

Method 2

Under method 2, the goods will be credited at their *cash sales value* to sales account. Total interest will be credited to an interest suspense account. The total of both cash sales value and interest is debited to the account of the purchaser. As each instalment is received, it will be debited in the cash book and credited to the purchaser's account.

At balancing time a portion of the interest suspense account will be transferred to the profit and loss account as a realized gain. At the termination of the period of payment, the interest suspense account will be completely extinguished.

Solution: Method 2

The journal entry would be—

JOURNAL

		Dr	*Cr*
Year		£	£
1	The X Co. Ltd.	3,003	
	Sales		2,600
	Interest Suspense A/c . . .		403
	For wagons sold on the instalment-payment system.		

The purchaser's account and the interest suspense account are—

LEDGER

THE X CO. LTD.

Year		£	Year		£
1	Sundries	3,003	1	Cash	600
				Balance c/d	2,403
		3,003			3,003
2	Balance b/d	2,403	2	Cash	600
				Balance c/d	1,803
		2,403			2,403
3	Balance b/d	1,803	3	Cash	600
				Balance c/d	1,203
		1,803			1,803
4	Balance b/d	1,203	4	Cash	600
				Balance c/d	603
		1,203			1,203
5	Balance b/d	603	5	Cash	603

INTEREST SUSPENSE ACCOUNT

Year		£	Year		£
1	P. & L. A/c	130	1	X Co. Ltd.	403
	Balance c/d	273			
		403			403
2	P. & L. A/c	106	2	Balance b/d	273
	Balance c/d	167			
		273			273
3	P. & L. A/c	82	3	Blance b/d	167
	Balance c/d	85			
		167			167
4	P. & L. A/c	56	4	Balance b/d	85
	Balance c/d	29			
		85			85
5	P. & L. A/c	29	5	Balance b/d	85

(*b*) Hire purchase

The usual method of accounting for hire purchase maintains three basic accounts—

1. Hire Purchase Trading Account. This is debited with sales at cost and credited with instalments due from customers at selling price. The instalments not yet due are carried forward at cost valuation and the account shows the gross profit due on hire purchase for the period.

2. Hire Purchase Sales Account. This account is debited with the selling price value of instalments due from customers and credited with the sales value of sales to customers. The instalments not yet due are carried forward at selling price.

3. Hire Purchase Customers' Account. These personal accounts are debited with the selling price value of sales and credited with cash received from customers. The balances carried forward will be instalments. They may or may not be due and the two balances should be distinguished.

It is also possible to have advance receipts which would show as a credit balance. Where self-balancing ledgers are used this account will be called the Hire Purchase Sales Ledger Control Account. The following example illustrates the procedure—

Example 5

From the following details set out the hire-purchase account in the books of a trader who sells numbers of articles of comparatively small value on the hire-purchase system, showing his profit of the business for the year ended 31st December, 1965. For the purpose of charging his hire-purchase customers, he adds 60 per cent to the cost price of the goods.

1965			£
Jan	1	Stock in customers hands at selling price	1,620
Dec	31	Sales of goods during year at selling price . . .	6,534
		Cash received from H.P.	
		Debtors	2,100
		Stock in customers hands at selling price	5,674

(*London Chamber of Commerce.*)

Solution 5

The value of stock in hand at selling price, £1,620 represents cost plus 60 per cent. The cost value is therefore $£1,620 \times \frac{100}{160} = £1,012$. The three accounts will show the following opening balances—

Hire Purchase Trading A/c . .	Debit . .	£1,012
,, ,, Sales A/c . .	Credit . .	£1,620
,, ,, Customers' A/c .	Debit . .	£1,620

Since the second and third balances cancel out, the effect is to show the instalments due at cost in the books.

The cost value of £6,534 sales is £4,084, and the cost value of the closing stock is £3,546. As can be seen in the accounts below, the Hire Purchase Customers' Accounts show a discrepancy which is assumed to be instalments due but not actually received.

A Contingency Provision may be made for bad debts on these instalments by debiting Hire Purchase Trading Account and crediting a Provision Account.

HIRE PURCHASE TRADING ACCOUNT

	£		£
Instalments not yet due at cost brought forward . . .	1,012	Hire Purchase Sales Account— Instalments for year . .	2,480
Cost of sales during year . .	4,084	Instalments not yet due at cost carried forward . .	3,546
Gross Profit for year carried to Profit and Loss A/c . .	930		
	6,026		6,026
Instalments not yet due at cost brought forward . .	3,546		

HIRE PURCHASE SALES ACCOUNT

	£		£
Hire Purchase Trading Account— Instalments due for year	2,480	Instalments not yet due at selling brought forward . . .	1,620
Instalments not yet due at selling carried forward . .	5,674	Sundry Hire Purchasers . .	6,534
	8,154		8,154
		Instalments not yet due at selling brought forward . . .	5,674

SUNDRY HIRE PURCHASE CUSTOMERS' ACCOUNTS

	£			£
Balances brought forward—		Cash		2,100
Instalments not due . .	1,620	Balances carried forward—		
Hire Purchase Sales . .	6,534	Instalments due .	380	
		Instalments not due	5,674	
				6,054
	8,154			8,154
Balances brought forward—				
Instalments due . .	380			
Instalments not due . .	5,674			

Second Method of Dealing with Hire-purchase Accounts (Goods Out on Stock System, at Cost). Where numbers of articles of much smaller value are being sold daily on the hire-purchase system, a simpler method is adopted.

The cardinal feature of this system is to consider all the goods out on hire as stock. To keep a full record of goods out on hire purchase, it is necessary to have ledger accounts of the customers, but these accounts are not part of the ordinary double-eutry system, although the principle of double-entry may be employed in balancing the accounts.

The procedure may be outlined as follows—

1. *Debit* hire-purchase trading account and credit purchases account with *cost* price of goods sent to customers on hire purchase. At the same time each customer's (*memorandum*) account will be debited with the *sale price* of such goods.

2. Returns from customers. Debit Purchases or Returns Account and Credit H.P. Trading Account with cost price of goods and credit the customers account with the agreed (sales price) value of returns.

3. The instalments paid will be *debited* to cash and credited to hire-purchase trading account. At the same time, the customer's (*memorandum*) account will be *credited.*

4. The instalments due and unpaid will be debited to instalments due account and credited to hire-purchase trading account.

5. The stock "out," i.e. the same proportion of the cost of the goods sent as the amount of unaccrued instalments bears to the total amount of the instalments, is credited to hire-purchase trading account and debited to hire-purchase stock account.

6. The *memoranda* accounts will show the balances against the customers, but not being part of the double entry are not brought into the trial balance. Thus, the customers' accounts are "reference" accounts only. A transfer may be made similar to that in (4).

The gross profit is the excess of the sum of instalments due and paid, plus stock out on hire purchase at the end of the period, over the stock out on hire purchase at the beginning, plus goods sent to customers during the period, less returns, at cost.

In account form this will be—

HIRE-PURCHASE TRADING ACCOUNT

	£		£
Stock at Cost b/d		Instalments Paid	
Goods sent to Customers at Cost . .		" Due	
Gross Profit		Stock at Cost c/d	
Stock at Cost[1] b/d			

[1] Or transferred to and from a separate stock account (see Example 4).

Before illustrating the working of the above a simple example is given to show the computation of the value of the stock out on hire-purchase.

Example 6

Goods costing £10 are sent to B. Brown on hire-purchase, the price being £20, payable in twenty instalments of equal intervals. At the end of the accounting period of the hire vendor, five instalments are yet unpaid (fifteen having been paid at due dates).

Solution 6

The stock in the hands of the customer is valued as follows—

$$\frac{5}{20} \times £10 = £2{\cdot}50$$

Assuming, further, that (for sake of simplicity) it is the only transaction of the period, the hire-purchase trading account would appear as below—

HIRE-PURCHASE TRADING ACCOUNT

	£		£
Goods at Cost	10·00	Instalments Paid	15·00
Gross Profit	7·50	Stock	2·50
	17·50		17·50

HIRE-PURCHASE STOCK ACCOUNT

	£		
Hire-purchase Trading A/c	2·50		

In the Memorandum Hire Purchase Ledger—

B. BROWN

	£		£
Goods	20·00	Cash (detailed as each payment is made)	15·00
		Balance c/d	5·00
	20·00		20·00
Balance b/d	5·00		

The balances on the customers' accounts do not appear as part of double-entry accounting and hence do not form a part of the trial balance. *Practically*, these memoranda accounts are vital, but from a *double-entry* point of view entirely unnecessary, as the hire-purchase trading account gives the necessary results and forms an integral-part of the double entry.

Subsidiary books employed will be the day books, the cash book and, supplementary to the double entry, the memorandum ledger.

The day books, as to sales and returns inwards, will usually contain supplementary columns in order to fulfil the functions of the double entry *and* to furnish the necessary data from which may be compiled the memoranda accounts, i.e. there will be a column for the purpose of the double entry and others recording the detail necessary for the compilation of the memoranda accounts. The columns in the sales day book, apart from date and folio columns, are usually necessary to record—

1. Cost price of the goods sold.

2. Sale price of the goods sold.
3. Number of amounts of instalments.
4. Periodicity of instalments.
5. Any other information that circumstances require.

Column 2 provides the data for entering up the memoranda accounts. The total of column 1 will be debited to the hire-purchase trading account and to the credit of purchases account. The individual items in column 2 will be posted to the debit of the customers' accounts in the memorandum ledger. It is usual to total column 2 and post this to a memorandum ledger adjustment account, the entries being credited. This gives a control on the accuracy of the postings.

Returns inwards (at cost) will be dealt with conversely. Column 1 is totalled and the total debited to purchases account and credited to hire-purchase trading account as part of the ordinary double entry. The details of returns (at selling price) will be posted from column 2 to the credit of the respective customers' accounts in the memorandum ledger, and if a memorandum ledger adjustment account is employed, the total of column 2 will be posted to the debit of this account.

The other columns call for no special mention as they are self-explanatory. It may here be mentioned that as the accounts of customers are very numerous, the card ledger system is frequently employed.

With regard to cash received, the entries will be made in the cash book in the usual way, but such entries fulfil a twofold function: (i) for the double entry, (ii) for writing up the memoranda accounts. The total of cash received from hire-purchase customers is posted (as part of the double entry) to the credit of hire-purchase trading account, whilst the individual receipts are posted to the credit of the customers' accounts in the memorandum ledger. If a memorandum ledger adjustment account is employed the total of such receipt will be posted to the debit thereof.

The memorandum ledger adjustment account, when totalled, will have the balance on the opposite side to the detailed balances in the memorandum ledger. Thus the system is to adapt the double-entry idea in the verification of the memorandum ledger total by means of the adjustment account, but still it is quite independent of the formal double entry accounting.

Lastly, any instalments actually due and unpaid will be ascertained from the memorandum ledger, and these will be credited to the hire-purchase trading account and debited to a separate account called Instalments Due Account. Frequently the latter are ignored for the purpose of the hire-purchase trading account, in which case the cost equivalent of the unpaid instalments will be included in stock.

The balance of the hire-purchase trading account will be transferred to the trading account, subject to suitable provision for losses, depreciation, and the like.

Example 7

Jones Ltd. forward a piano to A. Alan on the hire-purchase system, the cost being £100 and the selling price £200; payable in fifty monthly instalments of £4 each, commencing from 31st August. The sale takes place on 31st August, 19..; the instalments are regularly paid. Accounts are drawn up to 31st December.

On 1st October, 19.., a similar sale is made to B. Bloom, the cost price being £78, the sale price £104 payable in weekly instalments of £2, commencing from 1st October; the instalments are paid regularly. Show the various entries necessary in the books of the hire vendor.

HIRE-PURCHASE STOCK SCHEDULE

Contract No.	Name	No. of Instalments	No. of Instalments Paid	No. of Instalments Unpaid	Cost Price	Proportion of Cost Price
					£	£
1	A. Alan	50	5	45	100	90
2	B. Bloom	52	14	38	78	57
					178	147

The total of the cost price column (as part of the double entry) is posted to the debit of the hire-purchase trading account. If such an account is to be drawn up to 31st December, 19.., the cash received and the value of the stock in the hands of customers will be found as follows—

1. Cash received from—

   Alan—£20, i.e. 5 payments of £4. Bloom—£28, i.e. 14 payments of £2.

2. Stock "out"—

   Instalments outstanding × Cost

$$\begin{aligned} & && \pounds \\ \text{Alan} &= \tfrac{45}{50} \times \pounds 100 = && 90 \\ \text{Bloom} &= \tfrac{38}{52} \times \pounds 78 = && 57 \\ & && \underline{\underline{147}} \end{aligned}$$

Ordinarily, *in practice*, a schedule will be prepared for the purpose of arriving at the valuation of the hire-purchase stock out, thus—

HIRE-PURCHASE SALES DAY BOOK

Date	Particulars	No. of Instalments	Period of Instalments	Amount of Instalment	Cost Price	*Fol.*	*Selling Price*
19..				£	£		£
Aug 31	A. Alan	50	monthly	4	100	*1*	*200*
Oct 1	B. Bloom	52	weekly	2	78	*2*	*104*
					178		*304*

(The end column shows the hire-purchase stock "out," the total of which is incorporated into the double-entry accounts, as below.)

HIRE-PURCHASE TRADING ACCOUNT

	£		£
Goods at Cost (*Cr. Purchases*)	178	Instalments Paid (*Dr. Cash*)	48
Gross Profit transferred to Trading A/c	17	Stock (as above or transferred to Hire-purchase Stock A/c) c/d	147
	195		195
Balance—Stock b/d	147		

The separate instalments of cash, detailed above, will be entered in the cash book (in practice a separate subsidiary cash book will be employed). The debit entry will thus occur in the cash book, the totals (daily, weekly, monthly, as required) of which will be credited to the hire-purchase trading account. In this case £48 is the sum to be so treated.

The above entries complete the formal double entry, but entries are also made in respect of cash received in the memorandum books. The individual items in the selling price column of the hire-purchase sales day book will be debited to the personal accounts in the memorandum ledger and the total will be posted to the credit of the memorandum ledger adjustment account, if one be employed.

The cash received will be posted in individual items, as recorded in the cash book, to the credit of the individual accounts in the memorandum ledger, and in total to the debit of the memorandum ledger adjustment account.

MEMORANDUM HIRE-PURCHASE LEDGER

No. 1 A. ALAN

19..		£	19..		£
Aug 31	Goods	200	Dec 31	Cash	20
				Balance c/d	180
		200			200
19.1					
Jan 1	Balance b/d	180			

No. 2 B. BLOOM

19..		£	19..		£
Oct 1	Goods	104	Dec 31	Cash	28
				Balance c/d	76
		104			104
19.1					
Jan 1	Balance b/d	76			

It is again emphasized that the cash book fulfils the dual function (*a*) of supplying the double entry, and (*b*) of supplementing the memoranda accounts, which are completely outside the double entry.

ACCOUNTING BY THE FINANCE COMPANY

(*a*) Credit sale and hire purchase

Many traders find the considerable work involved in hire-purchase trading a drawback to such schemes, but the method of trading is so widespread that they cannot insist on cash terms. Many of the smaller firms would find the capital required for hire-purchase trading difficult to raise.

In such cases, finance companies who specialize in hire-purchase facilities are only too eager to take over the work. Both parties benefit from this arrangement, which allows both parties to specialize in the work they know best. The trader actually effects the sale, collects the deposit money (if any) and gets the customer to complete the forms. The transaction is then handed over to the finance company, which pays the trader the balance of the cash price and collects the instalments from the customers. For the trader, the sale is much the same as a cash sale, except that the agreement gives the finance company the right to return to him any goods of which possession has been taken on default. Such returns are valued at cash price less the proportion paid, as in Example 6.

A similar arrangement is sometimes made with manufacturers of products for which hire-purchase terms are advertised nationally, e.g. vacuum cleaners. In these cases there is no question of the trader having to accept returns. He makes a sale and retains the customer's deposit. The manufacturer then takes over the transaction and pays the trader the balance of the cash price. The customer pays his instalments to the manufacturer or his agent.

Example 8

A finance company offers to take over the financing of a trader's hire-purchase trade. The trader is to obtain a deposit of at least 10 per cent on all transactions, and the finance company will pay the balance of the cash price monthly. In the first month (January) the trader's sales are £60,000, of which £40,000 are hire-purchase sales. 10 per cent deposit was obtained in all cases, except for £4,000 sales on which £1,000 was paid. Show the trader's accounts.

Cash Account

19..		£			
Jan 1–31	Cash Sales	20,000			
	H.P. Sales (deposits)	4,600			

Hire-purchase Sales

			19..		£
			Jan 1–31	Cash Deposits	4,600
			31	Finance Co.	35,400

Cash Sales

			19..		£
			Jan 1–31	Cash	20,000

Finance Company

19..		£			
Jan 31	H.P. Sales for month	35,400			

Example 9

On 30th November, after some months of trading, goods of cash sale value £200 were recovered by the finance company. Out of 24 instalments, 6 had been paid. Record the return in the trader's books.

RETURNS ON HIRE-PURCHASE SALES

19..			£				
Nov 30	Finance Co. . . .		150				

FINANCE COMPANY

				19..			£
				Nov 30	Returns		150

To illustrate the case where the manufacturer takes over hire-purchase contracts, a more complicated example is taken below.

Example 10

A. Manufacturer markets a vacuum cleaner, cash price £30, on which retailers are allowed $33\frac{1}{3}$ per cent trade discount. If the customer wishes to pay by instalments, the manufacturer takes over the transaction and there is an additional charge of £3 to the cost. The customer pays a deposit of £5 to the dealer, and the balance of the hire-purchase price in seven monthly instalments to the manufacturer. The dealer receives the balance of full cash selling price from the manufacturer.

The following transactions were recorded in two months—

	Number Sold to A. Dealer	Number Sold by A. Dealer *For Cash*	Number Sold by A. Dealer *On Hire-purchase*
19..			
March	3,000	2,800	100
April	4,000	3,200	300

Cash received from A. Dealer—

	£
March	57,500
April	72,500

To record the transaction in the dealer's books requires several steps—

1. Purchases are recorded in the usual way by debiting purchases account, crediting A. Manufacturer's account with the cost price of £20 (cash price £30 *less* trade discount £10).

2. Cash sales are debited to cash and credited to cash sales account at £30 per article.

3. Hire-purchase sales involve two parts—

(*a*) The deposit is debited to cash, credited to hire-purchase sales account.

(*b*) The balance of cash price payable by Manufacturer is debited to his account and credited to hire-purchase sales.

4. Payments to Manufacturer will be debited to his account, credited to cash. It is clear that the trader settles promptly at the month end.

(*a*) The Books of A. Dealer

PURCHASES

19..		Units	£			
Mar	A. Manufacturer	3,000	60,000			
Apr	" "	4,000	80,000			

A. MANUFACTURER

19..		£	19..		£
Mar	H.P. Sales	2,500	Mar	Purchases	60,000
	Cash	57,500	Apr	"	80,000
Apr	H.P. Sales	7,500			
	Cash	72,500			

CASH SALES

			19..		£
			Mar	Cash	84,000
			Apr	"	96,000

CASH ACCOUNT

19..		£	19..		£
Mar	Cash Sales	84,000	Mar	A. Manufacturer	57,500
	H.P.Sales (Deposits)	500			
Apr	Cash Sales	96,000	Apr		72,500
	H.P. Sales (Deposits)	1,500			

HIRE-PURCHASE SALES

			19..		£
			Mar	Cash	500
				A. Manufacturer	2,500
			Apr	Cash	1,500
				A. Manufacturer	7,500

The manufacturer is entitled to regard all his sales as completed credit sales to the dealers until he is notified that some are, in fact, on hire-purchase. He may then reverse the entries and treat the hire-purchase stock as stock-on-hire. A memorandum account will be opened for each hire-purchase customer.

The steps in recording the transactions are—

1. *Dr.* dealers account } with the selling price to retailers, i.e. £20.
   Cr. Sales account }

2. On notification of hire-purchase sales, several adjustments must be made.

(*a*) Transfer the hire-purchase sales to hire-purchase trading account from sales account.

(*b*) The stock-on-hire account must be debited with the amount outstanding from customers (this will be supported by a memorandum account for each customer), that is—

	£	
Cash price	30	
Add Charges	3	
	33	
Less Deposit paid to dealer	5	
		£28

The corresponding credits are—

£25 due to dealer, balance of cash price; £3 hire-purchase charges.

Hire-purchase Sales

			19..			£
			Mar	Sales		2,000
			Apr	,, ...		6,000

Sales

		Units	£			Units	£
19..				19..			
Mar	H.P Sales. . . .	100	2,000	Mar	A. Dealer	3,000	60,000
Apr	,, ,, ...	300	6,000	Apr	,, ,, ...	4,000	80,000

A. Dealer

		Units	£			Units	£
19..				19..			
Mar	Sales	3,000	60,000	Mar	Stock-on-hire . . .	100	2,500
					Cash	—	57,500
Apr	,, ...	4,000	80,000	Apr	Stock-on-hire . . .	300	7,500
					Cash	—	72,500

Stock-on-Hire

		Units	£				
19..							
Mar	H.P. Charges and A. Dealer . . .	100	2,800				
Apr	H.P. Charges and A. Dealer . . .	300	8,400				

Hire-purchase Charges

						Units	£
				19..			
				Mar	. . . .	100	300
				Apr	. . . .	300	900

Cash Account

		£			
19..					
Mar	A. Dealer	57,500			
Apr	,, ,, ...	72,500			

Two further steps may be involved—

3. Any cash paid by hire-purchase customers will be debited to cash, credited to stock-on-hire account.

4. At the end of the period, the proportion of hire-purchase charges realized will be transferred to profit and loss account, and the balance

unrealized carried forward (see Example 7). This balance must be deducted from the value of stock-on-hire in the balance sheet, e.g.—

	£
Stock-on-hire	11,200
Less hire-purchase charges . .	1,200
Stock	10,000

As the sale does not take place until the hirer exercises his option to purchase, the goods remain the legal property of the vendor until that time. Accordingly, the amount set aside for trading profit not yet earned is sometimes computed by reference to the gross trading profit percentage appropriate to the cash price of the goods in question. The Balance Sheet of a Hire Purchase firm should show the total amounts outstanding after provision for bad debts under hire-purchase agreements and Credit Sale agreements.

Example 11

A. Manufacturer, in the above example, received 250 instalments of £4 in April for his hire-purchase sales, and the appropriate proportion of charges was transferred to profit and loss account.

STOCK-ON-HIRE

19..		*Units*	£	19..		£
Mar	H.P. Charges and A. Dealer . .	100	2,800			
Apr	H.P. Charges and A. Dealer . . .	300	8,400	Apr	Cash	1,000

HIRE-PURCHASE CHARGES

19..		£	19..		*Units*	£
Apr	P. & L. A/c	107	Mar	. . . . .	100	300
	Balance c/f	1,093	Apr	. . . . .	300	900
		1,200				1,200
			Apr	Balance b/f		1,093

It should be noted that the trader takes full benefit for the normal gross profit in this period (see hire-purchase sales account). Only the hire-purchase charges are apportioned. These charges are £3, and seven instalments are payable. That is £$\frac{3}{7}$ = £0·43 (approximately) per payment, of which there are 250.

5. The proportion of profit earned on hire-purchase sales can be calculated on the hire-purchase trading account. If in our example Manufacturer makes a normal profit of £2 on sale to Dealer, his normal cost of sales is £18, and the hire-purchase trading account may be completed as follows—

HIRE-PURCHASE TRADING ACCOUNT

19..		Units	£	19..		Units	£
Mar	Cost of Sales . .	100	1,800	Mar	Sales	100	2,000
Apr	" " " . .	300	5,400	Apr	"	300	6,000
	Gross profit on H.P. Sales . . .		800				
			8,000				8,000

Alternatively, the hire-purchase sales figure may be transferred to trading account with the cash sales figure.

Problems of Determining the Income of Finance Companies. The finance company's gross profit arises from the difference between the amount of money which it originally spends in the purchase of goods or contractual rights and the total sum which it receives in instalments. A further source of profit is purchase option fees which become payable at the conclusion of agreements when hirers exercise their option to purchase. This is usually brought into account when it is received.

The charges made by finance companies are designed to produce a surplus after meeting the costs of arranging, administering and financing agreements. Since these costs do not accrue evenly over the life of an agreement the basic adopted for allocating income from finance charge is of prime importance.

The basis adopted for computing income yet to mature under the instalment credit agreements should be appropriate to the type of business carried on and ideally should neither anticipate nor duly defer income.

The actuarial and sum of the digits methods are the most suitable theoretical basis for computing income not yet matured. The amount carried forward as deferred or unearned income should not in any case be less than any rebates which would be allowable if all agreements were discharged and settled on the day immediately following the balance sheet.

PROVISION FOR BAD DEBTS

It is not sufficient to have regard only to overdue accounts, since indication that an agreement will not be fully discharged may appear before repayments fall into arrears. There are two methods which may be used to determine the provision for bad debts: one involves the individual assessment of accounts, and the other involves the application of percentages, based on experience, to the totals of balances outstanding.

ROYALTY ACCOUNTS

A royalty is an amount payable to the owner of an asset in exchange for the right to use it, the payment varying with the usage. The term originated in the royal right over minerals (especially) which was granted to an individual or corporation. In return for the privilege of working the minerals, the lessees paid a royalty which varied in proportion to production or the use made of the asset. The term also includes sums paid to a patentee for the right to use a patent and to an author or artist for the right to copy his work. Authors' royalties are usually calculated on the number of books sold.

Whilst coal mining rights were acquired by the State, when the coal-mining industry was nationalized, other royalties still exist.

The terms under which royalties are paid are decided by the parties concerned but, especially where mineral rights are involved, agreement may be made to pay a minimum rent.

Minimum Rent. This is a guaranteed minimum amount which the landlord, or owner of the copyright, is to receive. It is often payable only in the first years of the agreement when actual production may not have reached normal levels. It may also be a safeguard against a company acquiring rights which it does not intend to use.

Short-workings. The amount by which the minimum rent exceeds the royalties actually payable (calculated at the agreed rate per unit) is known as short-workings.

Right to Recoup Short-workings. Where short-workings arise through normal difficulties in starting production, the producer may obtain the right to recoup short-workings, say, within three years. In such cases, of course, he may only recoup himself from the amount by which the royalties exceed the minimum rent.

The right may be unlimited and the producer may then recoup short-workings from any later excess royalties over the minimum rent.

If the right is limited, the limitation may operate within a stated time—
(*a*) from the commencement of the agreement, or
(*b*) from the date of the short-workings.

Example 12

A. Landlord gives AB Ltd. the right to work minerals on his land at a royalty of 10p per ton mined. In the first three years, production is 2,000, 5,000 and 7,000 tons respectively. Show the accounts of AB Ltd.

Solution 12

ROYALTY ACCOUNT

Year		£	Year		£
1	A. Landlord . . .	200			
2	„ . . .	500			
3	„ . . .	700			

A. LANDLORD

Year		£	Year		£
			1	Royalties	200
			2	„	500
			3	„	700

A. Landlord's account would be discharged each year by cash payment.

The royalty account would be closed by a transfer to manufacturing account or production account, that is—

Dr. Manufacturing (or production) account
Cr. Royalties account

in respect of each annual amount.

If the landlord has a right to minimum rent, an account should be opened for the minimum rent and for the short-workings. The entries are—

Dr. Minimum rent *Cr.* Landlord	with the amount payable.
Dr. Royalties account *Cr.* Minimum rent account	with the actual royalties earned.
Dr. Short-workings account *Cr.* Minimum rent account	with the balance of minimum rent (which is the short-workings).

Example 13

If, in Example 12, the landlord had the right to minimum rent £550, the accounts would be—

Solution 13

ROYALTY ACCOUNT

Year		£	Year		£
1	Minimum Rent . . .	200			
2	,, ,, . . .	500			
3	A. Landlord . . .	700			

MINIMUM RENT ACCOUNT

Year		£	Year		£
1	A. Landlord . . .	550	1	Royalties . . .	200
				Short-workings . .	350
2	,, . . .	550	2	Royalties . . .	500
				Short-workings . .	50

SHORT-WORKINGS ACCOUNT

Year		£	Year		£
1	Minimum Rent . . .	350			
2	,, ,, . . .	50			

A. LANDLORD

Year		£	Year		£
			1	Minimum Rent . . .	550
			2	,, ,, . . .	550
			3	Royalties . . .	700

Where short-workings cannot be recovered they should be written off to profit and loss account. Where there is a right to recoup short-workings, they will be written off only if they have not been recovered by the end of the period agreed.

Recovery of Short-workings. In a year when short-workings are recoverable, the royalties must exceed the minimum rent. The minimum rent account is not used and the royalties earned are debited to royalties account and credited to the landlord.

Any short-workings recoverable will be standing on the debit of short-workings account and they are transferred to the landlord's account, i.e.—

Dr. A. Landlord's account.
Cr. Short-workings account.

Any balance irrecoverable is written off to profit and loss account, whilst any recoverable balance is carried forward.

Example 14

If we assume on the figures in our previous examples that short-workings are recoverable for two years after the year in which they arise, the accounts will be—

Solution 14

ROYALTIES ACCOUNT

Year		£	Year		£
1	Minimum Rent . . .	200			
2	" " . . .	500			
3	A. Landlord . . .	700			

SHORT-WORKINGS ACCOUNT

Year		£	Year		£
1	Minimum Rent . . .	350	3	A. Landlord . . .	150
2	" " . . .	50		P. & L. A/c . . .	200
				Balance c/d . . .	50
		400			400
4	Balance b/d . . .	50			

MINIMUM RENT ACCOUNT

Year		£	Year		£
1	A. Landlord . . .	550	1	Royalties . . .	200
				Short-workings . . .	350
2	" . . .	550	2	Royalties . . .	500
				Short-workings . . .	50

A. LANDLORD'S ACCOUNT

Year		£	Year		£
1	Cash	550	1	Minimum Rent . . .	550
2	,, ...	550	2	,, ,, . . .	550
3	,, ...	550	3	Royalties	700
	Short-workings .	150			

N.B. Of the balance on short-workings account after the maximum recovery has been made, £200 is written off to profit and loss as irrecoverable, £50 is carried forward as recoverable.

Example 15

In the fourth year of account, royalties are £900. The accounts for the year will be—

Solution 15

ROYALTIES ACCOUNT

Year		£			
4	A. Landlord . . .	900			

SHORT-WORKINGS ACCOUNT

Year		£	Year		£
4	Balance b/f . . .	50	4	A. Landlord . . .	50

A. LANDLORD'S ACCOUNT

Year		£	Year		£
4	Short-workings . .	50	4	Royalties	900
	Cash	850			

ACCOUNTING FOR CONTAINERS AND CASES

The treatment of the costs of containers, packages, and cases in which goods are despatched to customers varies according to the type of product, the nature of the packing case, and the manufacturing or trading policy of the individual firm. Some firms make their own packages and regard them as an inherent part of the cost of manufacture, others use returnable cases and crates which may even cost more than the product which is packed in them.

Non-returnable Containers

The cost of such containers is usually included in the sales price of the goods, and the cost of manufacture included with other costs. If they are purchased from outside, the treatment is similar to that of stock and loose tools, that is—

Opening stock *plus* purchases, *less* closing stock gives the cost of containers used.

The cost of containers may be treated as a separate item, in which case the sales day book is ruled with an extra column to record sales of containers. Any profit or loss on containers is transferred to profit and loss account at the end of the period.

Returnable Containers

Several problems arise in accounting for returnable containers.

(*a*) No Charge to Customers

1. The closing stocks will be held partly in the warehouse and partly in the hands of customers.
2. Each container will, presumably, have a limited life, and a reasonable allowance for depreciation must be made. This may involve keeping a record of each container used.
3. It is likely that some containers will be reported lost or damaged beyond repair.
4. Some of the damaged containers may be repaired from time to time.

The treatment of these problems may be illustrated in the case of returnable containers for which no charge is made to customers. The only account required is a Containers Stock Account. It is usual to provide a column for quantities in this account.

Example 16

Packen Ltd. opens the year with 1,000 containers, valued at £0·50 each. During the year a further 2,000 are purchased, 20,000 issues to customers are made, and 18,500 are returned. 20 cases were damaged, of which 10 were repaired at a cost of £0·10 per container. The purchase price of containers is £1, but stocks are valued at £0·50 to allow for depreciation.

Solution 16

CONTAINERS STOCK ACCOUNT

			Quantity	£			*Quantity*	£
1st Yr.								
Jan	1	Stock	1,000	500	Dec 31	P. & L. A/c (depreciation)		966
		Purchases	2,000	2,000		P. & L. A/c (damaged, written off)	10	10
		Cash (repairs)	—	1		Stocks in hands of customers	1,500	750
						Stocks in warehouse c/d	1,490	745
			3,000	£2,501			3,000	£2,501
2nd Yr.								
Jan	1	Stock b/d—						
		Customers	1,500	750				
		Warehouse	1,490	745				

The closing stock is calculated as follows—

Opening stock		1,000
Purchases		2,000
		3,000
Sent to customers	20,000	
Less Returns	18,500	
Stock in hands of customers	1,500	
Damaged stock written off	10	
		1,510
∴ Closing stock		1,490

Whilst no charge is made to customers for containers in this case, it is usual to rule extra columns in the ledger accounts of the customer so that the numbers of containers held and returned can be recorded. If each container has a serial number, this may be recorded on the invoice, and in the day book and ledger column provided on the debit side. The numbers of returned containers are recorded in a column on the credit side.

(*b*) A Charge Made to Customers

The additional problems which arise when containers are charged to customers are—

5. Profit may arise if the price charged to customers is above cost.
6. A further profit may arise if the allowance made on return is less than the price charged.
7. A time limit may be set for return, after which containers in hands of customers will be written off.

A *containers or packages stock account* is opened and debited with the value of stocks brought forward. Purchases of additional containers or their cost of manufacture is debited to this account. The closing stocks in warehouse and in the hands of customers are carried forward at the end of the period.

Additional columns to record the issue and return of containers are provided in the sales day book and the returns inwards books.

Customers are debited with the value of containers sent to them and credited with the value of returns.

A *containers suspense account* is opened, which is credited with the value of containers issued to customers and debited with the value of returns. The value of returnable containers held by customers at the end of the period is carried down to the credit of this account. This amount should be deducted from the value of debtors shown in the balance sheet. If a balance remains on this account, it will be a profit or loss which should be carried to profit and loss account.

Example 17

Packen Ltd. buys containers for £1 which it charges out at £1·25, allowing £0·75 on return. All stocks are valued at £0·50 at stocktaking.

On 1st January, the stock at warehouse was 8,000, and 16,000 were in the hands of customers. During the year 12,000 were purchased, 26,000 sent to customers and 19,000 returned. 200 were destroyed or lost and 100 were sold for scrap, £20. At the end of the period 14,000 were in the hands of customers (return period unexpired). Show the ledger accounts for the year ended 31st December 19..

Solution 17

CONTAINERS STOCK ACCOUNT

		Units	£			Units	£
19..				19..			
Jan 1	Stocks—			Dec 31	Containers lost	200	
	In Warehouse	8,000	4,000		Containers sold	100	20
	With Customers	16,000	8,000		Containers Suspense A/c—		
	Purchases (@ £1)	12,000	12,000		Profit @ £0·50 on issues to customers		13,000
	P. & L. A/c (profit on containers)		9,120		Retained by customers	9,000	6,750
					Closing Stocks—		
					In Warehouse @ £0·50	12,700	6,350
					With Customers @ £0·50	14,000	7,000
		36,000	£33,120			36,000	£33,120
19..							
Jan 1	Stocks—						
	In Warehouse	12,700	6,350				
	With Customers	14,000	7,000				

CONTAINERS SUSPENSE ACCOUNT

		Units	£			Units	£
19..				19..			
Dec 31	Containers Stock A/c— Profit of £0·50 on issues to customers		13,000	Jan 1	Containers in Customers' hands @ £0·75	16,000	12,000
	Sundry Debtors— Containers returned @ £0·75	19,000	14,250		Sundry Debtors— Containers issued at £1·25 per case	26,000	32,500
	Containers Stock A/c— Retained by customers @ £0·75	9,000	6,750				
	Balance— Containers in customers' hands @ £0·75	14,000	10,500				
		42,000	£44,500			42,000	£44,500

QUESTIONS

1. What are hire-purchase accounts? Explain the entries to be made: *(a)* in the buyer's books, *(b)* in the seller's books. How is depreciation dealt with? What other method is there of dealing with hire-purchase accounts?

2. What are credit sales? How do they differ from hire-purchase? What entries are necessary: (*a*) in the buyer's books, (*b*) in the seller's books?
3. What is a royalty? Why is a minimum rent often agreed?
4. List the entries to be made in accounting for containers.
5. What are the three basic methods of accounting for Hire Purchase?

EXERCISE 12

1. John commences trading on 1st January, 1965 selling television sets and washing machines both for cash and on hire purchase. Hire purchase sales are made on the basis of a 20 per cent deposit with the balance to be paid in four quarterly instalments. The first instalment is payable at the beginning of the next calendar quarter following the sale. The hire purchase agreements provide that any person wishing to do so may complete the purchase by paying off the balance due when the second instalment is made, thereby obtaining a 5 per cent refund of the initial hire purchase sales price.

The following information is extracted from John's books for the year ended 31st December, 1965—

	£
Cash sales	6,274
Purchases	8,700
Hire purchase instalments received, including complete payments	608
Hire purchase deposits received	648
Cash from the sale of goods returned	100

Sales under hire purchase agreements for the year were—

	At cost	At hire purchase sales price
	£	£
February	160	250
April	300	430
June	175	280
July	460	700
September	240	370
November	380	560
December	420	650

Included in these were—

(1) April sales of £150 (cost £110) were returned from hire in September, after only one instalment had been paid in July, and were sold finally in October for £100 cash;

(2) June sales of £200 (cost £130) were paid for completely in October;

(3) July sales of £250 (cost £180) were returned in November, no instalments having been paid and valued for stock at £140.

A contingency provision of 20 per cent on instalments due but not yet received, is to be made.

At 31st December, 1965 stock, excluding goods returned from hire, was valued at £1,760.

You are required to prepare for the year's trading the following—

(*a*) hire purchase trading account;
(*b*) general trading account;
(*c*) hire purchase sales ledger control account;
(*d*) statement of closing stock valuation.

(*Cost and Management Accountants.*)

2. On 1st January, 1962, S. Edge purchased a lorry for £2,180 and entered into a hire purchase agreement with a finance company under which he paid £440 as deposit, the balance, plus hire purchase charges of £240 being payable by equal monthly instalments over a period of 3 years commencing 1st January, 1962.

Provision for depreciation is made at 20 per cent of the cost of the lorry each year by means of a Depreciation Account, the Asset Account for the lorry showing the cost only.

The Hire Purchase charges are to be regarded as having accrued in equal monthly instalments over the period of the agreement.

You are required to prepare a schedule showing the figures appearing in Edge's Balance Sheets as at 31st March, 1962, 1963, 1964, 1965, 1966, 1967 for—

(1) The Lorry Account.
(2) Lorry Depreciation Account.
(3) Hire Purchase Account.
(4) The Hire Purchase Interest charged in the Profit and Loss Account for the year ending on those dates. (*A.C.C.A.*)

3. A. Dee acquired two Motor Vans under Hire Purchase Agreements as follows—

Registration Number . . .	264 DE	456 FA
Date of Purchase . . .	30th June, 1963	31st January, 1964
Cash Price . . .	£850	£910
Deposit	£94	£118
Interest (assumed to accrue evenly over the period of the agreement .	£108	£144

Both Agreements provided for payment to be made in thirty-six equal monthly instalments, commencing on the last day of the month following purchase.

On 1st August, 1964, Van 264 DE was totally destroyed in an accident. On 10th August, 1964—

(i) The insurance company paid £700 in settlement, and
(ii) The hire-purchase company accepted £500 in full satisfaction of the agreement.

Dee made up his Accounts annually to 28th February and provided depreciation on a straight line basis at 20 per cent for these vehicles with a full year's depreciation in the year of purchase and no depreciation in the year of disposal.

All instalments were paid on the due dates.

You are asked to record the foregoing transactions in the following Accounts—

(*a*) Motor Vehicles.
(*b*) Depreciation.
(*c*) Hire Purchase Company.

showing the Balances on 28th February, 1965.

(*A.C.C.A.*)

4. Cee Dee Ltd. closes its books on 31st December for the preparation of the annual accounts. A motor vehicle, the cash price of which was £2,120, was purchased from Motor Traders Ltd. on 1st July, 1964 under a hire purchase agreement. Cee Dee Ltd. paid £800 by way of a deposit and the agreement provided for the balance to be settled by 12 equal quarterly instalments of £140, payable on 1st October, 1st January, 1st April, and 1st July, in each year. Cee Dee Ltd. duly paid the instalments as they became payable. The vehicle was sold for £950 on 30th June, 1966, and Motor Traders Ltd. agreed to accept a payment of £610 to terminate the hire purchase agreement and this was paid on that date.

The motor vehicle was brought into the books of Cee Dee Ltd. at its cash price, and it was decided to spread the charge for interest evenly over the three-year period of the hire-purchase agreement. Depreciation was written off the vehicle as from the date of purchase at the rate of 25 per cent per annum on the cash price.

Show the accounts for (1) the Motor Vehicle, (2) Motor Traders Ltd., and (3) Hire Purchase Interest Suspense recording the above-mentioned transactions in the books of Cee Dee Ltd. *(A.C.C.A.)*

5. Casson & Co., printers and publishers, publish a book written by H. G. Sell to whom a royalty of 5p a copy is payable on every copy sold. The publishers pay all production and distribution costs, which costs are included in general debits to various expense accounts; 4,000 copies are printed, and an investigation disclosed that the costs of production included in the general debits to the accounts named below were the amounts set opposite the accounts named—

	£
Printing wages	120
Paper	190
Binding materials	110
Advertising	40

During the first year after publication, 200 free copies were issued to reviewers, libraries, etc., and 2,500 copies had been sold at a net price of 30p each, and Casson & Co. sent the author a cheque for the royalty due to him.

It is desired to know what profit has been made on this particular book during the first year. Make journal entries for all transactions that may be necessary to attain this object, and post to a publication of book account any items necessary to ascertain the profit on the book, closing the account and ascertaining the profit.

Assuming that in the second year the whole of the remaining books were sold at the same price, except 100 that were sold as remainders at 15p each, and that no further costs were incurred, except the royalty, which was paid on all books sold whether at the original price or as remainders, complete the account of the book for the second year. *(West Riding of Yorkshire.)*

6. (*a*) Explain in principle the difference between a hire-purchase transaction and a sale for settlement by instalments.

(*b*) On 30th June, 19.., Blanktown Garage supplied to Mr. X a motor-car on hire-purchase terms. The cost of the car to the garage had been £660, the cash sale price was £845, and the contract signed by X provided that he should pay £440 down and 22 monthly instalments of £20 each. All payments under the contract were made on the due dates.

How would you suggest that the garage, for which a hire-purchase transaction is a rarity, should record the matter in: (i) its books, and (ii) its annual accounts drawn up to 31st December, 19.. ? *(R.S.A.)*

7. A summary of A. Jackson's Balance Sheet as on 31st May, 1965, is as follows—

	£		£	£
A. Jackson—Capital Account	6,000	Plant and Machinery *less* Depreciation		3,600
Sundry Creditors	1,600	Stock on hand	1,400	
		Sundry debtors	2,000	
		Cash at bank	600	
				4,000
	7,600			7,600

After charging £550 for depreciation, the profit for the year ended 31st May, 1965, was £1,200. The basis of the charge for depreciation is 10 per cent of the cost of the plant and machinery and it is agreed that this basis is appropriate for all plant.

On going through the books it is found that—

(1) Included in the sales ledger balances there are accounts the balances on which, amounting to £360, represent goods in the hands of customers on sale or return. Such goods had been charged out at cost plus 33⅓ per cent.

(2) An amount of £312 is included in repairs and renewals which sum represents the deposit of £72 on the purchase of a machine being bought under a hire-purchase agreement and four equal monthly instalments. In the agreement the cash price of the machine is stated to be £720 and the transaction is to be completed in twelve months.

It can be assumed that interest accrues evenly over the whole of the period of the contract.

Show (1) what adjustments require to be made to the year's profit, and (2) draw up an amended Balance Sheet as on 31st May, 1965.

(A.C.C.A.)

8. On 30th June, 19.., X Ltd. paid a deposit of £5,000 on a linotype machine delivered to it on that day by Y Ltd. A hire-purchase agreement was signed under which X Ltd. undertook to pay, in addition to the deposit, five half-yearly instalments of £3,500 each, commencing on 31st December, 19... The cost of the machine to Y Ltd. was £18,000 and the "cash-sale" price £20,200.

Both companies prepare accounts annually to 31st December, and all instalments were paid on the due dates.

X Ltd. treated the difference between the hire-purchase price and the cash-sale price as interest, calculated at the rate of 10 per cent per annum (to the nearest £) and provided depreciation at the rate of 5 per cent per annum by the "straight line" method. Y Ltd. treated as profit in each year the proportion of the aggregate expected profit obtained by dividing the instalments (including deposit) received during the year by the total amount receivable under the contract.

You are required to show—

(*a*) the ledger entries in the books of X Ltd. up to 31st December, 19.1, and

(*b*) the position at 31st December, 19.1, as reflected in the balance sheets of both companies.

(R.S.A.)

9. A firm carrying on business as domestic appliance manufacturers make their own packing cases, which are charged to customers at 100 per cent on cost, but are returnable, full credit then being given. The following are the items relating thereto in respect of the year ended 31st December, 1965—

	£
Stock of cases in the factory at 1st January, 1965	596
Cases in the hands of customers as per ledger balances at 1st January, 1965	840
Cases charged to customers	3,140
Materials used	38
Wages paid for making and repairing cases	156
Cases returned by customers	3,260
Cases kept by (i.e. sold to) customers	140
Stock of cases in the factory at 31st December, 1965	280

Cases in the hands of customers are valued at cost, less 20 per cent.

You are required to write up Cases Stock and Cases Reserve Accounts in respect of the foregoing items in the books of the firm, and to state how the balances remaining would be dealt with in the Balance Sheets at 31st December, 1964, and 1965.

(*L.C.C.*)

10. F. Smith sold a product which required expensive containers. These cost £4 each and were invoiced to customers at £7 each on the basis of sale or return within three months.

In his impersonal ledger, Smith maintained a "containers stock account" together with a "containers suspense account" showing the unrealized profit on containers in the hands of customers.

On 1st July, 19.., there were 100 containers in stock, and in addition 80 containers were in the hands of customers.

During the six months ended 31st December, 19.., 450 containers had been dispatched to customers and 350 had been returned within three months; 50 containers which had not been returned had been duly paid for by the customers. 140 containers had been purchased, 36 had been scrapped after return and sold for cash in December, 19.., at £1·50 each. Repairs to other containers returned cost £38, paid in cash.

You are required to—

(*a*) write up the accounts in Smith's impersonal ledger recording these transactions, bringing down the balances as on 31st December, 19..;

(*b*) prepare a statement showing the net profit or loss in respect of containers for the six months ended 31st December, 19.., and

(*c*) state the amount at which containers in stock and with customers should be shown in the balance sheet as on that date.

Ignore depreciation on containers. (*Chartered Accountants* (*modified*).)

11. On 30th June, 19.., the Blanktown Gazette Ltd., which prepares accounts annually to 31st December, acquired a printing machine on hire-purchase terms. The cash price of the machine was £14,000 and the terms set out in the contract provided for an immediate payment of £3,000 and six instalments of £1,997 each, payable half-yearly on 31st December, 19.., 30th June, 19.1, and so on up to 30th June, 19.3. These instalments were calculated on the basis of taking into account interest at the rate of 5 per cent per annum.

The first four instalments were all paid on their due dates but the fifth was not paid till 10th January, 19.3.

The Blanktown Gazette Ltd. provided depreciation on the machine at the rate of 10 per cent per annum, using the "straight line" method and taking no account of any possible scrap value.

Write up the ledger accounts concerned in the company's books, up to 31st December, 19.2, and show how the position would be reflected in the balance sheet as on that date. (*R.S.A.*)

12. O. Watt commenced to trade in electrical goods on 1st January, 1964. Purchases during the year ended 31st December, 1964, amounted to £6,500 and ordinary sales to £7,400. He also made sales under hire-purchase arrangements, the details of which are as follows—

	Cost	Sale price	Deposit paid	Monthly instalments	Number of instalments paid in the year
	£	£	£		
Vacuum cleaner . . .	40	80	8	18 of £4	6
Combined television and radio set . . .	105	140	14	21 of £6	5
Spin dryer . . .	30	50	5	9 of £5	3

The customer was unable to keep up the instalments on the spin dryer and it was returned on 20th December, 1964.

On 31st December, 1964, stock-in-trade, apart from the returned spin dryer, was valued at £800.

Prepare the Hire-purchase trading account, the Hire-purchase sales account and the General trading account for the year ended 31st December, 1964.

Interest is to be ignored. *(A.C.C.A.)*

13. A firm carrying on business as pottery manufacturers make their own packing cases, which are charged to customers at 100 per cent over cost, but are returnable, full credit being given. The following are the items relating thereto in respect of the year ended 31st December, 19..—

	£
Stock of cases, 1st January, 19..	596
Cases in hands of customers, as per ledger balances, 1st January, 19..	840
Cases charged to customers	3,140
Materials used	38
Wages paid for making and repairing cases	156
Cases returned by customers	3,260
Cases paid for by customers	140
Stock of cases in factory, 31st December, 19..	280

The cases in the hands of customers were valued at cost less 20 per cent.

You are required to show, by means of ledger accounts, how the foregoing items should appear in the books of the firm and to state how the balances remaining would be dealt with in the balance sheet. *(R.S.A.)*

14. A mining company leased a mine at a royalty of 5p a ton of ore raised from 1st January, 19... The minimum rent was £600 a year payable 31st December, and there was a right to recoup short-workings within five years of acquisition. The quantities of ore raised in those years were—

Year 1	5,600 tons
„ 2	11,000 „
„ 3	15,000 „
„ 4	17,000 „
„ 5	19,000 „

You are required to prepare and close off the owner's, minimum rent, royalty, and short-workings accounts for the five years as they would appear in the company's books. Ignore income tax. Payments were made regularly to the owner.

(Cost and Management Accountants.)

15. Traders Ltd. delivers goods to customers in wooden cases. The customer is charged with the case at 30p each, and is credited on the return at 20p. On 1st January, 19.., there were 5,000 cases in the warehouse and 10,500 cases in the hands of customers. During the year ended 31st December, 19.., the following transactions took place—

7,500 cases purchased at 25p each;
16,000 charged out to customers;
11,500 returned by customers;
400 scrapped.

On 31st December, 19.., 9,500 cases, for which the return period has not expired, were in the hands of customers. The cases purchased prior to 1st January, 19.., cost 15p each. Closing stocks are to be valued on the "first in, first out" principle.

(*a*) Prepare a statement in quantities only showing cases in stock at 31st December, 19.., and the number of cases in customers' hands for which the return period has expired.

(*b*) Prepare the cases stock account.

(*c*) Prepare the cases trading account showing separately the profit on the sale of cases and the profit on the hire of cases. (*Cost and Management Accountants.*)

16. On 1st April, 19.., Mainsprings Ltd., patentees of a new type of alarm clock, granted to Timekeepers Ltd. a licence to manufacture and sell clocks.

By the terms of the licence, Timekeepers Ltd. were to pay a royalty of 25p per clock sold, subject to a minimum payment of £2,000 per annum, to be paid annually on 31st March. Should the royalties, calculated on the number of clocks sold, be less than £2,000 in any year, the deficiency could be set off against royalties in excess of £2,000 in either of the next two succeeding years.

The number of clocks sold was as follows—

Year to 31st March, 19.1	6,000
" " " " 19.2	7,200
" " " " 19.3	9,600

Payments to Mainsprings Ltd. were made punctually on the due dates. The annual accounts of Timekeepers Ltd. are made up to 31st March in each year.

You are required to show the entries in the ledger of Timekeepers Ltd. (*Chartered Institute of Secretaries.*)

17. Shoes Ltd. on 1st January, 19.., leases a machine to Footwear Ltd. on the terms that the charge for royalty be 1·25p per 1,000 stitches with a minimum monthly payment of £12, with right to recoup "short-workings" over the three months immediately succeeding the month of shortage. The number of stitches for each month are—

19..

Jan	450,000	April	1,400,000
Feb	650,000	May	1,000,000
Mar	825,000	June	1,200,000

Show the monthly ledger (not cash book) entries required in the books of Footwear Ltd., for the six months to 30th June, 19.., assuming payment to be made on the last day of each month. (*Cost and Management Accountants.*)

18. A manufacturer markets a domestic appliance through dealers who sell it to their customers either for cash or on hire-purchase terms. Where the sale is for cash the customer pays the dealer in full. Where hire-purchase terms are taken, the customer pays the deposit to the dealer and pays the hire-purchase instalments to the manufacturer, who takes over the transaction from the dealer by paying him the balance of the full cash selling price.

Using the undernoted information, you are required to write up the appropriate accounts (including cash) in the books of the manufacturer. You are also required to show how the position shown by these accounts at 31st March would be disclosed on a balance sheet prepared at that date.

(i) Cash price of product	£15
(ii) Discount allowed to dealer	$33\frac{1}{3}$%
(iii) Additional charge for hire-purchase facilities . . .	£1·50
(iv) Hire-purchase deposit	£2·50
(v) Period of hire-purchase repayment	7 months
(vi) Number sold to dealers—	
January	2,000
February	2,400
March	3,000
(vii) Number sold by dealers—	
For cash—	
January	1,800
February	2,100
March	2,500
On hire-purchase—	
January	100
February	300
March	400
(viii) Cash received from dealers—March	£18,900
(ix) Hire-purchase instalments received—	
February—	
January agreements	80
March—	
January agreements	10
February agreements	280

(*Cost and Management Accountants.*)

19. J. Burnhill & Co. Ltd. manufacture an article which requires to be packed in specially fitted cases. The company buys these cases at £3 each and charges them out to customers, on the basis of sale or return within three months, at £4 each. A case ledger is kept in which the transactions with customers as regards cases are recorded. A case ledger control account, together with a "cases stock account" is maintained in the nominal ledger and there is also a "cases suspense account" which shows the unrealized profit on cases in the hands of customers.

On 1st April, 19.., there were 90 cases in stock and 80 cases were in customers' hands.

During the year ended 31st March, 19.1, 900 cases had been bought, 1,500 had been sent to customers, and 1,100 were returned. Twenty cases, purchased prior to 1st April, 19.., had become very dilapidated and upon return were sold as scrap in March, 19.1, £5 being received. The cost of repairs to cases amounted to £60. Customers had paid for 60 cases which they had failed to return within the stated time limit.

Provision for depreciation of cases is to be made at the rate of 10 per cent per annum calculated on the cost of cases in stock and in customers' hands at the beginning of the year.

Show the record of these transactions in the nominal ledger accounts mentioned above and prepare a statement to show the net charge to the profit and loss account in respect of cases for the year ended 31st March, 19.1.

(*Certified and Corporate Accountants.*)

20. A. Ltd., a mining company, works minerals under a lease, for a period of 10 years from 1st January, 19.., from B. Ltd.

By the terms of the lease, a royalty of 25p per ton is payable to B. Ltd., subject to a minimum rent of £5,000 a year.

A. Ltd. granted a sub-lease, for the same period, to C. Ltd. The sub-lease provided for a royalty of 37½p per ton, subject to a minimum rent of £2,400 a year.

Both the lease and the sub-lease provided that, should the royalties for any calendar year be less than the minimum rent, the deficiency (short-workings) could be recouped out of royalties, in excess of the minimum, of the two immediately following calendar years.

The output for the three years from the commencement of thel ease was as follows—

	By A. Ltd.	*By C. Ltd.*
	tons	tons
19..	10,400	5,600
19.1	14,800	8,000
19.2	12,800	7,600

All payments, under both lease and sub-lease, were made annually on 31st December.

You are required to show the accounts in the ledger of A. Ltd. necessary to record these transactions for the years 19.., 19.1, and 19.2, closing the accounts on 31st December in each year. Ignore taxation. (*Chartered Institute of Secretaries.*)

21. Green and Brown commenced trading as equal partners on 1st June, 19.., as selling and distributing agents of a detergent. The partnership commenced with a capital of £1,500, of which £1,000 was contributed by Green and £500 by Brown.

It was agreed that the capital accounts should remain fixed and that interest on the capital should be paid at the rate of 5 per cent per annum.

On 1st June, 19.., hire-purchase agreements were entered into for the purchase of two delivery vans, the agreements stating that the cash price of each vehicle was £750 and the hire-purchase price £810. A deposit of £252 was paid on each vehicle and the balance was payable in 18 equal monthly instalments, the first instalment being paid on 30th June, 19... All other instalments were paid on the last day of each month.

The detergent was purchased in bulk at a cost of 25p per gallon, being stored in tanks which the partners had installed at a cost of £200. It was sold in either 1-gallon tins at 50p per tin, the tins being non-returnable, or in 50-gallon returnable drums at 40p per gallon. The drums were charged out and credited on return at £8 per drum.

During the year ended 31st May, 19.1, 12,000 gallon tins were purchased at 7½p per tin, and 60 drums at £6 per drum.

24,000 gallons of detergent were purchased during the year, and 11,000 gallons were sold in gallon tins, and 12,000 gallons sold in 50-gallon drums.

During the year ended 31st May, 19.1, the following payments had been made—

	£
Rent, rates, and insurance	540
Printing, stationery, and office expenses	170
Office salaries	340
Motor expenses	430
Partners' drawings—	
Green	600
Brown	600

At 31st May, 19.1—

Sundry creditors amounted to £740 (including £60 for motor expenses and £20 for stationery).

Sundry debtors amounted to £1,100 (including £240 in respect of drums in customers' hands).

The stock consisted of 980 gallons of detergent, 1,000 1-gallon tins and 30 drums (20 used, 10 new). The cost of the drums in use is to be written off over their estimated life of three years, a full year's depreciation to be charged in the year in which they were brought into use.

Motor vans are to be depreciated at the rate of 25 per cent per annum and storage tanks at 15 per cent per annum.

You are required to prepare a profit and loss account for the year ended 31st May, 19.1, and balance sheet as at that date. The profit and loss account is to be in tabular form and is to show the cost of detergent and the cost of packing materials included in sales. *(Certified and Corporate Accountants.)*

22. AB & Co. Ltd. started a hire-purchase side of the business for which they keep separate books and a hire-purchase trading account, the profit shown on which is to be transferred to general trading account at the year end.

In 19.. the following transactions were entered into—

	Customer	Item	Cost £	Sale Price £	Deposit £	Monthly Instalments
1st Jul	A	Radiogram	50	75	15	12 at £5
1st Aug	B	Refrigerator	65	90	18	18 at £4
1st Sep	C	Washing machine	40	60	12	12 at £4
1st Nov	D	Suite	100	136	28	18 at £6
1st Dec	E	Radiogram	55	75	15	12 at £5

Deposits are paid on date of purchase and instalments are due at the end of each month, the first at the end of the month in which the deposit is paid. At 31st December, A is two instalments, and C one instalment in arrears.

You are required to write up the individual ledger accounts, to prepare the hire-purchase trading account to 31st December, 19.., and show the relevant balance sheet entries at that date.

(Calculations to nearest £.) *(Cost and Management Accountants.)*

CHAPTER 13

DEPARTMENTAL ACCOUNTS

"... double-entry bookkeeping is born of the same spirit as the system of Galileo and Newton. . . . With the same means as these, it orders the phenomenon into an elegant system, and it may be called the first cosmos built upon the basis of a mechanistic thought. Double-entry bookkeeping discloses to us the cosmos of the economic world by the same method as later the cosmos of the stellar universe was unveiled by the great investigation of natural philosophy."

WERNER SOMBART (1902)

DEPARTMENTAL accounts are accounts relating to the several departments, or divisions, of a business, and are used when it is desired to ascertain the trading results of each department, or class of goods, separately.

Analytical Purchases and Sales Books. It may be desirable to keep analytical purchases and sales books. The following are specimens—

DEPARTMENTAL PURCHASES BOOK

Date	Name	Led. Fol.	Total	Dept. 1	Dept. 2	Dept. 3	Dept. 4

DEPARTMENTAL SALES BOOK

Date	Name	Led. Fol.	Total	Drapery	Hosiery	Out-fitting	Boots

The headings of the columns vary; sometimes the departments are lettered, e.g. "A," "B," "C," etc., sometimes numbered, sometimes named, as in the two examples. Whenever analysis is resorted to, there must always be a "total" column. The object of this is to afford a check upon the arithmetical accuracy of the tabular columns. By means of cross casting it is possible to see whether the total of the analysis columns is equal to the sum of the total column. This will also prove whether any item has been omitted in the analysis.

Similar rulings will be required for the purchases returns book and the sales returns book.

Accounting Procedure. One of the simplest ways of establishing departmental results is to maintain a Trading Account for each department.

"A" Department Trading Account

Stock		Sales	
Purchases		Returns Outwards . . .	
Carriage		Stock c/d	
Returns Inwards . . .			
Wages.			
P. & L. A/c (gross profit)			
Balance b/d			

Where a more analytical account is required, the ledger accounts will be more elaborate. It will be necessary to open separate stock, purchases, sales, returns, and wages accounts for each department or class of goods, and this is most easily accomplished by using analytical rulings as follows—

Stock

Date	Particulars	Dept. A	Dept. B	Total	Date	Particulars	Dept. A	Dept. B	Total

Specialized machines are available for organizations such as Department Stores who have a large number of departments. Another possibility where the departments are very numerous, is to maintain a separate ledger in respect of each department.

Advantages of Departmental Accounts. By means of departmental accounts it becomes possible, at balancing time, to ascertain the *gross* profit of each department or class of goods. Some businesses are content with this. Others go further and analyse all the expenses as well, in order to arrive at the *net* profit of each department or class of goods. The business, taken as a whole, might be yielding a satisfactory net profit, and yet one particular department might be running at a loss. Departmental profit and loss accounts will reveal this fact. Further, the results of different years may be collected and compared, and much valuable information gained therefrom. The decided advantages, therefore, may compensate for the extra cost involved in analysing the transactions, and in keeping additional ledger accounts.

Inter-Departmental Transactions. Purchases from, and sales to, other departments must be carefully recorded. They are sometimes added to the respective purchases and sales accounts, and sometimes dealt with in separate accounts. Much depends on the price at which such transfers are charged, whether at cost, or at cost plus a small departmental profit. When such transfers of goods are made at cost, they should certainly not be credited as sales by the issuing department. It is better to credit them to a separate account entitled "Goods issued to Other Departments." At balancing time, these transfers must be debited to the trading account of the receiving department, and credited to the trading account of issuing department, if they have not already been merged in the departmental purchases and sales accounts.

Allotment of Indirect Expenses. Indirect or selling expenses may be allotted to the departments in a number of different ways and our examples show four of these: (1) by means of direct analysis; (2) according to the amount of floor space occupied by each department; (3) in proportion to the turnover of each department; (4) according to the number of articles sold. It is seldom possible to arrive at the exact amount by means of direct analysis, and the method chosen should be that which gives the fairest results, bearing in mind the fact that the great majority of overhead expenses are fixed charges.

Different Methods of Allotment for Items in the same Trading and Profit and Loss Account. Sometimes the allotment of expenses is dealt with before the trading accounts are prepared. This is generally the case where different methods of allotment are used for different items. Thus, rent, rates, and taxes may be apportioned according to the floor space occupied by each department. Wages and salaries are generally analysed directly. Insurance premiums may be apportioned according to the ratio that each department's stock bears to the total departmental stocks insured. Workmen's compensation insurance may be divided in the ratio that each department's wages and salaries bear to the total departmental wages and salaries. The allotment of printing and stationery is generally the result of direct analysis, the amounts issued being charged to the departments by the store-keeper. Carriage, postage, repairs, and office expenses are sometimes apportioned according to the results of direct analysis, and sometimes apportioned in fixed or agreed proportions. The amount of discounts allowed, including reserves for such discounts, is often apportioned between the departments in the ratio that each department's sales bear to the total departmental sales for the year. The amount of discounts received, including the reserves for such discounts, is then, likewise, apportioned between the departments in the ratio that each department's purchases bear to the total departmental purchases for the period. Depreciation can, sometimes, be charged direct to the departments according to the value of the assets held by them. Often, however, depreciation, interest on capital, legal expenses, bank charges, and other items of a similar nature cannot be satisfactorily apportioned. In such cases, they are usually included in the cost of floor area occupied.

Example 1

1. Allocation of Expenses by Means of Direct Analysis

X, Y, and Z are equal partners in a business, and according to the articles of partnership are entitled to interest at 5 per cent per annum on their respective capitals before the division of profits.

All other adjustments have been made, and from the following particulars you are requested to draw up trading and profit and loss accounts and balance sheet, showing the gross and net profits of each department, and the percentages of gross and net profit on turnovers respectively—

	£
Cash at bankers	2,030
Cash in hand	620
Cash creditor	1,500
Motor vans	625
Fixtures, fittings, etc.—	
A Dept.	4,726
B Dept.	3,842
Capital—	
X (1st Jan.)	25,970
Y (1st Jan.)	18,432
Z (1st Jan.)	15,617
Drawings—	
X	2,500
Y	1,750
Z	1,540

	A Department	B Department
	£	£
Stock (1st Jan.)	37,418	7,672
Purchases	65,158	38,516
Sales	89,527	47,733
Trade expenses	12,107	5,463
Discounts allowed	2,517	1,743
Discounts received	2,067	1,169
Housekeeping expenses	1,975	1,268
Sundry creditors	6,162	4,568
Sundry debtors	16,703	4,572
Stock, 31st December	35,463	9,872

The working of this example appears on pp. 1305–7.

Solution 1

Trading and Profit and Loss Accounts
For the Year Ended 31st December, 19..

	A Dept.	B Dept.	Total		A Dept.	B Dept.	Total
	£	£	£		£	£	£
Stock, 1st January	37,418	7,672	45,090	Sales	89,527	47,733	127,260
Purchases	65,158	38,516	103,674	Stock, 31st December	35,463	9,872	45,335
Balance (Gross Profit)	22,414	11,417	33,831				
	124,990	57,605	182,595		124,990	57,605	182,595
Trade Expenses	12,107	5,463	17,570	Gross Profit b/d	22,414	11,417	33,831
Housekeeping Expenses	1,975	1,268	3,243	Discounts Received	2,067	1,169	3,236
Discounts Allowed	2,517	1,743	4,260				
Balance (departmental profits)	7,882	4,112	11,994				
	24,481	12,586	37,067		24,481	12,586	37,067

General Profit and Loss Account
For the Year Ended 31st December, 19..

	£	£		£	£
Interest on Capital—			Departmental Profits—		
X: 5% £25,970	1,298		"A" Dept.	7,822	
Y: 5% £18,432	922		"B" Dept.	4,112	
Z: 5% £15,617	781				11,994
		3,001			
Balance to Capital—					
X: ⅓	2,998				
Y: ⅓	2,998				
Z: ⅓	2,997				
		8,993			
		11,994			11,994

Percentage of Gross Profit on Turnover: "A" Dept., 25·04; "B" Dept., 23·92 (22,415 × 100 ÷ 89,528 and 11,416 × 100 ÷ 47,733).
" " Net " " " "A" " 8·80; "B" " 8·61 (7,882 × 100 ÷ 89,528 and 4,111 × 100 ÷ 47,733).

Solution 1

Balance Sheet
As at 31st December, 19..

Liabilities	£	£	*Assets*	£	£
Sundry Creditors—			Cash at Bank	2,030	
"A" Dept.	6,162		Cash in hand	620	
"B" Dept.	4,568				2,650
		10,730	Sundry Debtors—		
Cash Creditor		1,500	"A" Dept.	16,703	
Capital—			"B" Dept.	4,572	
X, 1st Jan.	25,970				21,275
Add Interest	1,298		Stock—		
Add Share of Profit	2,998		"A" Dept.	35,463	
			"B" Dept.	9,872	
	30,266				45,335
Less Drawings	2,500		Fixtures & Fittings—		
		27,766	"A" Dept.	4,726	
Y, 1st Jan.	18,432		"B" Dept.	3,842	
Add Interest	922				8,568
Add Share of Profit	2,998		Motor Vans		625
	22,352				
Less Drawings	1,750				
		20,602			
Z, 1st Jan.	15,617				
Add Interest	781				
Add Share of Profit	2,997				
	19,395				
Less Drawings	1,540				
		17,855			
		78,453			78,453

Departmental
For the Half-year

	No. 1 Dept.	No. 2 Dept.	No. 3 Dept.	No. 4 Dept.	No. 5 Dept.	Total
	£	£	£	£	£	£
Stock, 1st July	326	458	426	501	673	2,384
Purchases	1,217	1,417	973	763	1,930	6,300
Balance (being Gross Profit c/d)	229	320	355	346	391	1,641
	1,772	2,195	1,754	1,610	2,994	10,325

Departmental Profit
For the Half-year

	No. 1 Dept.	No. 2 Dept.	No. 3 Dept.	No. 4 Dept.	No. 5 Dept.	Total
	£	£	£	£	£	£
Sundry Expenses	80	112	144	176	208	720
Rent	13	19	24	29	35	120
Depreciation	6	9	11	14	16	56
Departmental Profits to General P. & L. A/c	130	180	176	127	132	745
	229	320	355	346	391	1,641

Example 2

2. Apportionment of Expenses according to Floor Space Occupied

Reed and Stevens commenced a retail cash business on 1st July with a stock of goods divided as follows: No. 1 Dept. £326; No. 2 Dept. £458; No. 3 Dept. £426; No. 4 Dept. £501; No. 5 Dept. £673. They also had cash £556; fixtures and fittings £560; and equal amounts of capital.

On 31st December the summary of the cash book for the half-year was as follows—

	£		£
Sales—		Purchases—	
No. 1 Dept.	1,256	No. 1 Dept.	896
No. 2 Dept.	1,578	No. 2 Dept.	792
No. 3 Dept.	1,156	No. 3 Dept.	814
No. 4 Dept.	1,237	No. 4 Dept.	516
No. 5 Dept.	2,178	No. 5 Dept.	1,704
		General Expenses . . .	720
		Drawings—	
		Reed	250
		Stevens	250

The following purchases are unpaid on 31st December: No. 1 Dept. £321; No. 2 Dept. £625; No. 3 Dept. £159; No. 4 Dept. £247; No. 5 Dept. £226. Six months' rent, £120, is also outstanding. The stocks on

TRADING ACCOUNTS
Ended 31st December, 19..

	No. 1 Dept.	No. 2 Dept.	No. 3 Dept.	No. 4 Dept.	No. 5 Dept.	Total
	£	£	£	£	£	£
Sales	1,256	1,578	1,156	1,237	2,178	7,405
Stock, 31st Dec. . .	516	617	598	373	816	2,920
	1,772	2,195	1,754	1,610	2,994	10,325

AND LOSS ACCOUNTS
Ended 31st December, 19..

	No. 1 Dept.	No. 2 Dept.	No. 3 Dept.	No. 4 Dept.	No. 5 Dept.	Total
	£	£	£	£	£	£
Gross Profit b/d . .	229	320	355	346	391	1,641
	229	320	335	346	391	1,641

hand at the same date are: No. 1 Dept. £516; No. 2 Dept. £617; No. 3 Dept. £598; No. 4 Dept. £373; No. 5 Dept. £816.

Draw up departmental trading and profit and loss accounts, adding to the expenses 20 per cent per annum for depreciation of fixtures. Divide the expenses thus: No. 1 Dept. $\frac{5}{45}$ths; No. 2 Dept. $\frac{7}{45}$ths; No. 3 Dept. $\frac{9}{45}$ths; No. 4 Dept. $\frac{11}{45}$ths; No.5 Dept. $\frac{13}{45}$ths. Draw up also a balance sheet, allowing interest on capital at 5 per cent per annum, and dividing profits equally.

Solution 2

GENERAL PROFIT AND LOSS ACCOUNT
For the Half-year Ended 31st December 19..

	£	£		£	£
Interest on Capital—			Departmental Profits—		
Reed, 2½% £1,750	44		No. 1 Dept.	130	
Stevens 2½% £1,750	44		No. 2 Dept.	180	
		88	No. 3 Dept.	176	
Balance (net profit)—			No. 4 Dept.	127	
Reed, Capital ½	328·50		No. 5 Dept.	132	
Stevens, Capital ½	328·50				
		657			745
		745			745

Balance Sheet
As at 31st December, 19..

Liabilities	£	£	*Assets*	£	£
Creditors		1,578·00	Cash		2,019·00
Outstanding Rent		120·00	Stock—		
Capital—			No. 1 Dept.	516·00	
Reed, 1st July	1,750·00		No. 2 Dept.	617·00	
Add Interest	44·00		No. 3 Dept.	598·00	
Add Share of Profit	328·50		No. 4 Dept.	373·00	
			No. 5 Dept.	816·00	
	2,122·50				2,920·00
Less Drawings	250·00		Fixtures & Fittings	560·00	
		1,872·50	*Less* Depreciation	56·00	
Stevens, 1st July	1,750·00				504·00
Add Interest	44·00				
Add Share of Profit	328·50				
	2,122·50				
Less Drawings	250·00				
		1,872·50			
		5,443·00			5,443·00

Note 1. The original capital is arrived at as follows: stock £2,384 + cash £556 + fixtures £560 = £3,500 = £1,750 each partner.

Note 2. The final cash balance is obtained as follows: balance 1st July £556 + receipts £7,405 − payments £5,942 = £2,019.

Note 3. The creditors are composed of the amounts owing for the unpaid purchases of the different departments at 31st December, which when totalled amount to £1,578.

Example 3

3. Apportionment of Expenses According to Turnover

From the following particulars prepare departmental trading and profit and loss accounts for the year ended 31st December, 19.., apportioning the expenses between the departments in proportion to their respective turnovers—

	£
Stock (Raw materials and finished goods)—	
A Dept., 1st January	7,954
B Dept., 1st January	6,987
Purchases (raw materials), A Dept.	19,846
Purchases (raw materials), B Dept.	14,895
Sales A Dept.	48,994
Sales B Dept.	32,662
Exhibition expenses	1,915
Wages A Dept.	3,987
Wages B Dept.	1,989
Travellers' commission and expenses	5,376
Rent, rates, and taxes	987
Furniture and fixtures	1,275
Salaries	3,579
Working plant and utensils	55,595
Insurance (£35 of this is prepaid)	808
Bad debts provision, 1st January	748
Motor vans and vehicles	7,987
Directors' fees	2,025
Sundry debtors	22,953
Postage, telegrams, and bill stamps	917
Difference in exchange (*Dr.* balance)	38
Sundry expenses	2,796
Bad debts	828
Stationery, sample books, and catalogues (£345 of these are still in stock)	3,376
Debenture interest	630
Discounts on purchases	1,748
Discounts on sales	3,268
Motor expenses	637

Depreciate working plant, etc., 10 per cent; motor vans, etc., 20 per cent; furniture $2\frac{1}{2}$ per cent. Make a reserve of 5 per cent on Sundry debtors, for bad debts. Stock of raw materials and finished goods on 31st December, 19.., was—

A Dept. £9,895; B Dept. £7,958

Approximation. Apportionment is, in its nature, an *approximate* process. Whilst it is *fair* to share expenses between departments, no one can pretend that it is absolutely accurate. For this reason, elaborate methods of calculation are not recommended. Such methods merely give an appearance of exactness to an inspired guess and they can mean a fruitless waste of time. The turnover of two or more departments rarely gives an easy proportion, but this can be obtained by rounding off the figures. In

Solution 3

Trading and Profit and Loss Account

For the Year Ended 31st December, 19..

	A Dept.	B Dept.	Total		A Dept.	B Dept.	Total
	£	£	£		£	£	£
Stock 1st January	7,954	6,987	14,941	Sales	48,994	32,662	81,656
Purchases	19,846	14,895	34,741	Stock, 31st December	9,895	7,958	17,853
Wages	3,987	1,989	5,976				
Balance (Gross Profit)	27,102	16,749	43,851				
	58,889	40,620	99,509		58,889	40,620	99,509
	$\frac{3}{5}$	$\frac{2}{5}$					
Travellers' Commission & Expenses	3,226	2,150	5,376	Balance (Gross Profit)	27,102	16,749	43,851
Rent, Rates & Taxes	592	395	987	Discounts on Purchases	1,049	699	1,748
Salaries	2,147	1,431	3,579				
Insurance (£808 — £35)	464	309	773				
Directors' Fees	1,215	810	2,025				
Postage, Telegrams & Bill Stamps	550	366	917				
Exhibition Expenses	1,149	766	1,915				
Sundry Expenses	1,677	1,118	2,796				
Stationery & Samples (£3,376 — £345)	1,818	1,212	3,031				
Discounts on Sales	1,961	1,307	3,268				
Motor Expenses	382	254	637				
Debenture Interest	378	252	630				
Difference in Exchange	23	15	38				
Bad Debts	497	331	828				
Bad Debts Provn. (£1,147 — £748)	239	159	399				
Depreciation							
Working Plant, 10% £55,595	3,335	2,223	5,559				
Motors, etc., 20% £7,987	958	638	1,597				
Furniture, $2\frac{1}{2}$% £1,275	19	12	31				
Balance (Net Profit)	7,521	3,700	11,213				
	28,151	17,448	45,599		28,151	17,448	45,599

Note—
"A" Dept. = $\frac{3}{5}$ or 60%
"B" Dept. = $\frac{2}{5}$ or 40%

our example, the turnover of Department A may be taken as £48,000, and for Department B £32,000. Both are divisible by 16, giving a proportion of 3:2. Department A will bear three-fifths, Department B two-fifths of the expenses to be apportioned.

The solution to example 3 appears on p. 1310.

Example 4

4. Apportionment of Expenses According to Number of Articles Sold

The Toilet Requisites Co. manufacture two specialities, namely, "Venus" soap and "Hebe" scent. From the following particulars draw up the company's trading and profit and loss accounts for the year ended 30th June—

	£
Stocks of raw materials, soap (1st July)	1,200
" " " " (30th June)	1,800
" " " scent (1st July)	900
" " " " (30th June)	1,100
" manufactured soap (1st July)	1,000
" " " (30th June)	1,600
" " scent (1st July)	800
" " " (30th June)	900
" labels, boxes, bottles, etc., soap (1st July)	300
" " " " " " (30th June)	400
" " " " " scent (1st July)	350
" " " " " " (30th June)	260
Purchases of raw materials, soap	1,020
" " " scent	1,700
" labels, boxes, bottles, etc., soap	600
" " " " " scent	500
Wages, Soap Dept.	1,100
" Scent "	2,300
Manufacturing Expenses, Soap Dept.	150
" " Scent "	750
Salaries	1,050
Advertising	9,240
Printing and stationery	1,400
Postage	910
Rent, rates, and taxes	2,100
Sundry expenses	700
Sales of soap, 360,000 @ ·05p.	
" scent, 60,000 @ ·25p.	

The undivided expenses are to be apportioned between the two departments according to the *number* of cakes of soap or bottles of scent sold.

Apportionment of Expenses According to the Number of Articles Sold. In the example given, the quantities of the two articles sold are in the proportion 360,000:60,000, i.e. 6:1. In practice, of course, the proportion will almost certainly be found not to work out so easily and it will be necessary to round off the figures until a reasonable proportion is reached. Students are advised to familiarize themselves with modern processes and up-to-date methods in commercial arithmetic.

The solution to example 4 appears on p. 1312.

Solution 4

TRADING AND PROFIT AND LOSS ACCOUNT
For the Year Ended 30th June, 19..

	Soap	Scent	Total		Soap	Scent	Total
	£	£	£		£	£	£
Stocks, 1st July				Sales			
Raw Materials	1,200	900	2,100	360,000 Cakes of Soap @ ·05p	18,000		
Manufactured Goods	1,000	800	1,800	60,000 Bottles of Scent @ ·25p		15,000	33,000
Labels, Bottles, Boxes, etc.	300	350	650	Stocks, 30th June			
Purchases				Raw Materials	1,800	1,100	2,900
Raw Materials	1,020	1,700	2,720	Manufactured Goods	1,600	900	2,500
Labels, Bottles, Boxes, etc.	600	500	1,100	Labels, Bottles, Boxes, etc.	400	260	660
Wages	1,100	2,300	3,400				
Manufacturing Expenses	150	750	900				
Balance (Gross Profit)	16,430	9,960	26,390				
	21,800	17,260	39,060		21,800	17,260	39,060
Salaries	900	150	1,050	Gross Profit	16,430	9,960	26,390
Advertising	7,920	1,320	9,240				
Printing & Stationery	1,200	200	1,400				
Postage	780	130	910				
Rent, Rates, and Taxes	1,800	300	2,100				
Sundry Expenses	600	100	700				
Balance (Net Profit)	3,230	7,760	10,990				
	16,430	9,960	26,390		16,430	9,960	26,390

Separate Trading Accounts for Each Department. Where the same item of expenditure or charge is common to each department, a tabular trading and profit and loss account as shown on p. 1312 may be used. But where different expenses and charges are incurred in the various departments separate trading accounts must be prepared for each.

Example 5

From the following particulars of the Motor Car Engineering Works Ltd. prepare departmental trading accounts and a general profit and loss account for the year ended 31st December, 19. .—

	£
Fixtures and fittings	75
Loose plant and tools	225
Sundry debtors	2,925
Cars bought for resale	12,500
Carriage on cars sold	115
Management expenses	510
Profit and loss account (undistributed balances, 1st Jan.)	650
Bad debts	50
Petrol, oil, etc., used	625
Charged to customers for hire of cars	405
Sales of motor-cars	14,750
Charged to customers for repairs to cars	950
Accessories (tyres, tubes, etc.) used	2,350
Stock of cars for hiring out	650
Stock of accessories (tyres, tubes, petrol, oil, etc.) at end of current year	375
Expenses of hire cars	225
Sales of petrol, oil, etc.	975
Garage rents received	90
Debenture interest	125
Repairs to plant, etc.	27
Sales of accessories (tyres, tubes, etc.)	2,735
Wages in yard	156
Cost of repairs to cars (wages, materials, etc.)	875
Bad debts provision, 1st Jan.	120
Sundry receipts (washing cars, charging batteries, etc.)	166

The following adjustments are necessary—bad debts reserve: 5 per cent debtors; depreciation: loose plant and tools 20 per cent; fixtures and fittings: 5 per cent; cars for hire: 20 per cent; the manager is entitled to a commission of 5 per cent of the net profit after charging this commission.

Solution 5

MOTOR CARS TRADING ACCOUNT

For the Year Ended 31st December, 19. .

	£		£
Purchases	12,500	Sales	14,750
Balance (Gross Profit)	2,250		
	14,750		14,750

Accessories Trading Account
For the Year Ended 31st December, 19..

	£		£
Accessories used	2,350	Sales of Accessories	2,735
Petrol, Oil, etc., used	625	Sales of Petrol, Oil, etc.	975
Balance (Gross Profit)	735		
	3,710		3,710

Repairs Trading Account
For the Year Ended 31st December, 19..

	£		£
Cost of Repairing Cars	875	Amounts Charged to Customers for Repairs to Cars	950
Balance (Gross Profit)	75		
	950		950

Hire Cars Trading Account
For the Year Ended 31st December, 19..

	£		£
Expense of Hire Cars	225	Charges to Customers for Hire of Cars	405
Depreciation of Hire Cars, 20%, £650	130		
Balance (Gross Profit)	50		
	405		405

Profit and Loss Account

		£		£
Carriage on Cars sold		115	Trading A/cs (gross profits)—	
Management Expenses		510	Motor Cars	2,250
Bad Debts		50	Accessories	735
Repairs to Plant, etc.		27	Repairs	75
Debenture Interest		125	Hire Cars	50
Wages in Yard		156	Garage Rents	90
Bad Debts Provn.—			Sundry Receipts	166
5% £2,925	£146			
Less Old Provn.	120			
		26		
Depreciation—				
Loose Tools & Plant, 20% £225		45		
Fixtures, etc., 5% £75		4		
Manager's Commission $\frac{5}{105}$ of £2,308		110		
Balance (Net Profit) to Appropriation A/c		2,198		
		3,366		3,366

Manager's Commission. This is an item over which students constantly stumble. As the net profit is not yet known, the calculation must be made on the gross amount distributable, namely, $\frac{5}{105}$ of £2,308; which, as can be seen, is equal to $\frac{5}{100}$ of £2,198.

QUESTIONS

1. Explain what is meant by "departmental" accounts.
2. Submit rulings of a purchases book suitable for a business having four departments.
3. Submit rulings of a sales book suitable for a business dealing in tea, coffee, cocoa, and sugar, each of which is a separate department.
4. Explain how the ledger is affected by the keeping of "departmental" accounts. Give examples.
5. State briefly the advantages to be derived from a system of "departmental" accounts.
6. Are "departmental" accounts adopted with a view to ascertaining the *gross* or the *net* profit of each department?
7. What difficulties are there in the way of arriving at the "net" profit of each department?
8. What is meant by the phrase "allocation of indirect expenses"?
9. What methods may be used with reference to the allocation of indirect expenses as between different departments? Which is considered to yield the fairest result?
10. When it is not possible to make a tabular trading account of several departments owing to the item being different in each, what procedure must be resorted to?

EXERCISE 13

1. A manufacturer, whose business is divided into the three departments of knitted mufflers, sailors' jerseys, and woollen gloves, adopts the following method of recording his sale transactions. When goods are dispatched, an invoice is made out in an invoice carbon copy book, and sent to the purchaser. The carbon copy book is then handed to the ledger clerk, who writes the ledger folio of the customer's account under the total of the copy invoice, and posts the item to the debit of the customer's account in the ledger thus—

		Invoice No.	
April 1, 19..	To	Goods, N.B. 0001 . . .	£59

Does this method appear to you to provide an adequate record for book-keeping purposes? If not, what would you suggest, and with what object? (*R.S.A.*)

2. Explain briefly and comment upon some system of departmental accounts with which you are familiar.

3. The Needlebore Trading Co. manufactures and sells linoleum and carpets. From the following particulars prepare trading and profit and loss accounts, apportioning the undivided expenses in proportion to the turnovers of the departments—

	Linoleum Dept. £	Carpet Dept. £
Stocks (1st Jan.)	1,956	2,285
Purchases (net)	8,385	3,649
Wages	3,958	2,017
Manufacturing expenses (including depreciation of plant)	2,075	1,474
Sales (net)	21,446	10,723
Stocks (31st Dec.)	1,754	2,071

Salaries £3,068; rent, rates, and taxes £1,789; general expenses £916.

4. Jeffrey, Slater and Gibbs are equal partners in a business, and are entitled to interest at 5 per cent per annum on their respective capitals before division of profits. All other adjustments have been made. From the following particulars for the year ended 31st December, draw up trading and profit and loss account, showing the gross and net profit of each department, and the percentage of gross and net profit on turnovers respectively—

	£		£
Cash at bank	1,987	Capital (1st Jan.)—	
Cash in hand	520	Jeffrey	23,516
Cash creditor	2,000	Slater	16,379
Motor-car	752	Gibbs	13,176
Fixtures, fittings, etc.—		Drawings	
"A" Dept.	3,985	Jeffrey	2,750
"B" Dept.	4,106	Slater	2,000
		Gibbs	1,650
"A" Dept.		**"B" Dept.**	
Stock, 1st Jan.	32,516	Stock, 1st Jan.	7,497
Purchases	61,987	Purchases	36,518
Sales	81,082	Sales	46,916
Trade expenses	9,027	Discounts allowed	1,628
Discounts allowed	2,016	Discounts received	1,534
Discounts received	1,856	Trade expenses	4,159
Housekeeping expenses	1,632	Housekeeping expenses	1,079
Sundry creditors	4,438	Sundry debtors	4,178
Sundry debtors	14,891	Sundry creditors	3,987
Stock, 31st Dec.	31,678	Stock, 31st Dec.	8,918

5. Davis & Smith commenced a retail cash business on 1st July with a stock of goods divided as follows: No. 1 Dept. £373; No. 2 Dept. £478; No. 3 Dept. £402; No. 4 Dept. £537; No. 5 Dept. £667. They also had cash £773, fixtures and fittings £616; and equal amounts of capital. On 31st December, the summary of their cash book for the half-year was as follows—

	£		£
Sales—		Purchases—	
No. 1 Dept.	1,309	No. 1 Dept.	773
No. 2 Dept.	1,572	No. 2 Dept.	770
No. 3 Dept.	1,638	No. 3 Dept.	852
No. 4 Dept.	1,719	No. 4 Dept.	917
No. 5 Dept.	2,082	No. 5 Dept.	1,262
		General Expenses	816
		Drawings—	
		Davis	300
		Smith	300

On 31st December the following purchases were unpaid: No. 1 Dept. £353; No. 2 Dept. £539; No. 3 Dept. £446; No. 4 Dept. £355; No. 5 Dept. £340. One quarter's rent, £115, is also outstanding. Stocks on hand at this date are: No. 1 Dept. £427; No. 2 Dept. £531; No. 3 Dept. £457; No. 4 Dept. £567; No. 5 Dept. £757. Draw up departmental trading accounts, adding to the expenses 20 per cent per annum for

depreciation of fixtures. Divide the expenses in the following proportions: No. 1 Dept. 3; No. 2 Dept. 5; No. 3 Dept. 7; No. 4 Dept. 9; No. 5 Dept. 11. Draw up also a profit and loss account and balance sheet as at 31st December, allowing interest on capital at 5 per cent per annum, and dividing profits equally.

6. The Toilet Specialities Co. manufacture and sell two popular articles, "Excelsior" hair cream and "De Luxe" tooth powder respectively. From the following particulars draw up the company's trading and profit and loss accounts for the year ended 30th June—

	£
Stock of raw materials, hair cream (1st July)	807
,, ,, ,, ,, ,, (30th June)	616
,, ,, ,, tooth powder (1st July)	316
,, ,, ,, ,, ,, (30th June)	361
Stock of manufactured hair cream (1st July)	713
,, ,, ,, ,, (30th June)	543
,, ,, tooth powder (1st July)	307
,, ,, ,, (30th June)	378
,, bottles, boxes, labels, etc., hair cream (1st July)	307
,, ,, ,, ,, ,, ,, (30th June)	238
,, ,, ,, ,, tooth powder (1st July)	246
,, ,, ,, ,, ,, ,, (30th June)	247
Purchases of raw materials, hair cream	727
,, ,, ,, tooth powder	517
,, bottles, boxes, labels, etc., hair cream	518
,, ,, ,, ,, tooth powder	323
Manufacturing expenses, hair cream	268
,, ,, tooth powder	243
Wages, hair cream dept.	707
,, tooth powder dept.	734
Salaries	427
Advertising	5,896
Postage	506
Rent, rates, and taxes	722
Sundry expenses	317
Sales of hair cream, 75,000 bottles @ 10p per bottle.	
,, tooth powder, 500,000 boxes @ 2½p per box.	

The undivided expenses are to be apportioned between the two departments according to the *number* of bottles of hair cream or boxes of tooth powder sold.

7. From the following particulars of the Luxworth Motor Car Works Ltd. draw up departmental trading accounts, and a profit and loss account, for the year ending 31st December, 19...

	£
Fixtures and fittings	110
Loose plant and tools	378
Sundry debtors	3,026
Cars bought for resale	15,725
Carriage on cars sold	129
Management expenses	487
Profit and loss account—*Cr.* bal. 1st Jan.	706
Bad debts	110
Petrol, oil, etc., used	657
Charged to customers for hire of cars	467

	£
Sales of motor-cars	18,950
Charged to customers for repairs to cars	906
Accessories (tyres, tubes, etc.) used	2,418
Hire cars	574
Stock of accessories (tyres, petrol, oil, etc.) as at 31st December, 19..	356
Expenses of hire cars	208
Sales of petrol, oil, etc.	1,026
Garage rents received	110
Debenture interest	125
Repairs to plant, etc.	29
Sales of accessories (tyres, tubes, etc.)	2,907
Wages in yard	148
Cost of repairs to cars (wages, materials, etc.)	816
Bad debts provision, 1st January	140
Sundry receipts (washing cars, charging batteries, etc.)	175

The following adjustments are necessary—bad debts provision: 5 per cent on debtors; depreciation: loose tools: 20 per cent; fixtures and fittings: 5 per cent; hire cars: 20 per cent; the manager is entitled to a commission of 5 per cent of the net profit after charging this commission.

8. Smith, Brown & Johnson are equal partners in a business, and are entitled to interest at 5 per cent on their respective capitals before the division of profits. All other adjustments have been made, and from the following particulars you are requested to draw up trading and profit and loss accounts and balance sheet, showing the gross and net profits of each department, and also the percentages of gross and net profit on turnovers respectively—

	£		£
Capital—		Stock (1st Jan.)	74,837
Smith (1st Jan.)	51,942	Purchases	130,316
Brown (1st Jan.)	36,865	Housekeeping expenses	3,951
Johnson (1st Jan.)	31,234	Discounts allowed	5,034
Drawings—		Discounts received	4,135
Smith	5,000	Trade expenses	24,215
Brown	3,500	Stock, 31st Dec.	70,927
Johnson	3,080		
Cash at bank	4,059	No. 2 Dept.	
Cash in hand	1,241	Sundry debtors	9,144
Fixtures, fittings, etc.—		Sundry creditors	9,137
No. 1 Dept.	9,453	Sales	95,465
No. 2 Dept.	7,682	Stock (1st Jan.)	15,345
Vehicles	1,251	Purchases	77,032
Cash creditor	3,000	Housekeeping expenses	2,536
No. 1 Dept.		Discounts allowed	3,486
Sundry debtors	33,407	Discounts received	2,339
Sundry creditors	12,325	Trade expenses	10,925
Sales	179,055	Stock, 31st Dec.	19,743

9. Hammond & Nelson commenced a retail cash business on 1st July with a stock of goods divided as follows: A Dept. £653; B Dept. £916; C Dept. £853; D Dept. £1,003; E Dept. £1,346. They also had fixtures and fittings £1,121; equal amounts of capital; and cash £1,104.

The following was the summary of their cash book for the half-year ended 31st December—

Sales—	£	Purchases—	£
A Dept.	2,512	A Dept.	1,792
B Dept.	3,156	B Dept.	1,585
C Dept.	2,313	C Dept.	1,628
D Dept.	2,475	D Dept.	1,033
E Dept.	4,357	E Dept.	3,406
		General Expenses	1,441
		Drawings—	
		Hammond	500
		Nelson	500

The following purchases are unpaid on 31st December: A Dept. £641; B Dept. £1,250; C Dept. £318; D Dept. £493; E Dept. £452. One quarter's rent, £240, is also outstanding. The stocks on hand at 31st December are: A Dept. £1,033; B Dept. £1,234; C Dept. £1,197; D Dept. £747; E Dept. £1,633.

Draw up departmental trading accounts, adding to the expenses 20 per cent per annum for depreciation of fixtures. Divide the expenses thus: A Dept. 5 parts; B Dept. 7; C Dept. 9; D Dept. 11; E Dept. 13 parts. Draw up also a profit and loss account, and balance sheet, allowing interest on capital at 5 per cent per annum, and dividing profits equally.

10. From the following particulars prepare departmental trading and profit and loss accounts for the year ended 31st December, apportioning the expenses between the two departments in proportion to their respective turnovers—

	£
Stock (raw materials and finished goods)—	
X Dept. (1st Jan.)	15,909
Y Dept. (1st Jan.)	13,975
Purchases (raw materials), X Dept.	39,693
Purchases (raw materials), Y Dept.	29,791
Sales, X Dept.	97,988
Sales, Y Dept.	65,325
Exhibition expenses	3,831
Wages, X Dept.	7,975
Wages, Y Dept.	3,979
Travellers' commission and expenses	10,753
Rent, rates, and taxes	1,975
Fixtures and fittings	2,550
Salaries	7,159
Working plant and utensils	111,190
Insurance (£70 of this is prepaid)	1,617
Bad debts provision, 1st Jan.	1,497
Motor vans and vehicles	15,974
Directors' fees	4,050
Sundry debtors	45,907
Postage, telegrams, and bill stamps	1,834
Difference in exchange (*Dr.* balance)	77
Sundry expenses	5,592
Bad debts	1,657
Stationery, sample books, and catalogues (£690 of these are still in stock)	6,753
Debenture interest	1,260
Discounts on purchases	3,497
Discounts on sales	6,537
Motor expenses	1,274

Depreciate working plant 10 per cent; motor vehicles 20 per cent; furniture 2½ per cent. Make a provision of 5 per cent on sundry debtors. Stock of raw materials and finished goods on 31st December was—

X Dept. £19,791; Y Dept. £15,917

11. The Table Delicacies Co. manufacture and sell two specialities, namely, "Tip Top" fish paste and "A 1" sauce. From the following particulars draw up the company's trading and profit and loss accounts for the year ended 30th June—

	£
Stocks of raw materials—	
Fish paste (1st July)	1,251
Fish paste (30th June)	1,652
Sauce (1st July)	469
Sauce (30th June)	550
Stocks of manufactured fish paste (1st July)	1,074
Stocks of manufactured fish paste (30th June)	1,744
Stocks of manufactured sauce (1st July)	433
Stocks of manufactured sauce (30th June)	533
Stocks of bottles, pots, labels, etc., paste (1st July)	270
Stocks of bottles, pots, labels, etc., paste (30th June)	414
Stocks of bottles, pots, labels, etc., sauce (1st July)	344
Stocks of bottles, pots, labels, etc., sauce (30th June)	270
Purchases of raw materials, fish paste	1,033
Purchases of raw materials, sauce	815
Purchases of bottles, pots, labels, etc., paste	647
Purchases of bottles, pots, labels, etc., sauce	487
Wages, fish paste dept.	1,046
Wages, sauce dept.	1,205
Manufacturing expenses, paste dept.	113
Manufacturing expenses, sauce dept.	396
Salaries	652
Advertising	7,239
Printing and stationery	894
Carriage on sales	653
Rent, rates, and taxes	1,331
Sundry expenses	558
Sales of fish paste, 700,000 pots @ 5p per pot.	
Sales of sauce, 150,000 bottles @ 12½p per bottle.	

The undivided expenses are to be apportioned between the two departments according to the *number* of pots of fish paste or bottles of sauce sold.

12. Goods supplied to the various departments of PQ Ltd., a retail store, are debited to departmental stock accounts at cost plus a fixed percentage thereof to give the normal selling price. This fixed percentage, which is known as "mark up" is credited to a departmental mark up account. The departmental stock accounts and mark up accounts are adjusted for any subsequent reductions in normal selling prices (known as "mark down") and for sales. The mark up in 1964 and in 1965 is 25 per cent for department A and 33⅓ per cent in the case of department B.

	Department A	Department B
Book stocks at 1st January, 1965—	£	£
At normal selling prices less any mark down	10,000	15,500
At cost	8,500	12,000
Purchases at cost	47,000	82,500
Sales	59,000	110,500

You are informed that—

(*a*) Goods which cost £1,200 in 1964 and which had not been marked down were transferred from department A to department B but the transfer had not been recorded in the books. These goods were sold during the year after adjustment of the mark up to department B's normal selling price.

(*b*) Goods bought in 1965 were marked down as follows—

	Cost	Mark down
	£	£
Department A	6,000	600
Department B	15,000	3,000

With the exception of items costing £7,500 which were still in stock in department B at the year end and which are at the marked down price, all these items were sold.

(*c*) Physical shortages at the year end which had to be written off at cost totalled £400 for department A and £750 for department B.

(*d*) All goods in stock at the beginning of the year were sold in 1965.

You are required to—

(*a*) Calculate the value at cost of the stocks on hand at 31st December, 1965.

(*b*) Prepare trading account for the year 1965 for each department for which purpose stocks are to be valued at cost.

(*c*) Prepare "mark up" accounts for both departments.

(*Cost and Management Accountants.*)

13. S. Forest carries on business as an ironmonger and timber merchant. The following is the trial balance extracted from his books as on 31st March, 1962.

	Dr	*Cr*
	£	£
Purchases—Shop	4,800	
Yard	5,160	
Wages and Salaries—Shop	590	
Yard	1,480	
Sales—Shop		6,560
Yard		7,737
Expenses of Administration	650	
S. Forest—Capital Account as at 31st March, 1961		4,750
Drawings	1,530	
Purchase ledger balances		1,490
Plant and Machinery at cost—Yard	320	
Furniture, Fixtures and Fittings at cost—Shop	80	
Provision for depreciation—		
Plant and Machinery		303
Furniture, Fixtures and Fittings		36
Motor Vehicles—At cost 31st March, 1961	1,500	
Provision for depreciation		900
Sales and purchases during the year	620	
Stocks on hand on 31st March, 1961—		
Shop	1,180	
Yard	1,620	
Balances on Sales ledgers—		
Shop	380	
Yard	790	
Cash at Bank	1,100	
Provision for yard doubtful debts		24
	21,800	21,800

The following further information is given which is to be taken into account—

(1) During the year plant was made in the timber yard for its own use, materials used amounted to £90 and the labour involved to £60.

The yard also carried out repairs to the shop involving £18 for materials and £15 for labour.

(2) The yard purchased goods from the shop amounting to £20.

(3) The amount for sales and purchases of motor vehicles during the year covers the purchase of a new vehicle costing £1,000, less a deduction of £380 allowed for a vehicle traded in which originally cost £750 and in respect of which relative provision for depreciation was £355. The motor vehicles are used only by the yard.

(4) S. Forest has decided to grant bonuses to his staff as follows: Shop £70, Yard £100.

(5) Included in the Yard sales ledger balances is a debt of £50, which is regarded as bad and is to be written off, and a specific reserve is to be made for a further debt of £20. 5 per cent is to be provided against the remainder of debtors. It is not thought necessary to make any provision as regards the shop balances.

(6) Depreciation for the year, based on cost at the end of the year, is to be provided as follows—

	per cent
Plant and Machinery	10
Furniture, Fixtures and Fittings	5
Motor Vehicles	10

(7) Stocks on hand on 31st March, 1962, were valued at: Shop £1,450, Yard £2,210.

(8) The expenses of administration are to be apportioned equally between the shop and the yard.

You are requested to prepare (1) Trading and Profit and Loss Accounts for the year ended 31st March, 1962, in a form to show separately the net results of both the shop and the yard; and (2) a Balance Sheet as on that date.

14. A. F. Walters and J. B. Smith are in partnership as pipe manufacturers; they also rent and work a retail shop. Profits or losses are shared as follows: A. F. Walters two-thirds, J. B. Smith, one-third. The shop manager sends in weekly returns of all transactions, and these returns are duly incorporated in the books of the head office. You are required to prepare a trading and profit and loss account for the year ended 28th February, and a balance sheet as on that date; a separate trading account is also required showing the working results of the shop.

The following is a list of the ledger balances as extracted by the head clerk of the firm as on 28th February—

	£		£
A. F. Walters, capital . . .	6,200	Stock on hand, 1st March (factory)	3,828
J. B. Smith, capital . . .	3,500	" " " (shop)	747
Plant and machinery . . .	3,280	Cash purchases (shop) . . .	62
Fixtures and fittings (factory) .	620	Sundry creditors . . .	2,428
Purchases	16,780	Traveller's commission (factory)	152
Sales (factory)	24,353	Salaries (factory) . . .	2,280
" (shop)	12,538	Office expenses, postage, etc. (factory)	395
Manufacturing wages . . .	8,433	Law expenses and audit fee (factory)	41
" expenses . . .	891		
Rent, rates, taxes, light, and insurance (factory) . . .	360		
(shop) . . .	423		

	£		£
Bad debts written off (factory) .	8	Bills payable	78
Discount, *Cr.* balance (factory) .	282	Salaries of manager and assistant at shop	1,266
Provision for bad debts as on 1st March	74	A. F. Walters (drawings) . .	1,212
Sundry debtors	2,520	J. B. Smith (drawings) . .	606
Furniture, fixtures, and fittings (shop)	980	Cash at bank	2,512
Bills receivable	2,000	„ in hand (factory) . .	7
		„ „ „ (shop) . .	50

Before preparing the annual accounts, the following adjustments are necessary—

Interest is to be credited upon the capital accounts at 5 per cent.

Provide for: rent, rates, etc., account (factory) for rent accrued due 28th February, £78; rent, rates, etc., account (shop) two months' rent due to 28th February (the annual rent of the shop is £360); audit fee, £36.

The manager of the shop is entitled, under his agreement, to a commission of 2 per cent on the gross profit realized by the shop.

Plant and machinery are to be depreciated at 10 per cent. Fixtures and fittings are to be depreciated at 5 per cent.

Provision for bad and doubtful debts is to be made at 2½ per cent.

The stock on hand as on 28th February was valued as follows—

	£
Factory	3,105
Shop	470

The goods supplied by the factory to the shop during the year were priced out at £4,199 cost price. (*London Chamber of Commerce.*)

15. The sales ledgers of a trading concern are divided alphabetically and kept on a "self-balancing" basis. The following were the data from which the A–D sales ledger adjustment account in the nominal ledger was written up for March.

Balances in A–D ledger on 28th February (agreeing with adjustment account): Debtors £2,459; creditors £47.

	£
Sales during month	3,589
Sales returns during month	108
Cash received during month	2,891
Discount allowed during month	93
Bills receivable received during month	250
Bad debts written off	15

Miss D. Peter's account, having a debit balance of £9, was transferred to the A–D ledger, she having married a Mr. Cunningham.

A credit balance of £21 appearing on M. Brown's account in the bought ledger was set off against his account in the sales ledger.

The list of balances extracted from the A–D sales ledger at the end of March showed total debtors £2,664, and creditors £43.

Write up the adjustment account from the particulars given, ascertain the "difference," and state the most important of the figures you would first check in order to find it. (It may be assumed that a trial balance of the nominal ledger agrees and all the other ledgers balance.) (*R.S.A.*)

CHAPTER 14

BRANCH ACCOUNTS

The Government are very fond of statistics.
They add them and they multiply them and they subtract the square root and they make beautiful charts about them. But you must always remember that in the first instance they are dependent on the village watchman who just puts down what he damn well pleases.

JOSIAH STAMP

Divisions of the Subject. Branch accounts are generally divided into three main classes—

1. Where the branch book-keeping is done at the head office, the branch supplying the necessary information, or, making returns.
2. Where the branch keeps its own books, and at balancing time forwards a copy of its trial balance for incorporation in the head office books.
3. Foreign branches.

Accounting treatments may vary according to whether the branch is retail or wholesale. Moreover, the kind of business itself exercises an important influence upon the method of accounting. In some trades the stock is of a perishable nature, in others it remains good indefinitely; obviously, therefore, it cannot be dealt with in the same way in both cases.

1. BOOKS KEPT BY HEAD OFFICE

Transfer of Stock to Branches. When a branch is opened and stock is transferred to it from the head establishment, this transfer should not be treated as a sale; for it is merely an issue of goods. The value of the goods should be debited to a branch account, and credited to a special account entitled "Goods Sent to Branches." At balancing time this latter account is closed by transfer to trading account.

Example 1

On 1st January a branch establishment was opened, and stock value £1,000 was transferred thereto. Show the journal and ledger entries recording this transaction.

JOURNAL

		Dr	*Cr*
19..		£	£
Jan 1	Branch A/c	1,000	
	Goods sent to Branches		1,000

LEDGER

Branch Account

Date		Particulars	£	Date		Particulars	£
19..							
Jan	1	Goods to Branches .	1,000				

Goods Sent to Branches

Date		Particulars	£	Date		Particulars	£
19..				19..			
Dec	31	Trading A/c . .	1,000	Jan	1	Branch A/c . .	1,000

Trading Account

Date		Particulars	£	Date		Particulars	£
				19..			
				Dec	31	Sales (say) . . .	15,460
						Goods to Branches .	1,000

The goods sent to the branches thus appear in the trading account as a separate item. Otherwise, comparison of turnover may be undermined, since the goods are valued at cost and have not yet been sold.

Branch Supplies Book. Where there are several branches, each supplied with goods from the head establishment, a tabular "Goods Sent to Branches" or "Branch Supplies" book is employed. The totals of the columns are debited periodically to the separate branch accounts and credited to a "goods sent to branches" account. The following is a facsimile of the ruling—

Date	Particulars	Fo.	Total	Branch A	Branch B	Branch C

How Goods are Invoiced to the Branch. When branches are opened, the goods supplied to the branches may be charged out to them (according to the nature of the business)—

1. At cost.
2. At a fixed percentage on cost.
3. At selling price.

In the "multiple shop" system, that is, where there is one head establishment with numerous selling depots, the goods are charged to the branches at selling price. This procedure establishes a definite check upon such branches. What a branch cannot produce in money, it must have in stock (taken at selling price); and frequent stock-taking will reveal whether there is any leakage or not.

Where goods are charged to the branches at a price other than actual cost, i.e. at a percentage on cost, or at selling price, the branch supplies book would be ruled with duplicate columns for each branch. One column would record the cost price, for the purpose of the trading account; the other column would contain the invoice price, so as to facilitate the debiting of the respective branches therewith. The following is a specimen of such ruling—

Date	Particulars	Total		Branch A		Branch B	
		Cost Price	Invoice Price	Cost Price	Invoice Price	Cost Price	Invoice Price

Branch Receipts and Payments. The money received by the branch for the cash sales, and on ledger accounts where goods are also sold on credit, is either paid in daily at some local bank to the credit of the head office account, or else remitted every day direct to head office. The expenses of the branch, such as rent, rates and taxes, wages, petty charges, etc., are paid, in some cases, by cheque direct from the head office, and, in other cases, by means of the imprest system; whatever the branch spends for such purposes out of the original sum advanced to it is repaid to the branch by the head office. In a few instances, however, the wages and expenses are paid out of the cash takings, and only the balance remitted to the head establishment. The cash book kept by the head office generally contains extra columns on each side to record the receipts from, and payments to, the various branches, the totals of these columns being posted periodically to the branch accounts. The branch itself is provided with a small cash book for the purpose of recording its daily takings and any petty disbursements.

Branch Returns. In most cases, the branch is called upon by the head office to make periodic "returns." Where the branch sales are exclusively cash, the branch would simply make returns of—

1. Its daily takings, with a departmental analysis of such cash sales if necessary;
2. Its wages and other expenses, likewise dissected if desired;

3. Any commission that had accrued to the assistants or manager; and
4. Such statistical information respecting its present stock and future requirements as the head office may direct.

But where the sales are partly cash and partly credit, additional particulars have to be furnished, i.e. in connexion with the debtors—

5. What accounts have been settled since the last return;
6. The cash received, the discounts, returns, and allowances in connexion with such settlements;
7. What debts have become doubtful or bad;
8. Particulars of the credit sales since the last return;
9. The debtors outstanding at the date of the current return.

The branch itself usually keeps a small ledger for the debtors' accounts. From the information thus furnished by each branch, the head office is enabled to write up the various branch accounts.

A suitable form of weekly return for a leather shop is shown in Figure 14.1.

1. a. Retail Branches

(i) Goods to Branches at Cost Price

Example 2

From the following particulars prepare the branch account as it would appear in the head office books. The branch sales are for cash only, and the goods sent to the branch have been invoiced at cost price—

	£
Goods from head office	5,360
Returns to „ „	47
Rates, taxes, and insurance paid	75
Wages paid	365
Cash remitted to head office	6,650
Stock, 1st January	750
Rent paid	130
Stock, 31st December	790
Sundry expenses paid	80

BRANCH ACCOUNT

19..			£	19..		£
Jan	1	Balance	750	Dec 31	Cash	6,650
Dec	31	Goods from Head Office	5,360		Returns to Head Office	47
		Cash (Wages)	365		Stock c/d	790
		„ (Rent)	130			
		„ (Rates, Taxes & Insurance)	75			
		„ (Sundry Expenses)	80			
		P. & L. A/c (profit)	727			
			7,487			7,487
19..						
Jan	1	Balance b/d	790			

(ii) Goods to Branches at Cost Price Plus Fixed Percentage

Whenever goods are invoiced to the branch at a percentage on cost price, this percentage must be taken into account at balancing time, that

KALAMAZOO LEATHER SHOPS LTD.

For . . . . shop

. . . . Week/Month ending . . . . . .

Takings	Till No. 1	Till No. 2
Total week taking — Mon		
Tue		
Wed		
Thurs		
Refunds from suppliers — Fri		
Sat		
Total takings		
Total		

Banked			Office banking	
			Tuesday	
			Wednesday	
			Thursday	
			Friday	
			Saturday	
			Monday	
			Total banked	

Cash payments

			Salaries	For office use only
			Fares & Expenses	
			Cleaning & Laundry	
			Casual labour	
			Cash purchases for resale	
			Refunds	
			Sundries	
			Total cash payments	
			Total bank	
			Total week's takings	

Weekly till balance

			Till No. 1	Till No. 2
		This week's reading		
		Last week's reading		
		Balance		

Cash register balance

	Error plus		
	Error minus		
Total No. sales			
Total No. of customers	Date	Lid No.	Lid No.

Signed Manager

This sheet must be entered daily and forwarded to head office on Saturday night each week

FIG. 14.1

is to say, the branch purchases, and opening and closing stocks, must be reduced to cost in order to arrive at the correct profit. In an office, the cost can be easily ascertained by reference to the cost price column in the branch supplies book; but, in exercises and examination work, the cost must be found by arithmetical calculation. The student must remember that, if a percentage has been added to the cost of goods, the *same* percentage taken off will not reduce the goods to their original value. For example, suppose that £600 worth of goods has been sent to a branch with $33\frac{1}{3}$ per cent added to the cost; the goods would then have been invoiced to the branch at £800. Now, $33\frac{1}{3}$ per cent taken off £800 will not reduce it to its original figure of £600. An exposition of the reasoning behind this can be found on p. 2918.

Example 3

From the particulars furnished hereunder, write up the branch account in the head office books. The branch sales are exclusively cash, and the goods sent to the branch have been invoiced at $33\frac{1}{3}$ per cent on cost—

	£
Goods sent to branch *less* returns	7,200
Wages and salaries paid	380
Cash remitted by branch	7,068
Stock, 1st January	900
Rates, taxes, and insurance paid	85
Rent paid	150
Stock, 31st December	1,020
Sundry expenses paid	42

Solution 3(a)

BRANCH ACCOUNT

19..		£	19..		£
Jan 1	Balance (Stock)	675	Dec 31	Cash	7,068
Dec 31	Goods from Head Office	5,400		Stock c/d	765
	Cash (Rates, Taxes & Insurance)	85			
	Wages & Salaries	380			
	Rent	150			
	Sundry Expenses	42			
	P. &. L. A/c (net profit)	1,101			
		7,833			7,833
19..					
Jan 1	Balance (Stock) b/d	765			

The goods received from head office, and also the stocks at the commencement and end of the trading period, have been decreased by one-fourth before being dealt with.

Branch Accounts with Double Money Columns. Where the ledger accounts contain double money columns, one to record the invoice price, and the other the cost price, such columns possess the great advantage of showing clearly, and at a glance, both the nominal and the actual gross profits. The percentage added to the cost price, when invoicing goods to the branch, is usually the estimated or expected rate of gross profit on cost. And when the branch trading account is made up at the actual invoice figures, both sides should, theoretically, agree. A balance, if any, indicates that more, or less, than the anticipated gross profit is being made. In the following Solution, which is a re-working of Example 3, but with double money columns, the actual gross profit is short of what it ought to be by the sum of £12. This fact would, in practice, lead to a search for a probable error, and possibly to an investigation as to whether the figures relating to the goods or money were being manipulated. (See p. 1411–13.)

Solution 3(b)

BRANCH ACCOUNT

		Invoice Price				Invoice Price	
19..		£	£	19..		£	£
Jan 1	Balance (Stock) .	900	675	Jan–Dec	Cash . .	7,068	7,068
Jan–Dec	Goods from Head Office . .	7,200	5,400	Dec 31	Stock c/d . .	1,020	765
Dec 31	Balance (gross profit)		1,758		Balance (apparent loss)	12	
		8,100	7,883			8,100	7,833
Dec 31	Rates, Taxes & Insurance .		85	Dec 31	Gross Profit . .		1,758
	Wages & Salaries .		380				
	Rent . .		150				
	Sundry Expenses .		42				
	P. & L. A/c (net profit) . .		1,101				
			1,758				1,758
19..							
Jan 1	Balance (Stock) .	1,020	765				

Branch Adjustment Account. Instead of employing double money columns to bring both sets of figures into account, the goods sent to the branch are sometimes posted to the ledger at the invoice price only. It then becomes necessary to open a "branch adjustment account" in addition to a "goods sent to branches account," if it is desired by means of double entry to ascertain the actual trading profit. This method, applied to the previous example (3), will provide the following ledger accounts—

Solution 3(c)

BRANCH ACCOUNT

19..			£	19..			£
Jan 1	Balance (Stock) . .	*a*	900	Jan–Dec	Cash remitted . . .		7,068
Jan–Dec	Purchases from Head Office	*d*	7,200	Dec 31	Stock c/d . .	*b*	1,020
					Branch Adjustment A/c (apparent loss) .	*c*	12
			8,100				8,100
19..							
Jan 1	Balance (Stock) b/d . .		1,020				

BRANCH ADJUSTMENT ACCOUNT

			£				£
19..				19..			
Dec 31	Balance (% on Stock) c/d	*b*	255	Jan 1	Balance (% on Stock) .	*a*	225
	Branch A/c (apparent loss)	*c*	12	Jan–Dec	Goods to Branches A/c (% on Goods) . . .	*d*	1,800
	Branch P. & L. A/c (gross profit)		1,758				
			2,025				2,025
				19..			
				Jan 1	Balance b/d . .	*e*	255

GOODS SENT TO BRANCHES ACCOUNT

			£			£
19..				19..		
Dec 31	Branch Adjustment A/c	*d*	1,800	Jan–Dec	Branch A/c. . . .	7,200
	Transfer to Trading A/c (Goods at cost) . .		5,400			
			7,200			7,200

The credit balance of £255 in the branch adjustment account would be set-off against the debit balance of £1,020 in the branch account, enabling the branch stock to be entered in the stock account and in the balance sheet at cost, namely, £765. The branch adjustment account shows a gross profit of £1,758, which amount would be taken to a branch profit and loss account. Against this gross profit would be debited the total of the branch expenses, viz. £657. This would leave a net profit of £1,101 to be carried to the general profit and loss account—the same result as by the previous method.

QUESTIONS

1. How are branch accounts divided? What subdivisions are there?
2. What entries are made when a branch is opened and goods transferred thereto from stock? Is it correct to treat such a transfer as a sale?
3. Submit rulings of a "branch supplies book," and explain its use.
4. In what three ways are goods invoiced to branches?
5. What object is sought by invoicing goods to branches at selling price? Explain the term "multiple shop system."
6. Explain the method of dealing with branch receipts and payments.
7. Explain the term "branch returns." What do they comprise in the case of a branch doing: (1) only a cash business, (2) both cash and credit business?
8. How may the invoice price be reduced to cost when a known percentage has been added? Give examples.
9. Explain the object of double money columns in the ledger records of branch accounts.
10. Explain and illustrate the use of a branch adjustment account.

Credit Sales by Branches. These are treated in different ways. Where the transactions are not very large or numerous, everything is passed through one branch account, the debtors being treated in the same way as stock at the commencement and close of the trading period. In some cases, however, a separate "branch debtors account" is opened in addition to a "branch account." Where the turnover is sufficiently large to warrant it, the branch account itself is often divided into two parts, a "branch goods account" and a "branch expenses account," in order to show both gross and net profits.

Example 4

From the particulars given below, draw up the branch account or accounts in the head office books. The goods sent to the branch have been invoiced at cost, and the branch makes both cash and credit sales—

	£
Goods from head office	2,540
Returns to head office	40
Stock, 1st January	750
Cash sales	1,675
Six months' credit sales to 30th June	2,995
Allowances to customers	16
Discounts allowed to customers	120
Bad debts	29
Rents, rates, and taxes	90
Returns from customers	28
Wages and salaries	297
Debtors, 1st January	1,310
Stock, 30th June	695
Sundry expenses	65
Cash received on ledger a/cs	2,459
Debtors, 30th June	1,651

Solution 4(a)

The simplest form would be the following, which is constructed on a *cash* basis, the debtors being treated as a form of stock—

BRANCH ACCOUNT

19..			£	19..			£
Jan 1	Balance—			Jan–Jun	Cash—		
	Stock	£750			Ledger A/cs		2,459
	Debtors	1,310			Cash Sales		1,675
			2,060		Returns to Head Office		40
Jun 30	Goods from Head Office		2,540	Jun 30	Balance c/d—		
	Rent, Rates, & Taxes		90		Stock	£695	
	Wages & Salaries		297		Debtors	1,651	
	Sundry Expenses		65				2,346
	P. & L. A/c (net profit)		1,468				
			6,520				6,520
Jul 1	Balance b/d		2,346				

Solution 4(b)

A more elaborate form would be as follows—

BRANCH GOODS ACCOUNT

19..		£	19..		£
Jan 1	Balance	750	Jun 30	Cash Sales	1,675
Jan–Jun	Goods from Head Office	2,540		Credit Sales	2,995
	Returns Inwards	28		Returns to Head Office	40
	Allowances	16		Stock c/d	695
	Branch P. & L. A/c (gross profit)	2,071			
		5,405			5,405
Jul 1	Balance (Stock) b/d	695			

Branch Expenses Account

			£				£
19..				19..			
Jun	30	Rent, Rates, etc.	90	Jun	30	Transfer to Branch P. & L. A/c	601
		Wages & Salaries	297				
		Sundry Expenses	65				
		Bad Debts	29				
		Discounts	120				
			601				601

Branch Debtors Account

			£			£
19..				19..		
Jan	1	Balance	1,310	Jan–Jun	Cash	2,459
Jan–Jun		Credit Sales	2,995		Discount	120
					Returns Inwards	28
					Allowances	16
					Bad Debts	29
					Balance c/d	1,653
			4,305			4,305
Jul	1	Balance b/d	1,653			

Branch Profit and Loss Account

			£				£
19..				19..			
Jun	30	Branch Expenses A/c	601	Jun	30	Branch Goods A/c (gross profit)	2,071
		Head Office P. & L. A/c (net profit)	1,468				
			2,071				2,071

Depreciation of Assets. Where a branch possesses fixed assets such as furniture, fixtures, and fittings, the depreciation is often dealt with in the head office depreciation account only, as assumed in the previous examples. In some cases, however, it is charged against each particular branch, as in the following examples.

Example 5

From the undermentioned particulars construct the branch accounts as they would appear in the head office books The branches are charged with the goods at selling price, the sales being exclusively cash. The rate of gross profit is 25 per cent *on selling price.*

	Branch A	Branch B
	£	£
Goods from head office	10,145	10,216
Returns to head office	48	46
Sales by branch	9,626	9,818
Stock, 1st January	1,275	1,684
Stock, 31st December	1,726	1,986
Allowances off selling price	29	39
Sundry expenses	95	120
Salaries and wages	237	316
Depreciation of furniture and fixtures	22	24
Rent, rates, and taxes	260	284
Excess in stock at close	9	
Shortage in stock at close		10

Solution

Notes on Example. The selling price of goods is often subject to variation, according to the quantity taken. For instance, articles retailed at 1p each may be sold at 4p a dozen and 38p a gross, and so on. A record is kept of these allowances off selling price, and the total is written off at the end of the period. Again, it occasionally happens that at stock-taking the stock is different from what it ought to be, being sometimes more, and sometimes less. These discrepancies must, of course, be adjusted at balancing time.

Branch "A" Expenses Account

		£			£
19..			19..		
Dec 31	Salaries & Wages	237	Dec 31	Transfer to Branch P. & L. A/c	614
	Rent, Rates, & Taxes	260			
	Sundry Expenses	95			
	Depreciation of Fixtures, etc.	22			
		614			614

Branch "B" Expenses Account

		£			£
19..			19..		
Dec 31	Salaries & Wages	316	Dec 31	Transfer to Branch P. & L. A/c	744
	Rent, Rates, & Taxes	284			
	Sundry Expenses	120			
	Depreciation of Fixtures	24			
		744			744

Goods to Branches

		£			£
19..			19..		
Jan–Dec	Branch "A" Returns	36	Jan–Dec	Branch "A"	7,609
	Branch "B" Returns	34		Branch "B"	7,662
Dec 31	Trading A/c	15,201			
		15,271			15,271

Branch Profit and Loss Account

		Branch "A"	Branch "B"			Branch "A"	Branch "B"
19..		£	£	19..		£	£
Dec 31	Branch Expenses	614	744	Dec 31	Branch A/cs (Gross Profit)	2,392	2,417
	Head Office P. & L. A/c (Net Profit)	1,778	1,673				
		2,392	2,417			2,392	2,417

(The branch accounts are shown overleaf.)

Monthly Stock Accounts. Where goods are charged out to branches at selling price, or at a fixed percentage on cost, there is, of course, an

Branch "A" Account

Date		Particulars	Invoice Price		Date		Particulars	Invoice Price	
19..			£	£	19..			£	£
Jan	1	Balance (Stock)	1,275	956	Jan–Dec		Cash	9,626	9,626
Jan–Dec		Goods to Branches	10,145	7,609			Returns to Head Office	48	36
Dec	31	Excess in Stock	9				Allowances off Selling Prices	29	
		Branch P. & L. A/c (gross profit)		2,392	Dec	31	Balance (Stock) c/d	1,726	1,295
			11,429	10,957				11,429	10,957
19..									
Jan	1	Balance (Stock) b/d	1,726	1,295					

Branch "B" Account

Date		Particulars	Invoice Price		Date		Particulars	Invoice Price	
19..			£	£	19..			£	£
Jan	1	Balance (Stock)	1,684	1,263	Dec	31	Cash	9,818	9,818
Jan–Dec		Goods to Branches	10,216	7,662			Returns to Head Office	46	34
		Branch P. & L. A/c (gross profit)		2,417			Allowances off Selling Price	39	
							Shortage in Stock	11	
							Balance (Stock) c/d	1,986	1,490
			11,900	11,342				11,900	11,342
19..									
Jan	1	Balance (Stock) b/d	1,986	1,490					

adequate check on the stock; but where goods are invoiced at cost, there is no such check. In order to provide one, approximate (or estimated) stock accounts are prepared monthly, and recorded in a book kept specially for this purpose. These accounts enable the proprietor or directors to know at any time the value, approximately, of the stock on hand without going through the long and tedious process of stock-taking. Where the rate of gross profit is a fixed percentage of the selling price, a fairly accurate result may be obtained by adding to the stock at the commencement the subsequent net purchases, and deducting from the total the net sales for the same period, after reducing them by the said percentage of gross profit. Below is a specimen of one of these accounts.

The illustrations so far used have all been simple but, as stated, the type of business may necessitate or permit of variations, either in the manner of dealing with cash and stock or the selling of goods on credit.

APPROXIMATE STOCK ACCOUNT

19..			£	19..		£
Jan	1	Stock	2,850	Jan 31	Sales (less Returns)	1,060
	31	Purchases (less Returns)	550		*Less* (say) 25%	265
						795
					Balance (estimated Stock) c/d	2,605
			3,400			3,400
Feb	1	Balance b/d	2,605			

It is obviously impossible and unnecessary in this volume to deal with these matters fully, but the following points should be considered.

Control of Cash. It has been stated that cash takings, either in full or after the deduction of certain outgoings, are paid into the bank for the credit of head office. This does not mean that the branch has a banking account. In order to maintain the strictest control, a matter which is vital when it is borne in mind that a company may have several hundred branches separated from the head office by as many miles, the best arrangement is that *all* takings should be paid in to a local bank for the credit of head office and *all* expenses except incidentals which are paid out of a petty cash imprest, should be paid by head office direct to the creditor. For example in the case of such items as rent, gas and electricity, the accounts will be rendered to the branch and after checking by the manager they will be forwarded to head office for payment. Wages cheques will also be sent each week to the branch managers who, by arrangement, can cash them at the local bank so that they do not need to use their takings.

Purchases by Branches. Under all normal circumstances head office would make all purchases in order to obtain the benefits consequent upon large-scale buying, but in some cases branch managers would be allowed a little freedom in this connexion. In the case of a provision business for example it may be policy to purchase eggs from the local poultry farm, as by so doing an additional customer might be obtained, whilst the produce itself would be fresher. They could still be invoiced to, and paid by, head office, but in order to keep such purchasing under control the branch should be supplied with a printed order book in triplicate so that a copy of every order could be sent to head office and a printed note at the foot of every order would keep the amounts within specified limits, such as: "No responsibility will be accepted for any order of more than £20 unless it is countersigned by the Secretary."

Credit Sales. It may be advisable to allow credit sales, even if only to meet competition from other houses, and if this is done a system of control will be necessary. Numbered invoice forms should be supplied to the branches in triplicate so that one copy can be sent to head office. If the accounts are kept at head office the statements will be rendered from there, leaving very little room for errors or discrepancies.

1. b. Wholesale Branches

Method of Keeping the Accounts. In wholesale branches, where the volume of trade is very much greater, and the transactions large and important in themselves, the accounts are kept in a manner somewhat similar to departmental accounts. Separate stock, purchases, sales, and returns accounts are opened for each branch, thus: Branch "A" Stock Account, Branch "B" Stock Account; Branch "A" Purchases Account, Branch "B" Purchases Account; Branch "A" Sales Account, Branch "B" Sales Account, etc. Expense accounts are kept for each branch, e.g. Branch "A" Wages, Branch "B" Wages; Branch "A" Rent, Rates, and Taxes, Branch "B" Rent, Rates, and Taxes; and so on. Separate ledgers also are kept for each branch. For example, Branch "A" debtors ledger would contain the personal accounts of branch "A" customers. Branch "A" general ledger would record the branch asset accounts, such as motor vehicles, fixtures and fittings, and also the nominal accounts, such as rent, rates and taxes, wages, discounts, bad debts, etc.

How the Buying is Done. The head office generally does all the buying; keeps the creditors' accounts in its own books, merely distributing the goods to its branches for sale. Sometimes, however, the branches are permitted to order, from outside, any goods they may require, the goods being sent direct to the branch, but invoiced to the head office.

How Goods Sold are Invoiced. When invoicing goods to customers, branches make out the invoice in triplicate; one copy is forwarded to the customer, one to the head office, and one retained by the branch for reference.

Example 6

From the undermentioned particulars relating to a head office and its two wholesale branches, prepare final accounts and balance sheet as they would appear in the head office books.

	Head Office	Northern Branch	Southern Branch
	£	£	£
Stock, 1st January	—	4,825	4,126
Debtors	—	17,346	14,986
Creditors	8,347	—	—
Discounts earned	—	527	408
Bad debts	—	633	524
Bills payable	2,694	—	—
Purchases *less* returns	—	11,876	9,756
Furniture, fixtures, and fittings	120	310	239
Motor vehicles	—	1,972	1,568
Salaries	985	—	—
Cash at bank	8,906	—	—
Share capital (24,000 shares of £1 each, fully paid)	24,000	—	—
Travellers' salaries and expenses	—	3,108	2,006
Directors' fees	500	—	—
Sales *less* returns	—	27,659	22,914
Wages	—	2,397	1,716
Interim dividend 8%	1,920	—	—
Stock, 31st December	—	5,802	4,950
Debenture interest	425	—	—
Reserve fund a/c	7,500	—	—
Discounts allowed	—	1,646	1,542
5% debentures	8,500	—	—
Carriage inwards	—	510	458
Depreciation	13	234	186
Sundry expenses	—	3,067	3,010
Rent, rates, and taxes	245	357	298
Motor vehicle expenses	—	327	256
Cash in hand	21	76	50
Reserve for bad debts, 5% debtors			

TRADING AND PROFIT AND LOSS ACCOUNT

For the Year Ended 31st December, 19..

	Northern Branch	Southern Branch	Total		Northern Branch	Southern Branch	Total
	£	£	£		£	£	£
Stock, 1st Jan	4,825	4,126	8,951	Sales (net)	27,659	22,914	50,573
Purchases (net)	11,876	9,756	21,632	Stock, 31st Dec	5,802	4,950	10,752
Carriage Inwards	510	458	968				
Wages	2,397	1,716	4,113				
Balance (Gross Profit) c/d	13,853	11,808	25,661				
	33,461	27,864	61,325		33,461	27,864	61,325
Discounts Allowed	1,646	1,542	3,188	Balance (Gross Profit) b/d	13,853	11,808	25,661
Bad Debts	633	524	1,157	Discounts Earned	527	408	935
Rent, Rates, and Taxes	357	298	655				
Travellers' Salaries and Expenses	3,108	2,006	5,114				
Sundry Expenses	3,067	3,010	6,077				
Motor Vehicle Expenses	327	256	583				
Depreciation	234	186	420				
Bad Debts Reserve	867	749	1,616				
Balance (net profit)	4,141	3,645	7,786				
	14,380	12,216	26,596		14,380	12,216	26,596

General Profit and Loss Account

For the Year Ended 31st December, 19..

	£			£
Rent, Rates, & Taxes	245	Branch Profits—		
Salaries	985	Northern Branch	£4,141	
Directors' Fees	500	Southern Branch	3,645	
Debenture Interest	425			7,786
Depreciation	13			
Balance (net profit for year)	5,609			
	7,786			7,786

Balance Sheet

As at 31st December, 19..

Liabilities		£	*Assets*		£
Share Capital—			Motor Vehicles, *less* depreciation		3,540
24,000 Shares of £1 each fully paid		24,000	Furniture, Fixtures, & Fittings, *less* depreciation		669
5% Debentures		8,500	Stock-in-trade		10,752
Reserve Fund A/c		7,500	Sundry Debtors	£32,332	
Sundry Creditors		8,347	*Less* Bad Debts Reserve	1,616	
Bills Payable		2,694			30,716
P. & L. A/c—			Cash in Hand	147	
Profit for year	£5,609		Cash at Bank	8,906	
Less Interim Dividend	1,920				9,053
		3,689			
		54,730			54,730

Where the head establishment is a manufacturing concern, e.g. a factory which invoices the goods to its branches at a profit, there would be an extra column in the trading account, in order to show the trading profit of the factory as well as the trading profits of the branches.

2. BOOKS KEPT BY THE BRANCHES

Where the branches are semi-independent trading establishments, they generally do their own book-keeping, and at the end of the financial period forward a copy of their trial balance for the trading results to be incorporated in the head office books.

Head Office Account. Inasmuch as the head office finances the branch and supplies it with the greater part of its goods, there is a constant state of indebtedness on the part of the branch to the head office. The position is almost that of ordinary debtor and creditor, and is evidenced in the head office books by the *debit* balance of the branch account, and in the branch books by the *credit* balance of the head office account. In the branch books the head office account takes the place of the capital account in an ordinary trader's books. Should a branch have opening entries to record in its ledger, the excess of assets over liabilities would not be shown as capital but as a debt due to the head office. The "head office account" is known by various names; sometimes it is called the "head office current account," and sometimes the "head office adjustment account"; while the "branch account" in the head office books is also called the "branch current account" or the "branch adjustment account."

Remittance Account. To reduce the amount of its indebtedness, the branch remits at intervals a round sum of money to the head office. This money is sometimes credited direct to the branch account, and sometimes put to the credit of an intermediate remittance account. Much depends on how frequently the branch remits. Where remittances are made in moderate sums, and are, therefore, fairly numerous, a separate remittance account is of great advantage, as it keeps unnecessary details out of the branch account, thereby simplifying matters and making it very much clearer. At balancing time, however, the total of the remittance account must be transferred to the credit of the branch account, in order to show the correct amount the branch owes to the head office at that date. In the branch books, the remittance account is designated "remittances to head office," the counterpart of this account in the head office books being styled "remittances from branch."

Goods and Remittances in Transit. It frequently happens at balancing time that the branch account, and also the remittance account, as shown by the branch trial balance, do not correspond with their respective amounts as shown by the head office trial balance. This may arise where the branch has forwarded a remittance to the head office on the last day of the trading period. The branch, of course, has debited its remittance account with amount remitted; but the head office, not having received it until the first day of the new trading period, has not credited its remittance account. It also occurs whenever the head office has forwarded goods to the branch on the last day of the trading period, and has debited the branch account. The branch, however, has not credited the head office, because it did not receive the goods on that date.

Before attempting the final entries, the balances of the current accounts and the remittance accounts must be made to agree. The amount of the goods received by the branch, after the close of the trading period, must be deducted from the branch account in the head office books and put to a goods in transit account. The value of the remittance received by the head office, after the close of the trading period, must likewise be deducted from the remittance account in the branch books and placed to a remittance in transit account. The adjustments will be effected by means of journal entries, and the transit items will then appear on the balance sheet. In the ensuing period the adjustments will be written back, i.e. fresh journal entries will be made reversing the previous ones, thus closing the transit accounts. A specimen is given below. For the sake of clearness, trading and profit and loss account items have been omitted and the other items summarized.

Head Office Trial Balance
31st December, 19..

	£	£
Sundry assets	12,621	
Capital		10,950
Sundry creditors		3,128
Branch current a/c	2,916	
(£250 of this is for goods sent on 31st Dec.)		
Remittances from branch		1,459
	15,537	15,537

Branch Trial Balance
31st December, 19..

	£	£
Sundry assets	1,457	
Sundry creditors		369
Head office current a/c		2,666
Remittances to head office	1,579	
(£120 of this represents a remittance made on 31st Dec.)		
	3,036	3,036

The effect of the adjustments is as follows—

Head Office Trial Balance
31st December, 19..

	£	£
Sundry assets	12,621	
Capital		10,950
Sundry creditors		3,128
Branch current a/c	2,666	
Goods in transit to branch	250	
Remittances from branch		1,459
	15,537	15,537

Branch Trial Balance
31st December, 19..

	£	£
Sundry assets	1,457	
Sundry creditors		369
Head office current a/c		2,666
Remittances to head office	1,459	
Remittances in transit to head office	120	
	3,036	3,036

Eliminating the *contra* current and remittance accounts, the head office balance sheet would be as under—

BALANCE SHEET AS AT 31ST DECEMBER, 19..

Liabilities	£	*Assets*	£
Capital	10,950	Sundry Assets	14,078
Sundry Creditors	3,498	Goods in transit to Branch	250
		Remittance in transit from Branch	120
	14,448		14,448

Alternative Method. The more simple alternative is to treat the stock and cash in transit as adjustments at the year end in the trading account in the same way as "accruals" and "prepayments" are provided for in the expense accounts. Applying this to Example 3 on p. 1406, and assuming the items in transit of stock and cash are £250 and £120 respectively, the result would be as follows—

Solution 3(d)

BRANCH ACCOUNT

		£			£
19..			19..		
Jan 1	Balance (Stock)	675	Dec 31	Cash received	7,068
Dec 31	Goods from Head Office	5,400		" in transit c/d	120
	Cash (Rates, Taxes & Insurance)	85		Stock c/d	765
	Wages & Salaries	380		" in transit c/d	250
	Rent	150			
	Sundry Expenses	42			
	P. & L. A/c (net profit)	1,471			
		8,203			8,203
19..					
Jan 1	Cash in transit b/d	120			
	Stock b/d	765			
	" in transit b/d	250			

This avoids the making of two sets of journal entries and the opening of "stock in transit" and "cash in transit" accounts.

Example 7

From the following trial balance of the branch books, prepare the necessary journal entries to incorporate the figures in the head office books, and show the final accounts in the branch ledger and also in the head office ledger.

BRANCH TRIAL BALANCE

31st December, 19..

	£	£
Motor vehicles	275	
Furniture and fixtures	76	
Sundry debtors	1,075	
Sundry creditors		211
Stock, 1st January	750	
Purchases from head office	2,856	
Sales		3,975
Discounts received		19
Rent, rates, and taxes	93	
Sundry expenses	65	
Depreciation	34	
Head office a/c		3,385
Cash in hand	127	
Carriage inwards	82	
Wages and salaries	369	
Bad debts	32	
Remittances to head office	1,680	
Discounts allowed	76	
	7,590	7,590

Stock, 31st December, £825.

Solution 7

HEAD OFFICE JOURNAL

			Dr	*Cr*
19..			£	£
Dec 31	Remittances from Branch		1,680	
	Branch A/c			1,680
	Balance transferred.			
31	Branch Trading A/c		3,688	
	Branch A/c			3,688
	Stock, 1st Jan.	£750		
	Purchases	2,856		
	Carriage Inwards	82		
	Balances transferred.			
31	Branch A/c		4,800	
	Branch Trading A/c			4,800
	Sales	£3,975		
	Stock, 31st Dec.	825		
	Balances transferred.			
31	Branch Trading A/c		1,112	
	Branch A/c		19	
	Branch Profit & Loss A/c			1,131
	Gross profit and discounts received transferred.			

HEAD OFFICE JOURNAL (*contd.*)

			Dr	Cr
19..			£	£
Dec 31	Branch Profit & Loss A/c		669	
	Branch A/c			669
	Wages & Salaries	£369		
	Rent, Rates, & Taxes	93		
	Discounts Allowed	76		
	Sundry Expenses	65		
	Bad Debts	32		
	Depreciation	34		
	Balances transferred.			
31	Branch Profit & Loss A/c		462	
	Head Office Profit & Loss A/c			462
	Net profit of Branch transferred.			

In Head Office Ledger

Remittances from Branch

		£			£
19..			19..		
Dec 31	Branch A/c	1,680	Jan–Dec	Cash	1,680

Branch Account

		£			£
19..					
Jan 1	Balance	3,385	Dec 31	Remittances from Branch	1,680
Dec 31	Branch Trading A/c	4,800		Branch Trading A/c	3,688
	Branch P. & L. A/c	19		Branch P. & L. A/c	669
				Balance c/d	2,167
		8,204			8,204
19..					
Jan 1	Balance b/d	2,167			

Branch Trading Account

		£			£
19..			19..		
Dec 31	Branch A/c—		Dec 31	Branch A/c—	
	Stock	750		Sales	3,975
	Purchases	2,856		Stock	825
	Carriage Inwards	82			
	Branch P. & L. A/c (gross profit)	1,112			
		4,800			4,800

Branch Profit and Loss Account

		£			£
19..			19..		
Dec 31	Branch A/c—		Dec 31	Branch Trading A/c (gross profit)	1,112
	Wages & Salaries	369		Branch A/c—	
	Rent, Rates, & Taxes	93		Discounts Received	19
	Discounts Allowed	76			
	Sundry Expenses	65			
	Bad Debts	32			
	Depreciation	34			
	Head Office P. & L. A/c (net profit)	462			
		1,131			1,131

In Branch Ledger

Remittances to Head Office

		£			£
19..			19..		
Jan–Dec	Cash	1,680	Dec 31	Transfer to Head Office A/c .	1,680

Head Office Account

		£			£
19..			19..		
Dec 31	Transfer from Remittance A/c	1,680	Jan 1	Balance	3,385
	Balance c/d . . .	2,167	Dec 31	P. & L. A/c (net profit)	462
		3,847			3,847
			19..		
			Jan 1	Balance b/d . .	2,167

Trading and Profit and Loss Account
For the Year Ended 31st December, 19..

	£		£
Stock, 1st Jan.	750	Sales	3,975
Purchases from Head Office	2,856	Stock, 31st Dec. . . .	825
Carriage Inwards	82		
Balance (goods profit) . . .	1,112		
	4,800		4,800
Wages & Salaries . . .	369	Gross Profit b/d . . .	1,112
Rent, Rates, & Taxes . . .	93	Discounts Received	19
Sundry Expenses . . .	65		
Bad Debts . . .	32		
Discounts Allowed . . .	76		
Depreciation . . .	34		
Head Office A/c (net profit transferred)	462		
	1,131		1,131

Balance Sheet
As at 31st December, 19..

Liabilities		£	*Assets*	£
Sundry Creditors		211	Cash	127
Head Office A/c—			Sundry Debtors	1,075
Balance, 1st Jan.	£529		Stock	825
Add Goods supplied by			Motor Vehicles (*less* depreciation)	275
Head Office . .	2,856		Furniture & Fixtures (*less* depreciation)	76
	3,385			
Less Remittances . .	1,680			
	1,705			
	1,705			
Add Profit	462			
		2,167		
		2,378		2,378

The foregoing method would apply to both retail and wholesale branches, the principal difference between the two being that, in the latter, the trade would assume much larger proportions, and the turnover might run into tens and hundreds of thousands with the figures for other items correspondingly large.

QUESTIONS

1. What methods are there of dealing with the record of *credit* sales in the case of branches?
2. How is depreciation dealt with in branch accounts?
3. How are variations in the selling price (according to quantity taken) dealt with in branch accounts where the goods have been invoiced to the branch at selling price?
4. Explain and illustrate the use of "monthly stock accounts."
5. Explain the method of keeping the accounts in the case of *wholesale* branches.
6. How is the buying usually done in wholesale branches? How are goods sold usually invoiced?
7. What difference is there in the book-keeping where branches keep their own books?
8. Explain the nature and *modus operandi* of the "head office account."
9. Explain and illustrate the use of a "remittance account."
10. Explain and illustrate the method of dealing with goods and remittances *in transit*.

Inter-branch Transactions. Where there are several branches, each permitted to have credit dealings with the others, they will keep a current account with one another as well as with the head office. At balancing time, the balances of these current accounts will be liabilities and assets of the branches, as between themselves, but not liabilities of the business as a whole. When the general balance sheet is prepared in tabular or columnar form, they must be shown in their proper columns, in order to make the vertical totals agree. A columnar balance sheet, however, is only for the benefit of the business, and when the general balance sheet is framed, the balances of the head office current accounts, the branch current accounts, and the inter-branch current accounts, being contras, can easily be eliminated.

Unrealized Profits. If goods are transferred between branches at selling price, the selling branch will show a profit, but the organization *as a whole* does not realize that profit until the goods are sold.

This is dealt with by a "provision for unrealized profit" which is made on the goods unsold at the end of the period. The provision is debited to profit and loss account and records the profit which would otherwise be shown. In the balance sheet it is deducted from the value of the stock (at selling price) to give a net figure of stock at cost price.

Example 8

A branch trial balance shows—

	£	£
Stocks at cost to branch	3,000	
Other assets	17,000	
Head office current a/c		5,500
Profit and loss a/c		8,000
Creditors		6,500
	20,000	20,000

Goods are sent to branch from head office at 20 per cent on cost.

Solution 8

The cost prices of stock is £3,000 *less* one-sixth = £2,500, and £500 provision is required.

The amended trial balance will be—

	£	£
Stocks at cost to branch	3,000	
Provision for unrealized profit		500
Other assets	17,000	
Head office current a/c		5,500
Profit and loss a/c		7,500
Creditors		6,500
	20,000	20,000

In the combined balance sheet of head office and branches the balance sheet entry will be—

Combined Balance Sheet on . . . . .

		£
	Head Office Stock	?
	Branch Stock	2,500

If goods are also purchased from outsiders, the provision must only be made on the proportion of stock received from head office. If one-third of the stock of £3,000 was purchased from outside, then the amount of the provision is arrived at as follows—

	£
Stock held	3,000
Less purchased outside	1,000
Received from head office	2,000

Provision for unrealized profit £2,000 × $\frac{1}{6}$ = £333·33.

Example 9

Three partners, B. Brown, J. Jones, and S. Smith, have branch businesses working independently in London, Birmingham, and Dundee. Brown manages the London business, and receives two-thirds of the profits therefrom, the balance being shared equally between Jones and Smith. Jones manages the Birmingham business, receiving half of the profits therefrom, the balance being shared equally between Brown and Smith. Smith manages the Dundee business, receiving one-third of the profits therefrom, the balance being shared equally between Brown and Jones.

The branches buy from, and sell to, one another at a small inter-branch profit.

From the following trial balances draw up a tabular trading and profit and loss account, and a balance sheet in (*a*) columnar form, (*b*) ordinary form. Credit each partner with interest on capital at 5 per cent per annum, and depreciate plant and machinery at the rate of 10 per cent per annum. Show also the partners' capital accounts, and the branch current accounts, in the respective branch ledgers.

Solution 9

London Trial Balance

31st December, 19..

	£	£
Plant and machinery	5,408	
Cash in hand	178	
Cash at bank	7,157	
Current a/cs—		
Birmingham	2,029	
Dundee	1,970	
Stock, 1st January	5,896	
Sundry debtors	11,392	
Sundry creditors		7,047
Purchases	36,421	
Purchases from branches	2,857	
Sales		54,821
Sales to branches		1,723
Capital—B. Brown		18,862
Drawings—B. Brown	2,500	
Trade expenses	172	
Wages	3,608	
Discounts allowed	507	
Discounts received		412
Printing and stationery	220	
Advertising	286	
Carriage inwards	526	
Carriage outwards	817	
Salaries	627	
Bad debts	294	
	82,865	82,865

Stock, 31st December, £5,650.

BIRMINGHAM TRIAL BALANCE

31st December, 19..

	£	£
Plant and machinery	4,187	
Cash in hand	94	
Cash at bank	5,063	
Current a/c—London		2,029
Dundee	864	
Stock, 1st January	4,563	
Sundry debtors	9,746	
Sundry creditors		4,976
Purchases	28,198	
Purchases from branches	2,673	
Sales		39,857
Sales to branches		3,163
Capital—J. Jones		12,183
Drawings—J. Jones	2,000	
Trade expenses	104	
Wages	2,417	
Discounts allowed	406	
Discounts received		357
Printing and stationery	107	
Advertising	216	
Carriage inwards	419	
Carriage outwards	796	
Salaries	508	
Bad debts	204	
	62,565	62,565

Stock, 31st December, £4,620.

DUNDEE TRIAL BALANCE
31st December, 19..

	£	£
Plant and machinery	3,158	
Cash in hand	76	
Cash at bank	4,586	
Current a/cs—London		1,970
Birmingham		864
Stock, 1st January	3,616	
Sundry debtors	7,658	
Sundry creditors		3,018
Purchases	23,839	
Purchases from branches	2,272	
Sales		32,759
Sales to branches		2,916
Capital—S. Smith		9,175
Drawings—S. Smith	1,500	
Trade expenses	78	
Wages	1,987	
Discounts allowed	314	
Discounts received		296
Printing and stationery	92	
Advertising	186	
Carriage inwards	386	
Carriage outwards	687	
Salaries	413	
Bad Debts	150	
	50,998	50,998

Stock, 31st December, £3,700.

General Trading and Profit
For the Year

	London	Birmingham	Dundee	Total
	£	£	£	£
Stock, 1st Jan	5,896	4,563	3,616	14,075
Purchases	36,421	28,198	23,839	88,458
Purchases from Branches	2,857	2,673	2,272	7,802
Wages	3,608	2,417	1,987	8,012
Carriage Inwards	526	419	386	1,331
Balance (Gross Profit)	12,886	9,370	7,275	29,531
	62,194	47,640	39,375	149,209
Discounts Allowed	507	406	314	1,227
Carriage Outwards	817	796	687	2,300
Bad Debts	294	204	150	648
Printing & Stationery	220	107	92	419
Advertising	286	216	186	688
Salaries	627	508	413	1,548
Trade Expenses	172	104	78	354
Interest on Capital	943	609	458	2,010
Depreciation of Plant & Machinery	540	418	315	1,273
Balance (Net Profit)	8,892	6,359	4,878	20,129
	13,298	9,727	7,571	30,596
B. Brown	5,928	1,590	1,626	9,144
J. Jones	1,482	3,179	1,626	6,287
S. Smith	1,482	1,590	1,626	4,698
	8,892	6,359	4,878	20,129

AND LOSS ACCOUNT
Ended 31st December, 19..

	London	Birmingham	Dundee	Total
	£	£	£	£
Sales	54,821	39,857	32,759	127,437
Sales to Branches . .	1,723	3,163	2,916	7,802
Stock, 31st Dec. . .	5,650	4,620	3,700	13,970
	62,194	47,640	39,375	149,209
Gross Profit b/d . .	12,886	9,370	7,275	29,531
Discounts Received . .	412	357	296	1,065
	13,298	9,727	7,571	30,596
Net Profit b/d . .	8,892	6,359	4,878	20,129
	8,892	6,359	4,878	20,129

Columnar Balance Sheet

	London	Birmingham	Dundee	Total
Liabilities	£	£	£	£
Sundry Creditors	7,047	4,976	3,018	15,041
Current A/cs—				
London	—	2,137	2,114	4,251
Birmingham	—	—	900	900
Dundee	—	—	—	—
Capital—				
B. Brown	26,449			26,449
J. Jones		17,079		17,079
S. Smith			12,831	12,831
	33,496	24,192	18,863	76,551

General Balance Sheet (Ordinary Form)

Liabilities	£	£
Sundry Creditors		15,041
Capital—		
B. Brown, 1st Jan.	18,862	
Add Interest	943	
Add Share of Profits	9,144	
	28,949	
Less Drawings	2,500	
		26,449
J. Jones, 1st Jan.	12,183	
Add Interest	609	
Add Share of Profits	6,287	
	19,079	
Less Drawings	2,000	
		17,079
S. Smith, 1st Jan.	9,175	
Add Interest	458	
Add Share of Profits	4,698	
	14,331	
Less Drawings	1,500	
		12,831
		71,400

AS AT 31ST DECEMBER, 19....

	London	Birmingham	Dundee	Total
Assets	£	£	£	£
Cash in hand	178	94	76	348
Cash at Bank	7,157	5,063	4,586	16,806
Sundry Debtors	11,392	9,746	7,658	28,796
Current A/cs—				
London	—	—	—	—
Birmingham	2,137	—	—	2,137
Dundee	2,114	900	—	3,014
Stock-in-trade	5,650	4,620	3,700	13,970
Plant & Machinery (*less* depreciation)	4,868	3,769	2,843	11,480
	33,496	24,192	18,863	76,551

AS AT 31ST DECEMBER, 19....

Assets	£	£
Cash in hand	348	
Cash at Bank	16,806	
		17,154
Sundry Debtors		28,796
Stock-in-trade		13,970
Plant & Machinery (*less* depreciation)		11,480
		71,400

In London Ledger

B. Brown Capital

			£				£
19..				19..			
Dec	31	Drawings	2,500	Jan	1	Balance	18,862
		Balance c/d	26,449	Dec	31	Interest	943
						Share of Profits—	
						London	5,928
						Birmingham	1,590
						Dundee	1,626
			28,949				28,949
				19..			
				Jan	1	Balance b/d	26,449

Birmingham Current Account

			£				£
19..				19..			
Jan	1	Balance	2,029	Dec	31	Jones—Share of London profit	1,482
Dec	31	Brown—Share of Birmingham profit	1,590			Balance c/d	2,137
			3,619				3,619
19..							
Jan	1	Balance b/d	2,137				

Dundee Current Account

			£				£
19..				19..			
Jan	1	Balance	1,970	Dec	31	Smith—Share of London Profit	1,482
Dec	31	Brown—Share of Dundee Profit	1,626			Balance c/d	2,114
			3,596				3,596
Jan	1	Balance /bd	2,114				

In Birmingham Ledger

J. Jones, Capital

			£				£
19..				19..			
Dec	31	Drawings	2,000	Jan	1	Balance	12,183
		Balance c/d	17,079	Dec	31	Interest	609
						Share of Profits—	
						Birmingham	3,179
						London	1,482
						Dundee	1,627
			19,079				19,079
				19..			
				Jan	1	Balance b/d	17,079

London Current Account

		£			£
19..			19..		
Dec 31	Jones—Share of London Profit	1,482	Jan 1	Balance	2,029
	Balance c/d	2,137	Dec 31	Brown—Share of Birmingham Profit	1,590
		3,619			3,619
			19..		
			Jan 1	Balance b/d	2,137

Dundee Current Account

		£			£
19..			19..		
Jan 1	Balance	864	Dec 31	Smith—Share of Birmingham Profit	1,590
Dec 31	Jones—Share of Dundee Profit	1,626		Balance c/d	900
		2,490			2,490
19..					
Jan 1	Balance b/d	900			

In Dundee Ledger

S. Smith, Capital

		£			£
19..			19..		
Dec 31	Drawings	1,500	Jan 1	Balance	9,175
	Balance c/d	12,831	Dec 31	Interest	458
				Share of Profits—	
				Dundee	1,626
				London	1,482
				Birmingham	1,590
		14,331			14,331
			19..		
			Jan 1	Balance b/d	12,831

London Current Account

		£			£
19..			19..		
Dec 31	Smith—Share of London Profit	1,482	Jan 1	Balance	1,970
	Balance c/d	2,114	Dec 31	Brown—Share of Dundee Profit	1,626
		3,596			3,596
			19..		
			Jan 1	Balance b/d	2,114

Birmingham Current Account

		£			£
19..			19..		
Dec 31	Smith—Share of Birmingham Profit	1,590	Jan 1	Balance	864
	Balance c/d	900	Dec 31	Jones—Share of Dundee Profit	1,626
		2,490			2,490
			19..		
			Jan 1	Balance b/d	900

3. FOREIGN BRANCHES

Before we proceed to treat foreign branches, it is necessary to deal briefly with the subject of foreign exchange.

Foreign Exchange. This term is used to describe the means by which nations discharge or settle the mutual indebtedness that arises out of their trading with one another. Since, however, foreign debts are usually paid by bills of exchange, the term is also used, in a narrow sense, to denote the principles governing the creation, negotiation, and payment of foreign bills of exchange.

Currency. This term signifies the circulating medium of a country by means of which trade is carried on. It may be metallic (copper, silver, etc.) or paper currency in the form of bank notes.

Unit of Currency. Each country has, of course, its own currency and its own special terms for expressing monetary value. Each country has, also, some standard unit of currency for the purpose of financial calculations. In this country the unit is the £ sterling; *sterling* means standard English money. In France, the unit is the franc, in Germany the mark, in the United States the dollar, in Russia the rouble, in Italy the lira, in India the rupee, in Japan the yen, and so on.

Legal Tender. Each currency is legal tender only in its own country. A creditor in the U.K. must accept sterling offered in settlement of a debt, but he is not obliged to accept, say French francs or Australian pounds. Similarly, a Swiss creditor can demand to be paid in Swiss francs.

Rate of Exchange. The rate of exchange is the rate at which the currency of one country can be converted into the currency of another. It consists of two terms, one fixed and the other fluctuating. Thus, in the exchange between London and Paris, the fixed term is the £1 sterling, and the fluctuating term is the varying number of francs and centimes given in exchange for the £1 sterling. In the exchange between London and India, the fixed term is the Indian rupee, and the fluctuating term is the varying amount of British pence given as an equivalent for the rupee. In quotations of "Rates of Exchange" only the fluctuating terms are, as a rule, stated, the fixed terms being understood.

How Rates of Exchange are Quoted. There is, of course, a market for foreign bills just the same as for other commodities. The market consists of all the main banks operating in the City of London, the London offices of overseas banks, and the merchant banks, and all firms must be authorized by the Bank of England to deal in foreign exchange. Firms which deal extensively in foreign exchange usually use a broker who acts as a middleman to negotiate a price satisfactory to both seller and buyer. The current rates of exchange can be seen on the financial page of almost every important daily paper.

There are two methods of quoting a foreign rate of exchange, namely—

(*a*) *Number of foreign units to the* £. Examples of countries quoted by this method are America, France, and Germany.

(*b*) *Number of new pence to the foreign unit.* Examples of countries quoted by this method are India and China.

Under (*a*) the pound remains *fixed*, while the number of dollars, francs, and marks varies; whilst under (*b*) the foreign unit remains *fixed* and the pound varies.

Up to going to press, most papers also quoted the Bank of England limits. The upper price is that at which the Bank of England will begin to sell currency to prevent the price rising further. At the lower limit, the Bank will begin to buy. At the time of writing, such limits are quoted only for the U.S. Dollar.

Conversion of Currency into Sterling. The calculation required will be either a division or multiplication sum, according to how the rate is quoted.

(*a*) When the Rate of Exchange states the equivalent of the foreign currency to the English unit, i.e. the £ sterling.

Rule. Divide the currency amount by the rate, after adding on noughts, if necessary, to clear any decimals in the divisor. The answer will be in pounds and decimals of a pound.

CONVERSION FROM AND INTO STERLING

Example 10

Find the value in sterling of U.S.A. \$10,351 at \$2·40 to the £.

Solution 10

$$\frac{10{,}351}{2{\cdot}40} = \frac{103{,}510}{24} = £4312{\cdot}91$$

Example 11

Convert into sterling 9,121 Canadian dollars 14 cents at 2·60 dollars to the £.

Solution 11

$$\frac{9{,}121{\cdot}14}{2{\cdot}60} = \frac{912{,}114}{260} = £3{,}508{\cdot}13$$

Example 12

Exchange into the sterling equivalent \$8,462·80 at \$2·60 to the £.

Solution 12

$$8{,}462{\cdot}80 \div 2{\cdot}60 = £3{,}254{\cdot}92$$

(*b*) When the Rate of Exchange states the amount of English new pence equivalent to the foreign monetary unit.

Rule. Multiply the currency amount by the rate and divide by 100. The answer will be in pounds and decimals of a pound.

Example 13

Find the sterling equivalent of 2,428 rupees at $7\frac{1}{2}$ new pence per rupee

Solution 13

$$\frac{2{,}428 \times 7{\cdot}5}{100} = \frac{2{,}428 \times 15}{100 \times 2} = £182{\cdot}10$$

FORMS OF FOREIGN REMITTANCES

Bank Draft, Commercial Bills. In the rates of exchange, two prices are quoted, one for bank drafts, the other for commercial or ordinary trade bills. The former is slightly dearer than the latter, as the banker has naturally a higher standing than an ordinary trader.

Telegraphic Transfer. This is a message sent by wire, ordering the transfer of a specified sum of money from one person to another by means of debit and credit of their respective accounts. Branch businesses and agents abroad often cable to headquarters for immediate funds. Headquarters then instruct their bankers to cable to the bank's representatives abroad to place a certain sum at the disposal of the branch or agency. This method of remittance is slightly dearer than a bill.

Sterling Bills on London. Persons abroad who owe money to the United Kingdom may prefer to remit sterling bills on London, rather than have London draw on them in their own currency. Thus, the U.K. draws few bills, but accepts very many. London being the most important banking centre of the world, having a rate of exchange with every commercial country of any importance, sterling bills on London are readily negotiated abroad. These bills are not remitted by the drawers direct to London, but are purchased by other countries having payments to make to this country. We thus receive payment in our own money for goods sold to foreign countries.

TRANSACTIONS IN CURRENCY

It is now proposed to give an example of the method of treating items in currency in the subsidiary books and ledger. Generally speaking, the English merchant will invoice to his foreign customer in *sterling*, in order to ensure payment of the exact amount of the invoice, thus leaving the customer to deal with any profit or loss on exchange. But there are cases where the reverse procedure is necessary in order to facilitate trade.

Example 14

A. Smith, of London, sold goods to R. Brown, of Chicago, as follows—

Solution 14

12 cases Fancy Vases @ \$8·35 per case.
12 ,, ,, Goods @ \$11·46 ,, ,,

The items were invoiced to Brown in currency and converted in Smith's books at the rate of \$4·00. Brown remitted a draft, which was cashed at the rate of the day on which it was received, viz. \$2·40. Show Smith's day book and ledger with reference to the above.

In Smith's Books

FOREIGN SALES BOOK

Date	Particulars	Ledger Folio	Currency		Sterling
			$	c	£
	R. Brown, Chicago—				
	12 cases Fancy Vases @ $8·35 . .		100	20	
	12 „ „ Goods @ $11·46 . .		137	52	
			237	72	59·43

FOREIGN SALES LEDGER

R. BROWN, CHICAGO

	$ c	£		$ c	£
Goods . . .	237 72	59·43	Draft . . .	237 72	99·05
Difference in Exchange (profit) .		39·62			
	237 72	99·05		237 72	99·05

QUESTIONS

1. What is meant by "inter-branch" transactions? How are they dealt with? Do the "inter-branch" balances affect the final balance sheet?
2. Define the term "foreign exchange."
3. Explain the meaning of the following: currency, metallic currency, paper currency, unit of currency, sterling.
4. What is meant by "rate of exchange"?
5. What are the Bank of England limits?
6. What organizations form the Foreign Exchange Market?
7. How do you account for varying rates of exchange? What is meant by rates being *favourable to* or *against* a country?
8. In what two ways are rates of exchange quoted? Give examples.

PROBLEMS OF CONVERSION OF DATA

Special Features. With both home branches and foreign branches the book-keeping will vary according to whether the detail is recorded in the head office books or the branch books only. The general book-keeping will, therefore, be similar to that outlined in the preceding pages. The special features are the conversion of the accounts from currency into sterling, and the difficulties arising from the fluctuations in the rate of exchange.

Fixed and Fluctuating Rates of Exchange. Where the rate of exchange is fairly stable, slight fluctuations are not taken into consideration at all, and the accounts,with the exception of the remittance account, are converted into sterling at a fixed rate of exchange.

In other cases, where the rate of exchange is subject to violent fluctuations, the conversion of the accounts into sterling at a uniform rate for each item would result in showing fictitious branch profits or losses. To obviate this, the accounts are converted at different rates, as under—

1. Remittances at the actual rate of the day when made or cashed.

2. Fixed assets, also additions thereto, at the rate of the day when purchased. Additions, however, are sometimes converted at the average rate for the year or period, especially if made at various dates throughout the year. Fixed liabilities (loans, mortgages, etc.) at the rate ruling on the day they were incurred.

3. Floating assets and liabilities at the current rate of exchange on the date of balancing the books.

4. Revenue items, i.e. those affecting the trading and profit and loss account, at the average rate for the year or period. If the branch trial balance discloses merely the profit or loss for the period, then there will be only this amount to convert at the average rate.

The fixed assets and liabilities will remain in the foreign books, and they should, therefore, appear from time to time at the same value. The floating assets and liabilities are converted at the current rate at the date of balancing, in order that the balance sheet may be an approximately correct representation of the state of affairs. The revenue items are converted at the average rate for the period, because they have been going on continuously throughout the year. The stocks at the commencement and close of the period, although they appear in the trading account, are converted at the current rate on the dates of balancing. Thus the stock at the commencement will appear in the current trading account at the same value as it appeared in the balance sheet of the previous period. If there is a permanent alteration in exchange, the values of fixed assets and capital may have to be adjusted to current rates.

Procedure in the Head Office Books. Where the whole of the bookkeeping is done by the head office the foreign branch ledger will be ruled with double columns, one for currency, and the other for sterling. Entries will be made from the periodical branch returns, the items being converted into sterling at once, if a fixed rate of exchange is employed, and at balancing time, if various rates are employed.

Where the branch forwards to the head office a copy of its trial balance in currency, the head office is obliged to convert the various items into sterling before it can bring them into account. This will be done either at one fixed rate or at various rates, as the case may be. The remittance account is, of course, already converted, the remittances having been cashed on the day they were received from the branch, or purchased on the day they were forwarded to the branch. The value in sterling of the head office account is also known, being the amount brought forward from the last balancing.

Difference in Exchange. If, after conversion into sterling, the two columns of the branch trial balance do not agree (and it may be taken they never will) the totals must be made to correspond, by writing the balance on the lesser side, designating it "difference in exchange." A debit balance will signify a loss, and a credit balance will denote a profit; this amount will be debited or credited to the branch profit and loss account in the same way as other gains and losses. Where, however, the items are all converted at the same fixed rate, there will be no "difference in exchange" except for that appearing in the remittance account. In some cases, the profit or loss on exchange is not shown as a separate item, but is apportioned among the various items of expenditure, thus making the latter proportionately less in the case of a profit on exchange, and proportionately greater in the case of a loss.

Depreciation. Some accountants do not convert depreciation at the average rate for the year, even though it is a revenue item, and prefer to convert fixed assets, and the depreciation of them, at the same rate. It should be noted that, in the case of foreign branches, depreciation is often dealt with exclusively by head office, and on the *sterling* figures. In such cases, the head office would make an adjusting entry in its Journal, thus—

Depreciation . . . . . *Dr.*
Branch Current A/c . . . . *Cr.*

sending a credit note for the amount to the branch, which would pass the item through the branch books by means of a journal entry similar to the following—

Head Office Current A/c . . . . . *Dr.*
Fixtures and Fittings for depreciation thereon . *Cr.*

QUESTIONS

1. What are the special features of "foreign" branches?
2. What rate of exchange is adopted for conversion of foreign branch accounts into sterling?
3. In the case of a foreign country with a very fluctuating rate of exchange, what different rates are used in the conversion of accounts, and why?
4. Explain the method of procedure in the head office books as regards the record of the branch transactions.
5. What is meant by the term "difference in exchange"? How does it arise? In what two different ways is it dealt with in the accounts?
6. How is depreciation of fixed assets dealt with in the case of foreign branches?

Mine, Plantation, Etc. In the case of a foreign mine or plantation (tea, cocoa, rubber, tobacco, etc.) making monthly returns of its cash expenditure on capital and revenue account, the head office books would be ruled with double columns, one for currency and one for sterling; and both sets of figures would be recorded. At balancing time, the conversion would take place—according to the special circumstances mentioned previously—either at a fixed rate or at varying rates. A remittance account is employed; but, in many cases, the remittances are from the head office to the branch, instead of, as in other cases, from the branch to the head office. The reason is that the head office has to finance the mine or plantation. The output or crop of the latter is forwarded to Europe for sale by auction, and the proceeds are remitted direct to the head office; the branch does not handle any of the money.

Example 15

The Ceylon Tea Plantation Co. Ltd. remits to its foreign manager exchange for £9,600 in rupees at £6 per 100 rupees. At the end of the month the manager makes the following return of cash expenditure to his head office—

	Rs.
Plantation wages (planting)	21,400
,, ,, (manufacturing)	5,000
Salaries	2,000
Hospital expenses	500
Machinery and plant	40,000
Buildings, etc.	50,000
Rates and taxes	500
General expenses	600
Tools and implements	30,000
Coolie brokerage and passage money	10,000
	160,000

You are required to show the records in the foreign books, and also in the head office books.

Solution 15

In Foreign Books

CASH BOOK

19..		Rupees	19..		Rupees
Jan	London Office	160,000	Jan	Planting Wages	21,400
				Manufg. ,,	5,000
				Salaries	2,000
				Hospital Expenses	500
				Machinery & Plant	40,000
				Buildings	50,000
				Rates & Taxes	500
				General Expenses	600
				Tools & Implements	30,000
				Coolie Brokerage & Passage Money	10,000

LEDGER

London Office

	19..		Rupees
	Jan	By Cash . . .	160,000

In Head Office Books

CEYLON JOURNAL

		Dr	Cr
19..		Rupees	Rupees
Jan 31	Planting Wages	21,400	
	Manufacturing Wages	5,000	
	Salaries	2,000	
	Hospital Expenses.	500	
	Machinery & Plant	40,000	
	Buildings	50,000	
	Rates & Taxes	500	
	General Expenses	600	
	Tools & Implements	30,000	
	Coolie Brokerage & Passage Money . .	10,000	
	Plantation Cash A/c		160,000
	For sundry disbursements during the month.		

INFLATION AND CURRENCY FLUCTUATION

Depreciated Paper Currency. Hitherto, only currencies have been dealt with whose exchange fluctuations could be treated satisfactorily by taking the average rate for the year or trading period. It is now proposed to consider the case of countries where the legal tender is a greatly depreciated paper currency, whose sterling equivalent is subject to violent changes, e.g. the paper peso (dollar) of Chile and Peru. A currency will retain its value only so long as its issue is strictly limited to actual business requirements. But the moment a paper currency becomes over-issued, the trading community cannot absorb it, and forthwith a heavy depreciation sets in.

How British Book-keeping is Affected. The connexion of British book-keeping with such matters arises from the fact that many British companies are formed and registered in London, which have often only their head office in London, the business or works being situated in one of these South American republics. The company's capital is raised in sterling and the results of the company's operations have naturally to be presented to the shareholders in sterling. Thus, to such companies, the question of fluctuating exchange and its proper treatment in the accounts is an all-important one.

Rates of Exchange and Procedure in the Books. The aim of the book-keeping procedure of the London office is to record the result of the foreign transactions in their approximate sterling equivalent. Owing to the incessant and violent fluctuations in the rate of exchange, the average rate for the year will not give satisfactory results. When the business is transacted or the work executed, the value of the peso may be 4p; when payment is received, it may be 6p; when the bank balance admits of a remittance (possibly containing the profit on such business or work) being made to the London office, the rate may have risen to 8p or have dropped to 3p, the value of the peso varying from day to day and even from hour to hour. The only satisfactory way of dealing with such variations is to take the average rate of exchange for short periods, say, each month. This will suffice for all revenue transactions, and also for capital expenditure in the form of wages on capital account expended continuously throughout the month. Capital expenditure in the shape of fixed assets will, of course, be converted at the rate ruling on the date the assets were purchased, so that they may appear in the books at their approximate sterling cost. In the branch books, all capital expenditure is transferred at balancing time to the London office account. The branch balance sheet thus shows only the floating assets and liabilities, which are valued at the current rate of exchange on the date of such balance sheet. The difference between the floating assets and liabilities is represented by the balance of the London office account, which is converted into sterling at the same rate. Remittances are made to the head office usually by means of sterling bills on London. In the foreign books, the London office account will contain a memorandum *sterling* column; and, in the head office books, the branch office account will be provided with a memorandum *currency* column. At balancing time, any difference between the *Dr.* and *Cr.* sides of the memorandum columns is written off as profit or loss on exchange.

QUESTIONS

1. Explain the method of keeping the accounts in the case of a head office, say in London, owning a foreign mine or plantation. Submit specimens of any special rulings of books that might be necessary.

2. Name and explain some of the principal forms of foreign remittances.

3. How are transactions in currency dealt with in books of account kept in sterling? Give examples.

4. Explain the method of converting accounts kept in a fluctuating paper currency into sterling.

5. How is capital expenditure at the branch dealt with: (*a*) in the foreign books, (*b*) in the London office books?

6. How are remittances from the branch to the head office dealt with: (*a*) in the foreign books, (*b*) in the London books?

EXERCISE 14

1. The turnover of a branch of a business for 1962 was £24,000, on which there was a gross profit of 25 per cent. Included in the turnover were extraordinary sales of £8,000, on which the gross profit was 15 per cent. When the trading account for 1963 was drafted the total turnover revealed was £28,000, on which the gross profit appeared

to be 20 per cent. Excluding extraordinary sales the gross profit on turnover should have been only 1 per cent less than in 1962. The branch manager admitted that the discrepancy in the rate of gross profit was due to his having embezzled regular unrecorded amounts of money throughout the year. Extraordinary sales included in the 1963 turnover were £4,000, on which the gross profit was 10 per cent.

Calculate the total amount of the discrepancy, showing your workings, which have to be made to the nearest £.

2. From the following particulars prepare the branch account as it would appear in the head office books. The branch sales are exclusively cash, and the goods sent to the Branch have been invoiced at cost price—

	£
Goods from head office	5,508
Returns to head office	42
Rates, taxes, and insurance paid	65
Wages paid	362
Cash remitted to head office	6,871
Stock, 1st January	816
Rent paid	140
Stock, 31st December	795
Sundry expenses paid	81

3. From the particulars furnished hereunder, write up the branch account in the head office books. The branch sales are exclusively cash, and the goods sent to the branch have been invoiced at 33⅓ per cent on cost—

	£
Goods sent to branch *less* returns	6,840
Wages and salaries paid	372
Cash remitted by branch	6,855
Stock, 1st January	920
Rates, taxes, and insurance paid	80
Rent paid	145
Stock, 31st December	895
Sundry expenses paid	39

Show, in connexion with the above exercise: (*a*) the advantage of double money columns, (*b*) how the books are reconciled when the branch account is written up from the above figures exactly as they stand.

4. From the particulars given below, draw up the branch account or accounts in the head office books. The goods sent to the branch have been invoiced at cost, and the branch makes both cash and credit sales—

	£
Goods received from head office	2,517
Returns to head office	42
Stock, 1st January	625
Ready money sales	1,608
Six months' credit sales to 30th June	2,976
Allowances to customers	13
Discounts allowed to customers	132
Bad debts	218
Rent, rates, and taxes	108
Returns from customers	28
Wages and salaries	294
Debtors, 1st January	1,475
Stock, 30th June	595
Sundry expenses	63
Cash received on ledger accounts	2,516
Debtors, 30th June	1,542

5. Counties, Ltd., carries on a business with branches at Northtown and Southtown and you are given the following information—

(1) Goods are invoiced to branches at selling price, i.e. cost plus 25 per cent.

(2) Branch trading is wholly for cash, takings being banked intact daily to the credit of Head Office.

(3) Payments are made from Head Office save for petty items.

(4) Head Office expenses are divided equally between the branches.

(5) At stocktaking, Northtown Branch Stock Account showed a surplus of £100, and Southtown Branch Stock Account a deficiency of £90, both at selling prices.

(6) During the year Northtown Branch sent goods to Southtown Branch to the value of £300 at selling prices.

(7) Depreciation on Fixtures and Fittings is at 10 per cent and on Vehicles at 20 per cent, each calculated on cost prices.

From the following information extracted at 31st March, 1961, prepare Cash Account, Branch Stock Accounts as they would appear in the books of Head Office, and Profit and Loss Account for the year to 31st March, 1961, and a Balance Sheet as at that date.

	Head Office	North-town	South-town
Stock, 1st April, 1960, at selling price		7,000	5,700
Goods to Branches at selling price		31,000	33,000
Sales		33,250	36,250
Purchases	53,600		
Head Office and Branch Expenses	2,410	2,550	3,000
Head Office and Branch Expenses—			
Petty Cash	290	240	248
Petty Cash Imprest, 1st April, 1960, and 31st March, 1961	10	7	8
Bank Balance, 1st April, 1960	17,254		
Trade Creditors, 1st April, 1960	4,200		
Trade Creditors, 31st March, 1961	3,975		
Stock, 31st March, 1961	2,400		
Freehold Premises at cost	7,500	8,500	9,500
Fixtures and Fittings, at cost	1,800	1,400	1,600
Depreciation to 31st March, 1960	500	400	600
Motor Vehicles at cost	2,400		
Depreciation to 31st March, 1960	480		
Share Capital, Authorized and Issued	42,000		
General Reserve	8,759		
Profit and Loss Account, 1st April, 1960	3,200		
Taxation (paid)	2,000		

Ignore comparative figures *(L.C.C.)*

6. The summarized balances of Summer Fashions Ltd., trading in London, on 1st January, 19.., were—

	£
Fixed assets	50,000
Stock	10,000
Debtors	8,000
Cash	12,000
Creditors	20,000

(*a*) Record this position in the books of the company.

(*b*) On 2nd January two branches were opened at Amersham and Bexhill, and £4,000 goods (at cost) were sent to each branch.

(*c*) On 3rd January London head office makes purchases valued £16,000.

(*d*) On 4th January, £4,000 goods sent to each branch.

(*e*) On 7th January the following information was recorded—

	Amersham	Bexhill
	£	£
Remittances	11,500	9,000
Allowances made	200	300
Returns made	150	350

Head office sales £18,000, expenses paid £3,000, of which £1,000 related to Amersham, and £800 to Bexhill.

(*f*) On 7th January the value of the assets transferred to each branch was recorded as: Amersham £20,000; Bexhill £15,000.

The closing stocks were—

Amersham £2,000; Bexhill £3,000; Head Office £1,000.

The normal rate of gross profit is 50 per cent on sales.

Record the above transactions, show the profit made by Amersham and Bexhill, and prepare a statement to check the values of the closing stock at branches.

7. A company with its head office in London operates a branch in Holland. The branch books are kept in the local currency, the florin. A trial balance taken from the branch book at 31st December, 19.. was—

	f	f
Head office account at 1st January, 19..		152,636
Remittances	95,000	
Fixtures and fittings	7,687	
Debtors	122,073	
Stock at 1st January, 19..	23,465	
Creditors		121,968
Purchases	168,350	
Sales		192,581
Expenses	10,510	
Cash	40,100	
	467,185	467,185

In the head office books the balance on the branch account at 1st January 19.. was £16,607, and the remittance account balance on 31st December. 19.., was £9,661. There was no cash in transit.

The branch stock was valued at f31,500 on 31st December, 19...

The rates of exchange were—

1st January, 19..	f9·50	= £1
31st December, 19..	f10·50	= £1
At the time of purchase of the fixed assets	f10·25	= £1

(*a*) Prepare a trial balance, in sterling, showing the rates of conversion and show the profit or loss made by the branch.

(*b*) Give the journal entries required to incorporate the year's results in the books of head office. (*Cost and Management Accountants.*)

8. From the following condensed trial balance prepare amalgamated balance sheet as at 31st December, 19..

HEAD OFFICE TRIAL BALANCE

31st December, 19..

	£	£
Sundry assets	12,317	
Sundry creditors		3,017
Capital		12,000
Branch current account (£250 of this is for goods sent on 31st December)	3,960	
Remittances from branch		1,260
	16,277	16,277

BRANCH TRIAL BALANCE

31st December, 19..

	£	£
Sundry assets	2,847	
Sundry creditors		457
Head office current account		3,710
Remittances to head office (£60 of this represents a remittance made on 31st December)	1,320	
	4,167	4,167

9. Three partners, F. Finch, G. Green, and R. Roberts, have branch businesses working independently in London, Edinburgh, and Dublin. F. Finch manages the London business and receives two-thirds of the profits therefrom, the balance being shared equally between Green and Roberts. Green manages the Edinburgh business, receiving half of the profits therefrom, the balance being shared equally between Finch and Roberts. Roberts manages the Dublin business, receiving one-third of the profits therefrom, the balance being shared equally between Finch and Green. The branches buy from, and sell to, one another at a small inter-branch profit.

From the following trial balance draw up a tabular trading and profit and loss account, and a balance sheet in: (*a*) columnar form, (*b*) ordinary form. Credit each partner with interest on capital at 5 per cent per annum, and depreciate plant and machinery at the rate of 10 per cent per annum. Show also the partners' capital accounts, and the branch current accounts in the respective branch ledgers.

London Trial Balance

31st December, 19..

	£	£
Plant and machinery	5,616	
Cash in hand	216	
Cash at bank	7,808	
Current accounts—		
Edinburgh	2,386	
Dublin	2,017	
Stock, 1st January	6,174	
Sundry debtors	12,206	
Sundry creditors		8,165
Purchases	37,856	
Purchases from branches	3,047	
Sales		54,719
Sales to branches		4,028
Capital, F. Finch		20,646
Drawings, F. Finch	3,000	
Trade expenses	197	
Wages	3,814	
Discounts allowed	627	
Discounts earned		488
Printing and stationery	256	
Advertising	297	
Carriage inwards	564	
Carriage outwards	925	
Salaries	732	
Bad debts	308	
	88,046	88,047

Stock, 31st December, £6,285.

EDINBURGH TRIAL BALANCE

31st December, 19..

	£	£
Plant and machinery	4,406	
Cash in hand	115	
Cash at bank	5,219	
Current accounts—London		2,386
Dublin	1,027	
Stock, 1st January	4,629	
Sundry debtors	9,847	
Sundry creditors		5,028
Purchases	29,085	
Purchases from branches	2,875	
Sales		40,207
Sales to branches		3,318
Capital, G. Green		14,172
Drawings, G. Green	2,500	
Trade expenses	134	
Wages	2,675	
Discounts allowed	457	
Discounts earned		377
Printing and stationery	229	
Advertising	236	
Carriage inwards	425	
Carriage outwards	814	
Salaries	596	
Bad debts	219	
	65,488	65,488

Stock, 31st December, £4,752.

DUBLIN TRIAL BALANCE

31st December, 19..

	£	£
Plant and machinery	3,417	
Cash in hand	89	
Cash at bank	4,723	
Current accounts—London		2,017
Edinburgh		1,027
Stock, 1st January	3,852	
Sundry debtors	8,806	
Sundry creditors		3,351
Purchases	24,678	
Purchases from branches	2,359	
Sales		34,447
Sales to branches		3,028
Capital, R. Roberts		10,276
Drawings, R. Roberts	2,000	
Trade expenses	86	
Wages	2,075	
Discounts allowed	357	
Discounts earned		300
Printing and stationery	126	
Advertising	195	
Carriage inwards	397	
Carriage outwards	692	
Salaries	438	
Bad debts	156	
	54,446	54,446

Stock, 31st December, £3,972.

10. Lunarkit Ltd., London, has a Southampton branch shop which is invoiced for goods dispatched at selling price, being cost plus 25 per cent thereon. The branch keeps its own customers ledger and pays in gross cash receipts to a local branch of the company's bank for head office account. London office reimburse Southampton branch for all branch payments on the imprest system. The branch sends monthly returns to head office for incorporation in head office books.

From the following transactions for last January show in head office ledger—

(*a*) The Southampton branch account.
(*b*) Branch debtors account.
(*c*) How you incorporate the branch gross profits.

	£
Goods received from head office	10,250
Sales—cash £7,000, credit £5,000	12,000
Goods returned to head office	250
Cash received from customers less discount £150	7,850
Shop expenses paid	120
Receipts on head office imprest	90

NOTE. (i) At 1st January branch stock at H.O. invoice price was £30,000; debtors £14,000; cash float £200.

(ii) Stock at H.O. invoice price on 31st January was £28,000 (wastage *nil*).

(*London Chamber of Commerce.*)

11. Four partners, A, B, C, and D, have businesses working independently in London, Swansea, and Glasgow. A and B manage the London branch, each receiving one-third of the profits from the London business, the balance being shared equally between C and D.

C manages the Swansea house, receiving half of the profits from the business there, the balance being shared equally between A, B, and D.

D manages the Glasgow business, receiving one-third of the profits arising therefrom, the balance being shared equally between A, B, and C.

At the end of each year a combined statement is prepared showing the general position of the firm and the condition of each partner's account.

From the following separate statements make up the combined account (without interest) and also the general balance sheet of the firm.

LONDON HOUSE

	£		£
Creditors	15,000	Debtors	23,000
Swansea House	3,000	Glasgow House	2,000
A's Capital	10,000	Stock	13,000
B's "	10,000	A's Drawings	1,000
Profit and Loss	9,000	B's "	1,000
		Cash	7,000
	47,000		47,000

SWANSEA HOUSE

	£		£
Creditors	9,000	Debtors	11,000
Glasgow House	4,000	London House	3,000
C's Capital	5,000	Stock	3,000
Profit and Loss	6,000	C's Drawings	1,000
		Cash	6,000
	24,000		24,000

GLASGOW HOUSE

	£		£
Creditors	7,500	Debtors	9,000
London House	2,000	Swansea House . . .	4,000
D's Capital	5,000	Stock	5,000
Profit and Loss . . .	7,200	D's Drawings	500
		Cash	3,200
	21,700		21,700

(*Chartered Accountants.*)

12. A. Rice and B. Sago are partners trading as Rice and Sago, retail cash grocers, and sharing all profits and losses, two-thirds and one-third respectively. Rice manages the head office in town whilst Sago manages the branch business in the country, each business keeping separate books and bank accounts. On 30th June, 19.., C. Rice was admitted as a partner to one-sixth share of the profits which share was to be provided out of A. Rice's share.

From the annual trial balances shown below at 31st December, 19.., and the notes attached, prepare the profit and loss account and balance sheet of the partnership.

TRIAL BALANCE, 31ST DECEMBER, 19..

	Head Office		Country Branch	
	£	£	£	£
Capital—A. Rice		30,000		
B. Sago		15,000		
Drawings	3,200		2,400	
Gross profits for year		12,000		9,000
Stock, 31st December, 19.. . . .	25,000		11,000	
Wages and salaries	4,500		2,700	
Rent, rates, etc.	550		280	
Post, stationery, and general expenses . .	475		175	
Maintenance and repairs	160		55	
Creditors		5,600		4,320
Fittings and equipment.	8,000		4,560	
Country branch account	12,410			
Head office account				11,850
Cash at bank	8,305		4,000	
	62,600	62,600	25,170	25,170

NOTES. (i) On 31st December, 19.., head office dispatched goods at cost £460 to country branch, which received delivery on 2nd January, 19.1. On 1st January, head office received delivery of goods returned by country branch on 30th December, 19.., at cost £100. Stocks were physically taken at the respective warehouses at the close of business on 31st December, 19.., and so included in the trial balances above.

(ii) Provide for 10 per cent depreciation on the value shown for fittings and equipment.

(iii) Partners are entitled to interest on capital accounts shown above at 5 per cent per annum.

(iv) Drawings accounts are analysed as follows: A. Rice £2,500; B. Sago £2,000; C. Rice £1,000. (*London Chamber of Commerce.*)

13. Spheroids Ltd. opened an overseas branch in Karibia on 1st January, 19.. The following trial balance in Karibian dollars (K$), local currency, at 31st December 19.., has been received at head office.

BRANCH TRIAL BALANCE, 31ST DECEMBER, 19..

		K$	K$
Gross Profit			100,000
Selling and delivery expenses		40,000	
General office expenses		30,000	
Vehicles—cost, 31st March, 19..		15,000	
Office equipment—cost, 1st January, 19..		10,000	
Stock, 31st December, 19..		80,000	
Debtors and creditors		70,000	50,000
Head office remittance account—			
Remittance, 1st January, 19..	K$100,000		
Remittance, 30th June, 19..	50,000		150,000
Cash at bank		55,000	
		300,000	300,000

NOTES. (i) Depreciation is to be provided on cost of the fixed assets, according to use, at the rate of 5 per cent per annum on office equipment and 20 per cent per annum on vehicles.

(ii) Rates of exchange, for conversion, to £1 sterling during 19.. were as under—1st January K$6; 31st March K$6; 30th June K$5·5; 30th September K$5·5; 31st December K$5; Average, 19.. K$5·25.

From the above information prepare the branch trial balance in £ sterling, incorporating depreciation. Show the rates used in your conversions and answer to the nearest £. (*London Chamber of Commerce.*)

14. The United Kingdom Trading Co. Ltd. has branches at Dundee and Dover with head office at York. No trading is done at the head office. The branches each keep a separate set of books which contain a complete record of their trading. The capital accounts and bank account are kept in another set of books at head office, the branches being supplied with working capital from head office. From the following trial balances supplied by the branches, and the trial balance of the head office books, prepare a trading account, showing the trading result of each branch, also a general profit and loss account for the year ended 31st March and the balance sheet of the company.

Provide for bad and doubtful debts £250.
Provide for discount, 2½ per cent on debtors.
Wages owing, £125.
Stock at 31st March, £2,960.
Credit Southern branch 2½ per cent allowance on £1,850.
Depreciation of plant 7½ per cent on £3,500 to be charged in branch trading account.

NORTHERN BRANCH

TRIAL BALANCE, 31ST MARCH, 19..

	£	£
Head office account (amount due for working capital)		2,663
Trading account, Stock, 1st April	2,879	
Purchases	8,368	
Sales		15,872
Trade expenses	754	
Wages	3,370	
Salaries	290	
Rates, rent, and taxes	455	
Debtors	3,784	
Creditors		1,532
Discount	67	
Returns and allowances	100	
	20,067	20,067

SOUTHERN BRANCH

TRIAL BALANCE, 31ST MARCH, 19..

	£	£
Head office account (amount due for working capital)		2,151
Trading account, Stock, 1st April	1,397	
Purchases	3,512	
Sales		8,806
Trade expenses	474	
Wages	2,860	
Rent, rates, and taxes	274	
Debtors	2,960	
Creditors		661
Discount		34
Salaries	175	
	11,652	11,652

Provide for discount $2\frac{1}{2}$ per cent on debtors.
Provide for bad debts £125.
Expenses owing, £75.
Stock on 31st March £1,564.
Debit Northern Branch, $2\frac{1}{2}$ per cent allowance on £1,850.
Depreciation of plant, $7\frac{1}{2}$ per cent on £2,500, to be charged in branch trading account.

Head Office

Trial Balance, 31st March, 19..

	£	£
Share capital issued, 13,000 shares of £1 each		13,000
Calls in arrear	245	
$4\frac{1}{2}$% debenture stock		5,000
Plant and Machinery, northern branch	3,500	
Plant and Machinery, southern branch	2,500	
Goodwill, northern branch	3,000	
Goodwill, southern branch	2,500	
Bank	2,661	
Expenses (head office)	460	
Reserve fund account		4,000
Profit and loss account		500
£3,000 $2\frac{1}{2}$% Consols @ 80% (reserve fund investment)	2,400	
Rent, rates, taxes, and insurance	249	
Northern branch account	2,663	
Southern branch account	2,151	
Debenture interest account (paid to 30th Sept. last)	112	
Bank charges	59	
	22,500	22,500

Expenses owing, £55. Interest due on Consols, 3 mos. less tax @ £0·25. Directors' fees owing £750. Prepaid rates £32. (*West Riding of Yorkshire.*)

15. Green Limited has an authorized share capital of £250,000 in shares of £1 each. 200,000 shares have been issued on which ·75p per share has been called up.

The company's head office is in London and it has a branch in Glasgow.

All goods are purchased by the head office and invoiced to the branch at cost price plus 20 per cent. The branch keeps its own complete set of books.

The following are the trial balances as on 31st December, 19.1—

	London	Glasgow
Debits—	£	£
Land and buildings, at cost	62,880	24,380
Plant and machinery, at cost	57,367	18,273
Goodwill, at cost	20,000	—
Stock-in-trade, at or under cost	22,431	—
" " at invoiced price		12,840
Quoted investments, at cost	4,000	—
Trade investments, at cost	16,000	—
Debtors	9,619	5,143
Bills receivable	896	634
Balance at bank	3,120	1,527
Cash in hand	344	233
Preliminary expenses	1,648	—
Current account with branch	45,705	—
	244,010	63,030

	London	Glasgow
Credits—	£	£
Share capital	150,000	—
Share premium account	16,000	—
Calls in advance	7,500	—
General reserve	5,000	—
Creditors and accrued expenses	4,137	1,131
Profits prior to incorporation	6,724	—
Depreciation to date on land and buildings	1,954	1,246
" " plant and machinery	4,252	1,948
Reserve for income tax, 19.1/.2	18,000	—
Profit and loss account. Balance 1st January, 19..	6,248	—
Profit for the year 19.1	24,195	13,946
Current account with head office	—	44,759
	244,010	63,030

Subject to the items mentioned below, and to the appropriation of profits, all the necessary closing entries have been made.

The difference between the current accounts arises from: (*a*) £400 remitted by the branch on 31st December, 19.1, which was not received by head office until 2nd January, 19.2, and (*b*) £546 for goods invoiced and dispatched to the branch by head office on 30th December, 19.1, which were not received by the branch until 4th January, 19.2.

There are bills under discount amounting to £2,000 in respect of which £500 is to be provided against a probable loss.

The quoted investments had a market value of £4,200 on 31st December, 19.1. The trade investments were not quoted but were considered to have a value in excess of their cost.

Income tax for the year 19.1/.2 had been finally agreed at £19,460; on the profits of the year 19.1 it is estimated to be £15,000. Profits tax for the year 19.. had been overestimated by £115 and the adjustment included in the profit figure for 19.1. Profits tax for the year 19.1 is estimated at £4,000.

The directors decide to appropriate £4,000 to general reserve, to write off the balance on preliminary expenses and to recommend a dividend on 5p per share, less income tax.

You are required to prepare the balance sheet of Green Limited as on 31st December, 19.1, in a form suitable for publication, restricting the information given to the minimum requirements of the Companies Act, 1967. The auditors' report is not required. (*Chartered Accountants.*)

16. Ampicade Limited operates three factories at London, Newcastle, and Bristol. The whole of the production of these factories is marketed by two companies who are subsidiaries of Ampicade Limited, namely Interline Limited and Weavacon Limited. The trial balances of the books at 30th September, 19.1, at each of the factories and the balances of the factory accounts at the head office of Ampicade Limited, are as follows—

TRIAL BALANCES

	London	Newcastle	Bristol
	£	£	£
Stock of raw materials at 1st October, 19..	8,750	12,300	5,400
Purchases of raw materials—			
from suppliers	27,840	46,200	18,700
,, London		2,400	1,600
,, Newcastle			1,500
Production wages	23,560	38,700	14,500
Factory supplies	2,420	5,640	3,100
Repairs and maintenance	5,700	3,900	6,400
Rates and insurance	2,100	2,750	1,840
Carriage inwards	3,460	2,520	1,960
Carriage outwards (including cost of operating vehicles)	4,650	5,920	3,840
Work-in-progress	5,860	11,340	2,760
Office wages	2,360	5,140	1,950
Management salaries	2,500	2,900	1,800
Power	1,820	2,440	1,290
Heating and lighting	850	1,210	760
Stock of finished goods	2,400	3,100	1,800
Ancillary wages	4,820	7,360	3,160
Office supplies	380	530	290
Interline Limited	7,960	14,320	6,410
Weavacon Limited	3,620	8,540	2,570
Head office account		1,260	
	111,050	178,470	81,630
	£	£	£
Inter-factory material sales	4,000	1,500	
Sales—Interline Limited	46,320	85,830	16,540
Weavacon Limited	55,290	89,020	60,830
Head office account	4,290		3,640
Rents from let property		380	
Rebates on raw material purchases	290	460	180
Provision for accrued charges	860	1,280	440
	111,050	178,470	81,630

Factory account balances in head office books—

	London	Newcastle	Bristol
	£	£	£
Debit balances	18,390	2,430	1,830

Taking into account the following information, you are required to prepare such accounts as are necessary to show the profit for each of the three factories for the year ended 30th September, 19.1, and how these profits are arrived at. You are also required to show the opening trial balance as at 1st October, 19.1, for each factory.

(i) The cost of the fixed assets at the factories and the rates of straight line depreciation to be written off, are as follows—

	London	Newcastle	Bristol
	£	£	£
Freehold buildings $2\frac{1}{2}$ per cent	30,000	50,000	20,000
Plant and machinery 10 per cent	16,000	21,000	11,000
Office equipment 20 per cent	1,500	2,200	1,000
Motor delivery vehicles $33\frac{1}{3}$ per cent	2,400	4,200	2,100

(ii) The cash balances remitted to head office by the factories on 30th September, 19.1, were—

	£
London	2,140
Newcastle	3,690
Bristol	1,800

(iii) Any difference remaining between head office and factory account balances is accounted for in the case of Bristol by a mis-posting at head office of an item which should have been posted to the London factory account, and in the case of the London factory by the payment in cash by head office for a bulk purchase of materials, the payment not having been advised to the factory.

(iv) In order to reduce the profit earned by Weavacon Limited, it was decided to increase the value of sales made to that company by 10 per cent.

(v) The stocks in hand at 30th September, 19.1, were—

	London	Newcastle	Bristol
	£	£	£
Raw materials	9,630	14,820	7,310
Work-in-progress	6,320	13,160	3,110
Finished goods	3,400	3,550	2,140

(vi) Materials supplied by one factory to another are priced so as to cover the cost of transport between factories. ***(Cost and Management Accountants.)***

17. The Vendome Trading Company of London has a branch at Crystol. The branch keeps its own books, and the respective trial balances as on 31st March, 19.1, were—

	London	Crystol
Debits—	£	£
Furniture and fixtures	2,630	1,170
Stock, 1st April, 19.., at cost	17,200	9,720
Debtors	4,092	2,571
Bank and cash balances	16,657	596
Remittances to head office	—	52,500
Purchases	100,843	—
Goods from head office	—	37,328
Rent and rates	5,636	2,216
Salaries	7,586	4,392
General expenses	6,678	3,150
Crystol branch current account	52,549	—
	213,871	113,643

Credits—	£	£
Goods to branch at cost	37,849	—
Remittances from branch	52,025	—
Sales	94,637	61,148
Creditors	7,238	467
Head office current account	—	52,028
Capital, 1st April, 19..	22,122	—
	213,871	113,643

(1) Stocks as on 31st March, 19.1, at cost, were—

	£
Head office	15,890
Crystol Branch	4,325

(2) Goods sent by head office to the branch on 28th March, 19.1, costing £521 were stolen in transit, and on 30th April, 19.1, the insurance company admitted in full the claim for the cost of the goods.

(3) Provision for depreciation of the furniture and fixtures is to be made at 10 per cent for the year to 31st March, 19.1.

(4) Bonuses to the staff at head office and at the branch are to be provided at the rate of 20 per cent of the respective profits before charging such bonuses.

You are required—

(*a*) to prepare the firm's trading and profit and loss accounts of both the head office and the branch for the year to 31st March, 19.1, and

(*b*) to complete the entries in the branch current account in the head office books, bring the balance down as on 1st April, 19.1, and show what this balance represents. (*Chartered Accountants.*)

18. The Coventry branch of a Birmingham business receives its supplies from Birmingham at cost plus a charge of 10 per cent to cover the cost of handling. Sales are mainly for cash. A few sales are made on credit but no provision is made at Coventry for keeping a formal record of these. All takings are paid into bank for the credit of Birmingham.

Show how the following transactions relating to Coventry would appear in the Birmingham books and close off the accounts—

	£
Stock, 1st January, 19.. (at branch cost)	4,400
Cash received during year	40,000
Debtors, 1st January, 19..	160
Supplies from Birmingham (at original cost)	28,000
Debtors, 31st December, 19..	200
Stock, 31st December, 19.. (at branch cost)	3,960

(*Cost and Management Accountants.*)

19. From the following Trial Balances, prepare the Draft Balance Sheet of Kinson, Ltd., as at 31st December, 1960—

UTOPIA BRANCH

	Dr Crowns	*Cr* Crowns
London Office—		
Account 1st January, 1960 = £3,500		56,875
Remittances during Year = £1,000		15,750
Land and Buildings	52,500	
Fixtures and Fittings	4,125	
Bank Balance	9,000	
Debtors	41,480	
Creditors		30,800
Stock	24,640	
Profit and Loss Account		28,320
	131,745	131,745

LONDON OFFICE

	Dr £	*Cr* £
Share Capital—Authorized and Issued		5,000
Fixtures and Fittings (cost £200)	160	
Stock	842	
General Reserve		1,000
Debtors	3,410	
Bank Balance	1,753	
Profit and Loss Account		2,100
Creditors		2,565
Utopia Branch—		
1st January, 1960 = 56,875 Crowns	3,500	
Remittances during Year = 15,750 Crowns	1,000	
	10,665	10,665

At 31st December, 1960, Crowns were 16 to the £ and the average rate during the year was $15\frac{1}{2}$ Crowns to the £. At the time the Fixed Assets were acquired the rate was 15 Crowns to the £. Write off Branch Fixtures and Fittings at the rate of 10 per cent and write down London Office Fixtures and Fittings by £20.

Any difference on exchange is to be carried forward. Calculations can be made to the nearest £. (*L.C.C.*)

20. X.Y. trades in London and at a foreign branch at Domenico. The following are the Trial Balances in the books at 31st December, 1963—

LONDON TRIAL BALANCE

	£	£
Property at cost	5,000	
Equipment at cost	7,200	
Stock, 1st January, 1963	3,650	
Purchases	55,615	
Goods sent to Domenico		43,260
Freight on Goods sent to Domenico	2,190	
Operating Expenses	4,200	
Domenico Branch Account	32,840	
Sales		27,618
Remittances from Domenico		42,650
Debtors and Creditors	5,320	7,460
X.Y. Capital Account 1st January, 1963		10,000
Bank	14,973	
	130,988	130,988

DOMENICO TRIAL BALANCE

	Dollars	Dollars
Property at cost	100,000	
Equipment at cost	24,000	
Bank	243,000	
Debtors and Creditors	69,000	75,000
Stock, 1st January, 1963	128,000	
Goods from London	1,258,400	
Remittances to London	1,206,400	
London Account		1,034,800
Sales		2,144,400
Operating Expenses	225,400	
	3,254,200	3,254,200

Cash in Transit from Domenico, 31st December, 1963, £800.

Stocks, 31st December, 1963—London, £4,800, Domenico, 240,000 Dollars.

Rates of Exchange: Dollars per £ at 1st January, 1963, and for property and equipment, 20; at 31st December, 1963, 30; average for year, 25.

Prepare Trading and Profit and Loss Accounts for the year ended 31st December, 1963, and a Balance Sheet as at that date. Write off 10 per cent of the cost of the equipment at London and Domenico. *(L.C.C.)*

21. The Southern Confectionery Co. Ltd., London, has a branch at Bristol. Goods are invoiced to the Bristol branch at selling prices, being cost plus 25 per cent. The Bristol branch keeps its own sales ledger and transmits all cash received to London daily. All expenses are paid from London. From the following details prepare a profit and loss account of the Bristol branch for the year.

	£		£
Stock, 1st Jan. (at invoice prices)	1,250	Cash received for ledger a/cs	3,300
Stock, 31st Dec. (at invoice prices)	1,500	Goods invoiced from London	9,100
Sundry debtors, 1st Jan.	700	Rent and rates (paid from London)	400
Sundry debtors, 31st Dec.	900	Wages (paid from London)	340
Cash sales for the year	5,400	Sundry expenses (paid from London	80
Credit sales for the year	3,500		

(*Chartered Accountants.*)

CHAPTER 15

COST ACCOUNTING

And, as it works, th'industrious bee
Computes its time as well as we.

ANDREW MARVELL

Cost Accounting is probably the field of accountancy which has developed most within the last half-century, and there can be no doubt about its growing importance. This is partly a reflection of the growing complexity of modern production methods, which result in greater capital investment and a higher proportion of indirect costs, and partly a reflection of growing competition and widening markets. All these factors necessitate the keeping of systematic and accurate records which will show the cost of goods produced or contracts fulfilled.

OBJECTS OF COST ACCOUNTS

The primary object of Cost Accounts is to show the total cost of the articles a manufacturer produces, and to analyse the composition of that cost so that effective control over each element of cost can be exercised.

The main objectives which may be achieved are:

1. To Measure Profit in Relation to Accounting Periods

(*a*) They show not only whether or not a profit has been made on the working of the business as a whole, but whether or not a profit has been earned on each department, or process, or job.

(*b*) Where for certain reasons an industry is required to adopt a general policy with regard to prices, government contracts or foreign sales, then uniform cost systems are designed which result in effective measurements of cost for comparative purposes.

2. To Provide Information for Management Control

Of Sales

(*c*) The selling price of goods can be fixed with greater certainty, in order to realize the desired percentage of profit.

(*d*) Management should be provided with a basis for pricing policy for which it may require information with regard to marginal cost or the calculation of the "break-even point."

(*e*) They provide valuable data for estimating, or tendering for important contracts; and for comparison of the results of different manufacturing periods.

Of Costs

(*f*) In certain factories a standard cost control system can be designed. Such a system is linked to budgetary control and the whole of the productive capacity of the factory controlled against predetermined standards. This results in more efficient administration and effective use of resources, when variations from standards are effectively investigated.

(*g*) Since cost control operates on a long-term basis, periodical reassessment of cost standards must be undertaken, often using advanced management techniques such as value analysis. Pressure on profit margins due to competition may also lead to cost reduction programmes.

(*h*) The most economical use of production capacity, particularly when business is good requires accurate knowledge of the costs of various operations, processes and products.

Of Stocks

(*i*) Accurate information on the cost of stocks is necessary not only for Balance Sheet purposes but also for management control of Working Capital requirements.

3. To Provide Information for Planning and Decision Making

Many difficult decisions arise as to whether to buy new equipment which will make new products or save costs; whether to make or buy components; whether to accept work at "cut-throat" prices. This often requires special cost analysis and studies.

Whilst the terms used in manufacturing accounts and cost accounts are not yet standard in the accountancy profession, considerable efforts have been made to obtain uniformity, and in this volume the terms used are those laid down by the Institute of Cost and Works Accountants. Alternative terms may be mentioned, where these are in common use.

ANALYSIS OF COST

Cost

The cost of an article, or of a volume of production, is the amount of expenditure which the article or volume of production has incurred.

The Elements of Cost. There are only three elements of cost:

Materials: the cost of commodities supplied to an undertaking.
Labour: the cost of remuneration.
Expenses: the cost of services supplied.

All expenditure may be analysed under one of these heads. A carpenter making a table is using *materials* in the form of wood, glue, etc. The cost of the *labour* is the wages which are paid to him whilst he is working on it. Any other item of cost, such as carriage on materials or his fares (if they are paid to him) constitute the *expenses*.

If all costs are incurred directly on a single product, this simple analysis into elements of cost would be quite useful for comparison purposes. In most production today, however, costs are involved which are far removed from the individual item of production, e.g. salaries of accountants, and administration and selling charges, and for this reason costs are further subdivided into Direct and Indirect costs.

Direct Cost is that expenditure which may easily be identified with a particular unit of output or with a particular section of the productive organization. If the direct costs of a unit of production are grouped together, they constitute **Prime Cost.** That is, Prime Cost is the total of Direct Labour, Direct Materials and Direct Expenses.

Indirect Cost is any cost which cannot easily be identified with a particular cost unit or cost centre.

Overhead is the term used to denote all those elements of cost which are indirect to the unit of production. Overhead consists of Indirect Materials, Labour and Expenses, and is usually subdivided into—

Factory Overhead;
Administration Overhead;
Selling Overhead;
Distribution Overhead.

The student should avoid the use of the term "oncost." Typical items of cost in each category of overhead are:

1. FACTORY OVERHEAD. This comprises the indirect costs involved in manufacture, such as rent of factory building, depreciation of plant, cost of fuel, royalties, the salary of the works manager, the cost of progress and planning sections, watchmen, storekeepers, insurances, repairs, renewals, etc. It may include costing, if the costing is purely a factory function.

2. ADMINISTRATION OVERHEAD. This comprises the cost of accounting and secretarial work, and the cost of costing and budgetary control if a full system is in operation. It may include financial charges such as debenture interest.

3. SELLING OVERHEAD comprises the cost of maintaining a selling organization, salaries and commission of salesmen, the cost of their offices, and other expenses. It may include advertising campaigns and market research.

4. DISTRIBUTION OVERHEAD covers the costs of warehousing and transport, materials handling and control of finished goods from the moment they leave the factory to the moment they are delivered to the customer. Distribution may not be separable always from selling overhead, but it should be separated if possible.

The analysis of cost is shown in the form of a table below. It is important to learn this table because it shows the sequence of costing generally used. If the cost of a product is being prepared, the information will generally follow the sequence given—

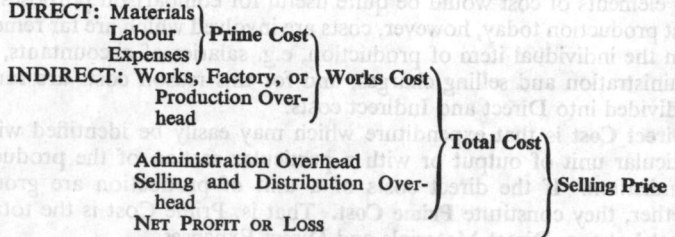

DIRECT: Materials Labour Expenses	Prime Cost	Works Cost	Total Cost	Selling Price
INDIRECT: Works, Factory, or Production Overhead				
Administration Overhead				
Selling and Distribution Overhead				
NET PROFIT OR LOSS				

Alternative Terms: Terminology is still not standard. The following alternatives to the I.C.W.A. terminology should be noted—

PRIME COST—Direct Cost, First Cost.

WORKS OR FACTORY COST—Manufacturing Cost, Production Cost.

TOTAL COST. May be called Cost of Sales or Selling Cost.

COST OF PRODUCTION (or Gross Cost). In some cases, these terms may be used to indicate works cost plus administration overhead.

The application of the analysis of cost to the final accounts of a firm is illustrated on p. 1601–2. The cost of an individual product will be presented, similarly, as follows—

COST SHEET FOR PRODUCT NO. . .

		£
Operatives' Wages		12·00
Direct Materials		13·00
Direct Expenses		2·00
	Prime Cost	27·00
FACTORY OVERHEAD		4·00
	Factory Cost	31·00
ADMINISTRATION OVERHEAD		3·00
SELLING AND DISTRIBUTION OVERHEAD		1·00
	Total Cost	35·00
PROFIT (10% of Cost)		3·50
	Selling Price	38·50

COMPARISON BETWEEN COST AND FINANCIAL ACCOUNTING

The strong division between cost and financial accounting is really historical. It so happens that financial accounting was well established with generally agreed procedures and objectives before the demand for cost accounting arose. For this reason, cost accounting, which has different objectives and, therefore, needs different procedures and methods, was forced to evolve as an independent system.

Costing is concerned with the revenue aspect of accounting, that is, the composition of cost and the sources of profit.

Financial accounting is concerned with the determination of profits, but not with how or where the profit arises.

The financial accounts also deal with the establishment of the Balance Sheet position and with appropriations of profit. The cost accounts are not concerned with these aspects.

It can be seen then, that all organizations need financial accounts of one kind or another, but cost accounts will only be found in larger organizations where it is essential to have control over costs.

SYSTEMS OF COST ACCOUNTING

Two main systems are found—

1. **Independent Cost and Financial Accounts.** The reason for this system is historical. A conventional set of financial accounts with appropriate subsidiary books is kept. Because the type of analysis used in the financial books is unsuitable for costing purposes, a second analysis of the basic data is made. From this, independent cost ledgers are posted. Such cost ledgers are made self-balancing by the use of control (or total) accounts. It must be emphasized, however, that there is no direct link with the financial books, which do *not* contain corresponding control accounts. The only link is a reconciliation statement which may be prepared periodically to reconcile the profit shown in the cost accounts with that disclosed in the financial accounts. This is the system generally found in British industry.

2. **Integrated Cost and Financial Accounts.** It is gradually coming to be recognized that a properly designed accounting system can achieve both cost and financial requirements together.

CLASSES OF COST ACCOUNTS

One of the main aims of costing is to relate costs to the object for which they have been expended. These objects may be expressed as Cost Units or Cost Centres.

A *Cost unit* is any quantity of product, service or time in relation to which costs may be ascertained or expressed. The same firm may use different units in different sections. Units may be by—

Number—e.g. persons employed, cases handled, animals loaded.
Length—feet of timber cut.
Area—square footage of floor cleaned.
Volume—cubic foot of building heated; gallons pumped.
Weight—ounce or lb. produced.
Value—capital value of buildings occupied, plant used.

Time—standard hours output; man/hours employed.

A *Cost Centre* is a location, person or item of equipment (or group of these) for which costs may be ascertained and used for the purposes of cost control. A cost centre may be personal or impersonal. Usually, the basic scheme of cost centres for a firm will be obtained from the organization chart. This implies subdividing each of the overhead divisions (factory, administration, selling and distribution) into sections, and establishing the cost of each section so that the person in charge may be given responsibility for controlling the costs. In some cases, however, it is desirable to treat a machine as a cost centre and to calculate a "machine-hour rate."

The class of cost accounts used in a particular firm will depend upon the type of production and the nature of the unit which it is most convenient (or traditional) to use. The main classes encountered are—

1. **Job Costing,** which relates costs to a single contract, or order. It may be subdivided into—

(*a*) *Terminal or Contract Costing*, which is used in building construction and civil engineering where a series of independent contracts are undertaken.

(*b*) *Job, Batch or Order Costing*. A job or order may be one unit or a group. A batch is a group of identical units produced together, but it may constitute only a part of the whole job or order; a separate cost for each is calculated. Much engineering work is costed in this way.

2. **Process Costing** is applied to operations of a continuous or mass-production nature when the units are indistinguishable one from the other. The costs of each stage of manufacture may be separated, e.g. production of gas, plating of components.

3. **Single or Output Costing.** This is used by firms supplying products of a uniform type, e.g. mines, quarries, breweries.

4. **Operating or Working Costing** is used by industries which supply a service and do not have a natural unit of output, e.g. railways, motor transport undertakings, etc. The following other methods may also be encountered—

(*a*) **Departmental Costing,** which is a system of costing by cost centres.

(*b*) **Multiple Costing,** which merely implies the use of different classes of costing within the same organization, e.g. batch costing with process costing for a rust-resistant treatment for all metal parts.

(*c*) **Class Costing,** where production is on fairly uniform lines, with a few distinguishable classes of product. Each class is treated differently in recovering overhead.

(*d*) **Test or Sample Costing.** Instead of costing all jobs or batches, only test or sample batches are costed, and from these costs a standard cost is established for succeeding batches.

There are really only three basic classes of costing: *Job, Process and Operating*. All others are variations on these.

COST ACCOUNTING PROCEDURE

Although individual systems vary considerably, it is normal to follow this procedure—

(*a*) All expenditure is analysed and classified into direct and indirect costs. The direct costs can be attributed to a particular job, process, or operation, and they are transferred to it.

(*b*) The indirect costs are placed to the relevant overhead account. If they can be placed to one particular account such as factory overhead, this is *allocation of overhead.* If they have to be divided between different overhead accounts, this is called *apportionment of overhead.*

(*c*) Of the factory overhead, some will relate to production departments (through which products pass); the rest will relate to service departments —non-production departments such as maintenance and steam-raising. The cost of service departments must be transferred to the production departments on a fair basis (preferably according to the use which is made of the service provided).

(*d*) Having established the overhead cost in each production department, the next problem is to charge each job, process or operation with its fair share, and this is called *recovery or absorption of overhead.*

Example 1

A company produces three products, Xray, Ynot and Zeddo. In one month, direct costs on each are—

	X	Y	Z
	£	£	£
Materials	1,000	2,000	3,000
Labour	1,500	2,500	4,000
Expenses	100	150	200

Factory Overhead is—

	Production Departments		Service	
	Dept. A	Dept. B	Maintenance	Steam-raising
	£	£	£	£
Allottable	3,000	2,000	500	800

Apportionable £8,200, between these four departments.

The cost accountant decides to apportion this as follows—

A	B	M	S
£	£	£	£
3,300	3,500	1,000	400

80 per cent of the steam is used by Dept. A, the rest by Dept. B. Maintenance is used: 60 per cent by A, 40 per cent by B. All products pass through Dept. A; X and Y pass through Dept. B. The time spent on them in each department is equal. Show the cost accounts.

PRODUCT X

	£		£
Direct Materials	1,000	Cost of Sales	8,490
" Labour	1,500		
" Expenses	100		
Overhead Recovery—			
Dept. A	2,720		
" B.	3,170		
	8,490		8,490

PRODUCT Y

	£		£
Direct Materials	2,000	Cost of Sales	10,540
" Labour	2,500		
" Expenses	150		
Overhead Recovery—			
Dept. A	2,720		
" B.	3,170		
	10,540		10,540

PRODUCT Z

	£		£
Direct Materials	3,000	Cost of Sales	9,920
" Labour	4,000		
" Expenses	200		
Overhead Recovery—			
Dept. A	2,720		
	9,920		9,920

STEAM-RAISING

	£		£
Indirect Material, Labour, and Expenses—		*Apportionment of Service Depts.—*	
Allocated	800	Dept. A 80%	960
Apportioned	400	Dept. B 20%	240
	1,200		1,200

DEPT. A

	£		£
Indirect Material, Labour, and Expenses—		*Overhead Recovery—*	
Allotted	3,000	Product X	2,720
Apportioned	3,300	„ Y	2,720
Apportionment of Service Depts.—		„ Z	2,720
Steam-raising	960		
Maintenance	900		
	8,160		8,160

DEPT. B

	£		£
Indirect Material, Labour, and Expenses—		*Overhead Recovery—*	
Allotted	2,000	Product X	3,170
Apportioned	3,500	„ Y	3,170
Apportionment of Service Depts.—			
Steam-raising	240		
Maintenance	600		
	6,340		6,340

MAINTENANCE DEPT.

	£		£
Indirect Material, Labour, and Expenses—		*Apportionment of Service Depts.—*	
Allotted	500	Dept. A	900
Apportioned	1,000	„ B	600
	1,500		1,500

OVERHEAD APPORTIONMENT

In drawing up a scheme of costing, one of the first steps must be to decide upon the *cost centres* which are to be used. Following this, those overheads which can be allotted are transferred to the relevant section. The others must be apportioned between the relevant departments. The method of apportionment will vary, but care is needed to select the fairest convenient method in the circumstances. The expenses may be apportioned in proportion to—

1. *Direct Wages Paid.* This may be used for items such as employers' liability insurance, but is otherwise unsatisfactory.

2. *Floor Area Occupied.* This is generally used for apportioning rent, rates and similar items. A centre occupying a greater area meets a greater share of the cost.

3. *Cubic Capacity Occupied.* This is similar to (2) but gives a more accurate basis for sharing such items as heating.

4. *Capital Employed.* Depreciation is an example of a charge which obviously varies in proportion to capital employed, and it should be apportioned accordingly. Rates and insurance may also be shared in this way. For costing purposes, the capital value may be the replacement of the asset rather than the written-down book value.

5. *Number of Employees.* Welfare and personal facilities may be shared in proportion to the numbers employed in a department.

6. *Measurement or Technical Estimate.* Electricity might be shared in proportion to the installed demand, e.g. the wattage of lamps in each section of an office. Power, steam, gas and water, are preferably metered, but alternatively a competent technical estimate of relative usages can be made, e.g. if two departments A and B have 10 h.p. and 20 h.p. installed, and A runs 1,000 hours, B, 2,000 hours, then we may take 10,000 and 40,000 h.p./hours for the purpose of assessing relative usage.

7. *Production Hours.* Some overhead may be apportioned in proportion to (*a*) direct labour hours, (*b*) machine hours.

In any case, the number of hours worked in each section is recorded and the expenses apportioned proportionately. Such items as management salaries, administration, supervision, research, and timekeeping, may be shared in this way.

Example 2

A company with departments A, B, C and D shows the following costs in a period—

	£
Rent	1,000
Depreciation of plant	450
Supervision	1,500
Canteen	150
Power	1,020

The following information is available—

	Department			
	A	B	C	D
Area sq. ft.	1,500	1,100	900	500
No. of employees	20	15	10	5
Plant value	£24,000	£18,000	£12,000	£6,000
Horse power	100	10	—	—
Machine hours	10,000	2,000	—	—

(*Cost and Works Accountants* (*modified*).)

Apportionment would be made as shown below—

Item	Total	A	B	C	D	Basis of Apportionment
	£	£	£	£	£	
Rent . .	1,000	375	275	225	125	Area
Depreciation .	450	180	135	90	45	Plant value
Supervision .	1,500	600	450	300	150	Number of employees
Power . .	1,020	1,000	20	—	—	Horse-power hours
Canteen . .	150	60	45	30	15	Number of employees
	4,120	2,215	925	645	335	

If Department D is a service department, it must be apportioned to production departments on one of the bases listed.

OVERHEAD ABSORPTION

Overhead recovery is also known as overhead *absorption*. It is the final step in accounting for overhead, when the job or product is charged with its fair share. It should not be confused with apportionment. The rates to be used for absorption are usually calculated at the beginning of a period. The cost of every job undertaken is calculated by recording the actual prime cost and then adding the overhead at the cost rates adopted. A different cost-rate must be adopted for each cost centre if accurate costs are to be obtained.

The rates which may be used are—

1. Percentage on cost

(*a*) **Percentage on prime cost.** If the anticipated costs are—

	£
Direct materials . . .	6,000
Direct wages . . .	2,000
Overheads . . .	10,000

the cost rate would be £$\frac{10000}{8000}$ × 100 = 125 per cent to be added to the prime cost of each job.

(*b*) **Percentage on Direct Wages.** The rate would be:

$$\frac{10,000}{2,000} = 500\% \text{ of wages.}$$

(*c*) **Percentage on Direct Materials.** The rate would be:

$$\frac{10,000}{6,000} = 166\% \text{ of material costs.}$$

These three rates are acceptable only if it can be shown that overhead varies in proportion to the element of cost taken, which is rarely the case. Nevertheless they are widely used because they are easy to apply. If prices of materials or wage rates vary, then the rates should be recalculated.

2. Rate per unit of production

This is suitable for process costs and single or output costs when uniform units are being produced. The rate is calculated—

$$\frac{\text{Anticipated overhead}}{\text{No. of units to be produced}} = \text{Rate per unit of production.}$$

A separate rate may be calculated for each process.

3. Rate per direct labour hour

This is calculated—

$$\frac{\text{Anticipated overhead}}{\text{Direct labour hours}} = \text{Rate per direct labout hour.}$$

This is an accurate rate where manual labour is employed and where proper records of the time spent on each job can be obtained. Naturally, an annual estimate of direct labour hours must take into account all holidays and other absences. It is not satisfactory where costly machinery is used.

4. Machine-hour rate

This is calculated—

$$\frac{\text{Anticipated overhead to machine (as a cost centre)}}{\text{Anticipated hours of machine operation}} = \text{Machine-hour rate.}$$

This method is very suitable for individual machines or for several machines performing similar work.

The anticipated overhead may include only machine overheads such as rent for area occupied, depreciation, maintenance, etc.; it may include also the wages of the operators if they are essential to machine running and the labour cannot be employed on other activities whilst the machine is running. In many workshops, an operative may tend several machines at once, in which case his labour should be costed separately.

5. Rate per production hour

This is a rate which includes in the overhead all the overhead of a production centre, and charges jobs with the number of hours in which they are in production (whether by hand or machine). It is used in steel production and similar processes. The calculation is—

$$\frac{\text{Anticipated overhead of cost centre}}{\text{Estimated number of production hours}} = \text{Rate per production hour.}$$

It is generally accepted that the best cost rates are those based on time or output, that is, rates numbered 2 to 5 above.

Under- and Over-absorption. If the cost rates are calculated at the beginning of a period and applied to all jobs during the period, then each job will have made a fair contribution to recovery of overhead. In practice, however, it is unlikely that the amount recovered will equal the actual overhead. This may be because overhead varies from the amount anticipated or because the base varies from the estimate. The result may be called under- or over-absorption or under- or over-recovery. This increases or decreases the actual profit realized.

Example 3

The following information relates to the activities of a production department of a factory for a certain period—

Material used	£3,600
Direct wages	£3,000
Labour hours worked	24,000
Hours of machine operation	20,000
Overhead chargeable to the department	£2,500

On one order carried out in the department during the period, the relevant data was—

Materials used	£200	Labour hours	1,650
Direct wages	£165	Machine hours	1,200

Calculate by the different methods the overhead which may be charged to the job. (*Cost and Works Accountants* (*modified*).)

Solution—

Item	Units	Overhead Recovered on Basis of				
		1 Machine Hours	2 Labour Hours	3 Direct Wages	4 Direct Materials	5 Prime Cost
Materials	£3,600					
Labour	£3,000					
Labour hours	24,000					
Machine hours	20,000					
Overhead	£2,500	$\frac{£2,500}{20,000}$	$\frac{£2,500}{24,000}$	$\frac{£2,500}{3,000} \times 100$	$\frac{£2,500}{3,600} \times 100$	$\frac{£2,500}{6,600} \times 100$
RATE		$12\frac{1}{2}$p per machine hr.	$10\frac{1}{2}$p per labour hr.	$83\frac{1}{3}$%	$69\frac{1}{2}$%	38%

Comparative Costs of Job No.................

	1	2	3	4	5
	£	£	£	£	£
Materials	200	200	200	200	200
Labour	165	165	165	165	165
Prime cost	365	365	365	365	365
Overhead	150	172*	138*	139*	139*
Factory cost	515	537	503	504	504

* The overhead is shown to the nearest £1. It can be seen what a remarkable difference may be made to cost.

DOUBLE-ENTRY COST ACCOUNTS

The double-entry aspect of costing is dealt with under the following headings—

(*a*) Cost Ledgers independent of Financial Accounts.
(*b*) Standard Costs.
(*c*) Integrated Cost and Financial Accounts.

(*a*) Cost Ledgers Independent of Financial Accounts

The ledgers required under this system are—

(i) *The Cost Ledger proper*. This is the costing impersonal ledger. All expenditure is recorded in an appropriate expense account in the Cost Ledger. Whilst the conventional form may be used, it is more usual to use a columnar form of account.

(ii) *The Stores Ledger*, which contains an account for each class of material and is usually ruled in columnar form to show receipts, issues and stocks in hand (balance). (See example on p. 1517.)

(iii) *The Job Ledger*, containing accounts for each job, order, or other cost unit. Each account is debited with direct materials, labour and expenses and, on completion, with appropriate amounts for overhead at the cost rates used. A columnar ruling is preferred, with columns for each element of cost, direct and indirect. (See example on p. 1518.)

(iv) *The Stock Ledger*, which contains an account for each class of finished goods, transferred from the job ledger.

Control Accounts. As explained previously, the costing ledgers are not connected with the financial accounts, but to make them self-balancing each has a control or total account which is kept in the cost ledger. If the books were strictly self-balancing, a control account would also be kept in each ledger, but this is not done. A complete trial balance can be extracted from the cost ledger.

(i) *Cost Ledger Control Account*. As the impersonal accounts are debited with expenses in the cost ledger, a corresponding *total* credit is made to control account. Similarly, when sales are made, stores returned or expenses transferred to jobs, the impersonal account is credited and control account debited. No personal accounts are kept in the cost accounts.

(ii) *The Stores Ledger Control Account*. When stores are received, the individual stores accounts are debited, at the same time the double entry is made in the Cost Ledger, which is self-balancing. The Stores Ledger Control A/c is debited and Cost Ledger Control A/c credited. (See Jan 1 below.)

(iii) *Job Ledger Control Account*. As individual jobs are debited with expenses and costs transferred from the Cost or Stores ledgers, the Job Ledger Control Account in the Cost Ledger is debited with the total. The corresponding entry would be a credit to the respective expense account or to Stores Ledger Control A/c. (See Jan 2 and 3 below.) Any balance carried forward on this account will be work-in-progress, and for this reason the control account is sometimes called work-in-progress account.

(iv) *Finished Stock Control Account*. When completed jobs are transferred to stock, the individual job accounts in the Job Ledger are credited and the relevant account in the Stock Ledger debited.

The double entry is completed by credit to Job Ledger Control Account and debit to Stock Ledger Control Account. (See Jan 10 below.)

Example 4

The following items are to be entered in appropriate accounts in the cost ledgers.

NOTE. To aid the student in following this example through, the entries required are stated. If the amounts are inserted and a narration added, the journal entry required may be seen.

19..	*Transaction*	£	*Entries Required*
Jan 1	Materials purchased for store	10,000	*Dr.* Stores ledger control a/c *Cr.* Cost " " "
2	Material purchased for special jobs	500	*Dr.* Job ledger control a/c *Cr.* Cost " " "
3	Materials issued from stores to production	8,000	*Dr.* Job ledger control a/c *Cr.* Stores " " "
4	Wages paid	12,000	*Dr.* Wages a/c *Cr.* Cost ledger control a/c
	Part of wages which were indirect— Factory Administration	 600 800	*Dr.* Factory overhead a/c *Dr.* Admin. " " *Cr.* Wages a/c
5	Direct wages charged to individual jobs	10,600	*Dr.* Job ledger Control a/c *Cr.* Wages a/c
	(It has been assumed, for simplicity, that the wages account is cleared.)		
6	Direct expenses on jobs	250	*Dr.* Job ledger control a/c *Cr.* Cost " " "
8	The overheads incurred for the period were— Factory Selling Administration	 3,000 2,000 2,500	*Dr.* Factory overhead a/c *Dr.* Selling " " *Dr.* Admin. " " *Cr.* Cost ledger control a/c
9	The overheads charged to jobs to date were— Factory overhead Administration overhead	 2,800 3,600	*Dr.* Job ledger control a/c *Cr.* Factory overhead a/c *Cr.* Administration overhead a/c
10	Cost of finished stock transferred	22,500	*Dr.* Stock ledger control a/c *Cr.* Job ledger control a/c
11	The cost of production of items sold was	19,900	*Dr.* Cost of sales a/c *Cr.* Stock ledger control a/c
	The selling overhead on the goods sold was	1,600	*Dr.* Cost of sales a/c *Cr.* Selling overhead a/c
	The actual sales figure was	27,500	*Dr.* Cost ledger control a/c *Cr.* Costing Profit and Loss a/c
	The balance on cost of sales a/c was transferred to costing profit and loss a/c		*Cr.* Cost of sales a/c } with cost of sales *Dr.* Costing profit and loss a/c }
	The difference between overhead recovery and actual were carried to costing profit and loss a/c		*Dr.* Costing profit and loss a/c *Cr.* Selling overhead a/c *Cr.* Factory " " *Dr.* Administration overhead a/c *Cr.* Costing Profit and loss a/c
	The balance on costing profit and loss a/c was credited to cost ledger control a/c, and the following balances were carried forward—		

	£	£
Stores ledger control a/c (stock of raw materials at cost)	2,000	
Cost ledger control a/c		7,850
Job ledger control a/c (stock of work-in-progress)	3,250	
Stock ledger control a/c (stock of finished goods)	2,600	

STORES LEDGER

(Name of Material or Article)..

Receipts									Issues								
Date	S.R. Book Folio	From Whom	Quantity				Price	Amount	Date	S.I. Book Folio	To Whom	Quantity				Price	Amount
			No.	cwt.	qr.	lb.						No.	cwt.	qr.	lb.		

NOTE 1. This ledger would be posted up daily from the stores received book and the stores issued book.
NOTE 2. The balance of the two sides should show the quantity of each article in stock at any time, and thus facilitate and check the process of stock-taking. Due allowance must, of course, be made for shrinkage and wastage.

JOB LEDGER

Job No...

Period Ending	Debits					Credits		Prime Cost	Establishment Charges	Total Cost
	Stores	Special Materials	Wages	Direct Expenses	Total	Stores Returned	Total			
	£	£	£	£	£	£	£	£	£	£

COST LEDGER CONTROL A/c

19..		£	19..		£
Jan 11	Cost of Sales A/c (actual sales figure)	27,500	Jan 1	Stores Ledger Control A/c	10,000
	Balance c/d	7,850	2	Job " " "	500
			4	Wages A/c	12,000
			6	Job Ledger Control A/c	250
			8	Factory, Admin., & Selling Overhead A/cs	7,500
			11	Costing P. & L. A/c (net profit for period)	5,100
		35,350			35,350
				Balance b/d	7,850

STORES LEDGER CONTROL A/c

19..		£	19..		£
Jan 1	Cost Ledger Control A/c	10,000	Jan 3	Job Ledger Control A/c	8,000
			11	Balance c/d	2,000
		10,000			10,000
Jan 11	Balance b/d	2,000			

JOB LEDGER CONTROL A/c

19..		£	19..		£
Jan 2	Cost Ledger Control A/c	500	Jan 10	Stock Ledger Control A/c	22,500
3	Stores " "	8,000	11	Balance c/d (Work-in-progress)	3,250
5	Wages A/c	10,600			
6	Cost Ledger Control A/c	250			
9	Factory Overhead A/c	2,800			
	Admin. " "	3,600			
		25,750			25,750
11	Balance b/d (Work-in-progress)	3,250			

STOCK LEDGER CONTROL A/c

19..		£	19..		£
Jan 10	Job Ledger Control A/c	22,500	Jan 11	Cost of Sales A/c	19,900
				Balance c/d (Stock-in-hand)	2,600
		22,500			22,500
Jan 11	Balance b/d (Stock-in-hand)	2,600			

WAGES A/c

19..		£	19..		£
Jan 4	Cost Ledger Control A/c	12,000	Jan 4	Factory Overhead A/c	600
				Admin. " "	800
			5	Job Ledger Control A/c	10,600
		12,000			12,000

FACTORY OVERHEAD A/c

19..		£	19..		£
Jan 4	Wages A/c	600	Jan 9	Job Ledger Control A/c	2,800
8	Cost Ledger Control A/c	3,000	11	Costing P. & L. A/c	800
		3,600			3,600

Administration Overhead A/c

19..		£	19..		£
Jan 4	Wages A/c	800	Jan 9	Job Ledger Control A/c	3,600
8	Cost Ledger Control A/c	2,500			
11	Costing P. & L. A/c	300			
		3,600			3,600

Selling Overhead A/c

19..		£	19..		£
Jan 8	Cost Ledger Control A/c	2,000	Jan 11	Cost of Sales A/c	1,600
				Costing P. & L. A/c	400
		2,000			2,000

Cost of Sales A/c

19..		£	19..		£
Jan 11	Stock Ledger Control A/c	19,900	Jan 11	Costing Profit and Loss (Cost of actual sales)	21,500
	Selling Overhead A/c	1,600			
		21,500			21,500

Costing Profit and Loss A/c

19..		£	19..		£
Jan 11	Cost of Sales A/c	21,500	Jan 11	Cost Ledger Control A/c (actual sales)	27,500
	Factory Overhead A/c	800		Admin. Overhead A/c	300
	Selling Overhead A/c	400			
	Cost Ledger Control A/c (Net profit for period)	5,100			
		27,800			27,800

The costing profit and loss account has been shown in conventional form, but it is usually prepared in a tabular form (see below). The net profit is credited to cost ledger control account. It will be seen that the balance on each overhead account has been written off. Factory and selling overhead were under-recovered, administration overhead over-recovered.

Tabular Form of Costing Profit and Loss for Period . . .

	£	£
Net profit on sales after deducting overhead recovered		6,000
Add Administration overhead over-recovered		300
		6,300
Deduct Factory overhead under-recovered	800	
Selling overhead under-recovered	400	
		1,200
Net profit (on costing data only)		5,100

This net profit must be adjusted in respect of items which differ with or do not appear in the financial accounts.

Scope of Cost Ledgers. It will be seen that the cost ledgers are concerned only with impersonal accounts showing revenue income and expenditure. They are not concerned with and do not show—

1. Personal accounts of debtors and creditors.
2. Assets and liabilities such as land and buildings, plant, capital, debentures, etc.
3. Appropriations of profit, debenture and other interest, bad debts provisions, dividends, tax, reserves, etc.

Reconciliation of Cost and Financial Accounts. Both the financial and cost accounts record the information from which the net profit may be calculated. It is imperative that a reconciliation be made between the two figures obtained, as a check.

The following modifications are usually necessary in the financial accounts—

(i) Wages account should be divided into direct and indirect wages.

(ii) Purchases account should be divided into purchases for store and purchases for special jobs.

(iii) Direct expenses on particular jobs should also be separately analysed.

(iv) Indirect expenses should be divided into separate sections for factory, administration, selling and distribution.

Causes of Disagreement. The main reasons for disagreement are—

(*a*) Certain items appear in both accounts but the amounts shown differ. This may be due to—

(i) *A difference in the accounting method.* Stocks may be valued at cost in the cost accounts but at a lower market value in the financial accounts. Depreciation may be on replacement values in the cost accounts.

(ii) *A difference in accounting period.* There may be a lag in posting items into the cost accounts, particularly in respect of indirect expenses.

(*b*) Certain items appear in one set of accounts but not in the other (see above).

Methods of Reconciliation. Reconciliation usually starts with the costing profit, obtained from the cost ledger control account and is shown in the form of a memorandum reconciliation account.

(*a*) *Differences in amounts shown in both sets of accounts.* The items shown in the control account are checked against the corresponding items in the financial books, with which they should agree. Any differences are noted and the costing profit and loss adjusted as follows—

		£
Costing profit		21,000
Difference in Stocks—		
Value in Cost A/cs	£8,000	
Value in Financial A/cs	6,000	
	deduct	2,000
		19,000
Difference in Depreciation—		
Amount in Cost A/cs	£15,000	
Amount in Financial A/cs	8,000	
	add	7,000
		26,000
Difference in Overhead—		
Charged in Cost A/cs	£10,000	
Recorded in Financial A/cs	11,000	
	deduct	1,000
Adjusted Profit		25,000

If there were no other adjustments, the adjusted profit would equal that shown in the financial accounts, but in practice, a further set of adjustments is usually necessary.

(*b*) *Differences due to items shown in only one set of accounts*. (i) Items included only in the financial accounts account for the bulk of these adjustments. These are too numerous to list but typical items are—

Non-operating items. Charitable donations, income from investments and rents, directors fees, capital gains and losses and legal fees.

Provisions and Reserves, etc. Provisions for bad debts, plant replacement and other reserves, sinking funds for redemption of capital.

Appropriations of profit. Corporation tax, dividends on shares and interest on debentures and tax withheld on these.

(ii) Items included only in the cost accounts may include notional rent (charged as an expense but not actually payable) interest on capital, over-recovery of overhead.

Example 5

MEMORANDUM RECONCILIATION ACCOUNT

	£	£		£	£
Financial—			Costing Profit		21,000
Depreciation	8,000		*Costing—*		
Overhead	11,000		Depreciation	15,000	
		19,000	Overhead	10,000	
Costing—					25,000
Stock		8,000	*Financial—*		
Amounts not charged in Cost A/c's—			Stock		6,000
			Amounts not credited in Cost A/c's—		
Loss on Sale of Plant	2,000		Bank Interest	150	
Interest on Debentures	100		Dividend	300	
		2,100	Rents Received	250	
Appropriation of Profits—					
Preliminary Expenses		500			700
Profit as per Finance A/c		23,100			
		52,700			52,700

(*b*) Standard Costs and Budgetary Control

It is a logical step from the costing procedures outlined, which already involve a considerable amount of prediction of future costs and recording of actual costs, to institute standard costs and budgetary control.

A *predetermined cost* is any cost which is computed in advance of production on the basis of a specification of all factors affecting cost.

The main factors are the level of expenditure on acquiring materials, labour and other resources and the efficiency with which those resources are used in production of saleable finished products.

A *standard cost* is a predetermined cost which is calculated from managements' standards of efficient operation and the relevant necessary expenditure.

A *cost variance* is the difference between a standard cost and the comparable actual cost incurred during a period of account. They may be favourable (actual cost being below standard) or unfavourable (actual cost exceeding standard).

So far as the accounting aspect is concerned, there is no difference between the under- and over-recovery arising from predetermined cost-rates and the variances arising from standard costs. The overhead accounts in Example 4 could be shown under Standard Costing as—

FACTORY OVERHEAD A/C

19..			£	19..			£
Jan	8	Cost Ledger Control A/c	3,000	Jan	9	Job Ledger Control A/c	2,800
					13	Factory Overhead Variance to Costing P. & L. A/c (unfavourable)	200

SELLING OVERHEAD A/c

			£				£
19..				19..			
Jan	8	Cost Ledger Control A/c .	. 2,000	Jan	11	Cost of Sales	. 1,600
					13	Selling Overhead Variance to Costing P. & L. A/c (unfavourable)	. 400

ADMINISTRATION OVERHEAD A/c

			£				£
19..				19..			
Jan	8	Cost Ledger Control A/c .	. 2,500	Jan	9	Job Ledger Control A/c .	. 3,600
		Admin. Overhead Variance to Costing P. & L. A/c (favourable)	. 1,100				

The important difference in the accounts is that every aspect of cost has a standard, and variances will therefore arise on wages (labour), materials and expenses. If in Example 4 the standard cost of labour in jobs during the period had been £10,800, the account would have been—

WAGES A/c

			£				£
19..				19..			
an	4	Cost Ledger Control A/c .	12,000	Jan	4	Factory Overhead A/c .	. 600
	13	Wages Variance (to P. & L. A/c)	200			Admin. Overhead A/c .	. 800
						Job Ledger Control A/c .	. 10,800

Variance Analysis. Whilst the principle of variances is simple, considerable complications arise in analysing the variances and bringing out the different factors which have contributed to an overall variance. For example, the wages variance shown above might be capable of analysis into many combinations of the following variances: rates of pay, substitution, gang, overtime, conditions, extra rate allowance, revisions, idle time, efficiency, etc. The other main variances are materials (price, usage, mix), expenses (price, usage, efficiency, capacity, volume, calendar) and yield (i.e. efficiency of the process).

In addition to these, there will be variances due to changes in methods and revisions of the standards during an accounting period. Since all standards are inter-locking, it is not possible to make a complete overhaul of the system every time a method changes. Thus, the old standard is retained and part of the variance is attributed to methods change or revisions.

Budgetary Control is the prediction of the levels of expenditure to be expected in a business within a period of time. Budgets are subdivided so that the executives responsible for different sections of the business may be given reports comparing actual expenditure with the budgets. Each executive is held responsible for implementing the business policy within the requirements set by the budgets. He is expected to take individual action to attain policy objectives, and this may lead to budget and/or policy revision.

(c) Integrated Cost and Financial Accounts

It has already been pointed out that the only part of the financial accounts which coincides with the cost accounts is that part which is concerned with the impersonal accounts and with determining profit. An integrated system eliminates this overlap. The nominal accounting is redesigned so as to meet the needs of both financial and cost accounting at the same time. Besides resulting in economy, the need for reconciliation is eliminated, and this saves considerable time and trouble at the year end.

The economy of the system may be seen by comparing the entries necessary under the usual cost accounting system with those needed when the system is integrated. For example—

(a) *Purchase of materials* £10,000

Normal entries—

Financial accounts—

Dr. Purchases account
Cr. Creditor

Cost accounts—

Dr. Stores ledger control account
Cr. Cost ledger control account

Integrated—

Dr. Stores ledger control account
Cr. Creditor

(b) *Sale of goods from finished stock* £6,000

Normal entries—

Financial accounts—

Dr. Debtor
Cr. Sales account

Cost accounts—

Dr. Cost ledger control account
Cr. Sales account (costing)
Dr. Cost of sales account
Cr. Finished goods control account

Integrated—

Dr. Debtor
Cr. Sales account
Dr. Cost of sales account
Cr. Finished goods control account

The following illustrates the principle—

Example 6

As at 30th November, 19.., the following balances existed in a company's integrated standard cost and financial accounts—

	£'000	
Balance Sheet Accounts—		
Capital and reserves	300	
Creditors and accruals	88	
Fixed assets	140	
Raw materials in store and process	80	(at standard)
Direct wages in process	20	(at standard)
Factory overhead in process	10	(at standard)
Finished stock	90	(at standard)
Debtors	100	
Cash at bank	10	

	£'000	
Trading Accounts—		
Budgeted sales	585	
Sales variance	12	(debit)
Standard factory cost of sales	493	
Materials variance	5	(credit)
Direct wages variance	7	(debit)
Factory overhead variance	2	(debit)
Administration and selling expense	14	

During December, 19.., the following transactions took place—

	£'000	
Budgeted sales	105	
Actual sales	98	
Cash received—from debtors	95	
Cash paid—to creditors	63	
Cash paid—direct wages	23	
Raw materials purchased	40	(actual cost)
Excess materials issued	1	(at standard)
Factory expenses incurred	17	
Administration and selling expense incurred	3	
Output finished (at standard cost)—		
Materials	50	
Direct wages	26	
Factory overhead	13	
Standard factory cost of actual sales	82	

The standard cost of materials purchased is £42,000.

The closing valuations of work-in-process accounts (which are debited at actual and credited at standard) are—

	£
Direct wages (at standard)	15,000
Factory overhead (at standard)	13,000

You are required to—

(*a*) write up and close off the ledger accounts, *and*
(*b*) prepare a trial balance of the closing balances.

Capital and Reserves A/cs

			19..		£'000
			Nov 30	Balances b/d	300

Sundry Creditors A/cs

19..		£'000	19..		£'000
Dec..	Cash	63	Nov 30	Balances b/d	88
31	Balances c/d	65	Dec..	Raw Materials	40
		128			128
			Dec 31	Balances b/d	65

Fixed Asset A/cs

19..		£'000			
Nov 30	Balances b/d	140			

Raw Materials in Store and Process A/c

19..		£'000	19..		£'000
Nov 30	Balance b/d	80	Dec..	Finished Stock	50
Dec..	Sundry Creditors	40	31	Material Variance (on issues)	1
31	Material Variance (on purchases)	2		Balance c/d	71
		122			122
Dec 31	Balance b/d	71			

Direct Wages in Process A/c

19..		£'000	19..		£'000
Nov 30	Balance b/d	20	Dec..	Finished Stock	26
Dec..	Cash	23	31	Variance	2
				Balance c/d	15
		43			43
Dec 31	Balance b/d	15			

Factory Overhead in Process A/c

19..		£ 000	19..		£'000
Nov 30	Balance b/d	10	Dec..	Finished Stock	13
Dec..	Cash	17		Variance	1
			31	Balance c/d	13
		27			27
Dec 31	Balance b/d	13			

Finished Stock A/c

19..		£'000	19..		£'000
Nov 30	Balance b/d	90	Dec..	Factory Cost of Sales	82
Dec..	Materials	50	31	Balance c/d	97
	Wages	26			
	Factory Overhead	13			
		179			179
Dec 31	Balance b/d	97			

SUNDRY DEBTORS A/c

19..		£'000	19..		£'000
Nov 30	Balance b/d	100	Dec..	Cash	95
Dec..	Sales	98	31	Balances c/d	103
		198			198
Dec 31	Balances b/d	103			

CASH AT BANK

19..		£'000	19..		£'000
Nov 30	Balance b/d	10	Dec..	Sundry Creditors	63
Dec..	Sundry Debtors	95		Direct Wages	23
31	Balance c/d	1		Factory Overhead	17
				Admin. & Selling Expenses	3
		106			106
			Dec 31	Balance (overdraft) b/d	1

BUDGETED SALES A/c

			19..		£'000
			Nov 30	Balance b/d	585
			Dec..	Sales and Variance	105

ACTUAL SALES A/c

19..		£'000	19..		£'000
Dec..	Budgeted Sales	105	Dec..	Sundry Debtors	98
				Sales Variance	7
		105			105

FACTORY COST OF SALES A/c

19..		£'000			
Nov 30	Balance b/d	493			
Dec..	Finished Goods	82			

SALES VARIANCE A/c

19..		£'000			
Nov 30	Balance b/d	12			
Dec..	Sales	7			

MATERIALS VARIANCE A/c

19..		£'000	19..		£'000
Dec..	Raw Materials	1	Nov 30	Balance b/d	5
31	Balance c/d	6	Dec..	Raw Materials	2
		7			7
			Dec 31	Balance b/d	6

DIRECT WAGES A/c

19..		£'000			
Nov 30	Balance b/d	7			
Dec..	Direct Wages	2			

FACTORY OVERHEAD VARIANCE A/C

		£'000	
19..			
Nov 30	Balance b/d	2	
Dec	Factory Overhead	1	

ADMINISTRATION AND SELLING EXPENSES A/C

		£'000	
19..			
Nov 30	Balance b/d	14	
Dec	Cash	3	

TRIAL BALANCE ON 31ST DECEMBER, 19..

	Dr £'000	*Cr* £'000
Capital and reserves		300
Creditors		65
Fixed assets	140	
Raw materials	71	
Direct wages	15	
Factory overhead	13	
Finished stock	97	
Debtors	103	
Cash at bank		1
Budgeted sales		690
Sales variance	19	
Factory cost of sales	575	
Materials variance		6
Direct wages variance	9	
Factory overhead	3	
Administration and selling expenses	17	
	1,062	1,062

DIRECT OR MARGINAL COSTING

Costs can be classified in three categories in terms of their behaviour in relation to changes in volume of production—

1. *Variable or direct costs* are those costs which change in direct proportion to the changes in production activity. If the cost of producing one unit is £1 then the cost of producing 100 units will be £100. The most obvious example of such direct costs is raw materials cost.

2. *Fixed or period costs* are those which are unaffected by changes in the volume of production. These costs are also known as constant, capacity or unavoidable costs. If a firm has period costs of £10,000 per month then these costs will be incurred whether production is undertaken or not. There will normally be a limit to the production which can be obtained from a given level of capacity provision.

3. *Semi-variable costs* are those costs which are not perfectly variable nor are they entirely fixed in relation to production volume. For instance, a cost might be at the level of £2,000 if 100 units are produced and rise to the level of £2,500 if 150 units are produced.

Semi-variable costs can, however, be analysed into two components one of which is variable and the other fixed.

TOTAL COST VARIATION

Costs vary in the way shown in Figure 15.1. At zero production costs are £2,000. At a production of 3,000 units the total costs are £5,000. Figure

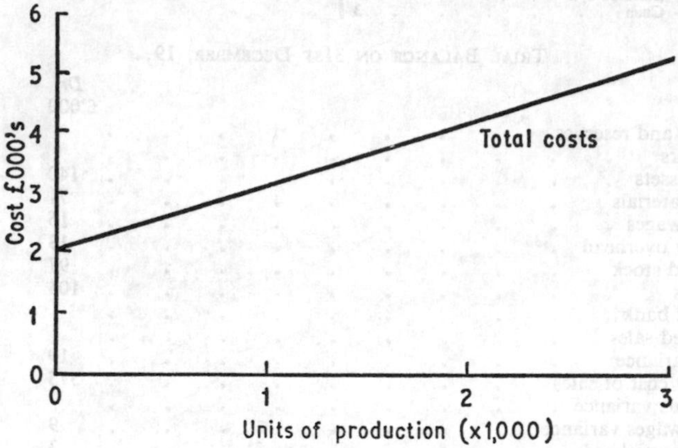

FIG. 15.1. Costs of XYZ Ltd. for one month

15.2 shows that total costs can be analysed into two components, fixed costs £2,000, variable costs £3,000 at 3,000 units, i.e. £1 per unit.

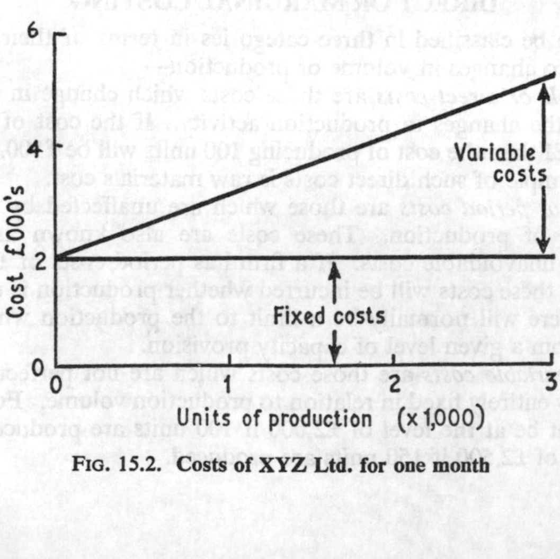

FIG. 15.2. Costs of XYZ Ltd. for one month

UNIT COSTS

Figure 15.3 shows the unit cost at various levels of production. At a production level of 1,000 units unit costs are £3, i.e. £2,000 fixed costs plus £1 a unit variable costs. At 2,000 units of production the unit costs will

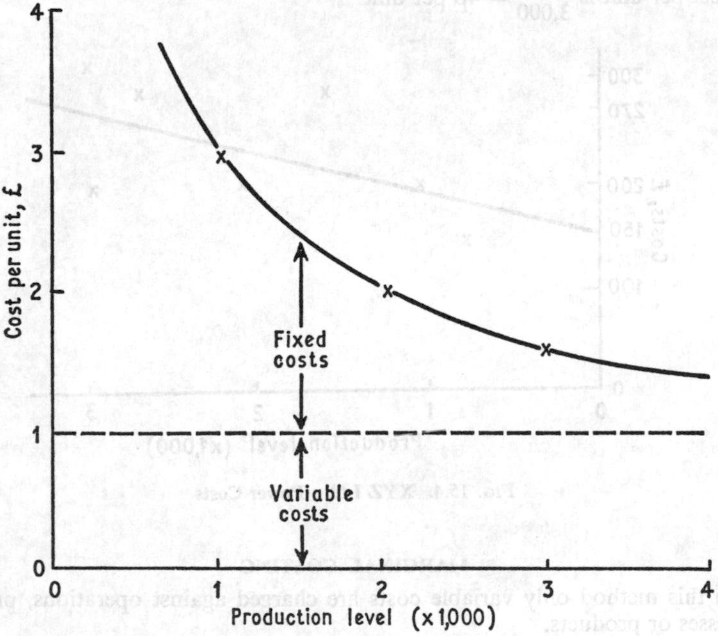

FIG. 15.3. **XYZ Ltd.: Unit cost at various levels of production**

be £2, i.e. fixed costs £2,000 plus variable costs of £1 per unit. The constant factor here is the variable cost. As the level of production rises the cost of each unit falls because the fixed costs of £2,000 are shared between a larger number of units.

ANALYSIS OF SEMI-VARIABLE COSTS

In Figure 15.4 the techniques by which a semi-variable cost can be split into its components is illustrated. The crosses indicate the information available on the power costs of XYZ Ltd. At 1,000 and 2,000 units of production £200 was spent. Similarly at 3,000 units £270 was spent, at 800 units, £150. Other costs at the various levels of production have also been plotted. A line of "best fit" can be calculated or drawn visually to show the line which is, in effect, the average of all the costs and production levels. In our illustration by extending the line to the base axis we find that the fixed component of this cost is approximately £150 and there is a variable component of £120 at the 3,000 production level. Variable cost per unit is $\frac{£120}{3,000}$ = 4p per unit.

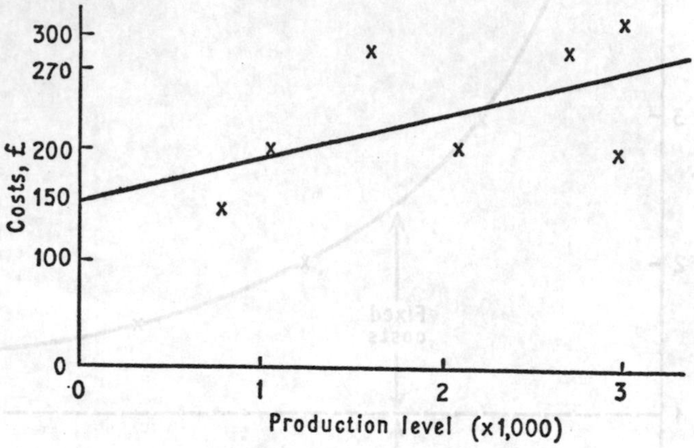

FIG. 15.4. XYZ Ltd.: Power Costs

MARGINAL COSTING

In this method only variable costs are charged against operations, processes or products.

Direct Costing also relates variable costs to products but may differ from Marginal Costing in charging some fixed costs to operations, processes or products.

COMPARISON WITH FULL COSTING

Figure 15.5 illustrates the difference in unit cost presentation. The total costs presentation shows a sales price per unit of £10 and total costs of £8 are deducted to show a profit per unit of £2.

Total cost presentation—	£	*Marginal cost presentation—*	£
Sales price per unit	10	Sales price per unit	10
Less Total costs	8	*Less* Variable or direct costs	4
Profit per unit	2	Contribution per unit	6

FIG. 15.5

The marginal cost presentation shows a sales price per unit of £10 less variable or direct costs of £4 leaving a contribution of £6 per unit.

Contribution is the difference between sales revenue and marginal or direct costs. Figure 15.6 shows that the difference is merely one of presentation if the budgeted level of production of 10,000 units is achieved

Full cost presentation—	£	*Marginal cost presentation—*	£
Sales	100,000	Sales	100,000
Less Total costs. . .	80,000	*Less* Direct costs . .	40,000
		Contribution . . .	60,000
		Fixed costs	40,000
Profit	20,000	Profit	20,000

FIG. 15.6. BUDGETED PRODUCTION 10,000 UNITS

The total contribution of £60,000 is applied firstly to meeting the fixed element of cost and the profit is the residue which remains after these costs have been met.

Figure 15.7 shows what happens if the level of production differs from

	£	£	Units
Actual Production level			8,000
Full cost			
Budgeted profit per unit		16,000	
Fixed costs	40,000		
Recovered 8,000 × £4	32,000		
Less Unrecovered fixed costs—		8,000	
Actual profit		8,000	
Marginal cost—			
Budgeted contribution (£6 × 8,000). . .		48,000	
Less Fixed costs		40,000	
Actual profit		8,000	

FIG. 15.7

the budgeted level. If it were true to say that the profit per unit was £2 then the profit on the sale of 8,000 units would be £16,000. However, there would be unrecovered fixed costs of £8,000 and the actual profit is £8,000. The marginal costing presentation shows that the contribution is as budgeted, £6 per unit and gives £48,000 which is applied to meeting the £40,000 fixed costs and leaves the residue, £8,000 profit.

Direct or marginal costing embodies an important generalization. The profit made on any unit of production depends upon *which* unit it is.

In the example every unit of production makes a contribution of £6, but the first 6,666 units are merely contributing to fixed costs. The 6,667th unit begins to contribute to profit and thereafter every unit produced increases profit by £6.

MANAGEMENT DECISIONS

It follows that a manager who had already produced 10,000 would be wrong to refuse production simply because it does not offer him a profit of £2 per unit. So long as his contribution has already covered his fixed costs then he would be justified in accepting any production which gives him some contribution. Indeed, in bad times it would be better to accept any job which offered more than £4 per unit since it would make some contribution to covering fixed costs. These costs will be incurred whether production is entered into or not. The minimum price for the unit would then be £4. At this point it would definitely not be worthwhile entering into production. The full cost presentation is misleading because it suggests that the minimum price should be £8.

Managers must consider, however, the long-term effect of the prices which they fix. In our example the manager has been required by the budget to look for a contribution of £6. He must understand that this is required to cover both his fixed costs and the profit to be made by his department or section. Whilst he may be justified in accepting a particular job which gives a lower rate of contribution in order to fill up his production capacity, he will be quite wrong to do this if it means that the long-term price of his product is going to be depressed. In the long run the contribution must recover all the fixed costs and make the profit requirements. If industry began to operate on the basis of simply covering its marginal costs then this would be uneconomic.

BREAK-EVEN ANALYSIS

The relationship between profits, the volume of production and the level of costs can best be shown in a break-even chart, as in Figure 15.8. The point at which sales revenue and costs intersect is the break-even point. At this point sales revenue is equal to the total cost and the company is neither making a loss nor a profit.

At levels lower than the break-even point the company will be making a loss and at higher levels it will begin to show a profit.

Figure 15.9 shows an alternative way of plotting the cost on the chart. In this illustration the total costs have been broken down to show the variable costs to which are added several "layers" of fixed costs. This shows a series of break-even points at which each type of fixed cost is being recovered. The break-even point for overall profitability is of course unaltered. The chart merely shows at what level each type of fixed cost will be covered.

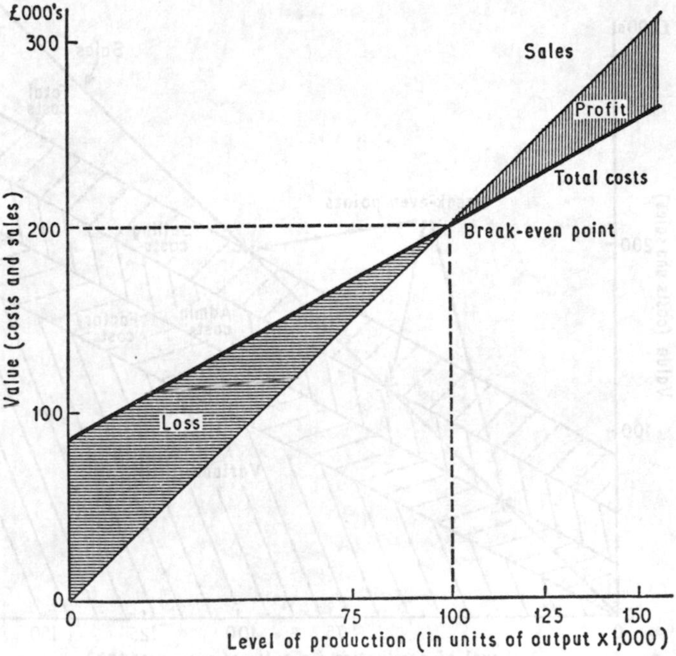

FIG. 15.8. ABC Ltd.: Break-even Chart

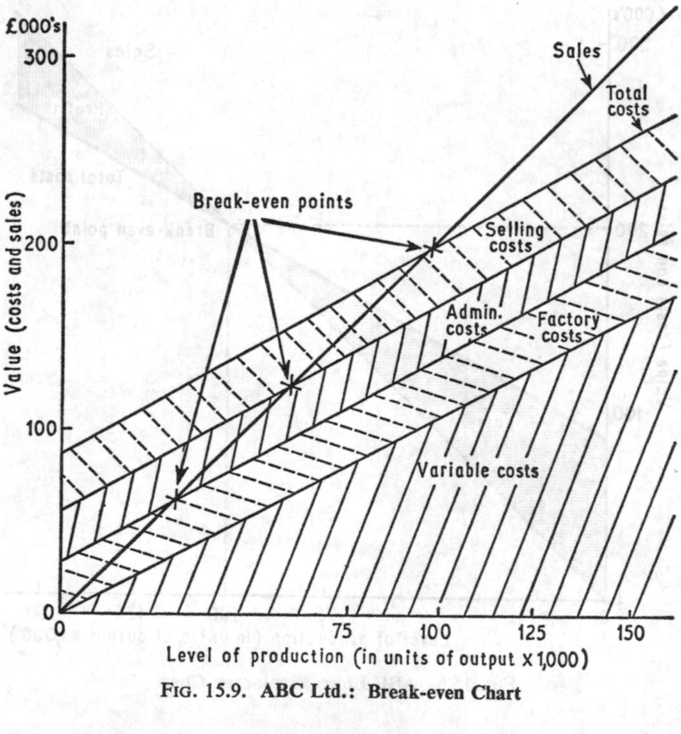

FIG. 15.9. ABC Ltd.: Break-even Chart

MARGIN OF SAFETY

The significance of the break-even chart may be that it shows whether a company has a low or a high break-even point. Figure 15.10 shows

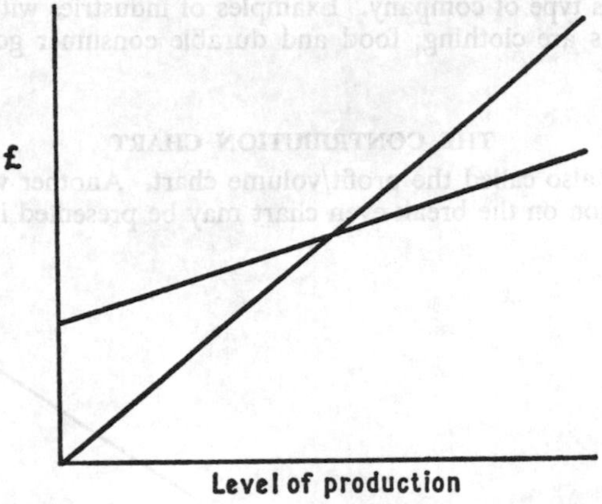

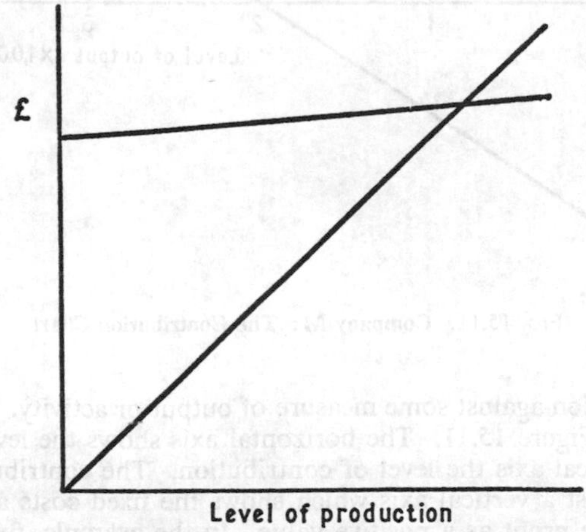

FIG. 15.10. Company X (Low); Company Y (High)

Company X with a low break-even point and Company Y with a high break-even point. In the event of recession, Company Y will become unprofitable sooner than X. In a boom it may be *more* profitable.

Company Y has relatively low variable costs but heavy fixed costs. Companies of this type offer "off-season" prices to improve profitability.

In the case of Company X the bulk of the costs are variable. Companies of this type tend to emphasize economies on operating cost. Close control of the use of labour and materials have a very great effect on the profitability of this type of company. Examples of industries with a low level of fixed costs are clothing, food and durable consumer goods (electric irons, etc.).

THE CONTRIBUTION CHART

This chart is also called the profit/volume chart. Another way in which the information on the break-even chart may be presented is by plotting

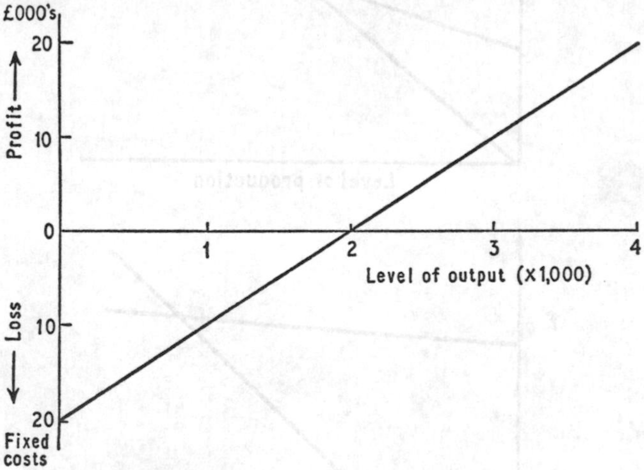

FIG. 15.11. **Company M: The Contribution Chart**

the contribution against some measure of output or activity. An example is shown in Figure 15.11. The horizontal axis shows the level of output and the vertical axis the level of contribution. The contribution can be plotted against a vertical axis which shows the fixed costs as a negative value and the profit as a positive value. In the example, fixed costs are £20,000 and the break-even point is at 2,000 units of production. The rate of contribution is therefore £10 per unit. At 4,000 units the total contribution would be £40,000. Deducting the fixed costs of £20,000 leaves a profit of £20,000.

The contribution chart is useful for control purposes since it may show a departmental manager the point at which he has begun to cover his fixed costs and the point at which he is making a profit. The contribution made by a section may be plotted in terms of the control period (for example monthly).

THE PROFIT/VOLUME RATIO

The profit/volume ratio is the relationship between the contribution and sales value. In Fig. 15.5 the profit volume ratio is

$$\frac{\text{contribution £6}}{\text{sales value £10}} \times 100 = 60\%$$

The profit/volume ratio is 60 per cent. This ratio is useful where a company has a mixture of products with varying rates of contribution. Products which offer a higher rate of contribution are normally preferred.

KEY-FACTOR ANALYSIS

However, in Fig. 15.12 the two products X and Y are shown each giving a different rate of contribution per unit.

	Product X	Product Y
	£	£
Sales prices	10	10
Less Variable costs	4	7
	6	3
Key factor of production—		
Labour, grade IV	6 hours	2 hours
Contribution per key factor unit	£1 per hour	£1·50 per hour
Available hours 120 *per week—*		
Contribution from product X	£1 per hour = £120	
Contribution from product Y	£1·50 per hour = £180	

FIG. 15.12

At first glance it would appear that product X is to be preferred since it gives a higher rate of contribution. This would only be true if both products used the same quantity of resources and capacity within the firm. When this is not the case the problem can be approached by identifying one factor which is in short supply. There will usually be one factor in production which prevents the company from taking more than a certain level of orders. This may be equipment or labour or availability of materials. Whichever factor this "key factor" may be, the contribution can be maximized if the contribution per key factor unit is minimized.

In the example the key factor of production is assumed to be a particular quality of labour and product X required six hours of this labour and product Y two hours. The contribution per key factor unit is so far £1 per hour on product X and £1·50 per hour on product Y.

The validity of this calculation can be seen by assuming that 120 hours of the labour is available within a working period. On this basis the contribution from product X would be £120 in a week whereas the contribution from product Y would be £180.

DETERMINATION OF THE OPTIMUM PRODUCT MIX

The optimum product mix can be calculated by taking available production in series. That is, as far as possible, filling production with the product which has the highest contribution per key factor and then working progressively down the list of products.

In the example given in Fig. 15.12 product X gives a contribution of £1 per key factor unit (Grade IV labour hours) and product Y gives £1·50 per key factor unit.

Whilst it is logical to argue that if the available hours are taken up by production of Y the overall contribution will be higher and, therefore, profits will be higher, the firm may not be able to do this because demand for Y is insufficient.

Suppose the firm has three products with the following contributions per key factor—

Product	X	Y	Z
Contribution per Grade IV labour hour	£1	£1·50	£1·25

If the effective demand for the products and the hours of labour required to produce a unit are—

Product	X	Y	Z
Demand in units	40	30	7
Hours of Grade IV labour per unit	6	2	4

Then, if the firm has only 120 hours of labour time available per week, the production should be taken up first with Y, then with Z and, finally, such amount of X which can be fitted in.

The production schedule would be—

	Total contribution £
30 units of Y = 60 hours	90
5 ,, ,, Z = 30 ,, ...	35
7 ,, ,, X = 28 ,, ...	30
	£155

It can be seen that two hours of production time are not used. In practice, these could be taken up by production of part of a unit of Y or X, on the assumption that time would be available for its completion later.

AN ANNUAL CONTRIBUTION CHART

For some businesses it may be possible to exercise control on the basis of an annual contribution chart. The company must specify what the level of fixed costs and expected profits will be and it can then state that the contribution required must be equal to that amount of money. Company M (see Fig. 15.11) has a profit requirement of £22,000 and fixed costs of £20,000. Its total contribution requirement therefore is £42,000 in a year. A chart can be drawn up as in Fig. 15.13 showing the expected

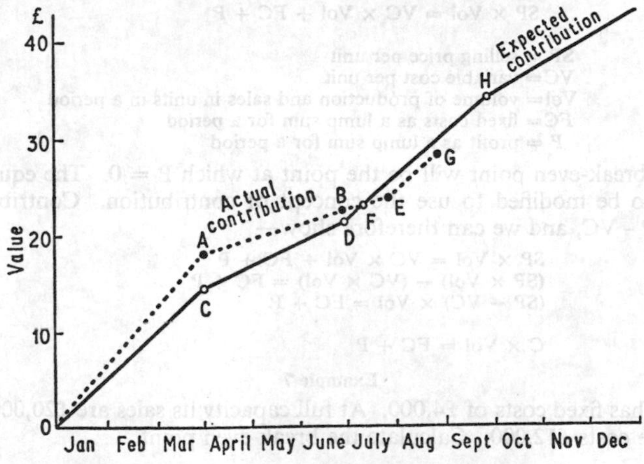

FIG. 15.13. **Annual Contribution Chart**

contribution on an annual basis. This is not a straight line since the business is seasonal. Month-to-month control can be exercised by plotting the actual contribution obtained from production against the expected contribution. Fig. 15.13 shows the way in which this may be done.

It can be seen from the chart that the actual contribution was higher in the first three months of the year than expected even though this is a very active period for the company. However the actual contribution between March and June was at a lower rate than had originally been anticipated. This can be seen because line AB is not parallel to line CD.

Another factor is that between June and August the company did not experience an expected recovery of sales activity. As a result line BE is the actual contribution crossing the expected contribution line and between point F and point G the company is falling below its expected contribution for the year. However it can be seen that sales began to recover sometime in July and that between point E and G that is July and August the level of contribution was as good as had been expected. In other words line EG is parallel to DH. It can be seen that this chart is a useful way of checking the progress of the company.

THE MONTHLY CONTRIBUTION CHARTS

The chart can be broken down into monthly periods and also sub-divided in sectional and departmental areas of responsibility so that the managers know their own expected and actual levels of contribution.

The cost-profit-volume relationship may be expressed—

$$\text{Sales} = \text{Variable costs} + \text{fixed costs} + \text{profit}$$

or

$$SP \times Vol = VC \times Vol + FC + P$$

where

SP = selling price per unit
VC = variable cost per unit
Vol = volume of production and sales in units in a period
FC = fixed costs as a lump sum for a period
P = profit as a lump sum for a period

The break-even point will be the point at which $P = 0$. The equation can also be modified to use the concept of contribution. Contribution C is SP − VC, and we can therefore show—

$$SP \times Vol = VC \times Vol + FC + P$$
$$(SP \times Vol) - (VC \times Vol) = FC + P$$
$$(SP - VC) \times Vol = FC + P$$

or

$$C \times Vol = FC + P$$

Example 7

A firm has fixed costs of £4,000. At full capacity its sales are £20,000 and variable costs £12,000. Calculate the break-even point.

Solution

At full capacity, the equation would show—

Contribution	= Fixed Cost	+ Profit
£8,000 (or £80 × 100%) =	£4,000	+ £4,000

The break-even point will be that percentage of production at which—

$$£80 \times \%\ \text{production} = £4{,}000, \text{ or } \%\ \text{production} = \frac{4{,}000}{80}$$

$\therefore$ Break-even point = 50% of production capacity.

JOINT COSTS

These are costs which arise in relation to two or more joint products. Products will be joint if in order to produce one we have to produce the other, e.g. coke and gas. One product is often considered the main and the others the by-products but any attempt to apportion the costs must be arbitrary. Such apportionment may be made on sales value, weight or other measure of volume. In some cases the sales value of by-products is deducted from the costs of the main product. Over a period of time, the by-product may become the main product and vice versa.

COMMON COSTS

These are costs which arise in relation to two or more products when the business has a free choice of which products it will make. A cost may represent a wide variety of different combinations of products.

In this case, the analysis of the costs of the various products is meaningful and costs can be measured in relation to output and activity.

PROBLEMS IN BREAK-EVEN ANALYSIS

There are a number of factors which affect the validity of a break-even chart and which therefore reduce its value in the business situation.

1. *The Break-even Chart Illustrates the Relationship between Sales, Volume of Production and Levels of Costs.* In practice it is difficult to collect these three factors in terms which make comparison easy and valid.

2. *The Division of Costs into the Three Categories of Fixed, Variable, and Semi-variable* with the latter type of costs being analysed into the two components of fixed and variable costs assumes that it is a practical possibility to make the division. However, many costs are semi-variable, and it is difficult to analyse such items as bonuses on wages and depreciation charges and cost of maintenance in an accurate way.

3. *The Sales Mix.* If a company has a number of different products or is engaged on a variety of contracts it is hard to find one factor which measures the amount of work done or the level of production accurately. As an example, a transport undertaking would find it difficult to relate costs to mileage if one journey was a short local journey and another was long range haulage. Although one may argue that these categories are fairly clear, in practice the lorry may undertake a variety of journeys and unless the underlying pattern is fairly regular it would not be realistic to show variable costs per mile. The introduction of multiple units such as the ton-mile or the passenger-mile helps but does not really solve the problem. For sales prices the break-even chart also assumes that sales prices will be constant whatever the volume of production. In fact this may not be the case and, as production rises, so prices may fall, so that the line would not be straight but would tend to flatten out. Any change of prices would, of course, affect the break-even position of the firm.

4. *Measures of Volume.* Some variable costs vary with factors such as the number of consignments handled or the length of time spent on an activity, or may be related to production output. The break-even chart must take one or other of these factors as a common measure of output. Whichever is taken, some of the variable expenses will not be truly variable in relation to that particular factor.

5. *The Break-even Chart shows the Fixed Costs as Unchanging* but, again, if the capacity is increased the fixed costs may rise also.

6. *The Technology of a Firm* may change and, clearly, the nature of variable and fixed costs would also change. It would then be necessary to construct new charts based on the new capacity available.

7. *Efficiency*. It is sometimes argued that the efficiency of the firm will decline as it increases in size. If this were the case then the cost line would curve upwards towards the end.

ASSUMPTIONS OF MARGINAL COSTING

These objections can be summarized in the form of assumptions which can be made to give a valid break-even chart. These are (1) that selling prices of products will not vary at different levels of output, (2) that the production capacity of the plant will remain fairly constant, (3) that efficiency of operation will be constant.

Despite the difficulties it is reasonably certain that this approach to costs is more useful than the full cost approach in *some circumstances*. For informed and intelligent management decisions it is necessary to keep both kinds of calculations in mind.

For a fuller treatment of this topic the reader is referred to the author's *Planning for Profits*, Gee & Co., 1967.

CAPITAL EXPENDITURE DECISIONS

The problem of identifying the costs when capital expenditure decisions are made is dealt with on p. 2943 *et seq*.

COST ESTIMATING AND PRICING

All estimates of cost must be based on the expected future costs of labour, materials, services and other overheads. Reliable estimates require a good knowledge of current costs which may then be adjusted for expected future conditions of production, changes in prices and wage rates, and other future circumstances.

One-off Jobs. Estimating the costs of a "one-off" (unique) job or contract is usually based on an analysis of the quantity of direct labour and materials required. Current standards of efficiency may be adjusted for improvements in productivity. Prices and wage rates are adjusted for the expected rates at the time when the work is expected to be done. Overheads should also be at estimated future levels, applied on the established bases for absorption, as discussed on pp. 1511–13. The costs of special jigs, tools, services, facilities and equipment are included, and these may be difficult to estimate if there is a possibility of repeat orders from the same or other customers.

A target price is frequently calculated by adding a percentage for profit, as in the following example.

Example 12

A company estimates for Job No. 555 which will require Direct Materials £50; Direct Labour; £60 in the machine shop, £100 on assembly, £10 on polishing.

Monthly departmental Direct Labour costs are: Machining £2,400, Assembly £6,000, Polishing £1,200. The normal monthly costs of factory production are Direct Labour £14,600, Direct Materials £2,440 and Departmental overheads £9,360, of which £1,200 is in the Machining department, £600 in Assembly and £240 in Polishing. General overhead of £3,960 is applied to all jobs on the basis of factory costs. Departmental overheads are applied only to those jobs actually going through the department on the basis of direct labour cost. Profit is added at the rate of 20 per cent on the target selling price.

Solution 12

COST ESTIMATE—JOB NO. 555

	£	£
Material		50
Wages: Machining	60	
Assembly	100	
Polishing	10	
		170
PRIME COST		220
Departmental overhead—		
(*a*) Machining—50% on wages	30	
(*b*) Assembly—10% on wages	10	
(*c*) Polishing—20% on wages	2	
		42
FACTORY COST		262
(*d*) General overhead 15% on Factory cost		40
Transport		19
TOTAL COST		321
Add Profit—20% on selling price		80
TARGET SELLING PRICE		£401
Say		£400

(*a*) $\frac{1,200}{2,400} = 50\%$ (*c*) $\frac{240}{1,200} = 20\%$

(*b*) $\frac{600}{6,000} = 10\%$ (*d*) £14,600 + £2,440 + £9,360 = £26,400

$$\frac{3,960}{26,400} = 15\%$$

The actual price agreed will depend on the prices offered by competitors, but should not be allowed to fall below the estimated marginal costs of production.

Repetitive Production. The costs of repetitive production depend very much on the volume of sales which can be expected. Since sales volume may also depend on the price set, cost estimating and pricing is a complex process, which is often handled by determining the target price and volume to achieve over the anticipated life of the products, which may be several years. Given the price and volume, it is then possible to forecast the methods of production and the allowable costs of materials, labour capital facilities and overheads, by breaking the product down into its various components and the work required from each function such as marketing, or department such as assembly or machining. Quality and efficiency standards must be specified and production is then engineered to meet the allowable costs. Again, the process is complicated by the fact that profit, as well as being calculated as a margin on price, must also give a reasonable return on the capital invested.

SUBSIDIARY BOOKS AND RECORDS IN A COSTING SYSTEM

Because of the great emphasis placed upon analysis of information in costing, considerable use is made of subsidiary records. The rulings are usually columnar and designed for the particular business using them. The following books of prime entry are usually found—

(i) *Stores Received Book*. A typical ruling is shown on p. 1547.

(ii) *Stores Issued Book*. A typical ruling of this book is also shown on p. 1547.

(iii) *Materials Transfer Journal*. The transfer of materials issued for one job to use on another must be carefully recorded, otherwise considerable errors in costing may arise.

(iv) *Stores Returned Book*. This book records the return stores issued for a job but not used on it.

(v) *Analytical Wages Book and Abstract*. A wages abstract as required for costing is shown on p. 1548. It is the document from which the cost ledger is finally posted.

(vi) *Direct Expenses Journal*. This book is used for recording those expenses which can be directly charged to jobs.

(vii) *Departmental Overhead Distribution Summaries*. This lists the expenses of the firm and shows the bases on which they have been apportioned to the various departments. A form similar to that used in Example 2 (*ante*) may be used.

(viii) *Overhead Summaries*. These summarize the overhead applicable to various sections of the firm, following the distributions shown in (vii).

(ix) *Job and Order Summaries*. These summarize the costs debited to each job or order, and indicate the results expected, as follows (p. 1549).

STORES RECEIVED BOOK

Date	Order No.	From Whom	Particulars	Stores Ledger Folio	Quantity				Price	Amount	Remarks
					No.	cwt.	qr.	lb.			
										£	

STORES ISSUED BOOK

Date	Requisition No.	Particulars	To Whom or for What Purpose	Stores Ledger Folio	Quantity				Price	Amount	Remarks
					No.	cwt.	qr.	lb.			
										£	

WAGES ABSTRACT

Contract 1		Contract 2		Contract 3		Contract 4		Contract 5		Expenses	Summary
No.	Amount	No.	Amount	No.	Amount	No.	Amount	No.	Amount		
	£		£		£		£		£	£	

	Job A	Job B	Job C	Total	Profit or Loss
	£	£	£	£	£
Cost of production	300	650	480	1,430	
Selling expenses	50	150	220	420	
Cost of sales	350	800	700	1,850	
Profit	+ 50		+ 150	150	+ 200
or Loss		− 50			−50
Selling price.	400	750	850	2,000	150

COST SHEETS

In addition to the above subsidiary books, the art of the cost accountant includes the preparation of many forms of cost report which may be presented to all levels of management. Some of these may be routine, presented regularly at specified times, but many are prepared and presented as reports on specific problems, showing particular cases of excessive costs. It is impossible to illustrate a full range of such reports, which, in any case, are best designed for the specific purpose in mind, but the following examples of cost sheets will illustrate the sort of report which is prepared—

COST OF PRODUCTION OF A STANDARD PRODUCT
(say) BESSEMER STEEL

	January, 19.. Output: 1,000 tons		
	Expenditure	Cost per Ton	Percentage on Selling Price
	£	£	
MATERIALS—			
Purchased direct (particulars from Analysis Purchase Book)	525	0·525	10·50
Requisitions of stores (particulars from Stores Requisition Book)	950	0·950	19·00
LABOUR— (Particulars from Wages Book analysed according to the various operations of labour)			
Operation No. 1	250	0·250	5·00
" " 2	304	0·304	6·08
" " 3	325	0·325	6·50
" " 4	287	0·287	5·75
" " 5	338	0·338	6·75
" " 6	305	0·305	6·08
" " 7	216	0·216	4·34
PRIME COST	3,500	3·500	70·00
DIRECT EXPENSES—			
1. Rent, Rates, Taxes, and Insurance of Works	25	0·025	0·50
2. Motive Power, Fuel, Gas. Water, Lighting	275	0·275	5·50
3. Royalty	50	0·050	1·00
4. Non-productive Wages and Salaries	150	0·150	3·00
5. Repairs, Depreciation, etc., of Plant and Machinery	100	0·100	2·00
6. Interest on Capital Outlay on Plant, etc.	25	0·025	0·50
	4,125	4·125	82·50
INDIRECT EXPENSES—			
1. Rent. Rates Insurance, etc., of Offices, Warehouses	12	0·0125	0·25
2. Lighting, Heating, Water	8	0·0083	0·16
3. Salaries of Office Staff, Manager	250	0·250	5·00
4. Bad Debts and Discounts	50	0·050	1·00
5. Depreciation of Fixtures, etc.	4	0·0041	0·09
6. Interest on Capital, Loans	51	·0·050	1·00
TOTAL COST	4,500	4·500	90·00
Percentage of Profit, 11⅑% (which gives a 10% profit on the Selling Price)		0·500	10·00
SELLING PRICE PER TON		5·000	100·00

The wages book should be so arranged that the workmen engaged on similar operations of labour are grouped together so that the total amount spent on each operation of labour can be extended in a separate column, as this information is necessary in preparing the cost accounts.

NOTE. The 11⅑ per cent added to cost in order to yield 10 per cent on return is arrived at as follows—

$$\frac{10 \times 100}{100 - 10} = \frac{\not{1}\not{0} \times 100}{\not{9}\not{0}_{\;9}} = 11\tfrac{1}{9}\% = \text{percentage required.}$$

Example 8

This example shows the analysis of the cost of gas and other products made by the Gas Boards.

COST OF GAS AND

	Scottish	Northern	North Western	North Eastern	East Midlands	West Midlands
	£	£	£	£	£	£
Process materials (including expenses thereon)—						
Coal	10,602,296	3,601,208	19,668,909	7,606,079	7,789,295	17,257,644
Coke	647,120	199,173	1,322,719	365,313	334,451	1,577,981
Oil	506,458	212,076	864,293	336,783	789,786	1,410,991
	11,755,874	4,012,457	21,855,921	8,308,175	8,913,532	20,246,616
Other process materials and services	574,538*	247,104	931,163	315,377	401,055	997,633
Process wages . . .	801,367	289,469	1,332,225	579,828	559,063	998,055
Repairs and maintenance of buildings and plant. .	992,890	419,504	1,019,477	669,332	765,224	1,783,242
General works charges .	717,875	445,235	1,461,052	510,177	811,659	1,494,121
Crude gas purchased (including expenses thereon)	882,762	1,327,989	619,664	26,982	1,790,809	218,311
Purified gas purchased (including expenses thereon)	43,326	1,915,563	—	568,775	3,149,501	345,661
Cost of gas and products .	**15,768,632***	**8,657,321**	**27,219,502**	**10,978,646**	**16,390,843**	**26,083,639**
1958–9 . . .	*17,086,466*	*9,295,577*	*29,027,913*	*11,800.603*	*16,077,662*	*26,049,035*

* The Scottish Board in addition include £2,091,122 under

PRODUCTS 1959–60

Wales	Eastern	North Thames	South Eastern	Southern	South Western	Total	*1958–9*
£	£	£	£	£	£	£	£
1,020,692	10,856,062	22,188,061	16,861,776	6,159,503	7,182,809	130,794,334	*143,798,964*
64,573	440,986	1,909,899	1,489,838	503,348	638,570	9,493,971	*9,597,134*
18,717	603,904	1,450,335	1,482,164	567,159	477,833	8,720,499	*8,281,276*
1,103,982	11,900,952	25,548,295	19,833,778	7,230,010	8,299,212	149,008,804	*161,677,374*
109,694	408,633	1,019,111	636,220	460,414	290,472	6,391,414	*6,360,726*
100,458	642,902	1,527,459	1,216,951	365,676	356,934	8,770,387	*9,640,402*
158,695	749,721	2,448,520	1,459,866	575,942	500,452	11,542,865	*12,495,953*
218,587	673,909	2,356,033	1,545,040	498,200	489,103	11,220,991	*11,957,224*
1,733,225	—	1,716,938	300,245	303,086	—	8,920,011	*7,454,280*
841,031	5,283	587,927	—	—	6,462	7,463,529	*6,719,423*
4,265,672	14,381,400	35,204,283	24,992,100	9,433,328	9,942,635	203,318,001	*216,305,382*
4,239,101	*15,046,900*	*38,599,971*	*27,832,829*	*10,339,980*	*10,909,345*	*216,305,382*	

these headings for fuel used in heating retorts.

Example 9

The costs set out in Example 9 are summarized by the Board in the way shown on p. 1552–3. Income from other products has been deducted so as to show the net cost of gas manufactured and purchased.

Example 10

The cost statement on p. 1555 gives a quarterly report on the actual costs of production in a paint works.

The section on the left, headed Quarterly Budget, is an example of the flexible budget and gives the budgeted expenditure on each item (wages, asbestos rope, etc.) according to the level of production, which is gauged

SUMMARY

Cost of Gas and Products

The gross cost of gas and products manufactured and purchased was £203·3 m. Deducting the net income from products other than gas (£82·4 m.) the net cost of gas manufactured and purchased becomes £120·9 m. Expressed as an average cost per therm of gass sold this is 4·67p compared with 4·82p in 1958–9. Details hereunder.

1958–59		1959–60
£m.		£m.
	Cost of raw materials for gas-making (including handling):	
143·8	Coal	130·8
9·6	Coke	9·5
8·3	Oil	8·7
161·7		149·0
14·2	Cost of gas purchased (crude and purified)	16·4
9·6	Process wages	8·8
12·5	Repairs and maintenance of buildings and plant (including wages)	11·5
18·3	Other charges (including wages)	17·6
216·3		203·3
	Deduct—	
90·6	Income from products (net)	82·4
125·7	Net Cost of Gas	120·9

by the number of machine-hours operated. Whilst the budgets cover a range from 27,000 to 39,000 machine-hours, the forecast level is 33,000 machine-hours, at which level 1,480 batches of paint would be produced in the quarter.

The section on the right, headed Actual Cost, shows the actual figures for the first three quarters of the year. The resulting variances for each quarter are analysed in the lower section.

Example 11

In addition to the quarterly reports on costs of production, the actual and standard cost of each batch may be recorded. The product batch cost sheet on p. 1556 illustrates a form which might be used.

In this case, the costs are analysed between Material Costs and Conversion Costs (the cost involved in converting the materials from the raw state into the finished product).

It will be observed that only three departments were concerned with this particular job.

Income tax has no bearing on the answer as it is an appropriation of profits and not a charge to cost of production.

WORKS BUDGET/ACTUAL COST STATEMENT

Quarterly Budget (F = Forecast)

Production Unit										
Machine-Hours	27,000		30,000		33,000 F		36,000		39,000	
Batches					1,480					
Expense	**Qty**	**£**	**Qty**	**£**	**Qty**	**£**	**Qty**	**£**	**Qty**	**£**
Wages—Supervision		350		350		350		350		350
Wages—General		2,300		2,500		2,700		2,900		3,100
Asbestos rope or substitute		110		130		150		170		190
Grinding media		500		560		620		680		740
Sundries		25		30		35		40		45
Mtce. materials		120		140		160		180		200
Mtce. labour	1,700	638	1,800	675	1,900	712	2,000	750	2,100	788
Electricity—Power	160,000	880	170,000	935	180,000	990	190,000	1,045	200,000	1,100
Steam process										
Water	150	7	150	7	150	7	150	7	150	7
Total (£)		4,930		5,327		5,724		6,122		6,520

Actual Cost

Production Unit	1st Quarter		2nd Quarter		3rd Quarter		4th Quarter	
Machine-Hours	31,424		28,438		28,665			
Batches	1,364		1,316		1,267			
Expense	**Qty**	**£**	**Qty**	**£**	**Qty**	**£**	**Qty**	**£**
Wages—Supervision		304		298		283		
Wages—General		2,877		2,717		2,459		
Asbestos rope or substitute		216		194		200		
Grinding media		600		560		200		
Sundries		37		23		12		
Mtce. materials		523		298		322		
Mtce. labour	2,940	1,176	2,700	1,080	2,322	929		
Electricity—Power	178,200	980	161,267	888	167,557	921		
Steam process								
Water	150	7	150	7	150	8		
Total (£)		6,720		6,065		5,334		

Budget submitted by . . . . .

Budget approved by . . . . .

Variances (Credits *Cr.*)		1st Quarter	Var.	2nd Quarter	Var.	3rd Quarter	Var.	4th Quarter	
Departmental Cost Variance	Actual direct cost as detailed above	6,720		6,065		5,334			
	Budgeted direct cost of actual production	5,521	1,199	5,130	935	5.152	182		
Production Variance	Budgeted direct cost of actual production	5,521		5 130		5,152			
	Amount recovered in product costs (actual production at std. rate)	5,190	331	4,834	296	4,787	365		
Net Variance (£)			1,530		1,231		547		

PRODUCT BATCH COST

Date	S/C	Unit	Batch	Product No.
Sep 57	11	LB	007	A 380–1781

Total Input	Std. 2280	Act. 2350	Unit Cost	Std. 17·1	Act. 1·85

MATERIAL ANALYSIS

	Material Codes	Std. lb.	Act. lb.	p per lb.	Std.—Unit Cost	— Act.
M	2815	34	34	3·25	·01	·01
D	622	36	36	12·4	·04	·04
R	3546	670	670	16·7	·98	·95
Z	4769	705	705	4·75	·29	·29
X	102–0773	235	235	6·05	·12	·12
X	102–0773	112	112	6·05	·06	·06
X	102–0773	4	4	6·05		
X	102–0773	34	34	6·05	·02	·02
L	1242	34	34	2·75	·01	·01
L	1743	388	388	4·65	·16	·15
L	1412	28	28	6·75	·02	·02
X	251–0012		34	56·05		·16
X	250–0009		26	4·6		·01
X	332–0000		10	8·65		·01

CONVERSION ANALYSIS

Code	Act. Units	Act Cost
311	20	23
311	1	21
253 (Tint)	4	9
456 (Test)	6	47

PRODUCTION ANALYSIS

	Units	Value
Ware-house		
Plant	2240	4426
Surplus		

MATERIAL COST

Total	Std.– 4018·50	Act 4325·99		
VARIANCE Total	Batch 307·49	% 7·65	Dr.*	
W.P.G.				
Mats.	307·49	7·65	Dr.*	

CONVER-SION COST

Total	Std. 300·00	Act. 100·14	
Variance	Batch 199.86	% 66·62	Cr.*

TOTAL ACTUAL COST	Unit 1·98	Batch 4426·13

Std. W.P.G.	Std. Loss 3·00 %	Act. Loss 4·68 %	Gain %
Act. W.P.G.	Tinters %	Surplus ·44 %	Others 2·63 %
	ADDITIONS		

†NOTE. In the case of Gallon Accounts the Total Standard Material Cost $= \frac{\text{Total Actual Input}}{\text{Actual W.P.G.}} \times$ Standard Material Cost per Gallon

Works Use

*Significant Variance Noted........................Plant Supt.

MATERIALS AND LABOUR IN A COSTING SYSTEM

Control of the cost of labour and materials is of fundamental importance to costing.

Materials

Reference should be made to the section on stock valuation and control in the previous chapter.

Labour

Control of labour cost has two main aspects—

1. Time. 2. Rates of pay.

1. Control of Time. This has two main aspects—

(*a*) *Time-keeping*, which implies establishing an efficient system for recording the arrival and departure of workers at the place of work.

(*b*) *Time-booking*, which implies an efficient system for recording the time actually spent by each worker on particular jobs. This is usually an essential for direct labour, if accurate costs are to be obtained.

2. Rates of Pay. There are many methods of paying labour in use, and it is important to choose the best method for the circumstances. Generally, the aim will be to reduce cost per unit of output, but this does not mean that the lowest rate of pay is the best. A high rate of pay may lead to improved quality, a saving on overheads and material wastage, and other economies which more than offset the rise of labour cost.

In choosing the method of paying labour, the factors to be considered include—

(*a*) *The effect of the method on the workers.* Will it provide an incentive which they understand? A complicated system may fail on this account.

(*b*) *The effect of the rate on production efficiency.* If the workers are given an incentive to concentrate on quantity of output, the quality may tend to fall. This may require the setting up of a stricter inspection system and a closer control of materials. Similarly, hurried work might lead to a misuse of tools.

(*c*) *The incidence of overhead in costs.* An increase in the volume of production will reduce the amount of fixed overhead incurred on each unit, but variable overheads may rise disproportionately.

METHODS OF WAGE PAYMENT

1. Time Rates. Workers are paid at hourly rates, with extras for overtime and holiday work. The payment is not related to output, and effective supervision may be needed to ensure that adequate work is done. On the other hand, time rates are generally used for highly skilled work, indirect workers, and supervisors, and for transport workers. where it is impossible to relate payment to output.

The high wage plan is a time rate, but workers are paid high wage rates as an inducement to accept high standards of performance on the job.

2. Piece Rates. In ordinary piece work, a fixed price is paid to the worker for each job or piece completed. Strict inspection is necessary.

In differential piece work, the price for the piece changes as the number of pieces completed increases. If the price per piece increases, then the differential is accelerating.

On a strict piece-work system, a worker who did not satisfactorily complete any work could receive no wages at all. The worker might have worked all the week and completed a fair number of pieces, none of which passed inspection. To avoid this situation, workers may be given a guaranteed daily or weekly wage.

3. Bonus Systems. Under these systems of payment of wages there is taken into consideration the ratio that "work done" bears to "time taken."

Two schemes under methods of remuneration are chosen for consideration, namely, the Halsey and Rowan systems. Other schemes are employed but they more or less approximate in effect to the two methods explained below.

Halsey Bonus Scheme. The Halsey scheme provides for a bonus of 50 per cent on hours saved at the usual rates per hour. The scheme works out as under—

Fourty-four hours were allotted for a piece of work at 50p per hour. The work was completed in 33 hours, with the following result—

		£
Time allowed	44 hours	
Time taken	33 hours @ 50p per hour	16·50
Time saved	11 hours	
Bonus will be earned on 11 × ½ = 5½ hrs. @ 50p . . .		2·75
	Total Wages . . .	18·75

Rowan Bonus Scheme. The Rowan scheme provides for a bonus of a percentage increase of pay equal to the percentage the hours saved bears to the hours allotted, which percentage will be added to amount earned on work done. Applying the above example, the result yields the following—

	£
Time taken, 33 hours @ 50p per hour	16·50
Bonus is arrived at one the following formula—	

$$\frac{\text{Time saved 11 hours} \times 100}{\text{Time allotted 44 hours}}$$

Reduction of above formula shows 25 per cent.	
Therefore, 25 per cent of £16·50 will be added	4·13
	20·63

4. **Efficiency Pay.** Efficiency pay is granted to employees beyond a day wage for their completion of skilled work in the minimum of time. The rate of increase moves within the margin of 5 per cent and 40 per cent, and is applied according to efficiency beyond the 65 and reaching toward the 100 per cent standard.

5. **Priestman Plan.** The Priestman plan is a bonus on output. It moves according to the following circumstance—

A standard output is agreed upon by the management and the employees' representatives. Now, according to output beyond the standard, a bonus "at the rate of increase" is granted to the employees.

6. **Profit-sharing Schemes** and co-partnership schemes are intended to develop a long-term co-operation between management, shareholders, and employees.

QUESTIONS

1. Mention the chief classes of cost accounts.
2. Explain three methods of remuneration of labour.
3. Define Overhead, Standard Costs, Job Costing.
4. Define Marginal Costing.
5. What methods are available for pricing materials drawn from stores?
6. What ledgers are needed in a cost accounting system?
7. Explain what is meant by Integrated Accounts.
8. What problems are involved in reconciling cost and financial accounts?
9. Explain fixed overhead, key factor, contribution.
10. Give three methods of overhead recovery and overhead apportionment.

EXERCISE 15

1. According to the factory job cost ledger, Job No. A8473 has incurred the following prime costs—

Materials (Direct)
  10 cwts @ £10 per cwt.
Wages (Direct)
  Department X 18 hours @ 50p per hour.
  Department Y 30 hours @ 60p per hour.

Budgeted overhead for the year, based on normal capacity, is as follows—

Variable overhead

Department X £6,000 for 9,000 direct labour hours.

Department Y £8,000 for 10,000 direct labour hours.

Fixed overhead

Total budgeted direct labour hours for whole factory 22,000.

Total budgeted expenditure £16,500.

You are required

(*a*) to calculate the cost of Job No. A8473.

(*b*) Estimate the % of profit obtained if the price quoted to the customer was £180.

(*A.C.C.A.*)

2. Draw up a form of weekly or monthly cost sheet adapted to one *only* of the following industries, and give specimen entries illustrating its working: (*a*) cotton-spinning mill, (*b*) iron foundry, (*c*) brewery. (*Chartered Accountants.*)

3. State the unit or units of output or earning generally in use for preparation of cost accounts of the following: (1) breweries, (2) brickworks, (3) iron and steel manufacturers, (4) water works. (*Chartered Accountants.*)

4. When auditing the accounts of a large factory where wages are paid by piece-work, you find on reference to the company's statistical results the following—

A. Dept.	Year (1)	% on Output	Year (2)	% on Output
Material	10,500	10·50	11,500	11·50
Wages	5,250	5·25	7,250	7·25
Packing	1,050	1·05	1,000	1·00
Supervision	525	0·52	500	0·50

What are your conclusions?

5. From the following information relating to a year's operations, you are required to compile and close off the cost and financial accounts of a company whose accounts are integrated, and prepare a final trial balance.

	Actual	Standard
Balances at beginning of period—	£	£
Customers	185,000	
Suppliers	84,000	
Cash	39,000	
Materials		40,000
Fixed assets	200,000	
Depreciation provision	94,000	
Work-in-progress		60,000
Investments	12,000	
Ordinary share capital	300,000	
Profit and loss account (credit)	58,000	
Transactions during year—		
Sales	404,000	385,000
Cost of sales		249,000
Wages (gross) (70% direct)	112,000	
Materials issued (85% direct)		106,000
Materials purchased	137,000	131,000
Materials returned	4,000	5,000

Cash paid—		
Wages	102,000	
Expenses	7,000	
Suppliers	125,000	
Interim dividend	23,000	
Cash received—		
From customers	416,000	
Income from investments	4,000	
Overhead allowance		65,000

Variances—adverse—

Direct wages—	
Rates	3% of actual.
Efficiency	4% " "
Methods	3% " "
Indirect materials—price	4% of standard.

Depreciation at 10 per cent per annum is to be charged to costs.

(Cost and Management Accountants.)

6. X Limited manufactures a number of products including product D which is sold under contract to J. Limited. Using the information given below:

(*a*) calculate the selling price of 100 units of D;
(*b*) evaluate 1,000 units of D held in stock by X Limited.

This valuation is for inclusion in the balance sheet. Give brief reasons in support of the method you recommend.

Standard production date for 100 units:

			£
Direct materials	200 lbs. of material Z	@	0·25 per lb.
Direct wages	50 hours	@	0·50 per hour
Variable production overhead			5·00
Machine hours	10		

Budgeted data for year:

	£000s
Production variable cost	1,000
Overhead: fixed production	400
administration	350
selling and distribution	700
Profit 20% of selling price	
Machine hours 100,000	

(Cost and Management Accountants.)

7. The Northern Foundry Co. Ltd. are manufacturers of steel castings. The company has instituted a system of costing; and you are requested to advise as to the basis on which standing charges and established expenses should be charged. The manufactures of the company vary greatly, some of the castings being of considerable size and weight, and others very small, but requiring intricate workmanship.

The points you have to deal with are—

(1) Foremen's wages, and wages of labourers and others not directly charged.
(2) Rent and rates.
(3) Travellers' salaries and expenses, and expenses of the forwarding department.
(4) General office expenses.
(5) Salaries of manager and managing director.

What would you advise? *(Chartered Accountants.)*

8. Explain five methods of remuneration of workmen in vogue in manufacturing industries. Discuss freely the merits and/or demerits of the methods. Also, state which method you more particularly favour, giving reasons in support of your preference.

9. Outline the means of control of "time" obtaining in most factories, and state one reason which—perhaps above many others—justifies the adoption of the system of time control you will have explained.

10. Sketch the form of a wages abstract and explain the purpose it serves in a costing system.

11. Draw up a chart which will show the way in which the elements of cost are compiled from prime to total cost.

12. A manufacturing company, having instituted stores accounts, finds that at the end of the first financial year there are considerable discrepancies between the values of the physical stock and the values as shown by the stores records. Investigation discloses that the differences in quantities are small and that they arise mainly in values.

Explain how this might happen, and suggest a system which, if used, should result in the values of the physical stock agreeing, within reasonable limits, with the values as disclosed by the stores records. *(R.S.A.)*

13. Describe a system of cost accounts suitable for use in any manufacturing business with which you may be familiar.

Submit an appropriate cost sheet, inserting details building up to total cost, and explain carefully the meaning and source of each item you insert. *(R.S.A.)*

14. To what extent do you consider that it is advisable to maintain agreement between the financial and costing records of a manufacturing business? Give reasons for your answer and explain, in particular, how you would deal with the records of purchases and wages. *(R.S.A.)*

15. The summarized revenue accounts of a business for the two years ended 31st December, 1962, show the following—

	1961	1962
	£	£
Sales	45,000	60,480
Factory cost of sales	30,000	32,500
Gross profit	15,000	27,980
Overheads	20,000	22,000
Profit	—	5,980
Loss	5,000	—

Towards the end of 1961 plans had been made to cut out waste and introduce new methods in the factory. These plans became effective on 1st January, 1962. As from that date selling prices were increased by 20 per cent.

Prepare a statement showing concisely how much of the increased gross profit is due to—

(*a*) the increased sales prices;
(*b*) changes in sales volume;
(*c*) the introduction of new methods in the factory. (*A.C.C.A.*)

16. Blu-Print Ltd. are asked to quote for supplying 5,000 or 25,000 or 50,000 booklets.

They normally expect a profit of 10 per cent on sales.

Costs are reckoned to be—

	£
Paper and other materials, per 1,000 copies	3
Wages, per 1,000 copies	2
Lay-out cost	50
Variable overhead, 120 per cent of wages	
Fixed overhead	20

Draft a cost computation, showing also selling prices (to the nearest £) that may be quoted per 1,000 copies in each of the three cases. (*A.C.C.A.*)

17. (*a*) Explain briefly the circumstances in which a machine-hour rate may suitably be used in cost accounting.

(*b*) Calculate from the following data the machine-hour rate for machine "A"—

Cost of machine	£21,000
Estimated scrap value	£1,000
Effective working life	20,000 hours
Running time per 4-weekly period	150 hours
Monthly amount payable under a maintenance agreement covering all repairs	£75
Standing charges allocated to machine per 4-weekly period	£30
Power used by machine	5 units per hour, at a cost of 6p per unit.

(*Chartered Accountants.*)

18. The balances shown in the cost books at 30th September, 1963, are as follows—

	£	£
Financial ledger adjustment A/c	34,800	
Stores ledger control A/c	1,848	
Work in progress A/c	3,195	
Wages control A/c (accrued wages)		311
Factory overhead control A/c (under-absorbed overhead)	168	
Finished goods stock A/c	12,000	
Prime cost of sales A/c	182,000	
Administration overhead control A/c	27,800	
Selling and distribution overhead control A/c	18,500	
Sales		280,000
	£280,311	£280,311

(*a*) You are required to open these accounts and enter the balances; and then pick up the following transactions for the month of October in so far as they affect the cost books (using the same accounts and any others you may deem necessary).

		£
Total goods received notes for materials (all materials pass through stores)		15,122
Total invoices for materials		15,122
Gross wages payable (including employers National Insurance £450)		8,900
Factory direct wages	£6,000	
Factory indirect wages	£2,900	
	£8,900	
Accrued wages 31st October		423
P.A.Y.E. (I. Tax) deductions		1,600
National Insurance deductions		500
Net wages cheque drawn		6,350
Materials issued to production		14,185
Wages allocated		
Factory direct wages—£6,000		
Factory indirect wages—£3,012		
Indirect materials issued to factory		870
Invoices for factory overhead expense		2,124
(N.B. Factory overhead is absorbed at the rate of 100 per cent on direct wages)		
Stores stock 31st October		1,915
Work in progress 31st October		4,380
Finished goods stock 31st October		14,000
Administration overhead incurred		3,100
Selling and distribution overhead incurred		2,050
Sales		32,000
Interim dividend paid (net)		8,000

(*b*) Extract the trial balance from the cost books as at 31st October.

(*A.C.C.A.*)

19. A factory is engaged in the production of washing machines. Two models are made, the "Standard" and the "Super," and the costing records consist of the monthly analysis as between the two models of direct wages and materials issued. All other factory expenses, classified as "works overhead," are allocated in proportion to the direct wages, and office and administration expenses, classified as "office overhead," in proportion to the total factory cost.

The whole of the materials required to complete a machine are issued from store on the day that assembly of the machine is commenced and it is assumed, as regards partly assembled machines, that, on the average, on any given date one half of the total wages required to complete have been expended.

The data for September, 19.., were summarized as follows—

	Standard Model Number	Super Model Number	Total Number
Quantities—			
Partly assembled on 31st August	40	16	56
Completed during September (including those commenced in August)	360	82	442
Partly completed on 30th September	60	12	72

	£	£	£
Financial Data—			
Direct wages	5,920	1,600	7,520
Material	9,044	2,652	11,696
Works overhead			1,504
Office overhead			1,036
			21,756

Calculate the unit cost of each type of machine. (*R.S.A.* (*modified*).)

20. From the following details calculate the labour cost chargeable to Job No. 873 in respect of an employee who is paid according to—
(*a*) The Rowan scheme.
(*b*) The Halsey 50 per cent scheme.

Job No. 873

Time allowed	5 hours 30 minutes
Time taken	4 hours 25 minutes
Rate of pay	£1 per hour

21. (*a*) Describe briefly the more usual bases for allocating works and factory expenses in Costing; and
(*b*) The Revenue Account of a business for the year to 30th September, 1963, is—

	£	£	£
Sales			122,475
Materials		51,650	
Labour—			
Dept. 1	7,500		
2	12,000		
3	10,500		
		30,000	
Carried forward		81,650	

	£	£	£
Brought forward		81,650	
Factory overhead			
Dept. 1	3,000		
2	7,200		
3	3,150		
	13,350		
Other overhead	19,000		
Profit	8,475		
		40,825	
			122,475

Opening and closing stocks may be ignored.

In October, 1963, a selling price is submitted for a particular job. It is shown below, the details as regards overhead and profit being based on the above Revenue Account.

	£
Materials	18
Labour—40 hours at £1	40
(Dept. 1, 20 hours; 2, 5 hours; 3, 15 hours)	
	58
Add 50 per cent on prime cost	29
	87

You are asked to submit a revised costing for the job, using a basis OTHER than prime cost for recovering overhead and profit, and adding to total cost 15 per cent for profit.

22. The following particulars are extracted from the books of a business—

	£
Sales	42,980
Purchase: raw materials	21,000
Opening stocks—	
Raw materials	1,750
Finished product	1,250
Closing stocks—	
Raw materials	1,400
Finished product	2,250
Direct wages	7,000
Salaries—	
Sales	1,700
Office and general	5,500
Carriage—	
Inwards	250
Outwards	400
Power, heat and light—	
Factory	400
Office and general	100

Draft a schedule showing—

1. Cost of raw materials used.
2. Cost of goods sold.
3. Profit.
4. Percentage added to the cost of goods sold to cover—

   (*a*) Sales expenses.
   (*b*) Office and general expenses.
   (*c*) Profit.

(*A.C.C.A.*)

23. A factory department—B.4—comprises five machines, each of the same type, size and capacity.

Two operators—a mechanic and his assistant—are employed on each of the machines.

A 40-hour week is worked, which includes 3 hours per week for adjustment and set-up time. This work is done jointly by the two machine operators. Their basic wages are: mechanic £1 per hour; assistant 60p per hour. The average bonus rate on basic wage is 12½ per cent.

The company's year is divided into four 13-week periods.

It is desired to recover both the direct labour cost and the factory overhead by the application of a single machine rate.

Factory overhead—

1. Machine set-up time as above.
2. Depreciation at 12½ per cent on machine cost (£8,000 per machine).
3. Maintenance and repairs: £5 per week per machine.
4. Consumable stores: £1 per week per machine.
5. Electric current: 4 units (at 5p per unit) per hour per machine.
6. Allocations to department B.4—
   Local rates: £320 per annum.
   Heat, light, etc.: £400 per annum.
   Foreman's salary: £1,440 per annum.

(*a*) Prepare a summary of the cost of operating ONE machine for a 13-week period; and

(*b*) Compute the hourly rate for operating ONE machine.

24. A chemical company owns two factories, identified for the purposes of this question as A and B. A manufactures a single product, X and B another single product, Y and B uses part of the output of A as its own raw material.

Accounts are being prepared for the year to 31st December, 19.1, and the following data are given—

	Factory A	Factory B
Financial Records—	£	£
Raw materials, Stocks on 31/12/.. plus purchases during 19.1	101,950	26,900
Raw materials, Stocks at 31/12/.1 at cost	750	600
Wages	35,200	17,400
Factory power and overheads	21,600	10,700
Sales (excluding inter-factory transfers)	146,000	98,790
Quantity Records—	Tons	Tons
Output of X and Y	960	420
Finished Stocks on hand at 31/12/..	None	None
do. 31/12/.1 X	40	None
Y	—	42

During the year Factory A had "sold" 200 tons of X to Factory B, charging it at the rate of £190 a ton.

You are required to calculate—

(*a*) the gross profit for the year shown by each factory's own records;

(*b*) the total value of the stocks (assumed all taken at cost) for inclusion in the company's balance sheet as on 31st December, 19.1; and

(*c*) the company's true gross profit for the year. (*R.S.A.*)

25. A chemical factory is designed to produce a standard (uniform) product at a rate of up to 100,000 tons per annum. The selling price is £120 a ton and the costs are estimated as follows—

	Per Ton of Output £	Total for a Year £
Prime costs—		
Materials	60	
Wages	20	
Direct expenses	5	
Factory overheads—		
Variable with production	7	
Fixed		60,000

	Per Ton Sold
	£
Selling and administration expenses—	
Variable with sales	3
Fixed	40,000

You are required to compute, assuming in each case that the total production is sold—

(*a*) the net profit or loss of the undertaking for a year, assuming production at the full rate;

(*b*) the same, assuming production as half the full rate; and

(*c*) the "break even" point. (*R.S.A.*)

26. You are accountant to a firm of engineers and the following is an analysis, arranged from a costing viewpoint, of the expenditure as disclosed by the accounts for the year to 31st December, 19..—

	£
Factory—	
Direct wages	41,000
Materials	80,920
Depreciation of machinery	19,550
Indirect wages	5,200
Other overheads	7,210
Selling and distribution	15,850
General administration	12,680

The basis on which individual costings are worked out is to apportion all factory overheads in proportion to the total of direct wages and machinery depreciation, and distribution and administration charges in proportion to total factory cost.

In January, 19.1, all the factory workers (but excluding office staffs, etc.) received a 10 per cent rise of pay; no other material changes as compared with 19.. have taken place or are anticipated in 19.1.

In April, 19.1, a customer asks for an estimate for a special job, and the following are the direct costs which it is estimated will be entailed in completing it—

	£
Direct wages	6,120
Materials	9,760
Depreciation of machinery	1,580

Allowance is to be made for selling and distribution expenses at half the average rate computed from the 19.. accounts and 10 per cent is to be added to the total cost for profit.

Work out the estimate for the selling price. (*R.S.A.*)

27. (*a*) Define marginal costing.

(*b*) Present the following information to show clearly to management the marginal product cost and the contribution per unit.

	Product	*£ per Unit*
Direct materials	A	10
	B	9
Direct wages	A	3
	B	2
Fixed expenses		£800
(Variable expenses are allotted to products as 100% of direct wages)		
Sales price	A	20
	B	15

(*Cost and Management Accountants.*)

28. For the two years ended 31st December, 1961, a summary of the operating expenses and profit of a business is as under—

	1960	1961
	£	£
Materials used	11,200	14,800
Direct labour	30,400	34,600
Overhead—		
Variable	18,000	24,800
Fixed	15,000	16,000
Profit	13,400	25,960

There were no opening or closing stocks of materials or of finished product.

It may be taken that as from 1st January, 1961—

(*a*) Selling prices were increased by 10 per cent.

(*b*) Material prices rose by 5 per cent and wage rates by 10 per cent.

(*c*) Of the variable overhead one-half comprises material, and one-half labour.

You are asked—

1. To draw up a statement in columnar form reconciling the increase in profit with changes in the various factors of cost; and
2. To comment briefly on possible explanations of such changes.

(*A.C.C.A.*)

29. From the following information relating to the first year's transactions, you are required to write up, close off, and balance the appropriate accounts in the self-balancing cost ledger of a manufacturer and prepare a trial balance of the closing balances.

	£
Freehold property at cost (depreciated in annual accounts at rate of 10 per cent)	85,000
Plant and machinery at cost (depreciated in annual accounts at rate of 20 per cent)	240,000
Office furniture and equipment at cost (depreciated in annual accounts at rate of 25 per cent)	5,000

DEPARTMENTS

	A	B	C	D	E	F	Stock
	£	£	£	£	£	£	£
Depreciation	8,000	14,000	4,000	16,000	2,000	1,000	
Net wages	35,000	46,000	20,000	65,000	73,000	40,000	
Deductions from wages	5,000	7,000	3,000	9,000	11,000	5,000	
Materials used	58,000	92,000	62,000	140,000	5,000	1,000	
Expenses	5,000	8,000	3,000	10,000	2,000	9,000	
Spoilage of work in departments	2,000	1,000	500				
Total cost of production transferred	*−83,000*	+34,000	+8,000	+41,000			
Total cost of production transferred		*−143,000*	+92,000	+15,000			
Cost of finished stock transferred			*−170,000*	*−300,000*			+470,000
Materials purchased							450,000

Material losses in stock were 4 per cent of purchases.

Cost of sales from stock was £450,000.

Sales invoiced to selling subsidiary company were £700,000.

Proceeds of sale of spoilage were £300.

Cost of department E is to be apportioned to departments A and B on the basis of wages.

Cost of department F is to be written off against profit.

(*Cost and Management Accountants.*)

30. The following is the trial balance of the head office general ledger of a company at the beginning of a trading period—

	£	£
Trade creditors		384,560
Trade debtors	693,800	
Bank		286,350
Glasgow (Factory current accounts)	265,000	
Manchester (Factory current accounts)	486,000	
Bristol (Factory current accounts)	195,000	
Watford (Factory current accounts)	90,000	
Stock in warehouses	295,000	
Private ledger account		1,353,890
	2,024,800	2,024,800

The following transactions took place during the subsequent trading period—

	Value of Goods Sent by Factories to Warehouses at Standard Cost	Payments Made Out of Head Office Bank on Account of Factories	Credit Purchases and Returns Made for Factories but Paid for at Head Office	
			Purchases	Returns
	£	£	£	£
Glasgow	196,540	85,000	133,690	8,650
Manchester	331,760	167,000	167,500	9,240
Bristol	96,410	50,000	29,600	1,690
Watford	58,220	25,000	38,200	2,480
	682,930	327,000	368,990	22,060

	£
Sales from warehouses to customers	975,600
Sales returns by customers	41,690
Payments made out of head office bank—	
To suppliers (discount received £2,640)	331,910
For warehouse salaries and expenses	25,000
For head office salaries and expenses	31,290
For an instalment of income tax	90,000
As a payment to account of London buildings	20,000
Payments into head office bank—	
From customers (discount £3,940)	895,220
From sundry revenues	14,860
The value of the stock at warehouses at the end of the trading period	308,000
The following variances arising at the factories during the trading period have to be written off—	
Glasgow—loss	2,350
Manchester—profit	3,990
Bristol—loss	1,284
Watford—loss	730

Charges accrued and unexpired have to be ignored.

You are required to—

(*a*) open and write up for the trading period the head office general ledger;
(*b*) prepare a profit and loss account for the trading period;
(*c*) prepare a closing trial balance of the head office general ledger.

(*Cost and Management Accountants.*)

31. During September, 19.., a factory department produced 7,800 units of finished product, of which 5,000 units were sold to an associated company at cost plus 20 per cent, and 2,400 to other customers at cost plus 30 per cent.

120 finished units were rejected on final inspection. Units rejected by customers (from September production) were—

Associated company 180.
Others 60.

All rejects were sold as scrap during September at 20p per unit.

The manager is entitled to a commission of 1 per cent of the monthly departmental profit, subject to a maximum allowance for rejects of 2 per cent of each month's quantity output.

The cost records for September, 19.., show the following—

	£
Wages	4,160
Materials used	2,860
Overhead allocation (to cover all other costs)	2,080

There were no opening stocks of the finished product, which is consistently valued for inventory purposes at prime cost.

Show in detail the profit and loss account of the department for the month as it will appear in the costing records, and calculate the manager's commission.

(*Certified and Corporate Accountants.*)

32. Kleenup Ltd. manufactures a vacuum cleaner of a uniform standard type selling at £22·50 and the costing data worked out for the month of October, 19.., were as follows—

Output 2,500 cleaners—Expenditure for the month—

	£
Raw materials consumed	17,760
Wages and salaries—	
Factory	7,363
Office	3,890
Showroom	1,410
Rent and rates—	
Factory	3,910
Office and showroom	1,410
Power	2,550
Heating and lighting—	
Factory	1,540
Office and showroom	660

Depreciation—	
Machinery	930
Office equipment	110
Showroom equipment	30

Estimates of expenditure not included above, for the full year—

Advertising	17,400
Miscellaneous expenditure—	
Factory	15,840
Office and showroom	20,160

It is estimated that one-third of all expenditure not directly apportioned between the office and showroom is attributable to the showroom and two-thirds to the office.

All office expenses are treated as administrative and the company's travellers receive a commission of 10 per cent on the sale price of all cleaners sold; 2,400 cleaners were sold during the month.

Draw up a cost statement showing the prime cost, factory cost and total cost (including administrative but excluding selling expenses) per cleaner and calculate the net profit realized per cleaner sold. (*Chartered Institute of Secretaries.*)

33. A manufacturing company of which you are the chief accountant produces three different products, X, Y, and Z. The processes by which they are produced are independent of one another, and in no case are the sales of any one product affected by prices or sales of the others.

The following budgeted profit and loss statement for the year ended 30th November, 19.., is presented to you by your assistant—

	Total £	X £	Y £	Z £
Sales	100,000	15,000	10,000	75,000
Variable production cost	60,000	8,000	4,000	48,000
Fixed production cost (apportioned to products)	20,000	1,000	3,000	16,000
	80,000	9,000	7,000	64,000
Gross profit	20,000	6,000	3,000	11,000
Variable selling cost	8,000	2,700	2,600	2,700
Fixed selling cost (apportioned to products)	2,000	700	700	600
	10,000	3,400	3,300	3,300
Net profit	10,000	2,600	—	7,700
Net loss	—	—	300	—

N.B. The bases of apportionment of fixed cost are known and acceptable to you.

Your assistant recommends that, to improve the profit position, product Y should be eliminated from the range of articles produced by the company, thus leaving only two articles to be produced.

You are required—

(*a*) to redraft the budgeted profit and loss statement to show the profit that would result if product Y were eliminated;

(*b*) to state whether or not you agree with your assistant's recommendation. Give brief reasons. (*Cost and Management Accountants.*)

34. Production costs of a factory for a year are as follows—

	£
Direct wages	80,000
Direct materials	120,000
Production overheads, fixed	40,000
Production overheads, variable	60,000

During the forthcoming year it is anticipated that—

(*a*) the average rate for direct labour remuneration will fall from 17p per hour to $15\frac{1}{2}$p per hour;

(*b*) production efficiency will be unchanged;

(*c*) direct labour hours will increase by $33\frac{1}{3}$ per cent;

(*d*) the purchase price per unit of direct materials, and of the other materials and services which comprise overheads will remain unchanged.

Compute a factory overhead rate for next year, the overheads being absorbed on a direct wages basis. (*Cost and Management Accountants* (*modified*).)

35. You are required to record the undernoted transactions in the accounts in the financial and cost ledgers which are affected by them. The cost and financial books are integrated. You are required also to prove the accuracy of your work by taking out a trial balance.

	£
Materials purchased during period—	
At cost	32,856
At standard	29,324
Salaries—	
Research and development	3,900
Production	5,400
Selling	3,800
Distribution	1,600
Administration	2,100
Wages—	
Research and development	950
Production	14,680
Selling	1,300
Distribution	4,920
Administration	1,150
Supplies—	
Research and development	940
Production	1,350
Selling	540
Distribution	2,920
Administration	750

Expenses—	
Research and development	1,800
Production	3,640
Selling	980
Distribution	430
Administration	1,340
Cheques drawn in favour of trade creditors	46,500
Cheques drawn for salaries, wages, supplies, and expenses	41,000
Deductions made from wages and salaries	4,900
Stock of materials on hand at beginning of period, at standard	10,640
Trade creditors at beginning of period	29,440
Cash at bank at beginning of period	56,820
Sales during period—	
At actual	97,500
At standard	72,100
Trade debtors at beginning of period	51,430
Cash received from trade debtors	48,600
Discount allowed to customers	1,250
Discount allowed by suppliers	1,890
Depreciation—	
Financial provision	4,200
Charge against costs	4,950
Research expenditure capitalized	2,000
Cost of work carried out on new factory extension by building maintenance department	2,600
Notional rent of freehold factory	1,000

(*Cost and Management Accountants.*)

36. A company is about to produce two articles whose prime cost is composed as follows—

	Cost per Dozen £
Product A	
Direct material cost	0·50
Direct wages, 4 hours at 30p per hour (including 2 machine-hours)	1·20
Prime cost	1·70
Product B	
Direct material cost	0·75
Direct wages, 2 hours at 45p per hour (including 1 machine-hour)	0·90
Prime cost	1·65

For the three months ending 30th September, 19.., the budget shows the following information—

Budgeted output of product A	1,000 dozen
,, ,, ,, B	2,000 ,,
,, overhead	£6,000

You are required—

(*a*) to name three cost rates by which overhead to be absorbed by each product could be calculated;

(*b*) to calculate the overhead to be absorbed by each product under each of the cost rates that you name.

Show your workings. (*Cost and Management Accountants.*)

37. Two businesses, AB Ltd. and CD Ltd., sell the same type of product in the same type of market.

Their budgeted profit and loss accounts for the year ended 30th June, 19.., are as follows—

	AB Ltd.		CD Ltd.	
	£	£	£	£
Sales		150,000		150,000
Less—				
Variable costs	120,000		100,000	
Fixed costs	15,000		35,000	
		135,000		135,000
Net profit budgeted		15,000		15,000

You are required to—

(*a*) calculate the break-even points of each business;

(*b*) state which business is likely to earn greater profits in conditions of—

(i) heavy demand for the product.

(ii) low demand for the product.

Give your reasons. (*Cost and Management Accountants.*)

38. The following is the general ledger control account in the cost ledger—

	£	£		£	£
Sales		60,000	*Opening Stock*—		
Closing Stock—			Materials	7,000	
Materials	7,300		Work-in-progress	4,000	
Work-in-progress	5,000		Finished goods	2,000	
Finished goods	2,500				13,000
		14,800			
			Purchases and Expenses—		
			Materials	10,000	
			Production Overhead	11,000	
			Administration Overhead	2,000	
			Selling and Distribution Overhead	4,000	
					27,000
			Wages, Salaries, etc.—		
			Direct	12,000	
			Indirect	5,150	
			Holiday Pay	250	
			National Insurance	500	
			Idle Time	300	
			Administration	2,900	
			Selling salaries, expenses, and commission	5,250	
					26,350
			Net profit per financial accounts		8,450
		74,800			74,800

Stores Issues direct materials	£8,500
" " consumable stores	£1,000
Overhead absorption: Production	150% of direct wages.
" " Administration	£5,000
" " Selling and Distribution	£9,000

From the above information, prepare control accounts for stocks, work-in-progress, and overheads, and the profit and loss account as they would appear in the cost ledger. (*Cost and Management Accountants.*)

39. The following is a summary of the trading and profit and loss account of AB Ltd. for the year ended 31st December,—

	£			£
Materials Consumed	68,500	Sales (60,000 units)		150,000
Wages	37,750	Finished stock (2,000 units)		4,000
Factory Expenses	20,750	Work-in-progress—		
Administration Expenses	9,560	Materials	£1,600	
Selling and Distribution Expenses	11,250	Wages	900	
Preliminary Expenses written off	1,000	Factory Expenses	500	
Goodwill written off	500			3,000
Net Profit	8,140	Dividends Received		450
	157,450			157,450

The company manufactures a standard unit.

In the cost accounts, factory expenses have been allocated to production at 20 per cent of prime cost, administration expenses at 15p per unit, and selling and distribution expenses at 20p per unit. The net profit shown by the cost accounts was £8,200.

Prepare—

(*a*) control accounts for factory expenses, administration expenses and selling and distribution expenses;

(*b*) a statement reconciling the profit disclosed by the cost records with that shown in the financial accounts. (*Cost and Management Accountants.*)

40. The following balances are extracted from a cost ledger as at 1st March—

	Dr £	*Cr* £
Stores ledger account	17,634	
Work-in-progress account	22,434	
Factory overhead account		436
Administration overhead account	106	
Finished stock account	12,629	
Cost ledger control account		52,367
	52,803	52,803

Further transactions took place during the ensuing six months, as follows—

	£
Goods finished (at cost)	84,260
Factory expenses incurred	4,318
Administration expenses allocated to production	3,210
Salaries and wages paid—	
Direct labour allocation	12,638
Factory salaries	5,210
Office salaries	1,624
Stores purchased	51,326
Administration expenses incurred	1,216
Goods sold (at cost)	85,615
Stores—production issues	61,434
Factory expenses allocated to production	8,884

(*a*) Construct the accounts in the cost ledger from the above information.
(*b*) Schedule the remaining balances as at 1st September.

41. Draft a form to illustrate the collection and distribution of overheads over a number of production cost centres, and show the basis of apportionment in respect of five different types of overhead. (*Cost and Management Accountants.*)

42. A price containing a very slender profit margin has been submitted for a tender, which it now appears is not competitive enough, and your company has been asked to requote. It is also apparent that owing to lack of orders your company may shortly revert to a four-day working week for a few months. Give the main points of a price advisory report to the general manager. (*Cost and Management Accountants.*)

43. Show journal entries (narratives are not required) to give effect to the double-entry principles of integral accounting in respect of the following—

	£
(*a*) Payment of—	
Net wages cheque	800
National Insurance cheque	100
and the deduction from wages of P.A.Y.E. tax	100
(*b*) Allocation of gross wages and National Insurance—	
Direct wages (in progress)	600
Departmental indirect wages	150
(Wages are paid a week in arrear)	
(*c*) Credit purchases of raw materials	2,000
and returnable packages	120
(*d*) Charging into departmental costs of a proportion of annually paid insurances	70
(*e*) Credit charging by outside engineers of departmental plant repairs	240
(*f*) Payment of suppliers' accounts (after £60 taken for cash discounts)	1,130
(*g*) Factory cost of production of finished stocks	10,000
(Ratios: direct materials 12, direct wages 2, factory overheads 6)	
(*h*) Factory cost of finished stocks sold	8,000
(*i*) Sale of finished stocks on credit (after allowing £370 sales rebates)	10,370
(*j*) Payment by customers of credit sales (after taking £120 in cash discounts)	13,380

(*Cost and Management Accountants.*)

CHAPTER 16

DETERMINATION OF MANUFACTURING AND CONTRACT PROFITS

Suddenly through the power of gold
Everything that seemed so hard to bear
In a gleaming golden glow is cloaked.
Sun is melting what was frozen
Every man fulfills his hopes.
Rosy beams light the horizon,
Look on high: the chimney smokes!

BERTHOLDT BRECHT

WHILST the trading and profit and loss account is a satisfactory form of final accounts for a trading business, it is not sufficiently explanatory for manufacturing firms.

Such firms usually prepare an additional account, the Manufacturing Account, which shows the factory or works cost of the goods produced. Where more than one product is produced a separate manufacturing account may be prepared for each product.

The factory cost calculated in this way is transferred to the trading account, replacing the purchases item in a trader's accounts and the cost of goods sold, and gross profit is then calculated in the usual way.

The particular form of manufacturing account adopted by any business will be designed to yield the maximum amount of information on the composition of the factory cost, and great stress is therefore laid on the sequence of the items and the way in which they are grouped together.

This sequence and grouping is generally that used in the costing system of the firm, and the manufacturing account is then merely an annual summary of the results of manufacturing activity which have been analysed in detail in the cost accounts.

This classification is reflected in the final accounts of a manufacturing firm in the following way—

MANUFACTURING ACCOUNT

Prime Cost + *Factory Overhead*	=	FACTORY COST OF PRODUCTION (transferred to Trading A/c)

TRADING ACCOUNT

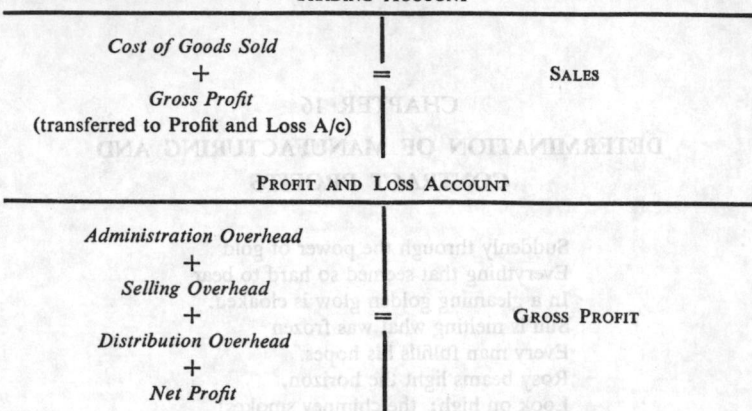

Cost of Goods Sold + *Gross Profit* (transferred to Profit and Loss A/c)	=	SALES

PROFIT AND LOSS ACCOUNT

Administration Overhead + *Selling Overhead* + *Distribution Overhead* + *Net Profit*	=	GROSS PROFIT

This is based on the classification of costs in the previous chapter.

With the above general classification in mind, the student should be able to work through a trial balance deciding under which heading each item must go and marking it in pencil accordingly, thus—

M—Manufacturing Account
T—Trading Account
P—Profit and Loss Account
B—Balance Sheet.

The items are presented in the order shown above and every opportunity of showing a significant sub-total should be taken.

Prime Cost—

(i) *Cost of Raw Materials Used*. This figure may be calculated in a separate account but it is more usual to show the calculation of the cost in the normal way—

	£
Raw Materials—	
Opening Stock	2,000
Purchases (less returns)	15,000
	17,000
Less Closing Stock	3,000
Cost of Raw Materials used	14,000

(ii) *Direct Labour*. This consists of the wages of all operatives and workers whose work is direct to the product.

(iii) *Direct Expenses*. May include such items as carriage, etc.

These three items are added to show the sub-total for prime cost.

Factory Overhead. A sub-heading is used and the items totalled to show the total of Factory or Works Overhead. These may include power, rent, rates, heating, lighting, depreciation, insurance, internal transport, works manager's salary, repairs, store-keeper, supervisors, etc. Some items, such as directors' remuneration, the costs of research and development, etc., may be apportioned between the Factory and Administration, Selling and Distribution. The method of dividing the amounts will usually be given (but see under Apportionment, previous chapter).

Gross Works Cost of Production. The total of prime cost and factory overhead, calculated as above, is sometimes called the Gross Works Cost of Production or Manufacture. This is because the above computation ignores the possible existence of work-in-progress.

Net Works Cost of Production—

(*a*) *Work-in-progress.* The time taken to complete a unit or batch of production varies considerably from industry to industry, but in very few cases is it possible for all work to be fully completed at the end of the financial year. Incomplete work is called work-in-progress. The principles on which it is valued are dealt with on p. 0701 et seq. Its effect on the manufacturing costs of a firm can be considerable, and the gross cost of manufacture must be adjusted for work-in-progress at the end and the beginning of the year.

The treatment is essentially the same as that for stock, viz.—

	£
Gross Cost of Production	50,000
Add Work-in-progress at start	8,000
	58,000
Deduct Work-in-progress at close	10,000
Net Works Cost of Production	48,000

See also the note below on Work-in-progress.

(*b*) *By-products, Scrap and Rejected Material.* A further adjustment may be made to net works cost of production in respect of by-products, scrap, rejected material, etc. The cost of all these items will, of course, be included in the gross cost of manufacture, yet all of them have a value (this may have to be estimated) which should be deducted from the Gross Cost of Production if an accurate figure of net cost of production is to be obtained.

Net Cost of Production transferred—

The Net Cost of Production is transferred to trading account by the usual double entry—

Credit manufacturing account
Debit trading account.

Cost of Goods Sold—

The cost of finished goods sold will be shown on the debit side of the trading account—

	£	£
Finished Goods		
Opening Stock	5,000	
Add Net Works Cost of Production transferred	48,000	
	53,000	
Less Closing Stock	6,000	
Cost of Goods Sold		47,000

Sales and Gross Profit. The sales, *less* returns, will be credited to trading account and the gross profit (or loss) in the trading account carried down to the credit (or debit) of the profit and loss account.

Profit and Loss Account. Whilst this is quite straightforward, it is desirable to use sub-headings for each part of the overhead shown in it. Students should also not forget the balance of those items, part of which has already been recorded in the manufacturing account.

Example 1

The following exemplifies the basic form of manufacturing, trading and profit and loss account.

Manufacturing Account for the Year Ended 31st December, 19..

		£	£		£
Raw Materials				Net Works Cost of Production (transferred to Trading Account) . .	42,500
Opening Stock .	£2,000				
Purchases (net) .	15,000				
	17,000				
Closing Stock .	1,500				
Cost of Direct Materials used		15,500			
Direct Labour					
Factory Wages . .		12,000			
Direct Expenses					
Carriage		500			
Prime Cost . .			28,000		
Factory Overhead					
Factory Rent .	£1,600				
" Repairs .	2,100				
Plant Repairs .	3,900				
Supervisors' Wages	5,000				
Works Manager's Salary . .	1,400				
Share of Directors' fees	2,000				
			16,000		
Gross Works Cost of Production			44,000		
Add Work-in-Progress at start		3,000			
Deduct Work-in-Progress at close		4,000			
			1,000		
			43,000		
Deduct Estimated Value of Scrap			500		
			42,500		42,500

TRADING ACCOUNT FOR THE YEAR ENDED 31ST DECEMBER, 19..

	£	£		£
Finished Goods			Sales *Less* Returns	60,000
Opening Stock	4,500			
Net Cost of Production	42,500			
	47,000			
Less Closing Stock	3,000			
Cost of Goods Sold		44,000		
Gross Profit		16,000		
		60,000		60,000

PROFIT AND LOSS ACCOUNT FOR THE YEAR ENDED 31ST DECEMBER, 19..

	£	£		£
Administration Overhead			Gross Profit	16,000
Salaries	2,000			
Other Expenses	3,000			
		5,000		
Selling Overhead				
Salaries	1,000			
Commission	500			
Advertising	2,500			
Other expenses	800			
		4,800		
Distribution Overhead				
Van expenses	900			
Wages	500			
		1,400		
Net Profit for Year		4,800		
		16,000		16,000

An alternative form of manufacturing account may be presented by dividing the account into two sections—

(*a*) Prime Cost Account.

(*b*) Cost of Production Account.

The above account would be presented in the following form—

Example 2

MANUFACTURING ACCOUNT

(*a*) Prime Cost Account

	£	£		£
Raw Materials			Prime Cost transferred to Cost of Production Account	28,000
Opening Stock	2,000			
Purchases	15,000			
	17,000			
Closing Stock	1,500			
Cost of Materials used		15,500		
Direct Labour				
Factory Wages		12,000		
Direct Expenses				
Carriage		500		
		28,000		28,000

MANUFACTURING ACCOUNT (*contd.*)

(*b*) Cost of Production Account

		£		£
Prime Cost of Goods Manufactured		28,000	Net Cost of Production (transferred to Trading Account)	42,500
Factory Overhead				
Factory Rent	£1,600			
,, Repairs	2,100			
Plant Repairs	3,900			
Supervisors' Wages	5,000			
Works Manager's Salary	1,400			
Share of Directors' Fees	2,000			
		16,000		
GROSS COST OF PRODUCTION		44,000		
Add Work-in-progress at start		3,000		
		47,000		
Less Work-in-progress at close		4,000		
		43,000		
Less Scrap (estimated value)		500		
		42,500		42,500

Transfer Pricing. In Example 1 it will be noticed that the goods produced have been transferred from the manufacturing account to the trading account *at cost price*.

This is the usual practice, and in such cases the manufacturing account will show neither profit nor loss. Alternatively, the manufacturing department may be put on a business basis, i.e. its output is charged to the selling department *at current trade prices* irrespective of cost. In other words, the selling department is not placed at a disadvantage by having to take over goods at a price higher than that at which they could be purchased from an outside manufacturer of such goods.

In this case the manufacturing account will show a balance, which will represent either profit or loss on production, and will be transferred to profit and loss account. By this means it will be seen whether the manufacturing department is a profitable one; and if not, it can be closed down, unless cost of production can be lowered by strict supervision and economies to cheapen production.

Work-in-progress—Alternative Treatment. In Example 1 above, the stocks of work-in-progress were treated as single items, without regard to their composition.

In most cases, however, the value of work-in-progress is composed partly of prime cost and partly of overhead, and if it is necessary that strictly accurate figures for prime cost and overhead are to be obtained, the adjustment in respect of work-in-progress should be made separately to each.

The use of this method is illustrated in the example which appears on the opposite page—

Example 3

MANUFACTURING ACCOUNT FOR YEAR ENDED 31ST DECEMBER, 19..

	£	£		£
Raw Materials			Trade Price of Goods Manufactured (transferred to Trading Account)	59,000
Opening Stocks	6,500			
Purchases	22,500			
	29,000			
Less Closing Stock	5,000			
Cost of Materials Used		24,000		
Prime Cost of Work-in-progress				
Add Opening Stock	8,000			
Deduct Closing Stock	10,350			
		2,350		
		21,650		
Direct Labour				
Manufacturing Wages		22,750		
Direct Expenses				
Carriage and Freight		450		
PRIME COST		44,850		
Factory Overhead		8,800		
Overhead on Work-in-progress				
Add Opening Stock	1,500			
Deduct Closing Stock	1,850			
		350		
NET FACTORY COST OF PRODUCTION		53,300		
Manufacturing Profit		5,700		
		59,000		59,000

TRADING ACCOUNT

	£	£		£
Finished Goods			Sales (*less* Returns)	75,000
Opening Stock	5,000			
Trade Price of Production transferred	59,000			
	64,000			
Less Closing Stock	5,900			
Cost of Goods Sold		58,100		
Gross Profit		16,900		
		75,000		75,000

PROFIT AND LOSS ACCOUNT

		£
	Manufacturing Profit	5,700
	Gross Trading Profit	16,900

Cost Price plus Fixed Percentage. The goods may also be transferred to trading account from manufacture at cost price plus a fixed percentage. If, in the above example, the goods were transferred at cost plus 10 per cent, the value of goods transferred would be £53,300 *plus* £5,330 = £58,630, and the manufacturing profit would be £5,330 (that is, the added percentage). The drawback of this system is that it credits manufacture with profit on a purely arbitrary basis.

Notional Expenses. In order to obtain an accurate cost of production, notional expenses may be charged in the manufacturing account. For instance, a firm may have two factories engaged on similar products. In one case, the factory may be rented; in the other, owned by the firm. Clearly, other things being equal, the second factory would be able to show more profit unless a charge were made in lieu of rent.

The solution is to calculate the appropriate amount of rent and to debit this to manufacturing account, under Factory Overhead, as if the amount had been paid.

The double entry is completed by crediting the amount to profit and loss account. Although the ultimate net profit is, therefore, unaltered, the net cost of production and the manufacturing profit are more accurately stated for comparison purposes.

Quantities. Manufacturing accounts and trading accounts are frequently provided with an additional column in which is recorded the quantity of goods involved in production.

The relationship between such *quantities* is the same as for *values*, i.e.—

Opening Stock + Input − Closing Stock = Output

If the information given is incomplete, any one of the items in the formula can be calculated, if the other items are known. For instance: 5,000 units are put into production, the opening stock is 500, the closing stock 600. The output may be calculated as—

$$500 + 5{,}000 - 600 = 4{,}900 \text{ units}$$

Losses may arise, however. If 4,800 units were transferred to trading account in the above example, then 100 units have been lost in production. Losses may be normal or abnormal and the treatment varies accordingly.

NORMAL LOSSES. Many processes of manufacture involve unavoidable losses, and there is no point in establishing the cost of such losses which, in any case, will bear a constant ratio to output.

ABNORMAL LOSSES may also arise due to spoilt work, defective materials, interruptions of production due to machine breakdown, etc. As it is assumed that abnormal losses *can* be avoided, the cost of them should be shown as an expense. The treatment is—

Credit manufacturing account with cost of abnormal losses.

Debit profit and loss account.

Quantities of raw materials and work-in-progress will appear only in the manufacturing account, but stocks of finished goods may be carried forward both in the manufacturing and trading account. In some firms, stocks of finished goods will be shown only in the trading account when they have been delivered to warehouse and are out of control of the works management. Any quantities of finished goods remaining in the factory will be shown in manufacturing account.

Example 4

The following information was extracted from the books of a manufacturing company on 31st December, 19.. Stocks of raw materials on 1st January, 19.., were 500 units value £6,000; purchases during the year £58,000 (enough for 5,000 units); closing stock value £5,800 (600 units) A normal loss of 50 units is expected. 4,600 units have been transferred to trading account, and 200 units carried forward in manufacturing account at cost. Show the manufacturing account for the year ended 31st December.

MANUFACTURING ACCOUNT FOR YEAR ENDED 31ST DECEMBER, 19..

	Units	£		Units	£
Raw Materials			Normal Loss in Production	50	—
Opening Stock	500	6,000	Abnormal Losses (transferred		
Purchases	5,000	58,000	to P. & L. A/c)	50	1,200
			Finished Goods		
	5,500	64,000	Transferred to Trading		
Closing Stock	600	5,800	Account	4,600	110,400
			Balance in Works c/f	200	4,800
Raw Materials Used	4,900	58,200			
Direct Labour		57,700		4,900	
Direct Expenses		500			
		116,400			116,400

N.B. Costs of production 4,900 units = £116,400. Deduct 50 units normal losses; thus 4,850 units must share £116,400 costs.

∴ Cost of abnormal losses is—

$$£116{,}400 \times \frac{50}{4{,}850} = £1{,}200$$

It may happen that finished goods are transferred to trading account at market price or at cost price plus a fixed percentage, whilst the stocks on manufacturing account are carried forward at cost. If, in the above example, goods were transferred to trading account at cost plus 20 per cent the result would be—

MANUFACTURING ACCOUNT FOR THE YEAR ENDED 31ST DECEMBER, 19..

	Units	£		Units	£
Raw Materials Used	4,900	58,200	Normal loss in production	50	—
Direct Labour		57,700	Abnormal losses	50	1,200
Direct Expenses		500	*Finished Goods*		
Manufacturing Profit		22,080	Transferred to Trading A/c	4,600	132,480
			Balance in Works c/f	200	4,800
	4,900	138,480		4,900	138,480

	£
Cost of Goods transferred	110,400
Add 20% profit	22,080
Value of goods transferred	132,480

CONTRACT ACCOUNTS

In civil engineering and building work it is common for a firm to be employed on several separate contracts at the same time and for these contracts to continue over a long period of years. As the firm may be tied to its estimate of the price at which it can complete the contract, it is essential that a close check be kept on the costs incurred on each contract and, eventually, on the profit actually realized. Also, it is necessary to establish rules for determining profits on uncompleted contracts.

To meet this problem, separate contract accounts are opened for each contract, and the cost of materials and wages debited to each account. All direct costs can be analysed and charged directly to each contract, and it is relatively simple to establish the prime cost of each contract.

Overhead. Any expenditure incurred on overhead is debited to an overhead account (subdivided if required, according to whether it is applicable to administration, estimating, etc.) and is then recovered by debiting each contract account with a fair share of the total incurred (overhead account is credited).

(Methods of deciding what is a fair share have already been dealt with under Overhead Recovery on p. 1511–3.)

Plant is frequently taken out on a contract for considerable periods of time. In such cases, the book value of the plant may be transferred to the contract when the plant is sent out. If the contract account is balanced at the end of a period, the value of any plant held must be carried down in the contract account. When the plant is returned it is revalued and the contract account credited with the current value. In this way, the contract bears the actual cost of depreciation.

Determination of Profit Realized on a Contract. Some of the contracts may take several years to complete, during which time a firm may receive some payment on account of the work done. Whilst permission may be obtained to pay interest on capital in such cases, most firms prefer to determine the amount of profit realized and to pay dividends accordingly.

Method of Payment for Large Contracts. Whilst a small contract may be paid for in one lump sum after the work is completed, in the case of larger contracts, the parties usually provide for payment to be made in stages.

Work Certified. The agent of the purchaser of the building or other work will inspect it at certain stages and will sign a certificate to state that certain parts of the work have been satisfactorily completed.

Profit on Work Certified. The profit on a contract is, of course, the contract price (equivalent to sales value) *less* the cost of completing the work.

The profit on work certified is the contract (or sales) value of the work completed *less* the cost of that work.

If a contract worth £200,000 is certified as 40 per cent complete, then the value of the completed work is £80,000. If total cost of the contract is to be £150,000, then we would expect the cost of the work completed to be about £60,000 (40 per cent of £150,000). Assuming that it is £60,000, the profit made would be £20,000.

PROPORTION OF PROFIT RESERVED. It is usual, however, to allow for unforeseen contingencies and to reserve, say, one-third of the apparent profit. In our example, the profit to date would be £20,000 *less* one-third = £13,333.

Retention Money. Although the purchasing firm may have certified 40 per cent of the work done they, also, must guard against contingencies. In some cases they are entitled to exact penalties if the contract is not completed on time. They will, therefore, retain part of the value of the work certified, say 10 per cent. This money is known as "retention money" and it will only be paid on satisfactory completion of the whole job. In our example the work certified is valued at £80,000, the retention of 10 per cent is £8,000 and the purchasing firm will pay out £72,000.

Profit Transferred to Profit and Loss Account. A further reduction is made in the profit to be taken to profit and loss account, in the same proportion as the retention money reduces the work certified. This is an additional reduction made after the profit taken has been reduced to allow for contingencies. In our example, then, the profit finally taken to profit and loss account would be £13,333 less £1,333 (10 per cent) = £12,000.

The following full example is a typical examination question—

Example 7

The following trial balance was extracted on 30th June, 19.1 from, the books of AB Ltd., contractors—

	£	£
Share capital—shares of £1		35,180
Profit and loss account, 1st July, 19..		2,500
Provision for depreciation on plant and tools		6,300
Cash received on account: Contract 7		128,000
Creditors		8,120
Land and buildings, cost	7,400	
Plant and tools, cost	5,200	
Bank	4,500	
Contract 7—		
Materials issued	60,000	
Direct labour	83,000	
Expenses	4,000	
Plant and tools on site, cost	16,000	
	180,100	180,100

Contract 7 was begun on 1st July, 19... The contract price is £240,000, and the customer has so far paid £128,000, being 80 per cent of the work certified. The cost of work done since certification is estimated at £1,600.

On 30th June, 19.1, after the above trial balance was extracted, plant costing £3,200 was returned to store, and materials then on site were valued at £2,700.

Provision is to be made for direct labour accrued due £600, and depreciation of all plant and tools at 12½ per cent on cost.

You are asked to—

(*a*) Write up the contract account.

(*b*) Show your computation of the profit (if any) for which credit may properly be taken.

(*c*) Submit the balance sheet of AB Ltd. on 30th June, 19.1.

(*a*) CONTRACT NO. 7 ACCOUNT

Date			£	Date				£
19.1				19.1				
Jun	30	Materials	60,000	Jun	30	Plant returned		2,800
		Direct Labour	83,600			Balance c/d—		
		Expenses	4,000			Materials	£ 2,700	
		Plant and Tools	16,000			Plant	11,200	
		P. & L. A/c— Profit on Contract	7,840			Cost of work not certified	1,600	
						Cost of work completed, certified (including profit)	153,140	
								168,640
			171,440					171,440
19.1								
Jun	30	Balance b/d—						
		Materials	2,700					
		Plant	11,200					
		Work-in-progress	154,740					

(*b*) COMPUTATION OF PROFIT TAKEN ON CONTRACT No. 7

	£	£
Materials	60,000	
Less Value on site	2,700	
		57,300
Direct labour	83,000	
Add Provision for amount accrued due	600	
		83,600
Expenses		4,000
Plant	16,000	
Less Amount returned to store at 87½ per cent of cost	2,800	
	13,200	
Less Value on site at 87½ per cent of cost	11,200	
Depreciation on plant		2,000
Total expenditure to date		146,900
Less Cost of work not yet certified		1,600
Cost of work certified		145,300
Profit to date		14,700
Value of work certified		160,000
Profit to date, less one-third for contingencies		£9,800
Proportion of cash received to work certified—80 per cent		
Proportion of profit credited to Profit and Loss Account— 80 per cent of £9,800		£7,840
Work in progress. Cost of work not certified		1,600
Cost of work certified		145,300
Profit taken		7,840
		£154,740

AB LIMITED

BALANCE SHEET AS AT 30TH JUNE, 19.1

		£		Cost £	Deprecia-tion £	£
Share Capital—						
Shares of £1 each		35,180	*Fixed Assets—*			
Revenue Reserve—			Land & Buildings	7,400		7,400
P. & L. A/c		9,690	Plant & Tools	21,200	8,950	12,250
		44,870		28,600	8,950	19,650
Current Liabilities—			*Current Assets—*			
Trade Creditors	£8,120		Stores		2,700	
Expense Creditors	600	8,720	Work-in-progress	154,740		
			Payment on Account	128,000		
					26,740	
			Bank		4,500	
						33,940
		53,590				53,590

WORKINGS

Profit and loss a/c—	
Balance per trial balance	2,500
Profit on Contract No. 7	7,840
	10,340
Depreciation on plant and tools, 12½ per cent on £5,200	650
	9,690

	Cost £	Depreciation £	
Plant and tools—			
Per trial balance	5,200	6,300	
Transfer from Contract No. 7	3,200	400	
On Contract No. 7	12,800	1,600	
Per profit and loss a/c		650	
	21,200	8,950	£12,250

EXERCISE 16

1. Crane, Derrick, & Co. Ltd. railway and general contractors, whose head offices and works are at Porthampton, are engaged on two large contracts, as follows—

No. 1 Contract. Light railway for the New Forest Light Railway Co. Ltd. at a contract price of £150,000.

No. 2 Contract. New hotel for the Sussex Development Co. Ltd. at a contract price of £210,000.

No. 1 Contract was commenced in January, and

No. 2 Contract in March.

On 31st December the following balances stood in the books of the company in respect of these contracts—

		£	
No. 1 Contract.	Plant and machinery	5,000	
	Purchases	30,000	
	Wages and salaries	43,000	
	Sundry expenses	2,500	
	Cash received on account		£60,000

		£	
No. 2 Contract.	Plant and machinery	3,500	
	Purchases	80,000	
	Wages and salaries	56,000	
	Sundry expenses	1,500	
	Cash received on account		£120,000

The value of materials on hand and work finished but not certified for was as follows: No. 1 Contract £2,500; No. 2 Contract £6,500. In the case of No. 1 Contract, 80 per cent of the amounts certified for was paid to the contractors, the remaining 20 per cent being retained until completion. In the case of No. 2 Contract the retentions amounted to £22,500.

Make out accounts in respect of each contract. Deal with the plant and machinery employed on the contracts in the way you consider best, stating your reason. Show the profit earned in respect of each contract, and say what you consider the company would be justified in carrying to profit and loss account in respect of them on 31st December. *(Chartered Accountants.)*

2. Healthy Dogs Ltd., manufactures dog foods and sells them in tins of one standard size. The books of the company reveal balances and information as follows—

	£		£
Stocks at Cost on 1st January, 1965—		Distribution Charges	1,500
Tinned Food	1,800	Selling Expenses	3,290
Ingredients	500	Advertising	3,225
Tins, Labels, etc.	350	Directors' Fees	1,000
Purchases—		Sales	30,000
Ingredients	6,190	Freight and Carriage Inwards	781
Tins, Labels, etc.	3,200	Stocks at Cost on 31st December, 1965—	
Manufacturing Wages	4,688	Ingredients	370
Factory Expenses	2,344	Tins, Labels, etc.	425
Factory Rent	1,562		

Certain ingredients purchased at £1·40 a cwt during the previous year proved unsuitable, and 50 cwt had been sold in the current year at £1·00 a cwt, the proceeds being included in sales; 50 cwt were still in stock on 31st December, 1965, when the market value was £1·10 a cwt.

The stock of tinned food on 31st December, 1965, was 50,000 tins (all produced during the year); in addition, 20,000 tins produced during the year were still held by consignees on 31st December. These had been invoiced at 5p a tin and treated as sales.

750,000 tins of food were produced during the year.

The directors decided that the charge to Profit and Loss Account for the year in respect of advertising should be 10 per cent of the total manufacturing cost.

Prepare from the above information, Manufacturing, Trading and Profit and Loss Accounts for the year ended 31st December, 1965.

3. A contract for the construction of a large block of offices was commenced by Speedwell Constructors Ltd., on 1st June, 1964, and in the period ended on 31st March, 1965, expenditure had been incurred as follows—

	£
Purchase of materials	21,562
Materials issued from store	1,738
Wages	9,861
Direct expenses	5,005
Administration expenses charged to the contract	2,142
Purchase of plant for the project on 1st June, 1964	12,000

The stock of materials on the site on 31st March, 1965, amounted to £1,828 and on that date there were wages accrued of £720.

A sum of £38,460 had been received by the company which was the amount for work completed to 31st January, 1965, less 10 per cent retention money, as certified by the architects.

The effective life of the plant is estimated to be four years. Other expenditure can be regarded as having been incurred evenly over the period.

The practice of the company is to take credit for no more than two-thirds of the profit on work certified (less retention).

1. Prepare a Contract Account in respect of the project for the period ended 31st March, 1965, and

2. Show how you arrive at the amount of profit taken to the credit of the Profit and Loss Account. *(A.C.C.A.)*

4. Bubble Cars Ltd. sell two types of small cars. (i) The PIP, (ii) The GLOBE. The PIP is exclusively produced in the company's factory. The GLOBE is purchased for resale.

From the following particulars of manufacturing—all PIP production—and of trading in both types of car during the three months to 31st March last prepare the following statements—

(*a*) Manufacturing Account for PIP production.

(*b*) Trading Accounts for the two types of car (combined totals not required), i.e. the PIP and the GLOBE; also

(*c*) Make any two *brief* comments on the results shown in (*a*) and (*b*).

PARTICULARS REFERRED TO ABOVE

	£	£
Purchases—		
Materials and Parts	25,000	
Works Fuel and Power	3,000	
Works Stores	7,000	
GLOBE cars	65,000	
		100,000
Factory Wages		22,000
Works Rent, Insurance, etc.		1,000
Works, Repairs		300
Depreciation of Factory Plant		2,500
Works Sundry Expenses		5,000
Sales—		
The PIP	90,000	
The GLOBE	80,000	
		170,000

	Jan 1	Mar 31
Stocks, per Inventories—	£	£
Materials and Parts	4,000	5,000
Works Stores	1,800	2,000
Work in Progress	13,000	12,000
PIP Cars—completed	24,000	30,000
GLOBE Cars	14,000	10,000
	56,800	59,000

(L.C.C.)

5. Snapshooters Ltd. manufacture cameras of one standard model.

The following trial balance at 31st December, 19.. was extracted from the company's books—

	£	£
Issued share capital		20,000
Plant and machinery, at cost *less* depreciation	18,000	
Debtors and creditors	12,000	11,000
Stock of materials, 31st December, 19..	2,170	
Manufacturing wages	49,000	
Materials used in factory	21,000	
Factory expenses, including depreciation of plant and machinery	14,000	
Stocks of finished cameras, 1st January, 19..—		
In factory (330 cameras)	3,960	
In warehouse (475 cameras)	7,125	
Sales (7,430 cameras)		133,740
Provision for unrealized profit on stock, 1st January, 19..		1,425
Administration and selling expenses	34,380	
Balance at bank	8,030	
Profit and loss account, 1st January, 19..		3,500
	169,665	169,665

(1) During 19.., the production of 7,000 cameras was completed. 7,200 cameras were transferred from the factory to the warehouse; these transfers are recorded in the manufacturing account and in the trading account at factory cost plus 25 per cent.

(2) Closing stocks of finished cameras in the factory are entered in the manufacturing account at factory cost. Closing stocks of finished cameras in the warehouse are entered in the trading account at factory cost plus 25 per cent, but they are shown in the balance sheet at factory cost.

(3) There are no stocks of partly finished cameras at either the beginning or end of the year 19...

You are required to prepare a manufacturing account and a trading and profit and loss account for the year 19.., and a balance sheet at 31st December, 19.. (not necessarily in a form for publication). ***(Institute of Bankers.)***

6. K. Kirk and C. Caldy commenced business in partnership as builders on 1st January, 19... Kirk brought in £6,000 and Caldy £2,000 and plant valued at £3,000, and it was agreed to share profits and losses equally.

At 31st December, 19.., the summary of the cash book was—

	£		£
Capital	8,000	Materials No. 1	4,530
Receipts No. 1 Contract	10,500	,, No. 2	6,789
,, No. 2 ,,	12,250	,, No. 3	6,091
,, No. 3 ,,	5,000	Wages No. 1	2,875
		,, No. 2	4,832
		,, No. 3	3,057
		Plant	1,000
		General Expenses	2,996
		Drawings—Kirk	1,200
		,, —Caldy	1,200
		Balance c/f	1,180
	35,750		35,750

At the end of the year, No. 1 contract had been completed and settled, No. 2 contract had been completed but a further £2,225 was to be received, and No. 3 contract was not yet completed, the work-in-progress being valued at £10,000, of which the £5,000 shown above had been received on account.

The plant was revalued on 31st December, 19. ., at £1,731.

Prepare separate contract accounts, the profit and loss account for the year ended 31st December, 19. . . and the balance sheet at that date. (*R.S.A.*)

7. The following information is taken from the books of a small brickyard at the close of a trading period—

	£	£	£
Capital: 200,000 ordinary shares of 25p each			**50,000**
Wages—			
Clay-getting	**830**		
Maintenance	**560**		
Boiler house	**160**		
Making	**180**		
Burning	**610**		
Drying and setting	**395**		
		2,735	
Debtors		**13,200**	
Creditors			**12,840**
Coal—			
Used for firing kilns	**425**		
Used for boiler	**80**		
		505	
Profit and loss account		**960**	
Land and buildings		**10,000**	
Salaries (office)		**980**	
Salaries (yard personnel only)		**300**	
Sales			**8,465**
Stock at beginning of period		**337**	
Works general expenses		**120**	
Royalties		**350**	
Power and lighting (office)		**47**	
Power and lighting (yard)		**30**	
Repair to kilns		**217**	
Rent, rates, and insurance (office)		**46**	
Rent, rates, and insurance (yard)		**30**	
Repair to machines		**83**	
Delivery expenses		**710**	
Depreciation—			
Kilns	**84**		
Plant and machinery	**70**		
		154	
Discounts		**146**	
Bad debts		**38**	
Telephone and telegrams		**73**	
Printing and stationery		**85**	
Kilns		**18,800**	
Plant and Machinery		**17,800**	
Cash		**3,559**	
		71,305	**71,305**

NOTES—

(*a*) The opening stock, valued at £337, comprised 750,000 bricks, and the production during the period, after allowing for spoilage, was 11,000,000. 10,500,000 bricks were sold during the period.

(*b*) A new kiln was constructed during the period by the yard's own employees, and included in maintenance wages is £140 paid for work done on the new kiln. 250,000 bricks were also taken from the period's production to build the new kiln.

(*c*) The closing stock was wholly made up of bricks produced during the period.

(*d*) Delivery expenses (£710) include £590 which has been re-charged to customers and is included in the total sales.

You are required to prepare, for internal use only, manufacturing, trading, and profit and loss accounts and balance sheet for the period. Your accounts must show—

(i) prime cost;
(ii) works expenses;
(iii) cost of sales;
(iv) administration expenses. *(Cost and Management Accountants.)*

8. Included in the activities of a Contracting Company for the year ended 31st December, 1963, is the following contract regarding which the appended information is available—

Contract No. 101. Commenced 1st May, 1963.

	£
Equipment transferred to Site	23,000
Cost of materials sent to Site	45,816
Paid to sub-contractors in period	9,220
Wages paid in period	65,305
Expenses paid in period	8,322
Due to sub-contractors for work done as at 31st December, 1963	4,100
Accrued wages, 31st December, 1963	2,520
Accrued expenses, 31st December, 1963	695
Total contract price	175,000
Expenditure included above in respect of unfinished part of contract	8,210
Amount due in respect of work completed	150,000
Cash received on contract	120,000
Depreciation to be provided on equipment at rate per annum	20%

Show the amount which would appear in the Contract Ledger in respect of Contract No. 101 for the year ending 31st December, 1963, including the amount which would be transferred to Profit and Loss Account for the year ending that date. It is the practice of the company as regards unfinished contracts not to take credit for more than two-thirds of any accrued profit and to reserve fully for any anticipated loss. All calculations may be made to the nearest £.

9. You are required to prepare from the following information final accounts for the year ending 31st December, 19.., of UX Ltd. Your accounts must clearly show—

Cost of materials consumed;
Cost of goods completed;
Cost of goods sold;
Prime costs of production;
Total factory overhead.

The balance sheet is for publication but not the accounts.

	£	£
Issued and authorized capital		150,000
General reserve		250,000
Trade debtors	112,460	
Carriage inwards	9,960	
Returns	12,200	
Loose tools purchased	10,600	
Trade creditors		61,400

	£	£
Cash at bank	36,000	
Purchases—raw material	221,600	
Works salaries	42,440	
Profit and loss account		26,445
Freehold buildings	41,500	
Wages—direct	350,000	
Plant and machinery	106,300	
Repairs to plant	19,750	
Sales		990,200
General expenses	5,430	
Power	65,300	
Fixtures and fittings	21,150	
Selling expenses	55,300	
Work-in-progress	20,000	
Stock—		
Raw material	28,740	
Finished goods	86,350	
Loose tools	15,860	
Manufacturing expenses	26,000	
Administration expenses	27,770	
AB Ltd.—current account	16,000	
Motor vehicles	5,400	
Shares in AB Ltd.	1,500	
Shares in PQ Ltd.	12,500	
Bank interest		65
Wages—indirect	128,000	
	1,478,110	1,478,110

NOTES—

(1) Stocks at 31st Dec., 19.. were—

	£
Finished goods	92,600
Raw materials	21,550
Loose tools	12,820
Work-in-progress	63,000

(2) Depreciation on reducing balance method is to be provided as follows—

Land and buildings	2 per cent
Plant and machinery	10 " "
Motor vehicles	20 " "
Fittings and fixtures	10 " "

(3) Provide £800 for doubtful debts.

(4) The original costs and accumulated depreciations are—

	Land and Buildings	Plant	Fixtures and Fittings	Motor Vehicles
	£	£	£	£
Cost	65,500	152,600	32,150	6,300
Depreciation	24,000	46,300	11,000	900
	41,500	106,300	21,150	5,400

(5) General expenses include £60 rent for the first quarter of 19.1.

(6) Commission of £840 is due but unpaid to salesmen.

(7) Allow £25,000 for Schedule D income tax on the year's profit and transfer £15,000 to reserve.

(8) Provide for a dividend of 5 per cent tax free.

(9) UX Ltd. owns 1,000 ordinary shares in AB Ltd., whose issued capital is 1,500 ordinary shares of £1 each, fully paid.

(10) PQ Ltd., is a trade investment of 10,000 ordinary shares of £1 each, fully paid. The market value is £11,000. (*Cost and Works Accountants.*)

10. An engineer's books give the following figures. For the first year: materials purchased £17,500; sales £30,000; wages £7,500; expenses £2,000. The stocks at the beginning of the year were: materials £6,000; finished work £4,000; and at the end of the year they were: materials £5,000; finished work £3,000. For the second year, the materials purchased were £14,000; wages £4,800; expenses £1,200; sales £17,000. The stock at the end of the second year is materials £7,000, and finished work £6,000. Prepare a statement showing each year (and also the average of the two years) what are the percentages of cost of materials, wages, expenses, and profit on the output. (*West Riding of Yorkshire.*)

11. The undermentioned figures have been extracted from the trial balance of the Blankshire Iron Co. Ltd., whose financial year closes on 30th June.

Prepare a furnaces account showing the cost per ton of the pig iron produced, a trading account and a profit and loss account.

	£
Coal purchased	7,320
Coke and limestone purchased	19,550
Ironstone purchased	7,461
Wages (furnace)	6,842
Sales of pig iron	62,446
Stock of pig iron (30th June)	9,402
Trade charges	5,424
Sales of waste materials and by-products	5,862
Office salaries	3,401
Directors' fees	1,500
Transfer fees	52
Depreciation	3,890
Interest received	321
Bad debts	1,680

The stock of pig iron in hand as on 30th June was valued at £9,221.

The pig iron produced during the year amounted to 18,600 tons. (*London Chamber of Commerce.*)

12. A manufacturer's books show the following figures for each item for two years: materials used, £22,389 and £21,427; wages £7,495 and £7,577; rent and power, £1,659 and £1,655; carriage, £513 and £494; trade expenses, £303 and £309; gas and water, £213 and £240; travellers, £719 and £763; repairs, £426 and £563; insurance, £78 and £78; depreciation, £600 and £580.

Goods produced (net), £36,468 and £36,261.

Prepare a statement showing for each year the various costs per cent on production. (*West Riding of Yorkshire.*)

13. Details of the assets and liabilities of C.D., a builder at 31st December, 1962, were as follows—

Debtors, £1,580; Stock of Materials on Contract, £2,430; Plant and Tools, £6,570; Yard and Offices, £3,050; Cost of Work-in-Progress, £3,840; Creditors for Materials, £1,230; Bank Overdraft, £2,850.

At this date C.D. had only one job on hand, a factory contract, for which his tender of £35,000 had been accepted and on which he had commenced work on 1st December, 1962.

His Cash Account for the period 1st January to 31st August, 1963, when he died, was as follows—

Receipts	£	*Payments*	£
Cash on account of Factory Contract . .	12,000	Factory Contract—	
Cash from Debtors at 31st December, 1962 . .	684	Materials . . .	6,840
Bank Drawn . . .	12,489	Wages . . .	5,958
Capital Introduced . .	8,000	General Expenses .	2,940
		Personal Withdrawals . .	4,820
		Bank Lodged . . .	12,530
		Cash on Hand at 31st August, 1963 . . .	85
	33,173		33,173

On 31st August, 1963, creditors for materials were £1,295, for wages £182 and for general expenses £240. The stock of materials at 31st December, 1962, had been completely used up and it was estimated that the factory would be completed by 31st October, 1963, with a further expenditure on materials of £3,140 (including the stock on hand at 31st August, 1963 of £1,840), on wages £2,640, and on general expenses £684.

Prepare a Working Account for the period 1st January to 31st August, 1963, and a Balance Sheet as at that date to show the position of C.D. assuming that the profit of the factory had to be treated as accruing evenly over the period of its erection. Provide for depreciation on the plant and tools at the rate of 10 per cent per annum. (*L.C.C.*)

14. A. Ltd., contractors, prepare Accounts half-yearly on 30th April and 31st October. On 1st May, 1962, the following particulars are extracted from their ledger—

Contract 123		Contract price £60,000
Balance on ledger account . . .		£8,500
being—	£	
Wages	8,400	
Materials used	6,050	
Expenses	2,750	
Plant, cost	3,300	
	20,500	
Less—Cash received . . .	12,000	
	8,500	

In respect of Contract 123, during the half year to 31st October—

(*a*) The Plant was transferred to another job on 2nd May.
(*b*) New Plant, costing £500, was installed on the same date.
(*c*) The following amounts were expended—

	£
Wages	7,600
Materials bought . . .	8,250
Expenses	650

(*d*) Cash was received from the customer—

	£
30th June . . .	7,500
30th September . . .	8,500

On 31st October, Contract 123 was estimated to be two-thirds completed. At that date the stock of materials, at cost, was £300. Provision for depreciation of Plant is to be made—£180 transferred Plant: £60 new Plant.

You are asked to—

(i) Write up the Contract account and the customer's account.

(ii) Submit a statement of the amount of profit, if any, which you think may properly be taken to Profit and Loss Account for the half year to 31st October, 1962.

(iii) Show how the position should be recorded in the Balance Sheet at that date in respect of Contract 123. (*A.C.C.A.*)

15. The Ay-one Construction Co. Ltd.—a public works contractor—commenced work on a contract (referred to in its books as Contract T.H.) on 1st May, 1961. In the period ended 31st January, 1962, expenditure incurred on the project was as follows—

	£
Purchase of plant for the project on 1st May, 1961 .	7,200
Purchase of materials	16,776
Materials requisitioned from store . . .	1,462
Wages	7,227
Direct expenses	4,483
Administration expenses charged . . .	1,972

The amount of work executed to 30th September, 1961, has been certified by the architects at £28,800 which was the figure after the deduction of 10 per cent retention money. The Ay-one Construction Co. Ltd. had received the sum so certified.

Wages accrued to and stock of materials on the site on 31st January, 1962, amounted to £620 and £1,040 respectively.

It can be assumed that the expenditure, other than as concerns the plant, was incurred evenly over the period. The effective life of the plant is six years.

Submit the Contract Account for the period ended 31st January, 1962, and give your computation of the profit taken to the credit of Profit and Loss Account. The company's practice is to limit the credit taken to two-thirds of the profit on work certified, that is after the deduction for retentions. (*A.C.C.A.*)

16. (*a*) What is the prime purpose of a Cost statement, and what rules should be borne in mind in its preparation?

(*b*) P. Barnes Ltd. manufacture a single product. Below is a summary of the manufacturing, etc., records for the three months ended 30th September, 1963.

	30th June £	30th Sept £
Sales		29,000
Raw materials bought . . .		8,300
Factory wages		5,500
,, heat, power and light . .		1,500
,, expenses		2,000
Stocks—		
Raw materials	900	700
Finished product	7,820	—
(tons 1,200)		(tons 800)

Production for the three months was 2,000 tons. Stock of finished product on 30th September is to be valued at prime cost of output for the three months to that date.

Prepare an Operating Account for the three months to show—

(i) Factory cost per ton of output for each item of cost given above.
(ii) Per cent manufacturing profit to Sales.
(iii) Average selling price per ton of Sales (to nearest £).

What further information would you suggest as being necessary to make this statement as useful as possible? (*A.C.C.A.*)

17. On 1st January, 1963, PQ Ltd., building and estate developers, purchased an area of land for development divided into plots of equal size. The company builds houses for sale on some of the plots, and leases certain plots to other builders on a 75 year lease at a ground rent of £45 per year cash. The company provides roads and service mains on the estate, the cost of which is charged to the estate account.

Development proceeds piecemeal. When building commences on a plot or number of plots an appropriate proportion of the balance on the estate account is transferred to work in progress and on the leasing of a plot a similar amount is transferred to a freehold ground rent asset account.

The company is responsible for final fencing and services, etc., and on the sale of a house or leasing of a plot the sum of £250 is debited to the appropriate account and credited to a provision for final services account. If the actual cost of providing final services exceeds the provision, the excess is written off against profit. The lessees are required to maintain the roads, fencing and service mains during the 75 years of their leases.

On 1st January, 1964 the following balances appeared in the accounts of the company—

	£
(i) Estate account—	
Land—cost of 150 plots neither leased nor sold . . .	33,000
Roads—Services—cost applicable to 150 plots	26,250
(ii) Freehold ground rent asset account—	
Estimated cost of land and services for 22 plots leased prior to 31st December, 1963	14,190

During 1964 the following transactions took place—

(i) Expenditure of £5,420 was incurred in providing final services for the last 20 plots sold or/leased in 1963.

(ii) 30 houses were commenced in March.

(iii) Leases of plots for 20 houses on normal terms were granted in April and May.

(iv) The last six of the houses commenced in 1963 and the first ten of the houses commenced in 1964 were sold.

(v) Freehold ground rents in respect of 10 plots granted in 1963 were sold for £12,000.

You are required to write up the following accounts for the year ended 31st December, 1964—

(*a*) the estate account;
(*b*) the provision for final services account;
(*c*) the freehold ground rent asset account. (*L.C.C.*)

18. Teleservices Ltd. operates a scheme whereby it undertakes, in consideration of a fee of £4 per annum paid annually in advance, to provide maintenance of television receivers for the first three years of the life of each receiver.

Experience has shown that the average cost of such maintenance is likely to be about £1·50 in the first year of a receiver's life, £3 in the second year, and £4·50 in the third, and it is desired to adjust the accounts in such a way that the profit on a completed three-year contract should be spread evenly over the three years.

The scheme started to operate on 1st January, 19.., and the following statement shows the receipts and expenditure in each of the first three years—

		Receipts	Cost of Service
		£	£
19..	All first-year contracts	9,600	3,462
19.1	Second-year contracts	8,800 }	11,432
	First-year contracts	12,800 }	
19.2	Third-year contracts	8,200 }	
	Second-year contracts	11,600 }	20,585
	First-year contracts	7,200 }	

All receipts are credited to a "T.V. Service Account" and the cost of maintenance debited to the same account, and no detailed records are kept beyond the names of subscribers and the dates of contracts. It is to be assumed (for simplicity) that all contracts run from 1st January in each year.

Write up the T.V. Service Account for the three years, showing the amounts to be taken to the credit of profit and loss in each year. (*R.S.A.*)

19. The following are the summarized Revenue Accounts of X. Ltd., for the two months ended 30th November—

	Oct.	Nov.		Oct.	Nov.
	£	£		£	£
Finished stock	19,200	12,600	Sales	24,800	22,000
Work in Process	7,700	7,000	Finished stock	12,600	10,350
Materials used	7,300	7,625	Work in Process	7,000	5,600
Wages	4,850	5,850			
Works expenses	750	800			
Depreciation	220	220			
Balance c/d	4,380	3,855			
	44,400	37,950		44,400	37,950
Salaries	1,160	1,160	Balance b/d	4,380	3,855
Office expenses	900	900			
Profit	2,320	1,795			
	4,380	3,855		4,380	3,855

Production capacity is 10,000 units per month.

All sales are made at £2 per unit.

The finished stock is valued throughout at £1·50 per unit.

The wages debit includes works office expenses amounting to £1,100 in October, and £1,000 in November. These items, as also works expenses, may be regarded as variable costs.

Prepare a statement of unit costs of OUTPUT and profit for each of the two months; and comment briefly on the results disclosed.

20. Chipperfield Ltd. is a company manufacturing a standardized product, and accounts for the year ended 30th June, 19.1, are in course of preparation. The following figures are extracted from the books—

	30th June, 19..	30th June, 19.1
	£	£
Stocks, etc., on hand—		
Raw materials	7,300	9,700
Work-in-progress	400	500
Finished goods	20,000	?

Revenue balances for the year, after all adjustments—

	£
Raw materials (purchases *less* returns)	178,500
Sales *less* returns	308,500
Manufacturing wages	51,700
Salaries and wages (supervision and administration)	18,900
Factory power	10,400
Sundry factory expenses	5,100
Depreciation of machinery	8,200

Two-thirds of the salaries and wages for supervision and administration are to be treated as a manufacturing charge.

8,000 units of the finished product were unsold at 30th June, 19.., production during the year amounted to 96,000 completed units (that is, taking no account of work-in-progress), and 92,000 units were sold, none having been lost or otherwise unaccounted for.

You are required—

(*a*) to ascertain the value (at factory cost) of the finished stock on hand at the end of the year, based on the average production cost for the year;

(*b*) to draw up the company's manufacturing and trading accounts for the year; and

(*c*) to calculate the average gross profit per unit sold during the year.

(*R.S.A.*)

21. The following figures were extracted from the books and records of Sarratt Ltd., a manufacturing business, the accounts of which are in course of preparation—

	31st March, 19..	31st March, 19.1
	£	£
Stocks, etc., on hand—		
Raw materials	8,800	6,200
Work-in-progress	500	600
Finished goods	11,500	to be ascertained

Revenue balances for the year ended 31st March, 19.1, after all adjustments—

	£
Raw materials (purchases *less* returns)	48,900
Sales, *less* returns (finished goods)	102,000
Manufacturing wages	19,600
Salaries and wages (supervision and administration)	4,500
Depreciation—machinery	6,150
Power	1,300
Rent and rates	3,000
Heating and lighting	800
Sundry factory expenses	450
Office and showroom expenses	1,450
Advertising	2,600
Bad debts	150
Discounts on sales	350

One half of the salaries and wages (other than manufacturing wages) is to be treated as a manufacturing charge, and of the rent, rates, heating and lighting, three-quarters is to be apportioned to the factory and one quarter to the office and showroom.

15,000 units of the finished product were unsold at 31st March, 19.., 105,000 units were completed during the year and 100,000 units were sold, none being lost or unaccounted for.

You are required to ascertain the value (taken at cost) of the finished product unsold at the end of the year, to draw up the company's manufacturing, trading, and profit and loss account for the year and to ascertain the gross profit per unit sold.

(*R.S.A.*)

22. At 31st March, 19.., the following trial balance of the XYZ Co. Ltd. was extracted—

	£	£
Share capital		100,000
Premium on forfeited shares		50
Goodwill	5,000	
Raw material stocks	32,452	
Work-in-progress	10,336	
Debtors	56,297	
Tools	654	
Office furniture	185	
Plant and machinery	12,510	
Leasehold buildings	6,140	
Mortgage on buildings		5,000
Creditors		26,200
Cash at bank	29,691	
Cash in hand	53	
Preliminary expenses	2,500	
Manufacturing wages	39,066	
Packing and carriage out	4,087	
Carriage inwards	638	
Sales		225,984
Sales returns	169	
Raw materials	148,308	
Repairs to machinery	844	
Office salaries	3,296	
Directors' fees	500	
Consumable tools	1,061	
Office sundries	128	
Legal and professional charges	250	
Rates— $\frac{1}{8}$ office, $\frac{7}{8}$ factory	120	
Mortgage interest	245	
Building repairs	53	
Factory sundries	311	
Works manager's salary	1,250	
Travelling and entertaining expenses	363	
Insurances—		
Factory	556	
Office	79	
Bank interest		53
Bank charges	145	
	357,287	357,287

The following final adjustments have to be made—

	£
1. Raw material stocks at 31st March, 19..	27,368
2. Work-in-progress at 31st March, 19..	15,209
3. Provision for bad and doubtful debts	1,000
4. Mortgage interest due	25
5. Wages accrued due	1,043
6. Insurance paid in advance—	
(a) Office furniture—7½ per cent	
(b) Plant and machinery—10 per cent	
8. Tools were valued at 31st March, 19.. at	550
9. Lease amortization—10 per cent	
10. Proposed dividend of 5 per cent	
11. £500 to be written off preliminary expenses	

Prepare manufacturing, trading, and profit and loss accounts for the year ended 31st March, 19.., and a balance sheet as at that date. Income tax is to be ignored. Commitments for capital expenditure at 31st March .19.., amounted to £7,500.

(*Cost and Management Accountants.*)

23. The following are details of a contract (No. 21A) undertaken by MN Ltd.—

Date commenced	1st July, 1965	
Date completed	31st October, 1966	
Contract price	£100,000	
Direct expenditure	1965	1966
	£	£
Materials	13,824	24,699
Wages	14,287	30,298
Expenses	944	1,324
	£29,055	£56,321
Plant purchased for cash at beginning of contract	12,000	—
Payments for plant on hire purchase		2,000
Penalty for failure to complete by 30th September, 1966		1,000
Cash received	36,000	63,000

The plant purchased for cash was sold for £3,250 on 31st October, 1966.

An initial deposit of £2,000 was paid on 1st March, 1966, for the plant acquired on hire purchase. The hire purchase agreement called for three further payments at six monthly intervals each of £2,000, which included interest at the rate of 10 per cent per annum. This plant, the cost price of which was £7,445, was used on the contract until 31st August when it was transferred to another contract, its value for depreciation purposes then being fixed at £5,800.

The cash received in each year represented the contract price of all work certified in that year less, in the case of uncompleted contracts 10 per cent for retention and in the case of the cash received in 1966 the penalty.

When the annual accounts for the year ended 31st December, 1965 were completed, it was expected that the contract would be completed by 30th September, 1966 when it was estimated that the realizable value of the plant would be £3,855 at 30th September, 1966, and that expenditure still to be incurred would total £53,000 but the necessity to hire plant in 1966 was not foreseen.

For the purpose of the annual accounts—

(*a*) all depreciation was charged to contracts by the straight line method and was calculated by reference to the expected market value of the plant at the completion of the contract;

(*b*) credit was taken for that proportion of the estimated profit on uncompleted contracts which the contract price of the work certified bore to the total contract price.

You are required to prepare the contract account for the years 1965 and 1966 showing the transfer to the profit and loss account.

Ignore taxation. (*L.C.C.*)

24. A contracting company requires a cost system installed to show costs and profits for each contract. You are required to—

(*a*) draft a suitable cost ledger card, *and*

(*b*) construct a control account from the following information—

			£
Dec	1	Balance b/f	22,346
	31	Site wages incurred	3,415
		Materials delivered direct to sites	12,221
		Progress payments received	18,000
		Supplies from own yard	1,504
		Sub-contractors' charges	546
		Plant hire	326
		Materials returned to yard	87
		Site erection expenses	87
		Site supervision salaries	210
		General overhead (Apportioned to contracts)	1,707
		Material prices overcharged	131
		Transport and delivery charges	134

State how the final balance is capable of arithmetical proof.

(*Cost and Management Accountants.*)

25. A public works contractor secured a contract at a price of £500,000. Work began on 1st July, 19.., and the contract ledger account showed the following items debited up to 31st March, 19.1—

	£
Materials	90,000
Wages	105,000
Direct charges	5,000
Plant	16,000

The measurement at 31st March, 19.1, read as follows—

		£
Total work done certified to date		240,000
Total work done per last measurement		210,000
Total work done for month		30,000
Less retention money 10 per cent		3,000
		27,000
Materials on site	£5,000	
Less 20 per cent	1,000	
		4,000
Amount payable		31,000

Prepare a *pro forma* account for the contract showing the profit earned to date and indicate by means of a note the basis on which you arrive at the amount which might be carried to profit and loss account. Allow for depreciation on the plant at 10 per cent per annum. (*Cost and Management Accountants.*)

26. William Duncan commenced business as a building contractor on 1st January, 19... At the completion of each contract, but not before, a sales invoice is rendered to the customer.

The following table shows the prime cost of all contracts commenced in 19.. and the price charged to customers for all contracts completed in that year.

	Cost of Materials Used	Wages	Sales Invoice
	£	£	£
Contract A	8,640	11,300	24,175
" B	10,170	14,580	31,500
" C	4,090	6,210	—
" D	1,830	1,550	—
	24,730	33,640	55,675

The following is a summary of Duncan's bank account for the year 19...

BANK SUMMARY

	£		£
Capital introduced	20,000	Purchases (materials)	22,000
Contract A	24,175	General expenses	3,915
" B	25,000	Fixed assets	7,000
" C	2,000	Cash	36,000
		Balance, 31st December, 19..	2,260
	71,175		71,175

All receipts had been paid into the bank.

Wages amounting to £640 were outstanding at 31st December, 19...

Wages amounting to £33,000 were paid out of the cash drawn from the bank, and the balance of the cash represents Duncan's drawings.

Purchases of materials during 19.. amounted to £26,535. No discounts were received. The stock of materials at 31st December, 19.., not charged to any contract, amounted, at cost, to £1,805.

Work-in-progress at 31st December, 19.. is to be valued at prime cost plus an addition of 25 per cent for overhead expenses and profit.

You are required to prepare a trading and profit and loss account for the year 19.. and a balance sheet as on 31st December, 19... Ignore depreciation of fixed assets. (*Chartered Institute of Secretaries.*)

27. Separate operating accounts are kept by A Ltd. for their factory and warehouse. Issues from the former are consistently charged to the latter at factory cost, plus 5 per cent.

For the purpose of these operating accounts finished stock in the warehouse, and any remaining in the factory, are consistently valued on the same basis, i.e., cost plus 5 per cent.

For the year ended 31st December, 1962, the following details are supplied—

			£
Factory			
Materials bought			30,000
Wages			16,000
Production overhead			10,600
Stocks—1st Jan., 1962	Materials		1,200
Stocks—31st Dec., 1962	Materials		1,400
	Finished stock: 100 units		
Issues to Warehouse: 4,600 units			
Warehouse			
Stocks—1st Jan., 1962			
	Finished stock: 200 units		2,730
Stocks—31st Dec., 1962			
	Finished stock: 350 units		
Sales (including opening stock): 4,450 units			80,100
Warehouse and selling overhead			8,800

Write up—

(*a*) Factory account.
(*b*) Warehouse account.
(*c*) Profit and Loss Account, including provision for a staff bonus of 5 per cent of the true profit. (*A.C.C.A.*)

28. The following are particulars of two contracts, Nos. 101 and 202 respectively, undertaken by C. Down, Ltd.—

	No. 101	No. 202
Date commenced	1st June, 1963	1st July, 1964
Date completed	30th November, 1964	30th April, 1965
Contract price	£100,000	£160,000

	1963	1964	1965
Direct Expenditure—	£	£	£
Materials	14,632	25,891	33,270
Wages	16,237	31,248	40,865
Expenses	866	1,215	1,624
Plant purchased for cash at commencement of contract	10,725	—	12,350
Payments for plant acquired on hire-purchase terms	—	5,200	2,600
Penalty for failure to complete Contract 101 by 31st October, 1964	—	500	—
Cash received	36,000	63,500	72,000

The plant purchased in 1963 for cash was sold, on 30th November, 1964, for £2,750.

As regards the plant purchased on hire-purchase terms, an initial deposit of £2,600 was paid on 28th February, 1964. The hire-purchase agreement called for two further payments of £2,600 each, which included interest at the rate of 12 per cent per annum; these payments were made on the due dates, viz.: 30th June, 1964, and 31st October, 1964. This plant, the cash price of which was £7,504, was used on Contract No. 101 until 30th June, 1964, when it was transferred to Contract No. 202. For depreciation purposes the value of this plant at the date of transfer was taken to be £6,000.

The cash received in each year represented the contract price of all work certified in that year, less, in the case of uncompleted contracts, 10 per cent retention money, and, in the case of cash received for Contract No. 101 in 1964, the penalty.

When the annual accounts for 1963 were prepared, it was expected that Contract No. 101 would be completed on 31st October, 1964, when the market value of the plant purchased for cash would be £3,925. At that time it was estimated that expenditure on Contract No. 101 in 1963 would amount to £39,000, but the acquisition of additional plant in 1964 was not then foreseen.

When the annual accounts for 1964 were prepared, it was expected that Contract No. 202 would be completed on 30th June, 1965, when the market value of the plant purchased for cash and of the plant transferred would be £9,000 and £4,250 respectively. At that time it was estimated that the further expenditure on Contract No. 202 would amount to £46,041.

The following principles were adopted for the purposes of the annual accounts—

1. All depreciation was charged to the contract by the straight line method, and was calculated by reference to the estimated market value of the relevant plant at the completion of each contract.

2. Credit was taken for that proportion of the estimated profit on each uncompleted contract, which the contract price of the work certified bore to the total contract price.

You are required to prepare summaries of the accounts for Contract No. 101 for the years 1963 and 1964, and for Contract No. 202 for the year 1964, showing in each case the transfer to Profit and Loss Account at the end of the year. (*L.C.C.*)

29. DEPARTMENT A

		Units	£			Units	£
Oct 1	Work in progress (30 per cent complete) .	200	170	Dec 31	Transfer to Finished Stores . . .	1,900	
Dec 31	Costs for the quarter—			Dec 31	Work in progress (60% per cent complete) .	300	
	Materials used .		5,962				
	Direct Labour .		3,836				
	Overhead . .		1,918				
			11,886				11,886

During the quarter 2,000 units were begun.

Complete the account, showing your workings clearly.

Ignore wastage, and treat the costs shown as accruing evenly over the three months. (*A.C.C.A.*)

30. Vita Ltd. manufacturers and markets through its retail branches a product "Vitabon" which is sold in tins of standard size at 30p per tin.

During the three months to 30th April, 1962, output was 38,600 tins of the finished product, and of these, 7,400 tins were in stock on that date.

The following particulars are extracted from the cost and other records—

	£
Purchases—	
Raw materials	3,900
Tins	460
Direct labour	2,895
Carriage inwards	160
Manufacturing expenses	1,930
Office and selling expenses allocated . . .	980
Sales	11,910

	1st Feb.	30th April
Stocks—	£	£
Raw materials, cost	2,500	3,000
Tins, cost	400	360
Finished product—		
8,000 tins "Vitabon" at prime cost . .	1,300	?

In December, 1961, 5,000 lbs of raw materials had been purchased at 5p per lb and formed part of the stocks on 1st February, 1962. These proved to be of substandard quality and the sales for the three months to 30th April, included 4,000 lbs of such materials at 3·75p per lb, the remainder being in stock (at cost) on that date. Its realizable value is estimated at 2½p per lb.

Prepare separate Manufacturing and Trading Accounts for the three months to 30th April, 1962, analysing unit costs in the clearest possible way to assist management. (*A.C.C.A.*)

CHAPTER 17

PARTNERSHIP ACCOUNTS

> However, it is always a good idea to close your books each year, especially if you are in partnership.
>
> As the proverb says: "Frequent accounting makes for lasting friendship."
>
> LUCA PACIOLI—*Treatise on Bookkeeping* 1494

LAW OF PARTNERSHIP

BY the Partnership Act, 1890, partnership is defined as "the relation which subsists between persons carrying on a business in common with a view of profit."

Relationships which are Not Partnerships. The relation between members of any company or association which is—

(*a*) Registered as a company under the Companies Act, 1862, or any other Act of Parliament for the time being in force and relating to the registration of joint stock companies (now Companies Acts, 1948 and 1967); or

(*b*) Formed or incorporated by or in pursuance of any other Act of Parliament or letters patent, or Royal Charter; or

(*c*) A company engaged in working mines within and subject to the jurisdiction of the Stannaries;

is not a partnership within the meaning of the Act.

Prohibition of Large Partnerships. No partnership consisting of more than twenty persons can be formed to carry on any business for gain without being registered as a company under Sect. 434 of the Companies Act, 1948. In the case of a banking business the number must not exceed ten (Sect. 429).

However, Sect. 119 of the Companies Act, 1967, gives the Board of Trade authority to approve the formation of a banking partnership of up to twenty persons. Each partner must be approved by the Board.

Sect. 120 of the Act exempts from the normal maximum of twenty persons partnerships of—

(*a*) *Solicitors*. Each partner must be a solicitor.

(*b*) *Accountants*. Each partner must be qualified for appointment as a company auditor under Sect. 161 of the Companies Act, 1948.

(*c*) *Stock Exchange Members*. Each partner must be a member (broker or jobber) of the same recognized Stock Exchange under the Prevention of Fraud (Investments) Act, 1958.

Other professions to which this privilege has been extended include patent agents, actuaries, chartered engineers and surveyors.

These exemptions apply to limited and general partnerships.

Firm and Firm-name. Persons who have entered into partnership with another are, for the purposes of the Partnership Act, 1890, called collectively a firm, and the name under which their business is carried on is called the firm-name.

By the Registration of Business Names Act, 1916, every firm having a place of business in the United Kingdom, and carrying on business under a name *which does not consist of the true surnames of all the partners*, must be registered. Particulars must be furnished of the business name, general nature of the business, principal place of business; the present Christian name and surname, any former Christian name and surname, nationality, and if that nationality is not the nationality of origin, the nationality of origin, usual residence, and the other business occupation (if any) of each partner. The names of the partners must also appear on the notepaper, catalogues, showcards, etc., issued by the firm.

Difference between an Ordinary Partnership and a Company. The following points should specially be noted—

1. The individuality of the members who form a company is entirely lost in the personality of the company itself, which is regarded in law as a separate and distinct entity. Thus, a member of a company may enter into contracts with the company itself in the same manner as any other individual.

2. In a company, the creditors can proceed against the property of the company only in case of necessity, and, ordinarily, there is no remedy beyond the amount of the nominal capital. In a partnership, the creditors may not only proceed against the property of the partnership, but also against the private property of each individual partner.

3. In a public company, shares may be transferred without the consent of the other members of the company, and without affecting its existence; this is not possible in a partnership.

4. In the case of a limited company, the liability of each shareholder is limited to the amount unpaid on the shares which he holds and, to a limited extent, for twelve months after sale. In a partnership each member is liable jointly for the whole of the debts of the firm, although the Limited Partnerships Act, 1907, affords provision for partners with limited liability.

5. In a partnership the number of members must not generally exceed twenty, or, in the case of a banking company, ten. In a public company there must not be less than seven persons, and in a private company not less than two nor more than fifty.

6. In a partnership, each general partner can take part in the management, and his actions are legally binding on the firm; but in a company, the rights of management are restricted to the directors and managers appointed by them.

7. In a partnership, the rights of the members are regulated by the deed of partnership, or the Partnership Act, and may be altered by mutual

agreement. In a limited company, the objects of the company are governed by the memorandum of association, which cannot be altered except by consent of the court; and the powers of the directors are regulated by the articles, which can be altered only by special resolution of the shareholders.

8. The law prescribes an annual audit for a limited company, but not for a partnership.

9. The capital of a partnership may be increased by additions and by profits, or decreased by withdrawals and losses, or altered by mutual agreement. The nominal capital of a company is fixed by the memorandum, is unaffected by trading profits or losses, and can only be increased or decreased in a special statutory manner.

Kinds of Partners. There are different kinds of partners, viz.—

Acting or active partner, one who actually takes part in the business; *dormant or sleeping partner*, one who has capital in the business, but is not actually engaged in it; *limited partner*, is a sleeping partner under the Limited Partnerships Act, whose liability for debts is limited; *quasi partner*, one who has retired from active participation in the business, but has left his capital in it as a loan, receiving interest on it varying with the profits, or who (although not a partner) incurs liabilities as if he were a partner by reason of the fact that he holds himself out or allows himself to be represented as such.

Power of a Partner to Bind the Firm. Every partner is an agent of the firm and his other partners for the purpose of the business of the partnership; and the acts of every partner who does any act for carrying on in the usual way business of the kind carried on by the firm of which he is a member bind the firm and his partners, unless the partner so acting has in fact no authority to act for the firm in the particular matter, and the person with whom he is dealing either knows that he has no authority, or does not know or believe him to be a partner.

Partner using Credit of Firm for Private Purposes. Where one partner pledges the credit of the firm for a purpose apparently not connected with the firm's ordinary course of business, the firm is not bound, unless he is in fact specially authorized by the other partners.

Liability of Partners. Every general partner in a firm is liable jointly with the other partners for all debts and obligations of the firm incurred while he is a partner; and after his death his estate is also severally liable in a due course of adminstration for such debts and obligations, so far as they remain unsatisfied, but subject to the prior payment of his separate debts.

Liability of Firm. (*a*) Where one partner acting within the scope of his apparent authority receives the money or property of a third person and misapplies it; and (*b*) where a firm in the course of its business receives money or property of a third person, and the money or property so received is misapplied by one or more of the partners while it is in the custody of the firm; the firm is liable to make good the loss.

Liabilities of Incoming and Outgoing Partners. By Sect. 17 of the Partnership Act—

(1) A person who is admitted as a partner into an existing firm does not thereby become liable to the creditors of the firm for anything done before he became a partner, unless it is quite clear from the agreement that he intended to make himself liable.

(2) A partner who retires from a firm does not thereby cease to be liable to outside parties for partnership debts or obligations incurred before his retirement.

(3) A retiring partner may be discharged from any existing liabilities, by an agreement to that effect between himself and the members of the firm as newly constituted and the creditors, and this agreement may be either express or inferred as a fact from the course of dealing between the creditors and the firm as newly constituted.

Variation of Terms of Partnership. The mutual rights and duties of partners, whether ascertained by agreement or defined by the Partnership Act, may be varied by the consent of all the partners, and such consent may be either express or inferred from a course of dealing.

Partnership Property. By Sect. 20 of the Partnership Act—

All property and rights and interest in property originally brought into the partnership stock or acquired, whether by purchase or otherwise, on account of the firm, or for the purposes and in the course of the partnership business, are called in this Act partnership property, and must be held and applied by the partners exclusively for the purposes of the partnership and in accordance with the partnership agreement.

Unless the contrary intention appears, property bought with money belonging to the firm is deemed to have been bought on account of the firm.

Rights and Duties of Partners. By Sect. 24 of the Partnership Act, the interests of partners in the partnership property, and their rights and duties in relation to the partnership, shall be determined, subject to any agreement express or implied between the partners, by the following rules—

(1) All the partners are entitled to share equally in the capital and profits of the business, and must contribute equally towards the losses whether of capital or otherwise sustained by the firm.

(2) The firm must indemnify every partner in respect of payments made and personal liabilities incurred by him—

(*a*) in the ordinary and proper conduct of the business of the firm; or,

(*b*) in or about anything necessarily done for the preservation of the business or property of the firm.

(3) A partner making, for the purpose of the partnership, any actual payment or advance beyond the amount of capital which he has agreed to subscribe, is entitled to interest at the rate of 5 per cent per annum from the date of the payment or advance.

(4) A partner is not entitled, before the ascertainment of profits, to interest on the capital subscribed by him.

(5) Every general partner may take part in the management of the partnership business.

(6) No partner shall be entitled to remuneration for acting in the partnership business.

(7) No person may be introduced as a partner without the consent of all existing partners.

(8) Any difference arising as to ordinary matters connected with the partnership business may be decided by a majority of the partners, but no change may be made in the nature of the partnership business without the consent of all existing partners.

(9) The partnership books are to be kept at the place of business of the partnership (or the principal place, if there is more than one), and every partner may, when he thinks fit, have access to and inspect and copy any of them.

It is essential to realize that the Partnership Act does not apply where there is a deed in existence dealing with any point in question.

Notice particularly that in view of Sect. 24 (3), it may be more advantageous to bring in further money as a *loan* than as additional capital.

Expulsion of Partner. No majority of the partners can expel any partner unless a power to do so has been conferred by express agreement between the partners.

Duration of Partnership at Will. Where no fixed term has been agreed upon for the duration of the partnership, any partner may determine the partnership at any time on giving notice of his intention so to do to all the other partners. Where the partnership has originally been constituted by deed, a notice in writing, signed by the partner giving it, is sufficient.

Where a partnership entered into for a fixed term is continued after the term has expired, and without any express new agreement, the rights and duties of the partners remain the same as they were at the expiration of the term, so far as is consistent with the incidents of a partnership at will. A continuance of the business by the partners or such of them as habitually acted therein during the term, without any settlement or liquidation of the partnership affairs, is presumed to be a continuance of the partnership.

Duties of Partners towards the Firm. Partners are bound to render true accounts and full information of all things affecting the partnership to any partner or his legal representatives.

Every partner must account to the firm for any benefit derived by him without the consent of the other partners from any transaction concerning the partnership, or from any use by him of the partnership property, name, or business connexion.

If a partner, without the consent of the other partners, carries on any business of the same nature as, and competing with, that of the firm, he must account for and pay over to the firm all profits made by him in that business.

Partnership Deed. There may be, and often are, "partnerships at will" without the existence of any deed or written agreement. Owing to the conflicting legal interpretations of the Partnership Act, however, a deed should be drawn up and the following matters dealt with specifically—

1. The amount of capital each partner is to contribute, and whether the amount is to be fixed or not.

2. How profits and losses, including capital profits and losses, are to be shared.

3. The amount each partner is to be allowed to draw.

4. Whether interest is to be allowed on capital and charged on drawings, and at what rate.

5. Whether drawings, profits and losses, and interest are to be dealt with in separate current accounts, or merged finally into the capital accounts.

6. Whether the balances of the partners' current accounts are to be charged or credited with interest, and at what rate.

7. That a profit and loss account and balance sheet be drawn up each year, and audited by a professional accountant; and that such balance sheets be signed by all the partners and be binding on them, unless a manifest error is discovered within six months afterwards.

8. In the case of policies of survivorship insurance being taken out, how the premiums are to be dealt with, and how the policy money is to be divided when received.

9. The method of arriving at the amount of goodwill in the case of the death or retirement of any of the partners.

10. The method of arriving at the amount payable on the death or retirement of a partner—whether he is to be entitled to his capital, as in the last balance sheet, plus a higher rate of interest to date of death or retirement in lieu of profits or whether fresh accounts are to be prepared up to date of death or retirement, and whether the partnership assets are to be revalued for this purpose.

11. That in the event of the death of a partner, his capital should remain in the business as a loan bearing interest, and be repayable by instalments, so as to prevent the business being crippled by a large withdrawal of funds.

QUESTIONS

1. What is the legal definition of "partnership"?
2. What is meant by partnership property?
3. What partnerships are prohibited by law?
4. Explain the meaning of the terms "firm" and "firm-name."
5. State briefly some of the differences between an ordinary partnership and a joint stock company.
6. Explain what is meant by the following: "active partner," "dormant partner," "limited partner," "*quasi* partner."
7. What power has a partner, as such, to bind his firm?

THE ACCOUNTS

Fixed Capital Accounts. In practice, it is usual for the amounts of the partners' capitals to be fixed by the partnership deed. The capital accounts, therefore, remain at the same figure during the partnership. Partners' salaries, profits, and interest on capital are not shown in the capital accounts but in separate current or drawings accounts, the balances of which are carried to the balance sheet, and in some cases bear interest. A distinction is thus made and maintained between original capital and undrawn profits. The difference between the two methods can easily be seen from the example on the next page, which represents the liabilities side of a balance sheet drawn up both ways.

Partner's Advances. Any further sums of money advanced by a partner to the firm will be by way of *loan* rather than *capital*, inasmuch as partners' loans have priority of repayment over partners' capital in the event of a dissolution. The interest on such loans, unless paid in cash, should, therefore, be credited to the partners' loan account or current account, and not to his capital account.

Partner's Salaries. Where some of the partners devote the whole of their time to the business while others do not, it is usual to allow the former a salary before ascertaining the net profit. The practice also obtains where there are junior partners who, having little or no capital in the firm and taking only a small share of the profits, would otherwise derive insufficient remuneration from the business for their services to it. The salary is sometimes drawn out in cash, and sometimes credited to the partner's capital account, according to the agreement.

Interest on Capital. In order to adjust the rights of partners, as between themselves, it is usual to allow interest on partners' capitals. Where partners share equally in the profits, but have unequal capitals, the partner with the smaller capital would otherwise get an advantage over the other; and where the partners have equal capitals but share profits unequally, the partner who takes the larger share of profits would otherwise gain at the expense of the other.

Drawings. Amounts taken out of the business by a partner during the year are drawings. They may be in cash or in kind.

TREATMENT OF CAPITAL

Partners' capital may be treated as fixed. In this case, profits and interest less drawings are accounted for in a Current Account. Alternatively, these items are carried to Capital Account. The difference can be seen in the example on p. 1708.

VARIATIONS IN CAPITAL AND PROFIT SHARES

The terms agreed between the partners will considerably affect their relative shares of the income from the business and the accountant must carefully consider the effect for his client under various alternatives.

Example 1

Unequal Capitals but Equal Shares of Profits—

		£
Capital—	A	4,000
	B	2,000

1. Fixed Capital Method

Liabilities	£	£
Bills Payable		1,656
Sundry Creditors		3,074
Outstanding Expenses		85
Loan A/c, Potts		2,000
Current A/c, Potts—		
Share of Profit	1,376	
Interest on Capital	350	
Interest on Loan	100	
	1,826	
Less Drawings	1,550	
		276
Current A/c, Kemp—		
Share of Profit	864	
Interest on Capital	150	
	1,014	
Less Drawings	850	
		164
Capital—		
Potts	7,000	
Kemp	3,000	
		10,000
		17,255

2. Alternative Method

Liabilities	£	£
Bills Payable		1,656
Sundry Creditors		3,074
Outstanding Expenses		85
Loan A/c, Potts	2,000	
Interest accrued	100	
		2,100
Capital—		
Potts, 1st Jan.	7,000	
Add Interest	350	
Add Share of Profit	1,376	
	8,726	
Less Drawings	1,550	
		7,176
Kemp, 1st Jan.	3,000	
Add Interest	150	
Add Share of Profit	864	
	4,014	
Less Drawings	850	
		3,164
		17,255

Net Profits before charging interest £1,100. Division of profits—

If interest at 5% charged				If no charged interest	
	£		£		£
A Interest	200	B Interest	100	A	550
Half net profits	400	Half net profits	400	B	550
	600		500		1,100

Example 2

Equal Capitals but Unequal Shares of Profits—

£

Capital—A 3,000 with $\frac{3}{5}$ profits.
B 3,000 with $\frac{2}{5}$ profits.

Net profits before charging interest at 5 per cent £1,100. Division of profits—

If interest at 5% charged				If no charged interest	
	£		£		£
A Interest	150	B Interest	150	A	660
Share of profits	480	Share of profits	320	B	440
	630		470		1,100

DETERMINING THE RATE OF INTEREST

The rate of interest to be allowed on partners' capital may take into account—

(a) *Minimum Return.* The rate should not be lower than that obtainable by investing in Government stock or leaving the capital on deposit at the Bank. The rate may vary from 2½ per cent to 8 per cent or more according to circumstances.

(b) *Compensation for Risk.* An additional percentage should be allowed for the fact that risk of losing capital may be higher in a business than in "gilt-edged" investment.

SUPER-PROFITS

If a fair salary is allowed to partners in respect of their work in the firm (what they could earn if working for someone else) and interest on capital is allowed, then the profit remaining is super-profit. It may be regarded as the pure return on the entrepreneurial risk carried by the partners. It is one basis for calculating the Goodwill.

Example 3

C and D are in partnership. C was previously employed at a salary of £4,000 per annum and D could earn £3,000 per annum working for C.

C provides capital of £10,000 and asks for interest of 8 per cent per annum calculated—

	per cent
Minimum return . . .	5
Return for risk . . .	3

What are the super profits if the firm earns £13,000 in the first year?

Solution—

	£	£	£
Profit on operation			13,000
Partners' salaries—			
C	4,000		
D	3,000		
		7,000	
Interest on Capital—			
C	800	800	
			7,800
Super-profits			5,200

Interest on Drawings. In many cases, interest is not chargeable on drawings, the reason being that the drawings are not out of *capital* but on account of *profits* that are accruing. Where, however, partners withdraw capital sums, interest is charged. In order to adjust the rights of the partners *inter se*, that is, to prevent one partner getting any advantage over the others, it is also necessary to charge interest on drawings where partners, who are equal as regards capital and share of profits, draw out *unequal* sums. The interest is debited, by means of a journal entry, to the drawings account and credited to an interest on capital account.

Drawings Account. The following is an example *without interest—*

Example 4

R. RUMLEY, DRAWINGS

19..			£	19..			£
Mar	1	Cash	60·00	Dec	31	Transfer to Current A/c .	240·00
Jun	1	Cash	50·00				
Sep	1	Cash	75·00				
Dec	1	Cash	55·00				
			240·00				240·00

The following is an example *with interest—*

Example 5

R. RUMLEY, DRAWINGS

19..			Interest £	£	19..			£
Mar	1	Cash . . .	2·50	60·00	Dec	31	Transfer to Current A/c .	245·44
Jun	1	Cash . . .	1·46	50·00				
Sep	1	Cash . . .	1·25	75·00				
Dec	1	Cash . . .	0·23	55·00				
	31	Interest . . .		5·44				
				245·44				245·44

If the Capital account is not fixed, the transfer may be direct to Capital A/c.

Current Account. Drawings may be debited directly to the Current Account, as follows—

Example 6

R. RUMLEY, CURRENT

			£				£
19..				19..			
Mar	31	Cash	120·00	Dec	31	Interest on Capital . .	250·00
Jun	30	Cash	80·00			Share of Profit . . .	365·82
Sep	30	Cash	65·00				
Dec	31	Cash	130·00				
	31	Balance transferred to Capital	220·82				
			615·82				615·82

Final Accounts of Partnerships. Preparation of the final accounts of a partnership differs from preparation of the accounts of a sole trader only in respect of the appropriation of the profit between the partners.

Example 7

The following trial balance was taken from the books of Gray and Brown, hire-car proprietors, as at 30th April, 1963, the end of their first trading year.

	£	£
Capital Accounts—		
Gray		1,600
Brown		200
Drawings—Gray	800	
Brown	240	
Hire Cars at cost on 1st May, 1962	1,800	
New car bought under Hire Purchase 30th October, 1962 (Cash Price)	920	
Cash at Bank	524	
Sundry Debtors for Hire	260	
Creditors for Repairs		296
Petrol, Oil and Grease	365	
Sales of Petrol		300
Spares and Repairs to Cars	426	
Rent and Rates	260	
Office Salaries	420	
Advertising and Stationery	126	
Car Licences and Insurance	220	
Receipts from Hire of Cars		3,400
Instalments on Hire-Purchase of Cars not yet due . .		640
Hire purchase Interest (including £25 on instalments not yet due)	75	
	6,436	6,436

Prepare a Profit and Loss Account for the year to 30th April, 1963, and Balance Sheet as at that date, making the necessary adjustments for the following—

Depreciation of cars at 25 per cent per annum—

	£
Stock of Spares	115
Stock of Petrol	50
Doubtful Debts	25

Interest on partners' capital at 5 per cent per annum.
(No interest is allowed on undrawn profits.)
Licences and insurance unexpired £120.
Commission due to staff at 5 per cent of hire receipts.
Parner's salary due to Gray £500 for management.
Net profits to be shared equally between the partners.

The depreciation to be allowed is—

	£
25 per cent of £1,800 for one year	450
25 per cent of £920 for six months . . .	115
Charge per Profit and Loss Account . . .	565

and the amount to be charged against profits in respect of the other adjustments is—

	Petrol, Oil and Grease	Spares and Repairs	Licences and Insurance	Office Salaries
	£	£	£	£
Per trial balance	365	426	220	420
Less: Stocks	50	115		
Less: Prepayments			120	
Add: Commission—5% of £3,400 .				170
Total per Profit and Loss Account .	315	311	100	590

and the final account and Balance Sheet is—

GRAY AND BROWN

Profit and Loss Account for the Year to 30th April, 1963

	£	£		£	£
Vehicle Costs—			Car Hire receipts . . .	3,400	
Petrol, Oil and Grease . .	315		Petrol sales	300	
Spares and Repairs . .	311				3,700
Licences and Insurance . .	100				
Depreciation at 25 % per annum	565				
		1,291			
Administration—					
Rent and Rates . . .	260				
Salaries and Commission. .	590				
Advertising and Stationery	126				
		976			
Finance—					
Hire-purchase interest . .	50				
Doubtful debts . . .	25				
		75			
		2,342			
Net profit for the year, c/d . .		1,358			
		3,700			£3,700

	£	£		£
Partners' Current Accounts—			Net profit, b/d	1,358
Gray—				
Interest on Capital . .	80			
Salary	500			
Half share of balance . .	384			
		964		
Brown—				
Interest on Capital . .	10			
Half share of balance . .	384			
		394		
		1,358		1,358

GRAY AND BROWN

Balance Sheet at 30th April, 1963

	£	£		£	£
Capital Accounts—			Fixed Assets—		
Gray	1,600		Hire Cars at cost. .	2,720	
Brown	200		*Less:* Depreciation to date	565	
		1,800			
Current Accounts—				2,155	
Gray—Share of profit . .	964		*Less:* Hire-purchase instalments not yet due .	615	
Less: Drawings . .	800				
		164			1,540
Brown—Share of profit .	394		Current Assets—		
Less: Drawings . .	240		Stocks of Spares and Petrol .	165	
		154	Trade debtors *less* provision for doubtful debts .	235	
			Payments in advance . .	120	
			Bank balance . . .	524	
		2,118			1,044
Current Liabilities—					
Trade creditors . . .	296				
Accrued commission . .	170				
		466			
		2,584			2,584

(*Certified Accountants.*)

Goodwill. This term has received various legal definitions, e.g. "Nothing more than the probability that the old customers will resort to the old place"; "The benefit arising from connexion and reputation." The goodwill may arise from the reputation of the article sold, the personality of the proprietor, monopoly, patents, trade marks, favourable locality, etc.

There are three classes of goodwill—

Personal or "Dog." This attaches to a proprietor and will move with him. It has little value to a purchaser, even if restrictive covenants are imposed on the seller.

Adherent or "Cat." This attaches to premises and will remain when a proprietor leaves. It is, therefore, of value to a potential purchaser.

Fugitive or "Rat." Some goodwill is neither personal nor adherent but will be dissipated if a business changes hands. Again, this has no value to a potential purchaser.

Adherent goodwill may have to be taken into consideration on the death of an existing partner or the admission of a new one, and also on the sale of the business.

Valuation of Goodwill. This involves calculating the value of the net adherent goodwill. To some extent, there will be a goodwill element in the value or rental of property since they will rise in accordance with the position of the property. More is paid for a position on a High Street or a site near a tube station.

The net goodwill will be that element of business which is worked up by continued personal effort by management.

No general rules apply since the price will be negotiated between the buyer and seller, but calculations may be based upon operating profits before partnership salaries, and interest on capital or super-profits. In either case, the valuation assesses the capital value of the future excess income due to the existence of goodwill. For instance, in the case of C and D, above (p. 1709), a buyer might offer two years purchase of the operating profits, £26,000, for goodwill. Alternatively, he might offer three to five years purchase of the super-profits, that is £15,600 to £26,000. In practice, the buyer might start at £15,600 and be prepared to go up to £26,000.

It is, however, important to remember that goodwill should never appear in the books of a business unless—

(*a*) It has been purchased.

(*b*) It is necessary to raise it in connexion with the introduction of a new partner.

(*c*) The death or retirement of an existing partner makes it necessary to arrive at the true value of such partner's shares.

Admission of Partners. It is usual to charge an incoming partner a premium for goodwill. The method of treating this item in the books of account varies considerably. There are five main ways of dealing with this matter, and they are as follows—

1. A goodwill account is raised, the amount being credited to the old partners in the proportion in which they share profits and losses.

2. The premium paid for a share of the goodwill by the incoming partner is drawn out again, in cash, by the old partners.

3. The premium paid for a share of the goodwill by the incoming partner is retained in the business; the sum so paid being credited in the proper proportions to the old partners' capital accounts.

4. The premium paid for a share of the goodwill by the incoming partner is paid to the old partners direct, no record being made in the firm's books.

5. An agreed amount of cash is withdrawn by the old partners and charged to a goodwill account.

It is to the advantage of the incoming partner that the payment of a premium for goodwill should be shown in the partnership books, and thus ensure there being a permanent record of it, in order to facilitate matters if he should retire and require payment to him of a similar sum. It is also, usually, to the advantage of the new partner that the premium he pays on admission should not be drawn out again, but should be left in the business, so that the latter shall derive some benefit from it.

Example 8

J. Rowell and M. Collado are in partnership, sharing profits and losses in the proportions of two-thirds and one-third respectively. They agree to admit C. Constant as a partner with a fifth share on condition that he brings in £2,000 capital, and that the old partners are credited with their respective shares of the goodwill estimated at £1,200. Rowell and Collado, as between themselves, are to share profits and losses in the same ratio as before. Make the necessary entries in the books, and state the partners' future proportions of profit respectively.

JOURNAL

		Dr	*Cr*
		£	£
	Goodwill	1,200	
	J. Rowell $\frac{2}{3}$		800
	M. Collado $\frac{1}{3}$		400
	For their respective shares of goodwill		

CASH BOOK

	£		£
C. Constant (Capital)	2,000		

As Constant takes one-fifth of the profits, four-fifths will remain, and the partners' shares will be as follows—

Rowell will receive $\frac{2}{3}$ of $\frac{4}{5}$ or $\frac{8}{15}$ths;
Collado " " $\frac{1}{3}$ of $\frac{4}{5}$ or $\frac{4}{15}$ths;
Constant " " $\frac{1}{5}$ or $\frac{3}{15}$ths.

Example 9

J. Judge and K. King are in partnership, sharing profits and losses in the proportions of three-fourths and one-fourth respectively. They agree to admit K. Kerry as a partner on condition that he brings into the business £1,500 capital and pays them a premium of £300 for a fifth share in the profits. Make the necessary entries in the books.

CASH BOOK

	£		£
K. Kerry (Capital) . . .	1,500		

As only £1,500 was brought into the business, a separate cheque would be handed to Judge and King for the premium.

Alternatively, the premium would appear on both sides of the cash book—

CASH BOOK

	£		£
K. Kerry (Capital) . . .	1,500	J. Judge	225
Premium—		K. King	75
J. Judge (Capital) . . .	225		
K. King (") . . .	75		

Example 10

O. Oldham and B. Barlass are in partnership, sharing profits and losses three-fifths and two-fifths respectively. They agree to admit W. Wheater as a partner on condition that he brings into the business £2,500, £500 of which is to be regarded as premium for admission. Make the necessary entries in the books.

CASH BOOK

	£		
W. Wheater (Capital). . .	2,000		
O. Oldham, Capital ($\frac{3}{5}$ of Wheater's premium) . .	300		
B. Barlass, Capital ($\frac{2}{5}$ of Wheater's Premium)	200		

In this case the money brought in by Wheater must be split up, the capital being separated from the premium, which belongs to the old partners, and must be credited to their capital accounts in the same proportion in which they are entitled to share profits.

Example 11

C. Coward agrees to admit F. Glen into partnership on the following terms: (*a*) that Glen brings £2,650 capital in cash into the business; (*b*) that £650 is to be paid out to C. Coward and is to appear in the books of the partnership as goodwill. Make the necessary entries in the books.

CASH BOOK

	£		£
F. Glenn (Capital)	2,650	Goodwill (amount paid out to C. Coward by way of premium)	650

QUESTIONS

1. How far is each partner liable for the obligations of the firm? Does this liability continue after his decease?
2. What is the liability of the firm with reference to money or property—

   (*a*) received by a partner who misapplies it?
   (*b*) received by the firm, and a partner misapplies it?

3. Explain what is meant by "holding out," and the liabilities attaching to it. Does the penalty apply to the continued use of the firm-name after the decease of any of the partners?
4. What are the liabilities of incoming and outgoing partners respectively? Can they be discharged from these liabilities by an agreement between all the partners?
5. Can partners vary their mutual rights and duties by means of a written agreement?
6. What are the mutual rights and duties of partners, as laid down by the Partnership Act, in regard to the following—

   (*a*) Sharing of profits or losses? (*b*) Payments made by a partner on account of the firm? (*c*) Advances to the firm by a partner? (*d*) Interest on capital? (*e*) Management of the business? (*f*) Remuneration of partners? (*g*) Introduction of new partners? (*h*) Disputes *re* partnership affairs? (*i*) Partnership books?

7. Can a partner be expelled by the other partners?
8. When does a partnership terminate? Under what circumstances is a "continuance" of a partnership presumed?

Adjustment of Assets on Admission of Partner, Amalgamation of Businesses. It often happens, when a new partner is admitted, that the assets of the business are revalued, any appreciation or depreciation being adjusted in the capital accounts of the old partners. A new partner may also bring into the partnership other assets besides cash, namely, book debts, plant, etc., and the goodwill of his own connexion.

Example 12

V. Evans and T. Taylor are partners in a coal business, sharing profits and losses equally. On 31st December their capitals stood at £3,500 and

£3,000 respectively. The firms' assets and liabilities on the same date were as follows: coal trucks £756; furniture and fittings £260; sundry creditors £1,140; cash at bank £1,325; plant and lorries £840; bills payable £1,068; sundry debtors £4,740; cash in hand £52; and stock of coal £735. They agree to take into partnership P. Primrose, a colliery agent, as and from 1st January, on the following terms: profits and losses to be shared, Evans two-fifths, Taylor two-fifths, and Primrose one-fifth. Primrose is to bring into the business sundry debtors amounting to £720 (less a reserve of 5 per cent for bad debts), and the goodwill of his connexion estimated at £400. His capital in the new business is to be £1,800, the balance of which he is to pay on 1st January, 19... It was also agreed between them that the following adjustments should be made as regards the business of Evans and Taylor: coal trucks to be taken at £955, and plant and lorries at £950, the values placed on them by a public valuer; a bad debts reserve of 5 per cent of the sundry debtors to be created; the goodwill to be valued at £1,250; and Evans to be paid out from the bank balance such a sum as will reduce his capital to the same amount as Taylor's. Make the necessary entries in the subsidiary books, and show the balance sheet of the new firm prior to commencing business.

In Evans and Taylor's Books

JOURNAL

		Dr	*Cr*
19..		£	£
Jan 1	Sundry Debtors	720	
	Goodwill	400	
	Bad Debts Reserve		36
	P. Primrose (Capital)		1,084
	For assets brought in by P. Primrose.		
1	Coal Trucks	199	
	Plant and Lorries	110	
	Goodwill	1,250	
	Bad Debts Reserve		237
	V. Evans (Capital)		661
	T. Taylor (,,)		661
	For net gain to Evans and Taylor on the revaluation of their assets.		

Note particularly that the sundry debtors must *not* be entered at the net figure of £684, as individual debts of a total value of £720 are actually in existence.

CASH BOOK

	£		£
Balance	1,325	V. Evans (Capital) (amount withdrawn by him to reduce his capital, £4,161 to the same amount as T. Taylor, £3,661) .	500
P. Primrose (Capital) (amount paid in by him to raise his capital from £1,084 to £1,800) .	716		

BALANCE SHEET AS AT 1ST JANUARY, 19..

Liabilities	£	*Assets*		£
Bills Payable	1,068	Cash in hand		52
Sundry Creditors	1,140	,, at Bank		1,541
Capital—		Debtors	£5,460	
V. Evans	3,661	*Less* Reserve	273	
T. Taylor	3,661		——	5,187
P. Primrose	1,800	Stock of Coal		735
		Coal Trucks		955
		Plant and Lorries		950
		Furniture and Fittings		260
		Goodwill		1,650
	11,330			11,330

Guarantee of Assets and Liabilities—Preferential Claim on First Year's Profits. It often happens that an incoming partner requires the assets and liabilities, as shown by the firm's balance sheet, to be guaranteed, in order to protect himself against errors that may subsequently be discovered. Should a liability have been omitted or underestimated, the loss arising from it will not then be borne by the new partnership, but solely by the old partners. Should discounts and bad debts arise in connexion with the debtors in excess of what has been provided, the new partnership will not share in such losses, which will be debited to the old partners' capital accounts, and not to the firm's profit and loss account.

On the other hand, there are sometimes profits accruing on work in progress, or orders in hand, which the old partners justly require to be reserved entirely for themselves. Such profits will be credited, in their proper proportions, to the capital accounts of the old partners, and not to the profit and loss account of the firm. In some cases, however, an arrangement is made whereby the old partners become, in respect of such accruing gains, entitled to a preferential claim of a fixed amount of the first year's profits.

Preparation of Final Accounts of a New Partnership. When a new partner has been admitted it frequently happens that the full implications have not been realized by the partners and the accounting treatment must be corrected to reflect the correct position.

The following example is a problem set by the London Chamber of Commerce—

Example 13

George and William are in partnership sharing profits equally after charging interest on capital at 5 per cent per annum. On 1st January, 1963 they agreed to take over the business of Bernard and to make him a partner on the following terms—

(*a*) The firm took over Bernard's assets at the following values—

	£
Goodwill	1,500
Motor Vehicles	820
Stock	3,200
Debtors	1,100
	6,620

(*b*) The new firm undertook to pay Bernard's creditors amounting to £1,260 and Bernard was to bring in cash to make his capital £6,000.

(*c*) The goodwill of the old firm was to be increased to £4,000.

(*d*) The partners of the new firm were to share profits in the proportion of 3:2: and 3, interest on capital being charged at 5 per cent per annum as before.

The Trial Balance at 31st December, 1963, shows the following balances—

	£	£
Capital Accounts at 1st January, 1963—		
George		8,150
William		4,500
Bernard		480
Current Accounts—		
George		920
William		364
Drawings—		
George	1,800	
William	1,420	
Bernard	1,500	
Goodwill	3,000	
Fixtures and Fittings	800	
Motor Vehicles (old firm)	1,750	
Stock 1st January, 1963 (old firm)	6,824	
Purchases	22,640	
Sales		39,400
Rent, Rates and Insurance	1,500	
Lighting and Heating	750	
Wages	4,920	
Office Salaries	420	
Motor Expenses	856	
Postages, Stationery and Telephone	220	
Trade Expenses	416	
Commission	1,200	
Provision for Bad Debts (old firm)		200
Cash at Bank	2,360	
Cash in Hand	280	
Sales Ledger Balances	3,250	
Bought Ledger Balances		1,892
	55,906	55,906

You are to prepare Trading and Profit and Loss Accounts for the year ended 31st December, 1963, and a Balance Sheet as at that date, taking into account the following adjustments—

(*a*) Stock at 31st December, 1963, £9,250.
(*b*) Provision for Bad Debts to be increased to £300.
(*c*) Depreciation to be written off—

	per cent
Motor Vehicles . . .	20
Fixtures and Fittings . .	10

The only entries that have been made in the books in respect of Bernard's Capital Account have been to credit him with the value of Debtors taken over, plus the cash brought in and to debit him with the Creditors paid on his behalf. Calculations may be made to the nearest £.

The first problem is to calculate how much cash Bernard brought in.

	£
The Assets taken over	6,620
Less: Creditors taken over	1,260
Net Assets taken over	5,360
Bernard has brought in cash	640
To make up Capital of	6,000

Since Bernard brings in goodwill of £1,500 and the goodwill of the old firm is to be increased to £4,000, the total goodwill will be £5,500. The increase of £1,000 in old goodwill is shared by the old partners equally, and the new capital account will be—

		Capital of the Old Partners	
1963		*George*	*William*
Jan 1	Balance	8,150	4,500
	Goodwill (share)	500	500
	Adjusted balance after taking over Bernard	8,650	5,000

Depreciation on fixtures and fittings is £80. Depreciation on vehicles can be calculated—

	£
Motor vehicles (old firm) . .	1,750
Bernard	820
	2,570
Depreciation at 20 per cent .	514

The Capital Account of the new partner, Bernard, shows a credit balance of £480. This represents—

	£
Debtors	1,100
Cash	640
	1,740
Less: Creditors paid	1,260
	480

To this must be added the balance of the assets—

	£
Goodwill	1,500
Vehicles	820
Stock	3,200
	5,520

Giving a total of £6,000 Capital.

The final accounts can now be prepared as follows—

GEORGE, WILLIAM & BERNARD, PARTNERSHIP

TRADING AND PROFIT AND LOSS ACCOUNT FOR THE YEAR ENDED 31ST DECEMBER, 1963

	£	£		£
Opening Stock—			Sales	39,400
(old firm)	6,824			
(Bernard)	3,200			
	10,024			
Purchases	22,640			
	32,664			
Closing stocks	9,250			
		23,414		
Cost of goods sold—				
Wages		4,920		
Gross profit		11,066		
		39,400		39,400
	£	£		£
Rent, Rates and Insurance		1,500	Gross profit	11,066
Lighting and Heating		750		
Office salaries		420		
Motor expenses		856		
Postages, stationery and telephone		220		
Trade expenses		416		
Commission		1,200		
Provision for Bad Debts	300			
Less: Old provision	200			
		100		
Depreciation—				
Motor vehicles	514			
Fixtures and Fittings	80			
		594		
Net Profit		5,010		
		11,066		11,066

APPROPRIATION ACCOUNT

	£	£		£
Interest on Capital at 5%			Net profit before interest on capital	5,010
George	433			
William	250			
Bernard	300			
		983		
Share of Profits—				
George	1,510			
William	1,007			
Bernard	1,510			
		4,027		
		5,010		5,010

BALANCE SHEET ON 31ST DECEMBER, 1963

		£	£
Goodwill			5,500
Fixed assets			
Fixtures and Fittings		800	
Less: Depreciation		80	
			720
Motor Vehicles		2,570	
Less: Depreciation		514	
			2,056
			8,276
Current assets			
Stock		9,250	
Debtors	3,250		
Less: Provision for Bad debts	300		
		2,950	
Cash at bank	2,360		
,, in hand	280		
		2,640	
		14,840	
Current liabilities			
Trade creditors		1,892	
Working Capital			12,948
Net assets employed			21,224

Represented by—

	George	William	Bernard	
	£	£	£	*Total*
Capital	8,650	5,000	6,000	19,650
Current Accounts—				
Opening balance . . .	920	364		
Add: Interest . . .	433	250	300	
,, Profit . . .	1,510	1,007	1,510	
	2,863	1,621	1,810	
Less: Drawings . . .	1,800	1,420	1,500	
Balance at 31st December, 1963	1,063	201	310	1,574
				£21,224

Guarantee of Minimum Profits. An established partner will often guarantee a minimum share of profits to a new partner. In this case, the share of profit is calculated in accordance with the agreed proportions and, if the new partner's profit is below the minimum, the amount necessary to make up the minimum is debited to the established partner and credited to the new.

Admission of an Employee. Where a new partner has previously been an employee, and is admitted to partnership during the year, it is necessary to apportion the profit between the pre- and post-partnership periods.

Example 14

Philip Lex and his son Basil Lex together with Thomas Pleed were in partnership as solicitors practising in the name of Lex and Pleed.

Francis Seal, the managing clerk, was admitted as a partner on 1st April, 1962.

The sharing of profits and losses in the new partnership were to be as follows: Philip Lex five-twelfths, Thomas Pleed four-twelfths, Basil Lex two-twelfths and Francis Seal one-twelfth. Basil Lex was also to receive £700 per annum by way of salary.

Prior to becoming a partner, Francis Seal had received a salary of £1,660 per annum together with a commission of 2 per cent of the net profits before a charge was made for any partner's salary but after charging his own salary and commission.

For the new partnership's first year it was agreed that any excess of his share of the profits, over and above what his remuneration would have been if he had continued as managing clerk plus an additional amount of £440, should be charged against Philip Lex's share.

After perusing the draft accounts for the year ended 31st March, 1963, as drawn up by their accountant, the partners agreed (1) to make provision for bonuses to the staff in the sum of £1,400, (2) that the following adjustments should be made—

(*a*) that Basil Lex should be credited with £400 of his father's share of the profit;

(*b*) that Arthur Pleed, son of Thomas Pleed, employed by the partnership, should be given an additional bonus of £250, the same to be charged against his father's share of the profit.

Before charging Basil Lex's salary and prior to making the abovementioned adjustments, the profit for the year was £35,700.

Prepare a statement of division of profits for the year ended 31st March, 1963. (*Certified Accountants.*)

The apportionment may be made along the following lines—

LEX & PLEED, SOLICITORS

Statement of Division of Profits for the Year Ended 31st March, 1963

		£	Philip Lex	Basil Lex	Thomas Pleed	Francis Seal
Profit-sharing ratio			5	2	4	1
			£	£	£	£
Profits for the year		35,700				
Less: Staff Bonus		1,400				
		34,300				
Less: Salary payable to Basil Lex		700		700		
Balance divisible in profit-sharing ratio		33,600	14,000	5,600	11 200	2,800
Transfer to Basil Lex			−400	+400		
Bonus payable to son, Arthur					−250	
			13,600	6,700	10,950	2,800
Excess of Seal's share over emoluments as managing clerk—	£					
Profits, less staff bonus	34,300					
Less: Salary	1,660	1,660				
	32,640					
Commission $\frac{2}{102}$ × £32,640	640	640				
		2,300				
Add: Increase		440				
		2,740				
Share of Profits		2,800				
Excess		60				
Adjustment: 6/11ths of excess charged to Philip Lex and credited to Basil Lex and Thomas Pleed in the proportion 4:2			−33	+11	+22	
		£				
Divisible between partners		34,050	13,567	6,711	10,972	2,800
Bonus to Arthur Pleed		250				
Staff Bonus		1,400				
		35,700				

QUESTIONS

1. What are the respective duties of partners towards the firm?
2. Can a partnership exist without a deed or written agreement? What are such partnerships then called?
3. Outline the principal points which should be specifically dealt with in a partnership deed, in view of the conflicting legal interpretations of the Partnership Act.
4. Explain what is meant by "fixed" capital accounts. What is the object of such? Draw up a balance sheet both ways in order to illustrate your answer.
5. Explain the nature and treatment of "partners' advances." Why are such sums not put in as additions to capital?
6. Explain the object and treatment of "partners' salaries." Is the salary always drawn out?
7. Why is it at times necessary to charge interest on capital in a partnership? How is such interest dealt with in the books?
8. When is it necessary in a partnership to charge interest on drawings, and when not? Give reasons in each case for your answer.
9. Submit *pro forma* drawing accounts of three kinds to illustrate actual business practice.
10. What is meant by partners' current accounts? How do they differ from partners' drawing accounts?

LIMITED PARTNERSHIPS

A limited partnership is a partnership formed under the Limited Partnerships Act, 1907, which came into operation on 1st January, 1908.

Meanings of Terms. By Sect. 3—

"Firm," "firm name," and "business" have the same meanings as in the Partnership Act, 1890.

"General partner" shall mean any partner who is not a limited partner as defined by this Act.

Constitution of a Limited Partnership. By Sect. 4—

(2) A limited partnership shall not consist, in the case of a partnership carrying on the business of banking, of more than ten persons, and, in the case of any other partnership, of more than twenty persons, and must consist of one or more persons called *general partners*, who shall be liable for all debts and obligations of the firm, and of one or more persons to be called *limited partners*, who shall at the time of entering into such partnership contribute thereto a sum or sums as capital or property valued at a stated amount, and who shall not be liable for the debts or obligations of the firm beyond the amount so contributed.

(4) A body corporate may be a limited partner.

See p. 1903 for modifications introduced by the Companies Act, 1967.

Limited Partner's Capital a Fixed Contribution. Sect. 4 (3) enacts—

A limited partner shall not during the continuance of the partnership, either directly or indirectly, draw out or receive back any part of his contribution, and if he does so draw out or receive back any such part shall be liable for the debts and obligations of the firm up to the amount so drawn out or received back.

Registration Required. By Sect. 5 of the Act it is enacted that—

Every limited partnership must be registered as such in accordance with the provisions of this Act, or in default thereof it shall be deemed to be a general partnership, and every limited partner shall be deemed to be a general partner.

The partnership must be registered by sending to the Registrar of Companies a statement, signed by all the partners, giving (Sect. 8), the following particulars—

1. The firm name.
2. The general nature of the business.
3. The principal place of business.
4. The full name of each of the partners.
5. The term, if any, for which the partnership is entered into, and the date of its commencement.
6. A statement that the partnership is limited, and the description of every limited partner as such.
7. The sum contributed by each limited partner, and whether paid in cash, or how otherwise.

Notice of any change of the above must be sent to the Registrar within seven days. A registration fee of £2 is payable, and an *ad valorem* stamp duty of £1 per cent on the amount introduced by the limited partner or partners, or any subsequent increase. Any person may inspect the Register of Limited Partnerships on payment of 5p, and may also obtain copies of any documents on payment of the prescribed fees.

Modifications of Partnership Law in the Case of Limited Partnerships. Sect. 6 enacts as follows—

(1) A limited partner shall not take part in the management of the partnership business, and shall not have power to bind the firm:

Provided that a limited partner may by himself or his agent at any time inspect the books of the firm and examine into the state and prospects of the partnership business, and may advise with the partners thereon.

If a limited partner takes part in the management of the partnership business he shall be liable for all debts and obligations of the firm incurred while he so takes part in the management as though he were a general partner.

(2) A limited partnership shall not be dissolved by the death or bankruptcy of a limited partner, and the lunacy of a limited partner shall not be a ground for dissolution of the partnership by the court unless the lunatic's share cannot be otherwise ascertained and realized.

(3) In the event of the dissolution of a limited partnership its affairs shall be wound up by the general partners unless the court otherwise orders.

Rights and Duties of Limited and General Partners. These are determined by Sect. 6 (5), which says—

Subject to any agreement express or implied between the partners—

(*a*) Any difference arising as to ordinary matters connected with the partnership business may be decided by a majority of the general partners.

(*b*) A limited partner may, with the consent of the general partners, assign his share in the partnership, and, upon such assignment, the assignee shall become a limited partner with all the rights of the assignor.

(*c*) The other partners shall not be entitled to dissolve the partnership by reason of any limited partner suffering his share to be charged for his separate debt.

(*d*) A person may be introduced as a partner without the consent of the existing limited partners.

(*e*) A limited partner shall not be entitled to dissolve the partnership by notice.

Application of General Partnership Law. Sect. 7 of the Act enacts as follows—

> Subject to the provisions of this Act, the Partnership Act, 1890, and the rules of equity and of common law applicable to partnerships, except so far as they are inconsistent with the express provisions of the last-mentioned Act, shall apply to limited partnerships.

Advantages and Disadvantages of Limited Partnerships. In the case of the limited partner the advantages are (1) that his liability is limited to the amount he has agreed to contribute, and (2) that he can share in the profits of the partnership without increasing this fixed liability. This enables a capitalist to provide funds for inventors to carry out their ideas, also friends to finance a young man setting up in business, and to share in any benefits accruing, without incurring any further risk beyond the fixed liability. The disadvantages are (1) the limited partner cannot withdraw any part of his capital, (2) he cannot take part in the management, (3) he cannot dissolve the partnership by giving notice, (4) other partners can be introduced without his consent, (5) there is publicity consequent upon registration and open inspection of the Register.

As regards the general partner the advantages are (1) fresh capital can be obtained without the expense and formalities of converting the business into a limited company, or without mortgaging his property, (2) the limited partner cannot interfere with the management of the business, (3) a new partner can be introduced without the consent of the limited partner, (4) there is no fear of capital being suddenly withdrawn, as the death or bankruptcy of the limited partner does not of itself dissolve the partnership, neither can the limited partner dissolve it by giving notice. The disadvantages to him are, chiefly, compulsory registration, and the consequent publicity through anyone being able to inspect the Register and obtain copies of any document.

Winding up of Limited Partnerships. The provisions of the Bankruptcy Act, 1914, apply to limited partnerships in like manner as if they were ordinary partnerships, and on all the general partners being adjudged bankrupt, the assets of the limited partnership vest in the trustee.

QUESTIONS

1. What is meant by "goodwill" in a partnership? How does goodwill arise? When is goodwill brought into the books, and when not?
2. How is the value of the goodwill of a business arrived at?
3. In what different ways is goodwill treated in the case of an incoming partner who pays a premium for a share therein?
4. When assets are revalued on admission of a new partner, how should any appreciation or depreciation thereof be treated in the books?
5. Explain the phrases "guarantee of assets and liabilities," and "preferential claim on profits." Under what circumstances do such things arise, and how are they dealt with in the books?
6. How is goodwill valued and treated in the case of an outgoing partner?

7. What is meant by "policies of survivorship assurance"? Explain their treatment in the books.

8. How is goodwill treated on the sale of a partnership business?

9. What various methods are there of repaying an outgoing partner his share in the partnership?

10. Explain the method of treatment in the books where an outgoing partner's share is being repaid by means of an annuity.

11. What are the advantages and disadvantages of limited partnerships?

JOINT VENTURES

A Joint Venture is a partnership without the use of a firm name, limited to a particular speculation in which the persons concerned agree to contribute capital and to share profits or losses.

Nature of Joint Ventures. A joint venture may consist of a joint consignment of goods, an underwriting transaction, a speculation in shares, or any similar form of enterprise.

Advantages of a Joint Venture. One party may be able to buy at much lower prices and on far better terms than others. Another party may be in a position to sell at exceptionally good prices. A third party, who may not be favourably circumstanced for either buying or selling, may however, have special financial resources. Thus, the combined services of the parties in a common venture may make it a highly remunerative one.

The Methods of Procedure. It is usual for one of the parties to be appointed to manage the joint venture, that is, to do all the buying and selling and to look after it. For these services he obtains an extra remuneration by being allowed to charge against the joint account a commission of so much per cent on the amount of the sales, and, in some cases, on the amount of the purchases, sales, and expenses. Under these circumstances a joint account is opened and debited with the cost of the goods. Each of the other parties then remits his proportion of the cost, which is placed to the credit of their personal accounts, as this amount is payable back again to them plus their share of profit, or less their share of loss, as the case may be. The joint account is also debited with all expenses, charges, and commission; it is likewise credited with all sales whether for cash or on credit. The balance of the account then represents profit or loss to be shared in the agreed proportions. When the goods have been sold and paid for, then a remittance to each of the parties for the amount due to him will close the speculation.

In other cases, each of the parties concerned opens in his books merely an account for the joint venture, to record such of the transactions as he is directly concerned with. A general statement, prepared from information supplied by the parties, is rendered showing the profit on the joint speculation. Each party then debits the joint account and credits his profit and loss account with his portion of such profit. There will then remain in one party's books a debit balance, and in the other party's books a credit balance, of the same amount. Payment of this balance by one party to the other will finally close the venture.

Sometimes, a separate joint banking account is opened, and a separate set of books kept for the venture. The transactions are then recorded like ordinary partnership transactions; and, in such cases, interest on capital is generally charged, particularly when the parties interested have advanced unequal amounts.

Example 15

Bought goods from Martin & Son £720, and took from stock goods value £220, for a joint speculation with S. Singleton, profits divisible equally. Received S. Singleton's share of speculation. Paid charges and expenses £71. Sold joint account goods for cash £1,220. Sent sight draft to Martin & Son. Charged as manager 5 per cent commission on sales. Rendered statement to Singleton with cheque for the amount due to him. Write up the subsidiary books and show the ledger accounts.

JOURNAL

	Dr	Cr
	£	£
Joint A/c	720	
Martin & Son		720
For goods bought for a joint speculation with S. Singleton.		
Joint A/c	220	
Goods on Joint A/c		220
For goods taken from stock for a joint speculation with S. Singleton.		
Joint A/c	61	
Commission		61
5% on sale of goods, £1,220, for the joint speculation with S. Singleton.		

CASH BOOK

	£		£
S. Singleton	470	Joint A/c	71
Joint A/c	1,220	Martin & Son	720
		S. Singleton	544

LEDGER

MARTIN & SON

	£		£
Cash	720	Joint A/c	720

Joint Account

	£		£
Martin & Son	720	Cash	1,220
Goods on Joint A/c	220		
Cash (Expenses)	71		
Commission	61		
Balance (Profit)—			
S. Singleton ½	74		
Profit and Loss ½	74		
	1,220		1,220

S. Singleton

	£		£
Cash	544	Cash	470
		Joint A/c (½ profit)	74
	544		544

Goods on Joint Account

	£		£
Trading A/c	220	Joint A/c	220

Commission

	£		£
P. & L. A/c	61	Joint A/c	61

Trading Account

			£
		Goods on Joint A/c	220

Profit and Loss Account

			£
		Joint A/c	74
		Commission	61

Example 16

On 1st February L. Wilson bought goods value £600 and consigned them to D. Bowden as a joint speculation, profits being divisible equally. On the same date he paid carriage and freight £40; insurance £20, and drew

IN WILSON'S LEDGER

JOINT CONSIGNMENT WITH D. BOWDEN

Date		Particulars	Amount	Date		Particulars	Amount
19..			£	19..			£
Feb	1	Goods	620	Feb	1	Bill Receivable at 2 m/d	310
		Carriage & Freight	40			Balance (due from Bowden) c/d	466
		Insurance	20				
	4	Discount on Bill	3				
		P. & L. A/c (share of profit)	93				
			776				776
Jul	31	Balance (due for Bowden) b/d	466	Jul	31	Cash	466

IN BOWDEN'S LEDGER

JOINT CONSIGNMENT WITH L. WILSON

Date		Particulars	Amount	Date		Particulars	Amount
19..			£	19..			£
Feb	1	Bill Payable, due 4th Apr	310	Jun	30	Gross Proceeds of Sale of Goods	1,000
Mar	1	Dock Dues & Cartage	16				
		Duty & Insurance	28				
Jun	30	Storage	25				
		Sundries, Brokerage, & Expenses of Sale	62				
		P. & L. A/c (share of profit)	93				
		Balance (due to Wilson) c/d	466				
			1,000				1,000
Jul	31	Cash	466	Jul	31	Balance (due to Wilson) b/d	466

on Bowden at two months for £310 on account, discounting the bill on 4th February for £307. On receipt of the goods on 1st March, Bowden paid dock dues and cartage £16, and government duty, insurance, etc., £28. On 31st July Wilson received an account sales showing that on 30th June the goods had realized gross £1,000, and that Bowden's disbursements made on the same date were storage £25, sundries, brokerage, and expenses of sale £62. Bowden also enclosed a sight draft for the amount due at 31st July. Prepare a general statement showing the result of the venture, and write up the accounts in Wilson's and Bowden's ledgers respectively.

Example 17

B. Black and W. White were partners in the following scheme, Black to take five-ninths and White four-ninths of the profits. They agreed to guarantee the subscription at par of 85,000 shares of £1 each in a company, and to pay all expenses up to allotment, in consideration of the company's issuing to them 11,500 other shares fully paid. Black provided cash for registration and fees £114; advertising £2,175; printing and prospectuses £225. White paid cash for rent of office £40; secretary, etc., £95; petty cash and sundries £25; stamps £78; solicitor's charges £240. Applications fell short of the 85,000 shares by 3,500, and White paid in full for that number on the joint account. The company handed Black and White the 11,500 shares. They then sold all their shares at £0·82 each, less brokerage 2p per share. White received the net proceeds of 5,000, Black of 10,000. Prepare joint account and the separate accounts of the partners, showing their shares of profit, and the amount due to each other in settlement.

JOINT VENTURE

	£		£
Black—		Black—	
Registration & Fees	114	Proceeds of Sale of 10,000	
Advertising	2,175	Shares @ £0·80 net	8,000
Printing & Prospectuses	225	White—	
White—		Proceeds of Sale of 5,000	
Rent of Office	40	Shares @ £0·80 net	4,000
Secretary, etc.	95		
Petty Cash & Sundries	25		
Stamps	78		
Solicitor's Charges	240		
White—Cash for shares not taken up	3,500		
Balance (Profit)—			
Black $\frac{5}{9}$ths	3,060		
White $\frac{4}{9}$ths	2,448		
	12,000		12,000

B. BLACK

	£		£
Joint A/c—		Joint A/c—	
Proceeds of Sale of 10,000		Registration & Fees	114
Shares @ £0·80 net	8,000	Advertising	2,175
		Printing & Prospectuses	225
		Joint A/c—	
		$\frac{5}{9}$ths of Profit	3,060
		Balance (due to W. White) c/d	2,426
	8,000		8,000
Balance (due to White) b/d	2,426		

W. WHITE

	£		£
Joint A/c—		Joint A/c	
Proceeds of Sale of 5,000 Shares @ £0·80 net	4,000	Rent of Office	40
Balance (due from B. Black) c/d	2,426	Secretary, etc.	95
		Petty Cash & Sundries	25
		Stamps	78
		Solicitor's Charges	240
		Joint A/c—	
		Cash for Shares not taken up	3,500
		Joint A/c—⅘ths of Profit	2,448
	6,426		6,426
		Balance (due from B. Black) b/d	2,426

QUESTIONS

1. Define a "joint venture." What does it consist of?
2. What advantages are there in a joint venture over a speculation on one's own account?
3. What methods of procedure are there in dealing with joint ventures from a book-keeping point of view? Outline briefly the most usual one.
4. When goods are taken from one's own stock for the purpose of a joint venture with others, how should they be dealt with in the books?
5. When different persons enter into a joint speculation, and each one takes some part in the transactions connected with it, how is the profit of the venture ascertained, and how is a final settlement between the parties effected?

EXERCISE 17

1. What constitutes a partnership, and can a partnership exist without each partner becoming personally liable for the firm's responsibilities to creditors?

John Leach and William Nash had carried on business as linen drapers for some years, but without any partnership deed, or without any arrangement as to the course to be adopted in the event of the death of either party. The business had been a profitable one, and the accounts had been made up yearly on the 31st December, and professionally audited by an auditor called in for the purpose. Leach died suddenly in July last, leaving his entire estate to his widow. What course would Nash have to adopt under the circumstances, and when would Leach's estate cease to have an interest in the profits of the business? *(London Chamber of Commerce.)*

2. Give the "drawings account" of John Robertson as it would appear in the firm's private ledger as on 31st December, under the following conditions—

His capital on 1st January was £5,000.

His drawings were: 1st May £250; 1st July £300; 1st November £200; 1st December £100.

His share of profits for the year was £795.

Interest is allowed by the firm's partnership articles on capital and charged on withdrawals at the rate of 5 per cent per annum. (*R.S.A.*)

3. A partnership consists of three partners whose capitals and profit-sharing ratios are given below, together with the balances standing upon their current accounts at the beginning of their trading year and the profit earned by each of the branches, which they respectively manage, during the year.

	Capital	P/S Ratio	Current Account at 1/4/. .	Profit—Year to 31/3/. 1	
	£	%	£		£
Bee . .	7,500	40	200 (*Cr*)	Bch R	1,980
Dee . .	4,000 (including £1,400 brought in 30/9/. .)	25	250 (*Cr*)	Bch S	1,380
Gee . .	3,000	35	120 (*Dr*)	Bch T	1,480

In addition to his capital contribution, Gee has £2,000 on loan to the firm at 5 per cent per annum interest. The profit figures above have been struck without making any provision for this interest or for any other matter touching upon the division of profits between the partners.

The partnership articles provide that—

(*a*) Each partner is to be entitled to a commission of 5 per cent of the profit earned by the branch managed by him, before making any other appropriation whatever.

(*b*) Dee is to be accorded a salary of £350 for general administration.

(*c*) Interest on capital is to be allowed at the rate of 6 per cent per annum, regardless of current account balances or drawings.

(*d*) The residue of profit is to be divided as shown above.

You are required to complete the firm's profit and loss account for the year and to write up the partners' current accounts. Drawings during the year have amounted to: Bee £2,320, Dee £1,610, Gee £1,180. (*London Chamber of Commerce.*)

4. Dickson and Bell, having capitals of £2,000 and £1,500 respectively, admit Peters into partnership on terms that he shall contribute £1,000 as capital, and pay them £1,400 as his share of the goodwill. Interest on capital to be at 5 per cent per annum (charged to profit and loss account) and profits to be shared in the proportion of capitals. Peters has only £1,000, which he pays in as capital; and in attempt to

PROFIT AND LOSS ACCOUNT

		£		£
Interest on Capital—			Profit	2,500
Dickson . . .	£140			
Bell	105			
Peters	50			
		295		
Profits divided—				
Dickson . . .	£980			
Bell	735			
Peters	490			
		2,205		
		2,500		2,500

meet the position, the partners raise a "goodwill account" for £1,400, which is credited, £800 to Dickson's capital and £600 to Bell's. You are called in at the end of the year, and find they have closed off the profit and loss account as shown above. Correct the error made by the partners, and the effect thereof, by journal entries (which should be fully explanatory). Show the true position of the partners' accounts.

5. The books of Black and White, who are equal partners, are balanced yearly as on 31st December. Before profits are ascertained and divided, 5 per cent interest is allowed upon partners' capital. Depreciation at the rate of 5 per cent is written off the plant account, and a provision of 5 per cent is made for bad and doubtful debts. One year's interest, at the rate of $4\frac{1}{2}$ per cent, is due upon the loan on mortgage, and has not yet been passed through the books. The stock on hand, as on 31st December, was valued at £3,225. The following are the final balances as on 31st December—

	£		£
Purchases	16,450	Trade charges	400
Manufacturing wages	2,150	Premium on lease (6 years unexpired as on 1st January)	2,400
Sales	24,800	Sundry creditors	15,345
Black's capital	5,000	Loan on mortgage	5,000
" drawings (including interest)	550	Freehold land and buildings	8,000
White's capital	2,000	Plant	4,000
" drawings (including interest)	350	Provision for bad and doubtful debts (as on 1st Jan.)	600
Stock (as on 1st January)	3,000	Sundry debtors	13,100
Salaries	820	Cash at bank	1,200
Rates and taxes	325		

Prepare a trading and profit and loss account for the year ended 31st December, and a balance sheet as on that date. (*London Chamber of Commerce.*)

6. Lion and Unicorn are in partnership as chemical manufacturers. Profits or losses are divided equally. Under the deed of partnership the following adjustments are necessary before the division of profits—

Five per cent interest is allowed on partners' capital; 10 per cent depreciation is to be written off plant and barges; 5 per cent provision is to be made for bad and doubtful debts.

On 31st December the ledger balances of the firm were as follows—

	£		£
Purchases	63,000	Sundry creditors	3,860
Barges	3,250	Insurance	265
Repairs and replacements	3,205	Bad debts	341
Freight and marine insurance	312	" " provision (1st January)	385
Allowances from creditors	2,420	Advertising	982
Coal	4,404	" suspense account	5,800
Gas and water	302	Cottage rents received	117
Machinery and plant	25,000	Cash in hand	325
Wages	6,221	R. Lion, capital	59,400
Land and buildings	13,840	" drawings (including interest)	4,250
Salaries	858	P. Unicorn, capital	30,000
Sundry debtors	7,940	" drawings (including interest)	2,050
Sales	74,441		
Cash at bank	2,185		
Stock (1st January)	25,220		
Rent, rates, and taxes	873		

Stock was taken as on 31st December, and was agreed at £30,342. It was also agreed to write off half the advertising suspense account, and to transfer to building account £3,000 from purchases account, and £250 from wages account, representing cost of material and labour spent upon new buildings erected during the year. Prepare trading and profit and loss accounts for the year ended 31st December and a balance sheet as on that day. *(London Chamber of Commerce.)*

7. Tupp and Sedge were partners in a retail business sharing profits and losses: Tupp two-thirds, Sedge one-third. Interest on fixed capital was credited at the rate of 5 per cent per annum. No interest was charged on drawings. Accounts were made up to 31st March each year.

On 1st January, 19.1, Palmer was admitted as a partner, and from that date all profits and losses were to be shared: Tupp six-tenths, Sedge three-tenths, Palmer one-tenth. Before ascertaining the partners' shares of profits or losses, Palmer was to be credited with a salary at the rate of £600 per annum. Provisions regarding interest on capital and drawings remained unaltered.

It was agreed that Palmer's total share of profits, including his salary and interest on capital, should be guaranteed by Tupp at a minimum rate of £1,500 per annum. Any apportionment of profit for a particular period should be made as to gross profit on the basis of sales and as to expenses, with the exception of general expenses, on the basis of time.

The trial balance extracted from the books on 31st March, 19.1, was as follows—

	£	£
Capital—		
Tupp		4,800
Sedge		2,400
Palmer (cash paid in 1st January, 19.1)		800
Drawings—		
Tupp	3,000	
Sedge	1,500	
Palmer	300	
Delivery van, at cost	1,000	
Provision for depreciation thereon at 31st March, 19..		400
Furniture and fittings, at cost	2,400	
Provision for depreciation thereon at 31st March, 19..		300
Sales (nine months to 31st December, 19.., £24,000)		33,600
Purchases	22,200	
Stock, 31st March, 19..	4,800	
General expenses (nine months to 31st December, 19.., £455)	1,040	
Salaries	2,400	
Heating and lighting	220	
Rent and rates	960	
Creditors		1,500
Debtors	2,000	
Balance at bank	1,980	
	43,800	43,800

On 31st March, 19.1, the stock was valued at £4,700 and rates paid in advance amounted to £60. £80 is to be provided for electricity consumed to that date.

Included in the sales and debtors was an amount of £600 for goods invoiced on sale or return on 1st February, 19.1, and which were still unsold on 31st March, 19.1. The cost price of these goods, which were not included in the stock, was £300.

Depreciation is to be provided at the rate of 20 per cent per annum on the cost of the delivery van and 2½ per cent per annum on the cost of furniture and fittings.

You are required to prepare—

(*a*) Trading and profit and loss accounts for the year to 31st March, 19.1, and
(*b*) a balance sheet as on that date.

Ignore taxation. (*Chartered Accountants.*)

8. X, Y, and Z are partners.

Their respective capitals in the business, as shown by their balance sheet on 31st December are: X, £3,000; Y, £2,200; Z, £800. The profit for the year, amounting to £1,600, has been credited to X, ½ share; Y and Z, ¼ each, and the books have been closed.

During the year they have withdrawn nothing beyond their salaries, which have already been charged to profit and loss account. It is found on 31st March next that interest on the partners' capital (5 per cent per annum), as provided by the partnership agreement, has been omitted.

Give the entries you would make in the books to correct this error.

(*West Riding of Yorkshire.*)

9. From the following particulars draw up the liabilities side of the balance sheet in two ways, in order to illustrate the difference in the presentation of accounts when the capitals are: (*a*) fixed, (*b*) not fixed—

Bills payable £1,706; sundry creditors £2,173; outstanding expenses £175; loan account R. Rudd, £1,500; capital accounts: R. Rudd £7,000; B. Butler £4,500; drawing accounts: Rudd £1,600; Butler £1,200; shares of profit: Rudd £1,473; Butler £1,157; interest on capitals: Rudd £350; Butler £225; interest on load: R. Rudd £75.

10. A. Bassett and P. Palmer are in partnership, sharing profits and losses two-thirds and one-third respectively. They agree to admit D. Dawson as a partner on condition that he brings into the business £1,500 capital and pays them a premium of £250 for a fifth share in the profits. Make the necessary entries in the books.

11. D. Dutton agrees to admit F. Fletcher into partnership on the following terms: (*a*) That Fletcher brings £2,300 capital into the business; (*b*) that £300 is to be paid out to Dutton and is to appear in the books of the partnership as goodwill. Make the necessary entries in the books.

12. The company of which you are chief accountant is considering the purchase of a partnership. It is agreed that a goodwill payment should be made, based on a three-year purchase of the weighted average profits over the past four years. The appropriate weights to be used are 1963: 1; 1964: 2; 1965: 3; 1966: 4.

The profits as shown by the accounts are—

		£
Year ended 31st July—	1966	23,470
	1965	20,137
	1964	12,721
	1963	15,100

You are asked to investigate the firm's books, which reveal—

(*a*) That goods costing £500 were delivered and taken into stock on 30th July, 1965, but included as purchases in the following year.

(*b*) That the method of valuing stock had been changed on 31st July, 1965, so as to include production overheads for the first time at the rate of 75 per cent on labour cost. It was agreed for goodwill calculations to reverse this decision. The labour content of stocks at 31st July, 1965, was £2,000 and at 31st July, 1966, £3,000.

(*c*) All plant in use at the end of each year had been depreciated at 10 per cent on the reducing balance method, but it was agreed that this should be adjusted to 20 per cent on the same basis. The book value shown on the latest balance sheet

was £18,000. There had been no sales over the period of the investigation; purchases were £3,800 in December 1965 and £5,600 in September 1963.

(*d*) In the stock sheets at 31st July, 1964, 100 tons of metal had been priced at £21 per ton instead of £12 per ton, and a sub-total of £374 had been carried forward as £437.

(*e*) In April 1964 a major repair to plant costing £1,600 had been charged to revenue, which it was agreed should be capitalized for goodwill calculations.

(*f*) The partners had made no charge for their own services, and it was agreed that an annual charge of £3,000 should be made to cover expected management costs, together with a bonus of 5 per cent of profits after charging the bonus.

Calculate the sum to be paid for goodwill. (*L.C.C.*)

13. Road, Lane and Street carry on business in partnership as retail drapers under an agreement which provides that—

(1) The partners are to be credited at the end of each year with interest at the rate of 5 per cent per annum on the balances at the credit of their respective capital accounts at the commencement of each year.

(2) No interest is to be charged on drawings.

(3) Profits and losses are to be shared in the proportions: Road 50 per cent, Lane 30 per cent, and Street 20 per cent. It is agreed, however, that Street's share of profit should be a minimum of £1,000 per annum, any deficiency to be borne by the other two partners in their profit-sharing ratios.

The Trial Balance of the partnership as at 31st December, 1960, is as follows—

	Dr £	*Cr* £
Partners' Capital Accounts at 1st January, 1960—		
Road		8,000
Lane		5,000
Street		3,000
Partners' Current Accounts at 1st January, 1960—		
Road		1,600
Lane		1,200
Street		800
Sales		44,500
Trade Creditors		3,700
Shop Fittings (cost 3,600)	2,200	
Freehold Premises at cost	6,000	
Leasehold Premises—		
Purchased during Year	4,500	
Additions and Alterations	2,500	
Purchases	28,000	
Stock at 1st January, 1960	4,200	
Salaries and Wages	6,400	
Office and Trade Expenses	4,520	
Rent, Rates and Insurance	1,050	
Professional Charges	350	
Debtors	2,060	
Provision for Doubtful Debts at 1st January, 1960		50
Bank Balance	4,370	
Drawings, other than monthly payments—		
Road	700	
Lane	600	
Street	400	
	67,850	67,850

You are given the following additional information—

(1) Stock at 31st December, 1960, is valued at £3,600.

(2) A debt of £60 is to be written off and the provision against the remaining debtors should be 5 per cent.

(3) Salaries and Wages include the following monthly drawings by the partners: Road, £50; Lane, £30; and Street, £25.

(4) Partners have, during the year, been supplied with goods from stock and it is agreed that these should be charged to them as follows: Road, £60; and Lane, £40.

(5) On 31st December, 1960, Rates paid in advance and Office and Trade Expenses owing are £250 and £240 respectively.

(6) Depreciation of Shop Fittings is to be provided at 5 per cent per annum on cost.

(7) Professional Charges include £250 fees paid in respect of the acquisition of the Leasehold Premises, which fees are to be capitalized.

(8) The cost of and the additions and alterations to the Leasehold Premises are to be written off over 25 years, commencing on 1st January, 1960, the period of the lease.

Calculations can be made to the nearest £.

You are required to prepare—

(*a*) the Trading and Profit and Loss Accounts for the year ended 31st December 1960;

(*b*) the Balance Sheet as at that date; and

(*c*) the Partners' Current Accounts in columnar form for the year ended 31st December, 1960. (*L.C.C.*)

14. Black and White, and Brown and Green, whose businesses are similar in character, decide to amalgamate and form a limited company to carry on the combined business, and they consult you upon the matter.

The respective Balance Sheets at 31st December, 1965, were—

	Black and White	Brown and Green
	£	£
Current Assets—		
Cash at Bank	5,250	2,175
Debtors, *less* Provision for Bad Debts	8,326	5,982
Stock	8,218	7,146
Fixed Assets, at Cost *less* Depreciation—		
Motor Vehicles	2,000	1,640
Fixtures and Fittings	1,049	1,629
Plant and Machinery	4,629	5,761
Freehold Premises	8,500	6,450
	37,972	30,783

	Black and White	Brown and Green
	£	£
Current Liabilities—		
Creditors	6,442	5,110
Accrued Charges	280	323
Current Accounts—		
Black	800	
White	450	
Capitals—		
Black	16,000	
White	14,000	
Brown		15,500
Green		9,850
	37,972	30,783

The profits for each of the three years to 31st December, 1965, after charging Depreciation but before charging Interest on Capital and ignoring Taxation, were—

	Black and White	Brown and Green
	£	£
1963	6,270	4,850
1964	8,100	5,250
1965	7,950	5,782

Black and White, share profits in the ratio of 8:7, and Brown and Green in the ratio of 3:2.

State briefly your suggestions as to—

(1) The basis for amalgamation; and

(2) The capitalization of the company and the division of the capital amongst the four partners.

15. George and Fred are in partnership sharing profits and losses two-thirds and one-third respectively. On 1st January, 1964, Mike is admitted as a partner bringing in £8,000 in cash, part as payment for goodwill and the balance as capital. He is to receive one-fifth of the profits, the old partners continuing in their existing ratios. The payment for goodwill is to be calculated at two years' purchase of the average profits (unweighted) over the last four years.

The unaudited profits as shared by the partners were—

	£
1960	4,500
1961	6,900
1962	5,100
1963	4,800

The unaudited profits for the year ended 31st December, 1964, were £6,500 and the capital accounts of the partners on 1st January, 1965, after being credited with their share of these profits and debited with drawings for the year were—

	£
George	9,600
Fred	5,900
Mike	6,400

At this date it is decided to have the accounts for the last five years audited and any discrepancies, including the calculation of goodwill for Mike's admission, adjusted.

The auditors discovered the following—

(1) In 1962 depreciation of £100 on plant had been charged instead of £1,000.

(2) Closing stocks were—

understated at 31st December, 1962 by £300
overstated at 31st December, 1963 by £600
understated at 31st December, 1964 by £150

(3) Provision created in 1963 for a claim by a customer for damages of £1,200 was found to be unnecessary, as the case was lost by the customer and the amount written back in 1964.

(4) An invoice for electricity amounting to £150 was omitted from the closing provisions for 1963.

(5) An item of plant costing £300 on which depreciation of 10 per cent should have been charged was written off as revenue in 1964.

You are required to show in columnar form—

(*a*) how Mike's £8,000 is dealt with on his initial entry into the business;

(*b*) starting with the balances shown above, the adjustments in the capital accounts in respect of the auditors' findings. (*L.C.C.*)

16. E. Helm and P. Porter are in partnership, sharing profits and losses equally. Helm agrees to buy out P. Porter, and the position of affairs on this date is as follows—

BALANCE SHEET AS AT 1ST JANUARY, 19..

Liabilities	£	*Assets*	£
Sundry Creditors	1,265	Cash	1,525
Capital—		Sundry Debtors	4,624
E. Helm	3,110	Office Furniture	336
P. Porter	2,110		
	6,485		6,485

Helm is to take over the office furniture at £310, to allow Porter £625 for his share of the goodwill, and to pay him his proportion as and when realized, interest to be taken into account at 5 per cent per annum. A loss of £224 is sustained on the sundry debtors; and a discount of £30 is obtained from the creditors. The latter were paid at an average date of four months, and the debtors were realized at an average date of eight months from the date of dissolution. Helm paid Porter £550 on 1st March, £650 on 1st June, £750 on 1st September, and the balance on 31st December. Draw up the account current between Helm and Porter, and show the final payment made to Porter on 31st December.

17. Fern, Moss and Hay carry on business in partnership and share profits and losses in the proportions of five-eighths, two-eights and one-eighth respectively.

The following is the Trial Balance extracted from the books as on 31st March, 1964—

	Debit £	Credit £
Bank Overdraft		6,280
Bank Charges	600	
Capital Accounts—Fern		8,200
Moss		3,000
Hay		1,600
Current Accounts—Fern		820
Moss		630
Hay	60	
Freehold Land and Buildings	14,000	
Incidental Trade expenses	280	
Loan Account—Fern		7,600
Machinery and Plant at cost	16,200	
Office Salaries	420	
Purchases	34,500	
Professional Charges	40	
Provision for depreciation on Machinery and Plant at 1st April, 1963		6,500
Provision for doubtful debts at 1st April, 1963		400
Rates, Telephone and Insurance	440	
Sales		54,340
Sundry Debtors	12,680	
Sundry Creditors		6,010
Stock on hand at 1st April, 1963	7,920	
Wages	8,180	
	95,380	95,380

Included in the item "machinery and plant" are payments duly made on the prescribed dates, under a hire-purchase agreement entered into on 30th November, 1963, from which the following information is obtained: cash price of machine £1,600, deposit £160, interest £180, payment to be made by 12 equal monthly instalments on the last day of each month, the first payment to be made on 31st December, 1963.

It is not desired that an interest Suspense Account should be opened and there is agreement between the partners for the interest to be apportioned equally over the term of the contract.

The following information is to be taken into account—

(1) Debts totalling £94, for which provision was made on 1st April, 1963, are to be written off and those which were considered to be doubtful on 31st March, 1964 amounted to £450.

(2) £168 was owing on 31st March, 1964 for professional charges.

(3) £26 was owing in respect of telephone charges and the annual premium £104 due 31st December, 1963, as regards comprehensive insurance had been paid on 10th January, 1964.

(4) Hay is to receive credit for salary £620.

(5) The loan from Fern was paid into the firm's bank account on 1st October, 1963.

(6) Provision for depreciation of machinery and plant is to be made at 10 per cent on cost.

(7) The valuation of the stock on hand at 31st March, 1964 was £8,300.

Prepare: Trading and Profit and Loss Accounts for the year ended 31st March, 1964 and draw up a Balance Sheet as on that date. (*A.C.C.A.*)

18. (*a*) The profits of the partnership of Austin, Bell & Cooper amounted, on 31st December, to £2,521·25. On 1st January the capitals of the partners were as follows: Austin £6,250; Bell £4,500; Cooper £4,500. The partners' drawings were: Austin *nil*; Bell £350; and Cooper £350. Interest is to be allowed on capital at 5 per cent per annum. Profits are divisible thus: Austin $\frac{3}{7}$; Bell and Cooper $\frac{2}{7}$ each. Draw up the profit and loss and capital accounts.

(*b*) On 1st January following they agree to take into partnership P. Peters, with an eighth share of the profits. What amount must he bring in to entitle him to such a share on a par with the capital of the others as at the previous 31st December, and what will be the new proportions for division?

19. D. K. Tooth, a dentist, became the lessee of a house on 1st January, 1965, at a rental of £420 per annum and paid a year's rent in advance. He entered into an agreement with A. Kinfoot, a chiropodist, to share the ground floor with him as from that date for their separate practices, and they engaged a joint receptionist at a salary of £35 per month. It was stipulated that the expenses and any income from the house should be shared as to D. K. Tooth three-fourths and A. Kinfoot one-fourth. The latter agreed to rent the garage as from 1st January, 1965, paying therefor £1·25 per week.

A joint bank account was opened with £1,000, D. K. Tooth paying in £600 and A. Kinfoot £400.

The first floor was let on 1st March, 1965, to a firm of stockbrokers at a rental of £204 per annum with an annual additional charge of £84 for services, such sums to be paid quarterly in advance on 1st March, 1st June, 1st September, and 1st December. The tenants were to pay their own rates. The second floor was converted into a flat, and a caretaker entered into occupancy of same on 1st April, 1965, living there free of rent and rates, and was paid a salary of £14 per month for the services of himself and his wife.

Payments out of the joint bank account, in addition to salaries to 31st December, 1965, were as follows—

	£
Fittings taken over	80
Cost of conversion of second floor	210
Rates on ground floor and second-floor flat including £30 for the half-year to 31st March, 1966	75
Cleaners	96
Repairs	23
General Expenses	50

The rent of the first floor was received on the due dates and paid into the joint bank account. At 31st December, 1965, A. Kinfoot was owing four weeks' garage rent.

By agreement D. K. Tooth took over fittings to the value of £30 and this amount was to be charged to him. It was decided to write £30 off the cost of conversion including the fittings.

Prepare—

(1) a summary of the joint bank account to 31st December, 1965;

(2) an Income and Expenditure Account for the year ended on that date, showing the cost to D. K. Tooth and A. Kinfoot of their rooms; and

(3) a Balance Sheet as on that date showing the capital invested by each in the venture. (*A.C.C.A.*)

20. *X*, *Y* and *Z* are in partnership sharing profits in the ratios 3:2:1 after salaries of £1,000 per annum to *Y* and £500 per annum to *Z*. Interest at 5 per cent per annum is allowed on Capital Accounts but no interest is allowed on Current Accounts or

charged on drawings. *X* has guaranteed that *Z*'s participation in profits in any year (including salary but excluding interest on capital) shall not be less than £2,000.

Their book-keeper extracted a Trial Balance as at 31st December, 1962, and presented draft accounts to you as follows—

DRAFT BALANCE SHEET

	£		£
Capital Account—*X*	16,000	Current Account at 31st December, 1961—*Z*	518
Y	10,000	Drawings—*X*	4,137
Z	4,000	*Y*	3,029
Current Accounts at 31st December, 1961—*X*	925	*Z*	1,965
Y	317	Stock at 31st December, 1962	3,684
Bad Debts Provision at 31st December, 1961	439	Debtors	10,019
		Freehold Premises at cost	12,200
		Plant at cost *less* Depreciation as at 31st December, 1961	3,619
Creditors	2,461	Cash at Bank	6,274
Unappropriated Profits	11,328	Cash in Hand	25
	45,470		45,470

DRAFT PROFIT AND LOSS ACCOUNT

	£		£
Stock at 31st December, 1961	2,613	Stock at 31st December, 1962	3,684
Purchases	35,967	Sales	61,572
Salaries and Wages	10,355	Bad Debts Recovered	54
Heat, Light and Power	1,449		
Machinery Maintenance	1,044		
Selling Expenses	964		
Bad Debts written off	340		
General Expenses	1,250		
Profit	11,328		
	65,310		65,310

Salaries and wages include the salaries (but not commissions) of *R* and *S* but not partners' salaries.

R and *S* are managers remunerated as follows—

(*a*) Salaries of £1,500 and £1,000 per annum respectively plus—

(*b*) Commissions of 2 per cent and 1 per cent respectively of the profits computed before making any transfers to the partners, before charging any managerial commission, but after charging all employees' salaries except the salary of the manager concerned.

The bad debts provision is to be 5 per cent of debtors.

Obsolete stock valued at £369 in the valuation as at 31st December, 1962, is to be written off.

Plant scrapped, having a depreciated value of £219 on 31st December, 1961, is to be written off.

Machinery maintenance is found to include the purchase of a new machine for £360.

Depreciation of plant is to be provided at 10 per cent of written-down value.

Unsold goods sent to customers on sale or return, invoiced *pro forma* at £219 (being cost plus 50 per cent) have been included in sales, although unsold at 31st December, 1962.

You are required to prepare—

(*a*) Trading and Profit and Loss Accounts for the year ended 31st December, 1962, and a Balance Sheet as at that date; and

(*b*) Partners' Current Accounts in columnar form. Ignore taxation.

(*L.C.C.*)

21. A, B, and C enter into partnership on 1st January. Each partner is to draw a like sum per annum for his services, and to share profits according to capital, and according to the time the capital is in the business. On 1st January, A pays in £5,000; on 1st April B pays in £4,000; on 1st June C pays in £4,000; on 1st November, A pays in a further £2,000. The net profits on 31st December amounted to £2,520. How much of the latter sum should each partner receive?

22. S. Simpson agreed to take W. Winder into partnership. Winder was to bring in £6,000. Of this, £2,205 was to be paid for a three-sevenths share of Simpson's profits, calculated at two years' purchase of their average amount, and the remainder was to be Winder's capital. Simpson was to leave one-half of this purchase money in the concern, in order to make his capital up to half as much again as that of Winder. What were Simpson's average profits, and what was his capital before the partnership?

23. X retires from business and agrees to dispose of it to Y. The assets are: plant £2,500; stock £3,750; debtors £4,520. The liabilities, which are to be discharged by Y, are: sundry creditors £3,750. Y brings in as his capital £3,500. The purchase money is to be paid by instalments of £1,000 each year, interest at 5 per cent per annum being charged on the unpaid balance. Y is also to pay £2,000 for goodwill out of the profits, at the rate of one-fourth of the profits each year, after charging interest on the unpaid purchase money. No interest, however, is to be charged on the sums due for goodwill. The profits for the next five years were as follows: 1st year £1,750; 2nd year £1,950; 3rd year £2,050; 4th year £2,500; 5th year £2,065. Show the profit and loss account, the business purchase account, and the goodwill account, all up to the completion of the latter.

24. A. Grant and his two sons John and Henry are in partnership as farmers. A. Grant is entitled to a half share of the profits up to a maximum of £1,000 per annum and interest on his loan in accordance with the Partnership Act, 1890, his sons sharing the remaining profits equally.

The Partners draw salaries for their services as agreed from time to time.

A full set of books is not kept but all receipts and payments are passed through a banking account.

From the following particulars prepare a Profit and Loss Account for the year to 31st March, 1964, and a Balance Sheet at that date.

STATEMENT OF AFFAIRS AT 31ST MARCH, 1963

	£		£
Creditor for Fertilizer	684	Implements	2,236
Loan from A. Grant	2,000	Livestock	7,132
		Produce	1,304
Capital Accounts			
A. Grant	7,000	Growing crops	1,046
J. Grant	3,300	Cash at bank	126
H. Grant	3,300	Debtor for Crops sold	4,440
	16,284		16,284

SUMMARY OF BANK ACCOUNT YEAR TO 31ST MARCH, 1964

	£		£
Balance 31st March, 1963	126	Livestock	2,400
Sales of Crops	9,484	Fertilizers	750
Sales of Livestock	5,954	Feeding Stuffs	1,524
Sales of Eggs	210	Seeds	262
Sales of Wool	102	Labour and National Insurance	4,925
Government Grant for Water Supply	400	Veterinary Services	32
Government Subsidy for Fertilizer	50	Accountancy and Audit	75
		New Water Supply	800
		Market Expenses	104
		Additions to Implements	624
		Tractor Expenses	712
		Partners' Salaries	
		A. Grant	1,500
		J. Grant	1,000
		H. Grant	1,000
		Balance 31st March, 1964	618
	16,326		16,326

From inspection of the vouchers you find that at 31st March, 1964, there were—

	£
Debtors for Crops sold	3,804
Debtors for Cattle sold	84
Creditors for Fertilizers	292
Creditors for Feeding Stuffs	844
Sales of Straw paid for by Contra against the local grocers' account for supplies to A. Grant's household	50

and that poultry and eggs from the farm had been consumed by the partners to the value of £52 by A. Grant, £26 by J. Grant and £26 by H. Grant.

A professional valuation at 31st March, 1964, showed the following—

	£
Livestock	9,128
Produce and Stores	1,752
Growing Crops	828
Implements	2,400
Water Supply	360

The licence and insurance of the tractor had been paid in advance to the extent of £20.

25. Briar and Thorne entered into a joint venture to buy and sell a quantity of smoking requisites. It was agreed that Briar should receive a commission of 2 per cent on all sales, in consideration for which he was to bear all losses from bad debts. Subject to this arrangement, profits and losses were to be shared equally.

On 2nd January, 1965, Briar purchased goods for £6,800 for which he paid £4,800 in cash, and accepted bills of exchange for £800 and £1,200.

On 3rd January, Briar sent to Thorne goods which had cost £2,750, and Thorne paid £3,500 to Briar.

On 9th January, Briar sold goods to Street for £420 and to Road for £250 and they accepted bills of exchange for the amounts respectively due from them. Briar endorsed both these bills over to Thorne, who discounted them. (Ignore discounting charges.)

On 3rd February, Briar sold goods for £1,800. On delivery the customer rejected goods invoiced at £90, and these goods were collected by Thorne, who sold them to another customer for £110.

On 11th February, Street met his bill, but Road's bill was dishonoured. Road was insolvent with no assets.

On 5th March, Thorne paid the bill for £800 which had been accepted by Briar, and Briar paid the second bill for £1,200.

During March, 1965, Briar sold the remainder of the goods in his possession for £2,910, and Thorne's sales amounted to £3,400. Bad debts (apart from the amount due from Road) were £42, of which £30 was in respect of sales by Briar, and £12 was in respect of sales by Thorne.

On 30th April, 1965, the venture was closed. Thorne took over the stock in his possession at a valuation of £500, and the sum required to settle accounts between the ventures was paid by the party accountable.

You are required to show—

(*a*) The accounts which would appear in the books of Briar and Thorne respectively to record the joint venture, and

(*b*) a memorandum Joint Venture account, showing the net profit.

(*L.C.C.*)

26. Powell and Johns entered into a joint speculation with the object of buying and selling second-hand motor vehicles. A joint banking account was not opened, and each of the parties made purchases, subsequently selling the vehicles and paying incidental expenses through his own separate business.

It was agreed that profits and losses should be shared equally and that each party should render to the other a quarterly statement of his transactions and expenses.

Any vehicles unsold at the end of each quarter were to be taken over by the party buying them, at their trade list price.

During the three months ended 31st March, 1964, the following transactions took place—

1964	
Jan 5	Powell bought two cars for £1,240 and paid storage rent £30.
Feb 6	Johns sold one of these cars for £1,420.
8	Powell sold the other for £150.
Mar 10	Johns bought a further four cars for £3,380 and paid £60 for cleaning and repairing them.
15	Powell sold two of these cars for £5,250 and paid commission and advertising £66.
31	Powell's travelling and hotel expenses were £240 for the quarter while Johns had paid out £160 for similar expenses.
	The trade list price of the two unsold cars was £1,800.

Assuming that the required statements have been exchanged, prepare an account giving the result of the joint venture as a whole and show how the foregoing transactions should be recorded in each party's books, settlement between them being effected by cheque on 30th April, 1964.

27. Rees and Ford are Iron and Steel merchants, each carrying on business on his own account. From time to time, however, they enter into joint transactions and share profits and losses equally, passing the entries through their own books of account and rendering each other statements of business done.

The following transactions took place during 1961—

January	Rees bought scrap for £2,480 and paid £60 for storage.
February	Ford sold part of his scrap for £2,840, Rees disposing of the rest for £300.
March	Ford bought steel for £6,760 and paid £120 for sorting and delivery.
	Rees sold half of this steel for £10,500 and paid commission and advertising £130, the remainder being taken into Ford's own stock at a value of £3,718.
	It was agreed that Rees and Ford should be allowed £480 and £320 respectively for general expenses of the venture.

Prepare a Statement showing the result of all these transactions and show the entries in each party's books.

28. J S, an estate agent, and H R, a plumber, decide to buy an old house, convert it into flats and then sell it.

The following receipts and payments arose—

	£
By J S—	
Purchase of the house, including legal charges	3,300
Payment of general and water rates	73
Payment of electricity and gas charges	60
Rents received from tenants	260
Amount realized from the sale of the property, less legal charges	6,590
By H R—	
Payment of the building contractors' accounts	1,400
Payment of a cleaner's wages	40
Proceeds received from the sale of scrap timber and piping	60
Rents received for lock-up garages at the premises	10

These additional matters should be taken into account—

(1) J S occupied part of the house during the conversion and he and H R have agreed that the value of this accommodation, which has not been included in the "rents received from tenants", is £35.

(2) One of the tenants left owing £18 in rent; as this person had been given his

tenancy on a reference provided by H R, it was agreed that this loss should be borne by him alone.

(3) The agreed value of the agent's fees for work done, without payment, by J S was £200 and the agreed value of plumbing work carried out by H R, also without payment, was £300. These items are to be credited to the respective joint-venturers in the final settlement.

(4) The profit or loss on the enterprise, including the rents less the expenses, are to be shared by J S and H R in the ratio of 3:2 respectively.

You are required to prepare—

(*a*) the joint venture accounts in the individual books of account of J S and H R;

(*b*) a memorandum joint venture account showing the profit or loss on the enterprise and its division between the joint-venturers.

29. Brown and Green, with their wives, went for a holiday together to Majorca. The fares and hotel expenses of the party were paid for beforehand through a travel agency and are not included in the figures dealt with below, which are concerned only with "spending money." It was agreed beforehand that all holiday expenses proper should be shared equally between the two families, whichever member of the party might make the individual payments, but that if any member of the party should spend anything on personal items (such as clothes or presents for friends) he or she should bear such expenditure personally, and to that end should keep a note of any such items. For accounting purposes between the members of the party all expenditure in pesetas (the currency in use in Majorca) was to be converted at 150 pesetas to the £, any differences on exchange being regarded as "joint" expenditure. The husbands were to be ultimately responsible for the whole of the holiday expenses and any final settlement was to be in sterling after the return to England.

The following statement shows the relevant particulars—

	Mr. Brown	Mrs. Brown	Mr. Green	Mrs. Green
Sterling	£	£	£	£
Cost of currency obtained from banks at home	75·00	*Nil*	30·00	*Nil*
Carried on leaving home	8·50	5·75	10·00	4·25
Travellers' cheques cashed	*Nil*	*Nil*	*Nil*	20·00
Remaining on return home	3·60	5·75	4·35	1·65
Proceeds of unspent pesetas	10·85	*Nil*	2·70	*Nil*
Personal expenses	*Nil*	*Nil*	*Nil*	3·00
Currency	*Pesetas*	*Pesetas*	*Pesetas*	*Pesetas*
Purchased in England	11,350	*Nil*	4,540	*Nil*
Proceeds of travellers' cheques cashed abroad	*Nil*	*Nil*	*Nil*	2,650
Unspent balances exchanged back into sterling	1,650	*Nil*	450	*Nil*
Personal expenses	*Nil*	1,700	350	900

Each husband had supplied his own wife with pesetas according to her requirements, and on return she handed back to him any unspent balances for inclusion in the amounts paid into the respective banks.

While in Majorca Mr. Green had lent Mr. Brown 1,200 pesetas (not repaid), the Brown family having underestimated their currency requirements.

Prepare a statement, in as simple a form as possible, to show the amount due (in sterling) from the one husband to the other on the final settlement and the amount due from each wife to her husband. (*R.S.A.*)

30. Duke and Lord entered into a joint venture to buy and sell second-hand cars. Profits and losses were to be shared: Duke two-thirds and Lord one-third.

On 16th August, 19.., Duke purchased two cars for £320 and £480 respectively. He incurred expenditure of £120 on repairs and on 1st September, 19.., sold one of the cars for £400 and on 10th September, 19.., the other car for £620.

On 12th September, 19.., he purchased a further car for £600 which was sold on 20th September, 19.., for £800, which amount was paid to Lord who paid it into his own bank account.

On 12th August, 19.., Lord purchased a car for £400 which he sold for £500 on the 15th August, 19.., having incurred expenses of £40 on it. This car was returned by the customer on 20th August, 19.., who was allowed £480 for it. As this car was still unsold on 30th September, 19.., it was agreed it should be taken over by Duke at a valuation of £450.

On 30th September, 19.., the sum required in full settlement as between Duke and Lord was paid by the party accountable.

You are required to prepare—

(*a*) the joint venture account as it would appear in the books of Duke recording his transactions with the joint venture, and

(*b*) a memorandum account for the joint venture, showing the net profit.

(*Chartered Accountants.*)

CHAPTER 18

DISSOLUTION OF PARTNERSHIP

The business man, the acquirer vast,
After the assiduous years surveying results, preparing for departure,
Devises houses and lands to his children, bequeaths stocks, goods, funds
for a school or hospital,
Leaves money to certain companions to buy tokens, souvenirs of gems
and gold.

WALT WHITMAN—*My Legacy*

When is a Partnership Dissolved? Subject to any agreement between the partners, a partnership is dissolved—

(*a*) If entered into for a fixed term, by the expiration of that term.

(*b*) If entered into for a single adventure or undertaking, by the termination of that adventure or undertaking.

(*c*) If entered into for an undefined time, by any general partner giving notice to the other or others of his intention to dissolve the partnership.

In the last-mentioned case the partnership is dissolved as from the date mentioned in the notice as the date of dissolution, or, if no date is so mentioned, as from the date of the communication of the notice.

Dissolution by Bankruptcy, Death, Charge, or Illegality. Subject to any agreement between the partners, every partnership is dissolved as regards all the partners by the death or bankruptcy of any partner.

A partnership may, at the option of the other partners, be dissolved if any partner suffers his share of the partnership property to be charged under the Partnership Act for his separate debt.

A partnership is in every case dissolved by the happening of any event which makes it unlawful for the business of the firm to be carried on or for the members of the firm to carry it on in partnership.

Dissolution by the Court. On application by a partner the court may decree a dissolution of the partnership in any of the following cases—

(*a*) When a partner is found lunatic by inquisition, or in Scotland by cognition, or is shown to the satisfaction of the court to be of permanently unsound mind, in either of which cases the application may be made as well on behalf of that partner by his committee or next friend or person having title to intervene as by any other partner.

(*b*) When a partner, other than the partner suing, becomes in any other way permanently incapable of performing his part of the partnership contract.

(*c*) When a partner, other than the partner suing, has been guilty of such conduct, as in the opinion of the court, regard being had to the nature of the business, is calculated to affect prejudicially the carrying on of the business.

(*d*) When a partner, other than the partner suing, wilfully or persistently commits a breach of the partnership agreement, or otherwise so conducts himself in matters relating to the partnership business that it is not reasonably practicable for the other partner or partners to carry on the business in partnership with him.

(*e*) When the business of the partnership can only be carried on at a loss.

(*f*) Whenever in any case circumstances have arisen which, in the opinion of the court, render it just and equitable that the partnership be dissolved.

Notice of Dissolution or Change. Where a person deals with a firm after a change in its constitution, he is entitled to treat all apparent members of the old firm as still being members of the firm until he has notice of the change.

An advertisement in the *London Gazette* as to a firm whose principal place of business is in England or Wales, in the *Edinburgh Gazette* as to a firm whose principal place of business is in Scotland, and in the *Dublin Gazette* as to a firm whose principal place of business is in the Republic of Ireland, shall be notice as to persons who had no dealings with the firm before the date of the dissolution or change so advertised. A firm whose principal place of business is in Northern Ireland is required to give notice in the *Belfast Gazette.*

Bearing in mind that this advertisement only serves as notice to those who have not had previous dealings, it is considered advisable for the retiring partner to circularize all creditors and obtain a written release from future debts from the other partners if he is to be sure of complete freedom from further liability.

Continuing Authority of Partners for Winding-up Purposes. After the dissolution of a partnership the authority of each partner to bind the firm, and the other rights and obligations of the partners, continue notwithstanding the dissolution so far as may be necessary to wind up the affairs of the partnership, and to complete transactions begun but unfinished at the time of the dissolution.

Provided that the firm is in no case bound by the acts of a partner who has become bankrupt; but this proviso does not affect the liability of any person who has after the bankruptcy represented himself or knowingly suffered himself to be represented as a partner of the bankrupt.

Rule for Distribution of Assets. By Sect. 44 of the Partnership Act, 1890, in settling accounts between the partners after a dissolution of partnership, the following rules must, subject to any agreement, be observed—

(*a*) Losses, including losses and deficiencies of capital, shall be paid first out of profits, next out of capital, and lastly, if necessary, by the partners individually in the proportion in which they were entitled to share profits.

(*b*) The assets of the firm including the sums, if any, contributed by the partners to make up losses or deficiencies of capital, shall be applied in the following manner and order—

(1) In paying the debts and liabilities of the firm to persons who are not partners therein.

(2) In paying to each partner *rateably* what is due from the firm to him for advances as distinguished from capital.

(3) In paying to each partner *rateably* what is due from the firm to him in respect of capital.

(4) The ultimate residue, if any, shall be divided among the partners in the proportion in which profits are divisible.

Formula for Treatment of a Dissolution of Partnership. For making the necessary entries in the books in connexion with an ordinary dissolution of partnership, the following formula will prove useful to the student—

1. Open a realization account and debit it with the total of the assets (except cash or a debit balance of any of the partners' capital accounts).

2. Open accounts for cash, creditors, partners' loans, partners' capitals, and enter therein the balances as in the balance sheet.

3. Debit cash and credit realization account with the proceeds of the sale of the assets. If any of the assets are not sold but are taken over by one of the partners, then debit that partner's capital account and credit realization account with the agreed value.

4. Credit cash and debit realization account with the expenses of winding up.

5. Pay off (*a*) creditors, (*b*) partners' loans, i.e. credit cash and debit these accounts.

6. Balance the realization account and transfer the balance, profit or loss as the case may be, to the partners' capital accounts. If, as the result of a loss on realization, the capital account of one of the partners is put temporarily in debit, that partner must bring in cash to repay to the firm his indebtedness; debit cash and credit partner's capital account. The deficiency may also be made good by transfer from such partner's loan account, if he has one.

7. Balance partner's capital accounts and divide the cash according to these credit balances of capital.

NOTE. Students often divide the cash between the partners in the same proportion as *profits and losses*, but this is quite wrong. The debit balance of cash at the close must be equal to the *total* of the credit balances of the capital accounts; and the cash paid out to each partner must be *the amount standing to the credit of his capital account*, no more, no less.

Garner *v.* Murray. Whenever a partner is unable to repay to the firm his indebtedness, the ruling of *Garner* v. *Murray* must be applied. This decision by Mr. Justice Joyce, in November, 1903, was "that the solvent partners are only liable to make good their share of the deficiency, and that the remaining assets should be divided among them in proportion to their capitals." In other words, the loss caused by the default of an insolvent partner is to be borne in proportion to *capital*, and not in the proportion that ordinary losses are to be borne. After considerable discussion and controversy, it is thought that the correct interpretation of this ruling is for the solvent partners *to bring in cash* to meet their share of the loss on realization.

For the benefit of accountancy students it may, perhaps, be as well to give a short summary of the *Garner* v. *Murray* case, and of the great controversy to which it gave rise amongst professional accountants.

Garner, Murray, and Wilkins entered into partnership under a parol agreement to contribute capital in certain unequal shares but to divide profits equally. On dissolution the assets realized sufficient to pay the creditors and advances of two of the partners, but were insufficient to repay the partners' capitals. The position was approximately as follows—

BALANCE SHEET

Liabilities	£	*Assets*	£
Capital—		Cash	1,916
Garner	2,500	Wilkins—Overdrawn	263
Murray	314	Deficiency of Firm	635
	2,814		2,814

Wilkins was insolvent, and unable to contribute anything. Mr. Justice Joyce held that a loss arising through the default of one of the partners must be distinguished from an ordinary trading loss or loss on realization. That, provided outside creditors' claims had been met, the liability of each separate partner was limited to making good *his* share of the deficiency. That, in the case in question, each partner should be treated as liable to contribute an equal third share of the deficiency, and that the assets should then be applied in paying each partner rateably what was due to him in respect of capital.

The decision caused great surprise in accountancy circles, which had not previously discriminated between an *internal* and an *external* loss, i.e. between a loss occasioned by the default of a partner, and an ordinary trading loss. As previously explained, under the old method the £263 would have been added to the £635, and the total loss of £898 would have been borne by the solvent partners in the same *relative* proportions in which they had previously shared profits, namely, 1:1, or one-half each. The effect of Mr. Justice Joyce's decision, however, was that the £635 should be shared by *all* the partners in the same way that they shared ordinary profits and losses, i.e. one-third each; but that Wilkins's £263 and share of deficiency should be borne by the solvent partners in the proportion of their capitals. For although the solvent partners are not liable to "make good" the insolvent partner's overdraft and share of deficiency, yet inasmuch as his default causes a deficiency of assets, it follows that the solvent partners actually *bear* the loss of this amount. And as this loss represents a deficiency of cash, it follows that the solvent partners bear this loss of cash in the same proportion in which they share the actual cash, namely, in proportion to their capital, i.e. in the ratio which each partner's capital bears to the total capital of the partners. This can be plainly seen from the worked example No. 4.

The decision occasioned much comment and discussion, which finally developed into a sharp controversy, raging chiefly round the precise meaning of the judge's words, "making good his share of the deficiency." Many accountants contended it meant that the solvent partner should bring in cash; others contended this was unnecessary, so long as there was a sufficient credit balance in his capital account to liquidate his share of the firm's deficiency. The arguments and counter-arguments are as follows—

1. The solvent partner should bring in cash, which should be debited to cash account and credited to the deficiency account, thus actually carrying out the letter of the law, and "making good" their shares of the deficiency. The arguments against this course are: (1) that it is unreasonable to ask a partner to bring in cash when he already has a credit balance in his capital account; (2) that it might be impossible, as the partner might have sunk the whole of his capital in the business; (3) that it is quite contrary to accountancy practice in other cases, where, if the result of a realization is to place a partner's account in debit, such deficit is often made good by transfer from his current account, and even from his loan account if he has one. In reply, it is urged that these objections are not points of equity but merely sentimental reasons and questions of convenience, which do not invalidate the argument that this method fulfils the letter of the law.

2. The solvent partners should have their shares of the deficiency debited to their capital accounts. In opposition to this course it is contended: (1) that debiting a loss to capital is not making it good; (2) that the capital accounts as per last balance sheet represent the partners' agreed shares of such capital, and are, according to the judgement, to form the basis for distribution of the assets; (3) that to debit the shares of deficiency to the capital accounts would alter the capital accounts and destroy the basis for the distribution of the assets; (4) that this flaw in fulfilling the conditions of the judgement vitiates this method.

3. The solvent partners should be shown on the balance sheet as debtors for their shares of the deficiency. This would prevent the capital accounts being altered. The objections raised to this course are: (1) that it is an attempt to carry out the judgement by means of a paper entry instead of an actual contribution; (2) that in the case of fixed capitals a partner who had a credit balance in his current account could offset it against this debit, and thus render this method futile.

1. Profit on Realization

Example 1

Long and Short are in partnership, sharing profits and losses two-thirds and one-third respectively. The state of affairs at the date of the dissolution is as follows—

BALANCE SHEET

Liabilities	£	*Assets*	£
Sundry Creditors	2,750	Cash	725
Capital—		Sundry Debtors	2,168
Long	3,540	Stock	4,029
Short	2,107	Fixtures & Fittings	1,475
	8,397		8,397

The fixtures and fittings are taken over by Long at the agreed price of £1,425. The debtors and stock realize £7,265, and the expenses of winding up are £115. Close the books of the firm, showing the ledger accounts.

REALIZATION ACCOUNT

		£		£
Sundry Assets		7,672	Cash	7,265
Cash (Expenses)		115	Long (Capital) Fixtures taken over as agreed	1,425
Balance (profit)—				
Long, $\frac{2}{3}$	£602			
Short, $\frac{1}{3}$	301			
		903		
		8,690		8,690

CASH BOOK

	£		£
Balance	725	Realization A/c (Expenses)	115
Realization A/c—		Sundry Creditors	2,750
Proceeds of Sale of Assets	7,265	Balance—	
		Long	2,717
		Short	2,408
	7,990		7,990

SUNDRY CREDITORS

	£		£
Cash	2,750	Balance	2,750

LONG, CAPITAL

	£		£
Fixtures, etc.	1,425	Balance	3,540
Cash	2,717	Realization A/c—	
		$\frac{2}{3}$ Profit	602
	4,142		4,142

SHORT, CAPITAL

	£		£
Cash	2,408	Balance	2,107
		Realization A/c—	
		$\frac{1}{3}$ Profit	301
	2,408		2,408

2. Loss on Realization

Example 2

Topping and Bottomly are in partnership, sharing profits and losses two-thirds and one-third respectively. The following is the state of affairs at the date of dissolution—

BALANCE SHEET

Liabilities	£	*Assets*	£
Sundry Creditors	3,344	Cash	638
Topping (Loan A/c)	1,200	Sundry Debtors	3,146
Capital—		Stock	4,285
Topping	4,025	Fixtures & Fittings	1,275
Bottomly	2,275	Goodwill	1,500
	10,844		10,844

The debtors, stock, fixtures, and fittings realize £8,426, and the expenses of winding up are £132. During the realization, events actualize a contingent liability of £125, which has, therefore, to be paid in addition to the other creditors. Close the books of the firm, showing the ledger accounts.

REALIZATION ACCOUNT

	£			£
Sundry Assets	10,206	Cash (Proceeds of Sale of Assets)		8,426
Cash (Expenses)	132	Balance (loss)—		
„ (Contingent Liability)	125	Topping, $\frac{2}{3}$	£1,358	
		Bottomly $\frac{1}{3}$,	679	
				2,037
	10,463			10,463

CASH BOOK

	£		£
Balance	638	Realization A/c (Expenses)	132
Realization A/c		Realization A/c (Contingent	
Proceeds of Sale of Assets	8,426	Liability)	125
		Sundry Creditors	3,344
		Topping (Loan A/c)	1,200
		Balance—	
		Topping	2,667
		Bottomly	1,596
	9,064		9,064

SUNDRY CREDITORS

	£		£
Cash	3,344	Balance	3,344

TOPPING, LOAN ACCOUNT

	£		£
Cash	1,200	Balance	1,200

TOPPING, CAPITAL

	£		£
Realization A/c, ⅔ Loss .	1,358	Balance	4,025
Cash	2,667		
	4,025		4,025

BOTTOMLY, CAPITAL

	£		£
Realization A/c, ⅓ Loss . .	679	Balance	2,275
Cash	1,596		
	2,275		2,275

3. Loss on Realization, necessitating the partners bringing in cash to meet the deficits, and so enabling the creditors to be paid in full

Example 3

High and Lowe are in partnership, sharing profits and losses three-fifths and two-fifths respectively. At the date of dissolution their capitals are High £765, and Lowe £430. The creditors amount to £2,750. The balance of cash in hand is £76, while the other assets realize £2,543, the expenses of winding up being £54. The partners bring in the cash to meet their respective deficits. Close the books ofthe firm, showing the ledger accounts.

CASH BOOK

	£		£
Balance	76	Realization A/c (Expenses) .	54
Realization A/c (Proceeds of Sale of Assets)	2,543	Sundry Creditors . . .	2,750
High, Capital (Cash brought in) .	63		
Lowe, Capital (Cash brought in) .	122		
	2,804		2,804

REALIZATION ACCOUNT

	£				£
Sundry Assets	3,869	Cash (Proceeds of Sale)			2,543
Cash (Expenses)	54	Capital (loss)—			
		High $\frac{3}{5}$		£828	
		Lowe $\frac{2}{5}$		552	
					1,380
	3,923				3,923

SUNDRY CREDITORS

	£		£
Cash	2,750	Balance	2,750

HIGH, CAPITAL

	£		£
Realization A/c ($\frac{3}{5}$ of Loss)	828	Balance	765
		Cash	63
	828		828

LOWE, CAPITAL

	£		£
Realization A/c ($\frac{2}{5}$ of Loss)	552	Balance	430
		Cash	122
	552		552

NOTE. With this example the student finds himself confronted at the outset with the difficulty of ascertaining the book value of the assets that were sold. Such a difficulty often presents itself in connexion with examination work. It is solved as follows: The total of the liabilities side of the balance sheet was £3,945 (£765 + £430 + £2,750). Inasmuch as the two sides of the balance sheet equal each other, the total value of the assets must have been £3,945; and since the cash in hand was £76, the book value of the other assets must have amounted to £3,869 (£3,945 less £76).

4. A Loss on Realization, some partners being solvent and some insolvent, necessitating the rule of Garner *v.* Murray being applied

Example 4

A, B, and C are in partnership, sharing profits and losses three-sixths, two-sixths, and one-sixth respectively. The state of affairs at the date of dissolution is as follows—

BALANCE SHEET

Liabilities	£	*Assets*	£
Sundry Creditors	3,875	Cash	986
A (Loan A/c)	250	Sundry Debtors	3,056
Capital—		Stock	1,844
A	1,520	Fixtures & Fittings	720
B	1,120	C, Capital (*Dr* balance)	159
	6,765		6,765

The assets other than cash realized £4,844, and the expenses of winding up are £52. A and B are solvent, but C is unable to bring in anything. Make the necessary adjustments, and draw up a balance sheet showing the position of affairs before applying the *Garner* v. *Murray* rule, after which close the books of the firm showing the ledger accounts.

CASH BOOK

	£		£
Balance	986	Realization A/c (Expenses)	52
Realization A/c (Proceeds of Sale of Assets)	4,844	Sundry Creditors	3,875
Deficiency A/c (Cash brought in)—		A (Loan A/c)	250
A	414	Balance c/d	2,343
B	276		
	6,520		6,520
Balance b/d	2,343		

REALIZATION ACCOUNT

	£			£
Sundry Assets	5,620	Cash (Proceeds of Sale)		4,844
Cash (Expenses)	52	Deficiency A/c (transfer)—		
		A, $\frac{3}{6}$	£414	
		B, $\frac{2}{6}$	276	
		C, $\frac{1}{6}$	138	
				828
	5,672			5,672

SUNDRY CREDITORS

	£		£
Cash	3,875	Balance	3,875

A, LOAN ACCOUNT

	£		£
Cash	250	Balance	250

DEFICIENCY ACCOUNT

	£		£
Realization A/c, loss b/f	828	Cash—	
		A	414
		B	276
		Balance c/d	138
	828		828
To Balance b/d	138		

The position of affairs before the solvent partners paid in their shares of the firm's deficiency was as follows—

BALANCE SHEET

Liabilities	£	*Assets*	£
Capital—		Cash	1,653
A	1,520	C—Overdrawn	159
B	1,120	Deficiency of Firm (loss on Realization)	828
	2,640		2,640

which subsequently becomes—

BALANCE SHEET

Liabilities	£	*Assets*		£
Capital—		Cash		2,343
A	1,520	C—		
B	1,120	Capital A/c Overdrawn	£159	
		Share of Deficiency	138	
				297
	2,640			2,640

Applying the *Garner* v. *Murray* rule, the solvent partners will receive and lose the following amounts—

A receives $\frac{1520}{2640}$ of £2,343 = £1,349 and loses $\frac{1520}{2640}$ of £297 = £171
B receives $\frac{1120}{2640}$ of £2,343 = £994 and loses $\frac{1120}{2640}$ of £297 = £126

The ledger accounts will be as follows—

A, Capital

	£		£
Cash	1,349	Balance	1,520
Transfer from C's A/c	171		
	1,520		1,520

B, Capital

	£		£
Cash	994	Balance	1,120
Transfer from C's A/c	126		
	1,120		1,120

C, Capital

	£		£
Capital (Overdrawn)	159	Transfer to—	
Share of Firm's Deficiency	138	A, Capital	171
		B, „	126
	297		297

CASH BOOK

	£		£
Balance	2,343	Capital—	
		A	1,349
		B	994
	2,343		2,343

Procedure prior to Garner *v.* Murray Decision. Prior to the *Garner* v. *Murray* decision, it was thought that the amount overdrawn by the insolvent partner, together with his share of the firm's deficiency, constituted a loss to be treated like ordinary partnership trading losses, i.e. to be borne by the solvent partners in the same *relative* proportions in which they shared profits. For the sake of illustration consider the previous example, the balance sheet of which would have appeared as follows—

BALANCE SHEET

Liabilities		£	*Assets*		£
Capital—			Cash		2,343
A		1,520	C. Capital—		
B		1,120	Overdrawn . .	£159	
			Share of Deficiency	138	
					297
		2,640			2,640

A and B share profits in the ratio of 3:2, and would therefore bear the loss of the £297 in the proportions of three-fifths and two-fifths. Thus, the final result would have been as under—

BALANCE SHEET

Liabilities		£	*Assets*	£
Capital—			Cash	2,343
A	£1,520			
Less $\frac{3}{5}$ of £297 . .	178			
		1,341		
B	1,120			
Less $\frac{2}{5}$ of £297 . .	119			
		1,001		
		2,343		2,343

Present Differences of Opinion re Garner *v.* Murray Decision. Many accountants do not even now admit the solvent partners' obligation to bring in cash to make good their shares of the firm's deficiency. They merely bring the partners' contributions *into account*, i.e. assume these amounts to be part of the cash available. It makes no difference to the final answer, as can be seen from the following, which represents their method of working the example in question. The position of affairs after realization was as follows—

BALANCE SHEET

Liabilities	£	*Assets*	£
Capital—		Cash	1,653
A	1,520	C, Capital—Overdrawn . .	159
B	1,120	Deficiency of Firm (Loss on Realization) . . .	828
	2,640		2,640

Bringing the contributions into account, we arrive at the following position—

BALANCE SHEET

Liabilities	£	*Assets*		£
Capital—		Cash		1,653
A	1,520	A's Contribution to Deficiency, $\frac{3}{6}$ of £828		414
B	1,120	B's Contribution to Deficiency, $\frac{2}{6}$ of £828		276
				2,343
		C—Overdrawn	£159	
		Share of Deficiency, $\frac{1}{6}$ of £828	138	297
	2,640			2,640

The amount of cash available has now been determined, and must be applied to the repayment of the partners' capitals *pro rata*. The final statement, showing how much each partner will receive, will be as follows.

FINAL STATEMENT

		£		£
Amounts due to Partners in respect of Capital—			Cash	1,653
A— $\frac{1520}{2640}$ of £2,343 =	£1,349			
Less Contribution due	414	935		
B— $\frac{1120}{2640}$ of £2,343 =	£994			
Less Contribution due	276	718		
		1,653		1,653

5. A Loss of Realization, and all the partners insolvent, the creditors being paid a dividend

Example 5

Jones and Brown are in partnership, sharing profits and losses two-thirds and one-third respectively. The following is the state of affairs at the date of dissolution—

BALANCE SHEET

Liabilities	£	*Assets*	£
Sundry Creditors	6,270	Cash	405
Capital—		Sundry Debtors . . .	2,342
Jones	2,100	Stock	2,070
Brown	1,200	Fixtures & Fittings . . .	1,486
		Goodwill	3,267
	9,570		9,570

The assets other than cash realize £4,465, and the expenses of winding up are £176. Close the books of the firm.

CASH BOOK

	£		£
Balance	405	Realization A/c (Expenses) .	176
Realization A/c—		Sundry Creditors—	
(Proceeds of Sale of Assets) .	4,465	Dividend of approx. £0·75 in the £ on £6,270 . .	4,694
	4,870		4,870

REALIZATION ACCOUNT

	£		£
Sundry Assets	9,165	Cash (Proceeds of Sale) . .	4,465
Cash (Expenses) . . .	176	Balance (loss carried to P. & L. A/c)	4,876
	9,341		9,341

SUNDRY CREDITORS

	£		£
Cash (Dividend of approx. £0·75 in £)	4,694	Balance	6,270
Balance transferred to P. & L. A/c	1,576		
	6,270		6,270

PROFIT AND LOSS ON REALIZATION ACCOUNT

		£			£
Realization A/c—			Balance from Sundry *Crs* .		1,576
(Balance b/f)		4,876	Capital—		
			Jones, ⅔ . .	£2,200	
			Brown, ⅓ . .	1,100	
					3,300
		4,876			4,876

JONES, CAPITAL

	£		£
P. & L. A/c	2,200	Balance	2,100
		Balance c/d	100
	2,200		2,200
Balance b/d	100	Brown Capital (transfer) . .	100

BROWN, CAPITAL

	£		£
P. & L. A/c	1,100	Balance	1,200
Balance c/d	100		
	1,200		1,200
Jones Capital (transfer) . .	100	Balance b/d	100

NOTE. In this case a profit and loss account is opened, debited with the loss on realization, and credited with the unpaid balance of the creditors' account, which makes a paper profit. The balance of the profit and loss account is carried to the capital accounts in the usual way. The capital accounts are then closed by transfer of their corresponding but opposite balances.

Alternative Form of Realization Account. In some cases, the asset accounts are not closed by transfer to a realization account, being left open. The cash received for the assets is debited in the cash book and credited to the various asset accounts, the balances of which, representing either gains or losses, are carried to a realization profit and loss account. The actual gain or loss on each asset is thus easily perceived. For examination purposes, the method already outlined is recommended.

Example 6

Smith and Roff are equal partners in a retail concern. They decide to retire, and sell their business on 31st December, the position of affairs on this date being as follows—

BALANCE SHEET AS AT 31ST DECEMBER, 19..

Liabilities	£	*Assets*	£
Sundry Creditors	720	Cash at Bank	620
Capital—		Sundry Debtors	1,670
Smith	3,500	Stock-in-trade	2,480
Roff	2,500	Lease	1,300
		Fixtures & Fittings	650
	6,720		6,720

The lease was sold for £1,650, fixtures and fittings for £725, and stock for £2,450. The book debts realized only £1,550, £45 being allowed for discount. The creditors were paid £700 in full settlement. The expenses of winding up were £55. Close the books of the firm, showing the result of the realization, and detailing the various ledger accounts. Show also the payment to each partner of the amount actually due to him.

LEASE

19..		£	19..		£
Jan 1	Balance	1,300	Dec 31	Cash	1,650
Dec 31	Realization A/c (gain)	350			
		1,650			1,650

FIXTURES AND FITTINGS

19..		£	19..		£
Jan 1	Balance	650	Dec 31	Cash	725
Dec 31	Realization A/c (gain)	75			
		725			725

SUNDRY DEBTORS

19..		£	19..		£
Jan 1	Balance	1,670	Dec 31	Cash	1,550
				Discount	45
				Bad Debts	75
		1,670			1,670

Stock

19..		£	19..		£
Jan 1	Balance . . .	2,480	Dec 31	Cash . . .	2,450
				Realization A/c (loss) .	30
		2,480			2,480

Sundry Creditors

19..		£	19..		£
Dec 31	Cash	700	Jan 1	Balance . . .	720
	Discount . . .	20			
		720			720

Bad Debts

19..		£	19..		£
Dec 31	Sundry Debtors . .	75	Dec 31	Realization A/c (loss) .	75

Discounts Received

19..		£	19..		£
Dec 31	Realization A/c (gain) .	20	Dec 31	Sundry Creditors .	20

Discounts Allowed

19..		£	19..		£
Dec 31	Sundry Debtors . .	45	Dec 31	Realization A/c (loss) .	45

Realization Profit and Loss Account

19..	*Losses*		£	19..	*Gains*	£
Dec 31	Stock . . .		30	Dec 31	Lease . . .	350
	Discounts Allowed .		45		Fixtures & Fittings .	75
	Bad Debts . . .		75		Discounts Received .	20
	Cash (Expenses) . .		55			
	Capital (net gain)—					
	Smith, ½ .	£120				
	Roff, ½ .	120				
			240			
			445			445

SMITH, CAPITAL

		£			£
19..			19..		
Dec 31	Cash	3,620	Jan 1	Balance . . .	3,500
			Dec 31	Realization A/c (½ profit) . . .	120
		3,620			3,620

ROFF, CAPITAL

		£			£
19..			19..		
Dec 31	Cash	2,620	Jan 1	Balance . . .	2,500
			Dec 31	Realization A/c (½ profit) . . .	120
		2,620			2,620

CASH BOOK

	£			£
Balance	620	Sundry Creditors . . .		700
Lease	1,650	Realization A/c (Expenses of Winding up) . .		55
Fixtures & Fittings	725	Capital—		
Sundry Debtors.	1,550	Roff . . .	£2,620	
Stock	2,450	Smith . . .	3,620	
				6,240
	6,995			6,995

Conversion of a Partnership into a Limited Company. **Please refer to p. 2505.**

QUESTIONS

1. In what three ordinary ways may a partnership be dissolved?
2. Explain what effect the following have upon the duration of a partnership (*a*) bankruptcy; (*b*) death; (*c*) charge; (*d*) illegality.
3. In what six cases can a dissolution of partnership be decreed by the court?
4. What notice must be given to creditors and others when a dissolution or change of partnership takes place?
5. Explain what is meant by the "continuing authority of partners for winding-up purposes."
6. State the legal rule for adjusting losses, and distributing assets, on the dissolution of a partnership, where no agreement to the contrary exists.
7. Submit a formula for dealing in the books with an ordinary dissolution of partnership.

8. When the result of a dissolution is to place a partner's capital account temporarily in debit, what is that partner's duty with reference thereto?

9. Explain briefly the *Garner* v. *Murray* decision, and the consequent treatment of accounts in the books.

10. When, on a dissolution of partnership, the assets realize only sufficient to pay the creditors a dividend, how are the accounts in the books closed?

Goodwill and Outgoing Partners. On the death or retirement of a partner, his share of the goodwill has to be valued, and the amount arrived at according to the terms of the partnership deed; or if no arrangement has been made, then the goodwill of the firm is valued, and of this amount a proportion, the same as that in which he shares profits, is then credited to his capital account. The amount is then debited to Goodwill Account or, if the new partners decide against raising a Goodwill Account, it is debited to their Capital Account in their new profit sharing proportions. Instead of the partner's share of the goodwill, an annuity, or a percentage of the profits for a certain number of years, is sometimes paid to the deceased partner's representatives.

Goodwill on Sale of a Partnership Business. When a partnership business is sold as a going concern, the amount obtained for the goodwill will be a profit, to be divided among the partners in the same proportion as they share profits on trading.

Policies of Survivorship Assurance. Partners often assure themselves either jointly or severally as a means of obtaining the necessary cash to pay out a deceased partner's share of the capital and goodwill. This prevents any financial difficulties when such a necessity arises. The premiums paid are debited to profit and loss as a business expense, and on the death of a partner, *the cash received for the policy is debited in the cash book and credited to the partners' capital accounts (including the account of the deceased partner), in the same proportion as they share profits.* The cash is then in hand with which to make the required payment. If desired, a policy account may be opened, and dealt with in a similar way to the insurance policy method of depreciation.

Example 7

A. Ashton and B. Beeching are in partnership, sharing profits and losses three-fifths and two-fifths respectively. In order to provide money for repayment of their share of the capital and goodwill in the event of death, they assure their lives jointly for £8,000, paying an annual premium of £300, which is debited to the firm's profit and loss account each December. Beeching dies on the last day of June, 19. .. The partnership deed provides that his representatives are to receive his capital, as per the last balance sheet, plus interest at 5 per cent per annum to date of death, and his share of the profits to date of death, estimated according to the profits of the preceding year. They are also to receive as his share of the goodwill an amount estimated at two years' purchase of his average net profits of the last three years, before charging the insurance premiums. The net profits for the last three years after charging the insurance premiums were £2,420, £2,800, and £2,310 respectively. Beeching's capital shown in the balance sheet was £2,620, and his drawings to date of death amount to £725. Make the necessary adjustments and draw up Beeching's account, showing the amount payable to his legal representatives.

The goodwill is calculated thus—

Average profit for the last three years before charging insurance premiums = (£2,720 + £3,100 + £2,610 ÷ 3) = £(8,430 ÷ 3) = £2,810.

Total goodwill on basis of two years' purchase of the average net profits = (£2,810 × 2) = £5,620.

Beeching's share of goodwill = $\frac{2}{5}$ of £5,620 = £2,248.

CASH BOOK

		£	
Assurance Policy—			
A. Ashton (Capital)	£4,800		
B. Beeching (Capital)	3,200		
		8,000	

B. BEECHING (DECEASED)

19..			£	19..			£
Jun	30	Drawings	725·00	Jan	1	Balance	2,620·00
		Balance c/d	7,870·50	Jun	30	Interest on above 6 mos. @ 5% p.a.	65·50
						Profits for 6 mos. $\frac{1}{2}$ of ($\frac{2}{5}$ of £2,310)	462·00
						Share of Goodwill	2,248·00
						Cash (Share of Assurance Policy).	3,200·00
			8,595·50				8,595·50
		Cash	7,870·50	Jun	30	Balance b/d	7,870·50

Revaluation of Assets. Retirement of a partner should also be accompanied by a revaluation of the assets which are taken over, since the value on the books may be greater or less than the current market value.

In this case, a Revaluation Account may be opened: in principle it is identical to the Realization Account and it is debited with decreases in asset values or increases in liabilities. It is credited with increases in asset values or decreases in liabilities. The corresponding entries are made in the asset and liabilities accounts.

The surplus or deficit on revaluation is credited or debited to the partners in their old profit-sharing proportions.

The following example is taken from a Certified and Corporate Accountants' paper—

Example 8

Ham, Bacon and Lamb were in partnership sharing profits and losses in the ratio of 5:3:2. A summary of the firm's balance sheet as on 30th September, 1963, was as follows—

	£	£		£	£
Capitals—			Freehold land and buildings		10,000
Ham	15,000		Machinery and plant		4,000
Bacon	7,000		Motor vehicles		1,600
Lamb	5,000		Stock on hand		6,800
		27,000	Sundry debtors	7,300	
Ham, Loan A/c		3,000	*Less* provision for doubtful debts	400	
Sundry creditors		5,000			6,900
			Cash at bank		5,700
		35,000			35,000

On 30th September, 1963, Ham retired from the firm. Bacon and Lamb decided to continue in partnership sharing profits as to Bacon three-fifths and Lamb two-fifths.

The partners agreed that, both as regards the dissolution and the continuing partnership, adjustments should be made in the September, 1963 balance sheet as follows—

(*a*) The value of freehold land and buildings should be put at £12,500 and machinery and plant at £3,600.

(*b*) A reduction of £500 should be made from the stock in respect of old and unsaleable items.

(*c*) An increase of £120 should be made in the provision for doubtful debts.

(*d*) An amount of £300, included in sundry creditors as a provision in respect of an alleged infringement of a patent, is no longer needed.

It was also agreed that one of the firm's motor vehicles should be taken by Ham at its books value of £650 and that he should also take items of machinery and plant at the amount of £1,100 included in the above-mentioned adjusted valuation for such items.

According to the provisions of the partnership agreement, the full value of goodwill on 30th September, 1963, was agreed at £18,800. Certain customers being retained by Ham, it was agreed that he should purchase a proportion of the goodwill paying therefor £3,800.

Bacon and Lamb decided that goodwill should not be brought into the books of the new partnership as an asset.

Since the continuing partners were unable to pay the amount owing to Ham immediately, he agreed to allow such amount to remain on loan account.

You are requested to prepare: (1) The Revaluation Account, (2) in columnar form the partners' Capital Accounts of the old and new firm, recording the transactions outlined, and (3) the opening Balance Sheet of the new firm.

Solution

HAM, BACON AND LAMB

REVALUATION ACCOUNT AT 30TH SEPTEMBER, 1963

	£	£		£
Machinery and plant—decrease in value		400	Freehold land and buildings—increase in value	2,500
Stock—reduction in respect of obsolete stock		500	Goodwill—valuation of	18,800
Doubtful debts provision—increase		120	Creditors—provision no longer required	300
Partners' capital accounts—shares of net surplus on revaluation—				
Ham—$\frac{1}{2}$	10,290			
Bacon—$\frac{3}{10}$	6,174			
Lamb—$\frac{1}{5}$	4,116			
		20,580		
		21,600		21,600

PARTNERS' CAPITAL ACCOUNTS

1963		Ham £	Bacon £	Lamb £	1963		Ham £	Bacon £	Lamb £
Sep 30	Assets taken over by Ham—				Sep 30	Balances brought forward	15,000	7,000	5,000
	Machinery and plant	1,100				Revaluation account	10,290	6,174	4,116
	Motor vehicle	650							
	Goodwill	3,800							
	Goodwill—balance written off—£18,800 – £3,800 = £15,000 in profit-sharing ratio		9,000	6,000					
	Transfer to loan account	19,740							
	Balances c/f		4,174	3,116					
		25,290	13,174	9,116			25,290	13,174	9,116

BACON AND LAMB

BALANCE SHEET AT 30TH SEPTEMBER, 1963

	£	£		£	£
Partners' Capital Accounts—			Fixed Assets—		
Bacon	4,174		At revaluation dated 30th September, 1963—		
Lamb	3,116		Freehold land and buildings	12,500	
		7,290	Machinery and plant	2,500	
Loan Account—Ham—			Motor vehicles	950	
Balance prior to retirement	3,000				15,950
Transfer from Capital Account	19 740		Current Assets—		
		22,740	Sundry debtors	7,300	
Sundry Creditors		4,700	*Less:* provision for doubtful debts	520	
				6,780	
			Stock on hand	6,300	
			Cash at bank	5,700	
					18,780
		34,730			34,730

Repayment of Outgoing Partner's Share by Instalments. On the death or retirement of a partner, his share of the capital and goodwill may, instead of being paid out immediately to his representatives, be treated as a loan, bearing interest, and repayable by fixed instalments.

Example 9

Assume that in example 7, B. Beeching's share of capital, profits, and goodwill, viz. £7,870, is payable by annual instalments of £1,500, interest at 5 per cent per annum being allowed on the outstanding balance. Show the ledger account in the firm's books.

B. BEECHING (DECEASED) LOAN

Year		£	Year		£
1	Cash (6 mos.)	750	1	Balance	7,870
	Balance c/d	7,317		Interest, 6 mos	197
		8,067			8,067
2	Cash	1,500	2	Balance b/d	7,317
	Balance c/d	6,183		Interest, 1 year	366
		7,683			7,683
3	Cash	1,500	3	Balance b/d	6,183
	Balance c/d	4,992		Interest, 1 year	309
		6,492			6,492
4	Cash	1,500	4	Balance b/d	4,992
	Balance c/d	3,742		Interest, 1 year	250
		5,242			5,242
5	Cash	1,500	5	Balance b/d	3,742
	Balance c/d	2,429		Interest, 1 year	187
		3,929			3,929
6	Cash	1,500	6	Balance b/d	2,429
	Balance c/d	1,050		Interest, 1 year	121
		2,550			2,550
7	Cash	1,103	7	Balance b/d	1,050
				Interest, 1 year	53
		1,103			1,103

Repayment of Outgoing Partner's Share with Interest from Date of Realization of Assets. Although, by law, interest ceases at the date of dissolution, yet it frequently happens that the continuing partner agrees to pay the outgoing partner his share by instalments with interest as and from the date of realization of the assets. In some cases the average date is ascertained, and interest calculated from this date. The account then takes the form of an account current.

Example 10

M. Lowther and A. Borchard are in partnership, sharing profits and losses equally. Lowther agrees to buy out Borchard, and the position of affairs on this date is as follows—

BALANCE SHEET AS AT 1ST JANUARY, 19..

Liabilities	£	*Assets*	£
Sundry Creditors	1,270	Cash	1,340
Capital—		Sundry Debtors	4,850
M. Lowther	3,090	Office Furniture	260
A. Borchard	2,090		
	6,450		6,450

Lowther is to take over the office furniture at £200, to allow Borchard £540 for his share of the goodwill, and to pay him his proportion as when realized, interest to be taken into account at 5 per cent per annum. A loss of £150 is sustained on the sundry debtors, and a discount of £30 obtained from the creditors. The latter were paid at an average date of *four* months and the debtors were realized at an average date of *eight* months from the date of dissolution. Lowther paid Borchard £550 on 1st March, £550 on 1st June, £550 on 1st September, and the balance on 31st December. Draw

PROFIT AND LOSS ADJUSTMENT ACCOUNT

19..		£	19..			£
Dec 31	Bad Debts (loss)	150	Dec 31	Discount on Creditors (gain)		30
	Furniture (loss)	60		Capital (net loss)—		
				Lowther, ½	£90	
				Borchard, ½	£90	
						180
		210				210

ADJUSTED BALANCE SHEET, 31ST DECEMBER, 19..

Liabilities	£	*Assets*	£
Creditors	1,240	Cash	1,340
Capital—		Debtors	4,700
M. Lowther	3,000	Office Furniture	200
A. Borchard	2,000		
	6,240		6,240

A. BORCHARD IN ACCOUNT CURRENT WITH M. LOWTHER

31st December, 19..

Date	Item	Amount	Days	Products	Date	Item	Amount	Days	Products
19..		£			19..		£		
Mar 1	Cash	550·00	305	167,750	Jan 1	Office Furniture ($\frac{2}{5}$ of £200) . . .	80·00	364	29,120
May 1	Sundry *Crs* ($\frac{2}{5}$ £1,240) .	496·00	244	121,024		Cash ($\frac{2}{5}$ of £1,340) .	536·00	364	195,104
Jun 1	Cash	550·00	213	117,150		Goodwill . . .	540·00	364	196,560
Sep 1	,, ...	550·00	121	66,550	Sep 1	Sundry *Drs* ($\frac{2}{5}$ of £4,700)	1,880·00	121	227,480
Dec 31	Balance of Products .			175,790		Interest on Balance of Products— $\frac{175,790 \times 10}{73,000}$	24·09		
	Balance c/d . .	914·09							
		3,060·09		648,264			3,060·09		648,264
Dec 31	Cash	914·09			Dec 31	Balance b/d . .	914·09		

Lowther owes Borchard as follows—

	£
Capital	2,000·00
Goodwill	540·00
Interest	24·09
	2,564·09

He pays as follows—

		£
Mar 1	Cash	550·00
Jun 1	Cash	550·00
Sep 1	Cash	550·00
Dec 31	Cash	914·09
		2,564·09

up the account current between Lowther and Borchard, and show the final payment made to Borchard on 31st December.

Although Lowther and Borchard share profits and losses, including profits and losses on realization of the assets, *equally*, yet the actual assets themselves, as in the balance sheet, belong to the partners in the proportion that their capitals bear to the total capital, three-fifths and two-fifths respectively.

Repayment of Outgoing Partner's Share by Means of an Annuity. On the death or retirement of a partner, his share of the capital and goodwill is sometimes paid out by means of an annuity for a limited number of years, or for his lifetime, or for the joint lives of himself and wife.

In such cases, the total amount due will be credited to a separate account in the name of the annuitant and debited to a goodwill account. This separate account will be credited each year with interest at an agreed rate on the diminishing balance, and debited each year with the payment of the annuity. The amount of the latter will be ascertained from annuity tables. If before the expiration of the annuity, this account is extinguished, all future payments of the annuity will be debited to profit and loss account as a sustained loss; on the other hand, if the annuity terminates before this credit sum is exhausted, the balance will be transferred to the goodwill account in reduction thereof. Until the annuity account is finally closed, the balance of it will appear each year on the liabilities side of the balance sheet. An alternative method would be simply to debit a goodwill account each time the annuity is paid.

EXERCISE 18

1. Messrs. Black and White were equal partners in a retail boot shop. They decided to retire and dispose of their business as on 31st December. At the close of the year their balance sheet was as follows—

	£		£
B. Black, Capital	3,050	Lease	1,250
W. White ,,	960	Fixtures	220
Sundry Creditors	480	Sundry Debtors	840
		Stock	2,060
		Cash at Bank	120
	4,490		4,490

The lease and fixtures were disposed of for £2,700, and the cash duly received. The book debts were collected, and realized £752. The stock was sold by auction, and produced £1,340 after payment of commission and expenses. The sundry creditors were paid off, £38 being allowed for discount. The expenses of realization amounted to £87.

As book-keeper to the firm, prepare whatever accounts may be necessary to show the result of the realization and the amount receivable by each partner.

(*London Chamber of Commerce.*)

2. Black and White are equal partners, and their balance sheet stands as follows—

Assets: Cash £400; debtors £2,000; stock £1,500; machinery £2,000.
Liabilities: Creditors £1,800; Black's capital £2,900; White's capital £1,200.

They decide to dissolve partnership, and the assets realize the following amounts: debtors £1,880; stock £1,200; machinery £1,800. They receive £100 as discounts from creditors, and the expenses of realization amount to £230. Prepare ledger accounts showing the result of the winding up.

3. Black and White have been in business together for three years ending 31st December, at which date they agree to dissolve partnership. Black takes over the business and agrees to pay White £1,800 for his share of the goodwill.

Black has drawn out £500 each year and White £650 each year. Black's capital at the start was £3,000 and White's £4,000.

The profits of each year were £1,000, £1,200, and £1,350 respectively. There was no deed of partnership and no arrangement as to interest on capital. Draft capital accounts (in White's show the amount he will receive on going out), profit and loss account in Black and White's books, and goodwill account in Black's books.

4. The position of a business firm is as follows—

BALANCE SHEET

Liabilities	£	*Assets*	£
Creditors	2,020	Cash at Bank	1,530
Capital—		Debtors	2,466
Robinson	3,120	Stock	3,754
Larkin	2,760	Goodwill	2,300
Sparrow	2,150		
	10,050		10,050

The partnership is dissolved, the assets realized, and the creditors duly discharged. What will be the share of each partner—

(*a*) If the assets realize their book value, and the partners share profits equally?

(*b*) If the debtors realize £2,400; stock £3,800; goodwill £2,500; and partners share profits in the proportions of 5, 4, and 3?

(*c*) If the debtors realize £2,200; stock £3,198; and the partners share profits equally?

5. Hawker and Haigh are in partnership, sharing profits and losses $\frac{4}{5}$ths and $\frac{1}{5}$th respectively. They dissolve partnership, and their capitals on this date are: Hawker £3,700; and Haigh £550. The other liabilities of the firm amount to £6,000, which includes £1,500 due to Hawker for advances, and £250 due to Haigh for advances. The assets of the firm realize net £7,230. Draw up accounts, showing the final result of the realization and the amounts receivable by the respective partners.

6. Bean, Gonne, and Dunnit are partners who share profits and losses equally. After realization of the assets upon dissolution of the partnership, the position was as follows—

	£
Capital accounts—	
Bean	8,000 *Cr*
Gonne	5,000 *Cr*
Dunnit	3,500 *Dr*
Cash at bank	6,500

Dunnit had no financial resources. You are required to show the entries necessary to close the above accounts of the partnership. (*Cost and Works Accountants.*)

7. Black and White are accountants sharing profits and losses equally after payment of a salary of £500 per annum to White.

The trial balance on the 31st December, 1965, was—

	£		£
Drawings—Black	1,500	Capital—Black	3,500
White	1,200	White	1,750
General Expenses	2,500	Loan (Black, advanced 1st January, 1965)	1,200
Salaries (including £500 to White)	5,500	Bills rendered	15,000
Furniture and equipment at cost	750	Clients' disbursements recovered	1,050
Goodwill	1,500	N.B. There were no amounts owing to clients on 31st December, 1965	
Debtors	3,060		
Work in progress 31st December, 1964	2,100		
Cash at Bank	1,740		
Clients disbursements—			
Balance 31st December, 1964	1,400		
Expenditure during year	1,250		
	22,500		22,500

On the 31st December, 1965, the outstandings were: work in progress £1,800, disbursements for clients recoverable but not yet rendered £1,520 and expenses accrued £360. No provision is to be made for depreciation and any difference on client's disbursements account is to be treated as irrecoverable.

On 31st December, 1965, the partnership was dissolved on the following terms.

(1) Black is to take over the furniture and equipment at a valuation of £600, also the tenancy of the office for a sum of £250.

(2) The debtors, work in progress and disbursements recoverable, to be taken over by the partners subject to an allowance of 10 per cent to cover the costs of collection and contingencies; the agreed gross amounts were—

	Black	White
	£	£
Debtors	1,800	1,260
Work in progress	760	1,040
Disbursements recoverable	850	670

The loan of White was repaid on 1st January, 1966, and expenses accrued were discharged in cash for the exact amount provided.

All transactions were completed and all amounts receivable or payable were settled in cash in January, 1966.

Prepare—

(*a*) The balance sheet on the 31st December, 1965, with profit and loss account for the year ended on that date. The accounts are not to include differences or allowances arising on realization.

(*b*) The Realization account, and

(*c*) In columnar form, the partners' capital accounts for the year ended 31st December, 1965, bringing down the balances on that date, subsequent to final settlement. Any balances on Drawings account are to be transferred to capital accounts on 31st December, 1965. (*L.C.C.*)

8. Wood, Harrison, and Batty are partners, and divide profits in the proportions of 4, 3, and 2 respectively. The partnership is dissolved, and the state of affairs on date of dissolution is as follows—

BALANCE SHEET

Liabilities	£	*Assets*	£
Creditors	2,755	Cash at Bank	475
Capital—		Bills Receivable	150
Wood	5,000	Debtors	8,420
Harrison	3,500	Stock	2,360
Batty	2,500	Plant	2,350
	13,755		13,755

The assets realize £437 less than their book value. The expenses of winding up are £85. What amounts are payable to the partners respectively?

9. Partridge and Paterson entered into partnership for five years, and shared profits and losses as 2 to 1. Partridge's initial capital was £3,500 and Paterson's £850. The partnership deed provided that on termination the proceeds of realization, after liquidating the creditors' claims, should be divided according to the partners' shares and interests therein. Accounts have been drawn up annually, and profits, losses, and drawings have been duly adjusted. At the end of the fifth year, Partridge's capital is £4,000 and Paterson's £450. The balance of cash remaining after paying all expenses and the creditors amounts to £2,020. Adjust the partners' capital accounts.

10. Walker, Skipper and Hopper were in equal partnership which was terminated on 31st March, 1966. Skipper and Hopper decided to continue in a new equal partnership and take over the assets and liabilities of the old firm and pay out Walker in cash. The following was the final Balance Sheet of the old firm.

Liabilities	£	£	*Assets*	£
Sundry Creditors		4,000	Plant and Machinery	4,000
Capital Accounts—			Stock-in-Trade	14,400
Walker	10,500		Sundry Debtors	7,600
Skipper	7,250		Cash at Bank	3,000
Hopper	7,250			
		25,000		
		£29,000		£29,000

The assets were taken over at amounts as follows—

Plant and Machinery £3,600, Stock-in-Trade £13,800 and the Sundry Debtors at their book value less 5 per cent.

Goodwill was valued under the provisions of the old partnership deed at £10,800.

You are required to give the realization account of the old firm and to prepare the balance sheet of the new firm, assuming that the amount to be paid out to Walker was borrowed from the bank. *(A.C.C.A.)*

11. X, Y, and Z dissolve partnership, and, after realization, the following is the position of affairs—

BALANCE SHEET

Liabilities	£	*Assets*	£
Creditors	464	Cash at Bank	11,550
Capital—		Z, Capital—Overdrawn	434
X	6,000		
Y	5,000		
Profit on Realization	520		
	11,984		11,984

The partners share profits and losses as follows: X $\frac{1}{2}$; Y $\frac{3}{10}$; and Z $\frac{1}{5}$. Z is quite unable to contribute anything. Draw up the final accounts.

12. The partnership of X, Y, and Z came to an end on 25th April. X's capital was £6,600; Y's £4,400; while Z had overdrawn to the extent of £350. Profits and losses were shared in the proportions of 3, 2, and 1. The assets were: cash at bank £425; bills receivable £950; debtors £6,730; plant £3,500; stock £3,500. The liabilities were: bills payable £805; bank overdraft £2,000; creditors £1,650. Z is insolvent, but his partners recover £90 from his separate estate. The assets realized the following sums: bills receivable £925; debtors £6,500; plant £3,000; stock £3,300. The expenses of winding up amounted to £185. Draw up the final accounts, and show what each partner will receive.

13. The partnership A, B, and C came to an end on 31st December. The capital of A was £5,000, and of B £4,000, while C's account was overdrawn to the extent of £500, and he had no outside means. Profits and losses were shared in the proportions of A $\frac{1}{2}$, B $\frac{1}{3}$, and C $\frac{1}{6}$. Their assets amounted to £8,870, and their liabilities to £370. The business was sold for £10,000. Show the partners' accounts after the sale had been effected. (*Chartered Accountants.*)

14. Briar, Poulsen, and Rose had been trading in partnership, sharing profits and losses in the proportion of 6, 5, and 4 respectively, and the firm's balance sheet as on 30th June, 19.., was as follows—

	£		£
Capital—		Goodwill	2,300
Briar	14,480	Lease	750
Poulsen	5,260	Furniture & Fittings	1,200
Rose	4,380	Stock	15,870
Creditors	670	Debtors	3,040
		Bank	1,630
	24,790		24,790

The partners decided to dissolve the partnership as on 1st July, 19.., Briar and Poulsen retiring and Rose continuing as a sole trader. Rose agreed to take over the goodwill and lease, part of the furniture and fittings, and part of the stock at valuations of £1,500, £950, £850, and £7,300 respectively, and he undertook to collect the debtors on behalf of the firm and to pay the creditors. As consideration for getting in the debts he was to receive a commission of $2\frac{1}{2}$ per cent on all amounts collected.

The remainder of the furniture, fittings, and stock was sold by auction, the net proceeds, £8,272, being paid into the firm's banking account.

During the following six months, Rose collected £2,680 of the debtors, paying the proceeds into his own banking account, and out of this sum had paid all the creditors. The remaining debtors, some of which were doubtful, he agreed to take over at a valuation of £100. On 31st December, 19.., the partners had a settlement, Briar agreeing to leave £10,000 of his capital as a loan to Rose.

Set out the realization account, the partners' capital accounts, and the closing cash book entries. (*R.S.A.*)

15. Brown, Jones, and Robinson were in partnership as coal merchants. On 31st December their balance sheet showed the following position of affairs—

Liabilities		£	*Assets*	£
Sundry Creditors		3,000	Cash in hand and at Bank	1,400
Loan on Mortgage		400	Sundry Debtors	4,000
Brown—Capital	£2,500		Stock	1,500
Drawings	1,000		Motor Lorries, etc.	500
		3,500	Freehold Property	1,000
Jones—Capital	£1,500		Robinson—Overdrawn	500
Drawings	500			
		2,000		
		8,900		8,900

They shared profits and losses in the proportions of Brown one-half, Jones one-third, Robinson one-sixth. It was decided to dissolve the partnership as at the date of the above balance sheet. The freehold property realized £1,300. Bad debts and discounts allowed amounted to £500. The stock realized £1,200, and the motor lorries, etc., £300. The mortgage on the property was duly paid off. The creditors were also paid, less discounts amounting to £100. The costs of realization amounted to £300. After the assets had been realized and all the liabilities discharged, Robinson became bankrupt, and a claim was made against his estate for the amount due from him to the firm on the dissolution, and a dividend thereon at the rate of 33·3p in the £ was received. Write up the realization account; the cash account, and the capital and drawing accounts of the partners, and close the books of the firm.

(*Chartered Accountants.*)

16. Morgan and Newell are in partnership, sharing profits and losses two-thirds and one-third respectively. The following is the state of affairs at the date of dissolution—

BALANCE SHEET

Liabilities	£	*Assets*	£
Sundry Creditors	12,000	Cash	900
Capital—		Sundry Debtors	4,082
Morgan	4,720	Stock	4,320
Newell	2,462	Fixtures & Fittings	3,080
		Goodwill	6,800
	19,182		19,182

The assets, other than cash, realize £8,600, and the expenses of winding up are £300. Close the books of the firm. It is assumed that nothing is forthcoming from the private estates of the partners.

17. Wyatt and Dawson are equal partners in a retail concern. They decide to retire, and sell their business on 31st December, the position of affairs on this date being as follows—

BALANCE SHEET

Liabilities	£	*Assets*	£
Sundry Creditors	900	Cash at Bank	1,000
Capital—		Sundry Debtors	1,900
Wyatt	6,000	Stock	5,000
Dawson	4,000	Fixtures & Fittings	1,000
		Lease	2,000
	10,900		10,900

The lease was sold for £3,000, fixtures for £1,100, and stock for £4,600. The book debts realized only £1,800, £60 being allowed for discount. The creditors were paid £860 in full settlement. The expenses of winding up were £64. Close the books of the firm, showing the result of the realization, and detailing the various ledger accounts. Show also the payment to each partner of the amount actually due to him.

18. Lamb and Crow have carried on business in partnership as Estate Agents, for many years, sharing profits and losses two-thirds and one-third respectively, the business being conducted from offices at London and Brighton.

It was agreed that as from 31st March, 1964, the partnership should be dissolved, Lamb taking over the London connection and Crow taking the Brighton business.

Their Balance Sheet at that date was as follows—

BALANCE SHEET 31ST MARCH, 1964

	£		£
Creditors	2,150	Goodwill	2,000
		Furniture	1,800
Capital Accounts—		Debtors—	
Lamb	10,000	London	2,000
Crow	2,650	Brighton	1,000
		Cash at Bank	8,000
	14,800		14,800

The Goodwill and Furniture were revalued as follows—

		£
Goodwill—	London	1,600
	Brighton	800
Furniture—	London	850
	Brighton	720

Each partner also took over the book debts of his connection at their book value less 5 per cent as a provision for bad debts. Lamb undertook to pay the creditors of the firm.

The costs of the dissolution were £250 which were paid by the partnership and it was also agreed that sums of £500 and £50 should be allowed to Lamb and Crow respectively towards the future cost of repairs to the premises previously occupied by the partnership.

Prepare a Cash Account, Realization Account and Capital Accounts of the Partners, assuming that all the foregoing transactions were duly completed.

(*A.C.C.A.*)

19. Duke and Earl carried on business in partnership sharing profits and losses as to Duke $\frac{3}{5}$ths, Earl $\frac{2}{5}$ths. The summarized balance sheet of the partnership as on 31st March, 1964, was as follows—

	£	£		£	£
Capital Accounts (fixed)—			**Fixed Assets**		**9,000**
Duke	**7,000**				
Earl	**5,000**				
		12,000	**Current Assets—**		
Current Accounts—			**Stock**	**4,800**	
Duke	**3,000**		**Sundry debtors** . . .	**8,400**	
***Less:* Earl** . . .	**1,200**		**Cash at bank** . . .	**1,600**	
		1,800			**14,800**
Loan—Earl . . .		**4,000**			
Sundry Creditors . . .		**6,000**			
		£23,800			**£23,800**

Two motor cars are included in the item "fixed assets," the book values being £900 and £800.

The partners have decided to retire and have accepted an offer from Lords Ltd., to take over the fixed assets (excluding the motor cars) and the stock at an inclusive figure of £21,000. This consideration was to be satisfied by the allotment by the company to the partners of 6,000 5 per cent £1 preference shares, valued at 15s. each, a payment of £7,500 in cash and the balance by the allotment by the company to the partners of 30,000 ordinary shares of a nominal value of 4s. each.

£7,800 was received in settlement of sundry debtors and £5,500 was paid out in settlement of sundry creditors.

On dissolution of the partnership, the partners agreed that the basis of distribution should be as follows—

(*a*) One motor to be taken over by Duke at £1,400 and the other by Earl at £1,000.

(*b*) Earl's loan to be repaid by the allotment to him of preference shares to the value of the loan, Duke being allotted the remainder.

(*c*) The allotment of the ordinary shares to be in the proportion of the fixed capitals.

(*d*) Cash to be taken in settlement of balances remaining.

Prepare (1) the Realization Account, (2) the Bank Account, and (3) the Capital Accounts of the partners showing how the final settlement between them was effected.

(A.C.C.A.)

20. Brick and Stone were in partnership sharing profits and losses three-fifths and two-fifths respectively, and their Balance Sheet at 31st December, 1964, was summarized as follows—

BALANCE SHEET

	£	£		£
Capital Accounts—			Buildings, Equipment and two	
Brick . . .	8,915		Motor Cars . . .	7,400
Stone . . .	4,600		Investments at cost . .	3,200
		13,515	Stock of Materials . .	3,575
Loan from—			Debtors . . .	4,370
Stone . . .	1,000			
Interest . . .	100			
		1,100		
Creditors . . .		2,330		
Bank Overdraft . .		1,600		
		18,545		18,545

It was agreed that the partnership be dissolved and that an offer from Walls Ltd., to purchase the buildings, equipment and stock of materials should be accepted, on the following terms—

(1) The total purchase price to be £20,000, payable as to £12,000 in cash and the balance by the issue to the partners of 15,000 fully paid Ordinary Shares of 10s. each in Walls Ltd.

(2) Of the motor cars, which were excluded from the sale, one was to be taken over by Brick at £845, and the other by Stone at £320.

(3) The loan from Stone was to be transferred to his Capital Account together with the interest due.

(4) The investments were all sold and realized £2,900.

(5) The Debtors realized £4,110 only, due to bad debts, but allowances of £80 were obtained from the Creditors.

(6) Costs of £210 were incurred and paid by the partnership.

(7) It was agreed that the partners would divide the shares from Walls Ltd., in proportion to their Capital Accounts after completion of the realization, and that their final balances be paid in cash.

Prepare—

(*a*) The Realization Account.
(*b*) The Bank Account.
(*c*) The Partners' Capital Accounts, including the final settlement between them.
(*A.C.C.A.*)

21. A partnership between G., K. and N. was dissolved on 31st December, 1962. At that date a balance sheet was made up and agreed showing that G.'s capital was £5,500, K.'s £5,500 and that N. was overdrawn to the extent of £350.

Trading profits and losses were shared in the ratio of 3, 2 and 1, respectively, but there was no partnership deed.

The assets were—

	£
Motor Vehicles	820
Sundry Debtors	6,860
Plant	3,000
Stock	4,000

and the liabilities—

Hire-purchase Instalments on Vehicles	400
Bank Overdraft	1,980
Trade Creditors	1,650

N. in unable to contribute anything towards his share of any deficiency

The assets realize the following amounts—

Motor Vehicles (taken over by G.)	795
Debtors	6,630
Plant	2,500
Stock (taken over by K.)	3,800

G. also took over the hire-purchase liability on the vehicles.

The expenses of winding-up amounted to £185.

Prepare the ledger accounts showing how much each partner should have received assuming that all receipts had been collected and all payments made by 31st March, 1963. (*A.C.C.A.*)

22. Hardy and Ivor are in partnership, sharing profits and losses as to two-thirds and one-third respectively. At 31st August, 19.., their position was—

BALANCE SHEET

Liabilities	£	*Assets*	£
Creditors	3,459	Cash	200
Capital—		Debtors	215
Hardy	708	Stock	860
Ivor	408	Fixtures	1,900
		Motor vehicles	1,400
	4,575		4,575

Dissolution takes place, the assets (other than cash) realize £2,040, expenses of realization being £39. Neither partner has any other assets. Close the books of the firm, indicating the dividend paid to the creditors. (*Institute of Book-keepers.*)

23. Grove and Lane were developing in partnership an invention which had been patented. They shared profits in the ratio of 2 to 1. The following was their balance sheet as on 30th June, 1961.

	£		£
Capital Account, Grove	5,600	Goodwill and Patents	21,000
Loan Account, Grove	9,000	Stock on hand	1,200
Central Bank Ltd.	6,500	Sundry Debtors, *less* provision for doubtful debts	3,000
Sundry Creditors	7,000	Capital Account, Lane	2,900
	28,100		28,100

There was every prospect that the business could be made very successful but for this more working capital was required, which the partners were unable to find. They approached Holloway Ltd. as to it acquiring the business. The company made an offer to take over, as on 30th June, 1961, the goodwill, patents and stock at an inclusive figure of £34,300 leaving the partnership to deal with the debtors and creditors. In settlement of the purchase price, £10,000 in 6 per cent £1 Preference shares and 8,000 £1 Ordinary shares were to be allotted to the partners and £14,300 paid in cash. The offer was accepted and it was decided that Grove should be appointed a director of Holloway Ltd. Lane chose to retire and by agreement he was to receive £1,300 from Grove such to be effected by adjustment on capital accounts. In addition, 400 Ordinary shares were to be allotted to Lane, any balance being paid to him in cash.

The partnership business ceased and all the transactions were duly carried through. The sundry debtors realized £2,700 and the creditors were settled for £6,800.

Prepare Realization Account, Bank Account and give, in columnar form, the partners' capital accounts showing the completion of the transactions.

(*A.C.C.A.*)

24. Cole and Porter have traded as engineers for several years, sharing profits and losses as to three-fifths and two-fifths respectively and at 31st March, 1963, their Balance Sheet was as follows—

	£	£		£	£
Trade Creditors .		13,250	Freehold Factory .		3,000
Capital Accounts			Plant . . .		12,000
Cole . . .	15,000		Stock . . .		20,500
Porter . . .	15,000		Debtors . . .	8,000	
		30,000	*Less* Reserve . .	250	
Undrawn Profits—					7,750
Cole . . .	2,000		Bank . . .		4,000
Porter . . .	2,000				
		4,000			
		£47,250			£47,250

They agreed to sell the business as a going concern to Rich Ltd., for the sum of £35,000 excluding the premises and bank balance, and received in exchange 30,000 shares of £1 each in Rich Ltd., fully paid, and £5,000 in cash. The company also undertook to pay the trade creditors. Cole purchased the factory from the partnership for £5,000 and later leased it to the company. The costs of dissolution, amounting to £150, were paid by the partnership.

In the absence of any provision in the partnership deed, Porter suggested that the profit on the sale should be divided in proportion to the partners' capital accounts as they stood at 31st March, 1963.

Prepare accounts showing the result of the dissolution and state your reasons for accepting or rejecting Porter's suggestion. *(A.C.C.A.)*

25. Corn, Rice and Oates were partners in the firm of Farmer & Co., sharing profits and losses in the proportions of three-sixths, two-sixths and one-sixth respectively. Accounts were prepared annually to 31st October. Oates died on 30th April, 1962.

On the death of a partner, the partnership agreement provided that his personal representatives should be entitled to receive the amounts appearing to his credit on the last balance sheet prior to his death less subsequent drawings, and in addition, to—

(*a*) any salary and interest on capital from the date of the last balance sheet to the date of death;

(*b*) an additional 7 per cent per annum on his capital for a like period in lieu of share of profits;

(*c*) his share of the goodwill of the partnership which was to be computed at one and a half year's purchase of the average profits for the three years ended prior to the date of death, such profits to be those before charging interest on capital and partners' salaries.

The share of goodwill so ascertained was to be purchased by the remaining partners in accordance with the proportions in which they shared profits. Payment of the balance found to be due to the deceased partner's estate was to be made by three equal instalments, the first instalment to be paid two months after the date of death, the other two at four-monthly intervals from that date. Interest at the rate of 5 per cent per annum from the date the first instalment became due was also to be paid on the outstanding balances.

The balances to the credit of capital and current accounts on 31st October, 1961, were as follows—

	Capital Account	Current Account
	£	£
Corn	6,300	500
Rice	4,200	440
Oates	2,400	300

Interest on capital at the rate of 5 per cent per annum was credited to each partner's current account but no interest was charged on drawings. Oates was in receipt of a salary of £40 per month.

The surviving partners duly paid cash for their shares of Oates' goodwill and the first two instalments of the balance due to his estate were paid by the firm on their due dates.

The following were the profits before charging interest on capital and Oates' salary—

	£
Year to 31st October, 1959	1,900
Year to 31st October, 1960	3,200
Year to 31st October, 1961	4,500
Year to 31st October, 1962	5,204

During the period from 31st October, to the date of his death Oates' drawings, including his salary, amounted to £284.

It is requested that you prepare (1) an account showing how the profit for the year ended 31st October, 1962, should be allocated, and (2) Oates' account and that of his personal representatives in the books of the firm for the year ended 31st October, 1962, including the entries necessary consequent upon his death.

N.B.: Any question of income tax is to be ignored. (*A.C.C.A.*)

26. Up to 31st March, 19.., Henry, John, and Kenneth had been trading in partnership and sharing profits in the respective proportions of 8, 7, and 5, and the firm's balance sheet drawn up as on that date was as follows—

		£		£
Capital—			Freehold Property	5,500
Henry	£17,000		Other Fixed Assets	4,100
John	14,000		Stock	26,600
Kenneth	12,000		Debtors	10,700
		43,000		
Creditors		3,200		
Bank Overdrawn		700		
		46,900		46,900

Henry having given notice that he wished to retire on the date mentioned, and it having been determined to admit Lambert as a new partner on the following day, the following terms were agreed—

(1) The balance sheet was to be revised, before the change, by writing up the book value of the freehold property to £7,500, and £200 was to be set aside as a provision against doubtful debts.

(2) Henry was to be credited with £3,000 for his share of goodwill. He was to be paid £5,000 out of money to be brought in by Lambert, and agreed to leave the balance of the sum remaining due to him as a loan to the firm.

(3) Lambert was to bring in £7,000 in cash and to be entitled to one-fifth of the profits, the other partners, as between themselves, sharing the balance in the same proportion as before.

(4) Finally, adjustments were to be made between the partners' capital accounts to give effect to their agreement that Lambert should purchase one-fifth of the firm's goodwill, which was to be valued for this purpose at £9,000. No goodwill account was to appear in the books of the new firm.

Write up the partners' capital accounts, showing the entries recording the foregoing, and draw up an initital balance sheet for the new firm. (*R.S.A.*)

27. (*a*) O. Brown and P. Crew are in partnership, sharing profits and losses three-fifths and two-fifths respectively. In order to provide money for repayment of their share of the capital and goodwill in the event of death, they assure their lives jointly for £8,000, paying an annual premium of £310, which is debited to the firm's profit and loss account each December. Crew dies on the last day of June, 19... The partnership deed provides that his representatives are to receive his capital as per the last balance sheet, plus interest at 5 per cent per annum to date of death, and his share of the profits to date of death, estimated according to the profits of the preceding year. They are also to receive his share of the goodwill, estimated at two years' purchase of the average net profits of the last three years before charging the insurance premiums. The net profits for the last three years after charging the insurance premiums were £2,073, £2,458, and £2,024 respectively. Crew's capital as per last balance sheet was £3,000, and his drawings to date of death amount to £720. Make the necessary adjustments and draw up Crew's account, showing the amount payable to his legal representatives.

(*b*) Assuming that P. Crew's share of the capital and goodwill is payable by annual instalments of £2,000, interest at 5 per cent per annum being charged on the outstanding balance. Show the ledger account in the firm's books.

CHAPTER 19

COMPANIES: FORMATION AND CAPITAL

Mrs. Bertram—"That sounds like nonsense, my dear."
Mr. Bertram—"May be so, my dear, but it may be very good law for all that."

SIR WALTER SCOTT—*Guy Mannering*

A COMPANY is a legal person or entity created by the association of a number of persons in accordance with the law, for the purpose of a defined object.

The formation of companies in England, for trading and other purposes, dates back for more than three centuries. We see some notable examples in the seventeenth century in the East India Company, the Hudson's Bay Company, the New River Company, and the Bank of England, which were incorporated by Royal Charter or by special Acts of Parliament. Incorporation otherwise than by these two methods was not possible until 1844; while the principle of "limited liability" was not recognized till 1855. The Act of 1862 opened up a new era in the history of companies, and there was further important legislation in 1908. The whole of the statute law relating to companies was consolidated by the Companies Act, 1929, which governed companies in Great Britain until the Companies Act, 1947, revised the law. The Companies Act, 1948, which consolidated the 1929 and 1947 Acts, and the Companies Act, 1967, which introduced important amendments, now govern companies in Great Britain. Insurance Companies are governed by the Insurance Companies Act 1958, as amended by the Companies Act 1967.

Prohibition of Large Partnerships. Companies not incorporated are, in the eyes of the law, nothing more than private partnerships.

In general, a partnership having the acquisition of gain as its object is limited to a maximum of twenty partners (ten in the case of a banking business) but, as stated on p. 1701, larger partnerships may be formed by accountants, solicitors, stockbrokers and jobbers, patent agents, actuaries, chartered engineers and surveyors, subject in some cases to the approval of the Board of Trade.

Kinds of Companies. There are three kinds of companies which may be constituted and incorporated under the Companies Acts, 1948 and 1967.

1. COMPANY LIMITED BY SHARES. This is a company having the liability of its members limited by the memorandum to the amount, if any, unpaid on the shares respectively held by them. Once the capital is fully paid up, there is no further liability resting on the shareholder. The majority of

companies are limited by shares, and it is proposed therefore to deal mainly with such companies.

2. Company Limited by Guarantee. This is a company having the liability of its members limited by the memorandum to such amount as the members may respectively thereby undertake to contribute to the assets of the company in the event of its being wound up. There are only a few companies of this class in existence.

3. Unlimited Company. This a company not having any limit on the liability of its members. Every shareholder is liable for the debts of the company as in ordinary partnership. Such a company possesses, however, two advantages: (*a*) The liability of each member ceases at the end of a year from the time he ceases to be a member; (*b*) the shares of the company are transferable; (*c*) the company does not have to file accounts with the Registrar of Companies.

Number of Persons. The legal minimum number of persons that can form a public company is seven, or in the case of a private company, two. The maximum number of members for a private company is fifty. If a company carries on business for more than six months after the number of its members has been reduced below seven, or two, as the case may be, every member cognizant of the fact is personally liable for the whole of the debts of the company contracted after the period of six months.

Public Company. A public company is any company which is not a private company and is therefore free to offer its shares to the public for subscription.

Private Company. By Sect. 28 of the Companies Act, 1948, a private company is one which by its articles—

1. Restricts the right to transfer its shares.

2. Limits the number of its members (exclusive of persons who are in the employment of the company and ex-employees) to fifty.

Where two or more persons hold one or more shares jointly, they are, for the purposes of this section of the Act, to be treated as a single member.

3. Prohibits any invitation to the public to subscribe for any shares or debentures of the company.

Unless the memorandum or articles expressly forbid it, a private company may turn itself into a public company by passing a special resolution, and filing with the registrar of companies the prescribed statement in lieu of prospectus, together with the prescribed statutory declaration.

Advantages of a Private Company. A private company is exempt from several of the obligations and restrictions imposed on a public company—

1. The minimum number of members may be two instead of seven. (Sect. 1, Companies Act, 1948.)

2. It is not obliged to file a statement in lieu of a prospectus. (Sect. 48 (3).)

3. The restrictions put upon the commencement of business, namely, the obtaining of the minimum subscription, waiting for the certificate entitling it to commence, etc., do not apply. (Sect. 109 (7).)

4. The restrictions placed on the allotment of shares (Sect. 48 (3)), and on the appointment of directors (Sect. 181 (5)) do not apply.

5. It is not obliged to hold a statutory meeting or forward to the members, or to file with the registrar of companies, the statutory report. (Sect. 130.)

Exempt Private Company. Before the Companies Act, 1967, came into force some private companies were not required to include a copy of their accounts in the Annual Return filed with the Registrar of Companies. This status was abolished by the 1967 Act.

Re-Registration of Companies—Unlimited to Limited. Under Sect. 44 of the Companies Act, 1967, it is possible for an unlimited company to become limited but without prejudice to debts and obligations incurred before the change in status. This clause replaces Sect. 16 of the 1948 Act.

Limited to Unlimited. Under Sect. 43 of the 1967 Act a new provision is made for a limited company to abandon that status and become unlimited. This arises from the abolition of the exempt private company which, under the 1948 Act, exempted small family businesses from disclosure of their accounts. Such businesses may now only obtain privacy from their trading results if they are also prepared to accept the risks of unlimited status. In 1969, there were just over 4,000 such companies.

Disclosure of Accounts. Limited status requires full disclosure except in the case of Discount companies under Sect. 175 of the 1948 Act and Insurance companies under Sect. 433, provided they are recognized as such by the Board of Trade. The specific exemptions are given in Schedule 2 of the 1967 Act which also extends some exemptions to Shipping companies recognized by the Board of Trade. Exemption was withdrawn from London Clearing and some Scottish Banks in 1970.

Difference between a Company and a Partnership. The following differences should be carefully noted—

1. The individuality of the members who form a company is entirely lost in the personality of the company itself, which is regarded in law as a separate and distinct entity. Thus a member of a company may enter into contracts with the company itself in the same manner as any other individual.

2. In a limited company, the creditors can proceed only against the property of the company in case of necessity, and, ordinarily, there is no remedy beyond the amount of the fixed capital, which is, in fact, the total amount of the property of the legal person. In a partnership or unlimited company the creditors may not only proceed against the property of the partnership, but also against the private property of each individual partner or member.

3. In a public company, shares may be transferred without the consent of the other members, and without affecting its existence: this is not possible in partnerships or private or unlimited companies.

4. In the case of a limited company, the liability of each shareholder is

limited to the amount unpaid on the shares which he holds; in a partnership and an unlimited company, each member is liable jointly for the whole of the debts of the firm.

5. The minimum number of members is two for a partnership or private company and seven for a public company. The maximum number is generally twenty for a partnership (ten in the case of banks) but may be increased for a few professions, subject to Board of Trade approval in some cases. For a private company the maximum is fifty (except for employees). There is no maximum for a public company as to the number of shares issued.

6. In a partnership, each partner can take part in the management, and his actions are legally binding on the firm; but in a company, the rights of management are restricted to a special body, selected by the shareholders, called *directors*.

7. In a partnership the rights of the members are regulated by the deed of partnership, and may be altered by mutual agreement. In a limited company, the powers of the company are governed by the memorandum of association, which can be altered only to a limited extent, as laid down in the Companies Act, 1948; and the powers of the directors are regulated by the articles, which can only be altered by special resolution of the shareholders.

8. The law prescribes an annual audit for a company, but not for a partnership.

9. The capital of a private firm is decided by the partners and may be altered by mutual agreement. The capital of a company is *fixed* by the memorandum, and can only be increased or decreased in a special statutory manner.

FORMATION OF COMPANY

Any seven or more persons (or, where the company to be formed will be a private one within the meaning of the Act, any two or more persons) associated for any lawful purpose may, by subscribing their names to a memorandum of association, and otherwise complying with the requirements of the Act in respect of registration, form an incorporated company.

The steps in the formation of a company are briefly as follows—

1. Promoter devises a scheme of capitalization bearing in mind—

(*a*) Price to be paid if for an existing business.
(*b*) Assets to be purchased.
(*c*) Cost of formation.
(*d*) Working capital.

2. Promoter approaches financiers with a view to underwriting (if there is to be an issue of shares to the public).

3. Solicitor prepares any contracts in connexion with the purchase of

assets and underwriting, but in particular the following documents to be filed with the Registrar of Companies—

(*a*) Memorandum of association,
(*b*) Articles of association,
(*c*) Statement of nominal capital,
(*d*) Declaration of compliance with the requirements of the Companies Act,

and if the company is a public one—

(*e*) A list of persons who have consented to become directors,
(*f*) Individual contracts agreeing to act as directors,
(*g*) Individual undertakings to acquire qualification shares (if any).

These documents, when stamped, are all lodged with the Registrar and within two or three days a certificate of incorporation will be issued.

Scheme of Capitalization. When the promoters of a company wish to raise money from the public, the offer is not likely to meet with success unless investors can be attracted.

Types of Invested Capital. There are three main types of invested funds—

1. *Debentures.* Loans for a fixed period carrying a fixed rate of interest.
2. *Preference Shares.* Shares carrying limited voting rights but with a fixed percentage rate of dividend.
3. *Ordinary Shares or Equity.* Shares normally carrying full voting rights and the entitlement to the residual earnings out of which the directors may propose dividends.

Each type is dealt with more fully later. The factors attracting different types of investor are as follows—

1. *Priority.* The claim of the investors is in the order of priority shown above. Ordinary shares have the lowest priority in claiming dividends and for repayment of capital in the event of liquidation.
2. *Risk.* The risk of non-payment follows the order of priority.
3. *Share of Income.* Debentures and Preference shares are limited in their participation in profits. Ordinary shares are not.
4. *Control.* Control of the company normally lies with the equity or ordinary shares.

Gearing. The relationship between fixed return and ordinary share capital is called the gearing of the company. This is considered fully in the chapter on interpretation at the end of the book. A company promoter will arrange a gearing which attracts sufficient capital of each type.

Underwriting, Commissions and Discounts. Underwriting is insurance against the risk that shares or debentures offered to the public for subscription may not be taken up, the underwriters guaranteeing to take up those shares or debentures for which the public fail to subscribe. In return for this they are paid a commission either in cash or in shares. An agreement to *place* shares, however, is not an underwriting agreement. By Sect. 53 of the Act, it is lawful for a company to pay a commission to any person in consideration of his subscribing or agreeing to subscribe, whether absolutely or conditionally, for any shares in the company, or procuring or agreeing to procure subscriptions, whether absolutely or conditionally, for any shares in the company, if the payment of the commission is authorized by the articles, and the commission paid or agreed to be paid does not exceed 10 per cent of the price at which the shares are issued, or the amount or rate authorized by the articles, whichever is the less, and—

(*a*) In the case of shares offered to the public for subscription, disclosed in the prospectus; or

(*b*) In the case of shares not offered to the public for subscription disclosed in the statement in lieu of prospectus, or in a statement in the prescribed form signed in like manner as a statement in lieu of prospectus and filed with the Registrar of Companies, and, where a circular or notice, not being a prospectus, inviting subscription for the shares is issued, also disclosed in that circular or notice.

Where a company has paid any sums by way of commission or allowed any sums by way of discount in respect of any shares or debentures, the total amount so paid or allowed, or so much thereof as has not been written off, must be stated in every balance sheet of the company until the whole amount has been written off.

Commission may also be paid by the underwriters to sub-underwriters for placing blocks of the underwriting, or to brokers or banks for placing shares. This is known as an "overriding" commission.

In addition to this a company usually pays brokerage. Stockbrokers and bankers are naturally in close touch with the investing public and where shares are applied for by their clients they receive a small commission if application forms bear their name and address. There is, of course, no question of underwriting in this case.

Registration of a Company. This third step in the formation of a company is almost entirely secretarial work and will therefore form a separate part of the studies of the accountancy student. Nevertheless a certain general knowledge of these matters is required and they are therefore dealt with quite briefly.

Memorandum of Association of a Company. The memorandum must state—

1. The name of the company, with "Limited" as the last word in its name, if it is limited.
2. Whether the registered office of the company is to be situated in England or in Scotland.
3. The objects of the company.
4. That the liability of the members is limited, if it is not to be unlimited.
5. The amount of the share capital with which the company proposes

to be registered, and the division thereof into shares of a fixed amount, unless it is limited by guarantee.

No subscriber to the memorandum may take less than one share, and each subscriber must write opposite to his name the number of shares he takes.

Articles of Association. Companies which are limited by guarantee, and unlimited companies, *must* register articles of association along with the memorandum. These are a set of rules or bye-laws drawn up to govern the internal working of a company. They regulate the issue of capital, the transfer and forfeiture of shares, the holding of meetings, prescribe for the keeping of the accounts and the audit thereof, define the powers and duties of directors, the rights of shareholders *inter se*, etc. The First Schedule to the Companies Act, 1948, Table C, contains a model set of articles suitable for adoption by a company limited by guarantee.

Where a company limited by shares does not frame articles of its own, a model set of articles, called Table A, provided in the Companies Act, 1948, applies automatically to the company. Even if articles are registered by a company limited by shares, Table A will still apply so far as its provisions are not inconsistent with the Articles, unless it is expressly excluded or modified by the Articles.

By Sect. 9, articles must (*a*) be printed, (*b*) be divided into paragraphs numbered consecutively; (*c*) be signed by each subscriber to the memorandum of association. Sect. 10 allows a company, by special resolution, to alter or add to its articles. Any article is null and void in so far as it conflicts with the memorandum of association or with the law. Any special resolution altering the articles must be printed and forwarded to the registrar of companies to record within fifteen days. An exempt private company need not print the resolution but must forward a copy to the registrar in a form acceptable by him. Such special resolution must also be embodied in or annexed to every copy of the articles issued subsequently.

Registration of Memorandum and Articles. The memorandum and the articles (if any) must be signed by each subscriber in the presence of at least one witness, who must attest the signature. They must then be forwarded to the Registrar of Companies for that part of the United Kingdom in which the registered office is stated by the memorandum to be situate; and he will retain and register them.

Registration Fees. Registration stamps are necessary, in the case of a company having a share capital, according to the following scale—

	£
Where the nominal share capital does not exceed £2,000 . .	20·00
Where the nominal share capital exceeds £2,000, the following fees according to the amount of nominal share capital—	
For every £1,000 or part of £1,000 up to £5,000 . .	1·00

	£
For every £1,000 or part of £1,000 after the first £5,000 up to £100,000	0·25
For every £1,000 or part of £1,000 after the first £100,000 .	0·05
For any increase of share capital after the first registration, the same fees per £1,000 or part of £1,000 as would have been payable if the increased share capital had formed part of the original share capital.	
No company to pay in respect of nominal share capital on registration, or afterwards, any greater amount of fees than	68·00
For re-registration of a limited company as unlimited .	5·00
For registration of annual accounts of overseas companies	3·00
For registration of a change of name	10·00

There is also capital duty of £0·50 per cent imposed by the Finance Act, 1933.

A company not having share capital pays a minimum registration fee of £20 and a maximum of £38 if it has 3,000 or more members. Capital fee is not payable.

A company limited by guarantee pays whichever would be higher if it were limited by shares or had no share capital.

The fees payable on the first registration are generally included in the item "preliminary expenses."

Re-Registration as an Unlimited Company. Re-registration of a limited company as unlimited requires preparation of a revised Memorandum and Articles of Association in accordance with Table E of the Companies Act, 1948. These are similar to those for a limited company except—

(*a*) Clauses 4 and 5 of the limited company Memorandum should be excluded. These are the statement that the liability of members is limited and the statement of share capital;

(*b*) Three new paragraphs should be inserted at the Share Capital section of the Articles. Paragraph 1 states the number of members proposed to be registered and that any future increases must be notified. Paragraph 3 is a substitute for paragraphs 40 to 46 of Table A.

Printed copies must be forwarded with the application together with the following forms:

R.1: Application for re-registration, to be signed by an officer of the company.

R.2: Members' assent to the re-registration, giving full names and addresses of *all* members and to be signed by *all* members (or their Attorneys).

R.4: Directors' declaration as to the members' assent, to be signed by all directors before a Commissioner for Oaths.

Preliminary Expenses. These include the law costs, registration fees, and other expenses incidental to the formation or promotion of a company.

Hence they are also called *formation expenses* and *promotion expenses*. Such expenditure is, of course, capital expenditure; but it is usually written off to revenue over a period of years, three, five or seven, according as the amount is small, large, or very large. The balance of the account appears each year on the assets side of the balance sheet until the amount is finally extinguished.

Promoter. This is the person who does the necessary preliminary work in forming or floating a company. The promoter stands in a fiduciary relationship towards the company he is floating, and must not, therefore, use his position to make any secret profit at the expense of the company. The promoter is personally liable for any acts done before the company is registered, and the company cannot subsequently ratify such acts.

Certificate of Incorporation. On the registration of the memorandum of association of a company the Registrar certifies under his hand that the company is incorporated, and, in the case of a limited company, that the company is limited. From the date of incorporation mentioned in the certificate of incorporation the subscribers to the memorandum, together with such other persons as may from time to time become members of the company, form a body corporate by the name contained in the memorandum, capable forthwith of exercising all the functions of an incorporated company, and having perpetual succession and a common seal, with power to hold lands, and with such liability on the part of the members to contribute to the assets of the company, in the event of its being wound up, as is mentioned in the Act.

The certificate of incorporation given by the registrar in respect of any association is conclusive evidence that all the requirements of the Act in respect of registration, and of all matters precedent and incidental thereto, have been complied with, and that the association is a company authorized to be registered and duly registered under the Act. If the company is a private one, it is at liberty to commence business forthwith; but a public company cannot proceed further than the issue of its prospectus inviting the public to apply for its shares or debentures until it obtains a certificate entitling it to commence business. (See p. 1911.)

Prospectus. This is a document issued by public companies inviting the public to subscribe for shares or debentures of the company. Every prospectus issued by or on behalf of a company, or in relation to any intended company, must be dated, and such date will, unless the contrary be proved, be taken as the date of publication of the prospectus. A copy of every such prospectus, signed by every person who is named therein as a director or proposed director of the company, or by his agent authorized in writing, must be filed for registration with the Registrar of Companies on or before the date of its publication, and no such prospectus must be issued until a copy of it has been so filed for registration. Every prospectus must state on the face of it that a copy has been filed for registration.

All matters required by law to be stated in a prospectus are set out in the Fourth Schedule to the Companies Act, 1948. This is unaffected by the Misrepresentation Act, 1967.

Statement in Lieu of Prospectus. A company which does not issue a prospectus on or with reference to its formation, must not allot any of its shares or debentures unless, at least three days before the first allotment of either shares or debentures, there has been filed with the Registrar of Companies a "Statement in Lieu of Prospectus" signed by every person who is named therein as a director or proposed director of the company, or by his agent authorized in writing, in the form and containing the particulars set out in the fifth schedule of the 1948 Act. This does not apply to a *private* company.

Allotment of Shares and Restrictions on Allotment. Allotment signifies the distributing of the shares in response to the applications made for them, or in pursuance of contracts agreeing to take them. A *letter of allotment* (see p. 1925) is sent to each allottee informing him of the numbers of the shares allotted to him. An application for shares is an offer to contract, and the posting of the letter of allotment is an acceptance of such offer. If no allotment is made a Letter of Regret (see p. 1926) is forwarded.

Minimum Subscription. By Sect. 47 of the Act—

1. No allotment shall be made of any share capital of a company offered to the public for subscription unless the amount stated in the prospectus as the minimum amount which, in the opinion of the directors, must be raised by the issue of share capital in order to provide for the matters specified in para. 4 of the Fourth Schedule to this Act has been subscribed, and the sum payable on application for the amount so stated has been paid to and received by the company.
2. The amount so stated in the prospectus shall be reckoned exclusively of any amount payable otherwise than in cash and is, in this Act, referred to as "the minimum subscription."
3. The amount payable on application on each share shall not be less than 5 per cent of the nominal amount of the share.

If the above conditions have not been complied with on the expiration of forty days after the first issue of the prospectus, the directors of the company must, within forty-eight days after the issue of the prospectus, refund to the applicants all moneys received from them. Beyond this period, the directors of the company would be liable to pay 5 per cent interest on amounts to be refunded to the applicants.

The above regulations, except (3), do not apply to any allotment of shares subsequent to the first allotment of shares offered to the public for subscription.

Where a company does not issue a prospectus there must be delivered to the Registrar of Companies a statement in lieu of prospectus, three days prior to proceeding to allot shares offered to the public for subscription.

Restrictions on Commencement of Business. By Sect. 109, a company must not commence any business or exercise any borrowing powers unless—

(*a*) Shares held subject to the payment of the whole amount thereof in cash have been allotted to an amount not less in the whole than the minimum subscription; and

(*b*) Every director of the company has paid to the company on each of the shares taken or contracted to be taken by him, and for which he is liable to pay in cash a proportion equal to the proportion payable on application and allotment on the shares offered for public subscription, or in the case of a company which does not issue a prospectus inviting the public to subscribe for its shares, on the shares payable in cash; and

(*c*) No money is liable to be repaid to applicants for shares or debentures by reason of failure to apply for or to obtain permission for the shares or debentures to be dealt with on any stock exchange; and

(*d*) There has been filed with the Registrar of Companies a statutory declaration by the secretary or one of the directors, in the prescribed form, that the aforesaid conditions have been complied with; and

(*e*) In the case of a company which does not issue a prospectus inviting the public to subscribe for its shares, there has been filed with the Registrar of Companies a statement in lieu of prospectus.

On the filing of the statutory declaration, and the statement in lieu of prospectus where necessary, the Registrar of Companies issues a certificate that the company is entitled to commence business. This section does not apply to a *private* company.

Return as to Allotments. By Sect. 52, whenever a company limited by shares makes any allotment of its shares, the company must within one month thereafter file with the Registrar of Companies—

(*a*) A return of the allotments stating the number and nominal amount of the shares comprised in the allotment, the names, addresses, and descriptions of the allottees, and the amount (if any) paid or due and payable on each share; and

(*b*) In the case of shares allotted as fully or partly paid up otherwise than in cash, a contract in writing constituting the title of the allottee to the allotment together with any contract of sale, or for services or other consideration in respect of which that allotment was made, such contracts being duly stamped, and a return stating the number and nominal amount of shares so allotted, the extent to which they are to be treated as paid up, and the consideration for which they have been allotted.

Certificates of Shares or Stock. Every company must, within two months after the allotment of any of its shares, debentures, or debenture stock, and within two months after lodgement of the transfer of any such shares, debentures or debenture stock, complete and have ready for delivery the certificates of all shares, the debentures, and the certificates of all debenture stock allotted or transferred, unless the conditions of issue of the shares, debentures, or debenture stock otherwise provide. A certificate, under the common seal of the company, specifying any shares or stock held by any member is prima facie evidence of the title of the member to the shares or stock. The certificates are issued in exchange for the allotment letters and the bankers' receipts for money paid on application and allotment.

Nature of Shares and of Money Due on Them. The shares or other interest of any member in a company are personal estate, transferable in the manner provided by the articles of the company. Each share in a company having a share capital must be distinguished by its appropriate number, unless it belongs to a class, all issued shares of which are fully paid and rank *pari passu.* A company cannot purchase its own shares. Any money due from a member of the company in respect of his shares is of the nature of a specialty debt, that is, recoverable any time within twelve years.

Transfer of Shares. Unless the articles restrict or forbid it, shares are transferable either by deed or by an instrument in writing signed by the transferor and the transferee, and such transfer must be sent to the company's office for registration. The transferee then has the right to have his name entered on the Register of Members as the holder of the shares. Any transfer of the shares of a deceased member by his personal representative—executor or administrator—or by the trustee in bankruptcy is valid. Some companies charge a fee of 12½p for registering transfers although the Stock Exchange recommend dropping the charge. These fees are posted to a separate account under the heading of "transfer fees," and carried to the credit of the profit and loss account. When partly paid shares are transferred, the transferor may still be liable for the amount due on them within a period of one year from the time at which he ceased to be a member, that is, if the transferee fails to pay the amount.

Office and Seal of Company. Every company must have a *registered* office to which all communications and notices may be addressed. Notice of the situation of the registered office, and of any change therein, must be given to the Registrar of Companies.

Every company must also possess a *common seal,* which must be used for the authentication of all important documents.

Meetings—Annual General Meeting. A general meeting, which is specified as the annual general meeting of a company, must be held once at least in every calendar year, and not more than fifteen months after the holding of the last preceding general meeting. If default is made in holding such a meeting, the Board of Trade may, on the application of any member, call or direct the calling of a general meeting of the company.

Statutory Meeting and Statutory Report. By Sect. 130 of the Act, every company limited by shares and every company limited by guarantee and having a share capital shall, within a period of not less than one month nor more than three months from the date at which the company is entitled to commence business, hold a general meeting of the members of the company which is to be called the statutory meeting. The directors must, at least fourteen days before the day on which the meeting is held, forward a report (in the Act called the *statutory report*) to every member of the company. The statutory report must be certified by not less than two directors of the company.

This must give specific information as set out in full in the section of the Act referred to. For specimen see next page.

A copy of this report must be filed with the Registrar of Companies. The provisions as to the statutory meeting and the statutory report do not apply to a *private* company.

Different Amounts Payable on Shares. A company, if so authorized by its articles, may—

1. Make arrangements on the issue of shares for a difference between the shareholders in the amounts and times of payment of calls on their shares.

2. Accept from any member the whole or a part of the amount remaining unpaid on any shares held by him, although no part of that amount has been called up.

3. Pay dividends in proportion to the amount paid up on each share where a larger amount is paid up on some shares than on others.

Alteration of Share Capital. By Sect. 61 a company limited by shares, if so authorized by its articles, may alter the conditions of its memorandum, that is to say, it may—

(*a*) Increase its share capital by the issue of new shares of such amount as it thinks expedient.

(*b*) Consolidate and divide all or any of its share capital into shares of larger amount than its existing shares.

(*c*) Convert all or any of its paid-up shares into stock, and reconvert that stock into paid-up shares of any denomination.

(*d*) Subdivide its shares, or any of them, into shares of smaller amount than is fixed by the memorandum, so, however, that in the subdivision the proportion between the amount paid and the amount (if any) unpaid on each reduced share shall be the same as it was in the case of the share from which the reduced share is derived.

(*e*) Cancel shares which, at the date of the passing of the resolution in that behalf, have not been taken or agreed to be taken by any person, and diminish the amount of its share capital by the amount of the shares so cancelled.

Every copy of the memorandum issued subsequently must be in accordance with the alteration. Notice of any such increase, consolidation, division, conversion, or reconversion must be given to the Registrar of Companies.

Reduction of Share Capital. A company limited by shares may, if so authorized by its articles, by special resolution confirmed by an order of the court, modify the conditions contained in its memorandum so as to reduce its share capital in any way. An office copy of any such order must be filed with the Registrar of Companies before the resolution can take effect.

WALDRON MANUFACTURING AND TRADING COMPANY
Limited
STATUTORY REPORT OF THE DIRECTORS

PURSUANT to Section 130 of the Companies Act, 1948, your Directors beg to report as follows—

(*a*) The total number of shares allotted is 60,000, of which 20,000 are allotted as fully paid up, in part consideration of the goodwill and assets of the business, and upon each of the remaining shares the sum of £0·50 has been paid in cash.

(*b*) The total amount of cash received by the company in respect of the shares issued wholly for cash is £20,000.

(*c*) The receipts and payments of the company to 20th March, 19.., are as follows—

Particulars of Receipts	£	Particulars of Payments	£
Application and Allotment Instalments—		Vendor (part payment of purchase price)	10,000
Ordinary Shares	5.000	Preliminary Expenses	3,000
Preference Shares	15,000	Printing and Stationery	120
Debentures	10,000	Balance at X Bank	16,880
	30,000		30,000

The preliminary expenses of the company are estimated at £4,000.

(*d*) The following are the names, addresses, and descriptions of the Directors, Auditors, Manager, and Secretary of the company—

Directors

FRANK T. WALDRON, Merchant, 1 Penley Mansions, Sidcup.
THOMAS RETROP, Solicitor, 2 Lucas Street, Bexley.
ALBERT O. COOPER, Gentleman, The Cedars, Farnham.
JAMES F. LONGLEY, Gentleman, 8 Park Drive, Bromfield.

Auditors

FREDERICK SHARPE & CO., Chartered Accountants, 67–9 Temple Avenue, Holborn, London, E.C.2.

Manager

FRANK T. WALDRON, Merchant, 1 Penley Mansions, Sidcup.

Secretary

THOMAS DUNSCOMBE MATTHEWS, Chartered Secretary, 27 Finsbury Park Road, London, N.22.

(*e*) Particulars of contracts, the modification of which is to be submitted to the meeting for its approval, together with the particulars of the modification or proposed modification.

We hereby certify that this report is correct.

FRANK T. WALDRON } *Directors*
THOMAS RETROP }

Auditors Report

We hereby certify that so much of this report as relates to the shares allotted by the company and to the cash received in respect of such shares, and to the receipts and payments of the company on capital account, is correct.

F. SHARPE & CO., Chartered Accountants } *Auditors*

Dated this 20th day of March, 19...

Reserve Liability of Limited Company. A limited company may by special resolution determine that any portion of its share capital which has not been already called up shall not be capable of being called up, except in the event and for the purposes of the company being wound up. The object of this is to increase the confidence of creditors in the financial stability of the company, but it is rarely done nowadays.

Mortgages, Charges and Debentures. By Sect. 95 of the Act—

(*a*) a charge for the purpose of securing any issue of debentures;
(*b*) a charge on uncalled share capital of the company;
(*c*) a charge created or evidenced by an instrument which, if executed by an individual, would require registration as a bill of sale;
(*d*) a charge on land, wherever situate, or any interest therein;
(*e*) a charge on book debts of the company;
(*f*) a floating charge on the undertaking or property of the company;
(*g*) a charge on calls made, but not paid;
(*h*) a charge on a ship or any share in a ship;
(*i*) a charge on goodwill, on a patent or a licence under a patent; on a trade mark or on a copyright or a licence under a copyright;

shall, so far as any security on the company's property is thereby conferred, be void against the liquidator and any creditor of the company, unless the prescribed particulars of the charge, together with the instrument (if any) by which the mortgage or charge is created or evidenced, are delivered to or received by the Registrar of Companies for registration in the manner required by the Act within twenty-one days after the date of its creation.

The Registrar shall keep, with respect to each company, a register in the prescribed form of all the charges created by the company, and requiring registration under this section, and shall, on payment of the prescribed fee, enter in the register with respect to every such charge, the date of creation, the amount secured by it, short particulars of the property charged, and the names of the persons entitled to the charge. The register shall be open to inspection by any person on payment of a fee not exceeding 1s. for each inspection.

The Registrar shall give a certificate under his hand of the registration of any mortgage or charge registered in pursuance of this section stating the amount thereby secured. The company shall cause a copy of every certificate of registration to be endorsed on every debenture or certificate of debenture stock which is issued by the company, and the payment of which is secured by the charge so registered.

It shall be the duty of the company to send to the Registrar for registration the particulars of every charge created by the company, and of the issues of debentures of a series, requiring registration under this section. Every company must keep a copy of every such instrument, and a copy of one such debenture, at its registered office.

Perpetual Debentures. A condition contained in any debentures, or in any deed for securing any debentures, is not invalid by reason only that thereby the debentures are made irredeemable or redeemable only on the happening of a contingency, however remote, or on the expiration of a period, however long.

Power to Reissue Redeemed Debentures. Where a company has redeemed any debentures previously issued, the company, unless the articles or conditions of issue expressly otherwise forbid, has power to keep the debentures alive for the purposes of reissue, and may either reissue the same debentures or issue others in their place. Where a company has deposited any of its debentures to secure advances from time to time, on current account or otherwise, the debentures are not deemed to have been redeemed by reason only of the account of the company having ceased to be in debit whilst the debentures remained so deposited.

Trust Deed. The property of the company comprised in the charge is frequently conveyed by way of mortgage to a trustee or trustees for the debenture holders. Such an instrument is called a "trust deed," and reference to such trust deed and conditions is made on every debenture covered by it.

Floating Charge. If the property mortgaged consists of assets other than freeholds and leaseholds, such as stock, book debts, etc., the charge is called a "floating charge," and the company is able to deal with its movable property in the ordinary course of business. A floating charge attaches to the assets in the varying condition they may happen to be from time to time, and remains dormant all the while the company is a going concern, or until after default in payment of interest.

Rights of a Debenture Holder. A debenture holder who has a charge upon the company's property may—

1. Sue for repayment of the principal and any interest which is owing.
2. Present a winding-up petition against the company.
3. Prove for the debt in the winding up.
4. Appoint a receiver.

The last right is the one most frequently exercised; for a company may be only temporarily embarrassed, and a little careful management may lift it out of its difficulties.

Auditors and Audit. Every company must have an annual audit, and the auditors must report to the members on the accounts examined by them, and on every balance sheet, every profit and loss account and all group accounts laid before the company in general meeting during their tenure of office. The report shall be read before the company in general meeting and shall be open to inspection by any member.

The report shall state whether in the auditors' opinion the company's balance sheet and profit and loss account and the group accounts have been properly prepared in accordance with the provisions of the 1948 and 1967 Acts. Whether in their opinion a true and fair view is given—

(i) in the case of the balance sheet, of the state of the company's affairs at the end of its financial year;
(ii) in the case of the profit and loss account (if it be not framed as a consolidated profit and loss account), of the company's profit or loss for its financial year;
(iii) in the case of group accounts submitted by a holding company, of the state of affairs and profit or loss of the company and its subsidiaries dealt with thereby, so far as concerns members of the company.

It is the duty of the auditors of a company, in preparing their report under this section, to carry out such investigations as will enable them to form an opinion as to—

(*a*) Whether proper books of account have been kept by the company and proper returns adequate for audit have been received from branches not visited.
(*b*) Whether the company's balance sheet and (unless it is framed as a consolidated profit and loss account) profit and loss account are in agreement with the books of account and returns.

If not the auditors must state that fact in their report. Every auditor of a company has a right of access at all times to the books and accounts and vouchers of the company, and is entitled to require from the officers of the company such information and explanation as he thinks necessary for the purposes of his duties.

If the auditors fail to obtain all the information and explanations which, to the best of their knowledge and belief, are necessary for the purposes of their audit, they must state that fact in their report.

The auditors of a company are entitled to attend any general meeting of the company and to receive all notices of, and other communications relating to, any general meeting which any member of the company is entitled to receive, and to be heard at any general meeting which they attend on any part of the business of the meeting which concerns them as auditors.

Companies Established Outside the United Kingdom. By Sect. 407 every company incorporated outside Great Britain which establishes a place of business within Great Britain must, within one month from the establishment of the place of business, file with the Registrar—

(*a*) a certified copy of the charter, statutes, or memorandum and articles of the company, or other instrument constituting or defining the constitution of the company, and, if the instrument is not written in the English language, a certified translation thereof;

(*b*) particulars of the directors and secretary of the company;

(*c*) the names and addresses of some one or more persons resident in the United Kingdom authorized to accept on behalf of the company service of process and any notices required to be served on the company.

In the event of any alteration being made in any such instrument or in the directors or secretary or in the names or addresses of any such persons as authorized, the company must within the prescribed time file with the Registrar a notice of the alteration. Every such company must file with the Registrar each year the prescribed statement in the form of a balance sheet and profit and loss account or a certified translation thereof.

CAPITAL

Share Capital is the total amount "paid up" on all classes of shares of a company. (See Paid-up Capital.)

Authorized Capital is the amount stated in the memorandum of association as the amount of capital to be issued and upon which stamp duty has been paid.

Nominal Capital. The face value of a share must be stated when it is issued. It may be £0·25 or £1 or £10 and this is the nominal value. The total of the nominal value of all shares is the nominal capital. Nominal means "in name only" and the market value of shares will usually be greater than their nominal value.

Registered Capital is also another name for the authorized capital.

Issued and Subscribed Capital. This is the part of the authorized capital which has been issued to the public for cash, and to the vendors as fully or partly paid.

Called-up Capital is the amount of money which the holders of the shares—issued or subscribed—have been required to pay. A company does not necessarily require the full amount at once on the shares it has issued, and, therefore, *calls up only* such as it needs, hence the use of the term.

Paid-up Capital is the amount of the called-up capital that has actually been *paid up* by the shareholders, some of whom sometimes fail to pay the sums due from them when a call is made, the amounts thus owing being known as "calls in arrear" or "calls unpaid." It also includes the amount of the shares issued as fully or partly paid to the vendor and others.

Uncalled Capital is the difference between the nominal value of the shares actually issued to the public, the vendors and others and the called-up capital.

Unissued Capital is the amount of the authorized capital which has not yet been issued to the public, or subscribed capital which has not yet been called up.

Example. A company was formed with a capital of £100,000 in shares of £1 each, and duly incorporated. It issued to the vendors 30,000 shares of £1 each as fully paid, in part payment of the purchase consideration. It also offered to the public 50,000 shares, payable £0·125 per share on application, £0·125 per share on allotment, £0·25 per share one month later, and the balance as and when required. All the money was duly received with the exception of the call of £0·25 on 200 shares. Give the various kinds of capital.

	£	£
Authorized or Registered Capital—		
100,00 Ordinary share of £1 each		100,000 N
Issued Capital—		
80,000		80,000 N
Called-up Capital—		
50,000 £0·50 called-up	25,000	
30,000 Ordinary Shares of £1 each fully paid	30,000	
		55,000
Paid-up Capital—		
Called-up capital	55,000	
Less calls in arrear	50	
		54,950
Uncalled Capital—		
Issued capital	80,000 N	
Called-up	55,000	
		25,000
Un-issued Capital—		
Authorized capital	100,000 N	
Issued	80,000 N	
		20,000 N

The items marked N are all in nominal terms.

SHARES

A share is the individual portion of the joint stock company's capital owned by a shareholder. Shares are divided into different classes according to their respective rights.

Ordinary Shares are normally those which hold the voting control of the company and the right to participate in the profits.

Preferred Ordinary Shares are those which have a right to a fixed dividend after payment of dividend to the preference shareholders.

Deferred Ordinary Shares are those which rank for dividend after the preferred ordinary shares, and which are usually entitled to the profits then remaining.

Non-voting Ordinary Shares. During the 1950's, many companies issued ordinary shares without voting rights, especially as a consequence of take-over bids. The Stock Exchange will not now permit quotations of new issues of such shares and many companies have, accordingly, ceded full voting rights to such shares. This is called enfranchisement.

Preference Shares are those which have a prior claim on any profits available for dividend. They *may* also have a prior claim to repayment of capital in the event of a winding up. If the shares are not cumulative preference shares, the preference dividend is payable only *out of the profits of each year*; and if not paid then, the preference shareholder cannot claim to receive it out of profits in subsequent years.

Cumulative Preference Shares are those on which the fixed dividend accumulates until it is all paid, the arrears of any one year being carried forward as a charge upon the subsequent year's profits. There is, however, no obligation to pay until a resolution has been passed declaring a dividend. The arrears are, therefore, shown on the balance sheet by way of note only. Unless the articles expressly or impliedly provide otherwise, preference shares are always cumulative as to dividend, but not preferential as to capital.

Redeemable Preference Shares are a class of share which, by the Companies Act, 1948 (Sect. 58), a company may issue if authorized by its articles. The company may provide for their repayment by creating a "reserve fund" built up of "profits" which, otherwise, would have been available for dividends, or alternatively by an issue of new shares for this express purpose. No such shares can be redeemed unless fully paid.

Deferred, Founders', or Management Shares. These are shares which have to wait for their dividend until all other classes of share have participated in the profits. They are often taken by the founders or promoters of the company, and sometimes by the vendors. They are generally entitled to the whole or a very large portion of the surplus profits after payment of all prior claims.

Difference between Shares and Stock. Shares are units of capital transferable only in their entirety. Stock on the other hand is the mass of the capital of the company, any part of which is transferable; subject to any limitation in the memorandum or articles any fractional part of a pound may be transferred. Shares may be only partly paid, but stock must always be fully paid. Shares are usually numbered while stock is not identified in this way.

STATUTORY AND STATISTICAL BOOKS

The term *statutory books* merely means those which, by law, i.e. the Companies Act, 1948, every company must keep.

Books of Account. Sect. 147 of the Companies Act requires that every company shall cause to be kept proper books of account with respect to—

(*a*) all sums of money received and expended by the company and the matters in respect of which the receipt and expenditure takes place;
(*b*) all sales and purchases of goods by the company;
(*c*) the assets and liabilities of the company.

It will be seen that no particular books are specified, but whatever books are kept (cash book, sales and sales returns book, purchases and purchases returns book, and ledgers) must be such as to give a true and fair view of the state of the company's affairs and explain its transactions.

Books of Record. In addition to the above financial books, the law as contained in the Companies Acts makes the keeping of the following books compulsory—

1948 Act
Sect. 110. Register of Members (including a copy of any Dominion Register).
" 200. Register of Directors and Secretaries.
" 104. Register of Mortgages and Charges.
" 145. Minute Book.
1967 Act
Sect. 27–29. Register of Directors' Shareholdings and interest in Debentures.

Many other books are necessary if complete records are to be kept of the numerous details connected with the business operations, but they are optional.

However, Sects. 109–118 of the 1967 Companies Act give the Board of Trade wide powers to inspect the books and papers of companies and corporate bodies. These papers include accounts, deeds, writings and documents, even if they are in the possession of some other person.

Board of Trade Rights to Litigate. The Board has the right to appoint inspectors to investigate the affairs of companies under Sect. 165 of the 1948 Companies Act and sections of the 1967 Act 109 to 118 and sections 109 to 118 of the 1967 Act give wide powers to inspect books and documents. If criminal offences have been committed the inspector's reports may be referred to the Director of Public Prosecutions. The Board may also petition for liquidation of the companies and sue in its name to recover its property or for damges. Under Section 116, however, solicitors and bankers are exempted from producing privileged documents.

They are all statistical books and those generally to be found are—

1. Application and Allotments Book.
2. Call Books.
3. Share Certificate Books.
4. Registers of Transfers.

5. Debenture Interest Book.
6. Dividend Books.
7. Seal Register.
8. Register of Probates.
9. Directors' Attendance Book.
10. Agenda Book.
11. Register of Debenture Holders.

The keeping of all these books is almost entirely secretarial work, but as questions are set upon some of the more important in many accountancy examination papers, further consideration must be given to them.

Register of Mortgages and Charges. This is another tabular book in which are entered all charges specifically affecting the property of the company, and all floating charges on the undertaking or any property of the company, and should show the date the charge was created, the mortgagee's name and address, the amount of the charge, short particulars of the property charged, and the rate of interest.

An example of a suitable ruling is given below—

REGISTER OF CHARGES

No. of Charge	Date Charge Created	Mortgagee's		Amount of Charge	Particulars of Property Charged	Rate of Interest	Remarks
		Name	Address				
	19.. Jan. 1	Series of 100 debentures of £100 each, secured by a trust deed of which the following are trustees— John Wilson, The Lodge, Derby. Fred Smith, Red Gable, Leeds.		£ 10,000	The whole of the undertaking of the company, both present and future, including its uncalled capital for the time being.	% 4	

Application and Allotments Book. This is ruled in tabular form and sets out the names, addresses, and occupations of all applicants for shares, the number of shares applied for, the amount paid on application, the number of shares allotted, the distinctive numbers of such shares, the amount due on application and allotment, the balance due on allotment, the cash paid on allotment, cash returned on shares applied for and not allotted, the numbers of the share certificates issued, and a remarks column. It is used to record the details stated in respect of each applicant, and the register of members is compiled from it. Separate books or sheets are kept for each class of share.

All persons who are allotted shares must have some form of evidence of ownership, and this is the letter of allotment to which reference is made on p. 1910.

There is no one form, but a representative specimen appears on p. 1925.

Where the shares are eagerly sought after it may not be possible to allot shares to all applicants, so that some will have to be repaid the money deposited at the time of application; and as a matter of form a letter of regret (see specimen on p. 1926) is sent with the warrant or cheque.

The amount paid on application and allotment is usually only a part of the nominal value of the shares, the balance being received by the company in the form of calls spread over a period as stated in the prospectus. It would seem, then, that once a person has been allotted shares, the calls must be paid, usually to the full nominal value; the shares may, of course, be issued at a premium. After allotment any change of ownership can take place only by means of a transfer. In practice transfers would cause an enormous amount of work, at least until the shares had "settled down" on the market, but for an arrangement now to be described.

It must be remembered that in possibly the majority of share issues there are large numbers of persons who do not receive any allotment and who, in their desire to become shareholders, immediately turn to the Stock Exchange with a view to making a purchase. This demand, following the rule of supply and demand, will result in a price in excess of the amount paid on application and allotment and the shares are said to be at a premium. This may take place quite a long time before any calls are due and therefore at a time when those who are prepared to sell have only letters of allotment as evidence of their ownership.

To prevent the execution of a transfer which, besides causing the company a lot of work, would be expensive, most allotment letters are provided on the reverse side with a form of renunciation and acceptance. The holder of the letter of allotment has only to renounce his right to the share by signing the renunciation portion, whilst the buyer signs the form of acceptance, as the result of which the shares change hands. The period during which this may be done must, of course, be limited, and is usually fixed at not more than one month, after which shares can change hands only by transfer deeds. Opposite is a specimen of a Letter of Renunciation and Acceptance.

Many thousands of entries must obviously be made to record the cash in connexion with share issues, and in order to relieve the general cash book of all this detail, special subsidiary cash books are used, only the totals being transferred to the main book. The company's bankers also keep separate pass books to correspond. Much depends upon the size of the issue whether or not this is done, and in small companies it would no doubt be sufficient to record the details in an inner column of the general cash book, extending only the daily totals into the bank column.

The following example is typical and will show the relation of the cash books to the share ledger and application and allotment sheets.

ORDINARY SHARE APPLICATION AND ALLOTMENT BOOK

No. of Application	Name	Address	Occupation	No. of Shares Applied For	Amount Paid on Application
					£
1	Archer, Arthur	Green Hollow, Leeds	Iron merchant	500	125
2	Arnold, Benjamin	The Wave, Torquay	Barrister	1,000	250
3	Brown, Joseph	The Firs, Guiseley, Leeds	Stockbroker	1,000	250

[Left-hand side]

ORDINARY SHARE APPLICATION AND ALLOTMENT BOOK (*cont.*)

No. of Shares Allotted	Distinctive No.		Share Ledger Folio	Amount Due on Application and Allotment	Balance Due on Allotment	Cash Paid on Allotment	Cash Returned	No. of Share Certificate	Remark
	From	To							
				£	£	£	£		
							125		
800	1	800		400	150	150			
1,000	801	1,800	3	500	250	250			

[Right-hand side]

WALDRON MANUFACTURING AND TRADING COMPANY
Limited
(Incorporated under the Companies Act, 1948)

LETTER OF ALLOTMENT

No............... REGISTERED OFFICE,

....19....

Sir or Madam,

In accordance with your application for shares in the above company, I have to inform you that the directors have allotted you....................preference shares of £1 each. The amount payable on application and allotment in respect of the said shares is— £

You have paid on application £

Leaving a balance due from you of £

which sum must be paid to the company's bankers, THE METRO BANK LIMITED, Annon Street, London, S.W.32., on or before the........................instant.

Yours faithfully,

To....................................

....

.... SECRETARY

This form must be forwarded ENTIRE, together with remittance, to the company's bankers.

WALDRON MANUFACTURING AND TRADING COMPANY
Limited

BANKER'S RECEIPT

Received this............................day of..., 19....
from..
the sum of...
being.......................per share payable on allotment of.........................preference shares of £.........................each in the above company.

For THE METRO BANK LIMITED

.... Stamp ....

£ CASHIER

This receipt, when returned by the bankers, must be preserved and exchanged in due course for share certificate.

WALDRON MANUFACTURING AND TRADING COMPANY
Limited
(Incorporated under the Companies Act, 1948)

LETTER OF REGRET

No.................. REGISTERED OFFICE,

...................................19....

Sir or Madam.

With reference to your application for shares in the above company, I have to inform you that because of an over-subscription, the directors regret they are unable to make you any allotment.

I therefore enclose a cheque for £ . , being the amount deposited by you on application for the said shares, and shall be obliged if you will kindly sign and return the receipt at the foot of this form.

Yours faithfully,

To.................................
....
.... SECRETARY
....

WALDRON MANUFACTURING AND TRADING COMPANY
Limited

RECEIPT

No..................

...................19...

RECEIVED of the above-named company the sum of..................................
....being refund of amount paid on application for...........................preference shares in the above company not allotted.

Signature.............................. | *Stamp* | ....

£

WALDRON MANUFACTURING AND TRADING COMPANY
Limited
(Incorporated under the Companies Act, 1948)

LETTER OF RENUNCIATION

To the Directors of
THE WALDRON MANUFACTURING AND TRADING COMPANY LTD.

I hereby renounce my right to the allotment of..................................shares of £.......................each in the above company, and request you to allot the said shares to my nominee:

Name..

Address..

....

Occupation ....

(*Signed*)..

Dated this....................day of..................19....

WALDRON MANUFACTURING AND TRADING COMPANY
Limited
(Incorporated under the Companies Act, 1948)

LETTER OF ACCEPTANCE

To the Directors of
THE WALDRON MANUFACTURING AND TRADING COMPANY LTD.

I hereby agree to accept the..................................shares of £...........each in the above company renounced by..in my favour. I undertake to pay the calls which may be made thereon. I also hereby request you to enter my name on the Register of Members in respect of the said shares.

Dated this......................day of...........................19...

Signature..

Address ....

....

Occupation ....

Example 1

The Waldron Manufacturing and Trading Co. Ltd. was registered with a capital of £100,000, consisting of 50,000 ordinary shares of £1 each, and 50,000 6 per cent preference shares of £1 each. The objects of the company were *inter alia* to acquire the goodwill and assets of the business of Frank T. Waldron. The purchase price was to be paid as to £10,000 in cash, and as to £20,000 in fully-paid ordinary shares of the company, allotted either to the vendor or to his nominees. Ten thousand of the ordinary shares were offered on 1st January for public subscription, payable £0·13 per share on application, £0·37 per share on allotment, and the balance in calls not exceeding £0·25 per share.

Applications were received, and allotments made, as under—

			No. of Shares applied for	No. of Shares allotted
Jan	2	Matthew B. Barker, solicitor, 71 Lime Street, Barnes, London, S.W.13 (including 1 share as signatory of the memorandum)	2,500	2,000
	3	Edward Clarke, solicitors' clerk, 420 Mare Street, Hackney, London, E.8 (signatory)	1	1
Jan	4	John F. Dalton, H.M.C.S., 194 Mildmay Park, London, N.18 (signatory)	1	1
		Fred Evans, solicitors' clerk, 96 Rood Lane, Brixton, London, S.W.2 (signatory)	1	1
	6	Isaac L. Mensper, surveyor, 25 Leyton Street, Boro, London, S.E.1 (signatory)	1	1
		Ernest O. Prince, accountant, 12 Temple Chambers, Holborn, London, E.C.1 (signatory)	1	1
	7	Thomas P. Retrop, solicitor, 2 Lucas Street, Bexley, Kent (including 1 share as signatory)	3,000	2,495
		Arthur Holdfast, cotton merchant, 726 Lime Street, Liverpool	500	*nil*
	8	James F. Longley, gentleman, 6 Park Drive, Bromfield, Salop	10,000	5,500
		Mrs. Ruth Oliver, widow, Halstead Park, Framley, Bucks	500	*nil*

Allotments were made on 15th January in order of application, and the shares numbered from 1 upwards. No allotments were made to A. Holdfast and Mrs Oliver, whose deposits were duly returned in full with letters of regret, Nos. 1 and 2. The moneys due on allotment were payable by 20th January, by which date they were all received.

Allotments were also made to the vendor and his nominee as follows—

Frank Waldron, merchant, 1 Penley Mansions, Sidcup, Kent, 15,000 shares (4,501 to 19,500).

Ellen Goode, spinster, 114 High Road, Sydenham, London S.E.26, 5,000 shares (19,501 to 24,500).

Write up the application and allotments book, and shareholders' cash book, recording the above particulars. (See pp. 1930–31.)

The work entailed in the making of calls on shares or debentures is almost identical with that already described in connexion with an original issue. Call sheets or books in tabular form are used, together with a separate cash book and pass book, the cash eventually being posted to the capital account. The cash entries are given fully in the next chapter.

The share certificates having been issued, all future changes in ownership must take place as the result of a formal transfer. All changes must eventually be recorded in the register of members, but for this purpose, although some companies post direct from the transfer form, it is still quite customary to have a subsidiary book—a Register of Transfers.

Register of Transfers. This is a book ruled in tabular form. There is no standard ruling, but the book usually contains columns to record the names and addresses of both transferor and transferee, the number of shares transferred, their distinctive numbers and the amount paid up thereon, the date the transfer was registered, and the number of new share certificates issued to the transferee. Other columns are also met with in some companies' books, viz. date the transfer was lodged with the company, number of old share certificate to be cancelled, number of balance certificate issued to transferor, amount of consideration received by transferor, date, and number of minute passing the transfer, etc.

In large companies, separate transfer registers are kept for each class of shares, also a separate department and staff. In small companies, one register frequently suffices, transfers of ordinary shares being entered in black ink, and transfers of preference shares in red; while in many such companies the register of transfers is frequently bound up with the share ledger, and thus forms part of it.

A suitable ruling is illustrated on pp. 1934.

The transfer deed has to bear an *ad valorem* stamp duty based on the market price of the shares or stock changing hands. There are, however, many occasions when it is necessary for such securities to be transferred without a purchase or sale taking place. In these cases instead of the true value being entered in the transfer deed as the *consideration*, a "nominal" figure is used, often as low as 25p, and the stamp duty is then only 50p, however great the value of the shares may be.

This fixed duty of 50p is applicable when the transaction falls within one of the following descriptions—

(*a*) Vesting the property in trustees on the appointment of a new trustee of a pre-existing trust, or on the retirement of a trustee.

(*b*) A transfer, as for a nominal consideration, to a mere nominee of the transferor where no beneficial interest in the property passes.

(*c*) A transfer by way of security for a loan; or a re-transfer to the original transferor on repayment of a loan.

(*d*) A transfer to a residuary legatee of stock, etc., which forms part of the residue devisable under a will.

(*e*) A transfer to a beneficiary under a will of a specific legacy of stock, etc.

(*f*) A transfer of stock, etc., being the property of a person dying intestate to the party or parties entitled to it.

(*g*) A transfer to a beneficiary under a settlement on distribution of trust funds of stock forming the share of the funds to which he is entitled.

(*h*) A transfer on the occasion of marriage to trustees of a settlement made in consideration of marriage.

(*i*) A transfer by a liquidator of stocks forming part of the assets of a company to shareholders in that company in satisfaction of their rights on winding up.

If a transfer, however, is made on a sale, or in liquidation of a debt, or in exchange for other securities, *ad valorem* duty is payable on the value, or agreed value, of the consideration.

Registration of Transfers. Each transfer has to be forwarded, together with the share certificate concerned, to the company's registered office for approval and registration. The transfer is examined with respect to stamp duty, date, signatures, etc., and the distinctive numbers[1] of the shares mentioned therein are compared with the numbers stated in the share certificate, also with those in the shareholder's account in the share ledger. The signature of the transferor is compared with his signature on previous transfers or on application forms. In some cases the transferor is notified by the company of the lodgement of the transfer, as a precaution against forgery. The transfer is then submitted to the board of directors. If they approve it, a resolution is passed and recorded in the directors' minute book. Particulars are then entered in the register of transfers, the transfers being numbered in consecutive order. A new share certificate is made out

[1] If all the issued shares, or all those of a particular class, are fully paid up and rank equally for all purposes, none of those shares needs a distinguishing number.

41 REGISTER OF TRANSFERS

No. of Transfer	Date Transfer Registered	Transferor's				
		S.L. Folio	Name	Address	S.L. Folio	Name
	19..					
1	Jun 25	101	Barker, M. B.	71 Lime St., Barnes	105	Mensper, I. L.
2	Jul 15	101	,, ,,	,, ,, ,,	106	Prince, E. O.
3	Aug 4	110	Longley, J. F.	6 Park Drive, Bromfield	107	Retrop, T. P.
4	Sep 15	110	,, ,,	,, ,, ,,	103	Dalton, J. F.
5	Nov 10	110	,, ,,	,, ,, ,,	111	Johnson, Henry A.
6	Dec 15	110	,, ,,	,, ,, ,,	112	Thorpe, Fritz B.

for the transferee. If the shares transferred form only part of a shareholder's holding, it is the practice to issue a balance certificate to the transferor. A fee of £0·125 is sometimes charged in respect of each transfer.

Example 2

The following transfers of ordinary shares were made, approved, and duly registered in the books of the Waldron Manufacturing and Trading Co. Ltd.—

25th June, 500 shares (1–500) from M. B. Barker to I. L. Mensper; No. of transfer deed, No. 1.
15th July, 500 shares (501–1,000) from M. B. Barker to E. O. Prince.
4th August, 1,000 shares (24,501–25,500) from J. F. Longley to T. P. Retrop.
15th September, 200 shares (25,501–25,700) from J. F. Longley to J. F. Dalton.
10th November, 500 shares (25,701–26,200) from J. F. Longley to Henry A. Johnson, 65 Old Steine, Brighton.
15th December, 500 shares (26,201–26,700) from J. F. Longley to Fritz B. Thorpe, 9 Minstrel Street, Hastings.

Write up the company's register of transfers. (See below.)

Blank Transfer. A blank transfer is one signed by the transferor, but in which the name of the transferee and the date of execution are not filled in. It is usually deposited with the lender, together with the share certificate concerned, as security for a loan. The company will not, of course, recognize a blank transfer; but it gives the holder an equitable right to the shares mentioned therein. If desired, the necessary particulars are filled in and the transfer duly registered, thus giving the holder the legal title.

Certification of Transfers. This is a practice that has grown up owing to the exigencies of Stock Exchange procedure. If a seller's share certificate includes more shares than he wishes to dispose of, he cannot hand it over to the buyer along with the transfer deed; so he takes his certificate and the transfer to the company's office, and has his transfer "certificated."

(ORDINARY SHARES) 41

Transferee's Address	Shares Transferred No.	Distinctive Numbers From	Distinctive Numbers To	Amount Paid Up	No. of New Certificate	Remarks
				£		
25 Leyton St., Boro, S.E.1	500	1	500	375	11	
12 Temple Chambers, E.C.1	500	501	1,000	375	12	
2 Lucas Street, Bexley	1,000	24,501	25,500	750	13	
194 Mildmay Park, N.18	200	25,501	25,700	150	14	
65 Old Steine, Brighton	500	25,701	26,200	375	15	
9 Minstrel St., Hastings	500	26,201	26,700	375	16	

If the documents are in order, the secretary writes or stamps on them a note similar to the following—

Certificate No.....216....for.........500........Shares of........£1....................each, ...£0·75....per share paid up, numbered........781........to...........1280........... inclusive, lodged at the Company's registered office this............14*th*............ day of *September*. ....19.... ....*A. Briller*............ Secretary

The buyers and their brokers then act on the faith of this certification just the same as if the certificate had been lodged with themselves. No fee is charged for certification. The object of it is to satisfy the transferee that the transferor can give a good title to the shares mentioned in the transfer. The old certificate is at once cancelled, a new certificate is eventually forwarded to the transferee, and a balance certificate to the transferor. Under Sect. 79 of the Companies Act, 1948, the certification of a transfer is a representation by the company that there have been produced to the company such documents as on the face of them show a prima facie title to the shares. The certification does not represent that the transferor has any title to the shares but if any person acts on the faith of a certification made negligently by the company, the company will be under the same liability as if it had been made fraudulently.

Forged Transfers. If a forged transfer is passed by the directors, the transferee acquires no rights to the shares mentioned therein, even though he may have received a share certificate from the company; and his name may be removed from the register of members. The company remains liable to the true owner for any dividends he may have lost through their action, and it can be compelled to re-enter his name on the register of members in respect of such shares. The Forged Transfers Acts, 1891 and 1892, give power to joint stock companies, local authorities, incorporated friendly societies, and building or other provident societies to charge an additional fee on each transfer registered in order to provide a fund out of which to compensate the *transferee* for any loss sustained under a forged transfer.

Scrip. This term is a Stock Exchange contraction for the word "subscription." It denotes a *provisional* certificate for shares or debentures in a joint stock company, or bonds of a Government loan. The scrip certificate is issued when the allotment money is paid, and is exchanged in due course for the share certificate or bond when all the instalments have been paid. *The terms "scrip" and "share certificate" are often used, however, as if synonymous.*

The difference between a share certificate and a scrip certificate will be seen by reference to the illustrations on pp. 1935 and 1936 respectively.

On the back of the scrip certificate will appear the dates of the various payments, similar to the following—

Date	Description of Payment	Rate	Amount Paid	Signature of Secretary
19..			£	
Feb 15	Application	10%	10	*T. Briller*
25	Allotment	20%	20	*T. Briller*
May 15	First Call	30%	30	*T. Briller*
Sep 15	Second Call	40%	40	*T. Briller*

Register of Members. This is a book ruled in tabular form, and, in addition to stating the name and address of each shareholder, and the date of becoming and ceasing to be a member, contains the number and distinctive numbers of shares acquired and transferred, the amount paid or agreed to be considered as paid on the shares of each member. Where shares are partly paid a cash account for each member showing amounts called and paid up is incorporated, forming the share ledger. There is no standard ruling. For a specimen see p. 1937. The total of the balances in this register should always agree with the capital account in the double entry books.

Separate registers are usually kept for each class of share.

Further Statutory Provisions. By the Companies Act, 1948, no notice of any trust is to be entered on the register of members. The register must be kept at the registered office of the company, except that—

1. If the work of making up is done at another office it may be kept at that office.

2. If the company arranges with another person to make up the register it may be kept at the office of that person.

It must be open to the inspection of any member gratis, and to the inspection of any other person on payment of a fee not exceeding 5p. This right of inspection applies only to a "going" concern; after liquidation has been decided upon, application must be made to the court. Any member or other person may acquire a copy of the register, or of any part of it, on payment of the prescribed fee. Circular-advertising agencies generally avail themselves of this privilege in order to obtain lists of the investing public. A company may, on giving notice by advertisement in some paper circulating in the district in which the registered office is situate, close the register for any time or times not exceeding in the whole thirty days in each year. The court has power to rectify the register in case of mistakes or omissions. The register of members is prima facie evidence of any matters directed or authorized by the Act to be inserted therein. A company whose objects comprise the transaction of business in a colony may, if so authorized by its articles, keep a branch register of members in that colony, and such dominion register is deemed to be part of its principal register. A copy of each entry must be transmitted to the registered office in order that duplicate of such register may be kept.

REGISTER OF TRANSFERS, ORDINARY SHARES

No. of Transfer	Date Transfer Regis- tered	Transferor's			Transferee's			No. of Shares	Shares Transferred			No. of New Certificates	Remarks
		Fo.	Name	Address	Fo.	Name	Address		Dist. Nos. From	Dist. Nos. To	Amount Paid Up		
	19..										£		
1	Mar 15	8	Pearce, Stanley	14 Brewerton Lane, Bradford, Yorks.	97	Bucknall, Fred	Westgarth, Baildon, Staffs.	2,000	2,301	4,300	2,000	138	

REGISTER OF TRANSFERS, PREFERENCE SHARES

No. of Transfer	Date Transfer Regis- tered	Transferor's			Transferee's			No. of Shares	Shares Transferred			No. of New Certificates	Remarks
		Fo.	Name	Address	Fo.	Name	Address		Dist. Nos. From	Dist. Nos. To	Amount Paid Up		
	19..										£		
2	Mar 15	79	Honey, Timothy	Brevity St., Morley, Derbyshire	171	Carreras, Peter	Charles Street, Beverley, Yorks.	1,000	5,764	6,763	1,000	321	
3	28	33	Tushingham, George	17 George St., Liverpool	172	Dawson, Arthur	69 West Lane, Dinnington, Sheffield	500	571	1,070	500	322	

No........................

WALDRON MANUFACTURING AND TRADING COMPANY
Limited

(Incorporated under the Companies Act, 1948)

CAPITAL £100,000

50,000 ORDINARY SHARES OF £1 EACH
50,000 6% PREFERENCE SHARES OF £1 EACH

SHARE CERTIFICATE

THIS IS TO CERTIFY that..

of ....

is the Registered Proprietor of........................6 per cent Preference Shares of £1 each, numbered........................to........................inclusive in the WALDRON MANUFACTURING AND TRADING COMPANY LIMITED, subject to the provisions of the Memorandum and Articles of Association of the Company, and that there has been paid in respect to each of the said shares the sum of

....

....

GIVEN UNDER THE COMMON SEAL of the Company this ....day of.................................19........

....
.... } DIRECTORS

Seal.

....

SECRETARY

No transfer of the above shares can be made without the production of this certificate.

WALDRON MANUFACTURING AND TRADING COMPANY
Limited

(Incorporated under the Companies Act, 1948)

ISSUE OF £10,000 DEBENTURES in BONDS of £100 EACH, bearing interest at £5 per cent per annum on the amount for the time being paid up thereon.

SCRIP CERTIFICATE

No.....127.......

THIS IS TO CERTIFY that..

of ....

is entitled upon payment of all instalments when due, and subject to surrendering all receipts for such instalments, and also this SCRIP CERTIFICATE, to.................. DEBENTURES of £.................. each in the above-named company.

On completion of the payments this certificate is to be surrendered to the company to be exchanged for definitive debentures.

This certificate is issued subject to the conditions contained in the prospectus dated the......................day of................................19.......

GIVEN UNDER THE COMMON SEAL of the company this.......................day of.................................19........

.... } DIRECTORS
.... }

Seal

....
SECRETARY.

N.B. The instalments paid will be endorsed on the back hereof by the company on production of the bankers' receipts.

REGISTER OF MEMBERS AND SHARE LEDGER

Name: Brown, Joseph. *Date Entered as a Member*: 12th November, 19..

Address: The Firs, Guiseley, Leeds. *Date Ceased to be a Member*:

CASH ACCOUNT

Date	Particulars	Folio	Amount Called Up Per Share	Total Amount Called Up	Date	Particulars	Folio	Total Amount Paid Up
19..			£	£	19..			£
Nov 12	Application	1	0·25	250·00	Oct 16	Cash		250·00
	Allotment	1	0·25	250·00	Nov 16	Cash		250·00
19..					19..			
Jan 4	Call		0·25	375·00	Jan 4	Cash		375·00

[*Left-hand side*]

REGISTER OF MEMBERS AND SHARE LEDGER (*cont.*)

SHARE ACCOUNT

Shares Acquired						Shares Transferred						Balance	
Date	Folio	No. of Shares	Distinctive No. From	Distinctive No. To	Amount Paid Up	Date	Folio	No. of Shares	Distinctive No. From	Distinctive No. To	Amount Paid Up	No. of Shares	Amount Paid Up
19..					£						£		£
Nov 12	1	1,000	801	1,800	250·00	19..							
16					250·00	Dec 12		200	801	1,000	100·00	800	400·00
Dec 28		700	2,001	2,700	350·00							1,500	750·00
19..													
Jan 4					375·00							1,500	1,125·00

[*Right-hand side*]

Posting of Share Ledger. The register of members and share ledger will be posted up in stages as follows—

1. The names, addresses, number of shares, distinctive numbers, amount due on application and allotment will be entered up from the application and allotments book (or sheets) into the various shareholders' accounts. The cash received on application and allotment will be posted from the shareholder's cash book to the same accounts.

2. The amounts due on calls from time to time will be posted from the call book to the debit of the individual shareholders' accounts, and the cash received on account of calls will be credited from the shareholders' cash book to the same accounts.

3. The shares transferred from time to time will be posted from the register of transfers to the shareholders' accounts concerned.

A debit balance in the cash account of any shareholder will indicate calls in arrear; while a credit balance therein will denote calls paid in advance.

At balancing time the total of the balances in the various shareholders' accounts should equal the total amount of called-up capital after adjustment of any calls in advance and calls in arrear.

Folios. In the posting of the share ledger folio numbers must, of course, be inserted in order to facilitate subsequent reference. In the statutory and statistical books shown in the worked examples, and which have been posted to the share ledger, the first page of each book has not been numbered page 1, but *distinctive* folios have been adopted, viz. 21, 41, and so on. This has been done in order to make the posting clearer to the student, and to enable him to trace the posting references immediately. With a set of model books all numbered page 1, there would, to the student, be no ready or definite clue as to which book was referred to. In actual practice, however, the first page of each book would of course commence at page 1, no matter how many books there were.

Register of Stockholders. Where shares have been converted into stock, the register of members will show the amount of stock held by each member instead of the particulars of shares held. As stock must be fully paid the register of members may be simplified as shown on the next page.

Calls. The call book or sheets are in tabular form and a suitable ruling is given on p. 1943. A notice of the call to the shareholders is frequently dispensed with when the calls making the shares fully paid are made in quick succession in accordance with the terms of the prospectus. Receipt forms are attached at the foot of the letters of allotment and these should act as a sufficient reminder. Where the shares remain partly paid for any length of time, notices of calls *must* be sent out.

The clerical work follows closely that described in connexion with application and allotment, as will be seen from the example that follows.

REGISTER OF STOCKHOLDERS

NAME ....

ADDRESS...

....

OCCUPATION ....

Date entered as a Member ....

Date ceased to be a Member ....

Stock Acquired					Stock Transferred				Balance	
Date	Folio	Amount	No. of Certificate	Transferor's Folio in Register	Date	Folio	Amount	Transferee's Folio in Register	Date	Amount

71 SHAREHOLDERS' CASH BOOK 71

(ORDINARY SHARES)

Date		Receipts	Folio	Amount	Date	Payments	Folio	Amount
19..				£	19..			£
Jan	2	Application A/c—			Jan 15	Application A/c—		
		Barker, M. B.	101	325·00		Holdfast, A.	c	65·00
	3	Clarke, E.	102	0·13		Oliver, Mrs. R.	c	65·00
	4	Dalton, J. F.	103	0·13		Balance	c/f	2,015·65
		Evans, Fred	104	0·13				
	6	Mensper, I. L.	105	0·13				
		Prince, E. O.	106	0·13				
	7	Retrop, T. P.	107	390·00				
		Holdfast, A.	c	65·00				
	8	Longley, J. F.	110	1,300·00				
		Oliver, Mrs. R.	c	65·00				
				2,145·65				2,145·65

1 APPLICATION AND ALLOTMENTS

No. of Application	Name	Address	Occupation	No. of Shares Applied for	Amount paid on Application	No. of Shares Allotted
					£	
1	Barker, Matthew B.	17 Lime Street, Barnes, S.W.13	Solicitor	2,500	325·00	2,000
2	Clarke, Edward	420 Mare Street, Hackney, E.8	Solicitors' Clerk	1	0·13	1
3	Dalton, John F.	194 Mildmay Park, N.18	H.M.C.S.	1	0·13	1
4	Evans, Fred	96 Rood Lane, Brixton, S.W.2	Solicitors' Clerk	1	0·13	1
5	Mensper, Isaac L.	25 Leyton Street, Boro, S.E.1	Surveyor	1	0·13	1
6	Prince, Ernest O.	12 Temple Chambers, Holborn, E.C.1.	Accountant	1	0·13	1
7	Retrop, Thomas P.	2 Lucas Street, Bexley, Kent	Solicitor	3,000	390·00	2,495
8	Holdfast, Arthur	726 Lime Street, Liverpool	Cotton Merchant	500	65·00	—
9	Longley, James F.	6 Park Drive, Bromfield, Salop	Gentleman	10,000	1,300·00	5,500
10	Oliver, Mrs. Ruth	Halstead Park, Framley, Bucks	Widow	500	65·00	—
				16,505	2,145·65	10,000

NOTE. The shares allotted to the vendor and his nominee have, in this case, been entered from the book, in order to

72 SHAREHOLDERS' CASH BOOK 72

(ORDINARY SHARES)

Date	Receipts	Folio	Amount	Date	Payments	Folio	Amount
19..			£	19..			£
Jan 15	Balance . .	b/f	2,015·65	Jan 20	Transfer to General Cash Book .		5,000·00
20	Allotment A/c—						
	Barker, M. B.	101	675·00				
	Clarke, E. . .	102	0·37				
	Dalton, J. F.	103	0·37				
	Evans, Fred .	104	0·37				
	Mensper, I. L. .	105	0·37				
	Prince, E. O. .	106	0·37				
	Retrop, T. P. .	107	857·50				
	Longley, J. F. .	110	1,450·00				
			5,000·00				5,000·00

BOOK (ORDINARY SHARES) 21

Distinctive Numbers From	Distinctive Numbers To	Share Ledger Folio	Amount due on Application and Allotment	Balance due on Allotment	Cash paid on Allotment	Cash returned	No. of Share Certificate	Remarks
			£	£	£	£		
1	2,000	101	1,000·00	675·00	675·00		1	Signatory
	2,001	102	0·50	0·37	0·37		2	„
	2,002	103	0·50	0·37	0·37		3	„
	2,003	104	0·50	0·37	0·37		4	„
—	2,004	105	0·50	0·37	0·37		5	„
—	2,005	106	0·50	0·37	0·37		6	„
2,006	4,500	107	1,247·50	857·50	857·50		7	„
—	—	—	—	—	—	65·00	—	Letter of Regret, No. 1
24,501	30,000	110	2,750·00	1,450·00	1,450·00		10	
—	—	—	—	—	—	65·00	—	Letter of Regret, No. 2
			5,000·00	2,984·35	2,984·35	130·00		

journal into the share ledger; some accountants, however, enter them in the application and allotments have a complete record.

The call must be made by a resolution of the board of directors, evidence of which is contained in the directors' minute book.

Interest on Calls. Columns are provided, in the call book, for interest. Some shareholders may not be able to pay the whole of the amount due from them within the time stipulated by the call notice. In such cases, an extension of time is granted to such shareholders on condition that they pay interest on the sum due up to the actual time of payment. Again, some shareholders pay their shares in full, not wishing to be troubled by constant calls. In these cases, interest may be allowed by the company. (See regulations 18 and 21 of Table A.)

Example 3

On 5th May the directors of the Waldron Manufacturing and Trading Co. Ltd. made a first call of £0·25 per share on the ordinary shares. The call was payable by the 20th May, and the following amounts were received—

19..				£
May	9	E. Clarke	1 share	0·25
	11	F. Evans	1 ,,	0·25
	13	T. P. Retrop	2,495 shares	123·75
	14	E. O. Prince	1 share	0·25
	15	J. F. Dalton	1 ,,	0·25
	17	J. F. Longley	5,500 shares	1,375·00
	18	M. B. Barker	2,000 ,,	250·00
	20	I. L. Mensper	1 share	0·25

Barker and Retrop were allowed till 20th June to pay the balance, plus interest at 5 per cent, on which date the sums due (including interest thereon) were duly received. Write up the call book. (See p. 1943.)

Debenture Application and Allotments Book. This is a book ruled in tabular form to record the names and addresses of all applicants for debentures, the number of debentures applied for, and the amount deposited with such applications. Additional columns are also provided to record the number of debentures actually allotted, their distinctive numbers, the balance due on allotment, and the amounts subsequently received thereon.

Procedure in Connexion with Applications and Allotment of Debentures. The procedure in connexion with applications for debentures and allotments thereof is very similar to that adopted with respect to shares. A printed form is filled in, and the requisite money forwarded to the company's bankers. Allotments are then made, and the further sums payable duly remitted to the company's bankers. If any applications are not accepted, the deposit money is returned in full.

Dividend Book. This is a book, ruled in tabular form, which records at balancing time the names of the shareholders, the amount paid up on the shares held by each individual, the gross amount of dividend due, the

61 **CALL BOOK (ORDINARY SHARES)** 61

FIRST CALL OF £0·25 PER SHARE MADE MAY 5TH AND PAYABLE BY MAY 20TH

S.L. Folio	Name	Address	No. of Shares Held	Amount Due	Amount Paid	Arrears			Calls Paid in Advance	Remarks
						Amount Due	Days	Interest		
				£	£	£		£	£	
101	Barker, M. B.	71 Lime Street, Barnes, S.W.13	2,000	500·00	250·00	250·00	31	1·04		Paid June 20th
102	Clarke, E.	420 Mare Street, Hackney, E.8	1	0·25	0·25					
103	Dalton, J. F.	194 Mildmay Park, N.18	1	0·25	0·25					
104	Evans, F.	96 Rood Lane, Brixton, S.W.2	1	0·25	0·25					
105	Mensper, I. L.	25 Leyton Street, Boro, S.E.1	1	0·25	0·25					
106	Prince, E. O.	12 Temple Chambers, Holborn, E.C.1	1	0·25	0·25					
107	Retrop, T. P.	2 Lucas Street, Bexley	2,495	623·75	123·75	500·00	31	2·08		Paid June 20th
110	Longley, J. F.	6 Park Drive, Bromfield	5,500	1,375·00	1,375·00					
			10,000	2,500·00	1,750·00	750·00		3·12		

amount of tax (if any) deductible, and the net amount of dividend payable to each shareholder.

Separate books are kept for the dividends on different classes of shares, ordinary, preference, deferred, etc.

Example 4

The directors of the Waldron Manufacturing and Trading Co. Ltd. resolved to pay a dividend of 10 per cent on the ordinary shares for the year ending 31st December, according to the amounts paid up thereon.

From the particulars furnished in the register of ordinary shares, write up the ordinary share dividend book.

ORDINARY SHARE DIVIDEND BOOK

31ST DECEMBER, 19..

O.S.L. Folio	Name	Amount Paid Up on Shares	Amount of Dividend at 10%	Amount of Tax at 45%	Net Dividend	Remarks
		£	£	£	£	
101	Barker, M. B.	750·00	75·00	33·75	41·25	
102	Clarke, E.	0·75	0·08	0·04	0·04	
103	Dalton, J. F.	150·75	15·08	6·78	8·30	
104	Evans, Fred	0·75	0·08	0·04	0·04	
105	Mensper, I. L.	375·75	37·58	16·91	20·67	
106	Prince, E. O.	375·75	37·58	16·91	20·67	
107	Retrop, T. P.	2,621·25	262·13	117·96	144·17	
108	Fairleaf, Frank	15,000·00	1,500·00	675·00	825·00	
109	Goode, Ellen	5,000·00	500·00	225·00	275·00	
110	Longley, J. F.	2,475·00	247·50	111·38	136·12	
111	Johnson, H. A.	375·00	37·50	16·88	20·62	
112	Thorpe, F. B.	375·00	37·50	16·88	20·62	
		27,500·00	2,750·03	1,237·53	1,512·50	

Register of Directors and Secretaries. This is one of the statutory books. The Companies Act, 1948, Sect. 200, requires every company to keep at its registered office a register containing the names, addresses, and occupations and other particulars of its directors and the name and address of its secretary, and to send to the Registrar of Companies a copy thereof, and from time to time to notify to the Registrar any change among its directors or secretaries.

Register of Directors' Share and Debenture Holdings and Dealings and Options. Sect. 29 of the Companies Act, 1967, requires every company to keep a register showing the number, description and amount of any shares in or debentures of the company (or its holding or subsidiary company) held by each director (including those held in trust for him or of which he has the right to become the holder).

A suitable form for a register is shown on p. 1947 (*a*).

Under Sect. 27 the director must notify the company in writing of the number of shares or amount of debentures he holds and whenever he

REGISTER OF DIRECTORS AND SECRETARIES

PARTICULARS OF DIRECTORS

Present Christian Name or Names and Surname	Any Former Christian Name or Names or Surname	Nationality	Usual Residential Address	Business Occupation and Particulars of other Directorships	Date of Birth

PARTICULARS OF THE PERSON WHO IS SECRETARY

Present Christian Name or Names and Surname	Any Former Christian Name or Names and Surname	Usual Residential Address

acquires or relinquishes such interest including an option to buy shares or debentures in his own or associated companies. The price paid must also be included. An interest includes trusts and other indirect holdings and extends to the holdings of his wife and children.

The company should therefore maintain a register of notifications under Sect. 27 and a suitable form is shown on p. 1948 (*b*).

Minute Book. This is another of the statutory books. The Companies Act, Sect. 145, enacts that every company must cause minutes of all proceedings of general meetings and (where there are directors or managers) of its directors and managers to be entered in books kept for that purpose. Any such minute if purporting to be signed by the chairman of the meeting at which the proceedings were had, or by the chairman of the next succeeding meeting, is evidence of the proceedings.

In most companies two books are kept: one, called the Shareholders' or General Minute Book, to record the proceedings of the members in general meetings; and the other, called the Directors' Minute Book, to record the proceedings of board meetings. The books should preferably be provided with an alphabetical index, in order to facilitate reference.

Share Warrant Register. This is a register giving particulars of the share warrants which have been issued by the company. It is ruled in tabular form.

Share Warrant. This is a document under the seal of the company, which entitles the holder of it to the shares specified therein. It is subject to a stamp duty equal to three times the amount of the *ad valorem* duty chargeable on a deed transferring shares of the same nominal value, i.e. £6 per cent. It is transferable by mere delivery; and this fact makes it a very convenient instrument, particularly in the case of companies having foreign shareholders. A specimen is shown below.

The bearer of a share warrant is, subject to the articles of the company, entitled on surrendering it for cancellation, to have his name entered as a member in the register of members. The date of such surrender must also be entered in the register as if it were the date at which a person commenced to be a member.

No........................

ZENO TRADING COMPANY LIMITED

(Incorporated under the Companies Act, 1948)

CAPITAL £100,000

50,000 ORDINARY SHARES OF £1 EACH
50,000 6 PER CENT PREFERENCE SHARES OF £1 EACH

Stamp

SHARE WARRANT

THIS IS TO CERTIFY that the Bearer of this Warrant is the proprietor of........... fully paid-up 6 per cent Preference Shares of £1 each, numbered ....to............ inclusive in the ZENO TRADING COMPANY LIMITED, subject to the provisions of the Memorandum and Articles of Association of the Company.

GIVEN UNDER THE COMMON SEAL of the Company this.............................. day of.................................19.......

....
.... } DIRECTORS

SEAL

....

SECRETARY

Statutory Provisions. Sect. 83 of the Companies Act enacts as follows—

1. A company limited by shares, if so authorized by its articles, may, with respect to any fully paid up shares, issue under its common seal a warrant stating that the bearer

Name of Director..

Date of Event	Name of Company and Description of Holding	Name of Registered Holder	Name and extent of interest	Event notified Grant and exercise of rights	Price or Consideration	Date of Notification	Date of entry in Register

Notes—

1. "Director" includes any person in accordance with whose directions or instructions the directors of a Company are accustomed to act.

2. All information received from a Director under s. 27 of the Act must be entered in this register. The Company must also on its own initiative enter details of any grant to a Director of a right to subscribe for shares or debentures, and the exercise of any such right (s. 29 (2)). The entries in respect of each director must appear in chronological order, and be made within three days.

3. Nature and Extent of Interest of the Director in any shares, stock or debentures must be recorded if that director so requires.

FIG. 19.1

THE COMPANIES ACT, 1967

Notification by Director of occurrence of an event affecting his interest in Shares or Debentures Pursuant to Sections 27 (1) (*b*) and 31 of the Act

Name of Director..

Date of Event	Name of Company[1]	Description of holding[2]	Name of Registered holder	Nature of Event[3]	Additional Statements[3]

Dated.......................... Signed.. To...Limited

[1] Insert name of Company whose shares or debentures are involved being either the Company, its subsidiary or holding company or any subsidiary of its holding company.

[2] Insert number or amount, and class, of shares or debentures involved.

[3] *See* note 1, p. 1949.

Section 25 (5) of the Act provides that the nature and extent of a director's interest must be recorded in the register if he so requires. State details in this column, if so required.

of the warrant is entitled to the shares therein specified, and may provide, by coupons or otherwise, for the payment of the future dividends on the shares included in the warrant.

2. Such a warrant as aforesaid is in this Act termed a "share warrant."

3. A share warrant shall entitle the bearer thereof to the shares therein specified, and the shares or stock may be transferred by delivery of the warrant.

Register of Probates and Letters of Administration. The Probate is the official evidence that the person named therein is the executor of a deceased shareholder, and Letters of Administration authorize the person named therein to administer the estate of a shareholder who has died intestate. Both documents bear the seal of the Court of Probate.

When a shareholder dies leaving an executor, or if, for any reason, there is no executor and the court appoints an Administrator, the probate or Letters of Administration are lodged at the company's office by the executor or administrator. Such person, being the legal personal representative, has two alternatives—

1. He may (unless the articles give the company the right to insist upon a personal representative becoming registered as a member or selling the shares) content himself with simply registering his right to deal with the deceased shareholder's stocks and shares in the company.

2. He may, when lodging the probate or letters of administration, ask to be registered as a member.

If the first course is adopted the secretary of the company makes a memorandum in the share register against the deceased shareholder's name.

Probate or
Letters of administration granted on..

to..of etc., Executor or
Administrator.

Date.......................................

He makes a similar memorandum on the back of the share certificate and returns it endorsed to the executor or administrator. The advantages of this procedure to the executor are—

(*a*) He is liable only to the extent of the estate for any calls on the shares.

(*b*) He can transfer the shares by virtue of Sect. 76 of the Companies Act.

If the second alternative is adopted by the executor and he desires to become registered as a member, the secretary closes the deceased shareholder's account in the share register and opens a new account in the name of the executor, who becomes thereby responsible *personally* for any uncalled liability on the shares. The procedure necessarily depends on the articles of association. Sometimes, a "letter of request" is all that is required, but in many cases the directors insist upon a transfer from the personal representative *as executor* to the personal representative *personally*.

In large companies, a register is frequently kept, giving the deceased shareholders' names and folios in the share ledger, the names and addresses of the executors or administrators, date of death, date of probate, date probate was registered, and any further particulars that may be thought desirable.

Annual Return. Sect. 124 (1) of the Companies Act, 1948, directs that—

Every company having a share capital shall, once at least in every year, make a return containing with respect to the registered office of the company, registers of members and debenture holders, shares and debentures, indebtedness, past and present members and directors and secretary, the matters specified in Part I of the Sixth Schedule to this Act, and the said return shall be in the form set out in Part II of that Schedule or as near thereto as circumstances admit:
Provided that—

(*a*) a company need not make a return under this subsection either in the year of its incorporation or, if it is not required by Sect. 131 of this Act to hold an annual general meeting during the following year, in that year;

(*b*) where a company has converted any of its shares into stock and given notice of the conversion to the Registrar of Companies, the list referred to in para. 5 of Part I of the Sixth Schedule must state the amount of stock held by each of the existing members instead of the amount of shares and the particulars relating to shares required by that paragraph;

(*c*) the return may, in any year, if the return for either of the two immediately preceding years has given as at the date of that return the full particulars required by the said para. 5, give only such of the particulars required by that paragraph as relates to persons ceasing to be or becoming members since the date of the last return and to shares transferred since that date or to changes as compared with that date in the amount of stock held by a member. . . .

Part I of the Sixth Schedule requires that the Annual Return shall contain—

1. The address of the registered office of the company.

2. (1) If the register of members is, under the provisions of this Act, kept elsewhere than at the registered office of the company, the address of the place where it is kept.
(2) If any register of holders of debentures . . . is . . . kept . . . elsewhere than at the registered office of the company, the address of the place where it is kept.

3. A summary, distinguishing between shares issued for cash and shares issued as fully or partly paid up otherwise than in cash, specifying the following particulars—

(*a*) the amount of the share capital of the company and the number of shares into which it is divided;
(*b*) the number of shares taken from the commencement of the company up to the date of the return;
(*c*) the amount called up on each share;
(*d*) the total amount of calls received;
(*e*) the total amount of calls unpaid;
(*f*) the total amount of the sums (if any) paid by way of commission in respect of any shares or debentures;
(*g*) the discount allowed on the issue of any shares issued at a discount or so much of that discount as has not been written off at the date on which the return is made;

(*h*) the total amount of the sums (if any) allowed by way of discount in respect of any debentures since the date of the last return;

(*i*) the total number of shares forfeited;

(*j*) the total amount of shares for which share warrants are outstanding at the date of the return and of share warrants issued and surrendered respectively since the date of the last return, and the number of shares comprised in each warrant.

4. Particulars of the total amount of the indebtedness of the company in respect of all mortgages and charges which are required (or, in the case of a company registered in Scotland, which, if the company had been registered in England, would be required) to be registered with the Registrar of Companies under this Act. . . .

5. A list—

(*a*) containing the names and addresses of all persons who, on the fourteenth day after the company's annual general meeting for the year, are members of the company, and of persons who have ceased to be members since the date of the last return or, in the case of the first return, since the incorporation of the company;

(*b*) stating the number of shares held by each of the existing members at the date of the return, specifying shares transferred since the date of the last return (or, in the case of the first return, since the incorporation of the company) by persons who are still members and have ceased to be members respectively and the dates of registration of the transfers;

(*c*) if the names aforesaid are not arranged in alphabetical order, having annexed thereto an index sufficient to enable the name of any person therein to be easily found.

6. All such particulars with respect to the persons who at the date of the return are the directors of the company and any person who at that date is the secretary of the company as are by this Act required to be contained with respect to directors and the secretary respectively in the register of the directors and secretaries of the company.

There shall be annexed to the annual return—

(*a*) A written copy, certified both by a director and the secretary of the company to be a true copy, of every balance sheet laid before the company in general meeting during the period to which the return relates (including every document required by the law to be annexed thereto (Sects. 127; 149; 156).

(*b*) A copy, certified as aforesaid, of the report of the auditors on, and of the report of the directors accompanying, each such balance sheet. (Sect. 127.)

The documents to be annexed to the balance sheet are the profit and loss account and any group accounts (Sect. 156).

A private company must send with the return—

1. A certificate signed by a director and by the secretary that the company has not since the date of the last return (or in the case of the first return since the incorporation of the company) issued any invitation to the public to subscribe for any shares or debentures of the company.

2. If the number of members, as shown by the return, exceeds fifty a certificate signed by a director and the secretary that the excess consists of employees of the company or past employees who were members whilst in the employment of the company and have since continued to be members.

QUESTIONS

1. What books is a company compelled by law to keep?
2. What statistical books are usually kept by a company?

3. Explain the nature and use of an application and allotments book.
4. Explain the following and their use: (*a*) letter of allotment, (*b*) letter of regret.
5. Explain the following: (*a*) letter of renunciation, (*b*) return of allotments.
6. What subsidiary cash books are used in connexion with the receipt of money on shares? What objection is raised against them? What alternative procedure is there?
7. Explain the nature and use of a call book.
8. How are calls made? What is a notice of call?
9. How does the question of interest arise in connexion with calls, and how is it treated?
10. Submit *pro forma* ruling of a call book, and enter therein six specimen entries.
11. Explain the nature and use of a register of transfers.
12. Submit *pro forma* ruling of a register of transfers and enter therein six specimen entries.
13. What are the provisions of the Companies Act with regard to share certificates?
14. What is a "scrip" certificate? What stamp does it require?
15. Explain the nature and use of the register of members and share ledger. What are the statutory requirements in connexion therewith?
16. What date should be entered in the register of members as date of entry?
17. State briefly some of the statutory provisions with respect to the register of members. Can a company keep a dominion register?
18. How are share ledgers indexed?
19. State briefly the various steps by which the share ledger is posted.
20. What does: (*a*) a *debit* balance, (*b*) a *credit* balance in the cash account of any shareholders' accounts signify?
21. How can the balances in the share ledger be agreed with those in the financial books?
22. Explain the use of the "balance" column in a share ledger account.
23. Submit *pro forma* ruling of a register of members and share ledger, and enter therein six specimen entries; also *pro forma* ruling of a register of stockholders.
24. Explain the nature and use of a register of charges. Submit *pro forma* ruling.
25. Submit *pro forma* ruling of a register of debenture holders, and enter therein six specimen items; also *pro forma* ruling of a register of debenture stockholders.
26. Explain the nature and use of a dividend book. Submit *pro forma* ruling, and enter three specimen items therein.
27. Describe briefly the nature and use of the following: (*a*) register of directors and secretaries, (*b*) minute book, (*c*) share warrant and share warrant register, (*d*) register of probates.
28. Give some particulars regarding a company's annual return.

EXERCISE 19

1. On 20th January, the Eastwood Timber Co. Ltd. allotted 500 ordinary shares of £1 each number 18,500 to 18,999, to Ernest Willington, 33 Rayleigh Street, E.C.4, and on the same day they sent him a letter of regret with reference to the further 500 shares for which he had applied.

E. Willington paid for the shares allotted to him as follows: 11th January, 25p per share on application; 20th January, 25p per share on allotment; and 50p per share (final call) on 20th February.

On 28th February, E. Willington purchased a further 500 shares, Nos. 1 to 500, on the Stock Exchange, for which he paid £1·05 per share. The transfer was lodged and approved on 6th March. These shares were purchased from R. Gee, 14 High Street, Burnham.

On 31st March, E. Willington sold 100 shares, Nos. 1 to 100, to Peter Robinson 14 Dowgate Street, Southminster, at £1·25 per share, the transfer being lodged on 1st April and approved on 3rd April.

Show the transactions as they would appear in the statistical books of the Eastwood Timber Co. Ltd. Ignore all questions of brokerage, stamps, and transfer fees. (*R.S.A.*)

2. Give suitable rulings for the share ledger of a limited company and enter therein the following particulars—

John Smith, cork merchant, 440 Austin Friars, E.C.2, applied, on 2nd January, for 150 ordinary shares of £1 each, and forwarded the necessary 13p per share with his application.

On 12th January, John Smith forwarded a further 12p per share on being informed by the company that 150 ordinary shares (numbered 1 to 150) had been allotted to him.

On 10th March, a call of 25p per share was notified by the company, and was duly paid by John Smith on his holding on 15th March.

On 3rd April, John Smith sold 100 of his shares (numbered 1 to 100) to William Brown, hatter, 486 Bond Street, W.1, at 63p per share, the transfer being in due course accepted by the company. (*London Chamber of Commerce.*)

3. The Companies Act, 1948, enacts that every public limited company shall make an "annual return." Give an example of such a return, including in it all the details necessary to meet the requirements set out in Part I of the Sixth Schedule to the Act.

4. The undermentioned persons applied for shares in the X Y Z Manufacturing Co. Ltd. The shares offered for subscription were shares of £1 each, payable £0·25 per share on application, £0·375 on allotment, and the balance as an when required. The distinctive numbers of the shares allotted ran from No. 1 upwards. The list was closed on 1st February, and some of the allotments made were as under—

	Shares Applied for	Shares Allotted
Arthur Roberts, wool merchant, 10 Finsbury Street, Burnton	4,000	3,000
Henry P. Richards, gentleman, The Grange, Lynford, Hants.	3,000	2,000
Lucas Norton, iron manufacturer, 114 Princes Street, Sheffield	5,000	4,000
Ellen Allerton, spinster, Park Grove, Finchley	200	nil
Norman Princeton, stockbroker, 120 Lombard Street, London, E.C.3	5,000	4,000
George L. Lloyd, lace manufacturer, 178 High Road, Nottingham	500	500

All moneys due on allotment were received by 15th February. Write up the application and allotments book for the above.

5. The Pneumatic Tyre Co. Ltd. on 1st March, allotted to Robert Essley, merchant, of 115 Walkley Road, Thornheath, 500 ordinary shares of £1 each, number 721 to 1,220 inclusive, upon an application dated 23rd February, Essley having on that day paid to the company's bankers a deposit of £0·125 per share on 100 shares. The amount due on allotment was £0·25 per share, which was duly paid on 10th March. On 1st May the company made a first call of £0·25 per share, which was duly paid on the 15th May. On 25th June, Essley purchased from Thomas King, surveyor, of 14 The Lanes, Farnham, the last 100 of King's 500 shares (numbered 1 to 500 inclusive), upon which £0·625 per share had been paid up; the transfer was registered on 1st July. On 31st August the company made a further call of £0·125 per share, which was

duly paid on 15th September. On 1st October, Essley sold to John Tinton (a new shareholder), merchant, of 115 Lime Street, Halifax, 80 shares, numbered 801 to 880 inclusive, £0·75 per share paid up, the transfer being registered on 12th October. On 15th October the company called up the remaining £0·25 per share, which was duly paid on 25th October. On 25th November, Essley sold to Philip Brown (a new shareholder), engineer, of 9 Lupus Street, Benfield, the remainder of his shares, the transfer being registered on 2nd December. Write up the above transactions in the company's share ledger, showing the accounts of Essley, King, Tinton, and Brown.

6. Referring to the previous exercise, enter the transfers therein mentioned into the company's transfer register, assuming the numbers of the transfer deeds and of new certificates.

7. On 5th May, the directors of the Auto Brake Co. Ltd. made a first call of £0·25 per share on the ordinary shares. The call was payable by the 20th May, and the following amounts were received—

				£
May	9	R. T. Lake	2,000 shares . .	300·00
	11	A. F. Brown	1 share . .	0·25
	13	F. Cassell	1 share . .	0·25
	14	T. O. Neller	1 share . .	0·25
	15	N. P. Locksley	1 share . .	0·25
	17	E. Chalmers	1 share . .	0·25
	18	F. T. Bullen	2,495 shares . .	323·75
	20	J. P. Silverlock	5,500 shares . .	1,375·00

Lake and Bullen were allowed till 20th June to pay the balance, plus interest at 5 per cent, on which date the sums due (including interest thereon) were duly received. Write up the call book and the subsidiary cash book.

8. The Auto Brake Co. Ltd. having taken power in its memorandum of association to issue £10,000 debentures in bonds of £100 each, offered the same for public subscription on 1st March, payable 40 per cent on application and 60 per cent on allotment. Applications were received, and allotments made, as under—

			Applied for	Allotted
Mar	2	Robert E. Adams, baker, 61 Carnaby Street, Birmingham	30	20
	4	Alfred Brady, surveyor, 17 Seaford Road, Liverpool .	10	10
		William S. Cooper, butcher, 21 Regent Street, Leeds .	6	nil
		Charles T. Dawson, architect, 44 Windsor Road, Manchester	10	5
	5	Henry Ellis, solicitor, 21 Crofton Street, Warwick .	6	5
		Philip O. Foster, artist, 12 Penton Road, Nottingham .	6	5
	6	Edward Goodwin, journalist, 75 Percy Street, Reading.	10	10
	7	Catherine E. Howard, spinster, 25 Burnaby Gardens, Winchester	25	20
		Walter Irving, engineer, 112 Brockley Road, Southampton	10	5
	8	Thomas D. Jeffries, merchant, 29 Granville Street, London, W.2	5	nil
		Matthew Lockwood, barrister, 108 Westbourne Grove, Windsor	5	5
		Lionel F. Taylor, gentleman, 76 Stewart Road, London, W.16	20	15

Allotment was made on 10th March in order of application, the numbers of the debentures running from 1 upwards. No allotment was made to Cooper and Jeffries, whose deposits were duly returned with letters of regret, Nos. 5 and 6. The moneys payable on allotment were all received by 20th March. Write up the debenture applications and allotments book and subsidiary cash book.

9. The following transfers of debentures were made, approved, and duly registered in the books of the Auto Brake Co. Ltd.—

May 15 5 Debentures (1–5) from R. E. Adams to C. T. Dawson; No. of transfer deed, No. 101.
Jun 10 5 debentures (56–60) from C. E. Howard to H. Ellis.
15 5 debentures (86–90) from L. F. Taylor to P. O. Foster.
25 5 debentures (61–65) from C. E. Howard to H. Ellis.
Jul 9 5 debentures (6–10) from R. E. Adams to James Burnaby, merchant, 112 Leman Street, Northampton.
Aug 22 5 Debentures (91–95) from L. F. Taylor to Rupert Armstrong, engineer, 95 Bromley Road, Newcastle.

Write up the debenture transfer register.

10. A friend desires you to advise him as to whether he should invest £1,000 (which he has free) in—

(*a*) Ordinary shares of a company would yield 2 per cent per annum on the basis of the present price and dividends paid the last three years; or

(*b*) In 6 per cent cumulative preference shares of the same company; or

(*c*) In 4 per cent debentures of the same company.

How would you advise him? (*U.L.C.I.*)

CHAPTER 20

COMPANIES: RAISING OF CAPITAL

ISSUE OF SHARES AND DEBENTURES

Scale of issue

THE level of capital issues and redemptions in the United Kingdom between 1965 and 1970 can be judged from the following table—

Capital Issues and Redemptions in the United Kingdom
(excluding British Government and nationalized industries)

	Gross issues	Gross redemptions	United Kingdom	Overseas
	M£	M£	M£	M£
1965	779·2	150·1	657·0	−27·9
1966	1,050·9	205·0	889·8	−43·9
1967	908·6	204·0	698·4	6·1
1968	1,050·5	334·2	759·8	−43·5
1969	1,039·6	355·3	692·3	−8·0
1970	810·7	447·2	376·0	12·4

Source: Monthly Digest of Statistics—H.M.S.O.

The Overseas issues are issues in the United Kingdom on behalf of foreign governments and enterprises (largely governments).

Types of issue

The net issues (gross less redemptions) were broken down between the different types of investment in the following way, between 1959 and 1970.

New Issues in the United Kingdom
Percentage of Total Funds raised

	Ordinary Shares	Preference Shares	Loan Stock Debentures
1959–64	58·7%	2·0%	39·3%
1965–70	27·1%	1·4%	71·5%

Source: Midland Bank Review

It can be seen that whereas in 1959–64 most issues were of Ordinary shares, in subsequent years more Loan Capital was issued. The proportion of Preference shares was small and it fell in the years after 1965.

Terms of issue

Shares and debentures may be issued in different ways both as regards terms of payment and also as regards price.

1. **As Regards Price.** Shares and debentures may be issued *at par*, that is, at a price *equal* to their nominal value, as, for instance, a £1 share for £1, or a £50 debenture bond for £50. They may likewise be issued *at a premium*, that is, at a price *above* their nominal or face value, as, for instance, a £1 share for £1·25, or a £100 debenture bond for £105. They may also be issued *at a discount*, that is, at a price *below* their nominal value.

2. **As Regards Terms of Payment.** Shares and debentures may be issued payable in full on application. They may also be issued payable by instalments as and when the money is required by the company.

3. **Convertible Loan Stock.** Debentures may be issued to the public with the right to convert the loan stock to shares at a later date on specified terms. Investors may be more willing to buy such stocks which initially offer a sure income and a later opportunity to share the full earnings if the company is successful.

ACCOUNTING FOR ISSUES

The methods of accounting for issues are dealt with in the following pages in eight sections:

1. Shares and debentures payable in full.
2. Shares and debentures payable by instalments.
3. Convertible Loan Stock.
4. Shares over-subscribed.
5. Calls in arrear and advance.
6. Forfeiture of shares.
7. Preliminary expenses.
8. Debentures as collateral security for loan.

1. Shares and Debentures Payable in Full

(*a*) Shares and Debentures at Par

When shares and debentures are issued payable in full on application, a separate account must be opened for each class of shareholders or debenture holders, and also for each kind of share capital or debentures. The people who take the ordinary shares will be called ordinary shareholders, and the money they pay for these shares will be called ordinary share capital, and similarly with debenture holders and preference share holders.

Example 1

A limited company issued at par 30,000 ordinary shares of £1 each, and £10,000 4½ per cent debentures in bonds of £50 each; which were all subscribed and fully paid up. Make the necessary journal and cash book entries, post to ledger, extract trial balance, and draw up the company's balance sheet.

Solution 1

JOURNAL

	Dr	Cr
	£	£
Ordinary Shareholders	30,000	
Ordinary Share Capital		30,000
30,000 shares of £1 each.		
Debenture Holders	10,000	
Debentures		10,000
200 bonds of £50 each.		

CASH BOOK (*Dr.* side)

Receipts	Bank
	£
Ordinary Shareholders	30,000
Debenture Holders	10,000

LEDGER

Ordinary Shareholders

	£		£
Ordinary Share Capital	30,000	Cash	30,000

Ordinary Share Capital

			£
		Ordinary Shareholders	30,000

Debenture Holders

	£		£
Debentures	10,000	Cash	10,000

Debentures

			£
		Debenture Holders	10,000

Trial Balance

	£	£
Ordinary share capital		30,000
Debentures		10,000
Cash at bank	40,000	
	40,000	40,000

BALANCE SHEET

	£		£
Issued Share Capital—		Cash at Bank	40,000
Ordinary Share Capital—			
30,000 Shares of £1 each .	30,000		
Long-term Liabilities—			
Debentures—			
200 Bonds of £50 each. .	10,000		
	40,000		40,000

Treatment of Details. The details as to the individual shareholders, the particular shares held, and the respective amounts paid on them, are omitted in the journal, cash book, and general ledger; they are not, however, ignored altogether, but are entered into the various statistical books explained in the previous section.

(*b*) Shares and Debentures at a Premium

A separate account must be opened in the ledger for the premium. A premium on the issue of *shares* must be treated in accordance with Sect. 56, Companies Act, 1948, as a capital reserve which can be used only for the following purposes—

(i) In issuing fully paid bonus shares.
(ii) Writing off preliminary expenses.
(iii) Writing off expenses of issuing, and commissions paid or discounts allowed on shares or debentures.
(iv) Providing for a premium on redeemable preference shares or debentures.

Example 2

A limited company issued 20,000 preference shares of £1 each at £1·125 per share, and £10,000 4½ per cent debentures, in bonds of £50 each, at a premium of 5 per cent; which were all subscribed and fully paid up. Make the necessary journal and cash book entries, and show also the company's balance sheet.

Premiums on Debentures. Premiums received by a limited company on the issue of its debentures are *capital* profits, i.e. not profits available for dividend, and are retained in the business. Unless, however, the articles of association expressly forbid it, there seems nothing to prevent a company from taking such profits to its profit and loss account as divisible profits, although such a practice is strongly condemned by all the leading accountants. The term "capital profits" is used in contradistinction to "revenue profits," which are gains by trading.

These premiums are usually transferred to a capital reserve account, and are then available for writing off capital losses, or for writing down the

Solution 2

JOURNAL

	Dr	Cr
	£	£
Preference Shareholders	22,500	
Preference Share Capital		20,000
20,000 Shares of £1 each.		
Share Premium A/c		2,500
£0·125 per share on 20,000 shares.		
Debenture Holders	10,500	
Debentures		10,000
200 bonds of £50 each.		
Debenture Premium		500
5% on £10,000.		

CASH BOOK (*Dr.* side)

Receipts	Bank
	£
Preference Shareholders	22,500
Debenture Holders	10,500

BALANCE SHEET ON . . .

	£		£
Issued Share Capital—		Cash at Bank	33,000
................Ordinary Shares .	?		
20,000 £1 Preference Shares .	20,000		
Capital Reserves—			
Share Premium A/c .	2,500		
Debenture Premium A/c[1]	500		
Long-term Liabilities—			
$4\frac{1}{2}$% Debentures			
200 Bonds of £50 each . .	10,000		
	33,000		33,000

[1] The company is not obliged to place the premium on debentures to capital reserve, but would probably do so as a matter of prudence.

value of intangible assets, such as goodwill. The ordinary reserve fund is often drawn upon for the purpose of dividends, hence the necessity for putting such profits to a *special* reserve account. The expenses of issue (if any) are a first charge against the premium before it is transferred to a capital reserve account. Where the debentures are redeemable, the premium is often transferred to a debenture redemption account, thus forming the nucleus of the fund for repayment.

(*c*) Shares and Debentures at a Discount

Shares may only be issued at a discount if of a class already issued and if the issue otherwise complies with Sect. 57 of the Companies Act, 1948, which stipulates—

(*a*) The issue of the shares at a discount must be authorized by resolution passed in general meeting of the company, and must be sanctioned by the court.

(*b*) The resolution must specify the maximum rate of discount at which the shares are to be issued.

(*c*) Not less than one year must at the date of the issue have elapsed since the date on which the company was entitled to commence business.

(*d*) The shares to be issued at a discount must be issued within one month after the date on which the issue is sanctioned by the court or within such extended time as the court may allow.

Also, every prospectus relating to the issue of shares and every balance sheet must contain particulars of the discount allowed on the shares, or of so much of that discount as has not been written off at the date of the issue of the document in question.

The discount must be separated from the amount payable on the shares and debentures; it must be posted to a separate account in the ledger, as it forms no part of the shares and debentures, but is merely a loss sustained by the company in issuing the shares and debentures.

Example 3

A limited company, having complied with the regulations as contained in the Companies Act, 1948 (Sect. 57), issued 10,000 shares of £1 each at a discount of 5 per cent, which were all subscribed and fully paid. Make the necessary journal, cash book, and ledger records; also show the company's balance sheet.

Solution 3

JOURNAL

		Dr	Cr
		£	£
	Sundry Shareholders	9,500	
	Share Discount	500	
	Share Capital		10,000
	Issue of 10,000 shares of £1 each at a discount of 5%.		

CASH BOOK (*Dr.* side)

Receipts	Bank
	£
Sundry Shareholders	9,500

LEDGER

SHARE CAPITAL

			£
		Balance b/d	10,000
		Sundry Shareholders . .	9,500
		Share Discount . . .	500

SUNDRY SHAREHOLDERS

	£		£
Share Capital	9,500	Cash	9,500

SHARE DISCOUNT

	£		
Share Capital	500		

BALANCE SHEET

	£	£		£
Nominal Capital—			Sundry Assets	10,000
20,000 Shares at £1 each . . .	20,000		Cash at Bank	9,500
			Share Discount . . .	500
Issued Capital—				
20,000 Shares of £1 each . . .		20,000		
		20,000		20,000

Discount on Debentures. The discount allowed by a limited company on the issue of its debentures is a *capital* loss. The latter term is used in contradistinction to "revenue loss," which is a loss sustained by trading.

Example 4

A limited company issued £10,000 4½ per cent debentures, in bonds of £50 each, at £45 per bond; which were all subscribed and fully paid up. Make the necessary journal and cash book entries, and show also the company's balance sheet.

Solution 4

JOURNAL	Dr	Cr
	£	£
Debenture Holders	9,000	
Debenture Discount	1,000	
Debentures		10,000
Issue of 200 Bonds of £50 each at a discount of £5 per bond.		

CASH BOOK (*Dr*. side)

Receipts	Bank
	£
Debenture Holders	9,000

BALANCE SHEET ON . . .

	£		£
4½ % Debentures—		Cash at Bank	9,000
200 Bonds of £50 each . .	10,000	Debenture Discount . . .	1,000
	10,000		10,000

Writing off Discount on Debentures. The 2nd Schedule of the Companies Act, 1967, states that the amount of such discount must be separately stated on the balance sheet until the whole is written off. If the debentures are irredeemable, the amount of such discount should, none the less, be gradually written off like preliminary expenses but over a long period. Where the debentures are redeemable, the amount of such discount is generally written off over the period of the debenture loan, e.g. if the debentures are payable at the end of five years, then one-fifth of the discount will be written off each year. Where, however, the debentures are redeemable by annual drawings of a fixed amount, the discount must be written off each year in proportion to the amount of debentures outstanding; so that those years which enjoy the larger portion of the debentures shall bear the larger portion of the discount. The debentures themselves will be shown on the balance sheet at their nominal or face value.

Example 5

A limited company issued £8,000 debentures at a discount of 5 per cent, repayable at the end of five years. Show the discount account in the ledger for this period.

Solution 5

DEBENTURE DISCOUNT

Year		£	Year		£
1	Debentures	400	1	P. & L. ($\frac{1}{5}$ of £400) . . .	80
				Balance c/d	320
		400			400
2	Balance b/d	320	2	P. & L. ($\frac{1}{5}$ of £400) . . .	80
				Balance c/d	240
		320			320
3	Balance b/d	240	3	P. & L. ($\frac{1}{5}$ of £400) . . .	80
				Balance c/d	160
		240			240
4	Balance b/d	160	4	P. & L. ($\frac{1}{5}$ of £400) . . .	80
				Balance c/d	80
		160			160
5	Balance b/d	80	5	P. & L. ($\frac{1}{5}$ of £400) . . .	80

Example 6

A limited company issued £8,000 debentures at a discount of 5 per cent, repayable by annual drawings of £1,600. Show the discount account in the ledger for the period of duration of the debentures.

Solution 6

	£
The debentures outstanding 1st year will be . .	8,000
,, ,, ,, 2nd ,, ,, ,, . .	6,400
,, ,, ,, 3rd ,, ,, ,, . .	4,800
,, ,, ,, 4th ,, ,, ,, . .	3,200
,, ,, ,, 5th ,, ,, ,, . .	1,600
	24,000

Therefore $\frac{80}{240}$ths of the discount must be written off in the first year, $\frac{64}{240}$ths the second year, and so on. Or, more shortly, the discount must be written off in the ratio of the years taken backwards. Now $5 + 4 + 3 + 2 + 1 = 15$; and the proportions will therefore be $\frac{5}{15}$, $\frac{4}{15}$, $\frac{3}{15}$, $\frac{2}{15}$, and $\frac{1}{15}$ respectively.

DEBENTURE DISCOUNT

Year		£	Year		£
1	Debentures	400·00	1	P. & L. ($\frac{1}{3}$ of £400) . . .	133·33
				Balance c/d	266·67
		400·00			400·00
2	Balance b/d	266·67	2	P. & L. ($\frac{4}{15}$ of £400) . . .	106·67
				Balance c/d	160·00
		266·67			266·67
3	Balance b/d	160·00	3	P. & L. ($\frac{1}{5}$ of £400) . . .	80·00
				Balance c/d	80·00
		160·00			160·00
4	Balance b/d	80·00	4	P. & L. ($\frac{2}{15}$ of £400) . . .	53·33
				Balance c/d	26·67
		80·00			80·00
	Balance b/d	26·67	5	P. & L. ($\frac{1}{15}$ of £400) . . .	26·67

2. Shares and Debentures Payable by Instalments

Shares and debentures are most frequently issued payable by instalments at certain intervals. In such cases a separate account is opened for the amount due on application and allotment and for each call.

(*a*) Shares at Par

Example 7

A limited company issued its full authorized capital of 50,000 ordinary shares of £1 each, payable £0·12 per share on application, £0·38 on allotment, and £0·25 on each of two subsequent calls, which were all subscribed and the money duly received. Make the necessary journal and cash book entries, post to ledger, and draw up trial balance and balance sheet.

Solution 7

JOURNAL

	Dr £	Cr £
Application & Allotment A/c (Ord. Shares) .	25,000	
Ordinary Share Capital		25,000
Allotment of 50,000 ordinary shares, payable £0·12 on application and £0·38 on allotment.		
First Call A/c (Ord. Shares)	12,500	
Ordinary Share Capital		12,500
£0·25 per share on 50,000 shares.		
Second Call A/c (Ord. Shares)	12,500	
Ordinary Share Capital		12,500
£0·25 per share on 50,000 shares.		

CASH BOOK (*Dr.* side)

Receipts	Bank
	£
Application & Allotment A/c (Ordinary Shares) (Application Money) .	6,250
Application & Allotment A/c (Ordinary Shares) (Amount due on Allotment) . . .	18,750
First Call A/c (Ordinary Shares)	12,500
Second Call A/c „ „	12,500

LEDGER

Application and Allotment Account (Ordinary Shares)

	£		£
Ordinary Share Capital . .	25,000	Cash (Application) . . .	6,250
		„ (Allotment) . .	18,750
	25,000		25,000

First Call Account (Ordinary Shares)

	£		£
Ordinary Share Capital . .	12,500	Cash	12,500

Second Call Account (Ordinary Shares)

	£		£
Ordinary Share Capital . .	12,500	Cash	12,500

Ordinary Share Capital

			£
		Application & Allotment .	25,000
		First Call	12,500
		Second Call	12,500

Balance Sheet

	£		£
Authorized and Issued Capital—		Cash at Bank	50,000
50,000 Ordinary Shares of £1 each . .	50,000		
	50,000		50,000

(*b*) Shares at a Premium

Example 8

A limited company issued 50,000 preference shares of £1 each at a premium of £0·125 per share, payable £0·25 per share on application, £0·375 on allotment (including the premium), and £0·25 per share on each of two later calls. The shares were all subscribed and the money duly received. Make the necessary journal and cash book entries.

Solution 8

JOURNAL

		Dr	*Cr*
		£	£
	Application & Allotment A/c (Pref. Shares)	31,250	
	Preference Share Capital		25,000
	Share Premium A/c		6,250
	Issue of 50,000 pref. shares of £1 each, payable £0·25 on application and £0·375 (including premium of £0·125) on allotment.		
	First Call A/c (Pref. Shares)	12,500	
	Preference Share Capital		12,500
	£0·25 per share on 50,000 shares.		
	Second Call A/c (Pref. Shares)	12,500	
	Preference Share Capital		12,500
	£0·25 per share on 50,000 shares.		

CASH BOOK (*Dr*. side)

Receipts	Bank
	£
Application & Allotment (Preference Shares)	12,500
Application & Allotment (including sum on account of premium)	18,750
First Call (Preference Shares)	12,500
Second Call " "	12,500

(*c*) Debentures at Par

Example 9

A limited company issued £100,000 4½ per cent mortgage debentures at par, payable 25 per cent on application, 25 per cent on allotment, and the balance three months later. All the money was duly received. Make the necessary journal and cash book entries.

Solution 9

JOURNAL

	Dr	Cr
	£	£
Application & Allotment A/c (Debentures)	50,000	
4½% Debentures		50,000
Issue of £100,000 debentures payable 25% on application and 25% on allotment.		
Call A/c (Debentures)	50,000	
4½% Debentures		50,000
50% of £100,000.		

CASH BOOK (*Dr.* side)

Receipts	Bank
	£
Application & Allotment (Debentures)	25,000
Application & Allotment "	25,000
Call A/c (Debentures)	50,000

(*d*) Debentures at a Premium

Example 10

A limited company issued £100,000 debentures in bonds of £100 each at a premium of £5 per bond, payable £30 per bond on application (including the premium), and the balance on allotment. The money was duly received. Make the necessary journal and cash book entries.

Solution 10

JOURNAL

	Dr	Cr
	£	£
Application & Allotment A/c (Debentures) .	105,000	
Debentures.		100,000
Debenture Premium A/c		5,000
£30 per bond (including £5 premium) on application and £75 per bond on allotment of 1,000 bonds of £100 each.		

CASH BOOK (*Dr.* side)

Receipts	Bank
	£
Application & Allotment (Debentures)	30,000
" " " "	75,000

(*e*) Shares and Debentures at a Discount, Payable in Instalments

Example 11

A limited company, having previously issued 10,000 £1 ordinary shares, takes the necessary steps and is empowered to issue 10,000 shares at a discount of 5 per cent; 20 per cent on application, 20 per cent on allotment and the balance on first call.

Solution 11

The journal, cash book, and ledger records will be—

JOURNAL

	Dr	*Cr*
	£	£
Application & Allotment A/c	4,000	
Ordinary Share Capital		4,000
Allotment of 10,000 ordinary shares of £1 each.		
First Call A/c	5,500	
Ordinary Share Discount.	500	
Ordinary Share Capital		6,000
£0·60 per share on 10,000 ordinary shares of £1 each, with 5 per cent discount.		

CASH BOOK (*Dr*. side)

Receipts	Bank
	£
Application & Allotment	4,000
First Call	5,500
	9,500

LEDGER

SHARE CAPITAL

			£
		Balance b/d	10,000
		Application & Allotment . .	4,000
		Call	5,500
		Share Discount	500

APPLICATION AND ALLOTMENT ACCOUNT (SHARES)

	£		
Share Capital	4,000		

SHARE DISCOUNT

	£	
Share Capital	500	

BALANCE SHEET ON . . .

	£		£
Issued Share Capital—		Sundry Assets	10,000
20,000 £1 Ordinary Shares fully		Cash	9,500
paid	20,000	Share Discount A/c[1] . . .	500

[1] The balance on the discount account is a *fictitious asset*. It appears on the assets side of the balance sheet because it is a debit balance, but is merely an expense not yet written off.

Example 12

A limited company issued 1,000 $4\frac{1}{2}$ per cent debenture bonds of £100 each at a discount of 5 per cent, payable 25 per cent on application, and the balance on allotment. The money was duly received. Make the necessary journal and cash book entries.

Solution 12

JOURNAL

		Dr	*Cr*
		£	£
	Application & Allotment A/c (Debentures) .	95,000	
	Debenture Discount	5,000	
	$4\frac{1}{2}$% Debentures		100,000
	Issue of 1,000 $4\frac{1}{2}$% debentures of £100 each at a discount of 5 per cent.		

CASH BOOK (*Dr.* side)

Receipts	Bank
	£
Application & Allotment (Debentures) (payable on application) . .	25,000
Application & Allotment (Debentures) (payable on allotment) . .	70,000

3. Convertible Loan Stock

Debentures issued with a later right to conversion to shares must be treated as debentures until the holders exercise their option to convert their holdings to shares.

Whilst debentures may be offered at a discount quite freely, it must be remembered that shares must be paid for in full unless the consent of the court is obtained for them to be issued at a discount. Care must be taken to see that the actual consideration paid for debentures issued at a discount equals or exceeds the nominal value of the shares issued. If it does not, then the shares are being issued at a discount.

(*a*) Debentures Issued and Converted at Par

Example 13

On 1st January, a company issued 10,000 5 per cent debentures of £5 at par, convertible after six months to £1 ordinary shares at par. All the holders exercised their option at six months. The authorized capital was £100,000, of which £50,000 had already been issued. Show the necessary journal and ledger entries and relevant balance sheets.

Solution 13

JOURNAL

			Dr	*Cr*
19..			£	£
Jan	1	Debenture Application & Allotment A/c . .	50,000	
		5% Debentures . .		50,000
		Issue of 10,000 5% convertible debentures of £5 each.		
Jul	1	5% Convertible Debentures . . .	50,000	
		Ordinary Share Capital . . .		50,000
		Conversion of 5% debenture stock.		

LEDGER

5% Convertible Debentures

19..			£	19..			£
Jul	1	Ordinary Share Capital	50,000	Jan	1	Debenture Holders .	50,000

Ordinary Share Capital

				19..			£
				Jul	1	Balance . . .	—
						Convertible Debentures	50,000

Balance Sheet on 1st January

		£		£
Authorized Capital . . .		100,000	Sundry Assets . . .	50,000
			Cash	50.000
Issued Share Capital—				
50,000 £1 Ordinary Shares fully paid . . .	50,000			
5% *Convertible Loan Stock—*				
10,000 £5 Debentures . .	50,000			
		100,000		100,000

BALANCE SHEET ON 1ST JULY

	£		£
Authorized and Issued Share Capital—		Sundry Assets (including cash) .	100,000
100,000 £1 Ordinary Shares fully paid	100,000		
	100,000		100,000

(*b*) Debentures Issued at a Discount, Converted to Shares at a Premium

Example 14

On 1st January, the company issued 10,000 5 per cent debentures of £5 at 95, convertible after six months to £1 ordinary shares at current market price. Other details as in (*a*) above. All the holders exercised their option to convert on 1st July, when the price of the ordinary shares was £1·25. Show journal and ledger entries and the relevant balance sheets.

Solution 14

JOURNAL

			Dr	*Cr*
19..			£	£
Jan	1	Debenture Application & Allotment A/c . .	47,500	
		Discount on Debentures	2,500	
		5% Debentures		50,000
		Issue of 10,000 5% debentures of £5 at 95.		
Jul	1	5% Debentures	50,000	
		Ordinary Share Capital		40,000
		Premium on Ordinary Shares		10,000
		Conversion of 5% debenture stock at current market price of £1·25 per share.		

LEDGER

5% CONVERTIBLE DEBENTURES

			£				£
19..				19..			
Jul	1	Ordinary Share Capital	40,000	Jan	1	Debenture Holders and Discount on Debentures . . .	50,000
		Share Premium . .	10,000				
			50,000				50,000

ORDINARY SHARE CAPITAL

				£
	19..			
	Jul	1	Balance . . .	50,000
			5% Convertible Debentures . . .	40,000

SHARE PREMIUM ACCOUNT

		19..	£
		Jul 1 5% Convertible Debentures . . .	10,000

BALANCE SHEET ON 1ST JANUARY, 19..

	£		£
Authorized Capital . . .	100,000	Sundry Assets	50,000
		Cash	47,500
Issued Share Capital—		Discount on Debentures . .	2,500
50,000 £1 Ordinary Shares fully paid	50,000		
5% Convertible Loan Stock—			
10,000 £5 Debentures . .	50,000		
	100,000		100,000

BALANCE SHEET ON 1ST JULY, 19..

	£		£
Authorized Capital . . .	100,000	Sundry Assets (including cash) .	97,500
		Discount on Debentures . .	2,500
Issued Share Capital—			
90,000 £1 Ordinary Shares fully paid	90,000		
Capital Reserves—			
Share Premium A/c . .	10,000		
	100,000		100,000

(*c*) Debentures Issued at a Discount, Converted to Shares at a Premium, but Option Only Partly Taken Up

Example 15

The company issued 10,000 5 per cent debentures of £5 at 90, convertible after six months to shares at the rate of 9 £1 shares to every two debentures. Of the Debenture holders 40 per cent exercised their right within the stipulated period. Show journal and ledger entries and the relevant balance sheets.

Solution 15

JOURNAL		Dr	Cr
19..		£	£
Jan 1	Debenture Application & Allotment A/c .	45,000	
	Discount on Debentures	5,000	
	5% Convertible Debentures		50,000
	Issue of 10,000 5% debentures of £5 at 90.		
Jul 1	5% Convertible Debentures	20,000	
	Ordinary Share Capital		18,000
	Shares Premium A/c		2,000
	Conversion of 5% debenture stock for those holders exercising option.		

LEDGER

5% Convertible Debentures

		£			£
19..			19..		
Jul 1	Ordinary Share Capital	18,000	Jan 1	Debenture Holders & Discount on Debentures .	50,000
	Share Premium . .	2,000			
	Balance c/d . .	30,000			
		50,000			50,000
			Jul 1	Balance b/d .	30,000

Ordinary Share Capital

				£
		19..		
		Jul 1	Balance .	50,000
			5% Convertible Debentures . .	18,000

Share Premium Account

				£
		19..		
		Jul 1	5% Convertible Debentures . .	2,000

Balance Sheet on 1st January

	£		£
Authorized Capital . . .	100,000	Sundry Assets	50,000
		Cash	45,000
Issued Share Capital— . .		Discount on Debentures . .	5,000
50,000 £1 Ordinary Shares .	50,000		
5% Convertible Loan Stock—			
10,000 £5 Debentures . .	50,000		
	100,000		100,000

BALANCE SHEET ON 1ST JULY

	£		£
Authorized Capital . . .	100,000	Sundry Assets (including cash) .	95,000
		Discount on Debentures . .	5,000
Issued Share Capital—			
68,000 £1 Ordinary Shares .	68,000		
Capital Reserves—			
Share Premium A/c . .	2,000		
5% Convertible Loan Stock—			
6,000 £5 Debentures . .	30,000		
	100,000		100,000

Note re Premiums and Discounts. The premiums and discounts are shown only in the journal, and are never mentioned in the cash book. As far as the cash book is concerned, the receipts in the case of a premium will be *more*, and in the case of a discount *less*, than the nominal value of the shares or debentures.

4. Shares Over-Subscribed

It frequently happens that more shares are applied for than there are shares to allot, and in such cases the shares are said to be *over-subscribed*. Those applicants to whom no allotment is made have their money refunded in full. But those subscribers who are allotted a smaller number of shares than they have applied for, do not have all the money returned to them; the amount they have overpaid on application is carried forward to the credit of the amount due from them on allotment.

Example 16

A limited company offered for subscription 50,000 shares of £1 each, payable £0·125 per share on application, and £0·25 per share on allotment. Applications were received for 60,000 shares. The deposits on 5,000 shares were returned to those applicants to whom no shares were allotted. The deposits on the other 5,000 shares were carried forward against the amounts due on allotment, these subscribers having paid for more shares than were allotted to them. The moneys payable on allotment were duly received. Make the necessary entries in the company's books to record the above transactions.

Solution 16

JOURNAL

		Dr	Cr
		£	£
	Application & Allotment A/c	18,750	
	Share Capital		18,750
	Allotment of 50,000 shares, payable £0·125 on application and £0·25 on allotment.		

CASH BOOK

Receipts	Bank	Payments	Bank
	£		£
Application & Allotment . .	7,500	Application & Allotment (deposits returned to non-allottees, £0·125 per share on 5,000 shares) . . .	625
Application & Allotment . .	11,875	Balance c/d . . .	18,750
	19,375		19,375
Balance b/d	18,750		

LEDGER

APPLICATION AND ALLOTMENT ACCOUNT

	£		£
Share Capital	18,750	Cash on Application .	7,500
Cash (returned)	625	Cash on Allotment . .	11,875
	19,375		19,375

SHARE CAPITAL ACCOUNT

			£
		Application & Allotment .	18,750

NOTE. The journal entry is made for the number of shares actually *allotted*, and not for the number of shares applied for. In the cash book, however, the exact amount of money received on application must, of course, be recorded, and when the cash is posted to the ledger the application and allotment account is over-credited. The cash returned to non-allottees is therefore posted to the debit of that account, thus closing it.

5. Calls in Arrear and in Advance

Calls in Arrear. Shareholders sometimes fail to pay the sums due from them on the shares they hold. The total of these amounts will constitute the calls in arrear, and may be carried down to the debit of the allotment or calls accounts *or* transferred to the debit of a calls in arrear account in the ledger. Failure to pay calls may lead to forfeiture of dividends and of the shares (see p. 2023). The articles of association generally give the directors power to charge interest on calls in arrear. (Clause 18 of Table A—see p. 2023–4—names 5 per cent per annum as the interest payable.)

Calls in Advance. Some shareholders, who do not wish to be troubled by repeated calls, pay their shares in full before the proper time. In such cases, the money received by the company in excess of what has been called up must be put to a separate "calls in advance" account. No dividend will be payable on this money, for it does not as yet form part of the company's capital. Most articles of association, however, give the directors power to pay interest on such calls received in advance. When the company does call up such money, a transfer must be made debiting the calls in advance account and crediting share capital account.

How Calls are Shown on the Balance Sheet. Although the calls in arrear and calls in advance are separate accounts in the ledger, yet the calls in arrear are not shown as a separate item on the assets side of the balance sheet, nor the calls in advance as a separate item on the liabilities side; the calls in advance being added, and the calls in arrear deducted, from capital account. Some accountants, however, show the calls in advance separately.

Nominal Capital Shown on Balance Sheet. When a limited company's shares are payable by instalments, the books at any date will record only such part of the capital as has been actually called up at this date. On the balance sheet, however, it is usual to show both the nominal and the issued capital, together with the amount called up on the shares so issued.

Example 17

A limited company with an authorized capital of £100,000, in shares of £1 each, issued 50,000 of such shares, payable £0·13 per share on application, £0·12 on allotment, £0·25 three months later, and the balance as and when required. All moneys payable on allotment were duly received. But when the call of £0·25 per share was made, one shareholder failed to pay the amount due on his 100 shares; and another shareholder, who held 75 shares, paid them in full. Make the necessary entries in the company's books to record the above transactions, and show the capital on the company's balance sheet.

Solution 17

JOURNAL

		Dr	*Cr*
		£	£
	Application & Allotment A/c	12,500	
	Share Capital		12,500
	Allotment of 50,000 shares, payable £0·13 per share on application and £0·12 on allotment.		
	First Call A/c	12,500	
	Share Capital		12,500
	£0·25 per share on 50,000 shares.		

6. Forfeiture of Shares

What Forfeiture Means. Should the shareholder not pay calls in arrear within a stipulated time, the directors generally have power conferred on

CASH BOOK (*Dr* side)

Receipts	Bank
	£
Application & Allotment	6,500·00
Application & Allotment	6,000·00
First Call (£12,500 — £25)	12,475·00
Calls in Advance (£0·50 per share on 75 shares)	37·50

BALANCE SHEET

	£	£
Authorized Capital—		
100,000 Shares of £1 each	100,000·00	
Issued Capital—		
50,000 Shares of £1 each, £0·50 per share called up	25,000·00	
Add Calls Paid in Advance	37·50	
	25,037·50	
Less Calls in Arrear	25·00	
		25,012·50

them by the articles of association to cancel such shares, after due notice has been given to the shareholder, and to appropriate to the company's own use any money already paid up on them. These shares are then said to be forfeited, and the shareholder ceases to be a member of the company. The articles must be strictly complied with, otherwise the forfeiture may not be valid; and particulars of all forfeited shares must be given in the annual return filed with the Registrar of Companies.

Provisions of Table A. As regards forfeiture of shares the following provisions of Table A, are typical of most articles of association:

33. If a member fails to pay any call or instalment of a call on the day appointed for payment thereof, the directors may, at any time thereafter during such time as any part of the call or instalment remains unpaid, serve a notice on him requiring payment of so much of the call or instalment as is unpaid, together with any interest which may have accrued.

34. The notice shall name a further day (not earlier than the expiration of fourteen days from the date of service of the notice) on or before which the payment required by the notice is to be made, and shall state that in the event of non-payment at or before the time appointed the shares in respect of which the call was made will be liable to be forfeited.

35. If the requirements of any such notice as aforesaid are not complied with, any share in respect of which the notice has been given may at any time thereafter, before the payment required by the notice has been made, be forfeited by a resolution of the directors to that effect.

36. A forfeited share may be sold or otherwise disposed of on such terms and in such manner as the directors think fit, and at any time before a sale or disposition the forfeiture may be cancelled on such terms as the directors think fit.

37. A person whose shares have been forfeited shall cease to be a member in respect of the forfeited shares, but shall, notwithstanding, remain liable to pay to

the company all moneys which, at the date of forfeiture, were payable by him to the company in respect of the shares, but his liability shall cease if and when the company shall have received payment in full of all such moneys in respect of the shares.

39. The provisions of these regulations as to forfeiture shall apply in the case of non-payment of any sum, which, by the terms of issue of a share, becomes payable at a fixed time, whether on account of the nominal value of the share, or by way of premium, as if the same has been payable by virtue of a call duly made and notified.

[NOTE RE 34 ABOVE. Students must not be of the opinion that—at the expiration of fourteen days—the secretary of the company must proceed to send a notice *re* calls in arrear with a view to their forfeiture. There may be considerable delay, and careful inquiry is prosecuted before the notice (hinting forfeiture) is sent.

Circumstances occasioning delay in payment of calls are often extenuating, and the secretary of a company is diffident of taking steps to enforce the payment of arrears.]

Liability of Ex-shareholder. The ex-shareholder is, strictly speaking, still liable, even after forfeiture, for the sum owing on the shares. But the amount is, for all practical purposes, a bad debt, and is usually written off. Moreover, a shareholder of substance cannot simply abstain from paying calls and expect his shares to be forfeited. It is the duty of the directors to compel payment if it can be obtained. The ex-shareholder's liability ceases, however, so soon as the company receives payment in full from a third party for the shares forfeited.

Entries Required when Shares are Forfeited. The amount called up on the shares has been credited to capital account and debited to allotment or call accounts in expectation of the money being paid. These entries must be cancelled by the following entries:

Dr. Share Capital A/C—with full amount called up on the shares
Cr. Call A/Cs—with amounts of unpaid calls
Cr. Forfeited Shares A/C—with amounts for which cash was received.

An alternative method is:

Dr Share Capital A/C Cr. Forfeited Shares A/C	with full amount called up on shares
Dr. Forfeited Shares A/C Cr. Calls A/Cs	with amount of unpaid calls.

Example 18

A limited company has an issued capital of £60,000 in shares of £1 each, £0·75 per share called up. The directors resolve that 160 shares, in which the first and second calls of £0·25 per share each had not been paid, should be forfeited. Make the necessary journal entries and show the effect on the company's balance sheet.

In the share ledger a note would be made *in red ink*, in the shareholder's account, stating that the shares were forfeited, and giving the date of the director's resolution.

What is Done with the Cash Received on Forfeited Shares. The money

Solution 18

First Method

JOURNAL

	Dr	Cr
	£	£
Share Capital (*full amount called up*) . .	120	
Forfeited Shares A/c (*amount paid*) . .		40
First Call A/c (*amount due*) . .		40
Second Call A/c (*amount due*) . .		40
160 Shares Nos..................to..................forfeited by order of the board for non-payment of calls. Resolution No................ dated....................		

Alternative Method

JOURNAL

	Dr	Cr
	£	£
Share Capital.	120	
Forfeited Shares A/c . . .		120
160 Shares of £1 each, £0·75 called up, forfeited, as per resolution dated..................		
Forfeited Shares A/c	80	
First Call A/c		40
Second Call A/c		40
Amount of unpaid calls written back.		

Both Methods

BALANCE SHEET

		£	£
Issued Capital—			
	60,000 Shares of £1 each, £0·75 called up . .	45,000	
Less	160 " " forfeited . .	120	
	59,840		44,880
Forfeited Shares A/c.			40

received on forfeited shares is, retained and is, of course, a profit to the company, credited to Forfeited Shares A/C but it is a *capital* profit which is not available for paying dividends, and must not be taken to profit and loss account. If the amount paid includes a premium, then an equivalent amount must be transferred back from the Share Premium A/C to the Forfeited Shares A/C as follows:

Dr. Share Premium A/C }
Cr. Forfeited Shares A/C } with premium already paid.

If it is proposed to reissue the shares, the amount is left in the forfeited shares account, to be dealt with whenever such reissue takes place. After reissue any balance remaining in the account represents a premium on the shares and must be transferred to the share premium account in accordance with Sect. 56 of the Companies Act, 1948.

Reissue of Forfeited Shares

Power to Reissue. As the forfeiture of shares is not a reduction of capital within the meaning of the Companies Act, the articles of association of a company usually give the directors power to reissue forfeited shares. Such shares may be issued at par, at a premium, or even at a reduced price. The reduction, however, should not exceed the amount already paid up on the shares, as otherwise this would be tantamount to the issue of shares at a discount, which is only legal under special conditions as stated on p. 2006.

Entries on Reissue. On reissue, a journal entry is made, debiting the person to whom the shares have been re-allotted with the amount he has agreed to pay for them, debiting forfeited shares account with the reduction in price (if any), and crediting share capital account with the called-up value of the shares. Any balance remaining on forfeited shares account after all shares have been reissued is transferred to share premium account.

Example 19

The directors of the aforesaid company resolved that the previously mentioned shares, namely 160 shares of £1 each, £0·75 per share called up £0·25 per share paid up, should be issued to John Smith, credited with £0·75 per share paid, for £100. Make the necessary entries in the company's books.

Solution 19

JOURNAL

		Dr	Cr
		£	£
	John Smith (*personal account in general ledger*) .	100	
	Forfeited Shares A/c	20	
	Share Capital		120
	Reissue of 160 shares of £1 each, credited with £0·75 per share paid, for £100, as per resolution No..................dated..................................		
	Forfeited Shares A/c	20	
	Share Premium A/c		20
	Premium on reissue of forfeited shares.		

CASH BOOK (*Dr.* side)

Receipts	Bank
	£
John Smith	100

Note. As £120 of capital (¾ of £160) is being issued for £100, the balance of £20 must be made good out of the forfeited shares account.

7. Preliminary Expenses

All expenses incidental to the formation, registration, incorporation, flotation, and commencement of business are, in the case of a joint stock company, debited to a special account entitled "preliminary expenses." They are also called "formation expenses" and "promotion expenses." They comprise the following—

1. Solicitors' fees for drawing up memorandum and articles of association.
2. Registration fees, stamp duties on the nominal capital.
3. Cost of printing memorandum and articles of association.
4. Cost of share registers, seal, etc.

How Dealt with in the Books. Where the preliminary expenses are not borne by the vendor, the amount will appear in the company's books. It is in *the nature* of capital expenditure, and it has been suggested that as a matter *of law* it might be upheld as an asset permanently. It is, however, the universal practice to write it off against revenue over a period of years, usually three to five, according to the amount.

In examination work, preliminary expenses should not be written off unless specific instructions are given to do so. The balance of the account not written off must be shown on the assets side of the balance sheet until the whole amount has been finally extinguished.

Costs of Issuing Shares and Debentures

Such expenses must be distinguished from preliminary expenses as they must be stated separately in the balance sheet until they are written off.

They comprise the following—

1. Accountants' and valuers' fees for preparing reports for the prospectus.
2. Solicitors' fees for drawing up the prospectus.
3. Costs of printing the prospectus, letters of allotment, letters of regret, call notices, etc.
4. Costs of advertising the issue.
5. Costs of preparing the debenture trust deed.

How Dealt with in the Books. Likc preliminary expenses, they should be written off over a period, usually three to five years.

8. Debentures as Collateral Security for Loan

A limited company had an authorized debentures issue of £80,000 in or secondary security, that is, a security in addition to the principal security. A collateral security is not intended to be realized except in the event of the principal security proving insufficient. Some companies issue debentures as collateral security for a bank overdraft or a bank loan.

Entries in the Books. The amount of the debentures so issued is entered "short" on the balance sheet, i.e. not extended into the money columns, and a note is added explaining that the debentures have been issued as security for a bank loan or overdraft as the case may be. It is the practice of some accountants to credit the amount of such debentures to the debentures account itself, and to debit it to a debenture suspense account, the latter appearing temporarily on the assets side of the balance sheet. When the loan has been repaid, or the overdraft extinguished, and the debentures released, then a journal entry is passed crediting the debenture suspense account, thus closing it, and debiting the debentures account, thus reducing the latter to its original amount.

Example 20

A limited company has an authorized debenture issue of £80,000 in bonds of £100 each. £50,000 of such bonds have been issued at par to the public, and the money has been duly received. £10,000 of the remainder has been issued to its bankers as collateral security for a loan of £8,000. How should these facts be recorded in the company's balance sheet?

Solution 20

BALANCE SHEET

	£
Debentures—	
500 Bonds of £100 each at par	50,000
Loan from Bankers (Secured by issue of £10,000 Debentures)	8,000

QUESTIONS

1. What companies enter the *nominal* capital in their books? Submit *pro forma* journal entries in such a case. What objection is raised to this practice?
2. What are calls in arrear and what entries are necessary in the books?
3. What are calls in advance and what entries are required in the books?
4. What is meant by "forfeiture of shares"? What is the ex-shareholder's liability for the money owing?
5. State briefly the provisions of Table A with reference to forfeiture of shares.
6. What entries are required in the books when shares are forfeited?
7. What happens to the cash which has actually been received on forfeited shares? Would it be correct to carry it to the profit and loss account as a divisible profit?
8. Can forfeited shares be reissued? If so, at what price? How should the balance (if any) on forfeited shares account after reissue be treated?
9. What entries are necessary in the books when forfeited shares are reissued?
10. What is a debenture? What entries are necessary to record it in the books?
11. State the conditions under which shares may be issued at a discount.
12. How should preliminary expenses be treated in the company's books?
13. What is meant by "debentures as collateral security for loan"? What entries are necessary in the company's books and balance sheet in such cases?
14. What is underwriting? Is an agreement to *place* shares an underwriting agreement? Under what conditions may a company pay commission to persons for procuring subscriptions to shares?
15. Must commission paid in respect of shares or debentures, or discount allowed on shares and debentures, be made known to the shareholders?
16. What statutory provisions are there with reference to the audit of a company? Must the auditor's report and balance sheet be published? Have debenture holders a right to receive and inspect the auditor's report and balance sheet?
17. What are the rights and duties of an auditor as laid down by the 1967 Act?

18. What is share capital? Explain the following terms with reference to a company's capital: Nominal, authorized, registered, issued, subscribed, called-up, paid-up, uncalled, reserve. Apply the above terms to the following example: A company was formed with a capital of £250,000 in shares of £1 each, and duly incorporated. It issued to the vendors 50,000 shares of £1 each as fully paid, in part payment of the purchase consideration. It also offered to the public 150,000 shares, payable £0·13 per share on application, £0·12 per share on allotment, £0·25 per share one month later, and the balance as and when required. All the money was duly received with the exception of the call of £0·25 on 300 shares.

19. What is a share? Explain the following kinds: ordinary, preferred ordinary, deferred ordinary, preference, cumulative preference, redeemable preference, deferred, founders', management.

20. Explain the following terms with reference to the issue of shares and debentures: at par, at a premium, at a discount, over-subscribed, calls in arrear, calls paid in advance.

EXERCISE 20

1. A limited company issued, at par, 200,000 ordinary shares of £1 each, and £80,000 debentures in bonds of £100 each; which were all subscribed and fully paid up. Make the necessary journal and cash book entries, post to ledger, draw out trial balance, and make a balance sheet.

2. A limited company issued 200,000 preference shares of £1 each at £1·125 per share, and £80,000 debentures at a premium of 5 per cent; which were all subscribed and fully paid up. Make the necessary journal, cash book, and ledger entries, and draw up trial balance and balance sheet.

3. A limited company issued £80,000 debentures in bonds of £100 each, at £95 per bond; which were all subscribed and fully paid up. Make the necessary journal, cash book, and ledger entries, and draw up trial balance and balance sheet.

4. A limited company issued 200,000 ordinary shares of £1 each, payable £0·125 per share on application, £0·375 per share on allotment, and £0·25 per share on each of two subsequent calls. All the money was duly received. Make the necessary journal and cash book entries, post to ledger, and show trial balance and balance sheet.

5. A limited company issued 200,000 preference shares of £1 each at £1·125 per share, payable £0·375 per share on application (including the premium), £0·25 per share on allotment, and the balance in two later calls each of £0·25 per share. Make the necessary journal, cash book, and ledger entries, and show trial balance and balance sheet.

6. A limited company issued, at par, £80,000 debentures in bonds of £100 each, payable 20 per cent on application, 30 per cent on allotment, and the balance three months later. All the money was duly received. Make the necessary journal and cash book entries, post to ledger and draw out trial balance, and show also the balance sheet.

7. A limited company issued £80,000 debentures in bonds of £100 each, at a premium of 10 per cent, payable 20 per cent on application (including the premium), and 90 per cent on allotment. All the money was duly received. Make the necessary journal, cash book, and ledger entries, and show also the trial balance and balance sheet.

8. A limited company issued £80,000 6 per cent first mortgage debentures in bonds of £100 each, at a discount of 10 per cent, payable £20 per bond on application, and the balance on allotment. All the money was duly received. Make the necessary journal and cash book entries, post to ledger, and draw up trial balance, and show also the company's balance sheet.

9. A limited company offered for subscription 200,000 shares of £1 each, payable £0·125 per share on application, and £0·25 per share on allotment. Applications were received for 230,000 shares. The deposits on 15,000 shares were returned to those persons to whom no shares were allotted. The deposits on the other 15,000 shares were carried forward to the allotment account, these subscribers having paid for more shares than were allotted to them. The moneys payable on allotment were duly received. Make the necessary entries in the company's journal, cash book, and ledger, to record the above transactions.

10. A limited company with a registered capital of £250,000, in shares of £1 each, issued 200,000 of such shares, payable £0·125 per share on application, £0·125 per share on allotment, £0·25 per share three months later, and the balance as and when required. All moneys payable on allotment were duly received. But when the call of £0·25 per share was made, one shareholder failed to pay the amount due on his 250 shares; and another shareholder, who held 200 shares, paid them right up in full. Make the necessary journal and cash book entries in the company's books to record the above transactions, and show the company's balance sheet.

11. Stockport Ltd. was incorporated on 1st January, 19.., and on that date invited applications for 100,000 shares of £1 each, at par, payable £0·25 per share on application, £0·25 on allotment, and £0·50 per share on 1st July, 19...

Applications for exactly 100,000 shares were received and the allotment was completed early in January. All amounts due on allotment were received with the exception of that due on 1,000 shares issued to John Bolton. These shares were forfeited by the directors on 25th March, 19...

During the three months to 31st March, 19.., Stockport Ltd. had—

(*a*) bought, and paid for, fixed assets at a cost of £50,000;

(*b*) purchased goods for resale and incurred general expenses amounting to £76,000, of which £6,000 remained unpaid at this date; and

(*c*) received £92,000 for cash sales.

You are asked to prepare—

(i) a total cash account for the three months to 31st March, 19.., and
(ii) a balance sheet at 31st March, 19...

A charge is to be made for depreciation on the fixed assets for the three months at the rate of 10 per cent per annum.

There are no transactions other than those of which details are given in this question and there was no stock-in-trade held on 31st March, 19... (*R.S.A.*)

12. On 1st May, Eldec Ltd. offer to the public 50,000 ordinary shares and 25,000 preference shares under a "package deal": two ordinary £0·25 shares at £0·75 each and one 6 per cent £1 preference share at £1 each. £2 is payable on application, being payment in full for the ordinary shares and £0·50 part payment for the preference shares, the balance being due on 1st August.

Applications are received for 30,000 lots of shares. Allotment is made and money refunded to unsuccessful applicants on 5th May. The final instalment is received from all except the holder of 2,000 shares. Following a minute of the directors, these shares are declared forfeit on 1st October, being re-issued at £0·75 per share on 20th October.

Give the ledger accounts required to cover these transactions.

(*Cost and Management Accountants.*)

13. The nominal capital of William Pearson & Co. Ltd. consists of 50,000 shares of £1 each. On 31st December, the ledger balances of the company were as follows—

	£		£
Share capital (Issued 30,000 shares of £1 each with £0·50 per share called up)	15,000	Manufacturing wages	12,450
Unpaid calls	150	Salaries	1,230
Cash in hand	190	Discount (*Cr.*)	48
Sundry creditors	1,960	Carriage and cartage	395
Sundry debtors	3,640	Rates and taxes	111
Cash at bank	1,150	Insurance	98
Reserve fund	4,000	Sales	62,850
Machinery and plant	6,000	Trade expenses	382
Mortgage debentures (45 debentures of £100 each at 5% interest)	4,500	Repairs	174
Freehold premises	11,500	Purchases	41,800
Stock (1st January)	8,800	Unpaid dividends	252
		Bad debts	191
		Office expenses	124
		Interest paid on debentures	225

Machinery and plant—original cost less sales was £10,434.

Stock was taken as on 31st December, and was valued at £6,820.

Before closing the accounts the following adjustments are necessary—

Make a provision of 5 per cent for bad and doubtful debts. Depreciation at the rate of 10 per cent is to be written off the machinery and plant account. Prepare trading and profit and loss accounts for the year ended 31st December. Take £1,000 to the reserve fund, and prepare a balance sheet as on that date.

(London Chamber of Commerce.)

14. On 1st August, 19.., Enix Ltd. made a public offer of 2,500 6 per cent debentures of £100 each at the price of £97 per debenture, £10 of which was payable on application, £37 on allotment, and the remaining £50 on 31st January, 19.1.

The application lists were closed on 5th August, by which date applications, with cheques to correspond, had been received for 3,760 debentures. Allotment took place on the following day, when applications for 900 debentures were accepted in full, applications for a further 2,400 scaled down by a third, and the remainder refused. Cheques to the unsuccessful applicants were posted on the following day.

By 31st March, 19.1, to which date the company made up its next annual accounts, all the allotment money had been received as well as the final instalment on all except eight of the debentures.

Record the foregoing, including all cash received and paid, in the form of journal entries. *(R.S.A.)*

15. In December, 19.., Tagetes Ltd., which at that time had an issued share capital of £200,000, all in £1 shares of one class, made a public issue of £100,000 6 per cent convertible loan stock. The stock was offered at the issue price of £98 per £100 of stock, of which £10 was payable on application and the balance on allotment, and the terms provided that holders should have the right, on giving notice in December, 19.3, to exchange their holdings for shares in the company on the basis of sixty-five shares for each £100 of Loan Stock.

The issue of loan stock was over-subscribed, applications for £350,000 being received on 19th December, 19... The excess application money was all retained and set off against the amount due on allotment: allotment took place on 21st December and the allotment money was all received by 30th December.

You are required to set out—

(*a*) the ledger accounts recording the issue of the loan stock (*not* including cash book entries);

(*b*) the position as reflected in the company's balance sheet as on 31st December, 19.. (the discount on the issue not having then been written off);

(*c*) supposing that holders of £60,000 of the loan stock exercised their right to convert in December, 19.3, the ledger entries recording that fact; and

(*d*) the position as reflected in the balance sheet as on 31st December, 19.3 (ignoring the discount on the original issue). (*R.S.A.*)

16. (*a*) Among the different types of share which a limited company may issue are the following—

1. cumulative preference,
2. non-cumulative preference,
3. participating preference with limited participating rights,
4. participating preference with unlimited participating rights.

Explain the meaning of each of the terms used, and distinguish between the rights of the holders in each case as compared with the others.

(*b*) The issued capital of Y Ltd. consists of 100,000 participating preference shares and 100,000 ordinary shares, all of £1 each, and such part of the profits of each year as it may be decided to distribute are applied in providing for dividends in the following order—

Firstly, 5 per cent on the cumulative preference shares;
Secondly, 10 per cent on the ordinary shares;
Thirdly, up to 2½ per cent rateably on both classes of shares;
Lastly, any further dividend to the holders of the ordinary shares only.

For the three years ended 30th June, 19.., 19.1, and 19.2 the total amounts distributed as dividend were £20,000, £17,000, and £23,000 respectively, i.e. £60,000 in all.

Draw up a statement to show how much each class of shareholder received for each year and the totals of the three years: also, show what difference it would have made to the final answer if £20,000 had been distributed in each of the three years. (*R.S.A.*)

17. From the following trial balance of the accounts of a manufacturing company (whose authorized capital consists of 15,000 ordinary shares of £10 each) prepare a trading account and a profit and loss account for the year ended 31st December, and a balance sheet as on that date.

	£		£
Capital issued and fully paid up, 9,000 shares of £10 each	90,000	Purchases returns	750
Stock (1st January)	32,000	Manufacturing charges	11,500
Cash in hand	150	Manufacturing wages	28,550
Cash at bank	2,900	Salaries	1,500
Purchases	52,350	Trade expenses	6,850
Sales	136,500	Rates and taxes	250
„ returns	400	Insurance	190
Bad debts	570	General expenses	2,640
Interest and bank charges	350	Discounts (balance) *Dr.*	1,800
Land and buildings	22,250	Patents	5,000
Machinery and plant	35.600	Bad debts provision (1st January)	2,600
Sundry debtors	52,500	Profit and loss (*Cr.* balance 1st January)	750
Sundry creditors	21,750	Reserve account	5,000

Charge depreciation on land and buildings account at 3 per cent per annum, and on machinery and plant account at 6 per cent. Make a provision of 5 per cent on the sundry debtors for bad debts; write down patents account by 10 per cent; carry forward £90 of insurance; and charge £500 as directors' fees. The value of the stock, as on 31st December, was agreed at £23,700. Charge 10 per cent on net profits as remuneration to the managing director, and appropriate £2,500 to the reserve account, carrying forward the balance. Assume your own figures for original cost of the fixed assets. (*R.S.A.*)

18. The Diamond Car Company Limited was registered as dealers in cars in 19.., with a nominal capital of £100,000 consisting of 200,000 shares of £0·50 each. The whole of the capital was offered and fully subscribed; £0·25 per share had been called and was fully paid up with the exception of the first call of £0·10 per share of 2,000 shares which remained unpaid. A holder of 4,000 shares had elected to pay up his shares in full. Under the articles of association, interest at 5 per cent was allowed on calls paid in advance, and 10 per cent interest was chargeable on calls in arrear. As at 31st December, 19.1, twelve months' interest had accrued in both the above cases, but no entries had been made in the books in respect of the interest due to and by the respective shareholders.

On 1st July, 19.1, 300 8 per cent debentures of £100 each were issued at 96 and were fully subscribed and paid up.

In addition to the ledger accounts necessary to record the above transactions, the following balances appeared in the books of the company as at 31st December, 19.1—

	£
Haulage charges	5,500
Motor lorries	2,540
Loose tools, 31st December, 19..	350
Purchases	55,341
Purchases returns	1,352
Sales	68,871
Sales returns	2,200
Showroom fixtures and fittings	1,500
Machinery and plant (repairing outfit)	1,562
Stock, 31st December, 19..	20,992
Office furniture	300
Rent and rates, showroom	1,685
Rent and rates, offices	200
Insurances	545
Motor lorries insurances	100
Machinery repairs	224
Leasehold showrooms	43,390
Directors' fees	500
Office salaries	1,286
Showroom salaries and commission	2,178
Office expenses	171
Legal expenses	90
Showroom expenses	424
Carriage inwards	922
Carriage outwards	624
Discount account, credit balance	356
Cash in hand	16
Cash at bank	12,280
Profit and loss account, debit balance 31st December, 19..	3,286

	£
Reserve for bad debts, 31st December, 19.	200
Sundry creditors	2,770
Sundry debtors	5,340
Licences	108
Drivers' salaries	1,925
Tuition fees received	1,200
Receipts for repair of cars	2,872
Mechanics' wages	1,142
Petrol, oil, and repairs for motor lorries	1,500

Prepare trading and operating accounts for year ended 31st December, 19.1 and balance sheet as on that date.

When preparing the above accounts, make the following adjustments—

(*a*) Depreciation is to be written off as follows—

Motor lorries	20 per cent.
Showroom fixtures and fittings	10 per cent.
Office furniture	5 per cent.

(*b*) The following valuations were made as at 31st December, 19.1—

	£
Machinery and plant	1,400
Loose tools	300
Stock in hand	19,240

(*c*) Provision for bad and doubtful debts is to be made of an amount equal to 5 per cent on the sundry debtors.

(*d*) The following items have been paid in advance—

	£
Rates—Showroom	120
Office	15
Insurances—General	65
Motor lorries	17

(*e*) An action against a haulage company, in respect of a damaged car, was settled on 28th December, the haulage company agreeing to pay £200 in respect of the car, and £72 law costs. No entries in respect of this settlement had been made.

(*f*) The interest due on the debentures, as at 31st December, 19.1, had not been passed through the books. (*Cost and Management Accountants.*)

19. The secretary of the Cheshire Manufacturing Co. Ltd. takes out his balances on 31st December, and submits to you the following particulars, from which prepare trading account, profit and loss account, and balance sheet—

Nominal capital £150,000, divided into 5,000 preference shares of £10 each, and 10,000 ordinary shares of £10 each.

	£		£
5,000 preference shares, £10 each, £2 paid	10,000	Purchases	43,249
10,000 ordinary shares, £10 each, £5 called up	50,000	Land and buildings	25,100
150 5% mortgage debentures of £100 each, issued at 95	15,000	Fuel	570
Cost of issue of debentures	750	Plant and machinery	5,620
		Repairs	445
		Loose tools (1st January)	1,752
		Office expenses	363

	£		£
Sales	53,847	Sundry debtors	24,300
Wages	9,371	Sundry creditors	9,160
Discounts received	324	Carriage inwards	220
Discounts allowed	517	Goodwill	10,000
Salaries	975	Carriage outwards	410
Bad debts	275	Debenture interest paid	375
Postage, etc.	86	Profit and loss account, balance of loss brought forward from last account	2,243
Rates, taxes, and insurance	524	Unpaid calls, ordinary shares	250
Travelling expenses	302	Bank overdraft	1,525
Interest and bank charges	75	Cash in hand	114
Directors' fees	550		
Stock (1st January)	11,420		

Accrued debenture interest £375. Accrued wages £50. Provide for bad debts £400; insurance prepaid £21. Depreciate land and buildings 1 per cent and plant and machinery 10 per cent. Provide for discounts, 5 per cent on sundry debtors and 2½ per cent on sundry creditors. Stock at 31st December, £18,763. Assume any other figures that may be necessary.

Value of loose tools at 31st December, £2,000. (*U.L.C.I.*)

20. The North London Engineering Co. Ltd. was registered on 1st January, with a nominal capital of £100,000, in ordinary shares of £1 each. It had power to issue £15,000 mortgage debentures of £100 each, bearing interest at 4 per cent per annum. It took over on that date an existing engineering business and commenced manufacturing. Stock was taken and the books balanced, and accounts prepared annually; and at the close of the year stock was taken and valued at £14,250. The following adjustments were necessary before closing the accounts—

(*a*) Depreciation to be written off plant and machinery at the rate of 10 per cent, and off patents account at 20 per cent.

(*b*) The half-year's debenture interest due on 31st December to be passed through the books.

(*c*) A 5 per cent provision for bad and doubtful debts to be made.

Make such adjustments and prepare a trading account, a profit and loss account, and a balance sheet from the following balances (31st December), after carrying £1,500 profit to the Reserve Account.

	£		£
Share capital 60,000 Shares of £1 each issued and £0·50 per share called up	30,000	Cash in hand	320
Unpaid calls	300	Sundry creditors	4,095
Patents	900	Sundry debtors	7,240
Mortgage debentures	9,000	Reserve account	8,500
Freehold buildings (1st January)	24,000	Machinery and plant	12,480
Stock (1st January)	17,200	Unpaid dividends	58
Manufacturing wages	22,100	Mortgage debenture interest	180
Salaries	2,400	Provision for auditors' fees	75
Carriage	560	Bad debts	578
Rates, taxes, and insurance	252	Interest and bank charges	138
Sales	121,580	Additions to buildings during the year	3,840
Trade expenses	721	Holdfast Bank Ltd. (overdraft)	4,200
Repairs	240	Bad debt reserve (1st January)	321
Rents receivable	374		
Purchases	84,604		

(*R.S.A.*)

CHAPTER 21

COMPANY EARNINGS

All men are ready to invest their money
But most expect dividends

T. S. ELIOT—*The Rock*

THE general rules followed in reporting company income are the same as those outlined in earlier chapters and internal income statements will be adapted to the type of business and company organization.

However, the determination of the profits available for distribution among the shareholders and the disposition or division proposed is particularly important for limited companies, as the shareholders, unlike partners or sole traders, do not have unlimited liability for debts of the firm. Once a dividend has been paid, it is beyond the reach of creditors. For this reason, the rules of law concerning divisible profits are quite strict in relation to a limited company.

Divisible Profits. In law, three broad principles govern the payment of dividends by a company—

1. The interest of outside creditors must be protected.
2. The shareholders' capital must not be used to pay a dividend.
3. There must be a bona fide profit from which to pay the dividend.

Effect of Articles. Both the memorandum and articles of association can *restrict* the company's power to declare dividends, but cannot extend it beyond the legal limits. The provisions of Table A of the 1948 Act are contained in clauses 114 to 122, and the main provisions are—

Clause 116. No dividend shall be paid otherwise than out of profits. (Note that this does *not* preclude the payment of dividends out of capital profits.)

Clause 117. The directors may transfer to reserve such sums as they think desirable before recommending a dividend.

Clause 114 vests the right in the members to declare dividends in general meeting, but does not allow a greater dividend to be declared than the directors recommend.

Clause 115 allows directors to pay such interim dividends as are justified by the profits.

Depreciation. The amounts allowed for depreciation may considerably affect the amount of profit available for dividend. Of course, each case will be considered on its merits, but, in general—

(*a*) It is *not* obligatory to provide for depreciation on fixed or wasting assets, provided that there are sufficient assets to cover the liabilities. Goodwill is a fixed asset (*Lee* v. *Neuchatel Asphalte Co. Ltd.*).

(*b*) It is obligatory to provide for the depreciation of current assets (*Verner* v. *General & Commercial Trust Ltd.*).

(*c*) If excessive depreciation has been written off an asset, it may be added back to profits provided a bona fide revaluation is made (*Stapley* v. *Read Bros. Ltd.*).

(*d*) If a debit balance on profit and loss has been created to some extent by depreciation on fixed assets, it is not necessary to make this part good before paying dividends from subsequent profits (*Ammonia Soda Co. Ltd.* v. *Chamberlain.*).

Capital Profits may be distributed if the following three conditions apply—

1. The articles do not forbid such distribution.
2. The profit must have been actually realized. It must not be a mere paper profit.
3. Only that portion of the profit which remains after a bona fide revaluation of all the assets may be used (*Lubbock* v. *British Bank of South America; Foster* v. *New Trinidad Lake Asphalte Co. Ltd.*).

An unrealized capital appreciation may, however, be distributed in the form of bonus shares (see p. 2118). Even a profit on forfeited shares may be distributed in this way.

Capital losses may be charged against current profits or, if the directors think fit, carried back against the profits of years in which the losses were incurred. Alternatively, they can be charged against future profits over several years.

Non-operating Profits and Losses. These may arise from a variety of sources such as outside investments or licensing fees. They may be credited or debited to profits in the year in which they arise. One example is profit on sale of investments. They are often called "other income."

Exposure draft ED7 of the A.S.S.C. states that accounting for extraordinary and prior year items through reserves or retained profits instead of through the profit and loss account can lead to anomalies in the reported annual results of business and to disparities in the reported results of similar businesses. This statement requires all extraordinary and prior year items, with rare exceptions, to be accounted for through the profit and loss account of the year and not through reserves. It does not deal with the timing and methods of computing such items but only with the manner in which they should be reported in the accounts.

Extraordinary items are those material items which derive from events or transactions outside the ordinary activities of the business and which are not expected to recur frequently. They do not include items which, though exceptional or abnormal on account of size or incidence (and which may therefore require separate disclosure), derive from the ordinary activities of the business.

Prior year adjustments are those rare adjustments arising from prior year items, the accounting effects of which could not be ascertained or estimated with reasonable assurance at the time of preparation of the accounts for the relevant period, usually because of some major uncertainty then existing. They do not include the normal recurring corrections and adjustments of accounting estimates made in prior years.

Provisions. A provision, according to Schedule 2 of the 1967 Companies Act is "any amount written off or retained by way of providing for depreciation, renewals or diminution in value of assets or . . . providing for any known liability of which the amount cannot be determined with substantial accuracy." Where the amount provided exceeds the amount, which in the opinion of the Directors is reasonably necessary, then the excess must be treated as a reserve.

Reserves. The 1967 Companies Act abandons the distinction between capital and revenue reserves which was established by the Companies Act, 1948, and adopts a negative definition of reserves as being retentions of profits which are not provisions and not in respect of liabilities. Reserves therefore include all profits retained or "ploughed back" into the business which are not provisions.

Writing-off Capital Expenditure. In the case of goodwill, leases, patents, trade marks, preliminary expenses and underwriting commissions, a proportion of the cost may be charged as a current expense until the item disappears from the Balance Sheet.

INTEREST

Interest is the service charge or expense incurred by the use of borrowed money.

(*a*) Debenture Interest

Debenture interest is usually paid half-yearly, and the company must normally deduct income tax at the current basic rate. It is very important to remember that, except in the case of income debentures, interest is payable whether there are profits or not. For this reason debenture interest is chargeable to profit and loss account and not to appropriation account.

Entries for Debenture Interest. The interest is debited to a separate debenture interest account. Entries are made as follows—

JOURNAL	Dr	Cr
	£	£
Debenture Interest	800	
Debenture Holders		560
Income Tax		240
Half-year's debenture interest, less tax at £0·30 in the £.		

The debenture interest account is closed, at balancing time, by transfer to profit and loss. The journal entry would be—

	£	£
Profit and Loss Account . .	800	
Debenture Interest . . .		800

Deduction of Income Tax. A limited company must deduct income tax at the current rate from all interest paid to debenture holders. The amount of the tax must be remitted direct to the Collector of Taxes within 14 days. However, the tax due may be offset against tax deducted on interest and annual payments received (but not on dividends received). The journal entry would be—

	£	£
Collector of Taxes . . .	240	
Cash		240

If offsetting tax suffered is available, then the amount would be less than £240.

How the Debenture Interest is Paid. In large companies a cheque is drawn for the net amount of the interest payable, and posted to the debit of the debenture holders account, thus closing it. The cheque itself is paid in to the credit of a separate debenture interest account at the company's bank, and a separate debenture interest pass book is kept. Cheques or warrants are then drawn on this account for each debenture holder's portion, and sent to the debenture holders concerned. When the debenture holders clear their cheques, the amount will be debited by the bank to this particular debenture interest account, and eventually this account will be closed. When the number of debenture holders is not very large a separate debenture interest bank account may not be opened; the debenture interest cheques or warrants may be drawn on the ordinary bank account. The journal entry would be—

	£	£
Debenture-holders . . .	560	
Cash		560

Unclaimed or Unpaid Debenture Interest. If at balancing time all the debenture holders have not cleared their interest cheques there will be an unpaid balance of debenture interest. Very often (especially in exercises and examination papers), there is no separate statement of cash; the money with which to pay this debenture interest is included in "Cash at Bank." If it is desired to show the unpaid balances, there are two ways this might be done. The first would be to journalize the cash payments to Debenture-holders only after the cheques are cleared. In our example, if £20 remains unclaimed, this method would be journalized—

	£	£
Debenture-holders . . .	540	
Cash		540

From a practical viewpoint, this is not a very satisfactory method. A better alternative is to journalize the whole payment of £560 when the cheques are made out and then to journalize an adjustment for the amount outstanding at the end of the period, thus—

	£	£
Cash (on Debenture interest account)		
Unclaimed	20	
Debenture Interest . .		20

Debenture Interest less Tax. In exercises and examination papers the student will, sometimes, find in the trial balance an item like the following—

Debenture Interest *less* tax at £0·30 . . £560

In the profit and loss account the debenture interest must be raised to the gross sum, as the full debenture interest is a charge against profits. The amount of the tax must be ascertained, added back to the debenture interest and credited to a Collector of Taxes Account. The amount of the tax is found by arithmetical process. If, for example, the tax is thirty per cent of the gross amount taxable, the amount stated as "debenture interest" is equal to 70 per cent of the full amount. To raise the amount to the proper sum, apply the formula: $£560 \times \frac{100}{70}$, which will yield the *gross* amount taxable, i.e. £800.

(*b*) Interest on Calls

Interest on Calls in Arrear. The articles of association usually empower the directors to charge interest on calls not paid within the specified time.

Provisions of Table A. Clause 18 of Table A, Companies Act, 1948, reads as follows—

> If a sum called in respect of a share is not paid before or on the day appointed for payment thereof, the person from whom the sum is due shall pay interest upon the sum from the day appointed for payment thereof to the time of actual payment at such rate not exceeding 5 per cent per annum as the directors may determine, but the directors shall be at liberty to waive payment of that interest wholly or in part.

The same or similar provisions are usually contained in special articles.

Entries in the Books. Where the share ledger does not contain any columns for interest, accounts will have to be opened in the general ledger for the shareholders concerned. The following journal entry will be necessary if £5 is due—

	£	£
Shareholder	5	
Interest Receivable . . .		5

The interest receivable will be taken as a profit to profit and loss account, and the shareholders will appear as debtors on the balance sheet. Where the share ledger account is in two parts, a cash account and a share account, the interest will be shown in the share ledger itself, being debited to the shareholders concerned from the interest column in the call book. In the general ledger the interest will be treated impersonally, i.e. the shareholders' names will not appear. The following journal entry will be required—

	£	£
Outstanding Interest . . .	5	
Interest Receivable . . .		5

The interest receivable will be treated as a profit in the profit and loss account, and the outstanding interest will appear as an asset in the balance sheet.

Interest on Calls paid in Advance. The Articles of Association usually give the directors of a company power to allow interest on calls paid in advance.

Provisions of Table A. Clause 21 of Table A, Companies Act, 1948, reads as follows—

> The directors may, if they think fit, receive from any member willing to advance the same, all or any part of the moneys uncalled and unpaid upon any shares held by him; and upon all or any of the moneys so advanced may (until the same would, but for such advance, become payable) pay interest at such rate not exceeding (unless the company in general meeting shall otherwise direct) five per cent per annum, as may be agreed upon between the directors and the member paying such sum in advance.

The same or similar provisions are usually contained in special articles.

Entries in the Books. Where the share ledger is not provided with columns for interest, accounts will be opened in the general ledger for the shareholders concerned. The following journal entry will be required if £10 becomes due—

	£	£
Interest Payable	10	
Shareholder		10

The interest payable will be a loss in the profit and loss account, and the shareholders will appear as creditors on the balance sheet. Where the share ledger account is in two parts, a cash account and a share account, the interest will be shown in the share ledger itself, being credited to the shareholders from the interest column in the call book. In the general ledger the interest will be treated impersonally, the following journal entry being made—

	£	£
Interest Payable	10	
Outstanding Interest . . .		10

The interest payable will be transferred to profit and loss as a loss, and the outstanding interest will be a liability on the balance sheet. In many cases, however, interest will be paid on the due date, and only the following cash book entry (payments side) will be required—

	£	£
Interest on Calls in Advance	10	
Cash		10

This amount will be transferred like other losses to profit and loss account at balancing time.

Interest on Bank Loans and Overdrafts. Since the charges for these items are debited directly to the company by the bank, it is customary for the gross interest to be charged and the effect of this is that the company is not required to deduct income tax on these items. As with other items of interest, the gross amount is chargeable as an expense against profits.

Interest on Capital, Paid out of Capital

Non-Revenue Earning Period. During the construction of works or buildings which take a long time to complete, a company is unable to earn any income with which to pay dividends on shares issued for this purpose. In such cases it is legal for companies to pay interest on these shares during this period, called the non-revenue earning period, and to capitalize the interest, i.e. treat it as part of the cost of the works or buildings so constructed. Certain restrictions are imposed.

Provisions of the Companies Act, 1948. The conditions to be complied with are laid down in Sect. 65, and may be summarized as follows—

1. The payment must be authorized by the articles or a special resolution, and must have the sanction of the Board of Trade, who determine the period and may obtain a report of the circumstances (at the company's expense).

2. The period cannot extend beyond the half-year following the half-year in which the work is completed.

3. The rate of interest cannot exceed 4 per cent except by order of the Treasury.

4. The payment of interest shall not reduce the amount paid up on shares.

Other Cases of Interest Paid out of Capital. Parliamentary companies, which are incorporated under special Acts of Parliament, usually have similar powers conferred on them. It is also legal (*Hinds* v. *Buenos Ayres Grand National Tramways Co. Ltd.*) for companies to capitalize debenture interest, or a portion of it, in those cases where the debentures have been issued for the purpose of raising money to defray the cost of construction of works or buildings, or the provision of plant which will not be ready for use until a much later period. The debenture interest capitalized is added to the value of the property or works account. Interest on calls in advance may be paid whether there are profits available or not.

Arguments "For." The arguments in favour of charging interest on capital to capital are briefly as follows—

1. If a company engages with a contractor to erect buildings for it for a certain price, the contractor will include in his price not only the actual cost of construction but also interest on the capital outlay up to date of settlement, and also his customary profit; and, therefore, if the company erects the buildings for itself, and the buildings cannot be made productive until they are finished, the company is entitled to charge to capital not merely the actual capital outlay, but also the interest paid on the capital during the period of construction.

2. That the payment to shareholders of a low rate of interest during the construction of the work is the least expensive method of financing it.

3. That as interest can be paid out of capital in the case of loans and debentures, it ought also to be payable in the case of shares.

4. That if interest has not been so charged a false idea is given of the cost of the undertaking. It can scarcely be fairly said that a concern has cost only £50,000 if the £50,000 has been outstanding for a period and interest has, therefore, been lost on it.

Arguments "Against." The counter-arguments, i.e. against charging interest on capital to capital, are the following—

1. The law makes a distinction between capital contributed by shareholders and capital obtained from lenders and debenture holders.

2. Interest on loans and debentures is rightly payable out of capital; for the company's capital exists for the purpose of paying its creditors.

3. Interest on capital during construction of works is not part of the cost of such works, but merely an expense in the obtaining of capital moneys; and should be treated in the same way as commission and brokerage on the placing of a company's shares, or discount on the issue of a company's debentures. That is, it should be temporarily capitalized, and written off against revenue periodically.

CORPORATION TAX

The way in which Corporation Tax is actually calculated and provided for is discussed in Chapter 28. For this chapter, a simple treatment is assumed in the examples so that the principles of accounting for company earnings may be illustrated.

Earnings or Appropriable Profits. The net profits which a company shows after deduction of expenses, provisions, interest and corporation tax are the earnings out of which dividends can be paid. After payment or provision for the preference share dividends and the claims of minority interests, the balance is the earnings of the equity or ordinary shares (and deferred or founders' shares, if any). See p. 2915 for Earnings per Share.

DIVIDENDS

A dividend (Latin *dividendum* from *dividere* = to divide) is a share of the profits of a company, the profits being *divided* among the shareholders. The term "dividend" is applied to the *total* sum divisible and also to the *portion* received by each individual shareholder. Dividends are proposed or recommended by the directors and declared by the company in general meeting, the shareholders having usually to pass a resolution sanctioning the proposed distribution. The dividend then becomes a liability to the shareholders as from the date of its declaration, but does not bear interest against the company.

Interim Dividend. An interim (Latin *interim* = in the meantime) dividend is a dividend declared before the close of the company's financial period, either out of profits that are accruing, or out of profits brought forward from a previous period.

DIVIDENDS (PAID AND PROPOSED). With one exception (see p. 2107), dividends can be paid only out of profits, and for this reason are declared at the end of the year, after profits for the year have been determined. The directors submit a recommendation to the shareholders' meeting for confirmation, but the shareholders cannot *increase* the dividend. Directors generally have the right to pay such interim dividends as appear to be justified by the profits, without obtaining the shareholders' sanction. The amounts shown are net, i.e. after deduction of tax. The book-keeping entries are dealt with later in this section. One other important point of difference between the interim and final dividends is in the entries to be made on the balance sheet. Interim dividends will have been paid and do *not* therefore, appear as liabilities on the balance sheet. Final dividends are only provided for, and not paid before the accounts are closed. They will, therefore, show on the balance sheet as "unpaid dividends" or "proposed dividends" under current liabilities.

DIVIDEND EQUALIZATION RESERVE. It is to the company's advantage that the price of its shares on the Stock Exchange shall not fluctuate unnecessarily. The regular payment of reasonably good dividends will assist in keeping them steady. By making a reserve in good years the directors may draw upon it should the profits fall below the average, and so be enabled to pay the same dividend as in a normal year.

Entries for a Dividend. When a dividend on any kind of shares is declared, the Profit and Loss Appropriation Account is debited and a numbered Dividend (or Shareholders) Account is credited with the net amount payable.

How the Dividend is Paid. In large companies a cheque is drawn for the net amount of the dividend (i.e. *less* tax), and the amount is posted to the debit of the dividend account (or shareholder's account, as the case may be). The cheque itself is paid in to the credit of a separate dividend account at the company's bank, and a separate dividend pass book is kept. Cheques, or *dividend warrants*, as they are called, are then drawn on this account for each shareholder's portion, and are sent to the shareholders concerned. When the shareholders clear their dividend warrants, the amounts will be credited to this particular dividend account, and a corresponding debit is made to the Dividend (or Shareholders) Account. When the number of shareholders is not very large, a separate dividend account may not be opened at the bank; the dividend warrants may be drawn on the ordinary bank account.

Unclaimed or Unpaid Dividends. If, at balancing time, there is any balance in the dividend pass book, it will arise from the fact that some of the shareholders have not presented their dividend warrants for payment.

The balance on the dividend account may be carried forward or transferred to an Unclaimed Dividend Account. The balance on the Dividend Bank Account may be carried forward on that account, transferred back to the general Bank Account or transferred to a Deposit Account for Unclaimed Dividends Account. The balance on the Unclaimed Dividends Account must be shown as a liability on the company's balance sheet; for the company will still be liable to pay the money, at any rate for a period of twelve years, after which time the dividends may be forfeited.

If the cash is retained in the Dividend Bank or Deposit Account, then this may be deducted from the liability on the Balance Sheet to show a zero net liability.

The Appropriation Account. Essentially, this is a sub-division of the profit and loss account which shows the way in which the disposable income or earnings (after meeting operating costs, depreciation, provisions for expenses and interest) has been divided between—

1. Taxation.
2. Dividends.
3. Retention of profit.

Example 1

During the year ended 31st December, 1971, Bruce Castle Limited had a total turnover of £690,000. The trading profit for the year was £80,000 after charging directors' salaries £8,000; directors' fees £2,000; depreciation on plant £7,200, and on fixtures and fittings £2,850. The auditor's fees amounted to £1,000. In addition to the trading profit the company had income from quoted investments of £1,100 and unquoted investments £1,900. The company paid debenture interest of £7,000 during the year and suffered Corporation Tax at the rate of 30 per cent on the profits. The ordinary dividend proposed for the year is £25,000. Profits retained from previous years amounted to £38,000 and there was over-provision of Corporation Tax in the previous year of £900.

Show the Profit and Loss Appropriation Account in a form suitable for publication.

Solution 1

BRUCE CASTLE LIMITED

PROFIT AND LOSS ACCOUNT FOR THE YEAR ENDED 31ST DECEMBER, 1971

	£	£	£
Turnover for the Year			690,000
Trading Profit after charging:			80,000
Directors Salaries	8,000		
Directors Fees	2,000		
		10,000	
Depreciation of Plant	7,200		
Fixtures and Fittings	2,850		
		10,050	
Auditors Fees		1,000	
Income from Investments:			
Quoted		1,100	
Unquoted		1,900	
			3,000
			83,000
Less Debenture Interest			7,000
Profit before Taxation			76,000
Corporation Tax on profit for the year (30%)			22,800
Profit for the Year after Taxation			53,200
Proposed Ordinary Dividend			25,000
Profit for the Year Retained in the business			28,200
Profit Retained from previous years brought forward		38,000	
Add Over-provision for Corporation Tax in previous year		900	
			38,900
Retained Profits carried forward			£67,100

Example 2

At 1st January, 19.., a company has a credit balance on appropriation account of £5,000, and the net profit for the year was £29,000. During the year a half-year's dividend was paid on £50,000 6 per cent preference shares, and the directors now propose that the balance available for distribution should be appropriated as follows—

1. To provide for 40 per cent Corporation Tax.
2. To pay the final dividend on the preference shares.
3. To pay a dividend of 10 per cent on the 100,000 ordinary shares.
4. To transfer £2,500 to staff welfare fund.
5. To write off the existing balance of goodwill—£5,000.
6. To transfer 50 per cent of any balance, after making the above provisions, to general reserve.
7. To carry forward the balance.

Draft the profit and loss appropriation account to give effect to the above, and carry the items to a skeleton balance sheet. Assume that base rate Income Tax is 30 per cent.

Solution 2

PROFIT AND LOSS APPROPRIATION ACCOUNT

FOR YEAR ENDED 31st DECEMBER, 19..

	£		£
Provision for Corporation Tax	11,600	Balance b/f	5,000
Interim Preference Share Dividend (net)	1,050	Net Profit b/d	29,000
Final Preference Share Dividend (net)	1,050		
Proposed Ordinary Share Dividend (net)	7,000		
Staff Welfare Fund	2,500		
Goodwill written off	5,000		
General Reserve	950		
Balance c/f	4,850		
	34,000		34,000

BALANCE SHEET

AS AT 31ST DECEMBER, 19..

	£	£		£	£
Authorized and Issued Capital—			Goodwill—		
50,000 6% Preference Shares of £1 each fully paid	50,000		Balance at 1st January, 19..	5,000	
100,000 Ordinary shares of £1 each fully paid	100,000		*Less* Written off	5,000	
		150,000			
Reserves—					
General Reserve		950			
Profit and Loss Balance c/f		950			
Staff Welfare Fund		2,500			
Provisions and Current Liabilities—					
Corporation Tax		11,600			
Proposed Dividends—					
Final Preference dividend (net)		1,050			
Ordinary Share dividend (net)		7,000			

Note particularly that the interim dividend does not appear as a liability as it has already been paid.

Dividend "Free of Tax." A notice sometimes appears to the effect that dividends are *free of tax*. This statement does not mean that such dividends are not taxed, but that the amount quoted is after deduction of tax. Thus a dividend of 10 per cent free of tax would be equivalent to one of 20 per cent subject to tax if tax were at the rate of £0·50 in the £.

Scrip Dividend. Financial and other companies sometimes take power in their articles to pay free of tax "scrip" dividends, that is, to distribute, by way of dividend, shares or debentures in other companies.

A company is obliged, under penalty of £10 for each offence (maximum £100), to issue with the dividend a statement in writing showing the gross dividend, the income tax deducted, and the net amount payable.

Example 3

The accounts of the Excelsior Trading Co. Ltd. show a net profit of £40,060 for the year ended 31st December and there is a balance of £6,000 brought forward. The directors resolve as follows—

1. To pay a dividend of 5 per cent (less tax at £0·30 in the £) on the preference shares (£80,000).
2. To pay a dividend of 10 per cent, free of base rate tax, on the ordinary shares (£100,000).
3. To transfer £3,000 to the reserve fund.
4. To transfer £2,000 to a dividend reserve fund.
5. To carry the balance forward.

Make the necessary entries to carry out the above, and show the ledger accounts affected. Corporation Tax on the profits should be provided for at the rate of 40 per cent.

Solution 3

JOURNAL

	Dr	Cr
	£	£
Profit & Loss A/c	40,060	
Appropriation A/c		40,060
Balance transferred.		
Appropriation A/c	2,800	
Preference Share Dividend (net) . . .		2,800
Appropriation A/c	10,000	
Ordinary Share Dividend (net) . . .		10,000
Appropriation A/c	3,000	
Reserve Fund A/c		3,000
Amount transferred.		
Appropriation A/c	2,000	
Dividend Reserve A/c		2,000
Amount transferred.		
Appropriation A/c	16,240	
Provision for Corporation Tax .		16,240
Amount transferred.		

CASH BOOK (*Cr.* side)

Payments	Bank
	£
Preference Shareholders	2,800
Ordinary Shareholders	10,000

LEDGER

PROFIT AND LOSS ACCOUNT

For the Year Ended 31st December, 19..

	£		£
Appropriation A/c . . .	40,060	Net Profit	40,060

APPROPRIATION ACCOUNT

	£		£
Corporation Tax . . .	16,240	P. & L.	40,060
Preference Share Dividend (net) .	2,800	Balance b/f	6,000
Ordinary Share Dividend (net) .	10,000		
Reserve Fund	3,000		
Dividend Reserve . . .	2,000		
Balance c/f	12,020		
	46,060		46,060

PREFERENCE SHARE DIVIDEND

	£		£
Cash	2,800	Appropriation . . .	2,800

ORDINARY SHARE DIVIDEND

	£		£
Cash	10,000	Appropriation . . .	10,000

RESERVE FUND ACCOUNT

			£
		Appropriation . . .	3,000

DIVIDEND RESERVE ACCOUNT

			£
		Appropriation . . .	2,000

PROVISION FOR CORPORATION TAX

			£
		Appropriation . . .	16,240

ARREARS OF DIVIDEND ON CUMULATIVE PREFERENCE SHARES

Treatment in Books and on Balance Sheet. A cumulative preference share is not only entitled to *preference*, i.e. to receive a fixed dividend before other shares receive any, but is entitled to carry forward its claim to dividends from one year to the next.

If current profits are insufficient, the cumulative preference dividend becomes a first charge on subsequent profits. The question then arises as to how such arrears of dividend should be treated. Should they be brought into the books as an ordinary liability, or should they be left until there are sufficient profits available to pay them? One method is to bring them into the books as an actual liability, and journalize them as follows—

Arrears of Preference Share Dividend . . *Dr.*
Outstanding Preference Dividend . . *Cr.*

The arrears then appear on the assets side of the balance sheet, as a loss carried forward, while the outstanding dividend figures on the liabilities side. When there are sufficient profits available to pay them, then the "arrears of preference share dividend account" will be closed by transfer to the appropriation account, and the payment of the arrears will be debited to the "outstanding preference dividend account," thus closing it. The most common method, however, is to make no entry in the books at all. The liability does not accrue until there are sufficient profits available to pay it and also in most cases until the dividend is actually declared. Therefore the arrears are best shown by way of a note in the balance sheet. To comply with the 2nd Schedule to the Companies Act, 1967, such note should show the amount of the arrears (before deduction of tax) and the period for which the dividends are in arrear.

PROFITS PRIOR TO INCORPORATION

A limited company frequently takes over a business from a date prior to the date of its own incorporation. If the company, and not the vendor, is entitled to any profits earned prior to its incorporation—and this is often the case in modern agreements—such profits are not available for dividend because they are capital profits. A company cannot legally earn profits before its official existence, and a public company not until it has a certificate entitling it to commence business.

How Dealt With. These profits should be put to a capital reserve account. They should not be transferred to the general reserve fund as they might then inadvertently be paid in dividends, and the directors would be liable to refund the money. Where the vendor has waived his claim to the profits earned prior to incorporation, he is usually entitled to interest on the purchase money until such time as it is actually paid. Such interest should certainly be a first charge on any profits prior to incorporation. The vendor might also require an additional payment in the purchase price, which would be reflected in the price paid for goodwill. Pre-incorporation profits could be used to reduce this goodwill or to reduce the book value of assets taken over.

How Ascertained. Ideally, the books would be balanced on the take-over date and the pre-acquisition profit accurately found. Usually this cannot be done, and approximate methods are used. The first year's trading must be divided into two periods, *before* and *after* incorporation. The profit of the first year may be apportioned either according to *time*, or according to *turnover*; that is, either in the ratio which each period of time bears to the total period of time, or in the ratio which each period's turnover bears to the total turnover for the year. The most accurate method, however, is to apportion each separate item in the profit and loss account on the basis which best applies to that item. Thus gross profit, travellers' commissions and delivery expenses will vary with turnover whereas rent and rates and similar charges vary directly with time. The profits available for distribution will be only such profits as have been earned *subsequent* to the date of incorporation.

Example 4

A company was incorporated on 1st May to take over a business as a going concern from 1st January of the same year. The total turnover for the year ended 31st December was £100,000, namely; £30,000 for the first period up to 1st May, and £70,000 for the following period. The gross profit is £35,000 and the profit and loss account is given below. How should the profits earned prior to incorporation be ascertained?

Profit and Loss Account

For the Year Ended 31st December, 19..

	£		£
Rent & Rates	1,620	Gross Profit b/d	35,000
Insurance	360		
Lighting & Heating	1,020		
Salaries	3,900		
Directors' Fees	1,000		
Commission	5,000		
Discounts	2,500		
General Office Expenses	1,200		
Carriage	1,500		
Bank Charges	210		
Repairs & Renewals	690		
Bad Debts	300		
Loan Interest	600		
Net Profit	15,100		
	35,000		35,000

Solution 4

Apportioning period expenses on a time basis we get $\frac{4}{12}$ prior to incorporation and $\frac{8}{12}$ after incorporation.

Apportioning sales expenses on the basis of turnover we get $\frac{3}{10}$ prior to incorporation and $\frac{7}{10}$ after incorporation.

The apportionment would therefore be as follows—

	Before Incorporation	After Incorporation	Total	Basis of Apportionment
	£	£	£	
Rent & Rates	540	1,080	1,620	Time
Insurance	120	240	360	„
Lighting & Heating	340	680	1,020	„
Salaries	1,300	2,600	3,900	„
Directors' Fees	—	1,000	1,000	Fees are only payable by the Company after incorporation
Commission	1,500	3,500	5,000	Turnover
Discounts	750	1,750	2,500	„
General Office Expenses	400	800	1,200	Time
Carriage	450	1,050	1,500	Turnover
Bank Charges	70	140	210	Time
Repairs & Renewals	230	460	690	„
Bad Debts	90	210	300	Turnover
Loan Interest	200	400	600	Time
Total Expenses	5,990	13,910	19,900	
Gross Profit	10,500	24,500	35,000	Turnover
Net Profit	4,510	10,590	15,100	Difference between Gross Profit and Total Expenses

LOSS PRIOR TO INCORPORATION

Where a company takes over a business from a date prior to its own incorporation, and the trading results for this prior period show a loss, such loss may be added to the goodwill as being in reality an increase of the purchase price. Should there be no account for goodwill, one may be opened and debited with this loss. Such loss could also be put to a special suspense account, and extinguished by capital profits, such as premiums on shares or debentures. The objection to this latter method is that the new company's profits would be used to make good a loss which they should not legitimately bear. It is consistent, that as a profit made before the company's incorporation is capital, a loss may be so treated, but some doubt has been expressed whether the company should not "err on the safe side," and write off such a loss over a period of years. A third alternative is to debit the loss against subsequent profits.

BONUS SHARES

Most successful companies do not distribute all their profits every year. They usually accumulate profits on the profit and loss account or in various reserve accounts.

The main reason for this is that profits are not always available in the form of surplus cash, especially if the company is expanding. Funds are needed to finance this expansion, and profits are "ploughed back," or retained in the company. The shareholder does not lose by this. Although his dividend is not as large as it might be, the asset value of the company increases and the value of a share in those assets is increased.

As an illustration, the balance sheet of a company is as follows—

Example 5

BALANCE SHEET OF XY LTD. ON..................................19........

	£		£
Share Capital—		Fixed Assets	50,000
60,000 £1 Ordinary Shares .	60,000	Current Assets . . .	40,000
Revenue Reserves	40,000	Cash	10,000
	100,000		100,000

It is clear that the company could not pay more than £10,000 in dividends (the amount of cash available) without borrowing.

On the basis of the book value of the assets, the value of each £1 share is—

$$\frac{\text{Total assets}}{\text{No. of shares}} \text{ i.e. } \frac{£100{,}000}{60{,}000} = £1{\cdot}66$$

If the directors of XY Ltd. see no long-term possibility of paying out these reserves in dividends, they may decide to *capitalize* them by issuing bonus shares. The balance sheet would then be—

BALANCE SHEET OF XY LTD. ON..................................19........

	£		£
Share Capital—		Sundry Assets . . .	100,000
100,000 £1 Ordinary Shares .	100,000		

Each shareholder has been given two bonus shares for every three shares he held previously. If Miss Spinks of Blackheath was the owner of 300 £1 shares, she is now the owner of 500 such shares (nominal value £500).

Advantages and Disadvantages

(*a*) As regards the company.

Advantages—

1. Profits can be distributed without affecting the bank balance, which therefore remains to be used as additional working capital.

2. If profits are fairly constant after the issue, the distribution over a larger number of shares will reduce the *rate* of dividend paid, and relate it to the capital actually employed. If XY Ltd. above had paid a dividend of £6,000 before the balance sheet was drawn up, this would represent 10 per cent on the original issued capital but only 6 per cent on the capital actually employed (£100,000).

3. To maintain the dividend at the same rate, and keep the market price

of shares steady, correspondingly increased profits must be earned. This is likely to be a more realistic target for the company. Failure to recognize this may lead to a take-over bid.

(*b*) As regards the shareholders.

Advantages—

1. No surtax is payable on a bonus share distribution.

2. The bonus may be applied to extinguishing the liability on uncalled capital, so that the shares become fully paid up without the shareholders' contributing further cash.

3. If immediate cash is preferred by individual members their shares can generally be disposed of on the Stock Exchange.

(*c*) Effect on market value of holding.

Prima facie the price *per share* must be less after the bonus issue; but in theory the total value of the old holding should equal that of the new, thus—

Price of shares before bonus issue, £1·20 (nominal £1).

Bonus issue of 1 new share for every 2 held.

Price of shares after bonus issue, £0·80, i.e. 2 shares at £1·20, or 3 shares at £0·80 = £2·40.

In practice, the value of the new holding will generally be higher than that of the old because of the expected higher level of dividends.

(*a*) Bonus Shares Issued at par

Example 6

A company with a paid-up capital of £200,000 in £1 shares, having accumulated a reserve of £70,000, resolves to capitalize £50,000 of it by issuing to the shareholders 50,000 bonus shares of £1 each fully paid, each shareholder to receive one bonus share for every four shares held in the company. Show the entries required to record the transaction.

This is assuming that the actual dividends paid do not increase.

If dividend was 10 per cent actual payment (on 4 shares) = £0·40.

New dividend rate 8 per cent actual payment (on 5 shares) = £0·40.

JOURNAL

		Dr	*Cr*
		£	£
	Reserve A/c	50,000	
	Bonus Share Dividend		50,000
	Bonus payable out of reserve in fully-paid shares as per resolution dated..........................		
	Bonus Share Dividend	50,000	
	Share Capital		50,000
	Issue of 50,000 bonus shares of £1 each in payment of bonus, at the rate of 1 bonus share for every 4 shares held in the company.		

Fractions. Obviously bonus issues frequently give rise to complications over fractions. If one bonus share is issued for every six held, then a shareholder with 100 shares is entitled to $16\frac{2}{3}$ bonus shares.

This difficulty may be dealt with in the following ways—

(i) The articles and the resolution making the bonus issue may provide for the shares representing all the fractions to be sold and the proceeds paid in cash to the shareholders concerned. In the case above, the shareholder would receive a certificate for 16 bonus shares, plus the cash value of two-thirds of a share.

(ii) A date is set by the company by which time shareholders must either dispose of their fractions or make them up to whole units. The secretary of the company may act as intermediary, the directors may arrange for certain shareholders to be ready to buy up surplus shares and, in the interim, "fractional certificates" may be issued. These are certificates of rights, and not share certificates. The shareholder entitled to $16\frac{2}{3}$ bonus shares might sell the $\frac{2}{3}$ or buy another $\frac{1}{3}$ (or more) to make up his bonus to a whole number.

(*b*) Bonus Shares Issued at a Premium

Example 7

A company with a paid-up capital of £120,000 in £1 shares decides to distribute a bonus, equal to 25 per cent of its capital. The reserve fund was £50,000; the market value of shares is £3. It is proposed to issue the shares at a premium of £2 per share, and to distribute them to shareholders as to one fully-paid share for every twelve shares held. Prepare the necessary journal entries for putting into effect the issue of the bonus shares on the terms stated.

JOURNAL

		Dr	*Cr*
		£	£
	Bonus Share Dividend	30,000	
	Share Capital		10,000
	Share Premium A/c		20,000
	Issue of 10,000 fully-paid shares, at a premium of £2 per share; distributed as to 1 share for every 12 held in the company.		

(*c*) Bonus Applied to Making Shares Fully Paid

Example 8

A company with a nominal and issued capital of £20,000 in £1 shares, £0·75 per share paid, declares a bonus out of the reserve fund, at the rate of $33\frac{1}{3}$ per cent on the paid-up capital, with the object of making the shares fully paid. Show the entries necessary to record the transaction.

JOURNAL

	Dr	Cr
	£	£
Final Call A/c	50,000	
Share Capital		50,000
Call of £0·25 per share on 200,000 shares, as per resolution dated............		
Reserve Fund A/c	50,000	
Bonus Share Dividend		50,000
Bonus of 33⅓% on £150,000 paid-up capital, payable out of the reserve fund, as per resolution dated		
Bonus Share Dividend	50,000	
Final Call A/c		50,000
Application of bonus to payment of final call, as per resolution dated		

In this case it is especially important to notice that the call must be made in the correct way by a resolution of the directors and the entries passed through the books, although the shareholders are not being called upon to pay it.

In addition to the simple entries shown in these three examples it will, of course, be necessary to prepare bonus share lists showing the numbers to which each member is entitled, from which the register of members can be posted.

Rights Issue of Shares. Successful, expanding companies may be in a position to issue bonus shares to their members and yet may at the same time require to raise further capital. The shares may have a high value on the Stock Exchange and may be very much in short supply.

In such cases, the directors may make a "rights" issue. New shares are issued, but the existing shareholders are given the right to subscribe in proportion to their existing holding.

For example, the £1 shares of a company may be valued on the Stock Exchange at £3. New shares might be offered to members at £1·50, which means they are being given a bonus of £1·50 since they could sell the share for £3. From the company's point of view, of course, these shares of £1 are issued at a premium of £0·50.

Shareholders who do not wish to take up the offer could sell their rights for £1·50 or thereabouts on the Stock Exchange.

Example 9

A company with issued capital of 200,000 £1 ordinary shares and reserves of £500,000 decides to make a rights issue to shareholders at the rate of one £1 share for every one held. The market price of the shares is £2·50 and they are to be issued at £1·25. The excess of market price over the issue price is to be treated as a bonus. All the rights were taken up.

The entries to be made are—

1. When the rights offer is made, debit sundry members with the market value £500,000 and credit nominal value £200,000 to Ordinary Share Capital and £300,000 to Share Premium Account.

2. When cash is received from members or their assignees, debit cash and credit Sundry Members Account with £250,000.

3. Debit the balance on Sundry Members Account to Bonus Share Dividend Account and credit the same amount £250,000 to Sundry Members Account, thus closing that account.

4. Transfer the Bonus Share Dividend from the General or Capital Reserve Account by crediting £250,000 to Bonus Share Dividend and debiting £250,000 to the Reserve Account.

ORDINARY SHARE CAPITAL

			£
		Balance	200,000
		Sundry Members	200,000

GENERAL RESERVE ACCOUNT

	£		£
Bonus Share Dividend	250,000	Balance	500,000
Balance c/d	250,000		
	500,000		500,000
		Balance b/d	250,000

SUNDRY MEMBERS ACCOUNT

	£		£
Ordinary Share Capital	200,000	Cash	250,000
Share Premium	300,000	Bonus Share Dividend	250,000
	500,000		500,000

BONUS SHARE DIVIDEND

	£		£
Sundry Members	250,000	General Reserve	250,000

SHARE PREMIUM ACCOUNT

			£
		Sundry Members	300,000

QUESTIONS

1. Explain the terms "dividend," "interim dividend." State briefly the provisions of Table A with reference to dividends.
2. What entries are required in the books when a dividend is declared and paid?
3. Explain the procedure adopted in paying dividends: (*a*) in large companies, (*b*) in small companies.
4. What deduction does a company usually make when paying dividends, and how does it deal with the amount so deducted?
5. Explain the meaning of "unclaimed" or "unpaid" dividends. How should they be treated in the company's balance sheet?
6. What is meant by the phrase "dividend free of tax"? What is the effect of such a dividend to the shareholder? What is a "scrip" dividend?
7. What is a "dividend equalization fund"? Does it serve a useful purpose?
8. Explain the meaning of the phrase "profits prior to incorporation."
9. How should profits prior to incorporation be dealt with?
10. What methods are there of ascertaining the profits earned prior to incorporation? What are the advantages of the different ways?
11. How should a loss prior to incorporation be dealt with?
12. What necessity is there at times to pay interest on capital out of capital?
13. What are the provisions of the Companies Act, 1948, with reference to the payment of interest out of capital?
14. In what other cases can interest on capital be paid out of capital? State briefly the arguments "for" and "against."

EXERCISE 21

1. (*a*) What is an "appropriation account"? Prepare such an account and enter therein items which in your judgement properly belong to it. In this connexion, would "preliminary expenses" and "amounts written off goodwill" be proper items to place on its debit side?

(*b*) Explain the following terms—

1. A charge against profits.
2. An appropriation of profits.

Support your explanations by practical examples of how accountants view and interpret their meaning.

2. After considering the audited accounts of the company for the year ended 31st December, the directors of the Rayon D'Or Publishing Co. Ltd. resolved as follows—

(1) To pay the 6 per cent dividend (less tax) due upon the preference stock (£50,000).

(2) To pay a dividend of 8 per cent (less tax) upon the ordinary share capital (£60,000).

(3) To transfer £1,500 to the renewals reserve account.

(4) To carry forward the balance.

The profits shown by the profit and loss account amounted to £20,000. Corporation Tax is 40 per cent.

Assume the rate of income tax payable to be £0·45 in the £. Show the entries necessary to carry out the above resolutions. (*R.S.A. modified.*)

3. The Welsh Manufacturing Co. Ltd. closed its books on 31st December, with the following balances—

	£		£
Stock at 1st January—		Due to the Ystwyth Banking Co.	2,478
Materials	6,420	Repairs to machinery	444
Finished goods	9,400	Wages	15,500
Sundries	530	Salaries	3,400
Materials purchased	38,000	Insurance	335
Coal and coke used	1,460	Sales	56,800
Rents, rates, and taxes	987	Fittings and fixtures	650
Sundries purchased (*less* returns)	580	Returns inward	1,740
Discount account *Dr.* balance	448	Travelling and exhibition expenses	948
Sundry debtors	4,300	Bad debts	542
Sundry creditors	2,870	Bad debts provision	500
Plant and machinery	11,750	General reserve	10,000
General expenses	2,007	Bills receivable	735
Premises	10,000	Bills payable	940
Share capital (60,000 shares at £1 each, £0·60 called on each share, and all paid)	36,000	Profit and loss account (1st January) *Cr.* balance	2,388
		Dividend paid (gross)	1,800

Stocks on hand 31st December—

	£
Materials	10,743
Finished Goods	19,430
Sundries	340

You are required to draw up a trial balance, a trading and profit and loss account, and balance sheet, as at 31st December, having made the following adjustments, assuming any other necessary figures—

Depreciate plant and machinery and fittings 10 per cent each, and the premises 2 per cent. Insurance paid in advance £93. Keep the bad debts provision at £500.

Comment upon the balance sheet as to whether you consider the company is in a healthy state, and give suggestions regarding the various items of expenditure, etc. Would you recommend a dividend; if so, how much?

(*Union of Educational Institutions.*)

4. The following balances were shown on the books of East & Ham Ltd. after closing the profit and loss account for the year ended 31st January, 19.1—

	£
Share capital—authorized, 20,000 shares of £1 each; issued, 18,000 shares	18,000
Premises at cost	10,000
Machinery at cost, less depreciation to date of £3,500	11,500
Creditors	2,588
Preliminary expenses	220
Stock as valued by the directors	5,796
Debtors	8,329
Share premium account	1,000
Profit and loss account—accumulated profit at 31st January, 19..	2,273
Debentures (secured on assets)	4,000
General reserve	5,000
Fixtures, etc., at cost, less depreciation to date £650	450
Balance with bank	5,364
Provision for bad debts	138
Profit for year to 31st January, 19.1	8,660

It was resolved that—

(*a*) preliminary expenses be written off;
(*b*) general reserve be increased to £7,500;
(*c*) a dividend of 15 per cent on the issued share capital be declared.

Prepare the company's appropriation account for the year ended 31st January, 19.1, and the balance sheet at that date. Ignore income tax. (*R.S.A.*)

5. Wildfire Ltd. was incorporated on 1st April, 19.., and took over the business of Hawk & Finch, partners, as from 1st January, 19... It was agreed that all profits made from 1st January should belong to the company and that the vendors should be entitled to interest on the purchase price from 1st January to the date of payment. The purchase price was paid on 30th April, 19.., including £840 interest.

The following profit and loss account for the year to 31st December, 19.., was prepared.

	£		£
Salaries of vendors	1,250	Gross profit	30,000
Wages and general expenses	7,980		
Rent and rates	620		
Commission on sales	1,500		
Bad debts	429		
Interest paid to vendors	840		
Directors' fees	2,775		
Depreciation of motor vans	500		
Directors' travelling expenses	276		
	16,170		
Net profit	13,830		
	30,000		30,000

You are given the following information—

(1) Sales amounted to £30,000 for the three months to 31st March, 19.., and £120,000 for the nine months from 1st April to 31st December, 19... Gross profit is at a uniform rate of 20 per cent of selling price throughout the year, and a commission of 1 per cent is paid on all sales.

(2) Salaries of £1,250 were paid to the vendors for their assistance in managing the business in the three months to 31st March, 19...

(3) The bad debts written off are—

(*a*) a debt of £121 taken over from the vendors, and
(*b*) a debt of £308 in respect of goods sold in July, 19...

(4) Three motor vans were taken over from the vendors, at a valuation of £2,000 and a fourth van was purchased on 1st July, 19.., for £1,000. Depreciation has been written off at the rate of 20 per cent per annum.

(5) Wages and general expenses amounted to £665 in each calendar month.

You are required: (*a*) to set out the profit and loss account, in columnar form, so as to distinguish between the period prior to the company's incorporation and the period after incorporation; and (*b*) to state how you would deal with the profit prior to incorporation.

NOTE. You are to assume that all calendar months are of equal length.

(*Institute of Bankers.*)

6. You are required to prepare from the following information the balance sheet at 31st December, 19.., and profit and loss account for the year ended on that date, for XY & Co. Ltd., in accordance with the Companies Act, 1948 (apart from comparative figures). The necessary notes to the balance sheet required to comply with the Act must be shown.

(*a*) TRIAL BALANCE—31ST DECEMBER, 19..

	£	£
5% cumulative preference shares of £1 each fully paid		300,000
Ordinary shares of £1 each fully paid		2,000,000
General reserve		800,000
Taxation		558,202
$4\frac{1}{2}$% debenture stock 1961–74		880,000
Freehold and leasehold land and buildings at cost	759,265	
Plant and machinery	2,641,647	
Goodwill	350,000	
Trade investments	586,826	
Quoted investments	150,000	
Stocks	631,760	
Directors' fees	8,500	
Directors' remuneration	31,425	
Preference dividend (net)	8,625	
Debenture interest (gross)	22,500	
Interim dividend (net) at 8%	92,000	
Investment reserve		280,000
Unclaimed dividends		2,200
Suspense		51,363
Depreciation—		
Freehold and leasehold land and buildings		183,860
Plant and machinery		1,037,813
Work-in-progress	2,475,015	
Progress payments against work-in-progress		895,245
Debtors	1,771,329	
Prepayments and deposits	21,340	
Provision for bad and doubtful debts		18,350
Bills receivable	433,202	
Tax reserve certificates	450,000	
Cash in hand	5,622	
Share premium		55,420
Debenture redemption reserve		110,456
Profit and loss account		487,242
Bank overdraft		122,864
Creditors and accrued liabilities		1,231,036
Investment income—		
Trade		25,925
Quoted		7,500
Trading profit		1,391,580
	10,439,056	10,439,056

(*b*) The following provisions are required—

	£
(i) Auditors' remuneration	2,100
(ii) Half-year's debenture interest (gross)	19,800
(iii) Depreciation of freehold and leasehold land and buildings	51,285
(iv) Depreciation of plant and machinery	271,542
(v) Additional provision for doubtful debts	9,320
(vi) Specific provision for loss on uncompleted long-term contract (included in work-in-progress)	22,000
(vii) Profits tax	138,000

(*c*) A reserve for income tax for 19.1/.2 is required . . . 433,000

(*d*) A final dividend of 12 per cent on the ordinary shares is to be paid.

(*e*) The following transfers from profit and loss account have been recommended by the directors—

Debenture redemption reserve	50,000
General reserve	100,000

(*f*) The suspense account is made up as follows—

Profit on sale of investments	£26,363	
Taxation refund relating to previous years	25,000	
		51,363

(*g*) Of the original issue of £1,000,000 4½ per cent debentures, £120,000 have been redeemed.

(*Cost and Management Accountants.*)

7. From the following information you are required to prepare the final accounts of Speedyclean for the year ended 31st March, 19.1—

	£	£
Cash at bank and on hand	13,856	
Maintenance of service equipment	943	
Petrol and oil	3,682	
Office expenses	1,965	
Rent, rates, and insurance	1,692	
Goodwill	2,000	
Cleaning charges		28,712
Debtors	1,925	
Capital accounts—Waters		11,600
Soper		8,200
Prepaid and accrued charges at 1st April, 19..	596	140
Motor vans	3,490	
Equipment	1,933	
Cleaners' wages	9,860	
Creditors		1,496
Drawings—Waters	1,300	
Soper	900	
Rent receivable		200
Van licences and insurance	730	
Maintenance of vans	850	
Office wages	780	
Furniture and fittings	1,230	
Cleaning materials	650	
Advertising	1,592	
Heating and lighting	374	
	50,348	50,348

(i) At 31st March, 19.1, the stock of petrol and oil was £75 and the stock of tyres was £82.

(ii) Van licences and insurance have been prepaid to 31st December, 19.1.

(iii) Rent of £1,200 per annum has been paid to 30th June, 19.1.

(iv) Amounts due and unpaid at 31st March, 19.1, are as follows—

	£
(*a*) Telephone	22
(*b*) Van maintenance	84
(*c*) Electricity	37
(*d*) Cleaners' wages	49

(v) Depreciation rates are as follows—

(*a*) Motor vans	20 per cent
(*b*) Equipment	15 " "
(*c*) Furniture and fittings	$7\frac{1}{2}$ " "

(vi) Partners' salaries to be charged are—

	£
Waters	1,200
Soper	900

(vii) Partners who share profits and losses equally are entitled to interest at 8 per cent on capital at the beginning of the year.

(viii) The prepaid and accrued charges at 1st April, 19.., in the list of balances include the following—

	Prepaid £	Accrued £
Van licences and insurance	296	
Rent	300	
Telephone		27
Electricity		33
Cleaners' wages		59
Office stationery		21
	596	140

(*Cost and Management Accountants.*)

8. Tyne and Weare Ltd. has an authorized capital of £100,000 divided into 30,000 ordinary shares, 30,000 6 per cent non-cumulative preference shares, and 40,000 5 per cent cumulative preference shares, all of £1 each, fully paid.

The balances on the books, after closing the profit and loss account for the year ended 31st December, 19.1, were as follows—

	£
Ordinary share capital	30,000
6 per cent non-cumulative preference shares	30,000
5 per cent cumulative preference shares	40,000
Freehold properties at cost	110,000
5 per cent debentures (secured on assets)	10,000
Debenture interest accrued	250
Office furniture, cost £1,200, *less* depreciation	960
Profit and loss account, balance at 31st December, 19.. (*Cr.*)	526
Debtors and payments in advance	2,465
Provision for bad debts	300
Balance at bank (*Dr.*)	8,872
General reserve	2,000
Cash in hand	110
Profit for year ended 31st December, 19.1	9,331

The directors recommend that—

(*a*) all dividends for the year 19.1 on the preference shares be paid;
(*b*) a dividend of 15 per cent be paid on the ordinary shares; and
(*c*) £1,000 be transferred to the general reserve.

Prepare—

(i) the above balances as a trial balance;
(ii) the appropriation account to show the proposed distribution; and
(iii) the balance sheet as at 31st December, 19.1, for submission to the members.

(*R.S.A.*)

9. From the following statement make out trading account, profit and loss account, and balance sheet for the Motor Manufacturing Company Limited, for the year ended 31st December.

Write off the whole of preliminary expenses and depreciate Plant and Machinery, office furniture, patterns and patents at a uniform rate of 7½ per cent per annum, assuming figures for original cost of these assets.

Add £2,000 to the sinking fund for redemption of debentures and leave the provision for bad and doubtful debts at 5 per cent on sundry debtors. Stock on hand at the above date was taken at £10,087.

	£		£
Nominal capital 80,000 shares of £1 each	80,000	Balance to credit of profit and loss (1st January)	890
Subscribed capital 60,000 shares of £1 each fully called	60,000	Bills payable	15,500
Calls in arrear	1,000	Sales	122,000
Freehold premises	18,000	Purchases	62,100
Plant and machinery	20,000	Provision for bad and doubtful debts	2,250
Interim dividend paid	2,000	Preliminary expenses	400
Debentures, 5%	20,000	Sinking fund for redemption of debentures	8,000
Stock (1st January)	18,750	N.B. This is represented by investments to an equivalent amount; and there is one year's interest on them at 3½% per annum due, but unpaid, at the date of making up these accounts.	
Office furniture	625	General expenses	475
Patterns	6,250	Discounts allowed	2,120
Patents	3,750	,, received	1,780
Goodwill	12,000	Directors' fees	525
Sundry debtors	37,500	Royalties paid	450
,, creditors	16,800	Interest on bank deposit	300
Cash in hand	150	Bad debts	150
Cash at bank current account	3,000	Debenture interest	1,000
Manufacturing wages	30,000		
Repairs and renewals	1,300		
Coal	2,225		
Gas and water	175		
Rates, taxes, and insurance	1,250		
Office salaries	1,000		
Travelling expenses	1,325		
Cash at bank on deposit	12,000		

10. Southport & Northwick Ltd. was formed with an authorized share capital of £20,000, divided into 10,000 ordinary shares and 10,000 6 per cent preference shares, all of £1 each.

The following balances were shown on the books after the profit and loss account had been completed at 31st December, 19..—

Ordinary share capital £10,000; balance at bank £13,800; expenses accrued £450; sundry debtors £7,200; plant and machinery £5,000 (cost £8,000 *less* depreciation £3,000); creditors £6,500; 5 per cent debentures (secured on land and buildings) £3,000; preliminary expenses £500; land and buildings £5,500 (cost); stock on hand

£5,250; general reserve £2,500; work-in-progress £2,125; preference share capital £5,000 (5,000 shares issued); fixtures and fittings £350 (cost £425, *less* depreciation £75) and accumulated profit to date £12,275.

It was resolved that—

(*a*) the preliminary expenses be written off;
(*b*) the general reserve be increased by £1,500;
(*c*) the dividend on the preference shares be provided for; and
(*d* a dividend of £0·25 per share on the ordinary shares be provided for.

Prepare the appropriation account of the company for the year ended 31st December, 19.., and the balance sheet at that date. Ignore income tax. (*R.S.A.*)

11. The directors of a limited liability company (having an authorized capital of £120,000), issue a prospectus inviting applications for 100,000 shares of £1 each, and stating that 10,000 shares will be issued in addition as fully paid to the vendor in part payment of purchase money. £0·125 per share is payable on application, £0·125 per share on allotment, £0·25 per share three months after allotment, and 10s. per share six months after allotment. The capital offered was over-subscribed by 10,000 (ten thousand) shares. The amount due on allotment was received in full. The sum of £24,000 was received in respect of the first, and £48,000 in respect of the second call. The purchase money is stated to be £80,000, viz.—

	£
Land and buildings	35,000
Stock and work-in-progress	15,000
Machinery and plant	20,000
Goodwill	10,000
	80,000

Make the journal entries necessary to open the books of the company, and to record the payment of the instalments, stating where the details of calls in arrear should be found. (*Chartered Accountants.*)

12. The Silver Ore Company Ltd. was formed on 1st April with an authorized capital of £60,000, divided into 30,000 ordinary shares of £1 each and 30,000 5 per cent cumulative preference shares of £1 each. The whole of the ordinary shares were issued and fully paid, but of the cumulative preference shares 22,000 only were issued, and of these 21,900 were fully paid, but on the remaining 100 shares £0·75 only had been paid. From the following trial balance prepare balance sheet, trading account, and profit and loss account on 31st March, following.

	£	£
Ordinary share capital		30,000
Preference share capital		21,975
Balance at bank	10,522	
Crushing plant and machinery	4,000	
Cost to date of sinking mine	2,000	
Land	20,000	
Expenses of promotion of company	600	
Royalties paid	1,000	
Silver sold (cash)		17,000
Other minerals sold (including coal used by the company)		950
Light railway, cost	1,200	
Wages of miners, etc.	6,900	
Wagons	500	
Bank interest		270

	£	£
Advertising	500	
Carriage paid on crushing plant and machinery	180	
Erection of sheds, etc..	1,500	
Legal expenses	100	
Oil	200	
Repairs to plant	90	
Coal bought	300	
,, used from own mines	150	
Office furniture	150	
Salaries	2,000	
Interim preference dividend, paid 2nd October, 5 per cent per annum, gross	548	
Cash in hand	55	
Directors' fees	700	
Investment in Rosario Tin Mines, 2,000 Ordinary Shares, £5 each, £4 paid	8,000	
Brokers' charges, etc., on same	100	
Dividend received thereon		320
Deposit A/c at bank, 3 per cent per annum	8,900	
Interest received to 31st December		120
Loose Tools	440	
	70,635	70,635

Depreciate plant and light railways at 15 per cent per annum. Wagons are valued at £400, and loose tools at £300. Promotion expenses to be charged over a period of three years. Value of silver on hand £1,500. On 21st December, the directors decided to forfeit the 100 shares on which only £0·75 had been paid up.

Do not provide for Corporation Tax. (*U.L.C.I., modified.*)

13. The issued capital of Greens Ltd. consists of 40,000 ordinary shares of £1 each. Annual accounts are prepared to 31st March.

On paying a dividend, the practice is to transfer the amount required to pay same to a special bank account opened for the purpose which is called "Dividend Bank Account No. ——." Any balance remaining on this account after twelve months is transferred to an account styled "Deposit Account for Unclaimed Dividends," the balance of the corresponding dividend account being then transferred to "Unclaimed Dividends Account." Warrants more than twelve months old, when presented for payment, are paid out of the ordinary bank account and at the end of the year the corresponding total is transferred to this account from the deposit account.

On 31st March, 1964 the balance standing on Dividend Account No. 16 was £63·60 and on Unclaimed Dividends Accounts £295·75. Dividend No. 17 of 12 per cent free of tax was declared payable on 15th June, 1964.

Warrant No. 16/254 for £14 was presented on 12th April, 1964 and Dividend Bank Account No. 16 was closed on 20th May, 1964. The balance on Dividend Bank Account No. 17 on 31st March, 1965 was £36. Warrants more than twelve months old presented during the year totalled £45·80.

You are required (1) to record the foregoing transactions in the ledger and special bank accounts, and (2) to set out the corresponding entries in the balance sheet of the company as on 31st March, 1965. (*A.C.C.A.*)

14. State whether, from the legal point of view, a company may distribute a dividend in each of the following circumstances—

(*a*) When there is a profit in Year 2 of £5,000 but a loss brought forward from Year 1 of £7,500.

(*b*) When the company itself has made a trading profit of £10,000 but its wholly owned subsidiary company has incurred a trading loss of £12,000.

(*c*) When, on trading alone, there is neither profit nor loss but certain fixed assets have been sold at a profit of £2,000.

Give full reasons for your answer and state whether the legal view is supported by modern accounting practice. (*L.C.C.*)

15. On 1st January the A Company Ltd. acquired a fifty-year lease of its business premises, paying therefore £10,000. It was decided to provide for depreciation by setting aside £90 per annum as a sinking fund, and on 31st December, the amounts so set aside had (with interest) accumulated to £2,400. On 31st December, twenty years later, the directors obtained from an insurance company a policy assuring them the payment of £10,000 at the end of thirty years, in consideration of an annual premium of £220, the first premium being paid upon that date; and having thus provided for the redemption of capital they gave instructions that the £2,400 accumulated during the past twenty years should be stated in the balance sheet dated 31st December, as "Reserve Fund."

Do you consider this treatment correct? Give reasons for your answer.

(*Chartered Institute of Secretaries.*)

16. Light Industries, Ltd., has an Authorized Share Capital of £1,000,000 divided into 250,000 6 per cent Cumulative Preference Shares of £1 each, 700,000 Ordinary Shares of £1 each, and 200,000 Ordinary Shares of £0·25 each. On 31st March, 1964, there have been issued 200,000 of the Preference Shares (all fully paid), 550,000 Ordinary Shares (400,000 fully paid and 150,000 on which £0·50 has been called up, but a call of £0·25 was outstanding on 600 of the latter) and all the Deferred Shares (fully paid).

The accounts for the year to 31st March, 1964, showed a disposable balance, after deducting the interim dividends paid, of £68,178, which was dealt with as follows—

(*a*) £25,000 was transferred to General Reserve, which previously stood at £125,000.

(*b*) Six months final dividend was paid on the Preference Shares, a final dividend of 6 per cent on the Ordinary Shares, calculated on the amounts called up, and a dividend for the year of 10 per cent on the Deferred Shares.

(*c*) The balance was carried forward.

In November, 1964, the Directors declared interim dividends of 3 per cent on the Preference Shares, and 4 per cent on the Ordinary Shares, calculated on the amounts called up.

Interest on calls in arrear was payable at the rate of 10 per cent per annum. In the accounts to the 31st March, 1964, the amount of such interest outstanding was calculated and brought into account, being for two years on the £0·25 calls on 600 shares. On 1st December, 1964, the calls in arrear were paid up with interest to date.

In addition to the balances disclosed by the above information, the following were standing in the company's books as on 31st March, 1965—

	£
Trade Debtors	95,347
Trade Creditors	14,748
Leasehold Property at cost	219,000
Leasehold Redemption Fund, 31st March, 1964	34,720
Leasehold Redemption Fund Policy, 31st March, 1964	34,720
Premiums paid on above during year	4,500
Machinery and Plant, 31st March, 1964 (cost £190,000)	124,800
Machinery and Plant bought during year	6,300

	£
Patents and Trade Marks at cost	230,000
Vans, Lorries and Cars, 31st March, 1964 (cost £10,000)	7,250
Vans sold during year (book value £580; cost £1,000)	423
Bank Overdraft (secured)	12,371
Loose Tools, 31st March, 1964, plus Purchases	1,742
Stock, 31st March, 1964	242,393
Cash in Hand	419
Purchases *less* Returns	326,623
Sales *less* Returns	558,105
Directors' Fees	5,000
Factory Power and Expenses	15,663
Office and Showroom Expenses	3,592
Salaries and Wages, Factory	132,646
Salaries and Wages, Office and Showroom (including Managing Director, £1,000)	6,375
Travellers' Salaries and Commission	10,974
Heating and Lighting	868
Discount (*Cr.* Balance)	2,332
Transfer Fees	34
Provision for Bad Debts, 31st March, 1964	1,750
Advertising	9,347
Legal Expenses and Audit Fees (315)	612

You are required to prepare the company's Manufacturing and Profit and Loss Accounts for the year ended 31st March, 1965, and a Balance Sheet as on that date. In preparing these accounts the following information and instructions are to be taken into account—

(*a*) The Stock-in-Trade on hand at 31st March, 1965, was valued at £238,689, the Loose Tools at £1,375, and the Vans, Lorries and Cars at £5,730.

(*b*) The Managing Director is entitled to a commission equal to 1 per cent of the net profit (calculated to the nearest £).

(*c*) The Bad Debts Provision is to be made up to £2,000.

(*d*) The Heating and Lighting is to be apportioned, four-fifths to the factory and one-fifth to the offices and showroom.

(*e*) The old Plant and Machinery is to be depreciated 10 per cent (on book value) and the new 4 per cent.

(*f*) Factory Wages were accrued and unpaid amounting to £123 and Heating and Lighting £272.

(*g*) The surrender value of the Policy at 31st March, 1965, was £39,521.

(*h*) £750 of the expenditure on Advertising is to be carried forward.

(*i*) Taxation to be ignored. (*L.C.C.*)

17. The Wye Co. Ltd., was registered with an authorized capital of £50,000 divided into 200,000 Ordinary Shares of £0·25 each and on 31st December, 1963 the following balances were taken from the company's books—

	£
Issued Share Capital—	
100,000 Ordinary Shares of £0·25 each (fully paid)	25,000
Cash in hand	280
Sundry Trade Creditors	1,440
Sundry Trade Debtors	5,585
Balance at Bank	1,725
Undistributed Profits	7,500

	£
Machinery at cost	10,344
5 per cent Debenture Stock	6,750
Premises at cost	18,500
Stock at 1st January, 1963	13,200
Manufacturing Wages	18,750
Office Salaries	1,860
Discounts on purchases	62
Sales Delivery expenses	586
Office Rent and Rates	162
Provision for Depreciation of Plant to 31st December, 1962	1,800
Insurance	147
Sales	92,600
Repairs to premises	268
Raw Materials purchased	62,750
Bad Debts written off	282
Office Expenses	182
Debenture Interest for the year (Gross)	337
Manufacturing Expenses	572
Unclaimed Dividends	378

The stock of raw materials at 31st December, 1963, was valued at £9,460.

Provision has to be made for doubtful debts of £270 and additional depreciation of £1,000 on Plant.

The Directors recommend a dividend of 5 per cent gross on the paid-up capital at the end of the year.

During the year £2,500 of the undistributed profits had been capitalized by the issue of 10,000 fully paid Ordinary Shares of £0·25 each at par.

Prepare a Trading and Profit and Loss Account for the year and a Balance Sheet as at 31st December, 1963.

Income Tax, Profits Tax and Corporation Tax are to be ignored.

(*A.C.C.A.*)

18. The Authorized Share Capital of R.S.T. Ltd., is £75,000 divided into 30,000 5 per cent Cumulative Preference Shares of £1 each, and 45,000 Ordinary Shares of £1 each; 20,000 Preference Shares and 30,000 Ordinary Shares have been issued and fully paid.

The balances on the books at 31st December, 1969, before the appropriation of the balance on the Profit and Loss Account, are as follows—

	£	£
Preference Share Capital		20,000
Ordinary Share Capital		30,000
Freehold Land and Buildings	20,025	
Machinery and Plant	56,088	
Furniture, Fixtures and Fittings	2,416	
Share Premium Account		7,000
General Reserve		13,000
Profit Prior to Incorporation		5,178
5 per cent Debentures (repayable after 1984; secured by a floating charge)		30,000
Quoted Investments at cost	4,892	
Sundry Debtors and Prepayments	14,276	
Creditors and Accrued Expenses		5,602
Stock on hand, at cost	23,129	

	£	£
Cash at Bank	5,164	
Cash in Hand	526	
Trade Investments, at cost	2,500	
Provision for Deferred Repairs		1,393
Debenture Redemption Reserve		2,000
Profit and Loss Account		14,843
	129,016	129,016

The balances shown for Freehold Land and Buildings, Machinery and Plant and Furniture, Fixtures and Fittings are the net amounts after providing for depreciation on the diminishing values up to 31st December, 1969. From the accounts for these items it is ascertained that the cost of the assets now in existence was: Freehold Land and Buildings, £23,920, Machinery and Plant, £116,490, Furniture, Fixtures and Fittings, £5,285. No disposal of any of these assets has been made during the year.

The Directors are of the opinion that the market value of the Stock on Hand and of the Trade Investments is in excess of cost. The market value of the Quoted Investments is £5,400.

Out of the balance of the Profit and Loss Account it has been decided to—

(*a*) appropriate £4,000 by way of Corporation Tax Reserve;
(*b*) increase the Debenture Redemption Reserve to £2,500;
(*c*) set aside £2,500 against a possible increase in the price of raw materials;
(*d*) pay a full year's dividend on the Preference Shares and to propose a dividend of 12 per cent on the Ordinary Shares (both dividends subject to Income Tax at £0·3875 in the £); and
(*e*) carry forward the balance.

Prepare for publication the Balance Sheet of the Company as at 31st December, 1969.

(*L.C.C., modified.*)

19. The Ess Co. Ltd. was registered with a nominal capital of 60,000 ordinary shares of £1 each and on 31st December, 1962, the balances in the company's ledger were as follows—

	£
Issued Share Capital—	
15,000 Shares of £1 each—fully paid (including bonus issue)	15,000
Cash in Hand	190
Sundry Creditors	960
Sundry Debtors	3,790
Cash at Bank	1,150
Undistributed Profits	5,000
Machinery at cost	6,000
5 per cent Debenture Stock	4,500
Freehold Factory and Offices at cost	11,500
Stock at 1st January, 1962	8,800
Productive Wages	12,450
Office Salaries	1,230
Discounts received	48
Sales Delivery Costs	395
Rent and Rates	111
Provision for Depreciation of Machinery to 31st December, 1961	1,200
Insurance	98
Sales	61,650

	£
Trade Expenses	382
Repairs to Premises	174
Raw Materials purchased	41,800
Unclaimed Dividends	252
Bad Debts	191
Office Expenses	124
Debenture Interest for the year	225

The stock of raw materials at 31st December, 1962, was valued at £6,820.

A provision has to be made for doubtful debts amounting to £182 and for 10 per cent depreciation on the cost of the machinery as an addition to the existing provision of £1,200.

During the year £5,000 of undistributed profits had been capitalized by the issue of 5,000 ordinary shares of £1 each as fully paid.

The directors recommend a dividend of 10 per cent on the capital paid up at the end of the year.

Prepare a Trading and Profit and Loss Account for the year and a Balance Sheet as at 31st December, 1962. Ignore Income Tax and Corporation Tax.

(*A.C.C.A.*)

20. H. Tonk Ltd., Music Publishers, after due formalities, carried out the following transactions in the year to 31st December, 1958. Give Journal entries with narratives for each transaction (including cash received or paid) adding "(P & L)" after each item affecting any section of the company's Profit and Loss Account. (Ignore Tax.)

1958		£
Jan 1	The company declared a bonus share dividend of 10s. per share on 40,000 existing £1 ordinary shares, from its General Reserve, which was applied in payment of the uncalled liability of £0·50 per share—making the shares fully paid.	
Feb 28	Received application monies for 50,000 5 per cent Debentures of £1 each—to be issued at a discount of 2½ per cent—at £0·50 per Debenture.	
Mar 1	Accepted applications for and issued 40,000 5 per cent Debentures (at 97½ per cent) pro-rata to amounts applied for on 28th February, excess application monies being retained.	
Mar 31	Received balance payable (in full) on 40,000 5 per cent Debentures.	
July 2	Paid Royalties to composers for half-year to 30th June	5,000
Aug 31	Paid Interim Dividend on 40,000 ordinary shares for 1958 at 10 per cent actual	4,000
Dec 31	Accrued Debenture Interest	1,500
	Accrued Royalties to Composers	6,000

(*L.C.C.*)

CHAPTER 22

THE PUBLISHED ACCOUNTS OF COMPANIES

"Let us sit on this log by the roadside" says I "and forget the inhumanity and ribaldry of the poets. It is in the glorious columns of ascertained facts and legalised measures that beauty is to be found."

"Go on Mr Pratt" say Mrs Samson. "Them ideas are so original and soothing. I think statistics are just as lovely as they can be."

O. HENRY—*The handbook of hymen*

In dealing with the accounts of limited companies the requirements of the Companies Act, 1948, as modified by the Companies Act, 1967, must be borne in mind. Whilst there is no fixed layout required by the Acts, the published accounts must give certain information.

The requirements embodied in earlier Acts were consolidated in the 1948 Act but that Act allowed some private companies to secure exemption from the requirements under certain conditions. At the end of 1966, out of approximately 550,000 companies registered, more than 400,000 were exempt. A committee under the chairmanship of Lord Jenkins produced the Jenkins Report in 1962 and many of its recommendations were included in the Companies Act, 1967.

The 1967 Act requires disclosure of much more information than did the previous Acts and the status of the exempt private company was abolished. However, the Act allows a limited company to re-register as an unlimited company if it wishes to preserve the confidentiality of its accounts, provided it is not a subsidiary of a limited company, a holding company or a Trading Stamp Company.

Date of Operation. The accounting and disclosure provisions of the 1967 Act came into force with the financial year ending on or after 27th January, 1968, except for the requirements to analyse profit and turnover under Sect. 17, which came into force on or after 27th July, 1968.

Perhaps the most important of all the provisions affecting the accounts is that contained in Sect. 149 (1) of the 1948 Act which states—

> Every balance sheet of a company shall give a true and fair view of the state of affairs of the company as at the end of its financial year, and every profit and loss account of a company shall give a true and fair view of the profit or loss of a company for the financial year.

Every balance sheet of a company shall be signed on behalf of the board by two of the directors of the company, or if there is only one director, by that director. There are special provisions for banking companies (Sect. 155).

Details of the information required to be given in the accounts are set out in the 2nd Schedule of the 1967 Act. A requirement of great practical importance is that both the balance sheet and the profit and loss account must show corresponding figures for the previous year in respect of all items.

The other main requirements are as follows—

All members of the company and debenture holders are entitled to receive copies of the accounts, auditors' report and directors' report. In addition, copies of the documents must be filed with the Registrar of Companies and are available for public inspection. In practice, most companies will freely supply them to anyone who requests a copy. The Board of Trade has power to modify the requirements and the information may be given in notes or annexed documents at the discretion of the Directors.

RECOMMENDATIONS ON ACCOUNTING PRINCIPLES

The Institute of Chartered Accountants in England and Wales publishes recommendations on accounting principles, from time to time. The recommendations are a valuable guide to good current practice in preparing accounts and all students should be familiar with them.

On the presentation of company accounts, the recommendations make the following main points, among others—

(i) "A true and fair view" implies the consistent application of generally accepted principles.

(ii) The use of general headings such as "liabilities" and "assets" is unnecessary.

RESERVES, PROVISIONS, AND CURRENT LIABILITIES

At one time, the terms Reserves, Provisions and Current Liabilities were regarded as interchangeable and the distinction still presents many difficulties.

The following definitions are based upon the Recommendations of the Institute of Chartered Accountants.

Reserves, provisions and current liabilities are all created by a debit to profit and loss account. Reserves are debited to profit and loss appropriation account. Provisions and current liabilities to the general profit and loss account.

(i) Reserves are free, provisions are for specific requirements.

(ii) Reserves are not intended to meet any contingency, liability or loss known to exist at the time of the balance sheet.

(iii) Provisions may be for specific items existing at the date of the balance sheet which *cannot* be closely estimated.

It follows that an excessive provision should, in fact, be treated as a reserve.

Current Liabilities are sums set aside to meet accrued charges and items which can be closely estimated, e.g. telephone bill, rates, proposed dividends, income tax due.

Provisions may be made for depreciation, bad debts, discounts on debtors, and repairs and renewals, and the student should refer to the examples of these given elsewhere in this book.

Capital Reserves are any reserves which are not available for distribution as dividends. They may be created—

(*a*) For statutory reasons (share premiums);
(*b*) Because the memorandum and articles so decide;
(*c*) For other legal reasons (see Divisible Profits);
(*d*) Because the directors so decide. In this case, the directors are quite free to transfer such profits to revenue whenever they wish.

The 1967 Companies Act abandons the distinctions between Capital and Revenue Reserves in the Balance Sheet but the two reserves required to be created under the 1948 Act are retained—

(i) Under Sect. 58 a capital redemption reserve fund must be created out of profits if preference shares are not redeemed from the proceeds of a new issue.
(ii) Premiums on shares issued must be shown separately in the Balance Sheet under Schedule 2 of the 1967 Act and can only be used for limited purposes under Sect. 56 of the 1948 Act.

Contingent Liabilities. A contingent liability will be a liability only if a certain event takes place. It may never arise; in fact, if it does the firm will have to meet a claim upon it. Many different transactions may give rise to contingent liabilities, such as commitments for capital expenditure, discounting bills of exchange, etc.

There is no entry in the books for contingent liabilities and, therefore, nothing in the balance sheet, but details should be added as a note.

DISTINCTION BETWEEN A PROVISION AND A RESERVE

Since the 1967 Act defines a provision but not a reserve, the underlying logic of the distinction is not very clear. However, suppose there is a charge which is difficult to determine, e.g. depreciation. If no estimated charge were made in the profit and loss account, this would result in higher profits being stated and, consequently, a greater distribution of income. To prevent such a result a provision is made by debiting the profit and loss account and crediting "provision for depreciation", thus reducing profits by the amount of the depreciation.

Calculation and allowance for provisions, then, makes for a more realistic estimate of operating profits and profits available for dividend.

It still does not follow that all the profit will be distributed.

If it is decided that it is inadvisable to spend all the profit by distribution to the owners of the business but rather to save some for a possible trade depression or even to strengthen the general financial stability of the business, this can be accomplished by carrying some of the profits to a Reserve.

A debit would be made in the profit and loss appropriation account and a credit to reserve account. At a later date such a sum may be distributed to the owners.

On the other hand assume a person borrows cash in order to commence a business, agreeing to repay the cash out of profits. He will be unable to spend all his profits and at the same time repay the loan out of profits. Effectively the same is true of a limited company, so appropriations for reserves of this nature may be for the repayment of capital sums and may be called capital reserves and are not free for distribution or spending.

RESERVE FUNDS

This term should not be applied to a reserve unless it is represented by specifically earmarked investments or other assets, realizable when required at not less than the amount of the fund. Exceptions arise in the case of the "capital redemption reserve fund" (see p. 2401). Whilst the Institute of Chartered Accountants recommend that where the term Fund is used the amount should be represented by an investment which is distinct from the ordinary cash resources of the business; in practice, the term is not always used in this sense. Sect. 58 of the Companies Act applies the term to the capital redemption reserve fund but does *not* require the setting aside of cash corresponding to the profits reserved (see p. 2401).

SECRET RESERVES

A secret reserve is a surplus, the existence of which is not shown on the balance sheet.

How Secret Reserves are Made. Secret reserves are made in various ways—

1. By excessive depreciation of assets, such as writing down premises, investments, etc., below their proper value.

2. By undervaluation or omission of assets. Assets may be shown at cost though they have greatly appreciated. Stock-in-trade may be valued much below its actual price. Some companies omit their goodwill, though it may be of enormous value, or even the value of premises.

3. By creating unnecessary or excessive reserves for bad debts, discounts, etc., or for fictitious liabilities.

4. By charging capital expenditure to revenue, as, for instance, debiting additions to buildings to the profit and loss account instead of to the

buildings account. On the balance sheet the buildings would thus appear at less than their proper value.

Advantages of Secret Reserves. The advantages claimed for them are—

1. They promote financial stability. Extraordinary losses can be met out of such "undisclosed" or "hidden surpluses" instead of out of revenue, thus preventing the dividend being reduced and public confidence shaken. Banks and insurance companies often have recourse to such methods.

2. They enable a normal rate of dividend to be maintained—not only for the above reason (1), but also because they enable unduly fluctuating profits to be controlled, and steady, progressive results to be shown.

3. They advance the interests of the undertaking. By means of secret or "inner" reserves, huge profits can be concealed from business rivals, whereas the publication of such profits would stimulate competition, and perhaps injure the company's trade.

Disadvantages of Secret Reserves. The objections raised against the practice of creating secret reserves are—

1. The shareholders have not a full knowledge of the company's affairs, inasmuch as the published accounts are inaccurate and misleading. The trading and profit and loss accounts do not show the true profits. The balance sheet is not a correct representation of the state of affairs, because some of the liabilities may be overstated, while some of the assets may be undervalued and even omitted altogether.

2. Secret reserves are dangerous resources. They may be utilized to meet exceptional losses sustained through depreciation of investments, etc.; they can, with equal facility, be used to conceal losses arising from bad management or reckless speculation.

3. Concealment of facts and manipulation of figures are bad in principle; and while they may, sometimes, serve the company's interests, they may also be, and frequently are by unscrupulous directors, used to the company's detriment. Suspicions may be aroused which will weaken or destroy confidence in the management much more quickly than a policy of straightforward dealing, even in adverse circumstances.

Whether or not a company is justified in creating secret reserves is a subject upon which much discussion has taken place and until recently, it was common practice in the case of banks and similar institutions. The practice of creating such reserves is now generally condemned. It would be unwise to dogmatize on the subject, as the position of each individual company must be considered, and it would have to be left to those who control the financial affairs of a business as to whether or not secret reserves should be created.

The practice of creating secret reserves must be reviewed in cases where limited liability companies are controlled under the Companies Acts, 1948 or 1967.

The Companies Act, 1948, 8th Schedule, para. 27 (2), introduced a check on the creation of undisclosed reserves, although certain types of secret reserve may exist in many companies operating under the Act. Reference should also be made to the well-known case of *R.* v. *Lord Kylsant and Morland*, 1931, better known as the Royal Mail Steam Packet Company case.

(v) *Amounts set aside for future income tax* should be shown separately and not grouped with reserves, however described. Current taxation is a current liability.

BALANCE SHEET REQUIREMENTS—SOURCES OF FUNDS

(*a*) **Share Capital.** There must be summarized—

(i) Authorized share capital.

(ii) Issued share capital.

(iii) The amount of redeemable preference shares issued and the latest and earliest date on which the company may redeem them; whether this is mandatory or optional and whether any premium is payable.

(iv) The share capital on which interest has been paid out of capital (under Sect. 65 of 1948) and the rate of interest.

(v) The number, description and amount of shares held by subsidiaries or their nominees. Generally such holdings are prohibited except for trustee holdings under Sect. 27 of the 1948 Act.

(vi) The number, description and amount of unissued shares under option, stating price and period of option.

(vii) The amount of arrears of fixed cumulative dividends before deduction of income tax (unless the dividends are tax free, when the fact should be stated). Show the period for which the dividends are in arrear.

These must be classified under separate headings appropriate to the company's business, unless the amounts are too small to be material.

(*b*) **Reserves.** A reserve shall not include—

(i) Amounts provided for depreciation, renewals or diminution in value of assets.

(ii) Amounts provided for known liabilities.

(iii) Amounts provided for equalizing tax charges against profits.

Any excess amounts provided under (i) and (ii) shall be treated as reserves.

The following reserves must be shown separately—

A Capital redemption reserve fund under Sect. 58 of the 1948 Act for redemption of preference shares.

A Share premium account created under Sect. 56 of the 1948 Act.

In addition, the document must show any material movements on reserves.

(*c*) **Liabilities,** if material, classified under appropriate headings and including—

1. Debentures held for the company by nominees or trustees.
2. Debentures of the company held by subsidiaries, stating the number, description and amount.
3. Redeemed Debentures available for re-issue under Sect. 90 of the 1948 Act.
4. Liabilities secured on the assets of the company.
5. Particulars of any liabilities of other persons secured on the assets of the company.
6. The aggregate of the bank loans and overdrafts.
7. Other borrowings repayable wholly or in part more than five years from the date of the Balance Sheet. The terms of the repayment and the rate of interest should also be stated.
8. *Inter-group indebtedness.* Amounts owing to subsidiaries and holding and fellow-subsidiaries distinguishing debentures from other indebtedness.
9. Recommended dividends must be shown, gross.

(*d*) **Provisions.** A provision is—

1. Any amount written off or detained by way of providing for depreciation renewals or diminution of assets.
2. Any amount retained by way of providing for any known liability of which the amount cannot be determined with substantial accuracy.

Known liabilities include all liabilities in respect of expenditure contracted for and all disputed or contingent liabilities.

If material, the following provisions must be shown—

1. Provision for corporation tax giving the basis on which it has been computed.
2. Amounts set aside for equalizing the charges on the company taxation.

Movements on provisions must show the source of any increase, and the application of any decrease in the aggregate, but not if the amount is immaterial.

(*e*) **Contingent Liabilities and Future Capital Expenditure.** If contingent liabilities are not provided for, the aggregate amount, if material, estimated if necessary, must be shown. Similarly, the estimated amount of capital expenditure contracted for but not provided for and authorized by the directors but not contracted for must be stated.

In both cases, the information may be given by way of note or statement annexed to the report.

BALANCE SHEET REQUIREMENTS—USES OF FUNDS

Assets must be classified under headings appropriate to the business unless the amounts are not material or the assets are not separable from those in another class.

The assets must be identified in three groups—

1. Fixed assets.
2. Current assets.
3. Assets which are neither fixed nor current.

The methods of arriving at the valuation of each class of assets must be stated, except where the amounts are not material.

(*f*) **Fixed Assets.** The normal method of stating fixed assets is to state—
1. *Aggregate cost* of the assets, or if the assets stand in the books at a valuation—
2. *Aggregate valuation;* and to deduct from the cost or valuation—
3. *Aggregate depreciation* written off.

If the figures before 1st July, 1948, or 27th January, 1967, cannot be obtained without unreasonable expense or delay, the net amount at which the assets stand in the books at that date may be treated as the amount of a valuation at either of these dates.

In practice as few accounts are made up to 1st July or 27th January, it is usual to treat the amount shown in the last balance sheet prior to those dates as the *net book amount.*

Exceptions to the Normal Method: 1. If the normal method would involve unreasonable expense or delay (e.g. where there are numerous small tools which cannot be listed individually).

2. If replacement is provided by making provision for renewals and charging the cost of replacement against it or by charging the cost of replacement direct to revenue.

In such case state—

(*a*) The means of providing for replacement.
(*b*) The amount of any provision not used.

3. For quoted investments the market value must be shown. For unquoted investments the value as estimated by the directors may be given.

4. Goodwill, patents and trade marks.

5. Investments in subsidiary companies.

Fixed Assets at Valuation, other than unquoted investments, must show each separate valuation, the year of the valuation and the amount. If the valuation was made during the accounting year the names or qualifications of the valuers and the basis of valuation used must be stated.

Movements on Fixed Assets, other than investments, must show the aggregate amounts of assets acquired or scrapped during the period.

The following items must be shown separately—

(i) *The value of land* (including buildings) distinguishing freehold, long-lease (50 years or over) and short-leases.

(ii) *Goodwill patents and trade-marks.* The aggregate amount in or ascertainable from the books or papers in possession of the company if not written off.

(iii) *Quoted investments.* The aggregate amount of investments quoted on a Stock Exchange of repute in (*a*) Great Britain or (*b*) abroad, at market value if this exceeds book value and at stock exchange value if this is lower than market value.

(iv) *Unquoted investments.* Aggregate valuation by the directors or the valuation at cost or valuation less the amount written off from the asset.

(v) *Unquoted investment in equity share capital.*

Where the directors estimate of value is not shown—

(*a*) The aggregate income for the year from them.

(*b*) The investing companies share of profits less losses *before tax* and *after tax.*

(*c*) The accumulated share of undistributed profit *less* losses.

(*d*) The way in which any losses have been dealt with in the investing companies' accounts.

(vi) *Shares in and aggregate amounts arising from subsidiaries* including loans, and distinguishing shares from indebtedness.

(vii) *Shares in fellow subsidiaries.*

(viii) *Other group indebtedness.*

(*g*) **Current Assets.** The directors must state if they are of the opinion that the realizable value of any of the current assets is less than the book amount.

The following items must be shown separately so far as they are not written off.

(i) *Loans to employees, salaried directors and their trustees* made for the purpose of purchasing fully paid shares in the company or its holding company.

(ii) *Loans to officers of the company* including those repaid during the year by the company, a subsidiary or a third party guaranteed by the company, except loans in the normal course of business and loans of less than £2,000 if in accordance with company practice as certified by the directors. Loans to directors are restricted by Sect. 190 of the 1948 Act.

(iii) Preliminary expenses.

(iv) Expenses of issuing shares or debentures.

(v) Sums paid by way of commission in respect of shares or debentures.

(vi) Sums allowed by way of discount in respect of any debentures.
(vii) Sums allowed by way of discount on any issue of shares.

The manner in which the stock-in-trade or work-in-progress is valued must be stated if the amount is material to an appreciation of the company's affairs.

GENERAL REQUIREMENTS

1. **Basis of Conversion of Foreign Currencies.** This must be stated where the amounts of assets or liabilities affected are material.

2. **Corresponding Amounts** for the preceding year must be shown for all items in the Balance Sheet but there is a transitional exemption for new items in the first Balance Sheet produced under the 1967 Act.

THE PROFIT AND LOSS ACCOUNT REQUIREMENTS

The items required to be shown in the profit and loss account are—

(*a*) **Revenues**

1. *Turnover* and how it has been arrived at. Banking and discounting activities may be excluded. Jenkins defined turnover as "the total amount receivable by a company . . . for goods sold or supplied by it as a principal and for services provided by it." Both turnover and profit must be broken down by class of business either here or in the directors' report.

If the turnover does not exceed £250,000 the company is exempt from this provision providing it is not a subsidiary or a holding company.

2. *Income from land* if a substantial part of the company's income. Outgoings such as rates and ground rents may be deducted.

3. *Investment income* distinguishing between quoted and unquoted investment sources.

(*b*) **Expenses**

4. *Directors' emoluments*, Sect. 196 of the Companies Act, 1948, requires *the accounts* to show.

(*a*) *The aggregate amount of directors' emoluments*—

(i) For services as a director either of the company or of a subsidiary.
(ii) For other services.

The term "emoluments" includes any sum paid by way of fees, percentages, expense allowance in so far as it is charged to U.K. income tax, contributions under pension schemes and benefits in kind.

(*b*) *The aggregate of directors' or past directors' pensions*, distinguishing pensions for—

(i) Services as a director of the company or of a subsidiary.
(ii) Other services.

Pensions receivable under a pension scheme the contributions to which are substantially adequate for its maintenance, shall not be included.

(*c*) *The aggregate amount of compensation to directors* or past directors in respect of loss of office, distinguishing—

(i) Compensation for the loss of office of director.
(ii) Compensation for the loss of any other office.

(*d*) Adjustments arising from expenses disallowed for tax or retention of emoluments for which the director was previously treated as accountable.

(*e*) The number of directors whose emoluments under (*a*) fall in each bracket of a scale in multiples of £2,500. Pension contributions are excluded.

(*f*) The emoluments in (*e*) of the highest-paid director(s) if they exceed those of the chairman.

(*g*) The number of directors waiving emoluments and the amount waived in the year.

Requirements (*a*) to (*f*) do not apply to directors employed entirely outside the United Kingdom.

Requirements (*e*) to (*g*) do not apply if the emoluments do not exceed £15,000 and the company is not a subsidiary or a holding company.

5. *Chairman's emoluments*, excluding pension contributions, must be stated provided he is not employed entirely outside the United Kingdom.

6. *Employees receiving more than* £10,000 *per annum* excluding pension contributions. The number in each bracket of £2,500, starting at £10,000, must be stated unless they work entirely outside the United Kingdom.

7. *Interest payable* must be divided between—

(*a*) Interest on bank loans, overdrafts and other loans repayable within 5 years, whether secured or not.

(*b*) Interest on other loans whether secured or not.

8. *Hire of plant and machinery*. If material, the amount paid must be shown.

PROFIT AND LOSS ACCOUNT

There must be stated separately—

9. *Provisions for depreciation*, renewals or diminution in value of fixed assets.

If depreciation or replacement of fixed assets is provided by some method other than a depreciation charge or provision for renewals, the method must be stated. If no depreciation is provided the fact should be stated.

Amounts charged for provision of renewal should be shown separately from depreciation or diminution provision.

If depreciation is not related to the valuation of the assets in the Balance Sheet the fact must be stated.

These provisions do not apply to shares in subsidiaries.

10. *Taxation*—

(*a*) The charge for U.K. Corporation tax (including tax imposed elsewhere to the extent of relief from U.K. income tax) and the basis of computation.

(*b*) The charge for U.K. income tax and the basis of computation.

(*c*) The charge for overseas tax on profits, income and capital gains (if charged to revenue).

(*d*) Any special circumstances affecting tax liability in the current or succeeding years.

11. Amounts provided for the redemption of share capital or loans.

12. *Reserves.* Amounts set aside or proposed to be set aside to or withdrawn from reserves.

13. *Provisions.* Amounts set aside to provisions (other than for depreciation, renewals or diminution in value of assets) and amounts withdrawn from provisions and not applied for the purposes thereof. The Board of Trade has power to dispense with this (cf. the power in connexion with the balance sheet).

14. *Aggregate Dividends* paid and proposed, gross of income tax.

15. *Auditors' Remuneration including Expenses.*

16. Any material aspects in which items shown in the profit and loss account are affected by transactions of a sort not usually undertaken by the company or by circumstances of an exceptional or non-recurrent character or by a change in the basis of accounting.

17. Any charges and credits relating to prior years must be stated separately if not included elsewhere.

General. As with the balance sheet, the corresponding items for the previous year must be shown, except for the first year of commencement of the Act.

Sect. 14 (6) of Schedule 2 requires shown "any material respects in which any items in the profit and loss account are affected—

(*a*) By transactions of a sort not usually undertaken by the company or otherwise by circumstances of an exceptional or non-recurrent nature.

(*b*) By any change in the basis of accounting.

In stating any of the items, all sums must be included whether paid by the company or by any other person. In the case of compensation the accounts must distinguish between amounts paid by the company, by a subsidiary or by any other person.

For the purpose of this section a subsidiary includes any company to which a director is *nominated* by the company whether it is a subsidiary or not for other purposes of the Act.

The Board of Trade may exempt companies trading overseas from any requirements which might be harmful to a company's or a group's interests.

LOANS TO OFFICERS

Sect. 197 of the Companies Act, 1948, requires the accounts to show:

1. Loans made during the company's financial year by the company, or by a subsidiary or under guarantee from the company or a subsidiary—

(*a*) To officers of the company.

(*b*) To any person becoming an officer after the loan was made, including loans repaid during the year.

2. Loans made before the commencement of the financial year and outstanding at the end of it.

The following are *not* to be included—

(*a*) Loans made in the ordinary course of business of the company or its subsidiary if such business includes the lending of money;

(*b*) Loan by a company or its subsidiary to an *employee* if the loan does not exceed £2,000 and is certified by the directors of the company or its subsidiary to be made in accordance with a practice adopted or about to be adopted with respect to loans to employees; not being in either case a loan made by the company on the guarantee of or on a security from a subsidiary, or vice versa.

The Board of Trade is given power to modify the requirements of the Act (except that requiring a true and fair view) as to matters to be stated in the accounts for the purpose of adapting them to the circumstances of a company. The consent of the company's directors is necessary. (Sect. 149 (4).)

Group Accounts. The requirements in respect of groups are dealt with in the chapter on Holding Companies (Chapter 25).

DIRECTORS REPORT

The 1948 Companies Act allowed any information required in the accounts to be included in the Directors Report which was required to be annexed to the balance sheet laid before the Annual General Meeting.

The 1967 Act considerably increased the amount of information to be included in the Directors Report. The information required is now—

1. *The recommended dividend.*
2. *Proposed transfer to reserve.*

These two requirements were imposed by the 1948 Act.

3. *Directors names* including anyone who served as such during the year.

Any significant changes during the year—

4. *Principal activities of the company.*

5. *Fixed assets.*

6. *Land held as fixed assets* (including buildings).

7. *Issues of shares or debentures* giving the number and amount of each class, the consideration received and the reasons for the issues.

8. *Directors options to acquire shares or debentures* to which the company is party, explaining the arrangement and the directors involved.

9. *Directors interest in shares or debentures* at the beginning of the year or date of appointment and at the end of the year.

10. *Directors' interest in contracts with the company* at any time in the year if the contract is significant to the company and his interest material. Indirect interests must be included, and the names of the parties and the directors, the nature of the contract and his interest. Interests as a director of another company and service contracts are excluded.

11. *Analysis of turnover and profit or loss before tax* of a company or group between substantially different classes of business stating—

(*a*) the proportions between each class and describing the classes;

(*b*) the extent in money to which each class has contributed a profit or loss before tax.

12. *Average number and remuneration of employees per week* if more than 100 of employees mainly in the United Kingdom. The sum of the number employed and all remuneration payable each week is to be divided by the number of weeks in the year.

13. *Political and charitable contributions* must be stated separately if they exceed £50. Any individual political contribution exceeding £50 must state the name of the person or party and the amount concerned.

14. *Exports.* Companies or groups which disclose their turnover must state the value of their exports as a principal or state that no goods were exported, unless the Board of Trade agrees that disclosure would be contrary to the national interest.

EXEMPTIONS FROM DISCLOSURE

Banking and Discount Companies may seek certain exemptions from the Board of Trade under Sect. 12 of the 1967 Act and Sect. 23 of Schedule 2.

Insurance Companies are given certain exemptions by virtue of Sect. 24 of Schedule 2 but the Board of Trade has power to revoke this.

Shipping Companies are given certain exemptions provided they satisfy the Board of Trade that it is in the national interest for them to be treated as such.

Exemptions do not prevent accounts providing a "true and fair view".

Overseas Companies having a place of business in Great Britain are subject to the requirements of the Act in respect of accounts, etc., to be deposited with the Registrar of Companies in English.

An illustration of a Directors Report, balance sheet and profit and loss account, drawn up to comply with the foregoing requirements, are set out in the following pages.

These are adapted from the Annual Report of Tate & Lyle, Ltd., 1967.

TATE & LYLE, LIMITED

REPORT OF THE DIRECTORS

Your Directors have pleasure in presenting their Annual Report and the Group Profit and Loss Account for the year ended 30th September, 1967, together with the Company's Balance Sheet and Group Balance Sheet as at that date.

Although the new requirements relating to accounts contained in the Companies Act, 1967, are not mandatory with respect to the accounts now presented, such requirements have largely been complied with, including comparative figures wherever possible.

The principal activities of the Group during the year again consisted of the growing of sugar cane and production of raw sugar; the manufacture, sale and distribution of refined sugar; trading in molasses; the shipping and lighterage of sugar; the manufacture of sugar machinery and the provision of technical consultancy services.

Subsidiary Interests

Under this section the report deals with the activities of subsidiaries throughout the world.

Loan Capital

Following negotiations during the latter part of the financial year the Company placed through J. Henry Schroder Wagg & Co. Limited early in October, 1967, an issue of £4,000,000 7¼ per cent Debenture Stock 1989/94 at a price of £97¾ per cent. The proceeds of the issue have been applied in repaying short-term borrowings.

Fixed Assets

Additions to Fixed Assets during the year net of disposals but including amounts charged to assets under construction, totalled £9,773,843, the significant changes being as follows—

	£'000s	£'000s
Raw Sugar Production—		
West Indies	725	
British Honduras	883	
Zambia	3,644	
		5,252
Manufacture and Distribution of Refined Sugar—		
United Kingdom	1,484	
Canada	254	
Africa	275	
		2,013
Molasses Storage and Distribution		546
Shipping		1,773
Miscellaneous		190
		9,774

Cumulative depreciation increased by £4,509,967 giving a net increase in Fixed Assets of £5,263,876.

GROUP PROFIT

The group profit for the year, before taxation totalled £9,508,436 compared with £7,396,714 in 1966. The following statement shows the contributions to group profit of the various trading activities together with an analysis of the total turnover.

		Profit before Tax 1967	Turnover 1967
		£	£'000s
Production of Raw Sugar—			
West Indies and British Honduras		(687,696)	17,104
Refining and Distribution—			
United Kingdom		5,674,423	115,814
Canada		2,281,920	15,628
Africa		346,821	5,887
Molasses Trading, Storage and Distribution		2,556,184	27,827
Shipping		1,761,645	6,650
Engineering and Miscellaneous		304,452	4,922
		12,237,749	
Deduct—			
Holding Company's Charges—			
Finance	2,080,695		
Administration	648,618		
		2,729,313	
		9,508,436	
Total Turnover			193,832
Aggregate value of goods exported from the United Kingdom			15,230

Total turnover represents the amount receivable by the group in the ordinary course of business for goods sold and services provided. Inter-group sales of materials are included where further processing is necessary.

TAXATION

The total charge for taxation in 1967 was £4,006,444 compared with £3,235,929 last year.

In estimating the charge for United Kingdom Corporation Tax on the profits of the year, account has been taken of the proposed increase in the rate from 40 per cent to 42½ per cent from 1st April, 1967.

NET PROFIT AND DIVIDENDS

The net profit after providing for taxation available to the Parent Company was £5,197,921 which together with the sum of £33,313 brought forward from 1966, gives a total of £5,231,234 dealt with as follows—

	£	£
Allocated to General Reserve		1,350,000
Dividends paid and proposed, less Income Tax—		
On the 6½ per cent Cumulative Preference Stock—		
Half-year to 31st March, 1967	45,710	
Half-year to 30th September, 1967	45,710	
On the Ordinary Stock—		
Dividends on account of the year ended 30th September, 1967—		
First Interim of 2 per cent	431,004	
Second Interim of 6 per cent	1,293,013	
Final of 2 per cent now recommended by the Directors and payable on or about 3rd April, 1968	431,004	
	2,246,441	
Income Tax deducted and payable to the Inland Revenue	1,577,289	
		3,823,730
Balance carried forward to the next account		57,504
		5,231,234

CONTRIBUTIONS FOR POLITICAL AND CHARITABLE PURPOSES

	1967 £
Political Purposes—	
British United Industrialists	6,250
Economic League	1,283
Conservative Industrial Fund	1,000
Cities of London and Westminster Conservative Association	63
Common Cause Limited	100
	8,696
Charitable Purposes	68,309

EMOLUMENTS OF DIRECTORS

	1967 £	1966 £
Pursuant to Companies Act, 1948, Section 196		
Fees	9,500	9,712
Fixed Remuneration and sundry benefits	85,847	92,758
Remuneration geared to profits	131,106	110,249
Pension Fund Contributions	50,538	22,841
	276,991	235,560
Pensions in respect of past Directors	9,191	12,593

Pursuant to Companies Act, 1967, Sections 6 and 7	1967
Chairman	£18,936
Other Directors—	Number
Up to £2,500	3
£2,501 to £5,000	—
£5,001 to £7,500	1
£7,501 to £10,000	1
£10,001 to £12,500	2
£12,501 to £15,000	9
£15,001 to £17,500	—
£17,501 to £20,000	1

One Director has waived his rights to receive emoluments of an aggregate amount of £6,000.

SALARIES, WAGES AND NUMBER OF EMPLOYEES

Pursuant to Companies Act, 1967,

Section 8

There were no employees of the Company whose emoluments exceeded £10,000.

Section 18

(i) Average number of persons employed by the Group in the United Kingdom 11,050

(ii) Aggregate remuneration paid or payable in respect of the year to the number of employees stated above . . £13,164,062

BOARD OF DIRECTORS

The names of the persons who were Directors of the Company at any time during the financial year are listed on p. 4.

The particulars of Directors' shareholdings, as required by the Companies Act, 1967, are contained in the appendix to this report.

AUDITORS

The Auditors, Messrs. Edmund D. White & Sons, having expressed their willingness to continue to act, will be re-appointed under the provisions of Section 159 of the Companies Act, 1948.

JOHN O. LYLE
Chairman

Appendix to the Report of the Directors

DIRECTORS' SHAREHOLDINGS at 27th October, 1967

	Tate & Lyle Limited		Canada and Dominion Sugar Company Limited	Caroni Limited	The West Indies Sugar Company Limited	Sundry Holdings
	Ordinary stock	6½% Preference stock	Shares of no par value	Ordinary stock units of 10p each	Ordinary shares of £1 each	
	£	£				
ir Ian D. Lyle .	119,778		616			
	286,593	1,040	140		21,696	
ohn O. Lyle . .	6,344					
	80,365	16,719	80			
ir Peter Runge .	39,099			900		
	435,949	1,040	31			
. H. Tate . .	73,500		1,000	12,500		
	26,500					
O. Whitmee .	3,218		954			£200 Tate & Lyle, Limited 5½% Debenture Stock
ord Lyle of Westbourne .	59,000	2,600		7,500		£1,475 } Caroni Limited
	2,008	4,153				£333 } 6% Preference Stock
I. D. Oliphant .	16,941		1			
	1,400					
/. R. Booth . .	3,556					400 Rhodesia Sugar Refineries Limited Ordinary Shares of £0.25 each
	24,000	2,000				
F. P. Tate . .	106,114			45,000		
olin Lyle . .	161,843		300		13,762	
	15,204		80			
. S. Wingate-Saul .	4,393					
axon Tate . .	38,070		1,500			
olin Rowan . .	6,200			5,875	500	
	961					
. E. Hobbs . .	1,641				450	
. A. C. Hugill .	140				213	
ordon L. Shemilt .	535		103			
he Earl of Perth .	1,200					£1,800 Tate & Lyle, Limited 6¾% Convertible Loan Stock
iscount Boyd of Merton . .	100					£1,000 Tate & Lyle, Limited 4¾% Debenture Stock

s Trustees of the Company's Staff Pension Funds the undermentioned Directors re also each deemed to be interested in the following holdings—

	Tate & Lyle, Limited		
M. D. Oliphant W. R. Booth Colin Lyle J. E. Hobbs	Ordinary Stock £57,800	5½% Debenture Stock £26,000	6¾% Convertible Loan Stock £17,050

Note: (i) Figures in italics are holdings in which a Director is interested as Trustee.
(ii) The requirement of the Companies Act, 1967, that Directors who have a joint interest shall be deemed each to have that interest, results in certain holdings above being duplicated.

TATE & LYLE, LIMITED AND SUBSIDIARY COMPANIES

GROUP PROFIT AND LOSS ACCOUNT

FOR THE YEAR ENDED 30TH SEPTEMBER, 1967

		1967
	£	£
TRADING PROFIT		12,192,827
Add—		
Claims under West Indies Sugar Industry Rehabilitation Funds	186,159	
Investment Revenue—		
Quoted Investments	57,887	
Unquoted Investments	104,410	
Profit on Redemption of Debentures	22,621	
Profit on Sale of Investments	20,893	
		391,970
		12,584,797
Deduct—		
Interest on—		
Debenture and Unsecured Loan Stocks	1,328,202	
Fixed loans repayable within five years	415,254	
Bank loans, overdrafts and other loans	1,862,255	
	3,605,711	
Capital Increase and Incorporation Expenses	33,728	
Loss on Disposal of Fixed Assets	115,150	
		3,754,589
		8,830,208
Add—		
Transfer from Investment Grants Equalization Account		
1966	244,752	
1967	433,476	
		678,228
PROFIT BEFORE PROVIDING FOR TAXATION		9,508,436
Deduct—		
Charge for Taxation		4,006,444
NET PROFIT AFTER PROVIDING FOR TAXATION		5,501,992
Deduct—		
Share of Minority Interests—		
Dividends Paid or Payable	359,943	
Retained in the Accounts of Subsidiaries	190,942	
		550,885
Carried Forward		4,951,107

	£	£
Brought Forward		
PROFIT OF THE YEAR ATTRIBUTABLE TO TATE & LYLE, LIMITED		4,951,107
Deduct—		
Amount dealt with in the accounts of Subsidiary Companies—		
Debenture Stock Sinking Fund	36,660	
General Reserve	60,000	
Losses less unappropriated profits	(343,474)	
		(246,814)
PROFIT OF THE YEAR DEALT WITH IN THE ACCOUNTS OF TATE & LYLE, LIMITED		5,197,921
Add—		
Balance brought forward from previous Account		33,313
		5,231,234
Transferred to Capital Reserve	—	
Allocated to General Reserve	1,350,000	
		1,350,000
		3,881,234
Dividends to Members Paid and Proposed—Gross—		
Preference	155,610	
Ordinary	3,668,120	
	3,823,730	
Income Tax deducted and retained	—	
		3,823,730
Balance carried forward to next Account		57,504

NOTES ON THE GROUP PROFIT AND LOSS ACCOUNT

1. TRADING PROFIT

There has been no change in the basis of valuation of stocks of sugar in the United Kingdom and Canada. In the United Kingdom a base stock of 300,000 tons has been valued at £23 per ton and in Canada 50,000 tons has been valued at £21 per ton.

The market price of raw sugar at 30th September, 1967, was £18 per ton.

The following items have been charged before arriving at the trading profit—

	1967 £
Audit Fee and Expenses	62,501
Depreciation of Buildings	790,407
Depreciation of Plant and Machinery	2,766,953
Depreciation of Ships, Tugs, Barges and Small Craft	1,305,251
Renewal of Plant and Machinery	1,774,291
	6,636,902

2. Sugar Industry Rehabilitation Funds

Of the total amount claimed during the year under the Sugar Industry Special Funds Ordinances of Jamaica and Trinidad a sum equal to 5 per cent of the amount claimed during the immediately preceding twenty years has been credited to Profit and Loss Account and the balance has been credited to Capital Reserve.

3. Charge for Taxation

	1967
Applicable to the profits of the period—	£
United Kingdom—Corporation Tax	3,252,953
Income Tax	3,161
Profits Tax	1,019
Overseas Tax	1,900,411
	5,157,544
Add— Adjustments (stated)	405,870
	5,563,414
Deduct— Adjustments (stated)	1,556,970
Net amount charged in Profit and Loss Account	4,006,444
The charge for Corporation Tax would have been greater, but for relief from Double Taxation, by	452,854

4. Dividends to Members Paid and Proposed

Preference—net	91,420
Ordinary—net	2,155,021
	2,246,441
Income Tax deducted and payable to the Inland Revenue	1,577,289
Income Tax deducted and retained	—
Gross Dividends	3,823,730

6. Foreign Currencies

These have been converted at the rates ruling at 30th September, 1967.

TATE & LYLE LIMITED AND SUBSIDIARY COMPANIES

BALANCE SHEETS at 30th September, 1967

	Notes	1967 Group £
CAPITAL EMPLOYED—		
Issued Share Capital of Tate & Lyle, Limited	1	39,075,200
Capital Reserves	2	11,136,660
Revenue Reserves	3	11,482,353
Investment Grants Equalization	4	999,671
Interest of Outside Shareholders of Subsidiary Companies		10,826,880
Debenture Stocks and Fixed Loans	5	30,928,361
Future Taxation	6	4,929,036
		109,378,161
REPRESENTED BY—		
Fixed Assets	7	95,914,332
Investments	8	6,873,571
Development Expenditure	9	1,337,510
Current Assets	10	63,948,546
		168,073,959
Current Liabilities and Provisions	11	58,695,798
		109,378,161

The Notes form an integral part of these Balance Sheets.

JOHN O. LYLE *Chairman*
F. H. TATE *Vice-Chairman*

NOTES TO THE BALANCE SHEETS

1. SHARE CAPITAL OF TATE & LYLE, LIMITED

	Authorized in Shares of £1 each £	Issued and Converted into Stock £
6½ per cent Cumulative Preference	2,394,000	2,394,000
Ordinary	43,606,000	36,681,200
	46,000,000	39,075,200

2. CAPITAL RESERVES

GROUP	Share Premium Account £	Debenture Stock Sinking Fund £	General £	Total £
Balances at 30th September, 1966	4,544,213	432,680	7,900,114	12,877,007
Transferred from Profit and Loss Account		36,660		36,660
Transferred from General Reserve			32,656	32,656
Transferred to Investment Grants Equalization Account			(446,293)	(446,293)
Capital Grants and net surplus on disposal of fixed assets			232,998	232,998
Adjustments due to changes in the Group			(94,855)	(94,855)
Amount written off Trade Investments			(199,725)	(199,725)
Adjustment for loss on termination of Chirundu Sugar Estates Limited including provision for contingent liabilities			(1,342,447)	(1,342,447)
Differences on Exchange			40,659	40,659
Balances at 30th September, 1967	4,544,213	469,340	6,123,107	11,136,660

NOTES TO THE BALANCE SHEETS—(*Cont'd*)

3. REVENUE RESERVES

	Future Crops Expenditure	Debenture Stock Redemption	General	Profit and Loss Account	Total
	£	£	£	£	£
GROUP					
Balances at 30th September, 1966	1,017,896	226,572	18,012,723	7,073,410	26,330,601
Retained Profit of the year			1,410,000	(319,283)	1,090,717
Transferred to Capital Reserve			(32,656)		(32,656)
Adjustments due to changes in the Group				(212,155)	(212,155)
Additional depreciation arising on sale of two ships at market value to partly owned Subsidiary Company			(440,000)		(440,000)
Differences on Exchange				26,265	26,265
	1,017,896	226,572	18,950,067	6,568,237	26,762,772
Deduct—					
Proportion included in Capital Reserves on Consolidation					15,280,419
Balance at 30th September, 1967					11,482,353

4. INVESTMENT GRANTS EQUALIZATION

	1967
	£
Transferred from Capital Reserve	446,293
Amount received in respect of expenditure during the year	1,231,606
Transferred to Profit and Loss Account	(678,228)
Balance at 30th September, 1967	999,671

5. DEBENTURE STOCKS AND FIXED LOANS

			1967
TATE & LYLE, LIMITED			£
Secured			
4½ per cent First Mortgage Irredeemable Debenture Stock			500,000
4¾ per cent Debenture Stock 1968/78	(a)		2,580,371
5½ per cent Debenture Stock 1980/85	(b)		4,666,162
Unsecured			
6¾ per cent Convertible Loan Stock 1985/90	(c)		10,554,300
FIXED LOAN	(d)		3,053,435
			21,354,268
SUBSIDIARY COMPANIES			
Secured			
3¾ per cent Debenture Stock	(e)		449,687
5¼ per cent Debenture Stock	(f)		2,000,000
Unsecured			
5 per cent Sinking Fund Debentures 1978	(g)		1,571,906
8½ per cent Guaranteed Convertible Loan Stock 1982/86	(h)	3,000,000	
Deduct—Held within the Group		1,447,500	
			1,552,500
FIXED LOAN	(i)		4,000,000
GROUP TOTAL			30,928,361

(*a*) Redeemable at the Company's option from 1st December, 1968, to 30th November, 1973, at £102 per cent; from 1st December, 1973, to 30th November, 1977, at £101 per cent and from 1st December, 1977, to 30th November, 1978, at par.

(*b*) to (*i*) Give details of the other loans.

6. FUTURE TAXATION

	1967
	£
Overseas Tax	156,043
Taxation Equalization Account, including tax deferred by accelerated capital allowances	4,772,993
	4,929,036

NOTES TO THE BALANCE SHEETS—(*Cont'd*)

7. **Fixed Assets**

	30th September, 1966 (*a*)	Additions	Disposals	30th September, 1967
LAND AND BUILDINGS				
Freehold	£	£	£	£
Cost	13,814,580	3,266,808	41,198	17,040,190
1948 Book Value	71,859		240	71,619
1956 Valuation	321,176		10,906	310,270
1962 Valuation	19,072,359		110,441	18,961,918
	33,279,974	3,266,808	162,785	36,383,997
Long Lease				
Cost	1,161,833	274,718	1,971	1,434,580
1962 Valuation	678,193		4,050	674,143
	1,840,026	274,718	6,021	2,108,723
Short Lease				
Cost	297,200	24,356	750	320,806
1962 Valuation	256,400			256,400
	553,600	24,356	750	577,206
TOTAL LAND AND BUILDINGS	35,673,600	3,565,882	169,556	39,069,926
Depreciation	3,913,852	792,552 (*b*)	22,852	4,683,552
	31,759,748			34,386,374
PLANT AND MACHINERY				
Depreciation Basis				
Cost	31,112,331	6,137,304	652,918	36,596,717
1948 Book Value	214,097		6,410	207,687
1956 Valuation	407,365		146	407,219
1962 Valuation	5,775,665		240,230	5,535,435
	37,509,458	6,137,304	899,704	42,747,058
Depreciation	15,075,414	2,860,032 (*b*)	560,663	17,374,783
	22,434,044			25,372,275
Renewals Basis				
Cost	1,934,370	672,857	147,798	2,459,429
Book Value	236,472			236,472
1962 Valuation	14,299,638		24,909	14,274,729
	16,470,480	672,857	172,707	16,970,630
SHIPS, TUGS, BARGES AND SMALL CRAFT				
Cost	10,243,339	70,576	32,115	10,281,800
1962 Valuation	7,148,667		579,432	6,569,235
1963 Valuation	2,981,896		144,500	2,837,396
	20,373,902	70,576	756,047	19,688,431
Depreciation	5,004,516	1,745,251 (*c*)	304,353	6,445,414
	15,369,386			13,243,017
ASSETS UNDER CONSTRUCTION at Cost	4,375,431	1,360,830		5,736,261
Other Assets at Valuation	241,367		35 592	205,775
TOTAL FIXED ASSETS				
Cost or valuation	114,644,238	11,807,449	2,033,606	124,418,081
Depreciation	23,993,782	5,397,835	887,868	28,503,749
	90,650,456			95,914,332

(*a*) These figures have been adjusted primarily to meet the requirements of the Companies Act, 1967, but also to take into account differences on exchange between 30th September, 1966 and 1967, and to exclude the assets of Chirundu Sugar Estates Limited which is not included in the 1967 consolidation.

(*b*) Includes £2,145 and £93,079 respectively which have been charged to Development Expenditure.

(*c*) Includes £440,000 provided out of General Reserve.

NOTES TO THE BALANCE SHEETS—*(Cont'd)*

8. Investments

GROUP	1967 £
Quoted—Market Value £1,567,900 (1966, £1,846,732)	1,729,822
Unquoted—Directors' Valuation £4,788,490 (1966, £2,342,782)	5,143,749
	6,873,571

Included above are Trade Investments with a Book Value of £5,662,386 (1966, £2,956,547)

9. Development Expenditure

Development expenditure will be written off against future earnings over an extended period of years when raw sugar production commences at Nakambala Estate, Zambia.

10. Current Assets

GROUP	1967 £
Stocks including Net Forward Commitments	30,819,580
Taxation on Stocks: Adjustment Account	(358,701)
Debtors and Prepayments	22,604,665
Future Crops Expenditure	1,520,471
Short Term Deposits	2,273,820
Notes and Bills Receivable	5,876,411
Cash at Banks and in Hand	1,043,074
Differences on Inter-Company Balances due to varying accounting dates	169,226
	63,948,546
Less: Current Liabilities (note 12)	51,815,572
NET CURRENT ASSETS	12,132,974

11. Current Liabilities and Provisions

GROUP	1967 £
Taxation	2,572,394
Bank Loans and Overdrafts	20,383,878
Short Term Loans	164,303
Bills Payable	6,660,592
Creditors and Accruals	19,092,585
Proposed Dividends—	
Outside Shareholders of Subsidiary Companies	7,324
Stockholders of Tate & Lyle, Limited: Ordinary—gross	2,934,496
Transitional relief under Finance Act, 1965	—
CURRENT LIABILITIES	51,815,572
DEFERRED LIABILITY	
Corporation Tax—payable after 30th September, 1968	3,032,356
PROVISIONS	
Replacement of Plant and Machinery	
Tate & Lyle Refineries Limited—net of tax	2,152,074
John Walker & Company (Sugar Refiners) Limited	272,196
These figures represent the excess, at 30th September, 1967, of amounts provided out of trading profits for the replacement of Plant and Machinery over the actual expenditure.	
Ships Surveys and Repairs	946,729
Contingent liabilities on termination of Chirundu Sugar Estates Limited	420,452
Pension Schemes	56,419
Following the establishment of a Sugar Workers' Pension Scheme in Trinidad £300,000 of the provision at 30th September, 1966, is included in Current Liabilities in 1967.	
	58,695,798

12. Assets Charged by way of security for Loans and Overdrafts

Bank overdraft and loan facilities totalling £588,204 to Rhodesia Sugar Refineries Limited are secured by mortgages over that company's industrial land and buildings and a collateral bond over movable assets. At 30th September, 1967, £340,063 had been advanced.

A loan of £35,003 from the Security Building Society to The Zambia Sugar Company Limited is secured by a first mortgage over certain of the residential property of that company.

NOTES TO THE BALANCE SHEETS—(*Cont'd*)

13. CONTINGENT LIABILITIES

There are Contingent Liabilities in respect of—

(*a*) Customs Bonds and Guarantees, Bills under Discount, and Guarantees under a scheme for purchase of houses by employees.

(*b*) The Guarantee of the principal plus a premium of 1 per cent and interest on the £5,000,000 5½ per cent Debenture Stock of Sugar Line Limited of which £2,000,000 is at present issued.

(*c*) to (*f*) list similar Contingent Liabilities under Guarantees.

(*g*) The uncalled liability totalling £49,900 on certain Investments.

14. CONTRACTS FOR CAPITAL EXPENDITURE

	Group £
Contracts for Capital Expenditure for which no provision is made in the Accounts are estimated at	**8,337,000**
Expenditure authorized by the Directors but not contracted for amounted to	**3,411,000**

15. FOREIGN CURRENCIES

These have been converted at the rates ruling at 30th September, 1967.

QUESTIONS

1. What are the requirements of the Companies Act, 1967, as to "fixed" and "current" assets?

2. How is stock and work in progress usually valued for balance sheet purposes?

3. The Companies Act, 1967, requires that certain assets, in so far as they appear in the books of a company, must be shown quite separately on the balance sheet. Enumerate these assets.

4. Say what you know of the legal requirements as to the signing and distribution of the balance sheet.

5. Whilst dividends may not be paid out of capital, there is, in fact, one exception to this rule. When is a company allowed to pay interest on its shares out of capital and who sanctions such payments?

EXERCISE 22

1. Explain as clearly as you can the meaning of each of the following terms, defining the distinction between each pair—

(*a*) interest: dividend;
(*b*) current liability: contingent liability;
(*c*) turnover in connexion with the 1967 Companies Act;
(*d*) reserve: provision (in connexion with the published balance sheet of a limited company). **(*R.S.A., modified.*)**

2. King and Town Limited have an authorized capital of £200,000 divided into shares of £1 each of which 125,000 shares have been issued.

The following balances remained on the books after the preparation of the profit and loss account for the year ended 30th September, 19. .

Share capital £125,000; debentures (secured on assets) £20,000; land and buildings at cost £30,750; goodwill at cost £10,000; share premium account £2,500; machinery at cost £80,580; provision for bad debts £1,620; balance with bank (*Dr*) £25,670; provision for dividend £12,500; general reserve account £26,000; debtors £81,700; creditors £79,950; profit and loss account: undistributed profit £25,600; provision for depreciation of machinery £21,830; stock on hand (as valued by officials of the company) £86,300.

(*a*) list the above balances in the form of a trial balance; and
(*b*) prepare the balance sheet of the company for presentation to the members.
(*R.S.A.*)

3. In the course of drawing up the balance sheet of a limited company you have to deal, among other items, with the following—

(*a*) an investment in a Government security, made with money temporarily in excess of requirements for working capital;

(*b*) a 25 year loan to another company with which your company has important trade connexions, but in which it holds no shares;

(*c*) a temporary loan to a company of which your company owns 75 per cent of the ordinary share capital;

(*d*) a contract between your company and another, signed before the balance sheet date, for the other company to supply yours with a quantity of valuable machinery, none of which had been delivered and for which no payment on account had been made.

State, as regards each item, the general heading, if any, under which it would appear and the wording you would use to describe it. (*R.S.A.*)

4. A draft balance sheet as at 31st December, 19.., shows the following items under the heading capital and liabilities—

	£
Reserve for depreciation	21,700
General reserve	70,000
Provision for doubtful debts	2,967
Undistributed profits	56,474

The ledger shows that—

(*a*) the depreciation reserve represents—

(i) depreciation of plant based on original cost, £16,700;

(ii) depreciation above what the directors consider necessary to replace existing plant, £5,000.

(*b*) the general reserve includes £20,000 premiums received on issue of shares;

(*c*) the provision for doubtful debts is made up of debtors known to be three or more months overdue in their payments;

(*d*) included in the undistributed profits is £25,000 being the difference between the book value on 1st January, 19.. and the amount of a professional valuation of the same date.

Redraft the balance sheet so far as these items are concerned to conform with the 1967 Act. State your reasons for making these amendments.

(*Cost and Management Accountants.*)

5. The following was extracted from the books of Corncrake Ltd.

TRIAL BALANCE, 31ST MARCH, 19.1

	£	£
Share capital, authorized and issued—		
25,000 ordinary shares of £1 each		25,000
Share premium account		2,000
Freehold properties, at cost less sales . . .	23,700	
5 per cent debentures (secured)		8,000
Interest paid	245	
Motor vans (cost £7,200)	4,320	
Debtors	9,880	
Gross profit on trading		22,350
Administration and selling expenses	11,630	
Directors' fees	3,000	
Balance at bank	7,880	
Carried Forward	60,655	57,350

	£	£
Brought Forward	60,655	57,350
Stock in trade, 31st March, 19.1	8,220	
Creditors		9,675
Profit and loss account, 31st March, 19.. . . .		1,850
	68,875	68,875

You are given the following information—

(1) The original cost of the freehold properties acquired by the company was £28,000. One of these properties (cost £3,000) was sold in May, 19.., for £4,300. The directors have decided that the remaining properties should be written up in the books to their estimated market value at 31st March, 19.1, £32,000.

(2) The interest paid (£245) represents the net amount, after deduction of income tax, of a full year's interest on the debentures and £15 interest on a bank overdraft.

(3) Provision is to be made for depreciation of the motor vans, at the rate of 20 per cent per annum, calculated on cost.

(4) On 1st April, 19.., the company had lent £2,000 to a director and the item "Debtors £9,880" includes £475 representing the outstanding balance of this loan.

(5) A reserve of £2,800, based on the profit of the year to 31st March, 19.1, is to be made for income tax, Schedule D, 19.1/.2.

(6) No dividend has been paid and none is proposed.

You are required to prepare a profit and loss account for the year to 31st March, 19.1, and a balance sheet at 31st March, 19.1, setting them out, as far as the information permits, in a form which is suitable for publication and which satisfies the requirements of the Companies Act, 1967, in respect of these items.

The profit and loss account should disclose no more than the minimum required to comply with the Act. In the balance sheet all credit balances representing profits legally available for dividend should be classified as revenue reserves.

Corporation Tax is $42\frac{1}{2}$%.

The auditor's report is not required. (*Institute of Bankers.*)

6. The following was extracted from the books of Beanstalk Ltd.—

Trial Balance, 31st December, 19.7

	£	£
Share capital, authorized and issued, 30,000 ordinary shares of £1 each		30,000
Share premium account		7,500
Plant, at cost, less depreciation to 31st Dec., 19.7 . .	8,000	
Stock-in-trade, 31st Dec., 19.7	17,600	
Debtors, *less* provision for bad debts	22,840	
Freehold property, at cost	35,000	
Profit on trading (after charging depreciation) . .		24,000
Profit on exchange, arising from the revaluation of a foreign currency		1,700
Creditors		25,200
Administration and selling expenses	8,750	
5 per cent debentures (issued, 31st Dec., 19.7) . .		5,000
Balance at bank	4,260	
Reserve for income tax, 19.7/.8		4,500
Interest on bank overdraft	50	
Bad debts (including £300 increase in provision) . .	600	
Directors' fees	2,200	
Profit and loss account, 1st Jan., 19.7		1,400
	99,300	99,300

The following matters are to be taken into account—

(i) The plant shown in the trial balance was purchased on 1st January, 19.., and depreciation has been written off each year at 10 per cent per annum on the straight-line method. In view of the enhanced cost of replacement, the directors propose to debit the profit and loss account of 19.7 with an additional amount of £2,000.

(ii) The item, directors' fees £2,200, is the balance after crediting the fees account with £1,000 for part of the fees for 19.6 which were waived.

(iii) During 19.7 the liability for income tax, 19.7/.8, has been agreed at £3,300. It is estimated that the liability for 19.8/.9 will be £6,300.

(iv) No dividend has been paid and none is proposed.

You are required to prepare a profit and loss account for the year 19.7 and a balance sheet at 31st December, 19.7.

The profit and loss account is to be divided into sections. The first section should be headed, "Not for publication" and should include all items, the disclosure of which is not required by the Companies Act, 1967. The rest of the account should be headed "For publication," and this, together with the balance sheet, should conform, as far as the information allows, with the requirements of the Act. The auditor's report is not required.

NOTE. Ignore income tax under Schedule A, and profits tax.

(Institute of Bankers.)

7. After the preparation of the profit and loss account of Red Tape Ltd. for the year to 28th September, 19.1, the following trial balance was extracted—

	£	£
Authorized and issued share capital (ordinary shares of £1 each, fully paid)		40,000
Share premium		3,000
Profit and loss account		7,800
Plant and machinery	19,200	
Stock-in-trade, 28th Sept., 19.1	34,350	
Trade debtors and creditors	21,600	33,400
Balance at bank	270	
Investments, at cost (£8,000 2½% Consols and 5,000 shares in X Ltd.)	8,780	
	84,200	84,200

(1) Depreciation of plant and machinery, which had been omitted from the profit and loss account, is to be charged at 10 per cent per annum, by the reducing balance method. The plant and machinery account is made up as follows—

PLANT AND MACHINERY

	£		£
Cost	36,000	Depreciation to 28th Sept. 19..	15,342
		Sale proceeds of one machine (cost £2,000)	600
		Loss on sale	858

(2) £5,000 (nominal) of the 2½ per cent Consols was purchased some years ago at 70, and the remaining £3,000 was purchased at the close of business on 28th September, 19.1, at 51. (Ignore brokerage.)

(3) X Ltd. was incorporated in September, 19.., and issued, at par, 12,000 shares of £1 each, 5,000 of which were allotted to Red Tape Ltd. Sales by Red Tape Ltd. to X Ltd. during the following year represented a substantial part of the turnover of Red Tape Ltd.

You are required to prepare the balance sheet of Red Tape Ltd. at 28th September, 19.1, in a form which complies with the requirements of the Companies Act, 1948.

The profit and loss account, comparative figures and auditor's report are not required.

Ignore taxation, dividends, and accruing investment income.

(Institute of Bankers.)

8. King & Lynn Limited has an authorized share capital of £30,000 divided into 20,000 ordinary shares of £1 each and 10,000 preference shares of £1 each.

The balances on the books of the company, after closing the profit and loss account for the year ended 31st March, 19.., were as follows—

	£
Ordinary share capital (10,000 shares issued)	10,000
6% preference share capital (10,000 shares issued)	10,000
Cash in hand	70
General reserve	7,000
Balance at bank	2,348
Debtors	10,605
Provision for bad debts	106
Stock on hand at 31st March, 19..	12,002
Profit and loss account—undistributed profit	5,606
Office furniture (cost £570)	450
Creditors	4,263
Plant and machinery (cost £5,256)	4,000
Freehold property at cost	4,500
Goodwill (cost £5,000)	1,000
Investment: 3 per cent British Guaranteed Stock at cost (market value at 31st March, 19.., £2,005)	2,000

It was resolved—

(*a*) that the dividend on the preference shares for the year to 31st March, 19.., be provided;

(*b*) that the balance of the goodwill account be written off;

(*c*) that a further £1,000 be transferred to the general reserve;

(*d*) that a dividend at the rate of 15 per cent on the ordinary shares be provided.

Prepare the balance sheet as at 31st March, 19.., for presentation to the members of the company. Ignore income tax. *(R.S.A.)*

9. The authorized share capital of the Excelsior Machine Co. Ltd. is £250,000 divided into 60,000 5 per cent preference shares of £1 each and 190,000 ordinary shares of £1 each: 40,000 preference shares and 60,000 ordinary shares have been issued and fully paid.

The balances on the books on 31st December, 19.., before the appropriation of the balance on the profit and loss account, are as follows—

	£	£
Preference share capital		40,000
Ordinary share capital		60,000
Freehold land and buildings	40,050	
Machinery and plant	112,176	
Furniture, fixtures, and fittings	4,832	
Premium on shares account		14,000
General reserve		26,000
Profit prior to incorporation		10,356
5% debentures (repayable after 19.2)		60,000
Carried Forward	157,058	210,356

	£	£
Brought Forward	157,058	210,356
Quoted investments, at cost	9,784	
Sundry debtors and prepayments	28,551	
Creditors and accrued expenses		11,203
Stock on hand, at cost	46,259	
Cash at bank	10,327	
Cash in hand	1,052	
Trade investments, at cost	5,000	
Provision for deferred repairs		2,786
Debentures redemption reserve		4,000
Profit and loss account		29,686
	258,031	258,031

The balances shown for freehold land and buildings, machinery and plant, and furniture, fixtures, and fittings are the net amounts after providing depreciation on the diminishing value up to 31st December, 19... From the accounts for these items it is ascertained that the cost of the assets now in existence was: freehold land and buildings £47,840; machinery and plant £232,980; furniture, fixtures, and fittings £10,570. No disposal of any of these assets has been made during the year.

The directors are of the opinion that the market value of the stock on hand and of the trade investments is in excess of cost. The market value of the quoted investments is £10,800.

Out of the profit and loss account balance it has been decided to—

(*a*) appropriate £8,000 by way of future tax reserve;
(*b*) increase the debenture redemption reserve to £5,000;
(*c*) set aside £5,000 against a possible increase in the prices of raw materials;
(*d*) pay a half-year's dividend on the preference shares and propose a dividend of 12 per cent on the ordinary shares (both dividends less income tax at £0·425 in the £);
(*e*) carry forward the balance.

Prepare for publication the balance sheet of the company as on 31st December, 19...

NOTE. Comparative figures are not required. A profit and loss account is not required. **(*R.S.A.*)**

10. On 31st December, 19.., a limited company owned machinery which appeared in its balance sheet drawn up as on that date as "at cost £97,300 *less* aggregate depreciation £51,770."

During 19.1 the company bought new machinery at a cost of £12,400 and sold old machinery which had originally cost £5,800 and in respect of which it had provided £4,900 (part of the £51,770 above) depreciation. The additional depreciation provided in respect of the year ended 31st December, 19.1, in respect of all the machinery in use at that date was £9,780.

Show how the machinery should appear in the company's balance sheet as on 31st December, 19.1, supposing that—

(*a*) the company wishes to disclose to its members information regarding additions to and disposals of machinery, and
(*b*) no more than the minimum statutory information is to be given.

(*R.S.A.*)

11. Show the entries that would appear in the published accounts of a limited company in relation to each of the following matters, at the same time indicating, as regards the balance sheet entries, under what general heading each would be included—

(*a*) an issue of 500 5 per cent debentures of £100 each made during the current financial year at an issue price of 96 per cent, the directors having decided that one half of the discount should be written off;

(*b*) 100 similar debentures held by the company's bankers as collateral security for an overdraft which amounted at the accounting date to £8,770;

(*c*) a guarantee limited to £20,000, given by the company as security for the bank overdraft of an associated company;

(*d*) a premium of £1,235 paid on a leasehold sinking fund policy, the surrender value of the policy (which is more than the aggregate premiums paid) being £13,200 at the previous balance sheet date and £14,850 at the date of the present balance sheet; (show the entries relating to the sinking fund as well as the policy);

(*e*) the charge against profits in respect of bad and doubtful debts of a sum of £770, of which £130 represents debtors' accounts actually written off, £240 is an estimate of actual doubtful debtors still standing on the books after the foregoing have been written off, and the remaining £400 is a precaution in order to bring in the debtors at a conservative figure. (*R.S.A.*)

12. You are accountant to a limited company which prepares accounts annually to 31st March, and which, on 31st March, 19.., owned machinery the aggregate cost of which was £17,800 and on which depreciation amounting in all to £8,450 had been written off.

During the year to 31st March, 19.1, new machinery was purchased at a cost of £1,900, and old machinery (original cost £1,350, book value at 31st March, 19.., £470) was sold for £590. Depreciation provided for the year to 31st March, 19.1, amounted to £2,360.

Your assistant, in the course of drafting the company's balance sheet as on 31st March, 19.1, set out the entry relating to the machinery as follows—

	£	£
Machinery, at cost per last balance sheet . . .	17,800	
Additions *less* sales	1,310	
	19,110	
Less depreciation	10,810	
		8,300

State with reasons whether you think this complies with the Companies Act. If, in your opinion, it does not, amend it. (*R.S.A.*)

13. Define the following and state how, in the course of audit of a limited company's accounts, you would deal with the items when they appear in the balance sheet for the first time—

(*a*) General Reserve;
(*b*) Plant Replacement Reserve;
(*c*) Debenture Stock;
(*d*) Capital Reserve. (*A.C.C.A.*)

14. The Companies Act, 1967, Schedule 2, requires that "any material respects in which any items shown in the Profit and Loss Account are affected—

(*a*) by transactions of a sort not usually undertaken by the company or otherwise by circumstances of an exceptional or non-recurrent nature; or (*b*) by any change in the basis of accounting," shall be stated by way of note if not otherwise shown.

Give four examples of items you would expect to find noted or shown in accordance with the requirements of the above paragraph. (*L.C.C.*)

15. The Directors of a manufacturing company which has incurred a considerable trading loss in the year to 31st December, 1962, propose to eliminate this loss by writing up the book values of the fixed assets, which it is contended appear in the books much below their current replacement values. Comment on this proposal. (*L.C.C.*)

16. The following is an extract from the draft Balance Sheet of Universal, Ltd., presented to you for approval—

1959			1960	
£	£	Fixed Assets—	£	£
163,000		Freehold Properties at cost . . .	163,000	
45,000	117,500	*Less* Depreciation to date . . .	49,000	114,000
390,000		Plant and Machinery at cost . . .	425,000	
128,000	262,000	*Less* Depreciation to date . . .	162,000	263,000
	379,500	Total Fixed Assets		377,000

The whole of the company's fixed assets have been revalued on the basis of the estimated present-day cost of those assets, reduced to take into account depreciation according to their respective ages.

The values of the fixed assets, on this basis, according to the report of the company's independent valuers are—

	£
Freehold Properties . .	225,000
Plant and Machinery . .	575,000

The directors propose to substitute these figures for those included in the draft accounts and ask you for your observations.

Submit your Report to the directors. (*L.C.C.*)

17. (*a*) Define the following terms used in the Companies Act, 1967—

(i) Reserve.
(ii) Provision.

(*b*) State, giving your reasons, in which of the above two categories each of the following items should be placed—

(i) The surplus arising on a professional revaluation of the company's properties.

(ii) The estimated cost of maintaining, for the remaining period of guarantee, machines sold during the year.

(iii) An amount, transferred from Profit and Loss Account, equal to a reduction in the agreed liability for taxation.

(iv) An amount, appropriated from profits, to provide for the increased cost of replacement of fixed assets. (*L.C.C.*)

18. At 31st March, 1964, Aybee Ltd., had an Authorized Capital of £35,000 divided into 10,000 7½ per cent non-cumulative preference shares of £1 each of which 5,000 Shares have been issued and fully paid and 50,000 Ordinary shares of £0·50 each, of

which 48,000 had been issued and £0·375 per share paid, the remaining £0·125 per share being due on 30th June, 1964.

In addition to any balances arising from the foregoing, the private ledger contained balances at 31st March, 1964 as follows—

	£
Stock on Hand at 1st April, 1963	14,200
Cash in Hand	50
Bank Overdraft	4,060
Purchases of Materials	67,280
Sales	97,650
Returns from Customers	420
Returns to Suppliers	240
Productive Wages	16,750
Net Cost of Tools used	476
Office Salaries	2,270
Sales Transport Costs	1,320
Rent and Rates	486
Insurance	480
General Expenses	286
Cash Discounts Allowed	360
Cash Discounts Received	240
Bad Debts Provision 1st April, 1963	220
Interest on Bank Overdraft	160
Freehold Land and Buildings, at Cost	10,500
Machinery at Cost	16,350
Trade Debtors	6,748
Trade Creditors	6,723
Goodwill at Cost	4,600
Accumulated provision for Depreciation of Machinery to 1st April, 1963	1,750
Loan to a Director	2,600
Directors' Remuneration	4,750
Undistributed Profits at 31st March, 1963	12,500
Reserve of Capital Profits	6,000
Preference Dividend for half year to 30th September, 1963 (less tax).	2,297

You are required to prepare a Trading and Profit and Loss Account for the year to 31st March, 1964, and a Balance Sheet at that date, after taking into account the following—

(1) A reserve for future taxation of £1,700.
(2) The dividend due on the preference shares for the half year to 31st March, 1964.
(3) Additional depreciation of Machinery of £500.
(4) A total provision for Bad Debts of £420.
(5) Insurance paid in advance of £60.
(6) Stock of Materials and Finished Goods at 31st March, 1964, £15,620.

(A.C.C.A.)

19. Discuss briefly the factors governing distribution of the profits of a limited company. The directors of a limited company, of which you are the auditor, seek your advice as to the distribution of surplus following a professional revaluation of their shop premises. Draft a report to them and include therein your opinion of the uses to which the surplus might be put.

(A.C.C.)

20. In what respects does the Companies Act, 1967, change the requirements concerning Directors' Reports?

21. From the information given you are required to prepare:

(*a*) the profit and loss account of AB Limited for the year ended 31st December, 1968, and balance sheet at that date in accordance with the Companies Acts 1948 and 1967 with the necessary notes provided to include movement of reserves;

(*b*) statement showing how the pre-tax trading profit was calculated.

Schedule "F" tax is to be ignored. Comparative figures and an auditor's report are not required. Particular attention should be given to layout.

AB Limited had an authorised capital of £1,200,000 in ordinary shares of £1 of which 900,000 were issued and fully paid and £500,000 in 6 per cent cumulative redeemable preference shares, issued and fully paid.

The trial balance at 31st December, 1968, is set out below:

	£	£
Ordinary share capital		900,000
6% Cumulative preference share capital		500,000
Share premium		132,000
Capital reserve		750,600
Retained profits, 1st January, 1968		605,000
8% Debenture (interest payable 30th June and 31st December)		500,000
Freehold properties	2,857,000	
Fixtures and fittings	303,000	
Stocks	826,900	
Debtors	355,300	
Hire purchase and other instalment debts	1,250,200	
Provision for unearned charges		127,400
Investments quoted at cost	180,400	
Investments unquoted at cost	60,100	
Cash at bank and in hand	185,300	
Creditors		781,000
Taxation		287,000
Sales		4,495,900
Cost of goods sold	3,253,900	
Wages and salaries	320,400	
Rates, repairs and maintenance	260,300	
Other expenses	38,400	
Directors' emoluments	15,800	
Income from quoted investments		9,500
Income from unquoted investments		3,200
Interest on debentures	40,000	
Preference dividend	30,000	
Provision for doubtful debts 1st January, 1968		46,100
Provision for depreciation:		
properties 1st January, 1968		427,000
fixtures 1st January, 1968		141,000
Suspense account		245,000
Provision for obsolete stock 1st January, 1968		26,300
	9,977,000	9,977,000

You are informed that:

1. On 31st December, 1968, the cumulative redeemable preference shares were redeemed at 102, and payment was to be made on 1st January, 1969. In addition there

was a bonus issue of £1 ordinary shares on the basis of 1 new share for every 3 held but no entries had been made in the books of account.

2. The freehold properties were revalued on 30th June, 1968, at £3,500,000 from which date depreciation was to be charged at the rate of 2% per annum but the revaluation had not been effected in the books.

3. The balance on suspense account was made up as follows:

	£
Proceeds of the sale of a freehold property on 1st July, 1968, which had been revalued at £100,000	120,000
Proceeds of first call of £0·25 in the £1 on a new issue of £500,000 second mortgage debenture @ 8½%	125,000
	245,000

4. The taxation balance was made up of £60,000 being tax equalisation reserve and £227,000 being the Corporation Tax on the profits for the year ended 31st December, 1967, which have since been agreed at £220,000.

5. The following provisions are to be made:

	£
Auditor's remuneration	2,500
Directors' fees	6,000
Doubtful debts	11,000
Obsolete stock	8,700
Corporation Tax on the 1968 profits (the tax equalisation reserve is unchanged)	215,000
Depreciation on fixtures and fittings	16,200
Dividend on ordinary shares (pre-bonus issue) of 15%.	

6. The market value of the quoted investments at 31st December 1968, was £196,000 and the directors' valuations of the unquoted was £57,000.

7. Capital expenditure commitments at 31st December, 1968, were:

	£
Contracts placed with suppliers	27,000
Authorised but not committed	32,000
	59,000

(*Cost and Management Accountants.*)

CHAPTER 23

COMPANIES: DEBENTURE REDEMPTION

FALSTAFF: I can get no remedy against this consumption of the purse. Borrowing only lingers and lingers it out, but the disease is incurable.

W. SHAKESPEARE—*King Henry IV, Part II*, Act I, Sc. II.

A DEBENTURE is an acknowledgement of a debt by a company, usually creating a charge on the undertaking or property of the company, bearing a fixed rate of interest, and either repayable within a fixed term of years or irredeemable during the existence of the company. Some debentures are convertible to shares at a later date.

The issue of a debenture or series of debentures is the most usual way in which a company borrows money for extending its business, apart from increasing its capital.

TYPES OF DEBENTURE

A debenture may be one of many types according to security, permanence, or priority.

1. As to Security—

(*a*) FIXED CHARGE, i.e. on specific assets constituting a mortgage to trustees with a deed of trust. In this case the company may not dispose of any part of the assets so charged or do anything which would jeopardize the security without first obtaining the sanction of the debenture holders through the trustee.

(*b*) FLOATING CHARGE, i.e. a charge on the undertaking as a whole. This does not prevent the company from dealing with the assets in the normal course of business.

(*c*) NAKED DEBENTURE. In this case the holders are given no security at all. Naturally, investors are not eager to lend money without security. In the past, under much more stable financial conditions, however, companies of undoubted standing have been able to borrow by this means.

2. As to Permanence—

(*a*) REDEEMABLE DEBENTURES. Debentures which are redeemable—

(i) by payment to the holders, either at par or at a premium, at the expiry of a specified period or at the company's option at any time within a specified period;

(ii) by purchase in the open market;

(iii) by annual drawings;

(iv) by conversion to Ordinary Shares (Convertible Debentures).

(*b*) IRREDEEMABLE DEBENTURES. As indicated by the name, no undertaking is given at the time of issue, as to redemption, in which case they are repayable only in the event of a winding-up or some serious default on the part of the company.

3. As to Priority—

Debentures may constitute a first or second charge on the property which is to be the security.

Debentures are also classified as—

1. DEBENTURES TO BEARER, that is, debentures payable to bearer, with or without power for the bearer to have them placed on a register or to have them at any time withdrawn from it. These are transferable by simple delivery.

2. REGISTERED DEBENTURES, that is, debentures payable to a registered holder with or without interest coupons payable to bearer. Any transfer of these must be registered with the company.

Difference between Debentures and Debenture Stock. A debenture is transferable only in multiples of its stated units. A person investing £10,000 in debentures might purchase 10,000 £1 debentures or 1,000 £10 debentures. In the first case he can sell his holding only in multiples of £1; in the second only in multiples of £10. If his holding were in debenture stock he may sell any part he wishes, even in *fractions* of a pound (unless this is specifically prohibited).

Debenture Interest is the interest usually payable yearly or half-yearly on the money borrowed.

Difference between a Shareholder and a Debenture Holder. A shareholder is an *inside* person, a member of the company; a debenture holder is an *outside* person, merely a loan creditor. A shareholder shares in the profits, getting a *dividend* on the money he has invested; a debenture holder receives *interest* on the money he has lent, charged as a working expense, even if there is not any profit.

This last point of difference is important and explains why debenture interest is charged to profit and loss account whilst dividends are debited to the appropriation account.

Generally speaking, a company wishing to raise fairly large sums of money has two main alternatives: (*a*) the issue of ordinary shares, and (*b*) the issue of debentures or preference shares. The reasons for choosing debentures are—

1. The security behind debentures is in itself an attraction and enables them to be issued at a lower rate of interest than preference shares.

2. Unlike shares, other than redeemable preference shares, the company can redeem them when it no longer requires the money. The alternative, a reduction of capital, is a costly business requiring the sanction of the High Court.

3. A lower annual rate of interest may be provided for by issuing debentures at a discount. They may then be redeemed at par on

the due date or purchased at a lower price on the market at an earlier date.

4. Redeemable preference shares are at a disadvantage compared with debentures, as the Companies Act, 1948, makes compulsory the raising and maintaining of a capital redemption reserve fund when they are repaid out of profits. This means that the profits so set aside are permanently capitalized.

5. Since preference shares are paid dividends, the company pays out of profits after Corporation tax. The company must therefore earn more to meet preference dividends than to meet debenture interest, which is deducted before Corporation tax is calculated.

It has already been stated that interest on debentures must be paid irrespective of whether or not there are sufficient profits, and this may sometimes be a disadvantage to the company. In fact, it may even lead to the appointment of a receiver for the debenture holders. One method of overcoming this difficulty is by the issue of income debentures still providing the holder with security but upon which interest is payable only if there are sufficient profits.

REDEMPTION OF DEBENTURES

There are four ways by which a company provides for the repayment of its debentures, and they are as follows—

1. Out of profits.
2. Out of capital.
3. By means of a sinking fund.
4. By means of an insurance policy.

Before proceeding to give the examples of the redemption of debentures, it must be emphasized that companies are empowered, under Sect. 90 of the Companies Act, 1948, to reissue redeemable debentures, but that the balance sheet of the company must give particulars of any redeemed debentures which may be reissued.

1. Out of Profits

Example 1

A limited company has a balance of £6,300 at the credit of its profit and loss account. Instead of declaring a dividend, it is resolved to utilize the profits to repay its £6,000 debentures now redeemable at a premium of 5 per cent. Make the necessary entries in the journal and cash book *and show the Appropriation Account.*

Solution 1

CASH BOOK

			£
		Debenture Holders . . .	6,300

JOURNAL

	Dr	Cr
	£	£
Profit & Loss A/c	6,300	
Appropriation A/c		6,300
Transfer of balance.		
Appropriation A/c	300	
Premium on Repayment of Debentures . .		300
Premium on repayment now provided.		
Debentures	6,000	
Premium on Repayment of Debentures . .	300	
Debenture Holders		6,300
Transfer of balances.		
Appropriation A/c	6,000	
General Reserve		6,000
Transfer of amount of profits equal to debentures repaid.		

APPROPRIATION ACCOUNT

	£		£
Premium on repayment of debentures	300	Balance	6,300
Transfer to General Reserve .	6,000		

Example 2(a)

A limited company has power under its articles of association to apply its profits in the purchase of its debenture stock in the open market and to cancel it. The amount standing to the credit of profit and loss account is £8,000, and to the credit of debenture stock account £40,000. The company's bank balance is £20,000. The directors decide to expend £8,000 in purchasing and cancelling further debenture stock, the market price of which, inclusive of all charges, is 92 per cent. Show the ledger accounts affected.

Solution

CASH BOOK

	£		£
Balance	20,000·00	Debenture Stock— £8,695·65 @ 92% . .	8,000·00

DEBENTURE STOCK

	£		£
Cash—		Balance . . .	40,000·00
£8,695·65 @ 92% . .	8,000·00		
Transfer to Reserve (profit on purchase) .	695·65		
Balance c/d . . .	31,304·35		
	40,000·00		40,000·00
		Balance b/d . . .	31,304·35

APPROPRIATION OF PROFIT ACCOUNT

	£		£
Transfer to Reserve . .	8,000·00	P. & L. A/c . . .	8,000·000

RESERVE ACCOUNT

			£
		Appropriation A/c . .	8,000·00
		Debenture Stock . . .	695·65
			8,695·65

The cash having, in each of the two examples, been paid away on account of debentures, it is not available to pay the profits by way of dividend, but the amount would be available for dividend if the company was in funds later, or for a bonus distribution in shares.

Treatment of Interest on own Debentures. If the company buys its own debentures on the open market, it will normally cancel them and interest will no longer be payable. However, some interest may have accrued at the time of purchase. The purchase of accrued interest allows cancellation of the claim for interest in the future. It is not a cost of the redemption. In fact, the cost of cancelling the Debenture capital is *reduced* by the amount of interest claim purchased and the profit on redemption is higher than it would otherwise appear.

Example 2(b)

If the interest accrued on the £8,695·65 of debentures purchased in example 2(*a*) is £400, show the ledger account for the transaction.

CASH BOOK

	£		£
Balance	20,000·00	Debenture Stock and account interest . . .	8,000·00

INTEREST ON DEBENTURES

	£		£
Cash (accrued interest on redemption)	400·00		

DEBENTURE STOCK

	£		£
Cash	7,600·00	Balance	40,000·00
(£8,695·65 at 92% cum interest)			
Transfer to Reserve . .	1,095·65		
Balance c/d . . .	31,304·35		
	40,000·00		40,000·00

RESERVE ACCOUNT

	£		£
		Appropriation . . .	7,600·00
		Debenture Stock . .	1,095·65

THE APPROPRIATION ACCOUNT

	£		£
Reserve Account . .	7,600·00	P & L account . . .	8,000·00

Note that the appropiration is reduced by the amount of accrued interest.

When at a later date, the interest on the Debentures is approriated, the interest account will be credited with the full amount accrued but the amount accrued on the redeemed stock will not be paid out.

Example 2 (c)

The Company provides for 10% interest on unredeemed Debenture Stock of £32,400 and for £400 interest on redeemed stock (up to the date of redemption). Show the entries.

APPROPRIATION ACCOUNT

	£		£
Debenture interest . . .	3,640		

INTEREST ON DEBENTURES

	£		£
Balance (accrued interest on redeemed stock) . . .	400	Appropriation Account . .	3,640
Cash (interest on outstanding stock)	3,240		

CASH ACCOUNT

	£		£
		Interest on outstanding stock .	3,240

Where a sinking fund is being built up, if the debentures have been acquired either out of the proceeds of sale of sinking fund investments or out of profit to the sinking fund, then, as such debentures will form part of the sinking fund investments, the interest will be credited to the fund exactly as though the investments were outside investments. The debit for such interest will be to profit and loss account.

2. Out of Capital

Example 3

A limited company issued £15,000 debentures at a discount of 5 per cent, repayable *at par* by annual drawings of £3,000. Make the necessary entries in the company's books for the first year.

CASH BOOK

		£	Year		£
			1	Debentures Redeemed .	3,000

LEDGER

DEBENTURES

Year		£	Year		£
1	Transfer from Debentures Redeemed . . .	3,000	1	Cash	14,250
	Balance c/d . . .	12,000		Discount . . .	750
		15,000			15,000
			2	Balance b/d . . .	12,000

DEBENTURES DISCOUNT

Year		£	Year		£
1	Debentures . . .	750	Year 1	P. & L. Appropriation	250
			1	Balance c/d . . .	500
		750			750

DEBENTURES REDEEMED ACCOUNT

Year		£	Year		£
1	Cash	3,000	1	Transfer to Debentures .	3,000

3. By Means of a Sinking Fund

The entries to create a sinking fund for the redemption of a loan are shown on p. 0625. As a debenture is merely a special form of loan they are not repeated here, but the student should revise the principles involved before going on.

The sinking fund entries may be summarized as follows—

1. *Debit* profit and loss appropriation account, *Credit* sinking fund account } with annual amount of profit set aside.
2. *Debit* sinking fund investment account, *Credit* cash account } with equivalent amount of cash invested.
3. *Debit* cash account, *Credit* sinking fund account } with interest received after the first year.
4. *Debit* sinking fund investment account, *Credit* cash account } with interest reinvested (this is combined with (2) above).

At the end of the funding period the entries are—

5. *Debit* cash account, *Credit* investment account } with amount realized on sale of investments.
6. *Debit* debentures account, *Credit* cash account } with cash paid on the redemption of the debentures.

This still leaves the sinking fund balance which is now available for dividends and is, therefore, transferred to general reserve—

Debit sinking fund account, *Credit* general reserve account } with accumulated provisions.

In addition, the following problems may arise—

(i) The debentures may have been issued at a discount; this must be written off at some stage.

(ii) The debentures may be redeemed at a premium.

(iii) Investments may be realized at a profit or a loss.

(iv) The debentures may not be paid off in cash: shares of equivalent value may be issued.

This problem is similar to that of convertible loan stock (see p. 2015).

(*a*) **Writing off Discount on Redeemable Debentures.** This may be done—

(*a*) By writing off a fixed amount annually over the life of the debentures.

(*b*) By writing off discount proportional to the outstanding debt at the end of the year.

Example 4. Method (a)

X Ltd. issues £20,000 5 per cent debentures at a discount of 2½ per cent repayable annually over five years.

5% DEBENTURES

		£			£
Year 1 (close)	Cash	4,000	Year 1 (start)	Cash	19,500
	Balance c/d	16,000		Debenture Discount	500
		20,000			20,000
Year 2 (close)	Cash	4,000	Year 2 (start)	Balance b/d	16,000
	Balance b/d	12,000			
		16,000			16,000
			Year 3	Balance b/d (and so on.)	12,000

DEBENTURE DISCOUNT

		£			£
Year 1 (start)	5% Debentures	500	Year 1 (close)	P. & L. A/c	100
				Balance c/d	400
		500			500
Year 2 (start)	Balance b/d	400	Year 2 (close)	P. & L. A/c	100
				Balance	300
		400			400
Year 3 (start)	Balance	300			

and so on to the end of the life of the debentures.

Example 4. Method (b)

In this case, the amount to be written off is calculated—

Year	*Amount outstanding* £		*Proportion*		£
1	20,000	=	$\frac{20,000}{60,000} \times 500$	=	166·67
2	16,000	=	$\frac{16,000}{60,000} \times 500$	=	133·33
3	12,000	=	$\frac{12,000}{60,000} \times 500$	=	100·00
4	8,000	=	$\frac{8,000}{60,000} \times 500$	=	66·67
5	4,000	=	$\frac{4,000}{60,000} \times 500$	=	33·33
	60,000				500·00

(*b*) Redemption of Debentures at a Premium—

Example 5

£50,000 5 per cent debentures redeemable at 6 per cent premium, all of which were redeemed at the end of ten years.

5% Debentures

		£			£
Year 10	Cash	53,000	Years 1–10	Balance . . .	50,000
			Year 10	Premium on Redemption	3,000

Premium on Redemption of Debentures

		£			
Year 10	5% Debentures . .	3,000			

Although this is called a premium, it is an *expense* to the company. It is a premium *paid*, *not* (as in the case of a share premium) a premium *received*. This premium may be written off to profit and loss account or written off against reserves (to which the sinking fund, if any, will have been transferred).

(*c*) **Loss on Realization of Investments.** Changes in stock market prices may considerably affect the amount actually realized when the investment is sold. Whilst these profits or losses are of a non-trading or capital nature, they can be used quite freely in any way the directors may decide.

As they arise out of the sinking fund, however, it is best to combine them with that fund.

Example 6

Investments on a sinking fund of £10,000, realized at a loss of £500.

SINKING FUND INVESTMENTS ACCOUNT

	£		£
Balance	10,000	Cash	9,500
		Loss transferred to Sinking Fund	500
	10,000		10,000

SINKING FUND ACCOUNT

	£		£
Sinking Fund Investments . .	500	Balance	10,000
Balance transferred to General Reserve	9,500		
	10,000		10,000

If a profit was made the entries would be—

Debit sinking fund investments account } with profit made on
Credit sinking fund account } realization.

(*d*) Shares of Equivalent Value issued to Redeem Debentures—

Example 7

At the end of ten years, X Ltd. redeem £10,000 5 per cent debentures at a premium of 5 per cent, meeting the price entirely by the issue of its own £1 ordinary shares, which have a market value of £1·25.

It should be noted that there are two premiums here—

(*a*) Five per cent premium paid on redeeming the debentures;
(*b*) Twenty-five pence premium received on issuing the shares.

5% DEBENTURES

Year		£	Years		£
10	Ordinary Share Capital .	8,400	1–10	Balance . . .	10,000
	Share Premiums . .	2,100	Year		
			10	Premium on Redemption of Debentures .	500
		10,500			10,500

£1 ORDINARY SHARE CAPITAL

			Years		£
			1–10	Balance . . .	—
			Year		
			10	5% Debentures . .	8,400

PREMIUM ON SHARES

			Year		£
			10	5% Debentures . .	2,100

PREMIUM ON REDEMPTION OF DEBENTURES

Year		£			
10	5% Debentures . .	500			

The premium is calculated as follows—

	£
Nominal value of debentures to be redeemed	10,000
5% premium payable on redemption	500
Total value of shares to be issued	10,500

Value of £1 shares is £1·25 of which—

	£
£1 (or $\frac{4}{5}$) is nominal value ($\frac{4}{5}$ of £10,500)	8,400
£0·25 ($\frac{1}{5}$) is premium ($\frac{1}{5}$ of £10,500)	2,100
	10,500

4, By Means of an Insurance Policy

This is very similar to the sinking fund method but, unlike that, there is no interest receivable during the period. Of course, the premiums payable total less than the amount obtained at the end of the policy's life and the difference is, in fact, the interest earned (with bonuses). The advantage is that it is safe, and the sum required is assured when it is needed. Many policies also pay substantial bonuses. On the other hand, a loss will be suffered if the policy is surrendered before its term is up.

Example 8

Ushant Ltd. issue 10,000 5 per cent debentures on 1st January, 19. ., the terms of which include that the company must provide a sinking fund for redemption on 31st December, 19.3 (three years later). The directors decide to take out an insurance policy to provide the necessary cash, the annual premium being £3,141·07, on which the return is 3 per cent per annum compound interest. Show ledger accounts.

5% Debentures

		£			£
Year 3 (end)	Cash	10,000·00	Year 1 (start)	Cash	10,000·00

Cash (*re* Redemption)

		£			£
Year 3 (end)	Debenture Redemption Policy	10,000·00	Year 3 (end)	5% Debentures . .	10,000·00

Debenture[1] Redemption Account

		£			£
			Year 1 (end)	P. & L. Appropriation	3,141·07
				Debenture Redemption Policy—Interest at 3% p.a. on £3,141·07 for one year . . .	94·23
					3,235·30
			2 (end)	P. & L. Appropriation	3,141·07
				Debenture Redemption Policy—Interest at 3% p.a. on £6,376·38 for one year . . .	191·30
					6,567·67
Year 3 (end)	General Reserve . .	10,000·00	3 (end)	P. & L. Appropriation	3,141·07
				Debenture Redemption Policy—Interest at 3% p.a. on £9,708·74 for one year . . .	291·26
		10,000·00			10,000·00

Debenture[1] Redemption Policy Account

		£			£
Year 1 (start)	Cash—Premium . . .	3,141·07			
	Debenture Redemption Interest . . .	94·23			
		3,235·30			
Year 2 (start)	Cash—Premium . . .	3,141·07			
	Debenture Redemption Interest . . .	191·30			
		6,567·67			
Year 3 (start)	Cash—Premium . . .	3,141·07	Year 3 (end)	Cash	10,000·00
	Debenture Redemption Interest . . .	291·26			
		10,000·00			10,000·00

These accounts will be balanced off yearly in the usual way.

CONVERSION INTO NEW DEBENTURES

When a company finds it necessary to borrow money at a time when interest rates are high, it is obviously the duty of the directors to relieve the company of this heavy burden, if and when, at some later date, rates become lower. Assuming that the company has power to redeem during the life of the debentures, the method adopted will be to redeem them out of the proceeds of a further issue carrying a lower rate of interest. The book-keeping entries in this case are merely the entries appertaining to (*a*) the redemption of debentures followed by those required for (*b*) an issue of debentures.

CONVERSION OF DEBENTURES INTO SHARES

It will be remembered that whilst debentures may be issued at a discount, shares can be so issued only in special circumstances. (Sect. 57, Companies Act, 1948.)

The courts will not permit the evasion of this restriction by the conversion into an equal number of fully-paid shares, of debentures previously issued at a discount. But even when debentures have not become repayable, they may be converted into the same number of shares (representing the nominal value of the debentures) if they are partly paid to the extent of the cash originally paid for the debentures, or even into fully-paid shares on a basis that their number is in the same proportion that the cash paid on the original debentures bore to their nominal value.

Example 9

A company issued £10,000 debentures at 95. On what basis can they be converted into shares?

1. If they have become due for repayment, 10,000 shares of £1 each fully paid may be issued in exchange.

2. 9,500 shares of £1 each fully paid (i.e. 19 shares of £1 each fully paid for £20 debentures) or 10,000 shares of £1 each £0·95 paid (i.e. one share of £1 each, £0·95 paid for every £1 debenture) if such debentures have not reached maturity.

A full treatment of the entries for convertible loan stock will be found on p. 2015 *et seq*.

A premium received on issue of debentures is legally available for distribution as dividends unless prohibited by the articles. Although this is the case the practice is not considered sound finance.

DEBENTURES ISSUED TO A BANK

The entries in connexion with the issue of debentures have already been considered in a previous section in so far as they are issued in the normal way, and irrespective of the type of debenture. There is one further type which it is essential to deal with for examination purposes. A company does not always need to raise money on debentures if it has a good sound financial foundation, as it is then a comparatively simple matter to obtain a bank overdraft. Many of these overdrafts are granted without any security whatever, but where security is called for by the banker, debentures often serve this purpose. Such debentures are then said to be issued as *collateral security* for the overdraft or loan. A collateral security is one which can be realized by the party in possession in the event of the original loan not being repaid at the due date or other breach of agreement between the parties. On repayment of the borrowed money the collateral security is at once released.

Sect. 90 of the Companies Act, 1948, provides that debentures issued as security for a bank overdraft shall not be considered to have been redeemed by reason only of the account of the company having ceased to be in debit whilst debentures still remain deposited.

No entry whatsoever is made in the financial books in respect of such debentures, their existence being recorded simply by a note on the balance sheet under the liability secured.

Example 10

A. Co. Ltd. obtains an overdraft from its bankers of £10,000, giving as collateral security £15,000 debentures. The balance sheet will appear as follows—

BALANCE SHEET
AS AT..19........

	£
Current Liabilities—	
Bank Overdraft, N. Bank Ltd.	10,000
Secured by an issue of £15,000 debentures.	

QUESTIONS

1. In what different ways may debentures be redeemed?
2. Explain briefly the procedure at the end of the period when debentures are redeemed by means of a sinking fund.
3. Can a company issue perpetual debentures? Has a company power to reissue redeemed debentures?
4. Explain the terms "trust deed," "trustee for debenture holders," "floating charge." What are the particular advantages of the last-named?
5. What is the difference between debentures and debenture stock?
6. What is the relationship of a debenture holder to the company?
7. Briefly outline the advantages and disadvantages from the company's point of view of issuing debentures.
8. May debentures be converted into shares? If so under what conditions?
9. When are debentures issued as collateral security and what entries are made in the books and on the balance sheet?

EXERCISE 23

1. A company borrowed £18,000 on debentures, at a discount of 5 per cent, repayable *at par* at the end of ten years, and decides to provide for redemption by means of an annual sinking fund at 5 per cent compound interest. Show the subsidiary book entries, the ledger account affected, and explain the procedure at the end of the period.

The annual instalment required to produce £1 in 10 years at 5 per cent is £0·079504.

2. A limited company has a balance of £10,500 at the credit of its profit and loss account, and instead of declaring a dividend, it resolves to use the profits to pay off

£10,000 debentures, now due, at a premium of 5 per cent. Make the necessary journal and cash book entries and show the ledger accounts affected.

3. A limited company issued £15,000 debentures at a discount of 5 per cent, repayable *at par* by annual drawings of £1,875. Show the cash book and the ledger accounts.

4. The following balances stood in the books of a company on 31st December, 19..—

	£
5 per cent Mortgage Debentures	50,000
Debenture Redemption Fund	52,100
Debenture Redemption Fund Investments—	
£26,400 4 per cent Funding Loan	25,000
£28,000 3½ per cent War Stock	27,100

On 28th February, 19.1, the investments were sold (the Funding Loan at 110 and the War Stock at 99), and the debentures paid off at 102 together with accrued interest. The interest has been paid up to 31st December, 19...

Write up the ledger accounts concerned, ignoring brokers' charges.

Calculate income tax on the debenture interest at £0·25 in £. *(R.S.A.)*

5. Some years ago Z Ltd. made an issue of 5 per cent debentures, repayable by periodical drawings or by purchase in the market. Appropriations to a debenture redemption reserve have been made year by year. Interest is payable on 31st March and 30th September, and had been paid up to date. On 31st March, 19.., the debentures in issue amounted to £57,000 and the redemption reserve stood at £38,500. On 1st May, 19.., Z Ltd. purchased in the market for cancellation £2,000 of the debentures at a cost of £1,943 and on 1st December a further £2,000 at a cost of £1,871. Interest on the debentures remaining in issue was paid on 30th September, 19.., and 31st March, 19.1, and on the latter date £3,750 was transferred to the credit of the debenture redemption reserve.

Set out the ledger accounts recording the above transactions, excluding the cash book and ignoring income tax. *(R.S.A.)*

6. The following is a summary of the balance sheet of AB Ltd. at 31st March, 19..—

	£		£
Share capital (shares of £1 each) .	100,000	Fixed assets	114,000
Debenture redemption reserve .	25,000	Investment on account of debenture redemption, at cost .	24,000
P. & L. A/c	17,000	(Market value, £20,800)	
5% debentures (redeemable at a premium of 4%) . . .	30,000	Current assets	62,000
Current liabilities . . .	28,000		
	200,000		200,000

In January, 19.., the debenture holders were notified that the debentures would be redeemed on 1st April, 19... They were given the option of: (*a*) repayment in cash or (*b*) satisfaction by the issue of four shares of £1 each, fully paid, for every £5 of debentures.

Holders of £20,000 debentures elected to take shares, and the others were repaid in cash. The cash was provided by the sale, at the market value shown above, of a part of the investment, which produced exactly the required amount. All these transactions were completed on 1st April, 19...

Show the entries in the journal of the company to record the above matters and set out a summary of the balance sheet as it should appear on 1st April, 19.., after completion of the above.

Cash is to be journalized. *(Institute of Bankers.)*

7. A limited company in 1944 made an issue of 2,000 7 per cent debentures of £100 each. Interest was payable half-yearly on 30th June and 31st December, and the issue was repayable at par on 31st December, 1964. The company reserved the right, however, on giving due notice, to redeem the issue on any interest date after 31st December, 1956, at 105 per cent. On 31st December, 1957, there was a debenture redemption fund amounting to £108,500, represented by investments which had cost that amount. The directors gave notice to repay the issue on 30th June, 1958, in accordance with the terms of issue, at the same time offering the holders the right, instead of taking cash, to receive a £100 $4\frac{1}{2}$ per cent debenture and £7 cash for each existing debenture.

Holders of 1,400 debentures accepted this offer and the remainder were paid out in cash. The cash was provided by the company partly out of current funds and partly by the sale of a portion of the investments which realized £58,700 (book value £51,000). Set out the ledger accounts affected by these transactions.

The cash book entries are not required and interest payments are to be ignored. *(R.S.A.)*

8. On 1st July, 1957, Sparkes Limited issued 10,000 6 per cent debentures of £10 each at 95 per cent, repayable on 30th June, 1977, at par. £6 per debenture was payable on application and the balance on allotment. Interest was payable on the full nominal amount as from 1st September, 1957.

Applications were received for 15,000 debentures. All allotments were made proportionately, over-subscriptions being applied to the balance due on allotment, which took place on 31st August, 1957. All sums due on allotment were received by 14th September, 1957.

Assuming that the discount is to be written off evenly over the whole period, you are required to draft journal entries to record—

(*a*) the issue of debentures, and

(*b*) the charges to the profit and loss account for the year ended 30th June, 1958. *(Chartered Accountants.)*

9. Tarrant, Ltd., had issued £10,000 3 per cent Debentures. The Debenture Trust Deed provided that—

(1) A Sinking Fund for redemption of these Debentures was to be built up by annual appropriations of £500 which, together with any interest received on the investments of the Sinking Fund, were to be invested on 31st December in each year;

(2) Sinking Fund Investments could be realized at any time to purchase Debentures in the open market at or below par for immediate cancellation; and

(3) Interest was payable on 30th June and 31st December.

You ascertain that—

(i) At 1st January, 1961, £10,000 Debentures were outstanding;

(ii) The balance on the Sinking Fund stood at £1,450 on 1st January, 1961;

(iii) Sinking Fund Investments were realized on 30th April, 1961, for £195 (cost £180) and the proceeds were used to purchase Debentures of a nominal value of £200; and

(iv) Interest on Sinking Fund Investments for the year ended 31st December, 1961, amounted to £78 on which date the available funds were duly invested.

You are required to write up the ledger accounts for the year 1961, for (*a*) Sinking Fund; (*b*) Sinking Fund Investments; and (*c*) Redemption of Debentures. Ignore taxation. *(L.C.C.)*

10. In 1943, Northern Ltd. offered for subscription at par, £30,000 5 per cent Debentures, repayable at par on 31st December, 1962. Interest was payable half-yearly on 30th June and 31st December. The issue was fully subscribed and all expenses in connexion therewith were written off out of revenue during the first five years

of the currency of the issue. By the terms of issue, the Company agreed to set aside a minimum sum of £976 out of profits to form a Sinking Fund for the redemption of the Debentures, such sums to be invested in gilt-edged securities, together with any interest arising therefrom. On 31st December, 1961, the book value of the investments stood at £25,274, and on 1st January, 1962, a further £976 was duly invested. During the year ended 31st December, 1962, the net income arising from the Sinking Fund Investments amounted to £1,154, and this was set aside together with a further appropriation of £976, but these two amounts were not invested. At 31st December, 1962, all the Sinking Fund Investments were sold, realizing £29,700, and the Debentures were repaid.

Prepare the following on 31st December, 1962—

1. Debentures Account.
2. Sinking Fund Account.
3. Sinking Fund Investments Account.

How do you consider the balances of the two latter accounts should be dealt with after the above transactions have been recorded? *(L.C.C.)*

11. Omega Ltd. has outstanding £250,000 5½ per cent debenture stock, repayable at par in 1975, or on 31st December in any earlier year from 1955 onwards at a premium of 5 per cent.

The company has given notice to repay the debentures on 31st December, 1959, at the premium stated above, and has arranged to finance the repayment partly by making an issue of £200,000 new 4½ per cent debentures at a discount of 2 per cent, finding the balance of cash out of its existing resources. In allotting the new debentures, preference is to be given to holders of the existing debentures up to the nominal value of debentures now held: applications from other persons are to be accompanied by a remittance of 10 per cent, the balance of 88 per cent being payable on allotment.

The lists were closed on 20th December, by which date conversion applications had been received from holders of £105,000 of the existing debentures and cash applications for £172,000. The conversion applications were accepted in full: as regards the cash applicants, applications for £34,000 were refused and the application money returned on 22nd December, while the remainder were suitably scaled down. All allotment money due was received by 31st December, on which day the company repaid the amount due to the old debenture holders who had not converted, as well as the cash differences due to those who had converted.

Show the ledger accounts and cash book entries recording these transactions. (Interest is to be ignored.) *(Chartered Institute of Secretaries.)*

12. The books of the British Manufacturing Co. Ltd., at the end of its first year's business on 31st December, showed the following balances, the stock-in-trade at that date amounting to £6,000.

	£		£
Share capital	40,000	Discounts *Dr.*	200
5% debenture stock . . .	10,000	Preliminary expenses . .	500
Interest on debenture stock paid		Purchases	49,000
less tax	475	Sales	70,000
Buildings (cost £27,000) . .	20,000	Wages	15,000
Machinery (cost £32,500) . .	25,000	Cash in hand	3,525
Office and general repairs . .	1,500	Debtors	6,000
Directors' Fees	300	Creditors	1,500

Write off preliminary expenses £500; depreciation on buildings £400; and on machinery £1,000. Prepare a trading and profit and loss account for the year ended 31st December. *(Chartered Accountants.)*

13. A company made an issue of £100,000 debenture stock, secured by trust deed on all the fixed and floating assets of the company. Of this amount £50,000 was

subscribed at a premium of £2 per cent, £30,000 was subscribed at par, and £20,000 was issued to the company's bankers by way of collateral security for a loan of £15,000. Give the entries which should appear in the company's balance sheet to record these transactions. *(Chartered Accountants.)*

14. Premiums on shares of a company having been carried to a reserve fund, a portion in a bad year's trading is transferred to profit and loss account in order to pay its preference dividend. Would you see any objection to this course? *(Chartered Accountants.)*

15. A company is about to repay its £300,000 7 per cent debentures at par. The debenture holders have the option of converting into an equal amount of 6 per cent debentures repayable by annual drawings over ten years at 104. The holders of £200,000 7 per cent debentures exercise their option. The company offers the remaining 6 per cent debentures to the public who apply for £200,000 nominal. Applications for £50,000 nominal are from existing debenture holders. The terms of issue of the debentures to the public are 25 per cent on application, 25 per cent on allotment, and two calls of 25 per cent each. Allotment is made in full to existing holders; no allotment is made to applicants for £500 and less (these amount to £25,000 nominal); other allotments are made *pro rata*.

You are required to journalize the whole of these transactions (including cash) up to the final repayment of the 6 per cent debentures. The ten yearly repayments may be shown as one repayment. *(Cost and Management Accountants.)*

16. The following is the balance sheet of the Northern Iron Co. Ltd., as at 30th September, 19..—

	£	£
Assets—		
Freehold Land, at cost		20,000
Buildings, at cost	39,000	
Additions, at cost	2,000	
	41,000	
Depreciation	1,000	
		40,000
(*subject to mortgage, per contra*)		
		60,000
Fixed Plant and Machinery, value as taken over by the Company	140,000	
Additions at cost	17,000	
	157,000	
Depreciation	7,000	
		150,000
Loose Plant, Tools, and Patterns, as valued by the Company's Managers		50,000
Stock-in-trade, as taken and valued by the Company's Managers		80,000
Sundry Trade Debtors	110,000	
Less Provision for bad Debts and Discounts	5,500	
		104,500
Goodwill		40,000
Preliminary and Formation Expenses		10,500
		495,000

	£	£
Capital and Liabilities—		
Nominal Capital, £500,000 divided into 200,000 6% Cumulative Preference Shares of £1 each, and 300,000 Ordinary Shares of £1 each.		
Paid-up Capital—		
200,000 Ordinary Shares of £1 each	200,000	
100,000 6% Cumulative Preference Shares of £1 each	100.000	
		300,000
First Mortgage Debentures		75,000
Mortgage on Freehold Land and Buildings, *contra*		20,000
County Bank for Overdraft		5.000
Sundry Trade Creditors		60,000
Reserve Fund		20,000
P. & L. A/c		15,000
		495,000

Remodel above Balance Sheet in conformity with regulations contained in the Companies Act, 1967. (*Chartered Accountants.*)

17. Karnatic Ltd. has issued £500,000 of debentures at par on the condition that it opens up and invests a sinking fund. During the life of the fund the annual contributions have amounted to £485,000 and interest and dividends on the investment have totalled £9,975. Under the terms of the issue £50,000 of debentures have been purchased on the open market for £47,860, which was raised by selling investments (costing £37,556) for that amount.

The company is now exercising its option to redeem the rest of the debentures at 102 per cent, and the remaining investments are sold for £488,419.

Set out and close off the ledger accounts in which these transactions should be recorded. (*Certified and Corporate Accountants.*)

CHAPTER 24

COMPANIES: REDEEMABLE PREFERENCE SHARES

Shares. O mighty Shares! To set those blaring images so high, and to cause us smaller vermin, as under the influence of henbane or opium, to cry out night and day, "Relieve us of our money, scatter it for us and sell us, ruin us, only we beseech ye take rank among the powers of the earth and fatten on us."

CHARLES DICKENS—*Our mutual Friend*

As shown on p. 2001, the volume of Preference Shares issued in 1965–70 fell to 1·4 per cent of total capital issues. During the same period, there was a considerable amount of preference share capital redeemed.

The important restrictions as to both the issue and the redemption of a class of share which, like a debenture, could be redeemed and reissued, are contained in Sect. 58 of the Companies Act, 1948. The provisions, in so far as they affect the accounts, are as follows—

1. The issue must be authorized by the articles.
2. No such shares may be redeemed except (*a*) out of profits otherwise available for dividend, or (*b*) out of the proceeds of a fresh issue made for the purposes of the redemption.
3. They must be fully paid before they can be redeemed.
4. Where any such shares are redeemed otherwise than out of the proceeds of a new issue, there must be transferred from the profits to a capital redemption reserve fund a sum equal to the nominal amount of the shares redeemed.
5. The premium, if any, payable on redemption must have been provided for out of the profits of the company or out of share premium account before the shares are redeemed.
6. A statement must appear in the balance sheet, specifying what part of the issued capital consists of such shares and the earliest date and latest date on which the company has power to redeem the shares.
7. A new issue may be made to provide the money for redemption as if the shares to be redeemed had not been issued, and accordingly the share capital shall not for the purposes of stamp duty be deemed to be increased provided the old shares are redeemed within one month of the new issue.
8. The redemption of preference shares does not reduce the company's authorized capital.
9. The capital redemption reserve fund may be applied in paying up unissued shares to be issued to members of the company as fully paid bonus shares.

FORMULAE FOR BOOK-KEEPING ENTRIES REQUIRED ON THE REDEMPTION OF REDEEMABLE PREFERENCE SHARES

At Par	At a Premium	At a Discount	By an Issue of Shares for the Purpose
Debit Redeemable Preference Share Capital A/c. *Credit* Bank A/c. Cash to holders of.................. shares redeemed.	*Debit* Redeemable Preference Share Capital A/c. *Credit* Preference Capital Redemption A/c. For amount of shares being redeemed.	*Debit* Redeemable Preference Share Capital A/c. *Credit* Preference Capital Redemption A/c. For nominal amount of shares being redeemed.	*Debit* Redeemable Preference Share Capital A/c. *Credit* { (*a*) Cash. (*b*) Preference Capital Redemption A/c. } For amount of shares being redeemed. (*a*) If redeemed at par. (*b*) If redeemed at a premium.
Debit Profit and Loss Appropriation A/c. *Credit* Capital Redemption Reserve Fund. Transfer to Reserve of amount redeemed.	*Debit* Profit and Loss Appropriation A/c. *Credit* Preference Capital Redemption A/c (*a*). *Credit* Capital Redemption Reserve Fund (*b*). For transfer of premium to (*a*) and transfer of amount redeemed to (*b*).	*Debit* Profit and Loss Appropriation A/c. *Credit* Capital Redemption Reserve Fund. For nominal amount of shares redeemed.	*Debit* Profit and Loss Appropriation A/c. *Credit* Preference Capital Redemption A/c. Transfer of premium (if any).
NOTE The normal entries relating to an issue of shares will also arise when shares are redeemed by an issue of shares.	*Debit* Preference Capital Redemption A/c. *Credit* Bank A/c. Cash to holders of.................. shares redeemed.	*Debit* Preference Capital Redemption A/c. *Credit* Bank A/c. Cash to holders of.................. shares redeemed.	*Debit* { (*a*) Redeemable Preference Share Capital A/c. (*b*) Preference Capital Redemption A/c. } *Credit* Bank A/c. Cash to holders of.................. shares redeemed. (*a*) If redeemed at par. (*b*) If redeemed at a premium.
		Debit Preference Capital Redemption A/c. *Credit* Discount on Redemption of Shares A/c.	

The statement on the next page summarizes the book-keeping entries for the redemption of shares, and students are advised to study the formulae it contains.

The two outstanding points of importance to the examinee, the committing to memory of which is important, are—

1. If redeemed out of profits a capital redemption reserve fund must be created in a sum equal to the nominal amount of the shares redeemed.

2. If the shares are being redeemed at a premium, a transfer must be made from the profits or from an existing share premium account of an amount equal to the premium on redemption.

The term reserve *fund* normally implies the existence of equivalent, earmarked investments. However, it must be used because the Companies Act specifies it in this case, even if there are no corresponding investments.

Redemption partly from New Issue, partly from Reserves

Example 1

In 1955 the Turnover Trading Co. Ltd. made a public issue of 8 per cent redeemable preference shares of £1 each, repayable at £1·10 on the company giving six months' notice. 124,500 of these shares were subscribed and fully paid.

With a view to the redemption of the above in April, 1959, the company, having at the time a general reserve fund of £90,000, offered for subscription at par 75,000 6 per cent preference shares of £1 each, payable in full on application. 61,320 of these were taken up and allotted. Immediately afterwards the company redeemed the whole of the 8 per cent shares in accordance with the terms of the issue.

NOTE. Profits equal to the nominal value of the redeemed shares must be transferred to capital redemption fund only if they are not redeemed from the proceeds of a new issue.

The capital is still retained in the business—

	£
6% preference shares (proceeds of new issue)	61,320
Capital redemption reserve (equivalent reserve for balance) . .	63,180
Nominal value of 8% preference shares (redeemed) . . .	124,500

8% REDEEMABLE PREFERENCE SHARES

1959		£	1959		£
Apr	Cash	136,950	Apr	Balance	124,500
				Premium on Redemption of Shares A/c . . .	12,450
		136,950			136,950

PREMIUM ON REDEMPTION OF SHARES

1959		£		1959			£
Apr	Redeemable Preference Shares	12,450		Apr	General Reserve		12,450

GENERAL RESERVE FUND

1959		£	1959			£
Apr	Premium on Redemption of Shares	12,450	Jan	1	Balance	90,000
	Capital Redemption Reserve Fund	63,180				
	Balance	14,370				
		90,000				90,000

CAPITAL REDEMPTION RESERVE FUND

			1959		£
			Apr	General Reserve Fund	63,180

PREFERENCE SHARE APPLICATION AND ALLOTMENT ACCOUNT

1959		£	1959		£
Apr	Preference Share Capital	61,320	Apr	Cash	61,320

6% PREFERENCE SHARES CAPITAL

			1959		£
			Apr	Application & Allotment A/c	61,320

Redemption partly from New Issue, partly from Profits

Example 2

10,000 6 per cent redeemable preference shares of £1 each fully paid in A Ltd. are outstanding on 1st January, 19... This being the date of redemption, the shares are redeemed at £1·10 each. 4,000 ordinary shares of £1 each are issued at £1·05 for cash for the purpose of redemption. Show ledger entries, assuming that the balance of profit and loss appropriation account is £24,600.

6% REDEEMABLE PREFERENCE SHARES

19..			£	19..			£
Jan	1	Cash	11,000	Jan	1	Balance	10,000
						Premium on Redemption of Shares	1,000
			11,000				11,000

PREMIUM ON REDEMPTION OF SHARES

19..			£	19..			£
Jan	1	Redeemable Preference Shares	1,000	Jan	1	P. & L. Appropriation A/c	800
						Share Premium A/c.	200
			1,000				1,000

ORDINARY SHARE CAPITAL

			19..		£
			Jan 1	Cash	4,000

ORDINARY SHARE PREMIUM ACCOUNT

19..		£	19..		£
Jan 1	Premium on Redemption of Shares	200	Jan 1	Cash	200

CAPITAL REDEMPTION RESERVE FUND

			19..		£
			Jan 1	P. & L. Appropriation A/c	6,000

PROFIT AND LOSS APPROPRIATION ACCOUNT

19..		£	19..		£
Jan 1	Premium on Redemption of Shares	800	Jan 1	Balance	24,600
	Capital Redemption Reserve Fund	6,000			
	Balance	17,800			
		24,600			24,600

Redemption partly from New Issue, with issue of Bonus Shares

Example 3

A company issued 25,000 7 per cent redeemable preference shares of £1 each at par. At 30th June, 19.., the shares are to be redeemed at £1·10 a share, and for the purpose of assisting the redemption 15,000 ordinary shares of £1 each were issued at par. On the above date 1,000 of the redeemable preference shares had been forfeited for non-payment of the last call of £0·25, 800 of which had been reissued as fully paid for £0·60 a share. The balance of profit and loss account was £12,100 and the general reserve £3,000. On the same day as the redemption took place a bonus share dividend was declared of £12,500.

ORDINARY SHARE CAPITAL

19..		£	19..		£
Jun 30	Balance c/d	27,500		Cash	*15,000*
			Jun 30	Bonus Share Dividend Account	12,500
		27,500			27,500
			Jul 1	Balance b/d	27,500

FORFEITED SHARES ACCOUNT

		£			£
19..			19..		
Jun 30	Reserve	150		*Balance b/d* . . .	150

PREMIUM ON SHARES REISSUED

		£			£
			19..	*Balance b/d* . . .	280

PROFIT AND LOSS APPROPRIATION ACCOUNT

		£			£
19..			19..		
Jun 30	Redeemable Preference Shares—Premium . . .	2,480		*Balance b/d* . . .	12,100
	Capital Redemption Reserve Fund . . .	9,620			
		12,100			12,100

7% REDEEMABLE PREFERENCE SHARES

		£			£
19..			19..		
Jun 30	Cash	27,280	Jun 30	7% Redeemable Preference Shares Capital .	24,800
				P. & L. Appropriation A/c—Premium on Redemption . . .	2,480
		27,280			27,280

CAPITAL REDEMPTION RESERVE FUND

		£			£
19..			19..		
Jun 30	Bonus Share Dividend Account . . .	9,800	Jun 30	P. & L. Appropriation A/c . . .	9,620
				Reserve A/c . . .	180
		9,800			9,800

RESERVE ACCOUNT

		£			£
19..			19..		
Jun 30	Capital Redemption Reserve Fund . . .	180	Jun 30	*Balance* b/d . . .	3,000
	Bonus Share Dividend Account . .	2,700		Forfeited Shares A/c . .	150
	Balance . . .	270			
		3,150			3,150
			Jul 1	Balance b/d . . .	270

BONUS SHARE DIVIDEND ACCOUNT

		£			£
19..			19..		
Jun 30	Ordinary Share Capital .	12,500	Jun 30	Capital Redemption Reserve Fund . .	9,800
				Reserve Account . .	2,700
		12,500			12,500

CASH

		£			£
19..			19..		
	Balance b/d . . .	40,330	Jun 30	Redeemable Preference Shares—Redemption of 24,800 Shares of £1 each at £1·10 a Share . .	27,280
	Ordinary Share Capital .	15,000		Balance c/d . . .	28,050
		55,330			55,330
Jun 1	Balance b/d . . .	28,050			

QUESTIONS

1. What are the regulations governing the issue by a company of redeemable preference shares?

2. From the point of view of the book-keeping entries required, what is the main point of difference between a redemption of redeemable preference shares: (*a*) out of accumulated profits, and (*b*) out of the proceeds of a new issue of shares?

3. Within what time must shares be redeemed after the issue of new shares placed on the market for that purpose?

4. Why is the redemption of redeemable preference shares not looked upon as a reduction of capital?

EXERCISE 24

1. Redheads Ltd., has an authorized share capital of £150,000 and its summarized Balance Sheet as on 31st March, 1965 was as follows—

	£		£	£
Share capital—				
Issued and fully paid—		Fixed assets . .		75,000
20,000 6% Redeemable Preference Shares of £1 each	20,000	Current assets—		
50,000 Ordinary Shares of £1 each	50,000	Stock-in-trade .	35,000	
		Sundry debtors .	10,000	
		Investments . .	15,000	
	70,000	Cash at bank .	14,000	
Share premium account . .	17,000			74,000
General Reserve . . .	30,000			
Profit and Loss Account . .	20,000			
Sundry creditors . . .	12,000			
	149,000			149,000

The preference shares are redeemable at £1·10 per share and it was decided to redeem them on 1st April, 1965.

In order to provide the necessary funds for the redemption, the investments were sold and realized £15,200.

On 1st June, 1965, a bonus issue of ordinary shares was made, out of reserves, of nine new shares for every ten then held.

Give the journal entries of these transactions (including those relating to cash) and prepare the Balance Sheet as it would appear after the transactions had been completed. (*A.C.C.A.*)

2. A company had in issue 50,000 6 per cent redeemable preference shares of £1 each, which were fully paid. Under the terms of the issue, the company had the option of redeeming these shares at a premium of 5 per cent, and decided to exercise this option on 1st January, 19...

In order to provide £20,000 of the money required, a fresh issue of 5 per cent redeemable preference shares of £1 each (payable in full on application) was made and was fully subscribed.

The 6 per cent shares were forthwith redeemed, the balance required being provided out of profits.

Show, by journal entries, how these transactions should be recorded in the company's books. (*R.S.A.*)

3. A company had in issue 200,000 6 per cent redeemable preference shares of £1 each. Under the terms of the issue redemption was to take place on 1st September, 19... A general reserve of £125,000 had already been built up out of past profits. For the purpose of the redemption 75,000 new 5 per cent preference shares of £1 each were offered to the public at £1·50 payable in full on allotment. All were taken up and paid for. The 6 per cent redeemable preference shares were thereupon redeemed.

Show the ledger entries to record the above.

4. 6,000 5 per cent redeemable preference shares of £1 each fully paid in Semmonds Ltd. are outstanding at the 31st March, 19.. The shares, being due for redemption at that date, are redeemed at £1·10 each, the balance standing to the credit of the profit and loss appropriation account being £11,500.

You are required to show the ledger accounts in the books of Semmonds Ltd., giving effect to the above redemption. (*Corporation of Certified Secretaries.*)

5. The following is a summary of the balance sheet of A.B. Ltd. as on 31st March, 19..—

	£		£
Authorized and Issued Share Capital—		Fixed Assets	53,000
		Investments	13,000
50,000 £1 Ordinary Shares .	50,000	Stock-in-trade . . .	21,000
20,000 6 % Redeemable Preference Shares of £1 . .	20,000	Debtors	23,000
P. & L. A/c	17,000	Balance at Bank . . .	8,000
Current Liabilities . . .	31,000		
	118,000		118,000

The preference shares were redeemed on 1st April, 19.., at a premium of 5p per share.

To finance the redemption, the investments were sold on the same day for £11,000 and 8,000 ordinary shares were issued at par and paid up in full.

You are required to prepare a summary of the balance sheet on 1st April, 19.., after the completion of the above matters. Assume that the company had no other transactions on 1st April. Show your workings. (*Institute of Bankers.*)

6. The share capital of Tarran Feather Co. Ltd. consisted of 200,000 ordinary shares of 25p each and 30,000 6 per cent redeemable preference shares of £1 each. The company decided to redeem the preference shares at a premium of 15p each on 1st January, 1960, partly from the proceeds of an issue of 60,000 ordinary shares at

a price of 30p each, and the balance from its reserve fund. On 1st January, 1960, the balance of the reserve fund was £40,000, and that on the profit and loss account was £21,000.

Show the ledger entries necessary to record this redemption, and how the capital and reserves of the company would appear on the balance sheet after redemption had taken place.

7. A company offered for sale for subscription at par 300,000 7 per cent Redeemable Preference Shares of £1 each, repayable at £1·10 per share after 10 years. 249,000 of these Shares were duly subscribed and fully paid.

Ten years later, in order to provide part of the necessary funds, the company offered for subscription at par 150,000 6 per cent Preference Shares of £1 each, payable in full on application. 122,640 of these Shares were taken up and allotted, and the whole of the 7 per cent Shares duly redeemed.

Assuming that the General Reserve stood at £180,000 at the date of redemption, show the entries in the ledger necessary to record all the foregoing transactions.

(*L.C.C.*)

8. In January, 1952, The Overton Co. Ltd. offered for sale 150,000 7½ per cent Redeemable Preference Shares of £1 each, repayable at £1·10 per share after 10 years. 124,500 of these shares were duly subscribed and fully paid.

In May 1962, in order to provide part of the necessary funds the company offered for subscription at par 75,000 6 per cent Preference Shares of £1 each, payable in full on application

61,320 of these shares were taken up and allotted, and the whole of the 7½ per cent shares duly redeemed.

Assuming that the General Reserve stood at £90,000 in January 1962, show the ledger and Cash Book entries necessary to record all the foregoing transactions.

9. The following is the balance sheet of Excelsior Ltd. on the 31st March, 1966.

	£		£
Capital issued and fully paid		Sundry assets . . .	200,000
100,000 Ordinary shares of £1 each	100,000	Bank balance . . .	85,000
50,000 redeemable preference shares of £1 each . .	50,000		
Profit and loss account . .	60,000		
Sundry creditors . . .	75,000		
	285,000		285,000

Under the powers contained in its Articles the company resolves to redeem the preference shares out of profits at a premium of 10p per share.

Prepare the ledger accounts necessary for recording the transactions, and a summarized balance sheet showing the position on completion of redemption.

(*L.C.C.*)

10. On 1st June, 1964 a company has outstanding 15,000 6 per cent Redeemable Preference Shares of £1 each, fully paid. In accordance with the original terms of issue, these shares are redeemed at £1·10 each on that date.

In order to provide the necessary funds the company issued 40,000 Ordinary Shares of 25p each at 30p per share and £5,000 6 per cent Debenture Stock at par.

Show the ledger and cash book entries to record all these transactions, assuming that the company had undistributed profits of £24,000 on 1st June, 1964.

(*A.C.C.A.*)

CHAPTER 25

BUSINESS SALES, PURCHASES, TAKE-OVERS, MERGERS, RECONSTRUCTIONS

When bad men combine, the good must associate; else they will fall, one by one, an unpitied sacrifice in a contemptible struggle.

EDMUND BURKE

THERE are many circumstances which involve, for the purposes of accounting treatment, the sale and purchase of a business. This chapter considers a few examples.

GROUP ACCOUNTS AND CONSOLIDATION

In other circumstances, companies enter into continuing relationships which may create a group. These relationships involve the sale and purchase of shares in a company and they may also involve the formation of a new Holding Company. This chapter considers some examples and also the additional requirements concerning publication of the annual report and accounts laid down by the 1948 and 1967 Companies Acts.

PURCHASE OF A BUSINESS

Vendor, Purchase Price, Going Concern. In numerous cases a company is formed for the purpose of acquiring and working an old-established business. The person who sells the business to the company is termed the *vendor*, and the money paid for the business is called the *purchase price*. The purchase price is generally paid, partly in cash, and partly in shares. If the prospectus showed that the vendor was taking the purchase price wholly in cash, it would give rise to suspicions on the part of the public; it would look as if the vendor had little faith in his own business, and was glad to be rid of it. In a good business, therefore, it will generally be found that the vendor takes a large number of shares in the company, thereby fostering the confidence of the general public. The shares issued to the vendor may be valued either at par or at a premium, according to the agreement made with him. When such shares are allotted to the vendor they may be either fully or partly paid (usually the former). Sometimes, the business is taken over by the company as a *going concern*, i.e. exactly as it stands, all the assets including the cash, and all the liabilities, and without any stoppage of business. Sometimes, the cash of the old business is not taken over; sometimes, the liabilities are not taken over, but left for the vendor himself to discharge. These matters, however, are arranged by agreement.

Goodwill. A company usually purchases, not only the assets, but also the goodwill of the business, that is, the right to the good name and connexion of the business. In some cases the amount paid for goodwill is stated, in other cases it has to be ascertained. If the company takes over only the assets, then the goodwill will be the excess of the purchase price over the value of the assets. Thus, if the assets amounted to £10,000, and £15,000 was paid for the business assets and goodwill, then £5,000 would denote the value of the goodwill. If the company takes over both assets and liabilities, the difference between the assets and liabilities will show the net asset value of the business. The excess of the purchase price over the net asset value of the business will give the amount paid for goodwill. Thus, if the assets amount to £15,000 and the liabilities to £6,000, then £9,000 is the net asset value of the business. If the purchase price of the business is £13,000, then £4,000 would be the amount to debit to a goodwill account.

Business Purchase Account. In accounting for the purchase of a business, a Business Purchase Account is debited in the new ledger with the purchase price of the business, and the account of the vendor is credited with the same. All the assets, including the amount for goodwill, are then debited to their respective accounts, and the total credited to the business purchase account. The business purchase account is then debited with the total of the liabilities taken over, and the liabilities are credited to their particular accounts. When these entries are posted, the business purchase account will be found to balance; and all the assets and liabilities will have been brought into the books. It is possible, of course, to avoid these *three* entries and to show the transaction by means of *one* journal entry, namely, by *debiting* all the assets, including the goodwill, and *crediting* the liabilities and also the amount due to the vendor. Students, however, are so often confused when they attempt this method, that it is advisable to follow the business purchase account method for preference. Another very good method is to have *one* journal entry for the asset accounts and *one* for the liability accounts. This is very simple and leaves the vendor's account in credit for the amount due to him.

Formula for Purchase of a Business. The following detailed steps should prove useful to the student—

1. *Debit* business purchase account and *credit* vendor with the agreed purchase price.
2. *Debit* each asset, including goodwill, and *credit* business purchase account with the total.
3. *Debit* business purchase account with the total of the liabilities taken over, and *credit* each separate liability.
4. *Debit* vendor, and *credit* share capital account and debentures account, with the shares and debentures issued to him in part payment of the purchase price of the business.
5. *Debit* application and allotment account (or shareholders and

debenture holders account) with the amounts due from shareholders and debenture holders, and *credit* share capital account and debentures account.

6. *Debit* cash account with the balance taken over (if any) and the amounts received from shareholders and debenture holders; *credit* cash account with any sums paid to the vendor.

Example 1

A company with an authorized capital of £150,000, consisting of 75,000 ordinary shares of £1 each, and 75,000 6 per cent preference shares of £1 each, and also £30,000 debentures in bonds of £100 each, purchased as a going concern for £100,000 the business of Rowell & Co., whose balance sheet was as below—

BALANCE SHEET

	£		£
Capital	70,000	Freehold Premises	30,000
Sundry Creditors	15,000	Plant & Machinery	15,000
Bills Payable	5,000	Furniture & Fixtures	2,000
		Stock	12,000
		Book Debts	26,500
		Bills Receivable	1,500
		Cash	3,000
	90,000		90,000

The purchase price was to be paid thus: £25,000 in fully-paid ordinary shares, £25,000 in fully-paid preference shares, £25,000 in debentures, and the balance in cash. The remainder of the shares and debentures were offered to the public, and were all subscribed and fully paid up. Make the necessary journal and cash book entries, and show the purchasing company's balance sheet.

Solution 1

JOURNAL

		Dr	*Cr*
		£	£
	Business Purchase A/c	100,000	
	Vendors		100,000
	Purchase price of business as per agreement dated.........		
	Cash	3,000	
	Bills Receivable	1,500	
	Sundry Debtors	26,500	
	Freehold Premises	30,000	
	Plant & Machinery	15,000	
	Stock	12,000	
	Furniture & Fixtures	2,000	
	Goodwill	30,000	
	Business Purchase A/c		120,000
	Sundry Assets acquired as per Agreement dated.........		

JOURNAL (*contd.*)

	Dr	Cr
	£	£
Business Purchase A/c	20,000	
Bills Payable		5,000
Sundry Creditors		15,000
Sundry liabilities as per agreement dated...........		
Rowell & Co. (Vendors)	75,000	
Ordinary Share Capital		25,000
(25,000 shares of £1 each.)		
Preference Share Capital . .		25,000
(25,000 shares of £1 each.)		
Debentures		25,000
(250 bonds of £100 each)		
Shares and debentures issued as fully paid in part payment of the purchase price, as per agreement dated..		
Ordinary Shareholders	50,000	
Ordinary Share Capital		50,000
50,000 Shares of £1 each.		
Preference Shareholders	50,000	
Preference Share Capital . . .		50,000
50,000 Shares of £1 each.		
Debenture Holders	5,000	
Debentures		5,000
50 Bonds of £100 each.		

CASH BOOK

Receipts	Bank	Payments	Bank
	£		£
Balance	3,000	Rowell & Co.	25,000
Ordinary Shareholders . .	50,000	Balance c/d	83,000
Preference Shareholders . .	50,000		
Debenture Holders . . .	5,000		
	108,000		108,000
Balance b/d	83,000		

BALANCE SHEET

	£		£
Authorized & Issued Capital—		*Fixed Assets—*	
75,000 Ordinary Shares of £1 each	75,000	Goodwill at cost	30,000
75,000 Preference Shares of £1 each	75,000	Freehold Premises at cost	30,000
Debentures—		Plant & Machinery at cost	15,000
300 Bonds of £100 each	30,000	Fixtures & Fittings at cost	2,000
Sundry Creditors	15,000	*Current Assets—*	
Bills Payable	5,000	Stock	12,000
		Sundry Debtors	26,500
		Bills Receivable	1,500
		Cash at Bank	83,000
	200,000		200,000

CONVERSION OF A PARTNERSHIP INTO A LIMITED COMPANY

In law, what happens in this case is that the partnership comes to an end and the business is sold as a going concern to the new company.

The partners become shareholders and, probably, directors in the new company, but their relationship to the concern and to each other is fundamentally changed.

The entries in the new company's books will follow the example given above. The partnership books will be closed and the final entries will record the realization of the firm. Examples of partnership realization are given on pp. 1805–19, but in this case the problem of how to divide the shares and cash arises.

In the absence of agreement the fairest way is to divide the shares out first in the same ratio as profits and losses are shared, thus giving the partners the same right to any profit on the sale as if they had remained partners. The cash is then paid out to balance their capital accounts.

Example 2

R, S, and T, partners, share profits and losses in the ratio of 3:2:1. Their balance sheet at 31st December, 19.., is—

BALANCE SHEET
As at 31st December, 19..

	£	£		£	£
Capital—			Sundry Assets		10,650
R	5,500		Sundry Debtors	3,000	
S	3,000		*Less* Bad Debts Reserve	300	
T	2,000				2,700
		10,500	Cash at Bank		300
Sundry Creditors		3,150			
		13,650			13,650

They have agreed to convert the partnership into a Limited Company. The business is valued at £13,500, payable as to £1,500 in cash; balance in shares worth £1 each. The creditors are to be taken over by the company, as also is the cash at bank.

Solution 2

REALIZATION ACCOUNT

Date			£	£	Date		£
19..					19..		
Jan	1	Sundry Assets		10,650	Jan 1	Sundry Creditors	3,150
		Sundry Debtors		3,000		Bad Debts Reserve	300
		Cash at Bank		300		Purchasing Company	13,500
		Profit on Realization—					
		R $\frac{3}{6}$	£1,500				
		S $\frac{2}{6}$	1,000				
		T $\frac{1}{6}$	500				
				3,000			
				16,950			16,950

PURCHASING COMPANY

Date			£	Date		£
19..				19..		
Jan	1	Realization Account— Purchase Price	13,500	Jan 1	Shares	12,000
					Cash	1,500
			13,500			13,500

CAPITAL—R

Date			£	Date		£
19..				19..		
Jan	1	Shares	6,000	Jan 1	Balance	5,500
		Cash	1,000		Share of Profit on Realization	1,500
			7,000			7,000

CAPITAL—S

Date			£	Date		£
19..				19..		
Jan	1	Shares	4,000	Jan 1	Balance	3,000
					Share of Profit on Realization	1,000
			4,000			4,000

CAPITAL—T

Date			£	Date		£
19..				19..		
Jan	1	Shares	2,000	Jan 1	Balance	2,000
		Cash	500		Share of Profit on Realization	500
			2,500			2,500

SHARES IN NEW COMPANY ACCOUNT

			£				£
19..				19..			
Jan	1	Purchasing Company	12,000	Jan	1	Capital—	
						R $\frac{3}{6}$	6,000
						S $\frac{2}{6}$	4,000
						T $\frac{1}{6}$	2,000
			12,000				12,000

Example 3

X and Y trading in partnership share profits and losses equally. On 30th September, 19.., they sold their business to P Ltd.

Their balance sheet at this date was—

BALANCE SHEET

As at 30th September, 19..

		£		£
Capital—			Sundry Assets	16,350
X	£5,280		Cash	470
Y	4,560		Current A/c: X	500
		9,840		
Current A/c: Y		480		
Loan A/c: X		2,100		
Creditors		4,900		
		17,320		17,320

The purchasers agree as follows—

(*a*) To pay deposit of £5,000 immediately so that the firm could discharge its liabilities.

(*b*) To give £3,000 for goodwill and £15,920 in cash for the remaining assets (excluding cash which is not taken over).

(*c*) To pay interest on the balance of purchase price at 5 per cent per annum, full completion to be made on 31st December, 19...

X and Y are to be allowed interest on their capitals at 5 per cent per annum, and X to be allowed interest on his loan at 4 per cent per annum till settlement. Ignore tax.

Show accounts in the books of the vendors.

The items in italics (disposing of the balance sheet items) should *first* be inserted so as to commence "in balance."

Solution 3

Realization Account

19..			£	19..		£
Sep 30	Assets		*16,350*	Sep 30	P. Ltd.— Purchase Consideration	18,920
	Expenses		*?*			
	Profit—					
	X	£1,285				
	Y	1,285	2,570			
			18,920			18,920

Cash

19..		£	19..		£
Sep 30	Balance b/d	*470*	Sep 30	Expenses of Realization	*?*
Oct 1	P. Ltd.	5,000	Oct 1	Creditors	*4,900*
Dec 31	" " : Balance	14,094	Dec 31	Loan A/c	2.121
				Capital—	
				X	6,146
				Y	6,397
		19,564			19,564

P Ltd.

19..		£	19..		£
Sep 30	Realization— Purchase Consideration	18,920	Oct 1	Cash: (Deposit)	5,000
Dec 31	Interest on Balance— £13,920 at 5% per annum for 3 months	174	Dec 31	Cash: Balance	14,094
		19,094			19,094

Capital Accounts

		X	Y			X	Y
19..		£	£	19..		£	£
Dec 31	Cash	6,146	6,397	Sep 30	Balances b/d	*5,280*	*4,560*
					Current A/cs	785	1,765
				Dec 31	Interest on Capital	66	57
					Interest A/c— Balance	15	15
		6,146	6,397			6,146	6,397

Current Accounts

		X	Y			X	Y
19..		£	£	19..		£	£
Sep 30	Balance b/d	*500*		Sep 30	Balance b/d		*480*
	Capital	785	1,765		Profit on Realization	1,285	1,285
		1,285	1,765			1,285	1,765

LOAN ACCOUNT, X

19..		£	19..		£
Dec 31	Cash	2,121	Sep 30	Balance b/d	*2,100*
			Dec 31	Interest on Loan	21
		2,121			2,121

INTEREST ACCOUNT

19..			£	19..		£
Dec 31	Interest on Capital—			Dec 31	P. Ltd.	174
	X	£66				
	Y	57				
		—	123			
	Interest on Loan X		21			
	Balance: Capital Accounts—					
	X: ½	£15				
	Y: ½	15				
		—	30			
			174			174

NOTE 1. The order of payment should be carefully observed. If the balance of current account of X had still remained in debit after balancing realization account it would have been set off against his loan account.

AMALGAMATION OF LIMITED COMPANIES

In the years 1954–8 there were 292 mergers and amalgamations (involving £16·2 million) in the United Kingdom and this rose to 885 (involving £332 million) in 1963.

For a purchaser, an amalgamation may arise from the desire to diversify, the need to find an outlet for surplus funds; buying out a competitor; rationalizing production; marketing and sales rationalization or reducing research and development costs.

For a seller, estate duty factors often force a sale and joining a group may mitigate these; family dissension or illness may force a crisis and lack of a successor may persuade the founder of a business to sell out on retirement. A more common reason is the desire to expand, since joining a group may give access to new facilities.

The principal forms of amalgamation are—

1. FORMATION AND PROMOTION OF A NEW (PURCHASING) COMPANY to take over the assets, etc., of two or more existing companies, the latter being wound up on completion of the transfer. Alternatively, the new company may become a "holding company", i.e. it acquires and holds the shares of the existing companies, who retain their separate existence.

2. Amalgamation by Absorption, where one existing company purchases and takes over the entire business of another company, and the latter is wound up.

3. Amalgamation by the Acquirement of a Controlling Interest, where one company purchases not less than fifty per cent of the issued capital of another company, and both companies retain their separate existence. (This may mean a take-over bid.)

4. Share Exchange; two companies simply exchange shares in each other and there are no changes in the formal structure of each.

5. Reconstruction, which may be of two kinds—

(*a*) *External;* a new company is formed with identical objects but a new capital structure to replace an existing company.

(*b*) *Internal;* the capital structure is reorganized but without forming a new company. This is also called *Reorganization.* It may also include a scheme of capital reduction.

AMALGAMATION BY FORMATION OF A NEW COMPANY, THE OLD COMPANIES BEING WOUND UP

A striking example of this method of amalgamation was the combination of the British Motor Corporation and Leyland Motors Ltd. into The British Leyland Motor Corporation. The old companies ceased to exist, and the new company issued fresh stock certificates to the shareholders of the old companies in accordance with the terms arranged.

In the amalgamation of limited companies, it is necessary first to obtain the shareholders' sanction to the scheme of amalgamation and the sale of the assets to the new company; and then to appoint liquidators whose duty it is (*a*) to carry the scheme into effect, and (*b*) to wind up the vendor companies. The liquidators, however, really act as the vendor to the new company, from whom they receive the purchase consideration (usually fully-paid shares of the new company, but sometimes partly cash and partly shares or debentures). The cash and/or shares, etc., is distributed to the shareholders of the old companies.

Closing the Books of the Old Companies. The precise procedure varies in accordance with the terms arranged for the transfer of the old companies' businesses, e.g. whether the new company takes over the cash as well as the other assets and discharges the liabilities, etc., or otherwise. The following formula, which is expressed in general terms, may be found useful—

1. Open a business realization account, *debiting* this account with the assets taken over and *crediting* it with the liabilities transferred. The contra entries appear in the various assets and liabilities accounts, which are now closed.

2. *Debit* the new company and *credit* business realization account with the amount of the consideration, the balance of the latter account being

transferred to a sundry shareholders account. A credit balance indicates a profit on realization, whilst a debit balance represents a loss. In some cases, however, the net assets are taken over at the book values and thus neither a profit nor a loss occurs.

3. Open a shares account, *debiting* it with the value of the shares received from the new company. If the purchase consideration includes cash or debentures, additional accounts are opened as they are required.

4. Close the share capital account, reserve account (if any), and profit and loss account by transfer to the sundry shareholders account.

5. *Debit* the sundry shareholders account with the amount of shares, debentures or cash distributed to the shareholders and *credit* shares, debentures or cash account, as the case may be.

6. Where the old company retains its cash balance, discharges its liabilities, and pays its own expenses, these transactions are passed through the cash account, the expenses incurred being debited to the business realization account.

Fractional Certificates. Occasionally the allotment of shares in the new company involves the issue of fractional certificates. The solution of this problem is dealt with on p. 2121.

Distribution of Shares, etc., to the Old Shareholders. The liquidators of the old companies prepare a share distribution list, showing the names and addresses of the old shareholders, and particulars of their shareholding in the old and new companies. If fractional certificates are involved, or if the purchase consideration includes the issue of debentures or a cash payment to the old shareholders, additional columns must be provided for these particulars. A duplicate of this list is handed to the new company, and forms the basis of the allotment and entries in the new share registers, etc. (See illustrations on following page.)

New Company's Books. The entries to be made in the new company's books are as follows—

1. *Debit* each asset account, including goodwill, and *credit* business purchase account, with the total.

2. *Debit* business purchase account with the total of the liabilities taken over, and *credit* the separate liability accounts.

3. *Debit* business purchase account, and *credit* the liquidators of the vendor companies with the agreed purchase price.

4. *Debit* the liquidators of the vendor company with the total allotment of shares, debentures, or cash paid (as the case may be) in satisfaction of the purchase price. Shares capital, debentures or cash account are credited.

5. Where the new company obtains the benefit of any reserves or undivided profits, the business purchase account will show a credit balance as the total value of the assets transferred will be in excess of the combined total of the liabilities and purchase price. This balance should be transferred to the credit of a capital reserve account; it is not permissible to

use it for revenue purposes. Payments for liquidation or preliminary expenses in connexion with the acquirement of the business may be debited to this account, and the balance utilized for the reduction of goodwill.

6. If the combined total of the liabilities taken over and the purchase price is in excess of the total value of the assets, the difference is debited to goodwill.

7. In some cases, the new company makes a further capital issue to provide additional working capital. The entries required for such issue will be identical with the entries for new companies discussed earlier in the chapter.

SHARE DISTRIBUTION LIST

LEFT-HAND RULING.

Old Share Led. Fo.	Name		Address	Shares in Old Company			
	Surname	Christian Names		Old Cert. No.	No. of Shares	Distinctive Numbers From	Distinctive Numbers To

RIGHT-HAND RULING.

Shares in New Company				New Share Led. Fo.	Cash Payment		Remarks
New Cert. No.	No. of Shares	Distinctive Numbers From	Distinctive Numbers To		Chq. No.	Amount	
						£	

Example 4

The Bat Co. Ltd. and the Cedo Co. Ltd. agree to combine and form a new company under the title of the Batcedo Co. Ltd, with a capital of £300,000 in £1 shares to acquire their businesses. The sale contract provides that the new company is to take over the whole of the assets and liabilities of both companies, the consideration being the issue to the Bat Co. of £200,000, and to the Cedo Co. of £75,000 in fully-paid £1 shares, the latter company also to receive £7,500 in cash.

The new company is to pay the liquidation expenses of the Bat Co. (£900) and Cedo Co. (£600), and its own formation expenses of £1,800, these amounts to be charged against the capital reserve account.

The balances in the books of the vendor companies at the date of the amalgamation were as shown opposite.

	Bat Co.		Cedo Co.	
	Dr	*Cr*	*Dr*	*Cr*
	£	£	£	£
Issued share capital		150,000		75,000
Goodwill	25,000		10,000	
Freehold and leasehold property	95,600		45,280	
Plant and machinery	35,250		21,560	
Stock-in-trade	18,760		12,685	
Sundry debtors	12,655		6,525	
Sundry creditors		8,620		5,680
Mortgage on property				10,000
Bank balances	27,605		3,130	
Reserve		50,000		5,000
Profit and loss balances		6,250		3,500
	214,870	214,870	99,180	99,180

Assume that the amalgamation was duly completed, the mortgage paid off and the sundry assets of Cedo Ltd. were revalued and entered in the books of Batcedo Co. Ltd. as follows—

	£
Freehold and leasehold property	140,700
Plant and machinery	55,500
Stock	31,000
Sundry debtors	18,935

Prepare—

1. The liquidators' closing accounts for the old companies, and
2. The opening accounts and the first balance sheet of the new company.

Books of the Bat Co. Ltd.

The principal ledger accounts are as follows—

BUSINESS REALIZATION ACCOUNT

	£		£
Sundry Assets	214,870	Creditors	8,620
		Batcedo Co.	200,000
		Sundry Shareholders (Balance written off)	6,250
	214,870		214,870

BATCEDO CO. LTD.

	£		£
Business Realization A/c (Agreed purchase price)	200,000	Shares	200,000

SHARES ACCOUNT

	£		£
Batcedo Co. Ltd. (Shares received)	200,000	Sundry Shareholders (Distribution of shares)	200,000

SHARE CAPITAL

	£		£
Sundry Shareholders	150,000	Balance b/f	150,000

RESERVE ACCOUNT

	£		£
Sundry Shareholders	50,000	Balance b/f	50,000

PROFIT AND LOSS ACCOUNT

	£		£
Sundry Shareholders	6,250	Balance b/f	6,250

SUNDRY SHAREHOLDERS

	£		£
Shares Distributed	200,000	Capital	150,000
Business Realization A/c	6,250	Reserve	50,000
		P. & L.	6,250
	206,250		206,250

Books of the Cedo Co. Ltd.

BUSINESS REALIZATION ACCOUNT

	£		£
Sundry Assets	99,180	Creditors	5,680
		Mortgage	10,000
		Batcedo Co. Ltd.	82,500
		Sundry Shareholders (Balance written off)	1,000
	99,180		99,180

MORTGAGE ACCOUNT

	£		£
Business Realization A/c	10,000	Balance b/f	10,000

BATCEDO CO. LTD.

	£		£
Business Realization A/c (Agreed purchase price)	82,500	Shares	75,000
		Cash	7,500
	82,500		82,500

SHARES ACCOUNT

	£		£
Batcedo Co. Ltd. (Shares received)	75,000	Sundry Shareholders (Distribution of Shares)	75,000

SHARE CAPITAL

	£		£
Sundry Shareholders	75,000	Balance b/f	75,000

RESERVE ACCOUNT

	£		£
Sundry Shareholders . .	5,000	Balance b/f	5,000

PROFIT AND LOSS ACCOUNT

	£		£
Sundry Shareholders . .	3,500	Balance b/f	3,500

SUNDRY SHAREHOLDERS

	£		£
Shares Distributed . . .	75,000	Capital	75,000
Cash	7,500	Reserve	5,000
Business Realization A/c .	1,000	P. & L.	3,500
	83,500		83,500

Books of the Batcedo Co. Ltd.

BUSINESS PURCHASE ACCOUNT

(i) Purchase of Bat Co. Ltd.

	£		£
Trade Creditors . . .	8,620	Sundry Assets . . .	214,870
Vendor (Bat Co. Ltd.) .	200,000		
Balance (to Capital Reserve) .	6,250		
	214,870		214,870

(ii) Purchase of Cedo Co. Ltd.

	£		£
Trade Creditors . . .	5,680	Sundry Assets . . .	97,000
Mortgage	10,000	Balance (to Goodwill) . .	1,180
Vendor (Cedo Co. Ltd.) . .	82,500		
	98,180		98,180

VENDOR (LIQUIDATOR OF THE BAT CO. LTD.)

	£		£
Shares issued in Payment of Purchase	200,000	Business Purchase A/c . .	200,000
	200,000		200,000

VENDOR (LIQUIDATOR OF THE CEDO CO. LTD.)

	£		£
Shares issued in Part Payment	75,000	Business Purchase A/c	82,500
Cash—Balance of Purchase Price	7,500		
	82,500		82,500

SUNDRY ASSETS ACCOUNTS (EXCLUDING GOODWILL)

	£		
Business Purchase A/c	189,870		
" " "	87,000		

SHARE CAPITAL

			£
		Bat Co.	200,000
		Cedo Co.	75,000

GOODWILL ACCOUNT

	£	
Balance	35,000	**NOTE. The goodwill may be offset against the capital reserve.**
Business Purchase A/c	1,180	

MORTGAGE ACCOUNT

	£		£
Cash	10,000	Business Purchase A/c	10,000

CAPITAL RESERVE ACCOUNT

	£		£
Cash—		Bat Co.	6,250
Bat Liquidation Expenses	900		
Cedo Liquidation Expenses	600		
Preliminary Expenses	1,800		
Balance c/d	2,950		
	6,250		6,250
		Balance b/d	2,950

CASH ACCOUNT

	£		£
Cash transferred from—		Cedo Co., Mortgage paid off	10,000
Bat Co.	27,605	Cedo Co., Balance of Purchase	
Cedo Co.	3,130	Price	7,500
		Liquidation Expenses—	
		Bat Co.	900
		Cedo Co.	600
		Preliminary Expenses	1,800
		Balance c/d	9,935
	30,735		30,735
Balance b/d	9,935		

BALANCE SHEET OF THE BATCEDO CO. LTD.

	£		£
Authorized Share Capital, 300,000 Shares of £1 each	300,000	Goodwill	36,180
		Freehold & Leasehold Property	140,700
		Plant & Machinery	55,500
Issued Share Capital: 275,000 Shares of £1 each, fully paid	275,000	Stock-in-trade	31,000
		Sundry debtors	18,935
Capital Reserve A/c	2,950	Cash	9,935
Sundry Creditors	14,300		
	292,250		292,250

AMALGAMATION BY FORMATION OF A "HOLDING COMPANY"

This method is a variation of the preceding one; the old companies continue their separate existence, and the new company either—

(*a*) Purchases the shares of the old companies for cash, in which case the entries required are a debit to investment account and a credit to cash for the amount paid for the shares; or

(*b*) Allots and issues its own shares in exchange for the shares of the old companies. By this method, the entries required are a debit to investment account and a credit to share capital account.

Whichever method is adopted, the financial books of the old companies are not affected; all that occurs is a change of shareholders, and this change is effected by the execution of transfer deeds in the usual manner; the entries recording the transfers being made in the register of transfers and share ledger.

The new "holding" company makes a public issue of capital to provide itself with the necessary funds; the financial books recording this issue being written up in the ordinary way. Nominally, the assets of the new company consist of shares in the old companies, but, in reality, the "holding" company is the absolute owner of the old companies' businesses.

AMALGAMATION BY ABSORPTION

Where one company acquires the business of another, the latter company going into liquidation and its separate existence being terminated, the transaction is described as "amalgamation by absorption." Usually, the purchasing company acquires the entire undertaking, i.e. it takes over the whole of the assets and also discharges the liabilities, but in some cases, only the assets are transferred, the liabilities being paid by the vendor company.

A practical point which arises for consideration is that the vendor company's business may be a valuable one and the sale, consequently, results in a profit to the shareholders, such profit arising (*a*) from a higher price being paid for goodwill than the amount at which it stands in the company's books, (*b*) the reserves being no longer required, and (*c*) the market value of the purchasing company's shares (which form part of the sale of consideration) being greater than their nominal value. In some cases the market price of the shares may be at a discount, but as this probably will be taken into consideration when fixing the purchase price for the absorbed company's business, the absorption may still show a profit to the shareholders. In order to show the transaction in its true aspect, the vendor company should pass the shares received through its books at their market value.

With the purchasing company, however, different considerations arise. and the shares issued in payment (or part payment) must be dealt with on the basis of their nominal value. Thus, if company A, whose £1 shares stand at a premium of 50p per share, purchases the undertaking of company B, for £150,000, payable in fully-paid £1 shares, and the net assets acquired (i.e. the excess of total assets over liabilities) are valued at £230,000 the purchasing company apparently makes a profit of £80,000, as it acquires assets worth that amount in excess of the purchase price. The real effect of the transaction is, however, that company A issues shares of the total nominal value of £150,000 at a premium of £80,000, and the latter amount must be credited to a premium on shares account. The true intrinsic value of a share is not its nominal value but its market value, i.e. the price at which it may be bought or sold; and it will be seen that the shareholders of the vendor company receive, approximately, the true value of the assets transferred.

Generally, the purchase price is fixed after a detailed valuation of the assets and liabilities has been agreed upon but, in some cases, the practice obtains of settling the purchase price on the basis of the market value of the vendor company's shares. For example, if company C, whose shares stand at 25p per share premium, has an issued capital of £80,000, this indicates that the market estimates the total value of the net assets, in round figures, at £100,000. Now, if the undertaking is absorbed by company D on this basis, the purchase price payable is £100,000, whatever the book value of the assets may be. Usually, they are somewhat less, and the purchasing company must revalue the assets and make the necessary adjustments. Floating assets and liabilities must appear at their actual value, whilst the surplus of the purchase price over the book value of the remaining assets is attributable either (*a*) to an increase in value of some of the fixed assets (land, property, etc.), or (*b*) to the value of the goodwill.

Example 5

The balance sheet of Dale Co. Ltd. at 31st December, 19.., is as follows—

	£		£
Capital—		Land & Buildings	75,000
120,000 shares of £1 each fully paid	120,000	Plant & Machinery	36,450
Reserve Fund	60,000	Stock-in-trade	45,575
P. & L. A/c—		Sundry Debtors	38,250
Balance at Credit	6,528	Cash at Bankers	12,380
Sundry Creditors	21,250	Cash in hand	123
	207,778		207,778

The entire undertaking is acquired—as on the above date—by Somerton Co. Ltd. the agreed purchase consideration being the payment in cash of £100,000 and the allotment of two fully paid £1 shares (market value £1·25 per share) of Somerton Co. in exchange for each three shares of Dale Co. The liquidation expenses of the vendor company amount to £1,500, the balance of the cash consideration being distributed *pro rata* amongst the shareholders.

Close the books of the vendor company and show the opening entries in the books of the purchasing company to record the acquisition of the business.

Solution

Books of Dale Co. Ltd.

JOURNAL

	Dr	Cr
	£	£
Realization A/c	207,778	
Sundry Assets		207,778
Being total value of assets disposed of.		
Sundry Creditors	21,250	
Realization Account		21,250
Being amount of liabilities.		

JOURNAL (*contd.*)

		£	£
	Somerton Co. Ltd.	200,000	
	Realization A/c		200,000
	Being agreed purchase price.		
	Shares A/c	100,000	
	Cash A/c	100,000	
	Somerton Co. Ltd.		200,000
	Being receipt of purchase consideration; £100,000 in cash, and 80,000 shares of £1 each fully paid, valued at £1·25 per share.		
	Realization A/c	1,500	
	Cash		1,500
	Being payment of liquidation expenses.		
	Share Capital	120,000	
	Reserve Fund	60,000	
	P. & L. A/c	6,528	
	Sundry Shareholders		186,528
	Being transfer of balances.		
	Business Realization A/c	11,972	
	Sundry Shareholders		11,972
	Being transfer of profit on realization.		
	Sundry Shareholders	198,500	
	Shares		100,000
	Cash		98,500
	Being distribution of £0·83 in the £ in shares and £0·82 in the £ in cash.		

The two principal ledger accounts are as follows—

REALIZATION ACCOUNT

	£		£
Sundry Assets	207,778	Creditors	21,250
Liquidation Expenses . . .	1,500	Somerton Co.	200,000
Transfer to Sundry Shareholders	11,972		
	221,250		221,250

SUNDRY SHAREHOLDERS

	£		£
Shares—		Share Capital . . .	120,000
80,000 £1 shares at £1·25	100,000	Reserve Fund . . .	60,000
Cash	98,500	P. & L. A/c . . .	6,528
		Realization	11,972
	198,500		198,500

Books of Somerton Co. Ltd.

JOURNAL

	Dr	*Cr*
	£	£
Land & Buildings	75,000	
Plant & Machinery	36,450	
Stock-in-trade	45,575	
Sundry Debtors	38,250	
Cash at Bankers	12,380	
Cash in Hand	123	
Liquidator of Dale Co. Ltd.		207,778
Being value of assets acquired.		
Liquidator of Dale Co. Ltd.	21,250	
Sundry Creditors		21,250
Being liabilities taken over.		
Liquidator of Dale Co. Ltd.	186,528	
Share Capital		80,000
Being allotment of 80,000 shares of £1 each, fully paid.		
Cash		100,000
Premium on Shares A/c		6,528
Being excess value of the net assets over the nominal value of shares and cash paid.		

The ledger account for the liquidator of Dale Co. will appear as follows—

LIQUIDATOR OF DALE CO. LTD.

	£		£
Sundry Creditors	21,250	Sundry Assets	207,778
Share Capital	80,000		
Cash	100,000		
Premium on Shares	6,528		
	207,778		207,778

AMALGAMATION BY THE ACQUISITION OF A CONTROLLING INTEREST

Under this form of amalgamation, an existing company purchases a sufficient number of shares of another company so as to obtain a controlling interest in the latter concern; the shares being acquired either by agreement with the shareholders or by purchase in the open market. The Companies Act, 1948, provides that a three-fourths majority of the shareholders, present either personally or by proxy at an extraordinary general meeting, is needed to pass certain resolutions effecting any important alterations in the constitution—or the regulations—of the company. To ensure effective control, therefore, the shares acquired must be not less than three-fourths of the issued capital.

The entries required in the books of the purchasing company are a debit to investment account (shares in . . . Co. Ltd) and a credit to cash for the cost of the shares purchased; the investment appearing as an asset in the balance sheet. The financial books of the company whose shares are purchased are not affected; all that occurs is a change of shareholders, the new shareholders being either the purchasing company itself or its nominees; the only entries made are in the transfer register and the share ledger recording the transfer of the shares.

Both companies continue their separate existence, but, usually, the purchasing company nominates, wholly or partially, a fresh directorate and thereby obtains day-to-day control over the other company's activities.

Take-over Bids. The "take-over bid" is a term used after World War II to describe the acquiring of a controlling interest in a company by a new group of shareholders.

In many cases, such take-over bidders have offered to buy shares at much higher prices than those prevailing on the Stock Exchange, sometimes with the support of the directors of the company. In such cases, the Stock Exchange price has been based on the *dividends paid* by the company. The take-over valuation has been based on the net value of the assets of the company. The gap between the two valuations has often been great because of rising price levels and because the balance sheets have stated historical cost and not current value of assets.

The conduct of take-over negotiations is now governed by The City Code on Take-overs and Mergers ("the Green Book") and supported by recommendations jointly issued by the City Take-over Panel and the I.C.A. of E. & W.

Share valuation is dealt with more fully on p. 2942.

RECONSTRUCTION

The term "reconstruction" is commonly used to describe a scheme under which a company goes into liquidation for the express purpose of selling its assets to a new company for partly-paid shares carrying a further liability. Usually, the liquidating company has exhausted its working capital and, by means of such a scheme, the company is reconstructed and reconstituted so as to form a new company with precisely the same objects, the same or a similar name, and composed of the same shareholders, who are called upon to provide additional working capital.

Reconstruction schemes may also be initiated for the purpose of—

1. Widening the company's sphere of operations by enlarging the powers contained in its memorandum of association;

2. Changing the domicile of the company, e.g. a Scottish company registered at Edinburgh wishing to become an English company with a London registration; or

3. Carrying into effect a compromise with its creditors and/or members, by which the creditors will accept shares or debentures in satisfaction of their debts; this is called an external reconstruction.

The term "reconstruction" is also used in connexion with schemes for reduction of capital; this is called an internal reconstruction and is dealt with on p. 2526.

Entries in the Books. The entries in the financial books of the old company are similar to those for the liquidation of a vendor company in an amalgamation. For the new company, the entries are upon the same lines as for a new company acquiring a vendor's business in exchange for shares credited as fully or partly paid.

When partly-paid shares are issued, the entries for the additional capital called up are made in the ordinary manner. (See p. 2002.)

REORGANIZATION

This term is generally used to denote the rearrangement of a company's share capital, either by the consolidation of shares of different classes, or by the subdivision of the shares into different classes. Simple consolidation of shares and their division into shares of larger amount than existing shares, or the subdivision of shares into shares of smaller amount, is sanctioned by Sect. 61 of the Companies Act, 1948, and such alterations must be notified to the Registrar of Companies within one month of their being put into effect.

Where the rearrangements involve the revision of preferential or deferred rights possessed by certain classes of shareholders, such revision must be sanctioned by the shareholders and may require to be confirmed by the court in the manner provided for by Sect. 72 of the 1948 Act.

Reorganization differs from Reconstruction in that the latter usually involves the liquidation and winding up of the original company, a new company taking over its entire undertaking, whilst reorganization does not involve liquidation, the company continuing its separate existence with a rearrangement of its capital and possibly the revision of the rights of different classes of shareholders. It does not imply inability to raise working capital and merely involves a rearrangement of the capital structure.

Entries in the Books. In most cases, the only entries required are the closure of the old share capital accounts, and the opening of new accounts to correspond with the revised capital.

Example 6

A company has issued 100,000 ordinary shares of £1 each, and it decides to divide these shares into two classes, viz. 50,000 preferred ordinary shares of £1 each (with prior rights as to dividend and return of capital in a winding-up) and 50,000 deferred ordinary shares of £1 each. The journal entry to record this rearrangement will be as shown in the following way—

		Dr	Cr
		£	£
	Ordinary Share Capital . . . . Dr	100,000	
	Preferred Ordinary Share Capital . . .		50,000
	Deferred Ordinary Share Capital . . .		50,000
	Being the division of the company's paid-up share capital into two classes in accordance with special resolution passed on ....19.......		

Share Conversion List. The members' accounts in the share ledger for the ordinary shares are closed and new accounts opened for the preferred and deferred ordinary shares. To facilitate the entries in the new share ledgers and the exchange of the old share certificates for the new certificates, a share conversion list is compiled in the following or similar manner.

SHARE CONVERSION LIST

LEFT-HAND RULING.

Old Share Led. Fo.	Name		Address	Old Ordinary Shares			
	Surname	Christian Name		Old Cert. No.	No. of Shares	Distinctive Numbers	
						From	To

RIGHT-HAND RULING.

New Preferred Ordinary Shares				New Share Led. Fo.	New Deferred Ordinary Shares				New Share Led. Fo.	Remarks
Cert. No.	No. of Shares	Distinctive Numbers			Cert. No.	No. of Shares	Distinctive Numbers			
		From	To				From	To		

The conversion of share capital into stock or vice versa, and other re-arrangements of capital are effected in a similar manner.

REDUCTION OF CAPITAL

Provisions of the Companies Act. By Sects. 66 and 67 of the Companies Act, 1948, it is enacted as follows—

Subject to confirmation by the court, a company limited by shares . . . may, if so authorized by its articles, by special resolution reduce its share capital in any way, and in particular, without prejudice to the generality of the foregoing power, may—

(*a*) Extinguish or reduce the liability on any of its shares in respect of share capital not paid up; or

(*b*) Either with or without extinguishing or reducing liability on any of its shares, cancel any paid-up share capital which is lost or unrepresented by available assets; or

(*c*) Either with or without extinguishing or reducing liability on any of its shares, pay off any paid-up share capital which is in excess of the wants of the company,

and may, if and so far as is necessary, alter its memorandum by reducing the amount of its share capital and of its shares accordingly. (Sect. 66.)

Where a company has passed a resolution for reducing share capital, it may apply to the court for an order confirming the reduction. (Sect. 67.)

Where the reduction involves repayment to or diminution of liability of shareholders or in any other case if the court directs, creditors may object to the reduction and the court may order the debts of such creditors to be paid or secured. The order of the court must also be produced to the Registrar of Companies before it takes effect.

Limited and Reduced. When the court has made an order confirming the reduction—which may include such terms and conditions as it may think fit—it may, by Sect. 68 (2)—

(*a*) if for any special reason it thinks proper so to do, make an order directing that the company shall, during such period, commencing on or at any time after the date of the order, as specified in the order, add to its name as the last words thereof the words "and reduced"; and

(*b*) make an order requiring the company to publish, as the court directs, the reasons for reduction. . . .

Meaning of Reduction of Capital. Reduction of capital means a diminution in the nominal amount of the share capital of a company; it also means a reduction in the paid-up capital of a company.

Circumstances Leading to a Reduction of Capital. A company might require to reduce its capital in the following circumstances—

(*a*) If there is an accumulation of trading losses representing the result of several years of adverse fortune in the prosecution of its business;

(*b*) If there are capital losses of an extensive nature requiring drastic revaluation of the assets of the company;

(*c*) If the cash resources of the company are such that there seems no likelihood of that cash ever being required for the business.

Methods of Effecting the Reduction of Capital. There are several ways by which a company may give effect to the reduction of its capital. Of the cases (*a*), (*b*), and (*c*) above, the most usual form of reduction of capital is that which arises out of the paid-up capital having been lost, or the capital being unrepresented by available assets, i.e. (*a*) or (*b*).

At the same time as the resolution reducing the capital it is usual to pass a resolution increasing the authorized capital to the original amount—i.e. the amount on which stamp duty has been paid.

1. Writing off Losses

Example 7

A limited company, having sustained heavy losses obtained the sanction of the court to reduce its capital from 100,000 shares of £1 each, fully paid, to 100,000 shares of £0·50 each fully paid. Make the necessary journal entry to effect this change of the company's capital, and state how the share ledger and certificates will be adjusted.

JOURNAL

	Dr	Cr
	£	£
Share Capital	50,000	
Profit & Loss A/c		50,000
Reduction of 100,000 shares of £1 each, fully-paid, to 100,000 shares of £0·50 each, fully-paid, as per order of the court dated		

It is of the utmost importance that the carrying into effect of a "reduction" does not create a further liability on the shareholders as regards their holdings. For instance, if an attempt be made to reduce the paid-up capital, say, from £0·50 paid up to £0·25 paid up on the individual shares—without reducing the nominal amount of the share—the company would not be acting according to the intention of the Act, which is to limit the liability of the shares to the amount for which they were issued, and the arrangement indicated above would defeat that object.

In the share ledger, each page will be impressed with a rubber stamp referring to the resolution and its effect. The share certificates will either be dealt with in a similar manner or new ones will be issued to replace them.

2. Existinguishing Losses and Writing down Assets

(This illustrates the most common type of capital reduction scheme.)

Example 8

Overleaf is the balance sheet of the Thetis Co. Ltd. as at 31st December, 19...

	£		£
Authorized Capital—		Freehold Land & Buildings	25,000
240,000 Shares of £1 each . . . £240,000		Machinery & Plant .	55,420
		Patents .	67,000
		Stock	8,250
		Sundry Debtors	4.738
Issued Capital—		Preliminary Expenses	5,000
100,000 Ord. Shares of £1 each	100,000	Cash in hand .	60
80,000 Pref. Shares of £1 each	80,000	P. & L. A/c—	
Bank Overdraft	4,000	Balance at debit .	30,532
Sundry Creditors	12,000		
	196,000		196,000

Resolutions were passed—

1. That the £1 preference and ordinary shares be reduced to the same number of fully-paid shares of £0·75 and £0·50 for the respective classes of shares;

2. That the sum thus rendered available be applied as follows—

(*a*) The balances to the debit of profit and loss and preliminary expenses to be written off;

(*b*) the machinery and plant to be reduced to £40,000;

(*c*) £1,000 to be written off the stock;

(*d*) the balance to be utilized to reduce the patents account;

3. That the authorized capital be increased to £240,000 made up of 300,000 ordinary shares of £0·50 and 120,000 Preference Shares at £0·75 each.

Make the necessary journal entries, and draw up the new balance sheet.

Solution 8

JOURNAL

	Dr £	*Cr* £
Preference Share Capital .	20,000	
Capital Reduction A/c .		20,000
80,000 preference shares of £1 each, fully paid, reduced to 80,000 shares of £0·75 each, fully paid, as per resolution dated........................		
Ordinary Share Capital .	50,000	
Capital Reduction A/c .		50,000
100,000 shares of £1 each, fully paid, reduced to 100,000 shares of £0·50 each, fully paid, as per resolution dated........................		
Capital Reduction A/c	70,000	
Profit & Loss A/c		30,532
Preliminary Expenses A/c		5,000
Machinery & Plant A/c		15,420
Stock A/c .		1,000
Patents A/c		18,048
Amounts written off, as per resolution dated........................		

LEDGER

CAPITAL REDUCTION ACCOUNT

		£			£
19..			19..		
Dec 31	P. & L. A/c	30,532	Dec 31	Preference Share Capital	20,000
	Preliminary Expenses	5,000		Ordinary Share Capital	50,000
	Machinery & Plant	15,420			
	Stock	1,000			
	Patents	18,048			
		70,000			70,000

PREFERENCE SHARE CAPITAL

		£			£
19..			19..		
Dec 31	Capital Reduction	20,000	Dec 31	Balance	80,000
	Balance c/d	60,000			
		80,000			80,000
			Dec 31	Balance b/d	60,000

ORDINARY SHARE CAPITAL

		£			£
19..			19..		
Dec 31	Capital Reduction	50,000	Dec 31	Balance	100,000
	Balance c/d	50,000			
		100,000			100,000
			Dec 31	Balance b/d	50,000

BALANCE SHEET OF THE THETIS COMPANY LIMITED AND REDUCED

		£		£
Authorized Capital—			Freehold Buildings	25,000
300,000 Ord. Shares of £0·50	£150,000		Plant & Machinery	40,000
120,000 Pref. Shares of £0·75	90,000		Patents	48,952
	240,000		Stock	7,250
			Sundry Debtors	4,738
			Cash in hand	60
Issued Capital				
100,000 Ord. Shares of £0·50		50,000		
80,000 Pref. Shares of £0·75		60,000		
Bank Overdraft		4,000		
Sundry Creditors		12,000		
		126,000		126,000

The student's attention is especially drawn to the fact that whilst, in this example, the preference shareholders have been called upon to forfeit £0·25 of the capital value of their shares, the ordinary shareholders have suffered a loss of £0·50 per share. Generally speaking, this is always the case in a reduction of capital, although it is clear that, as the circumstances which bring about the reduction vary widely in each individual case, so will the rights of the various classes of shareholders be affected to a different degree. Whether or not it is equitable is a matter for the court to decide.

But this is the guiding principle. During the better years of the life of the company, the equity holders—usually the holders of ordinary shares—benefit by the larger dividends paid, and on this basis should expect to suffer to a greater extent should a reduction become necessary.

From a shareholder's point of view, a capital reduction might appear to be somewhat of a tragedy, but it may, in fact, be a blessing in disguise. **The main purpose of a reduction is to eliminate the debit balance of the profit and loss account from the books, so making possible a resumption of dividends.**

In almost every case the necessity is forced upon the company as the result of a number of very bad years, and if this is so, it is reasonable to assume that the market value of the shares is reflected in a very low price. The shareholder has therefore, in fact, already lost his capital if he wishes to dispose of his shares. One of the most likely results of a capital reduction is an early resumption of dividends, the effect of which will be to improve the prospects in the share market and in the long run carry them to a higher figure than that at which they stood when they were of a higher nominal value.

Reference to a capital reduction which was of wide public interest at the time will bear out and amplify the above remarks.

The following are extracts from a financial paper in which the details were published—

AMALGAMATED ANTHRACITE SCHEME

The scheme of arrangement which the board of Amalgamated Anthracite Collieries is presenting to shareholders is necessarily somewhat drastic. To secure a firm basis for the scheme, the directors have obtained an independent valuation of the chief assets. And to enable the assets to be written down to that valuation, a capital cut of over 50 per cent is required. The present issued capital of £9,105,098 is to be reduced by £4,918,339 to £4,581,660.[1] The scheme itself is somewhat complicated and, *as is right and proper*, the ordinary shareholders make the greatest sacrifice.

---

[1] The apparent discrepancy in these figures is due to the fact that the scheme also includes an increase of capital for the purpose of capitalizing the preference dividend arrears.

The ultimate effect of the scheme can be summarized as follows—

Existing Holding	*Holding under Scheme*
100 preference £1 "original issue" .	100 "A" preference shares of £0·50 each.
	100 "B" preference shares of £0·50 each.
	100 ordinary £0·20 shares.[1]
100 preference £1 "1937 issue" .	100 "A" preference shares of £0·50 each.
	100 "B" preference shares of £0·50 each.
	75 ordinary £0·20 shares.
100 ordinary £1 shares . .	100 ordinary £0·20 shares.

The ability of the company to earn profits depends entirely on trade conditions, but the directors are satisfied that the present scheme *brings the payment of dividends* on all classes of shares very much nearer.

3. Return of Capital not Required

A reduction by the repayment of unrequired capital is naturally in an entirely different category. The nominal capital is not reduced in this case but by the repayment the shares are reduced to a lower paid-up value, so that should use be found for the money at a later date it is only necessary to make a call; a much cheaper and quicker operation than making a new issue.

The entries would consist of—

1. *Dr.* capital a/c.
   Cr. return of capital a/c (or capital reduction a/c).
2. *Dr.* return of capital a/c.
   Cr. cash.

A reduction of capital may also be effected by a company in the following circumstances—

(*a*) Forfeiture of shares for non-payment of calls;

(*b*) Surrender of shares by a member in circumstances which entitle the company to forfeit his shares for non-payment of calls;

(*c*) Cancellation of unissued shares.

GROUP ACCOUNTS

Section 150 of the 1948 Companies Act requires the preparation of group accounts where a company has a subsidiary at the end of its financial year and is not a wholly-owned subsidiary of another company incorporated in Great Britain.

HOLDING COMPANIES

A holding company is defined by the Companies Act, 1948, Sect. 154 (4), as follows—

A company shall be deemed to be another's holding company if, but only if, that other is its subsidiary.

---

[1] The receipt of shares of a nominal value of £1·20 per £1 share is due to the fact that as a part of the scheme arrears of preference dividends amounting to £591,104 are being cancelled. This represents about £0·25 per share.

A holding company then is briefly one which has acquired control over one or more other companies.

Subsidiary Company. Sect. 154 of the Companies Act, 1948, states—

> (1) . . . a company shall . . . be deemed to be a subsidiary of another if, but only if—
>
> (*a*) that other either:
>
> (i) is a member of it and controls the composition of its board of directors;
>
> or
>
> (ii) holds more than half in nominal value of its equity share capital; or
>
> (*b*) the first-mentioned company is a subsidiary of any company which is that other's subsidiary.

In determining whether a company is a subsidiary of another company shares held by a nominee or by a subsidiary company of that other company shall be treated as being held by that company, but shares held in a fiduciary capacity shall not be treated as held by that company.

Advantages of the "Holding" System of Control. (*a*) The subsidiary companies so held remain separate entities, and practically no disturbance takes place in their *modus operandi*.

(*b*) The goodwill of the subsidiary companies represented by trade marks and trade names remains intact.

(*c*) Whilst the holding company has a controlling interest in the subsidiary companies, and a central policy is possible, the subsidiaries prosecute their several business policies as determined by their own managements, who are in the best position to judge local conditions and requirements, etc.

(*d*) Financial and statistical results being separately prepared for each unit, comparisons of results are easier to follow and understand than when merged into one huge set of figures as obtains for a concern with a head office and branches (i.e. the multiple shop system).

(*e*) Financial arrangements as regards reserves for contingencies and trading reserves, also control of working capital, are best arranged by each subsidiary company, whose management would be fully cognizant of all the circumstances involved in such matters.

(*f*) The capital resources, or means of creating them, are enhanced by the "holding" company, which can arrange for seasonal capital to its subsidiaries; also permanent capital is provided by the "holding" company, whose status in the money market is a guarantee of its strength, whereas not one of the subsidiaries may be strong in this way.

Disadvantages of the "Holding" System of Control. A disadvantage of this system is the power which the directors have to mislead shareholders; also the facility given to the manipulation of inter-company transactions with the intention of concealing the true state of affairs, which is a practice that may be carried out by unscrupulous directors, although the Companies Act, 1948, has done much to reduce this danger.

Group Accounts—Provisions of the Companies Act, 1967. The following additional information must be given in the accounts of companies which are members of groups—

1. The identity of the company regarded by the directors as the ultimate holding company unless the subsidiary trades overseas and the Board of Trade agree that disclosure would be harmful to any company in the group.

2. Where a company has subsidiaries or holds more than one-tenth of the equity in terms of nominal value of issued shares or where the shares' value constitutes more than one-tenth of the total assets of the investing company then it must state—

(*a*) the name of the company or subsidiary;

(*b*) the country in which incorporated if not Great Britain;

(*c*) whether it is registered in England or Scotland if the companies are not registered in the same country;

(*d*) the description and proportion of the nominal value of each share class held.

The Board of Trade may agree to exemption on the grounds that it would be harmful to the companies.

If the directors consider the details of non-subsidiaries to be of excessive length and the profit and loss account is not principally affected, the details may be omitted but they must be included in the next annual return.

Direct holdings must be distinguished from indirect holdings through other subsidiaries or their nominees.

The 2nd Schedule to the Companies Act, 1967, makes it obligatory for holding companies to set out separately in their accounts the following information—

1. The aggregate amount of shares in subsidiaries.
2. The aggregate of amounts owing by subsidiaries to the company.
3. The aggregate of indebtedness to subsidiaries of the company.
4. The number, description and amount of shares in or debentures of the company held by its subsidiaries or their nominees (excluding shares held on trust, provided the company or its subsidiaries are not beneficially interested).

The method used to arrive at the value of the shares which are fixed assets must be stated, but the requirements of the 2nd Schedule as to the method of stating fixed assets (i.e. at cost less aggregate depreciation) or investments do not apply.

In addition to the above information, unless the company is a wholly-owned subsidiary of another company incorporated in Great Britain, group accounts must be laid before the company in general meeting with the company's own balance sheet.

Group Accounts shall be in the form of *Consolidated Accounts* comprising a consolidated balance sheet and a consolidated profit and loss account dealing with the affairs of the company and all its subsidiaries. (Sect. 151 (1) of the 1948 Companies Act.)

If, however, the company's directors are of opinion that it is *better* for the purpose—

(*a*) of presenting the same or equivalent information about the company and its subsidiaries,

(*b*) of so presenting it that it may be readily appreciated by the company's members,

the group accounts may be prepared in another form (Sect.151 (2)).

Omission of a subsidiary from group accounts may be authorized by the Board of Trade if, in the opinion of the directors, its inclusion—

(*a*) is impracticable;

(*b*) would be of no real value in view of the insignificance of the amounts;

(*c*) would involve undue expense or disproportionate delay;

(*d*) would be misleading or harmful;

(*e*) is undesirable because the businesses of holding and subsidiary company are so different.

If these apply to all subsidiaries, group accounts are not required.

Thus, more than one set of consolidated accounts may be prepared dealing with different groups of companies, or separate accounts of each subsidiary or of statements expanding the information about subsidiaries in the company's own accounts, or any combination of these.

The group accounts may be wholly or partly incorporated in the company's own balance sheet and profit and loss account (Sect. 151 (3)).

The group accounts must give a true and fair view of the state of affairs and profit or loss of the company and its subsidiaries, and for this purpose the directors of the holding company are to secure that, except where there are good reasons against it, the financial years of the holding company and its subsidiaries shall coincide.

Consolidated accounts are to comply with the provisions of the 2nd Schedule so far as applicable, i.e. the form of accounts and the information given must be similar to that of the holding company's own balance sheet and profit and loss account.

The following requirements must be met for the holding company but not for the Group—

1. Directors' emoluments, compensation and pensions.
2. Loans to officers.
3. Investments in other companies.
4. Employee emoluments over £10,000 per annum.

Where group accounts are not submitted, the company must annex to the balance sheet a statement showing—

(*a*) the reasons why subsidiaries are not dealt with in group accounts;

(*b*) the net aggregate amount attributable to members of the holding company, both—

(i) dealt with;
(ii) not dealt with in the company's accounts;
(iii) for the respective financial years of the subsidiaries ending with or during the financial year of the company; and
(iv) for the previous financial years since they respectively became the holding company's subsidiary;

(*c*) the net aggregate amount of the subsidiaries' profits after deducting the subsidiaries' losses (or vice versa)—

(i) for the respective financial years of the subsidiaries ending with or during the financial year of the company;
(ii) for their other financial years since they respectively became the holding company's subsidiary;

so far as those profits *are* dealt with, or provision is made for those losses, in the company's accounts;

(*d*) any qualifications in the report of the auditors of the subsidiaries on their accounts for their respective financial years ending as aforesaid, and any note or saving contained in those accounts to call attention to a matter which, apart from the note or saving, would properly have been referred to in such qualification, in so far as the matter which is the subject of the qualification or note is not covered by the company's own accounts and is material from the point of view of its members;

or, in so far as the information required by this sub-paragraph is not obtainable a statement that is not obtainable. (Part II of Eighth Schedule, para. 15 (4).)

The statement must also show in relation to the subsidiaries whose financial years did not end with that of the company (*ibid.*, para. 6)—

(*a*) The reasons why the company's directors consider the subsidiaries' financial years should not end with that of the company; and

(*b*) the dates on which the subsidiaries' financial years ending last before that of the company respectively ended or the earliest and latest of those dates.

Accounts of Subsidiary Companies. The balance sheet of a company which is a subsidiary of another company must show—

1. The aggregate amount of its indebtedness to all companies of which it is a subsidiary or a fellow subsidiary.
2. The aggregate amount of the indebtedness of all such companies to it, distinguishing between indebtedness in respect of debentures and otherwise.
3. The name and place of incorporation of its ultimate holding company.

Book-keeping Entries in the Case of the Holding Company. On the purchase of the shares the holding company will debit shares in subsidiary company account and credit cash, share capital, or debentures account, according to the method of purchase adopted.

Consolidated Accounts. Consolidated accounts may be regarded as the accounts of the holding company and its subsidiaries combined into one business under the name of the holding company.

Unless the directors believe there are good reasons against it, all members of a group shall end their accounting years on the same date. If the financial years differ, the group accounts must deal with the last results before the holding company balance sheet date. In this case, the directors of the holding company must state the earliest and latest closing dates of subsidiary accounts and their reasons for not securing co-termination.

PREPARATION OF THE CONSOLIDATED BALANCE SHEET

There are well-established principles which are followed in consolidation and, once the student has mastered them he will experience little difficulty.

In the ensuing examples, the rule is stated and then illustrated. Throughout the examples H Ltd. is the holding company and S Ltd. the subsidiary.

Rule 1. Consolidation is the adding together of the balance sheets of the holding company and its subsidiary. The investment in the subsidiary will appear on the holding company's balance sheet as "Investment in Subsidiary, at cost." If the whole share capital has been acquired and there are no reserves, the ordinary share capital on the liabilities side of the subsidiary's will correspond to the holding company's investment. As these items are equal and on opposite sides, they may be eliminated and the consolidated balance sheet will still have equal assets and liabilities.

Example 9

Holding Co. Ltd. acquired the share capital of S Ltd. for £20,000 on 1st July 19.. Show the consolidated balance sheets.

Solution 9

BALANCE SHEET OF HOLDING CO. LTD. ON 1ST JULY, 19..

	£		£
Ordinary Share Capital	100,000	Sundry Assets	110,000
Trade Creditors	30,000	Investment in S (cost)	20,000
	130,000		130,000

BALANCE SHEET OF S LTD. ON 1ST JULY, 19..

	£		£
Ordinary Share Capital	20,000	Sundry Assets	30,000
Trade Creditors	10,000		
	30,000		30,000

CONSOLIDATED BALANCE SHEET OF HOLDING CO. LTD.
AND ITS SUBSIDIARY S LTD.

	£		£
Ordinary Share Capital	100,000	Sundry Assets	140,000
Trade Creditors	40,000		
	140,000		140,000

The above illustration is the simplest possible case. In practice, the cost per share of an investment in a subsidiary will rarely coincide with the value appearing in the subsidiary's balance sheet. Most established companies will have some reserves accumulated, and it is likely that the price paid will also exceed the book value of the company as shown in the balance sheet.

The net asset value of a company is the total assets less the total liabilities to outsiders. It shows the book value of the business to its shareholders. (See overleaf for its calculation.)

Goodwill on consolidation is the excess of the cost of a holding company's share in a subsidiary over the net asset value of that share.

Capital reserve on consolidation is the excess of the net asset value of a holding company's share in a subsidiary over the price paid for that share.

Rule 2. The net asset value of the subsidiary must be found. If the price paid for the investment in S exceeds the net asset value, *goodwill* arises on consolidation. If the net asset value exceeds the price paid, a *capital reserve* arises.

Example 10

The balance sheet of H Ltd. is the same as above, but the balance sheet of S Ltd. is as follows—

BALANCE SHEET OF S LTD. ON 1ST JULY, 19..

	£		£
Ordinary Share Capital	10,000	Sundry Assets	25,000
Revenue Reserves	5,000		
Sundry Creditors	10,000		
	25,000		25,000

The net asset value is—

	£
Gross assets	25,000
Less Gross liabilities	10,000
Net Asset Value	15,000

Alternatively, this may be calculated as—

	£
Capital	10,000
Add Reserves	5,000
Net Asset Value	15,000

If the price paid exceeds net asset value, the balance is goodwill.

If the price paid is less than net asset value, the balance is capital reserve.

If the price is £20,000, the goodwill is £5,000 and the result is—

CONSOLIDATED BALANCE SHEET OF H LTD. WITH S LTD.

		£			£
Ordinary Share Capital		100,000	Goodwill arising on consolidation		5,000
Trade Creditors—			Sundry Assets—		
H Ltd.	£30,000		H Ltd.	£110,000	
S Ltd.	10,000		S Ltd.	25,000	
		40,000			135,000
		140,000			140,000

The holding company does not always acquire all the shares of a subsidiary. It has no need to acquire non-voting preference or deferred shares, and it need only acquire 50 per cent + 1 share of the ordinary share capital. Any such shares not acquired (and, therefore, held by outsiders) are called the Minority Interest.

Rule 3. The claims of the minority shareholders must be deducted from the net asset value before the value of the holding company's interest and the amount of goodwill or capital reserve can be calculated.

Preference, deferred and other non-controlling shares, are not normally entitled to more than their nominal interest. Minority ordinary shareholders are entitled to a proportionate share of all reserves.

Example 11

Let us assume that the investment in S Ltd. which cost £20,000 in Example 9 represents 15,000 ordinary shares. Assume also that the balance sheet of H Ltd. is the same, but that of S Ltd. is as follows—

BALANCE SHEET OF S LTD. ON 1ST JULY, 19. .

	£		£
10,000 £1 5% Preference Shares	10,000	Sundry Assets	44,000
20,000 Ordinary Shares	20,000		
Revenue Reserves	4,000		
Trade Creditors	10,000		
	44,000		44,000

	£
Gross Assets	44,000
Less Creditors	10,000
Net Assets are	34,000

The claim of preference shareholders on these is £10,000, leaving for ordinary shareholders £24,000. Of this—

$\frac{15000}{20000}$ i.e. 75 per cent belongs to H Ltd. = £18,000
$\frac{5000}{20000}$ i.e. 25 per cent belongs to minority shareholders in S Ltd. = £6,000

This may also be calculated—

	£
75 per cent ordinary shares	15,000
75 per cent of reserves	3,000
Holding Company's interest	18,000

Similarly with the minority interest.

As H Ltd. paid £20,000 for £18,000 net assets, there is goodwill on consolidation of £2,000. The balance sheet of S Ltd. may be amended ready for consolidation as follows—

BALANCE SHEET OF S Ltd.
(ready for consolidation)

	£		£
Holding Company Interest	20,000	Goodwill on consolidation	2,000
Minority Interest—		Sundry Assets	44,000
Preference Shareholders	10,000		
Ordinary Shareholders	6,000		
Trade Creditors	10,000		
	46,000		46,000

The holding company interest may be eliminated and the investment in S Ltd. eliminated from H Ltd.'s balance sheet with the following result—

CONSOLIDATED BALANCE SHEET OF H LTD. WITH S LTD.

		£			£
Ordinary Share Capital		100,000	Goodwill		2,000
Minority Interest in Subsidiaries—			Sundry Assets—		
Preference Shareholders in S Ltd.	£10,000		H Ltd.	£110,000	
Ordinary Shareholders in S Ltd.	6,000		S Ltd.	44,000	
		16,000			154,000
Trade Creditors		40,000			
		156,000			156,000

Rule 4. All mutual indebtedness between the holding company and its subsidiaries must be eliminated from the consolidated balance sheet.

Such indebtedness may take the form of loans, debentures, interest and dividends due, bills of exchange, etc. Such items should always be equal and on opposite sides, and elimination simply involves striking out the appropriate items before consolidation.

Example 12

H Ltd. has two subsidiaries, S Ltd. and T Ltd. Below are the balance sheets of these companies on the same date.

BALANCE SHEET OF H LTD.

	£		£
Ordinary Share Capital	90,000	Sundry Assets	100,000
Reserves	55,000	Investment in S Ltd. (1)	40,000
Debentures	50,000	T Ltd. (2)	50,000
Trade Creditors (6) (inc. £500 owing to S Ltd.)	5,000	Debentures in S Ltd. (3)	5,000
		Loan to T Ltd. (4)	2,000
		Sundry Debtors (5) (inc. £1,000 Bill Receivable from T Ltd.)	3,000
	200,000		200,000

BALANCE SHEET OF S LTD.

	£		£
Ordinary Share Capital (1)	30,000	Sundry Assets	60,000
P. & L. A/c (1)	10,000	Sundry Debtors (6)	7,000
Debentures (3)	20,000		
Trade Creditors (7) (inc. £1,000 owing to T Ltd.)	7,000		
	67,000		67,000

BALANCE SHEET OF T LTD.

	£		£
Ordinary Share Capital (2) .	35,000	Sundry Assets . . .	53,000
Reserves (2)	15,000	Sundry Debtors (7). . .	3,000
Loan from H Ltd. (4) . .	2,000		
Trade Creditors (5) (inc. Bills Payable)	4,000		
	56,000		56,000

To guide the student, the corresponding items have been numbered—

(1) and (2), the investments in subsidiaries in H Ltd. equal the share capital and reserves in S Ltd. and T Ltd.

(3) Of £20,000 debentures in S Ltd., H holds £5,000. The £5,000 is eliminated from H Ltd. and the net liability of S Ltd. becomes £15,000.

(4) A straightforward elimination of £2,000 asset in H Ltd., £2,000 liability in T Ltd.

(5) Eliminate £1,000 from bills receivable of H Ltd., which makes debtors £2,000, and from trade creditors of T Ltd., which leaves £3,000.

(6) Eliminate £500 from trade creditors of H Ltd., which leaves £4,500 and from sundry debtors of S Ltd., which leaves £6,500.

(7) The mutual indebtedness of subsidiaries is also eliminated. Trade creditors of S Ltd. become £6,000, sundry debtors of T Ltd., £2,000.

In preparing a large consolidated balance sheet it is easy to omit an item on first working. If a full page is taken, and plenty of space left between sub-headings, such omissions may be corrected without spoiling the appearance of the answer.

CONSOLIDATED BALANCE SHEET OF H LTD. WITH ITS SUBSIDIARIES S LTD. AND T LTD.

		£			£
Ordinary Share Capital . .		90,000	Sundry Assets—		
Reserves		55,000	H Ltd. . .	£100,000	
Debentures—			S Ltd. . .	60,000	
H Ltd. . .	£50,000		T Ltd. . .	53,000	
S Ltd. . . .	15,000				213,000
		65,000	Sundry Debtors—		
Trade Creditors—			H Ltd. . .	£2,000	
H Ltd. . .	£4,500		S Ltd. . .	6,500	
S Ltd. . . .	6,000		T Ltd. . .	2,000	
T Ltd. . . .	3,000				10,500
		13,500			
		223,500			223,500

Rule 5. Revenue from subsidiary companies may be credited to the profit and loss account of the holding company in the same way as dividends received from any other investment, provided those profits have been earned since the date of acquisition. Any pre-acquisition profits received as dividends must be treated as a return of capital and deducted from the cost of the investments in the subsidiary.

Example 13

H Ltd. acquired its control of S Ltd. on 1st January 19... The following balance sheets are to be consolidated on 31st December of the same year.

BALANCE SHEET OF H LTD. ON 31ST DECEMBER, 19..

	£		£
Ordinary Share Capital	90,000	Sundry Assets	100,000
P. & L. A/c[1]	30,000	Investment in S Ltd.	40,000
Trade Creditors	20,000		
	140,000		140,000

[1] This includes £3,000 dividend received from S Ltd.

BALANCE SHEET OF S LTD. ON 31ST DECEMBER 19..

		£		£
Ordinary Share Capital		30,000	Sundry Assets	50,000
P. & L. A/c—				
Balance on 1st Jan	£8,000			
Profit for year	2,000			
	10,000			
Dividend paid on 31st Dec.	3,000			
		7,000		
Trade Creditors		13,000		
		50,000		50,000

As the balance sheet is for 31st December, the net asset value of S Ltd. on acquisition can only be calculated by reference to the position at the date of take-over, i.e.—

	£
Ordinary Share Capital	30,000
Profit and Loss Account on 1st January	8,000
Net Asset Value	38,000
Goodwill is therefore	2,000
Purchase Price	40,000

However, of the dividend £3,000 paid by S Ltd., only £2,000 represents earnings since acquisition.

THE CORRECTED BALANCE SHEET OF H LTD.

	£			£
Ordinary Share Capital	90,000	Sundry Assets		100,000
P. & L. A/c	29,000	Investment in S Ltd.	£40,000	
Trade Creditors	20,000	*Less* Dividend from pre-acquisition profits	1,000	
				39,000
	139,000			139,000

The goodwill is still £2,000. If the purchase price is reduced to £39,000 because of the dividend the net asset value also falls to £37,000.

CONSOLIDATED BALANCE SHEET OF H LTD. WITH S LTD.

		£			£
Ordinary Share Capital		90,000	Sundry Assets—		
P. & L. A/c		29,000	H Ltd.	£100,000	
Trade Creditors—			S Ltd.	50,000	
H Ltd.	£20,000				150,000
S Ltd.	13,000		Goodwill on consolidation		2,000
		33,000			
		152,000			152,000

The purpose of a company acquiring a controlling interest in another is often to secure outlet for goods or sources of raw materials. A subsidiary may, therefore, be selling goods at a profit to a holding company and vice versa. Such inter-company profits, however, are not *realized* until the goods are sold to outsiders. The value of stocks in the consolidated balance sheet will be overstated unless such inter-group profits are eliminated. However, only the holding company's share of such profits need be eliminated. So far as minority shareholders are concerned, such profits have been realized.

Rule 6. Eliminate the holding company's share of unrealized profits on inter-group transactions by crediting the appropriate asset and debiting profit and loss.

Example 14

BALANCE SHEET OF H LTD.

	£		£
Ordinary Share Capital	90,000	Sundry Assets	95,000
Reserves and P. & L. A/c	29,000	Investment in S Ltd. (25,000 Ord. Shares)	39,000
Trade Creditors	20,000	Stocks (inc. £2,000 from S Ltd.)	5,000
	139,000		139,000

BALANCE SHEET OF S LTD.

	£		£
Share Capital— 30,000 £1 Ordinary Shares	30,000	Sundry Assets	50,000
P. & L. A/c	6,000		
Trade Creditors	14,000		
	50,000		50,000

S Ltd.'s rate of gross profit is $33\frac{1}{3}$ per cent of selling price. The gross profit on £2,000 stock sold to H Ltd. is therefore £$\frac{2000}{3}$ = £667, of which $\frac{25000}{30000}$, i.e. $\frac{5}{6}$, relates to the holding company (£556), and $\frac{5000}{30000}$ i.e. $\frac{1}{6}$, relates to the minority interest (£111). Therefore, the amount to be eliminated from the holding company's profit is £556.

The calculation of goodwill is—

	£
Ordinary Share Capital	30,000
Profit and Loss Account	6,000
Net Asset Value	36,000
Deduct $\frac{1}{6}$ minority interest	6,000
Holding Company Interest	30,000
Goodwill is therefore	9,000
Purchase Price	39,000

The amended consolidated balance sheet will be—

CONSOLIDATED BALANCE SHEET OF H LTD. WITH S LTD.

		£			£
Ordinary Share Capital		90,000	Sundry Assets—		
P. & L. A/c	£29,000		H Ltd.	£95,000	
Less unrealized profit	556		S Ltd.	50,000	
		28,444			145,000
Minority Interest in S Ltd.		6,000	Goodwill on Consolidation		9,000
Trade Creditors—			Stocks	£5,000	
H Ltd.	£20,000		*Less* Unrealized profit	556	
S Ltd.	14,000				4,444
		34,000			
		158,444			158,444

CONSOLIDATED PROFIT AND LOSS ACCOUNT

The purpose of the consolidated profit and loss account is to give a true and fair view of the profits and losses of the group and the final balance must represent the group profits available for dividend.

Following the rules given above, the following adjustments must be made—

1. The holding company's share of pre-acquisition profits must be transferred to capital reserve. Pre-acquisition losses are put to goodwill.
2. The proportion of profits or losses attributable to minority shareholders must be transferred to them.
3. The holding company share of unrealized profits must be eliminated, and transferred to write down the appropriate asset.
4. Inter-company dividend payments must be eliminated.

Example 15

The profit and loss accounts of White Ltd. and its subsidiary Black Ltd. on 31st December, 19.., are as follows—

	White Ltd.	Black Ltd.		White Ltd.	Black Ltd.
	£	£		£	£
Interim Dividends paid	4,000	2,000	Balance b/f.	12,000	4,000
Proposed Final Dividend	6,000	3,000	Net Profit for year	16,000	6,000
Balance c/f	19,500	5,000	Interim Dividend received from Black Ltd.	1,500	
	29,500	10,000		29,500	10,000

White Ltd. acquired its holding of 6,000 ordinary shares out of 8,000 issued in Black Ltd. on 1st January two years earlier, when Black Ltd. had a credit balance of £3,600. The stock of Black Ltd. includes £480 for goods invoiced by White Ltd. at cost plus $33\frac{1}{3}$ per cent.

CONSOLIDATED PROFIT AND LOSS ACCOUNT OF WHITE LTD. (WITH BLACK LTD.)
For the Year Ended 31st December, 19..

		£			£
Transfer to Minority Interest—			Balance b/f—		
Balance b/f	£1,000		Black Ltd.		4,000
Share of profit for year	1,500		White Ltd.		12,000
		2,500	Net Profit for year—		
Interim Dividends paid—			Black Ltd.		6,000
Black Ltd.	£2,000		White Ltd.		16,000
Less—			Interim Dividend from		
Minority Interest	500		Black Ltd.	£1,500	
White Ltd. (contra)	1,500		*Less* Set-off (contra)	1,500	
		—			—
White Ltd. (paid)		4,000			
Transfer to Capital Reserve ($\frac{3}{4}$ of £3,600)		2,700			
Transfer to Stock— $\frac{3}{4}$ of £120 (25% of £480)		90			
Proposed Final Dividend, White Ltd.		6,000			
Balance c/f—					
Black Ltd.	£5,000				
Add Proposed Dividend	3,000				
	8,000				
Less Minority Interest	2,000				
	6,000				
Less Reduction due to transfers to Capital Reserve and Stock	2,790				
	3,210				
White Ltd.	19,500				
		22,710			
		38,000			38,000

QUESTIONS

1. Explain the terms "vendor," "purchase price," "going concern." How is the vendor usually paid?
2. How is goodwill ascertained when a company takes over: (*a*) only assets (*b*), both assets and liabilities?
3. What is the object and use of a "business purchase account"? Submit a formula for the purchase of a business.
4. What statutory powers has a company with reference to: (*a*) the alteration of share capital, (*b*) the reorganization of share capital?
5. What is meant by the reserve liability of a limited company?
6. What are the principal forms under which limited companies may amalgamate their businesses? Discuss their principal features.
7. Explain how fractional parts of a share are dealt with in an amalgamation, reconstruction, or reorganization, etc.
8. Outline a scheme of "amalgamation by absorption."
9. How is a "controlling interest" in a company acquired?
10. Define the terms "reconstruction" and "reorganization." What is the distinctive difference between a reconstruction scheme and a reorganization scheme?
11. In what ways may capital be reduced in a limited company?
12. Define a "holding company." What is the nature of the principal assets of a holding company?
13. What do you understand by a "parent" company?
14. State briefly the advantages and disadvantages of the "holding" system of control.
15. Tabulate the rules for the preparation of a consolidated balance sheet.

EXERCISE 25

1. The Rendick Manufacturing Company Ltd. takes over the following assets and liabilities standing in the books of a private business on 1st January, 19..—

	£
Freehold Property	6,000
Plant and Machinery	2,000
Stock	7,600
Office Furniture	200
Sundry Debtors—	
A. Arnold	450
N. Norman	550
Cash in hand	500
Sundry Creditors—	
K. Kirkdale	700
N. Norton	500

The purchase consideration is £20,000, and it is discharged by the issue to the vendor of—

10,000 ordinary shares of £1 each, fully paid.

1,000 5 per cent preference shares of £5 each, fully paid, and the balance in cash.

The company valued the freehold property at £5,500, the stock at £7,000, and created a provision for bad debts equal to 5 per cent of the sundry debtors. The cash balance of £500 is not taken over.

Show the journal entries in the books of the Rendick Manufacturing Co. Ltd. on 1st January, 19.., to carry through the foregoing (including the cash paid, which is provided by means of an overdraft). (*Faculty of Teachers in Commerce.*)

2. On 31st December, 19.., the balance sheet of Bartons Ltd. was as follows—

	£			£	£
Capital		*Fixed Assets—*			
Authorized—		Patents and Trade Marks at Cost		50,750	
200,000 Shares of £1 each £200,000		Plant & Machinery:			
Issued:		At Cost	£29,312		
120,000 Shares of £1 each, fully paid	120,000	Aggregate Depn.	7,638		
Less—				21,674	
P. & L. A/c Balance	30,156				72,424
	89,844	*Current Assets—*			
		Stock		15,306	
Current Liabilities—		Sundry Debtors	£23,124		
Sundry Creditors	24,725	*Less* Provision for Bad Debts	1,382		
				21,742	
		Balance at Bank		227	
					37,275
		Capital Expenditure not written off—			
		Preliminary Expenses			4,870
	114,569				114,569

A resolution for the voluntary winding up of the company having been passed, the assets (with the exception of the cash) were sold to another company. The purchasers agreed to take over the liabilities of the vendor company and to allot to the liquidator 40,000 fully-paid ordinary shares of £1 each. These arrangements were duly carried out.

Make the journal entries necessary to record the transactions in the books of the purchasing company.

3. On the 31st March, 19.., George Ridley's balance sheet contained the following itemt—

ASSETS

Stock £8,500; debtors £7,000; bills receivable £1,500; business premises £10,000; plant and machinery £7,500; office fittings £800; motor lorries £1,200; cash £28; bank £536.

LIABILITIES AND CAPITAL

Sundry trade creditors £8,200; creditors for expenses £120; loan from T. Jones £1,000; capital £27,744.

On the same date, at the figures shown in the balance sheet, the business was converted into a private limited company called George Ridley Ltd. with a nominal capital of 50,000 £1 ordinary shares. The purchase price of the business was £30,000, payable as to £25,000 in ordinary shares and the balance in cash. The ordinary shares were duly issued to Ridley at par, and 10,000 to other shareholders for cash at par. The purchase was then completed by the payment of £5,000 to Ridley at the end of April, 19... The loan from T. Jones was repaid in June, 19.., together with £20 interest.

In addition to the balances arising from the foregoing, the following appeared in the company's books at 31st March, 19.1. You are required to prepare: (*a*) a trading account, (*b*) a profit and loss account, both for the year ended 31st March, 19.1, and (*c*) a balance sheet at that date.

	£
New plant and machinery, purchased 30th September, 19..	2,500
New motor lorries, purchased 30th September, 19..	1,000
New office fittings, purchased 1st April, 19..	500
Cash in hand	52
Cash in bank	2,264
Debtors	8,200
Creditors	4,315
Bills receivable	1,200
Purchases (net)	22,000
Sales (net)	35,955
Carriage on purchases	220
Carriage on sales	188
Manufacturing wages	3,200
Bad debts	115
Office salaries	720
Travellers' salaries and commission	630
Rates and insurance (factory, £231; office, £89)	320
Office expenses	478
Factory lighting, cleaning, heating and repairs	372
Motor lorries' running expenses for deliveries	235
Preliminary expenses of company formation	800

Adjustments, 31st March, 19.1 (not entered in books)—

Stock at 31st March, 19.1, £9,600.

Depreciation—plant and machinery at 10 per cent per annum; motor lorries at 20 per cent per annum; office fittings at 4 per cent per annum—to include purchases of these assets.

Provide 5 per cent on sundry debtors for bad debts.

Expenses due but unpaid—travellers' commission £120; factory repairs £72; office expenses £16.

Insurances paid in advance—factory £25; office £10.

Directors' fees due £200.

Write off one-half of preliminary expenses and one-third of goodwill.

(*Faculty of Teachers in Commerce.*)

4. The books of the Autogowell Motor Co. Ltd. contained the following balances at the 31st March, 19..—

Debits	£	*Credits*	£
Land and buildings	30,000	Ordinary shares of £1	100,000
Plant and machinery	20,000	Preference shares of £1	50,000
Motor vehicles	2,000	6% debentures	20,000
Stock	74,000	Sundry creditors	61,394
Sundry debtors	35,000		
Formation expenses	6,000		
Profit and loss account	64,000	NOTE. All the authorized capital was issued.	
Calls in arrear—			
Ordinary shares	294		
Preference shares	100		

It was resolved and subsequently approved by the court that the ordinary shares should be reduced to 100,000 shares of 37½p each, fully paid. The preference shares were reduced to 50,000 shares of 75p each, fully paid. The amount written off the capital was applied in writing off the formation expenses and profit and loss account and the balance in reducing the stock-in-trade.

You are required to show the ledger accounts giving effect to the above reduction and the balance sheet after it has taken place.

5. The following is the balance sheet of Structures Ltd. as at 31st December, 19..—

		£			£	£
Capital—			*Fixed Assets—*			
Authorized and Issued:			Freehold Premises at Cost		40,000	
100,000 Shares of £1 each, fully paid		100,000	Plant & Machinery at Cost	£90,000		
Less: P. & L. A/c		42,500	Aggregate Depn.	40,000		
		57,500			50,000	90,000
Long-term Liability—			*Current Assets—*			
6% Mortgage Debentures (secured by a floating charge)	£50,000		Stock		14,700	
Interest Outstanding	3,000		Work-in-progress		8,350	
		53,000	Sundry Debtors		15,280	
			Cash at Bank		1,970	
						40,300
Current Liability—						
Sundry Creditors		19,800				
		130,300				130,300

The debentures are held by Erectors Ltd., which company also holds 25,000 of the shares (such shares being acquired a year before at a cost of £17,500).

Agreement was reached between the two companies (necessary resolutions being duly passed) whereby Erectors Ltd. absorbed Structures Ltd. on the following terms—

(*a*) That Erectors Ltd. take over the assets and liabilities of Structures Ltd. as at 31st December, 19.., at their book figures, subject to reduction of freehold premises by £5,000, and plant and machinery by £2,500.

(*b*) That the capital and interest due on debentures be considered as part of the purchase consideration, such debentures to be cancelled on completion of the absorption.

(*c*) That the outside shareholders in Structures Ltd. be allotted £1 shares in Erectors Ltd. at par (but considered to be worth 25p each), the shares in Structures Ltd. to be taken as of the value of 50p each.

Show (in journal form) the entries required to close the books of Structures Ltd. and to record the transaction in the books of Erectors Ltd.

6. Bee Limited was incorporated on 1st March, 1964, to acquire a steel merchant's business. The purchase price was agreed at £6,000 to be satisfied by the issue of—

(*a*) 3,000 Ordinary Shares of £1 each fully paid; and
(*b*) £3,000 6 per cent Debentures.

The following are the Trading and Profit and Loss Accounts for the year ended 31st December, 1964—

	£		£
Cost of Goods sold	7,740	Sales	15,000
Gross Profit	7,260		
	15,000		15,000
Management Salaries	3,000	Gross Profit	7,260
Office Expenses	250		
Selling Expenses	820		
Carriage on Sales	170		
Rent and Rates	200		
Debenture Interest	135		
Dividend	300		
Directors' Fees	200		
Formation Costs	287		
Interest on Purchase price	90		
Balance	1,808		
	7,260		7,260

You are also informed that—

(i) The total value of the sales for January and February, 1964, was only one-tenth of the value of the sales for the remainder of that year.

(ii) The shares and debentures were all issued to the Vendor on 1st April, 1964.

(iii) Interest at 6 per cent per annum was paid on the purchase price from 1st January, 1964, to the date of settlement.

You are required to prepare a Statement in tabular form, apportioning the balance of the Profit and Loss Account between the periods before and after incorporation of Bee Limited.

Ignore Income Tax. *(A.C.C.A.)*

7. X and Y carried on their business as engineers. They sold this business to the Rapid Engineering Co. Ltd. on 1st January, 19.., on which date their balance sheet showed the following assets and liabilities—

ASSETS

	£
Cash at bank	300
Sundry debtors	5,500
Bills receivable	500
Stock-in-trade	7,000
Plant and machinery	3,500
Land and buildings	3,000
Patterns and models	1,000
Loose tools, etc.	800

LIABILITIES

	£
Sundry creditors	3,500
Provision for bad debts	500
Bills payable	400
Loan on mortgage of land and buildings	2,200

(X and Y's capitals were in equal shares.)

The purchase price was agreed at £18,500, and the discharge by the company of all the liabilities as shown above, the company to have the benefit of any reserves.

This purchase price was paid to the vendors by the allotment of—

12,000 ordinary shares in the company of £1 each at par.

5,000 5½ per cent cumulative preference shares of £1 each, and the balance in cash.

Show the details of the purchase in the company's journal and cash book, and prepare the balance sheet after the allotment of shares to the partners has been completed. (*Faculty of Teachers of Commerce.*)

8. A B Ltd. was registered with an authorized capital of £50,000, divided into 50,000 ordinary shares of £1 each, to acquire the business of A B as from 1st January, 19... A B's capital in the business at the date of sale was £18,000, and the sale agreement provided that he should receive in consideration of the sale 21,000 fully paid shares of £1 each in the company, which took over all assets and liabilities.

The sale agreement also provided that A B should guarantee that the liabilities as shown in his balance sheet at the date of sale would not exceed the amount disclosed and that the debtors would realize the amount shown.

In addition to the shares issued to A B as fully paid, 10,000 shares were issued at par, and 10s. per share had been called up on them.

No entries in respect of the share transactions (other than the receipt of cash) had been put through the financial books of the company during the year ended 31st December, 19.., on which date the trial balance was—

	£	£
A B, Capital		18,000
Cash received for shares		4,500
Plant and machinery, as on 1st January, 19..	6,750	
Plant and machinery, purchased 1st October, 19...	600	
Fixtures and fittings	1,280	
Office and management salaries	2,780	
Rates and insurance	496	
Repairs	207	
Freehold premises	9,850	
Trading account balance		19,498
Bad debts	92	
Bills receivable and payable	219	422
Sundry debtors and creditors	9,840	3,200
Factory charges		850
Stock, 31st December, 19..	6,745	
Office expenses, stationery, etc.	988	
Delivery expenses	210	
Advertising	1,750	
Discount account		318
Preliminary expenses	396	
Cash at bank	3,295	
Cash in hand	15	
Interim dividend paid free of tax	1,275	
	46,788	46,788

You are required to prepare profit and loss account for the year ended 31st December, 19.., and a balance sheet as on that date, taking the following into consideration—

(*a*) Plant and machinery to be depreciated by 10 per cent per annum and fixtures and fittings by 5 per cent. Assume figures for original cost.

(*b*) Included in the item Repairs is an amount of £57 for repairs executed prior to 1st January, 19.., for which no provision had been made at the date the company purchased the business.

(*c*) Included in the item Bad Debts is a debt of £45, which was one of those guaranteed by A B.

(*d*) A provision for bad debts to be created equal to 5 per cent of sundry debtors, and a reserve for income tax of £3,500.

(*e*) The amount appearing under the heading of factory charges is the amount charged in the trading account to cover rent, etc., of the factory.

(*f*) Preliminary expenses: one-half to be written off. (*C.I.S.*)

9. A company, after a series of trading losses, resolved to reduce its capital of 60,000 shares of £1 each fully paid to 60,000 shares of 25p each fully paid.

The balance sheet of the company prior to the reduction of capital was as follows—

	£		£
Capital—		Goodwill	10,000
Authorized and Issued:		Freehold Property . . .	9,030
60,000 Shares of £1 each,		Plant & Machinery. . .	19,240
fully paid	60,000	Stock	20,470
Premium on Shares A/c . .	600	Sundry Debtors . . .	21,290
Sundry Creditors . . .	40,350	Cash	670
		P. & L. A/c	20,250
	100,950		100,950

It was resolved to eliminate the premium on shares account and to allocate the amount then available upon reduction of capital as follows—

(*a*) To write off the debit balance of the profit and loss account.
(*b*) To write off entirely the value of goodwill.
(*c*) To reduce the value of plant and machinery by £9,240.
(*d*) To reduce the value of the stock by 20 per cent.
(*e*) To provide a provision for bad debts of £1,500.
(*f*) To use any available balance to reduce the book value of the freehold property.

You are required to give the journal entries necessary to give effect to the above and to show the balance sheet of the company after the reduction of capital. (*C.I.S.*)

10. A company, not wishing to deplete its cash resources but anxious to maintain its dividend history, decides to distribute profits by means of bonus shares.

(i) What are the advantages and disadvantages of this from the point of view of the company and the shareholders?

(ii) Illustrate your answer with the entries necessary when the distribution is one share of £1 for every ten shares of £1 each on an issued capital of £100,000. (*R.S.A.*)

11. D. Fence, carrying on a trading business, wishes to expand. To provide the finance for this purpose he decided to convert his business into a limited company as on 31st March, 1965 and issue shares for cash.

The following is the balance sheet of the business as on 31st March, 1965—

	£		£	£
Capital Account	15,701	Fixed Assets at cost *less* depreciation to date—		
Sundry Creditors.	736	Freehold Premises . . .	7,450	
		Furniture, Fittings and Equipment . . .	3,240	
				10,690
		Current Assets—		
		Trading stock . . .	3,396	
		Sundry debtors . . .	1,487	
		Cash at bank . . .	864	
				5,747
	16,437			16,437

For the transfer to the company the value of the following assets was fixed as follows—

Goodwill £12,000, freehold premises £14,000, furniture, fittings and equipment £4,800, trading stock £3,163 and, as regards the sundry debtors, £150 was allowed as a provision for doubtful debts. The cash at bank was retained by Fence and he discharged the sundry creditors.

The company, in the name of Fence & Co. Ltd., was incorporated on 1st April, 1965, with an authorized capital of £50,000 divided into 50,000 shares of £1 each. In satisfaction of the assets acquired by the company, Fence received fully paid shares at par, the remainder of the share capital being issued at £1·30 per share for cash, payable on application.

On 12th April, 1965, applications were received for 48,100 shares and *pro rata* allotments were made on 26th April, 1965.

Fence personally paid all costs of the transaction.

It can be assumed that no trading transactions were carried out between 31st March, 1965, and 27th April, 1965.

Give the journal entries necessary to close Fence's books and prepare the Balance Sheet of Fence & Co. Ltd., as on 27th April, 1965. (*A.C.C.A.*)

12. Grand Ltd. and Palace Ltd. carry on businesses of a similar nature, and it is agreed that they should amalgamate. A new company Grand Palace Ltd. is to be formed to which the assets and liabilities of the existing companies, with certain exceptions, are to be transferred. At the date of the amalgamation the Balance Sheets of the two companies were as follows—

	Grand £	Palace £		Grand £	Palace £
Shares (£1 each)	7,500	4,000	Freehold Property at cost	5,250	3,000
General Reserve	4,000	—	Plant and Machinery at cost, less depreciation	1,250	750
Profit and Loss Account	1,000	1,000			
5 per cent Debentures	—	3,000	Motor Vehicles	500	—
Creditors	3,750	1,600	Stock	3,000	3,900
			Debtors	4,100	1,050
			Bank	2,150	900
	16,250	9,600		16,250	9,600

Assets and liabilities are to be taken at book value, with the following exceptions—

Goodwill of Grand Ltd. and Palace Ltd. is to be valued at £4,000 and £1,500 respectively.

Motor Vehicles of Grand Ltd. are to be valued at £1,500.

The Debentures in Palace Ltd. are to be discharged by the issue of 6 per cent. Debentures in Grand Palace Ltd. at a premium of 4 per cent.

The Debtors and Bank of Palace Ltd. are to be retained by the liquidator and the Sundry Creditors are to be paid from the proceeds.

You are required to compute the basis on which Shares in Grand Palace Ltd. will be issued to shareholders in the existing companies and to draw up a Balance Sheet of the new company immediately after the completion of the amalgamation. (*L.C.C.*)

13. On 1st March, 1965 A and B (trading in partnership as A & B and making up their accounts to 31st December) executed an agreement for the sale to a new company A.B. Ltd., as at 1st January, 1965, of the following assets, for a consideration of £135,000, allocated as under—

	£
Goodwill	30,000
Freehold land and buildings	60,000
Plant and machinery	35,000
Stocks	10,000

The partnership would retain the debtors and creditors at 31st December, 1964.

The company was incorporated on 1st March, 1965, with an authorized capital of £250,000 in ordinary shares of £1 each, of which £135,000 were issued forthwith in satisfaction of the purchase consideration. The business was deemed to have been carried on by the vendors on behalf of the purchasers from 1st January, 1965, and A & B continued their book-keeping records to 31st March, without regard to the sale of the assets, although for the month of March sales had been invoiced, and purchases made, in the name of A.B. Ltd.

The trial balance in the books of A & B at 31st March, 1965 was as follows—

	£	£
Goodwill	10,000	
Freehold land and buildings	25,000	
Plant and machinery	20,500	
Stock—31st December, 1964	9,500	
Debtors	7,300	
Creditors		6,300
Capital account A		32,000
,, ,, B		25,000
Current account A		80
,, ,, B		70
Wages and salaries	18,600	
Directors' fees	300	
Purchases	20,500	
A.B. Ltd.	1,050	
Expenses	2,400	
Cash at bank	—	
Sales		52,300
Discounts	600	
	115,750	115,750

Stocks at 31st March were valued at £8,200. The balance of A.B. Ltd.'s account represented preliminary and formation expenses. Debtors included debts outstanding at 31st December, 1964, of £1,300 which are considered good. Creditors included items unpaid at 31st December of £800 which are still unpaid. There were no sales or purchases for cash, and you are to assume that trading profits accrued regularly over the period.

You are required to prepare—

(*a*) the journal entries necessary to open the books of A.B. Ltd.;

(*b*) an interim trading and profit and loss account for A.B. Ltd., for the three months ended 31st March, 1965, and the balance sheet at that date, ignoring depreciation and taxation;

(*c*) the account of A & B as it would appear in the books of A.B. Ltd.

14. P Ltd. is a public company having an issued capital of £1,000,000 in fully paid £1 shares, all of one class, and Q Ltd. is another public company having an issued share capital of £200,000 divided into shares of 25p each, all fully paid and of one class.

P Ltd. decides to attempt to obtain a controlling interest in Q Ltd., at a time when the market quotations of the shares of the two companies are $37\frac{1}{2}$p and $17\frac{1}{2}$p respectively, and to this end makes an offer to the members of Q Ltd. to purchase their shares on the following alternative terms—

(1) To issue one fully paid share in P Ltd. for each six shares of Q Ltd.;

(2) To issue one fully paid share in P Ltd., plus 80p in cash for each ten shares of Q Ltd.

The offer is accepted by the holders of 150,000 shares of Q Ltd. on the basis of the first alternative and a further 530,000 shares on the basis of the second alternative.

Record the carrying out of these transactions in the form of journal entries, on the basis that the new shares of P Ltd. are valued at £1·20 at the time of issue, and show how the position would be reflected in the next published balance sheet of P Ltd.

(*R.S.A.*)

15. The Birget Engineering Co. Ltd. purchased certain patents from Short & Sharp, under an agreement dated 30th June, at a cost of £40,000. £1,000 of this sum was to be paid to the vendors in cash, and the balance in fully-paid £10 ordinary shares.

Including the shares allotted as fully paid to the vendors, the company issued capital to the extent of £75,000, consisting of £50,000 in ordinary shares of £10 each (£1 on application, £4 on allotment, and £5 at the end of three months), and £25,000 in 5 per cent preference shares of £5 each (£1 on application, £2 on allotment, and £2 at the end of three months).

Under the agreement with Short and Sharp, the patents passed to the company on 9th July, which date was also the date of allotment.

All the shares issued to the public were fully subscribed and duly paid for with the exception of £200 calls in arrear on the preference shares. All cash was paid direct to the company's bankers.

Make the necessary entries in the books of the company to give effect to the above transactions, and show how they would appear in the company's first balance sheet.

(*London Chamber of Commerce.*)

16. Black is in business. His assets, apart from goodwill, are valued at £30,000, and his liabilities are £2,000. White is in business, and his assets, apart from goodwill, are valued at £20,000, and his liabilities are £1,500. Their profits for the last three years have been—

Black,	£600 first year;	£700 second year;	£800 third year.
White,	£400 ,, ;	£500 ,, ;	£600 ,,

They agree to sell their businesses to a limited company to be formed with a nominal capital of £100,000, divided into 60,000 5 per cent preference shares of £1 each and 40,000 ordinary shares of £1 each, the company taking over the assets and the liabilities. It is also agreed that Black and White shall each receive fully-paid preference shares in consideration of goodwill (based on 2 years' purchase price of average of past 3 years' profits); the balance of purchase money to be paid in cash. The public subscribe and pay in full for 20,000 preference shares and 35,000 ordinary shares. The company paid preliminary expenses, £1,500. Show the vendors' accounts in the company's ledger and the balance sheet of the company after these transactions have been completed.

(*Institute of Book-keepers.*)

17. The John Smith and Steel Bin Co. Ltd. was registered on and took over the premises of John Smith as from 1st January. John Smith sold his business to the company upon the following valuation—

	£
Buildings (on leasehold premises with 21 years to run from 1st January)	7,500
Machinery and plant	11,650
Stock and materials	3,872
Goodwill	10,000

The company took over the book-debts, which John Smith guaranteed, while he discharged the liabilities existing on 31st December last. The company was registered with a nominal capital of £80,000 divided into 80,000 shares of £1 each. Of these 25,000 fully paid shares were allotted to the vendor as part consideration for the sale of the business, the balance being paid to him in cash. 20,000 shares were offered to subscribed, and fully paid by the public, with the exception of 200 shares, on which 50p per share had been paid, and which were forfeited during the year by resolution of the boards of directors, owing to the non-payment of the final call of 50p per share. The books were closed on 31st December, and stock taken as on that date, amounting to £6,760.

You are required to write off one-twentieth of the value of the buildings (to provide for the expiration of the lease); 8 per cent of the machinery and plant (as depreciation); one-fourth of the preliminary expenses; and 5 per cent from the book-debts (as provision against bad and doubtful debts); and then to prepare the company's trading account and profit and loss account for the year to 31st December, and balance sheet as on that day. The balances of the ledger accounts then, in addition to those resulting from the above transactions, were—

	£		£
Purchases	35,720	Office expenses	1,006
Rent	76	Directors' fees	200
Rates and taxes	211	Sundry debtors	12,380
Wages	8,241	,, creditors	4,467
Salaries	917	Preliminary expenses	400
Manufacturing expenses	2,163	Bad debts (of which £187 were in respect of the debts guaranteed by John Smith, and are payable by him)	206
Sales	49,798	Cash at bank	3,599
Returned purchases	311	Auditors' fees	100
Discounts allowed (of which £239 were allowed on debts, which were guaranteed in full by John Smith, and are payable by him)	1,033	Returned sales	763
		Discounts received	561

State what dividend you would recommend to be paid to the shareholders, and what balance of profit and loss account would be carried forward to the next year.

(*R.S.A.*)

18. A. Edwards & Co. sold their business to a company for the sum of £220,000, to be paid for by 125,000 £1 ordinary shares and £95,000 in cash. Their assets consisted of—

	£
Freehold land and buildings, valued at	28,000
Machinery and plant, etc., valued at	25,000
Book debts, certified by the auditors at	45,000
Stocks and materials in progress, valued at	140,000
Advertising plates, etc.	25,000

And their liabilities were—

	£
Trade creditors	40,000
Loans on mortgage	45,000

The capital of the company was £250,000, consisting of 125,000 ordinary shares of £1 each, and 125,000 6 per cent preference shares of £1 each, issued at £1·05 a share. The preference shares were subscribed by the public as follows—

On application 5p per share; on allotment 12½p per share.
On first call 50p per share; on second call 37½p per share.

Make the journal entries for the above transactions in the company's books, and set out the balance sheet thereafter. (*Chartered Accountants.*)

19. A and O, trading in partnership, and sharing profits and losses in the proportions of two-thirds and one-third respectively, sold their business to J. S. & Co. Their balance sheet showed as follows—

	£		£
Creditors	3,750	Plant	2,000
A's Capital	6,000	Fixtures & Furniture	650
O's Capital	4,000	Stock	7,500
		Book Debts	2,500
		Bills Receivable	500
		Cash at Bank	600
	13,750		13,750

The purchasers agreed to give £2,000 for goodwill, but would only take over the stock at £7,000, and the plant at £1,700. Make up the capital accounts of A and O, carrying out the terms of sale. (*Chartered Accountants.*)

20. R and J, equal partners, agree to amalgamate with F, a sole trader, to form a new company called Z Ltd., having an authorized capital of 100,000 ordinary shares of 25p each.

The respective balance sheets at 31st December, 1965 were as follows—

	R and J £	F £
Capital accounts R	5,850	
J	4,760	
F		5,000
Current accounts R	1,770	
J	2,155	
Creditors	3,065	2,400
Bank		1,700
	17,600	9,100
Freehold buildings	3,280	1,790
Plant	2,660	2,960
Vehicles	1,560	800
Investments	2,500	
Debtors	3,200	2,350
Stock	2,000	1,200
Bank	2,400	
	17,600	9,100

Under the terms of the amalgamation the following were agreed—

(1) Goodwill of R and J to be valued at £3,000 and F at £1,600.

(2) Investments to be taken over by R at £2,800.

(3) A potential bad debt of £150 to be written off F's debtors and then a bad debt provision of 2½ per cent on all debtors to be created.

(4) Other assets to be valued at—

	R and J £	F £
Freehold buildings	4,000	2,000
Plant	2,500	3,000
Vehicles	1,400	700
Stock	1,800	1,200

(5) Z Ltd., to issue 43,400 shares as total consideration, to be allotted to R, J and F *pro rata* to the amounts due to them.

You are required to present—

(*a*) journal entries closing the books of F;

(*b*) the realization account and partners' capital accounts of the partnership, so as to close their books, and show how many shares in Z Ltd. each receives;

(*c*) the opening balance sheet of Z Ltd. following the amalgamation.

(*L.C.C.*)

21. Two companies decide to amalgamate and form a new company. The Balance Sheets of the two companies A. Ltd. and B. Ltd. at the date of the amalgamation were as follows—

	A. Ltd. £	B. Ltd. £		A. Ltd. £	B. Ltd. £
Share Capital—			Goodwill		12,000
50p Shares fully paid .	100,000		Freehold Premises . .		44,000
£1 Shares fully paid . .		80,000	Plant and Machinery . .	40,000	28,000
Loan on Mortgage . .		40,000	Stock-in-Trade . .	75,000	25,000
Sundry Creditors . . .	45,000	30,000	Sundry Debtors . . .	70,000	20,000
General Reserve . . .	40,000		Cash at Bank . . .	15,000	3,000
Profit and Loss Account .	15,000		Profit and Loss Account		18,000
	200,000	150,000		200,000	150,000

The new company is incorporated under the name of A.B. Ltd., the Share Capital to be divided into shares of 50p each.

The shareholders in A. Ltd. are to be credited with £20,000 for Goodwill and the Goodwill in B. Ltd.'s Balance Sheet is to be regarded as valueless.

Prepare the Balance Sheet of A.B. Ltd. and state what proportion of the share capital of the new company will be received by the shareholders of the two merging companies. (*L.C.C.*)

22. The directors of Large Ltd. ask you to draft a Consolidated Balance Sheet of the whole undertaking by amalgamating the assets and liabilities of the subsidiary companies, S. Ltd. and T. Ltd. with those of Large Ltd.

Your detailed workings should be shown.

The following is an abstract of the Balance Sheets of the three companies as on 31st December, 1965.

	Large Ltd. £	£	S. Ltd. £	T. Ltd. £	£
Share Capital, Authorized and Issued—					
Ordinary Shares of £1 each, fully paid		100,000	40,000		30,000
Share Premium Account (Premium on issue of 20,000 Shares issued in payment for 30,000 Shares in S. Ltd.) .		10,000			
Sundry Creditors		19,000	20,000		3,000
Bills Payable (all issued to Large Ltd.).			18,000		
Profit and Loss Account—					
Balance brought forward . .	5,000			6,000	
Add Interim Dividend from T. Ltd. .	6,000				
Profit for year to date . .	12,000			12,000	
		23,000		18,000	
Deduct Interim Dividend of 30 per cent per annum .				9,000	
					9,000
		152,000	78,000		42,000

Note. Large Ltd. had a contingent liability in respect of bills discounted £10,000. Sundry creditors of S. Ltd., £20,000, includes £15,000 owed to Large Ltd.

	Large Ltd.		S. Ltd.		T. Ltd.
	£	£	£	£	£
Goodwill at cost . . .				6,000	
Land, Buildings, Plant and Machinery at cost . . .		25,000		30,000	20,000
Investments, at cost—					
30,000 Ordinary Shares in S. Ltd. .	30,000				
20,000 Ordinary Shares in T. Ltd. .	40,000				
		70,000			
10,000 Ordinary Shares in T. Ltd. .				20,000	
Stocks		10,000		3,000	8,000
Sundry Debtors . . .	10,000			2,000	7,000
Advance to S. Ltd. . . .	15,000				
		25,000			
Bill Receivable (accepted by S. Ltd.) .		8,000			
Balances at Bankers . . .		14,000		10,000	7,000
Profit and Loss Account— . .					
Balance brought forward . .			4,000		
Deduct Interim Dividend from T. Ltd.			3,000		
			1,000		
Add Loss for year to date . .			6,000		
				7,000	
		152,000		78,000	42,000

On 1st January, 1964, the date when Large Ltd. purchased the 30,000 shares in S. Ltd., the debit balance on the latter company's Profit and Loss Account was £1,000. Large Ltd. and S. Ltd. both purchased their shares in T. Ltd. on 1st January, 1965.

(*L.C.C.*)

23. Pink and Green were trading in partnership, sharing profits in the ratio of three and two, and the firm's balance sheet drawn up as on 30th June, 19.., was—

	£		£	£
Capital and Current A/c's—		Fixed Assets—		
Pink	45,500	Motor Vans (at cost)	4,800	
Green	28,500	*Less* depreciation	2,100	
				2,700
	74,000	Furniture & Fittings (at cost) .	5,600	
Creditors	2,850	*Less* depreciation	2,400	
				3,200
				5,900
		Current Assets—		
		Stocks	46,500	
		Debtors . . .	16,300	
		Bank . . .	8,150	
				70,950
	76,850			76,850

On 31st March, 19.1, the business was converted into a private limited company, incorporated on that day under the name of Dianthus Ltd. with an authorized capital of £100,000. The company took over all the firm's assets and liabilities for £74,000, issuing as consideration 20,000 7 per cent preference shares and 54,000 ordinary shares (all of £1 each), the profit earned during the nine months since the date of the firm's last balance sheet, so far as undrawn, belonging to the partners. The ordinary shares were to be divided between the partners in their profit-sharing proportion and the preference shares in such proportion that neither partner should be indebted to the other. Both partners became directors and each was entitled to director's fees at the rate of £1,200 per annum.

The company kept the partnership books in use, and no record of the formation of the company was made except as regards the payment of the formation expenses. Accounts are in course of being prepared to 30th June, 19.1, and a trial balance has been drawn up (after closing the trading account) as follows—

	Dr £	*Cr* £
Capital and current accounts, 30th June, 19..—		
Pink		45,500
Green		28,500
Motor vans (at cost)	4,800	
„ „ depreciation to 30th June, 19..		2,100
Furniture and fittings (at cost)	5,600	
„ „ „ depreciation to 30th June, 19..		2,400
Stock, 30th June, 19.1	47,460	
Debtors and creditors	17,320	3,170
Drawings (including Directors' fees)—		
Pink	1,800	
Green	1,600	
Gross Profit for the year		12,800
Sundry expenses	4,200	
Formation expenses	360	
Bank balance	11,330	
	94,470	94,470

Depreciation is to be provided at 20 per cent on the motor vans and 5 per cent on the furniture and fittings, calculated in each case by reference to the original cost to the partnership.

You are required to set out—

(*a*) a statement showing how the two classes of shares were divided between the partners;

(*b*) the journal entry to be put through to record the sale of the business by the partners to Dianthus Ltd.;

(*c*) a statement showing the apportionment of the profit for the year;

(*d*) the partners' personal accounts, including the closing entries, and

(*e*) the company's balance sheet showing the position before appropriations.

(*R.S.A.*)

24. A owns 200,000 shares in AB Limited. He offers these shares of £1 each to CD Limited at 62½p each, the consideration to be satisfied either by: (*a*) cash, or (*b*) the issue of fully-paid £1 ordinary shares in CD Limited, at the value of £1·25 each, or (*c*) partly by cash and partly by ordinary shares in CD Limited, at the price stated.

The directors of CD Limited decide to accept the offer, and to satisfy the consideration due to A, as to £50,000, by the issue to him of 40,000 shares, and as to the balance, in cash.

For the purpose of providing the cash necessary, CD Limited issue a further 60,000 ordinary shares of £1 each at 25p premium. Such issue is fully subscribed and the liability to A is settled.

Show the journal entries in respect of these transactions as they appear in the books of CD Limited. (*R.S.A.*)

25. Chatenays Ltd. was registered with a nominal capital of £200,000, comprising 100,000 each of ordinary and 6 per cent preference shares of £1 each to purchase the old-established business of Abel Chatenay. The purchase price was agreed at £120,000, payable as to £30,000 in cash; £40,000 in ordinary shares of £1 each, and £50,000 in 6 per cent preference shares of £1 each. The company was to discharge the liabilities of the old firm. The balance sheet of Abel Chatenay as on the date of purchase was as follows—

SUMMARIZED BALANCE SHEET

	£		£
Capital	100,000	Freehold Works . . .	36,000
Creditors	14,040	Machinery & Plant. . .	37,860
Bank Loan	2,000	Sundry Debtors . . .	18,764
		Stock	22,440
		Cash in hand	976
	116,040		116,040

The balance of both classes of shares was issued to the public and fully subscribed and paid up.

Prepare the accounts necessary to record the above purchase in the company's books, and give the initial balance sheet of the new company. (*R.S.A.*)

26. Stone and Rock carried on business in partnership as builders, sharing all profits and losses: Stone two-thirds, Rock one-third.

They agreed with Flint, who was in business on his own account, to amalgamate their businesses as on 31st March, 19. . .

The summarized balance sheets of the two firms as on that date were as follows—

		Stone and Rock £	Flint £			Stone and Rock £		Flint £
Capital—				Freehold Premises . .		8,000		
Stone . . .	£21,000			Plant & Equipment .		7,000		5,000
Rock	8,000					15,000		5,000
		29,000		Work-in-progress		17,000		7,000
Flint			7,000	Debtors. .	£2,750		2,800	
Trade Creditors . . .		9,000	4,000	*Less* Provision	750		500	
Bank Overdraft . . .			3,300			2,000		2,300
				Balance at Bank . .		4,000		
		38,000	14,300			38,000		14,300

The terms on which the businesses were amalgamated were as follows—

(1) Profits were to be shared: Stone one-half, Rock one-quarter, and Flint one-quarter.

(2) The value of goodwill of the two firms was agreed at Stone and Rock £12,000, Flint £6,000. (No account for goodwill was to be opened in the books, but adjusting entries for transactions between the partners were to be made in the partners' capital accounts.)

(3) The new firm was to take over all the assets and discharge all the liabilities of Stone and Rock, but assets were to be revalued as follows—

	£
Freehold premises	11,000
Plant and equipment	6,250
Work-in-progress	18,500
Debtors	2,750

(4) Flint was to collect his own debts and pay his trade creditors. The new firm was to take over his plant and equipment for £5,000 and his work-in-progress for £7,500 and to pay off his bank overdraft.

(5) The capital of the firm was to be £40,000, contributed in profit-sharing ratios. The balance due to be paid in or withdrawn by each partner was to be entered in a current account.

You are required to show—

(*a*) the partners' capital accounts in columnar form recording these transactions, and

(*b*) the opening balance sheet of the new firm. (*Chartered Accountants.*)

27. AB & Co. Ltd. decided to write up its assets as at the 31st December, 19.., following a revaluation carried out on 30th September, 19...

The increases in values were as follows—

	£
Land and buildings	50,000
Plant and machinery	30,000
Fixtures and fittings	5,000

A capital reserve is to be created.

The directors decided to distribute out of this increase a bonus issue of one £1 ordinary share for each of the 75,000 ordinary shares of £1 each which have been issued.

Show the journal entries required to record these transactions.

(*Cost and Management Accountants.*)

28. The following are the trial balances of Needles Ltd. and its subsidiary company, Pins Ltd. as on 31st December, 19.1—

Needles Ltd.	£	£
Authorized and issued share capital (ordinary shares of £1 each, fully paid)		30,000
Cost of goods sold	87,000	
Fixed assets	18,175	
General expenses	23,000	
Debtors and creditors	6,125	5,550
Balance at bank	8,930	
Stock, 31st December, 19.1, at cost	7,320	
12,000 ordinary shares in Pins Ltd., at cost	16,600	
Profit and loss account—		
Balance at 31st December, 19..		3,600
Sales (including sales to Pins Ltd. £8,400)		128,000
	167,150	167,150

Pins Ltd.	£	£
Authorized and issued share capital (ordinary shares of £1 each, fully paid)		15,000
Stock, 31st December, 19.1 (at cost) (including goods purchased from Needles Ltd. for £2,400)	4,180	
Fixed assets	16,500	
Cost of goods sold	27,320	
Sales		36,000
Debtors and creditors	3,750	2,960
General expenses	5,440	
Balance at bank	770	
Profit and loss account—		
Balance at 31st December, 19..		4,000
	57,960	57,960

Needles Ltd. acquired the shares in Pins Ltd. on 31st December, 19..

The cost to Needles Ltd. of the goods sold to Pins Ltd. was 30 per cent below the price at which they were sold to the subsidiary. These goods have been included in the amounts shown in the trial balance of Pins Ltd. as "stock" and "cost of goods sold" at their cost to Pins Ltd.

No dividends were paid by either company during 19.1. It is proposed that Pins Ltd. should pay a dividend of £1,500 for 19.1.

You are required to prepare a consolidated trading and profit and loss account for the year 19.1 and a consolidated balance sheet as on 31st December, 19.1.

Ignore taxation and depreciation of fixed assets.

(*Chartered Institute of Secretaries.*)

29. The summarized balance sheets of Wheat Ltd. and its subsidiary companies, Corn Ltd. and Straw Ltd. at 31st December, 19.1, were as under—

WHEAT LTD.

	£		£
Issued Share Capital (100,000 shares of £1 each)	100,000	Freehold Properties	70,000
P. & L. A/c (including dividend from Corn Ltd.)	33,000	Current Assets	43,000
Trade Creditors	22,000	12,000 Shares in Corn Ltd., at cost	24,500
		15,000 Shares in Straw Ltd., at cost	14,500
		£3,000 5% Debentures of Corn Ltd., at cost	3,000
	155,000		155,000

CORN LTD.

		£		£
Issued Share Capital (12,000 shares of £1 each)		12,000	Freehold Properties	18,000
P. & L. A/c—			Current Assets	12,000
At 31st Dec., 19..	£4,000			
Add Net Profit 19.1	5,200			
		9,200		
5% Debentures		4,000		
Debenture Interest accrued		200		
Trade Creditors		4,600		
		30,000		30,000

STRAW LTD.

		£		£
Issued Share Capital (20,000 shares of £1 each)		20,000	Freehold Properties	17,000
P. & L. A/c—			Current Assets	16,400
At 31st Dec., 19..	£1,600			
Less Loss 19.1	1,200			
		400		
Trade Creditors		13,000		
		33,400		33,400

Wheat Ltd. acquired the shares and debentures in Corn Ltd. and the shares in Straw Ltd. on 31st December, 19...

The profit and loss account of Corn Ltd. for the year 19.. was debited with a proposed dividend of £3,000, and this was paid on 1st February 19.1. No other dividend was paid by any of the companies in 19.1, and none is proposed.

No entry has been made in the books of Wheat Ltd. in respect of the debenture interest due from Corn Ltd.

You are required to prepare the consolidated balance sheet of the group at 31st December, 19.1.

You are to show, as a schedule to the consolidated balance sheet, a short summary of your calculations of all the items therein, except share capital, freehold properties, current assets, and trade creditors. Ignore taxation.

30. The summarized balance sheets of Westward Ltd. and its subsidiary companies Eastward Ltd., and Southward Ltd., at 31st December, 19.1, were as follows—

WESTWARD LTD.

		£			£
Issued Share Capital—			Fixed Assets		88,000
200,000 Ordinary Shares of £1 each		200,000	Shares in Subsidiary Companies, at cost—		
P. & L. A/c (including dividend from Southward Ltd.)		31,000	75,000 Ordinary Shares in Eastward Ltd.	£93,400	
Current Liabilities		24,800	15,000 Ordinary Shares in Southward Ltd.	21,600	
					115,000
			Current Assets		52,800
		255,800			255,800

EASTWARD LTD.

		£		£
Issued Share Capital—			Fixed Assets	69,000
75,000 Ordinary Shares of £1 each		75,000	Current Assets	38,000
P. & L. A/c—				
At 31st Dec., 19..	£9,250			
Add Net Profit, 19.1	7,000			
		16,250		
Current Liabilities		15,750		
		107,000		107,000

SOUTHWARD LTD.

	£		£
Issued Share Capital—		Fixed Assets . . .	18,000
20,000 Ordinary Shares of £1 each	20,000	Current Assets . . .	26,000
4,000 6% Preference Shares of £1 each	4,000		
	24,000		
P. & L. A/c	4,560		
Proposed Dividends . . .	2,240		
Current Liabilities . . .	13,200		
	44,000		44,000

The following is a summary of the profit and loss account of Southward Ltd.—

		£		£
Proposed Dividends—			Net Profit, 19.1 . . .	2,800
Ordinary . .	£2,000		Balance 31st December, 19.. .	4,000
Preference . .	240			
		2,240		
Balance c/f . . .		4,560		
		6,800		6,800

Westward Ltd. acquired the shares in both subsidiaries on 31st December, 19...

The profit and loss account of Southward Ltd. for 19.. was debited with a proposed ordinary dividend of £1,600 and a proposed preference dividend of £240. Both these dividends were paid early in 19.1

You are required to prepare a consolidated balance sheet as on 31st December, 19.1. Show your calculations. (*Chartered Institute of Secretaries.*)

31. Beach Ltd. was incorporated in December, 19.., and issued 50,000 ordinary shares of £1 each, at a premium of 10p each. These shares were fully paid up in cash on 31st December, 19.., and the company commenced business on 1st January, 19.1.

Beach Ltd. paid preliminary expenses £400 and paid £40,000 for fixed assets, which were retained throughout the year 19.1.

In January, 19.1, Beach Ltd. acquired the whole issued share capital of Shingle Ltd. (22,000 ordinary shares of £1 each) at a valuation of £1·25 per share. The purchase consideration was satisfied by the issue of 25,000 fully paid ordinary shares in Beach Ltd.

In March, 19.1, Beach Ltd. lent £10,000, free of interest, to Shingle Ltd.

Shingle Ltd. was wound up and, after paying all creditors in full, the liquidator, on 30th June, 19.1, made a first and final payment, on account of share capital, to Beach Ltd., amounting to £34,000.

The net trading profit of Beach Ltd. for the year 19.1 amounted to £12,650, after charging £6,000 for depreciation of fixed assets.

Except for £9,470 owing to trade creditors, all purchases and expenses (other than depreciation) were paid in cash and all sales were for cash.

On 31st December, 19.1, stock-in-trade amounted to £11,230 at cost.

You are required—

(*a*) to show your calculation of the net trading receipts of Beach Ltd. for the year 19.1;

(*b*) to prepare a summary of the company's cash account for the year 19.1; and

(*c*) to set out the balance sheet of the company (not necessarily in a form for publication) at 31st December, 19.1.

Ignore taxation. (*Institute of Bankers.*)

32. The Cee Tee Co. Ltd. was incorporated with a view to acquiring as on 1st April, 1964, the business previously carried on by C. Tree. The authorized capital of the company was £150,000 divided into 105,000 Ordinary Shares of £1 each and 45,000 6 per cent Preference Shares of £1 each.

C. Tree's balance sheet as on 31st March, 1964 was as follows—

	£		£
C. Tree, Capital Account . .	54,030	Freehold Land and Buildings .	18,000
Trade creditors and accrued expenses	12,830	Plant and Machinery . .	33,600
Overdraft at Southern Bank .	6,640	Stock on hand . . .	9,000
		Sundry Debtors . . .	12,900
	73,500		73,500

The company acquired all the assets and undertook to discharge all the liabilities. For the purpose of acquisition it was agreed that the values of the assets should be taken as follows—

Freehold land and buildings £22,000, plant and machinery £30,000, stock on hand £8,500 and the debtors at book value with a deduction of 5 per cent to cover doubtful debts.

The bank agreed to the transfer of the overdraft to the company provided that a debenture for £7,500, secured on the freehold land and buildings, was issued to the bank. The purchase consideration fixed at £70,000 was settled by a cash payment of £20,000 and the issue at par, of 30,000 Ordinary Shares and 20,000 Preference Shares both fully paid. Provincial Investments Ltd. agreed to take up 75,000 ordinary shares at par and they were issued for cash on 1st April, 1964, such cash being paid the same day into The Cee Tee Co. Ltd.'s account with the Northern Bank.

The formation expenses £1,760 were paid by the Cee Tee Co. Ltd.

Give the journal entries, including those relative to cash, to close C. Tree's books and prepare the Balance Sheet of The Cee Tee Co. Ltd. as it would appear immediately after the completion of all the transactions mentioned. (*A.C.C.A.*)

33. The summarized balance sheets of Gleam Ltd. and its subsidiary companies Glitter Ltd. and Sparkle Ltd. at 31st December, 19.1, were as under—

GLEAM LTD.

	£		£
Issued Share Capital—		Fixed Assets	85,000
175,000 Ordinary Shares of £1 each	175,000	50,000 Ordinary Shares in Glitter Ltd., at cost . .	57,200
P. & L. A/c (including dividend received from Sparkle Ltd.) .	17,000	12,000 Ordinary Shares in Sparkle Ltd., at cost . .	23,400
Trade Creditors	15,600	Current Assets	42,000
	207,600		207,600

GLITTER LTD.

		£		£
Issued Share Capital—			Fixed Assets . . .	52,000
50,000 Ordinary Shares of £1 each		50,000	Current Assets. . .	19,000
P. & L. A/c—				
At 31st Dec., 19. . .	£5,300			
Add Net Profit, 19.1	1,000			
		6,300		
Trade Creditors. . .		14,700		
		71,000		71,000

SPARKLE LTD.

		£		£
Issued Share Capital—			Fixed Assets . . .	13,500
15,000 Ordinary Shares of £1 each		15,000	Current Assets. . .	28,500
5,000 6% Preference Shares of £1 each . . .		5,000		
		20,000		
P. & L. A/c—				
At 31st Dec., 19. . .	£6,000			
Add Net Profit, 19.1	3,800			
	9,800			
Less Proposed Dividends—				
Ordinary . £900				
Preference . 300	1,200			
		8,600		
Proposed Dividends . . .		1,200		
Trade Creditors. . .		12,200		
		42,000		42,000

Gleam Ltd. acquired the shares in both subsidiaries on 31st December, 19. .

Glitter Ltd. paid no dividend for 19. ., and none is proposed for 19.1.

The profit and loss account of Sparkle Ltd. for 19. . was debited with a proposed ordinary dividend of £750 and a proposed preference dividend of £300. Both these dividends were paid in January, 19.1.

You are required to prepare the consolidated balance sheet on 31st December, 19.1. Show the composition (by way of a note) of those items which are calculated. Ignore taxation. (*Institute of Bankers* (*modified*).)

34. The balance sheet of AB Ltd., at 31st December, 1964 was as follows—

Share capital—			Fixed assets—	Cost	Depn.	
		£		£	£	£
Authorized		450,000	Freehold property .	58,000	7,000	51,000
			Plant . . .	118,000	28,000	90,000
			Patents . . .	25,000	—	25,000
Issued—						
240,000 7% cum. red. preference shares of £1		240,000		201,000	35,000	166,000
200,000 ordinary shares of £1 each 75p paid		150,000	Subsidiary company—			
			Shares at cost .		90,000	
		390,000	Loan . .		35,000	
Deduct—						125,000
Profit and loss account debit balance .		161,000				
			Current assets—			
		229,000	Stocks at cost .		95,000	
Current liabilities—			Debtors . .		70,000	
Creditors . . .	£144,000					165,000
Bank overdraft . .	83,000					
		227,000				
		456,000				456,000

Arrears of preference dividend amounted to £84,000. The following capital reconstruction scheme, to take effect from 1st January, 1965, was duly approved and authorized—

(1) The unpaid capital on the ordinary shares to be called up immediately.

(2) The ordinary share capital of £200,000 to be written down to £22,500 in shares of 5p each.

(3) All arrears of preference dividend to be cancelled, and each preference shareholder to surrender one out of every three shares held, thereby reducing the preference share capital to £160,000.

(4) The freehold property is to be written up from £51,000 to £80,000 following an independent valuation.

(5) New capital is to be contributed, in cash at par in each case, as follows—

	£
(*a*) 7½ per cent debenture stock secured on the freehold property and fixed plant	80,000
(*b*) Each preference shareholder to subscribe for three new preference shares for each eight held	60,000
(*c*) Each ordinary shareholder to subscribe for two new ordinary shares for every one held	45,000

(6) The debit balance on profit and loss account and the patents are to be written off completely, while £80,000 is to be written off the shares in the subsidiary, and £20,500 off plant and machinery.

(7) A resolution has been approved restoring the authorized capital to its original amount.

You are required to prepare—

(*a*) the capital reduction and re-organization account;

(*b*) the balance sheet of the company as it would appear immediately after the reconstruction. (*Cost and Management Accountants.*)

35. The following are the balance sheets of B Ltd. and W Ltd. as at 31st March, 1966—

	B Ltd.	W Ltd.
	£	£
Ordinary shares of £1 each fully paid	10,000	
Ordinary shares of 25p each fully paid		5,000
Reserves and surplus	6,000	3,000
Creditors	4,000	3,000
	20,000	11,000
Freehold buildings	4,000	2,000
Plant and machinery	5,000	3,000
2,000 ordinary shares in W. Ltd. at cost	1,000	—
Stock	2,700	1,500
Debtors	6,000	2,000
Balance at bank	1,300	2,500
	20,000	11,000

It was decided that, on 1st April, 1966, both companies should go into liquidation and that a new company N Ltd. should be formed with an authorized capital of £50,000 divided into 100,000 shares of 50p each, to take over all the assets and liabilities of both companies at book values subject to the following adjustments—

(1) The freehold buildings of both companies are to be increased by 50 per cent.
(2) The stock of B Ltd. is to be reduced by £200.
(3) B Ltd. is to receive £2,500 for goodwill and W Ltd. £1,700.
(4) The debtors of W Ltd. are to be valued at £1,800.
(5) A 5 per cent discount is receivable from the creditors and suitable adjustment is to be made before liquidation.
(6) The expenses of the amalgamation paid by N Ltd. amount to £750.

You are to show—

(*a*) the journal entries closing the books of B Ltd;
(*b*) a statement of the shares allotted to the shareholders of each company;
(*c*) the balance sheet immediately after the amalgamation has been completed.
(*Cost and Management Accountants.*)

36. Breezi Ltd. entered into an agreement with Bright Ltd. whereby the latter undertook to acquire the goodwill and assets, apart from cash, of the former as on 31st December, 1961. A summary of Breezi Ltd.'s balance sheet as on that date was as follows—

	£		£
Share Capital, in shares of £1 each	66,000	Freehold Premises and Machinery and Plant	63,000
General Reserve including Profit and Loss Account	10,800	Goodwill	6,000
6 per cent Debentures	12,000	Stock on hand	11,500
Sundry Creditors	1,200	Sundry Debtors	2,700
		Cash at bank	6,800
	90,000		90,000

For the purpose of the acquisition the freehold premises and machinery and plant were valued at £82,000 and stock on hand at £12,000. The sundry debtors were taken over at their book value subject to an allowance of 5 per cent in respect of any that might prove to be doubtful. Breezi Ltd. were to discharge the liabilities other than the debentures. In consideration of the acquisition Bright Ltd. undertook—

(*a*) to issue 80,000 of their £1 shares, fully paid, at £1·20 per share;

(*b*) to issue, in discharge of the 6 per cent Debentures of Breezi Ltd. at a premium of 5 per cent, such an amount of fully paid 5 per cent Debentures at a discount of 4 per cent as would be sufficient for the purpose;

(*c*) to pay cash equivalent to 15p per share in respect of the shares in Breezi Ltd.

Give the journal entries to record the above-mentioned transactions in the books of Bright Ltd. and state what course you would suggest as regards the discount on the 5 per cent debentures issued. (*A.C.C.A.*)

37. The Wynne Co. Ltd. and the Garde Co. Ltd. agree to amalgamate and to promote a new company, to be registered as the "Wyngarde Co. Ltd." with a capital of £400,000 in £1 shares, to take over their respective undertakings. The balances in the books of the respective companies at the date of amalgamation were as follows—

	Wynne Co.		Garde Co.	
	Dr	*Cr*	*Dr*	*Cr*
	£	£	£	£
Issued Capital—				
Wynne Co., 150,000 shares of £1 each		150,000		
Garde Co., 100,000 " "				100,000
6 per cent debentures		50,000		
Goodwill	25,000		12,000	
Land and buildings	75,230		42,650	
Plant and machinery	35,400		18,745	
Stock-in-trade	42,676		26,520	
Sundry creditors		35,628		19,958
Sundry debtors	48,524		23,234	
Bills Receivable	15,620		4,257	
Balances at bank	18,902		1,234	
Reserve		20,000		5,000
Profit and loss account		5,724		3,682
	261,352	261,352	128,640	128,640

The consideration for the sale of the respective undertakings to the new company is—

Wynne Co.: the allotment of 150,000 fully paid shares of £1 each, a payment of £30,000 in cash and the discharge of the debenture debt at a premium of 5 per cent.

Garde Co.: the allotment of 100,000 fully paid shares of £1 each, and the payment of £10,000 in cash.

The old companies each pay their liquidation expenses, which amount to £600 for the Wynne Co. and £450 for the Garde Co. The formation expenses of the new company amount to £1,260.

The new company makes a public issue of 100,000 shares to provide additional working capital; the issue is fully subscribed and paid for in full on allotment. Close the books of the old companies and open the new company's books, drafting the first balance sheet.

38. The Ess Co. Ltd. had an issued capital of £95,000, consisting of 50,000 ordinary shares of £1 each, fully paid, and 45,000 7 per cent cumulative preference shares of £1 each, fully paid.

The Tee Co. Ltd. had an issued capital of £30,000 consisting of 30,000 ordinary shares of £1 each, fully paid.

These two companies decided to amalgamate their businesses, and for this purpose a holding company, called the Unit Co. Ltd. was registered on 1st July, 19.., with a capital of £150,000 in £1 shares. This company was to purchase all the ordinary shares of both the above companies. B., the managing director of the Ess Co. Ltd., and F., the managing director of the Tee Co. Ltd., each took up and paid for 1,500 shares.

The purchase was arranged on the following terms: the shareholders of the Ess Co. Ltd. received one £1 share, fully paid, in the Unit Co. Ltd. in exchange for each of their ordinary shares. The shareholders of the Tee Co. Ltd. received one and a half £1 shares, fully paid, in the Unit Co. Ltd. in exchange for each of their ordinary shares.

The expenses incidental to the formation of the Unit Co. Ltd. amounted to £2,000, and were paid out of cash.

Make the necessary entries in the books of the various companies to give effect to the arrangements outlined above, and draw up the opening balance sheet of the Unit Co., Ltd.

39. The following are the summarized balance sheets of Alpha Ltd., Beta Ltd., and Gamma Ltd., as at 31st March, 19.7—

	Alpha Ltd.	Beta Ltd.	Gamma Ltd.
	£	£	£
Ordinary share capital in fully paid £1 shares	100,000	50,000	32,000
Preference share capital in fully paid £1 shares	—	10,000	—
Share premium account	—	—	8,000
Capital redemption reserve fund	—	—	16,000
P. & L. A/c	80,000	40,000	20,000
	180,000	100,000	76,000
4,000 ordinary shares in Gamma Ltd.	6,000	—	—
5,000 preference shares in Beta Ltd.	5,500	—	—
40,000 ordinary shares in Beta Ltd.	60,000	—	—
24,000 ordinary shares in Gamma Ltd.	—	60,000	—
Other net assets	108,500	40,000	76,000
	180,000	100,000	76,000

Alpha Ltd. and Beta Ltd. purchased their ordinary shares in Gamma Ltd. on 31st March, 19.., and 31st March 19.5, respectively, when the latter's balance sheets were as follows—

	Gamma Ltd. 31st March 19..	Gamma Ltd. 31st March 19.5
	£	£
Redeemable preference share capital	16,000	—
Ordinary share capital	32,000	32,000
Share premium account	8,000	8,000
Capital redemption reserve fund	—	16,000
P. & L. A/c	4,000	12,000
Net Assets	60,000	68,000

When Alpha Ltd. purchased both its holdings of preference and ordinary shares in Beta Ltd. on 31st March, 19.2, the latter's balance sheet showed—

	£
Ordinary share capital	50,000
Preference share capital	10,000
P. & L. A/c.	20,000
Net assets	80,000

The preference shares carry no right to participate in profits beyond a fixed preferential dividend, and at 31st March, 19.2, the dividends had been paid up to date.

You are required to prepare a consolidated balance sheet of the group at 31st March, 19.7, not necessarily for publication. Show all workings and ignore dividends and taxation. (*Certified and Corporate Accountants.*)

40. With a view to reducing establishment expenses and generally to effect economy in working, the A Co. Ltd. was taken over by the B Co. Ltd. as from 1st January, upon the following terms—

(i) The B Co. to assume the liabilities and take over the assets at book values.
(ii) The B Co. to discharge the debentures in A Co. at 105 by the issue of new debentures at 6 per cent in the B Co.
(iii) The B Co. to pay the shareholders in A Co. 50p per share, and to give three 50p shares in the B Co. for every £1 share in the A Co. The 50p shares were considered as being at par.

The following balance sheet of the A Co. was prepared as on 31st December, 19. .

Liabilities	£	*Assets*	£
Nominal Capital: 50,000 shares of £1 each	50,000	Goodwill	35,000
		Freehold Land & Buildings	15,650
		Machinery & Plant	3,210
Issued: 47,500 shares of £1 each	47,500	Fixtures & Fittings	850
5% Debentures	12,000	Sundry Debtors	10,990
Reserve Fund	15,000	Stock	4,660
Sundry Creditors	7,650	Investments	14,650
P. & L. A/c, balance at credit	4,960	Cash at Bank and in Hand	2,100
	87,110		87,110

Give the entries necessary to close off the books of the A Co., and show how the acquisition of the business would be recorded in the books of the B Co.

(*Chartered Accountants.*)

41. The following was the balance sheet of the X Manufacturing Co. Ltd. (in which there were five shareholders with equal holdings), as on 31st December—

Liabilities	£	*Assets*	£
Nominal Capital: 20,000 Ordinary Shares of £1 each	20,000	Land & Buildings	2,300
		Plant & Machinery	2,108
		Furniture & Fittings	415
Issued: 18,000 Ordinary Shares of £1 each, fully paid	18,000	Stock	3,691
		Sundry Debtors	12,674
Sundry Creditors	5,674	Investments	16,420
Reserve Fund	15,000	Cash at Bank	8,502
P. & L. A/c, balance at credit	7,450	Cash in hand	14
	46,124		46,124

It was decided to form a new limited company to take over the business as a going concern as on the above date, the new company bearing the same name, and having a nominal capital of £75,000 in ordinary shares of £1 each. The consideration for the sale of the business was 50,000 fully-paid shares in the new company, and the balance of the profit and loss account in cash, the new company taking over all assets (as set out in the old company's balance sheet) with the exception of the investments; and undertaking to pay the sundry creditors and the liquidation expenses (estimated at £200), with the exception of £43 contributed by the old company.

The new company had fresh valuations made of the following assets, viz.:

Land and buildings which were valued at		£5,000;
Plant and machinery	" "	£3,500; and
Furniture and fittings	" "	£500

Draft the initial balance sheet of the new company as on 1st January. Give the entries necessary to close the books of the old company and state what each shareholder would receive. Investments were not realized, but were distributed *pro rata* to the shareholders. (*Chartered Accountants.*)

42. The balance sheets of the A Co. Ltd., and the D Co. Ltd. at 31st December were as follows—

Liabilities	A Co. £	D Co. £	*Assets*	A Co. £	D Co. £
Ordinary Capital in £1 shares	50,000	20,000	Land & Buildings	40,000	
Preference " "	50,000		Machinery	60,000	
Debentures	25,000	5,000	Patent Rights		20,000
Creditors	5,000	1,000	Debtors	20,000	5,000
Reserve	10,000		Investments	10,000	
P. & L. A/c. balances at credit	10,000	1,000	Bank	20,000	2,000
	150,000	27,000		150,000	27,000

The ordinary shares of the A Co. Ltd., were quoted at £1·50 per share, and the preference shares at par. They agreed to buy the patent rights of the D Co., Ltd. for £40,000, the book debts at their face value, and to give £10,000 for the goodwill. The consideration was to be the allotment of 20,000 ordinary shares and 25,000 preference shares—and the D Co. Ltd. was put into liquidation accordingly.

Make the necessary journal entries in the books of the A Co. Ltd., and show the balance sheet after the purchase. (*Chartered Accountants.*)

CHAPTER 26

BANKRUPTCY, STATEMENT OF AFFAIRS, DEFICIENCY ACCOUNT, TRUSTEE'S ACCOUNTS

Chatterton, the young poet who was soon to commit suicide, arrived in London and was taken up by Beckford, the Lord Mayor of London, who gave him the opportunity of writing a whole issue of John Wilkes' paper, the *North Briton*. Just as Chatterton thought his fortune was made, Beckford died and the deal fell through.

Chatterton wrote in his diary:

"... thrown out of the *North Briton* June 21 on account of the Lord Mayor's death.

	£	s.	d.
Lost by his death on this essay	1	11	6
Gained in elegies	2	2	0
Gained in essays	3	3	0
Am glad he is dead by	3	13	6"

BANKRUPTCY

Bankruptcy Laws and their Objects. The law that governs bankruptcy proceedings is the Bankruptcy Act, 1914, which is a consolidation of the Bankruptcy Acts, 1883 and 1890, and of the bankruptcy part of the Bankruptcy and Deeds of Arrangement Act, 1913, and which came into operation on the 1st January, 1915. A more recent Act relating to bankruptcy is the Bankruptcy (Amendment) Act, 1926. The object of bankruptcy laws is to extricate a debtor who has become hopelessly involved in financial difficulties, by distributing his estate equitably among his creditors, and releasing him from all further liability in respect of his past debts.

Courts of Bankruptcy. Proceedings must be taken in the County Court of the district in which the debtor has resided or carried on business for the longest period during the six months preceding the bankruptcy. The County Court must be one of those that have had bankruptcy jurisdiction conferred upon them. If the debtor has resided or carried on business for the longest period during these six months in the metropolitan district, or if he is resident abroad, or if his residence is unknown, then proceedings must be taken in the High Court. The Board of Trade has important powers in controlling and supervising bankruptcy proceedings. (Sects. 96, 97, 98, and 99).

Persons who may be Made Bankrupt. In general, any debtor who has committed an act of bankruptcy may be made bankrupt. Exceptions to this rule, however, exist in the case of companies registered under the Companies Act, 1948 (which must be wound up), and in certain circumstances lunatics and foreigners. Partnerships (including limited partnerships) can be made bankrupt, and a married women is now in the same position as if she were unmarried. A deceased debtor cannot be made bankrupt, but his estate may be administered in bankruptcy. (Sects. 126, 127, and 130.)

Petition. Bankruptcy proceedings are commenced by the presentation of a petition for a Receiving Order to be made against the debtor. A petition may be made by the debtor himself, who must allege inability to pay his debts, or by one or more creditors. By Sect. 4 of the Act, a creditor is not entitled to present a bankruptcy petition against a debtor unless—

(*a*) The debt owing by the debtor to the petitioning creditor or, if two or more creditors join in the petition, the aggregate amount of debts owing to the several petitioning creditors, amounts to fifty pounds; and

(*b*) The debt is a liquidated sum, payable either immediately or at some certain future time; and

(*c*) The act of bankruptcy on which the petition is grounded has occurred within three months before the presentation of the petition; and

(*d*) The debtor is domiciled in England, or within a year before the date of the presentation of the petition has ordinarily resided, or had a dwelling-house or place of business, in England, or (except in the case of a person domiciled in Scotland or Ireland, or a firm or partnership having its principal place of business in Scotland or Ireland) has carried on business in England, personally or by means of an agent or manager, or (except as aforesaid) is or within the said period has been a member of a firm or partnership of persons which has carried on business in England by means of a partner or partners, or an agent or manager.

If the debtor is the petitioner, the court will make the order at once, unless it is merely an attempt on his part to evade a committal order. If the petition is made by a creditor, a copy must be served on the debtor, and not less than eight days after such service the court will hear the petition. It may then either make the receiving order or dismiss the petition as it thinks fit. Whoever presents the petition must pay the stamp duty, and make the deposit required by the Bankruptcy Rules.

Receiving Order. If the court is satisfied as to the alleged act or acts of bankruptcy on the part of the debtor, it will forthwith make a receiving order against him, and this fact will be duly advertised in the *Gazette*. The effect of the receiving order is to constitute the Official Receiver the receiver of the debtor's property, and to stay any proceedings against the debtor by his creditors, although a secured creditor may still realize or otherwise deal with his security. (Sect. 7.)

Statement of Affairs. This is the statement of an insolvent debtor's assets and liabilities, prepared for submission to the Official Receiver and creditors. Particulars are given, in an inner column, of all secured debts and of the securities in connexion with them. The assets available for the general creditors are estimated at their realizable value and placed on one side of the statement; the liabilities to be paid out of these assets are placed on the other side. The excess of the liabilities over the assets then shows the estimated *deficiency*. The statement must be submitted within three days of the receiving order if made on the debtor's petition, or within seven days if made on a creditor's petition. It must also be prepared on the official forms. (Sect. 14.)

Meeting of Creditors. The creditors meet to discuss the statement of affairs submitted by the debtor, together with the Official Receiver's observations on it, and to consider which of the following will be most expedient. (Sect. 13)—

1. To accept a composition in satisfaction of their debts.
2. To agree to a scheme for the arrangement of the debtor's affairs.
3. That the debtor shall be adjudged bankrupt; that a trustee be appointed to administer the estate; that a committee of inspection be appointed to assist the trustee.

In each case the consent of the court is necessary. If either of the first two courses is approved, the receiving order is rescinded. In the last case the debtor is adjudged bankrupt by the court, and notice thereof advertised in the *Gazette*. Almost without exception, a debtor against whom a receiving order has been made is required to undergo a public examination.

Composition. This is a legal arrangement between a debtor and his creditors, whereby each creditor agrees to accept a part of his debt in full settlement of the whole of it.

Deed of Arrangement. This is a deed embodying an arrangement arrived at between a debtor and his creditors to assign all his property to a trustee for their benefit, to compound with them, and, in certain circumstances, where the creditors obtain control over the debtor's property or business. Such a deed, if it is made for the benefit of creditors generally or, if the debtor is insolvent, for the benefit of any three or more of them, is governed by the Deeds of Arrangement Act, 1914. It enables a debtor to escape the publicity and stigma of the Bankruptcy Court; while the creditors obtain a larger dividend, as the expenses consequent on bankruptcy are avoided. Such an arrangement, however, constitutes an act of bankruptcy, and a dissentient creditor may present a bankruptcy petition against the debtor founded on the deed. Should the debtor be declared bankrupt within three months of the execution of the deed, the latter becomes void against the trustee in bankruptcy. Owing to this contingency, the trustees under such deeds generally allow three months to elapse before distributing any of the assets realized.

Committee of Inspection. This is a small number of creditors, not more than five and not less than three, appointed by the whole body of creditors to supervise the winding-up of a debtor's affairs under the trustee in bankruptcy or Official Receiver. When there is no committee of inspection, its functions are exercised by the Board of Trade.

Public Examination. The examination is held in open court as soon as possible after the debtor has furnished his statement of affairs, unless the receiving order has been rescinded. Questions may be put to the debtor, by either the Official Receiver or the creditors, as to his conduct, his business affairs, and his property.

Discharge. When the public examination is concluded, the debtor may apply to the court for an order of discharge. The court has power to grant it, refuse it, or to suspend it for a time, as it thinks fit, taking into consideration all the circumstances of the case. By Sect. 26 (2), the court must refuse the discharge in all cases where the bankrupt has committed any misdemeanour under the Bankruptcy Acts, or in connexion with his bankruptcy, or any felony connected with this bankruptcy (unless for special reasons the court otherwise determines). It may also (i) refuse the discharge, (ii) suspend it for not less than two years, or (iii) suspend it until a dividend of £0·50 in the £ has been paid to the creditors, or (iv) require the debtor, as a condition of his discharge, to consent to judgment being entered against him for the unsatisfied balance of the debts proved in the bankruptcy.

This latter only applies under certain circumstances as mentioned in the Section.

Effect of the Order of Discharge. As soon as the debtor has obtained his order of discharge, he is released from all debts provable in the bankruptcy, except—

1. Debts to the Crown.
2. Debts incurred through fraud, or through a fraudulent breach of trust.
3. Judgment debts in an action for seduction, in affiliation proceedings, or in a matrimonial cause. (Sect. 28.)

QUESTIONS

1. What are the laws that govern bankruptcy? What is the object of bankruptcy laws?
2. Where must bankruptcy proceedings be taken?
3. What persons and bodies may be made bankrupt? Can a joint stock company be made bankrupt?
4. Explain the terms "bankruptcy notice" and "petition." Who presents the petition, the debtor or the creditor?
5. Explain the terms "receiving order," "fraudulent conveyance," "statement of affairs," "composition," "deed of arrangement."
6. What three courses are open to a meeting of creditors?
7. What is meant by the terms "committee of inspection," "bankrupt's public examination"?
8. What is meant by the "discharge" of a bankrupt? What are the conditions governing it?
9. From what debts does a bankrupt's discharge: (*a*) release him, (*b*) not release him?

Undischarged Bankrupt. This is an insolvent debtor who has not succeeded in obtaining his discharge. By Sect. 155—

Where an undischarged bankrupt—

(*a*) Either alone or jointly with any other person obtains credit to the extent of ten pounds or upwards from any person without informing that person that he is an undischarged bankrupt; or

(*b*) Engages in any trade or business under a name other than that under which he was adjudicated bankrupt without disclosing to all persons with whom he enters into any business transaction the name under which he was adjudged bankrupt; he shall be guilty of a misdemeanour.

The maximum penalty, under Sect. 164, is two years' imprisonment.

Annulment of Adjudication. The court has power to annul any receiving order that has been made on improper grounds. Where a bankrupt subsequently makes a satisfactory arrangement with his creditors, or afterwards pays his debts in full, the court may annul the bankruptcy. If this happens, the debtor is restored to his original position before the bankruptcy proceedings.

Joint and Separate Estates. By Sect. 33 (6) it is enacted as follows—

In the case of partners, the joint estate shall be applicable in the first instance in payment of their joint debts, and the separate estate of each partner shall be applicable in the first instance in payment of his separate debts. If there is a surplus of the separate estates, it shall be dealt with as part of the joint estate. If there is a surplus of the joint estate, it shall be dealt with as part of the respective separate estates in proportion to the right and interest of each partner in the joint estate.

Small Bankruptcies. By Sect. 129, it is enacted—

Where a petition is presented by or against a debtor, if the court is satisfied by affidavit or otherwise, or the Official Receiver reports to the court that the property of the debtor is not likely to exceed in value three hundred pounds, the court may make an order that the debtor's estate be administered in a summary manner, and thereupon the provisions of this Act shall be subject to the following modifications—

(i) If the debtor is adjudged bankrupt, the Official Receiver shall be the trustee in the bankruptcy;

(ii) There shall be no committee of inspection, but the Official Receiver may do, with the permission of the Board of Trade, all things which may be done by the trustee with the permission of the committee of inspection;

(iii) Such other modifications may be made in the provisions of this Act as may be prescribed by general rules with the view of saving expense and simplifying procedure; but nothing in this section shall permit the modification of the provisions of this Act relating to the examination or discharge of the debtor.

Provided that the creditors may at any time, by special resolution, resolve that some person other than the Official Receiver be appointed trustee in the bankruptcy, and thereupon the bankruptcy shall proceed as if an order for summary administration had not been made.

Administration Order. In small cases of insolvency, where the total liabilities do not exceed £50, bankruptcy proceedings are not possible, and the court is empowered to make an Administration Order, and compel the debtor to pay the whole or a portion of his debts either at once, or by stated instalments, out of his earnings. (B.A. 1883, Sect. 122, which is not repealed by the 1914 Act.)

Keeping Books. Unless a debtor can show his liabilities do not exceed £500 on the occasion of his first bankruptcy (subsequent bankruptcies £100), or the omission was honest and excusable, failure to keep books in certain circumstances amounts to misdemeanour. (Bankruptcy (Amendment) Act, 1926.)

STATEMENT OF AFFAIRS

Official Forms. On pp. 2608–14 will be found reduced facsimiles of the prescribed forms, Lists A to K, List L, and Front Sheet (or Statement). Each list has to be signed by the debtor and dated, thus—

Signature..

Dated..19....

The details may assume somewhat formidable proportions, but the principle involved is extremely simple and, once the elementary rules are thoroughly assimilated, no difficulty should be experienced in the working of examination problems on this subject. The procedure is as follows—

1. A rough statement should be prepared with assets on the right-hand side and liabilities on the left, in ordinary balance sheet form.

2. Each item must appear on the *same* side in the statement of affairs or deficiency account as it appears in the rough balance sheet.

The estimated value of each asset will appear on the right-hand side of the statement of affairs.

The estimated amount of each liability will appear on the left-hand side of the statement of affairs.

The estimated loss (the excess of book value over estimated realizable value of an asset, or the increase in the amount of liability over the book value) will appear on the right-hand side of the deficiency account.

The estimated gain (the excess of estimated realizable value over the book value of an asset, or the decrease in the amount of liability over the book value) will appear on the left-hand side of the deficiency account.

3. Any item not in the rough balance sheet must appear both in the statement of affairs and in the deficiency account, but on reverse sides; in other words, there must be double entry therefor.

4. The capital account must be accounted for in the deficiency account on the same side as it appears in the balance sheet. Certain adjustments are required in connexion with the capital account, as will be noticed presently, but the rule herein will, nevertheless, be followed.

5. The balance of the statement of affairs and deficiency account will be equal and closed by a cross transfer.

These rules may be summarized—

(*a*) Every item in the balance sheet must be accounted for directly or indirectly on the corresponding side of the statement of affairs or the deficiency account.

(*b*) Any item not in the balance sheet must directly or indirectly appear both in the statement of affairs on the one side and in the deficiency account on the opposite side.

List 'A', Unsecured Creditors. On this list appear the names of all cash and trade creditors who have merely a claim upon the general assets of the estate. Creditors on promissory notes and bills payable are unsecured creditors, these documents not being documents of title. The balances of debts that exceed the preferential limit (rent, wages, salaries, etc., as per Lists F and G) are also shown on this list. On the printed form will be found notes respecting the treatment of contra accounts and the particulars required of any bills of exchange held by creditors.

List 'B', Fully Secured Creditors. On this list appear the names of creditors who hold a covering security for their debts, such as a mortgage, charge, or lien upon any property of the debtor. The holder of an absolute bill of sale is also a secured creditor as regards the chattels mentioned therein. Goods sent on approval, or on sale or return, remain the property of the owner unless they are in the order and disposition of the debtor (Sect. 38 (2) (*c*)), and do not form part of the bankrupt's estate. A banker may be also a secured creditor in respect of an overdraft, inasmuch as he has a lien on the securities in his possession, unless they have been deposited with him merely for safe custody. A creditor may realize his security and prove for the balance of his debt (if any), or he may surrender his security and prove for the whole of the debt. Should, however, the security in the creditor's possession realize more than the amount of the debt, the creditor must hand over the balance for the benefit of the general creditors. Any estimated surplus from securities in the hands of fully secured creditors must be shown on the assets side of the statement of affairs. With mortgage securities, interest will be payable up to date of repayment; for a mortgage is not a first charge in respect of principal and a second charge in respect of interest, but a joint charge in respect of both. Where there are first, second, or third charges on the same property in respect of different debts, the surplus from the first debt will be carried forward to the second, and so on. It should be noted that where the security does not belong to the debtor himself the creditor proves for the full amount.

List 'C', Creditors Partly Secured. This list contains the names of creditors who have a charge on some part of the debtor's property which, when realized, will pay off only a portion of the debt, the balance of which must, therefore, rank against the estate for dividend. On the statement of affairs, the value of the security is deducted from the amount of the debt and only the balance extended.

List 'D', Liabilities of Debtor on Bills Discounted Other than his Own Acceptances for Value. The debtor's own acceptances for value, i.e. his

In the High Court of Justice

IN BANKRUPTCY

No. of 19

Re

N.B.—You are required to fill up carefully and accurately this sheet, and such of the several sheets, A, B, C, D, E, F, G, H, I, J, and K as are applicable showing the state of your affairs on the day on which the Receiving Order was made against you, viz.—the day of 19. . .

Such sheets when filled up will constitute your statement of affairs and must be verified by oath or declaration.

STATEMENT OF AFFAIRS

At 19 , date of Receiving Order.

Gross Liabilities	Liabilities (as stated and estimated by Debtor)	Expected to Rank	Assets (as stated and estimated by Debtor)	Estimated to produce
£		£		£
	Unsecured creditors as per list (A)		Property as per list (H) viz.—	
	£		(*a*) Cash at bankers . . .	
	Creditors fully secured as per list (B) . . .		(*b*) Cash in hand . . .	
	Estimated value of securities . . .		(*c*) Cash deposited with Solicitor for costs of petition . . .	
			(*d*) Stock-in-trade (cost £).	
			(*e*) Machinery . . .	
	Surplus		(*f*) Trade Fixtures, Fittings, Utensils, etc.	
	Less amount thereof carried to sheet (C) .		(*g*) Farming Stock . . .	
	Balance thereof to contra £		(*h*) Growing Crops and Tenant Rights . . .	
			(*i*) Furniture . . .	
			(*j*) Life Policies . . .	
	Creditors partly secured as per list (C) .		(*k*) Stocks and Shares . .	
	Less estimated value of securities . .		(*l*) Reversionary or other Interests under Wills . .	
	Liabilities on Bills discounted other than Debtor's own acceptances for value as per list (D), viz.—		(*m*) Other Property, viz.—	
			Total as per list (H). .	
	On accommodation bills as Drawer, Acceptor, or Endorser . . . £		Book debts, as per list (I), viz.— Good . . . . £	
			Doubtful	
	On other bills as Drawer or Endorser . . . £		Bad	
	Of which it is expected will rank against the estate for dividend			
	Contingent or other liabilities as per list (E) . . £		Estimated to produce	
	Of which it is expected will rank against the estate for dividend		Bills of exchange or other similar securities as per list (J) . . . £	
	£		Estimated to produce	
	Creditors for rent, etc., recoverable by distress as per list (F). . .		Surplus from securities in the hands of creditors fully secured (per contra) . . .	
	Creditors for rates, taxes wages, etc., payable in full as per list (G) .		£	
	Sheriff's charges payable under Sect. 41 of the Bankruptcy Act, 1914, estimated at . . .		Deduct creditors for distrainable rent, and for preferential rates, taxes, wages, Sheriff's Charges, etc. (per contra.) . .	
	£		£	
	Deducted contra . £			
	Surplus explained in statement (K)		Deficiency explained in statement (K)	
	£		£	

I of
in the County of make oath and say that the above statement and the several lists hereunto annexed, marked A, B, C, D, E, F, G, H, I, J, and K, are, to the best of my knowledge and belief, a full, true, and complete statement of my affairs on the date of the above-mentioned Receiving Order made against me.

Sworn at
in the County of
this day of 19 } (Signature)
Before me

LIST 'A'. UNSECURED CREDITORS

The Names to be arranged in alphabetical order and numbered consecutively, Creditors for £10 and upwards being placed first

No.	Name	Address and Occupation	Amount of Debt	Date when Contracted		Consideration
				Month	Year	

NOTES—(1) When there is a contra account against the Creditor less than the amount of his claim against the estate, the amount of the Creditor's claim and the amount of the contra account should be shown in the third column, and the balance only be inserted under the heading "Amount of Debt," thus—

Total amount of claim . . . . £
Less contra account . . . . £
—————— £

No such set-off should be included in sheet 'I'.
(2) The particulars of any Bills of Exchange and Promissory Notes held by a Creditor should be inserted immediately below the name and address of such Creditor.

LIST 'B'. CREDITORS FULLY SECURED

No.	Name of Creditor	Address and Occupation	Amount of Debt	Date when Contracted		Consideration	Particulars of Security	Date when given	Estimated Value of Security	Estimated Surplus from Security
				Month	Year					

LIST 'C', CREDITORS PARTLY SECURED

No.	Name of Creditor	Address and Occupation	Amount of Debt	Date when Contracted		Consideration	Particulars of Security	Month and Year when given	Estimated Value of Security	Balance of Debt Unsecured
				Month	Year					

LIST 'D', LIABILITIES OF DEBTOR ON BILLS DISCOUNTED OTHER THAN HIS OWN ACCEPTANCES FOR VALUE

No.	Acceptor's Name, Address, and Occupation	Whether Liable as Drawer or Endorser	Date when Due	Amount		Holder's Name, Address, and Occupation (if known)	Amount Expected to Rank against Estate for Dividend
				Accommodation Bills	Other Bills		

LIST 'E', CONTINGENT OR OTHER LIABILITIES

Full particulars of all Liabilities not otherwise Scheduled to be given here

No.	Name of Creditor or Claimant	Address and Occupation	Amount of Liability or Claim	Date when Liability Incurred		Nature of Liability	Amount Expected to Rank for Dividend
				Month	Year		

LIST 'F', CREDITORS FOR RENT, ETC., RECOVERABLE BY DISTRESS

No.	Name of Creditor	Address and Occupation	Nature of Claim	Period During which Claim Accrued Due	Date when Due	Amount of Claim	Amount Recoverable by Distress	Difference Ranking for Dividend (to be Carried to List A)

LIST 'G', PREFERENTIAL CREDITORS FOR RATES, TAXES, WAGES, ETC.

No.	Name of Creditor	Address and Occupation	Nature of Claim	Period During which Claim Accrued Due	Date when Due	Amount of Claim	Amount Payable in Full	Difference Ranking for Dividend (to be Carried to List A)

LIST 'H', PROPERTY

Full particulars of every description of property in possession and in reversion as defined by Sect. 167 of the Bankruptcy Act, 1914, not included in any other list, are to be set forth in this list.

Full Statement and Nature of Property	Estimated to Produce
(*a*) Cash at Banker	
(*b*) Cash in hand	
(*c*) Cash deposited with Solicitor for Costs of Petition	
(*d*) Stock-in-trade at (cost £)	
(*e*) Machinery at	
(*f*) Trade Fixtures, Fittings, Utensils, etc., at	
(*g*) Farming Stock at	
(*h*) Growing Crops and Tenant Right at	
(*i*) Household Furniture and Effects at	
(*j*) Life Policies	
(*k*) Stocks and Shares	
(*l*) Reversionary or other Interests under Wills, etc.	
(*m*) Other Property (state particulars), viz.	

LIST 'I', DEBTS DUE TO THE ESTATE

No.	Name of Debtor	Residence and Occupation	Amount of Debt			Folio of Ledger or other Book where Particulars to be Found	When Contracted		Estimated to Produce	Particulars of any Securities Held for Debt
			Good	Doubtful	Bad		Month	Year		

NOTE.—If any debtor to the estate is also a creditor, *but for a less amount than his indebtedness*, the gross amount due to the estate and the amount of the contra account should be shown in the third column, and the balance only be inserted under the heading "Amount of Debt," thus—

	£
Due to estate	
Less contra account . . .	

No such claim should be included in sheet 'A'.

LIST 'J', BILLS OF EXCHANGE PROMISSORY NOTES, ETC., AVAILABLE AS ASSETS

No.	Name of Acceptor of Bill or Note	Address, etc.	Amount of Bill or Note	Date when Due	Estimated to Produce	Particulars of any Property Held as Security for Payment of Bill or Note

LIST 'K', DEFICIENCY ACCOUNT

	£	£		£	£
Excess of Assets over Liabilities on the[1]............ day of..19.... (if any)			Excess of Liabilities over Assets on the[1]........... day of..19.... (if any)		
Net profit (if any) arising from carrying on business from the[1]...........day of..................... 19...., to date of Receiving Order, after deducting usual Trade Expenses . . .			Net loss (if any) arising from carrying on business from the[1]..........day of..................... 19...., to date of Receiving Order, after deducting from Profits usual Trade Expenses		
Income or profit from other sources (if any) since the[1]............day of.............................. 19....			Bad Debts (if any) as per Schedule "I"[2] . .		
			Depreciation of Machinery		
			Depreciation of Trade Fixtures, Fittings, etc. .		
			Expenses incurred since the[1]...........day of ....19...., other than usual Trade Expenses, viz.: Household and Personal Expenses of self and[3]......................		
			Other losses and expenses (if any)[4]—		
			Surplus as per Statement of Affairs (if any) .		
Total amount to be accounted for[5] .			Total amount accounted for[5] .		

NOTES.—[1] This date should be 12 months before date of Receiving Order, or such other time as Official Receiver may have fixed.
[2] This Schedule must show when debts were contracted.
[3] Add "Wife and Children" (if any), stating number of latter.
[4] Here add particulars of other expenses or losses (if any), including liabilities (if any) for which no consideration received.
[5] These figures should agree.

LIST 'L',

(In substitution for such of the Sheets named 'A–J' as will have to be returned blank.)

LIST	PARTICULARS AS PER FRONT SHEET	DEBTOR'S REMARKS
A	Unsecured Creditors	
B	Creditors fully secured	
	etc.	

ordinary bills payable, will be included in List A. On List D the debtor must furnish particulars of all unmatured bills of exchange to which he is a party as either drawer or endorser. The *acceptor* of a bill is, of course, the person primarily liable for payment, yet, if he makes default, the liability attaches to every endorser and also to the drawer. All unmatured bills receivable discounted with bankers or bill brokers, or endorsed on to creditors, must, therefore, be entered on this list; but only those that the acceptor is expected to dishonour will be shown as liabilities of the estate *ranking for dividend*, though the *total* will be shown in the "Gross Liabilities" column.

Accommodation bills must also be shown on this list, but in a separate column. On these bills the debtor may be liable not only as drawer or endorser but also as accommodation *acceptor*. He is not liable to the drawer unless he has shared the proceeds, but he is liable to any third party who is a holder for value. Where the debtor is the acceptor, such bills should be extended as liabilities of the estate. Where, however, he is liable merely as drawer or endorser, only those bills expected to be dishonoured should be shown as ranking against the estate for dividend.

List 'E', Contingent or Other Liabilities. On this list must be entered all liabilities as surety or guarantee for others, the balance due on shares not fully called up, liabilities in respect of any uncompleted contracts or a repairing lease, etc., and sums due to deferred creditors.

Postponed or Deferred Creditors. Certain of the creditors entered on List E are called postponed or deferred creditors, because their claims are not considered unless and until all the other creditors have been paid in full. These are—

1. Loans for business purposes from the debtor's spouse where the debtor is a sole trader. If the husband is a partner in a firm, and the wife has lent money to the firm, she can claim as an ordinary creditor. (Sect. 36.)

2. Loans for business purposes at a rate of interest varying with the profits.

3. Amount due to seller of the goodwill of a business in consideration of a share of the profits.

The last two are governed by the Partnership Act, 1890, Sect. 3.

These debts are not in any way distinguished on the Statement of Affairs as the question of postponement will arise when proofs of debt are dealt with for voting and dividend purposes.

List 'F', Creditors for Rent, etc., Recoverable by Distress. If the landlord distrains within three months before the date of the receiving order, he can be called upon to pay the preferential creditors out of the proceeds, becoming a preferential creditor himself for any loss he thereby sustains. (Sect. 33 (4).) Should he distrain after the commencement of the bankruptcy, he is entitled to only *six months'* rent due before the date of the adjudication order, the balance ranking for dividend as an unsecured creditor. (Sect. 35.) Gas, water, and electric light corporations often have power of distraint in respect of their particular charges, and would, in such cases, also appear on this list.

List 'G', Preferential Creditors for Rates, Taxes, and Wages. By Sect. 33 (1) of the Bankruptcy Act, 1914, and other Acts, certain classes of preferential creditors rank before others and are, in consequence, known as pre-preferential creditors. The following is a list of these debts—

PRE-PREFERENTIAL—

1. Funds belonging to a friendly society or trustee savings bank, which are in the hands of the debtor as an officer of the society.
2. The proportion of an articled clerk's premium, as the trustee shall decide, where the employer becomes bankrupt, and the trustee does not transfer the articles to some other person.
3. Reasonable funeral and testamentary expenses in the case of a deceased insolvent debtor.
4. The expenses properly incurred by the trustee under a deed of arrangement which was avoided by the subsequent bankruptcy.

PREFERENTIAL—

1. Assessed rates for the twelve months preceding the receiving order.
2. Assessed taxes up to the 5th April preceding the receiving order, not exceeding one year. The Crown is not preferential in respect of debts arising in the course of trading. The Inland Revenue is preferential for one year only *prior* to the making of the receiving order. Where several years are outstanding the Revenue may choose the largest, the remaining years being included in the unsecured creditors.
3. Wages and salaries of a clerk for four months, not exceeding £200.
4. Wages of workmen and labourers for four months, not exceeding £200.
5. Where any labourer in husbandry has contracted for wages in a lump sum, he has priority for the whole or a part of such sum, as the court may decide to be due, proportionate to the time of service expired.
6. All contributions due by the employer under the National Insurance Acts during the twelve months preceding the receiving order.

The mere fact of obtaining judgment or a garnishee order does not enable the creditor to rank preferentially.

List 'H', Property. On this list must be entered all the debtor's belongings in the shape of goods, money, real and personal property wherever situate. The printed list sets out what details are required. Only those assets should be included here which are absolutely unfettered. Where assets are pledged or mortgaged as security for debts or loans, the assets appear under such debt or loan as "Value of Security" on the liabilities side, and *not* on the assets side. The surrender value of the life insurance policy (if any) must be shown.

Under "Other Property" are included reversionary interests, leases, stocks and shares, jewellery, and, in the case of a partnership bankruptcy, the surplus (if any) from the partners' separate estates.

Property Retained by Bankrupt. By Sect. 38, the property of the bankrupt divisible amongst his creditors does not comprise the following—

1. Property held by the bankrupt on trust for any other person;
2. The tools (if any) of his trade, and the necessary wearing apparel and bedding of himself, his wife and children, to a value inclusive of tools and apparel and bedding, not exceeding £20 in the whole.

List 'I', Debts Due to the Estate. As can be seen from the printed form, the debts have to be classified into good, doubtful, and bad. The doubtful debts have to be estimated, and the estimated value treated as an asset in the statement of affairs. The prescribed form contains a note respecting the treatment of contra accounts (if any).

List 'J', Bills of Exchange, Promissory Notes, etc., Available as Assets. On this list must be furnished particulars of all bills of exchange, promissory notes, etc., held by the debtor. Such documents, are, of course, handed over to the Official Receiver immediately the receiving order is made.

List 'L', in Substitution for such of the Sheets Named A-J as will have to be Returned Blank. The object of this list is to avoid, in the case of small bankruptcies, having to file a number of blank forms. The debtor fills in the letter of each form, and writes the word "nil" opposite to the forms that he returns blank.

Front Sheet. The totals of the various lists have to be transferred to the "Front Sheet" or summary. The assets are entered as on the lists H, I, and J, H being copied in detail; then follows the surplus (if any) from securities in the hands of fully-secured creditors; and the addition of these four gives the total of the *gross* assets. The liabilities are entered from the lists A to E, and the proper amounts are extended into the column headed "Expected to Rank." The liabilities as on lists F and G, and the sheriff's charges (if any) are then entered, but only in the inner column, added up, and the total deducted from the total of the gross assets on the opposite side. The balance gives the total of the *net* assets, and this total subtracted from the total of the liabilities ranking for dividend shows the estimated deficiency, which must agree with the deficiency shown in list K.

Example 1

From the following particulars draw up the statement of affairs to be furnished to the creditors of A. O. Lovejoy—

28th September, 19..	£
Unsecured creditors—	
Bills payable	1,856·75
Household debts	128·84
Trade accounts	9,037·29
Fully-secured creditors (holding security estimated to produce £9,000)	8,000·00
Liability on bills discounted, List D (£53·5 of which is expected to rank)	557·73
Creditors for distrainable rent	100·00
Preferential creditors for rates, taxes, wages, etc.	122·73

28th September, 19..	£
Cash in hand	10·63
Cash at bank	60·29
Stock-in-trade (estimated to produce £2,500)	4,060·91
Furniture and fixtures (estimated to produce £600)	1,080·64
Household furniture and effects (estimated to realize £220)	450·53
Book debts—	
Good	2,678·77
Doubtful £526·58 expected to produce half; Bad £487·74.	
Bills of exchange, good	237·91

(See p. 2619.)

Example 2

From the following particulars prepare statement of affairs of Messrs. Rupert and Larkin as at 30th June—

Plant and machinery £30,000; expected to realize £25,000. Stock-in-trade £12,000; expected to produce £7,000. Patents £5,000; estimated to realize £3,000. Furniture and fixtures £625; expected to produce £400. Cash in hand £10. Cash at bank £120. Bills receivable £2,514, all good. Bills payable £4,035. Loans £20,000, having a first charge on the plant and machinery. Liability for damages awarded to injured workman under the Workmen's Compensation Act, 1925, £100, not covered by insurance. Creditors £33,406, £8,000 of which has a second charge on the plant and machinery. Rent owing 1 year, £620. Rates and taxes, 1 year, £85. Preferential wages and salaries £80. Book debts £10,816; good £7,068, subject to 5 per cent cash discount; doubtful £2,020, expected to produce 25 per cent; and the remainder bad. Liabilities on bills discounted £1,856, of which £104 is expected to rank. L. Larkin's private estate shows an expected surplus of £60, and R. Rupert's a deficiency of £146.

How much in the £ does the estate show? (See p. 2621.)

QUESTIONS

1. Explain the term "undischarged bankrupt." What disabilities attach to such a person?
2. Can a bankruptcy be afterwards annulled? How are joint and separate estates of partners to be treated?
3. How are small bankruptcies dealt with? What is an "administration order"?
4. Give short particulars of the creditors who have to be entered on Lists A, B, and C respectively.
5. Give short particulars of the creditors who have to be entered on Lists D, E, and F respectively.
6. What is meant by "postponed" or "deferred" creditors? Give examples.
7. What are "preferential" creditors, and on what list are their claims entered?
8. What property is entered on List H? What property is retained by the bankrupt?
9. What debts are entered on Lists I and J, and how have they to be classified?
10. What is the purpose of List L, and "Front Sheet"? What is the procedure with the latter?

Difference between a Statement of Affairs and a Balance Sheet. This is a favourite examination question, and the student should, therefore, carefully note the four principal differences—

1. A balance sheet is prepared from the figures in the books and shows, on the assets side, the whole of the assets including such items as are being

Solution: Example 1

STATEMENT OF AFFAIRS
OF A. O. LOVEJOY, 28TH SEPTEMBER, 19..

Gross Liabilities	Liabilities		Expected to Rank	Assets		Expected to Produce
£		£	£		£	£
11,022·88	Unsecured Creditors (A)		11,022·88	Property (H)—		
8,000·00	Fully Secured Creditors (B) .	8,000·00		Cash in hand		10·63
	Value of Security . . .	9,000·00				
	Surplus to contra . . .	1,000·00		Cash at Bank		60·29
557·73	Liabilities on Bills Discounted (D)	557·73	53·51	Stock-in-trade	4,060·91	2,500·00
				Furniture and Fixtures	1,080·64	600·00
100·00	Creditors for Rent (F) . .	100·00		Household Furniture and Effects . .	450·53	220·00
122·73	Preferential Creditors for Rates, Taxes, Wages, etc. (G)	122·73		*Total* . . .		3,390·92
	Deducted in full per contra .	222·73		Book Debts (I)— Good		2,678·77
				Doubtful	526·58	
				Bad.	487·74	
					1,014·32	263·29
				Bills of Exchange (J)		237·91
				Surplus from Securities in hands of Fully Secured Creditors as per contra . . .		1,000·00
				Total Assets		7,570·89
				Deduct Creditors for Rent and Preferential Creditors, as per contra		222·73
				Net Assets		7,348·16
				Deficiency		3,728·23
19,803·34			11,076·39			11,076·39

carried forward to be written off in subsequent years; a statement of affairs shows only those "free" assets that are available for the general creditors, assets mortgaged or pledged as security for debts being shown underneath the debts themselves.

2. A balance sheet shows the book value of the assets; a statement of affairs shows their estimated realizable value as well.

3. In a balance sheet the preferential creditors are included in the total of the liabilities; in a statement of affairs they are deducted from the assets.

4. A balance sheet shows a trader's capital, profit or loss, and drawings; a statement of affairs excludes all these items.

DEFICIENCY ACCOUNT

The object of this form, List K, is to explain the deficiency as shown in the statement of affairs, i.e. to show by means of figures how it has been brought about. Starting from a given date—at least twelve months before the date of the Receiving Order—the initial capital (if any) should be shown on the one side, and all subsequent trading profits and any other sources of income. On the other side should be detailed trading losses, losses by bad debts, and all expenses or losses other than trade expenses, viz. household expenses of self, wife, and children; the difference between premiums paid on life policies and the surrender value of such policies; medical attendance; gambling or stock exchange losses; damages and costs in actions at law; loss through dishonoured bills or accommodation bills expected to rank; and the estimated losses on realization. The balance of this account must agree with the balance shown by the statement of affairs.

Adjustment of Profits and Losses. In exercises and examination work, the profits and losses are often given *after* charging interest on capital. In such cases, the profits and losses must be adjusted in order to eliminate this interest from the deficiency account. Thus, the profits must be *increased* and the losses *decreased* by the amount of such interest; and, in some cases, a small loss may be converted into a profit by means of this adjustment. When partners' salaries have been credited to capital, i.e. not drawn out in cash, the profits and losses must be adjusted in a similar manner, in order to avoid showing the salaries in the deficiency account as having increased the capital. When the partners' salaries have been drawn out in cash, the capital account will not have been affected, and, consequently, the profits and losses will not require adjustment.

Example 1(a)

Referring to Example 1, draw up from that and the following particulars the deficiency account of A. O. Lovejoy—

Capital at commencement £5,000. Trading results: 1st year, profit £1,678·21; 2nd year, loss £869·44; 3rd year, loss £660·38. Damages and costs in unsuccessful action at law £4,000. Drawings, 3 years @ £600 per annum.

Solution: Example 2

STATEMENT OF AFFAIRS
OF RUPERT AND LARKIN, 30TH JUNE, 19..

Gross Liabilities	Liabilities		Expected to Rank	Assets		Expected to Produce
£		£	£		£	£
29,752	Unsecured Creditors (A)[1]		29,752	Property (H)—		
20,000	Fully Secured Creditors (B)	20,000		Cash in hand		10
	Value of Security	25,000				
	Surplus to List "C"	5,000		Cash at Bank		120
8,000	Partly Secured Creditors (C)	8,000		Stock-in-trade	12,000	7,000
	Value of Security	5,000	3,000	Furniture and Fixtures	625	400
1,856	Liability on Bills Discounted (D)	1,856	104	Patents	5,000	3,000
310	Creditors for Rent (F)	310		Surplus from private estate of L. Larkin		60
265	Preferential Creditors[2] for Rates, Taxes, Wages, etc. (G)	265		*Total*		10,590
		575		Book Debts (I)— Good	7,068	6,715
				Doubtful	2,020	
				Bad	1,727	
					3,748	505
				Bills of Exchange (J)—	2,514	2,514
				Total Assets		20,324
				Deduct Creditors, for Rent, Rates, Taxes, Wages, etc., as per contra		575
				Net Assets		19,749
				Deficiency		13,108
60,183			32,856			32,857

[1] Bills Payable, £4,035; Trade Accounts, £25,406; Rent, £310.
[2] Damages to Workman, £100; Taxes, £85; Wages and Salaries, £80.
(Estate shows (£19,749 ÷ £32,857) £0·60 in the £, subject to expenses of winding up.)

Solution 1(a)

DEFICIENCY ACCOUNT

28th September, 19..

		£			£
Capital at commencement		5,000·00	Trading Losses—		
Trading Profit, 1st year		1,678·21	2nd year	£869.44	
Deficiency as per Statement of Affairs		3,728·23	3rd year	660·38	
					1,529·82
			Drawings, 3 yrs. at £600 p.a.		1,800·00
			Bad Debts		751·03
			Damages and costs in unsuccessful action at law		4,000·00
			Estimated Losses on Realization—		
			Stock	£1,560·91	
			Furniture	480·64	
			Household Furniture	230·53	
					2,272·08
			Liability on Bills discounted, expected to rank		53·51
		10,406·44			10,406·44

Example 2(a)

Referring to Example 2, draw up from that and the following particulars the deficiency account of Rupert and Larkin—

Capital at commencement £10,000. Trading results: 1st year, profit £1,116; 2nd year, loss £1,887; 3rd year, profit £587; 4th year, profit £316; 5th year, loss £2,872. Partners' drawings: Rupert, £900 per annum; Larkin, £500 per annum. The above profits and losses are after charging interest on capital at £500 per annum.

Solution 2(a)

DEFICIENCY ACCOUNT

30th June, 19..

		£			£
Capital at commencement		10,000	Losses by Trading—		
Profits by Trading—			2nd year	£1,387	
1st year	£1,616		5th year	2,372	
3rd year	1,087				3,759
4th year	816		Drawings, 5 years at £1,400 p.a.		7,000
		3,519	Bad Debts		3,242
Surplus from L. Larkin's private estate		60	Estimated Losses on Realization—		
Deficiency as per Statement of Affairs			Stock	£5,000	
		13,104	Fixtures	225	
			Plant & Machy.	5,000	
			Patents	2,000	
			Discount on Debtors	353	
					12,578
			Liability on Bills discounted expected to rank		104
		26,683			26,683

Firm Bankruptcy. The position dealt with so far has been confined to a sole trader. Where, however, there is a firm bankruptcy the problems are a little more complicated. It should be remembered that statements of affairs will be required both for the firm and for its constituent members.

Subject to certain exceptions, the private creditors have recourse only to the private estate, and the partnership creditors to the firm estate, generally referred to as the joint estate. Another confusing point arises where joint property is pledged as security for a private debt of one of the partners, in which case the private creditor is not a secured creditor, because he has not obtained the property of the debtor as security, but that of the joint estate. Examples are shown to illustrate the principles involved.

Example 3

A and B are partners and the position is as follows—

BALANCE SHEETS

FIRM

Liabilities	£	*Assets*		£
Creditors	600	Stock		300
		Debtors		100
		A	£120	
		B	80	
				200
	600			600

A

Liabilities	£	*Assets*	£
Creditors	250	Furniture	300
Surplus	30	Sundry Assets	100
Firm	120		
	400		400

B

Liabilities	£	*Assets*	£
Creditors	900	Furniture	600
Firm	80	Life Policy	250
		Deficiency	130
	980		980

It is assumed that all assets are worth book value save that stock is estimated to realize £140. Prepare draft statements of affairs and joint deficiency account.

STATEMENT OF AFFAIRS

Joint

	£		£
Creditors	600	Stock	140
		Debtors	100
		Sundry Assets (A's Estate) . .	150
			390
		Deficiency	210
	600		600

A

	£		£
Creditors	250	Furniture	300
Surplus	150	Sundry Assets	100
	400		400

B

	£		£
Creditors	900	Furniture	600
		Life Policy	250
		Deficiency	50
	900		900

Joint Deficiency Account

	£			£
A—Surplus	150	Excess of Liabilities over Assets of—		
Deficiency as per Statement of Affairs	210	A	£120	
		B	80	
				200
		Depreciation of Stock . . .		160
	360			360

Each statement of affairs is separately compiled and each deficiency or surplus is separately ascertained. Any surplus introduced from a separate estate to the joint estate (not being in the original balance sheet of the firm) must have its double entry. It has already been stated that as regards creditors, each "set" proves against the particular debtor, i.e. separate against separate, joint against joint, but it should be observed that the surplus of A, i.e. £150, is now available for the joint creditors.

Where in a partnership a partner has given security for a firm debt, the joint estate has first claim on such security: any surplus goes to the separate estate of that partner, the reverse applying when joint property is given as security to separate creditors.

Example 4

The creditors are—

	£		£
Joint . . .	3,000	Assets . . .	1,600
A . . .	500	" . . .	400
B. . . .	600	" . . .	640

The £640 asset of B has been placed as security for a loan of £500 to the firm included in the figure £3,000. The joint assets are estimated to realize £1,800. Prepare statements of affairs.

Solution 4

STATEMENTS OF AFFAIRS

JOINT

Liabilities	£	*Assets*	£
Unsecured Creditors . . .	3,000	Assets	1,800
		Deficiency . . .	1,200
	3,000		3,000

A

Liabilities	£	*Assets*	£
Creditors	500	Assets	400
		Deficiency	100
	500		500

B

Liabilities	£	*Assets*	£
Creditors	600	Surplus from Security held by Joint Creditors . . .	440
		Deficiency . . .	160
	600		600

The joint creditor of £500 would get (as the other joint creditors) £0·60 in the £ dividend = £300, i.e. $\frac{18}{30}$ × £500. Hence there is a shortage of £200. He recoups this from the £640 asset of B, leaving still a surplus of £440 which is now available for B's creditors.

This may be further proved as follows. This joint creditor has £640 security of B against the partnership debt £500, leaving £140 surplus. The dividend £300 received from the joint estate is now due to B's separate estate, since the £500 debt has been satisfied in full. B's estate thus receives £440 from the asset £640.

TRUSTEE'S ACCOUNTS

Trustee in Bankruptcy. This is a person elected by the creditors of a debtor who has been adjudged a bankrupt, to take over his property. The appointment is subject to the approval of the Board of Trade. The trustee's duties are to realize the debtor's estate, and distribute the proceeds, after paying the preferential claims, among the unsecured creditors.

Trustee's Cash Book. The trustee must keep a cash book, the prescribed form of which is as shown on the next page, also a trading account if he carries on business.

Trustee's Account of Receipts and Payments. The trustee must also render to the Board of Trade an account of his receipts and payments, the prescribed form of which is as shown on p. 2627. (Sect. 92.) This is audited by the Board of Trade, and an audited copy is kept for the inspection of the creditors or of the bankrupt.

Record Book. This is a book that must be kept by the trustee in bankruptcy. It contains records of the minutes of all meetings, the resolutions passed, and particulars, in order of date, as to how the estate has been administered. (Sect. 86.)

Bankruptcy Estates Account. This is an account kept by the Board of Trade with the Bank of England, and every trustee in bankruptcy, or under any composition or scheme of arrangement, must pay all moneys received by him into this account. He may, however, with the sanction of the Board of Trade, if the balance of cash is small, and if such procedure is to the obvious advantage of the creditors, make his payments into and out of some local bank. The account must be opened in the name of the debtor's estate, and any interest received thereon will form part of the general assets of the estate. A trustee must not pay any sums received by him as trustee into his own private banking account. If at any time he retains for more than ten days a sum exceeding £50, he is liable for interest thereon at the rate of 20 per cent per annum, and also for any expenses occasioned by his default, and may be removed from office. (Sect. 89.)

TRUSTEE'S CASH BOOK

Dr RECEIPTS — PAYMENTS

Date	Particulars	Total	Drawn from Bank	Debts Collected	Property Realized	Receipts from Securities Held by Creditors	Other Receipts	Date	Particulars	Voucher Nos. (in red)	Total

PAYMENTS (*cont.*) *Cr*

Paid into Bank	Costs of Realization								Allowance to Debtor	Preferential Creditors (Section 33) and Rent	Payments to Redeem Securities	Dividends Paid	Other Payments
	Board of Trade and Court Fees	Law Costs of Petition (including £5 stamp)	Law Costs after Receiving Order	Commission on Realization and Distribution		Charges of Auctioneer, Accountant, Shorthand Writer, &c., as taxed	Notices in *Gazette* and Local Paper	Incidental Expenses, including Possession					
				Board of Trade	Trustee								

BANKRUPTCY ACT, 1914

In the Court holden at No. of

In the matter of under Receiving Order dated day of 19...

Dr Statement, showing position of Estate at date of application for Release of Trustee Cr

	Estimated to Produce per Debtor's Statement	Receipts			Payments
To Total receipts from date of Receiving Order, viz.— (See list "H")			By Board of Trade and Court Fees (including Stamps of £5 on petition)		
Receipts per Trading Account . . .			Law Costs of Petition		
Other Receipts			Other Law Costs		
			Trustees' Remuneration as fixed by the Committee of Inspection, viz.—		
			per cent on £..........assets realized . .		
			per cent on £..............assets distributed in dividend		
			Special Manager's Charges		
			Person appointed to assist Debtor under Sect. 74 of the B.A., 1914		
			Auctioneer's Charges as Taxed		
			Other Taxed Costs.		
			Costs of Possession		
Total			Costs of Notices in *Gazette* and Local Papers		
			Incidental Outlay		
Less—			Total Cost of Realization		£
Deposit returned to Petitioner					
Payments to redeem Securities			Allowance to Debtor		
Costs of Execution					
Payments per Trading Account			*Creditors viz.*—		
	£		Preferential		
			Unsecured: Final Dividend now declared of.......... in the £ on...................... . . .		
			Dividends previously declared		
			The Debtor's estimate of amount expected to rank for dividend was	£	
			Balance		
Net Realizations	£				£

Power to Disclaim Onerous Property. By Sect. 54 (1)—

Where any part of the property of the bankrupt consists of land of any tenure burdened with onerous covenants, of shares or stock in companies, of unprofitable contracts, or of any other property that is unsaleable, or not readily saleable, by reason of its binding the possessor thereof to the performance of any onerous act, or to the payment of any sum of money, the trustee, notwithstanding that he has endeavoured to sell or has taken possession of the property, or exercised any act of ownership in relation thereto, but subject to the provisions of this section, may, by writing signed by him, at any time within twelve months after the first appointment of a trustee or such extended period as may be allowed by the court, disclaim the property.

A trustee is not, however, usually entitled to disclaim a lease except by consent of the court.

Powers of Trustee to Deal with Property. By Sect. 55 of the Act, it is enacted—

Subject to the provisions of this Act, the trustee may do all or any of the following things—

1. Sell all or any part of the property of the bankrupt (including the goodwill of the business, if any, and the book debts due or growing due to the bankrupt), by public auction or private contract, with power to transfer the whole thereof to any person or company, or to sell the same in parcels.
2. Give receipts for any money received by him, which receipts shall effectually discharge the person paying the money from all responsibility in respect of the application thereof.
3. Prove, rank, claim, and draw a dividend in respect of any debt due to the bankrupt.
4. Exercise any powers, the capacity to exercise which is vested in the trustee under this Act, and execute any powers of attorney, deeds and other instruments for the purpose of carrying into effect the provisions of this Act.
5. Deal with any property to which the bankrupt is beneficially entitled as tenant in tail in the same manner as the bankrupt might have dealt with it.

Powers Exercisable by Trustee with Permission of the Committee of Inspection. By Sect. 56, the trustee may with the permission of the committee of inspection do all or any of the following things—

1. Carry on the business of the bankrupt, so far as may be necessary for the beneficial winding up of the same;
2. Bring, institute, or defend any action or other legal proceedings relating to the property of the bankrupt;
3. Employ a solicitor or other agent to take any proceedings or do any business which may be sanctioned by the committee of inspection;
4. Accept as the consideration for the sale of any property of the bankrupt a sum of money payable at a future time, subject to such stipulations as to security and otherwise as the committee think fit;
5. Mortgage or pledge any part of the property of the bankrupt for the purpose of raising money for the payment of his debts;
6. Refer any dispute to arbitration, compromise any debts, claims, and liabilities, whether present or future, certain or contingent, liquidated or unliquidated, subsisting or supposed to subsist between the bankrupt and any person who may have incurred any liability to the bankrupt, on the receipt of such sums, payable at such times, and generally on such terms as may be agreed on;

7. Make such compromise or other arrangement as may be thought expedient with creditors, or persons claiming to be creditors, in respect of any debts provable under the bankruptcy;

8. Make such compromise or other arrangement as may be thought expedient with respect to any claim arising out of or incidental to the property of the bankrupt, made or capable of being made on the trustee by any person or by the trustee on any person;

9. Divide in its existing form amongst the creditors, according to its estimated value, any property which from its peculiar nature or other special circumstances cannot be readily or advantageously sold.

With the permission of the committee of inspection, he may also appoint the bankrupt to superintend the management of the property, or to carry on the business, and may also make him an allowance for the support of himself and family, or in consideration of his services. (Sects. 57 and 58.)

Remuneration of Trustee. By Sect. 82 (1)—

Where the creditors appoint any person to be trustee of a debtor's estate, his remuneration (if any) shall be fixed by an ordinary resolution of the creditors, or, if the creditors so resolve, by the committee of inspection, and shall be in the nature of a commission or percentage, of which one part shall be payable on the amount realized by the trustee, after deducting any sums paid to secured creditors out of the proceeds of their securities, and the other part on the amount distributed in dividend.

Distribution of Dividends. Sect. 62 enacts as follows—

1. Subject to the retention of such sums as may be necessary for the costs of administration, or otherwise, the trustee shall, with all convenient speed, declare and distribute dividends amongst the creditors who have proved their debts.

2. The first dividend, if any, shall be declared and distributed within four months after the conclusion of the first meeting of creditors, unless the trustee satisfies the committee of inspection that there is sufficient reason for postponing the declaration to a later date.

3. Subsequent dividends shall, in the absence of sufficient reason to the contrary, be declared and distributed at intervals of not more than six months.

Rights of Creditor who has Not Proved his Debt. By Sect. 65—

Any creditor who has not proved his debt before the declaration of any dividend or dividends shall be entitled to be paid out of any money for the time being in the hands of the trustee any dividend or dividends he may have failed to receive before that money is applied to the payment of any future dividend or dividends, but he shall not be entitled to disturb the distribution of any dividend declared before his debt was proved by reason that he has not participated therein.

Interest on Debts. Sect. 66 (1) provides as follows—

Where a debt has been proved, and the debt includes interest, or any pecuniary consideration in lieu of interest, such interest or consideration shall, for the purposes of dividend, be calculated at a rate not exceeding 5 per cent per annum, without prejudice to the right of a creditor to receive out of the estate any higher rate of interest to which he may be entitled after all the debts proved in the estate have been paid in full.

Bankrupt's Right to a Surplus. This is provided for by Sect. 69—

The bankrupt shall be entitled to any surplus remaining after payment in full of his creditors, with interest, as by this Act provided, and of the costs, charges, and expenses of the proceedings under the bankruptcy petition.

Unclaimed Funds or Dividends. By Sect. 153 (1)—

Where the trustee, under any bankruptcy composition or scheme, pursuant to this Act or any enactment repealed by this Act, has under his control any unclaimed dividend which has remained unclaimed for more than six months, or where, after making a final dividend, he has in his hands or under his control any unclaimed or undistributed money arising from the property of the debtor, he shall forthwith pay it to the Bankruptcy Estates Account at the Bank of England. The Board of Trade shall furnish him with a certificate of receipt of the money so paid, which shall be an effectual discharge to him in respect thereof.

Any person claiming to be entitled to any moneys in the bankruptcy Estates Account may apply to the Board of Trade for them; and if the Board of Trade is satisfied as to the validity of his claim, they order payment to be made to him.

Example 5

From the following particulars make out the trustee's Account of Receipts and Payments to date of first and final dividend.

RECEIPTS

Cash deposited with solicitor £10; cash in hand £15; cash at bank £104; stock £8,750; furniture and fixtures £320; patents £2,500; book debts £7,426; bills of exchange £2,420.

PAYMENTS

Board of Trade and court fees £153; law costs of petition £45; taxed costs of accountant and shorthand writer £256; guarantee premium £13 (authorized by the committee to be paid out of the assets); cost of notices in *Gazette* and local newspapers £5; incidental outlay: postages, stationery, etc., £43; allowance to debtor £100; preferential creditors for rent £300; and rates, taxes, and wages £240; trustee's remuneration (as fixed by the committee of inspection), 3 per cent on £18,997. Assets realized, and 2 per cent on dividend distributed to unsecured creditors, whose debts amounted to £38,861.

QUESTIONS

1. Explain the difference between a statement of affairs and a balance sheet.
2. What is the object of a deficiency account? What are its usual contents?
3. What adjustments of profits and losses are sometimes required when preparing a deficiency account?
4. What is a trustee in bankruptcy? How is he appointed?
5. What books and accounts must a trustee keep? What is a record book?
6. Explain the Bankruptcy Estates Account. Can a trustee pay his receipts into any bank he prefers? What penalties attach to a trustee with regard to the keeping of a large cash balance?
7. What power has a trustee with regard to onerous property? Does this power apply to a lease? Name some of the powers of a trustee with regard to property generally.

8. State briefly some of the powers a trustee may exercise with the permission of the committee of inspection.

9. How is the trustee remunerated? How are dividends to be distributed by him? What are the rights of a creditor who has not proved his debt?

10. What provision is made by the Bankruptcy Act, 1914, with respect to the following?—

(*a*) Interest on debts;
(*b*) surplus;
(*c*) unclaimed dividends or funds.

EXERCISE 26

1. From the following particulars make out the statement of affairs of Thos. F. Sellers for submission to his creditors—

	£		£
Good book debts	3,872	Partially-secured creditors . £872	
Doubtful „	1,500	Estimated value of securities 550	
Bad „	2,500		322
Unsecured creditors	7,278	Creditors fully secured (estimated value of securities, £2,500)	2,200
Bills payable	1,200		
Stock	1,200		
Fixtures	300		
Cash at bank	150		
Preferential creditors	267		

Make out his statement of affairs, assuming that the stock, doubtful debts, and fixtures will realize 50 per cent of the value mentioned above.

Solution: Example 5

TRUSTEE'S ACCOUNT OF RECEIPTS AND PAYMENTS

Dr — To Date of First and Final Dividend — *Cr*

Receipts	Amount	Payments	Amount
	£		£
Cash deposited with Solicitor	10	Board of Trade and Court Fees	153
Cash in hand	15	Law Costs of Petition	45
Cash at Bank	104	Trustee's Rumeration (as fixed by Committee of Inspection)—	
Stock	8,750		
Furniture & Fixtures	320	3% on £18,997 assets realized	569
Patents	2,500	2% on £19,430 assets distributed[1]	388
Book Debts	7,426	Taxed Costs of Accountant and Shorthand Writer	256
Bills of Exchange	2,420	Guarantee Premium	13
		Costs of Notices in *Gazette* and local newspapers	5
		Incidental Outlay— Postages, Stationery, etc.	43
		Total Costs and Charges	1,472
		Allowance to Debtors	100
		Preferential Creditors—	
		Rent	300
		Rates, Taxes, & Wages	240
		First and Final Dividend of 50p in the £ on £38,861 to Unsecured Creditors	19,433
	21,545		21,545

[1] Ascertained by calculating $\frac{2}{102}$ of £19,819, the *gross* amount distributable between unsecured creditors and trustee.

2. Richard Humphrey's balance sheet on 31st January was as follows: *Assets:* sundry debtors £106; stock at cost £395; cash in hand £11; shop fittings at cost £173. *Liabilities* bank overdraft £241; trade creditors £378; John Joker, for rent, £15; capital £40 Being pressed by creditors, he filed his petition in bankruptcy. On going through the list of debtors, he found that of the amount entered in the books, £60 was irrecoverable, and that accounts amounting to £10 were disputed. He estimated that the stock, if sold by auction, should realize £315, and that the shop fittings would realize £45. His household furniture was estimated at £280. He owed to sundry tradesmen £55, and a year's rent for his dwelling-house at £35 per annum. He also owed £2 income tax, and £8 for rates. The shop assistant had not received her wages for the previous two weeks at £5 a week. Prepare statement of affairs. *(U.L.C.I.)*

3. Prepare a statement of affairs from the following particulars of Jonas Johnson, manufacturer, Burnley, on 18th March.

	£
Unsecured creditors	22,100
Fully-secured creditors	9,870
Partly-secured creditors	4,764
Securities held by creditors, fully secured, valued at	12,107
Securities held by creditors, partly secured, valued at	2,321
Creditors for rents, rates, taxes, and wages (of which £600 only is preferential)	850
Plant: book value £12,600, estimated to produce only one-third of this sum	
Office furniture, estimated to realize	50
Cash in hand	5
Book debts—	
Good, expected to realize	3,000
Doubtful, £500, expected to realize	200
Bad, £300, expected to realize	*nil*
Life policy on the life of Jonas Johnson, in the Atlas Assurance Co., paid 20 annual premiums of £24 each. Estimated surrender value is $\frac{3}{8}$ of the amount paid in premiums.	

How much in the £ does the estate show? *(U.L.C.I.)*

4. From the following particulars prepare a statement of affairs and deficiency account as on 31st December, for the information of the creditors of Black & White, who are insolvent: cash in hand £200. Book debts: good £2,000; doubtful £300 (estimated to produce £100); bad £500. Stock-in-trade valued at £1,900. Freehold property cost £3,000, estimated to produce £2,500; this property is assigned to creditors for £2,300. Shares held £150: these are given as security for a debt of £400. Creditors: unsecured on open account £5,000; on bills payable £1,000; partially secured by shares £400; fully secured on freehold property £2,300; preferable claims for taxes, wages, and salaries £100. Black's drawings £2,000; White's drawings £2,850. The business commenced on 1st January, three years ago. Black put into it £2,500 and White £2,900. The first year showed a profit of £3,000, but the next two years showed a loss of £4,300. No provision was made for bad debts.

5. Thomas Jones having been adjudicated bankrupt, the following balances appear in his books—

Cash in hand £20; overdrawn at bank £150; stock-in-trade (cost £800) estimated at £500; machinery (cost £500) estimated at £400; trade fixtures (cost £300) estimated at £120; book debts: good £500 (estimated to produce £500); doubtful £250 (estimated to produce £100); bad £250; unsecured creditors £2,500; creditors fully secured £500; estimated value of security £600; liabilities on bills £400; creditors for half-year's rent £50; rates and taxes (12 mos.) £10; domestic servant's wages £30.

Arrange the above in the form of a statement of affairs for presentation to the first meeting of creditors.

6. Prepare statement of affairs of Winter & Co., shippers, who filed their petition on 29th September.

Books of partnership showed that there was owing £9,610; included in this are creditors for £2,560, who hold stock valued at £3,000, and also creditors for £1,000 who hold stock valued at £565. The assets consist of cash in office £10; at bank £400. Stock-in-trade £2,000 (estimated to produce £1,200). Land and buildings £1,500 (estimated to realize £1,000). Furniture, etc., £500 (estimated to produce £250). Preferential creditors for wages and taxes £90. Good book debts £500. Doubtful debts £250 (estimated to realize £100).

7. Samuel Hobson, in business in the city, finds himself insolvent. From the various books and papers in his possession the following particulars as to his financial position are forthcoming—

	£
Sundry debtors: good £1,280; doubtful £2,800 (estimated to produce £1,000); bad £700	4,780
Sundry freehold houses, etc. (estimated to produce £2,000)	3,300
Shares: 1,000 ordinary shares in the Cable Telegraph Co. valued at par	1,000
Mining and railway shares (£2,500 are held as security by partly-secured creditors and the balance by fully-secured creditors)	9,450
Loss through the unsuccessful defence of an action at law	5,420
Business expenses	3,200
Creditors—	
Unsecured	16,740
Partly secured	5,420
Fully secured	3,110
Preferential claims for salaries and rent	500
Private drawings	1,200
Samuel Hobson: capital account	3,800
Cash at bank	420
Bills receivable: good	800

Prepare the statement of affairs for submission to his creditors and a deficiency account in the ordinary form. (*London Chamber of Commerce*.)

8. Charles Jackson guarantees a loan of £200 for a friend. Hearing that this friend was in financial difficulties and only able to pay about 50p in the £ if made bankrupt, and being himself pressed by creditors, he decided to file his petition.

He had a works which had cost recently £1,000, but on this there was a mortgage of £800; cash at the bank £140; cash in hand £11 out of which he gave his solicitor £10 on account of costs. His stock-in-trade had cost £398, but he did not think that on forced realization it would bring in more than £275; his machinery, etc., he thought, ought to sell for £200, and the fittings, etc., for £50; after considering his book debts carefully, he thought that £118 was good, £296 bad, and £76 doubtful, perhaps worth £30; he had also a bill of exchange for £87.

He had unsecured creditors for £753; he had accepted two accommodation bills of £100, and on reference to his bill book found that he had two months before endorsed over William Fletcher's 3 months' bill for £167 to a creditor.

He owed £10 for house rent, £20 for income tax, £29 for rates, and £26 for wages. He had also household furniture worth £175, and a gold watch and chain worth £15. Make out in proper form, Charles Jackson's statement of affairs. (*U.L.C.I.*)

9. Fred Jackson, on the 31st March, unable to meet his engagements, requires a statement of affairs for submission to his creditors. Prepare the same from the following—

	Book Value £	Estimated to Realize £
Leasehold premises held for 99 years, subject to payment of ground rent £100 per year	10,000	9,000
Book debts—		
Good	6,650	6,000
Doubtful	500	250
Bad	750	
Fixed plant and machinery	4,000	3,000
Stock-in-trade	2,000	1,400

Cash in hand, £10. Life insurance policy for £2,500 at death, subject to a premium of £50 a year due and paid 28th February last, and held by insurance company for a loan of £200; surrender value £500. Household furniture and effects £360. Private and household debts £290. 600 shares in Cooper & Co. Ltd. of £1 each: 50p paid up, now quoted at 62½p per share. Loan of £5,000, secured by a first mortgage on the leasehold at 4½ per cent, the interest being paid to the 31st March. Unsecured creditors £15,000. Bankers for overdraft and interest £5,000, holding as security a second mortgage on leasehold of £4,000. Loan from E. Taylor £400 at 5 per cent per annum, interest being paid to 31st March, who holds as security second charge on life insurance policy. Ground rent of leasehold accrued since 31st December last.

With the following additional information, prepare a deficiency account—

On 1st April, three years ago, he had a capital of £12,000, in addition to household furniture. His private drawings, as shown in the cash book, were as follows—

	£
For the first year ended 31st March	4,905
" " second " " "	4,000
" " third " " "	5,000

He made a profit in his business in the first year of £5,000, and, in the subsequent years, losses of £3,000 and £935 respectively. (*U.L.C.I.*)

10. A Liverpool merchant, trading to the West Coast of Africa, finding himself, on 1st July, unable to meet his engagements, asks you to make up a statement of affairs for submission to his creditors. You find his books disclose—

	£
Unsecured creditors	8,830
Fully-secured creditors	2,352
Who hold security to the cost value of £2,630.	
Partly-secured creditors	37,697
Who hold securities of the cost value of £18,098.	
Preferential creditors	822
Bills payable	20,066
" receivable (discounted) (expected to rank, £1,000)	5,833
Book debts in England—	
(Good)	1,341
(Doubtful) £170, estimated to produce	85
(Bad) £34, of no value	—

	£
Stock in Liverpool at cost, £1,306, estimated at	1,200
,, and book debts, *less* sundry liabilities, at four stations on the coast	36,584
Of which it is estimated there will be a loss on realization of stock of £5,638, and of book debts of £7,586.	
Four station buildings, plant, steamer, and carrying craft, £40,000, expected to realize	20,000
Office furniture, £289, estimated to realize	200
Cash in hand	4
,, at bankers	80

Show his position, and make out his Deficiency Account from 1st July, five years ago, when he had a capital of £42,000. Profits appear from the books to have been made in first and second years of £5,000 and £4,000 respectively, and losses in the three subsequent years of £2,100, £2,600, and £3,031 respectively, after allowing £2,000 a year for interest upon capital, and his withdrawals having been at the rate of £4,500 a year. (*Chartered Accountants.*)

11. Prepare statement of affairs on 9th July of "The Sandy Freehold Land Society." Unsecured creditors £200,000; creditors fully secured £6,000; property held by secured creditors £12,000; creditors for rates, taxes, and wages (preferential) £300; bills of exchange (good) £22; book debts £27,000 (Good £1,000, doubtful £25,000, produce £2,000, remainder bad); Property £56,000; loans on mortgage (produce £60,000) £170,000; office furniture, etc., £100; cash at bankers £900; at office £100. (*Chartered Accountants.*)

12. Prepare statement of affairs and deficiency account as on 10th October, of William Corby.

Cash in hand £85; book debts £3,472 (estimated to produce £2,869); unfinished contract in hand (estimated to produce £3,000 over and above the cost of completing it); plant, tools, etc., cost £1,880 (estimated to realize £500); office furniture (estimated to realize £25); stock-in-trade valued at £1,900; investments valued £6,200, of which are deposited with bankers as security for loan £5,460; life policies for £2,000, of the estimated surrender value of £1,470, subject to advances made by the insurance company, amounting to £1,420; unsecured creditors on trade account £4,140; unsecured creditors for cash advanced £5,308; W. Smith for two months' wages due to him as clerk £100; A. Compton, six months' salary due to him at £45 per month; rent recoverable by distress £45; bankers for loans partly secured, £10,134 (estimated value of securities held by bankers £7,460, viz.: investments, £5,460, and lease £2,000); capital account on 1st January, as shown by the books, £189; loss on trading from 1st January to 10th October, £374; loss on sale of investments made on 13th June, £200; drawings £750. (*Chartered Accountants.*)

13. Prepare statement of affairs and deficiency account of Jones & Co., on 31st December.

The firm commenced business on 1st January, five years ago, with a capital of £25,000. The trading, after charging interest upon capital at £1,000 a year, resulted in a profit for first year of £602, and in losses in the subsequent respective years of £370, £450, £500, and £700. The drawings of the partners were at the rate of £900 a year; and £1,500 had been expended during the five years upon patents and experiments, and at the date of bankruptcy stood in the books at that sum. Unsecured creditors £15,050; creditors partly secured £19,080 (holding security, as stated by the books, of the value of £18,100, but which is only estimated to realize £6,000); creditors for wages, taxes, etc., £500; bills receivable discounted £2,060 (upon which it is estimated there will be a liability of £280); stock-in-trade £10,100 (which is estimated to realize £8,000); book debts, good £7,860; doubtful and bad £650 (estimated to realize £178);

land and buildings £8,000 (estimated to realize, £5,000); machinery and plant £12,500 (estimated to realize, £5,500); cash in hand £2. (*Chartered Accountants.*)

14. A filed his petition on 31st December, and his statement of affairs was composed of the following figures—

	£
Creditors—	
Unsecured	75,000
Partly secured by lien on shares	40,000
Fully secured by lien on stock	100
Liability on bills receivable (estimated to rank, £3,500)	7,000
Mortgage on mill	10,000
Creditors payable in full	3,000
Book debts—	
Good	20,000
Doubtful and bad (estimated to produce £2,000)	10,000
Consignments, good	5,000
Stock (estimated to realize £40,000)	60,000
Shares (cost and estimated to realize)	16,000
Cash at bankers	100
Bills of exchange	1,400
Mill of the value of	11,000
Machinery (estimated to realize £12,000)	15,000
Fixtures (estimated to realize £1,500)	3,000
Cottages (estimated to realize £3,000)	3,500

On 1st January, six years ago, he had a capital of £50,000. Profits were made in the six years of £20,500, after allowing interest on capital £10,000, and withdrawals amounted to £63,600.

Prepare the statement of affairs and deficiency account.

(*Chartered Accountants.*)

15. John Howson is unable to meet his engagements. His liabilities are—

	£
Underbank Banking Co. Ltd.	1,200
(As security for which they hold £1,500 debenture stock of the Berkshire Haulage Co.)	
Unsecured creditors	4,000
His father	3,000
(Who holds a mortgage on the premises.)	
Wages	100
Chief rent (half-year)	15
Bills discounted	500
(One-half of which will probably rank against the Estate.)	

And his assets are—

	£
Buildings, of the value of	2,000
Machinery, of the value of	1,500
Fixtures, etc., of the value of	200
Debenture stock of the Berkshire Haulage Co., value	1,500
Stock, estimated to realize	1,500
Book debts—	
Good	1,000
Doubtful (estimated to realize £100)	200
Bad	150
Cash	15

Prepare the statement for submission to his creditors.

(*Chartered Accountants.*)

16. Prepare statement of affairs of John Mason from the following particulars at 31st March—

	£		£
Freehold land and buildings	5,000,	estimated to produce	4,500
Book debts—			
Good	1,000		
Doubtful	300	„ „ „	100
Bad	500	„ „ „	*nil*
Stock-in-trade	1,500	„ „ „	1,000
Plant and machinery	1,200	„ „ „	600
Cash in hand	25		
Household Furniture and effects	300	„ „ „	180

Mortgage on the above freehold land and buildings, £3,500, at 5 per cent. The interest was paid to 31st December last. Trade creditors unsecured £2,500. Cash creditors unsecured £1,000. Bank overdraft £1,000 (the bank holding as security a policy for £2,000, payable at death: premium £50 per annum; surrender value, 31st March, £600). Preferential creditors for rent, rates, taxes, and wages, £300.

(Charterea Accountants.)

17. Henry Jones filed his petition in bankruptcy on 30th June. His books showed the following balances—

	£	£
Cash in hand	10	
Fixtures and fittings	250	
(Estimated to produce £80).		
Stock-in-trade	1,800	
(Estimated to produce £1,200).		
Sundry creditors—		
Open accounts		2,000
Bills payable		2,200
Sundry debtors	5,000	
Good, £1,000		
Doubtful, £2,000 (estimated at 50 per cent)		
Bank overdraft		1,200
Capital		1,660
	7,060	7,060

Liability on bills discounted, £500; £100 expected to rank.

His household furniture, etc., was valued at £750.

He owned the house he lived in—it was valued at £4,750—and he had a mortgage on it of £3,600 at 4 per cent. Interest paid to 31st December last.

Preferential creditors amounted to £35 (included in Sundry Creditors), and £45 for rates on his house.

Prepare a statement of affairs. *(Chartered Accountants.)*

18. A finds, by the following summary of assets and liabilities of his business, that he is insolvent, and on 15th October files his own petition in bankruptcy. Prepare his statement of affairs for presentation to his creditors.

The bank's overdraft is secured by the deposit of deeds representing his freehold property (valued for the purposes of the statement at £6,000), and dock warrants for stock of the value of £2,383. W. Smith's loan is secured by an assignment of a policy on A's life valued at £100. There are contingent liabilities on bills discounted amount ing to £589, of which the sum of £229 is expected to rank. Of the book debts, A states that £144 are bad and £365 doubtful; he estimates the value of the latter at £178. Of the bills receivable, he estimates that £283 is bad. A has private debts amounting to £389, and has private assets consisting of the above-named policy and household furniture valued at £585.

SUMMARY OF ASSETS AND LIABILITIES

Liabilities	£	*Assets*	£
Sundry Creditors	23,598	Cash in hand	29
Bank Loan	6,897	Petty Cash in hand . .	4
W. Smith: Loan	589	Stock at Cost	9,852
H. Jones: 9 months' Rent to 29th Sept. last	150	Fixtures and Fittings . .	329
		Office Furniture . . .	262
Rates: 6months to 31st March last	32	Motor Vehicles	682
		Sundry Debtors . . .	5,289
		Bills Receivable . . .	4,283
		Freehold Property . . .	6,589
	31,266		27,319

(*Chartered Accountants.*)

19. Catchem & Cheetam filed their petition in bankruptcy on 31st December. Their books showed that they owed £50,000 to unsecured creditors, £30,000 to creditors holding lien on goods for £10,000; £10,000 mortgage on the works, and £1,000 for salaries and rates. Bills of exchange for £10,000 had been discounted with their bankers, and it was estimated that there was a liability in respect of them of £3,000.

Their assets were—

Consignments £20,000 (estimated to realize £2,000). Good book debts £18,000; doubtful debts £6,000 (estimated to realize £3,000); bad debts £15,650. Works, cost £100,000 (depreciated out of profit and loss to £75,000), estimated to realize £50,000. Furniture and fittings £2,000 (estimated to realize £1,000). Stocks and work-in-progress £25,000 (estimated to realize £18,000). Cash and bills £1,350.

They commenced business on 1st January, five years ago, with a capital of £83,000. After charging annually £5,000 for depreciation of the works, £4,000 for interest on capital, and £1,500 for partners' salaries, the trading showed profits of £6,500 in first year and £5,000 in second year; and losses of £6,000 in third year, £7,000 in fourth year, and £9,500 in fifth year; while the withdrawals of the partners averaged £5,500 a year.

Draw up statement of affairs, and prepare deficiency account.

(*Chartered Accountants.*)

20. A trader files his petition in bankruptcy on 30th June, and you are instructed to prepare his statement of affairs. The information you are able to obtain as to his position is as follows—

The stock-in-trade at cost is £7,200, of which £600 worth is in the hands of a creditor for £1,000, who is entitled to exercise a lien. Book debts: good £9,750; doubtful £120 (worth 33p in the £); bad £150; fixtures and fittings (after depreciation) £230; cash in hand £10. Bills receivable £1,100 (held by bankers against overdraft of £4,000, the balance of which is secured by a second charge on debtor's freehold property and by the guarantee of his brother). Customers' bills under discount £1,500 (of which £200 is ascertained to be bad and £100 is doubtful). Freehold property £3,000 (subject to a first mortgage of £2,000). The unsecured creditors amount to £29,800, in addition to claims for rates, taxes, and wages amounting to £240. The stock-in-trade and the book debts (outside the bills) are estimated to be worth 75 per cent of their face value and the freehold property (which cost £2,800) is valued at £2,200. Subject to the modifications above stated, the assets are worth their book values.

You learn that the debtor had a surplus of assets of £5,000 on 1st January, two and a half years ago, since when he has withdrawn £3,000 per annum in equal monthly instalments. His profits for year ended 31st December (first year) were £2,100, and for second year £420, since which time he has not made up his books.

From these details you are required to prepare, as nearly as may be in statutory form: (*a*) statement of affairs; (*b*) deficiency account.

21. Prepare statement of affairs and deficiency account of Alfred Sykes, on 31st December. Good book debts in England £6,650; doubtful £5,000; bad £4,500. Properties: stock and book debts in Brazil £32,000; warehouse in England £26,000; stock in warehouse £1,000; and at bleachers and finishers, £4,750. Fixtures, hoist, etc., £500. Cash at bank £1; in hand £5. Creditors £65,000 (of which £250 is for wages and taxes, £20,000 is in respect of a mortgage on the warehouse building, and £7,500 is for bleaching and finishing). Bills payable £14,500; and there is a liability of £3,000 in respect of bills receivable, which, however, is not expected to rank. Assume that stock, doubtful debts, and fixtures in England will realize two-thirds, and the properties, stock, and book debts abroad one-half of their face-value. On 1st January, five years ago, he had a capital of £30,000. After charging interest thereon at the rate of £1,500 a year, and paying £800 a year for interest upon the warehouse mortgage, in the first three years he made profits of £4,200, £3,700, and £800 respectively; and in the last two years losses of £6,400 and £7,894. His withdrawals amounted to £6,200 a year. (*Chartered Accountants.*)

22. Prepare statement of affairs of Nathan Thorpe, engineer, on 20th March.

	Book Values	Estimated to Produce
	£	£
Leasehold premises held for 99 years at £50 a year . .	5,000	4,500
Fixed machinery and plant on the said premises . .	2,000	1,000
Loose tools, plant, etc.	700	350
Stock-in-trade	1,000	600
Book and other debts—		
Good (*less* 5 per cent).	300	285
Doubtful	800	200
Bad	2,000	

Cash in hand £5. 500 £1 shares in the Hole Mine Co. Ltd., 25p per share paid (balance called up); in liquidation, no return expected. Household furniture and effects £250; life insurance policy for £2,000 at death, subject to premium £35 a year, due 30th December, held by insurance company for loan of £180. Surrender value £200 (*less* loan).

Liabilities: Creditors for unsecured trade debts £3,000; private and household debts £150; loan of £2,000 at 4 per cent secured by first mortgage on leaseholds, interest paid to 20th May last; bankers for overdraft secured by second mortgage on leaseholds £2,500; loan of £1,000 at 5 per cent secured by third charge on leaseholds, and second charge on life insurance policy. Interest paid to 20th September last; ground rent of leaseholds accrued since 25th March last had not been paid; rent of dwelling house, £30 for half-year due 25th December last; taxes due 1st January last £20; local rates £25; liability on shares of Hole Mine Co. Ltd., above mentioned; omit calculations of income tax. (*Chartered Accountants.*)

23. Johnson & Caley, merchants, are unable to meet their obligations. From their books, papers, and information supplied by them, the following particulars relative to their affairs are ascertained—

	£
Cash in hand	250
Debtors—good £1,250; doubtful £600 (estimated to produce £200); bad £1,000	2,850

	£
Shares in the Straights Shipping Co. Ltd., of par value .	5,000
Property, estimated to produce £9,000	14,000
Bills receivable (good)	4,250
Other securities—£3,000 pledged with partly-secured creditors, and the remainder with fully-secured creditors	28,000
Johnson's drawings	9,000
Caley's "	8,400
Sundry losses	13,500
Trade expenses	7,400
Creditors—	
Unsecured	25,000
Partly secured	23,900
Fully secured	17,000
Preferential claims—wages, salaries, and taxes	750
Johnson—capital	10,000
Caley "	16,000

Prepare a statement of affairs, showing the assets, with respect to their realization; also a deficiency account in respect of the deficiency shown by the statement of affairs.

(*Chartered Accountants.*)

24. Prepare the respective balance sheets of the firm of Robinson Bros., and of the several partners—Alfred, Benjamin, and Charles; after which prepare the respective statements of affairs of the firm and the several partners, giving effect to the rights of holders of securities; accepting the values of assets as given on 3rd April—

	£
Trade creditors, joint estate, unsecured	31,280
Cash " " " "	6,642
" " " " collaterally partly secured by policies of assurance—	9,015
On the life of Alfred, worth	1,615
" " Benjamin, worth	738
Cash creditors, joint estate, fully secured	10,435
They holding securities belonging to the firm worth	14,395
Liabilities on bills discounted, considered good	1,340
Preferential creditors of joint estate	2,128
Tradesmen's claims on separate estate of Alfred	697
Cash creditors on separate estate of Alfred	2,578
They holding as security freehold property of his, worth	3,000
Tradesmen's claims on separate estate of Benjamin	119
" " " " " Charles	190
Cash creditors of Charles, unsecured	510
" at bank at credit of joint estate	1,050
" in hand " " " "	843
Debtors " " " "	2,975
Stock " " " "	30,155
Fixtures and furniture at credit of joint estate	1,400
Household furniture, separate estate of Alfred	1,000
" " " " " Benjamin	1,000
" " " " " Charles	500
Reversionary interest under will of John Smith, deceased, separate estate of Charles, worth	200
Alfred had overdrawn his account with the firm by	4,500
Benjamin " " " " " " " "	3,000
Charles " " " " " " " "	1,182

(*Chartered Accountants.*)

25. A business carried on under the style of Wood & Smith finds itself in difficulties and instructs you to prepare a statement of affairs for submission to a private meeting of the creditors.

The following particulars are obtained from the books, as at 1st February—

	£	£
Unsecured creditors		23,000
Loan from A		2,000
Creditors partly secured	4,600	
Estimated value of security	4,000	
Preferential claims		240
Stock-in-trade		1,500
Cash at bank		270
Cash in hand		65
Fixtures		400
Debtors—		
Good	820	
Bad	72	
Doubtful	41	

As regards the separate estates, Wood had no creditors nor assets, and Smith was a limited partner with £1,000 in the business. With respect to the loan, A had lent the £2,000 without security, and under an arrangement whereby he was to receive interest varying with the profits.

(*a*) Prepare statement of affairs allowing 15 per cent off stock, 10 per cent off good book debts (assuming that the bad and doubtful debts realized *nil*), and 50 per cent off fixtures.

(*b*) Append to statement any comments upon transactions, which, in your opinion, require special consideration.

26. A and B carried on business in partnership as ironmongers, and on 31st December, being in financial difficulties, they called their creditors together and laid before them the following statement of affairs—

Creditors	£	£	*Assets*	£
Unsecured Creditors		1,200	Cash in hand	10
Bank for Overdraft—			Stock-in-trade (cost £1,000) estimated to produce	750
Unsecured		600	Book Debts—Good, £300 do.	300
Secured Creditor—			„ „ Doubtful, £100 do.	50
Loan on Mortgage	800		„ „ Bad, £150 do.	—
Value of Property *contra*	1,000		Fixtures & Fittings (cost £500) do.	100
Estimated Surplus to *contra*	200		Property valued at £1,000 subject to Mortgage for £800 *contra*—Estimated Surplus	200
Preferential Creditors for Rent, Wages, etc., to *contra*	160		A's Estate—Estimated Surplus	150
				1,560
			Deduct Preferential Creditors	160
				1,400
			Deficiency	400
		1,800		1,800

B's estate showed a considerable deficiency.

The creditors agreed to accept 62½p in the £1, and appointed M as trustee to realize the estate and pay the dividend, his remuneration to be 5 per cent on the amount realized and 5 per cent on the amount distributed. The legal and other costs amounted to £35.

On realization, the stock produced £800; the book debts £335; the fixtures and fittings £115; the surplus from the property was £150; and the surplus from A's estate £120.

Draw up the trustee's final statement of account showing the disposition of the estate. (*Chartered Accountants.*)

27. Prepare from the following figures and particulars, a trustee's cash account showing the position of the estate of Tant & And, against whom a receiving order was made on 19th October, and first and final dividend paid on 28th September following.

The chief assets were book debts, which the debtors estimated to produce £2,144, but which realized £2,135, and two life policies which the debtors stated were worth £472, but which realized £565, out of which the trustee had to pay £375 to redeem the security. The cash in hand and at bank amounted to £4; some small investments stated to the worth £55 realized £40. The miscellaneous receipts were £8 and £5 deposit on creditors' petition.

There were nine preferential creditors' claims amounting to £26, and a dividend of £0·1375 in the £ was paid to the unsecured creditors, whose claims amounted to £13,250.

The other payments amounted to £504, including trustees' remuneration £206; Board of Trade and court fees £123; law costs £60; auctioneers' charges and incidental outlay.

28. A trustee of a bankrupt estate, with liabilities of £18,000, has completed his realization of the estate, and prepares to close the matter. His receipts have been—

	£		£
From stock-in-trade	1,250	From trading	7,000
„ book debts	3,100	„ household furniture	450
„ jewellery pledged	700	„ freehold buildings	3,000

His payments have been—

	£		£
Costs of petition	40	Mortgage on freehold	2,000
Auctioneers' costs	180	Board of Trade fees	80
Shorthand writers' charges	15	Notices in *Gazette*, etc.	5
Trading payments	6,250	To redeem jewellery	400

The committee allow the remuneration of the trustee at a commission of 5 per cent on assets realized and 3 per cent on assets distributed. Without providing for further payments, you are required to write up the estate cash book, showing the final close of the estate. You must assume that all items have been received from or paid to bank, but analysis columns may be dispensed with.

29. The following are the balances extracted from the books of the Ideal Newspaper Co. Ltd. on 31st December, from which you are required to prepare revenue account and balance sheet; nominal capital £100,000, divided into 40,000 preference shares of £1 each, and 60,000 ordinary shares of £1 each.

	£		£
Issued—40,000 cumulative preference shares of £1 each, 37½p paid	15,000	Additions to plant and Machinery, made 30th June	980
Issued—60,000 ordinary shares of £1 each, 25p called up	15,000	Stock, 1st Jan.	1,750
Calls in advance	150	Investments at cost	6,340
Calls in arrear	75	Profit & Loss A/c, 1st Jan. *Cr.*	7,320
Freehold Property, 1st Jan.	28,000	Motor-cars, vans, etc., 1st Jan.	845
Plant and machinery, 1st Jan.	9,500	Motor-cars, vans, etc., additions made on 30th June	90
Sundry creditors	7,300	Purchases of paper	8,250
Returns and unsolds	2,650	Purchases of ink	475
Reserve, 1st Jan.	10,000	Salaries	9,230
Dividends accrued on investments	300	Wages	1,000
Cash in hand	130	Trade charges	7,860
Liverpool Banking Co. Ltd.	5,295	Correspondence	4,365
Sales (cash and credit)	22,650	Discounts allowed	855
Advertisements	*Cr* 19,090	Commission	380
Debtors	5,800	Printing and stationery	110
Linotype installation, 1st Jan.	1,300	Free copies	695
Linotype installation, additions made on 30th June	135	Bad debts	75
		Bank interest, dividends, etc. *Cr.*	130
		Repairs	155

Provision for wages £48; discounts £350; bad debts £200. Depreciate freehold property at the rate of 1 per cent per annum, plant and machinery 7½ per cent per annum; linotype installation 10 per cent per annum; motor-vans 15 per cent per annum.

The amount received for advertisements includes £180 for advertisements which will not run off until next year. The sales include papers prepaid for next year amounting to £350. Stock-on-hand, 31st December, £1,646. (*U.L.C.I.*)

CHAPTER 27

LIQUIDATION

For War's a Banker, flesh his gold.
There by the furnace of Troy's field,
Where thrust meets thrust, he sits to hold
His scale and watch the spearpoint sway;
And back to waiting homes he sends
Slag from the ore, a little dust
To drain hot tears from hearts of friends;
Good measure, safely stored and sealed
In a convenient jar—the just
Price for the man they sent away.

AESCHYLUS—*Agamemnon*, *The oresteian trilogy*

THE machinery of bankruptcy was set up for individuals and partnerships as explained in the previous chapter. These rules also apply to the winding up or liquidation of companies.

In the liquidation of companies there are three parties concerned: (*a*) the company—which by law is a separate entity, (*b*) the creditors, and (*c*) the shareholders, who in winding up are referred to as contributories. In an Unlimited Company the liabilities of members are similar to those of partners.

Board of Trade. In addition, under Sect. 169 of the Companies Act, 1967, the Board of Trade may petition for winding up a company whose affairs have been investigated or in order to give relief to oppressed minority shareholders.

There are two main forms of liquidation and each is sub-divided into two types—

1. VOLUNTARY LIQUIDATION

(*a*) **Members.** If the directors, or a majority of the board, make a statutory declaration that, in their opinion, the company will be able to pay its debts in full within twelve months of the commencement of the liquidation, it is a Member's Voluntary Liquidation.

(*b*) **Creditors.** If the directors are unable to make the declaration that the company will be able to pay its debts in full within twelve months, then it is a Creditors' Voluntary Liquidation and they then have the right to be consulted in the appointment of the liquidator and to appoint from among themselves persons to act on the Committee of Inspection to control the liquidator.

Grounds for Voluntary Liquidation. A company may wind up voluntarily—

(*a*) on any event or expiry of time which the Articles state shall lead to dissolution;

(*b*) by special resolution of the members;

(*c*) by extraordinary resolution if it cannot continue in business because of its liabilities.

2. LIQUIDATION BY THE COURT

(*a*) **Liquidation Supervised by the Court.** This is like a members' voluntary liquidation and may be conducted in cases where there is no question of the company being unable to meet its debts.

(*b*) **Compulsory Liquidation.** This follows the procedure for bankruptcy as embodied in the legislation for bankruptcy but adapted to take account of the contributories (the shareholders).

Grounds for Liquidation by the Court. A company will be wound up by the Court if—

(*a*) The company has requested this by special resolution;

(*b*) Default is made in holding the statutory meeting or delivering the statutory report;

(*c*) The company does not carry on business for a year;

(*d*) The number of members falls below the minimum;

(*e*) The company is unable to pay its debts;

(*f*) The court considers winding up just and equitable.

Differences between Liquidation and Bankruptcy. The main differences are—

1. Bankruptcy always indicates insolvency. Liquidation may not indicate this as the winding up may be for quite a different purpose.

2. In a liquidation separate statements of affairs must be prepared as regards creditors and contributories.

3. The balances of the statement of affairs as regards creditors and the deficiency account are transferred to the statement of affairs as regards contributories.

4. A company may have issued debentures giving a floating charge, a position impossible in the case of an individual.

5. The deficiency account contains details of (i) expenses, divided into those paid and unpaid, (ii) directors' fees, (iii) dividends paid (whereas in bankruptcy such account merely contains the net loss or profit) and the period covered is three years prior to the winding-up order, or from the formation of the company if it has not been in existence for three years. On the other hand, the deficiency account in bankruptcy commences at a date twelve months prior to the receiving order, unless the Official Receiver otherwise orders.

Compulsory Liquidation. Compulsory liquidation by the Court is dealt with first since this is the most typical case. Other forms of liquidation follow the same basic pattern.

The principal forms required by the Companies (Forms) Order, 1949, in the case of a compulsory winding-up, illustrations of which are set out in the following pages, are as follows—

1. Statement of Affairs.

2. Deficiency or Surplus Account (List F)—where winding-up order made within three years of the formation of the company.

3. Lists A to E containing details of assets and liabilities in support of the Statement of Affairs (not illustrated).

One further point should be considered before passing to the accounts. Debenture holders are secured creditors, and trustees are appointed to protect their interests when the debenture deed is executed.

In the event of the company failing to pay interest on debentures, the debenture holders have the right to appoint a receiver or the trustees to take over control of the company. This does not necessarily imply that the company will be put into liquidation: if the company is able to meet the interest payments, control will be relinquished to the directors by the receiver.

THE PREPARATION OF A STATEMENT OF AFFAIRS IN COMPULSORY LIQUIDATION

This must be prepared and submitted to the Official Receiver within fourteen days from the date of the winding-up order, or of the appointment of a Provisional Liquidator, by the directors or secretary or other chief officer of the company.

Example 1

On 1st April, 19.2, a compulsory order for winding up was made against Youngs Ltd., the following particulars being disclosed—

	£	£	(Estimated to Produce) £
Cash in hand		5	5
Debtors		200	180
Land and buildings		3,000	2,400
Fixtures		1,000	1,000
Unsecured creditors	1,000		
Debentures—			
Fixed (secured on land and buildings)	2,100		
Floating	500		
Preferential creditors	300		
Share capital (£1 fully paid)	16,000		

Estimated liabilty for bills discounted £300, estimated to rank at £300. Other contingent liabilities £600, estimated to rank at £600.

The company was formed on the 1st October, 19.., and has made losses of £15,695.

Prepare statement of affairs and deficiency account.

The rough balance sheet is—

	£		£
Share Capital	16,000	Assets (as question) . . .	4,205
Creditors	3,900	P. & L. A/c . . .	15,695
	19,900		19,900

The items of £300 and £600 would appear as footnotes in the balance sheet of the company, and when brought into the statements will require double entry.

The question of debenture interest has been ignored in the above illustration, but the rule is that debenture interest is payable up to and including the date of repayment of the debenture *in the case of a company which is* SOLVENT, otherwise interest ceases at the commencement of the liquidation.

Solution 1

The worked statement of affairs and deficiency account appears on pp. 2705–6.

SETTLING THE LIST OF CONTRIBUTORIES

The operation of the principle of limited liability on the part of a shareholder is seen clearly when a company whose shares are only partly paid goes into liquidation.

Uncalled capital may be called up by the liquidator for the purpose of paying the creditors. The sale of partly-paid shares does not relieve the seller from his liability to pay the remaining calls for twelve months if the money cannot be collected from the person to whom he sold them. This is the reason for having the A and B lists, the B contributories being those contributories who have ceased to be members within one year from the date of the commencement of the liquidation, while the A list gives the present members.

Example 2

In a liquidation which commenced on 1st February, 19.1, the unsecured creditors were £13,000.

The following are the material details of the contributories appearing on the B list—

	No. of Shares	Date of Ceasing to be Member	Creditors Outstanding at Date of Ceasing to be Member
			£
A	1,000	1st August, 19..	500
B	1,500	1st September, 19..	750
C	300	1st October, 19..	800
D	200	15th December, 19..	950

Solution 1 (see p. 2704)

YOUNGS LIMITED (IN LIQUIDATION)

STATEMENT AS AT 1ST APRIL, 19.2, SHOWING ASSETS AT ESTIMATED REALIZABLE VALUES AND LIABILITIES EXPECTED TO RANK

	Estimated Realizable Values
	£
Assets not specifically pledged—	
Balance at bank	—
Cash in hand	5
Marketable securities	—
Bills receivable	—
Trade debtors	180
Loans and advances	—
Unpaid calls	—
Stock-in-trade	—
Work-in-progress	—
Freehold property	—
Leasehold property	—
Plant and machinery	—
Furniture, fittings, utensils, etc.	1,000
Patents, trade marks, etc.	—
Investments other than marketable securities	—
Other property, etc.—	—

Assets specifically pledged—	(a) Estimated Realizable Values	(b) Due to Secured Creditors	(c) Deficiency Ranking as Unsecured	Surplus Carried to Last Column	
	£	£	£	£	
Freehold property	2,400	2,100	—	300	
Estimated surplus from Assets specifically pledged					300

Estimated Total Assets available for Preferential Creditors, Debenture Holders secured by a Floating Charge, and Unsecured Creditors

Summary of Gross Assets	£
Gross realizable value of Assets specifically pledged	2,400
Other Assets	1,185
Gross Assets	3,585

(carried forward)	1,485

Solution 1 (*continued*)

(e) Gross Liabilities £			Estimated Realizable Values £
	Brought forward		1,485
	Liabilities (to be deducted from surplus or added to deficiency as the case may be)		
2,100	*Secured Creditors* to extent to which claims are estimated to be covered by Assets specifically pledged (item (*a*) or (*b*) whichever is the less). [Insert in "Gross Liabilities" column only.]		
300	*Preferential Creditors*		300
	Estimated balance of assets available for Debenture Holders secured by a floating charge and Unsecured Creditors		1,185
500	*Debenture Holders* secured by a floating charge . . .		500
	Estimated *Surplus/Deficiency* as regards Debenture Holders		685
		£	
	Unsecured Creditors—		
	Estimated unsecured balance of claims of Creditors partly secured on specific assets, brought from (*c*)	—	
1,000	Trade Accounts	1,000	
	Bills Payable	—	
	Outstanding Expenses	—	
600	Contingent liabilities: Legal costs . .	600	
300	Bills discounted . .	300	1,900
		£	
	Estimated Deficiency as regards Creditors being the difference between:		
	Gross Assets (*d*)	3,585	
4,800	and *Gross Liabilities* (*e*)	4,800	1,215
	Issued and Called-up Capital— 16,000 shares of £1 each		16,000
	Estimated Deficiency as regards Members		17,215

The above creditors had received no payment at the date of the liquidation.

The shares are of £1 each, £0·60 paid.

Assuming that the contributories on the A list completely default, and that the liquidator realizes a further £1,148·33, show the amount of the dividend to the unsecured creditors. Ignore expenses, costs, and remuneration of the liquidator.

Solution 2

The B contributories duly fulfil their obligations.

STATEMENT OF LIABILITY OF B CONTRIBUTORIES

Creditors Outstanding	A Shares	A £	B Shares	B £	C Shares	C £	D Shares	D £	Cash £
	1,000		1,500		300		200		
(1) . £500	(a)	166·67		250·00		50·00		33·33	500·00
(2) . 250				187·50		37·50		25·00	250·00
(3) . 50						30·00		20·00	50·00
(4) . 150	(b)							1·67	1·67
Total 950									801·67

NOTES. (*a*) The liability in each case is in proportion to the shareholding as at the date of ceasing to be members in respect of debts outstanding on that date, e.g. in (*a*) the liability of each B contributory is $\frac{10}{30}$; $\frac{15}{30}$; $\frac{3}{30}$; and $\frac{2}{30}$ of £500.

(*b*) Although the amount required to be contributed solely by D appears to be £150 (the others not being liable because they were not members at the 15th December, 19.., the date of the extra £150 outstanding) yet the sum claimable from him is £1·67, inasmuch as his maximum liability to the company is £80, being £0·40 in the £ on 200 shares; and having already contributed £78·33 [items 1, 2, and 3] he can be called upon to pay only £1·67.

It may be noted that C's maximum liability is £0·40 in the £ on 300 shares, viz. £120, so that whatever be the amount of the creditors in item 3, the liquidator could have claimed from C only £32·50, i.e. £120 less already contributed £87·50 [items 1 and 2].

The cash received into the *general* funds of the company is £801·67, which together with £1,148·33 makes £1,950 available for unsecured creditors of £13,000, i.e. £0·15 in £.

LIQUIDATOR'S CASH ACCOUNT

The preparation of a Liquidator's Cash Account calls for no detailed explanation, but the following matters require the attention of the student—

1. There is no double entry required.
2. The sequence of items should correspond with that of the official form.
3. The rights of various classes of shareholders (particularly if there is a surplus) require careful consideration.

Preference shares may have preference in winding-up and their claims must then be met in full before any payment is made to ordinary shareholders. Surpluses will normally be attributable to the ordinary shareholders unless other classes of shares are given rights to participate in them.

4. The remuneration of the liquidator may be a commission on collections plus a further commission on dividends paid.

5. The form of cash book for liquidations differs from that required for bankruptcies. (A statement of the receipts and payments must be furnished by a trustee in bankruptcy.)

The main outlines of the forms are given below.

Example 3

A liquidator has £11,220 to pay £20,000 creditors. After he has received his commission on collections, he is entitled to a further 2 per cent on dividends paid. What will he receive?

If he pays £100 he receives £2, thus absorbing £102.

Hence he receives $\frac{2}{102} \times$ £11,220 = £220, leaving £11,000 for distribution.

Example 4

The following are the balances of X Ltd., which decides to wind up voluntarily on 1st January, 19...

BALANCE SHEET

Liabilities	£	*Assets*	£	Estimated to Produce £
Share Capital (£1 fully paid)	2,000	Cash	60	
Creditors	4,900	Stock	1,700	1,680
		Debtors	4,790	4,495
		P. & L. A/c	350	
	6,900		6,900	

Creditors include preferential creditors £210.

The liquidator's remuneration is to be 4 per cent on amounts collected and 2 per cent on dividends paid to unsecured creditors. Liquidation expenses are £40. Show liquidator's cash account (calculate to nearest £). (See page 2710.)

STATEMENT OF AFFAIRS AND DEFICIENCY ACCOUNT

The prescribed form for the statement of affairs is shown on p. 2705-6 and the deficiency account is set out on p. 2709.

STATEMENT OF AFFAIRS—LIST 'F'

LIST 'F'—DEFICIENCY OR SURPLUS ACCOUNT

The period covered by this Account must commence on a date not less than three years before the appointment of the Receiver or, if the company has not been incorporated for the whole of that period, the date of formation of the company, unless the Receiver otherwise agrees.

		£
ITEMS CONTRIBUTING TO DEFICIENCY (OR REDUCING SURPLUS):		
1. Excess (if any) of Capital and Liabilities over Assets on the ....19........as shown by Balance Sheet (copy annexed)		
2. Net dividends and bonuses declared during the period from ....19........to the date of the Statement . . .		
3. Net trading losses (after charging items shown in note below) for the same period		
4. Losses other than trading losses written off or for which provision has been made in the books during the same period (give particulars or annex schedule) . .		
5. Estimated losses now written off or for which provision has been made for the purpose of preparing the Statement (give particulars or annex schedule)		
6. Other items contributing to Deficiency or reducing Surplus:		
	£	£
ITEMS REDUCING DEFICIENCY (OR CONTRIBUTING TO SURPLUS):		
7. Excess (if any) of Assets over Capital and Liabilities on the..........................19........as shown on the Balance Sheet (copy annexed) . . .		
8. Net trading profits (after charging items shown in note below) for the period from the...............19....... to the date of the Statement		
9. Profits and income other than trading profits during the same period (give particulars or annex schedule).		
10. Other items reducing Deficiency or contributing to Surplus:		
DEFICIENCY/SURPLUS as shown by STATEMENT .		£

NOTE AS TO NET TRADING PROFITS AND LOSSES:

Particulars are to be inserted here (so far as applicable) of the items mentioned below, which are to be taken into account in arriving at the amount of net trading profits or losses shown in this Account—

	£
Provisions for depreciation, renewals, or diminution in value of fixed assets	
Charges for United Kingdom income tax and other United Kingdom taxation on profits. . . .	
Interest on debentures and other fixed loans	
Payments to directors made by the company and required by law to be disclosed in the accounts . .	
....	
Less: Exceptional or non-recurring receipts—	
....	
Balance, being other trading profits or losses . .	
Net trading profits or losses as shown in Deficiency or Surplus Account above	£

Signature **Dated** **19**

Dr **LIQUIDATOR'S CASH ACCOUNT** Cr

Receipts	£	£	*Payments*	£	£
Balance		60	Law Costs	?	
Sale of Assets—			Auctioneer's Charges	?	
Stock	1,680		Incidental Expenses	?	
Debtors	4,495				40
		6,175	Liquidator's Remuneration—		
			4% on Amounts Collected	247	
			2% on Dividends to Unsecured Creditors[1]	98	
					345
			Preferential Creditors		210
			Dividend of £1 in £ to Unsecured Creditors		4,690
			Return to Contributories— £0·48 in £ on 2,000 Shares of £1 each, fully paid		950
		6,235			6,235

[1] Where there is insufficient cash left to pay the unsecured creditors *in full*, the calculation will be not 2 per cent. but $\frac{2}{102}$, e.g. assuming the unsecured creditors to be £4,690 and after all obligations have been discharged (except the liquidator's "dividend" remuneration of 2 per cent), there is a cash balance of £2,870·28, the respective payments to the liquidator and unsecured creditors will be—

Liquidator	$\frac{2}{102}$ × £2,870·28 = £56·28
Unsecured creditors	$\frac{100}{102}$ × £2,870·28 = £2,814

The liquidator thus receives 2 per cent of £2,814.

QUESTIONS

1. What do you understand by the term "liquidation"?
2. There are three accounts prepared in liquidation as compared with two in bankruptcy. Why is this necessary?
3. Up to what date is debenture interest payable in liquidation?
4. What do you understand by the 'A' and 'B' list of contributories?
5. State briefly the statutory forms required in compulsory liquidation.
6. What are the differences between the deficiency account in bankruptcy and that in compulsory liquidation?

EXERCISE 27

1. The Express Parcels Service Co. Ltd. went into voluntary liquidation on 29th February, 19... From the following particulars prepare a statement of affairs to be submitted to meetings of creditors and contributories. The authorized share capital which had been fully subscribed consisted of 10,000 7 per cent cumulative preference shares of £1 each and 5,000 ordinary shares of £1 each. The dividend on the preference shares had not been paid in the previous year. The assets and liabilities were as under—

	Book Value £	Estimated Value £
Land and buildings	4,500	3,000
Motor vans	5,650	3,200
Machines and tools	1,200	500
Furniture and fittings	975	325
Stores and spares	1,460	810
Debtors—		
Good	600	600
Doubtful	500	300
Bad	150	
Bank overdraft (secured by deposit of the deeds of land and buildings)		3,250
Unsecured creditors		6,130
Preferential creditors		80

(*Chartered Institute of Secretaries.*)

2. Prepare the statement of affairs of Unsound Ltd., which has just passed a resolution for voluntary liquidation. The books disclose the following balances—

	£
Goodwill	5,000
Freehold property	45,600
Plant and machinery	8,800
Fixtures and fittings	750
Investments	500
Bank overdraft (unsecured)	270
Cash in hand	10
Book debts	5,730
Stock-in-trade	2,020
Mortgage of freehold property	20,000
Interest accrued thereon	500
Authorized and issued capital—	
5,000 preference shares of £1 each	5,000
5,000 ordinary shares of £1 each	5,000
Unsecured trade creditors	59,100
Preferential creditors	710

It is estimated that the assets will produce the following sums—

	£
Goodwill	*nil*
Freehold property—	
The amount shown by the books.	
Plant and machinery	2,070
Fixtures and fittings	290
Investments	510
Book debts—	
Good	3,440
Bad and doubtful	860
Stock-in-trade	1,250

(*Institute of Book-keepers.*)

3. Preston & Co. Ltd. went into voluntary liquidation on 1st January, 19.., the balance sheet being as follows—

Liabilities	£	£	*Assets*	£
Capital, Authorized and Issued—			Land & Buildings	2,500
5,000 Ordinary Shares of £1			Plant & Machinery	3,125
each fully paid		5,000	Stock-in-trade	2,875
Sundry Creditors—	£		Sundry Debtors	2,598
Preferential	433			
Unsecured	8,626		Cash at Bank	87
		9,059	P. & L. A/c	2,874
		14,059		14,059

The liquidator's remuneration was fixed at 3 per cent on the amount realized by him and 2 per cent on the amount distributed to the unsecured creditors. The liquidator realized the assets as follows—

	£
Land and buildings	2,128
Plant and machinery	1,824
Stock-in-trade	1,457
Sundry debtors	2,186

The expenses of the liquidation amounted to £94, the preferential creditors were repaid in full, and a first and final dividend was paid to the unsecured creditors.

You are required to prepare the liquidator's Final Account. (*C.C.S.*)

4. A company went into voluntary liquidation on 30th June, 19.., when the liabilities were as follows—

	£
5 per cent debentures giving a floating charge over all assets	10,000
Unsecured creditors	6,750
Preferential creditors	370

Interest on the debentures had been paid to previous 31st March.

The assets (apart from the cash in hand at the commencement of the liquidation, £50) realized as follows—

	£
Stock	5,650
Book debts	9,850
Plant, etc.	1,250

The debenture liability was discharged on 30th September, 19.., and a first and final dividend distributed, the costs of the liquidation being £486.

Prepare the Liquidator's Final Account, showing the dividend distributed, assuming that his remuneration had been fixed at 3 per cent on the amount realized, and 2½ per cent on the amount distributed to unsecured creditors. (*R.S.A.*)

5. Frederick Ayling files his petition in bankruptcy. His assets include his freehold house, valued at £1,600. The house originally cost £2,000, of which sum he had borrowed £1,200 on first mortgage and £500 on second charge. Both mortgages are still outstanding in full.

Set out the entries appearing in Ayling's Statement of Affairs, arising out of the above information. Assume that interest on the mortgages has been fully paid. (*Institute of Book-keepers.*)

6. The position of S. Broke on 1st April was as under: business premises £1,000, estimated to realize £800; fixtures and fittings £150, estimated to realize £50; stock £1,600, estimated to realize £800; book debts £450, estimated to realize £380. There was a mortgage on the business premises of £900. Other creditors amounted to £2,200, of whom £200 were preferential. A year previously his capital was £800, the net profit for the year was £40, and his drawings amounted to £740. Prepare statement of affairs and deficiency account for submission to his creditors. (*U.L.C.I.*)

7. From the following particulars prepare the balance sheet of the business of James Gibson as on 1st July, 19.., and, in view of a receiving order having been made against him, also a statement of affairs. Sundry creditors £1,242. Owing £1,000 to bank, who hold a second mortgage of premises. Cash £17. Premises valued in books at £2,500 (subject to first mortgage of £1,750), estimated to realize £2,400. Stock, book value, £725, estimated to produce £420. Sundry debtors £650, of which £200 was estimated to be good, £150 doubtful, estimated to produce £100. Goodwill £800, estimated to produce *nil*. Fixtures and fittings £300, estimated to produce on a sale £125. Gibson had no assets outside his business except his household furniture, which was estimated to be worth £100. He had guaranteed a load for a friend, and expected to have to find £30 in respect of it.

NOTE. A deficiency account is not required.

(*Faculty of Teachers in Commerce.*)

8. A receiving order in bankruptcy was made against William Gimblett on 15th January, 19... The following are the particulars as to his position: owing to bank £3,860 secured by the deposit of deeds of freehold property valued at £4,000; unsecured creditors £3,720; preferential creditors for rent, etc., £90; loan by relative £300, who held shares belonging to bankrupt worth £250. B/R discounted £150;

policy of assurance in mortgage to company for £350 had a surrender value of £500; bankrupt's loan to a friend secured by P/N £200; household furniture, half of which belonged to his wife, was valued at £300; book debts £1,420, of which £240 was bad and £120 doubtful, estimated to produce £60. Prepare statement of affairs and calculate the probable dividend (to the nearest penny) after charging £120 for the expenses of the bankruptcy. (*Faculty of Teachers in Commerce.*)

9. The Asta Co. Ltd. decided to reduce its capital, and reorganize as at the 30th June, 19. . .

The following is the balance sheet as at the 30th June.

Liabilities	£	*Assets*	£
20,000 Ordinary Shares of £1 each, fully paid	20,000	Land & Buildings	18,000
15,000 7% Preference Shares of £1 each, fully paid	15,000	Plant & Machinery	7,000
£10,000 4% Mortgage Debenture Stock	10,000	Stock in hand	9,000
Reserve Account	7,000	Sundry Debtors	19,000
Sundry Trade Creditors	20,000	P. & L. A/c.	19,000
	72,000		72,000

The court and the debenture holders agreed to the company reducing its capital on the above date, the following being the particulars of the scheme—

(*a*) The ordinary shares to be reduced to 37½p each, fully paid.

(*b*) The preference shares to be reduced to 50p each, fully paid.

(*c*) Each £1 of mortgage debenture stock to be exchanged for one preference share of 50p each and for 50p of new debenture stock bearing 5 per cent interest.

(*d*) The reduction of capital and the reserves are to be applied in writing off the adverse balance of profit and loss account and the balance, if any, in writing down the land and buildings.

Show the balance sheet as it would appear after the above reorganization has taken place. (*C.C.S.*)

10. Z Ltd. passed a resolution on 1st July, 1963, to wind up voluntarily. The company's Balance Sheet as on 30th June, 1963, is summarized as follows—

	£		£
Share Capital—		Fixtures, Fittings and Equipment	25,600
5% Preference shares of £1 each fully paid	13,000	Stock on hand	12,400
Ordinary shares of £1 each fully paid	24,000	Sundry Debtors	20,220
6% Debentures	7,000	Cash in hand	180
Sundry Creditors	22,700	Profit and Loss Account	8,300
	66,700		66,700

The stock and the fixtures, fittings and equipment realized £36,220 and the debtors, apart from one for £840 which was irrecoverable, were collected in full. Creditors were paid in full, £680 of the total amount owing being preferential. The debentures were repaid, with interest £210, on 30th September, 1963. A clause in the Articles of Association provides as follows—

> "The preference shares shall confer on the holders the right to have their capital and any arrears of dividend outstanding at the date of the commencement of the winding-up (but not thereafter) paid in priority to the holders of ordinary shares."

The amount of such arrears of dividend on 30th June, 1963, was £1,625.

The liquidator's remuneration was agreed at the rate of 2¼ per cent on the amounts realized and 2½ per cent on the dividend paid to the ordinary shareholders. The costs of the liquidation amounted to £769.

Prepare the liquidator's account of receipts and payments.

Income tax is to be ignored. *(A.C.C.A.)*

CHAPTER 28

ACCOUNTING FOR TAXES, LEVIES, ALLOWANCES AND GRANTS

Well, fancy giving money to the Government!
Might as well have put it down the drain.
Fancy giving money to the Government!
Nobody will see the stuff again.
Well, they've got no idea what money's for—
Ten to one they'll start another war.
I've heard a lot of silly things, but, Lor!
Fancy giving money to the Government.

A. P. HERBERT—*Too Much*

TAXATION of businesses and individuals has two purposes: fund raising and regulation.

Fund-raising. The traditional system of taxation was evolved as a means of providing revenues for the King and his Government and this purpose is still important.

In 1968, 34·4 per cent of gross national product in the United Kingdom was taken as taxes or income and expenditure.

Comparable figures for other countries are shown in the following table.

TOTAL TAXES (INCLUDING SOCIAL SECURITY CONTRIBUTIONS) AS A PERCENTAGE OF GNP AT MARKET PRICES IN 1968

	Total taxes and contri-butions	Taxes on income on house-holds	on corpora-tions	total	Taxes on expen-diture	Social security contributions	*of which, paid by employers*
Belgium	33·0	8·1	2·1	10·2	13·3	9·5	6·0
France	36·9	4·7	1·8	6·5	15·9	14·5	10·8
Germany	34·2	8·1	2·1	10·2	12·9	11·1	n.a.
Italy	30·4	5·0	1·7	6·7	12·5	11·2	n.a.
Netherlands	37·8	10·4	2·8	13·2	11·2	13·4	9·9
EEC average	34·4	7·3	2·1	9·4	13·2	14·9	n.a.
United Kingdom	34·4	10·6	2·5	13·1	16·2	5·1	2·6
Norway	38·2	12·3	1·5	13·8	15·2	9·2	4·7
Denmark	34·7	15·3	1·0	16·3	16·5	1·9	n.a.
Sweden	42·3	18·6	1·6	20·2	13·9	8·2	4·3
USA	30·0	10·9	4·7	13·7	9·1	5·3	2·8
Japan	18·9	3·9	4·0	7·9	7·5	3·5	3·2

Regulation. The second purpose of taxation is to regulate individual business activities and this may involve the imposition of *penalties* in the form of taxes or the provision of *incentives* in the form of allowances or grants.

In this sense every tax may be a penalty or dis-incentive. Examples of incentives are Government grants for expenditure on training and capital grants.

In some cases, such as Redundancy Payments, the Government may establish separate funds for specific purposes and relate grants and benefits to the amounts contributed.

DIRECT AND INDIRECT TAXES

Direct taxes are assessed on an individual basis on individuals and corporate bodies and they include income tax, surtax, corporation tax, capital gains tax and estate duty. In the United Kingdom, responsibility for these taxes is largely in the hands of the Board of Inland Revenue. These taxes must be separately accounted for by the individual or company.

Indirect taxes are levied on expenditures or revenues (turnover) and they include value added tax, tariffs and customs duties, stamp duties and Redundancy payments. Responsibility for them is shared between various Ministries. These taxes are treated by and allowed as expenses to the individuals or firms paying them, but firms collecting such taxes become accountable for them to the Customs and Excise.

GRANTS AND ALLOWANCES

Incentives may take the form of grants or allowances. For instance, up to 1970, the Board of Trade paid cash grants of 45 per cent of capital expenditure on manufacturing plant installed in Development Districts.

Since October 1970, plant is eligible to a 60 per cent first year allowance from the Inland Revenue. This has the effect of reducing the corporation tax payable by a company or income tax of an individual.

A grant is received in cash and is valued at its face value. An allowance against tax is not received in cash. Its value is dependent on the firm or person making a profit; and it may be zero if there is no profit. Otherwise, it is worth the amount stated times the tax rate. If corporation tax is 40 per cent then a Capital Allowance of £10,000 is worth £4,000, but only if the firm would otherwise show a profit.

Complexity of the Tax System. Prior to the 1967 Budget, the Association of Certified and Corporate Accountants submitted a memorandum to the Chancellor of the Exchequer which started with the following words—

"This Association has often drawn attention to the growing complexity of taxation. It is not just that the accounting and clerical processes of collecting and paying taxes are increasing in cost: much more important, tax complexities are hampering the formulation of business policy and hence the improvement of economic growth. Too much of senior executives' time is taken up on tax problems. Too much ingenuity of a high intellectual order is spent on tax avoidance which might be better applied to raising industrial efficiency. Too often the real issues involved in important business decisions are obscured by uncertainty over future tax policies, or the possible administrative interpretation of tax measures already in force."

The Chartered and Cost Accountants made the same point in their submissions.

This chapter concentrates on the accounting treatment of tax and, unless otherwise stated, deals with taxes in force in 1971. Students should endeavour to keep informed on current rates and laws, since they change frequently. However, students must recognize that if they wish to give advice on tax it will be necessary to specialize in taxation.

ACCOUNTING FOR INDIRECT TAXES

These taxes may be raised in cash or by stamps.

Collected in Cash. Where a business is responsible for raising indirect tax in cash the tax is stated on invoices to customers and the amount so raised is paid to the Customs and Excise or Inland Revenue within a stipulated time.

Example 1

If goods are liable to purchase tax of 10 per cent on wholesale value, the sale of goods for £100 will suffer tax of £7·50 if the wholesale price is £75.

The invoice will state—

	£
To goods	100
plus Purchase tax	7·50
Total price	107·50

The accounting entries will be—

	£	£
Debit Customer	107·50	
Credit Sales		100
Purchase Tax Account		7·50

When the amount is paid to the Customs and Excise Department the entries will be—

	£	£
Debit Purchase Tax Account	7·50	
Credit Cash		7·50

When the final accounts are prepared the indirect taxes raised in cash, such as purchase tax, will not be treated as income nor will the payments be regarded as expenses, in determining income subject to direct taxation (income, surtax and corporation tax).

This ensures that the business does not pay tax on revenues raised on behalf of the tax authorities.

Collected by Stamp. Contributions to the National Health Service, National Insurance, Industrial Injuries Insurance, Selective employment tax and Redundancy fund are all collectable through a single stamp.

The amounts payable for National Health, National Insurance and Industrial Injuries in September 1971 were—

1. Employees not contracted out.

	Paid by Employee	Paid by Employer	Total
	£	£	£
Men . . .	0·88	2·15	3·03
Women . .	0·75	1·40	2·15

2. Contracted-out employees.

	Paid by Employee	Paid by Employer	Total
	£	£	£
Men . . .	1·00	2·27	3·27
Women . .	0·83	1·48	2·31

If employees earn less than £6 per week, the employer's proportion is increased. For men over 65 and women over 60, the employer's proportion is increased and the total payable is also reduced. Self-employed and non-employed persons pay at lower rates.

Contracted Status. This refers to the employee's status in relation to graduated National Insurance contributions. Most employees are not contracted out: those who may be are persons paid less than £9 per week; under 18 or over 70 (65 women); or retired over 65 (60 women); some company directors; and employees operating their own P.A.Y.E. deduction cards. Graduated pensions contributions are collected with P.A.Y.E. and are dealt with under Schedule E.

Selective Employment Tax (S.E.T.). The amount payable for S.E.T. was £2·40 per week for men; 62½p for women and boys under 18; and 40p for girls under 18.

Redundancy Fund. The amount payable was 6p for men and 3p for women, weekly. Under 18-year-olds were exempt, as were over 65's (60's for women) generally.

The combined contributions for men and women were, therefore—

		National Health, etc.	SET	Redundancy Fund	Total
		£	£	£	£
Not Contracted out	Men	3·03	2·40	0·06	5·49
	Women	2·15	0·625	0·03	2·805
Contracted out	Men	3·27	2·40	0·06	5·73
	Women	2·31	0·625	0·03	2·965

Purchase of Stamps. The employer will normally purchase a stock of stamps from which the employees' cards will be stamped weekly.

Example 2

If an employer 100 men and purchases stamps every four weeks, then he will buy a stock costing 400 × £5·49, that is £2,196.

The accounting entries will be—

	£	£
Debit National Insurance Stamps	2,196	
Credit Cash		2,196

When the transaction occurs which incurs tax or requires contribution by stamp, for example if 100 men are paid their week's wages, the entries will be complicated by the fact that part of the cost of the stamp is employer's contribution; part is the employees' contribution; part is S.E.T. and part is Redundancy Fund.

It is a misnomer to continue to call the stamp a National Insurance stamp but, at the time of going to press, no alternative name was available.

Example 3

If the National Insurance element alone is considered and if the 100 men in the example are paid £20 per week, then the respective payments between employer and employee are—

	£
Employer 100 @ £2·15 . .	215
Employee 100 @ £0·88 . .	88
	303

The net pay of the employees is reduced from £2,000 (100 @ £20 per week) to £1,912 (100 @ 19·12 per week) and the accounting entries will be—

	£	£
Debit Wages Account	2,000	
Debit Employer's Contribution to National Insurance .	215	
Credit Cash (net wages paid)		1,912
Credit National Insurance Stamps Account . . .		303

When the final accounts are prepared, the gross wages and the employer's contributions will appear as expenses and are allowable deductions in calculating the income for direct taxation purposes.

Redundancy Payments Scheme

Under the Redundancy Payments Act, 1965, employers must make lump-sum compensation payments, called "redundancy payments," to employees who are dismissed because of redundancy. It also requires these payments to be made in certain circumstances to employees who have been laid off or kept on short-time for a substantial period. The amount of the payments is related to pay, length of service with the employer and to age.

The Act also established a Redundancy Fund, financed by contributions collected with the employer's flat-rate National Insurance contribution. Employers who have to make redundancy payments as required by the Act may claim a rebate of part of the cost (ranging from two-thirds to just over three-quarters) from the Fund.

The Act provides for disputes about entitlement to redundancy payments or about claims for rebate from the Fund to be settled by Industrial Tribunals under The Industrial Training Act, 1964.

The Act covers all employees in all kinds of employment but not partnerships, independent contractors, freelance agents or those working on contracts *for* service.

To qualify, employees must—

(*a*) have 104 weeks' continuous service;
(*b*) work 21 hours per week or more;
(*c*) be under 65 (60 for women).

Specific employees who are excluded from the Act are—

1. Registered dock workers.
2. Fishermen paid by share of catch.
3. Crown servants and National Health employees.
4. Husbands or wives of the employer.
5. Domestic servants who are close relatives.
6. Some fixed-contract employees.

Dismissal for Redundancy. An employee is dismissed because of redundancy where the whole or main reason for his dismissal is that his employer's needs for employees to do work of a particular kind have diminished or ceased. It makes no difference why the employer needs fewer employees—this may be, for example, because he is closing down, either altogether or in a particular area, or because of a trade recession, or because of a change in production arrangements. In all these cases, if the result is that the employer needs fewer employees, then those employees who have been dismissed, have been dismissed because of redundancy. Any dispute about the cause of dismissal will have to be settled by the tribunal. In any tribunal hearing on such a dispute, the onus of proof will be on the employer to establish that the employee was not redundant.

Short-time or Lay-off. The employee may become entitled to redundancy payments if he is laid off or kept on short time involving less than half-pay for a substantial period. This is four weeks or six weeks within a 13-week period.

Contributions. Employers make weekly contributions to the Redundancy Fund of 6p in respect of employed men, 3p in respect of employed women (there is no contribution in respect of employees under age 18). These contributions are collected with the flat-rate national insurance contributions and are accordingly payable in respect of employees who are over 65 (60 for women) or who work for less than 21 hours a week.

Contributions are allowable as an expense for tax purposes.

Benefits for Employees. Years of service will count for payment as follows—

1. For each year of employment between ages 18 and 21 inclusive—half a week's pay.
2. For each year of employment between ages 22 and 40 inclusive—one week's pay.
3. For each year of employment between ages 41 and 64 (59 for women) inclusive—one and a half week's pay.

Reckonable service, i.e. which excludes weeks which do not count but which do not break continuity, must be aggregated to make complete years. No payment is due for a fraction of a year, but excess reckonable service in a higher age bracket will count towards service in the bracket immediately below. Weeks which do not count must be excluded from the service within each age bracket before the reckonable service in that bracket can be calculated.

The chart in Fig. 28.1 shows how many weeks' pay is due at different ages and for different service.

Calculating a Week's Pay. This depends on the status of the employee.

Time Workers are paid by hourly time rates or fixed wage or salary and the week's pay means earnings for normal weekly working hours including fixed overtime.

Piece-workers are paid according to work done and earnings mean normal weekly working hours at an average rate for a 4 week period up to the service of statutory notice of dismissal, but excluding any week in which no work was done. Hours worked include overtime but not hours paid for under a guaranteed-week agreement. All hours are calculated at ordinary rates (excluding overtime premiums).

Shift-workers work at varying hours according to the type of shift cycle and their rate may vary according to the time of day or day of the week. A more complicated formula is used to determine their week's pay.

No Normal Working Hours. If employees have no normal working

Service

Age (Years)	2	3	4	5	6	7	8	9	10	11
20	1	1	1	1	—					
21	1	1½	1½	1½	1½					
22	1	1½	2	2	2	2				
23	1½	2	2½	3	3	3	3	—		
24	2	2½	3	3½	4	4	4	4	—	
25	2	3	3½	4	4½	5	5	5	5	—
26	2	3	4	4½	5	5½	6	6	6	6
27	2	3	4	5	5½	6	6½	7	7	7
28	2	3	4	5	6	6½	7	7½	8	8
29	2	3	4	5	6	7	7½	8	8½	9
30	2	3	4	5	6	7	8	8½	9	9½
31	2	3	4	5	6	7	8	9	9½	10
32	2	3	4	5	6	7	8	9	10	10½
33	2	3	4	5	6	7	8	9	10	11
34	2	3	4	5	6	7	8	9	10	11
35	2	3	4	5	6	7	8	9	10	11
36	2	3	4	5	6	7	8	9	10	11
37	2	3	4	5	6	7	8	9	10	11
38	2	3	4	5	6	7	8	9	10	11
39	2	3	4	5	6	7	8	9	10	11
40	2	3	4	5	6	7	8	9	10	11
41	2	3	4	5	6	7	8	9	10	11
42	2½	3½	4½	5½	6½	7½	8½	9½	10½	11½
43	3	4	5	6	7	8	9	10	11	12
44	3	4½	5½	6½	7½	8½	9½	10½	11½	12½
45	3	4½	6	7	8	9	10	11	12	13
46	3	4½	6	7½	8½	9½	10½	11½	12½	13½
47	3	4½	6	7½	9	10	11	12	13	14
48	3	4½	6	7½	9	10½	11½	12½	13½	14½
49	3	4½	6	7½	9	10½	12	13	14	15
50	3	4½	6	7½	9	10½	12	13½	14½	15½
51	3	4½	6	7½	9	10½	12	13½	15	16
52	3	4½	6	7½	9	10½	12	13½	15	16½
53	3	4½	6	7½	9	10½	12	13½	15	16½
54	3	4½	6	7½	9	10½	12	13½	15	16½
55	3	4½	6	7½	9	10½	12	13½	15	16½
56	3	4½	6	7½	9	10½	12	13½	15	16½
57	3	4½	6	7½	9	10½	12	13½	15	16½
58	3	4½	6	7½	9	10½	12	13½	15	16½
59*	3	4½	6	7½	9	10½	12	13½	15	16½
60	3	4½	6	7½	9	10½	12	13½	15	16½
men only 61	3	4½	6	7½	9	10½	12	13½	15	16½
men only 62	3	4½	6	7½	9	10½	12	13½	15	16½
men only 63	3	4½	6	7½	9	10½	12	13½	15	16½
men only 64*	3	4½	6	7½	9	10½	12	13½	15	16½

Weeks of Pay

* For women aged between 59 and 60, and men aged between 64 and 65, the cash amounts due to be reduced by one-twelfth for every complete month by which the age exceeds 59 or 64 respectively.

FIG. 28.1. READY RECKONER

(Years)

Age (Years)	12	13	14	15	16	17	18	19	20
20									
21									
22									
23									
24									
25									
26	—								
27	7	—							
28	8	8	—						
29	9	9	9	—					
30	10	10	10	10	—				
31	10½	11	11	11	11	—			
32	11	11½	12	12	12	12	—		
33	11½	12	12½	13	13	13	13		
34	12	12½	13	13½	14	14	14	14	—
35	12	13	13½	14	14½	15	15	15	15
36	12	13	14	14½	15	15½	16	16	16
37	12	13	14	15	15½	16	16½	17	17
38	12	13	14	15	16	16½	17	17½	18
39	12	13	14	15	16	17	17½	18	18½
40	12	13	14	15	16	17	18	18½	19
41	12	13	14	15	16	17	18	19	19½
42	12½	13½	14½	15½	16½	17½	18½	19½	20½
43	13	14	15	16	17	18	19	20	21
44	13½	14½	15½	16½	17½	18½	19½	20½	21½
45	14	15	16	17	18	19	20	21	22
46	14½	15½	16½	17½	18½	19½	20½	21½	22½
47	15	16	17	18	19	20	21	22	23
48	15½	16½	17½	18½	19½	20½	21½	22½	23½
49	16	17	18	19	20	21	22	23	24
50	16½	17½	18½	19½	20½	21½	22½	23½	24½
51	17	18	19	20	21	22	23	24	25
52	17½	18½	19½	20½	21½	22½	23½	24½	25½
53	18	19	20	21	22	23	24	25	26
54	18	19½	20½	21½	22½	23½	24½	25½	26½
55	18	19½	21	22	23	24	25	26	27
56	18	19½	21	22½	23½	24½	25½	26½	27½
57	18	19½	21	22½	24	25	26	27	28
58	18	19½	21	22½	24	25½	26½	27½	28½
59*	18	19½	21	22½	24	25½	27	28	29
men only 60	18	19½	21	22½	24	25½	27	28½	29½
men only 61	18	19½	21	22½	24	25½	27	28½	30
men only 62	18	19½	21	22½	24	25½	27	28½	30
men only 63	18	19½	21	22½	24	25½	27	28½	30
men only 64*	18	19½	21	22½	24	25½	27	28½	30

Weeks of Pay

To Use the Table: Read off employee's age and number of complete years' service over age 18. The table will then show *how many weeks' pay* the employee is entitled to.

FOR REDUNDANCY PAYMENTS

Service

Age (Years)	2	3	4	5	6	7	8	9	10	11
20	⅔	⅔	⅔	⅔	—					
21	⅔	1	1	1	1	—				
22	⅔	1	1⅓	1⅓	1⅓	1⅓	—			
23	1	1⅓	1⅔	2	2	2	2	—		
24	1⅓	1⅔	2	2⅓	2⅔	2⅔	2⅔	2⅔	—	
25	1⅓	2	2⅓	2⅔	3	3⅓	3⅓	3⅓	3⅓	—
26	1⅓	2	2⅔	3	3⅓	3⅔	4	4	4	4
27	1⅓	2	2⅔	3⅓	3⅔	4	4⅓	4⅔	4⅔	4⅔
28	1⅓	2	2⅔	3⅓	4	4⅓	4⅔	5	5⅓	5⅓
29	1⅓	2	2⅔	3⅓	4	4⅔	5	5⅓	5⅔	6
30	1⅓	2	2⅔	3⅓	4	4⅔	5⅓	5⅔	6	6⅓
31	1⅓	2	2⅔	3⅓	4	4⅔	5⅓	6	6⅓	6⅔
32	1⅓	2	2⅔	3⅓	4	4⅔	5⅓	6	6⅔	7
33	1⅓	2	2⅔	3⅓	4	4⅔	5⅓	6	6⅔	7⅓
34	1⅓	2	2⅔	3⅓	4	4⅔	5⅓	6	6⅔	7⅓
35	1⅓	2	2⅔	3⅓	4	4⅔	5⅓	6	6⅔	7⅓
36	1⅓	2	2⅔	3⅓	4	4⅔	5⅓	6	6⅔	7⅓
37	1⅓	2	2⅔	3⅓	4	4⅔	5⅓	6	6⅔	7⅓
38	1⅓	2	2⅔	3⅓	4	4⅔	5⅓	6	6⅔	7⅓
39	1⅓	2	2⅔	3⅓	4	4⅔	5⅓	6	6⅔	7⅓
40	1⅓	2	2⅔	3⅓	4	4⅔	5⅓	6	6⅔	7⅓
41	1⅓	2	2⅔	3⅓	4	4⅔	5⅓	6	6⅔	7⅓
42	1⅚	2½	3⅙	3⅚	4½	5⅙	5⅚	6½	7⅙	7⅚
43	2⅓	3	3⅔	4⅓	5	5⅔	6⅓	7	7⅔	8⅓
44	2⅓	3½	4⅙	4⅚	5½	6⅙	6⅚	7½	8⅙	8⅚
45	2⅓	3½	4⅔	5⅓	6	6⅔	7⅓	8	8⅔	9⅓
46	2⅓	3½	4⅔	5⅚	6½	7⅙	7⅚	8½	9⅙	9⅚
47	2⅓	3½	4⅔	5⅚	7	7⅔	8⅓	9	9⅔	10⅓
48	2⅓	3½	4⅔	5⅚	7	8⅙	8⅚	9½	10⅙	10⅚
49	2⅓	3½	4⅔	5⅚	7	8⅙	9⅓	10	10⅔	11⅓
50	2⅓	3½	4⅔	5⅚	7	8⅙	9⅓	10½	11⅙	11⅚
51	2⅓	3½	4⅔	5⅚	7	8⅙	9⅓	10½	11⅔	12⅓
52	2⅓	3½	4⅔	5⅚	7	8⅙	9⅓	10½	11⅔	12⅚
53	2⅓	3½	4⅔	5⅚	7	8⅙	9⅓	10½	11⅔	12⅚
54	2⅓	3½	4⅔	5⅚	7	8⅙	9⅓	10½	11⅔	12⅚
55	2⅓	3½	4⅔	5⅚	7	8⅙	9⅓	10½	11⅔	12⅚
56	2⅓	3½	4⅔	5⅚	7	8⅙	9⅓	10½	11⅔	12⅚
57	2⅓	3½	4⅔	5⅚	7	8⅙	9⅓	10½	11⅔	12⅚
58	2⅓	3½	4⅔	5⅚	7	8⅙	9⅓	10½	11⅔	12⅚
59*	2⅓	3½	4⅔	5⅚	7	8⅙	9⅓	10½	11⅔	12⅚
60 (men only)	2⅓	3½	4⅔	5⅚	7	8⅙	9⅓	10½	11⅔	12⅚
61 (men only)	2⅓	3½	4⅔	5⅚	7	8⅙	9⅓	10½	11⅔	12⅚
62 (men only)	2⅓	3½	4⅔	5⅚	7	8⅙	9⅓	10½	11⅔	12⅚
63 (men only)	2⅓	3½	4⅔	5⅚	7	8⅙	9⅓	10½	11⅔	12⅚
64* (men only)	2⅓	3½	4⅔	5⅚	7	8⅙	9⅓	10½	11⅔	12⅚

Weeks of Pay

* For women aged between 59 and 60 and men aged between 64 and 65, the amount of payment due is to be reduced—*see* footnote to Appendix C. Where such a reduction applies, the rebate will be seven-ninths of the reduced amount.

FIG. 28.2. READY RECKONER

(Years)

Age (Years)	12	13	14	15	16	17	18	19	20
20									
21									
22									
23									
24									
25									
26	—								
27	4⅔	—							
28	5⅓	5⅓	—						
29	6	6	6	—					
30	6⅔	6⅔	6⅔	6⅔	—				
31	7	7⅓	7⅓	7⅓	7⅓	—			
32	7⅓	7⅔	8	8	8	8	—		
33	7⅔	8	8⅓	8⅔	8⅔	8⅔	8⅔	—	
34	8	8⅓	8⅔	9	9⅓	9⅓	9⅓	9⅓	—
35	8	8⅔	9	9⅓	9⅔	10	10	10	10
36	8	8⅔	9⅓	9⅔	10	10⅓	10⅔	10⅔	10⅔
37	8	8⅔	9⅓	10	10⅓	10⅔	11	11⅓	11⅓
38	8	8⅔	9⅓	10	10⅔	11	11⅓	11⅔	12
39	8	8⅔	9⅓	10	10⅔	11⅓	11⅔	12	12⅓
40	8	8⅔	9⅓	10	10⅔	11⅓	12	12⅓	12⅔
41	8	8⅔	9⅓	10	10⅔	11⅓	12	12⅔	13
42	8½	9⅙	9⅚	10½	11⅙	11⅚	12½	13⅙	13⅚
43	9	9⅔	10⅓	11	11⅔	12⅓	13	13⅔	14⅓
44	9½	10⅙	10⅚	11½	12⅙	12⅚	13½	14⅙	14⅚
45	10	10⅔	11⅓	12	12⅔	13⅓	14	14⅔	15⅓
46	10½	11⅙	11⅚	12½	13⅙	13⅚	14½	15⅙	15⅚
47	11	11⅔	12⅓	13	13⅔	14⅓	15	15⅔	16⅓
48	11½	12⅙	12⅚	13½	14⅙	14⅚	15½	16⅙	16⅚
49	12	12⅔	13⅓	14	14⅔	15⅓	16	16⅔	17⅓
50	12½	13⅙	13⅚	14½	15⅙	15⅚	16½	17⅙	17⅚
51	13	13⅔	14⅓	15	15⅔	16½	17	17⅔	18⅓
52	13½	14⅙	14⅚	15½	16⅙	16⅚	17½	18⅙	18⅚
53	14	14⅔	15⅓	16	16⅔	17⅓	18	18⅔	19⅓
54	14	15⅙	15⅚	16½	17⅙	17⅚	18½	19⅙	19⅚
55	14	15⅙	16⅓	17	17⅔	18⅓	19	19⅔	20⅓
56	14	15⅙	16⅓	17½	18⅙	18⅚	19½	20⅙	20⅚
57	14	15⅙	16⅓	17½	18⅔	19⅓	20	20⅔	21⅓
58	14	15⅙	16⅓	17½	18⅔	19⅚	20½	21⅙	21⅚
59*	14	15⅙	16⅓	17½	18⅔	19⅚	21	21⅚	22⅓
60	14	15⅙	16⅓	17½	18⅔	19⅚	21	22⅙	22⅚
61	14	15⅙	16⅓	17½	18⅔	19⅚	21	22⅙	23⅓
men only 62	14	15⅙	16⅓	17½	18⅔	19⅚	21	22⅙	23⅓
63	14	15⅙	16⅓	17½	18⅔	19⅚	21	22⅙	23⅓
64*	14	15⅙	16⅓	17½	18⅔	19⅚	21	22⅙	23⅓

Weeks of Pay

To Use the Table: **Read off employee's age and number of complete years service over age 18. The table will then show the number of weeks of pay which may be claimed as rebate.**

FOR REBATES

hours, their average weekly pay will be calculated over a 12-week instead of 4 week period.

Maximum Earnings. The maximum qualifying earnings are £40 per week. Payments received by employees are not taxable.

Rebates for Employers. Any employer who makes a redundancy payment as required by the Act may claim a rebate from the Fund of part of the cost. The amount of rebate due in respect of a particular redundancy payment will depend on how that payment is made up, as follows—

1. Where the payment (or part of it) is in respect of years of service between ages 18 and 40 inclusive, rebate will be two-thirds of the payment (or of that part of it).
2. Where the payment (or part of it) is in respect of years of service above age 40 (i.e. at age 41 or above), rebate will be seven-ninths of the payment (or that part of it).

Fig. 28.2 shows the amount of rebate in terms of number of weeks pay by different lengths of service.

Reductions of Benefits

Age. Payments of benefits for men over 64 (women 59) are reduced by one-twelfth for each complete month over that age.

Superannuation. The employer may reduce redundancy payments if he provides a pension or lump-sum superannuation payment.

Payments in lieu of notice; arrears of wages; accrued holiday pay and payments under the Contract of Employment Act cannot be deducted from Redundancy payments.

Early Termination. An employee leaving employment earlier than the redundancy date may lose all or part of his benefit if the employer does not agree to early termination. The employee may appeal against withholding of payments.

Reductions of Rebate. Rebates to employers will be reduced *pro rata* with any reduction of payments to the employee.

Payments to Employees. When the redundancy occurs, the following timetable must be followed—

Note: "D" below means the date of discharge of redundant workers.

When action is needed	Action to be taken by Employer
D minus a period exceeding 21 days	Identify among the workers to be made redundant those who will qualify for redundancy payments. Obtain a supply of the necessary forms from the employment exchange. If it is intended to offset pension payments the employment exchange should be advised.

When action is needed	Action to be taken by Employer
	If redundancy payments will be due to ten or more employees, complete forms RP1 in respect of all of them and send the forms to the employment exchange at least 21 *days* before D.
D minus a period exceedings 14 days	If redundancy payments will be due to less than 10 employees, the completed forms RP1 should reach the employment exchange at least 14 *days* before D.
	In all cases where it is not possible to complete column (8) of form RP1 send particulars to the employment exchange as soon as possible.
	Note: Employees under notice of dismissal may give the employer written notice of their intention to leave before the employer's notice expires. If the employer does not agree to the premature termination he must serve a written request on the employee to withdraw his notice, stating that unless he does so the employer will contest any liability to pay a redundancy payment to him. This request must be served before the employee's notice expires.
Remaining period before D . . .	Calculate the amounts of individual payments due and, wherever possible, tell the employees how much they will receive, so that any queries can be cleared before the payments are made.
	Any offer of re-engagement on the same, or alternative terms, should be made in writing to the employees concerned before D.
D	Make redundancy payments to each employee concerned and obtain receipt on form RP3.
Within D plus 6 months	Make claim for rebate by completing forms RP2 and send with the relevant form RP3 to the employment exchange named on form RP2. REBATE MAY BE WITHHELD IF A CLAIM IS NOT MADE WITHIN SIX MONTHS OF THE DATE OF THE REDUNDANCY PAYMENT.

Copies of the forms and explanatory leaflets are available from the local employment exchange.

Accounting for Redundancy Payments

Contributions. Since these are included in the flat-rate National Insurance contribution stamp, these may not be given separate accounting treatment.

Example 4

£6·00 will be payable for 100 men at 6p each.

In this case, the entries for National Insurance already given in Example 3 on p. 2805 will be modified to read—

	£	£
Debit Wages Account	2,000	
Debit Employer's contribution to National Insurance .	215	
Debit Redundancy Fund Contributions . . .	6	
Credit Cash		1,912
Credit National Insurance stamp A/c		309

At the end of the accounting period, the wages and contributions for the period will appear as expenses and any stock of stamps in hand will appear as a current asset in the Balance Sheet.

Redundancy Payment and Rebates

The accounting treatment must take into account—

1. payment of benefit to redundant employees;
2. claim for rebate;
3. receipt of rebates;
4. charging of payments and rebates against profits;
5. providing for disputed payments withheld;
6. award of payment after appeal;
7. payment of the award.

Example 5

Wilson and Jenkins Ltd. declared two employees redundant.

(*a*) Brown was paid off on 1st July and he was entitled to ten weeks' pay at £30 per week and, as he was 35 years old, the company was entitled to rebate of two-thirds which was duly claimed on 1st July and received on 10th November.

The accounting for this will be—

1. Payment of Benefit—

	£	£
Debit Redundancy Payments	300	
Credit Cash		300

2. Claim for Rebate—

	£	£
Debit Department of Employment and Productivity . .	200	
Credit Redundancy Rebates		200

3. Receipt of Rebates—

	£	£
Debit Cash	200	
Credit Department of Employment and Productivity . . .		200

The ledger accounts will then show—

REDUNDANCY PAYMENTS

		£			£
Jul 1	Cash (Brown) . . .	300			

CASH

		£			£
			Jul 1	Redundancy Payments .	300

REDUNDANCY REBATES

		£			£
			Jul 1	Department of Employment and Productivity .	200

MINISTRY OF LABOUR

		£			£
Jul 1	Redundancy Rebates Receivable . . .	200	Nov 10	Cash	200

4. **Charging Payments and Rebates against Profits.** At the end of the accounting period, the payments may be charged against profits and the rebates credited, and the entries will be—

	£	£
Debit Profit and Loss Account	300	
Credit Redundancy Payment		300
Debit Redundancy Rebates	200	
Credit Profit and Loss Account		200

If these are offset, the debit side of the Profit and Loss Account will show—

	£	£
Redundancy payments	300	
Less Rebates	200	
	—	100

(*b*) Walker was paid off on 10th August, 1969. He was 55 years old and was entitled to 20 weeks' pay. His average weekly pay was £45 per week.

Whilst under redundancy notice he left the company against their wishes and they therefore withheld redundancy payment and he appealed. The company were of the opinion that, on appeal, Walker might obtain a 50 per cent payment, but on 15th February, 1970, he was awarded 70 per cent of his entitlement. The company paid on 1st March and claimed rebate of seven months on that date. The cash was received on 8th June. The company accounting year ends on 31st December.

5. **Providing for Payments withheld if Disputed.** The accounting treatment will be, first, to provide on 10th August for the liability which the company considers is likely to arise, which at the minimum is 50 per cent of the redundancy payment of 20 weeks at £40 per week (maximum eligible), i.e. 50 per cent of £800—

	£	£
Debit Redundancy Payments	400	
Credit Redundancy Payments withheld pending appeal . .		400

If 100 per cent payment is provided for the amount would be £800.

At the end of the accounting year on 31st December, the Redundancy Payments will be charged to Profit and Loss Account as in (4) above and the Balance Sheet will show a liability, Redundancy Payments withheld pending appeal.

This may be offset against the Department of Employment (rebates receivable account) at the end of the year.

6. **Award of Payment after Appeal.** When the award is made, the accounting entries will be, in respect of the amount already provided for—

	£	£
Debit Redundancy Payments withheld	400	
Credit G. Walker		400

and in respect of the additional 20 per cent awarded,

	£	£
Debit Redundancy Payments	160	
Credit G. Walker		160

The entries to G. Walker's account can, of course, be combined. If 100 per cent had been provided for, the surplus provision of 30 per cent (£240) would be credited back to Profit and Loss.

7. **The Payment of the Award.** This may be accounted for by debiting G. Walker and crediting Cash or Bank with £560.

The claim and receipt of rebate will be for seven-ninths of the amount awarded, i.e. seven-ninths of £560 = £435·55 and the entries are as shown in (2) and (3) above. The charge against profits will be the difference between the award of £560 and the rebate of £435·55, i.e. £124·45.

Selective Employment Tax

Until the introduction of V.A.T., selective employment tax was payable by all employers with the weekly flat-rate National Insurance contribution in one combined stamp.

Under the Selective Employment Payments Act, 1966, *premiums* consisting of a refund of the tax that had been paid plus an additional sum could be paid to employers in industries classified as "manufacturing."

Refunds, without addition, were made to employers in the fishing, mining and quarrying, transport and communication, agriculture, horticulture and forestry industries; and also to local authorities (for whom special arrangements were made), to charities and to persons who employed domestic or nursing help in certain private households which included sick or aged persons or young children whose only parent was at work.

The Finance Act, 1967, provided that from 4th September, 1967, refunds of tax paid could be made as follows—

(*a*) half the tax paid in respect of certain part-time workers; and

(*b*) the full amount of tax paid in respect of persons employed abroad, after qualifying period.

Partial Refunds in Respect of Part-time Workers. An employer may claim a refund of half the tax paid for any employee in each week in which various conditions were satisfied.

Accounting for S.E.T.

Payments of Tax. Since S.E.T. was included in the flat-rate National Insurance contribution stamp, no separate accounting treatment may be given, as in the case of the Redundancy Fund contributions. This treatment was not recommended, however, since S.E.T. was a tax and the rate might have been varied from time to time. So, also, might the rate and conditions of refund. If S.E.T. was not isolated in the accounts, the result could be a loss of comparability between different periods.

Example 6

100 men would be liable at the rate of £2·40 per head per week and the amount paid would, therefore, be £240. The entries already given for National Insurance and Redundancy Fund Contributions will be modified to read—

	£	£
Debit Wages Account	2,000	
Debit Employer's Contribution to National Insurance .	215	
Debit Redundancy Fund Contribution	6	
Debit Selective Employment tax	240	
Credit Cash		1,912
Credit National Insurance Stamps Account . . .		549

Where a business is not eligible for refund of S.E.T. the tax will be shown as an expense in the profit and loss account for the period.

Refund of S.E.T.

Where the business is eligible for refund, there are three ways the tax might be treated—

1. **On an Actual Receipts and Payments Basis.** In this method, only actual payments made and receipts of refunds and premiums received are recorded. Refunds and premiums due are disregarded.

2. On an Accrual of Refund Basis. The Ministry of Employment are treated as debtors for the refund of tax due, but premiums receivable are ignored. When premiums are received they are treated as income.

3. On an Accrual of Refund and Premium Basis. The Ministry is regarded as a debtor for both refunds and premiums.

Example 7

A company's year ends on 31st December. During 1968 it is liable to S.E.T. of £500 monthly and the tax is paid by N.I. stamps. Immediately payment is made, a refund of the tax plus an extra refund of 30 per cent is claimed and this is paid by the Ministry after one month.

Whatever method is used, the payments of tax will be accounted for by—

	£	£
Debit S.E.T. (monthly)	500	
Credit National Insurance Stamps		500

Method 1—Actual Basis

At the end of the year this would charge 12 monthly payments of S.E.T. to Profit and Loss Account—

		£	£
Dec. 31st 1968	*Debit* Profit and Loss Account . . .	6,000	
	Credit S.E.T.		6,000

No entries would be made unless premiums were actually received, and these would be at the rate of £1,500 quarterly refund plus 30 per cent premium of £450. The entries would be—

		£	£
Apr 30	*Debit* Cash	1,950	
	Credit S.E.T. Refund and Premium . . .		1,950
Jul 31	*Debit* Cash	1,950	
	Credit S.E.T.		1,950
Oct 30	*Debit* Cash	1,950	
	Credit S.E.T.		1,950

At the end of the year three quarterly refunds would be credited to Profit and Loss account as follows—

	£	£
Debit S.E.T. Refund and Premium A/c	5,850	
Credit Profit and Loss A/c		5,850

The net charge to Profit and Loss account would be—

	£
S.E.T. paid	6,000
Less Refunds and Premiums	5,850
Net S.E.T.	150

If refund of premium is to be relied on, this method is unsatisfactory, since it takes no account of accrued refunds not yet received.

Method 2—Refund Accrual Basis

When the claims for refund of £1,500 and premiums of £450 were submitted, the following entries would be made—

		£	£
Mar 31	*Debit* Ministry of Employment	1,500	
	Credit S.E.T. Refund		1,500

No entry is made in respect of the premium receivable. Similar entries would be made on 30th June, 30th September and 31st December. When the refunds and premiums were received, the entries would be—

		£	£
Apr 30	*Debit* Cash	1,950	
	Credit Ministry of Employment		1,500
	Credit S.E.T. Premium		450

Similar entries would be made on 31st July and 30th October.

At the end of the year four quarterly refunds claimed would be credited to Profit and Loss account as follows—

	£	£
Debit S.E.T. Refund	6,000	
Credit Profit and Loss A/c		6,000

In addition, the three premiums actually received would also be carried to Profit and Loss—

	£	£
Debit S.E.T. Premium	1,350	
Credit Profit and Loss A/c		1,350

There would, therefore, be a net credit to Profit and Loss account as follows—

	£
S.E.T. Refunds receivable .	6,000
S.E.T. Premiums received .	1,350
	7,350
Less S.E.T. paid . . .	6,000
Net premium received . . .	1,350

The refund receivable of £1,500 would appear as a current asset in the Balance Sheet, but this method does not show the single premium receivable of £450 at the end of the year.

Method 3—Refund and Premium Accrual Basis

If both refund and premiums are accounted for, then when the claims for refund and premium were made the entries would be—

		£	£
Mar 31	*Debit* Ministry of Employment	1,950	
	Credit S.E.T. Refund and Premiums . . .		1,950

Similar entries would be made on 30th June, 30th September and 31st December. When the refunds and premiums were received the entries would be—

		£	£
Apr 30	*Debit* Cash	1,950	
	Credit Ministry of Employment . . .		1,950

and similar entries would be made on 31st July and 30th October.

At the end of the year, the full premiums and refunds receivable would be credited to Profit and Loss Account as follows—

	£	£
Debit S.E.T. Refund and Premiums . .	7,800	
Credit Profit and Loss Account . . .		7,800

and the net credit to Profit and Loss Account would be—

	£
S.E.T. Refund and Premium receivable . . .	7,800
Less S.E.T. paid	6,000
Net premiums receivable	1,800

Both the refunds and premiums claimed but not yet received would appear in the Balance Sheet as—

Current Assets—

	£
Ministry of Employment (S.E.T. Premiums and Refunds receivable) . . .	1,950

The third method is the most satisfactory.

INDUSTRIAL TRAINING LEVIES AND GRANTS

Under the Industrial Training Act, 1964, all commercial and industrial firms were to be subject to an Industrial Training Board which had the power to impose a levy on undertakings within its industry. By October 1969, twenty-eight Boards and one voluntary Board had been set up and all except four imposed a levy as a percentage of emoluments paid. The other four levied a lump sum per employee.

The Boards may also pay grants if firms undertake approved industrial training. Some Boards collect the levy and then pay out the grants.

Others provide for an offset: levy is assessed but not paid until grants have been agreed and the firm then pays or receives the difference.

Levy may be assessed quarterly, half-yearly or annually and grants may be receivable at similar periods. But these do not always coincide. One Board, the Engineering Industry Board, in 1966–7 established the following timetable—

Levy Base Year. Levy is assessed at 2½ per cent of total emoluments for the year from 6th April, 1966, to 5th April, 1967. This coincides with the Income Tax Year 1966–7.

Grant Year. The grant year runs from 1st September, 1966, to 31st August, 1967. Some training undertaken in that year may be eligible for a *specific* grant: other training gives the basis for assessing a *general* grant which is expressed as a percentage of levy.

Payment of Levy Only. If a company does not claim a grant then it must only provide for the levy payable. If a company's accounting year ended on 31st December, 1966, the provision would be on the emoluments paid in that accounting year. Of this, the levy for the nine months April to December would not yet have been paid.

The profit and loss account will be debited with the levy at the appropriate rate and a Provision for Training Levy credited.

When the levy notice is received, the Board should be credited and Provision debited. When the levy is paid, Cash will be credited and the Board debited. If no entry is made when the levy notice is received, the Provision will be debited when the cash is paid. Any balance of Provision will be shown under current liabilities in the Balance Sheet.

Example 8

Brown Engineering paid £100,000 in emoluments for the accounting year ended 31st December, 1966. On 1st December, 1966, they received a notice of training levy at the rate of 2½ per cent on emoluments for the year 1965–6 (ending on 1st April, 1966). Emoluments for the accounting year 1965 amounted to £90,000 and provision of 2½ per cent for training levy had already been made. The levy was paid on 20th December.

The ledger accounts will show—

(*a*) If the Levy is Entered when Notice Received—

PROVISION FOR TRAINING LEVY

		£			£
1966			1966		
Dec 1	E.I.T.B. . . .	2312·50	Jan 1	Balance b/d . .	1687·50
,, 31	Balance c/d . .	1875·00	Dec 31	Profit and Loss A/c .	2500·00
		4187·50			4187·50
			1967		
			Jan 11	Balance b/d . .	1875·00

ENGINEERING INDUSTRY TRAINING BOARD

1966		£	1966		£
Dec 20	Cash (levy)	2312·50	Dec 1	Provision for Training levy	2312·50

CASH A/c

			1966		£
			Dec 20	E.I.T.B.	2312·50

(b) If no Entry is made on Receipt of Notice—

PROVISION FOR TRAINING LEVY

1966		£	1966		£
Dec 1	Cash	2312·50	Jan 1	Balance b/d	1687·50
Dec 31	Balance c/d	1875·50	Dec 31	Profit and Loss A/c	2500·00
		4187·50			4187·50
			1967		
			Jan 1	Balance b/d	1875·00

The opening provision represents $2\frac{1}{2}$ per cent on emoluments for April to December, 1965, and the closing provision $2\frac{1}{2}$ per cent of the nine months April to December, 1966.

The levy required by the Board should be—

	£
1965	
Apr–Dec—$\frac{3}{4}$ of £90,000	67,500
1966	
Jan–Apr—$\frac{1}{4}$ of £100,000	25,000
Total emoluments	92,500
$2\frac{1}{2}$ per cent	£2,312·50

The entries for a company which does claim grants is best illustrated by assuming that Brown Engineering have commenced training in September, 1966. They will then be eligible for grant in 1966–7.

Since grants are receivable in respect of the last quarter of 1966 some estimate of the value should be made. If it is estimated that the training grant will be at the level of 100 per cent of levy, then one-quarter of the £2,500 levy provided for may be taken as receivable in grants, i.e. £625.

The additional entries are—

TRAINING GRANTS RECEIVABLE

1966		£			
Dec 31	Profit and Loss A/c	625			

PROFIT AND LOSS A/c

			£
		Training Grants Receivable	625

In the Profit and Loss account the grants receivable may be deducted from the levy provided for as follows on the debit of the profit and loss account—

	£
Training levy payable 1966	2,500
Less Grants receivable	625
Net training levy expense	1,875

The Balance Sheet items may also be offset. In this case, the liabilities side will show—

	£
Provision for Training levy	1,875
Less grants receivable	625
	1,250

Example 9

Brown Engineering paid £120,000 in emoluments for the accounting year ended 31st December, 1967. A return of emoluments for the levy year 1966–7 was submitted in May 1967 and a general grant was claimed in October 1967 for the training between September 1966 and August 1967 at the rate of 100 per cent of the levy. The E.I.T.B. undertook to offset grants against levy, but for firms claiming grants was unable to assess grants before February or March 1968. Provide for levy and grants receivable.

Solution 9

The accounts will show—

PROVISION FOR TRAINING LEVY

			1967		£
			Jan 1	Balance	1875·00
			Dec 31	Profit and Loss A/c	3000·00

TRAINING GRANTS RECEIVABLE

1967		£			
Jan 1	Balance b/d	625·00			
Dec 31	Profit and Loss A/c	3000·00			

The profit and loss account could, of course, be by-passed by debiting grants receivable and crediting the Levy Provision but this is undesirable: the effect of the Act should be shown even if it is nil.

The Balance Sheet would now show—

		£
Provision for Training levy 1966		1,875
" " " " 1967		3,000
		4,875
Training Grants receivable 1966	625	
" " " 1967	3,000	
		3,625
Net levy provided for		1,250

Example 10

On 20th March, 1968, Brown Engineering received notice of award of grant, the first instalment payable on 30th April at the rate of 90 per cent of levy. Final payment was due in September 1968.

Employers receiving less than 100 per cent grant are required to pay the difference between the grant and the levy in two equal instalments.

For this company, the levy would be assessed on emoluments paid in the year ending 5th April, 1967 as follows—

	Emoluments	Levy at 2½%
	£	£
1966 Apr–Dec —¾ of £100,000	75,000	1,875·00
1967 Jan–Mar —¼ of £120,000	30,000	750·00
Levy assessment		2,625·00
The grant at 90 per cent is therefore		2,362·50
and the difference payable		262·50
in two instalments of		131·25

The entries required are debit Levy Provision and credit the Training Board with the levy £2,625 when assessed. Credit the Grants Receivable and debit the Board with the amount of grants £2,362·50. If a payment is due to the Board credit cash and debit the Board. Since the full amount is due, this should clear the Board account when the second instalment is paid.

The accounts will then show—

Provision for Training Levy

		£			£
1968			1968		
Mar 20	E.I.T.B.	2,625·00	Jan 1	Balance	4,875·00

TRAINING GRANTS RECEIVABLE

			£				£
Jan	1	Balance . .	3,625·00	Mar	20	E.I.T.B. . .	2,362·50

ENGINEERING INDUSTRY TRAINING BOARD

			£				£
Mar	20	Training Grants Receivable .	2,362·50	Mar	20	Levy Provision .	2,625·00
Apr	30	Cash . . .	131·25				
Sep	30	Cash . . .	131·25				

CASH

							£
				Apr	30	E.I.T.B. . .	131·50
				Sep	30	,, . .	131·50

A further adjustment is required since the grant receivable is 90 per cent and not the 100 per cent anticipated. The amount of grant previously considered receivable and now not receivable must be written off. For 1966 £625 was expected, and only 90 per cent, £562·50, has been received. The entry is—

	£	£
Debit Profit and Loss Account . .	62·50	
Credit Training Grants Receivable . . .		62·50

For 1967, in respect of the nine months to the end of August, three-quarters of £3,000 was expected, i.e. £2,250, and £2,025 has been received. The difference of £225 must be debited to Profit and Loss account and credited to Training Grants Receivable.

If it is considered that 90 per cent is a more realistic estimate then 10 per cent must also be written off the amount accounted for as receivable in respect of the final three months of 1967.

Where payment is due from the Board, the entries will be the same except that cash is debited and the Board credited on the receipt of cash.

VALUE-ADDED TAX (V.A.T.)

In 1973, purchase tax and selective employment tax were replaced by V.A.T. The general principles of accounting for the tax follow the A.S.S.C. exposure draft ED10 where applicable.

Essentially, value-added tax is like a tax on sales and it is always charged to the ultimate consumer of goods and services. Unlike a sales tax, however, the value-added tax is not collected solely at the final point of retail sale. Value-added tax is added and collected at each stage of production and distribution when goods pass from one firm to another. At each stage, a trader must charge the tax to his customer at the stipulated rate, but he may deduct from the tax collected any tax which he himself has borne on goods and services supplied to him.

Example 11

Goods supplied to the public at a price of £500, are sold at intermediate stages as follows:

	Cost	*Cumulative*
	£	£
Stage 1	140	140
Stage 2	160	300
Stage 3	200	500

The Government is considering applying a sales tax of 20 per cent or a value-added tax of 20 per cent. What will be the tax paid at each stage under the two alternatives?

	Sales tax 20%	*Value-added tax* 20%
	£	£
Stage 1	Nil	28
Stage 2	Nil	32 (£60 less £28)
Stage 3	100	40 (£100 less £60)
Total	100	100

The tax paid will be identical under Sales Tax and V.A.T., but under the value-added tax (V.A.T.) each dealer will pay net tax only on the value added at his stage.

It can be seen that V.A.T. will be handled by many more traders than a sales tax and in this respect it will be more expensive to collect. Experience has shown, however, that a sales tax is more open to abuse and avoidance. V.A.T. makes every dealer into an agent for collection, and since his ability to claim refunds of tax paid depends upon his ability to produce evidence of payment, gives him a strong incentive to demand proper invoices from suppliers.

Methods of Accounting for V.A.T.

From the point of view of the firm, the method of accounting for V.A.T. is to record the tax paid at the same time as purchases are made and the tax receivable from customers at the time a sale is made.

Invoices will have to be retained as evidence of the amounts received and paid.

Sales

When sales are made, an invoice is raised for the price of the goods and V.A.T. at the proper rate is added. The accounting entries will be:

Debit Cash or Customer with price plus V.A.T.
Credit Sales with price of goods.
Credit V.A.T. Account with value-added tax charged.

Purchases

When goods are purchased, the entries will be:

Debit Purchases or expense account with cost price of goods.
Debit V.A.T. Account with value-added tax paid.
Credit Cash or Supplier with cost price of goods plus V.A.T.

Settlement

Settlement dates are staggered throughout the year, but after the initial period, settlement is quarterly, except that traders whose V.A.T. paid is regularly greater than their V.A.T. collected, may be allowed monthly settlement. If the amount collected exceeds the amount paid, then at the end of the period, the entries will be:

Debit V.A.T. Account with net tax payable.
Credit Cash with net tax paid.

Refund of V.A.T. If a firm is liable to V.A.T. but has paid more than it has collected from its customers, then it may be eligible for a refund of V.A.T. When this is received, the entries will be:

Debit Cash with refund received.
Credit. V.A.T. account with tax refund received.

This position will normally apply to firms which are zero-rated for V.A.T. They apply a zero rate to their sales but are eligible for refund on their payments for goods and services. All exports are also zero rated.

At the end of the accounting period the balance on V.A.T. account is V.A.T. payable or receivable (Customs and Excise as creditor or debtor).

Exemption from V.A.T. Some firms may be exempt from V.A.T. This means that they do not need to charge V.A.T. to their customers but it also means that they cannot claim a refund of the tax they pay on materials and supplies which they buy. Such firms should normally include V.A.T. in the cost of materials and supplies purchased or they may, as above, debit the tax paid to a V.A.T. account. At the end of the accounting period, the net tax paid will then be shown as an expense in the Profit and Loss Account, except that tax on assets is included in their cost. Where the expense is allowable as a business expense, an exempt firm may include V.A.T. as an expense. Traders with a turnover less than £5,000 per annum may choose to be exempt and certain other types of business are exempt. When the final accounts of an exempt firm which records V.A.T. on purchases and supplies are prepared, the entries will be:

Debit Profit and Loss account with net V.A.T. payable.
Credit V.A.T. account with net V.A.T. payable.

Where goods and services may be used for both business and private purposes, such as business entertaining, the claim for V.A.T. refund may be limited or disallowed.

Partial exemption. Many taxable firms, such as retailers and banks, deal in some goods or services which are taxable and others which are exempt. Unless the proportion of exempt supplies is insignificant, that is less than 5 per cent and under £5,000, such business may claim refund of a proportion of V.A.T. suffered.

The V.A.T. recoverable is calculated:

$$\text{V.A.T. on supplies} \times \frac{\text{Taxable outputs (sales)}}{\text{Total outputs (sales)}}$$

Where taxable goods are bought for sale purely in trade, that is, they are sold in the same state, without processing or performance of any operations on them, then full credit will be allowed for such sales and the above proportion will only be applied to the rest of the sales.

In either case, the proportions are calculated on a quarterly basis and then revised at the end of the year.

Mixed Ratings

Retailers have a particular problem in calculating the amount of V.A.T. on sales when some goods are zero rated and others standard rated, but they are both sold over the same counter. Of course, separate calculations and records of V.A.T. charged may be kept, but this may be difficult and expensive. Various methods of calculating the tax may be used, based on an analysis of the purchase (as between zero- or full-rated goods), and opening and closing stocks. A similar calculation to the one above is then used, for example:

$$\text{Total outputs (sales)} \times \frac{\text{Taxable inputs}}{\text{Total inputs}} \times \text{Tax rate}$$

Example 12

During the three months of its V.A.T. accounting period, a firm had the following transactions: Purchases of stock for trade, £10,000; cleaning materials, £50; fuel oil for heating (zero rated), £200; business entertaining £100 (V.A.T. disallowed); accountants fee, £250; purchase of adding machine, £80; postage and stamps (exempt), £40; returns to suppliers £120; telephone bill, £150; wages and salaries, £6,000; Export Sales, £12,000; Home Sales, £50,000. Show the V.A.T. account for the period. V.A.T. is at the rate of 10 per cent.

V.A.T. ACCOUNT

	£		£
Cash and Sundry Creditors (Purchases £10,000)	1,000	Cash and Sundry Debtors (£50,000 Home Sales)	5,000
Cash (Telephone (£150)	15	Sundry Creditors (Returns £120)	12
Sundry Creditors (Adding-machine £80)	8		
Accountants (Fee £250)	25		
Cash (Cleaning Materials £50)	5		
Balance (net Tax payable)	3,959		
	£5,012		£5,012
Cash (Customs and Exise)	3,959	Balance (net Tax payable)	3,959

DIRECT TAXES

Income tax is a levy on income arising within the United Kingdom or on income arising outside the United Kingdom if the person receiving the income is resident within the United Kingdom.

Surtax was an additional tax raised on higher incomes prior to 5th April 1973.

Incomes and Residence. Both these concepts are difficult to define: they do not coincide with the normal definitions.

Persons Liable to Income Tax. All persons ordinarily resident in the United Kingdom, whether British subjects or not, are liable to assessment; and also all persons not resident in the United Kindom (whether British subjects or not) in so far as they derive income from property, trade, or employment in the United Kingdom.

Taxation of Income at the Source. So far as possible, income is taxed *at its source*, the person who pays the income at the fountain head being liable to the income tax authorities for tax thereon or for any tax that should be deducted therefrom.

The Income Tax Acts. Income Tax law was consolidated by the Income and Corporation Taxes Act 1970 and the Taxes Management Act 1970, completing a process started with the Capital Allowances Act 1968.

Normally, changes in the provisions for income tax are made every year, and these changes are brought into effect by an annual Finance Act. The three consolidating acts together with the Acts for subsequent years, are collectively known as "The Income Tax Acts".

Schedules of Income Tax. Although there is only one income tax, it is levied under six schedules according to the nature and source of income and different rules apply to each schedule. The schedules are as follows—

Schedule A: Income from the ownership of land, in the United

Kingdom. It was abolished by the 1963 Finance Act, but revived in 1970 as the successor to Schedule D Case VIII.

Schedule B: Income from the occupation or use of land.

Schedule C: Income from Government and public stocks.

Schedule D: Divided into six cases as follows—

Case I: Profits from any trade.

Case II: Profits from any profession or vocation.

Case III: Interest, annuities, annual payments, discounts and profits on certain securities.

Case IV: Interest from securities outside the United Kingdom.

Case V: Income from possessions outside the United Kingdom.

Case VI: Specified income and any taxable income not assessable under any other case or schedule.

Up to 1970, there were two other cases.

Case VII: Gains on the disposal of assets held for not more than a year. Since 1970–71, this case has been replaced by the capital gains tax.

Case VIII: Income from land (including buildings) in the United Kingdom. Since 1970, this is replaced by Schedule A.

Schedule E: Income from an office, employment or pension.

Schedule F: Dividends, including capital dividends, and other distributions of companies resident in the United Kingdom (except any charged under Schedule D or Schedule E).

Administration of Income Tax. General control lies with the Commissioners of Inland Revenue who constitute the Board of Inland Revenue. They collect the taxes and advise the Government on tax matters.

Since April 1965, the Inspectors of taxes are responsible for the assessment of income-tax liability and the Commissioners hear the appeals against these assessments.

Income Tax Commissioners. Income Tax Commissioners are of two kinds: General or District Commissioners, and Special Commissioners.

General Commissioners are part-time honorary officials. Once they have determined an appeal it cannot be heard by the Special Commissioners.

Special Commissioners are highly trained officials before whom difficult cases of law can be heard. The taxpayer may elect the group of commissioners to which he wishes his appeal to go.

Appeals. Notices of assessment are issued in September and October and the taxpayer must appeal within 30 days, stating his grounds for doing so. In practice, most appeals are settled with the Inspector of Taxes.

If an appeal goes to the Commissioners, and is determined by them, it cannot be re-opened subsequently. On questions of fact, the decision of the Commissioners is final, there is no appeal; but on questions of law, an appeal can be made to the High Court and thence to the Court of Appeal, and to the House of Lords, against the decision of either the Special or the General Commissioners. The Commissioners of Inland Revenue are *ex-officio* Special Commissioners.

The Income Tax Year of Assessment. The year of assessment runs from 6th April of one year to 5th April of the next year, and is designated accordingly, i.e. 6th April, 1969, to 5th April, 1970, is the 1969–70 Income Tax Year.

Income Tax Returns. The onus for making returns is on the taxpayer. Early in April of each year the Inspector issues the well-known Form No. 1 to firms, companies, corporations, societies, and other bodies of persons, and Form No. 11 to individuals, having untaxed income liable under Schedule D. He also issues Form No. 12 to all individuals liable under Schedule E. Forms Nos. 11 and 12, in addition to the sections dealing with the various sources of income, contain also sections relating to the various allowances and reliefs which may be claimed by individuals. The forms must be completed and returned within twenty-one days. Every person, whether liable to tax or not, must make a return when called upon to do so (Income and Corporation Taxes Act, 1970, Sect. 5), and the onus is upon the taxpayer to obtain such a form if one is not received from his or her Inspector of Taxes. Where a person has a business address as well as a private residence, e.g. an employer or a partner in a firm, double forms may be received (1A, 11A, 12A, issued by assessors). Only one form need be filled up. On the second form it is sufficient merely to sign the declaration that a full return has been made elsewhere, and add the address of the business, or private residence, as the case may be. The inspector's duty is to supervise the returns of taxpayers and the assessments made by the assessors before they are allowed by the commissioners. He is also empowered to fill in omissions, amend assessments, and to make surcharges. The amount of the assessment can always be satisfactorily arranged with the Inspector if proper accounts are furnished. Notice of appeal against an assessment must be forwarded in writing, within thirty days of the date of the assessment notice, to the Inspector of Taxes, who will appear before the District or Special Commissioners in support of the assessment if there is an appeal.

Rates of Income Tax.[1] Until the year 1920–1 the rates of income tax were graduated according to the total income of the taxpayer. By the Finance Act, 1920, however, and all subsequent Finance Acts, a *standard rate* was fixed, with the proviso that a certain portion of taxable income should be charged at a reduced rate.

Unified Income Tax. A new system was introduced in April 1973 which unified the income and surtax by establishing a basic rate on the first £5,000 of taxable income and a number of higher rates which were fixed on the following scale—

[1] Certain examples io this chapter have used a rate of 50p in the £ to render illustration easier.

Basic rate—	30%	on first £5,000 of taxable income
Higher rates—	40%	on next £1,000 " "
	45%	" " £1,000 " " "
	50%	" " £1,000 " " "
	55%	" " £2,000 " " "
	60%	" " £2,000 " " "
	65%	" " £3,000 " " "
	70%	" " £5,000 " " "
	75%	on the remainder

DEFINITION OF INCOME

Statutory Income. The statutory income of a person is his total income from any, or if he has more than one, from every source, stated in accordance with the provisions of the Income Tax Acts.

Assessable Income. The assessable income of a person is his total statutory income less the allowance made in respect of certain annual charges.

Taxable Income. The taxable income of a person is his assessable income (or his statutory income if he has no earned income), less the personal allowances made for himself, housekeeper, dependent relatives, and, if married, his wife and children, etc.

Earned Income. This includes remuneration from office or employment, pension, superannuation, deferred pay and compensation (but not usually lump sums). It also includes payments for the past services of a deceased person and income from property attached to an employment or office. Provided a person takes an active part, it includes income from trades, professions and vocations, and the salaries and interest on capital paid to partners. Sleeping partners receive unearned income.

The precedent active partner of a firm has to make a declaration as to whether each partner is a "sleeping" or "active" partner.

Unearned or Investment Income. Under this heading will be included all income obtained without personal service or effort, such as rents from the ownership of land, houses, etc., dividends from investments, interest on money lent, profits from business or trade in the case of a dormant or sleeping partner.

Investment Income Surcharge. All income which is not earned income will be treated as investment income and is subject to a surcharge of 15 per cent if the investment income exceeds £2,000. Apart from personal reliefs and allowances, other deductions from total income may be charged against investment income to reduce the liability to surcharge.

Personal Allowances. The personal allowances which may be deducted from the assessable income are varied from time to time. For instance, the allowances in the tax year 1973–4 were—

	£
Single person's allowance	595
Married man's allowance	775
Children aged up to 11	200
Children aged up to 11–15	235

	£
Children aged up to 16 or over in full-time education	265
Additional personal allowance	100
Dependent relative allowance	100
(£45 for a woman, other than a married woman living with her husband.)	
Housekeeper's allowance	100
Daughter's services allowance	55
Blind person's allowance	130
Wife's earned income relief . . . . Maximum	595

Reliefs for the elderly—

Age exemption . .	no tax payable unless total income exceeded £700 (married couple £1,000).
Life assurance . .	normally 50% of premiums.
Retirement annuities (for non-employees) . .	up to £1,500 premiums or 15 per cent earned income.

Schedule A

Schedule A taxes incomes of landlords and owners of property and it was abolished in 1963, only to be brought back in 1969. It has covered five main classes of income:

1. Rents, Premiums on Leases, and certain other receipts from property which were charged under Schedule D Case VIII from 1963–9. This is now the main class of income under Schedule A.

2. Land Tax was abolished in 1963: it was a minor, ancient tax.

3. Tithe Annuities. Tithes were ancient taxes payable to the Church and they were largely abolished in 1936 by means of annuities providing for redemption. These annunities are allowable as expenses of those paying them.

4. Mineral Rights Duties were abolished after 1966–7 up to which time they were 1s. in the £ on mineral rights rents.

5. Royalties Welfare Levy is still made at the rate of 5p in the £ on mineral rights rents, for the benefit of the Miners Welfare fund.

Chargeable Incomes. Rents arising under any leases, rent charges, ground annuals, feu duties, other annual receipts arising from ownership of an estate or interest in land will all be chargeable under Schedule A.

Allowable Deductions. Payments for maintenance, repairs, rates, rents or other annual payments may be allowed as expenses deductible from the chargeable incomes, as may capital allowances on plant and machinery provided for repairs and maintenance.

Schedule B: Income from Occupation of Certain Woodlands

Originally applying to the occupation of nearly all land, income tax under Schedule B is now charged only in respect of the occupation of woodlands managed on a commercial basis where the occupier has not elected to be charged under Schedule D instead. Tax is charged on one-third of the annual value of the land as if it were let in its natural and unimproved state.

Schedules C and F: Income from British Government Securities and Dividends

Schedules C and F cover the taxation of interest and dividends received respectively and they are therefore considered together. Where such items accrue incidentally to business, they may be included in assessments under other schedules, and, especially, Schedule D Case III, which deals specifically with interest and dividends.

Exemptions. Some receipts are exempt from tax, such as receipts from national savings certificates, tax reserve certificates, the first £21 trustee savings bank interest and bonuses and interest under the Save-as-you-earn scheme.

Most building societies take part in the special arrangement whereby their interest is specially exempt from income tax but no repayment claim may be made in respect of tax paid by the society.

Taxed Income. Dividends and interest are normally received after income tax or Advanced Corporation Tax (A.C.T.) at the standard rate have been deducted. If the recipient is not liable for tax, a refund may be claimed. The payer must account to the Inland Revenue for the tax withheld from the payees.

Untaxed Income. Some interest and dividends, whilst liable to tax, are paid gross. Examples are 3½ per cent War Loan, 3 per cent Defence Bonds, Bank interest, co-operative bank interest, interest on private loans, small government dividends and local housing bonds.

Franked Income and Dividends. Since 1966, companies have been liable to deduct income tax at the standard rate from all dividends paid and to remit this to the Inland Revenue, monthly. Where a company receives income from other companies who have already deducted tax, this is called *franked investment income* and the tax thus paid may be deducted from the tax payable on the company's own dividends. From 1973–4, the system changed again. Accounting for Corporation tax is dealt with later.

Schedule D: Business and Professional Profits, Interest, Income from Abroad, Short-term Capital Gains, Rents, etc.

Case I

The profits of a trade (including commerce, industry, transport, finance, and agriculture) are assessed under Case I. The normal basis of assessment is the profit made in the trader's accounting year ending in the preceding year of assessment, but special rules apply where a new business is started, a business is discontinued, or the accounting date is changed. The profits of a trade carried on by a partnership are assessed in one sum on the partnership: each partner includes his share of the partnership assessment in his return of total income.

Broadly, the profit is the difference between the gross receipts and the expenses incurred wholly and exclusively for the purposes of the business.

No deduction may be made for interest on capital or other capital charges, lost capital, depreciation, reserves, losses unconnected with the business, expenditure on certain business entertaining and gifts, and private and domestic expenditure. Certain specific allowances for capital expenditure and depreciation are, however, available (see below). As part of the system of collection of income tax at the source no deduction is allowed for interest on borrowed money (except certain interest payable abroad), any annuity or other annual payment payable out of the profits, or any patent royalty. The total profit assessed thus includes these charges, but the trader is entitled to deduct income tax at the standard rate when he pays them: he thus recovers the tax relating to that part of his total profit which he has paid away by these charges.

Case II

The rules for the assessment of profits and the relief of losses of a profession or vocation under Case II are the same as those for Case I.

Case III

The tax on interest and other payments assessable under Case III is based on the income of the preceding year, except that where a source of income is newly acquired or is disposed of the basis is the income of the current year.

An individual (and also, if he is married, his wife separately) is entitled to exemption from income tax (but not surtax) on the first £15 of the total interest on ordinary deposits (but not investment deposits) with the Post Office Savings Bank, on deposits with a seaman's savings bank or the Savings Department No. 2 of the Birmingham Municipal Bank, and on ordinary deposits (but not Special Investment Department deposits) with a trustee savings bank.

Interest from certain British Government securities (e.g. 3½ per cent War Loan) is not chargeable to tax where the securities are in the benficial ownership of a person not ordinarily resident in the United Kingdom.

Case IV

Tax under Case IV in respect of income from securities out of the United Kingdom is charged on the full amount of income arising in the preceding year, whether remitted to the United Kingdom or not; the assessment is on the income of the current year, however, when a source of income is acquired or disposed of.

A person who is not domiciled in the United Kingdom, or a British subject who is not ordinarily resident here, is liable to tax only on the basis of the amount of income received in the United Kingdom. A person who is not resident here is not liable to tax under Case IV.

Case V

Tax on income arising abroad directly from trades, professions or pensions is charged under Case V (unless chargeable under Case I or Case II of Schedule D) on the amount of income received in the United Kingdom in the preceding year, except that where receipts from a particular source begin or cease the charge is on a current-year basis.

Tax on income from other possessions abroad is also charged under Case V, but by reference to the full amount of income arising in the preceding year (or in the current year when the source is acquired or disposed of).

A person who is not domiciled in the United Kingdom, or a British subject who is not ordinarily resident here, is liable to tax under Case V only on the basis of the amount of income received in the United Kingdom, whatever the nature of the possession. A person who is not resident here is not liable to tax under Case V.

Case VI

Income not chargeable under any other Case of Schedule D or under any other Schedule (including a number of particular types of income specifically assigned to Case VI by law) is generally assessed on the actual income of the year of assessment.

Case VII

Short-term gains, that is, gains arising from the disposal of chargeable assets (other than gains accruing as profits of a trade, profession, vocation, office or employment) within months of their acquisition, charged to tax under Case VII until 1970–1 when the gains were put within the scope of the Capital Gains tax.

Case VIII

Rents and other receipts from land (including buildings) in the United Kingdom were chargeable under Case VIII until 1969 when they were put under the scope of Schedule A.

Schedule E

Under this Schedule, all remuneration from employments is taxed. This covers all who are not in a profession or business on their own account, and includes managers, directors, civil servants and pensioners.

Mode of Assessment. Tax under Schedule E is chargeable on the emoluments of the year of assessment, that is, on the actual income in the years ended 5th April.

Formal assessment may not be necessary if the actual tax deducted under the PAYE scheme is very near to the tax due, but the taxpayer may request such an assessment. If payments such as bonuses are received in a later year an assessment will be made relating the income to the fiscal year to which it relates.

Allowable Expenses. Only a restricted number of expenses may be claimed under Schedule E and only if the money is "wholly, exclusively and necessarily incurred in the performance of duties." This does not include travelling to or preparation for duties.

Items which may be allowed are compulsory and other approved superannuation contributions, national insurance, overalls and clothing, tools and since 1958–9 subscriptions to professional societies.

It is sometimes possible to claim hotel and travelling expenses, servants' wages, the study of a clergyman and the cost of a *locum tenens* but not where the expense arises out of circumstances personal to the employees.

SURTAX

Surtax was a deferred instalment of income tax chargeable up to 1972–3 on total income from all sources in excess of £2,000 with special exemption for incomes below £2,500. In general the definition of net income chargeable to surtax follows that used for income tax, but certain exemptions and deductions allowable for income tax were not allowed for surtax and vice versa.

DOUBLE TAXATION RELIEF

Comprehensive arrangements for the relief of double taxation have been made with many other countries. These arrangements, while varying in detail, follow a general pattern. They provide for the exemption of some classes of income from tax in the country in which the income arises—for example, shipping or air transport profits arising in one country to a concern resident in the other are exempted from tax in the former country. Other classes of income remain taxable in both countries, sometimes, however, at a reduced rate in the country of origin, but the country in which the taxpayer is resident is required to allow relief from its own tax on the doubly taxed income. This is the way in which relief is given, for example, for the double taxation of the profits of trading concerns (other than those engaged in shipping or air transport) which are resident in one country and have branches in the other. These arrangements may apply to income tax, surtax, corporation tax, capital gains tax and estate duty.

Arrangements are also in force with a number of countries for reciprocal exemption from income taxes in respect of certain limited classes of income, for example, shipping profits, air transport profits and certain profits arising through agencies.

There is a special arrangement with the Republic of Ireland under which residents in the Republic (unless also resident in the United Kingdom) are totally exempt from United Kingdom income tax, and United Kingdom residents are similarly exempted from Irish income tax. Where a person is resident in both countries each country gives relief on doubly taxed income at one-half of the lower of the two "appropriate rates" of tax. There is a separate agreement dealing with the taxes which are levied on companies.

Where there is no comprehensive agreement with another country, relief is given by the United Kingdom unilaterally against the United Kingdom tax on the doubly charged income for corresponding overseas taxes. With minor exceptions, this relief is given only to residents of the United Kingdom on income arising abroad.

CORPORATION TAX

The General Scope of the Tax. The corporation tax falls on the income and the chargeable gains, collectively described as the "profits," of companies. A company means any body corporate or unincorporated association. It includes authorized unit trusts but does not include a partnership or a local authority or local authority association in the United Kingdom.

In the case of a resident company the charge is on all income and capital gains wherever arising and whether or not remitted to this country.

In the case of a non-resident company, the charge is on companies carrying on a trade in the United Kingdom through a branch or agency here and is on any income attributable to the branch or agency and on any capital gains on the disposal of assets in the United Kingdom used for the purpose of the trade or attributable to the branch or agency.

Profits Chargeable to Corporation Tax. The basic rule for the computation of *income* for corporation tax purposes is that, apart from certain special rules, it is to be computed in accordance with income-tax principles under the rules of the Schedules and Cases governing income tax. The several amounts of income so computed plus any capital gains are added together to provide the total profits on which the single corporation tax assessment is to be made.

Capital gains of companies for corporation tax purposes are computed in accordance with the principles applying for capital gains tax.

In arriving at the amount on which corporation tax is assessed, deductions are allowed for capital allowances applying the income tax rules with some modifications of detail. Relief is allowed also for annual interest paid and other "charges on income" and, in the case of investment companies, for expenses of management. There are special provisions for relief for trading losses against current profits (and to a limited extent against past profits) and against future trading income. Subject to certain conditions a trading loss by one company in a group may be set off against current profits of another company in the group.

CAPITAL GAINS TAX

When they accrue to individuals or to certain other unincorporated persons, gains on the disposal of all firms of property, with some exceptions such as motor cars, a private residence and chattels worth less than £1,000 and so on are chargeable to capital gains tax. When they accrue to companies, they are chargeable to corporation tax. The scope of the charge, and the rules for computing the gains, are broadly the same for both individuals and companies.

All persons, including companies, who are resident or ordinarily resident in the United Kingdom are liable to tax in respect of gains which accrue on the disposal of chargeable assets wherever situated except that there is no charge when disposals do not exceed £500 in one year. An individual who is not also domiciled in the United Kingdom is liable in respect of gains accruing on the disposal of assets situated abroad only to the extent that the gains are remitted to the United Kingdom. Persons who are neither resident nor ordinarily resident in the United Kingdom, but who carry on a trade in the United Kingdom through a branch or agency, are nevertheless liable on gains which accrue to them from the disposal of assets situated in the United Kingdom which are used for the purposes of that trade or branch or agency. Certain persons resident in the United Kingdom are exempt from the tax in whole or in part; they include local authorities, approved superannuation funds, friendly societies, registered trade unions, and other persons who qualify for exemption from income tax.

Disposal. Capital gains tax is chargeable on gains accruing on the disposal of assets. Disposal includes sale, exchange and gift and generally any occasion when the owner of an asset derives a capital sum from it. Assets are deemed to have been disposed of at their owner's death and there are notional disposals in certain circumstances, e.g. on the part of trustees on the termination of a life interest.

Assets include all forms of property, or interests or rights in or over property. The main exemptions from capital gains tax relate to the disposal of a principal private residence which has been occupied as such, together with not more than one residence similarly occupied by a dependent relative; tangible movable property worth £1,000 or less; normal life assurance policies on surrender or maturity; savings certificates, premium bonds, defence bonds and national development bonds; private motor cars; important works of art and other objects of national, scientific, historic or artistic interest (subject to certain undertakings by the beneficiary); gifts and bequests of land and buildings to the National Trust and similar bodies; and gifts of assets which would otherwise be chargeable provided that their value does not exceed £100 in one year.

Other exemptions and reliefs relate to gains accruing at death (the first £5,000 of which are exempt), on the disposal of a business by sale or gift on the retirement of the owner at the age of sixty or more, and on the sale of certain business assets when the proceeds are reinvested in comparable business assets. There are special reliefs which apply to certain government and Government-guaranteed stocks issued at a discount before 6th April,

1965, and on the disposal of units in authorized unit trusts schemes and shares in approved investment trust companies.

Calculation of Gains. In general, gains are computed as the difference between the cost of acquisition (together with expenses of acquisition and disposal and certain other allowable expenditure) and the consideration received for the disposal (or market value at date of disposal if there is no consideration or the transaction is not at arm's length). Any amount charged to or taken into account as a receipt in calculating income tax or corporation tax is excluded from the consideration. Losses are usually allowable if a gain in the same transaction would have been chargeable; they are set primarily against any gains accruing in the same year and any net losses for a year may be carried forward without time limit and set against gains of later years. On a disposal on or after 6th April, 1967, of land in the United Kingdom with development value, capital gains tax is normally computed by reference only to the current use value of the land.

The tax is not retrospective and gains are only chargeable in so far as they are attributable to the period after 6th April, 1965. In the case of assets held at that date and disposed of subsequently, there are rules by which the appropriate proportion of any gain or loss is determined, either by reference to market value at 6th April, 1965 (but not so as to exceed the gain or loss accruing over the whole period of ownership of the asset) or by a process of time apportionment under which the gain is treated as spread evenly over the whole period of ownership.

Capital gains are taxable under three separate heads, viz—

(i) Corporation tax is payable upon the capital gains realized by companies (except that for the year of assessment 1965–6 the realized capital gains of certain companies which had not come within the charge to corporation tax were charged with capital gains tax).

(ii) Capital gains tax is payable upon capital gains realized by individuals.

Capital gains tax assessments are made for a year of assessment beginning on 6th April. They are normally made in the period following the end of the year of assessment. Thus, apart from a few exceptional cases in which assessments were made earlier, assessments for the year of assessment 1965–6, the first year of the tax, began to be made in the year 1966–7.

In 1971, Capital gains tax was normally charged at a flat rate of 30 per cent on net chargeable gains (i.e. chargeable gains less allowable losses) but, if it was to an individual's advantage, he was charged on an alternative basis under which tax was charged as if one half of the net gains up to £5,000 and the whole of the excess over £5,000 were added to his total income for the year and assessed to income tax and surtax.

There are detailed special rules on the application of the tax in particular circumstances, e.g. bonus and rights issues, options, company reorganizations and mergers, trusts and wasting assets (including short leases).

The administration provisions for income tax are applied to capital gains tax with such adaptations as are necessary.

ESTATE DUTY

Estate duty is payable on the passing of property on death. It was imposed by the Finance Act, 1894, and is leviable under the provisions of that Act as varied from time to time by subsequent Finance and other Acts.

In general, estate duty is chargeable on the value of all property which changes hands or is deemed to pass on death. The charge to duty is thus not limited to property owned by the deceased, but may extend to other property, e.g., to trust funds where the deceased was entitled to the income during his lifetime and to gifts (with certain exceptions such as out-and-out gifts not exceeding £500) made by the deceased within seven years of his death (one year in the case of a gift for public or charitable purposes).

Broadly speaking, all property situate in Great Britain is liable to duty irrespective of the domicile of the deceased, and the property abroad is liable if the deceased died domiciled in Great Britain. The main exemptions from estate duty are—

(*a*) estates not over £15,000 are exempt;

(*b*) settled property which bore estate duty (or which would have borne it but for the exemption limit) on the death of a husband or wife is exempt from duty on the death of the surviving spouse unless that spouse was competent to dispose;

(*c*) certain Government securities carry exemption from estate duty when the deceased holder of such securities was neither domiciled nor ordinarily resident in the United Kingdom.

Estate duty is payable at a graduated scale according to the value of the estate at the death. The general rule is that all the liable property, settled or not settled, in which the deceased had an interest is aggregated and this value determines the rate of duty payable. If, however, the value of the deceased's own property is not more than £10,000, it is not aggregated with other settled property; instead, it and the other settled property are treated as two separate estates and each is charged to duty at the rate (if any) appropriate to itself. Similar treatment is given to certain life assurance policies. Any capital gains tax payable in consequence of death is deducted from the value of the assets for estate duty purposes.

Estate duty on personalty is payable on the date of death and on realty it becomes payable twelve months after death. Simple interest at 2 per cent per annum is normally charged on arrears of estate duty.

Provisions exist for the avoidance of double death duty taxation either by double taxation agreements or by unilateral relief. In 1967 there were reciprocal arrangements between the United Kingdom and Canada, France, India, the Irish Republic, Netherlands, Pakistan, South Africa, Sweden, Switzerland and U.S.A.

Unilateral relief is allowed in respect of deaths after 9th April, 1962, where property situated abroad is liable to estate duty in this country and to a death duty in the country of situation. The duty payable abroad is allowed as a credit against the duty payable in this country.

DIRECT TAXES ON BUSINESSES

Businesses will be taxed in accordance with the type of ownership.

1. **Sole Traders and Partnerships.** The net taxable income is liable to tax under Schedule D as the income of the individual owner or partners (shared according to the partnership rules). The total tax liability will include income tax and surtax.

2. **Open Companies.** The general liability is to Corporation Tax on the taxable profits, but all companies must account separately on a monthly basis for income tax deducted from dividends, interest and similar payments or receipts.

3. **Close Companies.** A close company is, broadly, one which is controlled by its directors or by five or fewer shareholders, and in which the public do not hold an interest of at least 35 per cent. These companies are subject to special rules, the main effect of which is to—

(*a*) restrict the amount of directors' remuneration which can be deducted;

(*b*) treat certain payments by the company (for example, interest paid to certain directors) as distributions, and require the company to account for income tax on loans to shareholders;

(*c*) require the company to account for income tax on its "shortfall," that is, the amount by which its actual distributions fall short of its "required standard." The required standard depends in the first instance on the nature and amount of a company's income after corporation tax, under a calculation which brings together the whole of the income from investments and, in the case of a trading or property-holding company, 60 per cent of the income from those activities; but if such a company shows that it could not distribute that amount without prejudicing the requirements of its business (including not only current requirements, but also requirements that may be necessary or advisable for the maintenance and development of the business), the required standard is abated accordingly. The amount of the company's income on which income tax is charged in this way can be treated as income of its members for surtax, even though undistributed; this surtax is payable by the company.

DIRECT TAX ON EMPLOYEES

The P.A.Y.E. Scheme. *Pay as You Earn.* From 6th April, 1944, income tax of employees has been deducted from pay under the P.A.Y.E. scheme. The tax due in respect of any pay is deducted from that pay as it is paid, so that in general the whole of the tax due on the year's earnings has been paid by the end of the income tax year. The tax deducted is remitted periodically to the tax collector by the employer.

The scheme is concerned with collection of tax and not with assessing it. The P.A.Y.E. Scheme is discussed more fully below

Graduated National Insurance Contributions. The P.A.Y.E. system is also used to collect contributions under the Graduated National Insurance Scheme.

Since October, 1966, a confusing feature of the scheme is that *all* employees must pay contributions whether they are contracted out of the scheme or not. The scheme is detailed on p. 2850.

EMPLOYER'S NORMAL RIGHT OF DEDUCTION. It is the employer's responsibility to pay both his own and the employee's graduated contribution, but he is entitled to deduct the employee's contribution from the particular payment on which that contribution has been calculated.

THE P.A.Y.E. SCHEME

Code Numbers. Up to 1973, we showed lists of codes, but these are now unnecessary, since the code number is now simply the amount of allowances against pay, without the last digit. For example: Allowances £2,000 code 200; Allowances £1,358, code 136. If there are no allowances, the code is 0 and if allowances are between £1 and £9, the code is 1.

Code Prefix. Some codes have a prefix D, followed by a number between 1 and 8. The D indicates that the higher rates of tax are payable and the 1 to 8 indicates which higher rate is applicable. For these, tax table D is provided.

Code Suffixes. Those codes which do not have a prefix will have the suffix H, L, or T. H or L indicates if the person is married or single and enables rapid changes to be made if the rates of personal allowance are changed. Taxpayers who do not wish their status to be known by their employer may obtain code T.

Tax Tables. Employers are supplied with monthly and weekly tax tables which show the tax due to date on the cumulative wages paid. New tables are published each year.

The pay due in the current month or week is added to the gross wages already paid. Table A shows the "free pay" to date for the employee's code number.

For instance, Table A for week 52 in 1965–6 showed—

Code	Total free pay to date		Decimal Equivalent
	£	s	£
675	995	16	995·80
676	1006	4	1006·20
677	1016	12	1016·60
678	1027	0	1027·00
679	1037	8	1037·40
680	1047	16	1047·80
681	1058	4	1058·20
682	1068	12	1068·60
683	1079	0	1079·00
684	1089	8	1089·40
685	1099	16	1099·80
686	1110	4	1110·20
687	1120	12	1120·60
688	1131	0	1131·00
689	1141	8	1141·40
690	1151	16	1151·80
691	1162	4	1162·20
692	1170	0	1170·00
693	1180	8	1180·40
694	1190	16	1190·80

If, in our example, the man with a code number of 688 had been paid £1,250 by week 51 and he is to be paid £25 in week 52, then his total pay up to week 52 is £1,275. His "free pay" is £1,131 so that his taxable pay is the difference, £144.

Table B shows the total tax due to date and, if the tax already deducted in previous periods is taken away from this, the balance is the tax due in the current period.

The following is an extract from Table B for 1965–6—

Total Taxable Pay to date		Total Tax Due to date		Total Taxable Pay to date		Total Tax Due to date	
£	s	£	s	£	s	£	s
142	0	23	2	172	0	30	2
	10	23	5		10	30	5
143	0	23	7	173	0	30	7
	10	23	9		10	30	9
144	0	23	12	174	0	30	12
	10	23	14		10	30	14
145	0	23	16	175	0	30	16
	10	23	19		10	30	19

Decimal Equivalent

Total Taxable Pay to date	Total Tax Due to date	Total Taxable Pay to date	Total Tax Due to date
£	£	£	£
142·00	23·10	172·00	30·10
0·50	23·25	0·50	30·25
143·00	23·35	173·00	30·35
0·50	23·45	0·50	30·45
144·00	23·60	174·00	30·60
0·50	23·70	0·50	30·70
145·00	23·80	175·00	30·80
0·50	23·95	0·50	30·95

The notes refer to the form P3 (1974) (PAYE Coding Guide) enclosed or sent with a previous notice of coding.

See note	**Coding allowances**	£
10	Expenses, etc.	46
12	Building Society interest payable	822
12	Loan, etc. interest	
13	Personal	595
13	Wife's earned income	
13	Additional personal	130
13	Children Including reduced allowance £	530
13	Dependent relatives	
14	Life insurance	313
	Total allowances due	2436
	Less	
17	**Family allowance deduction**	
16	**Allowances given against other income**	
	Untaxed interest	
	National Insurance Benefits	
	Occupational pensions	
17	Family allowance	
	Net allowances	
	Less	
18	**Tax unpaid for earlier years**	
	19 – £ *equivalent to a deduction of*	
	1973–74 £ *(estimated) equivalent to a deduction of*	
19-21	**Other adjustments**	
	Allowances given against pay	2436

Your code for 1974-75 is ▶ 243 | L

Keep this notice for future reference

HPB 52-7891

FIG. 28.3

In the example, the taxable pay was £144 and it was liable to tax of £23·60, then, if £22·50 had already been deducted, the tax deducted in week 52 would be £1·60.

If earnings fall, the total tax due to date may fall below the tax already paid. In this case, the balance will be credited back to the earnings.

Tax Deduction Cards. These are supplied to the employer although alternative forms may be used, subject to the agreement of the Inland Revenue.

The cards also provide for the employees' contribution to the Graduated pension fund to be recorded. A specimen Tax deduction card is shown in Fig. 28.4.

Form P60. At the end of the tax year the employer must notify the employee of the gross remuneration and the total tax deducted, and the Revenue will supply the necessary forms. Fig. 28.5 is an example.

The Earnings-related Short-term Benefits Scheme. An earnings-related supplement is payable to a person who is sick or unemployed and

1. is aged 18 or over and under minimum pension age (65 for a man, 60 for a woman); and
2. is entitled to flat-rate sickness or unemployment benefit (or to widow's benefit that allows her to choose whether or not to pay full flat-rate National Insurance contributions).

The supplement can be paid to a person receiving the higher rate benefit payable under the Industrial Injuries scheme instead of flat-rate sickness benefit.

Amount of Supplement. The earnings-related supplement is at the rate of one-third of that part of "average weekly earnings" which falls between £9 and £30. It is paid in addition to flat-rate sickness or unemployment benefit, including increases for dependants, subject to a maximum total benefit of 85 per cent of average weekly earnings.

Claims. The claimant is not required to make a separate claim for earnings-related supplement but he will at some time be asked to make a declaration of his earnings and to produce in support of this the Certificate of Pay and Tax Deducted issued to him by his employer at the end of the tax year, that is, his P60.

Form P45. When an employee changes employment he must receive Parts 2 and 3 of Form P45 showing his code, his gross pay to date and the tax deducted. Part 1 of the form goes to the local Revenue office. An unemployed person can claim repayment of tax weekly, as his liability declines, from the Tax office. His new employer will send Part 3 of the form to them when he takes on the new employee.

The illustration in Fig. 28.6 shows Part 3.

Part 2 is identical with Sections 1 to 6 of Part 3 above. Part 1 also contains the information given in Sections 1 to 6 above and, in addition, the information given in Fig. 28.7.

Employee's National Insurance No.						1968-69 Deduction Card

Employee's Surname	Christian Name(s) or other Forenames

Nature of Employment	Works No.	Branch, Dept., Contract, etc.	CODE. WEEKS 36 ONWARDS.	
			Code (or amended Code)	Week No. in which amended Code applied
Employer				
HENDON District		322 / District Refce,		

MAKE ENTRIES FROM 6 APRIL 1968, TO 6 DECEMBER 1968, OVERLEAF

NAT. INSCE. Employee's Graduated Contributions (1)			Week No.	Gross pay in the week (2)			Total gross pay to date (3)			Total free pay to date as shown by Table A (4)		Total taxable pay to date (5)		Total tax due to date as shown by Table B (6)		Tax deducted in the week (7)		Tax refunded in the week (8)	
£	s.	d.		£	s.	d.	£	s.	d.	£	s.	£	s.	£	s.	£	s.	£	s.
			B.F. from Wk. 35																
			36																
			37																
			38																
			39																
			40																
			41																
			42																
			43																
			44																
			45																
			46																
			47																
			48																
			49																
			50																
			51																
			52																
			§																

Total of col. (1)						
	If employee engaged during year, deduct pay in respect of previous employment(s)		If employee engaged during year, deduct tax in respect of previous employment(s)		§ If the Pay Day is on 5 April 1969, complete the line marked § as instructed in Note 4 on the BLUE CARD	
	Pay in respect of this employment		Tax deducted (or refunded) in respect of this employment. If a refund, mark entry "R"			

For official use

NATIONAL INSURANCE Graduated Contributions.
The amount to be remitted to the Collector is TWICE the amount entered in col. 1.

INCOME TAX				
	Amount of employee's Superannuation Contributions (if any) for the year in respect of this employment	£	s.	d.
	Holiday pay paid but not included in col. 2	£	s.	d.

Amounts paid on behalf of the employee or given otherwise than in money (see Employer's Guide to Pay As You Earn paras. 52A, 54, 55A and 115)

£ s d

Description of payment ....

FIG. 28.4

Certificate of pay and tax deducted **Year 1967-68**

Employee's National Insurance No.	Code No. at 5 April 1968 ▶ (*Enter "E" if an Emergency Code is in use at 5 April 1968*)	
Employee's Surname		District Reference /
Christian or other Forenames (or Initials)		Works No. (*if any*)

	Pay £	s.	d.	Tax £	s.	d.
1. Pay and tax in respect of previous employment(s) in 1967-68 taken into account in arriving at the tax deductions made by me/us						
2. Pay and tax in my/our employment						

I/We certify that the particulars given above include the total amount of pay (including overtime, bonus, commission, etc.) paid to you by me/us in the year ended 5 April 1968, and the total tax deducted by me/us (less any refunds) in that year.

Employer's Name (*in full*)

Address (*in full*)

Date

TO THE EMPLOYEE *Keep this certificate. It will help you to check any Notice of Assessment which the Tax Office may send you in due course. It will also be needed if you claim National Insurance sickness or unemployment benefit.*

P 60 (1967)

FIG. 28.5

INLAND REVENUE

INCOME TAX

NEW EMPLOYEE

PART 3

Particulars of old employment

1. Employee's National Insurance No.

2. Employee's Surname | Mr. Mrs. Miss etc | Initials

3.

This information is for official use only

4. | Day | Month | Year

5. Code No. at date of leaving
"E" is Emergency Code
"X" indicates Week 1 (Month 1) basis | Code No.

6. Last entries on Deduction Card | Week or Month No. | Week | Month

except where "E" or "X" is entered at item 5 | Total gross pay to date | £ | s. | d.

Total tax to date | £ | s.

NEW EMPLOYER – Please complete items 7 to 15 and send this form to your Tax Office IMMEDIATELY. Please also read the instructions on Part 2:

7. Employer's P.A.Y.E. Reference Number

8. Date employment commenced (Enter in figures) | Day | Month | Year 19

9. Enter "✓" if you require these items to be shown on Deduction Cards etc. | "✓" | Works No. | Branch, Dept.

10. Enter "S" if this employee will be in a Superannuation scheme by the next 5 April

For Tax Centre Use | N/D | P47 | M/E | DOM | H.P.

11. Enter "P" if this employee will not be paid by you between date shown at item 8 and the next 5 April

12. Employee's private address ....

13. If tax entered at item 6 does not agree tax entered on Deduction Card from the Tax Tables, state Tax Table figure here | £ | s.

14. Nature of employment

15. Declaration
I have prepared a * Deduction Card in accordance with the above particulars.

For Tax Centre Use | Ind. Cd. | T

Employer....................

Address....................

....

.... Date ....

P45

* State whether "Weekly" or "Monthly"

FIG. 28.6

7. Emergency Code • or Week 1 (Month 1) basis applies	Total gross pay in this employment	£	s.	d.
	Total tax deducted in this employment	£	s.	
8. Works No.		9. Branch, Dept., Contract, etc.		

10. Employee's private address --

11. I certify that the particulars entered at items 1 to 9 above are correct·

Employer --

Address --

-- Date ------------------------

FIG. 28.7

Simplified Scheme. It is possible to obtain Revenue permission to operate a simplified scheme.

Small Wages. Where wages or salaries are less than £5·25 per week or £22·75 per month, no tax deduction is made. However, if the employee has other employment, the amounts are £1 per week and £4 per month.

Annual Returns. The employer must supply details of gross pay and tax deducted and send the tax deduction cards to the Revenue by 19th April each year. Wages sheets and records are open to inspection. A special return is required by 5th May in respect of directors and certain employees. This return includes expenses, emoluments and payments in kind.

Employer's Liability. The employer is liable for the correct amount of deductions, except for errors made in good faith. Tax for the previous 12 months is a preferential debt in liquidation or bankruptcy.

GRADUATED NATIONAL INSURANCE CONTRIBUTIONS

On or after 21 September, 1971, contributions are on a scale starting at £0·01 on £9·01 and rising to £1·47 (contracted in) and £1·08 (contracted out) on £42 per week. A few typical weekly rates are given below:

Gross pay	Not contracted out	Contracted out
£	£	£
9·01	0·01	0·01
12·00	0·15	0·02
15·00	0·30	0·04
20·00	0·54	0·15
30·00	0·97	0·59
40·00	1·41	1·02
42·00 or more	1·47	1·08

Monthly tables are also available.

Persons for whom Graduated Contributions must be Paid

In general, graduated contributions must be paid by both employer and employee for any employee (other than a national insurance retirement pensioner) aged between 18 and 70 (65 for a woman) whose pay in his employment, before deductions, exceeds £9 in any income tax week. On and after 5th October, 1966, there is liability for graduated contributions even though the employee is contracted out—but at a lower rate than for employees who are not contracted out.

Gross Pay. The gross pay on which graduated contributions are calculated is in general the same as that taken for P.A.Y.E. purposes, as entered on the deduction card. Some of the items to be included, and some of those not to be included, in the gross pay figure, are set out below.

Items Included in Gross Pay. Among the items *to be included* by the employer in the gross pay figure are—

(*a*) Salary or wages.

(*b*) Overtime pay, commissions, fees and bonuses.

(*c*) Amounts set aside out of the employee's pay throughout the year to be paid out to him at a certain time (e.g. at Christmas or for his annual holiday); these should be included in the gross pay figure at the time they are set aside, if they form part of his assessable emoluments for income tax at that time.

(*d*) Holiday pay.

(*e*) Pay continuing during sickness or other absence from work.

(*f*) Pay received by the employee after the employment has ended.

(*g*) Payments instead of benefits in kind, e.g. board wages.

(*h*) Gratuities paid out by the employer (e.g. from a "service charge").

Items not Included in Gross Pay. Among the items *not to be included* by the employer in the gross pay figure (even though, in some cases, they may affect the yearly tax liability) are—

(*a*) Benefits in kind, e.g. free board and lodging on the employer's premises.

(*b*) Specific and distinct payments of, or contributions towards, expenses actually incurred by the employee in carrying out his employment.

(*c*) Payments of amounts which have already been included in the gross pay figure (e.g. holiday pay).

(*d*) Holiday pay under the scheme in the building and civil engineering industries, and similar schemes, where a number of employers contribute to a central holiday pay fund. Neither the holiday pay itself (whether paid directly from the fund, or by an employer who is reimbursed for it out of the fund), nor the amounts used to buy the special stamps which build up entitlement under the scheme are included in the gross pay figure.

(*e*) Wages in lieu of notice.

(*f*) Gratuities received by the employee directly, or through a "tronc" operated independently of the employer.

(*g*) Payments made to or by trustees—as under certain profit-sharing schemes—where the amount allocated to each person is or may be at the trustees' discretion, and where the trustees do not ordinarily make more than two such payments a year to any person.

ACCOUNTING TREATMENT OF P.A.Y.E.

Deduction of Tax. The amount of tax to be deducted will vary according to the personal circumstances of the employee and the amount he has earned so far during the tax year. The individual amounts will be recorded on each employee's tax deduction card and the total deducted will be deducted from the net wages paid.

The gross amount of wages is debited to wages account and cash is credited with the net amount paid. The tax deducted is credited to P.A.Y.E. Tax (or Collector of Taxes) account.

Graduated National Insurance Contribution. The deduction card will also record the employees' contributions under the graduated scheme. At £20 per week, these are 54p per head if they are not contracted out. To this must be added the employer's contribution of a like amount. The entries required are similar to those already illustrated for the flat-rate scheme. That is, the employees' contributions are deducted from the net pay, but the employer's contributions are debited as an additional expense.

Since the amount is payable to the Revenue with the P.A.Y.E. deducted, then the total of the two contributions may be credited with the P.A.Y.E. to the Collector of Taxes Account. The title may be amended to read P.A.Y.E. and Graduated Contributions (or Collector of Taxes P.A.Y.E. and Graduated Contributions). Alternatively, separate accounts may be maintained.

Example 13

The entries can best be illustrated by using the example used earlier in relation to National Insurance. If the amount of P.A.Y.E. tax deducted from the 100 men is £300; S.E.T. is £240; Redundancy Fund contributions £6; employer's contribution to the flat-rate National Insurance £215, and Graduated contributions are 100 at £0·54 = £54 from both employer and employee.

The entries will be—

	£	£
Debit Wages Account	2,000	
Debit Employer's contribution to N.I.—		
flat-rate	215	
graduated	54	
Debit Redundancy Fund contribution	6	
Debit S.E.T.	240	
Credit Cash		1,558
Credit N.I. Stamps		549
Credit N.I. Graduated contribution		108
Credit P.A.Y.E.		300
	2,515	2,515

The net amount payable to employees before P.A.Y.E. and Graduated contributions was:

	£	£
Net amount payable to employees before P.A.Y.E. and graduated pensions		1,912
P.A.Y.E. deducted	300	
Employees' graduated contribution	54	
		354
Net sum of wages payable		1,558

The student who contemplates going into business may well be deterred by the complexities he faces in simply paying wages to his employees. He may also consider that fact that, in our example, the gross cost to the firm of wages paid was £2,254. Out of this the employees have been left with £1,573 in the form of take-home pay.

This example also ignores training levy.

PAYMENT OF TAX TO THE COLLECTOR

Monthly Remittances. The total of the P.A.Y.E. deducted, less any tax refunded, during an income-tax month must be paid to the Collector within fourteen days of the end of that month. It is sufficient to send a single remittance to cover this tax payment and any graduated National Insurance contributions which may be due. The Remittance Card (P30), which should be sent to the Collector with each payment, should show how the total payment is made up between income tax and graduated National Insurance contributions.

Refunds Exceeding Deductions. If the amount of tax refunded to employees during any month exceeds the amount deducted during that month, the employer may deduct the excess from the tax to be paid to the Collector for the following month, or he may apply to the tax office for reimbursement.

ERRORS IN DEDUCTING OR REFUNDING TAX

Check the Entries on the Cards. It is very important that the entries on the Deduction Cards should be made correctly, and a check of the additions and subtractions on the cards is desirable. The tax which the employer is liable to pay over is the total tax deductible as shown by the Tax Tables.

Errors Discovered during the Year. If the employer finds during the course of the year that an error has been made in deducting tax in an earlier week or month of the year, the matter should be put right in the week or month in which the error is discovered.

Large Under-deductions of Income Tax. No attempt should be made to adjust an under-deduction if it is so large that it cannot be put right in the week or month in which it is discovered. Any such case should be reported at once to the tax office, which will give any instructions necessary.

Entries on Payment of Tax and Graduated Contributions. The total amount payable should be debited to P.A.Y.E. and Graduated Contributions or Collector of Taxes' Account and credited to cash.

Example 14

In Example 11 the amount would be the deductions and contributions for the month. If these are P.A.Y.E. and contributions for five weeks the entries would be—

		£	£
(*a*)	*Debit* P.A.Y.E.	1,500	
	Debit Graduated Contributions	270	
	Credit Collector of Taxes		1,770
(*b*)	*Debit* Collector of Taxes	1,770	
	Credit Cash		1,770

Since the tax is payable monthly in arrears, the Collector of Taxes Account will normally show a credit balance which will appear as a current liability in the Balance Sheet.

TREATMENT OF CORPORATION TAX

Employees assessed under Schedule E pay tax under the P.A.Y.E. scheme and have no problem in providing for tax, as it is deducted from their pay before they receive it.

The employer deducting the tax is liable for this to the Inland Revenue and the accounting treatment has been outlined under the section in accounting for P.A.Y.E. and deductions.

Businesses liable for tax under the other schedules and for Corporation Tax, however, are called upon to pay the tax on their income in the year following that in which they earn it. In consequence, the problem of how to provide for tax arises. If tax were at 50p in the £, a firm or a person making a profit of £2,000 in 1969–70 would be called upon to pay £1,000 tax in the year 1970–1, and the date for paying this would be 1st January, 1971. There is no legal requirement, of course, as to where the money is to come from, and the firm or person could, if they wished, pay the tax out of their earnings for 1970–1. In so doing they are meeting their legal liability for tax in 1970–1. However, if this policy is followed consistently throughout the firm's life it may have serious consequences if the firm's profits fall or if the firm ceases business. If the firm's profits fall, the smaller profit will have to meet a demand for tax arising from the larger profits of the previous year. A similar position may occur at the end of the firm's life when the Revenue have the option of assessing profits to attract the maximum tax.

Example 15

The Alpha Co. Ltd. meets its liability out of current profits. Corporation Tax is at 50 per cent and profits in the years ended on 31st December are as follows—

Year Ended	Profits	Tax Liability	Available for Dividends
	£	£	£
31st December, 1970	2,000	*Nil* (first year)	2,000
1971	3,000	1,000	2,000
1972	4,000	1,500	2,500
1973	2,000	2,000	*Nil*

As the company is debiting the profit and loss account with the amount *payable* each year instead of the amount *arising* from the profits made, the amount of profit available for dividends bears little relationship to the profitability of the company. Although profits in 1971 and 1972 increase to twice the 1970 level, the amount available for dividend is increased by only one-quarter. In 1973 a reduced profit of £2,000 has to bear tax on £4,000, with the result that no profit at all is available for dividend!

Provision for Tax. The prudent policy to follow is, clearly, to set aside an amount from each year's profits sufficient to meet the liability which is likely to arise on them in the next tax year. The general principles for making Provisions are dealt with on p. 0220. A simple Provision for Corporation Tax may be made or a Sinking Fund may be set up and an amount corresponding to the provision invested outside the firm, or in tax reserve certificates.

Provisions for Tax. Up to 1965, companies were liable to Income Tax and Profits Tax, but since that date they have been made subject to Corporation Tax which is levied on the profits of an accounting period. Since April 1973 this is payable under the imputation system.

The Corporation Tax on current profits will normally be payable until the following year, but full provision should be made for the tax when the profit arises. Failure to do this could give rise to serious difficulties in a year when profits fall. Where the appropriate rate is not known, the current rate should be used.

The Companies Act provides that any sum set aside to prevent undue fluctuations in charges for taxation (Tax Equalization Provision) shall not be treated as a reserve unless the amount set aside exceeds the amount which the directors consider to be reasonable necessary.

Example 16

The Alpha Co. Ltd. decided to make provision for Corporation Tax out of current profits at the rate of 50 per cent. Show the profit and loss and corporation tax accounts for the years 1969–73, if profits and liability are as shown in Example 1.

Solution 16

PROFIT AND LOSS ACCOUNT TO 31ST DECEMBER, 19..

	£		£
Year 1969–70			
Provision for Tax	1,000	Net profit	2,000
Balance c/f	1,000		
	2,000		2,000
Year 1970–1			
Provision for Tax	1,500	Balance b/f	1,000
Balance c/f	2,500	Net profit for year	3,000
	4,000		4,000
Year 1971–2			
Provision for Tax	2,000	Balance b/f	2,500
Balance c/f	4,500	Net profit for year	4,000
	6,500		6,500
Year 1972–3			
Provision for Tax	1,000	Balance b/f	4,500
Balance c/f	5,500	Net profit for year	2,000
	6,500		6,500

The result may be summarized as follows—

Year Ended	Profits	Tax Provided	Available for Dividends
	£	£	£
31st December, 1970	2,000	1,000	1,000
1971	3,000	1,500	1,500
1972	4,000	2,000	2,000
1973	2,000	1,000	1,000

NOTE. For the purposes of simplicity, the law relating to the tax payable on new businesses has been ignored in these examples.

CORPORATION TAX ACCOUNT

			£				£
Year 1969–70							
	Balance c/d	. . .	1,000	Dec 31	P. & L. A/c .	. .	1,000
Year 1970–1							
Dec 31	Balance c/d .	. .	2,500	Jan 1	Balance b/d .	. .	1,000
				Dec 31	P. & L. A/c .	. .	1,500
			2,500				2,500
Year 1971–2							
Jan 1	Cash .	. .	1,000	Jan 1	Balance b/d .	. .	2,500
Dec 31	Balance c/d .	. .	3,500	Dec 31	P. & L. A/c .	. .	2,000
			4,500				4,500
Year 1972–3							
Jan 1	Cash .	. .	1,500	Jan 1	Balance b/d .	. .	3,500
Dec 31	Balance c/d .	. .	3,000	Dec 31	P. & L. A/c .	. .	1,000
			4,500				4,500
Year 1973–4							
Jan 1	Cash .	. .	2,000	Jan 1	Balance b/d .	. .	3,000

Example 17

If Alpha Co. Ltd. decided to put aside an amount of money in investments corresponding to the provision for tax, additional entries would be needed as follows—

CASH ACCOUNT

		£			£
			1970 Dec 31	Tax Reserve Investments A/c	1,000
			1971 Dec 31	" " " "	1,500
1972 Jan 1	Interest on Tax Reserve Investments A/c[2]	40	1972 Dec 31	" " " " .	2,000
1973 Jan 1	Interest on Tax Reserve Investments A/c	60	1973 Dec 31	" " " "	1,000

TAX RESERVE INVESTMENTS ACCOUNT

		£			£
1970 Dec 31	Cash	1,000			
1971 Dec 31	"	1,500			
1972 Dec 31	"	2,000	1972 Jan 1	Income Tax A/c[1] . . .	1,000
1973 Dec 31	. . . .	1,000	1973 Jan 1	" " " . . .	1,500

[1] The corresponding debit in the Income Tax A/c would read "Tax Reserve Investments A/c". instead of "Cash" as shown in Example 2.
[2] The rate of interest is taken at 4 per cent.

Deduction of Tax at Source. In principle, tax must be deducted at source. A person making a payment which is in the nature of annual income is responsible for deducting tax at the full standard rate. This principle is generally found when debenture interest, royalties and ground rent are paid. The payer retains tax at the basic rate and must account to the Inland Revenue for the amount so deducted.

This affects the company in two different ways—

1. Payments of Income. If the company pays interest on debentures or other loans, it must deduct the tax before payment.

2. Receipts of Income. If the company receives income in the form of debenture interest, the payer will already have deducted tax. The tax paid on this franked income may be offset against the tax deducted from payments.

The Imputation System. The imputation system of Corporation Tax is intended to work so that a single rate of tax is paid on the company's profits irrespective of whether they are paid out as dividends or retained.

Advanced Corporation Tax (A.C.T.). Whenever a company pays a dividend, it is required to make, within one month, a payment of Corporation Tax in advance (A.C.T.).

A.C.T. is calculated in such a way that the actual dividend paid is treated as if it had been paid after deduction of the tax.

Example 18

A company pays dividends of £23,800 and A.C.T. is payable at 30 per cent. The amount of A.C.T. is $\frac{3}{7}$ of £23,800 (not $\frac{3}{10}$)—

Dividends paid	£23,800
A.C.T. three-sevenths of £23,800 .	£10,200

The total cash paid by the company is thus £34,000.

The accounting entries are—

	£	£
Dr. Ordinary Share Dividends .	23,800	
Dr. Advance Corporation Tax .	10,200	
Cr. Cash		34,000

Due Date for Corporation Tax. Apart from the payments in advance, Corporation Tax becomes payable within nine months of the end of a company's year, or one month after an assessment of the Corporation Tax payable is determined.

Recovery of A.C.T. When A.C.T. has been paid, because of dividends, it may be deducted from the company's total liability for Corporation Tax on its income only. This is not the total Corporation Tax payable, because a company is liable for Corporation Tax both on its income and on its capital gains.

Surplus A.C.T. The deduction of A.C.T. is limited to a maximum of 30 per cent of the trading income. Any A.C.T. disallowed in the current year is surplus A.C.T. The company may claim to spread such surplus back over Corporation Tax paid in the previous years or it may be carried forward indefinitely.

Example 19

During an accounting period, a company paid A.C.T. of £9,060, of which £6,000 was allowed against Corporation Tax due on the taxable income. The entries required would be—

	£	£
Dr. Surplus A.C.T. . . .	3,060	
Dr. Corporation Tax . .	6,000	
Cr. Advance Corporation Tax .		9,060

Mainstream Corporation Tax (M.C.T.). The net liability to tax which remains after A.C.T. has been deducted from the Corporation Tax liable on the trading income is called the Mainstream Corporation Tax. When Corporation Tax is at the rate of 50 per cent, the net liability for M.C.T. is therefore 20 per cent minimum.

Debenture and Loan Interest Paid. The treatment of these items is that the company will debit the gross amount to the general profit and loss account, and is obliged to pay the recipient only the *net* amount.

Example 20

In 1969–70 Beta Company Ltd. have a net profit of £20,000, after having deducted £200 gross interest paid on debentures. The basic rate of tax is 30 per cent. Show the appropriate entries.

Although the gross amount of debenture interest has been deducted, the amount paid would be after deduction of tax at basic rate. The entries would be—

	£	£
Dr. Debenture Interest . .	200	
Cr Collector of Taxes . . .		60
Cr. Debenture-holders . . .		140

DIVIDENDS AND INTEREST RECEIVED

Dividends and interest received which have suffered deduction of income tax or Corporation Tax, if applicable, are known as "franked investment income." Advanced Corporation Tax cannot be refunded but the income tax may be offset against the company's deduction of income tax from its own interest and dividend payments.

Example 21

Beta Company Ltd., as above, have also received £70 net dividends at the end of 1969. Show the accounting entries.

The appropriate entries would be—

	£	£
Dr. Cash	70	
Dr. Advance Corporation Tax .	30	
Cr. Dividends received . .		100

Surplus Franked Income. If a company suffers a greater deduction of tax on the franked investment income which it *receives* than it is able to deduct from its payments, then the surplus can be carried forward to another year.

Example 22

In 1970, Ceta deducted income tax of £80 from dividends and interest paid. The following year it deducted £200 because of higher dividends. It suffered deductions of £110 on franked investment income in each year. Show the accounts for the Collector of Taxes.

Solution 22

COLLECTOR OF TAXES ACCOUNT

			£				£
1970				1970			
Dec	31	Dividends and Interest received	110	Dec	31	Dividends and Interest paid	80
						Balance c/f	30
			110				110
1971				1971			
Jan	1	Balance b/f	30	Dec	31	Dividends and Interest paid	200
Dec	31	Dividends and Interest received	110				
	31	Balance c/f	60				
			200				200
1972				1972			
Jan	14	Cash	60	Jan	1	Balance b/f	60

Treatment of Corporation Tax. Corporation tax is assessed and charged on the full amount of a company's profits arising in its accounting period. Profits are to be computed by aggregating the company's income from all sources, together with its long-term capital gains.

Normally, the income of a company for corporation tax purposes is to be computed in the same way as for income tax. The computation and assessment are made under the same Schedules and Cases as for income tax and in accordance with the rules applicable to those Schedules and Cases.

Example 23

A company has a total income and chargeable gains of £60,000 in the year ended 31st December, 1975, of which £26,000 is trading income and £34,000 chargeable gains. Against this, it has charges allowable of £6,000. Included in the income are dividends received of £2,660 net.

During the year, the company paid dividends of £23,800. A.C.T. is payable at 30 per cent and Corporation Tax at 50 per cent.

Calculate the Corporation Tax payable and the surplus or deficit on A.C.T.

The following calculation may be made—

Solution 23

	£	*Corporation Tax at 50%*
Income—Trading	26,000	
Chargeable	34,000	
Less Charges	6,000	
Total Income liable to Corporation Tax	54,000	
Dividends Paid, £23,800		
A.C.T. three-sevenths of £23,800	10,200	
Dividends Received £2,660		
A.C.T. three-sevenths of £2,660	1,140	
Net A.C.T. payable	9,060	
Total Corporation Tax £54,000 × 50%	27,000	
Corporation Tax on chargeable gains £34,000 × 50%	17,000	17,000
Corporation Tax on trading income	10,000	
Minimum M.C.T. 20% of £26,000*	4,000	4,000
Maximum M.C.T. allowed against A.C.T.	6,000	
Net A.C.T. paid	9,060	Corporation Tax payable:
Allowed against Corporation Tax on the trading income	6,000	9 months after end of year £21,000
Surplus A.C.T.	£3,060	

* This assumes that the £6,000 charges are freely deductible from Corporation Tax on income.

Recoverable Surplus A.C.T. Where surplus A.C.T. arises because A.C.T. in one tax year would reduce Mainstream Corporation Tax to below 20 per cent in that year, then, in the first place it may be recovered from Corporation Tax suffered in the previous two years. Of course, recovery is only possible up to the limitation that Corporation Tax must be at least 20 per cent of the trading income in each year.

Example 24

Suppose, in our example, that £2,000 of Surplus A.C.T., £3,060, is recoverable against previous years, the entries would be—

	£	£
Dr. Corporation Tax . . .	2,000	
Cr. A.C.T.		2,000

There remains £1,060 Surplus A.C.T. If it is anticipated that there is a reasonable chance of recovering this against Corporation Tax in subsequent years, then it may be carried forward to the next year.

Irrecoverable Surplus A.C.T. If it is anticipated that Surplus A.C.T. is not likely to be recovered in later years, then the balance in the Surplus A.C.T. account should be written off to Profit and Loss Appropriation account.

Example 25

Suppose the remaining Surplus A.C.T. of £1,060 cannot be expected to be recovered in later years, then the entries will be—

	£	£
Dr. Profit and Loss Appropriation	1,060	
Cr. Surplus A.C.T.		1,060

ACCOUNTING FOR CAPITAL ALLOWANCES AND INVESTMENT GRANTS

Capital Allowances. The Capital Allowances Act 1968, as modified by subsequent Finance Acts, states the allowances which may be made in respect of some (but not all) capital expenditure and how they are to be calculated. These allowances apply to trades and businesses (whether incorporated or not) but only some of them apply to professions and employments.

The effect of the allowances is that depreciation is not allowed as a deduction from trading profits. Instead, capital allowances are calculated and allowed as a deduction in charging the profits (excluding depreciation) for the year.

Relevant Grants. The principal forms of relevant grants are grants in respect of machinery or plant paid by the Board of Trade under the Industrial Development Act, 1966; by the Government of Northern Ireland under the Capital Grants to Industry legislation; and grants to be paid by the Ministry of Agriculture, Fisheries and Food towards the cost of tractors and combine harvesters. Grants are deducted from expenditure before allowing capital allowances and certain forms of allowance may not be given.

Classes of Allowance

The allowances differ for different classes of expenditure, and some details are set out under the headings below. As regards machinery or plant, the system applies also to professions and employments.

Investment Allowances. For expenditure incurred before 17th January, 1966 (and also expenditure on assets contracted for before that date and brought into use not later than 16th January, 1968, unless a relevant grant was paid in respect of such expenditure) the system also provided for "investment" allowances. The essential feature of the investment allowance was that it was given *in addition to* the ordinary capital allowances (which normally amount to the full net cost of the asset).

Industrial Buildings. The initial allowance at the rate of 15 per cent was given only for expenditure on the construction of industrial buildings or structures, not for expenditure on the purchase of a used building. The writing-down allowance was normally 2 per cent of the cost of construction in the case of expenditure incurred on or before 5th November, 1962, (but could be at a different rate if the building changed hands) and was given until any initial allowance and the writing-down allowances had together written off the cost of construction (or, in the case of a building erected before 6th April, 1946, until it was fifty years old). The cost of preparing, cutting, tunnelling or levelling land in connexion with the construction of an industrial building was included as from 6th April, 1956, in the expenditure ranking for the allowances. On the sale or scrapping of an industrial building within the fifty-year period, a balancing allowance could be claimed if the proceed were less than the unallowed expenditure; if the proceeds exceed the unallowed expenditure a balancing charge was made.

The writing-down allowance in respect of expenditure incurred after 5th November, 1962, was normally 4 per cent of the expenditure. The period in which a balancing charge or allowance may be made in connexion with such expenditure was twenty-five years.

These allowances were in 1968, in general, confined to buildings used in manufacturing, processing or extractive industry, and in transport, water or power undertakings. Allowances for capital expenditure on dredging were given at the same rates as for industrial buildings if, broadly, the expenditure was incurred for the purposes of productive industry.

Machinery or Plant. The initial allowance at the rate of 30 per cent was given where due on the cost of new or secondhand machinery or plant (other than ordinary motor cars). Writing-down allowances for new plant or machinery on which expenditure was incurred after 5th November, 1962, were in the main at one of three rates; 15 per cent (the minimum rate), 20 per cent, or 25 per cent, according to the type of plant concerned. These rates continue to apply to machinery or plant if it changes hands. For expenditure incurred on or before 5th November, 1962, the writing-down allowances vary according to the type of plant concerned; a "basic rate" of allowance is computed so as to write the cost of the plant down to 10 per cent at, broadly speaking, the end of its estimated working life and allowances are given at five-fourths of the basic rate. There was a balancing allowance or charge when the asset was sold or scrapped.

Rates of Initial and Investment Allowances

Year of Expenditure	1957–8 from 10 Apr. 1957	1958–59 from 15 Apr. 1958	1959–60 to 1962–3 from 8 Apr. 1959	1963–4 and 1964–5; 1965–6 To 16 Jan. 1966	1965–6 From 17 Jan. 1966(*i*)	1966–7
Initial Allowances—	%	%	%	%	%	%
New industrial buildings	10	15				
Insulation of industrial and agricultural buildings .	—	15(*a*)	5	5	15	15
Dredging	10	15				
New ships	—	—	—	—(*k*)	—(*k*)	—(*k*)
New mining works	40	40	20	20(*h*)	40	40
Fuel-saving plant	—	30(*a*)	10	10	30	30
Private cars and second-hand plant and ships .	20	30	30(*f*)	30(*f*)	30(*j*)	30(*j*)
Other new plant and machinery . . .	20	30	10	10(*h*)	30(*j*)	30(*j*)
Investment Allowances on New Assets—						
Industrial buildings, and agricultural and forestry buildings and works	—	—				
Insulation of industrial and agricultural buildings .	10	10(*a*)	10(*g*)	15	—	—
Dredging	—	—				
Ships	40	40	40	40	—	—
Mining works	—	—				
Scientific research assets(*d*)	20	20	20(*g*)	30	—	—
Fuel-saving plant	20	20(*a*)				
Other plant and machinery(*e*)	—	—				

(*a*) Either the initial allowance or the investment allowance may be claimed but not both.

(*b*) Relates to expenditure in the basis period for 1956–7 assessments.

(*c*) Expenditure on the construction of new ships ordered before 11th April, 1951, continued to qualify for an initial allowance of 40 per cent if the investment allowance was not claimed.

(*d*) Expenditure on assets for scientific research has never qualified for the initial allowance; from 1949–50 until 5th November, 1962, the annual allowance in the first year was 60 per cent, followed by 10 per cent in each of the succeeding four years. From 6th November, 1962, the expenditure is allowed wholly in the first year.

(*e*) Including new plant and machinery on the renewals basis but excluding ordinary motor cars.

(*f*) For cars costing more than £2,000 acquired after 16th April, 1961, the initial allowance is restricted. There is no allowance for cars acquired after 6th April 1965.

(*g*) From 6th November, 1962, the 10 per cent and 20 per cent rates were increased to 15 per cent and 30 per cent respectively.

(*h*) Free depreciation is allowed for capital expenditure incurred after 3rd April, 1963, on certain new plant and machinery for use in Northern Ireland and the development districts designated by the Board of Trade, and in mining works there. Free depreciation was extended to new ships from 1965–66. Free depreciation (except for new ships) was withdrawn from 17th January, 1966.

(*i*) Under the Industrial Development Act, 1966, new plant and machinery in manufacturing industry will qualify for a grant of 20 per cent of expenditure (40 per cent in development areas) instead of investment and initial allowances. For the two years 1967 and 1968, from 1st January, 1967, the rates are increased to 25 per cent and 45 per cent respectively. Only the net expenditure after deduction of grants will qualify for capital allowances.

(*j*) No allowance for private cars or for plant and machinery qualifying for Investment Grants.

(*k*) Free depreciation from 6th April, 1965.

In certain instances a "renewals allowance" was given in place of the writing-down allowances, the cost of renewing the asset, excluding any element of betterment, being allowed as a deduction in computing the profits.

The Finance Act 1971 made radical changes in the system of capital allowances by introducing a "first-year allowance" and the "pooling system" for subsequent allowances.

FIRST-YEAR ALLOWANCE. This allowance is given in the year in which plant and machinery is acquired, generally at the rate of 60 per cent (raised to 80 per cent in July 1971) but at 100 per cent in development areas and Northern Ireland. In the case of motor vehicles, only *commercial* vehicles are eligible for the first-year allowance.

THE POOLING SYSTEM. Instead of considering each asset separately in calculating capital allowances, the pooling system puts together all expenditure on plant and machinery eligible for allowances and from this is deducted all the first year allowances and the total value of all disposals or withdrawals from use during the period. The balance remaining will then attract an annual allowance of 25 per cent. Private cars costing more than £4,000 are not admitted to the pool.

This procedure eliminates balancing allowances. Balancing charges will only arise if the proceeds from disposals in any year exceed the qualifying expenditure or when the business ends.

CLAIM TO PART ALLOWANCES. A company may disclaim or claim only part of a first-year allowance during any two-year period following acquisition of the asset.

Individuals may similarly claim a reduced annual writing-down allowance (there is no time limit in this case).

The effect of these rights is to allow postponement of the allowances when a company or individual has insufficient profits against which to offset them.

Mining Assets. Initial allowance at the rate of 40 per cent and writing-down allowances (computed by reference to the rate of exhaustion of the mineral deposit, subject to a minimum rate of 5 per cent) were given on capital expenditure on the construction of mining works. Writing-down allowances were also given in respect of expenditure on mineral exploration and discovery, and, since 6th April, 1949, in respect of capital expenditure on overseas mineral rights. Since the year 1963–4 allowances have been given in respect of expenditure incurred by a mining operator in acquiring a source of mineral deposits in the United Kingdom. There are balancing allowances or charges when mining assets are sold by the business as a going concern, or (in the case of allowances for mineral rights) when the operator ceases to work the source.

Patent Rights. Relief is given in respect of capital expenditure on the acquisition of patent rights provided that the rights were acquired for the purposes of a trade which was liable to United Kingdom tax, or the buyer would be liable to United Kingdom tax on any income from the rights.

Expenditure on Scientific Research. Capital expenditure incurred by a trader on scientific research related to his trade was allowed as a deduction in computing his profits. A trader could also deduct from his taxable profits payments to approved scientific research associations, universities, etc., for research related to his trade.

Losses

A loss in trade could be carried forward and set off against future profits of the same business. A loss in the last year of a business which had been discontinued could in certain circumstances be carried back and set off against profits of that business for the three preceding years. Alternatively, a loss could be set off against other income of the year in which the loss is incurred or the following year, but only if the trade was being carried on on a commercial basis and with a view to the realization of profit (there were certain restrictions to this right of set-off where a farmer or market gardener incurs a succession of losses).

A loss was computed in the same way as a profit except that, subject to certain conditions, account may also be taken of allowances for capital expenditure.

The allowances may be summarized as on pp. 2864–5.

INVESTMENT GRANTS

Under the Industrial Development Act, 1966, the Board of Trade made cash grants for capital expenditure incurred from 16th January, 1966 to 27th October, 1970 to individuals, partnerships and companies, including foreign firms, investing in plant and machinery in qualifying industrial processes. The grants also varied according to the area in which plant was located.

Qualifying Industrial Processes. The definition of processes was obscure but included manufacturing; quarrying, mining and extractive processes; construction and scientific research relating to these.

Qualifying Assets. Irrespective of the process, computers, ships and hovercraft were eligible for grants.

Qualifying Areas. The grants did not apply to Northern Ireland, which had a more generous scheme.

In *development areas* the grants in respect of processes were at a higher level. The qualifying assets were not subject to different grants in development areas.

Level of Grants. In general the grants were 20 per cent of the capital expenditure; 40 per cent in development areas, but these were raised to 25 per cent and 45 per cent respectively for the two calendar years 1967 and 1968.

Ineligible Assets. Certain assets, wherever employed, were ineligible for the grants. These were office furniture and equipment, canteen and welfare equipment; aircraft; road vehicles; and buildings.

Minimum expenditure of £25 had to be incurred.

Conditions and Repayments. The assets had to be brought into use within six months and had to be owned and used for three years from the date of application for grant or from completion of installation or construction. Where construction extended over a period, instalments on the grants were paid by the Board.

In the case of new ships, the period of use was five years.

Applications and Certification. Applications had to be made on the prescribed forms to the local Investment Grant Office of the Board of Trade and must be accompanied by a certificate from an accountant recognized as an auditor by the Board of Trade.

Tax Status. Since they were in the nature of capital receipts, capital grants were not taxable but they are deducted from the cost of the asset in calculating capital allowances.

Accounting Treatment of Investment Grants. The accounting of governments grants has varied in the past, but with the advent of regional development grants under the Industry Act 1972, the Accounting Standards Steering Committee (A.S.S.C.) proposed that a standard treatment should be adopted.

Their exposure draft ED9 states that three main ways of accounting for grants may be considered:

1. Credit the grant to Profit and Loss account immediately.
2. Credit the grant to a non-distributable reserve, i.e. a capital reserve.
3. Credit the grant to revenue over the useful life of the asset, in one of two ways—

(*a*) Reducing the cost of the asset (the net cost basis) on acquisition.

(*b*) Treating the grant as a deferred credit and transferring part to the credit of Profit and Loss account each year.

Accounting Entries. If we take as an example a machine acquired for £100,000 for which a grant is payable of £20,000 and which has a five-year life, at the end of which it has no residual value, the entries to be made under each method will be—

Acquisition of asset. If we assume that the grant is received at some time after the date of acquisition of the asset, then all methods will record the acquisition:

Dr. Asset account . . .	£100,000	
Cr. Cash (or creditor) . .		£100,000

Receipt of or accrual of grant. All methods will involve the same debit:

Dr. Cash or Grants receivable	£20,000

The difference between the methods lies firstly in the credits, which will be as follows:

Method 1	
Cr. Profit and Loss account	£20,000
Method 2	
Cr. Capital (or non-distributable) Reserve .	£20,000
Method 3 (*a*)	
Cr. Asset account	£20,000
Method 3 (*b*)	
Cr. Deferred Investment Grants . . .	£20,000

Effect on Reported Earnings and Balance Sheets. Each method will result in some differences in the reported profits and the value of the asset as shown on the Balance Sheets, as follows:

Arguments For and Against. *Method* 1. Treats the receipt of grant as an exceptional item of revenue in the year of receipt or accrual. Since grants have been varied considerably from year to year, the current effect of current grants is shown. However, like Method 2, it shows no correlation between the accounting treatment of the grant and the related expenditure.

Method 2. Treats the grant as a contribution to the capital fund of the firm, which arguably, the grant is rather than a contribution to revenue which the other methods assume. An additional objection to this method is that it will retain the Reserve on the Balance Sheets indefinitely into the future.

Method 3(*a*). Treats the grant as a reduction of the cost of the asset and, like 3(*b*), matches the grants to the expenditures. However, it understates the cost of the asset and if grants change the apparent cost of otherwise identical assets may be different. Moreover, control of expenditures and calculation of capital allowances is based on the gross cost of assets before grants.

Method 3(*b*). Treats the grants as revenue and matches this with the life of the asset.

Recommended standard. Method 3(*b*) has been recommended for adoption. If material, the amount of deferred credit to Profit and Loss should be disclosed and the Balance Sheet should show the deferred amounts under a separate heading.

The entries required under each method are shown on p. 2870.

CAPITAL ALLOWANCES AND DEPRECIATION

The capital allowances for tax purposes do not necessarily coincide with the commercial charge for depreciation. The treatment of capital expenditure on assets for income tax purposes is governed by the Capital Allowances Act 1968, and in the cases of patent, the Income and Corporation Tax Act 1970, as modified by subsequent Finance Acts. Generally these provisions apply to trades and businesses and not to professions and employment, but some provisions *do* apply to these income sources.

As from 1961–2 capital allowances for machinery and plant were

	Profit and Loss Accounts: Debits	Profit and Loss Accounts: Credits	Balance Sheets: Assets side	Balance Sheets: Liabilities side
Method 1	Depreciation £20,000 per annum for 5 years.	Grant £20,000 in Year 1.	*Year 1* Assets at cost . £100,000 *Less* Depreciation 20,000 Net book value . 80,000 *Year 2* Net book value . 60,000 and so on.	*Year 1* Retained earnings increased by £20,000. *Years 2–5* No effect.
Method 2	Depreciation £20,000 per annum for 5 years.	None.	As in Method 1.	*Year 1* Capital (non-distributable) Reserve increases to £20,000. *Year 2 onward* The £20,000 will remain in reserve.
Method 3 (*a*)	Depreciation £16,000 per annum for 5 years.	None.	*Year 1* Assets at cost . £100,000 *Less* Grants . 20,000 Net cost . . 80,000 *Less* Depreciation 16,000 Net book value . 64,000 *Year 2* Net book value . 48,000 and so on.	No effect.
Method 3 (*b*)	Depreciation £20,000 per annum for 5 years.	Investment Grant £4,000 per annum for 5 years.	*Year 1* Assets at cost . £100,000 *Less* Depreciation 20,000 Net book value . 80,000 (as in Method 1) and so on.	*Year 1* Deferred Investment Grants £20,000 *Less* Credits to P. & L. 4,000 Deferred at end of year . 16,000 *Year 2* Deferred at end of year . 12,000 and so on.

given to life assurance companies, investment companies, savings banks and certain industrial and provident societies.

The Basis Period. Under Sect. 72 of the 1968 Act, the allowance and charges are provided for in the year of assessment during the "basis period" giving rise to the charge or allowance. The "basis period" is usually the accounting period on which the assessment has been made, e.g. if accounts are prepared annually on 31st December, the accounts for the year ending 31st December, 1969, will provide the basis for assessment in 1970–1. Special provisions for new and discontinued businesses and for changes of accounting date ensure that no period is used as a basis more than once.

The basis period no longer applies to companies for whom the allowances are given in relation to the accounting year.

Computation of Business Profit. The profit and loss account of a business shows the profit which is available for dividends, and will normally make adequate allowance for depreciation. The directors of the firm will decide, in the light of financial policies and normal accounting principles, what an adequate allowance may be in the circumstances.

In adjusting accounts for income-tax purposes, we have to add back all items of depreciation and claim the reliefs to which the business may be entitled in accordance with the Acts, as already outlined.
Before 1971, the reliefs would be:

1. (*a*) Initial Allowances on the first cost, or
   (*b*) Investment Allowance.
2. Annual Allowance.
3. Balancing Allowances and Charges.

Annual Allowances. These allowances are equivalent to Depreciation and are normally calculated by the diminishing balance method.

In respect of machinery and plant, the normal allowance will be a percentage (fixed by the Commissioners of Inland Revenue) of the written-down value. An alternative method is provided by Sect. 21 of the 1968 Act, whereby a percentage (fixed by the Commissioners) of the original cost is written off each year.

Balancing Allowances and Charges. When industrial buildings, plant and machinery and mines, etc., are disposed of by sale, or are discarded by reason of obsolescence, there is to be a review of the total capital expenditure in relation to the allowances which have been granted in respect of it together with the amount realized by sale. For example—

	£
Capital expenditure on plant and machinery	8,000
Initial allowance and annual allowances	6,500
Balance unallowed	1,500
Amount realized (in year ended 31st December, 19. .)	450
Difference (balancing allowance)	1,050

In this case it will be seen that the amount unallowed is greater than the proceeds realized on discarding the assets. There will be a balancing allowance of £1,050 in the year of assessment 19.1/.2.

If the amount realized had been £2,000 instead of £450, we should have—

	£
Amount unallowed	1,500
Amount realized	2,000
Difference (balancing charge)	500

Here the trader has realized more than the cost of the plant as written down by the allowances, and there will be a balancing charge on £500.

There is a limitation on the amount of any balancing charge: it is not to exceed the amount of the initial allowance (if any) together with the aggregate of all annual allowances, in the case of buildings, or wear and tear allowances in the case of plant or machinery.

It should be noted that a balancing allowance may be claimed even though the machinery or plant is not replaced. If the taxpayer does replace the machinery or plant, he has an option to secure reductions in the amount of the balancing charge, if he thinks it will pay him to do so. It will be simpler to indicate the option by figures.

	£
Balancing charge on	620
Expenditure in providing new machinery . . .	540
Difference	80

The taxpayer can elect to have the balancing charge reduced to a charge on £80 only. But in that event he must forgo any title to initial allowance, annual allowance or balancing allowance in respect of the new machinery.

Where the expenditure in providing the new machinery exceeds the amount for the balancing charge, e.g.—

	£
Balancing charge on	620
New expenditure	750
Difference	130

the taxpayer can elect to have the balancing charge withdrawn, in which case the initial allowance for the new machinery will be calculated on £130 only, as will the annual allowances.

The intention of the 1968 Act is to make provision for tax relief on capital expenditure over an appropriate period of years with a system of adjustment at the end to ensure that the taxpayer gets by way of allowances neither more nor less than the original cost less residual proceeds.

Example 26

In the example of the plant costing £80,000, if the annual allowance is 20 per cent, then the Capital Allowance for tax purposes is calculated as follows—

		£
Cost of asset (eligible for capital allowances)		80,000
Year 1	Annual Allowance (20 per cent of £80,000)	16,000
		64,000
Year 2	Annual Allowance (20 per cent of £64,000)	12,800
		51,200
Year 3	Annual Allowance (20 per cent of £51,200)	10,240
Tax Book value at end of Year 3		40,960

If the asset is disposed of for £30,000, there would be a Balancing Allowance of £10,960.

Taxable Profits. If, in our example, the profits over the years are stable the amount of taxable profit would be smaller in the early years than the later years since the amount of annual allowance declines. The taxable profits and the Corporation Tax payable at 40 per cent would be—

	Year 1	Year 2	Year 3
	£	£	£
Sales	1,000,000	1,000,000	1,000,000
Less Operating costs	870,000	870,000	870,000
Operating profit before tax and depreciation	130,000	130,000	130,000
Capital allowances	16,000	12,800	10,240
Taxable profit	114,000	117,200	119,760
Corporation tax at 40 per cent	45,600	46,880	47,904

It can be seen that the tax charge rises as the amount of the capital allowances falls.

Renewals Basis. Instead of claiming capital allowances, the cost of replacing plant and machinery might be deducted from income in computing profits, and this is called the "renewals" basis. The taxpayer may choose to apply this basis to all or any part of his assets.

First-year Allowances and Pooling. If assets are acquired and used in areas which attract 100 per cent first-year allowances, then it will be possible to claim the full amount of eligible capital expenditure in the year when it is incurred.

In other cases, 60 per cent (80 per cent from July 1971) of each year's capital expenditure, plus 25 per cent of the balance in the pool will be claimed.

Example 27

In 1971, a company acquired assets for £5,000; in 1972 assets for £8,000; in 1973, assets for £10,000; in 1974, assets for £12,000. The assets acquired in 1971 were disposed of for £2,000 in 1973. Show your computation of the claim for capital allowances in each year assuming that all assets are eligible for 60 per cent first-year allowance and that pooled costs attract an annual writing-down allowance of 25 per cent.

Year	*Acquisition cost*	60% *First year Allowance*		*Pooled cost*	25% *Writing down Allowance*
	£	£		£	£
1971	5,000	3,000		2,000	500
1972	8,000	4,800		3,200	
			b/f	1,500	
				4,700	1,175
1973	10,000	6,000		4,000	
			b/f	3,525	
				7,525	
		less disposals		2,000	
				5,525	1,380
1974	12,000	7,200		4,800	
			b/f	4,145	
				8,945	2,239
1975			b/f	6,706	

The calculation for 1973 can be shown as follows:

		£
Assets acquired during the year		10,000
less first-year allowance		6,000
Balance of cost to pool		4,000
	£	
Balance from previous year	4,700	
less	1,175	
		3,525
Pooled costs		7,525
less disposals		2,000
Costs eligible for writing-down allowance		5,525
Writing-down allowance at 25%		1,380

PROVIDING FOR DEFERRED TAXATION

The amount of tax payable on the profits of any particular period often bears little relationship to the profits shown. There are many causes, but these result in two kinds of difference.

1. Permanent Differences. Permanent differences arise because some income is tax-free and some expenditures are not allowed for tax purposes. These differences are not usually accounted for because they are permanent. Their effect on the reported profits of any year must simply be accepted.

2. Timing Differences. Timing differences arise because some items are dealt with for tax purposes in one period and for business purposes in another period. Perhaps the most obvious timing differences arises from the differences between capital allowances and depreciation charges, but there are many other examples. For instance, a firm may make provisions for bad debts, thus reducing the reported profits, but for tax purposes only bad debts actually incurred will be allowed. Some companies may report income on an accruals basis but be taxed on a receipts and payments basis. In these, and many other cases, timing differences arise.

Changes in Tax Rates. One problem in accounting for the differences between the tax actually paid and that attributable to the profits for a period is that tax rates may change from time to time. Since provisions for differences must be made before future rates of tax are known, it is usual to calculate tax at the current rate. Thus, if the present rate of Corporation Tax in 50 per cent, provision will be made on this basis. If, however, the future rate of tax turns out to be 53 per cent, then the differences will have been underestimated.

Deferred Taxation. This is the taxation due to timing differences. It is accounted for by carrying timing differences to a Deferred Taxation account. These amounts are then carried forward to the period to which they are related and charged against Profit and Loss account. There may be both deferred credits and deferred debits.

Proposed Standard Method. Exposure draft 11 of the A.S.S.C., issued in May 1973, suggests that deferred taxation on all material timing differences should be accounted for, basing calculations either on each individual item or on groups of items giving rise to timing differences. Our next example illustrates the method proposed.

Example 28

A company buys Machine A in Year 1, for £10,000. The Corporation Tax rate is 50 per cent and a first capital allowance of 80 per cent is claimable, although depreciation is charged at 25 per cent on cost. In Year 2, the company buys Machine B for £20,000 and claims a first-year allowance of 100 per cent for tax purposes. During this and subsequent years, a writing down allowance is claimed on Machine A at 25 per cent of written down value (w.d.v.).

During the period, the company earns £50,000 per annum operating profit before charging depreciation and tax. Calculate the reported earnings, the actual Corporation Tax payable and the debits or credits to deferred taxation in each year.

Reported Earnings. The reported earnings are calculated by charging depreciation against the operating profits and the charging of the balance with Corporation Tax at the current rate. The calculations in Example 28 would show:

	Year 1	2	3	4
	£	£	£	£
Operating Profit before depreciation and tax	50,000	50,000	50,000	50,000
Depreciation: A	2,500	2,500	2,500	2,500
B	—	5,000	5,000	5,000
Profits after depreciation. . . .	47,500	42,500	42,500	42,500
Notional Corporation Tax 50%. . .	23,750	21,250	21,250	21,250
Reported Earnings	23,750	21,250	21,250	21,250

Corporation Tax Payable. The Corporation Tax payable is calculated by charging the capital allowances against the operating profits and then charging Corporation Tax on the balance at the current rate. The results for our example would be:

	Year 1	Year 2	Year 3	Year 4
	£	£	£	£
Operating Profit before capital allowances and tax	50,000	50,000	50,000	50,000
Capital Allowances: A	8,000	500	375	281
B	—	20,000	—	—
Taxable Profits	42,000	29,500	49,625	49,729
Corporation Tax at 50%	21,000	24,750	24,812	24,860

Deferred Taxation. There will be a credit to deferred taxation in any year that the notional Corporation Tax exceeds the actual tax payable. In our example, there are credits in the first two years because in those years 80 per cent of the cost of Machine A and 100 per cent of the cost of Machine B is allowable for tax, whilst only 25 per cent is charged for depreciation. Debits to deferred taxation arise in the next two years when actual tax exceeds the notional, as can be seen below:

	Year 1	Year 2	Year 3	Year 4
	£	£	£	£
Notional Corporation Tax	23,750	21,250	21,250	21,250
Actual Corporation Tax	21,000	14,750	24,812	24,860
Credited to Deferred Taxation	2,750	6,500	—	—
Debited to Deferred Taxation	—	—	3,562	3,610

The accounts for the four years will be as follows:

MACHINE A

	£		£
Year 1 Cash	10,000	Year 1 Profit and Loss Account (Depreciation)	2,500
		„ 2 „ „	2,500
		„ 3 „ „	2,500
		„ 4 „ „	2,500
	10,000		10,000

Machine B

		£			£
Year 2	. . . .	20,000	Year 2	Profit and Loss Account (Depreciation) .	5,000
			" 3	" " .	5,000
			" 4	" " .	5,000
			" 4	Balance carried down .	5,000
		20,000			20,000
Year 5	Balance brought down .	5,000			

Deferred Taxation

		£			£
			Year 1	Profit and Loss Account	2,750
Year 2	Balance carried down .	9,250	" 2	" " " .	6,500
		9,250			9,250
Year 3	Profit and Loss Account	3,562	" 3	Balance brought down	9,250
	Balance carried down .	5,688			
		9,250			9,250
Year 4	Profit and Loss Account	3,610	" 4	Balance brought down	5,688
	Balance carried down .	2,078			
		5,688			5,688
			" 5	Balance brought down	2,078

Corporation Tax Account

			Year 1	Profit and Loss Account	21,000
			" 2	" " "	14,750
			" 3	" " "	24,812
			" 4	" " "	24,860

The Corporation Tax shown in the Profit and Loss account each year will be the notional Tax. The Deferred Taxation balance will be shown as a separate item on the balance sheet if it is a material amount.

THE TREATMENT OF TAX IN COMPANY ACCOUNTS

A company has the same rights and obligations as the individual firm so far as the provision of tax is concerned, but as the rights of shareholders and creditors may be affected by the policy which the directors decide to follow in the treatment of tax, the following requirements are laid down by the Companies Act, 1967 (Second Schedule)—

Taxation shown must distinguish between—

(*a*) Charge to revenue for U.K. corporation tax and the amount before deduction of any double taxation relief and the basis of computation of the charge.

(*b*) Charge for U.K. income tax showing the basis of computation.

(*c*) Charge for overseas taxation of profits, income and capital gains so far as the latter are charged to revenue.

(*d*) Any special circumstances affecting liability in respect of taxation of profits, income or capital gains for the financial year or succeeding financial years.

THE CLASSIFICATION OF INCOME TAX IN THE BALANCE SHEET

Any liability for tax which is due but not paid should be shown as a current liability, but it is usually shown as a separate item from trade and other creditors.

If amounts have been set aside for tax which is not yet due although the amount may be known, there is considerable controversy about whether these amounts should be shown as reserves or provisions for tax, and considerable variation exists in practice. Many published balance sheets show an item "Amounts set aside for Taxation," which is classified neither as a reserve nor a provision.

The argument in favour of calling the amounts reserves is that these amounts are appropriations of profits and amounts taken from the appropriation account are invariably designated as reserves.

The argument in favour of calling them provisions is that they are amounts set aside to meet a specific liability, the amount of which cannot be determined with substantial accuracy (the legal definition of provisions).

ADJUSTMENT OF ACCOUNTS FOR ASSESSMENT OF INCOME TAX

The adjustment of accounts for income tax purposes is governed by considerations which may be presented as five rules. Commencing with the profit arrived at by the preparation of a profit and loss account—

1. Add any capital expenditure which has been charged against revenue and deduct any capital receipts for which credit has been taken.
2. Add back any personal expenses of the proprietor if any so charged.
3. Add any expenses not exclusively incurred in earning profits.
4. Add back any payments, such as royalties, from which tax has been deducted at the time of payment.
5. Add back any items carried to a reserve except a "specific" bad debts reserve.

Two Methods in Use. There are two methods of ascertaining the amount of profit assessable for income tax purposes—

1. To take the net profit shown by the profit and loss account, *add* back all those deductions which are not allowed by the income tax authorities, and *deduct* such items as are not taxable or have already been taxed.

2. To take the gross profit shown by the trading account and construct a new profit and loss account, including only such profits as are taxable, and only those losses and expenses which are allowed by the revenue authorities to be deducted. If this procedure is adopted it must be borne in mind that the trading account itself may contain inadmissible items, e.g. royalties, which must not be overlooked.

The student should accustom himself to both methods, although Method 2 is rarely operative except in cases where the book-keeping is defective.

Example 29

The following is the profit and loss account of Robert Reynolds, manufacturer, for the year ended 31st December, 19...

PROFIT AND LOSS ACCOUNT

		£		£
Bank Interest & Charges		20	Gross Profit as per Trading A/c	2,368
Subscriptions & Donations to Charities		15	Discounts Received	85
Trade Expenses		128	Profit on Sale of Investments	45
Income Tax. Sch. D		74	Dividends, *less* tax	24
Salaries		426		
Discounts Allowed		120		
Proprietor's Salary		260		
Repairs		32		
Bad Debts		87		
Bad Debts Reserve	£180			
Less Old Reserve	140			
		40		
Fire Insurance		18		
Office Expenses		37		
Loss by Cashier's Embezzlement (not covered by insurance)		60		
Depreciation—				
Lease		80		
Goodwill		35		
Plant & Machinery		46		
Interest on Loan		24		
Interest on Capital		120		
Ground Rent		25		
Balance (Net Profit)		875		
		2,522		

The inspector agrees to capital allowances of £25 on plant and machinery, and is prepared to admit as an expense £5 subscription to a local hospital at which employees receive treatment. R.R. claims £23 for life assurance premium.

Make up R. Reynolds's return for assessment for the current year.

First Method

PROFIT AND LOSS ADJUSTMENT ACCOUNT

	£		£
Deduction of Items—		Net Profit as per P. & L. A/c	875
Dividends (taxed)	24	Deductions not allowed, added back—	
Profit on Sale of Investments	45	Subscriptions & Donations	10
Balance (Assessable Profit)	1,520	Income Tax	74
		Proprietor's Salary	260
		Bad Debts Reserve	40
		Depreciation	161
		Interest on Loan	24
		Interest on Capital	120
		Ground Rent	25
	1,589		1,589

Second Method

PROFIT AND LOSS ADJUSTMENT ACCOUNT

	£		£
Bank Interest & Charges	20	Gross Profit as per Trading A/c	2,368
Subscription to Hospital	5	Discounts Received	85
Trade Expenses	128		
Salaries	426		
Discounts Allowed	120		
Repairs	32		
Bad Debts	87		
Fire Insurance	18		
Office Expenses	37		
Cashier's Embezzlement	60		
Balance (Assessable profit)	1,520		
	2,453		2,453

	£
The profit for current year's assessment is—	1,520
Deduct Capital Allowances	25
	1,495

Tax at the full standard rate will be chargeable on £1,495. Tax at the full rate will be allowed in respect of two-ninths of £1,495 (earned income); of the personal allowances and life assurance relief; also at the reduced rates within the prescribed limits.

PARTNERSHIP

Partners and Income Tax. The assessment is made on the firm. The allowances to which the partners may be individually entitled will be made on the firm's assessment.

The partners make separate returns for the purpose of claiming allowances or any other personal relief.

Example 30

Jones, Barron and Keery are in partnership sharing profits and losses equally. Jones receives a salary of £500, Barron £400, and Kerry £300 per annum. The capitals of the partners are: Jones £5,000, Barron £4,000, Kerry £3,000; and by the partnership deed each of the partners is entitled to interest on his capital at 5 per cent per annum. The firm's assessable profits for the previous year, as agreed with the inspector, were £8,253. The partners have no other source of income. Draw up a statement showing how the tax payable by the firm should be allocated among the partners. What difference would it make if the charge for income tax was merely debited to the rates and taxes account as an ordinary business expense?

Solution 30

STATEMENT ALLOCATING ASSESSABLE PROFIT BETWEEN PARTNERS

	Total	Jones	Barron	Kerry
	£	£	£	£
Interest on capital	600	250	200	150
Partnership salaries	1,200	500	400	300
Share of assessable profit divisible as profits and losses	6,453	2,151	2,151	2,151
	8,253	2,901	2,751	2,601

Each partner would claim the allowances to which he is entitled.

When the tax is paid, the best method of dealing with it is to charge each partner's share direct from the cash book to his drawing account. If the tax is debited to the profit and loss account and borne in the same ratio as general profits and losses, the result in the present case would be that each partner would thus bear one-third of the tax; Jones would be undertaxed, Barron would be properly taxed, and Kerry would be overtaxed (i.e. Kerry would be bearing a portion of the tax on Jones's profits).

Example 31

Scott, Russell, and Smith are partners in a business and share profits and losses four-ninths, three-ninths, and two-ninths respectively. Their capitals are: Scott £7,000, Russell £6,000, Smith £4,000. The partners draw salaries as follows: Scott £450 p.a., Russell £350 p.a., and Smith £200 p.a. They are also entitled to interest on their capitals at the rate of 5 per cent per annum. Scott has a private income from house property assessed under Schedule A at £300 net. Russell has one child under eleven at the commencement of the year of assessment, and pays a life assurance premium of £55 per annum. His wife has an income of £200 gross from investments. Smith pays an annual life assurance premium of £30. The assessable business profits, as agreed with the inspector, were £4,469.

Make up the firm's return for assessment, and show the allocation of the tax amoung the partners for the year 1959–60.

Solution 31

The firm's assessment will, therefore, be £4,469 *less* the allowances to be made to the partners individually.

STATEMENT ALLOCATING ASSESSABLE PROFIT BETWEEN PARTNERS

	Total £	Scott £	Russell £	Smith £
Interest on partners' capital	850	350	300	200
Partnership salaries	1,000	450	350	200
Share of assessable profit divisible in same ratio as profits and losses	2,619	1,164	873	582
	4,469	1,964	1,523	982

Scott's total income is £1,964 plus £300 (already taxed), viz. £2,264. In 1959–60 he would have claimed earned income relief at two-ninths in respect of £393, and the personal allowance.

Russell's total income is £1,523 plus his wife's income £200 (already taxed), viz. £1,723. If his allowances are earned income relief, £305; personal allowance, £180; allowance for child, £60; insurance premiums on his own life, £55, then he will pay tax on £1,723 less £600.

Smith's total income is £982. If £196 is allowed as earned income relief and Smith claims personal allowance, and allowance for insurance premiums, then the firm's assessment will be as shown—

		£
Assessable Business Profits		4,469
Less Allowances—		
Earned Income Relief:		
Scott	£393	
Russell	305	
Smith	196	
		894
Personal Allowance:		
Scott (say)	140	
Russell	240	
Smith (say)	140	
		520
Child's Allowance:		
Russell		100
Life Assurance Relief:		
Russell	55	
Smith	30	
Two-fifths allowable	$\frac{2}{5} \times 85 = 34$	34
		1,548
		2,921

Tax would be chargeable at the standard rate upon £4,469. Tax would be allowed at the standard rate upon £1,548, and there would be a deduction for the reduced rates.

Partners and Surtax. The following illustration, adapted from a circular issued by the Clerk to the Special Commissioners, should be studied—

Example 32

A firm consisting of three members (A, B, and C) might have—

		£
Partnership profits as assessed for the year 1961–2 (say)		20,000
Partnership income receivable in the year from: (*a*) dividends upon investments; (*b*) interest; (*c*) rents; (*d*) annual value of premises; and (*e*) any other sources of taxed income (say)—		
Dividends upon investments	£2,500	
Interest upon loans	2,500	
Rents	5,000	
		10,000
Total income for income-tax purposes		30,000
If the firm made any payments to third persons in respect of, for instance: (*a*) ground rents, (*b*) annual interest on mortgage or other loans to the firm, (*c*) annuities payable out of profits, these should be claimed as deductions from the above, as follows (say)—		
Ground rents	1,000	
Annual interest	1,000	
Annuities payable out of profits	1,000	
		3,000
Leaving		27,000

This represents the sum which for surtax purposes is to be treated as divisible among the partners in the firm.

Supposing, therefore, that for the year 1961–2, under the deed of partnership, partner B is entitled to a salary of £1,000 as a first charge in the partnership profits, and that the capital of the firm, amounting for that year to (say) £60,000, held equally by the partners, is next directed to be credited with interest at 5 per cent per annum, and that the balance of the profits is divisible in the proportion of: A, five-tenths; B, three-tenths; C, two-tenths; then the income from the partnership of each member of the firm for surtax purposes in respect of the year 1961–2 would be as shown hereunder—

		£
Partnership income for surtax purposes, as shown above		27,000
Less—		
Managing partner's salary	£1,000	
Interest on partners' capital (£60,000 at 5%)	3,000	
		4,000
Amount proportionally divisible among the partners		23,000

A	£	B	£	C	£
Interest on capital	1,000	Interest on capital	1,000	Interest on capital	1,000
Five-tenths profits	11,500	Three-tenths profits	6,900	Two-tenths profits	4,600
		Salary	1,000		
	12,500		8,900		5,600

£27,000

These sums of £12,500, £8,900, and £5,600 represent the amounts such partners A, B, and C respectively are for surtax purposes to be considered to have derived from this business, and should be entered by them when they are making their several returns.

Each partner would be able to claim two-ninths earned income relief, and the further earned income relief of £2,000, as well as national insurance allowance and any charges on income paid by him personally.

QUESTIONS

1. What is income tax? What persons are liable to it?
2. What is meant by taxation of income "at source"? Give examples.
3. Enumerate the schedules under which income tax is levied. What is the official year of assessment?
4. What income is taxable under Schedule E? Is it earned or investment income?
5. What is the mode of assessment under Schedule E?
6. What taxable income is comprised under Schedule D? Is it earned or investment income?
7. What is the mode of assessment under Schedule D? What is meant by "statutory" income under this schedule?
8. What is surtax? On whom is it levied?
9. What is the mode of assessment for surtax? By whom is the assessment made?
10. How is income tax collected from the partners in a partnership? Can the partners claim to be separately assessed for the purpose of obtaining the abatements, allowances, and relief to which they may be individually entitled?
11. How are the assessable profits adjusted in order to arrive at a partner's income: (*a*) for income tax, (*b*) for surtax?
12. What is the distinction between direct and indirect taxes?
13. Give examples of two direct and two indirect taxes.
14. How are National Insurance Contributions collected?
15. What is the difference between a Capital Allowance and an Investment Grant?

EXERCISE 28

1. What are the two purposes of taxation?

2. A company sells goods on 5th August to Brown for £200 and they are liable for Purchase Tax at 20 per cent. Tax is paid to the Customs and Excise on 1st September. Brown pays on 17th September. Show the accounting entries.

3. Robinson employs 150 men and on 1st January he buys four weeks' stock of stamps (covering National Insurance and other Social Security payments) which cost £5 per employee per week. Of this, £4 is the employer's contribution.

On 7th January, he pays £3,000 in gross wages. Show the accounting entries and the relevant items which would appear on a Balance Sheet drawn up on 8th January.

4. It has been the custom of a company, whose employment you enter, to charge corporation tax against the profits of the year in which it was paid. The company's financial year ends on 30th September, and, for example, income tax paid on 1st January, 19.1, for 19../.1 is charged against the profits of the year to 30th September, 19.1.

Do you consider this method correct? If so, give your reasons, but if you do not approve, suggest an alternative method which you think would be more correct.

5. The following items appear in the profit and loss account of a limited company—

(i) Income tax.
(ii) Loss on sale of a motor-car.
(iii) Debenture interest.
(iv) Depreciation of plant.
(v) Directors' fees.
(vi) Donation to the building fund of a hospital.
(vii) Premium on loss of profits policy.
(viii) Defalcation by cashier.

Would these items be allowed as deductions for income tax purposes? Give your reasons for allowance or disallowance. (*R.S.A.*)

6. The following items appear as expenses in the profit and loss account of a limited company—

	£
Directors' fees	1,000
Commissions	675
Rent	1,500
Interest on debentures	800
Discount	371
Depreciation of plant	419
Goodwill written off	500
Bad debts written off	286
Bad debts provision	250
Subscriptions and donations	37

State which of these items would be disallowed as an expense in computing the company's liability for income tax, explaining shortly in each case the principle underlying the disallowance. (*R.S.A.*)

7. Wilkinson employs 200 men and on 5th June he purchases a stock of National Insurance stamps sufficient for eight weeks. The stamps cost £6·66 of which £1 is the employees' contribution to National Insurance. The Selective Employment tax element is £1·50 per head and the Redundancy Fund payment £0·10 per head. On 12th June he pays a total of £4,500 out in gross wages. Show the accounting entries.

8. A company's year ends on 31st December and during 19.1 it is liable to S.E.T. of £1,000 monthly which it pays in National Insurance stamps. The company is eligible for refund of the tax plus 50 per cent and this is paid by the Ministry of Employment and Productivity one month after the quarterly claim has been submitted.

Show the accounting entries for the payment and refunds for the year and the charge or credit to Profit and Loss account assuming that the company uses (1) the actual basis, (2) the refund accrual basis, and (3) the refund and premium accrual basis.

9. Wilson Engineering Co. Ltd. paid emoluments of £200,000 in the year ending 31st December, 19.1, and £250,000 in the year ending 31st December, 19.2. On 5th December, 19.2, they received notice of a Training Levy of 1 per cent on emoluments for the year 19.1–2 (ending on 1st April, 19.2). Provision for a 1 per cent levy had been made in 19.1 and the levy was paid on 23rd December. Show the ledger accounts.

10. B, J, and K are in partnership sharing profits and losses equally. The capitals of the partners are: B £5,000, J £4,000, and K £3,000. Each partner draws a salary equal to one-tenth of capital held, also 5 per cent interest is credited annually to each partner's capital.

The assessable profits were £9,000. Draw up a statement showing how the tax payable by the firm should be allocated among the partners, if there is earned income relief of $\frac{2}{9}$ths, a personal allowance of £140 and tax is payable at £0·0835 on the first £60, £0·2105 on the next £150, £0·3105 on the next £150 and the standard rate is £0·3875 in the £.

11. (i) What, in your opinion, should be the basis of reserving for corporation tax in the accounts of a trading company? Take, as an example, the case of a company the accounts of which show—

	£
Year ended 31*st December*, 19..—	
Profit after charging:	
Debenture Interest, £500 (gross)	3,000
Year ended 31*st December*, 19.1—	
Profit, after debiting similar charges . . .	1,000

You may assume that during the year 19.1 a dividend, in respect of the 19.. profits, amounting to £2,000 gross was paid, but that no dividend payment is contemplated in respect of the 19.1 profits.

(ii) Do you consider there is any inequality of treatment for persons assessed under Schedule E as compared with those assessed under Schedule D, in regard to the deduction of expenses for income tax purposes. Explain the reasons for your view.

12. Robert Laws has been surcharged by the Inspector of Taxes with the undermentioned items in reference to his assessment under Schedule D—

(*a*) 5 per cent depreciation only, instead of the 10 per cent claimed, has been allowed;
(*b*) Interest on loan from J. Smithers disallowed;
(*c*) Cost of removing offices to new buildings disallowed;
(*d*) Subscription to local hospital disallowed.

Has Robert Laws any right of appeal against these surcharges? If so, what course is open to him, and what chance of success has he in respect of the above items? (*R.S.A.*)

13. The undermentioned items appeared in the annual accounts of a limited company. State briefly how they should be treated when preparing the company's return for corporation tax purposes—

(*a*) 5 per cent reserve on total sundry debtors as a provision for bad and doubtful debts.
(*b*) Interest received on deposit account with the Dresdner Bank, Old Broad Street, E.C.5.
(*c*) Premiums received on an issue of new shares.
(*d*) Loss by embezzlement by one of the company's travellers. (*R.S.A.*)

14. The undermentioned items appeared in the accounts of the Pleasure Steamers Co. Ltd. How should you deal with them when preparing the company's return for corporation tax purposes?
(*a*) Profit of £1,500 realized by the sale of stock, which formed part of the reserve fund investments.
(*b*) £150 written off during the year, representing one-fifth of the preliminary expenses account.
(*c*) Depreciation, at the rate of 6 per cent, written off the cost price of the company's steamers.
(*d*) 3,000 fully-paid shares of £1 each, received as part purchase price from a subsidiary company and distributed, by way of bonus, to the Pleasure Steamers Co. shareholders. (*R.S.A.*)

15. M, N, & P carry on business in partnership, sharing profits and losses in the following proportions—

M, seven-fifteenths; N, five-fifteenths; P, three-fifteenths.

Their profit and loss account for the past year was as follows—

	£		£
Salaries	304	Gross Profits	1,920
Trade Expenses	80		
Bad Debts	26		
Interest on Loan	25		
„ on Capital M	50		
„ on Capital N	30		
P's salary	350		
Goodwill written off	50		
Charitable Subscriptions	28		
Net Profit	977		
	1,920		1,920

Prepare return for income tax for the year ending 5th April next, showing on what amount the firm would be assessed.

16. Southern Ltd. has an issued capital of £240,000 in Ordinary Shares of £1 each, fully paid.

For the year ended 31st March, 1970, all closing entries have been made with the exception of those for taxation and the appropriation of profits. The following are the balances relating to the Profit and Loss Account—

	£	£
Trading Profit		43,154
Dividends on Investments (net)		690
Directors' Fees	500	
Debenture Interest (net)	2,300	
Reserve for Future Corporation Tax		1,150
Loss on Exchange	852	
Interim Dividend at 5 per cent (gross)	3,900	
Profit on Sale of Investments		1,456
Transfer Fees		42
Auditors' Remuneration	630	
Profit and Loss Account at 1st April, 1959		25,274

The following have been charged before arriving at the Trading Profit: Depreciation of Fixed Assets, £5,460; Manager's Remuneration, £10,520; Managing Director's Remuneration, £5,000; and Provision for Doubtful Debts, £600.

The credit on the Reserve for Future Corporation Tax is the balance remaining of the £18,000 reserved at 31st March, 1969, after payment of the tax due on 1st January, 1970.

The Auditors' Remuneration has been fixed at £630, including expenses, at the Annual General Meeting held on 15th June, 1969.

Corporation Tax assessable on the profits for the year ended 31st March, 1970, is estimated at £17,100.

It is proposed to pay a final dividend of 10 per cent gross.

You are required to prepare the Profit and Loss Appropriation Account in vertical narrative form. Income Tax may be calculated at 42½p in the £.

(*L.C.C., modified.*)

17. On 1st January, 19.3 Wilson Engineering had a provision for training levy of £1,875 on the books. On that date, they also had Training Grants receivable of 80 per cent of the levy.

On 1st April they received notice that grants to the company would be at the rate of 90 per cent and the accounts were adjusted accordingly. The grants were received on 1st June and levy of £2,475 was paid on 10th November.

At 31st December it was decided to provide £2,400 for levy for the year and for grants at the 90 per cent rate. Show the accounting entries.

18. The following is the trial balance as at 31st March, 19.6, of AB. Ltd.—

	£	£
Share capital: authorized and issued in £1 shares		120,000
6 per cent debentures outstanding (secured by floating charge)		40,000
Capital reserve		10,000
Investments at cost	29,745	
Goodwill at cost	25,000	
Debtors	44,100	
Creditors		33,763
Leasehold property at cost	60,000	
Leasehold amortization		6,000
Furniture and fixtures	39,940	
Provision for doubtful debts		760
Income tax		1,240
Trading profit for year		49,619
Stock at 31st March, 19.6	68,200	
Directors' fees	500	
Directors' salaries	5,000	
Cash at bank and in hand	3,740	
Profit and loss account, balance at 31st March, 19.5		15,219
Interest on bank overdraft	295	
Interest on 4 per cent government stock (net)		259
Dividend on shares in XY Ltd. (net)		470
Debenture interest (£1,410 paid net *less* provision from previous year of £600 gross)	810	
	277,330	277,330

You are informed that—

(1) The original value of the debentures issued was £60,000 and the issue is being redeemed by market purchases on 2nd January of each year. All debentures so redeemed are available for re-issue. Interest is payable half yearly on 1st July and 1st January each year. On 2nd January, 19.6 the company had purchased for redemption £9,000 of its debentures for £8,465 and debited this amount to investments account.

(2) The balance on the investments account consists of £11,000 4 per cent Government Stock (m.v. £9,400), 12,850 shares of £1 each of XY Ltd. a private company, issued at par on which 16s. has been paid, and the purchase price of the debentures redeemed in the year.

(3) The balance on the furniture and fixtures account is made up as under—

	£	£
Cost		73,200
Less depreciation at 31st March, 19.5	29,620	
Written-down value at 31st March, 19.5 of items scrapped at end of year	3,640	
		33,260
		39,940

The fixtures scrapped were purchased in December 19.1. Depreciation has been and is to be provided at 12½ per cent of cost with no allowance for residual value, a full year's depreciation being provided in the year in which the expenditure was incurred.

(4) The balance on the income-tax account represents an over-provision of income tax 19.5/.6.

(5) The following provisions are to be made—

	£
(*a*) Corporation tax @ 40 per cent	15,000
(*b*) Provision for doubtful debts to be 5 per cent of the book value	—
(*c*) Slow-moving stocks	3,000
(*d*) Leasehold amortization	1,500
(*e*) Audit fees	500

(6) A dividend of 10 per cent is to be recommended.

You are required to prepare the balance sheet as at 31st March, 1966 and the profit and loss account for the year ended on that date.

Comparative figures and an auditors' report are not required.

Workings to the nearest £.

Income tax to be provided @ £0·4125 in the £.

(*Cost and Management Accountants, modified.*)

19. Ceesden Ltd. has issued 100,000 shares of £1 each upon which 75p per share has been called up and paid.

Among the balances included in the Trial Balance as on 31st December, 19.2, are the following—

	Debit £	*Credit* £
Sales		285,462
Purchases	186,024	
Wages and other works expenses	22,717	
Works indirect expenses	1,438	
Depreciation for the year on—		
Plant and Machinery	2,988	
Office Fixtures, fittings and equipment . . .	279	
Stock on hand @ cost at 31st December, 1961—		
Raw Materials	37,032	
Finished Goods	12,643	
Selling and distribution expenses	9,820	
Office and Administration expenses . . .	4,965	
Management remuneration	7,000	
Interest received (net) from trade investments . .		1,380
Professional Charges other than audit fee . . .	1,060	
Interest (net) paid on debentures for half-year to 30th June, 1962	360	
Profit and Loss Account—Balance at 31st December, 1961		12,345

Management remuneration includes works manager's salary £2,500 and directors' salaries £4,500.

On 31st December, 19.2, stock on hand, valued at cost, was—

	£
Raw materials	44,526
Finished goods	14,756

Provision is to be made for: doubtful debts £194, directors' fees £1,500, half-year's debenture interest due 31st December, 19.2 auditors' remuneration £651 (fixed at the last annual general meeting) and corporation tax.

The liability for corporation tax 19.2/3, has been agreed and was less than the amount reserved by £1,164. Taxation based on the profit for the year ended 31st December, 19.2, is estimated as £21,860. The directors decide to transfer £10,000 to General Reserve, £3,000 to a Reserve for future fluctuations in raw material prices, to recommend a dividend of 2s. per share gross and to carry forward the balance on Profit and Loss Account. The standard rate of income tax is 40p in the £.

You are requested to prepare in vertical form a Trading and Profit and Loss Account for the year ended 31st December, 1962, in detail for submission to the Board showing the net profit before making a charge for taxation, and a form which conforms with the requirements of the Companies Act.

(*A.C.C.A., modified.*)

20. William James has been carrying on business for many years as a general merchant. The following is a summary of the company's profit and loss account for the year ended 31st December, 1957—

	£			£
Travellers' salaries and commission	8,100	Trading Profit		32,650
Office salaries and national insurance	7,500	Agency commissions		1,250
Rent and rates	1,125	Investment income (gross)	£200	
Lighting and heating	200	*Less* income tax	85	
Repairs and renewals	875			115
General expenses	570			
Legal charges	105			
Audit fee	150			
Directors' fees	2,000			
Depreciation of office furniture and calculators	175			
Interest on bank overdraft	50			
Income tax on the profits of the year	5,900			
Drawings	1,150			
Balance	6,115			
	34,015			34,015

The following analyses are supplied—

(1) Repairs and renewals—

	£
Decorating offices	100
Extension to offices, including architect's fees	550
Replacement of furniture	125
Additional advertising sign	100
	875

(2) General expenses—

	£
Telephone charges	160
Postages and stationery	200
Trade subscriptions	105
Donation to political party funds	52
Sundry expenses (all allowable)	53
	570

(3) Legal charges—

	£
Renewal of office lease	50
Stamp duty and costs *re* new share issue	55
	105

James used calculating machines as follows—

	Machine "A"	Machine "B"	Machine "C"
	£	£	£
Bought—31.3.1954	240	320	
Bought—30.9.1955			480
Sold —30.9.1957		200	

Initial allowance on the machines bought in 1954, and investment allowance on the machine bought in 1955, both at 20 per cent, also annual allowances at the basic rate of 10 per cent, were claimed and allowed for income tax purposes. It has been agreed that furniture and fittings (including advertising signs) are to be dealt with on a renewals basis for income tax purposes.

You are required—

(*a*) to prepare a computation of the adjusted profit for income tax purposes for the year ended 31st December, 1957;

(*b*) to prepare a statement showing the capital allowances on the calculating machines for 1958–9; and

(*c*) to state the amounts of the assessments to be made on the company and the income tax payable thereon, for the fiscal year 1958–9, ignoring any investment income for that year.

The standard rate of tax was 42½p in the £ at this time. Ignore the possible personal allowances or reduced rates.

21. Plastics Ltd., an old-established manufacturing company whose accounts are made up to 31st December in each year, erected an industrial building during the year to 31st December, 1950, at a total cost (excluding the site) amounting to £20,000.

The building was in full use by 31st December, 1950, and during the year to 31st December, 1951, there was further capital expenditure on additions to the building costing £5,000.

The premises were in use by the company as an industrial building up to 30th September, 1954, when they were sold: the gross proceeds of sale, £19,600, were made up as follows—

	£
Building	18,600
Land	1,000
	19,600

You are required to prepare a statement showing the capital allowances (including initial allowances at 10 per cent) in respect of the building, for each year of assessment affected. (*Chartered Accountants.*)

22. Alpha and Beta have been trading in partnership for several years, sharing profits three-fifths and two-fifths after charging salaries of £1,250 and £1,000 per annum respectively.

The adjusted trading profits of the firm for income tax purposes for the year ended 31st March, 1958, were £12,000 and capital allowances £800 have been agreed for 1958–9. On 6th October, 1958, Delta, an employee of the firm at a salary of £900 per annum, was admitted to partnership, and the sharing of profits from that date was as follows—

	Share of Profits	Partners' Salaries (per annum)
		£
Alpha	Three-sixths	1,500
Beta	Two-sixths	1,300
Delta	One-sixth	1,000

The appropriate notice has been given to the effect that income tax assessments are to be made on the firm as if there had been no change in the partnership.

You are required to prepare a statement, showing the division of the firm's assessment for 1958–9 between the partners. (*Chartered Accountants.*)

23. (i) A company buys an asset for £200,000 which is eligible for an investment grant of 20 per cent. Show the accounting entries on acquisition on the four bases discussed in ED9. Assume a 10-year life with no residual value.

What difference does each basis make to the Balance Sheet?

(ii) If the Annual Allowance is 20 per cent, what will be the written-down value for tax purposes at the end of the third year?

24. A company earns £100,000 per annum operating profit before charging depreciation and tax. The company buys Machine A for £20,000 in Year 1 and Machine B for £40,000 in Year 2. For machine A there is a first-year capital allowance of 80 per cent, followed by a writing-down allowance of 25 per cent. For machine B there is a first-year capital allowance of 100 per cent. On both machines, depreciation is at 25 per cent per annum on cost. Calculate (*a*) the reported earnings, (*b*) actual Corporation Tax payable, and (*c*) show the Deferred Taxation account for years 1 to 4.

In all years, the Corporation Tax is expected to be 50 per cent.

CHAPTER 29

INTERPRETATION OF FINAL ACCOUNTS AND BALANCE SHEETS

Readers of this strange language,
We have come at last to a country
Where light equal, like the shine from snow, strikes all faces

Here you may wonder
How it was that works, money, interest, building, could ever hide
The palpable and obvious love of man for man.

STEPHEN SPENDER—*After they have tired*

THIS chapter is concerned with the question of what conclusions, if any, may be drawn from the information presented in the final accounts and balance sheet of a business. It is also concerned with the question of what additional information and explanations a prudent person would want to ask for *before* drawing conclusions.

The accountant frequently finds himself in the position where he must comment on final accounts and balance sheets prepared by himself or by other persons. Apart from the purely technical questions of form and accuracy of the figures given, he is expected to interpret their *significance*. In doing so he may find that the accepted form of accounts and balance sheet is not easily followed by the layman and he may wish to re-design the form so that the figures become more intelligible.

Before any interpretation of accounts is undertaken, the point of view of the person asking the questions must be understood. What is he driving at? What use is he going to make of the information he obtains? The answer to the same question may be very different for different persons. The interested parties may be—

1. Insiders—

(*a*) THE MANAGEMENT are mainly concerned with evaluating results and using the accounts as a guide in controlling the firm. They may also have a personal interest in the profits made.

(*b*) THE SHAREHOLDERS are usually concerned firstly with dividends, but are also interested in the amount of profits retained, the possibility of bonus shares and the prospects of growth, in value, of the firm. The various classes of shareholders may have differing interests.

(*c*) EMPLOYEES may hold shares if the firm has a profit-sharing scheme. Or they may be concerned with the relation between profits and their own wages. Through their trade unions, they may use information from the accounts in wage negotiations.

2. **Outsiders—**

(*a*) The Inland Revenue. The share of profits taken in tax is high and the determination of taxable profits is of great importance.

(*b*) Creditors—

(i) *Trade Creditors* are concerned about the financial stability of the firm and the prospects of their receiving payment for their debts.

(ii) *Debenture Holders* may have their debenture secured on a particular asset but they are, in any case, concerned with the likely realizable value of the assets.

(iii) *Bankers* are usually concerned with the accounts and balance sheet before they make a loan, and seek an assurance that they will recover money loaned under all circumstances.

(*c*) Potential Purchasers of a Business, a New Partner, etc., are concerned to discover what the true position is, rather than the book values shown in the balance sheet. The past record of earnings will be considered and, also, the possible existence of goodwill.

(*d*) Other Outsiders. Government bodies, research institutes, trade associations, etc., may use a group of accounts to draw conclusions about particular industries or products. Great care is needed to standardize information so that valid conclusions may be drawn.

It should be stressed that of these interests, only Management is in the position to demand all the information it requires, and even then there is a limit to the information which can be economically produced. The Inland Revenue also have considerable powers, but such interests as trade creditors may only be able to obtain the minimum legally required to be published.

The general tendency is for firms to publish only the minimum of information, although there is a growing number of larger firms who are prepared to publish information in excess of the legal minimum.

PRESENTATION OF THE REVENUE ACCOUNTS AND BALANCE SHEET

(*a*) General

A number of general rules may be followed in presenting data.

Columnar Form. A columnar presentation in which associated items are added or subtracted and significant totals and sub-totals clearly brought out is often an aid to comparison. The columnar form of balance sheet is illustrated on p. 0216. A similar form of revenue accounts is illustrated below.

Percentages. It is customary to present the profit and loss account figures as percentages of sales; the balance sheet items may be shown as percentages of total capital or the gross assets.

COMPARATIVE FIGURES. The Companies Act, 1948, requires companies to show comparative figures for the previous year in the published accounts and balance sheet, but to give a good picture of the trend of results, comparative figures for the previous five to ten years should be presented.

Example 1

(*b*) Revenue Accounts

The following example of a revenue account follows these general rules of presentation.

REVENUE ACCOUNTS FOR NUCLEAR LTD.

(000s omitted)

		This Year	%		*Last Year*	%
		£			£	
1. Sales		8,000	100		6,000	100
Opening stock	£3,000			£2,000		
Purchases	6,000			5,000		
	9,000			7,000		
Closing stock	3,500			3,000		
2. Cost of goods sold		5,500	68·75		4,000	66·7
3. Gross profit		2,500	31·25		2,000	33·3
		£	%		£	%
4. Expenses—						
Administration		800	10		550	9·2
Financial		200	2·5		200	3·3
Selling and distribution		600	7·5		350	5·8
		1,600	20		1,100	18·3
		£	%		£	%
5. Net profit before tax		900	11·25		900	15
		£			£	
6. Provision for tax		450	5·625		500	8·3
7. Net profit after tax		450	5·625		400	6·6
Preference dividends		100	1·25		100	1·6
Ordinary dividends		150	1·875		150	2·5
8. Added to carry forward		200	2·5		150	2·5
		450	5·625		400	6·6

The interpretation of these figures has two aspects—

(i) Noting the differences in the results of the two periods.

(ii) Discovering or suggesting explanations for these differences.

To aid the student, the differences are noted below and some possible explanations given. These are by no means exhaustive. In practice, of course, there should be a series of specific explanations which, taken together, will build up a clear picture of the company's operation.

DIFFERENCE	POSSIBLE EXPLANATIONS
1. *Sales* have increased by £2,000 ($33\frac{1}{3}$ per cent on last year).	(*a*) Increase in sales volume (possibly with a decrease in sales price). This may be permanent if: new markets opened; new product launched. Or temporary if: product satisfying accumulated demand; competitors temporarily out of production; seasonal factors affect sales. (*b*) Increase in sales price (possibly with decrease in volume).
2. *Cost of goods sold* has increased £1,500 (now 68·75 per cent compared to 66·7 per cent of sales last year). A greater proportional rise than sales.	(*a*) Increasing purchases leading to shortage of supplies and rising prices. (*b*) Inefficient buying. (Larger stocks may be held at market price below cost.) (*c*) A change in the nature of goods sold.
3. *Gross profit* has increased, but proportionally decreased (now 31·25 per cent compared to 33·3 per cent of sales last year).	This change is a consequence of the changes in sales and cost of goods sold. It may represent changes on the buying or selling side, or a combination of both.
4. *Expenses* have increased by £500, with a percentage increase from 18·3 per cent to 20 per cent of sales. Administration and selling costs have increased more than proportionally, but relatively financial costs have fallen.	The stability of the actual financial expenses is due to the fact that these are fixed charges such as debenture interest. The *proportional* fall illustrates the benefit of increased sales and reflects a better use of the capital available. Administration and selling costs may have risen because of increased sales effort. Overselling may have given rise to excessive bad debts. Increased commissions usually result from increased sales.

(*c*) Balance Sheets

The questions which arise from consideration of a balance sheet will be as various as those arising from the consideration of revenue accounts, and will be equally illuminating in disclosing the state of the business.

Before going further, we must be clear on what the balance sheet purports to show. In fact, the items may be considered in groups—

FIXED ASSETS. Most balance sheets show the fixed assets at cost, *less* depreciation. This may not give any idea of the current value which may be more or less than that shown. In the years following World War II, when prices rose steadily, it was common to find land and buildings valued, in balance sheets, far below the price which could be obtained for them on the open market. On the other hand, the specialized plant and equipment used in some trades may be of little more than scrap value if the firm should try to dispose of them.

CURRENT ASSETS consisting of stock, debtors and cash. Stock is valued at cost or market value, whichever is lower. Debtors may be valued below actual value if provision has been made for bad debts. These valuations should, therefore, be a more reliable guide to actual values. In the normal course of trade, current assets will turn into cash.

CAPITAL, RESERVES, AND PROFIT AND LOSS ACCOUNT BALANCES. These items represent amounts contributed to the capital of the firm and profits accumulated over the years. They represent the proportionate claim of shareholders on the assets of the firm when realized. As such, the claim is subject to the same doubts as the valuation of the fixed assets, always assuming that these form a substantial proportion of the assets of the firm.

LONG-TERM LIABILITIES, e.g. debentures, represent long-term loans to the firm and a claim on the assets, often secured on a specific fixed asset. Whilst they have a preferential claim on the assets, the claim is subject to the same reservations as that of the shareholders.

CURRENT LIABILITIES represent claims which must be paid within the next accounting period, usually from the proceeds of the realization of the current assets.

Clearly the items which will be most sensitive to reflect the changing fortunes of a firm are the current assets and current liabilities, and for this reason the working capital of a firm is considered a reliable indicator of its state of affairs.

WORKING CAPITAL is the current assets – current liabilities; e.g. if current assets are £70,000 and current liabilities are £30,000, then working capital is £40,000.

The following specific points must be considered in evaluating the position of a firm from the balance sheet—

1. The working capital should be calculated and, if possible, compared with previous figures. A decline in this respect may be the best indicator of a deterioration in the firm's trading position.

2. The equity or surplus of total assets over total liabilities is of little value in this connexion and may appear quite reassuring when the firm's position is, in fact, quite weak.

3. The reliability of the balance sheet figures should be checked and, if they are not audited, steps taken to obtain verification by a third party.

4. Previous balance sheets should be obtained and inquiries made to check whether the figures are representative. A balance sheet may be "window-dressed" by calling in cash or discharging loans for the day of the balance sheet only.

5. The actual method of valuing the current assets should be checked.

If these are not in accord with accepted practice, they should be recalculated and the balance sheet and working capital figures adjusted accordingly.

6. Any changes in the basis of valuation or in methods of accounting should be noted and, if possible, the effect on the results calculated.

7. The method used for valuing fixed assets and the basis on which depreciation (if any) has been charged should be checked. A reasonable computation should be made and the effects on profits calculated.

8. The existence of stocks and other assets should be verified and some assurance obtained, preferably from a disinterested party, that the condition of the assets warrants their valuation. They should be in suitable condition for effective production. A banker may try to get some idea of the "break-up" value of the assets (that is, a value based on the assumption that the business were broken up and the assets sold).

9. The extent to which specific assets have specific charges on them such as mortgages.

10. Intangible assets (e.g. goodwill, patents, and fictitious assets such as preliminary expenses, debit balance to profit and loss account) should be excluded from any calculations of asset values and working capital.

11. The amount and realizability of investments should be considered. Some of these may be included as "quick assets" in working capital. Others, such as trade investments, may be fixed assets.

12. The treatment of taxation should be considered. A firm may be distributing profits without regard to the income tax liability which it will incur in respect of them.

13. The extent of contingent liabilities should also be discovered. Shares may be held on which calls are likely to be made, and there may be discounted bills of exchange or commitments for capital expenditure which could place a severe strain on the firm's resources.

14. The amount paid to directors in fees and emoluments, the amount of dividends paid in a company, and the level of drawings of a sole trader or partnership, must be considered in the light of the information already gleaned and the earning capacity of the firm. This gives an indication of the prudence or imprudence of the directors or owners.

15. Finally, profit should be related to the capital employed or total assets to give an indication of managerial efficiency and to equity interest to indicate the earning capacity of the ordinary shares.

Example 2

The summarized balance sheet of Quick Results Ltd. as at 31st March, 1950, is given on the next page.

It was estimated that income tax for 1950–1, based on the profits of the year to 31st March, 1950, would amount to £5,000.

There follows a summary of the motor vans account in the company's ledger.

BALANCE SHEET. 31ST MARCH, 1950

	£	£		£	£
Issued Share Capital		10,000	Freehold Property, at cos		6,000
Profit & Loss A/c—			Motor Vans—		
As at 31st March 1949	1,000		At cost	6,500	
Add Net Profit for year	11,500		*Less* Depreciation	4,900	
	12,500				1,600
Less Income Tax, 1949–50	2,000		Stock		4,000
		10,500	Debtors		6,700
			Balance at Bank		7,050
Creditors		5,200	Deposit (10%) on proposed purchase of new Freehold Property		350
		25,700			25,700

MOTOR VANS

			£				£
1939				1939–50			
Apr 1	Cost of 20 Vans		5,000		Depreciation		4,900
1950				1950			
Mar 31	Cost of 2 Vans		1,500	Mar 31	Balance		1,600
			6,500				6,500
1950							
Mar 31	Balance		1,600				

In June, 1950, the directors informed you that in view of the exceptionally high profits of the year to 31st March, 1950, they proposed to pay a dividend of 40 per cent net (i.e. after deduction of income tax) for that year.

State, with reasons, whether or not you consider the *financial position of the company* would justify the proposed dividend.

(NOTES. You are not required to consider any question of law or national policy. Ignore Profits Tax.)

Solution

1. The payment of a dividend of 40 per cent after tax would amount to £4,000 and would be paid from cash.

2. Tax for 1950–1 should have been provided for from the profits, which would have left £5,500 available for dividends.

3. (*a*) From the motor vans account it can be seen that no depreciation had been allowed on the new vans. The balance of £1,600 was composed of £1,500 cost of 2 new vans, £100 residual value of 18 old vans.

(*b*) If the earning power of the firm depended on 20 vans, some provision for replacement was obviously due. The cost of 18 new vans would be 18 × £750 = £13,500, and it is clear that the directors should have used any available funds for this purpose rather than dividends.

4. *Contingent Liabilities.* Ten per cent deposit had been paid on freehold property, leaving a commitment to capital expenditure of £3,150. Cash or investments should have been held available to meet this, rather than paid out in dividends.

5. *Working Capital*—

	£
Current Assets—	
Stock	4,000
Debtors	6,700
Bank	7,050
	17,750

		£
Current Liabilities: creditors		5,200
		12,550
Less Tax liability	£5,000	
Capital expenditure . . .	3,150	
		8,150
NET WORKING CAPITAL		4,400

Whilst, superficially, there was sufficient working capital available, if the tax liability and capital expenditure were taken into account it became dangerously low. This was still ignoring the evident need for replacement of motor vans.

6. No consideration had been given to the question of stock valuation and provision for bad debts on the debtors but, on the other hand, the freehold property might have been worth much more than the value stated.

Conclusion. Far from warranting the directors paying a high dividend, the position seemed to warrant their reconsidering the whole question of their capital needs, and the firm might have been advised to raise more capital by issuing shares or debentures, or mortgaging the freehold property.

RATIOS CALCULATED FROM THE REVENUE ACCOUNTS AND BALANCE SHEET

The analysis suggested so far has consisted of comparing specific items in the balance sheet and final accounts and drawing conclusions from the changes which have taken place.

A firm is an organization of people working together towards a common aim. The actions of any one person in the organization inevitably affects the others—in a sense, the firm itself is a "living" thing. The fixed assets may be compared to the body of the firm, the working capital to its stock of food and air. The working capital constantly circulates, through the body and out into the air, repairing, replenishing and building up the body of fixed assets.

Figure 29.1 illustrates the relationships. The fixed assets determine the facilities available for production or trade and largely determine the firm's sphere of operation. The working capital will start in the form of cash. From this, raw materials are purchased or manufactured. Raw materials may also be obtained from creditors. Then finished goods are sold. If sales are for cash, a replenishment of cash takes place; if on credit, debtors arise for a time but are eventually turned into cash. The replenishment fund of cash may be used to settle creditors' claims. All these items form a continuous cycle.

Cash may be drawn out of circulation if interest, taxes or dividends are paid, or if the fixed capital is replenished by the purchase of assets. It may be augmented by the sale of assets or the raising of new capital. It will be decreased when long-term liabilities are repaid and increased by the retention of profits (this also leads to an increase in the ordinary shareholders' capital).

In a healthy firm we can expect the flow of funds to proceed evenly at all points. Expansion or contraction should, also, be even throughout. In fact a considerable change in *one* respect only often means that the firm is robbing Peter to pay Paul, and that policy leads to disaster.

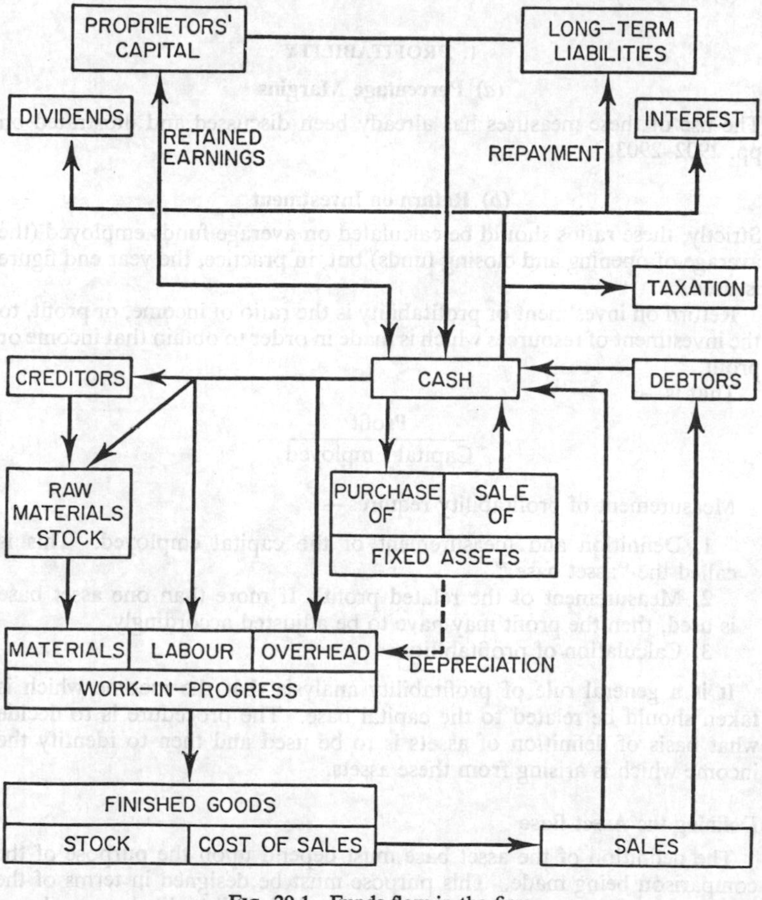

FIG. 29.1. Funds flow in the firm

The overall position of the firm, in this sense, can best be gauged by comparing the ratios between various connected items.

A ratio is one number expressed in terms of another. It will be meaningful only if there is an underlying relationship between the numbers compared. We will now consider some commonly used ratios which can be loosely grouped as measures of:

(1) profitability;
(2) liquidity or asset use;
(3) solvency.

1. PROFITABILITY

(*a*) Percentage Margins

The use of these measures has already been discussed and illustrated on pp. 2902–2903.

(*b*) Return on Investment

Strictly, these ratios should be calculated on average funds employed (the average of opening and closing funds) but, in practice, the year end figure is used.

Return on investment or profitability is the ratio of income, or profit, to the investment of resources which is made in order to obtain that income or profit.

That is—

$$\frac{\text{Profit}}{\text{Capital Employed}}$$

Measurement of profitability requires—

1. Definition and measurement of the capital employed. This is called the "asset base."
2. Measurement of the related profit. If more than one asset base is used, then the profit may have to be adjusted accordingly.
3. Calculation of profitability.

It is a general rule of profitability analysis that the income which is taken should be related to the capital base. The procedure is to decide what basis of definition of assets is to be used and then to identify the income which is arising from these assets.

Defining the Asset Base

The definition of the asset base must depend upon the purpose of the comparison being made. This purpose must be designed in terms of the decisions, which the person making the analysis will be likely to make.

There are several asset bases which may be used and, unfortunately, no generally agreed definitions. However, the following are the main ones used.

(*i*) **The Total Assets.** This figure can be obtained by taking the total of all the assets shown on the balance sheet, both fixed and current.

(*ii*) **The Total Assets Employed.** On this basis all the assets shown in the balance sheet but not, in fact, employed by management are eliminated from the base. Idle assets may include cash; outside investments; fixed assets acquired on take-over which the company intends to sell; and goodwill.

(*iii*) **The Assets Provided by Long-term Funds.** On this basis the current liabilities are deducted from the total assets or the total assets employed. Alternatively the total can be calculated by taking long-term debts *plus* all classes of shares *plus* all reserves *plus* retained earnings. This measures the funds provided by long-term investors in the company. The Institute of Cost and Works Accountants suggest this definition as the best for defining the total employment of capital by an organization.

(*iv*) **Proprietors' Capital.** If long- and short-term borrowings are deducted from total assets or total assets employed then what remains is the capital provided by all classes of shareholders (preference, ordinary and deferred).

(*v*) **The Assets Provided by Ordinary Shareholders.** This is also called equity since it is the amount of funds provided by the persons bearing the ultimate risk in a company. It can be calculated in two ways, either by taking total assets less all liabilities and preference shares or by taking the ordinary share capital paid up plus retained earnings and all reserves.

Defining the Return

The return of a company will be defined according to the asset base used but profit will usually be taken in all cases after adjusting cost of sales for stock and after deducting provisions such as depreciation on assets. Both these items affect the validity of profit figures.

(*i*) **Operating Profit before Interest, Corporation Tax and Dividends.** This is sometimes known as E.B.I.T. (earnings before interest and tax). This is the profit before any appropriations are made and it is therefore usually related to total assets, total assets employed or long-term funds (Bases 1, 2 and 3).

(*ii*) **Operating Profit after Interest and Corporation Tax.** This is the profit after meeting appropriations to outside interests (lenders and Inland Revenue) and it is used in calculating return to all capital provided by shareholders. (Base 4.)

(*iii*) **Operating Profit after Interest, Tax and Preference Dividends.** This is the earnings left to the ordinary shareholders, and it is therefore related to the assets provided by the equity. (Base 5.)

Example 3

The following figures are a simplified summary of the published balance sheet and profit and loss account of a company on 30th September, 19.1.

BALANCE SHEET ON 30TH SEPTEMBER, 19.1

	£	£	£,000
Sources of funds .			
6 per cent *Preference Capital*			1,300
Ordinary Shareholders' funds—			
£1 Ordinary shares		3,600	
Share premiums		700	
Capital reserves		800	
Revenue ,,		1,998	
Unappropriated profits		1,302	
			8,400
Debenture stocks and loans			700
Taxation equalization reserve			200
			10,600
Use of funds—			
Fixed assets (at cost less depreciation)			7,400
Goodwill, patents and trade marks			400
Trade investments			100
Net current assets—			
Stocks	2,600		
Debtors and prepayments	3,900		
Other investments	100		
Cash and Bank Balances	300		
		6,900	
Less Creditors and provisions	1,700		
Bank loans and overdrafts	1,800		
Taxation due	500		
Dividends unpaid	200		
		4,200	
			2,700
			10,600

PROFIT AND LOSS ACCOUNT FOR THE YEAR ENDED 30TH SEPTEMBER, 19.1

	£,000
Turnover	15,400
Less Operating costs and other expenses (including depreciation £656)	14,446
Profit on trading	954
Investment income	18
Carried forward	972

	£	£,000
Brought forward		
Operating profit before interest, tax and dividends		972
Interest payable		136
Operating profit before tax		836
Corporation tax		202
Profit after tax and interest		634
Profits brought forward from previous year		1,016
Profit available for appropriation		1,650
Dividends (gross)		
On preference shares	78	
On ordinary shares	270	
		348
Unappropriated profits carried forward		1,302

Some of the alternative calculations of profitability will be illustrated from these simplified accounts and balance sheet.

1. Total Asset Base

	£
Total assets are as follows—	
Fixed assets	7,400
Goodwill, etc.	400
Trade investment	100
Current assets	6,900
	14,800

The related profit is the operating profit before interest, tax and dividends of £972. Profitability is therefore—

$$\frac{£972}{£14,800} \times 100 = 6{\cdot}6 \text{ per cent}$$

2. Total Assets Employed Base. Let us assume that the investments are surplus. There are two items of £100 each (trade and other investments). The total assets employed are therefore—

	£
Total assets	14,800
Less Investments	200
	14,600

The related income from the idle assets must be eliminated.

The relevant profit is—

	£
Operating profit before interest, etc.	972
Less Investment income	18
	954

The profitability is—

$$\frac{£954}{£14{,}600} \times 100 = 6{\cdot}5 \text{ per cent}$$

Since this is less than the profitability on total assets, it follows that the outside investment is making a good contribution to the profitability of the company. Indeed, since £18,000 was made on outside investments of £200,000 the profitability of these investments was 9 per cent before tax.

3. Assets Provided by Long-term Funds. This figure of capital is—

	£
Total assets	14,800
Less Current liabilities	4,200
Assets provided by long-term funds	10,600

If the idle assets are eliminated, as above, the figure is—

	£
Assets provided by long-term funds	10,600
Less Idle assets	200
	10,400

The related profit, if the idle assets are not excluded, is £972 and the profitability is—

$$\frac{£972}{£10{,}600} \times 100 = 9{\cdot}2 \text{ per cent}$$

If the idle assets are eliminated the related profit is—

$$\frac{£954}{£10{,}400} \times 100 = 9{\cdot}2 \text{ per cent}$$

4. Equity or Assets Provided by Ordinary Shareholders. The capital base is the figure of ordinary shareholders funds, £8,400, to which may be added taxation equalization reserve £200, giving a total of £8,600.

The related profit is the profit after meeting interest and preference dividends—

	£
Profit after tax	634
Less Preference dividends	78
	556

The return to equity is therefore—

$$\frac{£556}{£8,600} = 6\cdot4 \text{ per cent}$$

The break-down of the profitability ratio between margin on sales and rate of asset turnover is dealt with under measures of solvency, ratio 2(*f*) and 2(*g*).

(*c*) Earnings per Share

This ratio compares the net earnings attributable to the shares to the number of shares issued. The operating profit is taken after deduction of interest, tax and, in the case of ordinary and deferred shares, any priority dividends but before any extraordinary items.

In the example there are 3,600,000 £1 shares.

$$\frac{\text{Operating profit after interest, tax and preference dividends}}{\text{Number of issued shares}} =$$

$$\frac{£556,000}{£3,600,000} = £0\cdot154 = 15\cdot4\text{p per share}$$

(*d*) Dividends per Share

A similar calculation can be made of the dividend paid in each share as follows—

$$\frac{\text{Total Dividends paid}}{\text{Number of issued shares}} = \frac{£270,000}{£3,600,000} = £0\cdot075 = 7\cdot5\text{p per share}$$

(*e*) The Price/Earnings Ratio

This ratio compares the average price of the share to the reported earnings per share. If the shares in the example are priced at £2·31 the calculation is—

$$\frac{\text{Market price per share}}{\text{Earnings per share}} = \frac{£2\cdot31}{0\cdot154} = 15\cdot1$$

(*f*) Dividend Yield

The dividend yield indicates the percentage of those dividends to the average price of the share.

$$\frac{\text{Dividends per share}}{\text{Price per share}} = \frac{0\cdot075}{2\cdot31} \times 100 = 3\cdot2 \text{ per cent}$$

2. LIQUIDITY OR ASSET USE

(*a*) WORKING CAPITAL RATIO indicates the ratio of current assets to current liabilities; for example—

$$\frac{\text{Current assets £6,000}}{\text{Current liabilities £3,000}} = \text{Working Capital Ratio 2·0}$$

A low ratio indicates lack of working capital, a very high ratio might indicate that too much capital is tied up in stocks or lying idle in the form of cash. A ratio of 2·0 is usually satisfactory.

No hard and fast rules can be laid down as to the *amount* of working capital which a firm requires, but it will be obvious that if current assets are insufficient to meet current liabilities, that is, there is *no* working capital, the firm will be unable to pay its debts as they arise and will be at the mercy of a creditor who might enforce its liquidation. A large surplus of total assets over total liabilities will not mean that the firm is stable, if there is a deficiency of working capital.

The working capital required, then, must be sufficient to enable a firm to conduct its normal trade without shortage of cash and to cover contingencies.

Overtrading. A firm with a deficiency of working capital is said to be overtrading. Small firms which expand too rapidly frequently fall into this difficulty. They become aware of it when, despite (or because of) excellent trade, they experience a sudden shortage of cash. So long as trade expands, little difficulty will be encountered, but as soon as a slight contraction takes place the firm may run into trouble.

The facts of each case must be considered, but the requirements for working capital can be determined, in view of the following factors—

1. The normal period of credit given on purchases and taken on sales.
2. The normal incidence of expenses, taking into account seasonal variations.
3. The rate of turnover of stock. Some businesses, must have more capital tied up in stock than others, e.g. a furniture shop holds stocks of higher value than a sweet shop.
4. The credit-worthiness of the proprietors in the case of sole trader, partnership and private limited companies.

(*b*) QUICK ASSET RATIO. The quick assets are those which will quickly turn into cash, e.g. debtors, cash, and investments. Their ratio to current liabilities indicates the potential ability of the firm to meet its current liabilities without sales of stock. The ratio should not be below 1, normally. For example—

$$\frac{\text{Quick assets (debtors and cash) £2,500}}{\text{Current liabilities £3,000}} = \text{Quick Asset Ratio 0·83}$$

This ratio is sometimes called the "Acid Test."

(*c*) AVERAGE TURNOVER PERIOD. This is the ratio between the average stock held and the turnover (sales) for the period, multiplied by 12 to give in months the period for which stock is held. Average stock may be taken as the average of opening and closing stocks if more complete figures are not available, but obviously it is better to take the average of as many figures as can be obtained, e.g. monthly or weekly stocks.

Turnover may be taken as Sales, but it is better to take cost of sales, particularly in comparison with stocks, as both will then be at a comparable valuation. For example—

$$\frac{\text{Average stock held (Closing stock £3,500 + Opening stock £3,000)}}{\text{Cost of Sales £5,500} \times 2^*} \times 12$$

$$= \frac{3,250}{5,500} \times 12 = \text{Average Turnover Period 7·1 months (approx.)}$$

* Average stock is $\frac{£3,500 + £3,000}{2} = £3,250$

(*d*) AVERAGE CREDIT ALLOWED. This ratio relates debtors to sales, to show the average period of credit, which is the ratio between debtors and sales, multiplied by 12 to give the months of credit allowed. For example—

$$\frac{\text{Debtors £1,500}}{\text{Sales £8,000}} \times 12 = 2\tfrac{1}{4} \text{ months}$$

(*e*) AVERAGE CREDIT PERIOD TAKEN. This ratio shows the average credit period taken from supplies. It is the ratio between creditors and purchases, multiplied by 12 to give the months of credit taken.

$$\frac{\text{Creditors £1,000}}{\text{Purchases £6,000}} \times 12 = 2 \text{ months}$$

The average debtors or creditors should be taken as follows—

$$\frac{\text{Opening and closing debtors or creditors}}{2} = \text{Average debtors or creditors}$$

Ratios (*c*), (*d*) and (*e*) can also be expressed in terms of days or weeks by multiplying by 365 or 52.

The profitability ratio can be broken down into two components by bringing sales into the calculations—

$$\frac{\text{Profit}}{\text{Capital employed}} = \frac{\text{Profit}}{\text{Sales}} \times \frac{\text{Sales}}{\text{Capital employed}}$$

(*f*) THE MARGIN ON SALES. This is the profit expressed as a percentage of sales. In the example, using the total asset base it is—

$$\frac{£972,000}{£15,400,000} \times 100 = 6·3 \text{ per cent}$$

Rate of Gross Margin on Cost or Sales Price. It is important that comparison is always on same basis but turnover can be taken at cost or selling price. Cost Price + Gross Margin = Selling Price. The three elements are connected; e.g. 5p cost, 10p S.P. = 100% on cost or 50% on S.P.

(*g*) RATE OF ASSET (OR CAPITAL TURNOVER). This is the Sales divided by the capital employed and it shows the number of times the asset value is recovered by Sales each year. In the example it is—

$$\frac{£15{,}400{,}000}{£14{,}800\ 000} = 1{\cdot}04 \text{ times}$$

Multiplying the margin by the rate of asset turnover gives the profitability or rate of return. In the example it is—

$$6{\cdot}3 \text{ per cent} \times 1{\cdot}04 = 6{\cdot}6 \text{ per cent}$$

The next stage of the breakdown may be to analyse assets between fixed and working capital and to analyse profits in terms of Sales—Costs, or to calculate the rate of turnover of fixed assets.

3. SOLVENCY

(*a*) **Capital Gearing Ratio.** The way in which the capital is geared may affect the dividend expectations of the ordinary shareholders. The gearing is the ratio between the fixed interest borrowing and the ordinary shareholders, whose dividend may vary with the earnings available for distribution. Capital is highly geared if a small change in revenue produces a large change in ordinary share dividends. This will be the case if the proportion of fixed interest borrowing is high.

The ratio may also take into account preference shares carrying fixed dividends by treating them as borrowing because of their fixed return.

The effect can best be seen from an example—

Example 4

	5% Debentures	Ordinary Shares	Profits Earned	Interest	Ordinary Dividend	
Year 1	£	£	£	£	£	Rate
Company A (high-geared) .	100,000	100,000	10,000	5,000	5,000	5%
Company B (low-geared) .	40,000	160,000	10,000	2,000	8,000	5%
Year 2						
Company A . . .			20,000	5,000	15,000	15%
Company B . . .			20,000	2,000	18,000	11¼%
Year 3						
Company A . . .			40,000	5,000	35,000	35%
Company B . . .			40,000	2,000	38,000	$23\frac{7}{10}$%

The ratio of long-term debt to ordinary shares is £100,000 to £100,000 or 1:1 in Company A and £40,000 to £160,000 in Company B.

In example 3, the preference shares of £1,300,000 will be added to the debenture stocks and loans of £700. Not all analysts would agree on the way to treat the taxation equalization reserve, but if it is added to the Ordinary Shareholders funds, the ratio of long-term debt to ordinary shares will be £2 million debt to £8·6 million ordinary shareholders' equity, or 1:4·3.

(*b*) **Capital Gearing Percentage.** Alternatively, the debt may be expressed as a percentage either of the total assets or of the assets provided by the long-term funds (see p. 2911). In example 3 the debt as a percentage of the assets provided by long-term funds is, for Company A

$$\frac{£100,000}{£200,000} = 50 \text{ per cent.}$$

For Company B it is

$$\frac{£40,000}{£200,000} = 20 \text{ per cent.}$$

In example 4, the percentage is

$$\frac{£2\text{m}}{£10{\cdot}6\text{m}} = 19 \text{ per cent.}$$

If the percentage of the total assets is to be calculated, note that the current debt should also be included in the calculation. In example 4, the current liabilities are £4·2 million, giving a total debt of £6·2 million. The total assets, fixed and current, come to £14·8m, which gives a gearing percentage of

$$\frac{£6{\cdot}2\text{m}}{£14{\cdot}8\text{m}} = 42 \text{ per cent.}$$

Compared to the 19% long-term percentage debt to equity, this percentage gives a much better idea of the extent to which this company is relying on borrowed money for its finances.

(*c*) **Geared Earnings Percentage.** The gearing and earnings may be related by showing the percentage of each accruing to each source of funds at various profit levels.

COMPANY A

		Debentures	Ordinary
Capital		50%	50%
Revenue	Year 1	50%	50%
	Year 2	25%	75%
	Year 3	12½%	87½%

COMPANY B

		Debentures	Ordinary
Capital		20%	80%
Revenue	Year 1	20%	80%
	Year 2	10%	90%
	Year 3	5%	95%

(*d*) **Times Interest Earned.** This ratio shows the number of times the operating profit before interest and corporation tax covers the interest payable on long-term loans and debentures. It may also be called the interest cover.

Operating profit before corporation tax is taken because interest is deductible from profit before the tax.

$$\frac{\text{Operating profit before interest, tax and dividends}}{\text{Interest on long-term loans}} = \frac{£972}{136}$$

$$= 7{\cdot}1 \text{ times covered}$$

(*e*) **Times Preference Dividend Earned.** This ratio is similar to the times interest earned ratio but the profit is taken after interest and tax, since these are prior charges on profits before a preference dividend becomes payable.

$$\frac{\text{Operating profit after interest and tax}}{\text{Preference dividend payable}} = \frac{£634}{78}$$

$$= 8{\cdot}1 \text{ times covered}$$

(*f*) **Times Fixed Charges Earned.** Where a company is leasing assets or has other similar fixed charges the ratio of the profit before deducting them may be compared to the cost of fixed charges. If the company has fixed charges totalling £243, then

$$\frac{\text{Operating profit before fixed charges, tax and dividends}}{\text{Fixed charges}} = \frac{£972}{243}$$

$$= 4 \text{ times covered}$$

These ratios measure the extent to which a company's income may decline before it becomes impossible to meet the various claims on that income.

(*g*) **The Dividend Cover.** Compares the earnings per share to the dividend per share and indicates the extent to which earnings are being retained and ploughed back into the company. It also indicates how far the earnings would have to fall before they were insufficient to cover the dividend.

$$\frac{\text{Earnings per share}}{\text{Dividends per share}} = \frac{£0{\cdot}154}{£0{\cdot}075} = 2{\cdot}1 \text{ times covered}$$

(*h*) **Book Valuation.** Shares may be valued in the light of their net asset value, and this method has been dealt with earlier.

Inter-firm Comparison

A number of schemes are run by individual industries and a Centre for Inter-firm Comparison was set up in 1959 by the British Institute of Management and the British Productivity Council.

Confidentiality. The Centre is independent and self-supporting and no information supplied to it by companies is passed to any other organization. The results of inter-firm comparisons are made available to participating companies only.

The comparative data for participating firms appears under code numbers, in ratio, percentage and similar statistical form. The comparative ratios are unlikely to be the same as those which might be calculated from published accounts, because some of the information on which the ratios are based is not given in published accounts, and because for the purpose of the comparison such key items as the figures of profit and assets (both fixed and current) are defined in a special way.

Comparability. In each comparison that it conducts the Centre makes special arrangements to enable participants to arrive at figures on an agreed uniform basis, and to enable firms to compare their figures with those of others with which they have some important features in common—such as similar products, similar processes and similar marketing problems.

Each firm in each group is sent a simple questionnaire on its costs, sales, assets, etc. Most of the information required can be taken straight from a firm's normal accounting records. Each participating firm receives a General Report showing how it compares and why it differs; and a confidential Individual Report on the firm's own performance.

The schemes are usually run on a non-profit-making basis.

Objectives of Inter-firm Comparison. Inter-firm comparison is intended to show the management of each firm taking part—

(*a*) how its profitability and productivity compare with that of other firms in the same industry;

(*b*) in what respects the firm is weaker or stronger than its competitors; and

(*c*) what specific questions of policy or performance should be tackled if the firm's profitability and productivity are to be raised.

Benefits. The information emerging from comparative surveys may throw new light on such points as the following—

(*a*) The actual rate of return on capital being achieved in the industry;

(*b*) The industry's cost structure;

(*c*) The main areas of weaknesses and strengths found in participating firms;

(*d*) The areas where there seem to be "bottleneck" factors inhibiting economic growth.

Comparisons may also provide realistic quantitative assessments of the scope for increased productivity and efficiency in the industry, by showing what could be achieved if the majority of firms could obtain the actual performance of the "better firms."

The Pyramid of Ratios. Most schemes use a system of interlocking ratios starting with the profitability or return on capital at the apex of the pyramid. This is broken down systematically so that sources of an unsatisfactory return can be identified.

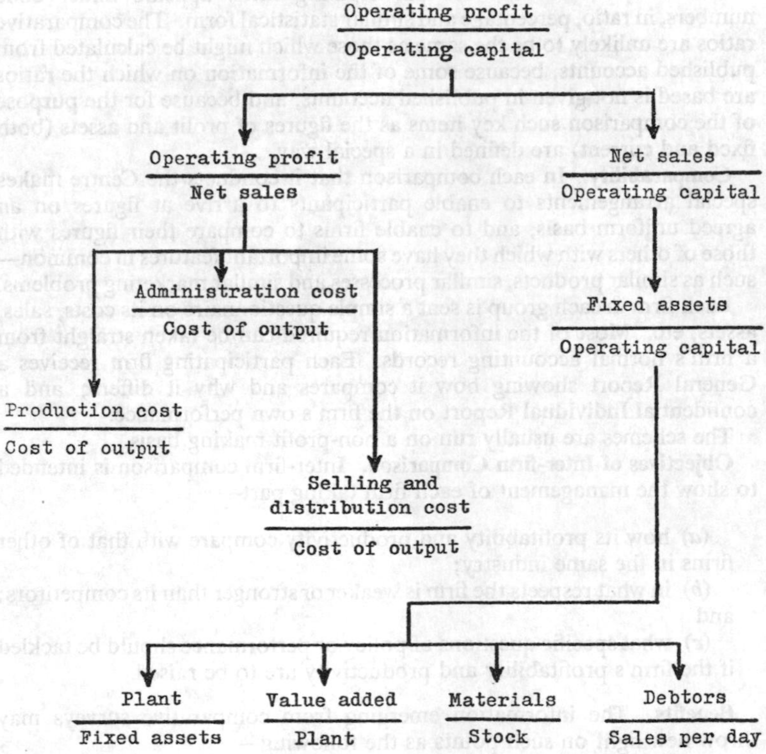

FIG. 29.2

For instance, the British Federation of Master Printers use the pyramid shown in Fig. 29.2.

STATEMENTS OF SOURCES AND DISPOSITION OF FUNDS

The analysis of two successive balance sheets may be carried a stage further by concentrating on the changes that have taken place and producing a statement which summarizes these changes. The effect is to show—

(a) SOURCES. Where extra funds have come from, whether from profits, borrowing, or issue of shares.

(b) DISPOSITION. What has been done with the extra funds raised, and whether they have increased the value of fixed or working capital.

The form adopted varies considerably, depending on the purpose of the statement and the amount of detail shown. Frequently the statement aims to explain the changes which have occurred in the working capital. This is, in fact, a reconciliation statement which reconciles the working capital shown on the opening balance sheet with that shown on the closing balance sheet. The following is an example—

Example 5

W.P.B. Ltd. presents the following balance sheet (simplified), p. 2924, to its shareholders on 31st July, 19.3.

It is clear from inspection that certain changes have taken place in the structure of the Balance Sheet and these may be clearly brought out by preparing a statement of Sources and Applications of funds.

The first step is to re-arrange the Balance Sheet in the vertical form, with the corresponding figures in two columns so that a third column may be used for the changes, as follows—

	31st July 1962	31st July 1963		Change
	£	£		£
Ordinary Share Capital	20,000	25,000		+5,000
Redeemable Preference Shares	10,000	Nil		−10,000
Capital Redemption Reserve Fund	Nil	5,000		+5,000
General Reserve	8,000	3,000		−5,000
Profit and Loss Account	2,000	9,000		+7,000
Trade Creditors	10,000	16,000		+6,000
	50,000	58,000		+8,000
Fixed Assets at cost	40,000	50,000		+10,000
Less Depreciation	10,000	14,000	(*less*)	+4,000
	30,000	36,000		+6,000
Investments	6,000	4,000		−2,000
Current Assets	14,000	18,000		+4,000
	50,000	58,000		+8,000

Since the liabilities represent sources of funds it follows that an increase in an item on the liabilities side of the Balance Sheet represents the flow of funds into the business—a source. The increase of an asset represents a flow of funds out of the business—an application.

Conversely the decrease of an item on the liabilities side must represent an application of funds and the decrease of an asset represents a source of capital.

BALANCE SHEET AT 31ST DECEMBER, 19.3

Corresponding Figures at End of previous Period			Corresponding Figures at End of previous Period		
£		£	£		£
20,000	Ordinary Share Capital . . .	25,000	40,000	Fixed Assets at cost	50,000
10,000	Redeemable Preference Shares . .	—	10,000	*Less* Depreciation	14,000
			30,000		36,000
	Capital Redemption Reserve Fund .	5,000	6,000	Investments at cost	4,000
8,000	General Reserve	3,000	14,000	Current Assets	18,000
2,000	Profit and Loss account . . .	9,000			
10,000	Trade Creditors	16,000			
50,000		58,000	50,000		58,000

Before we apply this simple logic, however, we must take a closer look at the sources of funds. How do funds come into a business? In the first place they may come from outside, from long-term sources such as the subscription of capital by shareholders or the loan of funds by debenture holders or a bank; alternatively they may come from short-term sources such as trade and expense creditors or bank overdrafts.

A further important source of funds to the firm, however, once it is established, is the funds it generates itself by its operations.

It is clearly desirable to show what funds have been obtained from each source and especially to show what flow has resulted from operations. This latter figure may have to be calculated by adding back to profits any non-cash debits such as transfers to Reserves or provisions such as depreciation.

Any analysis of sources of funds, then, must be presented to show clearly the total cash flow resulting from profits and this involves adding back to profits any "non-cash debits."

With this in mind, let us return to our Example 5, considering each item in the Balance Sheet in turn.

In Fig. 29.3 the transfer of each change to the Sources or Applications column has been charted.

(*a*) Ordinary Share Capital has increased by £5,000 and this is a source of funds.

(*b*) The Redeemable Preference Shares have been redeemed and this represents an application of funds of £10,000.

(*c*) Whilst the Capital Redemption Reserve Fund has increased by £5,000 the General Reserve has decreased by the same amount and this is simply a book transfer to comply with Section 58 of the Companies Act, 1948.

(*d*) Trade creditors have increased by £6,000, which is a source of funds.

(*e*) The cost of Fixed Assets has increased by £10,000 which means an application of funds.

(*f*) Depreciation has increased, but, of course, it is a deduction from the fixed assets. It is a source of funds, but as such it is a part of the cash flow from profits and it should be added back to the profit figure (see (*i*) below).

(*g*) Investments have decreased by £2,000 on cost, this is a source of funds. As we sold them for £2,000 we must have received this amount of cash back into the firm.

(*h*) Current assets have increased by £4,000, which is an application of funds.

(*i*) The profit figure is left to the last because it must be built up from various items on the Balance Sheet. In this case, only depreciation is

Item	Change		SOURCES	APPLICATIONS
	£		£	£
Ordinary Share Capital	+ 5,000		5,000	
Redeemable Preference Shares	- 10,000			10,000
Capital Redemption Reserve Fund	+ 5,000	Book Transfer		
General Reserve	- 5,000			
Profit and Loss Account	+ 7,000	+ 4,000	11,000	
Trade Creditors	+ 6,000		6,000	
	+ 8,000			
Fixed Assets at cost	+ 10,000			10,000
<u>less</u> Depreciation	+ 4,000			
	+ 6,000			
Investments	- 2,000		2,000	
Current Assets	+ 4,000			4,000
	+ 8,000		£24,000	£24,000

FIG. 29.3

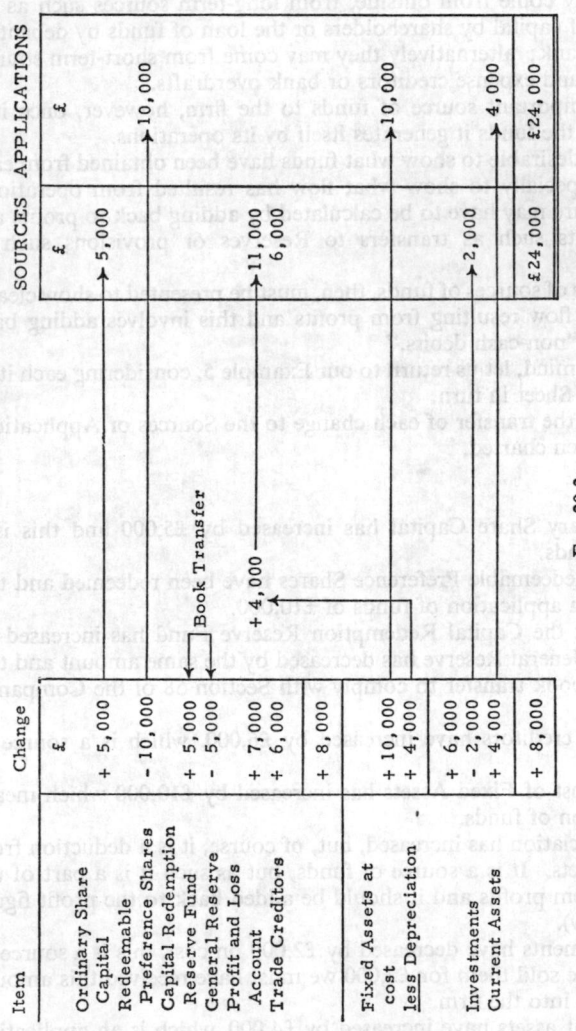

involved. Adding across, the source of funds from profits amounts to £11,000.

This information can now be presented in the usual form—

STATEMENT OF SOURCES AND APPLICATIONS OF CAPITAL FOR W.P.B. LTD. FOR THE PERIOD ENDED 31ST JULY, 1963

Sources. During the year, the company obtained funds from the following sources—	£	£
1. By the issue of 5,000 additional £1 Ordinary Shares	5,000	
2. From its own profit-earnings	11,000	
3. By increased borrowing from Trade Creditors	6,000	
4. By the sale of investments	2,000	
		24,000
Applications. These funds were applied to the following purposes—		
1. To the Redemption of Redeemable Preference Shares	10,000	
2. To the purchase of fixed assets	10,000	
3. To an increased investment in current assets	4,000	
		24,000

Example 6

From the following Balance Sheet of Southborne Ltd., prepare a statement to show the additional resources which became available during the year to 31st March, 1959, and how they were utilized, stating what you consider to be the value of this type of statement.

	At 31st March 1959	1958
	£	£
Issued Share Capital	100,000	75,000
Capital Reserve	20,635	16,000
Revenue Reserves—		
General	43,000	23,000
Taxation Equalization	18,000	16,000
Profit and Loss Account	21,290	19,680
	202,925	149,680
Future Income Tax	16,500	14,000
Mortgage Loans	28,000	30,068
Current Liabilities—		
Trade and Expense Creditors	65,000	48,000
Profits Tax to date	2,310	1,100
Proposed Dividend (net)	5,750	5,750
	320,485	248,598
Fixed Assets at cost	250,258	200,500
Less Depreciation	89,580	69,000
Carried forward	160,678	131,500

	At 31st March 1959	1958
	£	£
Brought forward	160,678	131,500
Trade Investments at cost	7,658	8,967
Current Assets—		
Stocks	41,924	29,280
Debtors	82,000	62,150
Cash in Hand	920	820
Balance at Bank	27,305	15,881
	320,485	248,598

NOTES: 1. Additions to Fixed Assets during the year amounted to £60,000, whilst assets which cost £10,242, book value £9,242, were sold for £13,877.

2. An investment which cost £6,612 was sold for £5,699, and the loss was written off to Profit and Loss Account.

3. A new investment was purchased for £5,303.

4. Accretions to the General and Taxation Equalization Reserves represented transfers from Profit and Loss Account.

5. Amounts charged to Profit and Loss Account for Taxation on current profits were: Profits Tax £2,310 and Future Taxation, £15,880.

(*London Chamber of Commerce. Higher Accounting paper Autumn* 1959.)

Following the method suggested, the changes in the Balance Sheet items are listed on the left and the columns for Sources and Applications drawn on the right of Fig. 29.4.

The individual items were calculated as follows—

(*a*) The increase in share capital was a source of £25,000 funds.

(*b*) The capital reserve presents a problem—how did it arise? The answer is that it is the profit made on the sale of assets for £13,877, which was a source of funds, and this is the amount which must be entered in the Sources column (£13,877). The balance of the proceeds is £9,242, which is the book value of the assets when they were sold. This book value represents the difference between the cost and depreciation provided of £1,000 and the profit on sale of £4,635 has been carried to Capital Reserve. But the fixed assets have increased by £49,758 according to the Balance Sheet. The difference arises from the purchase of assets for £60,000 in the year.

Similarly, the increase in the depreciation shown by the Balance Sheet is £20,580, but there was a decrease of £1,000 in the depreciation provision on account of the assets sold, so that the charge made against profits must have been £21,580. Since this represents a source of funds from profits, it is carried back to the profit and loss account.

(*c*) The General Reserve and the Tax Equalization Reserve have increased by £20,000 and £2,000 respectively and both these items should be carried back to the profit and loss account.

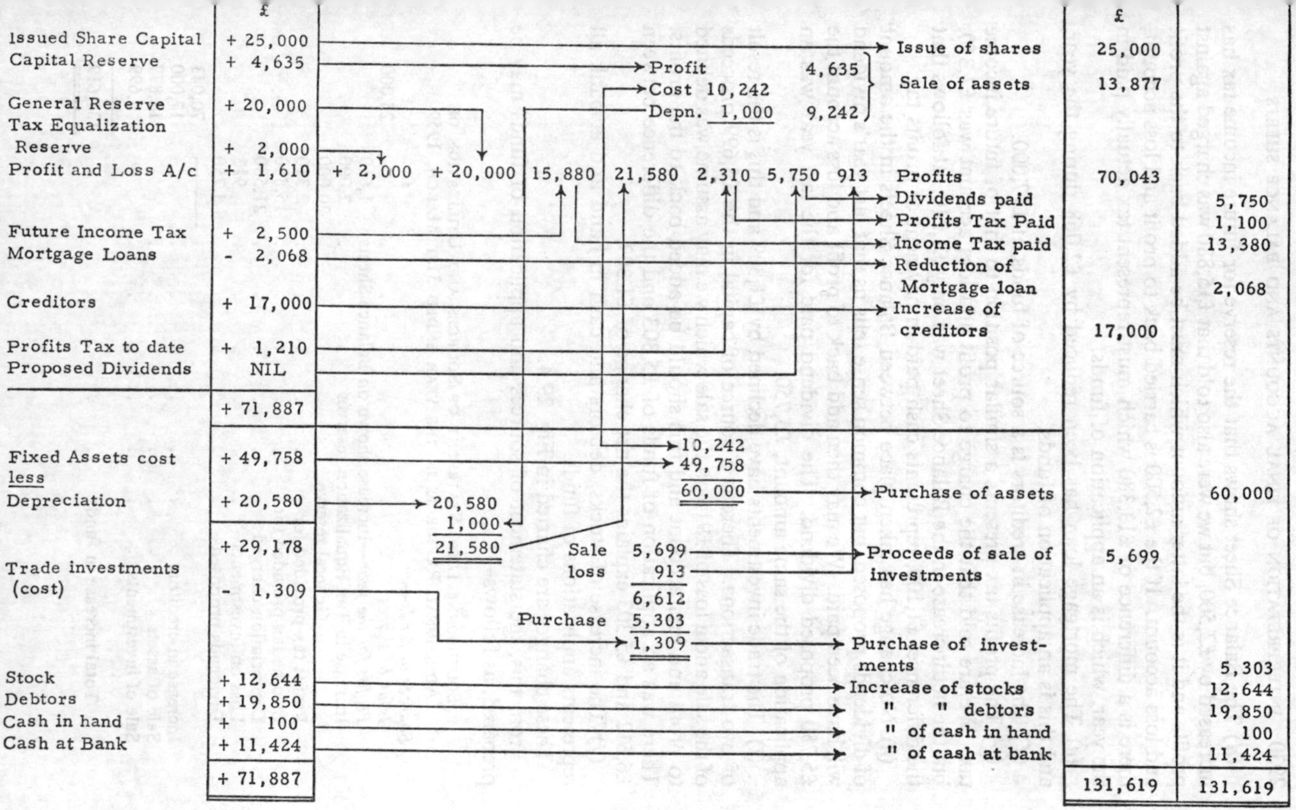
£
Issued Share Capital + 25,000
Capital Reserve + 4,635
General Reserve + 20,000
Tax Equalization Reserve + 2,000
Profit and Loss A/c + 1,610
Future Income Tax + 2,500
Mortgage Loans - 2,068
Creditors + 17,000
Profits Tax to date + 1,210
Proposed Dividends NIL
+ 71,887
Fixed Assets cost + 49,758
less
Depreciation + 20,580
+ 29,178
Trade investments (cost) - 1,309
Stock + 12,644
Debtors + 19,850
Cash in hand + 100
Cash at Bank + 11,424
+ 71,887
Profit 4,635
Cost 10,242
Depn. 1,000 9,242
+ 2,000 + 20,000 15,880 21,580 2,310 5,750 913
10,242
49,758
60,000
20,580
1,000
21,580
Sale 5,699
loss 913
6,612
Purchase 5,303
1,309
£
Issue of shares 25,000
Sale of assets 13,877
Profits 70,043
Dividends paid 5,750
Profits Tax Paid 1,100
Income Tax paid 13,380
Reduction of Mortgage loan 2,068
Increase of creditors 17,000
Purchase of assets 60,000
Proceeds of sale of investments 5,699
Purchase of investments 5,303
Increase of stocks 12,644
" " debtors 19,850
" of cash in hand 100
" of cash at bank 11,424
131,619 131,619

(*d*) The Balance Sheet shows that the reserve for future income tax has increased by £2,500, but we were also told that £15,880 was charged against profits and it is the latter amount which must be added back to the profit and loss account. If the £2,500 is carried back to profit and loss account, there is a difference of £13,380 which must represent tax actually paid in the year, which is an application of funds.

(*e*) The mortgage loan has been reduced by £2,068 during the year, and this is an application of funds.

(*f*) The increase in creditors is a source of funds of £17,000.

(*g*) The profits tax presents a similar position to that of future income tax. We are told that the charge to profit and loss account was £2,310, but the net increase in the Balance Sheet was only £1,210. It follows that the difference, £1,100, represents cash paid in payment of profits tax.

(*h*) No change has taken place between Balance Sheets in the amount of dividends proposed, but common sense tells us that last year's dividend will have been paid. We may then add back to profit and loss account the £5,750 proposed dividend. The dividend paid for the last year was an application of the same amount, £5,750.

(*i*) The trade investments have declined by £1,309 and this is the result of two transactions. There is a source of capital in the £5,699 proceeds of the sale and a loss of £913 on the sale which we may assume was debited to profit and loss account and this should be added back to the profits. There was an application of funds of £5,303 and the difference between £6,612 and £5,303 explains the net change of £1,309.

(*j*) The increase of stocks, debtors and cash in hand and at bank all represents applications of funds.

These changes are charted in Fig. 29.4.

From this, the statement of sources and application of funds may be prepared, as follows—

SOUTHBORNE LTD., STATEMENT OF SOURCES AND UTILIZATION OF ADDITIONAL RESOURCES IN THE YEAR ENDED 31ST MARCH, 1959

	£	£
Sources of funds—		
Issue of shares		25,000
Profits for the year—Increase shown on Balance Sheets	1,610	
Increase in Tax Equalization reserves	2,000	
,, ,, General reserve	20,000	
Profits tax provided for	2,310	
Income tax provided for	15,880	
Depreciation charged	21,580	
Loss on investments	913	
Dividends proposed	5,750	
		70,043
Increase in creditors		17,000
Sale of assets		13,877
Sale of investments		5,699
Total increase in funds		131,619

	£
Utilization of funds—	
Purchase of assets	60,000
Reduction of mortgage loan	2,068
Purchase of new investment	5,303
Increase of stock-holding	12,644
,, ,, debtors	19,850
,, ,, cash in hand	100
,, ,, cash at bank	11,424
Income tax paid	13,380
Profits tax paid	1,100
Dividends paid	5,750
Total of new funds utilized	131,619

From this statement we may see that all the increase of funds in the company during the year came from the owners of the firm, except for £17,000 provided by creditors, and more than half the increase came from profits.

The funds were used for substantial purchases of fixed assets but there was also a serious increase in current assets. The amount of £20,230 was paid out of the firm in tax and dividends.

Two main variations of the statement of sources and application of funds may be used. These relate the changes (*a*) to the cash position, so that the reasons for changes in cash are shown, or (*b*) to the working capital position.

The changes in Cash Statement, require little more than a re-arrangement of the figures. The change in cash is omitted and the statement commences with the opening cash. The remaining changes (sources or applications) are added or subtracted to arrive at the closing cash position.

The result is—

STATEMENT OF CHANGES IN THE CASH POSITION OF SOUTHBORNE LTD., IN THE YEAR ENDED 31ST MARCH, 1959

	£	£
Cash in hand and at bank at the start of the year		16,701
To which may be added funds obtained during the year—		
Shares issue	25,000	
Profits earned	70,043	
Increased borrowing from creditors	17,000	
Sale of fixed assets	13,877	
Sales of investments	5,699	
		131,619
Making available funds of		148,320
These were applied to—		
Purchase of assets	60,000	
Reduction of mortgage loan	2,068	
Purchase of new investments	5,303	
Increased stock-holding	12,644	
,, debtors	19,850	
Payments of tax	14,480	
,, of dividends	5,750	
		120,095
Leaving cash in hand and at bank at 31st March, 1959		28,225

The changes in Working Capital Statement are similar. The statement will start with the opening working capital position. The other items will show sources of capital which have increased the working capital, and applications of capital to fixed investment or to purposes such as dividend payments which have reduced the working capital. Finally, the statement will show the closing working capital.

If only the working capital form of statement is required, however, it may be simpler to draw up the chart in a slightly different way, starting with the calculation of the changes in net working capital.

The Vatter Method. An alternative and widely used method of solving problems of analysing funds flow has been developed by Professor William J. Vatter. This can be applied using any concept of funds, but will be used here to illustrate the preparation of statements of changes in Working Capital.

The procedure is as follows—

1. The Balance changes are analysed according to whether they represent increases on the debit or credit side of the accounts.

2. The current assets and the current liabilities changes are offset to give the change in Net Working Capital.

3. T accounts are opened for each balance sheet item for which a change has been identified.

4. The changes are entered in each T account as a debit or credit and a line is then drawn across the account below the change. The reason for this is that the analysis is retrospective (i.e. the purpose is to establish how the net change arose from the transactions in the past period). Each change is the final balance resulting from transactions affecting the account. Entries made below the line must eventually result in the net change shown above the line.

5. Where information is given on changes that have occurred during the year, the normal double entry is made in the T accounts. Entries affecting current assets or liabilities are debited or credited to Net Working Capital account.

6. When all the information given has been entered there may still be accounts showing changes, e.g. Fixed Assets may show an unexplained debit increase, debentures may show an unexplained credit increase. These changes show transactions which we have not been told. We may assume in the examples that fixed assets were purchased and debentures issued to the public. New T accounts may be required for transactions which were completed in the year, e.g. profits tax provided and paid.

7. The Sources of funds will be debits to the Net Working Capital and Applications will be credits. It is convenient to divide Sources into two types, operations and other sources, since some debits to Net Working Capital will be items such as annual depreciation and losses on sale of assets which have already been debited (and must therefore be added back) to reported profits for the year.

To illustrate the method, let us take Example 6 on p. 2927. The Balance Sheet changes in terms of debits and credits are as follows—

	Debit £	Credit £
Issued Share Capital		25,000
Capital Reserve		4,635
Revenue Reserves—		
General		20,000
Taxation Equalization		2,000
Profit and Loss Account		1,610
Future Income Tax		2,500
Mortgage Loans	2,068	
Fixed Assets	49,758	
Depreciation		20,580
Trade Investments		1,309
Net Working Capital	25,808	
	£77,634	£77,634

The change in Net Working Capital is calculated—

	1959 £	1958 £	Debit Increase
Current Assets	152,149	108,131	
Current Liabilities	73,060	54,850	
	£79,089	£53,281	£25,808

The T accounts can be worked as follows—

NET WORKING CAPITAL

	25,808		
Operations	£		£
(*b*) Loss on investment	913	(1) Fixed Asset Purchase	60,000
(*g*) Depreciation	21,580	(3) Investment Purchase	5,303
(*h*) Net Profit	47,550	(*c*) Profits tax paid	2,310
		(*d*) Income tax paid	13,380
		(*f*) Loan repayment	2,068
Other sources		(*h*) Dividend declared	5,750
(1) Proceeds of sale of assets (*a*)	13,877		
(2) Proceeds of investment sales (*b*)	5,699		(*i*) £88,811
(*e*) Issue of shares	25,000		
	(1) £114,619		

Issued Share Capital

			25,000
		(*e*) Issue of shares . . .	25,000

Future Income Tax

			2,500
(*d*) Net Working Capital Tax paid	13,380	(5) P & L A/c	15,880

Mortgage Loan

	2,068		
(*f*) Net Working Capital Repayment . . .	2,068		

Fixed Assets

	49,758		
(1) Net Working Capital Additions	60,000	(1) Sales (2)	10,242

Capital Reserve

			4,635
		(4) Profit on Asset Sale . .	4,635

General Reserve

			20,000
		(4) P & L A/c . . .	20,000

Taxation Equalization

			2,000
		(4) P & L A/c	2,000

PROFIT AND LOSS A/C

			1,610
(4) General Reserve	20,000	(h) Profit before tax and appropriations	47,550
Tax Equalization	2,000		
(5) Future Taxation	15,880		
Profits Tax (c)	2,310		
Dividends declared	5,750		

DEPRECIATION

			20,580
(1) Sale of assets	1,000	(g) Annual depreciation	21,580

TRADE INVESTMENTS

			1,309
(3) Purchases	5,303	(2) Sales (b)	6,612

Notes: (*a*) Sale of assets. The best method is to envisage the journal entry when an asset is sold. In the example it would be—

	Debit £	Credit £
Proceed of sale (Cash or NWC)	13,877	
Depreciation	1,000	
Fixed Assets (cost)		10,242
Profit on sale (Capital Reserve)		4,635
	£14,877	£14,877

Proceeds of sale would normally be debited to cash or debtors: in this case we debit Net Working Capital, since the proceeds are the flow of funds in this transaction.

If a profit or loss has been made on the sale, we would assume that these were shown in the Profit and Loss Account and have, therefore, decreased or increased the reported profits. The reported profits therefore under- or over-estimate the flow of funds from operations. A loss must be added back and a profit deducted from funds from operations.

However, in this case the Capital Reserve has increased by £4,635 so that the profit was obviously placed directly to that account.

(*b*) The journal entry for the sale of investments would be—

	Debit	Credit
	£	£
Proceeds of sale	5,699	
Loss on sale	913	
Investments		6,612
	£6,612	£6,612

(*c*) From the viewpoint of this analysis, provision for the tax amounts to a flow of funds.

(*d*) Since Future Income Tax has been credited with £15,880 but only showed a net change of £2,500, there must have been a payment of £13,380.

(*e*) There is an unexplained increase of £25,000 on the Share Capital A/c. It is assumed to be an issue.

STATEMENT OF THE CHANGES IN WORKING CAPITAL OF SOUTHBORNE LTD., IN THE YEAR ENDED 31ST MARCH, 1959

	£	£	£
Current Assets on 31st March, 1958	108,131		
Current Liabilities on 31st March, 1958	54,850		
Net Working Capital at 1st April, 1958			53,281
To which were added funds from—			
Operations—Net profit reported	47,550		
Add Depreciation	21,580		
Loss on investment	913		
		70,043	
Other Sources—Sale of assets	13,877		
Sale of investments	5,699		
Issue of shares	25,000		
		44,576	
			114,619
Working Capital available			167,900
From which the following applications were made—			
Purchase of fixed assets	60,000		
Purchase of investments	5,303		
Repayments on loan	2,068		
Profits tax provided	2,310		
Future Income Tax Paid	13,380		
Dividend declared	5,750		
			88,811
Leaving Working Capital on 31st March, 1959			£79,089

Current assets	152,149
" liabilities	73,060
	79,089

(*f*) The Mortgage Loan has a debit increase of £2,068. This is a repayment.

(*g*) Depreciation showed a net increase of £20,580 in the year although there was a decrease of £1,000 on the sale of the asset. The Profit and Loss Account must have been debited with an annual provision of £21,580.

(*h*) The net income from operations after depreciation but before tax and appropriations must have been £47,550 since there was a net increase of £1,610 after debits totalling £45,940. Dividends of £5,750 have been declared and are shown. The declaration represents a funds flow.

(*i*) Totalling the debits and credits to Net Working Capital shows that these result in a net change of £25,808.

The statement of Sources and Applications of funds can now be prepared in relation to Working Capital as on p. 2936.

A comprehensive example to illustrate these points is given below. The student is advised to go through it noting the possible explanations for the position shown. If possible, he should discuss the example with a fellow-student or a qualified man, and he may well be surprised by the variety of explanations which arise.

Example 7

Analysis of Final Accounts

THE COMPREHENSIVE CO. LTD.

(000s omitted)

REVENUE ACCOUNTS (SUMMARIZED) YEAR TO 31ST DECEMBER, 19..

	Last Year £	Last Year %	This Year £	This Year %
1. Sales	16,000	100·0	20,000	100·0
2. Cost of Goods Sold—				
Stock, 1st January	5,600		6,000	
Purchases	11,920		16,000	
	17,520		22,000	
Stock, 31st December	6,000		7,000	
Cost of goods sold	11,520	72·0	15,000	75·0
3. Gross profit	4,480	28·0	5,000	25·0
4. Expenses—				
Selling and distribution	450	2·9	550	2·7
Van depreciation	840	5·2	1,000	5·0
Administrative	1,720	10·7	1,850	9·3
Financial	400	2·5	600	3·0
	3,410	21·3	4,000	20·0
5. Net Profit before Tax	1,070	6·7	1,000	5·0
6. Provision for Tax	580		400	
7. Net Profit after Tax	490		600	
Preference dividend (*less* tax at 45p in the £)	110		110	
Ordinary dividend (*less* tax at 45p in the £)	198		198	
8. Added to carry forward	182		292	
	490		600	

COMPREHENSIVE CO. LTD.

(000s omitted)

BALANCE SHEETS (SUMMARIZED)

	Last Year £	%	This Year £	%	Change During This Year £
ASSETS AND LIABILITIES					
1. Current Assets—					
Bank			2,200	11·0	2,200
Debtors	2,600	18·9	4,400	22·0	1,800
Stock	6,000	43·6	7,000	35·0	1,000
	8,600	62·5	13,600	68·0	5,000
2. *Less* Current Liabilities—					
Bank Overdraft	1,850	13·5	—	—	−1,850
Creditors	2,000	14·5	3,040	15·2	1,040
Tax	400	2·9	560	2·8	160
	4,250	30·9	3,600	18·0	−650
3. Net Working Capital	4,350	31·6	10,000	50·0	5,650
4. Fixed Assets—					
Motor Vehicles:					
Cost at 1st January	4,440	32·3	4,440	22·2	
Additions			1,600	8·0	1,600
			6,040	30·2	
Less Depreciation	2,040	14·8	3,040	15·2	1,000
	2,400	17·5	3,000	15·0	
Premises	7,000	50·9	7,000	35·0	
	9,400	68·4	10,000	50·0	600
5. Total Assets *less* Current Liabilities	13,750	100·0	20,000	100·0	6,250
6. *Less* 5% Debentures	—		6,000	30·0	6,000
7. Total Assets *less* all Liabilities (EQUITY)	£13,750		£14,000		£250
OWNERS' INTEREST					
8. Preference Shareholders 5% cumulative shares	4,000	29·1	4,000	20·0	
9. Ordinary Shareholders (EQUITY)—					
Profit & Loss A/c	1,050	8·4	1,442	7·21	292
Future Taxation	514	4·1	518	2·59	−42
Reserve (General)	2,040	14·8	2,040	10·20	
Ordinary Shares	6,000	43·6	6,000	30·00	
	9,750	70·9	10,000	50·00	
	£13,750	100·0	£14,000	100·00	£250

Ratios that might be calculated from the foregoing balance sheet and revenue account are—

	Last Year	*This Year*
(*a*) Working capital ratio— $\frac{\text{current assets}}{\text{current liabilities}}$	$\frac{8{,}600}{4{,}250} = 2{\cdot}0$	$\frac{13{,}600}{3{,}600} = 3{\cdot}8$
(*b*) Quick asset ratio— $\frac{\text{debtors \& cash}}{\text{current liabilities}}$	$\frac{2{,}600}{4{,}250} = 0{\cdot}6$	$\frac{6{,}600}{3{,}600} = 1{\cdot}8$
(*c*) Average turnover period— $\frac{\text{average stock}}{\text{cost of sales}}$	$\frac{5{,}600 + 6{,}000}{2 \times 11{,}520} \times 12 = 6$ mos.	$\frac{6{,}000 + 7{,}000}{2 \times 15{,}000} \times 12 = 5{\cdot}2$ mos.

(*d*) Average credit periods—

(i) *allowed*—

$\frac{\text{average debtors}}{\text{sales}}$ $\quad \frac{2,600}{16,000} \times 12 = 2 \text{ mos.} \quad \frac{2,600 + 4,400}{2 \times 20,000} \times 12 = 2{\cdot}1 \text{ mos.}$

(ii) *taken*—

$\frac{\text{average creditors}}{\text{purchases}}$ $\quad \frac{2,000}{11,920} \times 12 = 2 \text{ mos.} \quad \frac{2,000 + 3,040}{2 \times 16,000} \times 12 = 1{\cdot}9 \text{ mos.}$

(*e*) Earnings rates on—

(i) *total assets*

$\frac{\text{net profit}}{\text{total assets}}$ $\quad \frac{1,070}{18,000} \times 100 = 5{\cdot}9\% \quad \frac{1,000}{23,600} \times 100 = 4{\cdot}2\%$

(ii) *equity interest*

$\frac{\text{profit (before tax)} - \text{perf. div. (gross)}}{\text{equity interest}}$

$\frac{1,070 - 200}{9,750} \times 100 = 8{\cdot}9\% \quad \frac{1,000 - 200}{10,000} \times 100 = 8\%$

A specimen statement of sources and distribution of funds is shown below.

STATEMENT OF SOURCES AND DISTRIBUTION OF FUNDS

	£	£
1. *Opening working capital*		4,350
2. Increase in profit and loss a/c (net)	250	
3. (*a*) *Add* Increase in capital— Debenture issue	6,000	
	6,250	
(*b*) *Deduct* new investment (vehicles)	600	
Net increase in working capital		5,650
Working capital at end of year		10,000

Alternatively, the quick asset increase can be explained—

	£	£
Increase in quick assets (net) during year—		
At close of year (£6,600 − £3,600)		3,000
At start of year (£2,600 − £4,250) deficiency		1,650
		4,650
This increase has been got—		
Long-term funds made available during year:		
Increase in revenue reserves		250
Debentures issued		6,000
		6,250
Less Disbursements—		
Additions to motor vehicles	1,600	
Less Obtained from depreciation for year	1,000	
	600	
Increase in stock	1,000	
		1,600
		4,650

THE CASH BUDGET, FORECAST OF TRADING ACCOUNT, PROFIT AND LOSS AND BALANCE SHEET

Many businesses today operate a system of Budgetary Control, specifying the expenditure to be incurred in different sections of a business and holding the head of a section responsible for keeping within his budget.

Even if the financial planning has not reached such a high level of control, however, cash budgets may be prepared periodically so that at least the cash position of the business is controlled. It is also customary to prepare a cash budget and profit and loss account for the first year of a business and the balance sheet expected at the end of the year, as a guide to the capital requirements.

Starting with a balance sheet, a cash budget may be prepared, say for the next twelve months, provided realistic assumptions may be made about the influx and outflow of cash.

Naturally, the form of cash budget will vary according to the circumstances, but in general a columnar form of presentation is to be preferred. Usually a cash budget is prepared annually, showing the cash position for each of the ensuing twelve months. It is not sufficient to show that the next annual cash balance will be healthy, because seasonal factors may affect the business and result in some "sticky" periods during the year when cash is very short.

In practice too, a cash budget is usually revised weekly or monthly.

Sources of Cash Budget—

1. Opening Cash Balance is obtained from the balance sheet at the commencement of the period.

2. Receipts—

(*a*) Sundry debtors: the net cash receivable in each period must be calculated from the anticipated sales. The average period of credit allowed must be calculated from the revenue accounts, or assumed (see Ratios). For example, if the period is two months, sales in January will be paid for in March. Trade and cash discounts must be deducted.

(*b*) Sales of capital assets will bring in additional cash, and any such anticipated sales should be brought into account.

(*c*) Issues of debentures or shares will also result in cash inflow and must be included.

(*d*) Miscellaneous income, such as rent receivable, transfer fees, etc., should be included.

3. Payments—

(*a*) The payment to creditors must be calculated in the same way as receipts from debtors, taking the anticipated purchases as the basis.

(*b*) Wages and expenses will be known or can be estimated if the composition of the cost of sales is known. Whilst wages are likely to be steady, expenses due may fluctuate widely if several expenses fall due at the same time.

(*c*) Profit appropriations shown in the final accounts may not have been paid in the period in which they arose. Interest and debentures and loans may arise and interim dividends be paid in the period.

(*d*) The purchase of assets and investments will result in cash outflow and must be budgeted for.

4. THE CLOSING BALANCE will be the result of the above factors.

Profit and Loss Forecast. Working on the same information as used in the cash budget, the trading and profit and loss accounts can easily be drawn up.

Balance Sheet. The information resulting will also allow a budgeted balance sheet for the last day of the period to be drawn up.

Example 8

The following information concerns Predigestion Ltd., and from it you are asked to prepare a cash budget for the next six months.

BALANCE SHEET OF PREDIGESTION LTD. ON 31ST DECEMBER, 19..

	£		£
Ordinary Share Capital	80,000	Fixed Assets	63,000
Long-term Liabilities—		*Current Assets—*	
5% Debentures	30,000	Stock	30,000
Current Liabilities—		Debtors	25,000
Trade Creditors	20,000	Cash	12,000
	130,000		130,000

(*a*) Sales are budgeted at £288,000 for the year, but sales in April to September are double the amount in other months.

(*b*) Each unit costs £2, which is split up as follows—

Raw Materials	45 per cent
Wages	30 per cent
Overhead	10 per cent

(*c*) Stocks of finished goods are £16,000 (at sales value). The rest are raw materials. Production and purchases are sufficient to maintain stocks.

(*d*) Suppliers allow one month's credit, and customers are given two months. You may assume that overhead is spread evenly throughout the year.

(*e*) Ignore work-in-progress.

(*f*) Debenture interest is payable in April and September.

NOTE—

Sales are £288,000 at £2 per unit = 144,000 units.

For six months sales are double "normal" level.

$\therefore$ Normal month's sales $\frac{144000}{18}$ = 8,000 per month

Sales in April, May, and June = 16,000 per month

Total sales for period = 72,000 units.

The cash budget and forecast trading and profit and loss account and balance sheet will appear as shown on p. 2942.

Valuation of Shares. Shares may need to be valued for various reasons. When one company absorbs another, the terms of the absorption will usually involve valuing the shares of both companies. Banks need to make a valuation of shares deposited with them as security. Many companies hold shares as investments and are required by the Companies Act to show

PREDIGESTION LTD.

	Jan	Feb	Mar	Apr	May	Jun
Sales in units	8,000	8,000	8,000	16,000	16,000	16,000
	£	£	£	£	£	£
CASH BUDGET						
Opening Balance—						
Dr	+12,000					
Cr		−1,900	−3,000	−600	−4,975	−16,175
Receipts—						
Debtors	12,500	12,500	16,000	16,000	16,000	32,000
	24,500	10,600	13,000	15,400	11,025	15,825
Payments—						
Wages	4,800	4,800	4,800	9,600	9,600	9,600
Overheads	1,600	1,600	1,600	3,200	3,200	3,200
Creditors (materials)	20,000	7,200	7,200	7,200	14,400	14,400
Debenture Interest (*less* tax at 10s.)				375		
Balance to next month c/f						
Dr						
Cr	−1,900	−3,000	−600	−4,975	−16,175	−11,375

Predigestion Ltd. will certainly need additional cash in the coming year. But should they try to obtain an overdraft or raise additional capital? That depends on whether their need for capital is temporary or permanent. The next six months of the cash budget may well give the answer to that question.

FORECAST TRADING AND PROFIT AND LOSS ACCOUNT FOR SIX MONTHS TO 30TH JUNE, 19..

	£	£		£
Raw materials—			Sales 72,000 units	144,000
Opening Stock	14,000		(Stocks of finished goods may be ignored as they are constant—see Raw Materials, of which the same is true.)	
Purchases	64,800			
Closing Stock	14,000	64,800		
Wages		43,200		
Overheads		14,400		
Debenture Interest (net)		375		
Net profit for period		21,225		
		144,000		144,000

BALANCE SHEET ON 30TH JUNE, 19..

	£		£	£
Ordinary Share Capital	80,000	*Fixed Assets*		63,000
Profit & Loss A/c balance	21,225	*Current Assets*		
Long-term Liabilities—		Stocks—		
5% Debentures	30,000	Raw Materials	14,000	
Trade Creditors	14,400	Finished Goods	16,000	
Cash (overdraft)	11,375			30,000
		Debtors		64,000
	157,000			157,000

the market value. In the case of companies and trusts whose main purpose is investment, the valuation of the shares held is of vital importance.

YIELD VALUATION. If shares are quoted on the Stock Exchange, then the price gives one valuation of the shares. Some examples of the calculations involved may be seen in Chapter 08 on Stock Exchange transactions and investment accounts. The Stock Exchange price is, generally speaking, based on the yield of the shares. If an investor expects 5 per cent return on his investment and he is offered three shares, all of the same nominal value, he will value them in proportion to the dividends paid—

1. £1 Ordinary share in A Ltd. Dividend 12 per cent.

Valuation $\frac{12}{5} \times £1 = £2{\cdot}40$

2. £1 Preference share in A Ltd. Dividend 7 per cent.

Valuation $\frac{7}{5} \times £1 = £1{\cdot}40$

3. £1 Ordinary share in XY Ltd. Dividend 17 per cent.

Valuation $\frac{17}{5} \times £1 = £3{\cdot}40$

The Stock Exchange valuation, however, fluctuates according to many factors. The past record of a company's dividends may not give a good indication of its future dividends. The dividends paid must also be compared with the earnings, because the company may be retaining large profits in order to expand and, ultimately, this may mean a much higher yield on the original investment.

CAPITAL EXPENDITURE DECISIONS

Capital expenditure decisions involve the disposition of large amounts of money, usually over a fairly long period of time.

Projects may be classified under four headings—

1. **No-return Projects.** These involve spending on facilities which, although they may be considered desirable in general terms for the sake of employee motivation and satisfaction, do not give rise to profits or cost savings to the firm. Such projects may be assessed in terms of cost-benefit analysis.

These projects may be optional or obligatory.

(*a*) *Optional.* In the case of optional projects a firm may consider, for instance, building a sports field but it has perfect freedom of choice on whether to do so or not.

(*b*) *Obligatory.* In the case of obligatory welfare spending the spending may be required by law, for instance, safety measures and other requirements imposed by the various Factory and Offices Acts. The only alternatives available are to withdraw from business or the country.

2. **Maintaining Old Business.** This category of expenditure is intended to maintain a going concern and it may not be possible to show that any

improvement of profits or reduction of costs will occur when the expenditure is made. On the other hand, failure to spend may undermine present profitability. Top management will generally act with restraint in making this kind of investment.

The First Lord of the Admiralty in 1866 said—"If we must needs keep up on old fleet we cannot expect a new one too. . . . Happy the nation that had no navy ten years ago! This is what has sent the Americans so far ahead. Every sixpence of their expenditure has been upon vessels of real and immediate efficiency."

3. **Cost Reduction.** This category of spending may result in savings of cost compared to present operation or some other alternative. The savings made can be compared to the capital investments required to obtain them to show whether the investment is worth-while. Especially where systematic value analysis and work study are used this category of investment may absorb a reasonable proportion of a firm's budgeted capital spending.

4. **New Projects.** This is the main category of investment projects. New projects may include new products, new designs and expansion of facilities to meet higher demands.

It has been said that the company which has too many no-return projects is "Wealthy but doomed."

Net Cash Investment and Returns. Evaluation of capital expenditure projects involves a comparison of the net cash returns to the net cash investment required to produce these returns.

The Net Cash Investment is the cash required at the start of a project to acquire the fixed assets and to provide working capital in the form of stocks, debtors, cash, etc.

If old assets are to be replaced, the cash proceeds of their sale can be deducted from the cash investment required for the new equipment. This gives the net additional cash investment required.

The Net Cash Returns are the cash earnings from sales of products or services less cash payments for running costs such as labour, materials and expenses. Depreciation and other book charges such as provisions for bad debts are *not* cash payments and should not, therefore, be deducted from sales revenue. Taxation, however, is a cash payment and must be deducted at the time when the actual payment is made.

The fixed and working capital in a project may have a realization value at the end of its life. For instance, if a project requires £75,000 worth of spares to be held throughout the life of the project, then in the final year of operation, when the project is run down, £75,000 should be returned to the company. Both fixed and working capital realization values at the end of the life of the project must be brought into account in assessing profitability.

Example 9

A project involves purchase of fixed assets costing £20,000 and the use of working capital to the amount of £4,000. The asset replaces an old piece of equipment which can be disposed of for £1,000 cash.

Net Cash Investment. The cost of fixed assets, £20,000, less proceeds of old assets replaced, £1,000, leaving £19,000 plus working capital required, £4,000, giving a total of £23,000 net cash investment.

Net Cash Returns. Sales of products will realize £40,000 per annum and costs on a normal accounting basis are £30,000 including a charge for depreciation of fixed assets of £6,000 and if the average rate of tax is 50 per cent then the calculation of the net cash returns will be as follows—

Net Cash Returns—

	£	£
1. Sales, annual		40,000
2. *Less* Costs	30,000	
3. *Less* Depreciation	6,000	
		24,000
4. Before tax cash flow		16,000
5. Taxable profit (1 minus 2)	10,000	
6. Tax at 50 per cent on £10,000		5,000
7. Net Cash Returns		11,000

The project has a life of ten years and the proceeds are as follows—

		£
Year 10	Sales of Fixed Assets	2,000
„ 10	Disinvestment of Working Capital	4,000

Time Scale. This information can be brought together in a simple way if we deal logically with the time scale. The convention adopted is to show the present time as Time Zero and to show subsequent returns as they occur at the end of year one, two, etc. The information can be presented in the manner shown below—

			Investment £	Returns £
Time	0	Net cash investment	23,000	
Year	1	Net Cash returns		11,000
„	2	„ „		11,000
„	3	„ „		11,000
„	4	„ „		11,000
„	5	„ „		11,000
„	6	„ „		11,000
„	7	„ „		11,000
„	8	„ „		11,000
„	9	„ „		11,000
„	10	„ „		11,000
„	10	Additional cash returns from sale of assets and disinvestment of Working Capital		6,000
		Totals	23,000	58,000

Various methods may be used to assess the project.

Comparative Cost. The first approach to any project may be to decide whether the comparative cost is within the resources of the firm. For instance, we may look at a project which involves the spending of £23,000, knowing that our firm has available or can obtain resources of this sort of size. The firm might not, however, be able to consider projects involving £230,000 or £2,300,000. This approach does not indicate whether the project is profitable or not, but only whether the firm can *afford* it.

Payback or Payout Method. The payback or payout is the length of time required for the cash returns of a project to equal the total cash outlay.

If the cash returns are at an annual uniform rate then the payback can be calculated as follows—

$$\frac{\text{Cash Outlay}}{\text{Annual cash return}} = \text{Payback period in years}$$

The payback on the project shown above is

$$\frac{£23{,}000}{£11{,}000} = 2{\cdot}09 \text{ years}$$

If the cash returns are not uniform, then the cash returns for each successive year are added until the total equals the initial cash outlay.

For example, a project involves the capital outlay of £100,000 and the returns in the first year are £30,000; in year two £40,000; in year three £60,000; in year four £80,000.

The total payback is £70,000 at the end of year two. In year three a further £60,000 is obtained making a total of £130,000. The payback must be between two and three years. If the £60,000 realized in year three is assumed to arrive at the uniform rate throughout the year we can assume that the £30,000 required to give complete payback would occur halfway through year three and the payback period is therefore 2½ years.

The fact that the payback method does not assess profitability may be seen if we compare two projects.

Example 10

		Project A	Project B
		£	£
Time 0	Cash outlays	100,000	100,000
Year 1	Cash returns	30,000	40,000
,, 2	,, ,,	40,000	60,000
,, 3	,, ,,	60,000	30,000
,, 4	,, ,,	80,000	20,000
	Payback	2½ years	2 years

It can be seen that project B gives a payback of two years compared with project A, which has a payback of 2½ years. Yet project A returns a total of £210,000 over its life compared to £150,000 which will come back from project B. There can be little doubt that project A is more profitable.

The payback in fact measures the risk of a project since it indicates the speed with which an initial investment is likely to be returned. Beyond this it does not effectively measure the profitability of alternatives.

The Accounting Assessment of Profitability. Although the accounting assessment of profitability is superior to the payback method it is still not satisfactory in discriminating between the projects which are truly most profitable to the firm. This can be shown by the following example.

Example 11

		Project C	Project D
		£	£
Time 0	Net cash investment	7,580	7,580
Year 1	Cash returns	3,000	1,000
,, 2	,, ,,	2,500	1,500
,, 3	,, ,,	2,000	2,000
,, 4	,, ,,	1,500	2,500
,, 5	,, ,,	1,000	3,000
		10,000	10,000

Both projects C and D are of a net cash investment of £7,580 and will secure returns of £10,000 over a five-year life.

The average profitability on an accounting basis would show—

	£
Net average annual cash returns	2,000
Less Annual Depreciation (20 per cent per annum)	1,516
Average annual net profit	484

This is on an original investment of £7,580 and it represents an average rate of return of 6·4 per cent. If the calculations were based on the average investment over the project life, assuming that there is no scrap value at the end of the life of the plant and equipment, the profitability would be 12·8 per cent.

A closer examination of the cash returns will show that project C is, in fact, preferable. It does, of course, have an earlier payback and would therefore be less risky, but also we can say that its profitability is greater since the value of money received in year one is greater than the value of the same amount of money received in year five.

The Time Value of Money. It is well known that money has a time value. We are all familiar with the idea of having money in a bank or building society and receiving interest. That interest is a compensation for our abstinence in not spending the money that we have available to us.

If the rate of interest is 10 per cent then £100 invested today will amount to £110 in a year's time and if we leave both interest and capital in the bank then at the end of year two we will have £110 plus £11 equals £121. This is the principle of compound interest.

Another way to look at this principle is to ask what amount of money invested today would bring £100 in two years' time if the interest rate is ten per cent? This can be calculated backwards. £100 at the end of year two is equivalent to

$$£100 - \left(\frac{10}{110} \times 100\right) = £91$$

at the end of year one.

If we have £91 at the end of year one this will be equivalent to

$$£91 - \left(\frac{10}{110} \times 91\right) = £82$$

at the present time.

This is the discounting principle. If I invest £82 today it will accumulate to £100 at the end of two years at a rate of interest of 10 per cent.

We may therefore say that £100 received in two years' time is equivalent to (has a present value of) £82 received at the present time at a rate of interest of 10 per cent.

The Discounted Cash Flow Method. The discounting principle can be used to evaluate the profitability of capital projects. Given that we have predictions of the present expenditures by way of net cash investment and the future returns by way of net cash returns, then we can evaluate the future return and determine what profitability may be represented.

To accomplish this task discount tables are used in which the present values of one pound received at a future time is given for a range of discount rates.

Table A Appendix I is the table of factors at interest rates of 1 to 50 per cent and for periods of time up to 50 years.

Table B Appendix I is a cumulative form of Table A.

Use of the Discount Tables. The following example shows the way in which project C can be evaluated using Table A.

Example 12

Project C		Column 1	Column 2 Factor at 10%	Column 3 Present value
		£		£
Time 0	Net cash outlay	7,580	1	7,580
Year 1	Net cash returns	3,000	0·909	2,727
,, 2	,, ,, ,, ...	2,500	0·826	2,045
,, 3	,, ,, ,, ...	2,000	0·751	1,502
,, 4	,, ,, ,, ...	1,500	0·683	1,034
,, 5	,, ,, ,, ...	1,000	0·621	621
				7,929

FIG. 29.5

In column 1 is shown the net cash investment and the cash returns. Column 2 shows the factor at 10 per cent taken from Table A. In column 3 the result of multiplying each of the amounts by the factor is shown. When these are totalled we have the *Present Value* of the receipts from the investment at a discount rate of 10 per cent, which is £7,925. Since this is greater than the net cash outlay it indicates that the profitability of the project is more than 10 per cent. If we are prepared to accept all projects which give a minimum return of 10 per cent then we would be prepared to accept project C. In the following table the same evaluation method has been applied to project D—

Project D		Column 1	Column 2 Factor at 10%	Column 3 Present value
		£		£
Time 0	Net cash outlay	7,580	1	7,580
Year 1	Net cash returns	1,000	0·909	909
,, 2	,, ,, ,, ...	1,500	0·826	1,239
,, 3	,, ,, ,, ...	2,000	0·751	1,502
,, 4	,, ,, ,, ...	2,500	0·683	1,707
,, 5	,, ,, ,, ...	3,000	0·621	1,863
				7,220

FIG. 29.6

The factors for discounting at 10 per cent are the same as were used in evaluating project C.

The present value of the cash flows in each year differs from those of project C except in year three in which both projects are expected to return £2,000 with a present value of £1,502.

Whereas the £3,000 in year one of project C has a present value of £2,727 the same amount of money received in year five of project D has a present value of only £1,863.

As a result the present value of the return from project D at 10 per cent is £7,220. This indicates that if we are not prepared to accept any projects with a rate of return of less than 10 per cent that we would not be prepared to accept project D, since the returns of £7,220 are less than the net cash for investments required, i.e. £7,580.

The method of applying the discounting concept is known as the *present value method*.

The Yield Method. The yield method carries the process of evaluation a stage further by finding the rate of interest at which the present value of the returns from a project is equal to the net cash investment or outlay required. This rate of return is the Yield or internal rate of return. It indicates the true profitability of a project.

For example, let us look at project D which we know has a rate of return of less than 10 per cent. Can we establish what the yield or internal rate of return is?

The procedure is to make a series of trials until the rate of discount at which the present value of the returns is equal to the present value of the net cash investment is discovered. This will be the internal rate of return of yield. The calculations are shown in the following table—

Project D		Net present value of returns				
		Trial 1	Trial 2		Trial 3	
		10%	6%		8%	
	£	£	Factor	P.V. £	Factor	P.V. £
Time 0 Net cash investment .	7,580					
Year 1 Cash returns .	1,000	909	0·943	943	0·926	926
,, 2 ,, ,, . .	1,500	1,239	0·890	1,335	0·857	1,285
,, 3 ,, ,, . .	2,000	1,502	0·840	1,680	0·794	1,588
,, 4 ,, ,, .	2,500	1,707	0·792	1,980	0·735	1,837
,, 5 ,, ,, . .	3,000	1,863	0·747	2,241	0·681	2,043
		7,220		8,179		7,679

FIG. 29.7

The first trial is the one made in Fig. 29.6. It gives a present value of £7,220, which is too low. The returns must be discounted at a *lower* rate. A second trial at 6 per cent gives a Present Value at £8,179, and this is in excess of the net cash investment of £7,580. The discount rate is therefore *too low*. The third trial is therefore made at 8 per cent. This gives a Present Value of £7,679 which is slightly in excess of the net cash investment. Our trials show that the rate of return of project D is just a little above 8 per cent.

Use of Table B. Table B shows the cumulative value of the sum of £1 received annually over the period of years. It is merely a cumulative version of Table A. This can be seen by checking the values of £1 at 10 per cent. Table A shows that the value of this at year one is 0·909 and this same value is given in Table B. In year two, Table A shows the value of £1 to be 0·826. Table B shows the value 1·736 and this is the sum of 0·909 plus 0·826 (there is a slight rounding error).

Table B is used when the same sum is received annually for a period of years. For instance, if a firm receives £1 for 10 years its value at a 10 per cent discount rate is £6·145.

Table 2 can also be used if the cash returns are uniform over the life of a project.

The method involves a factor which is obtained by calculating—

$$\frac{\text{Net cash outlays or investment}}{\text{Net annual cash return}} = \text{Factor (as in Table B).}$$

For example, a project involving investment of £6,000 can earn £1,500 per year. The factor is $\frac{£6,000}{1,500} = 4$.

The factor can be used in two ways—

(*a*) *If the life of the project is known* then the internal rate of return can be found by scanning Table B horizontally along the relevant row for the year until the factor is found. If a project has a life of five years, Table B at 5 years shows that the factor at 8 per cent is 3·993 and at 6 per cent 4·1. The rate of return is therefore a little *below* 8 per cent over five years.

(*b*) *If the discount rate is known* then it is possible to calculate the number of years a project must run if that rate of return is to be obtained. If, in the example, the project must earn at least 15 per cent then Table B shows that the project must have a life of nearly seven years. The six-year factor is 3·784 and the seven-year factor 4·160.

The fact that the discounting principle gives the compound interest rate of return can be proved by taking a simple example.

Example 13

If a project will require a cash investment of £9,948 and it gives annual cash returns of £4,000 for three years, then the rate of return is 10 per cent. The proof may be established by assuming that when the cash returns are received they are used first to meet the interest due at the stipulated rate and second, to repay the capital.

	Balance at investment at start of year	Cash Receipts	Interest at 10%	Repayment of Capital
	£	£	£	£
Time 0 . . .	9,948	—	—	—
Year 1 . . .		4,000	995	3,005
,, 2 . . .	6,943	4,000	694	3,306
,, 3 . . .	3,639	4,000	363	3,637*
			Total capital repaid =	9,948

* There is a slight error due to rounding.

THE IRRELEVANCE OF BOOK VALUES AND DEPRECIATION

There is no legal obligation for companies to charge depreciation on their assets against their profits, but, of course, if they do not do so, there will be no preservation of the capital in the business. A depreciation charge represents a recovery of part of the capital and any surplus remaining is true profit in the sense of a surplus return over and above the original investment (always assuming that the life of the investment covers the full term anticipated).

Example 14

Depreciation is calculated by taking the original cost of a machine, say £10,000, and estimating how long it will be in use and what value it will have on disposal at the end of its life. If at the end of ten years we can sell the asset for £1,000 then we can say that depreciation has been £9,000, that is £900 per year over ten years.

If the machine were the only asset held, and it earned revenues of £3,000 per annum, then the accounting profits would be reported each year as shown in the table below.

		Annual Earnings	Depreciation	Accounting Profit
	£	£	£	£
Time 0 Investment	10,000	—	—	—
Year 1		3,000	900	2,100
,, 2		3,000	900	2,100
,, 3		3,000	900	2,100
,, 4		3,000	900	2,100
,, 5		3,000	900	2,100
,, 6		3,000	900	2,100
,, 7		3,000	900	2,100
,, 8		3,000	900	2,100
,, 9		3,000	900	2,100
,, 10		3,000	900	2,100

If the estimates of life or disposal value of the asset are incorrect, then the profits reported in the early years will prove to have been incorrect. Suppose, in the example, the asset is disposed of at the end of three years for £1,000.

The table opposite shows the results.

The position, looking back, may be summarized by saying that using the asset cost £9,000 (original cost less disposal value). The earnings it brought in were £3,000 per annum for three years; i.e. £9,000. The project, therefore, showed neither a loss nor a profit.

However, because of our expectations, this was reported to shareholders for three years as a profit of £2,100 (total £6,300), followed by a loss in the final year of £6,300.

		Annual Earnings	Depreciation or Loss	Accounting Profit or Loss
	£	£	£	£
Time 0 Investment . .	10,000			
Year 1		3,000	900	2,100
" 2		3,000	900	2,100
" 3		3,000	900	2,100
				Profits 6,300
Equipment sold for . .	1,000		Loss 6,300	Loss 6,300
Total cost of asset . .	9,000		9,000	Nil

At the end of Year 3, the book value would be—

	£
Original cost	10,000
Less Three years' depreciation at £900 per annum . .	2,700
Book value	7,300

Given that revenues were £3,000 per year, the net cash outlays and returns were—

1. The original payment of £10,000.
2. The receipt of £3,000 per year in earnings for three years.
3. The receipt of £1,000 cash on sale of the equipment at the end of its life.

The investment was not successful.

The book value is irrelevant to decisions about the future: all that is relevant at the end of Year 3 is the £1,000 cash proceeds which the plant will bring if it is sold. These proceeds must include the cash value of any allowances for "tax losses."

The original predictions were that the asset would have a life of ten years, and the profitability then appeared satisfactory. At a stipulated rate of return of 20 per cent the project would have shown a Present Value profit of £2,995, as can be seen in table on p. 2954.

Example 15

At the end of Year 3, the firm is offered a new piece of equipment that promises to increase the savings to £5,000 per year, and which requires a capital investment of £6,000. The new equipment will have a life of seven years and will be disposed of at the end of that time for £2,000. If the old equipment is disposed of at the end of three years it will only fetch £1,000. We might, in fact, be tempted to say that since the new equipment will

			Investment	Annual Savings	Present value at 20%
			£	£	£
Time	0	Capital investment	10,000		
Year	1			3,000	
,,	2			3,000	
,,	3			3,000	
,,	4			3,000	
,,	5			3,000	
,,	6			3,000	
,,	7			3,000	
,,	8			3,000	
,,	9			3,000	
,,	10			3,000	
				30,000	12,576
		Scrap value of equipment		1,000	419
		Present value of returns at 20%			12,995

cost £6,000 and it could mean an accounting loss of £6,300, then it is not worth-while.

This approach is mistaken, because the problem of the new machine is not related to the depreciation, which merely tells us the way we have looked at our investment in the old machine. The new equipment must be appraised in relation to the possible cash flows or increases in cash flows which it will generate during its life if we buy it.

The correct appraisal (assuming that taxation has been taken into account) is—

New equipment costs £6,000. Increase in annual savings, £2,000. Anticipated scrap value at end of life, £2,000. Anticipated life, 7 years. See table on opposite page.

The earnings rate required is 20 per cent. At this rate the net investment of £5,000 will show a present-value profit of £767 and the old machine should be replaced.

Tax Considerations. As has been stated earlier taxation is a cash outflow which must be deducted from the return from the project before the net cash returns are identified.

Corporation Tax. Companies are liable for corporation tax. In 1971–2 the rate was 38·75 per cent of profits as calculated according to income tax rules. Individuals, sole traders and partnerships pay income tax at a standard rate subject to certain personal allowances and if their earned income exceeds about £5,000 they will be liable to pay surtax, in addition.

		Investment	Increase in Annual Savings	Present Value at 20%
		£	£	£
Year 3	Capital investment . . .	6,000		
	Less Disposal proceeds (old equipment) . . .	1,000		
		5,000		
Year 4	. . . . . .		2,000	
" 5	. . . . . .		2,000	
" 6	. . . . . .		2,000	
" 7	. . . . . .		2,000	
" 8	. . . . . .		2,000	
" 9	. . . . . .		2,000	
" 10	. . . . . .		2,000	
	New equipment sold . . .		2,000	
			16,000	
	Present value of returns at 20% .			5,767

Dividends. Dividends paid to shareholders, and in some cases the earnings which a company retains after the deduction of corporation tax, are subject to income tax at the prevailing rate. In 1967–8 this was £0·4125 in the £.

Investment Grants and Allowances. Certain types of capital expenditure attract cash grants from the Board of Trade and/or capital allowances from the Inland Revenue.

Cash grants are paid in relation to the spending; capital allowances are deducted from taxable income. When capital allowances are given on an asset which is eventually disposed of, then the total allowances are adjusted so that they equal the difference between original cost and the proceeds of the eventual disposal. A more detailed outline is given in the chapter on taxation.

Effect of Taxation. The effect of taxation on capital expenditure evaluation may be illustrated as follows.

Example 16

Suppose, in example 15, that tax had not been taken into account. What would be the change in the appraisal which would result from the tax allowances?

Let us suppose that the new machine attracts an investment grant of 25 per cent and an annual allowance of 25 per cent on the diminishing value, and that it is bought by a company paying corporation tax at

40 per cent. The book value of the old equipment for tax purposes is also relevant. Let us assume it is £800. Since the machine is sold for £1,000, there will be a balancing charge of £200.

A calculation of the capital allowances is shown below (a charge is shown in brackets).

			£	£
Start of project (Year 3) Balancing charge (old machine)				(200)
New Machine cost			6,000	
Investment grant (new machine)			1,500	
				1,500
Year	4	Capital allowance 25 per cent of Residual value	4,500	1,125
			1,125	
,,	5	Capital allowance 25 per cent of Residual value	3,375	844
			844	
,,	6	Capital allowance 25 per cent of Residual value	2,531	633
			633	
,,	7	Capital allowance 25 per cent of Residual value	1,896	474
			474	
,,	8	Capital allowance 25 per cent of Residual value	1,424	355
			355	
,,	9	Capital allowance 25 per cent of Residual value	1,069	267
			267	
,,	10	Capital allowance 25 per cent of Residual value	802	200
			200	
			602	

	£
Residual value sold for	2,000
Residual value	602
Balancing charge	(1,398)

If we assume that the benefit of both investment grants and capital allowances is received after one year's delay, the cash flows of the project can be calculated year by year.

	Before-tax Cash (Outlays) and Returns	Capital Allowances and (Charges)	Taxable Returns and (Allowances)	Tax at 40%	After-tax (Outlays) and Returns
	£	£	£	£	£
Year 3 .	(5,000)	—	—	—	5,000
Year 4 .	2,000	1,300	700	280	1,720
Year 5 .	2,000	1,125	875	350	1,650
Year 6 .	2,000	844	1,156	462	1,538
Year 7 .	2,000	633	1,367	547	1,453
Year 8 .	2,000	474	1,526	610	1,390
Year 9 .	2,000	355	1,645	658	1,342
Year 10 .	2,000	267	1,733	693	1,307
Year 11 .	—	(1,198)	(1,198)	(478)	(479)

	After-tax (Outlays) and Returns	20% Factor	Net Present Value	
	£	£	£	£
Year 4 .	1,720	0·833	1,430	
Year 5 .	1,650	0·694	1,145	
Year 6 .	1,538	0·579	890	
Year 7 .	1,453	0·482	700	
Year 8 .	1,390	0·402	560	
Year 9 .	1,342	0·335	450	
Year 10 .	1,307	0·279	365	
				5,540
Year 11 .	(479)	0·233	(111)	(111)
				5,429

The project is still worthwhile as it shows a net present-value profit at 20 per cent but this is reduced to £429, as compared to £767 in the appraisal before tax.

EXERCISE 29

1. The balance sheet of a limited company as on 31st December, 19.., was as follows—

	£		£
Issued Capital	100,000	Fixed Assets	72,300
Reserves	20,000	Stock	72,500
Debentures	50,000	Debtors & Prepayments	22,400
Current Liabilities	5,500	Bank	8,300
	175,500		175,500

(*a*) What was the amount of the company's working capital at that date?

(*b*) During the year ended 31st December, 19.1, the company earned a net profit of £19,700 after charging £4,800 for depreciation of the fixed assets, new fixed assets were bought at a cost of £18,600, and old ones sold for £1,300. Calculate the amount of working capital at the end of the year.

(*c*) The following appropriations are proposed out of the profit for 19.1: the transfer of £5,000 to general reserve and the declaration of dividends amounting to £7,500. What effect will each of these have on the working capital, and why?

(*R.S.A.*)

2. Gesprin Ltd. owns a factory turning out a standard product. The company can sell all it produces: the production (all sold) for 19.. amounted to 12,000 tons, and the following is a summary of the profit and loss account for that year, rearranged from a costing point of view—

	£		£
Raw Materials	120,000	Sales	360,000
Productive Wages	160,000		
Overheads varying in proportion to output	40,000		
Fixed Overheads	35,000		
Net Profit	5,000		
	360,000		360,000

The directors are considering the company's policy for 19.1 and to assist them in this they ask you to work out the following—

(*a*) What would have to be the weight of produce turned out (and sold) for 19.1 in order to double the company's profit for that year as compared with 19.., assuming no change in the costs or selling price?

(*b*) Assuming that the cost per ton of raw materials in 19.1 is 5 per cent less than in 19.. but that productive wages are increased by 10 per cent, what would have to be the selling price per ton in order that the company should secure the same net profit for 19.1 as for 19.., the output remaining at 12,000 tons?

Make these two calculations.

(*R.S.A.*)

3. The following balance sheet, with comparative figures, shows the position of a limited company at two consecutive accounting dates.

	31st December 19.1 £	£	19.. £	£
Fixed assets—				
At cost	**302,000**		**276,000**	
***Less* Depreciation**	**73,000**		**81,000**	
		229,000		**195,000**
Current assets—				
Stocks	**76,000**		**81,000**	
Debtors	**31,000**		**34,000**	
Bank balance	**18,000**		**—**	
		125,000		**115,000**
		354,000		**310,000**
***Less* Debentures**	**50,000**		**—**	
Bank overdraft	**—**		**19,000**	
Other current liabilities (including proposed dividend)	**37,000**		**39,000**	
		87,000		**58,000**
		267,000		**252,000**
Represented by—				
Issued capital—				
6 per cent preference shares	**50,000**		**50,000**	
Ordinary shares	**150,000**		**150,000**	
		200,000		**200,000**
Reserves		**67,000**		**52,000**
		267,000		**252,000**

The total ordinary dividend for 19.1 was at the rate of 5 per cent, and you are informed that, while the average unit cost of the commodities dealt in has decreased somewhat during the year, the volume of turnover has on the whole increased.

You are required to calculate—

(*a*) the amount of working capital at each accounting date;
(*b*) the book value of the ordinary shareholders' equity at each accounting date; and
(*c*) the ratio of the ordinary dividend to the balance of the year's profit available to pay the same.

Also, draw up a statement commenting on any inferences you are able to draw from the figures disclosed, dealing with any matters which you think might be referred to in the chairman's speech at the annual general meeting. (*R.S.A.*)

4. The following statement summarizes the trading and profit and loss accounts of Ampex Ltd., a company engaged in the wholesale trade, for the years ended 31st December, 19.. and 19.1—

	19.. £100s	19.1 £100s		19.. £100s	19.1 £100s
Opening Stock	800	1,200	Sales	5,000	5,500
Purchases	4,100	4,455	Closing Stock	900	1,200
Gross Profit	1,000	1,045			
	5,900	6,700		5,900	6,700
Administrative Salaries & Wages	245	310	Gross Profit	1,000	1,045
Travellers' Salaries, Expenses & Commission	240	260			
Rent & Rates	105	140			
Heat, Light, etc.	45	48			
Packing & Carriage Out	85	90			
Sundry Office Expenses	30	32			
	750	880			
Net Profit	250	165			
	1,000	1,045		1,000	1,045

Draft a report, to be submitted by yourself, as accountant, to the management, showing any comparative figures or percentages you consider significant and pointing out anything to which you think particular attention should be drawn. (*R.S.A.*)

5. A business friend of yours who does not know much about accountancy has a holding of 1,000 ordinary shares in a public company and asks you to explain certain points in connexion with the company's last balance sheet, a copy of which he has just received. The following is a summarized copy of the balance sheet in question.

	1,000s of £s		1,000s of £s
Capital issued and fully paid—		Fixed Assets	1,090
200,000 7% Cum. Pref. Shares of £1	200	*Less* Depreciation	420
2,000,000 Ordinary Shares of 25p	500		670
Debentures	250	Current Assets	1,580
Capital Reserves	300		
Revenue Reserves	650		
Provisions	60		
Current Liabilities	290		
	2,250		2,250

The questions your friend wants answered are the following—

(1) How do capital reserves differ from revenue reserves, and both from provisions?

(2) What is the value of his proportionate share of the company's net assets, based on the balance sheet figures?

(3) On the assumption that the ordinary shares of a well-managed company of this size, engaged in the industry in question, should have a market quotation such that the ratio of the balance of the company's annual earnings, after paying the preference

dividend, to the total market value of the ordinary shares should be 12½ per cent, what ought the company's profit (before tax) to be in order to justify a quotation of 90p?

(4) Assuming that the company's profit for the last year did in fact amount to the figure you calculate, what is the ratio of net profit to total capital employed in earning that profit as disclosed by the balance sheet? (*R.S.A.*)

6. You are investigating the position of a private limited company and among the documents produced for your inspection is a copy of the last balance sheet. One of the items appearing in this is "Goodwill £25,000."

Explain briefly what regard you would have to this, if you were acting on behalf of—

(*a*) a prospective lender of a substantial sum of money to the company (assumed to be short of working capital);

(*b*) a prospective shareholder who is negotiating with one of the existing members regarding the purchase price to be paid for a substantial block of shares in the company. (*R.S.A.*)

7. (*a*) Explain carefully what you understand by the expression "working capital."

(*b*) The following is a summary of the transactions during February, 19.., of Smith & Sons, a partnership engaged in wholesale trade—

	£
Sales for the month (all on credit: the cost of the goods sold amounted to £22,575)	27,982
Cash received from debtors	25,228
Cash discounts allowed	672
Debtors' accounts written off as bad	103
Trade purchases	21,351
Payments to suppliers	22,470
Expenses paid (including £1,595 outstanding on 31st January)	4,327
Expenses outstanding at 28th February (including all accruals)	1,422
Proceeds of sale of old motor van, standing in the books at the date of sale at £225	385
Cost of new van, bought in replacement of the foregoing	980
Partners' drawings	300

State (but without giving reasons), as regards each of the items enumerated, whether it increases or decreases the working capital, and by how much, or whether it does not affect it, and submit a statement showing the amount of the net increase or decrease of the firm's working capital during the month.

(*c*) State, giving the reason, whether depreciation on the fixed assets ought to be taken into account. (*R.S.A.*)

8. State briefly the circumstances in which you would expect to find goodwill appearing in the balance sheet of—

(*a*) a partnership,

(*b*) a limited company,

(*c*) the consolidated balance sheet of a group of companies. (*R.S.A.*)

9. A. Bow and C. Arrow are about to enter into partnership with a view to starting a wholesale business and have acquired a lease of suitable premises. They make the following estimates for the first year of trading—

(1) Fixed assets (office and showroom equipment and motor vans) will cost £3,500.

(2) The average monthly sales for the year should be £30,000, rising to £40,000 by the end of the year.

(3) The ratio of gross profit to sales should be 20 per cent.

(4) It will be advisable to hold enough stock to cover two months' sales.

(5) An average of one month's credit will be allowed by suppliers and to customers.

(6) Fixed overhead expenses (including £300 depreciation) will amount to £10,500 for the year and variable expenses are estimated at 12½ per cent of sales.

(7) Partners' drawings (combined) will be at the rate of £5,000 per annum, by regular monthly instalments at the end of each month.

You are required—

(*a*) to prepare an estimated trading and profit and loss account for the first year, ignoring possible discounts;

(*b*) to calculate the minimum amount of capital that should be provided by the partners (together) to avoid the necessity of borrowing; and

(*c*) to calculate (to the nearest 0·1 per cent) the ratio of the expected net profit to the capital employed, allowing £5,000 as the value of the partners' services for management and assuming that £50,000 capital is brought in at the start and the balance (as disclosed by your answer to (*b*) above) six months later. (*R.S.A.*)

10. The balance sheet of Sellers Ltd. at 1st October, 19.., was as follows—

Liabilities	£	*Assets*	£
Ordinary shares of £1 each	53,000	Buildings	8,000
General reserve	5,200	Plant	36,000
Mortgage	5,000	Lorries	3,000
Trade creditors	9,600	Stocks	16,000
		Trade debtors	5,600
		Cash	4,200
	72,800		72,800

Buyers Ltd., a company whose £1 preference shares are quoted at £1·175, and whose £1 ordinary shares are quoted at £1·425, agrees to acquire the assets of Sellers Ltd., except cash, and to take over the liabilities. The purchase consideration is to be discharged by the issue to the shareholders of Sellers Ltd. of 9,000 preference and 18,000 ordinary shares of Buyers Ltd., and the balance in cash.

On a valuation by Buyers Ltd., a reduction of £5,000 and £1,000 is made in the value of plant and lorries respectively. The costs of this arrangement, which were paid by Buyers Ltd., were £780.

You are required to record in the journal of Buyers Ltd. the transactions involved in the acquisition of the business of Sellers Ltd.

(*Cost and Management Accountants.*)

11. On 1st September, 19.., a company was incorporated and took over an existing business as from 1st January, 19.., the purchase price including £3,500 for goodwill. The accounts for the year ended 31st December, 19.., showed a net loss of £1,800; the sales from 1st January to 31st August amounted to £18,000, and from 1st September to 31st December were £12,000. How should the loss of £1,800 be treated when making up the accounts at 31st December, 19..? (*Cost and Management Accountants.*)

12. You are required to calculate from the following data, the number of ordinary shares in Investors Ltd. which would require to be allotted to the ordinary shareholders of Byusback Ltd. in exchange for the whole of their holding. A fair return for the type of businesses concerned is 10 per cent.

(*a*) BALANCE SHEET OF BYUSBACK LTD.

	£		£
Ordinary shares of 25p each	30,000	Goodwill at cost	5,000
Capital reserve	3,000	Fixed assets at cost *less* depreciation	33,000
Retained profits	15,000	Current assets	47,000
Current liabilities	39,000	Preliminary expenses	2,000
	87,000		87,000

Taxed profits and loss for the five years to the date of the above balance sheet are as follows—

£8,700; £9,400; £10,200; £2,700 (*loss*); £11,900.

Additional information—

(1) A revaluation of the fixed assets, subsequent to the date of the balance sheet, showed that they were undervalued by £22,000.

(2) Trade debts amounting to £1,000 are irrecoverable.

(3) The loss of £2,700 was due to the factory's being employed on development of new lines which the directors are certain will be as profitable as the old.

(*b*) BALANCE SHEET OF INVESTORS LTD.

	£		£
Ordinary shares of £1 each	100,000	Fixed assets, at valuation	207,000
Premium on issue of shares	3,000	Trade investments	53,000
Surplus on revaluation of fixed assets	100,000	Current assets	295,000
Retained profits	102,000		
6% debentures (new issue)	70,000		
Current liabilities	180,000		
	555,000		555,000

Taxed profits for the five years to the date of the above balance sheet, are as follows—

£52,000; £57,000; £54,000; £58,000; £62,000.

Additional information—

(1) The fixed assets were revalued during the year just ended.

(2) Since the date of the balance sheet, the buying price of the basic raw material has fallen by 5 per cent. This stock was valued at cost at £40,000 in the above balance sheet.

(3) Trade investments are permanent; they yield 4 per cent net annually.

(*Cost and Management Accountants.*)

13. You are required to prepare the accounts of Barrel and Bung Ltd. from the undernoted information—

	LEDGER ACCOUNT BALANCES 30th April, 19.8 £	30th April, 19.9 £
Balances on current account in favour of subsidiaries	552,808	—
Income from trade and general investments (net)	755,832	689,076
Interim dividend of 6 per cent *less* tax on ordinary stock	453,600	340,200
£841,085 stock in Cask and Bottle Ltd., at cost	614,594	614,594
Balance of profit unappropriated from previous year	1,157,005	849,603
Debtors less reserve	965,231	1,098,759
Land and buildings (19.8 shown net)	3,290,162	6,270,884
Plant replacement reserve	1,000,000	1,250,000
Profit remitted from subsidiary companies, *less* provision for loss	17,803	44,543
Shares in subsidiary companies at cost	593,756	463,571
Preference dividends for year *less* tax	25,294	25,294
Plant and machinery (19.8 shown net)	1,030,000	2,383,655
Stocks	3,873,047	4,848,898
Miscellaneous income	26,074	35,516
Reserve on shares in subsidiary companies after transferring £300,000 from liquidation surplus	45,000	315,000
Cash at bank, on deposit, and in hand	3,412,564	4,053,858

	Ledger Account Balances 30th April, 19.8	30th April, 19.9
	£	£
General reserve at 1st May	3,500,000	2,300,000
Transfer to general reserve from profits at 1st May.	1,500,000	—
Trade and sundry creditors	2,359,017	2,746,047
Motor vehicles, furniture and fittings (19.8 shown net)	645,000	1,843,155
7½ per cent cumulative preference shares of £5 each.	481,790	481,790
Provision for income tax made in previous years no longer required	—	200,000
Surplus on liquidation of subsidiary companies after transferring £300,000 to investment reserve	—	211,673
Balances on current account due by subsidiaries .	381,212	531,994
Trading profit	2,776,583	2,241,580
Accumulated depreciation (19.8 see assets) . .	—	3,379,280
Balance at credit of income tax provision account .	1,831,285	2,895,976
Investments	4,618,697	3,265,222
Ordinary shares of £5 each converted into stock .	5,400,000	8,100,000

Notes—

(i) A revaluation of fixed assets was made in 19.1. Subsequent additions have been debited at cost.

(ii) £1,150,000 has to be reserved to meet future taxation. £1,300,000 was reserved in 19.8.

(iii) The trading profit has been arrived at after charging depreciation and transfer to plant replacement reserve of £1,058,339 and directors' fees of £27,000. (£1,000,375 and £27,000 respectively in 19.8).

(iv) A reserve has already been provided on £3,265,222 of investments.

(v) It is proposed to transfer £1,000,000 to general reserve from profits, and to pay a final dividend of 6 per cent and a bonus of 7 per cent on the ordinary stock amounting in all to £737,100 (£604,800 was provided in 19.8).

(vi) The accumulated depreciation of £3,379,280 is made up of provisions of £1,072,270 on land and buildings, £1,018.855 on plant and machinery and £1,288,155 on motor vehicles, furniture, and fittings.

(vii) The balance of £2,300,000 of the general reserve has been arrived at after capitalizing £2,700,000 to increase the ordinary stock.

(viii) The authorized capital consists of 200,000 7½ per cent cumulative preference shares, 2,180,000 ordinary shares, and 1,620,000 ordinary shares converted into stock—all of £5 each.

(ix) Stocks are valued at or below cost.

(*Cost and Management Accountants* (*adapted*).)

14. The cash resources of a business have decreased during the last six months. From the following information show this decrease and state its causes—

Month	Sales	Debtors	Purchases	Creditors
	£	£	£	£
1	200,000	430,000	140,000	410,000
2	240,000	440,000	150,000	430,000
3	210,000	450,000	160,000	450,000
4	250,000	484,000	230,000	540,000
5	300,000	592,000	210,000	520,000
6	320,000	720,000	200,000	525,000
7	330,000	770,000	240,000	461,000
8	360,000	850,000	210,000	450,000
9	350,000	875,000	260,000	470,000

15. The following is the balance sheet of Madaloss Ltd.—

		£
Authorized and issued capital—		
600,000 8% cumulative preference shares of £1 each		600,000
400,000 ordinary shares of £1 each		400,000
		1,000,000
Profit and loss account		228,000
		772,000
Creditors		200,000
		972,000
Fixed assets—		
Freehold buildings at cost *less* depreciation	£200,000	
Plant and machinery at cost *less* depreciation	160,000	
		360,000
Investments at cost		340,000
Current assets—		
Stock	130,000	
Debtors	141,000	
Cash at bank	1,000	
		272,000
		972,000

A valuation of fixed assets shows the following values—

	£
Freehold buildings	180,000
Plant and machinery	120,000
The market value of the investments is	262,000
Stocks are shown to have been overvalued to the extent of	60,000

Authority is obtained for the following scheme of capital reduction—

(*a*) Preference shareholders are to receive for every three shares held, one 6 per cent cumulative preference share of £1 each, two 10 per cent preferred ordinary shares of £0·50 each, one ordinary share of £0·25.

(*b*) Arrears of preference dividend of £96,000 to be discharged by the issue of 96,000 ordinary shares of £0·25.

(*c*) Ordinary shareholders are to receive one ordinary share of £0·25 for each ordinary share held.

(*d*) The balance of the profit and loss account is to be written off.

(*e*) The revalued assets are to be written down to the new values.

You are required to record the foregoing in the form of journal entries and to show the balance sheet after giving effect to these entries.

(*Cost and Management Accountants.*)

16. You are required to prepare from the following information the accounts of Rigid Fluids Ltd. for the year to 31st August, 19.8—

(i) Ledger account balances—

	£
Cost of investment	120
Dividend bank account	215
Bank overdraft	12,030
Income from investment	7
Balance (loss) as at 31st August, 19.7	56,018
Four 5% convertible secured debentures	100,000

	£
Plant, machinery, fixtures and fittings	91,884
Trade and sundry creditors	68,796
Deposits	300
Stocks of materials, work-in-progress, and finished goods	101,281
Debenture interest	3,750
Directors' fees	343
Trade and sundry debtors	60,798
Unclaimed dividends	215
Leasehold property	3,323
Net profit on sale of fixed assets	97
Remuneration (executive directors)	3,970
Bills receivable	8,000
Interest receivable	47
Cash in hand	281
Ordinary shares of 10p each	150,000
Freehold land and buildings	75,000
Reserve for bad and doubtful debts	5,250
Net additions to plant, machinery, fixtures and fittings from 6th March, 19..	76,856
Motor vehicles	4,502
Depreciation provision as at 31st August, 19.7—	
On freehold land and building	1,874
On plant, machinery, fixtures and fittings	58,322
Goodwill, licences, and research	1
Transfer fees	38
Payments in advance	1,163
Capital reserve	25,597

(ii) Provisions to be made at 31st August, 19.8—

	£
Audit fee	315
Other expenses	14,195
Accrued income	1,584
Depreciation on fixed assets required to bring provision up to the following amounts—	
Freehold land and buildings	3,703
Leasehold property	173
Plant, machinery, fixtures and fittings	68,551
Motor vehicles	1,711
Debenture interest—3 months to 31st August, 19.8.	

(iii) Additional data—

The loss carried forward at 31st August, 19.8, is £26,478.

All taxable receipts and payments are shown gross.

The market value of the investment at 31st August, 19.8, was £112.

At 31st August, 19.8, the value of contracts for capital expenditure entered into by the company was £27,000.

The motor vehicles and leasehold property were purchased during the current year.

Freehold land and plant are shown at the value placed on them at 6th March, 19.., by Foot, Rule, and Partners.

A portion of the capital reserve had previously been used to write down the value of goodwill, etc.

The authorized capital of the company consists of 1,000,000 preferred ordinary shares of 10p as well as the issued ordinary shares.

The bank overdraft and the debentures are secured by a first and second charge respectively, on all of the assets and the uncalled capital.

(*Cost and Management Accountants* (*adapted*).)

17. A company has secret reserves which amount to £40,000 made up as follows—

	£
Deduction of 10 per cent from stock values	4,250
Motor van written off	750
Excessive reserve for income tax	2,500
Profit on sale of investments not transferred from investment account	5,000
Depreciation in excess of requirements written off machinery	27,500

It is decided by the board of the company that future balance sheets should be realistic, that the amount by which revenue has previously suffered should be placed to a dividend equalization reserve, and that the remainder should form the nucleus of a pension fund, a similar amount being invested to provide for pension payments. Record these transactions in journal form and state whether, and if so to what extent, the costs of the next period would be affected.

(Cost and Management Accountants.)

18. You are provided, by a person who does not disclose his interest, with the following financial statements of Broad and Narrow Ltd., a private limited company. You are required to restate this information in a form which you consider presents the position more clearly, and to set out for the guidance of your informant the features of the position disclosed by your examination of the information given to you.

	At 30th June, 19..	19.1
	£	£
Ordinary shares of £1 each	125,000	125,000
Capital reserves	6,900	6,900
Revenue reserves	15,900	15,600
6% Debentures	85,000	85,000
Trade creditors	91,250	80,050
Bank overdraft	—	72,000
Secured loans	7,000	7,000
Final dividend (gross)	6,250	6,250
	337,300	397,800
Fixed assets at cost	321,400	394,200
Less Depreciation	123,600	147,700
	197,800	246,500
Stock	45,000	67,500
Debtors	86,000	83,000
Investments	3,000	—
Cash	5,500	800
	337,300	397,800

(Cost and Management Accountants.)

19. Planners Ltd. was incorporated in December, 19... In that month, 50,000 shares of £1 each were issued and fully paid up in cash, and £20,000 was paid for fixed assets. It was proposed to commence a trading business on 1st January, 19.1.

It was estimated that sales would amount to £6,000 in January, 19.1, £10,000 in February, and £20,000 per month afterwards.

Gross profit (sale price, less purchase price of goods) was expected to be at a uniform rate of 25 per cent of selling price.

Purchasing was to be so arranged that, at the end of each month, the stock-in-trade would be exactly sufficient (and no more) to supply all the sales of the following month.

It was expected that every customer would pay for his goods on the last day of the second month after that in which the goods were sold: e.g. sales in January would be paid for on 31st March.

Trade creditors were to be paid on the last day of the month after that in which the goods were purchased.

It was expected that wages and salaries would amount to £1,000 in each month and would be paid on the last day of the month in which they were earned.

General expenses, estimated at £1,500 per month, were to be paid on the last day of the month after that in which they were incurred.

Any temporary excess of payments over receipts was to be financed by a bank overdraft.

You are required—

(*a*) to prepare the company's cash account and trading and profit and loss account for the *six months* to 30th June, 19.1, and balance sheet (not necessarily in a form for publication) on 30th June, 19.1, as they would appear if all the foregoing estimates and assumptions were correct, and

(*b*) to show the maximum bank overdraft during the period.

NOTES—

(i) Requirement (*b*) may be satisfied either by setting out the cash account in such a way as to disclose the required information, or by means of a separate statement.

(ii) Ignore depreciation of fixed assets, bank interest, and dividends.

(*Institute of Bankers.*)

20. On 1st January, 19.1, the whole issued share capital of Equinox Ltd. was acquired by Brown and Green. The former directors retired, and Brown and Green became directors.

The summarized balance sheets of the company at 31st December, 19.., and 31st December, 19.1, were as follows—

	19..	19.1		19..	19.1
	£	£		£	£
Issued share capital	20,000	20,000	Goodwill	8,000	8,000
P. & L. A/c	9,600	10,250	Freeholds, at cost	3,000	3,000
Income tax 19.1/.2	6,900	6,900	Motor vehicles at cost *less* depreciation	6,000	11,000
Income tax 19../.1	5,350	4,100	Stock-in-trade, at cost	28,500	36,400
Bank overdraft	1,150	7,800	Loans to directors	—	2,850
Trade creditors	23,500	39,500	Trade debtors	21,000	27,300
	66,500	88,550		66,500	88,550

The bank overdraft was secured by a mortgage on the freeholds, the market value of which, at 31st December, 19.1, was £10,000.

You are given the following particulars—

	19..	19.1
	£	£
Sales	203,000	208,000
Depreciation of motor vehicles charged in the profit and loss account	4,000	1,000
Directors' remuneration charged in the profit and loss account	2,500	6,500
Maximum bank overdraft	5,000	8,000
Minimum bank overdraft	*Nil*	4,600

The following is a summary of the stock in trade at the end of each of the years under review.

	31st December, 19.. Cost	31st December, 19.. Market Value	31st December, 19.1 Cost	31st December, 19.1 Market Value
	£	£	£	£
Group A	16,150	20,650	14,300	18,450
B	12,350	16,250	12,900	16,850
C	—	—	9,200	2,000
	28,500	36,900	36,400	37,300

In 19.1, the average selling price of the company's goods was 5 per cent higher than in the previous year.

The company paid no dividend in 19.1.

The directors have asked the bank manager to increase the overdraft limit from £8,000 to £15,000.

What, in your view, should the bank manager's answer be? Give your reasons, and set out your answer in the form of a report based on the figures and information given above.

You may assume that the trading results prior to 19.1 were satisfactory. Ignore profits tax. *(Institute of Bankers.)*

21. A Ltd. manufactures machinery, and its subsidiary company, B Ltd., produces a standard component part. The whole output of B Ltd. during the year 1953 (10,000 units) was sold to A Ltd. for £50 per unit, based on the following figures of costs and profit per unit:

	£
Materials	15
Manufacturing wages	20
Overhead expenses	10
Profit	5
Selling price	50

On 1st January, 19.1, the managing director of B Ltd. informed the directors of A Ltd. that the price of raw materials had been doubled, and he claimed that, to maintain his profit, the selling price of his company's output should be fixed at £65 a unit. The directors of A Ltd. agreed.

During 19.1, the cost to B Ltd. of materials remained stable at £30 per unit of output.

The following is a summary of the trading and profit and loss accounts of B Ltd. for 19.. and 19.1—

	19..	19.1		19..	19.1
	£	£		£	£
Stocks of materials (1st Jan.) at cost	100,000	100,000	Sales (10,000 units in each year)	500,000	650,000
Purchases	150,000	300,000	Stocks of materials (31st Dec.) at cost	100,000	200,000
Manufacturing wages	200,000	200,000			
Overhead expenses	100,000	100,000			
Net profit	50,000	150,000			
	600,000	850,000		600,000	850,000

It is suggested that these accounts prove that the increase in the price per unit charged to A Ltd. was excessive, and that, in the future, a price of £55 per unit will be sufficient to maintain the net profit of B Ltd. at £50,000 per annum.

Write a brief report, setting out your views. (*Institute of Bankers.*)

22. With the exception of one share held by his wife, John Dickinson held the whole share capital of AB Ltd., a manufacturing company, and he was the sole director of the company. The summarized balance sheets of the company at 31st December 19.., and 31st December, 19.1, and certain other particulars, are given below.

	19..	19.1		19..	19.1
	£	£		£	£
Issued share capital	28,000	28,000	Goodwill	6,000	6,000
P. & L. A/c	1,200	7,000	Plant and machinery, at cost, *less* depreciation	12,000	24,400
Loan by director		3,000			
Trade creditors	9,400	36,700	Stock and work-in-progress	11,600	24,900
Provision for current income tax		1,460	Trade debtors	8,850	14,750
			Balance at bank	150	6,110
	38,600	76,160		38,600	76,160

	19..	19.1
	£	£
Sales	94,000	185,000
Purchases	71,000	143,500
Net profit, after charging depreciation, director's remuneration and income tax, as given below	2,650	5,800
Depreciation (plant and machinery)	1,500	3,500
Director's remuneration	3,000	3,000
Income tax	—	1,460

The income tax charged in the accounts of 19.1 is the full amount of the company's liability for 19.1/.2, based on the profits of the year 19...

John Dickinson has asked his bank manager for an unsecured overdraft on the company's account, with a limit of £10,000. He has received a very large order from a buyer of first-class financial standing, and he needs an overdraft to finance the additional work which this order will involve. Dickinson has no substantial private resources.

You are required to write a report on the position of the company and the policy of the director, drawing reasonable inferences from the figures in the above balance sheets and giving your opinion of the proposal put before the bank manager.

Ignore profits tax. (*Institute of Bankers.*)

23. The summarized balance sheets of Y Ltd., on 31st March, 19.., and 31st March, 19.1, are as under—

31st March, 19..

	£	£		£	£
Share Capital and Reserves—			Fixed Assets, at cost	78,000	
Ordinary shares	50,000		*Less* Depreciation	20,000	
Redeemable preference shares	10,000				58,000
General reserve	12,000		Trade investment—		
P. & L. A/c	3,000		Shares in associated company, at cost		5,000
Reserve for Income Tax, 19../.1	18,000		Current assets		47,000
		93,000			
Current liabilities		17,000			
		110,000			110,000

31st March, 19.1

	£	£		£	£
Share Capital and Reserves—			Fixed assets, at cost . .	102,000	
Ordinary shares .	50,000		*Less* depreciation . .	28,000	
Capital Redemption Reserve Fund . . .	10,000				74,000
General Reserve . .	2,000		Trade investment— Shares in associated company, at cost		5,000
P. & L. A/c . . .	15,000		Loan to associated company . .		5,000
Reserve for Income Tax, 19.1/.2 . . .	8,000		Current assets . . .		31,000
		85,000			
Current liabilities		30,000			
		115,000			115,000

The final section of the profit and loss account of Y Ltd. for the year to 31st March, 19.1, is as follows—

	£		£
Reserve for Income Tax, 19.1/.2 (based on current profits) .	8,000	Net profit for year to 31st March, 19.1	20,000
Balance carried forward . .	15,000	Balance brought forward from 31st March, 19.. . . .	3,000
	23,000		23,000

You are approached by certain shareholders of the company, who are puzzled by the contrast between the two balance sheets in regard to working capital (i.e. excess of current assets over current liabilities), and seek an explanation. They are unable to reconcile the adverse change in regard to working capital with the fact that the company made a substantial profit of £20,000 in the year to 31st March, 19.1. The profit, they suggest, should be reflected by an increase in working capital.

You are required to prepare an explanatory statement, for the benefit of these shareholders, showing, *with figures*, the causes of the change in the company's position as regards working capital.

You are not required to comment on the financial policy of the company.

(*Institute of Bankers.*)

24. Estimators Ltd. was incorporated on 1st December, 19... It was proposed to issue a number of ordinary shares of £1 each on 1st January, 19.1, at par, to be paid up in full immediately, and to commence a trading business on the same day.

The number of shares to be issued was to be exactly sufficient to provide for the payment, on 1st January, 19.1, of (*a*) £1,600 for preliminary expenses, and (*b*) £14,000 for fixed assets, and, in addition, to produce the minimum sum necessary to ensure that, on the basis of the following estimates, the company would not overdraw its bank account or be compelled to borrow money at any time in the six months to 30th June, 19.1.

It was estimated that sales would amount to £8,000 in January, 19.1, £11,000 in February, and £14,000 in each subsequent month. It was expected that gross profit would be at a uniform rate of 25 per cent of selling price.

An initial stock of goods was to be purchased on credit on 1st January, 19.1, for £12,400, and subsequent purchasing was to be so arranged that the stock at the end of each month would amount to exactly £12,400 (at cost price).

Trade creditors were to be paid on the last day of the month after that in which the goods were purchased.

It was expected that payment for all sales would be received on the last day of the second month after that in which the goods were sold.

Wages and salaries, estimated at £1,000 per month, were to be paid on the last day of the month in which they were earned, and other expenses, estimated at £750 per month, were to be paid on the last day of the month after that in which they were incurred.

No discounts were to be allowed or received and all money received was to be paid into the bank.

You are required to prepare a summary of the company's bank account and trading and profit and loss account for the six months to 30th June, 19.1, and balance sheet at 30th June, 19.1, as they would appear if the company's transactions were in accordance with the foregoing plans and estimates.

The balance on the bank account at the end of each month is to be shown in a column provided for the purpose.

Ignore taxation and depreciation of fixed assets. (*Institute of Bankers.*)

25. The following were the balance sheets of Ono Ltd. as at 31st December, 19.. and 31st December, 19.1—

	19..	19.1
	£	£
Ordinary shares	50,000	50,000
Redeemable preference shares	20,000	15,000
Capital redemption reserve fund	—	5,000
Profit and loss account	40,000	45,000
	110,000	115,000
Fixed assets—		
Cost	120,000	97,000
Depreciation	40,000	24,000
	80,000	73,000
Net current assets	30,000	42,000
	110,000	115,000

During the year ended 31st December, 19.1—

(1) Fixed assets were sold for £10,000 (cost £30,000; depreciation accumulated £24,000). The surplus has been credited to profit and loss account.

(2) The redeemable preference shares redeemed were repaid to shareholders at a premium of 10 per cent of par value.

Prepare a statement showing: (*a*) the sources, and (*b*) the application, of working capital during 19.1. (*Corporation of Certified and Corporate Accountants.*)

26. During the year ended 31st December, 19.. the bank overdraft of PQ & Co. Ltd. has increased by £115,000. From the following balances at 1st January and 31st December prepare a statement which will enable you to show the directors why this increase has occurred.

	1st Jan. 19..	31st Dec. 19..
	£	£
Ordinary share capital	500,000	600,000
Share premium	—	25,000
General reserve	200,000	200,000
Profit on sale of plant	—	6,000
Profit and loss account—		
Balance brought forward	45,000	45,000
Profit for year after tax and proposed dividend	—	19,300
Creditors	258,000	323,000
Taxation	70,000	55,000
Unsecured loan	50,000	50,000
Proposed dividend (net)	23,000 (8%)	20,700 (6%)
Bank overdraft	132,000	247,000
	1,278,000	1,591,000

		1st Jan. 19.. £		31st Dec. 19.. £
Freehold and leasehold property		65,000		65,000
Plant and machinery at cost	310,000		380,000	
Less Depreciation to date	140,000		170,000	
		170,000		210,000
Shares in subsidiary company		50,000		50,000
Loan to subsidiary company		25,000		40,000
Trade investments		75,000		100,000
Stock-in-trade		185,000		290,000
Work-in-progress		283,000		347,000
Debtors		420,000		485,000
Cash in hand		5,000		4,000
		1,278,000		1,591,000

NOTES—

(*a*) During the year, plant costing £40,000 with a written down value of £10,000 was sold for £16,000 and this transaction has been taken into account in arriving at the above balances.

(*b*) The proposed dividend at 1st January 19.. of £23,000 was paid on 31st March, 19.. and taxation of £62,000 was paid during the year.

(*Cost and Management Accountants.*)

27. The summarized accounts of E. Farr, Ltd., for the calendar year 1964 and the preceding year were as follows—

	£	1964 £	1963 £
Profit and Loss Accounts			
Trading Profit (after depreciation of £6,000 and Directors' Remuneration of £4,000)		32,500	28,500
Less Loss on Sale of Plant (Cost, £1,500, depreciation, £1,250)		250	—
		32,250	28,500
Add Investment Income		450	450
Profit before Taxation		32,700	28,950
Less Taxation of Profits to date—			
Income Tax Estimated	17,125		14,575
Less Over-provided	1,000	16,125	—
		16,575	14,375
Add Balance b/f		12,625	6,000
		29,200	20,375

	1964 £	1963 £
Appropriated—		
Reserve	10,000	5,000
Dividend proposed	5,500	2,750
Carried forward	13,700	12,625
	29,200	20,375

	1964	1963
	£	£
Balance Sheets		
Fixed Assets at cost	52,500	40,000
Less Depreciation	19,750	15,000
	32,750	25,000
Current Assets—		
Investments (Temporary)	2,000	2,000
Stock	66,000	75,200
Debtors	57,500	50,000
Bank	9,000	—
	134,500	127,200
Total Assets	167,250	152,200
Less Current Liabilities—		
Bank Overdraft	—	13,375
Creditors	44,925	44,500
Income Tax due 1st January	14,625	11,450
Proposed Dividends	5,500	2,750
	65,050	72,075
Net Assets	102,200	80,125
Represented by—		
Share Capital	55,000	45,000
Revenue Reserve—		
General	20,000	10,000
Profit and Loss Account	13,700	12,625
	88,700	67,625
Future Income Tax	13,500	12,500
	102,200	80,125

Draw up a statement showing the additional resources which became available in the year 1964, and how they were utilized.

28. Describe five of the principal ratios which you consider significant when interpreting accounts and explain the inferences which may be drawn from their use.

29. At 31st December, 1963, the assets of a Manufacturing Company were as follows—

Fixed Assets at 1st January, 1963, £35,000. Additions during 1963, £5,500.
Current Assets, £14,500.

The liabilities at 31st December, 1963, were—

Sundry Trade Creditors, £26,500.
Profit and Loss Account, £6,000.
Issued Share Capital, £22,500.

You are asked to advise the directors why difficulty is experienced in financing the business and to prepare a Balance Sheet to support your answer.

30. The summarized Profit and Loss Accounts and Balance Sheets of Winton Ltd. are as follows—

PROFIT AND LOSS ACCOUNTS

31 Dec	1959 £	1960 £		1959 £	1960 £
Taxation	13,000	16,750	Balance b/f	8,250	12,750
Proposed Dividends	2,500	2,500	Trading Profit (after Depreciation, £10,000, and Directors' Remuneration, £2,500)	20,000	30,000
General Reserve	—	2,500	Profit on Sale of Investments	—	500
Balance c/f	12,750	23,000	Taxation Over-Provision	—	1,500
	28,250	44,750		28,250	44,750

BALANCE SHEETS

31 Dec	1959 £	1960 £		1959 £	1960 £
Share Capital	20,000	25,000	Fixed Assets (at cost)	20,000	25,000
General Reserve	2,500	5,000	Additions (at cost)	5,000	20,000
Profit and Loss Account	12,750	23,000			
Future Tax Reserve	8,750	13,750		25,000	45,000
Bank Overdraft	51,250	57,500	Depreciation	10,000	15,000
Trade Creditors	36,000	50,000			
Accrued Expenses	8,000	7,000		15,000	30,000
Provision for Taxation	5,000	7,250	Investments	4,500	—
Proposed Dividends	2,500	2,500	Stock	76,250	100,000
			Debtors	51,000	61,000
	146,750	191,000		146,750	191,000

The Trading Account for the year to 31st December, 1960, showed purchases of £300,000; sales, £350,000; wages and other expenses (excluding depreciation), £38,750.

Prepare—

(*a*) A summarized statement of receipts and payments for the year ended 31st December, 1960; and

(*b*) A statement showing the source of additional working capital which became available in that year, and the manner in which it was utilized.

31. Machinery can be purchased on payment of the following amounts—

(1) £2,000 on 1st January, 1964.
(2) £2,000 at the end of each of the next four years.
(3) £2,500 at the end of the fifth year.

Using the following tables, where appropriate, calculate the equivalent cash price which could be offered, if payment in full were to be made on 1st January, 1964, compound interest having been brought into account at 6 per cent per annum—

The cost of an Annuity of £1 for—

4 years is £3·4651;
5 years is £4·2124.

An Annuity of £1 per annum amounts to—

£4·3746 in 4 years;
£5·6371 in 5 years.

The present value of £1 is—

£0·79209 if payable 4 years hence;
£0·74726 if payable 5 years hence. (*A.C.C.A.*)

32. A project has a life of 10 years and involves the purchase of fixed assets for £100,000 and the use of £20,000 in working capital. If the assets are bought, an old machine can be disposed of for £5,000 cash. Sales are expected to be £200,000 per annum less accounting costs of £150,000 (including £30,000 depreciation). The company's average rate of tax is 50 per cent. The assets are expected to realize £10,000 at the end of 10 years.

Draw up a statement of the cash investment and returns.

33. Present the net outflow and inflow of cash from the project in Question 32 in terms of a logical times scale. Calculate the payback and the net present value at 10 per cent, and state whether the project is worth while at a 10 per cent required rate of return.

34. A project involves outlays of £37,900 and should secure returns of £5,000 in Year 1; £7,500 in Year 2; £10,000 in Year 3; £12,500 in Year 4; and £15,000 in Year 5.

Is the project worth while at 10 per cent? If not, at what rate of return is it worth while?

35. A project involves investment of £7,880 and returns of £2,630. If it has a life of seven years, what is the rate of return? What is the rate if its life is five years? How many years must the project last if the company requires a return of 25 per cent?

APPENDIX I

A—Annual present value

B—Cumulative present value

C—Capital recovery

D—Sinking funds

TABLE A
PRESENT VALUE FACTORS

To determine the present value of a single payment received "n" years from the present (or vice versa)

Years	1%	2%	3%	4%	5%	6%	7%	8%	9%	10%
1	·9901	·9804	·9709	·9615	·9524	·9434	·9346	·9259	·9174	·9091
2	·9803	·9612	·9426	·9426	·9070	·8900	·8734	·8573	·8417	·8264
3	·9706	·9423	·9151	·8890	·8638	·8396	·8163	·7938	·7722	·7513
4	·9610	·9238	·8885	·8548	·8227	·7921	·7629	·7350	·7084	·6830
5	·9515	·9057	·8626	·8219	·7835	·7473	·7130	·6806	·6499	·6209
6	·9420	·8880	·8375	·7903	·7462	·7050	·6663	·6302	·5963	·5645
7	·9327	·8706	·8131	·7599	·7107	·6651	·6227	·5835	·5470	·5132
8	·9235	·8535	·7894	·7307	·6768	·6274	·5820	·5403	·5019	·4665
9	·9143	·8368	·7664	·7026	·6446	·5919	·5439	·5002	·4604	·4241
10	·9053	·8203	·7441	·6756	·6139	·5584	·5083	·4632	·4224	·3855
11	·8963	·8043	·7224	·6496	·5847	·5268	·4751	·4289	·3875	·3505
12	·8874	·7885	·7014	·6246	·5568	·4970	·4440	·3971	·3555	·3186
13	·8787	·7730	·6810	·6006	·5303	·4688	·4150	·3677	·3262	·2897
14	·8700	·7579	·6611	·5775	·5051	·4423	·3878	·3405	·2992	·2633
15	·8613	·7430	·6419	·5553	·4810	·4173	·3624	·3152	·2745	·2394
16	·8528	·7284	·6232	·5339	·4581	·3936	·3387	·2919	·2519	·2176
17	·8444	·7142	·6050	·5134	·4363	·3714	·3166	·2703	·2311	·1978
18	·8360	·7002	·5874	·4936	·4155	·3503	·2959	·2502	·2120	·1799
19	·8277	·6864	·5703	·4746	·3957	·3305	·2765	·2317	·1945	·1635
20	·8195	·6730	·5537	·4564	·3769	·3118	·2584	·2145	·1784	·1486
21	·8114	·6598	·5375	·4388	·3589	·2942	·2415	·1987	·1637	·1351
22	·8034	·6468	·5219	·4220	·3418	·2775	·2257	·1839	·1502	·1228
23	·7954	·6342	·5067	·4057	·3256	·2618	·2109	·1703	·1378	·1117
24	·7876	·6217	·4919	·3901	·3101	·2470	·1971	·1577	·1264	·1015
25	·7798	·6095	·4776	·3751	·2953	·2330	·1842	·1460	·1160	·0923
26	·7720	·5976	·4637	·3607	·2812	·2198	·1722	·1352	·1064	·0839
27	·7644	·5859	·4502	·3468	·2678	·2074	·1609	·1252	·0976	·0763
28	·7568	·5744	·4371	·3335	·2551	·1956	·1504	·1159	·0895	·0693
29	·7493	·5631	·4243	·3207	·2429	·1846	·1406	·1073	·0822	·0630
30	·7419	·5521	·4120	·3083	·2314	·1741	·1314	·0994	·0754	·0573
31	·7346	·5412	·4000	·2965	·2204	·1643	·1228	·0920	·0691	·0521
32	·7273	·5306	·3883	·2851	·2099	·1550	·1147	·0852	·0634	·0474
33	·7201	·5202	·3770	·2741	·1999	·1462	·1072	·0789	·0582	·0431
34	·7130	·5100	·3660	·2636	·1904	·1379	·1002	·0730	·0534	·0391
35	·7059	·5000	·3554	·2534	·1813	·1301	·0937	·0676	·0490	·0356
36	·6989	·4902	·3450	·2437	·1727	·1227	·0875	·0626	·0449	·0323
37	·6920	·4806	·3350	·2343	·1644	·1158	·0818	·0580	·0412	·0294
38	·6852	·4712	·3252	·2253	·1566	·1092	·0765	·0537	·0378	·0267
39	·6784	·4619	·3158	·2166	·1491	·1031	·0715	·0497	·0347	·0243
40	·6717	·4529	·3066	·2083	·1420	·0972	·0668	·0460	·0318	·0221
41	·6650	·4440	·2976	·2003	·1353	·0917	·0624	·0426	·0292	·0210
42	·6584	·4353	·2890	·1926	·1288	·0865	·0583	·0395	·0268	·0183
43	·6519	·4268	·2805	·1852	·1227	·0816	·0545	·0365	·0246	·0166
44	·6454	·4184	·2724	·1780	·1169	·0770	·0509	·0338	·0226	·0151
45	·6391	·4102	·2644	·1712	·1113	·0727	·0476	·0313	·0207	·0137
46	·6327	·4022	·2567	·1646	·1060	·0685	·0445	·0290	·0190	·0125
47	·6265	·3943	·2493	·1583	·1009	·0647	·0416	·0269	·0174	·0113
48	·6203	·3865	·2420	·1522	·0961	·0610	·0389	·0249	·0160	·0103
49	·6141	·3790	·2350	·1463	·0916	·0575	·0363	·0230	·0147	·0094
50	·6080	·3715	·2281	·1407	·0872	·0543	·0339	·0213	·0134	·0085

TABLE A

To determine the present value of a single payment received "n" years from the present (or vice versa)

Years	11%	12%	13%	14%	15%	16%	17%	18%	19%	20%
1	·9009	·8923	·8850	·8772	·8696	·8621	·8547	·8475	·8403	·8330
2	·8116	·7972	·7831	·7695	·7561	·7432	·7305	·7182	·7062	·6940
3	·7312	·7118	·6931	·6750	·6575	·6407	·6244	·6086	·5934	·5707
4	·6587	·6355	·6133	·5921	·5718	·5523	·5337	·5158	·4987	·4820
5	·5935	·5674	·5428	·5194	·4972	·4761	·4561	·4371	·4190	·4020
6	·5346	·5066	·4803	·4556	·4323	·4104	·3898	·3704	·3521	·3351
7	·4817	·4523	·4251	·3996	·3759	·3538	·3332	·3139	·2959	·2791
8	·4339	·4039	·3762	·3506	·3269	·3050	·2848	·2660	·2487	·2331
9	·3909	·3606	·3329	·3075	·2843	·2630	·2434	·2255	·2090	·1938
10	·3522	·3220	·2946	·2697	·2472	·2267	·2080	·1911	·1756	·1615
11	·3173	·2875	·2607	·2366	·2149	·1954	·1778	·1619	·1476	·1346
12	·2858	·2567	·2307	·2076	·1869	·1685	·1520	·1372	·1240	·1122
13	·2575	·2292	·2042	·1821	·1625	·1452	·1299	·1163	·1042	·0935
14	·2320	·2046	·1807	·1597	·1413	·1252	·1110	·0985	·0876	·0779
15	·2090	·1827	·1599	·1401	·1229	·1079	·0949	·0835	·0736	·0649
16	·1883	·1631	·1415	·1229	·1069	·0930	·0818	·0708	·0618	·0541
17	·1696	·1456	·1252	·1078	·0929	·0802	·0693	·0600	·0520	·0451
18	·1528	·1300	·1108	·0946	·0808	·0691	·0592	·0508	·0437	·0376
19	·1377	·1161	·0981	·0829	·0703	·0596	·0506	·0431	·0367	·0313
20	·1240	·1037	·0868	·0728	·0611	·0514	·0433	·0365	·0303	·0261
21	·1117	·0926	·0768	·0638	·0531	·0443	·0370	·0309	·0259	·0217
22	·1007	·0826	·0680	·0560	·0462	·0382	·0316	·0262	·0218	·0181
23	·0907	·0738	·0601	·0491	·0402	·0329	·0270	·0222	·0183	·0151
24	·0817	·0659	·0532	·0431	·0349	·0284	·0231	·0188	·0154	·0126
25	·0736	·0588	·0471	·0378	·0304	·0245	·0197	·0160	·0129	·0105
26	·0663	·0525	·0417	·0331	·0264	·0211	·0169	·0135	·0109	·0087
27	·0597	·0469	·0369	·0291	·0230	·0182	·0144	·0115	·0091	·0073
28	·0538	·0419	·0326	·0255	·0200	·0157	·0123	·0097	·0077	·0061
29	·0485	·0374	·0289	·0224	·0174	·0135	·0105	·0082	·0064	·0051
30	·0437	·0334	·0256	·0196	·0151	·0116	·0090	·0070	·0054	·0042
31	·0394	·0298	·0226	·0172	·0131	·0100	·0077	·0059	·0046	·0035
32	·0355	·0266	·0200	·0151	·0114	·0087	·0066	·0050	·0038	·0029
33	·0319	·0238	·0177	·0132	·0099	·0075	·0056	·0042	·0032	·0024
34	·0288	·0212	·0157	·0116	·0086	·0064	·0048	·0036	·0027	·0020
35	·0259	·0189	·0139	·0102	·0075	·0055	·0041	·0030	·0023	·0017
36	·0234	·0169	·0123	·0089	·0065	·0048	·0035	·0026	·0019	·0014
37	·0210	·0151	·0109	·0078	·0057	·0041	·0030	·0022	·0016	·0012
38	·0190	·0135	·0096	·0069	·0049	·0036	·0026	·0019	·0013	·0010
39	·0171	·0120	·0085	·0060	·0043	·0031	·0022	·0016	·0011	·0008
40	·0154	·0107	·0075	·0053	·0037	·0026	·0019	·0013	·0010	·0007
41	·0139	·0096	·0067	·0046	·0032	·0023	·0016	·0011	·0008	·0006
42	·0125	·0086	·0059	·0041	·0028	·0020	·0014	·0010	·0007	·0005
43	·0112	·0076	·0052	·0036	·0025	·0017	·0012	·0008	·0006	·0004
44	·0101	·0068	·0046	·0031	·0021	·0015	·0010	·0007	·0005	·0003
45	·0091	·0061	·0041	·0027	·0019	·0013	·0009	·0006	·0004	·0003
46	·0082	·0054	·0036	·0024	·0016	·0011	·0007	·0005	·0003	·0002
47	·0074	·0049	·0032	·0021	·0014	·0009	·0006	·0004	·0003	·0002
48	·0067	·0043	·0028	·0019	·0012	·0008	·0005	·0004	·0002	·0002
49	·0060	·0039	·0025	·0016	·0011	·0007	·0005	·0003	·0002	·0001
50	·0054	·0035	·0022	·0014	·0009	·0006	·0004	·0003	·0002	·0001

TABLE A
PRESENT VALUE FACTORS

To determine the present value of a single payment received "n" years from the present (or vice versa)

Years	21%	22%	23%	24%	25%	26%	27%	28%	29%	30%
1	·8264	·8197	·8130	·8065	·8000	·7937	·7874	·7813	·7752	·7692
2	·6830	·6719	·6610	·6504	·6400	·6299	·6200	·6104	·6009	·5917
3	·5645	·5507	·5374	·5245	·5120	·4999	·4888	·4768	·4658	·4552
4	·4665	·4514	·4369	·4230	·4096	·3968	·3844	·3725	·3611	·3501
5	·3855	·3700	·3552	·3411	·3277	·3149	·3027	·2910	·2799	·2693
6	·3186	·3033	·2888	·2751	·2621	·2499	·2383	·2274	·2170	·2072
7	·2633	·2486	·2348	·2218	·2097	·1983	·1877	·1776	·1682	·1594
8	·2176	·2038	·1909	·1789	·1678	·1574	·1478	·1388	·1304	·1226
9	·1799	·1670	·1552	·1443	·1342	·1249	·1164	·1084	·1011	·0943
10	·1486	·1369	·1262	·1164	·1074	·0992	·0916	·0847	·0784	·0725
11	·1228	·1122	·1026	·0938	·0859	·0787	·0721	·0662	·0607	·0558
12	·1015	·0920	·0834	·0757	·0687	·0625	·0568	·0517	·0471	·0429
13	·0839	·0754	·0678	·0610	·0550	·0496	·0447	·0404	·0365	·0330
14	·0693	·0618	·0551	·0492	·0440	·0393	·0352	·0316	·0283	·0254
15	·0573	·0507	·0448	·0397	·0352	·0312	·0277	·0247	·0219	·0195
16	·0474	·0415	·0364	·0320	·0281	·0248	·0218	·0193	·0170	·0150
17	·0391	·0340	·0296	·0258	·0225	·0197	·0172	·0150	·0132	·0116
18	·0323	·0279	·0241	·0208	·0180	·0156	·0135	·0118	·0102	·0089
19	·0267	·0229	·0196	·0168	·0144	·0124	·0107	·0092	·0079	·0068
20	·0221	·0187	·0159	·0135	·0115	·0098	·0084	·0072	·0061	·0053
21	·0183	·0154	·0129	·0109	·0092	·0078	·0066	·0056	·0048	·0040
22	·0151	·0126	·0105	·0088	·0074	·0062	·0052	·0044	·0037	·0031
23	·0125	·0103	·0086	·0071	·0059	·0049	·0041	·0034	·0029	·0024
24	·0103	·0085	·0070	·0057	·0047	·0039	·0032	·0027	·0022	·0018
25	·0085	·0069	·0057	·0046	·0038	·0031	·0025	·0021	·0017	·0014
26	·0070	·0057	·0046	·0037	·0030	·0025	·0020	·0016	·0013	·0011
27	·0058	·0047	·0037	·0030	·0024	·0019	·0016	·0013	·0010	·0008
28	·0048	·0038	·0030	·0024	·0019	·0015	·0012	·0010	·0008	·0006
29	·0040	·0031	·0025	·0020	·0015	·0012	·0010	·0008	·0006	·0005
30	·0033	·0026	·0020	·0016	·0012	·0010	·0008	·0006	·0005	·0004
31	·0027	·0021	·0016	·0013	·0010	·0008	·0006	·0005	·0004	·0003
32	·0022	·0017	·0013	·0010	·0008	·0006	·0005	·0004	·0003	·0002
33	·0019	·0014	·0011	·0008	·0006	·0005	·0004	·0003	·0002	·0002
34	·0015	·0012	·0009	·0007	·0005	·0004	·0003	·0002	·0002	·0001
35	·0013	·0009	·0007	·0005	·0004	·0003	·0002	·0002	·0001	·0001
36	·0010	·0008	·0006	·0004	·0003	·0002	·0002	·0001	·0001	·0001
37	·0009	·0006	·0005	·0003	·0003	·0002	·0001	·0001	·0001	·0001
38	·0007	·0005	·0004	·0003	·0002	·0002	·0001	·0001	·0001	
39	·0006	·0004	·0003	·0002	·0002	·0001	·0001	·0001		
40	·0005	·0004	·0003	·0002	·0001	·0001	·0001	·0001		
41	·0004	·0003	·0002	·0001	·0001	·0001	·0001			
42	·0003	·0002	·0002	·0001	·0001	·0001				
43	·0003	·0002	·0001	·0001	·0001					
44	·0002	·0002	·0001	·0001	·0001					
45	·0002	·0001	·0001	·0001						
46	·0002	·0001	·0001	·0001						
47	·0001	·0001	·0001							
48	·0001	·0001								
49	·0001	·0001								
50	·0001									

TABLE A
PRESENT VALUE FACTORS

To determine the present value of a single payment received "n" years from the present (or vice versa)

Years	31%	32%	33%	34%	35%	36%	37%	38%	39%	40%
1	·7634	·7576	·7519	·7463	·7407	·7353	·7299	·7246	·7194	·7143
2	·5827	·5739	·5653	·5569	·5487	·5407	·5328	·5251	·5176	·5102
3	·4448	·4348	·4251	·4156	·4064	·3975	·3889	·3805	·3724	·3644
4	·3396	·3294	·3196	·3102	·3011	·2923	·2839	·2757	·2679	·2603
5	·2592	·2495	·2403	·2315	·2230	·2149	·2072	·1998	·1927	·1859
6	·1979	·1890	·1807	·1727	·1652	·1580	·1512	·1448	·1386	·1328
7	·1510	·1432	·1358	·1289	·1224	·1162	·1104	·1049	·0997	·0949
8	·1153	·1085	·1021	·0962	·0906	·0854	·0806	·0760	·0718	·0678
9	·0880	·0822	·0768	·0718	·0671	·0628	·0588	·0551	·0516	·0484
10	·0672	·0623	·0577	·0536	·0497	·0462	·0429	·0399	·0371	·0346
11	·0513	·0472	·0434	·0400	·0368	·0340	·0313	·0289	·0267	·0247
12	·0392	·0357	·0326	·0298	·0273	·0250	·0229	·0210	·0192	·0176
13	·0299	·0271	·0245	·0223	·0202	·0184	·0167	·0152	·0138	·0126
14	·0228	·0205	·0185	·0166	·0150	·0135	·0122	·0110	·0099	·0090
15	·0174	·0155	·0139	·0124	·0111	·0099	·0089	·0080	·0072	·0064
16	·0133	·0118	·0104	·0093	·0082	·0073	·0065	·0058	·0051	·0046
17	·0101	·0089	·0078	·0069	·0061	·0054	·0047	·0042	·0037	·0033
18	·0077	·0068	·0059	·0052	·0045	·0039	·0035	·0030	·0027	·0023
19	·0059	·0051	·0044	·0038	·0033	·0029	·0025	·0022	·0019	·0017
20	·0045	·0039	·0033	·0029	·0025	·0021	·0018	·0016	·0014	·0012
21	·0034	·0029	·0025	·0021	·0018	·0016	·0013	·0012	·0010	·0009
22	·0025	·0022	·0019	·0016	·0014	·0012	·0010	·0008	·0007	·0006
23	·0020	·0017	·0014	·0012	·0010	·0008	·0007	·0006	·0005	·0004
24	·0015	·0013	·0011	·0009	·0007	·0006	·0005	·0004	·0004	·0003
25	·0012	·0010	·0008	·0007	·0006	·0005	·0004	·0003	·0003	·0002
26	·0009	·0007	·0006	·0005	·0004	·0003	·0003	·0002	·0002	·0002
27	·0007	·0006	·0005	·0004	·0003	·0002	·0002	·0002	·0001	·0001
28	·0005	·0004	·0003	·0003	·0002	·0002	·0001	·0001	·0001	·0001
29	·0004	·0003	·0003	·0002	·0002	·0001	·0001	·0001	·0001	·0001
30	·0003	·0002	·0002	·0002	·0001	·0001	·0001	·0001	·0001	
31	·0002	·0002	·0001	·0001	·0001	·0001	·0001			
32	·0002	·0001	·0001	·0001	·0001	·0001				
33	·0001	·0001	·0001	·0001	·0001					
34	·0001	·0001	·0001							
35	·0001	·0001								
36	·0001									

TABLE B
CUMULATIVE PRESENT VALUE FACTORS

Years 0 to:	1%	2%	3%	4%	5%	6%	7%	8%	9%	10%
1	·990	·980	·971	·962	·952	·943	·935	·926	·917	·909
2	1·970	1·942	1·913	1·886	1·859	1·833	1·808	1·783	1·759	1·736
3	2·941	2·884	2·829	2·775	2·723	2·673	2·624	2·577	2·531	2·487
4	3·902	3·808	3·717	3·630	3·546	3·465	3·387	3·312	3·240	3·170
5	4·853	4·713	4·580	4·452	4·329	4·212	4·100	3·993	3·890	3·791
6	5·795	5·601	5·417	5·242	5·076	4·917	4·767	4·623	4·486	4·355
7	6·728	6·472	6·230	6·002	5·786	5·582	5·389	5·206	5·033	4·868
8	7·652	7·325	7·020	6·733	6·463	6·210	5·971	5·747	5·535	5·335
9	8·566	8·162	7·786	7·435	7·108	6·802	6·515	6·247	5·995	5·759
10	9·471	8·983	8·530	8·111	7·722	7·360	7·024	6·710	6·418	6·145
11	10·378	9·787	9·253	8·760	8·306	7·887	7·499	7·139	6·805	6·495
12	11·255	10·575	9·954	9·385	8·863	8·384	7·943	7·536	7·161	6·814
13	12·134	11·348	10·635	9·986	9·394	8·853	8·358	7·904	7·487	7·103
14	13·004	12·106	11·296	10·563	9·899	9·295	8·745	8·244	7·786	7·367
15	13·865	12·849	11·938	11·118	10·380	9·712	9·108	8·559	8·061	7·606
16	14·718	13·578	12·561	11·652	10·838	10·106	9·447	8·851	8·313	7·824
17	15·562	14·292	13·166	12·166	11·274	10·477	9·763	9·122	8·544	8·022
18	16·398	14·992	13·754	12·659	11·690	10·828	10·059	9·372	8·756	8·201
19	17·226	15·678	14·324	13·134	12·085	11·158	10·336	9·604	8·950	8·365
20	18·046	16·351	14·877	13·590	12·462	11·470	10·594	9·818	9·129	8·514
21	18·857	17·011	15·415	14·029	12·821	11·764	10·836	10·017	9·292	8·649
22	19·660	17·658	15·937	14·451	13·163	12·042	11·061	10·201	9·442	8·772
23	20·456	18·292	16·444	14·857	13·489	12·303	11·272	10·371	9·580	8·883
24	21·243	18·914	16·936	15·247	13·799	12·550	11·469	10·529	9·707	8·985
25	22·023	19·523	17·413	15·622	14·094	12·783	11·654	10·675	9·823	9·077
26	22·795	20·121	17·877	15·983	14·375	13·003	11·826	10·810	9·929	9·161
27	23·560	20·707	18·327	16·330	14·643	13·211	11·987	10·935	10·027	9·237
28	24·316	21·281	18·764	16·663	14·898	13·406	12·137	11·051	10·116	9·307
29	25·066	21·844	19·188	16·984	15·141	13·591	12·278	11·158	10·198	9·370
30	25·808	22·396	19·600	17·292	15·372	13·765	12·409	11·258	10·274	9·427
31	26·542	22·938	20·000	17·588	15·593	13·929	12·532	11·350	10·343	9·479
32	27·270	23·468	20·389	17·874	15·803	14·084	12·647	11·435	10·406	9·526
33	27·990	23·989	20·766	18·148	16·003	14·230	12·754	11·514	10·464	9·569
34	28·703	24·499	21·132	18·411	16·193	14·368	12·854	11·587	10·518	9·609
35	29·409	24·999	21·487	18·665	16·374	14·498	12·948	11·655	10·567	9·644
36	30·108	25·489	21·832	18·908	16·547	14·621	13·035	11·717	10·612	9·677
37	30·780	25·969	22·167	19·143	16·711	14·737	13·117	11·775	10·653	9·706
38	31·485	26·441	22·492	19·368	16·868	14·846	13·193	11·829	10·691	9·733
39	32·163	26·903	22·808	19·584	17·017	14·949	13·265	11·879	10·726	9·757
40	32·835	27·355	23·115	19·793	17·159	15·046	13·332	11·925	10·757	9·779

TABLE B
CUMULATIVE PRESENT VALUE FACTORS

Years 0 to:	11%	12%	13%	14%	15%	16%	17%	18%	19%	20%
1	·901	·893	·885	·877	·870	·862	·855	·848	·840	·833
2	1·712	1·690	1·668	1·647	1·626	1·605	1·585	1·566	1·546	1·528
3	2·444	2·402	2·361	2·322	2·283	2·246	2·210	2·174	2·140	2·106
4	3·102	3·307	2·974	2·914	2·855	2·798	2·743	2·690	2·639	2·589
5	3·696	3·605	3·517	3·433	3·352	3·274	3·199	3·127	3·058	2·991
6	4·230	4·111	3·998	3·889	3·784	3·685	3·589	3·498	3·410	3·326
7	4·712	4·564	4·423	4·288	4·160	4·039	3·922	3·812	3·706	3·605
8	5·146	4·968	4·799	4·639	4·487	4·344	4·207	4·078	3·954	3·837
9	5·537	5·328	5·132	4·946	4·772	4·607	4·451	4·303	4·163	4·031
10	5·889	5·650	5·426	5·216	5·019	4·833	4·659	4·494	4·339	4·192
11	6·206	5·938	5·687	5·453	5·234	5·029	4·836	4·656	4·486	4·327
12	6·492	6·194	5·918	5·660	5·420	5·197	4·988	4·793	4·610	4·439
13	6·750	6·424	6·122	5·842	5·583	5·342	5·118	4·910	4·715	4·533
14	6·982	6·628	6·303	6·002	5·724	5·468	5·229	5·008	4·802	4·611
15	7·191	6·811	6·463	6·142	5·847	5·576	5·324	5·092	4·876	4·676
16	7·379	6·974	6·604	6·265	5·954	5·668	5·405	5·162	4·938	4·730
17	7·549	7·120	6·729	6·373	6·047	5·749	5·475	5·222	4·990	4·775
18	7·702	7·250	6·840	6·468	6·128	5·818	5·534	5·273	5·033	4·812
19	7·839	7·366	6·938	6·550	6·198	5·877	5·584	5·316	5·070	4·844
20	7·963	7·469	7·025	6·623	6·259	5·929	5·628	5·353	5·101	4·870
21	8·075	7·562	7·102	6·687	6·312	5·973	5·665	5·384	5·127	4·892
22	8·176	7·645	7·170	6·743	6·358	6·011	5·696	5·410	5·149	4·910
23	8·266	7·718	7·230	6·792	6·399	6·044	5·723	5·432	5·167	4·925
24	8·348	7·784	7·283	6·835	6·434	6·073	5·746	5·451	5·182	4·937
25	8·422	7·843	7·330	6·873	6·464	6·097	5·766	5·467	5·195	4·948
26	8·488	7·896	7·372	6·906	6·490	6·118	5·783	5·480	5·206	4·956
27	8·548	7·942	7·409	6·935	6·513	6·136	5·797	5·492	5·215	4·964
28	8·601	7·984	7·441	6·961	6·533	6·152	5·810	5·502	5·223	4·970
29	8·650	8·022	7·470	6·983	6·551	6·166	5·820	5·510	5·229	4·975
30	8·694	8·055	7·496	7·003	6·566	6·177	5·829	5·517	5·235	4·979
31	8·733	8·085	7·518	7·020	6·579	6·187	5·837	5·523	5·239	4·983
32	8·768	8·112	7·538	7·035	6·590	6·196	5·844	5·528	5·243	4·986
33	8·800	8·135	7·556	7·048	6·600	6·203	5·849	5·532	5·246	4·988
34	8·829	8·157	7·572	7·060	6·609	6·210	5·854	5·535	5·249	4·990
35	8·855	8·176	7·586	7·070	6·616	6·215	5·858	5·538	5·251	4·992
36	8·878	8·192	7·598	7·079	6·623	6·220	5·862	5·541	5·253	4·993
37	8·900	8·208	7·609	7·087	6·629	6·224	5·864	5·543	5·255	4·994
38	8·918	8·221	7·619	7·094	6·634	6·228	5·867	5·545	5·256	4·995
39	8·936	8·233	7·627	7·100	6·638	6·231	5·869	5·547	5·257	4·996
40	8·951	8·244	7·635	7·105	6·642	6·234	5·871	5·548	5·258	4·997

TABLE B
CUMULATIVE PRESENT VALUE FACTORS

Years 0 to:	21%	22%	23%	24%	25%	26%	27%	28%	29%	30%
1	·826	·820	·813	·806	·800	·794	·787	·781	·775	·769
2	1·509	1·492	1·474	1·457	1·440	1·424	1·407	1·392	1·376	1·361
3	2·074	2·042	2·011	1·981	1·952	1·924	1·896	1·868	1·842	1·816
4	2·540	2·494	2·448	2·404	2·362	2·320	2·280	2·241	2·203	2·166
5	2·926	2·864	2·804	2·746	2·689	2·635	2·583	2·532	2·483	2·436
6	3·244	3·167	3·092	3·021	2·951	2·885	2·821	2·759	2·670	2·643
7	3·508	3·416	3·327	3·242	3·161	3·083	3·009	2·937	2·868	2·802
8	3·725	3·619	3·518	3·421	3·329	3·241	3·156	3·076	2·998	2·925
9	3·905	3·786	3·673	3·566	3·463	3·366	3·273	3·184	3·100	3·019
10	4·054	3·923	3·799	3·682	3·570	3·465	3·364	3·269	3·178	3·092
11	4·177	4·036	3·902	3·776	3·656	3·544	3·437	3·335	3·239	3·147
12	4·278	4·128	3·985	3·852	3·725	3·606	3·493	3·387	3·286	3·190
13	4·362	4·203	4·053	3·912	3·780	3·656	3·538	3·427	3·322	3·223
14	4·431	4·265	4·108	3·962	3·824	3·695	3·573	3·459	3·351	3·249
15	4·489	4·315	4·153	4·001	3·859	3·726	3·601	3·483	3·372	3·268
16	4·536	4·357	4·190	4·033	3·887	3·751	3·623	3·503	3·390	3·283
17	4·575	4·391	4·219	4·059	3·910	3·771	3·640	3·518	3·403	3·295
18	4·608	4·419	4·243	4·080	3·928	3·786	3·654	3·530	3·413	3·304
19	4·634	4·442	4·263	4·097	3·942	3·799	3·664	3·539	3·421	3·310
20	4·656	4·460	4·279	4·110	3·954	3·808	3·673	3·546	3·427	3·316
21	4·675	4·476	4·292	4·121	3·963	3·816	3·679	3·552	3·432	3·320
22	4·690	4·488	4·302	4·130	3·970	3·822	3·684	3·556	3·435	3·323
23	4·702	4·499	4·311	4·137	3·976	3·827	3·688	3·559	3·438	3·325
24	4·712	4·507	4·318	4·143	3·981	3·831	3·692	3·562	3·440	3·327
25	4·721	4·514	4·323	4·147	3·985	3·834	3·694	3·564	3·442	3·328
26	4·728	4·520	4·328	4·151	3·988	3·837	3·696	3·566	3·443	3·329
27	4·734	4·524	4·332	4·154	3·990	3·839	3·698	3·567	3·444	3·330
28	4·739	4·528	4·335	4·156	3·992	3·840	3·699	3·568	3·445	3·331
29	4·743	4·531	4·337	4·158	3·994	3·841	3·700	3·569	3·446	3·331
30	4·746	4·534	4·339	4·160	3·995	3·842	3·701	3·570	3·446	3·332
31	4·749	4·536	4·341	4·161	3·996	3·843	3·701	3·570	3·447	3·332
32	4·751	4·538	4·342	4·162	3·997	3·844	3·702	3·571	3·447	3·332
33	4·753	4·539	4·343	4·163	3·997	3·844	3·702	3·571	3·447	3·332
34	4·754	4·540	4·344	4·164	3·998	3·845	3·703	3·571	3·448	3·333
35	4·756	4·541	4·345	4·164	3·998	3·845	3·703	3·571	3·448	3·333
36	4·756	4·542	4·345	4·165	3·998	3·845	3·703	3·571	3·448	3·333
37	4·757	4·543	4·346	4·165	3·999	3·846	3·703	3·571	3·448	3·333
38	4·758	4·543	4·346	4·165	3·999	3·846	3·703	3·571	3·448	3·333
39	4·759	4·544	4·347	4·166	3·999	3·846	3·703	3·571	4·448	3·333
40	4·759	4·544	4·347	4·166	3·999	3·846	3·703	3·572	3·448	3·333

TABLE B
CUMULATIVE PRESENT VALUE FACTORS

Years 0 to:	31%	32%	33%	34%	35%	36%	37%	38%	39%	40%
1	·763	·758	·752	·746	·741	·735	·730	·725	·719	·714
2	1·346	1·332	1·317	1·303	1·289	1·276	1·263	1·250	1·237	1·224
3	1·791	1·766	1·742	1·719	1·696	1·674	1·652	1·630	1·609	1·589
4	2·130	2·096	2·062	2·029	1·997	1·966	1·936	1·906	1·877	1·849
5	2·390	2·345	2·302	2·260	2·220	2·181	2·143	2·106	2·070	2·035
6	2·588	2·534	2·483	2·433	2·385	2·339	2·294	2·250	2·209	2·168
7	2·739	2·677	2·619	2·562	2·508	2·455	2·404	2·355	2·308	2·263
8	2·845	2·786	2·721	2·658	2·598	2·540	2·485	2·431	2·380	2·331
9	2·942	2·868	2·798	2·730	2·665	2·603	2·544	2·486	2·432	2·379
10	3·009	2·930	2·855	2·784	2·715	2·649	2·587	2·526	2·469	2·414
11	3·060	2·978	2·899	2·824	2·752	2·683	2·618	2·555	2·496	2·438
12	3·100	3·013	2·931	2·854	2·779	2·708	2·641	2·576	2·515	2·456
13	3·130	3·040	2·956	2·876	2·799	2·727	2·658	2·592	2·528	2·468
14	3·152	2·061	2·974	2·892	2·814	2·740	2·670	2·602	2·538	2·478
15	3·170	3·076	2·988	2·905	2·825	2·750	2·679	2·610	2·546	2·484
16	3·183	3·088	2·999	2·914	2·834	2·757	2·685	2·616	2·551	2·488
17	3·193	3·097	3·006	2·921	2·840	2·763	2·690	2·620	2·554	2·492
18	3·201	3·104	3·012	2·926	2·844	2·767	2·693	2·624	2·557	2·494
19	3·207	3·109	3·017	2·930	2·847	2·770	2·696	2·626	2·559	2·496
20	3·211	3·113	3·020	2·933	2·850	2·772	2·698	2·627	2·560	2·497
21	3·215	3·116	3·022	2·935	2·852	2·773	2·699	2·628	2·561	2·498
22	3·217	3·118	3·024	2·937	2·853	2·774	2·700	2·629	2·562	2·498
23	3·219	3·120	3·026	2·938	2·854	2·775	2·701	2·630	2·563	2·499
24	3·221	3·121	3·027	2·939	2·855	2·776	2·701	2·630	2·563	2·499
25	3·222	3·122	3·028	2·939	2·855	2·776	2·702	2·631	2·562	2·499
26	3·223	3·123	3·028	2·940	2·856	2·777	2·702	2·631	2·564	2·500
27	3·224	3·123	3·029	2·940	2·856	2·777	2·702			
28	3·224	3·124	3·029	2·941	2·856	2·777	2·702			
29	3·224	3·124	3·029	2·941	2·856	2·777	2·702			
30	3·225	3·124	3·030	2·941	2·857	2·777	2·702			
31	3·225	3·124	3·030	2·941	2·857	2·778	2·703			
32	3·225	3·124								
33	3·225	3·125								
34	3·225	3·125								
35	3·225	3·125								
36	3·226	3·125								
37	3·226									
38	3·226									
39	3·226									
40	3·226	3·125	3·030	2·941	2·857	2·778	2·703	2·631	2·564	2·500

TABLE C
CAPITAL RECOVERY FACTORS

To determine the series of "n" payments which will be yielded by a given sum invested now

Years	1%	2%	3%	4%	5%	6%	7%	8%	9%	10%
1	1·0100	1·0200	1·0300	1·0400	1·0500	1·0600	1·0700	1·0800	1·0900	1·1000
2	·5076	·5155	·5226	·5305	·5376	·5455	·5529	·5606	·5685	·5760
3	·3401	·3466	·3534	·3604	·3671	·3741	·3811	·3880	·3951	·4021
4	·2564	·2625	·2691	·2755	·2820	·2886	·2952	·3019	·3086	·3155
5	·2062	·2121	·2183	·2246	·2309	·2374	·2439	·2505	·2571	·2638
6	·1724	·1786	·1846	·1907	·1970	·2034	·2098	·2163	·2229	·2296
7	·1486	·1546	·1605	·1666	·1728	·1792	·1855	·1921	·1987	·2054
8	·1307	·1365	·1425	·1485	·1547	·1610	·1675	·1740	·1807	·1874
9	·1167	·1225	·1284	·1345	·1407	·1470	·1535	·1601	·1668	·1736
10	·1056	·1113	·1172	·1233	·1295	·1359	·1424	·1490	·1558	·1627
11	·0964	·1022	·1081	·1142	·1204	·1268	·1334	·1401	·1469	·1540
12	·0888	·0946	·1005	·1066	·1128	·1193	·1259	·1327	·1396	·1468
13	·0824	·0881	·0940	·1002	·1065	·1130	·1197	·1265	·1336	·1408
14	·0769	·0826	·0885	·0947	·1010	·1076	·1143	·1213	·1284	·1357
15	·0721	·0778	·0838	·0899	·0963	·1030	·1098	·1168	·1241	·1315
16	·0679	·0736	·0796	·0858	·0923	·0989	·1059	·1130	·1203	·1278
17	·0643	·0700	·0759	·0822	·0887	·0955	·1024	·1096	·1171	·1247
18	·0610	·0667	·0727	·0790	·0855	·0924	·0994	·1067	·1142	·1219
19	·0580	·0638	·0698	·0761	·0827	·0896	·0968	·1041	·1117	·1195
20	·0554	·0612	·0672	·0736	·0802	·0872	·0944	·1018	·1095	·1175
21	·0530	·0588	·0649	·0713	·0780	·0850	·0923	·0998	·1076	·1156
22	·0509	·0566	·0627	·0692	·0760	·0830	·0904	·0980	·1059	·1140
23	·0489	·0547	·0608	·0673	·0741	·0813	·0887	·0964	·1044	·1126
24	·0471	·0529	·0590	·0656	·0725	·0797	·0872	·0950	·1030	·1113
25	·0454	·0512	·0574	·0640	·0710	·0782	·0858	·0937	·1018	·1102
26	·0439	·0497	·0559	·0626	·0696	·0769	·0846	·0925	·1007	·1092
27	·0424	·0483	·0546	·0612	·0683	·0757	·0834	·0914	·0997	·1083
28	·0411	·0470	·0533	·0600	·0671	·0746	·0824	·0905	·0988	·1074
29	·0399	·0458	·0521	·0589	·0660	·0736	·0815	·0896	·0981	·1067
30	·0387	·0447	·0510	·0578	·0651	·0726	·0806	·0888	·0973	·1061
31	·0377	·0436	·0500	·0569	·0641	·0718	·0798	·0881	·0967	·1055
32	·0367	·0426	·0490	·0560	·0633	·0710	·0791	·0875	·0961	·1050
33	·0357	·0417	·0482	·0551	·0625	·0703	·0784	·0869	·0956	·1045
34	·0348	·0408	·0473	·0543	·0618	·0696	·0778	·0863	·0951	·1041
35	·0340	·0400	·0465	·0536	·0611	·0690	·0772	·0858	·0946	·1037
36	·0332	·0392	·0458	·0529	·0604	·0864	·0767	·0853	·0942	·1033
37	·0325	·0385	·0451	·0522	·0598	·0679	·0762	·0849	·0939	·1030
38	·0318	·0378	·0445	·0516	·0593	·0674	·0758	·0845	·0935	·1027
39	·0311	·0372	·0438	·0511	·0588	·0669	·0754	·0842	·0932	·1025
40	·0305	·0366	·0433	·0505	·0583	·0665	·0750	·0839	·0930	·1023
41	·0299	·0360	·0427	·0500	·0578	·0661	·0747	·0836	·0927	·1021
42	·0293	·0354	·0422	·0495	·0574	·0657	·0743	·0833	·0925	·1019
43	·0287	·0349	·0417	·0491	·0570	·0653	·0740	·0830	·0923	·1017
44	·0282	·0344	·0412	·0487	·0566	·0650	·0738	·0828	·0921	·1015
45	·0277	·0339	·0408	·0483	·0563	·0647	·0735	·0826	·0919	·1014
46	·0272	·0335	·0404	·0479	·0559	·0644	·0733	·0824	·0917	·1013
47	·0268	·0330	·0400	·0475	·0556	·0642	·0730	·0822	·0916	·1011
48	·0263	·0326	·0396	·0472	·0553	·0639	·0728	·0820	·0915	·1010
49	·0259	·0322	·0392	·0469	·0550	·0637	·0726	·0819	·0913	·1009
50	·0255	·0318	·0389	·0465	·0548	·0634	·0725	·0817	·0912	·1009

TABLE C
CAPITAL RECOVERY FACTORS
To determine the series of "n" payments which will be yielded by a given sum invested now

Years	11%	12%	13%	14%	15%	16%	17%	18%	19%	20%
1	1·1100	1·1200	1·1300	1·1400	1·1500	1·1600	1·1700	1·1800	1·1900	1·2000
2	·5839	·5917	·5994	·6074	·6150	·6231	·6308	·6388	·6467	·6545
3	·4092	·4164	·4236	·4308	·4380	·4453	·4526	·4599	·4673	·4747
4	·3223	·3292	·3362	·3432	·3503	·3574	·3646	·3717	·3790	·3863
5	·2706	·2774	·2843	·2913	·2983	·3054	·3126	·3198	·3270	·3344
6	·2364	·2432	·2501	·2572	·2642	·2714	·2786	·2859	·2933	·3007
7	·2122	·2191	·2261	·2332	·2403	·2476	·2549	·2624	·2698	·2774
8	·1943	·2013	·2084	·2156	·2228	·2302	·2377	·2452	·2529	·2606
9	·1806	·1877	·1949	·2022	·2096	·2171	·2247	·2324	·2402	·2481
10	·1698	·1770	·1843	·1917	·1993	·2069	·2146	·2225	·2305	·2385
11	·1611	·1684	·1758	·1834	·1911	·1989	·2068	·2148	·2229	·2311
12	·1540	·1614	·1690	·1767	·1845	·1924	·2005	·2086	·2169	·2253
13	·1481	·1557	·1634	·1712	·1791	·1872	·1954	·2037	·2121	·2206
14	·1432	·1509	·1587	·1666	·1747	·1829	·1912	·1997	·2082	·2169
15	·1391	·1468	·1547	·1628	·1710	·1794	·1878	·1964	·2051	·2139
16	·1355	·1434	·1514	·1596	·1680	·1764	·1850	·1937	·2025	·2114
17	·1325	·1404	·1486	·1569	·1654	·1740	·1827	·1915	·2004	·2094
18	·1298	·1379	·1462	·1546	·1632	·1719	·1807	·1896	·1987	·2078
19	·1276	·1358	·1441	·1527	·1613	·1701	·1791	·1881	·1972	·2065
20	·1256	·1339	·1424	·1510	·1598	·1687	·1777	·1868	·1960	·2054
21	·1238	·1322	·1408	·1495	·1584	·1674	·1765	·1857	·1951	·2044
22	·1223	·1308	·1395	·1483	·1573	·1664	·1755	·1848	·1942	·2037
23	·1210	·1296	·1383	·1472	·1563	·1654	·1747	·1841	·1935	·2031
24	·1198	·1285	·1373	·1463	·1554	·1647	·1740	·1834	·1930	·2026
25	·1187	·1275	·1364	·1455	·1547	·1640	·1734	·1829	·1925	·2021
26	·1178	·1266	·1357	·1448	·1541	·1634	·1729	·1825	·1921	·2018
27	·1170	·1259	·1350	·1442	·1535	·1630	·1725	·1821	·1917	·2015
28	·1163	·1252	·1344	·1437	·1531	·1626	·1721	·1818	·1915	·2012
29	·1156	·1247	·1339	·1432	·1527	·1622	·1718	·1815	·1912	·2010
30	·1150	·1241	·1334	·1428	·1523	·1619	·1715	·1813	·1910	·2008
31	·1145	·1237	·1330	·1425	·1520	·1616	·1713	·1811	·1909	·2007
32	·1140	·1233	·1327	·1421	·1517	·1614	·1711	·1809	·1907	·2006
33	·1136	·1229	·1323	·1419	·1515	·1612	·1710	·1808	·1906	·2005
34	·1133	·1226	·1321	·1416	·1513	·1610	·1708	·1807	·1905	·2004
35	·1129	·1223	·1318	·1414	·1511	·1609	·1707	·1805	·1904	·2003
36	·1126	·1221	·1316	·1413	·1510	·1608	·1706	·1805	·1904	·2003
37	·1124	·1218	·1314	·1411	·1509	·1607	·1705	·1804	·1903	·2002
38	·1121	·1216	·1313	·1410	·1507	·1606	·1704	·1803	·1902	·2002
39	·1119	·1215	·1311	·1408	·1506	·1605	·1704	·1803	·1902	·2002
40	·1117	·1213	·1310	·1407	·1506	·1604	·1703	·1802	·1902	·2001
41	·1116	·1212	·1309	·1406	·1505	·1604	·1703	·1802	·1902	·2001
42	·1114	·1210	·1308	·1406	·1504	·1603	·1702	·1802	·1901	·2001
43	·1112	·1209	·1307	·1405	·1504	·1603	·1702	·1801	·1901	·2001
44	·1111	·1208	·1306	·1404	·1503	·1602	·1702	·1801	·1901	·2001
45	·1110	·1207	·1305	·1404	·1503	·1602	·1702	·1801	·1901	·2001
46	·1109	·1207	·1305	·1403	·1502	·1602	·1701	·1801	·1901	·2000
47	·1108	·1206	·1304	·1403	·1502	·1601	·1701	·1801	·1901	·2000
48	·1107	·1205	·1304	·1403	·1502	·1601	·1701	·1801	·1900	·2000
49	·1107	·1205	·1303	·1402	·1502	·1601	·1701	·1801	·1900	·2000
50	·1106	·1204	·1303	·1402	·1501	·1601	·1701	·1801	·1900	·2000

TABLE C
CAPITAL RECOVERY FACTORS
To determine the series of "n" payments which will be yielded by a given sum invested now

Years	21%	22%	23%	24%	25%	26%	27%	28%	29%	30%
1	1·2100	1·2200	1·2300	1·2400	1·2500	1·2600	1·2700	1·2800	1·2900	1·3000
2	·6625	·6705	·6785	·6865	·6944	·7025	·7105	·7187	·7266	·7348
3	·4822	·4897	·4972	·5047	·5123	·5199	·5275	·5352	·5429	·5507
4	·3936	·4010	·4085	·4159	·4234	·4310	·4386	·4462	·4539	·4616
5	·3417	·3492	·3567	·3642	·3719	·3795	·3872	·3949	·4027	·4106
6	·3082	·3158	·3234	·3311	·3388	·3466	·3545	·3624	·3704	·3784
7	·2851	·2928	·3006	·3084	·3163	·3243	·3324	·3405	·3486	·3569
8	·2684	·2763	·2843	·2923	·3004	·3086	·3168	·3251	·3335	·3419
9	·2561	·2641	·2723	·2805	·2888	·2971	·3056	·3140	·3226	·3312
10	·2467	·2549	·2632	·2716	·2810	·2886	·2972	·3059	·3147	·3235
11	·2394	·2478	·2563	·2648	·2735	·2822	·2910	·2999	·3087	·3177
12	·2337	·2423	·2509	·2597	·2684	·2773	·2863	·2953	·3043	·3134
13	·2292	·2379	·2467	·2556	·2646	·2736	·2826	·2918	·3010	·3102
14	·2256	·2345	·2434	·2524	·2615	·2706	·2799	·2891	·2984	·3078
15	·2228	·2317	·2408	·2499	·2591	·2684	·2777	·2871	·2965	·3060
16	·2204	·2295	·2387	·2479	·2572	·2666	·2760	·2855	·2950	·3046
17	·2185	·2277	·2370	·2464	·2558	·2652	·2747	·2843	·2939	·3035
18	·2170	·2263	·2357	·2451	·2546	·2641	·2737	·2833	·2930	·3027
19	·2158	·2252	·2346	·2441	·2537	·2633	·2729	·2826	·2923	·3021
20	·2147	·2242	·2337	·2433	·2529	·2626	·2723	·2820	·2918	·3016
21	·2139	·2234	·2330	·2426	·2523	·2620	·2718	·2816	·2914	·3012
22	·2132	·2228	·2324	·2421	·2519	·2616	·2714	·2812	·2911	·3009
23	·2127	·2223	·2320	·2417	·2615	·2613	·2711	·2810	·2908	·3007
24	·2122	·2219	·2316	·2414	·2512	·2610	·2709	·2808	·2906	·3005
25	·2118	·2215	·2313	·2411	·2510	·2608	·2707	·2806	·2905	·3004
26	·2115	·2213	·2311	·2409	·2508	·2607	·2705	·2804	·2904	·3003
27	·2112	·2210	·2309	·2407	·2506	·2605	·2704	·2804	·2903	·3002
28	·2110	·2208	·2307	·2406	·2505	·2604	·2703	·2803	·2902	·3002
29	·2108	·2207	·2306	·2405	·2504	·2603	·2703	·2802	·2902	·3002
30	·2107	·2206	·2305	·2404	·2503	·2603	·2702	·2802	·2901	·3001
31	·2106	·2205	·2304	·2403	·2503	·2602	·2702	·2801	·2901	·3001
32	·2105	·2204	·2303	·2402	·2502	·2602	·2701	·2801	·2901	·3001
33	·2104	·2203	·2303	·2402	·2502	·2601	·2701	·2801	·2901	·3001
34	·2103	·2203	·2302	·2402	·2501	·2601	·2701	·2801	·2901	·3000
35	·2103	·2202	·2302	·2401	·2501	·2601	·2701	·2801	·2900	·3000
36	·2102	·2202	·2301	·2401	·2501	·2601	·2701	·2800	·2900	·3000
37	·2102	·2201	·2301	·2401	·2501	·2601	·2700	·2800	·2900	·3000
38	·2101	·2201	·2301	·2401	·2501	·2601	·2700	·2800	·2900	·3000
39	·2101	·2201	·2301	·2400	·2501	·2600	·2700	·2800	·2900	
40	·2101	·2201	·2301	·2400	·2500	·2600	·2700	·2800		
41	·2101	·2201	·2300	·2400	·2500	·2600	·2700	·2800		
42	·2101	·2200	·2300	·2400	·2500	·2600	·2700			
43	·2101	·2200	·2300	·2400	·2500	·2600				
44	·2100	·2200	·2300	·2400	·2500					
45	·2100	·2200	·2300	·2400	·2500					
46	·2100	·2200	·2300	·2400						
47	·2100	·2200	·2300	·2400						
48	·2100	·2200	·2300							
49	·2100	·2200								
50	·2100	·2200								

TABLE C
CAPITAL RECOVERY FACTORS
To determine the series of "n" payments which will be yielded by a given sum invested now

Years	31%	32%	33%	34%	35%	36%	37%	38%	39%	40%
1	1·3100	1·3200	1·3300	1·3400	1·3500	1·3600	1·3700	1·3800	1·3900	1·4000
2	·7429	·7510	·7591	·7673	·7755	·7838	·7920	·8002	·8085	·8167
3	·5584	·5662	·5740	·5818	·5896	·5975	·6055	·6134	·6214	·6293
4	·4694	·4772	·4850	·4929	·5008	·5087	·5167	·5246	·5327	·5408
5	·4185	·4264	·4344	·4424	·4505	·4585	·4667	·4749	·4831	·4913
6	·3865	·3946	·4028	·4110	·4193	·4276	·4359	·4443	·4528	·4613
7	·3651	·3735	·3819	·3903	·3988	·4073	·4159	·4245	·4332	·4419
8	·3504	·3589	·3675	·3762	·3849	·3936	·4024	·4113	·4202	·4291
9	·3399	·3487	·3575	·3663	·3752	·3841	·3931	·4022	·4112	·4203
10	·3323	·3413	·3502	·3593	·3683	·3774	·3866	·3958	·4050	·4143
11	·3268	·3359	·3450	·3542	·3634	·3727	·3820	·3913	·4007	·4101
12	·3226	·3318	·3411	·3504	·3598	·3692	·3787	·3882	·3976	·4072
13	·3196	·3289	·3383	·3478	·3572	·3667	·3763	·3859	·3955	·4051
14	·3172	·3267	·3362	·3457	·3553	·3649	·3746	·3842	·3939	·4036
15	·3155	·3250	·3347	·3443	·3539	·3636	·3733	·3831	·3928	·4026
16	·3142	·3238	·3335	·3432	·3529	·3626	·3724	·3822	·3920	·4018
17	·3132	·3229	·3326	·3424	·3521	·3620	·3717	·3816	·3914	·4013
18	·3124	·3222	·3320	·3418	·3516	·3614	·3713	·3811	·3911	·4009
19	·3118	·3216	·3315	·3413.	·3512	·3610	·3709	·3808	·3907	·4007
20	·3114	·3213	·3311	·3410	·3509	·3608	·3707	·3806	·3905	·4005
21	·3111	·3209	·3308	·3407	·3506	·3606	·3705	·3805	·3904	·4004
22	·3108	·3207	·3306	·3405	·3505	·3604	·3704	·3803	·3903	·4002
23	·3106	·3205	·3305	·3404	·3504	·3603	·3703	·3802	·3902	·4002
24	·3105	·3204	·3304	·3403	·3502	·3602	·3702	·3802	·3902	·4001
25	·3104	·3203	·3303	·3402	·3502	·3602	·3701	·3801	·3901	·4001
26	·3103	·3202	·3302	·3402	·3501	·3601	·3701	·3801	·3901	·4001
27	·3102	·3202	·3302	·3401	·3501	·3601	·3701	·3801	·3900	·4000
28	·3102	·3201	·3301	·3401	·3501	·3601	·3700	·3800	·3900	·4000
29	·3101	·3201	·3301	·3401	·3501	·3600	·3700	·3800	·3900	·4000
30	·3101	·3201	·3301	·3401	·3500	·3600	·3700	·3800	·3900	·4000
31	·3101	·3201	·3300	·3400	·3500	·3600	·3700	·3800	·3900	
32	·3101	·3200	·3300	·3400	·3500	·3600	·3700			
33	·3100	·3200	·3300	·3400	·3500	·3600				
34	·3100	·3200	·3300	·3400	·3500					
35	·3100	·3200	·3300							
36	·3100	·3200	·3300							
37	·3100									

TABLE D

Annual Sinking Fund Instalments to Provide £1

Percentage

Year	0·5	1·0	1·5	2·0	2·5
1	1·00000	1·00000	1·00000	1·00000	1·00000
2	0·49875	0·49751	0·49628	0·49505	0·49383
3	0·33167	0·33002	0·32838	0·32675	0·32514
4	0·24813	0·24628	0·24444	0·24262	0·24082
5	0·19801	0·19604	0·19409	0·19216	0·19025
6	0·16460	0·16255	0·16053	0·15853	0·15655
7	0·14073	0·13863	0·13656	0·13451	0·13250
8	0·12283	0·12069	0·11858	0·11651	0·11447
9	0·10891	0·10674	0·10461	0·10252	0·10046
10	0·09777	0·09558	0·09343	0·09133	0·08926
11	0·08866	0·08645	0·08429	0·08218	0·08011
12	0·08107	0·07885	0·07668	0·07456	0·07249
13	0·07464	0·07241	0·07024	0·06812	0·06605
14	0·06914	0·06690	0·06472	0·06260	0·06054
15	0·06436	0·06212	0·05994	0·05783	0·05577
16	0·06019	0·05794	0·05577	0·05365	0·05160
17	0·05651	0·05426	0·05208	0·04997	0·04793
18	0·05323	0·05098	0·04881	0·04670	0·04467
19	0·05030	0·04805	0·04588	0·04378	0·04176
20	0·04767	0·04542	0·04325	0·04116	0·03915
21	0·04528	0·04303	0·04087	0·03878	0·03679
22	0·04311	0·04086	0·03870	0·03663	0·03465
23	0·04113	0·03889	0·03673	0·03467	0·03270
24	0·03932	0·03707	0·03492	0·03287	0·03091
25	0·03765	0·03541	0·03326	0·03122	0·02928
26	0·03611	0·03387	0·03173	0·02970	0·02777
27	0·03469	0·03245	0·03032	0·02829	0·02638
28	0·03336	0·03112	0·02900	0·02699	0·02509
29	0·03213	0·02990	0·02778	0·02578	0·02389
30	0·03098	0·02875	0·02664	0·02465	0·02278
31	0·02990	0·02768	0·02557	0·02360	0·02174
32	0·02889	0·02667	0·02458	0·02261	0·02077
33	0·02795	0·02573	0·02364	0·02169	0·01986
34	0·02706	0·02484	0·02276	0·02082	0·01901
35	0·02622	0·02400	0·02193	0·02000	0·01821
36	0·02542	0·02321	0·02115	0·01923	0·01745
37	0·02467	0·02247	0·02041	0·01851	0·01674
38	0·02396	0·02176	0·01972	0·01782	0·01607
39	0·02329	0·02109	0·01905	0·01717	0·01544
40	0·02265	0·02046	0·01843	0·01656	0·01484
41	0·02204	0·01985	0·01783	0·01597	0·01427
42	0·02146	0·01928	0·01726	0·01542	0·01373
43	0·02090	0·01873	0·01672	0·01489	0·01322
44	0·02038	0·01820	0·01621	0·01439	0·01273
45	0·01987	0·01771	0·01572	0·01391	0·01227
46	0·01939	0·01723	0·01525	0·01345	0·01183
47	0·01893	0·01677	0·01480	0·01302	0·01141
48	0·01849	0·01633	0·01438	0·01260	0·01101
49	0·01806	0·01591	0·01396	0·01220	0·01062
50	0·01765	0·01357	0·01357	0·01182	0·01026

TABLE D—(*Contd.*)

Year	3·0	3·5	4·0	4·5	5·0
1	1·00000	1·00000	1·00000	1·00000	1·00000
2	0·49261	0·49140	0·49020	0·48900	0·48780
3	0·32353	0·32193	0·32035	0·31877	0·31721
4	0·23903	0·23725	0·23549	0·23374	0·23201
5	0·18835	0·18648	0·18463	0·18279	0·18097
6	0·15460	0·15267	0·15076	0·14888	0·14702
7	0·13051	0·12854	0·12661	0·12470	0·12282
8	0·11246	0·11048	0·10853	0·10661	0·10472
9	0·09843	0·09645	0·09449	0·09257	0·09069
10	0·08723	0·08524	0·08329	0·08138	0·07950
11	0·07808	0·07609	0·07415	0·07225	0·07039
12	0·07046	0·06848	0·06655	0·06467	0·06283
13	0·06403	0·06206	0·06014	0·05828	0·05646
14	0·05853	0·05657	0·05467	0·05282	0·05102
15	0·05377	0·05183	0·04994	0·04811	0·04634
16	0·04961	0·04768	0·04582	0·04402	0·04227
17	0·04595	0·04404	0·04220	0·04042	0·03870
18	0·04271	0·04082	0·03899	0·03724	0·03555
19	0·03981	0·03794	0·03614	0·03441	0·03275
20	0·03722	0·03536	0·03358	0·03188	0·03024
21	0·03487	0·03304	0·03128	0·02960	0·02800
22	0·03275	0·03093	0·02920	0·02755	0·02597
23	0·03081	0·02902	0·02731	0·02568	0·02414
24	0·02905	0·02727	0·02559	0·02399	0·02247
25	0·02743	0·02567	0·02401	0·02244	0·02095
26	0·02594	0·02421	0·02257	0·02102	0·01956
27	0·02456	0·02285	0·02124	0·01972	0·01829
28	0·02329	0·02160	0·02001	0·01852	0·01712
29	0·02211	0·02045	0·01888	0·01741	0·01605
30	0·02102	0·01937	0·01783	0·01639	0·01505
31	0·02000	0·01837	0·01686	0·01544	0·01413
32	0·01905	0·01744	0·01595	0·01456	0·01328
33	0·01816	0·01657	0·01510	0·01374	0·01249
34	0·01732	0·01576	0·01431	0·01298	0·01176
35	0·01654	0·01500	0·01358	0·01227	0·01107
36	0·01580	0·01428	0·01289	0·01161	0·01043
37	0·01511	0·01361	0·01224	0·01098	0·00984
38	0·01446	0·01298	0·01163	0·01040	0·00928
39	0·01384	0·01239	0·01106	0·00986	0·00876
40	0·01326	0·01183	0·01052	0·00934	0·00828
41	0·01271	0·01130	0·01002	0·00886	0·00782
42	0·01219	0·01080	0·00954	0·00841	0·00739
43	0·01170	0·01033	0·00909	0·00798	0·00699
44	0·01123	0·00988	0·00866	0·00758	0·00662
45	0·01079	0·00945	0·00826	0·00720	0·00626
46	0·01036	0·00905	0·00788	0·00684	0·00593
47	0·00996	0·00867	0·00752	0·00651	0·00561
48	0·00958	0·00831	0·00718	0·00619	0·00532
49	0·00921	0·00796	0·00686	0·00589	0·00504
50	0·00887	0·00763	0·00655	0·00560	0·00478

TABLE D—(*Contd.*)

Percentage

Year	5·5	6·0	6·5	7·0	7·5
1	1·00000	1·00000	1·00000	1·00000	1·00000
2	0·48662	0·48544	0·48426	0·48309	0·48193
3	0·31565	0·31411	0·31258	0·31105	0·30954
4	0·23029	0·22859	0·22690	0·22523	0·22357
5	0·17918	0·17740	0·17563	0·17389	0·17216
6	0·14518	0·14336	0·14157	0·13980	0·13804
7	0·12096	0·11914	0·11733	0·11555	0·11380
8	0·10286	0·10104	0·09924	0·09747	0·09573
9	0·08884	0·08702	0·08524	0·08349	0·08177
10	0·07767	0·07587	0·07410	0·07238	0·07069
11	0·06857	0·06679	0·06506	0·06336	0·06170
12	0·06103	0·05928	0·05757	0·05590	0·05428
13	0·05468	0·05296	0·05128	0·04965	0·04806
14	0·04928	0·04758	0·04594	0·04434	0·04280
15	0·04463	0·04296	0·04135	0·03979	0·03829
16	0·04058	0·03895	0·03738	0·03586	0·03439
17	0·03704	0·03544	0·03391	0·03243	0·03100
18	0·03392	0·03236	0·03085	0·02941	0·02803
19	0·03115	0·02962	0·02816	0·02675	0·02541
20	0·02868	0·02718	0·02576	0·02439	0·02309
21	0·02646	0·02500	0·02361	0·02229	0·02103
22	0·02447	0·02305	0·02169	0·02041	0·01919
23	0·02267	0·02128	0·01996	0·01871	0·01754
24	0·02104	0·01968	0·01840	0·01719	0·01605
25	0·01955	0·01823	0·01698	0·01581	0·01471
26	0·01819	0·01690	0·01569	0·01456	0·01350
27	0·01695	0·01570	0·01452	0·01343	0·01240
28	0·01581	0·01459	0·01345	0·01239	0·01141
29	0·01477	0·01358	0·01247	0·01145	0·01050
30	0·01381	0·01265	0·01158	0·01059	0·00967
31	0·01292	0·01179	0·01075	0·00980	0·00892
32	0·01210	0·01100	0·01000	0·00907	0·00823
33	0·01133	0·01027	0·00930	0·00841	0·00759
34	0·01063	0·00960	0·00866	0·00780	0·00701
35	0·00997	0·00897	0·00806	0·00723	0·00648
36	0·00937	0·00839	0·00751	0·00672	0·00599
37	0·00880	0·00786	0·00701	0·00624	0·00555
38	0·00827	0·00736	0·00653	0·00580	0·00513
39	0·00778	0·00689	0·00610	0·00539	0·00475
40	0·00732	0·00646	0·00569	0·00501	0·00440
41	0·00689	0·00606	0·00532	0·00466	0·00408
42	0·00649	0·00568	0·00497	0·00434	0·00378
43	0·00611	0·00533	0·00464	0·00404	0·00350
44	0·00576	0·00501	0·00434	0·00376	0·00325
45	0·00543	0·00470	0·00406	0·00350	0·00301
46	0·00512	0·00441	0·00380	0·00326	0·00279
47	0·00483	0·00415	0·00355	0·00304	0·00259
48	0·00456	0·00390	0·00333	0·00283	0·00241
49	0·00430	0·00366	0·00311	0·00264	0·00223
50	0·00406	0·00344	0·00291	0·00246	0·00207

TABLE D—(*Contd.*)

Percentage

Year	8·0	8·5	9·0	9·5	10·0
1	1·00000	1·00000	1·00000	1·00000	1·00000
2	0·48077	0·47962	0·47847	0·47733	0·47619
3	0·30803	0·30654	0·30505	0·30358	0·30211
4	0·22192	0·22029	0·21867	0·21706	0·21547
5	0·17046	0·16877	0·16709	0·16544	0·16380
6	0·13632	0·13461	0·13292	0·13125	0·12961
7	0·11207	0·11037	0·10869	0·10704	0·10541
8	0·09401	0·09233	0·09067	0·08905	0·08744
9	0·08008	0·07842	0·07680	0·07520	0·07364
10	0·06903	0·06741	0·06582	0·06427	0·06275
11	0·06008	0·05849	0·05695	0·05544	0·05396
12	0·05270	0·05115	0·04965	0·04819	0·04676
13	0·04652	0·04502	0·04357	0·04215	0·04078
14	0·04130	0·03984	0·03843	0·03707	0·03575
15	0·03683	0·03542	0·03406	0·03274	0·03147
16	0·03298	0·03161	0·03030	0·02903	0·02782
17	0·02963	0·02831	0·02705	0·02583	0·02466
18	0·02670	0·02543	0·02421	0·02305	0·02193
19	0·02413	0·02290	0·02173	0·02061	0·01955
20	0·02185	0·02067	0·01955	0·01848	0·01746
21	0·01983	0·01870	0·01762	0·01659	0·01562
22	0·01803	0·01694	0·01590	0·01493	0·01401
23	0·01642	0·01537	0·01438	0·01345	0·01257
24	0·01498	0·01397	0·01302	0·01213	0·01130
25	0·01368	0·01271	0·01181	0·01096	0·01017
26	0·01251	0·01158	0·01072	0·00991	0·00916
27	0·01145	0·01056	0·00973	0·00897	0·00826
28	0·01049	0·00964	0·00885	0·00812	0·00745
29	0·00962	0·00881	0·00806	0·00736	0·00673
30	0·00883	0·00805	0·00734	0·00668	0·00608
31	0·00811	0·00737	0·00669	0·00606	0·00550
32	0·00745	0·00674	0·00610	0·00551	0·00497
33	0·00685	0·00618	0·00556	0·00500	0·00450
34	0·00630	0·00566	0·00508	0·00455	0·00407
35	0·00580	0·00519	0·00464	0·00414	0·00369
36	0·00534	0·00476	0·00424	0·00376	0·00334
37	0·00492	0·00437	0·00387	0·00343	0·00303
38	0·00454	0·00401	0·00354	0·00312	0·00275
39	0·00419	0·00368	0·00324	0·00284	0·00249
40	0·00386	0·00338	0·00296	0·00259	0·00226
41	0·00356	0·00311	0·00271	0·00236	0·00205
42	0·00329	0·00286	0·00248	0·00215	0·00186
43	0·00303	0·00263	0·00227	0·00196	0·00169
44	0·00280	0·00241	0·00208	0·00178	0·00153
45	0·00259	0·00222	0·00190	0·00163	0·00139
46	0·00239	0·00204	0·00174	0·00148	0·00126
47	0·00221	0·00188	0·00160	0·00135	0·00115
48	0·00204	0·00173	0·00146	0·00123	0·00104
49	0·00189	0·00159	0·00134	0·00113	
50	0·00174	0·00146	0·00123	0·00103	

TABLE D—(*Contd.*)

Percentage

Year	10·5	11·0	11·5	12·0	12·5
1	1·00000	1·00000	1·00000	1·00000	1·00000
2	0·47506	0·47393	0·47281	0·47170	0·47059
3	0·30066	0·29921	0·29778	0·29635	0·29493
4	0·21389	0·21233	0·21077	0·20923	0·20771
5	0·16218	0·16057	0·15898	0·15741	0·15585
6	0·12798	0·12638	0·12479	0·12323	0·12168
7	0·10380	0·10222	0·10066	0·09912	0·09760
8	0·08587	0·08432	0·08280	0·08130	0·07983
9	0·07211	0·07060	0·06913	0·06768	0·06626
10	0·06126	0·05980	0·05838	0·05698	0·05562
11	0·05252	0·05112	0·04975	0·04842	0·04711
12	0·04538	0·04403	0·04271	0·04144	0·04019
13	0·03945	0·03815	0·03690	0·03568	0·03450
14	0·03447	0·03323	0·03203	0·03087	0·02975
15	0·03025	0·02907	0·02792	0·02682	0·02576
16	0·02664	0·02552	0·02443	0·02339	0·02239
17	0·02354	0·02247	0·02144	0·02046	0·01951
18	0·02086	0·01984	0·01887	0·01794	0·01705
19	0·01853	0·01756	0·01664	0·01576	0·01493
20	0·01649	0·01558	0·01470	0·01388	0·01310
21	0·01471	0·01384	0·01302	0·01224	0·01151
22	0·01313	0·01231	0·01154	0·01081	0·01012
23	0·01175	0·01097	0·01024	0·00956	0·00892
24	0·01052	0·00979	0·00910	0·00846	0·00787
25	0·00943	0·00874	0·00810	0·00750	0·00694
26	0·00846	0·00781	0·00721	0·00665	0·00613
27	0·00760	0·00699	0·00643	0·00590	0·00542
28	0·00683	0·00626	0·00573	0·00524	0·00480
29	0·00614	0·00561	0·00511	0·00466	0·00425
30	0·00553	0·00502	0·00456	0·00414	0·00376
31	0·00498	0·00451	0·00408	0·00369	0·00333
32	0·00448	0·00404	0·00364	0·00328	0·00295
33	0·00404	0·00363	0·00326	0·00292	0·00262
34	0·00364	0·00326	0·00291	0·00260	0·00232
35	0·00329	0·00293	0·00260	0·00232	0·00206
36	0·00297	0·00263	0·00233	0·00206	0·00183
37	0·00268	0·00236	0·00209	0·00184	0·00162
38	0·00242	0·00213	0·00187	0·00164	0·00144
39	0·00218	0·00191	0·00167	0·00146	0·00128
40	0·00197	0·00172	0·00150	0·00130	0·00113
41	0·00178	0·00155	0·00134	0·00116	0·00101
42	0·00161	0·00139	0·00120	0·00104	
43	0·00145	0·00125	0·00108		
44	0·00131	0·00113			
45	0·00119	0·00101			
46	0·00107				
47					
48					
49					
50					

TABLE D—(*Contd.*)

Percentage

Year	13·0	13·5	14·0	14·5	15·0
1	1·00000	1·00000	1·00000	1·00000	1·00000
2	0·46948	0·46838	0·46729	0·46620	0·46512
3	0·29352	0·29212	0·29073	0·28935	0·28798
4	0·20619	0·20469	0·20320	0·20173	0·20027
5	0·15431	0·15279	0·15128	0·14979	0·14832
6	0·12015	0·11865	0·11716	0·11569	0·11424
7	0·09611	0·09464	0·09319	0·09177	0·09036
8	0·07839	0·07697	0·07557	0·07420	0·07285
9	0·06487	0·06351	0·06217	0·06086	0·05957
10	0·05429	0·05299	0·05171	0·05047	0·04925
11	0·04584	0·04460	0·04339	0·04222	0·04107
12	0·03899	0·03781	0·03667	0·03556	0·03448
13	0·03335	0·03224	0·03116	0·03012	0·02911
14	0·02867	0·02762	0.02661	0·02563	0·02469
15	0·02474	0·02376	0·02281	0·02190	0·02102
16	0·02143	0·02050	0·01962	0·01876	0·01795
17	0·01861	0·01774	0·01692	0·01612	0·01537
18	0·01620	0·01539	0·01462	0·01389	0·01319
19	0·01413	0·01338	0·01266	0·01198	0·01134
20	0·01235	0·01165	0·01099	0·01036	0·00976
21	0·01081	0·01016	0·00954	0·00896	0·00842
22	0·00948	0·00887	0·00830	0·00777	0·00727
23	0·00832	0·00776	0·00723	0·00674	0·00628
24	0·00731	0·00679	0·00630	0·00585	0·00543
25	0·00643	0·00595	0·00550	0·00508	0·00470
26	0·00565	0·00521	0·00480	0·00442	0·00407
27	0·00498	0·00457	0·00419	0·00385	0·00353
28	0·00439	0·00401	0·00366	0·00335	0·00306
29	0·00387	0·00352	0·00320	0·00292	0·00265
30	0·00341	0·00309	0·00280	0·00254	0·00230
31	0·00301	0·00272	0·00245	0·00221	0·00200
32	0·00266	0·00239	0·00215	0·00193	0·00173
33	0·00234	0·00210	0·00188	0·00168	0·00150
34	0·00207	0·00185	0·00165	0·00147	0·00131
35	0·00183	0·00162	0·00144	0·00128	0·00113
36	0·00162	0·00143	0·00126	0·00112	
37	0·00143	0·00126	0·00111		
38	0·00126	0·00111			
39	0·00112				
40					
41					
42					
43					
44					
45					
46					
47					
48					
49					
50					

TABLE D—(*Contd.*)

Percentage

Year	15·5	16·0	16·5	17·0	17·5
1	1·00000	1·00000	1·00000	1·00000	1·00000
2	0·46404	0·46296	0·46189	0·46083	0·45977
3	0·28661	0·28526	0·28391	0·28257	0·28124
4	0·19881	0·19738	0·19595	0·19453	0·19313
5	0·14685	0·14541	0·14398	0·14256	0·14116
6	0·11280	0·11139	0·10999	0·10861	0·10725
7	0·08898	0·08761	0·08627	0·08495	0·08364
8	0·07153	0·07022	0·06895	0·06769	0·06646
9	0·05832	0·05708	0·05587	0·05469	0·05353
10	0·04806	0·04690	0·04577	0·04466	0·04357
11	0·03995	0·03886	0·03780	0·03676	0·03576
12	0·03343	0·03241	0·03143	0·03047	0·02953
13	0·02813	0·02718	0·02627	0·02538	0·02452
14	0·02378	0·02290	0·02205	0·02123	0·02044
15	0·02017	0·01936	0·01857	0·01782	0·01710
16	0·01716	0·01641	0·01569	0·01500	0·01434
17	0·01464	0·01395	0·01329	0·01266	0·01206
18	0·01252	0·01188	0·01128	0·01071	0·01016
19	0·01072	0·01014	0·00959	0·00907	0·00857
20	0·00920	0·00867	0·00816	0·00769	0·00724
21	0·00790	0·00742	0·00696	0·00653	0·00613
22	0·00679	0·00635	0·00594	0·00555	0·00519
23	0·00585	0·00545	0·00507	0·00472	0·00439
24	0·00504	0·00467	0·00433	0·00402	0·00373
25	0·00434	0·00401	0·00371	0·00342	0·00316
26	0·00375	0·00345	0·00317	0·00292	0·00268
27	0·00323	0·00296	0·00272	0·00249	0·00228
28	0·00279	0·00255	0·00233	0·00212	0·00194
29	0·00241	0·00219	0·00199	0·00181	0·00164
30	0·00208	0·00189	0·00171	0·00154	0·00140
31	0·00180	0·00162	0·00146	0·00132	0·00119
32	0·00156	0·00140	0·00125	0·00113	0·00101
33	0·00135	0·00120	0·00108		
34	0·00116	0·00104			
35	0·00101				
36					
37					
38					
39					
40					
41					
42					
43					
44					
45					
46					
47					
48					
49					
50					

TABLE D—(*Contd.*)

Percentage

Year	18·0	18·5	19·0	19·5	20·0
1	1·00000	1·00000	1·00000	1·00000	1·00000
2	0·45872	0·45767	0·45662	0·45558	0·45455
3	0·27992	0·27861	0·27731	0·27601	0·27473
4	0·19174	0·19036	0·18899	0·18763	0·18629
5	0·13978	0·13841	0·13705	0·13571	0·13438
6	0·10591	0·10458	0·10327	0·10198	0·10071
7	0·08236	0·08110	0·07985	0·07863	0·07742
8	0·06524	0·06405	0·06289	0·06174	0·06061
9	0·05239	0·05128	0·05019	0·04912	0·04808
10	0·04251	0·04148	0·04047	0·03949	0·03852
11	0·03478	0·03382	0·03289	0·03199	0·03110
12	0·02863	0·02775	0·02690	0·02607	0·02526
13	0·02369	0·02288	0·02210	0·02135	0·02062
14	0·01968	0·01894	0·01823	0·01755	0·01689
15	0·01640	0·01573	0·01509	0·01447	0·01388
16	0·01371	0·01310	0·01252	0·01197	0·01144
17	0·01149	0·01094	0·01041	0·00992	0·00944
18	0·00964	0·00915	0·00868	0·00823	0·00781
19	0·00810	0·00766	0·00724	0·00684	0·00646
20	0·00682	0·00642	0·00605	0·00569	0·00536
21	0·00575	0·00539	0·00505	0·00474	0·00444
22	0·00485	0·00453	0·00423	0·00395	0·00369
23	0·00409	0·00381	0·00354	0·00329	0·00307
24	0·00345	0·00320	0·00297	0·00275	0·00255
25	0·00292	0·00269	0·00249	0·00230	0·00212
26	0·00247	0·00227	0·00209	0·00192	0·00176
27	0·00209	0·00191	0·00175	0·00160	0·00147
28	0·00177	0·00161	0·00147	0·00134	0·00122
29	0·00149	0·00136	0·00123	0·00112	0·00102
30	0·00126	0·00114	0·00103		
31	0·00107				
32					
33					
34					
35					
36					
37					
38					
39					
40					
41					
42					
43					
44					
45					
46					
47					
48					
49					
50					

TABLE D—(*Contd.*)

Percentage

Year	20·5	21·0	21·5	22·0	22·5
1	1·00000	1·00000	1·00000	1·00000	1·00000
2	0·45351	0·45249	0·45147	0·45045	0·44944
3	0·27345	0·27218	0·27091	0·26966	0·26841
4	0·18496	0·18363	0·18232	0·18102	0·17973
5	0·13307	0·13177	0·13048	0·12921	0·12795
6	0·09945	0·09820	0·09698	0·09576	0·09457
7	0·07624	0·07507	0·07392	0·07278	0·07167
8	0·05950	0·05841	0·05735	0·05630	0·05527
9	0·04706	0·04605	0·04507	0·04411	0·04317
10	0·03758	0·03667	0·03577	0·03489	0·03404
11	0·03025	0·02941	0·02860	0·02781	0·02704
12	0·02449	0·02373	0·02300	0·02228	0·02159
13	0·01992	0·01923	0·01858	0·01794	0·01732
14	0·01626	0·01565	0·01506	0·01449	0·01394
15	0·01331	0·01277	0·01224	0·01174	0·01125
16	0·01093	0·01044	0·00998	0·00953	0·00910
17	0·00899	0·00855	0·00814	0·00775	0·00738
18	0·00740	0·00702	0·00666	0·00631	0·00599
19	0·00611	0·00577	0·00545	0·00515	0·00486
20	0·00504	0·00474	0·00447	0·00420	0·00395
21	0·00417	0·00391	0·00366	0·00343	0·00322
22	0·00345	0·00322	0·00300	0·00281	0·00262
23	0·00285	0·00265	0·00247	0·00229	0·00213
24	0·00236	0·00219	0·00203	0·00188	0·00174
25	0·00196	0·00180	0·00166	0·00154	0·00142
26	0·00162	0·00149	0·00137	0·00126	0·00116
27	0·00134	0·00123	0·00112	0·00103	
28	0·00111	0·00101			
29					
30					
31					
32					
33					
34					
35					
36					
37					
38					
39					
40					
41					
42					
43					
44					
45					
46					
47					
48					
49					
50					

TABLE D—(*Contd.*)

Percentage

Year	23·0	23·5	24·0	24·5	25·0
1	1·00000	1·00000	1·00000	1·00000	1·00000
2	0·44843	0·44743	0·44643	0·44543	0·44444
3	0·26717	0·26594	0·26472	0·26350	0·26230
4	0·17845	0·17718	0·17593	0·17468	0·17344
5	0·12670	0·12547	0·12425	0·12304	0·12185
6	0·09339	0·09222	0·09107	0·08994	0·08882
7	0·07057	0·06949	0·06842	0·06737	0·06634
8	0·05426	0·05327	0·05229	0·05134	0·05040
9	0·04225	0·04135	0·04047	0·03960	0·03876
10	0·03321	0·03240	0·03160	0·03083	0·03007
11	0·02629	0·02556	0·02485	0·02416	0·02349
12	0·02093	0·02028	0·01965	0·01904	0·01845
13	0·01673	0·01615	0·01560	0·01506	0·01454
14	0·01342	0·01291	0·01242	0·01195	0·01150
15	0·01079	0·01035	0·00992	0·00951	0·00912
16	0·00870	0·00831	0·00794	0·00758	0·00724
17	0·00702	0·00668	0·00636	0·00605	0·00576
18	0·00568	0·00538	0·00510	0·00484	0·00459
19	0·00459	0·00434	0·00410	0·00387	0·00366
20	0·00372	0·00350	0·00329	0·00310	0·00292
21	0·00302	0·00283	0·00265	0·00248	0·00233
22	0·00245	0·00228	0·00213	0·00199	0·00186
23	0·00198	0·00185	0·00172	0·00160	0·00148
24	0·00161	0·00149	0·00138	0·00128	0·00119
25	0·00131	0·00121	0·00111	0·00103	
26	0·00106				
27					
28					
29					
30					
31					
32					
33					
34					
35					
36					
37					
38					
39					
40					
41					
42					
43					
44					
45					
46					
47					
48					
49					
50					

TABLE D—(*Contd.*)

Percentage

Year	26·0	27·0	28·0	29·0	30·0
1	1·00000	1·00000	1·00000	1·00000	1·00000
2	0·44248	0·44053	0·43860	0·43668	0·43478
3	0·25990	0·25754	0·25521	0·25290	0·25063
4	0·17100	0·16860	0·16624	0·16391	0·16163
5	0·11950	0·11720	0·11494	0·11274	0·11058
6	0·08662	0·08448	0·08240	0·08037	0·07839
7	0·06433	0·06237	0·06048	0·05865	0·05687
8	0·04857	0·04681	0·04512	0·04349	0·04192
9	0·03712	0·03555	0·03405	0·03261	0·03124
10	0·02862	0·02723	0·02591	0·02466	0·02346
11	0·02221	0·02099	0·01984	0·01876	0·01773
12	0·01732	0·01626	0·01526	0·01433	0·01345
13	0·01356	0·01264	0·01179	0·01099	0·01024
14	0·01065	0·00986	0·00912	0·00845	0·00782
15	0·00838	0·00770	0·00708	0·00650	0·00598
16	0·00661	0·00603	0·00550	0·00502	0·00458
17	0·00522	0·00472	0·00428	0·00387	0·00351
18	0·00412	0·00371	0·00333	0·00299	0·00269
19	0·00326	0·00291	0·00260	0·00232	0·00207
20	0·00258	0·00229	0·00202	0·00179	0·00159
21	0·00204	0·00180	0·00158	0·00139	0·00122
22	0·00162	0·00141	0·00123	0·00107	
23	0·00128	0·00111			
24	0·00102				
25					
26					
27					
28					
29					
30					
31					
32					
33					
34					
35					
36					
37					
38					
39					
40					
41					
42					
43					
44					
45					
46					
47					
48					
49					
50					

TABLE D—(*Contd.*)

Percentage

Year	31·0	32·0	33·0	34·0	35·0
1	1·00000	1·00000	1·00000	1·00000	1·00000
2	0·43290	0·43103	0·42918	0·42735	0·42553
3	0·24838	0·24616	0·24397	0·24180	0·23966
4	0·15938	0·15717	0·15500	0·15287	0·15076
5	0·10847	0·10640	0·10438	0·10240	0·10046
6	0·07647	0·07459	0·07277	0·07099	0·06926
7	0·05515	0·05349	0·05188	0·05031	0·04880
8	0·04040	0·03894	0·03754	0·03619	0·03489
9	0·02992	0·02866	0·02745	0·02630	0·02519
10	0·02233	0·02125	0·02022	0·01925	0·01832
11	0·01676	0·01584	0·01498	0·01416	0·01339
12	0·01263	0·01186	0·01114	0·01046	0·00982
13	0·00955	0·00890	0·00830	0·00774	0·00722
14	0·00724	0·00670	0·00620	0·00574	0·00532
15	0·00549	0·00505	0·00464	0·00427	0·00393
16	0·00418	0·00381	0·00348	0·00318	0·00290
17	0·00318	0·00288	0·00261	0·00236	0·00214
18	0·00242	0·00218	0·00196	0·00176	0·00158
19	0·00184	0·00165	0·00147	0·00131	0·00117
20	0·00141	0·00125	0·00110		
21	0·00107				
22					
23					
24					
25					
27					
27					
28					
29					
30					
31					
32					
33					
34					
35					
36					
37					
38					
39					
40					
41					
42					
43					
44					
45					
46					
47					
48					
49					
50					

TABLE D—(*Contd.*)

Percentage

Year	36·0	37·0	38·0	39·0	40·0
1	1·00000	1·00000	1·00000	1·00000	1·00000
2	0·42373	0·42194	0·42017	0·41841	0·41667
3	0·23755	0·23547	0·23340	0·23137	0·22936
4	0·14870	0·14667	0·14467	0·14270	0·14077
5	0·09856	0·09670	0·09488	0·09310	0·09136
6	0·06757	0·06593	0·06433	0·06278	0·06126
7	0·04733	0·04592	0·04454	0·04321	0·04192
8	0·03363	0·03243	0·03127	0·03015	0·02907
9	0·02413	0·02312	0·02216	0·02123	0·02034
10	0·01744	0·01660	0·01580	0·01504	0·01432
11	0·01266	0·01197	0·01132	0·01071	0·01013
12	0·00922	0·00866	0·00814	0·00764	0·00718
13	0·00674	0·00628	0·00586	0·00547	0·00510
14	0·00493	0·00456	0·00423	0·00392	0·00363
15	0·00361	0·00332	0·00306	0·00281	0·00259
16	0·00265	0·00242	0·00221	0·00202	0·00185
17	0·00194	0·00176	0·00160	0·00145	0·00132
18	0·00143	0·00128	0·00116	0·00104	
19	0·00105				
20					
21					
22					
23					
24					
25					
26					
27					
28					
29					
30					
31					
32					
33					
34					
35					
36					
37					
38					
39					
40					
41					
42					
43					
44					
45					
46					
47					
48					
49					
50					

TABLE D—(*Contd.*)

Percentage

Year	41·0	42·0	43·0	44·0	45·0
1	1·00000	1·00000	1·00000	1·00000	1·00000
2	0·41494	0·41322	0·41152	0·40984	0·40816
3	0·22737	0·22541	0·22347	0·22155	0·21966
4	0·13886	0·13699	0·13515	0·13334	0·13156
5	0·08966	0·08799	0·08635	0·08475	0·08318
6	0·05978	0·05835	0·05695	0·05558	0·05426
7	0·04068	0·03947	0·03830	0·03716	0·03607
8	0·02804	0·02704	0·02608	0·02516	0·02427
9	0·01950	0·01869	0·01791	0·01717	0·01646
10	0·01364	0·01299	0·01237	0·01178	0·01123
11	0·00958	0·00906	0·00858	0·00812	0·00768
12	0·00675	0·00634	0·00596	0·00561	0·00527
13	0·00476	0·00445	0·00415	0·00388	0·00362
14	0·00337	0·00312	0·00290	0·00269	0·00249
15	0·00238	0·00219	0·00202	0·00186	0·00172
16	0·00169	0·00154	0·00141	0·00129	0·00118
17	0·00119	0·00109			
18					
19					
20					
21					
22					
23					
24					
25					
26					
27					
28					
29					
30					
31					
32					
33					
34					
35					
36					
37					
38					
39					
40					
41					
42					
43					
44					
45					
46					
47					
48					
49					
50					

TABLE D—(*Contd.*)

Percentage

Year	46·0	47·0	48·0	49·0	50·0
1	1·00000	1·00000	1·00000	1·00000	1·00000
2	0·40650	0·40486	0·40323	0·40161	0·40000
3	0·21779	0·21594	0·21411	0·21231	0·21053
4	0·12981	0·12808	0·12639	0·12472	0·12308
5	0·08165	0·08015	0·07868	0·07724	0·07583
6	0·05296	0·05170	0·05048	0·04928	0·04812
7	0·03501	0·03398	0·03298	0·03202	0·03108
8	0·02342	0·02259	0·02180	0·02104	0·02030
9	0·01578	0·01514	0·01452	0·01392	0·01335
10	0·01070	0·01019	0·00971	0·00926	0·00882
11	0·00727	0·00689	0·00652	0·00617	0·00585
12	0·00496	0·00466	0·00439	0·00413	0·00388
13	0·00338	0·00316	0·00295	0·00276	0·00258
14	0·00231	0·00215	0·00199	0·00185	0·00172
15	0·00158	0·00146	0·00134	0·00124	0·00114
16	0·00108				
17					
18					
19					
20					
21					
22					
23					
24					
25					
26					
27					
28					
29					
30					
31					
32					
33					
34					
35					
36					
37					
38					
39					
40					
41					
42					
43					
44					
45					
46					
47					
48					
49					
50					

APPENDIX II

During the changeover period following 15th February, 1971, both £ s d and decimal coins are legal tender, at the following rates:

£ s d to Decimal	Decimal to £ s d
1d = $\frac{5}{12}$p	$\frac{1}{2}$p = 1·2d
3d = $1\frac{1}{4}$p	1p = 2·4d
6d = $2\frac{1}{2}$p	2p = 4·8d
1s = 5p	5p = 1s
2s = 10p	10p = 2s
	50p = 10s

If exact conversion is impossible, legal tender will be the next highest denomination provided change is not asked for.

For accounting and commercial purposes generally, however, there is no one universally applicable method of converting £ s d to decimal amounts and the parties involved in transactions and contracts must agree on how many decimal places are necessary for accurate conversion. The following table provides some guidance on possible conversion rates. In the text, various conversion rates are used. At the most accurate level, four places of decimals are used.

DECIMAL CONVERSION TABLE

£ s d	£ (Decimal)		£ s d	£ (Decimal)
	Correct to 4 places	Rounded to		
	0·0000	0·00		
1	0·0041	0·00	1 0	0·05
2	0·0083	0·01	2 0	0·10
3	0·0125	0·01	3 0	0·15
4	0·0166	0·02	4 0	0·20
5	0·0208	0·02	5 0	0·25
6	0·0250	0·03	6 0	0·30
7	0·0291	0·03	7 0	0·35
8	0·0333	0·03	8 0	0·40
9	0·0375	0·04	9 0	0·45
10	0·0416	0·04	10 0	0·50
11	0·0458	0·05	11 0	0·55
			12 0	0·60
			13 0	0·65
			14 0	0·70
			15 0	0·75
			16 0	0·80
			17 0	0·85
			18 0	0·90
			19 0	0·95
			2 6	0·13
			7 6	0·38
			12 6	0·63
			17 6	0·88
			3 4	0·17
			6 8	0·33
			13 4	0·67
			16 8	0·83

APPENDIX III

Selected Reading List

MANY students and others who read *Advanced Accounts* will wish to supplement their reading in certain topics or may wish to read more broadly. This bibliography cannot hope to be comprehensive, but it lists and comments on a few of the many good books which are available.

The list might make the nucleus of a small library in a college which is using *Advanced Accounts* as its textbook.

Three books, *Studies in Accounting Theory*, *Studies in the History of Accounting* and *Studies in Costing* would be essential in any collection. They in turn mention many titles which should lead the serious student to further readings.

ACCOUNTANTS INTERNATIONAL STUDY GROUP: *Accounting and auditing approaches to inventories in three nations*, 1968.

A review of the approaches to valuation of inventories in the U.K., the U.S.A., and Canada which brings out clearly the differences in national approaches and which also clarifies the basic problems in valuing inventories.

ALLAN, JAMES: *Speaking of Computers*. Accountants' Publishing Co., 1965.

A glossary of terms in narrative form and classified order, with an alphabetical index.

ALLAN, JAMES: *A Plain Man's Guide to Computers*. Accountants' Publishing Co., 1964.

An enlarged and consolidated 2nd edition brought up-to-date by the author from an original series of articles in The Accountants' Magazine. See *The Simple Computer*.

ALLAN, JAMES: *The Simple Computer*. Accountants' Publishing Co., 1969.

A successor to *A Plain Man's Guide to Computers*, 1964 this book is a compact treatment of the principles on which computers operate and are put to use. It combines the technical facts with a general appreciation of the computer and its applications to meet varied demands. Includes a glossarial index and two chapters on the teaching code "TAM."

ASSOCIATION OF CERTIFIED AND CORPORATE ACCOUNTANTS: *Capital Gains Tax*. The Provisions of the Finance Act, 1965, as amended by the Finance Acts, 1966 to 1969.

This booklet contains a detailed explanation of the taxation of short term and long term capital gains. It contains marginal references to the relevant sections and schedules of the Acts and over thirty practical examples.

See also a similar booklet published by the I.C.A. of E. & W.

ASSOCIATION OF CERTIFIED AND CORPORATE ACCOUNTANTS: *Corporation Tax*.

(1) *General Provisions* of the Finance Act, 1965, as amended by the Finance Acts, 1966 to 1969.

This is a detailed commentary on the sections and schedules of the Finance Act, 1965 and subsequent Acts dealing with the general provisions of the new Corporation Tax and is illustrated by over fifty practical examples.

(2) *Close Companies Provisions* of the Finance Act, 1965, as amended by the Finance Acts, 1966 to 1969.

This work deals with the arrangements for the taxation of close companies. It is annotated in detail and contains a large number of practical examples.

ASSOCIATION OF CERTIFIED AND CORPORATE ACCOUNTANTS: *Electronic Data Processing*. In five parts:

(I) *An Introduction* to Electronic Computers

This study forms the introduction to the series and deals with the principles of the subject with particular reference to certain aspects of Electronic Data Processing.

(II) *Management's Initial Considerations* when Planning for a Computer

The object of this booklet is to guide management to the stage when a decision will have to be made whether or not to acquire a computer or to make use of a commerical data-processing centre.

(III) *The Planning and Installation* of a Computer

This work deals with the careful planning which is essential once a decision has been made to proceed with the installation of a computer, and brings the series to the stage where the computer has been obtained, installed, and some initial data processing taken place.

(IV) *Management Control and Auditing*

This study deals with auditing problems and with the type of controls necessary in order to ensure that a high standard of management reporting and accuracy is maintained. In addition, the problems arising from changes in the conventional methods of keeping both accountancy and commercial records are also considered.

(V) *The Use of Computer Service Bureau*

This booklet deals with the more important considerations which have to be taken into account when making a decision as to whether or not time should be hired from a computer service bureau.

ASSOCIATION OF CERTIFIED AND CORPORATE ACCOUNTANTS: *Management Accounting. A concise appraisal.*

This work has been prepared for the accounting profession and executives to encourage the wider use of control accounting. The scope, objective and methods are examined in general terms.

ASSOCIATION OF CERTIFIED AND CORPORATE ACCOUNTANTS: *Management Accounting for the Small Business.*

The object of this publication is to demonstrate the increase in productivity which would accrue if smaller businesses were to make use of management accounting techniques. It has been written primarily for those who own such businesses, or who have the day-to-day responsibility for managing them. In this study examples of a business carrying on mixed engineering work and of an architectural practice are used to illustrate these techniques.

ASSOCIATION OF CERTIFIED AND CORPORATE ACCOUNTANTS: *Relief for Payment of Interest. The Provisions of the Finance Act*, 1969.

A detailed account of the changes in the treatment of Interest for the purpose of Income Tax and Corporation Tax, brought about by the Finance Act, 1969.

ASSOCIATION OF CERTIFIED AND CORPORATE ACCOUNTANTS: *Sources of Capital*, 1969.

A comprehensive summary about traditional and lesser-known sources of capital. Sections are devoted to permanent capital and long-term borrowing, special finance institutions, short-term finance, Government assistance for industry, agriculture and fishing and finance for exports and housing.

ASSOCIATION OF CERTIFIED AND CORPORATE ACCOUNTANTS: *The Modern Approach to Internal Auditing.*

The object of this study is to direct the attention of the accounting profession and of executives in commerce and industry to a wider concept of the function of the internal auditor. The study is explored in general terms and seeks to illustrate the value of development in this field of accounting.

ASSOCIATION OF CERTIFIED AND CORPORATE ACCOUNTANTS: *The Planning and Measurement of Profit.*

The purpose of this study is to outline the method of arriving at a consistent standard for assessing what profits should be earned in a given period, by any business, irrespective of size, and to enunciate a clear definition of profits which will be of practical application in connection with forward planning.

BAXTER, W. T. & DAVIDSON, S.: *Studies in Accounting Theory.* 2nd edn. Sweet & Maxwell, 1962.

A collection of important articles on problems of accounting theory such as the nature of depreciation, problems of stock valuation, and accounting for price level changes.

BROWN, R. G. & JOHNSTON, K. S.: *Pacioli on Accounting.* McGraw-Hill, 1963.

A new and highly readable translation of the first published treatise on book-keeping. Although it is nearly five hundred years since it first saw the light of day, much of it is still relevant today—sceptics should consider the quotations used at the beginning of some of our chapters; for instance, "Frequent accounting makes for good friendships." Recommended for students and teachers.

CARSBERG, B. V. & EDEY, H. C. (Eds): *Modern Financial Management.* Penguin Books, 1969.

A useful collection of important articles on financial problems The 18 articles cover problems of investment, valuation and income; pricing; long-range planning and control; problems in the public sector and mathematical methods in long-range planning and games theory.

CASTLE, E. F.: *Principles of Accounts*, 2nd edn, revised by D. Garbutt. University Tutorial Press, 1962.

A practical introductory textbook with many illustrations and exercises which covers the topics which may be studied before Carter is used. Recommended for students who find that Chapter I and II of *Carter* assume knowledge which they do not possess or as a textbook on preliminary courses.

CHAMBERS, R. J.: *Accounting, evaluation and economic behaviour.* Prentice-Hall, 1966.

Presents a model of accounting theory in a carefully contracted framework currently used in the study of social action. The role of the individual, of groups, of society, of business in the societal pricture is indicated and accounting theories developed to explain social action on the one hand; and social action shaping accounting theory on the other.

CHAMBERS, R. J.: *Financial management*. Law Book Co., of Australia, 1967.

An authoritative text which considers the aspects of business finance, management and accounting that provide top management with the information required for financial decision making.

CHAMBERS, R. J.: *Function and design of company annual reports*. Sweet & Maxwell, 1955.

Business communications are dealt with here as a means of informing not only the public at large, but also of informing potential and actual investors, employees, customers and critics. Financial information is examined in particular, and points of view are advanced with the intent of improving such communication by means of the Company Annual Report. A second part explains how this may best be achieved.

CHARTERED INSTITUTE OF SECRETARIES: *Business Aspects of Corporation Tax and Capital Gains Tax*.

The addresses delivered at the one-day conference held in Guildhall, 30th November 1965.

CUMMINGS, G.: *A Complete Guide to Investment*. Penguin 1963.

As its title claims this book reviews various kinds of investment and discusses the relative attractions of each type to different investors. Since tax affects the attractions of investments, readers should be sure that they buy the most recent edition.

DOWLING, J. T.: *Some auditing doubts and difficulties*. Institute of Chartered Accountants of Scotland.

Originally published in The Accountants' Magazine in 1954. A survey of the problems which face the auditor in practice.

DOWLING, J. T. & WALDIE, J.: *The Amalgamation of Companies*. Institute of Chartered Accountants Scotland, 1964.

Two papers in sequence, "The Accountant's Report on a Proposed Amalgamation of Companies" and "Study of a Proposed Amalgamation," originally published separately in The Accountants' Magazine in 1960 and 1961.

EDEY, H. C.: *An Introduction to Accountancy*. Hutchinson, 1966.

A modern academic introduction to accountancy suitable for university undergraduate courses and of interest to those who are looking for a revision textbook written from a more theoretical point of view. Strongly recommended for both teachers and students.

EDEY, H. C.: *Business Budgets and Accountants*. Hutchinson, 1966.

A rigorous review of the basic concepts of budgeting which is a useful introduction to the subject, or particular value to undergraduate students.

European Congress of Accountants, 1963: *Record of Proceedings*. Institute of Chartered Accountants of Scotland, 1964.

Published in English, French and German editions.

GIRDWOOD, D. G.: *Farm crops and livestock* (revised edn). Accountants' Publishing Co., 1965.

A glossary and guide, first published in the Accountants' Magazine in 1953 and 1954, revised by the author in 1965.

FERRIS, P.: *The City*. Rev. edn. Penguin, 1965.

An interesting account of the attitudes and outlook of the complicated network of financial institutions centred about the Bank of England and collectively called the City. Written by a highly skilled journalist, the book is very informative. Few readers will fail to glean new insights into the workings of the City.

FURNESS, H. J.: *The Cost of Labour Turnover*. Institute of Cost and Works Accountants, 1950.

A paper on labour turnover which discusses causes and calculates cost of labour turnover in relation to possible benefits.

GARBUTT, D.: *Planning for Profit*. Gee, 1967.

A deeper study and more comprehensive treatment of direct costing and the theory of cost behaviour then is given in *Carter*. One chapter is an extended introductory exercise and the final chapter describes the application of the principles of direct costing in a small clothing firm.

GARBUTT, D.: *A Simple Guide to Capital Expenditure Decisions*. Pitman, 1967.

A fuller exposition of the principles of evaluationg capital expenditure decisions than is given in *Carter* and a possible preliminary book for those who wish to read further on this subject.

GARBUTT, D.: *Training Costs under the Industrial Training Act* 1964. Gee, 1969.

Outlines the system established by the Industrial Training Act of 1964 and the application of accounting principles to ascertaining the costs of training; recording training activities and expenditures; budgeting for and controlling training and the use of cost-benefit analysis and break-even charts in the evaluation of training effectiveness.

GENERAL EDUCATIONAL TRUST OF THE INSTITUTE OF CHARTERED ACCOUNTANTS IN ENGLAND AND WALES: *Survey of published accounts* 1968–9. 1970.

Presentation and disclosure practices used in the annual accounts of 300 companies taken from the 1968–9 *Times* list of 500 largest industrial companies. Covers the general arrangement of accounts; profit and loss account; exceptional items; the Balance Sheet; and the Directors' report.

GILLETT BROTHERS DISCOUNT CO. LTD.: *The Bill of London.* Chapman & Hall, 1964.

A practical and fairly simple exposition of Bills of exchange of interest to students who may be working in this field and who wish to read more widely on the subject.

GOLDBERG, L.: *An outline of accounting*, 5th edn, revised. Law Book Co. of Australia, 1968.

First published 1939. Offers a logical and consistent approach to the study of accounting: its nature and scope; basic theory; practical everyday examples to illustrate the application of the theory.

INSTITUTE OF CHARTERED ACCOUNTANTS OF ENGLAND AND WALES: *Guide to the accounting requirements of the Companies Acts* 1948 and 1967. Gee, 1968.

Summary of the requirements of the Acts suitable for practitioners and advanced students.

INSTITUTE OF CHARTERED ACCOUNTANTS OF ENGLAND AND WALES: *Recommendations of accounting principles* 1969. Gee.

Section N of the members' handbook. Discusses problems, indicates acceptable accounting treatments and makes recommendations for members to follow.

INSTITUTE OF CHARTERED ACCOUNTANTS OF ENGLAND AND WALES: *Standard Costing*, 1969.

Clear and comprehensive exposition of the essentials of standard costing and a useful supplement to the brief reference in *Carter's Advanced Accounts* (*Carter*).

INSTITUTE OF CHARTERED ACCOUNTANTS OF ENGLAND AND WALES: *The history of the Institute of Chartered Accountants in England and Wales and its founder bodies* 1870–1965.

Describes the growth of the profession and its influence on public affairs.

INSTITUTE OF CHARTERED ACCOUNTANTS OF SCOTLAND: *A history of the Chartered accountants of Scotland from the earliest times to* 1954.

Published on the Institute's centenary in 1954, describes the foundation and growth of the oldest professional body of accountants in the world.

INSTITUTE OF CHARTERED ACCOUNTANTS OF SCOTLAND: *Sources of Financial and other statistics.* Accountants Publishing Co., 1967.

Lists useful publications under topics likely to be of interest to accountants, e.g. business ratios, company accounts, etc.

INSTITUTE OF CHARTERED ACCOUNTANTS OF SCOTLAND: *The Companies Act* 1967—*some requirements and implications.*

Gives a factual statement of the effect on company law of the requirements of the new Companies Act (except sections relating to insurance cos., bank, shipping and moneylenders) and then a number of authors consider specific problems.

INSTITUTE OF COST AND MANAGEMENT ACCOUNTANTS: *A Report On Marginal Costing*, 1961.

Defines marginal costing, and considers general applications, particular applications and the problem of assessing cost variability. The final chapters deal with practicability of marginal costing in assessing cost variability and the arrangement of cost accounts.

Appendices cover limiting factors; the break-even chart, presentation of results; joint product and gas industry costing and forms of marginal cost statement.

INSTITUTE OF COST AND MANAGEMENT ACCOUNTANTS: *Accountancy of Changing Price Levels.* I.C.M.A., 1965.

A useful exposition of various proposed methods of accounting for changing price levels. Discusses money and its functions, the effects of changing price levels, and the maintenance of real capital before viewing accountancy principles (on which recommendations are made) and going on to the problems of accounting for price-level changes.

INSTITUTE OF COST AND MANAGEMENT ACCOUNTANTS: *An Introduction To Business Forecasting*, 1960.

Deals with methods and problems in applying forecasting to sales; production; output; capital expenditures; the nature of forecasting of results; forecasting cash and standard costs.

INSTITUTE OF COST AND MANAGEMENT ACCOUNTANTS: *Costing Matters* (in conjunction with the British Productivity Council).

Deals in a clear and simple way with wages, machines, materials, overheads, budgetary control and standard costing.

INSTITUTE OF COST AND MANAGEMENT ACCOUNTANTS: *Cost Reduction.*

The importance of cost reduction. How to achieve management participation. Applications; methods; design; factory and marketing organisation; finance in a programme of cost reduction; value analysis.

INSTITUTE OF COST AND MANAGEMENT ACCOUNTANTS: *Introduction to Budgetary Control, Standard Costing, Material Control and Production Control.* I.C.M.A., 1966.

There is much useful material in this book, although it is rather complicated and only recommended for the more advanced student. Covers budgetary control and standard costing and the relationship between them. Includes a section on Production and Material Control. The appendix is a comprehensive set of budgets, costs, accounts, forms and statements and includes charts of standard cost accounting procedures and semi-variable overhead expenses.

INSTITUTE OF COST AND MANAGEMENT ACCOUNTANTS; *Management Information Systems and the Computer.* 1967. In two parts.

Part I discusses the design of a management information system; the design concepts; the impact of the computer; the place of M.I.S. in the organisational pattern of a company and the marshalling and handling of data. Two appendices contain helpful charts and diagrams.

Part II discusses computer application; the value of information; getting started; production planning and material control; payments; purchase analysis; invoicing; cash collection; complex product ranges and problem solving.

INSTITUTE OF COST AND MANAGEMENT ACCOUNTANTS: *Profitable Use of Capital in Industry.* I.C.M.A., 1966.

A concise review of the various methods of evaluating the profitable use of capital in industry, including discounted cash flow methods (yield and net present value), comparative cost, pay-back and four variants of return in investment.

Discusses capital, profit, measurement of the effective use of capital, planning and control of fixed and working capital.

INSTITUTE OF COST AND MANAGEMENT ACCOUNTANTS: *Selling and Distribution Cost Accounting.* 1961.

Outlining the problems of applying Cost Accounting to selling and distribution. Some forms are listed. Part D deals with methods of fixing selling prices; methods of marketing and trade associations.

INSTITUTE OF COST AND MANAGEMENT ACCOUNTANTS: *Terminology of Cost Accountancy*, revised. 1966.

Essential reading for students of I.C.M.A. examinations since their examinations are based on this terminology. An alphabetical list of definitions of terms ranging from *Absorbed overhead* to *Weighted Average Price.*

KOTAS, R.: *Accounting in the Hotel and Catering Industry*, 2nd edn. International Textbook, 1967.

A clear and comprehensive exposition of book-keeping and accounting principles in the hotel and catering industry. It covers both elementary topics and more advanced subjects such as budgetary control. Of particular value to managers and accountants in the hotel industry but of interest to accountants in other industries who wish to see how the principles are applied in another field.

LITTLETON, A. C. & TAMEY, B. S.: *Studies in the History of Accounting*. Sweet & Maxwell (out of print).

An authoritative collection of articles on the history of accounting which spans a period of two and a half thousand years, from 600 B.C. to the end of the Victorian era. It covers such topics as Greek and Roman Accounting developments prior to Luca Paciolo, the first English books on book-keeping and double-entry book-keeping in Japan.

LYNCH, T. D.: *The History of Income Tax*. Accountants' Publishing Co.

A concise survey covering the 15th to 20th centuries originally published in *The Accountants' Magazine* in 1962.

LYNCH, T. D. (Ed.): *Direct Taxation in the United Kingdom*. Accountants' Publishing Co., 1968.

A symposium by ten authors based on texts prepared by them for a five-day course on taxation organised by the Institute of Chartered Accountants of Scotland. It is intended to help not only the practising accountant but also the tax specialist and the student. General principles are illustrated by examples of common tax problems.

MATTESICH, R. V.: *Accounting and Analytical Method*, Measurement and Projection of Income and Wealth in the Micro- and Macro-economy. Irwin, 1964.

An important book which is difficult in parts. It aims to present a unified frame of accounting and to clarify accounting concepts as a prerequisite for the application of analytical methods used in the management sciences. It uses basic concepts from modern logic, mathematics and decision theory to improve accounting. Chapter 9 discusses budget models of the firm and a separate volume is available giving a fuller exposition and computer programme for a budget model.

MERRETT, A. J. & SYKES, A.: *Capital Budgeting and Company Finance.* Longmans, 1966.

Essential reading for advanced students and practitioners who wish to make use of the discounted cash flow appraisal methods. Incorporates a short-cut method for converting a before tax D.C.F. rate of return into an after tax rate under various tax rates and various scales of capital allowance.

MOST, K. S.: *Uniform Cost Accounting*. Gee, 1961.

A comprehensive study on the subject of uniform cost accounting. It discusses the nature and essentials of a uniform cost accounting plan, cost apportionment, overhead absorption and depreciation, classification and coding of accounts and the utilization of accounting figures.

PINKNEY, A.: *An Audit Approach To Computers.* Gee.

Provides an authoritative guide for all concerned in the task of controlling computerised accounting systems.

REECE, J. A.: *Statistics for The Cost Accountant*. I.C.M.A.

Discusses the meaning of statistics; the different parts of the subject; time series; average and dispersion; index numbers; economic statistics and statistical control.

RISK, J. M. S.: *The Classification and Coding of Accounts*, Occasional Paper No. 2. I.C.M.A., 1965.

A standard book on coding and classification of value to advanced students or practitioners. Discusses the history and nature of classification and symbolisation and their application to accounts coding.

SCHMALENBACH, E.: *Dynamic Accounting*, translated by G. W. MURPHY & K. S. MOST. Gee, 1959.

A classical German exposition of the basic concepts and problems of accounting which may, at first glance, appear deceptively simple and remote. In fact, it repays continued study since it returns again and again to the basic dilemmas of accounting.

SCOTT, J. A.: *Budgetary Control and Standard Costs*, 6th edn. 1970.

Covers the preparation of budgets and standard costs; budget and cost reports and accounts; advanced budgeting; financial control and control actions; long range planning and budgeting and mathematics and management.

SOLOMONS, D.: *Studies in Cost Analysis.* Sweet & Maxwell, 1968.

A collection of academic articles on problems of costing which should be read by all those who wish to specialize in this field.

THOMAS, A. J.: *The Accountant and Computers.* Pitman, 1969.

A useful introductory book for accountants who have little knowledge or experience of computers and whose interest may be stimulated by the references to computers in this edition of *Carter*.

WHEBLE, B. S.: *Documentary Credits; Uniform Customs and Practice.* Institute of Bankers.

Of particular value to students for the Institute of Bankers examinations or for those who are involved in using documentary credits since it describes currently accepted practices in this growing field.

WIGHTMAN, J.: *The Legal Life of David Fraser.* Institute of Chartered Accountants of Scotland, 1965.

Aspects of the law in action, illustrated for the C.A. apprentice. (Looseleaf publication.)

WILLIAMS, R. G. & MENDES, B.: *Comprehensive Aspects of Taxation.* Cassell, 1967.

A good textbook covering the essentials of taxation in one volume and useful as further reading for those who wish to know more about current tax rates and law.

SHORT ANSWERS

NOTE: A fully-worked *Key to Carter's Advanced Accounts* by Douglas Garbutt is available from the publishers.

EXERCISE 01

(1) (*a*) *Dr*. Carpets, *Cr*. Desks £120. (*b*) *Dr*. Typewriters £180, Loss £20, *Cr*. Safe £200. (2) To find *gross* amounts add back $\frac{1}{9}$, $\frac{1}{7}$, $\frac{1}{4}$, $\frac{3}{37}$, $\frac{1}{19}$, and $\frac{1}{3}$ respectively. (3) Bank balance £205·80 plus 3 cheques not cleared £391·50 less 2 cheques not presented £142·25. (4) Cash balance should be £973·25. Difference £5·10. (5) Cash balance £33, Bank £2,125. (6) *Dr*. Commission, *Cr*. Low £233·56. *Dr*. Solicitor's Charges £9·20, Cash £78·35. *Cr*. Smith £87·55. *Dr*. Assets. *Cr*. Harris £40. (7) R, N, N, N, R, R, N, P, P, P, P, R, N. (8) Raw Materials £2,019·98; Freight & Carriage £238·51; Light & Power £157·21; Rent £300; Telephone £22·25; Printing £27·39. (9) Bought £129 *Cr*., Sales £560 *Dr*. (10) U.K. £1,869, Abroad £1,336, Felt Hats £2,549, Helmets £656. (11) (*a*) Total payments £6·28. (12) Balance of cash £23·75. Overdraft £145·60. (13) Opening balance £25·30, closing £18·67. (14) Rent £3,583·33, Rates £1,966·00. (15) Closing balance Coal & Coke £15 *Dr*., Electricity £26 *Cr*. (17) Hughes £6·12, Elliott £3·08, Griffiths £4·85 (20) Original capital £655, stock £100, cash £70. Stop producing, start selling.

EXERCISE 02

(1) *A* is wrong. (2) Gross profit £5,217, Net £3,014, B/S totals £25,422. (3) Gross profit £5,873, Net £1,318·50, B/S totals £36,986, Interest £2·50. (4) Gross profit £5,750, Net £953, B/S totals £21,431. (5) Gross profit £7,362, Net £3,171, B/S totals £14, 331. (6) Gross profit £18,592, Net £11,058, B/S totals £34,841. (7) Gross profit £36,200, Net £16,950, B/S totals £109,040. (8) T.B. £61,784, Gross profit £7,610, Net £688, B/S totals £25,692. (10) (*a*) Profit and Loss *Cr*. £110 and £3·75. (*b*) Profit and Loss *Cr*. £113·75. (11) (*a*) Profit and Loss *Cr*. £187·82 and £4·99. (*b*) Profit and Loss *Cr*. £192·81. (12) Gross Profit £9,596, Net £4,480, B/S totals £8,774. (13) Gross Profit £6,425, Net £3,650, B/S totals £30,670. (14) Net profit after adjustments £2,905·14. (15) Rates owing £40·44. (16) Balance £3,190. (17) Gross profit £15,311, Net £8,665, B/S totals £35,951. (18) Gross Profit £28,000, Net £3,485, B/S totals £51,800. (19) Net trading profit £9,546, B/S totals £33,268. Loss on vehicle sale £215. (20) Gross profit £33,000, Net £862, B/S totals £59,852. (21) (i) Car expenses account balances *Dr*. £17, *Cr*. £61. (ii) Rent receivable account balances *Dr*. £150, *Cr*. £180.

EXERCISE 03

(1) Suspense A/c *Dr*. £9 and £4·75, *Cr*. £1·28 and £1. (2) Opening balance £77·40. (3) B/S totals £7,903. (4) Adj. net profit £3,926·61. (5) Difference £1·30. (6) (*a*) 33⅓%; (*b*) 50%; (*c*) 20%; (*d*) 20%. (8) Correct totals £16,010. (9) Net increase of profit £293·12. (11) Rates prepaid £29 *Dr*., outstanding £60 *Cr*. (12) (*a*) C; (*b*) R; (*c*) R; (*d*) C. (13) Net profit £7,718. (14) [2] Total £10,317. (15) (i) £277; (ii) Bank £399; (iii) Net profit £2,339. (16) Revised balance £882. (17) (*c*) and (*e*) have no effect. Debit (*a*) and (*d*). *Cr*. (*b*), (*f*), (*g*), (*h*). (18) Revised TB totals £16,970. (19) Correct balance £9,905.

EXERCISE 04

(2) [1] Interest £2·50. [3] Interest £1·25. [5] Interest £2·66. [6] Interest £3·50. [9] Interest £27·35. (3) (*a*) Bankers discount £1·09; (*b*) Bankers discount £1·35; (*c*) Bankers discount £0·54. (4) (*b*) Interest £8·25; (*c*) Balance c/d £114·13. (5) (*a*) 4th

April; (*b*) Discount £5. (6) £1·87 discount each. (7) Contingent liability £10,750 (note). (8) Interest £12·50. *Dr*. balance A's A/c £3,552·50. (9) Total Bills Receivable book £874·10. Discount £19·30. Total Bills Payable book £1,003·48. Discount £15·83. (10) (*a*) Interest £0·99; (*b*) £3·15. (11) Discount, negotiate (endorse) or hold. (12) Discount £1·25. (13) Bank overdraft £109·80. TB totals £844·65. (14) Totals £47·286. (15) Interest £25·00. Discount £40. (16) Bills Payable total £366,000. Bills Receivable total £194,000. (17) (*b*) Statement Goods £478, less Cash £200 and Bills Receivable £250. J.N. Creditor for £28. (18) Interest £9·75. (19) Discount £2·35. Cash £102·02. Bank £473·40. (20) Discount £250. Interest £100. (21) Balance Bank £181 on 1st September. Net Profit £37. Closing stock £164. (22) Discount £2·30. Interest £1·88.

EXERCISE 05

(1) to (3) See Chapter 05. (4) *Cr*. Balance £13,740. (7) TB totals £407. (8) Purchases *Dr*. balance £67, *Cr*. balance £5,478, Sales *Dr*. balance £9,931, *Cr*. balance £101. (9) TB totals £762. (10) TB totals £1,172. (11) TB totals £720. (12) Differences: 31st October Sec. 1 £11·75 too little, Sec. 3 £11·75 too much, Sec. 4 £3·90 short on debit. 30th November as above. 31st December Sec. 2 excess debits £5·85, Sec. 4 excess debits £6·10, Posting error £10. (13) TB totals £1,479 Bought ledger, TB total £2,223 Sales ledger, TB total £11,735 General ledger, Gross Profit £1,019, Net Profit £346. B/S totals £9,864. (14) Opening Journal total £5,955, TB totals £1,565, Bought ledger, TB totals £1,276, Sales ledger, TB totals £7,920 General ledger. (15) Purchases *Cr*. balance £7,265, Sales *Dr*. balance £10,829, Difference £5. (16) Cash balance £16,930. (17) Sales *Dr*. balance £2,682·32, Bought *Cr*. balance £1,352·80. (18) Sales *Dr*. balance £2,582, Private ledger *Cr*. balance £2,582. (19) Purchases *Cr*. balance £3,490.

EXERCISE 06

(1) Depreciation £110 per annum. (2) Final balance £534. (3) Final balance £2,732 (first), £2,677 (second), £2,696 (third). (4) Depreciation £346. Interest £100 falling to £16. (5) Profit and Loss debit £245 per annum. (8) Balance on R and R Provision £222. (10) Invest £188·40 per annum. (12) Loss £2,600. (14) Balance at end £1,747·50 at 5% or £1,590 at 7½%. (15) (i) £910; (ii) £1,914; (iii) Net Profit £412. (17) Loss on investment £10,030. (19) Depreciation balance £79,125. Renewals Reserve £11,580. (20) Plant balances (i) £16,095; (ii) £19,200. Loss on sale £400. Net book value at end £16,095. (21) Total depreciation £13,150, 19. . £257; 19.4 £95, 19.7 £20; 19.8 £132, 19.9 £312. (22) Results, Plant £307 loss; Car £12 profit; Office appliance £10 loss. (23) Gross profit £14,000, Net profit £2,547, B/S totals £15,959. (24) (*a*) 1961 £28,800, 1962 £30,000, 1963 £31,100, 1964 £32,400. (*b*) B/S value £153,900, Reserve £61,150. (25) Write off lease £175 per annum, Patent £85. (27) New B/S totals £14,700.

EXERCISE 07

(1) [1] 15s [2] £80,000. [3] Provide for loss. [4] Net loss £5,000. (2) (i) £4,900 or £4,350. (3) Profit and Loss 19. . £17,400, 19.1 £27,700, 19.2 £37,600, 19.3 £46,700. (4) Stock £3,985, Gross profit £9,450. (5) £10,000. (6) Gross profit £15,706. (7) Stock £17,361. (8) Claim £11,030. (9) Claim £1,960, Net profit £40, B/S totals £3,160. (11) Claim £4,746. (13) *A* £2,900, £2,617, £2,634. *B* £2,760, £2,920, £2,660. *C* £1,914, £1,820, £2,003. (14) Stock loss Music £3,000, Instruments £5,350. (15) Net profit £900. (16) Claim £240, Gross profit £199, Net Profit £88, B/S totals £718. (17) 30th June FIFO £297·50, AV £287. (18) Gross profit £150,632, Net profit £17,045, B/S totals £86,824. (19) Stock £18,904. (20) Closing balances *A* 400 yds £190, *B* 540 yds £432. (21) FIFO balance £70, 800 units, LIFO £75, 800 units.

EXERCISE 08

(1) £25. (2) £8. (3) £3·67. (4) 3·4%. (5) Loss 5p. (6) Increase £6·05. (7) Loss £60. (8) £3·86 per annum per £100. (10) Year 6 balance £1,636·85. (11) *Dr.* Balance 3rd April £859·99 Principal, *Cr.* Balance 3rd April £206·75 Interest. (12) Profit on sales £31·89. (13) *Dr.* Balance 30th September £946·64 Principal. (14) *Dr.* Balance 25th March £7,306·50. Principal, £26·75. Contango. (15) *Dr.* Balance 1st January £8,286·62. Principal, £49·48 Interest. (16) Balance £10,909·30 Principal. (17) 30th July Balances £7,050 Mexican £11,150 N.W., £225 Contango. (18) Net profit £1,400 income, £4,060 on sales. (19) 1st October balance £299 Capital *Dr.* (20) 1st April balance £9,425 Capital *Dr.*, Net profit £480.

EXERCISE 09

(1) First period profit £127, second period £22. (2) Net proceeds £17,311, Profit £8,641. (3) Profit £88. (4) Net proceeds £150. (5) Profit £8. (6) Profit on sales £2,207, on insurance £58. (7) First period profit £110, second period £74. (8) Profit £126·25. (9) Proceeds £4,100, Profit £890, Stock £428. (10) Profit £365. (11) Proceeds £311·80. (12) TB totals £14,056, Net profit £1,190, B/S totals £11,396. (13) Cash debits £170 and £50. James A/c total £520·50. (14) Proceeds £1,076·88. (15) New bill £578·85, Interest £16·85. (16) Proceeds £615. (17) Profit £903·59. (18) Loss £40. (19) Profit £237, Proceeds Rs 30,000, £2,250. (20) Profit £111·24 each.

EXERCISE 10

(2) Surplus £298, B/S totals £1,316, Cash £316 *Dr.* (3) Surplus £149, B/S totals £239, Expedition £168 surplus. (4) Profit £256 on Lucidity. Surplus £171, B/S totals £5,774, Capital £4,400. (5) Surplus £731, B/S totals £998. (6) Deficit £53, B/S totals £276. (7) Net profit £2,460, B/S totals £5,104. (8) Profit £110 on magazine, Surplus £112, B/S totals £4,055. (9) Profit £2,000, B/S totals £3,800. (11) Surplus £214. (12) Cash at end £274. (13) Surplus £288, B/S totals £3,156. (15) Deficit £200, B/S totals £1,903.

EXERCISE 11

(1) Gross profit £31,540, Net profit £6,220, B/S totals £267,205. (2) Net earnings £596 and £902. (3) Final Capital £14,110, Net profit £2,383, B/S totals £21,448. (4) Net profit £2,055, Statement total £5,792. (5) Net profit £3,208, Statement total £12,603. (6) Gross profit £613, Net profit £268, B/S totals £1,656. (7) Trading profit £2,755. (8) Gross profit £2,360, Net £1,015, B/S totals £2,397. (9) Gross profit £1,096, Net profit £300, B/S totals £1,206. (10) Gross profit £2,264, Net profit £1,078, B/S totals £5,217, Capital £3,880. (11) Net Sales £6,181. (12) Trading profit £1,392, B/S totals £6,433. (13) Gross profit £610, Net profit £424, B/S totals £876. (14) Gross profit £1,025, Net profit £642, B/S totals £1,273. (15) Adjusted profit £3,683, B/S totals £15,655. (16) Gross profit £2,085, Net profit £655, B/S totals £4,565. (17) Gross profit £8,550, Net profit £3,306, B/S totals £15,288. (18) Gross profit £7,034, Net profit £4,894, B/S totals £12,988. (19) Gross profit £382, Net profit £284, B/S totals £2,293. (20) £1,555 misappropriated.

EXERCISE 12

(1) (*a*) H.P. Gross profit £1,015, H.P. Trading profit £1,039. (*b*) General Gross profit £1,469. (*c*) Balances not due £1,654, due £30. (*d*) Stock value £2,978. (2) [1] £2,180 throughout. [2] £109, £545, £981, £1,417, £1,853, £2,180. [3] £1,595, £1,015, £435. [4] £20, £80, £80, £60. (3) (*a*) Vehicles balance £910 *Dr.* (*b*) Depreciation £364

Cr. (*c*) H.P. Co. £506 *Cr.* (4) Interest £360. (5) Year 1 Profit £314·50, Year 2 £160·50. (6) (*b*) Treat as credit sale. (7) Additional profit £126, B/S totals £7,726. (8) Overall Gross profit £4,500, taken £1,700. (9) Case Stock *Dr.* balances: In factory £280, with customers £232, Cases Reserve *Cr.* balance £580. (10) Containers Stock *Dr.* balances £416 (104 units) at warehouse, £520 (130 units) with customers. Suspense A/c *Cr.* balance £910 (130 units). (11) *Dr.* balance £10,500 on printing machine. *Cr.* £3,994 (less *Dr.* £1,997) for Machine Co. *Dr.* balance Interest Suspense A/c £49. (12) H.P. Trading Gross Profit £35, H.P. Sales balance £144 (*Cr.*), Gross profit £1,875. (13) Containers *Dr.* balances at warehouse £280, with customers £232. (14) Shortworkings Year 1 £320, Year 2 £50, Recoup £220 Year 3, Royalties paid Year 3 £630, Year 4 £950. (15) Net profit £1,815, Stock at warehouse £1,890, with customers £1,425. (16) Shortworkings 19.1 £500, 19.2 £200, Recouped in 19.3 £400. (17) Shortworkings Jan. £6·37, Feb. £3·87, March £1·69. Irrecoverable April £0·87, May £3·37. (18) B/S: Debtors £45,100 less unsold stock £2,000, Stock on hire £10,460 less unrealized charges £1,120. (19) Control A/c *Dr.* balance (with customers) £1,680, Suspense A/c *Cr.* balance £420, Stock A/c *Dr.* balance £1,710. (20) Shortworkings 19.. £1,000, Recoup 19.1 £700, 19.2 £100. Unrecoverable £200. Royalties receivable £2,400, £2,700 and £2,850. (21) Net profit £1,550, B/S totals £2,947. (22) Gross profit £51, B/S Stock on hire £190, H.P. debtors £265, less arrears £14.

EXERCISE 13

(1) Inadequate: use analysed sales book.

		Linoleum	*Carpet*
		£	£
(3)	Gross profit	6,826	3,369
	Net profit	2,977	1,445
		A	*B*
		£	£
(4)	Gross profit	18,257	11,819
	Net profit	7,438	6,487

Interest £2,654, Profit £3,757.

Percentage of gross profit to turnover *A* 22·5, *B* 25·1

Percentage of net profit to turnover *A* 9·2, *B* 13·8

(5) Total net profit £999 B/S totals £6,393.

		Excelsior	*De Luxe*
		£	£
(6)	Gross profit	4,850	10,800
	Net profit	3,823	3,959

(7) Net profit 3,317.

		Fish paste	*Sauce*
		£	£
(11)	Gross profit	33,376	15,954
	Net profit	24,048	13,955
		A	*B*
		£	£
(12)	(*a*) Stock	5,720	10,575
	(*b*) Gross profit	10,820	26,125
	(*c*) Balance	1,430 (*Cr.*)	2,025 (*Cr.*)
		Shop	*Yard*
		£	£
(13)	Gross profit	2,050	3,255
	Net profit	1,028	1,121 B/S totals £7,029

		Factory	Shop	General
		£	£	£
(14)	Gross profit	1,725	8,000	
	Net profit (loss)	(1,338)	6,106	4,779

B/S totals £15,073.

(15) Balance £2,632. Difference £11.

EXERCISE 14

(1) £1,760 Discrepancy. (2) Balance £795, Profit £736. (3) (*a*) Branch profit £1,070. (4) (*a*) Profit £1,221 on H.O. books. (*b*) Difference on debtors £2. Profit £2,038 in branch books. (5) Net profit £2,180 North, £2,030 South, B/S totals £60,144. (6) H.O. gross profit £8,500, net profit £7,300. Amersham Stock £2,000, net profit £4,650. Bexhill Stock £3,000, net profit £3,550. B/S totals £111,500. (7) TB total £47,481, Stock £3,000, Difference £1,268, Gross profit £2,953, Net profit £634. (8) TB totals H.O. £16,277. Branch £4,167, B/S totals £15,474.

		L	*E*	*D*
		£	£	£
(9)	Gross profit	13,577	8,588	8,086
	Net profit	9,130	5,132	5,482

Capitals: Finch £9,196, Green £5,915, Roberts £4,433. B/S totals: *L* £36,039, *E* £25,470, *D* £20,666.

(10) Branch profit £2,130. (11) General B/S totals £80,200. Profits: London £9,000, Swansea £6,000, Glasgow £7,200. (12) Net profit H.O. £5,515, Branch £5,334. Net profit Jan. to June £5,425, July to Dec. £5,424, B/S totals £60,169. Capital: A Rice £34,016, Sago £16,617, C. Rice £384 *Dr.* (13) Branch TB totals £58,958. Difference £3,694.

		Northern		Southern
		£		£
(14)	Gross profit	3,944		2,647
	Net profit	1,777		1,301
			£	
	General net profit		1,326	
	B/S totals		26,892	

(15) B/S totals £248,665.

		L	*N*	*B*
		£	£	£
(16)	Net cost of production	77,640	110,170	53,970
	Gross profit	30,500	74,030	29,820
	Net profit	19,510	57,700 (+380)	21,040
	TB total	38,600	66,980	29,420

		London	Crystal
		£	£
(17)	Gross profit	30,333	18,425
	Net profit	8,475	7,125
	TB totals	98,680	61,045

(18) (*a*) Stock balance £3,600, debtors £200, or (*b*) Stock £3,960, Branch Adj. £360 *Cr.* (19) TB totals £8,471, Difference £219, B/S totals £14,589. (20) TB totals £121,116, Stock £8,000, B/S totals £61,853.

	London	Domenico
	£	£
Gross profit	16,413	41,926
Net profit	11,493	32,790

(21) Branch gross profit £1,820, net profit £1,000.

EXERCISE 15

(1) Cost £125 13s. 10d., Profit £24 6s. 2d. (5) Total profit for year £132,660, TB totals £683,660. (6) (*a*) Selling price £262·50. (*b*) £800 marginal cost. (15) Prices £10,080, Sales volume £1,800, Increase in gross profits by new methods £1,100. (16) 5,000, £24 per 1,000; 25,000, £11 per 1,000; 50,000, £10 per 1,000. (17) £2·00 per hour. (18) TB totals £312,423. (19) Standard £45·15, Super £60·90. (20) (*a*) £5·29, (*b*) £5·125. (21) Cost £88·20, Price £101·43. (22) [1] £21·600; [2] £28,000; [3] £7,280; [4] (*a*) 7½%; (*b*) 20%; (*c*) 26%. (23) (*a*) £1468·20; (*b*) £3·05. (24) (*a*) £32,583, £15,630; (*b*) £16,665; (*c*) £47,705. (25) (*a*) £2,400,000; (*b*) £1,150,000; (*c*) Sales £480,000. (26) £22,780 (to nearest £10). (27) (*b*) Marginal cost A £16, B £13. Contribution A £4, B £2 per unit. (28) Sales price £10,560, Material price £672, Direct Labour Rates £3,648. Variable Overhead—Materials Price £540, Labour Price £1,080, Materials usage £688, Direct labour efficiency £5,528, Variable overhead efficiency £1,580, Fixed overhead volume £1,000, Profit £2,260. (29) Costing net profit £160,050 TB totals £595,750. (30) Standard gross profit £238,980, Actual net profit £220,876, TB totals £2,836,750 and £2,063,176. (31) Departmental profit £1,636, Commission £18 12s.

		£	£
(32)	Prime cost	25,123	10·0492 per unit
	Factory cost	35,373	14·1492 per unit
	Total cost	41,873	16·7492 per unit
	Net profit	5,711	2·284 per unit

(33) (*a*) £6,600 or £10,300 if fixed cost can be eliminated. (34) 120%. (35) TB totals £216,336. Private ledger £84,850. (36) Prime cost 120%, Direct wages 200%, Direct materials 300%, Machine hours £0·66 per hour, Labour hours £0·375 per hour. (37) (*a*) AB £75,000, CD £105,000, (*b*) (i) CD, (ii) AB. (38) Standard gross profit £23,000, Standard net profit £9,000, Actual net profit £8,450. (39) (*b*) Costing profit £8,200 + overhead over-recovered £1,250 — overhead under-recovered £260 + Dividends £450 — Preliminary expenses and Goodwill £1,500 = £8,140. (40) (*b*) TB totals £43,348.

EXERCISE 16

(1) No. 1 Profit taken £800, c/f £700, No. 2 Profit taken £6,368 c/f £4,869. (2) Manufacturing cost £18,750, Gross profit £10,150, Net Profit £2,450. (3) Contract profit £3,400 (⅔ of £5,100).

		PIP	*GLOBE*
		£	£
(4)	Cost of production	65,600	—
	Gross profit	30,400	11,000

(5) Factory cost of 7,200 units—£108,000, Gross profit £22,290, B/S totals £44,700. (6) Gross profits on No. 1 £3,095, No. 2 £2,854, No. 3 £284, Net profit £968, B/S totals £9,568. (7) (i) Prime cost £2,440; (ii) Works expenses £1,944; (iii) Cost of Sales £4,221; (iv) Admin. expenses £1,231, Net profit £2,119, B/S totals £63,999. (8) Profit taken £10,222, reserved £8,944. (9) Net factory cost of production £851,510, Gross profit £132,740, Net profit £38,700, B/S totals £527,385.

		Year 1	*Year 2*
(10)	Materials	66%	67%
	Wages	27%	27%
	Expenses	7%	6%

(11) Cost of production £35,311, Gross profit £21,530, Net profit £11,432. (12) Year 1 94·33%, Year 2 92·87% on Production. (13) Profit £1,323, B/S totals at start £17,470, at end £34,419. (14) (i) Customers A/c balance £28,000 (ii) Profit on contract £2,968; (iii) Fixed assets £440 plus current £300, plus work-in-progress £36,608 less cash £28,000. (15) Profit taken £2,400 (⅔ of £3,600). (16) (i) 8·75; (ii) 32%; (iii) £12 per

ton. (17) (*b*) £420 loss; (*c*) £5,550 profit. (18) *Cr.* Profit and Loss Year 1 £2,400, Year 2 £5,712, Year 3 £7,425. (19) Unit costs October £1·928 November £1·878. (20) (i) Closing stock £33,000; (ii) Gross profit £57,500; (iii) £0·625 average gross profit per unit sold. (21) Closing stock £16,000, Gross profit £21,788, Net profit £14,388. (22) Net factory cost transferred £194,745, Gross profit £31,070, Net profit £20,368, B/S totals £152,186. (23) 1965 Profit £3,767; 1966 Loss £963. (24) Balance £24, 273. (25) Profit to date £47,800, Profit taken £26,280. (26) Gross profit £14,405, Net profit £10,490, B/S totals £34,665. (27) Factory profit £2,820, Warehouse profit £15,020, Balance £16,815. (28) No. 101 Transfer 1963 £8,986, 1964 £9,054 (loss), No. 202 Transfer 1964 £16,550. (29) Equivalent units 2020, cost £5·8 per unit, Work-in-progress 300 cost £1,044. (30) Cost of production £8,685 at £0·225 per tin. Trading profit £1,960 at £0·050 per tin. Net profit £2,015.

EXERCISE 17

(2) Interest £17·92, Balance £177·08. (3) Current accounts: Bee *Dr.* £243, Dee *Cr.* £87, Gee *Cr.* £216. (4) Profit and Loss Adjustment £2,205. Debit Capitals old shares. Credit D £1,046, B £785, P £374. (5) Gross profit £6,425, Net Profit £3,650, B/S totals £30,670. (6) Gross profit £11,306, Net Loss £2,810 each, B/S totals £85,810. (7) Shares of profits: Tupp £3,640, Sedge £1,820, Palmer £120, B/S totals £10,880. (8) Capital *Cr* balances X £3,000, Y £2,235, Z £765. (9) (*a*) Current A/cs: Rudd £298, Butler £182; (*b*) Capital A/cs: Rudd £7,298, Butler £4,682. (10) *Dr.* Cash £1·500. (11) *Cr.* Fletcher Capital £2,300 (*Dr.* Cash). *Dr.* Goodwill £300 (*Cr.* Cash). (12) Weighted annual profit approx. £14,000, Goodwill on 3 years purchase £42,000. (13) Gross profit £16,000, Net profit £4,620, B/S totals £25,100, Current A/cs Credit Balances; Road £2,402, Lane £1,508, Street £1,250. (14) Approx. contribution Black & White 55% of assets, Brown & Green 45%. Partners take, Black 29%, White 26%, Brown 27%, Green 18%. Balance Sheet Net Asset value £56,600. On this basis B/S totals £68,755. (15) Adjusted balances: George £9,254, Fred, £5,727, Mike £6,439. (16) Cash £701. (17) Gross profit £20,220, Net profit £7,980, B/S totals £43,404. (18) (*a*) Austin *Cr.* Balance £7,316·25, Bell & Cooper *Cr.* £4,877·50. (*b*) Peters brings in £2,438·75. (19) Bank balance £268 *Dr.*, Cost of Rooms; Tooth £690, Kinfoot £230, B/S totals £518. (20) Gross profit £26,234. Managers commission; R £242, S £116, net profit after remuneration £10,242. Current A/cs: X £1,076 *Cr.*, Y £1,242 *Cr.*, Z £483 *Dr.* B/S totals £34,654. (21) A £1,260, B £709, C £551. (22) Profits £2,572, Simpson's capital was £4,590. (23) Business Purchase Balance £3,433. Net profit [1] £1,049. [2] £1,233. [3] £1,324. [4] £1,689. [5] £1,616. (24) Net profit £5,812, B/S total £18,994, Current A/cs AG £898, JG £630, H £630. (25) Net profit £2,074. (26) Net profit £1,722 each. (27) Net profit £3,504 each. (28) Net profit JS £960, HR £640. (29) Due to Brown £0·19 from Green. (30) Profit £330.

EXERCISE 18

(1) Profit on realization £186·50 each. (2) Loss on realization £375 each. (3) *Cr.* balances: Black £3,275, White £5,625. (4) (*a*) Capitals as stated, (*b*) R £75, L £60, S £45, (*c*) Capitals less £1,040·66. (5) Loss £3,020. Hawker receives advances of £1,500 plus £1,284 Capital. Haigh receives advances of £196. (6) Deficiency £1,000 each. Contributions to Dunnit, Bean £2,770, Gonne £1,730. Cash £5,230 to Bean. £3,270 to Gonne. (7) Net profit £6,760, B/S total £10,370, Loss on realization £2,038. Capital—Black £5,130, White £3,692. Cash—Black £192, White brings in £12. (8) Loss £522. W £4,768, H £3,326, B £2,384. (9) Loss Partridge £1,620, Paterson £810. (10) Profit £9,420. B/S total £35,420. (11) Z deficit £180 to X, £150 to Y. Cash £6,080 to X, £5,006 to Y. (12) X receives £5,760 net, Y £3,840 net. (13) Profit £1,500. C deficit £250. B receives £4,389. A receives £5,611. (14) Loss: Briar £630, Paulsen £525, Rose £420. Cash: Briar £3,850, Paulsen £4,735, Rose £1,317. (15) Loss £900. Brown receives £3,229. Jones £1,837. (16) Creditors receive 76p in £ or

£9,200 total. (17) Profit £576. Cash Wyatt £6,288, Dawson £4,288. (18) Loss £780. Lamb £7,780 Cash. Crow brings in £30. (19) Profit £9,500. Cash Duke £8,550, Earl £2,850. (20) (*a*) Profit £9,500, (*b*) Brick £8,970, Stone £5,980, (*c*) Shares: Brick £4,800, Stone £3,200. Cash: Brick £8,970, Stone £5,980. (21) Loss £1,140. Cash G £4,265, K £1,050. (22) Loss £2,374, Creditors receive £2,201. Hardy takes *Cr.* £36 from Ivor. Dividend 64p in the £. (23) Profit £12,000, Cash to Grove £1,800, to Lane £1,900. Consideration—£14,300 Cash, £10,000 Preference and £10,000 Ordinary shares. (24) Profit £9,850. Cole brings in £90, Porter receives £8,940. (25) Due to Oates £384, to his estate £40. Transferred to Reps. £3,600. *Cr.* balance on 31st October £1,200. (26) Henry, Loan £15,720. Capital A/c balances, John £13,930, Kenneth £11,950, Lambert £5,200. B/S totals £50,000. (27) (*a*) Balance £7,956; (*b*) Final payment Year 6 £80.

EXERCISE 19

Questions 1–9 are on statistical books and should follow the text. (10) Fixed interest safer. Ordinary shares better for growth, especially if inflation.

EXERCISE 20

(1) TB totals £280,000. Cash £280,000, Ordinary shares £200,000, Debentures £80,000. (2) TB totals £309,000. Premiums: on shares £25,000, on debentures £4,000. (3) Discount £4,000. B/S totals £80,000. (4) Application £25,000, Allotment £75,000, First Call £50,000, Final call £50,000. (5) Application £75,000, Allotment £50,000, First Call £50,000, Final Call £50,000. B/S totals £225,000. (6) Application £16,000, Allotment £24,000, Call £40,000. (7) Application £16,000. Premium £8,000. Allotment £72,000, B/S totals £88,000. (8) Application £16,000. Discount £8,000, Allotment £56,000, B/S totals £80,000. (9) Cash received £28,750 on Application, £48,125 on Allotment. Cash repaid £1,875. Balance £75,000. (10) Cash received on Application £25,000, on Allotment £25,000, on Call £50,037·50. (11) Cash received on Application £25,000, on Allotment £24,750. Cash balance £21,750. B/S totals £70,500. (12) Cash on Application: £45,000 Ordinary, £15,000 Preference. 1st August Call on Preference shares £11,500. 20th October Forfeited shares re-issued £1,500 Cash. Premium £500. (13) Gross profit £6,225, Net profit £2,956, B/S totals £28,518. (14) Cash received on Application and Allotment £37,600, Discount £7,500. Returned £4,600 cash. Balance on allotment £84,500. Call £125,000, Cash £124,600. In arrear £400. (15) (*a*) Discount £2,000. (*b*) B/S totals £300,000. (*c*) £60,000 Converted to £39,000 nominal, £21,000 Premium. (*d*) B/S totals £298,000. (16) (*b*) 19.. Preference £7,500, Ordinary £12,500. 19.1 Preference £6,000, Ordinary £11,000, 19.2 Preference £7,500, Ordinary £15,500. If £20,000 distributed each year Preference £22,500, Ordinary £37,500. (17) Gross profit £36,150, Net profit £18,262, Remuneration £1,826, B/S totals £136,262. (18) Operating profits: £2,776 Haulage, £1,294 £1,294 Repairs, £10,008 Car Trading, £5,691 Car Sales Net profit, £5,571 General Net profit. Interest: on calls in arrear £20, on calls in advance £50, B/S totals £87,075. (19) Gross profit £7,978, Net profit £872, B/S totals £85,631. (20) Gross profit £11,366. Net profit £5,507, B/S totals £61,240.

EXERCISE 21

(1) See pp. 1713 and 2109. (2) Corporation Tax £8,000, Preference Dividend £3,000 less tax £1,350, Ordinary share dividend £4,800 less tax £2,160, Balance £2,700. (3) TB totals £111,976. Gross profit £13,683, Net profit £3,225, B/S totals £56,101. Working capital ratio 4:1, Proposed dividend £1,800. Rise in stock levels affects profits. High bad debts provision. (4) Balance £5,513, B/S totals £41,301. (5) (*a*) Net profit £14,670, (*b*) £2,079 to be capitalized. (6) Net profit £986,533, balance after appropriations £539,150. B/S totals £7,336,591. (7) Gross profit £11,344, Net profit £5,071, Share of profit £693·50. B/S totals £24,359. (8) TB totals £122,647, Balance

on appropriation £557, B/S totals £122,107. (9) Gross profit £18,562. Net profit £9,000. Unappropriated £5,890. B/S totals £127,470. (10) Balance £7,475. Preference Dividend £300, Ordinary Share Dividend £2,500, B/S totals £39,225. (11) *Dr.* Business Purchase, *Cr.* Vendor £80,000. *Dr.* Assets, *Cr.* Business Purchase £80,000. *Dr.* Vendor, *Cr.* Share Capital £10,000. *Dr.* Application £12,500, Allotment £12,500, First Call £25,000, Final Call £50,000, *Cr.* Share Capital £100,000. *Dr.* Application, *Cr.* Allotment £1,250. *Dr.* Cash £97,000, *Cr.* Application £13,750, Allotment £11,250, First Call £24,000, Final Call £48,000. (12) Gross profit £10,900, Net profit £7,040, B/S totals £58,467. (13) Bank (*Dr.*) Unclaimed dividends (*Cr.*) £335·55. (14) (*a*) Yes, (*b*) Yes, (*c*) Only if asset revalued and Articles allow. (15) See p. 0617. (16) Gross profit £65,335, Net profit £26,222, Balance c/f £3,678. (17) Gross profit £5,788, Net profit £1,756. Unappropriated balance £8,006, B/S totals £39,756. (18) B/S totals £129,016, Unappropriated balance £1,843. (19) Gross profit £4,820, Net profit £1,756, B/S totals £27,468, Unappropriated £5,256. (20) *Dr.* General Reserve, *Cr.* Ordinary Share Capital £20,000. 28th Feb. Cash £25,000; 1st Mar. Cash £39,000, Discount £1,000. 31st Mar. £24,000 Cash. 2nd July *Dr.* Royalties, 31st Aug. *Dr.* Interim Dividend, 31st Dec. *Dr.* Debenture Interest £1,500, Royalties £6,000.

EXERCISE 22

(1) See p. 2203. (2) TB totals £315,000. B/S total £291,550. (3) (*a*) Current assets; (*b*) Fixed assets; (*c*) Current assets; (*d*) Note to B/S. (4) Deduct Depreciation from Fixed assets; Bad Debt provision from Debtors. Other items are reserves: Share premium and revaluation of assets excess are capital reserves. Revenue reserves total £86,474. (5) Available profit £4,365. B/S total £60,860. (6) Net profit on trading £18,950. Available profit £6,000, B/S totals £87,700. (7) B/S totals £82,280. (8) B/S totals £35,869. (9) B/S totals £257,456. (10) (*a*) At 31st Dec. 19.1 Cost £103,900, Depreciation £56,650, Book Value £47,250. (11) Sinking Fund Reserve £14,850 (Policy £14,850 fixed asset), Guarantee contingent liability £20,000. (12) (i) No; (ii) Show profit on sale separately. Cost £18,350 less Depreciation £9,930. (13) See text. (14) Sale of assets or know-how. Changes in method of accounting for stocks or depreciation. (15) Must publish names of valuers and qualifications. Surplus to reserve, not available for dividends. May meet losses due to excessive depreciation. (16) (i) Quite legal. (ii) May be desirable. (iii) Reserve £420,500. (iv) Excess depreciation may be taken back to Revenue reserves. (v) Dividends depend on cash availability. (17) See text. (18) Gross profit £13,884, Net profit £3,872. Total for appropriation £14,672, B/S totals £40,778. (19) Do not recommend cash distribution of capital profits. Better to issue bonus shares. (20) See p. 2213 of text. Companies Act, 1967, newly requires all but first two items.

EXERCISE 23

(1) Fund instalment £1,431, *Dr.* Profit and Loss, *Cr.* Redemption Fund; also *Dr.* Redemption Fund Investment, *Cr.* Cash. Interest £72 first year: rising annually to £789 in Year 10. (3) *Cr.* Debenture £14,250 Cash, £750 Discount. (4) Redemption Fund balance £55,760. Profit on 4% Funding £4,040, on 3½% War Stock £620. Debenture interest £417 less tax £104. Cash balance £5,447. (5) Debenture balance £57,000, Redemption reserve £42,461, Interest £2,725. (6) B/S totals £188,000. Capital £116,000, Share premium £3,600, Investments £12,000. (7) Cash £72,800, 4½% Debentures £140,000. Premium £12,800, Fund balance £103,400, Investment balance £57,500. (8) (*a*) £60,000 on application, £35,000 on allotment. Final receipts on allotment £5,000. (*b*) Ten months interest £5,000 less £2,125 tax, Discount w/o £250. (9) Profit and Loss A/c £490. Interest received £78. Invested £568. Profit on Redemption £7, on investment realized £15. (10) Sinking Fund Balance £27,404, on Investments £3,450. (11) Converted £105,000 plus £5,250 premium, Unconverted £152,250. Received on Application and Allotment £91,000. Unsuccessful cash

£34,000. Discount on issue £4,000. Premium on Redemption £12,500. (12) Gross profit £12,000. Net profit £7,600. (13) Premium £1,000. Stock £100,000, Bank loans £15,000. (14) See p. 2004. (15) Cash on Application £52,000. Cash returned £6,500. Calls in advance £7,000, First call £18,000 received, second £25,000. Premium on Redemption £4,000. (16) State Authorized Capital. Issued £300,000, Reserves £35,000, Long term liabilities £95,000, Current liabilities £65,000. Separate Goodwill £40,000, Group fixed assets (including loose tools) and current assets £184,500. Other debit balances £10,500. (17) Before option balance on Sinking Fund £457,419. Premium on Redemption £9,000. Profit on realization £31,000. Surplus assets £29,419.

EXERCISE 24

(1) Profit on realization £200 *Cr*. Investments £15,000 *Cr*. Cash £15,200 *Dr*. Redemption P.S. *Dr*. £20,000, Share Premium *Dr*. £2,000, *Cr*. Redemption £22,000. *Dr*. Redemption A/c *Cr*. Cash £22,000. *Dr*. General Reserve *Cr*. Redemption Fund £20,000. *Dr*. Redemption Fund £20,000, Share Premium £15,000, General Reserve £10,000, *Cr*. Bonus issue £45,000. *Dr*. Bonus Issue *Cr*. Share Capital £45,000. B/S totals £127,200. (2) *Dr*. Bank *Cr*. Redeemable Preference Capital £20,000. *Dr*. Bank £52,000 *Cr*. Redeemable Preference Capital £50,000 Premium £2,500 *Dr*. Profit and Loss *Cr*. Redemption Reserve Fund £32,500. *Dr*. Redemption Reserve Fund *Cr*. Premium A/c £2,500. (3) Reserve Fund £87,500 Premium on shares £37,500. (4) Premium £600, Reserve Fund £6,000. (5) B/S totals £104,000, Cash £6,000. Capital reserve £13,000. Profit and Loss balance £2,000. (6) Premium £3,000, Ordinary Shares £65,000, Reserve Fund £28,000, Profit and Loss Balance £16,500. (7) General Reserve Balance £28,740, Preference Shares £122,640, Redemption Reserve £126,360, Nominal redeemed £249,000. (8) General Reserve £14,370, Reserve Fund £63,180, Cash received Jan. £124,500, May £61,320. Paid May £136,950. (9) Premium £5,000. Reserve £50,000. (10) Premium £2,000 on issue £1,500 on redemption. Redemption Reserve £5,000.

EXERCISE 25

(1) Goodwill £5,550. (2) Value patents at £6,003. Write off Preliminary expenses £4,870. (3) Gross profit £10,110, Net profit £6,527 less interest £20, preliminary expenses £400 and goodwill £752. B/S totals £45,078. (4) B/S totals £156,000. Ordinary shares £37,206, Preference £37,400. (5) *Structures*—Sale price £122,800 less Creditors £19,800. Shares in E £37,500. Loss £7,500 on Realization. *Erectors*—Purchase price £103,000, Assets £122,800, Creditors £19,800. Share Premium £7,500, Cancel Debentures and Shares in Structures. Loss on investment £5,000. (6) Prior to incorporation, loss £65. After, profit of £1,873. (7) B/S totals £24,300. (8) Net profit £12,149, after appropriations £8,026, B/S £40,648. (9) B/S totals £55,350. (10) (i) See text. (ii) *Dr*. Reserves *Cr*. Share Capital. (11) Profit on realization £19,727. Pay £128 to Fence. B/S totals £54,410, Share Premium £4,410. (12) B/S total £30,400, Grand 7 for 3, Palace 615 for 400. (13) Gross Profit £30,500 for 15 months. £6,100 to A.B. Trading profit £8,900 for 15 months, £1,780 to A.B. Balance A.B. Ltd. £493. A.B. Ltd. B/S totals £141,980. Balance owing to A.B. £1,730. (14) [1] Shares £25,000 plus £5,000 premium, Cost of Control £3,750. [2] Shares £53,000 plus £10,600 premium, £42,400 cash, cost of control £13,250. Issued Capital £1,078,000. Cost of investment £136,000. (15) Ordinary Application £1,100, Allotment £4,400. Preference Application £5,000, Allotment £10,000. First call: Ordinary £5,500, Preference £10,000. (16) B/S totals £60,900. (17) Gross profit £6,110, Net profit £1,322, Dividend £1,120. B/S totals £50,689. (18) Goodwill £42,000. Preference Shares Application £6,250, Allotment £15,625, First call £62,500, Final call £46,875, Payment to vendor £95,000. B/S totals £341,250. (19) Profit on realization £1,200. Paid £6,800 to A and £4,400 to B. 20 (*a*) F profit on realization £1,545, Shares in Z £6,545. (*b*) R & J profit on realization £1,710 each, Shares in Z £6,530 R and £8,625 J. (*c*) Z B/S totals

£28,865. (21) B/S totals £340,000, A receives 1·75 shares in A.B. for every share held, B receives £5 for every £8 worth held. (22) £24,000 paid for Goodwill in T, £750 paid for Goodwill in S, B/S totals £176,750. (23) (*a*) Ordinary shares: Pink £32,400, Green £21,600. Preference shares: Pink £13,100, Green £6,900. (*c*) Profits £5,520 to partnership, £1,240 to Company. (*d*) Cash withdrawn £1,812 Pink, £908 Green. (*e*) B/S totals £78,410. (24) Cash £75,000, Share premium £10,000. (25) Goodwill £20,000. B/S totals £216,040. (26) Cash paid out Flint £1,450, Stone £2,500. Received £1,250 from Rock. B/S totals £51,000. (27) *Cr*. Capital Reserves £85,000. Bonus £75,000. (28) Net profit £21,240, Balance c/f £23,616, B/S totals £66,574. Cost of control in Pins £16,600. Unrealized profit in stock of Pins £576. (29) B/S totals £180,200, Goodwill in Corn £5,500, Capital Reserve for Straw £1,700. (30) B/S totals £303,350. Eastward Goodwill £9,150, Southward Goodwill £2,400. (31) Net Receipts £16,890, Cash balance £65,490. B/S totals £111,120. (32) Profit on sale of assets £15,970. B/S totals £144,470, Goodwill £16,715 Cash £53,240. (33) B/S totals £247,900. Sparkle Goodwill £6,000, Glitter Goodwill £1,900, Adjusted profit for Gleam £16,400. (34) B/S totals £511,500, Preference £220,000, Ordinary £67,500, Creditors £144,000. Cash £152,000. (35) To B 41,130, To W 19,170 shares allotted. 2,130 from W to B. Share capital £30,150, Fixed Assets £21,200, Current assets £14,850 less Creditors £6,650, Formation expenses £750. (36) Vendors £118,500: Cash £9,900, Share Capital £80,000, Premium £16,000. Debentures £13,125 (discount £525). Write off discount against Premium. (37) Price of Wynne £232,500, of Garde £110,000. Wyngarde B/S totals £405,586, Goodwill £45,094. (38) *Dr*. Investment *Cr*. Cash £1,500 (in each Company). B/S of Unit Co. £98,000 total. (39) B/S total £238,500, Goodwill, Beta £4,500, Gamma £14,000, Profit £102,800. (40) Profit on realization £27,540, Price paid £107,600. B pays £63,140 for Goodwill. (41) Each shareholder £10,000 in shares, £3,284 investments, £1,481 8s. cash. B/S totals £55,674. (42) B/S totals £205,000.

EXERCISE 26

(1) Deficiency £3,245. (2) Deficiency £62. (3) Deficiency £15,509, 37½p in £. (4) Deficiency £1,950. (5) Deficiency £1,400. (6) Deficiency £2,675. (7) Deficiency £9,820. (8) Surplus £163. (9) Deficiency £5,020. (10) Deficiency £3,769. (11) Deficiency £74,178. (12) Deficiency £3,368. (13) Deficiency £2,370. (14) Deficiency £19,600. (15) £750. (16) Deficiency £388·75. (17) Deficiency £927. (18) Deficiency £5,086. (19) Deficiency £650. (20) Deficiency £21,048. (21) Deficiency £21,761. (22) Deficiency £2,047. (23) Deficiency £18,700. (24) Deficiency of firm £4,723; surplus of Alfred £725; of Benjamin £881; Charles's statement balances. (25) Deficiency £23,292. (26) Balance due to A £70. (27) Balance £26. (28) First and final dividend of 32p in £. (29) Net profit £3,238; B/S totals £58,511.

EXERCISE 27

(1) Deficiency £725. (2) Deficiency £26,550. (3) Balance £2; total of liquidator's A/c £7,682. (4) Liquidator's remuneration £504 and £126; dividend £5,064. (6) Deficiency £1,070. (7) B/S totals £4,992; deficiency £660. (8) Dividend £0·41 in £. (9) B/S totals £45,000. (10) Ordinary shareholders £9,000 after remuneration of £225 to liquidator.

EXERCISE 28

(1) See p. 2801. (2) *Dr*. Brown £240 *Cr*. Purchase Tax £40, Sales £200. (3) Net wages £2,850, Employers contribution £600, Stock of stamps £2,250. (4) No. (5) (i) No, (ii) Sometimes, (iii) No, (iv) No, (v) Yes, (vi) No, (vii) No, (viii) Yes. (6) Debenture interest, Depreciation, Goodwill, Bad Debts Provision. Some subscriptions and donations. (7) N.I. stamps balance £9,240. Net wages £4,300, Employers N.I. £800, SET £300, Redundancy £20. (8) [1] *Actual* Refunds £3,000 quarterly plus

£900 premium. Profit and Loss debit SET £12,000 Credit £11,700. [2] *Refund Accrual* Profit and Loss debit SET nil, credit £2,700, Premiums £3,000 Refund Receivable. [3] *Premium and Refund Accrual* Profit and Loss Credit Premiums and Refunds £15,600 less £12,000. £3,900 receivable. (9) Opening provision £1,500, closing £1,875. Levy £2,125. (10) Assessable profit £9,000, Taxable £6,580, Partners liable for: B £839·625, J £795·175, K £748·950. (11) (i) Apportion tax payable on time basis to each financial year. (ii) Yes. (12) Yes on (*a*) and (*b*). (13) Add back (*a*) and (*d*). Deduct (*c*)—capital. (14) (*a*) and (*d*) capital. Add back (*b*) and 100% claimed for (*c*). (15) £1,510 before allowances. (16) Taxable profit £38,414, Profit after tax £22,770. Unappropriated profit £27,344, Profit on investments to Reserve. (17) Provision £1,800, Grants receivable £2,160, Cash paid £1,687. (18) Profit before tax £27,049, Corporation tax £15,000, Balance £7,508, B/S totals £239,715. (19) Gross profit £79,402, Net before tax £57,533, Unappropriated £26,182. (20) Gross income £14,307, Balancing charge £29, Taxable income £13,891. (21) Balancing allowance £2,000. (22) Assessable profit £11,200, Totals A £5,910, B £4,173, D £1,117. (23) (i) See p. 2868. (ii) £102,400. (24) (*a*) £47,500, £42,500, £42,500, £42,500. (*b*) £42,000, £29,500, £49,625, £49,719. (*c*) £5,500 credit, £13,000 credit, £7,125 debit, £7,219 debit.

EXERCISE 29

(1) (*a*) £97,700, (*b*) £104,900, (*c*) £97,400. No effect. (2) (*a*) 13,500 tons, (*b*) £30·66 per ton. (3) (*a*) 19.. £57,000, 19.1 £88,000; (*b*) 19.. £202,000, 19.1 £217,000; (*c*) 9·93 times. (4) Stock discrepancy Closing £900 net £1,200 (both years). Sales up 10%. Gross profit down to 19%. Net profit down to 3% of Sales. Expenses up to 16%. (5) [1] Not available for dividends; [2] 1,000 shares £725; [3] £2,250,000; [4] 10·62%. (6) (*a*) Irrelevant; (*b*) Value shares on yield. (7) (*a*) See p. 2905; (*b*) [1] Up £5,407; [3] Down £672; [4] Down £103; [7] Down £2,732; [8] Down £1,422; [9] Up £160; [10] Down £980; [11] Down £300. [2], [5] and [6] no effect. (*c*) No. (8) See text pp. 1709 and 2501 *et seq*. (9) (*a*) Gross profit £72,000, Net profit £16,500; (*b*) Cash required £57,700; (*c*) 21·6%. (10) Purchase price £54,000, Cash £8,775, Goodwill £6,000, Share premium £18,225 less expenses £780. (11) Add £1,080 to Goodwill. (12) (*a*) *B* Net assets £62,000, Average net profit £10,050, Super £3,850, Goodwill 5 years purchase £19,250, Price £81,250. (*b*) *I* Net assets £250,000, Average net profit £54,480, Goodwill (as for *B*) £147,400, Price £450,400. One £1 in Investors for 6⅜ 25p in *B*.

		19.9 £	*19.8* £
(13)	Profit for appropriation	2,241,580	2,776,583
	After appropriations	1,019,397	849,603
	B/S totals	21,995,310	19,424,303

(14) Increase in debtors £445,000 in Creditors £60,000. Longer credit given on sales. Shorter credit taken on purchases. Rise in stocks. Margins have fallen to 26·6%. (15) *Dr*. Cap. Reduction *Cr*. Assets £198,000. *Dr*. 8% Cum. Pref. £60,000 *Cr*. 6% Cum. Pref. £200,000 10% Preferred £200,000, 5s. Ordinary £74,000, Capital Reduction A/c £126,000. *Dr*. £1 Ordinary £400,000 *Cr*. 5s. Ordinary £100,000, Capital Reduction A/c £300,000. *Dr*. Capital Reduction £228,000, *Cr*. Profit and Loss, B/S totals £774,000. (16) Net profit £29,540, B/S totals £345,920 (or £372,398). (17) (*a*) *Dr*. Assets *Cr*. Div. Equalization Reserve £35,000, *Dr*. Investments *Cr*. Pension Fund £5,000. (*b*) Cost would rise. (18) Decrease of Net Working Capital £7,000. Loss £300. Assets purchased £48,700. (19) (*a*) Gross profit £24,000, Net profit £9,000, B/S totals £75,500. (*b*) Final balance £500, o/draft max. £4,500. (20) Insufficient security. Bad policy, poor management. Refuse. (24) Cash balance 30th June, 19.1, £3,500; gross profit £18,750; net profit £8,250; B/S totals £59,500. (27) *Uses* Assets £14,000, Debtors £7,500, Cash £9,000, Overdraft reduced £13,375, Dividends £2,750, Tax paid £11,950. *Sources* Shares issued £10,000, Profit £38,500, Investment income £450, Creditors £425, Stocks decreased £9,200. (28) See text. (29) Working capital deficiency £12,000.

Long-term finance needed. (30) (*a*) Total payments £356,250, receipts £350,000. Increase in overdraft £6,250. (*b*) *Sources* Share issue £5,000, Profits £33,250, Overdraft £6,250. *Uses* Dividends £2,500, Tax paid £8,000 Assets £20,000. Net Working Capital £94,250. (31) Equivalent cash price £10,798·35. (32) Net cash investment £115,000, returns £55,000 p.a. Year 10 £10,000 from Assets, £20,000 from Working. Capital. (33) N.P.V. at 10% £350,040. Pay back 2 years 33 days. (34) N.P.V. £36,100 at 10%. Not worthwhile. N.P.V. £38,395 at 8%. Not quite worthwhile. N.P.V. £40,895 at 6%. Worthwhile. (35) (*a*) About 27%, (*b*) About 20%, (*c*) 6½ years.

INDEX

ABSORPTION of companies, 2519–22
Acceptance, letter of, 1927
Accommodation bill, 0402, 0415
Account payee only, 0443
Accountancy charge, 0210
Accountants, partnerships, 1701
Accounting—
cost, 1501–57
cycle, 0216–17
definition, 0101
macro, 0101
methods, 0108
micro, 0101
principles, 0101
systems, 0501–34
Accounting Standards Steering Committee (A.S.S.C.), 0101, 2102, 2868
Accounts—
adjustment, 0504–07
book of, 1920
branch, 1401–44
business purchase, 2502
capital, 0201
consignment, 0901–13
consolidated, 2533–46
control, 0504–34
current, 1711
deficiency, 2620–5
definition, 0103, 0106
departmental, 1301–15
disclosure, 1903
drawing, 1710–11
final, 0104, 0201–2, 0305, 1711, 1719–24
fixed capital, 1706–7
group, 2501, 2531, 2533–5
head office, 1417–18
impersonal, 0106
interpretation, 0250–51
investment, 0815–26
manufacturing, 1601–9
nominal, 0106, 0502
partnership, 1701–34
period, 0202
personal, 0106, 0502
profit and loss, 0208–12, 1604, 2211–13, 2545–6, 2934
property, 0106
published, 2201–27
real, 0106, 0501
revenue, 0201
sales, 0903
sectional balancing, 0503
suspense, 0303–4
Accrual concept, 0104, 0204
Accruing income, 0218
Actuarial method of interest apportionment, 1208–11
Adjustment account, 0503–33
branch, 1407–8
Adjustments, trial balance, 0203
Administration order, 2605
Administration overhead, 1503
Advance—
calls in, 2021–2
payments in, 0217
Advance Corporation Tax (A.C.T.), 2858
Advances—
by partners, 1707
on consignment, 0902
Advertisements (Hire Purchase) Act, 1957, 1202
Advertising, 0210
Advice notes, 0117
Agency bills, 0404
Allotment—
book, 1922–30
letter of, 1925
Allowances—
capital, 2862–7
Allowances against tax, 2802–3
Amalgamation—
by absorption, 2519–22
of limited companies, 2509–22
Ammonia Soda Co. Ltd. v. *Chamberlain*, 2102
Amortization fund account, 0614
Annual Allowances, 2871
Annual contribution chart, 1541–2
Annual return, 1950–51
Annuity system of depreciation, 0611–12
Application and allotments book, 1922–29
Applications for debentures, 1942
Apportionments, 0218
Appreciation, 0602
Appropriation account, 2112–15
Arrears—
calls in, 2021
cumulative preference shares, 2115–16
payments in, 0217–18
Articles of association, 1907
Asset, financing acquisitions, 1201–1231
Assets—
acquisition, 0601
adjustment on admission of new partners, 1717
balance sheet, 0202–3, 2904–5, 2911–15
current, 0212
definition, 0212
depreciation, 0601–31, 1410–11
distribution on partnership dissolution, 1802–3
fictitious, 0213
fixed, 0212
incomplete records, 1101–12

Assets (*contd.*)—
intangible, 0213
liquid, 0213
provided by long-term funds, 2911, 2914
provided by Ordinary Shareholders, 2911, 2914–15
published accounts, 2201–27
revaluation, 1821
sale of, 0609
tangible, 0213
turnover rate, 2918
wasting, 0213
writing down, 2527–30
Association of Certified and Corporate Accountants, 0101
Audit, 1916
Audit fee, 0211–12, 2212
Authorized capital, 1918
Average price, stock valuation, 0705

BAD debts, 0212, 0248–9
hire purchase, 1212–13
Balance sheet, 0212–17
calls, 2021–3
consolidated, 2536–45
definition, 0102, 0202
errors, 0250
interpretation, 2904
preparation, 0212 *et seq.*
presentation, 2902–4
Balances—
credit, 0106
debit, 0106
Balancing—
allowances and charges, 2871–3
cash books, 0111
definition, 0103
investment accounts, 0817
Bank—
balances, 0113–14
cash books, 0112, 0509–19
charges, 0210
debentures issued to, 2314
drafts, 0431, 1438
giro, 0431–6
loans, 0213, 2107
notes, 0430–1
overdrafts, 2107
reconciliation, 0112–13
Banking and discount companies, 2214
Bankruptcy, 2601–31
administration order, 2605
annulment of adjudication, 2605
bills of exchange, 0401, 2607, 2617
committee of inspection, 2603
courts, 2601
creditors, 2606–7, 2615–16, 2629
creditors' meetings, 2603
deed of arrangement, 2603
deficiency account, 2602–5
discharged, 2604
dividend distribution, 2630
Bankruptcy (*contd.*)—
estates account, 2626–30
interest on debts, 2630
laws of, 2601
liabilities of debtors, 2607
partners, 1801, 2605
petitions, 2602
property, 2616, 2629
public examination, 2604
receiving order, 2602
small, 2605
statement of affairs, 2602, 2606–20
trustees account, 2626–31
unclaimed funds, 2631
undischarged, 2605
Base stock valuation, 0705
Batch processing, computer, 0129
Batching, apportionment of interest, 1215–16
Bear, 0810
Bearer cheque, 0439
Bill books, 0120, 0421, 0519, 0905
Bill of lading, 0424
Bill stamps, 0211
Bills of exchange, 0401–28
acceptance, 0403, 0406–8
acceptance honour *supra* protest, 0413–4
accommodation, 0402, 0415
advantages, 0402
agency, 0404
alteration, 0414
bank drafts, 0431
bankruptcy, 0407, 2607–8, 2617
books, 0120, 0421, 0519, 0905
cheques, 0439–49
commercial, 1438
consideration, 0410
damages on dishonour, 0413
dates of, 0404–5
days of grace, 0405
definition, 0401–2
delivery, 0408
discharge, 0415
dishonour, 0410–11, 0413, 0418–19
documentary, 0404, 0424, 0427–8
domicile, 0406
endorsement, 0408–9
fine bank, 0404
foreign, 0421, 0422–3
foreign domicile, 0404
forgery, 0414
form of, 0402, 0422
holder in due course, 0413
kinds of, 0402
letters of hypothecation, 0425
liability of parties to, 0403
lost, 0414
moratorium, 0415
negotiation, 0408
negotiation back, 0409
non-acceptance, 0407
non-payment, 0410–11

Bills of exchange (*contd.*)—
noting, 0411–12
overdue, 0405
parties to, 0402–3
payable at a future time, 0404
payable on demand, 0404
payment for honour *supra* protest, 0414
presentment for payment, 0410
protest, 0412
receivable book, 0520
recourse, 0408
referee in case of need, 0406
renewal, 0420
set, 0422
sola, 0422
stamp duty, 0403, 0423
sum payable, 0404
transactions, 0416
usance, 0423
Binary notation, 0126
Blank transfer, 1931
Bonus shares, 0819, 2004, 2118–22
Bonus system of wages, 1557–9
Book-keeping, definition, 0101
Books—
branches, 1417–35
of account, 1920
of record, 1921
statutory, 1920
value, 2952–7
Bought ledger, 0110, 0118, 0521–2, 1301–2
Brain, electronic, 0126
Branches—
accounts, 1401–44
adjustment account, 1407–8
books, 1417–35
buying, 1414
cash control, 1413
credit sales, 1408–10, 1414
depreciation of assets, 1410–11
foreign, 1436–43
interbranch transactions, 1424
invoicing, 1402–3, 1414–17
payments, 1403
purchases, 1413–14
receipts, 1403
retail, 1404–14
returns, 1403–4
stock accounts, 1411–13
stock transfer, 1401–2
supplies book, 1402
wholesale, 1414–17
Break-even analysis, 1534–6, 1542–4
British government securities, 2834
Brokerage, 1906
Brokers' commission, 0802–4
Brokers ledger, 0808–9
Budgetary control, 1524
Buildings, 0601
Bull, 0810
Business—
entity, 0102
purchase, 2501–9
purchase account, 2502
transactions, 0103
Buying, wholesale branches, 1414

CALLED-UP capital, 1918
Calls, 1938
in advance, 2021–2
in arrear, 2021–2
interest on, 2105–8
Capital—
accounts, 0201
allowances, 1204, 2862–69
authorized, 1918
called up, 1918
circulating, 0213
current, 0213
debenture redemption, 2305–6
definitions, 0213–14, 1918–20
equity, 0213
expenditure, 1544, 2943
expenditure, clubs, 1001
expenditure, managerial decisions, 2943–51
fixed, 0213
gearing, 2918–19
interest, 0218–19, 0235, 1707, 2107–8
invested, 1905
issued, 1918
loan, 0213
long term, 0213
paid up, 1918
partnership, 1703, 1707
personal, 0213
profits, 2102
receipts, clubs, 1003
recovery factors, Table C
reduction, 2526–31
registered, 1918
reserve on consolidation, 2537
share, 1920, 2206
trading, 0213
turnover, 2917
uncalled, 1919
unissued, 1919
working, 0214
Capital gains tax, 0821–6; 2838–41
Capital redemption fund, 2401
Capitalization, 1905
Card ledgers, 0130
Carriage, 0207–8
forward, 0207
paid, 0207
Cash account, liquidators', 2707–8
Cash books, 0111–12, 0121
balancing, 0111
incomplete records, 1111
posting, 0111
Cash budget, 2940
Cash control, branches, 1413
Cash discounts, 0111, 0207

Cash paid book, 0112
Cash received book, 0112
Cash reconciliation, 0112–13
Certificates—
fractional, 2121
of incorporation, 1909
of shares, 1911–2
of transfers, 1931–2
Characters, computer, 0127
Chargeable gains, 2838–41, 2860–1
Charges, register, 1922
Cheques, 0439–45
account payee only, 0443
alterations, 0440
bearer, 0439
books, 0444
cash books, 0111
crossed, 0440–2
dishonoured, 0444
endorsement, 0443
evidence of receipt, 0444
fictional payee, 0440
forgery, 0443
legal tender, 0443
lost, 0444–5
not negotiable 0441
open, 0440
order, 0439
post dated, 0440
Circulating capital, 0213
Class costing, 1506
Clients' ledger, 0807
Closing entries, 0235–6
Clubs, 1001–14
accounts, 1003
Cobol, 0129
Code numbers, 2844
Coding of securities, 0810–11
Collateral securities, debentures, 2027–8
Commercial bills, 1438
Commission—
accounts, 0210
consignments, 0901
errors, 0301–2
managers', 1315
underwriting, 1905–6
travellers', 0211
Committee of inspection, 2603
Common costs, 1543
Common seal, 1912
Companies—
absorption, 2519–22
acceptance of bills of exchange, 0407
amalgamation, 2509–24
articles of association, 1907
audit, 1916–17
capital raising, 2001–28
capitalization scheme, 1905
certificate of incorporation, 1909
debentures, 1915–6
redemption, 2301–15
definition, 1901
disclosure of accounts, 1903
Companies (*contd.*)—
formation, 1904–18
gearing, 1905
holding, 2518–19, 2531–6
income, 2101–23
kinds of, 1901–2
limited, 2505–23
meetings, 1912
memorandum of association, 1906–7, 1908
mortgages, 1915–6
number of persons, 1902, 1904
office and seal, 1912
partnerships, difference from, 1702–3, 1903–4
private, 1902–3
promoter, 1909
prospectus, 1909
public, 1902
published accounts, 2201–27
reconstruction, 2523–4
redeemable preference shares, 2401–7
register of members, 1937
registration, 1906
registration fees, 1907–8
reorganization, 2524–6
restrictions on commencement of business, 1911
seal, 1912
subsidiary, 2523, 2532
underwriting, 1905–6
Companies Act, 1948—
Sect. 1, 1902
Sect. 9, 1907
Sect. 10, 1907
Sect. 16, 1903
Sect. 27, 1944–5, 2206
Sect. 28, 1902
Sect. 47, 1910
Sect. 48, 1902, 1903
Sect. 52, 1911
Sect. 53, 1906
Sect. 56, 2203, 2206
Sect. 57, 2006, 2314
Sect. 58, 1920, 2203–4, 2206, 2401
Sect. 61, 1913, 2524
Sect. 65, 2107, 2206
Sect. 66, 2526
Sect. 67, 2526
Sect. 68, 2526
Sect. 72, 2524
Sect. 76, 1949
Sect. 79, 1932
Sect. 83, 1946
Sect. 90, 2207, 2315
Sect. 95, 1915
Sect. 104, 1921
Sect. 109, 1902, 1911
Sect. 110, 1921
Sect. 124, 1950
Sect. 127, 1951
Sect. 130, 1903, 1912
Sect. 131, 1950

Companies Act, 1948 (*contd.*)—
Sect. 145, 1921, 1945
Sect. 147, 1920
Sect. 149, 1951, 2201, 2213
Sect. 150, 2531
Sect. 151, 2534
Sect. 154, 2531–2
Sect. 155, 2201
Sect. 156, 1951
Sect. 165, 1921
Sect. 175, 1903
Sect. 181, 1903
Sect. 190, 2209
Sect. 196, 2210
Sect. 197, 2213
Sect. 200, 1921, 1944
Sect. 407, 1917
Sect. 434, 1701
Sect. 443, 1903
First Schedule, 1907
Second Schedule, 2203
Fourth Schedule, 1910
Sixth Schedule, 1950
Eighth Schedule, 2205
Companies Act, 1967, 2201, 2533
Sect. 12, 2214
Sect. 27, 1921, 1944
Sect. 28, 1921
Sect. 29, 1921, 1944
Sect. 43, 1903
Sect. 44, 1903
Sect. 109–18, 1921
Sect. 119, 1701
Sect. 169, 2701
Second Schedule, 2202, 2203, 2214, 2533, 2885
Compensating errors, 0301–2
Compulsory liquidation, 2702
Computer based direct debit service, 0446–9
Computers, 0125–9
analogue, 0126
digital, 0126
functions, 0126–7
input, 0127
languages, 0129
off-line, 0129
on-line, 0129
output, 0127
processing modes, 0129
programmes, 0129
real-time, 0129
storage, 0127–9
types, 0126
Confidentiality, 2921
Conservatism, 0105
Consignee, 0901
Consignment accounts, 0901–13
inwards, 0908–12
outwards, 0901–8
Consignor, 0901
Consistency, 0105
Consolidated accounts, 2533–46
Containers, 1235–8
Contango journal, 0810
Contra accounts, 0530
Contra adjustment accounts, 0507
Contra balances in ledgers, 0530–31
Contra entries, 0110
Contract profits, 1610–13
Contract stamp, 0801
Contribution chart, 1538–9
annual, 1541–2
monthly, 1542
Control account, 0503–4
cost ledgers, 1514
Control of Hiring Order, 1964, 1201
Control of Hiring (Rebates) Order, 1960, 1201
Controlling interests, 2523
Convertible loan stock, 2015–20
Copyrights, 0602
Corporation tax, 2109, 2303, 2854–62, 2954
Cost—
accounts, 1501–59
class, 1506
direct cost, 1529–30
double entry, 1514–29
job, 1506
marginal, 1532, 1544
multiple, 1506
operating, 1506
procedure, 1507–9
single, 1506
subsidiary books, 1544–5
system, 1505
test, 1506
analysis, 1502–4
centre, 1506
concept, 1506
definition, 0104
direct, 1503
estimating and pricing, 1544–6
indirect, 1503
ledgers, 1514–23
of goods sold, 0204–5
production, 1603
reduction, 2944
sheets, 1549–56
standard, 1523–4
unit, 1505–6
variation, 1530
volume-profit equation, 1542
Court liquidation, 2702
Courts of bankruptcy, 2601
Credit allowed, 2917
Credit balances, 0106
Credit note, 0117
Credit note book, 0120
Credit period taken, 2917
Credit sales, 1201, 1216–9
branches, 1408–10, 1414
Creditors' ledger, 0110, 0503–5, 0521–2
Creditors, provision for discount on, 0227

Crossed cheques, 0440
Cumulative preference shares, 1920
arrears in, 2116
Currency, 1436
account sales, 0903
conversion, 1437–8
paper, 1443–4
transactions, 1438–9
Current account, 1711
Current assets, 0212–13
balance sheet, 2904–5
Current capital, 0213
Current liabilities, 0213

DATA storage, computer, 0126–9
Day book, 0116–17
consignment, 0901
Death, dissolution of partnership, 1801
Debentures, 1915–16
application, 1942
as collateral security, 2027–8
at a discount, 2002, 2006–10, 2018–19, 2308–10
at a premium, 2004–5, 2013, 2310–11
at par, 2002–4, 2012–13, 2016
bearer, 2302
conversion, 2015–20, 2314
cost of issuing, 2027
definition, 0213
fixed charge, 2301
floating charge, 1916, 2301
holders' rights, 1916
instalments on, 2010–15
interest, 2103–9, 2302, 2305
irredeemable, 2302
issue, 2001–28, 2314–15
perpetual, 1916
redemption, 2301–13
reissue, 1916
trust deed, 1916
types, 2301–2
Debit balances, 0106
Debit note, 0117
Debit note book, 0119
Debiting, direct, 0433–6
Debtors, provision for discount on, 0220–7
Debtors' ledger, 0523–4
Debts, 0212, 0248–9
hire purchase, 1230
Decimal notation, 0126
Decisions, management, 1534
Deed of arrangement, 2603
Deferred creditors, 2615
Deferred ordinary shares, 1919
Deferred revenue expenditure, 1001–2
Deferred shares, 1920
Deferred taxation, providing for, 2875–8
Deficiency, definition, 0213
Deficiency account, 2620–5
Del credere commission, 0902–3
Delivery notes, 0117
Departmental accounts, 1301–15
Departmental costing, 1506
Departures, significant, 0101
Depletion unit method of depreciation, 0622–3
Depreciation, 0211, 0249–50, 2952
allowances against tax, 2862–75
annuity system, 0611–12
commercial, 2869–75
depletion unit method of, 0622–3
diminishing balance method of, 0605–6
foreign branches, 1436
fund principle, 0614–18
Institute of Chartered Accountants recommendations, 0623–4
insurance policy system, 0618–20
obsolescence, 0602
of assets, 1410–11
of fixed assets, 0601–31
paper currency, 1443
rates, 0624
repairs fund, 0621–2
revaluation method, 0620–1
sinking fund, 0614–18, 0625–6
wear and tear, 0602
Differences—
permanent, 2875
timing, 2875
Diminishing balance method of depreciation, 0605–6
Direct cost, 1529–30
Direct debit services, 0446–9
Direct debiting, 0433–6
Direct taxes, 2802, 2829–85
Directors—
attendance book, 1922
compensation for loss of office, 2211
emoluments, 2210–11
pension, 2210–11
register, 1921, 1945
reports, 2213–14
shareholdings, register of, 1921
Disclosure of accounts, 1903
exemptions, 2214–15
Discount and acceptance houses, 0403
Discounts, 0209–10
cash, 0111, 0209
on creditors, 0227
on debentures, 2006, 2007–10, 2014–15, 2017–20, 2309–10
on debtors, 0227
on shares, 2002, 2006–7, 2014–15
trade, 0209
Dishonour—
bills of exchange, 0413
cheques, 0444
Dismissal for redundancy, 2806–7
Dissolution of partnership, 1801–27
Distribution overhead, 1503
Dividend cover, 2920
Dividend yield, 2915
Dividends, 2109–16, 2955
Advanced Corporation Tax (A.C.T.), 2854–62

Dividends (*contd.*)—
  and rights, 0809
  appropriation account, 2112
  bankruptcy, 2630
  book, 1942, 1944
  cover, 2920
  equalization reserve, 2109–10
  free of tax, 2113
  income tax, 2110, 2860–1
  interim, 2109–10
  payment, 2109
  per share, 2915
  scrip, 1932–3, 2113
  taxation, 2110, 2113, 2858–62
  unclaimed, 2110
Divisible profits, 2101
Dock charges, 0207–8
Documentary bills, 0404, 0424, 0427 0902
Double entry—
  advantages, 0104
  book-keeping, 0108
  conversion of incomplete records, 1111–12
  cost accounts, 1514–30
Double money columns, 1406–7
Double taxation relief, 2837–8
Doubtful debts, 0212
Drawings account, 0235, 1710–11
Dual aspect concept, 0102
Duty, 0207–8

EARNINGS per share, 2915
Efficiency pay, 1559
Employees—
  admission to partnership, 1724
  and accounts, 2901–2
  loans to, 2213
Employers' Liability Act, 0210
Endorsement—
  bills of exchange, 0408–9
  cheques, 0443
Entity, business, 0102
Equal instalments method of interest apportionment, 1211
Equipment and machinery, 0602
Equity capital, definition, 0213
Errors—
  balance sheet, 0250
  correction of, 0301–9
  detection, 0531–3
  published accounts, 1004
  trial balances, 0115–16
Estate duty, 2841–2
Exchange rates, 1436–7, 1439–41, 1443–4
Expenditure, definition, 0104
Expenses, 0210–11, 1502–4
  accounts, 2210–11
  allowed for tax, 2837
  auditors, 2212
  departmental, 1303–12
  office, 0211

Expenses (*contd.*)—
  trade, 0211
  travelling, 0211
Exposure drafts (A.S.S.C.)—
  (ED3 Acquisitions and mergers)
  (ED6 Stocks and work-in-progress)
  ED7 Extraordinary items, 2102
  (ED8 Inflation)
  ED9 Government grants, 2868
  ED10 V.A.T., 2825
  ED11 Deferred taxation, 2876
  ED12 Treatment of tax under imputation system, 2858–62

FACTORY overhead, 1503, 1603
Fictitious assets, 0213
Fictitious bills, 0415
Fictitious payee, 0440
Final accounts, 0201, 0236
  errors, 0305
  incomplete records, 1105–10
  interpretation, 2901–57
  partnership, 1711, 1719–24
  preparation, 0104
  presentation, 2902–4
Finance—
  government control of, 1201
  misleading accounting for, 1210
Finance companies—
  accounting by, 1228–31
  determining income, 1234
Fine bank bills, 0404
Finished goods, 0202
Fire claims for stock, 0707–9
Fixed assets—
  balance sheets, 2208–9, 2904
  definition, 0212
  depreciation, 0602–31
  types, 0601–2
Fixed capital, 0213
Fixed capital accounts, 1706–7
Fixed charges—
  times earned, 2920
Fixed instalment method of depreciation, 0604
Floating charge, 1916
Folios, 1938
Forecast of trading account, 2940–3
Foreign bills, 0421
Foreign branches, 1436–44
Foreign currencies, conversion, 2210
Foreign domicile bills, 0404
Foreign exchange, 1436–44
Foreign promissory note, 0430
Forfeiture of shares, 2023–6
Forgery—
  bills of exchange, 0414
  cheques, 0443–4
  transfers, 1932
Form P45, 2850
Form P60, 2849
Fortran, 0129

Foster v. *New Trinidad Lake Asphalte Co. Ltd.*, 2102
Founders' shares, 1920
Fractional certificates, 2511
Franked income, 2834, 2860
Freight, 0207
Funds, statements and sources, 2922–39

Garner v. *Murray*, 1803–5, 1810–13
Gearing—
  percentage, 2919
  ratio, 2918–19
General ledger, 0110, 0503 *et seq.*
Giro, bank, 0431–6
Going concern concept, 0102
Goodwill, 1714, 1820, 2501–2
Graduated National Insurance Contribution, 2843
Grants, government, 2802–3
  investment, 2862–9, 2955
Gross loss, 0202
Gross pay, 2852–3
Gross profit, 0201
Ground rent, 0208–9
Group accounts, 2501, 2531, 2533–5
Guarantee, companies limited by, 1902

HEAD office—
  accounts, 1417–18
  foreign branches, 1436
Hind v. *Buenos Ayres Grand National Tramways Co. Ltd.*, 2108
Hire purchase, 1202
  bad debts, 1230–1
  buyers' books, 1204–9
  contracts, 1204
  government control, 1201
  income, 1211
  interest, 1211–16
  royalty accounts, 1231–35
Hire Purchase Acts, 1202–3
Holder in due course, 0413
Holding companies, 2518–19, 2531–6
Holiday pay, 2843
Hospital accounts, 1003
Hypothecation, letters of, 0425

IMPERSONAL account, 0106
Impersonal ledger, 0110, 0524–7
Imprest system of petty cash, 0116
Imputation system of Corporation Tax, 2858
Income, 0201–51
  accrued, 0104, 0211
  company reporting, 2101–24
  definition, 2832–3
  measurement, 0102
  statement, 0201–2
  statutory, 2832
  tax, 0235, 2829–38
    adjustment of accounts, 2879–85
    allowances, 2832–3, 2837
    appeals, 2830

Income (*contd.*)—
    capital gains tax, 0821–6, 2838–41
    classification in balance sheet, 2879
    code numbers, 2843–46
    companies, 2104
    corporation tax, 0202, 2303, 2838, 2854–62, 2954
    debenture profits, 2103–5
    depreciation allowance, 2862–75
    dividends, 2109, 2854–62
    double taxation relief, 2837–8
    estate duty, 2841–2
    expenses allowed, 2837
    investment income, 0618, 0627, 2834
    investment income surcharge, 2832
    P.A.Y.E., 2843, 2847
    partnerships, 2842, 2881–5
    personal allowances, 2832–3
    rates of, 2831–2
    returns, 2831
    Schedule A, 2829, 2833
    Schedule B, 2830, 2833
    Schedule C, 2830, 2834
    Schedule D, 2830, 2834–6, 2842, 2879–85
    Schedule E, 2830, 2836, 2843–4
    Schedule F, 2830, 2834
    statutory income, 2832
    surtax, 2837
    unearned income, 2832
    year of assessment, 2831
Incomplete records, 1101–12
Incorporation, profits prior to, 2116–18
Indexing ledger accounts, 0108
Indirect taxes, 2802
  accounts for, 2803–29
Industrial buildings, capital allowances, 2863
Industrial training levies, 2820–5
Initial allowances, 2871
Inland revenue and accounts, 2902
Input, computer, 0127
Instalment purchase, 1201, 1219–22
Instalments on shares, 2010–11, 2012–14
Institute of Chartered Accountants, 0101
  recommendations on depreciation, 0623–4
Institute of Cost and Management Accountants, 0101
Insurance, 0210
  companies, 2214
  fire claims, 0707–9
  policies—
    debenture redemption, 2310–12
    method of depreciation, 0618–20
Intangible assets, 0213
Inter-branch transactions, 1424
Inter-departmental transactions, 1303
Inter-firm comparison, 2920–2
Interest—
  definition, 2103
  in hire-purchase accounts, 1211–16
  investment loans, 0210

Interest (*contd.*)—
on calls, 2105–9
on capital, 0218, 0235, 1707, 2107–8
on debentures, 2103–4, 2302, 2305
on debts, 2630
rates, 1709
taxation, 2859–60
times earned, 2920
Interim dividend, 2109
Interpretations of accounts, 0250–1, 2901 *et seq.*
Inventory, 0701
Investments—
accounts, 0815–26
allowances, 2955
capital gains tax, 0821–6
cash, 0614
grants, 2862–9, 2955
interest, 0210, 0618, 0627
ledger, 0809, 0821–6
purchase of, 0815–6
sale of, 0816
tax, 0618, 0627, 0821–6
Invoice, 0117
pro forma, 0902
Invoicing—
branches, 1402–3
wholesale branches, 1414–17
Inwards consignments, 0908–12
IOU, 0437
Irrecoverable surplus A.C.T., 2862
Issue of shares and debentures, 2001–28, 2314–15
Issued capital, 1918

JOB costing, 1506
Jobbers ledger, 0808
Joint costs, 1542
Joint ventures, 1729–36
Journal, 0116–17, 0512–14
contango, 0810
errors, 0303
Stock Exchange, 0809

KEY-FACTOR analysis, 1539–40
Kites, 0415

LAND, 0601
income from, 2210
Law, partnership, 1701–6
Lease, 1202
Leaseholds, 0602
Ledgers, 0108–10
balances, 0106
balancing, 0110
card, 0129–30
consignment, 0901
impersonal, 0110
indexing, 0108
investments, 0809, 0821–6
loose leaf, 0122–30
Ledgers (*contd.*)—
private, 0110, 0503, 0533–5
purchase, 0110
sales, 0110
self balancing, 0503–7 *et seq.*
Lee v. *Neuchatel Asphalte Co. Ltd.*, 2102
Legal charges, 0210
Legal tender, 0431
Letters—
of acceptance, 1927
of allotment, 1925
of credit, 0403
of hypothecation, 0425
Liabilities—
balance sheet, 0214–17, 2904–10
current, 0213, 2202–3
definitions, 0213
incomplete records, 1111
long term, 0213
of debtor, 2607
of ex-shareholders, 2024
on bills, 0403
short term, 0213
Limited company—
amalgamation, 2509–23
conversion from partnership, 2505–9
Limited partnership, 1726–9
Liquid assets, 0213
Liquidation, 2701–10
Liquidators' cash account, 2707–8
Loan capital, 0213
Loan stock, convertible, 2015–21
Loans—
banks, 0213
to officers, 2213
Long-term capital, 0213
Long-term liabilities, 0213
Loose-leaf ledgers, 0129–30
Loose tools, 0206
Loss, 0208–12
on realization, 1807–16
prior to incorporation, 2118
Lubbock v. *British Bank of South America*, 2102

MACHINERY—
capital allowances, 2863
depreciation, 0602
Macro accounting, 0101
Magnetic Ink Character Recognition (MICR), 0127
Mainstream Corporation Tax (M.C.T.), 2859
Maintenance, depreciation fund, 0621–2
Management—
and accounts, 2901
decisions, 1534
shares, 1920
Manager's commission, 1315
Manual methods of accounts, 0107
Manufacturing account, 0202
Manufacturing charges, 0208
Manufacturing profits, 1601–9

Margin of sales, 2918
Marginal costing, 1532, 1544
Market value of stock, 0705–6
Matching revenue income and expenses, 0203
Materiality, 0105
Materials consumed, 0205–6
Mechanization, 0107
Meetings, 1912
Members, register of, 1933
Memorandum books, 0108
Memorandum of association, 1906–7 1908
Micro accounting, 0101
Mines, 1441–2
  capital allowances, 2866
Minimum profits, 1724
Minute book, 1945–6
Modes, computer processing, 0129
Money, as a common denominator, 0102
Monthly contribution charts, 1542
Mortgages, 1915
  register of, 1922
Multiple costing, 1506
Multiple posting, 0121

NAKED debentures, 2301
Names, firms, 1702
Narrations in journals, 0117
National Health Service, 1003
National Insurance, 0210
Natural resources, 0601
Negotiable instruments, 0408
Net asset value, 2920
Net-loss, 0202
Net-profit, 0202
Net-worth, 0213
New projects, 2944
Nominal accounts, 0106, 0501–2
Nominal ledger, 0110, 0524–8
Non-operating profits, 2102
Non-returnable containers, 1235–6
Non-voting ordinary shares, 1920
Not negotiable cheques, 0442
Notation—
  binary, 0126
  decimal, 0126
Noting, 0411–12
Notional expenses, 1608

OBSOLESCENCE, 0602
Odd and even day books, 0118–19
Office expenses, 0211
Officers of a company, loans to, 2213
Off-line computers, 0129
Omission, 0301–2
On-line computers, 0129
One-off jobs, 1544
Open cheque, 0440
Operating costing accounts, 1506
Operating expenses, 0202
Operating profit, 0202
  before interest, corporation tax and dividends, 2911
  after interest and corporation tax, 2911
  after interest, tax and preference dividends, 2911
Operations—
  arithmetic, 0126
  control, 0126–7
Optimum product mix, 1540
Order cheque, 0439
Order processing procedure, 0128
Orders in hand, 0206
Ordinary shares, 1919
Output cost accounts, 1506
Outwards consignments, 0901–8
Overdrafts, 0213
  interest on, 2107
Overheads, 1503–4, 1610
  absorption, 1511–13
  apportionment, 1509–11
  factory, 1503, 1603
Over-ordering of stock, 0711
Overtrading, 0216, 2905–8
Owners salaries, 0209, 0235

P45, 2850
P60, 2849
Packages, 0206
Paid up capital, 1918
Paper currency, fluctuation, 1443–4
Partners—
  acting, 1703
  advances, 1707
  annuity for outgoing, 1827
  bankruptcy, 2605
  drawings, 1707
  duties, 1704–5
  expulsion, 1705
  kinds of, 1703
  liabilities, 1703–4
  powers, 1703
  quasi, 1703
  rights, 1704–5
  salaries, 0209, 0235, 1707
  sleeping, 1703
Partnerships—
  accounts, 1701–36
  admission, 1714–17, 1724
  annual audit, 1703
  capital, 1703, 1707
  conversion to a limited company, 2505–9
  deed, 1705–6
  difference from a company, 1903–4
  dissociation, 1801–27
  duration, 1705
  income tax, 2842, 2881–5
  law, 1701–6
  limited, 1726–9
  prohibition, 1701, 1901
  property, 1704

Partnership (*contd.*)—
surtax, 2837
terms variation, 1704
Patent rights, capital allowances, 2866
Patents, 0602
Pay, gross, 2852–3
P.A.Y.E., 2847
Payee, fictitious, 0440
Payment, methods of, 0401–49
Payments—
in advance, 0217
in arrears, 0217
Period of accounts, 0248
Permanent differences, 2875
Perpetual debentures, 1916
Personal accounts, 0106, 0502
Personal allowances, tax, 2832–3
Personal capital, 0213
Petty cash book, 0116
Piece rates, wages, 1558
Piece rate workers, redundancy, 2807
Pilfering, 0710
Plant—
capital allowances, 2863–6
contract accounts, 1610
depreciation, 0602
Plantations, 1441–2
Pooling of tax allowances, 2874
Postage, 0211
Postponed creditors, 2615
Preference dividend—
times earned, 2920
Preference shares—
arrears of dividend, 2115
cumulative, 1920
definition, 1920
redemption, 1924, 2401–7
Preferred ordinary shares, 1919
Premium—
on debentures, 2004–6, 2013, 2310
on shares, 2004, 2012, 2017
Present value factors, Tables A, B
Prevention of Fraud (Investments) Act, 1958, 1701
Price earnings ratio, 2915
Prices of stock, 0704
Pricing, transfer, 1606
Pricing and cost estimating, 1544–6
Priestman plan, 1557
Principal books, 0108–16
Printing expenditure, 0210
Private companies, 1902–3
Private journal, 0513
Private ledger, 0110, 0503, 0533–5
Probates, register of, 1949–51
Procedure—
order processing, 0128
slip system of book-keeping, 0130 *et seq.*
slip system flow chart, 0134
Process costing, 1506
Processing modes, computer, 0129
Production unit method of depreciation, 0622–3
Profit—
capital, 2102
contract, 1610
debenture redemption out of, 2303–5
divisible, 2101
extraordinary items, 2102
guarantee of minimum, 1724
manufacturing, 1601–9
non-operating, 2102
on realization, 1805–6
prior to incorporation, 2116
prior year items, 2102
super, 1709
unrealized, 1424
Profit and loss account, 0208–12, 1604, 2211–13
consolidated, 2545–8
forecast, 2940
Profit-sharing schemes, 1559
Profit/volume ratio, 1539
Pro forma invoice, 0902
Programming, computer, 0129
Promissory notes, 0403, 0428–30
Promoter, 1909
Property, bankruptcy, 2616, 2629
Property accounts, 0106
Proprietors' capital, 2911
Prospectus, 1909–10
Provisions, 2202–7
Public companies, 1902
Published accounts, 2201–27
errors, 1004
Punched cards, 0121–5
Punched tape, 0121–5
Purchases—
balance sheet, 0206
books, 0118, 0515–16, 1301–2
branches, 1413–14
ledger, 0108, 0521–2
return book, 0119–20
Pyramid of ratios, 2922

QUALIFYING—
areas, 2867
assets, 2867
industrial processes, 2867
Quasi partner, 1703
Quick asset ratio, 2916

RATES, 0209
Rates of depreciation, 0624
Rates of exchange, 1436–7, 1443–4
Rates of interest, 1709
Ratios, 2908–20
profitability, 2910–15
liquidity or asset use, 2916–18
solvency, 2918–20
Raw materials, 0202, 0204
Real accounts, 0106, 0501
Realization concept, 0105, 0204
Realization, loss on, 1807–16
Realization, profit on, 1805–6
Receipts, branch, 1403

Receiving order, 2602
Reconciliation—
  bank, 0112–13
  cost ledgers, 1521
  statement, 0113
Reconstruction of companies, 2523–4
Records, incomplete, 1101–12
Recoverable surplus A.C.T., 2861–2
Recovery of A.C.T., 2858
Redemption—
  debentures, 2301–13
  fund account, 0614
  preference shares, 1924, 2401–7
Reduction of capital, 2526–31
Redundancy—
  fund, 2804–5
  payments—
    accounts, 2813–14
    payments scheme, 2806–16
    rebates, 2814–16
Referee in case of need, 0406
Register—
  of directors, 1944
  of directors' attendances, 1922
  of directors' shareholdings, 1921
  of members, 1933
  of mortgages and charges, 1922
  of probates, 1949–53
  of secretaries, 1944
  of stockholders, 1938
  of transfers, 1930–1
Registered capital, 1918
Registration fees, 1907–8
  share transfers, 0804
Registration of Business Names Act, 1916, 1702
Registration of companies, 1906
Regret, letter of, 1926
Remittance account, branch accounts, 1418
Renewal of fixed assets, 0602
Rent, 0208, 1232
  bankruptcy, 2615
  ground, 0208–9
Rental, 1202
Renunciation, letter of, 1927
Repairs, 0211, 0602
  depreciation fund, 0621–2
Repetitive production, 1545–6
Replacement of fixed assets, 0602–3
[illegible]serves, 2202–7
[illegible]cret, 2204–6
[illegible] branches, 1404–14
[illegible]ble containers, 1236–8
[illegible] investment, 2910–15
[illegible]nch, 1403–4
[illegible]method of depreciation,

Revenue (*contd.*)—
  published accounts, 2210
Rex v. *Lord Kylsant and Morland*, 2206
Rights—
  of debenture holders, 1916
  of partners, 1704–5
Rights issues, 0809, 0819–20
Royalties, 0208
  accounts, 1231–5

SAFETY margin, cost accounts, 1537–8
Salaries—
  accounts, 0207–8
  definition, 0209
  owners, 0209, 0235
  partners, 0209, 0235, 1707
  productive, 0207, 0209
Sale of assets, 0609
Sales—
  accounts, hire purchase, 1219
  book, 0118–19, 0517
    departmental accounts, 1301–2
  journal, 0119
  ledger, 0110, 0523–4
    adjustment account, 0503–7
    incomplete records, 1111
  returns book, 0120
  trading account, 0204
Sales tax and V.A.T., 2825–6
Sample costing, 1506
Schematic, computer, 0127
Scientific research, capital allowances, 2867
Scrip dividend, 1932, 2114–5
Secret reserves, 2204–6
Secretaries, register of, 1942
Sectional balancing, 0502
Securities, coding, 0810–11
Selective employment tax, 2804, 2816–21
Self-balancing ledgers, 0501–5 *et seq.*
Selling overhead, 1503
S.E.T., 2804, 2816–21
Share capital—
  alteration, 1913–5
  balance sheets, 2206
  definition, 1918
Share ledger, posting, 1938
Share warrant, 1946
Shareholders—
  and accounts, 2901
  and debenture holders, 2302–4
  liability, 1702
Shares—
  allotment, 1910
  at a premium, 2004–5, 2012, 2017
  at discount, 2002, 2006–7, 2014–15
  at par, 2002–4, 2010–11
  bonus, 0819, 2118–22
  certificates, 1911–12
  conversion from debentures, 2314
  cost of issuing, 2027
  cumulative preference, 1920, 2116

Shares (*contd.*)—
definition, 1919
difference from stock, 1920
exchange, 2510
forfeiture, 2023–6
founders', 1920
instalments on, 2010–11
issues, 2001–26, 2120–3
management, 1920
over subscribed, 2020–1
preference, 1920, 2116, 2401–7
rights issues, 2122–3
transfer, 1912
types of, 1919–20
valuation, 2942–3
Shift workers, redundancy, 2807
Shipping companies, 2214
Short-term liabilities, 0213
Short-time working, 2807
Short-workings, 1232
Single costing, 1506
Single entry, 0121–5
errors, 0302
incomplete records, 1102–5
Sinking fund—
debenture redemption, 2308–9
depreciation, 0614–17, 0625–6
instalments, Table D
Slide rule, 0126
Slip cash book, 0132
Slip day book, 0131–2
Slip ledger, 0130–1
Slip system, flow chart, 0134
Slip system of book-keeping, 0130–33
Societies, 1001–14
Sola draft, 0422
Sold ledgers, 0110
Solicitors, partnerships, 1701
Sources of funds, 2922
Stamp duty—
bills of exchange, 0403, 0423
contract, 0801
promissory notes, 0428
Stamps—
indirect tax, 2803–4
Standard costing, 1523–9
Stapley v. *Read Bros. Ltd.*, 2102
Statement of affairs, 2602, 2606–20
deficiency account, 2708–9
in compulsory liquidation, 2703–6
Statements—
monthly, 0117
reconciliation bank, 0112–13
Stationery expenditure, 0210
Statistical books, 0108, 1920–51
tabular, 0133
Statutory books, 1920–51
Stock, 0204–8
accounts, 1411–13
control, 0709–14
convertible loan, 2015–20
delivery, 0710
fire claims, 0707–9
Stock (*contd.*)—
losses, 0906–7
market value, 0705–6
over ordering, 0711
pilfering, 0710
prices, 0704
slow moving, 0710–11
transfer to branches, 1401–2
unused, 0211
valuation, 0701–14
Stock, difference from shares, 1920
Stock Exchange transaction, 0801–15
Stockbroker, 0801
commission, 0802–4
Stockholders, register of, 1938
Stock-taking, 0703, 0710–11
Storage, computer, 0127–9
Straight line method—
of depreciation, 0604
of interest apportionment, 1211
Subsidiary books, 0108, 0116–20
cost accounts, 1546–9
rulings, 0508–10
Subsidiary companies, 2532, 2535
Sum of the digits method of interest apportionment, 1215
Superannuation, 2812
Superfluity, depreciation, 0602
Super-profits, 1709
Supplies book, branches, 1402
Supplies, unused, 0211
Surplus A.C.T., 2858
Surplus franked income, 2860
Surtax, 2827
partnership, 2884–5
Survivorship assurance, 1820
Suspense account, 0303–4
Systems design, 0107–8

TABULAR system of book-keeping, 0133
Tabulation, punch card, 0125
Take over bids, 2523
Take up, 0810
Tangible assets, 0213
Taxable income, 2832
Taxable profits, 2854 *et seq.*
Taxes, 0209, 2801–85
capital gains, 0821–6, 2837–41
company accounts, 2884
corporation, 0202, 0235, 2840, 2842
deduction cards, 2846
depreciation, 0628
direct, 2802, 2829–85
equalization reserve, 2875–8
estate duty, 2841–2
income, 0202, 0235, 0618, 0627
indirect, 2802, 2803–29
tables, 2844–8
V.A.T., 2802, 2825–9

Telegraphic transfers, 1438
Test costing, 1506
Thieving, 0710

Time rates, wages, 1557–8
Time-sharing, computer, 0129
Timing differences, 2875
Tools, loose, 0206
Total account, 0503–8
Total Assets, 2910
  base (profitability), 2913
  employed, 2911
  employed base, 2913
Trade discounts, 0209
  definition, 0119
Trade expenses, 0211
Trading account—
  definition, 0202
  departmental, 1302, 1313–14
  difference from manufacturing account, 0202
  forecast, 2940
  hire purchase, 1219
Trading capital, 0213
Transactions, business, 0103
Transfers—
  blank, 1931
  certification, 1931–2
  forged, 1932
  of shares, 1912
  pricing, 1606
  register of, 1929–30
Travellers' commission, 0211
Travelling expenses, 0211
Trial balance—
  construction, 0114
  difference from balance sheet, 0203
  double entry, 0104
  errors, 0115, 0301–5
  incomplete records, 1112
Trust deed, 1916
Trustee in bankruptcy, 2626–31
Turnover period, 2917

UNCALLED capital, 1919
Unclaimed dividends, 2110
Underwriting, 1905–6
Undischarged bankruptcy, 2605
Unearned income, 2832
Unissued capital, 1919
Unit cost, 1531
Unrealized profits, 1424
Usance, 0423

VALUATION of stock, 0701–7
Value-added tax (V.A.T.), 2802, 2825–9
  accounting methods, 2826–9
  exemption, 2827–8
  mixed ratings, 2828–9
  puchases, 2827
  refund, 2827
  sales, 2826
  settlement, 2827
Value, book, 2920
Value factors, Tables A, B
Variance analysis, 1524
Verner v. *General Commercial Trust Ltd.*, 2102
Voluntary associations, 1001–14
Voluntary liquidation, 2701

WAGES—
  payments methods, 1557–9
  Priestman plan, 1559
  profit and loss account, 0208
  trading account, 0204–5
Warehouse notes, 0117
Wasting assets, 0213
Wear and tear, depreciation, 0602
Wholesale branches, 1414–17
Windmills, 0415
Woodlands, income tax, 2833
Work in progress, 0206, 1606–7
Working capital, 0214
Working capital ratio, 2916
Working costing, 1506
Worksheet, 0233–5, 0239
Writing down assets, 2527–30

YIELD valuation, 2943